Information Technology Law in Ireland

Second Edition

For LD

Information Technology Law in Ireland

Second Edition

DENIS KELLEHER

BCL, H.Dip. Econ.Sc, Barrister-at-Law (Kings Inns),
Advisory Counsel,
Office of the Attorney General,
Government Buildings,
Dublin 2

and

Legal Counsellor,
Permanent Representation of Ireland to the EU,
Brussels,
Belgium.

KAREN MURRAY

BA(NUI), LL.B(NUI), LL.M(QUB), Barrister-at-Law (Kings Inns),
Lecturer in law, National College of Ireland, IFSC, Mayor Street, Dublin 1.

Published by
Tottel Publishing Ltd
Maxwelton House
41–43 Boltro Road
Haywards Heath
West Sussex
RH16 1BJ

Tottel Publishing Ltd
Fitzwilliam Business Centre
26 Upper Pembroke Street
Dublin 2

ISBN: 978-1-84592-111-8
© Denis Kelleher & Karen Murray
First edition 1997

British Library Cataloguing-in-Publication Data
A catalogue record for this book is available from the British Library

Typeset by Marlex Editorial Services Ltd., Dublin, Ireland
Printed and bound in Great Britain by
Athenæum Press Limited, Gateshead, Tyne & Wear

Preface

A decade has passed since the first edition of this work was published. In that time technology has changed dramatically, as has Ireland's society and its economy. To reflect these changes, we have rewritten this edition in its entirety; none of the text from the first edition has been replicated. This complete rewrite has been forced by the very extensive changes that have occurred in both information technology and the laws that apply to it.

Information technology is no longer a novelty, nor is the idea that the law will apply even to the furtherest recesses of the Internet. This book again attempts to analyse how the law applies to technology, and how technology has changed the law. Information technology law is not a clear and distinct discipline of the law in the manner of tort, equity or contract law. Information technology law is an amalgam of all those disciplines. The implementation, adaptation and use of information technology is an important and growing function of Irish life. The object of this book is to examine how the law will apply to those processes.

This book was primarily written over a number of years, but came together in the final year before publication. During that time we were lucky to have the help and support of family, friends and work colleagues. We would like to thank John Gormley, Liam O'Daly, Jennifer Payne, Christopher O'Toole, Ruth O'Flaherty, Michael Kirwan, Laura Byrne, Therese Fanning and Sinead Melvin. We would also like to thank Conor McGuire, Richard Mitten, and the library staff at the National College of Ireland, in particular, Mary Buckley, Jordi Gil Sala and Tim Lawless. Thanks to all the staff at Tottel Publishing in particular to Amy Hayes for all her patience, persistence and her dedicated professionalism; Sandra Mulvey, Jennifer Lynch and Marian Sullivan for typesetting. Finally, thanks to Daisy.

This book is written in a personal capacity, it does not represent the views of either authors' employers, in particular it does not represent the views of the Attorney General or those of his Office.

Denis Kelleher

Permanent Representation of Ireland to the European Union, Rue Foissart 89 – 93, 1040 Brussels, Belgium.

Karen Murray

National College of Ireland, IFSC, Major Street, Dublin 1.

October 2007.

Contents

PART II: PATENTS

PART V: PRIVACY

PART VI: ECOMMERCE

PART VII: CONTENT

PART VIII: CYBERCRIME

PART IX: IT IN THE WORKPLACE

Chapter 33   Privacy at Work

Chapter 34   IT Misuse at Work

Chapter 35   Restraint of Trade Clauses

Table of Cases

D

E

O

P

Table of Statutes

Ireland

Copyright and Related Rights Acts 2000–2004 (contd)

Bunreacht na hÉireann

European Legislation

Other Jurisdictions

Statutory Instruments

PART I: COPYRIGHT AND RELATED RIGHTS

Chapter 1

Subsistence of Copyright, Authorship, Duration and Enforcement

Introduction

[1.01] Copyright is a trade-off: it encourages the public good of creativity by permitting the public bad of allowing authors and artists to monopolise the reproduction and exploitation of their work. As Macaulay said:

> 'It is good that authors should be remunerated; and the least exceptionable way of remunerating them is by a monopoly. Yet monopoly is an evil. For the sake of the good we must submit to the evil; but the evil ought not to last a day longer than is necessary for the purpose of securing the good'.[1]

[1.02] Copyright is a far from perfect system for encouraging the development of new works. *It's a Wonderful Life* is the classic example of what can happen to a work that escapes the confines of copyright protection. The film disappointed its audience upon release and, although nominated for an Oscar was quickly forgotten. Thanks to the vagaries of the US copyright process and a failure to renew its copyright, the film moved into the public domain in the 1970s. This gave *It's a Wonderful Life* a quality that overrode any of the original doubts about its artistic merit: *It's a Wonderful Life* could be shown by US television stations for free. As a result it became a staple of the schedules of US television, and through repeated showings attained the 'classic' status that it now holds. Whatever its faults, copyright exists and there is no question that it has been very successful in generating the cornucopia of fresh copyright works that surround us today. Hence the significance of copyright law and the significance of the rights that flow from it. Copyright may be unsatisfactory, but a successful system has yet to be designed that will reward the activities of authors and artists adequately or at all.[2]

The subsistence of copyright

[1.03] Section 17(1) of the CRRA 2000–2004 provide a concise summary of the essentials of copyright law:

> 'Copyright is a property right whereby, subject to this Act, the owner of the copyright in any work may undertake or authorise other persons in relation to that work to undertake certain acts in the State being acts which are designated by this Act as acts restricted by copyright in a work of that description.'

---

[1] Macaulay, House of Commons, 5 February 1841. Macaulay was speaking in a debate on a Bill to extend copyright to sixty years. Quoted in p 8, para 33 of Houses of Parliament (UK) All Party Parliamentary Internet Group, 'Digital Rights Management', June 2006.

[2] 'only one in forty digital songs are being paid for, digital music is ... essentially free', Keen, *The Cult of the Amateur* (Nicholas Brealey Publishing, 2007), p 108.

Copyright subsists in—

    (a)   Original literary, dramatic, musical or artistic works,[3]

    (b)   Sound recordings, films, broadcasts or cable programmes,

    (c)   The typographical arrangement of published editions, and

    (d)   Original databases.[4]

[1.04] Although the term 'works' only appears in the first of the above categories, this is the term used to refer to anything which is protected by copyright. This position is made clear by the CRRA 2000–2004 which provide that 'work' means:

> 'a literary, dramatic, musical or artistic work, sound recording, film, broadcast, cable programme, typographical arrangement of a published edition or an original database and includes a computer program except … where 'work' means 'literary, dramatic, musical or artistic work or film'.[5]

These categories may not be exclusive; for example, a film such as *The Sound of Music* contains a large number of musical works in the form of songs. There may also be considerable overlap between the components of the above categories so a film or sound recording might become the principle component of a broadcast or cable programme. The Act stipulates that certain works can only belong to a particular category. A literary work cannot be a dramatic or musical work or an original database and a photograph cannot be part of a film.[6] But different types of work may co-exist on the one page. However, once you can be certain that something is protected by copyright, it may not matter which of the above categories it falls into. Of course, this is not strictly true in every situation. One important difference is that while literary, dramatic, musical and artistic works and databases must be 'original' there is no similar requirement for sound recordings, films, broadcasts, cable programmes and typographical arrangements.

Originality

[1.05] Literary, dramatic, musical or artistic works and databases are only protected if they are original. The CRRA 2000–2004 contain no general definition as to what constitutes originality. In *University of London Press v University Tutorial Press*,[7] Peterson J stated that:

> 'The word original does not … mean that the work must be the expression of original or inventive thought. Copyright Acts are not concerned with the originality of ideas, but with the expression of thought, and, in the case of 'literary work', with the expression of thought in print or writing. The originality which is required relates to the expression of

---

3   Somewhat confusingly all categories of copyright are described as 'works', a term which is defined as: 'a literary, dramatic, musical or artistic work, sound recording, film, broadcast, cable programme, typographical arrangement of a published edition or an original database and includes a computer program except in CRRA 2000–2004, Part II, Chapter 7 where 'work' means "literary, dramatic, musical or artistic work or film".

4   CRRA 2000–2004, s 17(2).

5   CRRA 2000–2004, s 2(1).

6   CRRA 2000–2004, s 2(1).

7   *University of London Press Ltd v University Tutorial Press Ltd* [1916] 2 Ch 601.

thought. But the Act does not require that the expression be in an original or novel form, but that the work must not be copied from another work – that it should originate from the author'.[8]

University of London Press v University Tutorial Press involved the copying of mathematic questions, which were held to be original for the purposes of copyright law. At its most basic level, originality means that a work has not been copied and it is open to question whether the term has any meaning greater than this for the purposes of copyright law. The leading Irish case on this point is the decision of the Supreme Court in *Gormley v EMI Records (Ire) Ltd*,[9] in which Barron J came to the conclusion that:

> 'originality does not require the work to be unique, merely that there should have been original thought. Where there is treatment of materials already in existence it is necessary to show some new approach. It cannot be copied directly. The work must truly belong to the person claiming to be the author.'[10]

[1.06] In *Gormley v EMI Records (Ire) Ltd* the plaintiff had been a pupil in a Dublin national school in the 1960s. Her teacher, Mrs Cunningham, told her pupils many Bible stories and her pupils would recount various stories into a tape recording machine. She created a large number of such tapes containing literally hundreds of stories retold by her pupils. The plaintiff told the story 'And then there were twelve' in 1961. Many years later, the defendants gained access to Mrs Cunningham's material and selected stories were made into a tape called 'Give Up Yer Aul Sins'. The plaintiff's story was included as one of these, but while the defendants received the permission of Mrs Cunningham, they did not seek the permission of the children. The plaintiff lost in the High Court, and appealed that decision to the Supreme Court. The question that arose on appeal was whether 'the words of the story as recited by the plaintiff on the tape constitute an original literary work'.[11]

The Supreme Court dismissed the appeal stating that:

> 'It is not the words used which make the work original nor create the copyright. Where, as here material was copied it is necessary to show the necessary skill, labour and judgement to create a truly new work. It is this for which the plaintiff contends. None of this is apparent in what occurred. The plaintiff was not seeking to produce a new work but to show that she knew the story by reproducing what she had been told as faithfully as possible. It is clear that much skill, judgment and labour had been used by Mrs. Cunningham to reduce these stories to the level where they would be understood by children.'[12]

[1.07] In assessing the originality of a copied work, the Supreme Court took the view that notice must be taken of the skill, labour and judgment used to create a truly new

---

[8]   [1916] 2 Ch 601 at 608–609, cited by Reid LJ in *Ladbroke (Football) Ltd v William Hill (Football) Ltd* [1964] 1 WLR 273 at 277. Cited by Barron J in *Gormley v EMI Records (Ire) Ltd* [2000] 1 IR 74 at 90 together with *Interlego AG v Tyco Industries Inc* [1989] 1 AC 217 and *Joy Music Ltd v Sunday Pictorial Newspapers* (1920) Ltd [1960] 2 QB 60.

[9]   *Gormley v EMI Records (Ire) Ltd* [2000] 1 IR 74, [1999] 1 ILRM 178.

[10]   [2000] 1 IR 74 at 93.

[11]   [2000] 1 IR 74 at 86.

[12]   [2000] 1 IR 74 at 93.

work and not the actual work itself. The court also viewed the motivation and intention of a person as being important, since it looked at why the plaintiff recited the work and her desire to show that she knew it.

> 'It seems to me unlikely that a six-year-old would be in a position to exercise any original thought capable of being expressed when her sole purpose was to repeat the story which had been told to her by her teacher ... I do not suggest that a six-year-old can never have independent thought nor exercise sufficient skill or judgment for the purposes of obtaining a copyright. If the purpose is to copy, then a six-year-old would never have had sufficient independent originality to realise or to intend to give a different slant to the particular story which she had been told so as to make it a different thing.'[13]

The above should not be read as depriving every six-year old of the possibility that they might author a work in which copyright may subsist. But every case depends upon its facts and in this case Barron J was satisfied that the plaintiff did not have the necessary capacity for creative thought.

> 'It is not the language which creates the copyright, it is the creativity. In general originality would relate to the story rather than to the words in which it is expressed. Yet reducing words to a language which can be understood by the readers can be original: so the manner in which the language of the Bible was explained by Mrs Cunningham can be original.'[14]

This view that it is creativity which is important is consistent with decisions in England relating to disputes between possible joint authors. In *Flyde Microsystems v Key Radio Systems Ltd*[15] which concerned computer software, Laddie J held that the author must have contributed 'the right kind of skill and labour'.[16]

[1.08] Although skill and labour must be expended to produce a work, it is not necessary for a work to be 'novel' or absolutely new and it is important not to confuse the Copyright Act's requirement of originality with the Patent Act's requirement of novelty. In *Sands v McDougall Proprietary Ltd*,[17] the Australian High Court held that the word 'original' does not imply inventive originality when used in the context of copyright. It was held to be sufficient that the work be the production of something in a new form as a result of the skill, labour and judgement of the author.[18] Similarly, just writing down a note of somebody else's speech can be sufficient to give rise to copyright.[19] However, the fact that skill and labour has been expended may not be sufficient. In *Exxon Corp v*

---

13 [2000] 1 IR 74 at 93.
14 [2000] 1 IR 74 at 94.
15 *Flyde Microsystems v Key Radio Systems Ltd* [1998] FSR 449.
16 *Flyde Microsystems v Key Radio Systems Ltd* was followed in *Hadley v Kemp* [1999] EMLR 589. Park J stated that: 'contributions by the plaintiffs, however significant and skillful to the performance of the musical works are not the right kind of contributions to give them shares in the copyrights. The contributions need to be the creation of the musical works, not to the performance or interpretation of them'.
17 *Sands v McDougall Proprietary Ltd* [1917] 23 CLR 49.
18 Approved in *Express Newspapers v News (UK) Plc* [1991] FSR 36. See also *Radio Telefís Éireann v Magill TV Guide Ltd (No 2)* [1989] IR 554, [1990] ILRM 534 and *Allied Discount Card Ltd v Bord Fáilte Éireann* [1991] 2 IR 185, [1990] ILRM 811.
19 *Walter v Lane* [1900] AC 539.

Exxon Insurance Consultants[20] the Court of Appeal held that although a considerable amount of research had gone into selecting the name 'Exxon' it still was not protected as a literary work.

The fixation requirement

[1.09] The CRRA 2000–2004 provide that 'Copyright shall not subsist ... until that work is recorded in writing or otherwise'.[21]

Copyright law will only apply to one of these works if it has been recorded or fixed in some way. Therefore, if you simply think of a poem or hum a tune it will not receive the protection of copyright law, it must be recorded. The requirement of fixation is necessitated by the need for evidence, so that the existence of a particular work at a particular time can be proven. Copyright law confers a monopoly and 'there must be certainty in the subject matter of such monopoly in order to avoid injustice to the rest of the world'.[22] As was stated by Barron J in *Gormley v EMI Records (Ire) Ltd* 'the work must be recorded in order to determine the date on which it is made'.[23]

The requirement of fixation caused the Supreme Court some difficulty in *Gormley v EMI Records (Ire) Ltd*. That case considered the fixation requirement under the Copyright Act 1963, which required that a literary work be 'recorded, in writing or otherwise'.[24] The court had to decide whether a tape recording, which was basically a magnetic trace on a metal strip, could amount to 'writing' for those purposes. The court concluded that:

> 'proper construction of the provision must allow other material form to apply also to literary work. Nor is there any distinction in principle between taking down speech in shorthand and recording it on tape. Yet, in my view, the symbol which comprises the notation must be capable, without more, of being understood. This is not so with a magnetic trace. As a result, it is not entitled to protection as a literary work'.[25]

[1.10] It has to be doubtful that the Supreme Court's view of literary work in *Gormley* could apply to the CRRA 2000–2004 . By the year 2000 the Oireachtas would have been well aware of the existence of information technology and indeed makes the text available electronically itself. A work dictated to a stenographer will acquire protection from the time the shorthand note is taken down[26] and the protection available to a speech taken down in shorthand was acknowledged in *Gormley*. Copyright will subsist in a lecture given by a professor or a judgment given in court but only if it is recorded with the consent of the author. Consent may be implied: the professor will assume that his students will take notes; the judge will similarly assume that counsel will note his

---

[20] *Exxon Corpn v Exxon Insurance Consultants* [1982] RPC 69.
[21] CRRA 2000–2004, s 18(1).
[22] Per Farwell LJ in *Tate v Fullbrook* [1908] 1 KB 821 at 832–833, approved in *Green v Broadcasting Corporation of New Zealand* [1989] 2 All ER 1056 and [1989] RPC 700.
[23] *Gormley v EMI Records (Ire) Ltd* [2000] 1 IR 74 at 89. This does create a problem for works of folklore, which may only exist in an oral tradition; see CRRA 2000–2004, s 92.
[24] Copyright Act 1963, s 3(2).
[25] *Gormley v EMI Records (Ire) Ltd* [2000] 1 IR 74 at 89–90.
[26] *Donoghue v Allied Newspapers Ltd* [1938] Ch 106.

judgment. There may be limits to this consent: a student will not have the right to publish his class notes regardless of whether they are summaries[27] or verbatim transcripts.[28]

[1.11] The status of works which are recorded for the first time without the consent of the author may give rise to an interesting question as to whether they are protected under the CRRA 2000–2004.[29] This view is strengthened by the fact that although this provision of the Act is very similar to that in the UK's 1988 legislation there is no equivalent of the UK provision[30] which provides that copyright will apply to a recording of a work regardless of whether the recording was carried out with the permission of the author.[31] The introduction of a specific requirement of fixation is a change from the situation which existed under the 1963 Act, but it was a requirement of the Berne Convention[32] and the Rome Convention.[33] A performer will have the protection of copyright law, but professors and judges may not come within the Act's definition of performers as 'actors, singers, musicians, dancers or other persons who act, sing, deliver, declaim, play in, interpret or other wise perform ... works'.[34] This question may be resolved if it is kept in mind that original works are mental creations and are only recorded in a physical form. The fact that the Act will not protect something until it is recorded suggests that works can exist prior to the point at which they are recorded. This view is consistent with the provision that copyright protects expression and not ideas; until a work is recorded it exists as an idea. So the author or creator of a work will have the right to control such unauthorised first-time recordings and the copying or other dealings with them. However, their rights with regard to the term of copyright or indeed ultimate ownership of the work will not be prejudiced by this unauthorised recording. At the same time the person who does the recording of a work will be entitled to copyright in that recording. The CRRA 2000–2004 provide that copyright may subsist in a work that is recorded and also subsist in the recording of that work,[35] which may suggest that these two rights can subsist simultaneously. In *Walter v Lane*,[36] it was held that a journalist who transcribed a public speech was entitled to copyright in his record of that speech and he was successful in his action against the defendant who had given the original speech and who had copied the plaintiff's report.[37]

---

27   *Caird v Sime* [1887] 12 App Cas 327.
28   *Nichols v Pitman* [1884] 24 Ch 274.
29   CRRA 2000–2004, s 18(1).
30   UK Copyright, Designs and Patents Act 1988, s 3(2).
31   UK's CDPA 1988, s 3(3) reads 'it is immaterial for the purposes of sub-s 2 whether the work is recorded by or with the permission of the author and where it is not recorded by the author, nothing in that subsection affects the question of whether copyright subsists in the record as distinct from the work recorded.'
32   Berne Convention, art 2(2).
33   Rome Convention. For example arts 13 and 14.
34   CRRA 2000–2004, s 202(1). Section 202(2) states that a performance of a literary work includes a reading or recitation.
35   CRRA 2000–2004, s 18(3).
36   *Walter v Lane* [1990] AC 539.
37   The decision was endorsed in *Express Newspapers Plc v News (UK) Ltd* [1990] FSR 359. See also *Sands McDougall v Robinson* [1917] 23 CLR 49.

Literary works

[1.12] Copyright will subsist in a literary work, the CRRA 2000–2004 define a literary work as 'a work, including a computer program, but does not include a dramatic or musical work or an original database, which is written, spoken or sung.'

This definition would appear to be deliberately vague; its application will vary from case to case depending upon the individual facts. It may be tempting to try and formulate some concise definition of what exactly constitutes a literary work, but this would be inappropriate and unwise. The Oireachtas has never given a clear definition and courts appear unwilling to give anything more than direction limited by the facts of any individual case. In *Exxon Corp v Exxon Insurance Consultants International,* the English Court of Appeal approved the following quotation 'a literary work is intended to afford either information or instruction or pleasure in the form of literary enjoyment.'[38]

[1.13] In *RTÉ & Ors v Magill TV Guide Ltd & Ors,*[39] Lardner J offered the following definition:

> 'Literary work cannot in my judgment be confined to a work exhibiting literary art or style. Rather it has the broad sense of any written or printed composition'.[40]

[1.14] This definition is consistent with the view that the quality of a literary work is not important. In *University of London Press v University Tutorial Press*[41] Peterson J stated:

> 'the words 'literary work' cover work which is expressed in print or writing, irrespective of the question of whether the quality or style is high. The word literary seems to be used in a sense somewhat similar to the use of the word 'literature' in political or electioneering literature and refers to printed matter'.[42]

[1.15] A wide variety of material has been held to be a literary work for the purposes of copyright law, including the law list,[43] tallies for bridge parties,[44] stud books[45] and telegraph codes.[46] In *Hodges v Walsh,*[47] it was held that law digests and reports were protected and in *RTÉ and Ors v Magill TV Guide Ltd & Ors*[48] the Supreme Court held that RTÉ's radio and television schedules were literary works for the purposes of the Copyright Act 1963.

---

[38] *Hollinrake v Truswell* [1894] 3 Ch 420, per Davy LJ. But this definition is too wide to be conclusive or useful, see Laddie, p 34 and *Apple Computer v Computer Edge* [1984] FSR 496.

[39] *RTE and ors v Magill TV Guide Ltd & Ors* [1989] IR 554.

[40] *RTE and ors v Magill TV Guide Ltd & Ors* [1989] IR 554 at 563.

[41] *University of London Press v University Tutorial Press* [1916] 2 Ch 601.

[42] [1916] 2 Ch 601 at 608–609. Approved by the House of Lords in *Ladbroke (Football) Ltd v William Hill (Football) Ltd* [1964] 1 WLR 273 at 277.

[43] *Stevens & Sons v Waterlow Sons Ltd* [1877] 41 JP 37.

[44] *Stevenson v Crook* [1938] Ex (Can) 299.

[45] *Weatherby & Sons v International Horse Agency* [1910] 2 Ch 297.

[46] *Anderson & Co v Lieber Code Co* [1917] 2 KB 469.

[47] *Hodges v Walsh* [1840] 2 IR Eq R 266.

[48] *RTÉ & ors v Magill TV Guide Ltd & Ors* [1989] IR 554, [1990] ILRM 534.

[1.16] One good reason for rejecting qualitative tests is that standards change with the passage of time.[49] The European Union rejected efforts to introduce the qualitative standards into copyright law with the passing of the Directive on the Legal protection of Computer programs.[50] One motivation for this enactment was that German courts had started to develop what they termed the 'average programmer test'[51] under which a software program would only receive copyright protection if it was of a standard higher than that which might be produced by the average programmer. So the Directive on the Legal protection of Computer programs provides that 'no tests as to the qualitative or aesthetic merits of the program should be applied'.[52] However, *Fornet v Pearson*[53] suggests that a literary work must at least be the product of some rational mental process and not just a drunken scrawl. On the other hand, the meaning of a work does not have to be apparent to everyone. In *DP Anderson & Co v Lieber Code Co*[54] it was held that a complex code for sending telegrams was protected by copyright as a literary work although the code would have appeared as a meaningless collection of letters to anyone but those who had access to the means to decipher it.[55]

Descriptive titles and advertising slogans

[1.17] One important limitation on the application of copyright law is that a single word or a very short sequence of words will not be protected by copyright. The leading case on this point is the English Court of Appeal in *Exxon Corpn v Exxon Insurance Consultants* where it was held that the single word 'Exxon' was not a literary work. The English courts have also refused applications to protect the titles of books, newspapers and other works as copyright works themselves.[56] So newspaper titles using words such as 'Times',[57] 'Star',[58] and 'Herald'[59] have all been refused copyright protection. Although in *News Group Newspapers Ltd v Mirror Group Newspapers*[60] it was assumed that the mast head of *The Sun* tabloid could be protected as an artistic work. Of course, the newspaper owners could all have had other remedies available to them under the laws of passing off and trademarks. The reason for rejecting the applications in respect of

---

[49] *Sinanide v La Maison Kosmeo* [1928] 139 LT 365, CA is a relatively obscure example of a case where a judge came close to refusing copyright protection on qualitative grounds.

[50] Directive 250/91 on the Legal protection of Computer programs [1991] OJ L122/42.

[51] Hoeren, *Copyright, Software Protection in the EC*, Jongen and Meijboom (eds) (Klower Law and Taxation Publishers), p. 76.

[52] Directive 250/91, Recital 8.

[53] *Fornet v Pearson* [1897] 14 TLR 82.

[54] *DP Anderson & Co v Lieber Code Co* (1917) 2 KB 469.

[55] Similarly, in *Express Newspapers v Liverpool Daily Post and Echo Plc* [1985] 3 All ER 680 cards which were distributed with a newspaper contained letters which were arranged in a 5 X 5 pattern were held to be literary works.

[56] See *Coppinger on Copyright* p 970. Of course, protection may well be available under the law of passing-off and trademarks if the owner has been prudent in registering their title.

[57] *George Outram & Co Ltd v The London Evening Newspapers Co Ltd* [1911] 27 TLR 231.

[58] *Morning Star Co-Operative Society ltd v Express Newspapers Ltd* [1979] FSR 113.

[59] *Tamworth Herald Co Ltd v Thomson Free Newspapers Ltd* [1991] FSR 337.

[60] *News Group Newspapers Ltd v Mirror Group Newspapers* [1989] FSR 126.

these titles was they were all wholly or partially descriptive. Similarly, the title of a television or radio programme cannot be copyrighted[61] or the title of a book[62] or song[63] although issues of misrepresentation may arise.[64]

[1.18] The copying of advertising slogans is probably better dealt with by the law of passing off and trademarks. Those who have tried to protect such slogans by way of copyright law appear to have met with little success. The slogan 'youthful appear is a social necessity not a luxury'[65] was refused the protection of copyright law and it has been argued that the courts appear to be denying protection on the grounds that the slogans and titles at issue are too short.[66] However, in *Kirk v Fleming*[67] a slogan containing four sentences and 28 words did not qualify for copyright protection.[68] A further issue here is that courts may reject protection for short phrases as they lack the necessary skill and judgment. This may be unfair as advertising copyrighters may put extraordinary amounts of work, research and creativity into selecting and drafting a particular slogan; however, in the *Exxon* case the plaintiffs had also done a large amount of research but still failed to qualify for protection.[69]

Computer programs[70]

Musical works

[1.19] The CRRA 2000–2004 define a musical work as 'a work consisting of music, but (that) does not include any words, or action, intended to be sung, spoken or performed with the music'.[71] So the melody of a song will be protected but not the lyrics or the choreography which accompanies it. The Act contains no requirement that music be recorded in writing or other notation, although it must be fixed in some form. It would seem that how music is heard is more important than how it is recorded or stored. In

---

61 *Green v Broadcasting Corpn of New Zealand* [1989] RPC 469.
62 *Dicks v Yates* [1881] 18 Ch 76.
63 *Francis Day & Hunter Ltd v Twentieth Century Fox* [1940] AC 112.
64 *Chappell v Sheard* [1885] 2 K & J 117and *Willard King Organisation v United Telecasters (Sydney) Ltd* [1981] 2 NSWLR 547.
65 *Sinanide v La Maison Kosmeo* [1928] 139 LT 365.
66 Laddie, p 51.
67 *Kirk v Fleming* [1928–35] MCC 44.
68 See also *Noah v Shuba* [1991] FSR 14.
69 The Misleading Advertising Directive 84/450 (1984) OJ L250/17 as amended by Directive 97/55 (1997) OJ L 290/18 appears to create an exception from intellectual property law for comparative advertising. Recital 15 states that '…such use of anothers trademark, tradename or other distinguishing marks does not breach this exclusive right in cases where it complies with the conditions laid down by this Directive, the intended target being solely to distinguish between them and thus to highlight differences objectively Therefore, the imitation of a title or slogan for the purposes of the comparative advertising under the Directive is exempted by this Directive. This exemption applies not just to trademarks but also to 'trade names' which might be protected by copyright.
70 See Chapter 4.
71 CRRA 2000–2004, s 2(1).

Austin v Columbia[72] new arrangements in an opera were created by the plaintiff, which proved very popular. The defendant employed a composer to make his own arrangements from old tunes, which sounded similar to the plaintiff's work. In view of the fact that the defendant's piece had been derived from the plaintiff's and sounded similar, the fact that the notes used were not precisely the same was no defence.[73] The use of what might be termed the 'hearing' test may serve to resolve a potential difficulty in distinguishing between the protection afforded to computer programs and musical works stored on a computer in formats such as MP3. A computer program can be written which will create sounds in the same way as an MP3 file and it would appear to be inconsistent to protect one work as a program because it is written in JAVA and protect another as a musical work because it is saved as an MP3 file. Both types of work are stored electronically as a stream of 0s and 1s, however, the program may operate to cause figures to appear on the computer's VDU and the music file will cause a song to be played on its speakers. It is true that the MP3 file cannot be played without the intervention of a computer program but application programs such as Microsoft Word will not run unless an operating system such as Windows 98 is also in use. The difference between the protection of computer programs (which are protected as literary works) and musical works is significant. Distinguishing between musical files and computer programs by converting them into their human readable form, some musical works should be capable of being reduced to a form of musical notation such as sheet music, which the computer program cannot. But that distinction might not apply in the case of music that was formulated exclusively on a computer, to which the conventional rules of composition and notation may not be applicable.

Artistic works

Photographs

[1.20] The copyright protection of photographs is discussed in Chapter 5.

Painting

[1.21] The Act contains no definition of the term 'painting', in view of the various modern schools of art; the courts would have to take a very broad view of what constitutes a painting. Although it would appear that some form of paint and canvas is necessary, the courts have been unwilling to stretch this definition to the application of make-up to the human face. In *Merchandising Corpn of America Inc v Harpbond Inc*[74] a pop singer[75] had created what he termed his 'Prince Charming' style. This particularly involved the application of make-up to his face to create a blue band between two red bands on one of his cheeks. The defendants had produced a poster which showed the plaintiff made up in this style; the plaintiff then sought an injunction claiming that the

---

72 *Austin v Columbia* (1917–1923) MCC 398.
73 See also *Francis Day Hunter v Bron* (1963) Ch 587.
74 *Merchandising Corpn of America Inc v Harpbond Inc* [1983] FSR 32.
75 Adam Goddard whose stage name was 'Adam Ant'.

application of make-up to his face was a 'painting'. His application failed, the court stating that:

> 'A painting must be on a surface of some kind. The surface upon which the startling make-up was put was Mr Goddard's face and, if there was a painting, it must be the marks plus Mr Goddard's face. If the marks are taken off the face there cannot be a painting. A painting is not an idea: it is an object; and paint without a surface is not a painting. Make-up, as such, however, idiosyncratic it may be as an idea cannot possibly be a painting for the purpose of the Copyright Act 1956.'

The apparent breadth of this statement has been criticised and it has been suggested that the proper grounds for this decision should have been that three coloured lines on a face were too trite to be an original painting and that the plaintiff should have failed because his alleged work lacked the necessary originality.[76] Still, if the above quotation were to be adopted by the Irish courts in relation to art work generated on a computer, it would support the proposition that a work generated exclusively in a computer's memory is not a painting as it lacks a 'surface'. But as suggested above to hold that paintings could not be generated on a computer would give rise to an anachronistic result.

Drawings, diagrams, maps, charts, plans

[1.22] The above terms are probably interchangeable as a map could also be a drawing or a plan or chart. A conflict has occurred between the protection available to design material and that available to drawings of designs. In the UK copyright protection had been extended to drawings for standard vehicle parts such as exhausts[77] and gear boxes.[78] However, the Oireachtas rejected this extension in the Copyright (Amendment) Act 1987 and s 79 of the 2000 Act now provides that commercially reproducing a three dimensional object from 'a work in two dimensions (other than a work relating to a work of architecture)' will not generally amount to an infringement in the copyright of the two dimensional work.

Engravings, etchings, lithographs, woodcuts, prints or similar works

[1.23] Engraving means to inscribe, cut or carve on a hard surface using a sharp implement whereas etching uses acid and a lithograph uses ink-rejecting substances to the same end.[79] A woodcut is an engraved wooden block. In the context of this section, prints may be simply the product of these now relatively obsolete printing processes. But there is no reason why the section should be read in this limited way and prints could be generated in any way such as using a laser or bubble jet printer. The use of the term 'similar works' should ensure that this section is interpreted broadly and it could be argued that a file of electronic data held on a computer which can instruct an attached printer to produce a print depicting a dog or other image has the same function as woodcuts, engravings or lithographs. But caution should be applied before taking this

---

[76] Laddie, p. 196.

[77] *British Leyland Motor Corporation v Amstrong Patents Co Ltd* [1982] FSR 481.

[78] *Nichols v Rees* [1979] RPC 127.

[79] The *Concise Oxford English Dictionary* (8th edn, 1990). See also the protection of currency engravings under Chapter 24 of the CRRA 2000–2004 .

sort of analogy too far. In *Wham-O Manufacturing Co v Lincoln Industries*[80] the New Zealand Court of Appeal held that a mould for a Frisbee was an engraving and the actual Frisbee was a print. This approach was rejected by the Australian courts in *Greenfield Products v Rover-Scott Bonnar Ltd*[81] and it has been suggested that the English courts would concur.

Collages

[1.24] The copyright protection of collages is discussed in Chapter 4.

Sculptures

[1.25] The Act simply defines a sculpture as 'including any cast or model made for the purposes of sculpture. It should come as no surprise that this category of work has been expanded far beyond the product of sculptors such as Henry Moore. Although, it has been held that toy soldiers[82] and the plaster shapes used to produce the mould of sandwich maker parts were held to be sculptures,[83] the Irish courts might be unwilling to hold that something of this nature could truly be described as an artistic work. These interpretations of the term may be contrasted with the dictionary definition of sculpture as 'the art of making forms, often representational, in the round or in relief by chiselling stone, carving wood, modelling wood, casting metal etc'.[84] Computer Assisted Design (CAD) programs that can be used to design three dimensional objects within a computers memory are now commonplace. If such a program is connected to an appropriate device such as a saw it may be used to produce an object such as an artistic sculpture. It may be anachronistic to extend protection to wooden casts or mouldings[85] and refuse it to data which is kept for the purpose of producing a sculpture when both processes have the same object. It will depend on the facts of any particular case as to whether the products of such a process are the product of the creative process necessary to make them artistic.[86]

Works of architecture

[1.26] Works of architecture can be either 'buildings or models for buildings'[87] and 'building' includes 'any structure'.[88] Although it has been held that a building means a block of brick or stone work covered in by a roof,[89] a garden has also been held to be a structure.[90] The question of creativity may be at issue in deciding eligibility for

---

[80] *Wham-O Manufacturing Co v Lincoln Industries* [1985]RPC 127.
[81] *Greenfield Products v Rover-Scott Bonnar Ltd* [1990] 17 IPR 417.
[82] *Britain v Hanks Bros* [1902] 86 LT 764.
[83] *Breville Europe plc & ors v Thorn EMI Domestic Appliances Ltd* [1995] FSR 77.
[84] The *Concise Oxford English Dictionary* (8th edn, 1990).
[85] As occurred in *Wham-O Manufacturing Co v Lincoln Industries* [1985]RPC 127 and *Greenfield Products v Rover-Scott Bonnar Ltd* [1990] 17 IPR 417.
[86] Laddie, p 204.
[87] CRRA 2000–2004, s 2(1).
[88] CRRA 2000–2004, s 2(1).
[89] *Moir v Williams* [1892] 1 QB 264.
[90] *Vincent v Universal* [1928–35] MCC 275.

protection and the broad definition of building as any structure means that some forms of sculpture might alternatively qualify for protection under this heading. Note that models are only protected where they are for buildings.

Works of artistic craftsmanship

[1.27] This category would appear to be a catch-all to protect works such as embroidery and pottery which might not be protected otherwise.[91] One type of art work which might come into this category is 'installation art' such as 'Carl Andre's bricks, in Stone Circles created by Richard Long, in Rachel Whiteread's house, in the living sculptures of Gilbert and George'[92] The definition of artistic craftsmanship is highly problematic, which means that creators of such works may prefer to rely upon categories such as collages and sculptures.

Dramatic works

[1.28] This term is defined as including 'a choreographic work or a work of mime'.[93] It is not necessary for any words to be spoken in order to qualify for protection but it is essential for the protection that the work be written down or recorded in some form. So improvisational comedy will not be protected unless it is video taped or recorded by taking notes.[94] Dramatic works are a separate category of works distinct from literary works and once a play is written down or otherwise recorded, that writing will be protected as a literary work. It is the performance that is protected as a dramatic work and converting the work from a dramatic work to a literary work and vice versa would give rise to a claim for infringement for adaptation.[95] In *Fuller v Blackpool Winter Gardens*,[96] it was held that singing 'Daisy, Daisy' while dressed as a cyclist was not a dramatic piece because no acting was required to present it. Television programs give rise to problems. In *Television NZ v Newsmonitor Services*[97] it was held that the news and current affairs programmes comprising video and discuss lacked the choreography to make them a dramatic work. In *Green v Broadcasting Corpn of New Zealand*,[98] the Privy Council stated that 'a dramatic work must have sufficient unity to be capable of performance and that the features claimed ... being unrelated to each other ... lack that essential characteristic In this case, the format of *Opportunity Knocks* which included using a clapometer, did not qualify as a dramatic work. In the Canadian case of *FWS*

---

[91] *Coppinger on Copyright* p 85.

[92] *Creation Records v News Group Newspapers* [1997] EMLR 444.

[93] CRRA 2000–2004, s 2(1). The 1963 Act defined dramatic works as including 'a choreographic work or entertainment in dumb show if reduced to writing in the form in which the work or entertainment is to be presented, but does not include a cinematograph film, as distinct from a scenario or script for a cinematograph film Section 2.

[94] See *Tate v Thomas* [1921] 1 Ch 503 where the creator of the scenes characters and some lines of a play was held not to be an author of the play as others had composed the major part of the lines, lyrics and music of the play. Also see *Tate v Fullbrooke* [1908] 1 KB 821.

[95] CRRA 2000–2004, s 43(2) (a)(ii).

[96] *Fuller v Blackpool Winter Gardens* [1895] 2 QB 429.

[97] *Television NZ v Newsmonitor Services* [1994] 2 NZLR 91.

[98] *Green v Broadcasting Corpn of New Zealand* [1989] 2 All ER 1056.

Joint Sports v Copyright Board,[99] a sports game was not protected as a dramatic work even though it contained choreographic elements.[100]

[1.29] In *Norowzian v Arks Ltd (No 2)*[101] it was held that 'a work of dance or mime must be capable of being danced or mimed'. This case related to the Guinness advertisement, *Anticipation,* which involved an actor dancing to music. At the time of hearing the case, the plaintiff had become a successful director of advertising films but in 1992 in an effort to get work he had created a show reel, entitled *Joy,* which he sent to advertising agencies. This film is 'a striking film which made a big impression on those to whom a copy of it was sent'. The defendants produced their own film using similar techniques including the 'jump cutting' editing technique employed by the plaintiff in producing their advertisement. The plaintiff sued for infringement of his dramatic work but failed, Rattee J stating:

> 'I accept that, had the finished film been a recording of the dance routine performed by the actor in *Joy* in front of the camera, it might well have presented a recording of a work of dance or mime and therefore, a dramatic work. It does not. A large, probably the major, part of the effect of the film is the 'quirky' or surreal effect produced by the editing techniques used by Mr Norowzian in the cutting room after shooting of the film was complete, and in particular, the technique of jump cutting. The finished result is something very different from a recording on film of the dance or mime routine performed by the actor. The result is that, when the film is known to the viewer, what he sees is a sequence of movements apparently performed by the actor, but which in reality was not, and could not physically have been, performed by any actor. For the effect of the editing techniques used by Mr Norowzian has been to excise certain parts of the sequence of movements performed by the actor and to join together the parts immediately preceding and immediately following the parts excised. The result is striking, but unreal. No human performer could have performed the routine displayed by the film. It would be a physical impossibility'.[102]

Although Rattee J concluded that this film did not constitute a dramatic work, he went on to examine whether it was possible that there had been copying between the two works. Having viewed the two films, he noted that although, the two dancers did employ similar individual movements, they were performed in different sequences in each film. But he found that 'what are much more strikingly similar between the two films, are the filming and editing styles used by the respective directors'.[103] Since these styles were not protected by copyright, there was no infringement.

---

99 *FWS Joint Sports v Copyright Board* [1991] 22 IPR 429.
100 Also *Seltzer v Sunbrook* 22 F Supp 622.
101 *Norowzian v Arks Ltd (No 2)* [1999] EMLR 67.
102 The decision of Rattee J was appealed, but the appeal was dismissed see 143 SJ LB 279, (1999) The Times 14 November.
103 'Both use a fixed or 'locked off' camera position. Both use varying camera speeds and, in editing, both use jump cutting techniques which, together with the varying speeds and the sepia tinted, colourless settings produce an effect of somewhat disturbing unreality or quirkiness

Films

[1.30] The CRRA 2000–2004 make it clear that all films are protected, not just original films.[104] It would appear that this has the effect of actually limiting the protection available since the creative process which may be a vital part of creating film is not protected. However, protection might be available for the script of the film. This limitation can be compared to the very broad protection available to computer programs and the preparatory work and design materials used to create them. The limitations of this protection are illustrated by the case of *Norowzian v Arks Ltd (No 1)*[105] where Steinfeld QC[106] held that 'you either copy the film or you do not'. These facts are the same as in *Norowzian v Arks Ltd (No 2)* above. The difference is that in the first case the plaintiff claimed copyright infringement in his film as opposed to his dramatic work. The allegation was that 'what the defendants have commissioned to be made is what I think called in the vernacular a re-shoot of the plaintiffs film but not copying a single frame Steinfeld QC considered that:

> 'a re-shooting of a film sequence in which not a single frame of the original copyright film has been included as is the case here, cannot in my judgement be said to be a copy of the film.'

[1.31] The defendants had been inspired by elements of the plaintiff's work, but had not copied it directly. Therefore the claim failed.[107] The CRRA 2000–2004 would appear to suggest that copyright may subsist separately in at least the screenplay, the dialogue and the music of the film as well as the film itself.

[1.32] Films are broadly defined as 'a fixation on any medium from which a moving image may, by any means, be produced, perceived or communicated through a device'.[108] So the definition is not limited to films shot on chemical film and would extend to a magnetic video tape or digital images stored on a computers hard drive. Computer games are now frequently of such high quality that they are indistinguishable from films or cartoons; an allegation that the defendant had infringed the plaintiff's film copyright in a computer game was made, but not argued, in *Nova Productions v Mazooma Games*.[109]

Sound recordings

[1.33] Copyright will not subsist in a sound recording until the first fixation of the sound recording is made.[110] The term 'sound recording' is defined as meaning 'a fixation of sounds, or of the representations thereof, from which the sounds are capable of being reproduced, regardless of the medium on which the recording is made, or the method by

---

[104] CRRA 2000–2004, s 17(1).

[105] *Norowzian v Arks Ltd (No 1)* [1998] FSR 394.

[106] Sitting as a deputy Judge in the English High Court.

[107] See also *Telmak Teleproducts Australia Pty Ltd v Bond International Pty Ltd* [1985] 5 IPR 203.

[108] CRRA 2000–2004, s 2(1).

[109] *Nova Productions v Mazooma Games* [2006] EWHC 24 (Ch), [2006] All ER (D) 131 (Jan).

[110] CRRA 2000–2004, s 19.

which the sounds are reproduced'.[111] This protection will be in addition to the protections available for musical works and performances although it does not extend to 'sound-alike' records.[112] The development of digital technologies has created a market for 'cleaned up' versions of old records without the hiss and static of the original recording medium. Such a cleaned up record would be protected by this provision.

Typographical arrangements

[1.34] The CRRA 2000–2004 provide that copyright subsists in 'the typographical arrangement of published editions'.[113] In *The Newspaper Licensing Agency Ltd v Marks & Spencer Plc*[114] the plaintiff owned the copyright in the typographical arrangements in a large number of newspapers. The defendants subscribed to a newspaper cutting agency which would provide it with copies of articles of interest from a wide variety of newspapers. The plaintiff sued claiming that these copies infringed their copyright. However the House of Lords held that since none of the cuttings copied by the defendant sufficiently reproduced the layout of any page to amount to a substantial part of its typographical arrangement, there was no breach of that copyright.

Databases

[1.35] The copyright protection of databases is discussed in Chapter 14.

Performers' rights

[1.36] The CRRA 2000–2004 creates rights for performers. The Act defines a performance as meaning:

> 'a performance of any actors, singers, musicians, dancers or other persons who act, sing, deliver, declaim, play in, interpret or otherwise perform literary, dramatic, musical or artistic works or expressions of works of folklore, which is a live performance given by one or more individuals, and shall include a performance of a variety act or any similar presentation.'[115]

A performance of a literary work will includes 'a reading or recitation'[116] and the performance of a dramatic work includes a 'a choreographic work or a work of mime'.[117] A recording of a performance means any fixation 'made directly or indirectly from the live performance ... made from a broadcast of, or cable programme including, the performance, or ... made directly or indirectly from another recording of the performance'.[118]

---

[111] CRRA 2000–2004, s 2(1).

[112] *Records Australia v Telmark Teleproducts (Aust) Pty Ltd* (1987) 9 IPR 440.

[113] CRRA 2000–2004, s 17(1), s 2(1), defines published edition in this context as meaning a published edition of the whole or any part of one or more literary, dramatic or musical works or original databases See *Machinery Market v Sheen publishing* [1983] FSR 431.

[114] *The Newspaper Licensing Agency Ltd v Marks & Spencer Plc* [2001] UKHL 38, [2003] 1 AC 551.

[115] CRRA 2000–2004, s 202(1).

[116] CRRA 2000–2004, s 202(2).

[117] CRRA 2000–2004, s 202(3).

[118] CRRA 2000–2004, s 202(4).

Authorship

[1.37] The whole purpose of copyright law is to encourage the creativity of authors. This makes the identification of the author a key function of copyright law. In general, the author of a copyright work will be the first owner and any subsequent owners will take their title from him or her.[119] The whole function of copyright is to confer certain rights, such as the ability to control copying or adaptation, on that owner. Even if the author does not retain ownership, his or her identity is important, as the date of their death will determine the date on which the copyright term expires.[120] The inclusion of moral rights in the Act means that the author will retain certain rights even if they do not retain ownership.[121] The CRRA 2000–2004 state that the term 'author' means 'the person who creates a work'.[122]

[1.38] Under the CRRA 2000–2004 the term author will include the following:

'(a)   in the case of a sound recording, the producer;

(b)   in the case of a film, the producer and the principal director;

(c)   in the case of a broadcast, the person making the broadcast or in the case of a broadcast which relays another broadcast by reception and immediate retransmission, without alteration, the person making that other broadcast;

(d)   in the case of a cable programme, the person providing the cable programme service in which the programme is included;

(e)   in the case of a typographical arrangement of a published edition, the publisher;

(f)   in the case of a work which is computer-generated, the person by whom the arrangements necessary for the creation of the work are undertaken;

(g)   in the case of an original database, the individual or group of individuals who made the database; and

(h)   in the case of a photograph, the photographer.'[123]

[1.39] As noted above, creativity is not novelty: a person can create a work through the expenditure of skill and labour as opposed to novel thought. The identification of the author of a work may not be straightforward. In *Cummins v Bond*,[124] a psychic medium wrote a work called *The Chronicles of Cleo Phas* during a séance. The defendant edited the work and then sought to publish it. The resulting litigation was complicated by the fact that 'the plaintiff and her witness and the defendant are all of opinion, and I do not doubt that the opinion is an honest one – that the true originator of all that is to be found in these documents is some being no longer inhabiting this world'.

However, Eve J held that he could only decide authorship with regard to those alive when the work first came into existence and held that the plaintiff was the author. This

---

[119] CRRA 2000–2004, s 17(4) provides that copyright will not subsist in a work unless the requirements for copyright protection specified in chapter 18 (sections 182-190) of Part II with respect to qualification are complied with.

[120] CRRA 2000–2004, Pt II Ch 3.

[121] CRRA 2000–2004, Pt II Ch 7.

[122] CRRA 2000–2004, s 21.

[123] *A & M Records Ltd v Video Collection International Ltd.*

[124] *Cummins v Bond* [1927] 1 Ch 167.

decision can be contrasted with the normal position that the person who merely takes down a work, such as a secretary, dictated by another will not be the author.[125] On the other hand, where a public speech is given, a reporter who takes down a note of the speech will be the author of his own work[126] and the speaker will be the author of his speech. This is acknowledged by the CRRA 2000–2004 which state that 'copyright may subsist in a work that is recorded and may subsist in the recording of a work'.[127]

[1.40] The reporter will have to do something more than merely taking dictation and would have to exercise some skill and judgment in creating his work. In some circumstances, a reporter could even become the entire author of a work. In *Donoghue v Allied Newspapers*,[128] a racehorse jockey recounted various stories to a journalist who then wrote a series of articles for the *News of the World*. In subsequent litigation it was held that the jockey was not the author of the articles, as the journalist had given the articles their literary form. In *Gormley v EMI Records (Ire) Ltd*, it was suggested that certain people might not have the capacity to be authors. Barron J stated

> 'It seems to me unlikely that a six-year-old would be in a position to exercise any original thought capable of being expressed when her sole purpose was to repeat the story which had been told to her by her teacher ... I do not suggest that a six-year-old can never have independent thought nor exercise sufficient skill or judgment for the purposes of obtaining a copyright. If the purpose is to copy, then a six-year-old would never have had sufficient independent originality to realise or to intend to give a different slant to the particular story which she had been told so as to make it a different thing.'[129]

It may seem unfair to refuse copyright protection to a six-year-old girl and grant it to computer-generated works in the 2000 Act. But the CRRA 2000–2004 state that the author of a computer-generated work is the 'person by whom the arrangements necessary for the creation of the work are undertaken'.[130] In *Gormley*, the Supreme Court appeared to view the plaintiff's teacher as being this person and the plaintiff as simply an automaton who reproduced her teacher's work.

---

[125] See *Donoghue v Allied Newspapers Ltd* [1938] Ch 106.

[126] *Walter v Lane* [1990] AC 539; *Express Newspapers Plc v News (UK) Plc* [1991] FSR 36.

[127] CRRA 2000–2004, s 18(3).

[128] *Donoghue v Allied Newspapers* [1938] Ch 106.

[129] *Gormley v EMI Records (Ire) Ltd* [2000] 1 IR 74 at 93. A cautious approach should be taken before applying this dictum to other cases. The events, which gave rise to the work, had occurred in 1961, the Supreme Court was trying to assess authorship in 1998. After 37 years the plaintiff must have had difficulty recollecting a school day when she was a six-year-old. The view of the Supreme Court would be consistent with the view that young children are doli incapax (Children's Act 2001, s 52) that is incapable of committing crime. It is also consistent with the decision in *Fornet v Pearson* [1897] 14 TLR 82 where it was held that a drunken scrawl was not protected by copyright, as the author's rational faculties were virtually non-existent at the time the writing was made.

[130] CRRA 2000–2004, s 21.

Sound recordings

[1.41] The CRRA 2000–2004 make it clear that where a sound recording is produced, it is the producer who is the author of the work.[131] This definition is consistent with the view of the Supreme Court in *Gormley v EMI Records (Ire) Ltd.*[132] Since the Act provides that copyright may subsist in a work that is recorded and in the recording of that work, it may be necessary to distinguish between the two. In this case, 'much of the emphasis placed on the plaintiff's work is the charm in the way the story is recited. Emphasis was placed on the Dublin pronunciation of the word 'certainly'. But that charm belongs to the sound recording and not to the literary work.'

Films

[1.42] Films are works of joint authorship by definition. The CRRA 2000–2004 state that the author of a film is the producer and principle director.[133] The producer is defined as 'the person by whom the arrangements necessary for the making of the ... film ... are undertaken'.[134] The Act does not define 'principle director' and of course they may be the same person. In *Adventure Film v Tulley*,[135] it was held that a person who had been engaged as cameraman and who might have contributed some element to the direction of the film was not an author. It is very expensive to make a film and copyright law may follow the money to identify the author of a film, as opposed to examining the creative

---

[131] The Acts define a producer of a sound recording as 'the person by whom the arrangements necessary for the making of the ... sound recording, ... are undertaken CRRA 2000–2004, s 2(1). The producer of the sound recording for copyright purposes may be a different person from the individual who is might be termed 'Producer' by the industry. In *A & M Records Ltd v Video Collection International Ltd* [1995] EMLR 25, a pair of ice skaters, wished to have two musical works recorded to accompany their ice-skating. A conductor was employed to produce this and he then employed an arranger, a dispute arose over which of these two men was in fact the person who had made the arrangements necessary for the making the recording. The conductor had done the following work:

> Commissioned and paid for the musical arrangements of the arranger.
>
> Booked and paid for the studio.
>
> Engaged and paid for the musicians.
>
> Engaged and paid for the scoring, a sound engineer and the fixer.
>
> Paid for all incidental expenses such as taxis and food.

However, he was held not be the producer. Rather it was the agent of the ice skater's production company who had originally arranged for the conductor carry out the above work. Of course, the copyrights in the performance recorded and the musical work performed may also exist in parallel with the copyright in the sound recording.

[132] *Gormley v EMI Records (Ire) Ltd* [1999] 1 ILRM 178.

[133] Minimum Notice and Terms of Employment Act 1973-2001, s 21(b).

[134] CRRA 2000–2004, s 2(1) in *Century Communications v Mayfair* [1993] EMLR 376, it was held that a company, which had initiated a film, organised and paid for it was the author and not a Chinese company which had helped in the shooting of the film.

[135] *Adventure Film v Tulley* (1982) The Times, 14 October 1982.

imputs. So *In re FG (Films) Ltd*,[136] the company which actually provided the finance, and not a shell company under its control, was held to be the author.[137]

Broadcasts and cable programmes

[1.43] The author of a broadcast is the person making the broadcast. In the case of a broadcast that relays another broadcast by reception and immediate retransmission, without alteration, then it will be the person making the first broadcast.[138] The CRRA 2000–2004 define the person making the broadcast as:

> 'the person transmitting the programme, where he or she has responsibility to any extent for its contents, and … any person providing the programme who makes the arrangements necessary for its transmission with the person transmitting that programme'.[139]

The author of a cable programme will be the person providing the cable programme service in which the programme is included.[140]

Photographs

[1.44] The CRRA 2000–2004 states that the photographer will be the author of a photograph.[141]

Computer-generated works

[1.45] A great number of works are generated by computer, which can range from literary works written on a word processing package to complex designs produced by CAD programs. Although the Act makes provisions for computer generated works it will not recognise an inanimate object as being the author. Instead, the Act states that where a work is computer-generated, the author will be the person by whom the

---

[136] *Re FG (Films) Ltd* [1953] 1 WLR 383.

[137] See also: *Beggars Banquet Records v Carlton Television* [1993] EMLR 349; *Secretary of State v Central Broadcasting* [1993] EMLR 253; but note that as these are interlocutory decisions both are somewhat unsatisfactory.

[138] CRRA 2000–2004, s 21(c).

[139] CRRA 2000–2004, s 6(1).

[140] CRRA 2000–2004, s 21(d).

[141] CRRA 2000–2004, s 21(h). See Garnett, *Copyright in Photographs,* EIPR, Vol 22 Issue 5. In *Creation Records v News Group Newspapers* [1997] EMLR 444 the scene for a photograph had been set or arranged by a member of the band Oasis and it was argued that therefore he was the author of a photograph taken without his or the bands consent and not the photographer. This was rejected by Lloyd J who stated that: 'it seems to be that ordinarily the creator of the photograph is the person who takes it. There may be cases where one person sets up the scene to be photographed (the position and angle of the camera and all the necessary settings) and directs a second person to press the shutter release button at a moment chosen by the first, in which case it would be the first, not the second, who creates the photograph. There may also be cases of collaboration between the person behind the camera and one or more others in which the actual photographer has greater input, although no complete control of the creation of the photograph, in which case it may be a work of joint creation and joint authorship In the present case it seems to be me unarguable that anyone other than [the photographer] is the creator of his photograph.'

arrangements necessary for the creation of the work are undertaken.[142] This would not necessarily be the programmer who wrote a program to generate works, but might be a person who bought a copy of that program and initiated the 'run' command. Presumably, the person who makes the arrangements to create a computer-generated work can be compared to the producer of a film or sound recording. This must be reconciled with s 2(1) of the CRRA 2000–2004 which defines computer-generated works as meaning 'that the work is generated by computer in circumstances where the author of the work is not an individual'.[143]

This appears to anticipate that the skill, labour and judgment used to create a work would be provided directly by a computer but that it will only be a tool of a living person. This point was at issue in *Express Newspapers Plc v Liverpool Daily Post & Echo Plc*[144] where the plaintiff ran a competition in which a reader could match letters in the paper with those on a card to win a prize. The defendants copied these letters and when sued argued that because the letters were generated by a computer program, neither the plaintiffs nor their employees were the authors. However, the court held that the computer program was merely a tool of the plaintiff's employee who had written it and who was the author of the work.

Databases

[1.46] Where an original database is created, then the individual, or group of individuals, who made the database will be the author.[145] The distinction between a database and its contents which may have separate authors, must be kept in mind.

Joint authorship

[1.47] The Act states that a work of joint authorship means 'a work produced by the collaboration of two or more authors in which the contribution of each author is not distinct from that of the other author or authors'.[146] It is important to distinguish between works of joint authors, such as songs created by a band together, and collective works such as encyclopaedias or any work written in distinct parts by different authors or in which works or parts of works of different authors are incorporated.[147] In *Navitaire Inc v*

---

[142] CRRA 2000–2004, s 21(f).

[143] CRRA 2000–2004, s 2(1).

[144] *Express Newspapers Plc v Liverpool Daily Post & Echo Plc* [1985] FSR 306.

[145] CRRA 2000–2004, s 21(g).

[146] CRRA 2000–2004, s 22(1).

[147] CRRA 2000–2004, s 16(5). A work of joint authorship cannot be a collective work see *Redwood Music Ltd v Feldman & Co Ltd* [1979] RPC 385. The CRRA 2000–2004 further state that a film will be treated as a work of joint authorship by the producer and principal director, unless they are the same person (s 22(2)). Similarly a broadcast will be treated as a work of joint authorship if more than one person makes the broadcast and the contribution of each person is not distinct from that of any of the others involved in making that broadcast (s 22(3)). Finally, it is made clear that references to the author of a work will, unless otherwise provided, be construed, in relation to a work of joint authorship, as references to all of the authors of the work (s 22(4)).

Easyjet Airline Co Bulletproof Technologies,[148] Pumfrey J ruled that a computer program 'did not have joint authors, since it is perfectly possible to distinguish the contributions of the various authors'.[149]

[1.48] There have been several English decisions on the issue of joint authorship and these are particularly useful as the UK Copyright Designs and Patents Act 1988 contains a provision that is identical to that in the CRRA 2000–2004. In *Ray v Classic FM*,[150] the plaintiff was very well known in the UK for his encyclopaedic knowledge of classical music, and had been engaged as a consultant music advisor. He advised on the categorisation of the defendant's catalogue and database of classical music. At the time of judgment this included some 50,000 tracks. The plaintiff maintained that he was the sole author of the music catalogue, which was then used to create an electronic database. Lightman J stated that:

> 'A joint author is accordingly a person (1) who collaborates with another author in the production of a work; (2) who (as an author) provides a significant creative input; and (3) whose contribution is not distinct from that of the other author. He must contribute to the 'production' of the work and create something protected by copyright, which finds its way into the finished work ... A joint author must participate in the writing and share responsibility for the form of expression in the literary work. He must accordingly do more than contribute ideas to an author: he must be an author (or creator) of the work in question.'

[1.49] Lightman J adopted the view of Laddie J in *Cala Homes (South) Ltd v Alfred McAlpine Homes East Ltd*[151] that there is no restriction on the manner in which a joint authors' contribution may be funnelled and in particular there is no requirement that each of the authors must have exercised penmanship.[152] But in Lightman J's opinion what is required is 'something which approximates to penmanship. What is essential is a direct responsibility for what actually appears on the paper.' He distinguished the *Cala* case because in that case a director of the plaintiffs had provided a very detailed input including many of the design features in which architects were instructed to prepare plans. These were regularly vetted to ensure that they concurred with the director's image and in this exceptional case Lightman J suggested that the architects were functioning as 'scribes' for the director. In *Ray v Classic FM* Lightman J rejected the suggestion of the defendants that the plaintiff was functioning as a scribe for the defendant's team and held that the defendant's input was insufficient to make the defendant a joint author. To merely contribute ideas is not sufficient to become a joint author and this is plain from s 17(3) which provides that copyright does not protect the

---

[148] *Navitaire Inc v Easyjet Airline Co Bulletproof Technologies* [2004] EWHC 1725 (Ch), [2006] RPC 111.

[149] [2004] EWHC 1725 (Ch), [2006] RPC 111, para 92.

[150] *Ray v Classic FM* [1998] FSR 622.

[151] *Cala Homes (South) Ltd v Alfred McAlpine Homes East Ltd* [1995] FSR 818.

[152] *Flyde Microsystems v Key Radio Systems* [1998] FSR 449 'First it is necessary to determine whether the putative author has contributed the right kind of skill and labour. If he has then it is necessary to decide whether his contribution was big enough. The latter issue in particular is a matter of fact and degree.'

ideas and principles that underlie any element of a work. It is not enough to think up the plot of a play or suggest a comic routine[153] or to reminisce to a ghostwriter.[154]

[1.50] Jamming or spontaneously devising songs on stage or in a recording studio may be creatively productive but legally inadvisable. In *Stuart v Barrett*[155]:

> 'someone started to play and the rest joined in and improvised and improved the original idea. The final piece was indeed the product of the joint compositional skills of the members of the group present at the time.'

However, caution is advised when analysing the authorship of works created in this way; Morison QC stated that it would not be sensible to lay down any general rules to apply to all group compositions. He said that it must depend entirely on the individual circumstances of the band and that ultimately 'the question of whether a person is a joint author … is a question of fact and degree.' A similar creative process was claimed by the unsuccessful plaintiffs in *Hadley & ors v Kemp & Another*,[156] in which the parties were members of the 1980's pop group *Spandau Ballet*. The plaintiffs claimed that that the first-named defendant would show up with the bare bones of a song but that each member of the band would then contribute creatively and collectively to changes, which would give rise to a new song of which they were all joint authors. On the facts however, Park J held that the first-named defendant would present a complete song to the band, few changes would be made prior to its recording and he would have the last word on those changes. He stated the law to be that there must be 'a significant and original contribution to the creation of the work'. He continued:

> 'There are four elements: (1) The claimant must have made a contribution of some sort. (2) It must have been significant. (3) It must have been original. (4) It must have been a contribution to the creation of the musical work. The last point is important … The putative author must have contributed 'the right kind of skill and labour In the present case, contributions by the plaintiffs, however, significant and skillful, to the performance of the musical works are not the right kind of contributions to give them shares in the copyrights. The contributions need to be to the creation of the musical works, not to the performance or interpretation of them.'[157]

This is consistent with the Supreme Court decision in *Gormley v EMI Records (Ire) Ltd* where the plaintiff's claim failed because as a six-year-old girl she did not have the creative capacity to create a work.

The consequences of joint authorship

[1.51] The CRRA 2000–2004 state that references to the author of a work means a reference to all joint authors of a work; each of the authors will jointly hold the exclusive rights, such as copying or adapting a work, set out in Chapter 4 of the Acts.[158] However,

---

153 *Tate v Thomas* [1921] Ch 503.
154 *Evans v E Hulton & Co Ltd* [1923-8] MCC 51.
155 *Stuart v Barrett* [1994] EMLR 448.
156 *Hadley & ors v Kemp & Another* [1999] EMLR 589.
157 The fact that the plaintiffs did not object to the defendant being listed as sole composer at the time did not help their case.
158 CRRA 2000–2004, s 22(4).

joint authors need to be careful how they treat their rights. In *Godfrey v Lees*,[159] the plaintiff was a classically trained musician who worked closely with a pop group on several songs which used an orchestral accompaniment. He provided the arrangements and conducted the orchestra as well as contributing other ideas and material. The plaintiff succeeded in his claim to be a joint author of six recorded tracks but it did him no good. This was because he was regarded as having impliedly licenced the group to exploit his copyright; the licence was gratuitous and in principle was revocable. Since he did nothing for fourteen years he was estopped from revoking it. On the other hand, if rights have not been impliedly licenced or given up in this way, merely because someone is a joint author does not give them the unilateral right to reproduce works. In *Ray v Classic FM*, the court held that the defendant was not a joint author and also that 'it is quite clear that even if the defendant was a joint author ... joint ownership could not without the consent of the plaintiff justify the making of copies for the purposes of exploitation of the copyright abroad'.[160]

Works created during employment

[1.52] The CRRA 2000–2004 provides that, in general, employees will not be the authors of works that they produce in the course of their employment.

> 'The author of a work shall be the first owner of the copyright unless ... the work is made by an employee in the course of employment, in which case the employer is the first owner of any copyright in the work, subject to any agreement to the contrary'.[161]

[1.53] This exception is quite limited. Firstly it must be shown that the author was an employee at the time the work was created and secondly, it must be shown that the work was created during the course of employment. This may be quite difficult since many creators and authors of works tend not to be tied into a lasting contract of employment but may work freelance or on short-term contracts for services. This makes it very important that those who commission works or who hire individuals such as record producers to produce works should include in their contracts clear terms setting out the ownership of any works that are created and the assignment of individual's copyright ownership if such exists.

The definition of an employee

[1.54] The Act offers no definition of the term employee,[162] but there are generally three categories of worker.

---

[159] *Godfrey v Lees* [1995] EMLR 307.

[160] See Cescinsky v George Routledge [1916] 2 KB 325. See also Marchese, 'Joint Ownership of Intellectual Property' [1999] EIPR 364. See also Simcoe and Ingram, 'Joint authorship – a question of joint effort or intent' Copyright World, March 2000, p 18 for a discussion on the position of joint authors in Canada following the decision in *Darryl Neudorf v Nettwerk Productions Ltd* (10 December 1999) Vancouver C950847 (BCSC).

[161] CRRA 2000–2004, s 23(1)(a).

[162] Irish legislation contains no satisfactory definition of an 'employee Under the Minimum Notice and Terms of Employment Acts 1973–2001 it is defined as 'an individual who has entered into or works under a contract with an employer, whether the contract be for manual labour, clerical work or otherwise, (contd/)

These are:

(a) a person employed under a contract of employment or service (an employee or servant);

(b) a person working under a contract for services (an independent contractor); and

(c) office holders (such as a company director or judge).

[1.55] The Supreme Court distinguished between an employee and an independent contractor in *Denny v The Minister for Social Welfare*.[163] This involved an issue of social welfare law, as to whether the appellant was liable to pay employee contributions for a shop demonstrator (Sandra Mahon). She had a written contract with the appellants which stated *inter alia* that she was responsible for her own tax affairs and was not an employee but rather an independent contractor. Although Keane J held that 'the written agreement was undoubtedly drafted with understandable care with a view to ensuring, as far as possible, that Ms. Mahon was regarded in law as an independent contractor', he found that this was 'by no means decisive of the issue'.[164] Keane J was of the view that it was:

'clear that, while each case must be determined in the light of its particular facts and circumstances, in general a person will be regarded as providing his or her services under a contract of service and not as an independent contractor where he or she is performing those services for another person and not for himself or herself. The degree of control exercised over how the work is to be performed, although a factor to be taken into account, is not decisive. The inference that the person is engaged in business on his or her own account can be more readily drawn where he or she provides the necessary premises or equipment or some other form of investment, where he or she employ others to assist in the business and where the profit which he or she derives from the business is dependent on the efficiency with which it is conducted by him or her'.[165]

Keane J held that although there was no continuous supervision of Ms Mahon this was not a decisive factor. He held that on the other hand the appellants provided Ms Mahon with clothing and equipment necessary to do her work and Ms Mahon's income was dependant on her complying with the instructions of the appellant. Ms Mahon was not in a position to by better management and employment of resources to ensure a higher profit from her activities, she could not routine engage assistants and if she was unable to work she would have to arrange for a substitute herself but the substitute would have to be approved by the appellant. Keane J held that Ms Mahon was an employee. Murphy J stated in his concurring opinion that the provisions of her contract which dealt

---

[162] (\contd) whether it be expressed or implied, oral or in writing, and whether it be a contract of service or of apprenticeship or otherwise, and cognate expressions shall be construed accordingly' and under the Employment Equality Acts employee is defined as a person who has entered into or works under (or, where the employment has ceased, entered into or worked under) a contract of employment

[163] *Denny v The Minister for Social Welfare* [1998] 1 IR 34.

[164] [1998] 1 IR 34 at 51.

[165] [1998] 1 IR 34 at 50.

with taxation, unfair dismissals law and the relationship between the appellant and Ms Mahon were of marginal importance.[166]

[1.56] When a work is created by an office holder such as the director of a company, then *prima facie* as they are not an employee of the company the copyright should vest in themselves. Again the decision of ownership will depend on the facts of the case and merely because a person is called a director may not mean that they are also an employee.[167] Even if a work is created by a director in his function as a director of a company, the director will still be bound by his duties to the company[168] and the company may prove to be the equitable owner of the work. Similarly, the issue of whether or not property created by members of a partnership belongs to the individual partner or is the property of the partnership as a whole may arise.

In the course of employment

[1.57] Works created 'in the course of employment' are works which are created by an employee pursuant to his contract of employment or 'within the scope of his duties' as an employee. In *Stephenson, Jordan and Harrison Ltd v Macdonald and Evans*,[169] a management consultant wrote a book on what he termed management engineering. The plaintiffs submitted that they were the owners of copyright as the consultant had drawn up notes whilst visiting the premises of the plaintiff's clients and, subsequently, he had created reports which were sent to the clients. All this work was done while working for the plaintiffs and one entire section of his book was taken from a report he had written as an employee. The court of appeal held that these notes and reports were created in the course of employment and therefore the copyright in them belonged to the plaintiff. Different rules may apply to different occupations; for example the Code of Conduct for the Bar of Ireland provides that the copyright in an opinion belongs to the lay client.[170]

Lecturers and researchers

[1.58] In *Stephenson, Jordan and Harrison Ltd v Macdonald and Evans*[171] a portion of a book written by an ex-employee was based upon lectures which were delivered by the ex-employee while he was employed as a management consultant by the plaintiffs. These lectures were held not to be created or delivered in the course of his employment and therefore the plaintiffs did not own the copyright. The Court of Appeal took the view that lecturers are employed to deliver lectures and not to create copyright works. The fact

---

[166] 'These terms are included in the contract but they are not contractual terms in the sense of imposing obligations on one party in favour of the other. They purport to express a conclusion of law as to the consequences of the contract between the parties. Whether Ms Mahon was retained under a contract of services depends essentially on the totality of the contractual relationship express or implied between her and the appellant and not upon any statement as to the consequence of the bargain' [1998] 1 IR 34 at 53.

[167] *Lee v Lee Air Farming Ltd* [1961] AC 12.

[168] See Keane, *Company Law* (4th edn, Tottel Publishing 2007).

[169] *Stephenson, Jordan and Harrison Ltd v Macdonald and Evans* [1952] 69 RPC 10.

[170] Bar Council, *Code of Conduct for the Bar of Ireland*, 13 March 2006, para. 3.5.

[171] *Stephenson, Jordan and Harrison Ltd v Macdonald and Evans* [1952] 69 RPC 10.

that a lecturer may type out his notes or lecture is ancillary to the main purpose of his employment, which is to deliver the lecture.

> 'Prima facie I should have thought that a man engaged on terms which include that he is called upon to compose and deliver public lectures or lectures to some specified class of persons, would in the absence of clear terms in the contract of employment to the contrary, be entitled to the copyright in those lectures. That seems to me to be both just and commonsense.'

As in any other contract of employment or service, attention will have to be paid to the actual terms of the contract to see what exactly any individual was paid to do.[172]

Employees and officers of the State

[1.59] A very large number of copyright works are created under the aegis of the stat.e Where a work is created by an officer or employee of the government or of the state in the course of his or her duties, the government will be first owner of copyright.[173] This copyright is known as 'government copyright'.[174] 'Oireachtas Copyright' also exists.[175]

Journalists

[1.60] The Acts provide that:

> 'Where a work, other than a computer program, is made by an author in the course of employment by the proprietor of a newspaper or periodical, the author may use the work for any purpose, other than for the purposes of making available that work to newspapers or periodicals, without infringing the copyright in the work'.[176]

As in all other cases it would be a matter of evidence whether a work is created in the course of a journalist's employment or not. If it is so created, then the proprietor of the newspaper will be first owner of copyright but the journalist will retain significant rights as the author. If he wishes to bring out a collection of the articles he has published in a newspaper, he will be able to do so. The sole limitation placed on employees of newspapers is that they cannot submit that work to other newspapers. Virtually all the major Irish newspapers and many if not all of the provincial newspapers have a significant online presence. This means that 'newspaper' would have to be interpreted as including those exclusively online and the online editions of existing newspapers. A significant issue is whether a newspaper has the right to include a journalist's articles in a database other than its own online newspaper. In *Tasini and ors v The New York Times Co, Newsday Inc and ors*,[177] it was held that newspapers could not licence articles

---

[172] So in *Goswami v Hammons* (29 October 1982, unreported) HC (Eng), it was held that where the plaintiff had been employed to do research by a university and where he submitted results of his research as a PhD thesis with the consent of the university, the plaintiff was entitled to copyright in the thesis as it was not created in the course of his employment.

[173] CRRA 2000–2004, s 191(1).

[174] CRRA 2000–2004, s 191(2).

[175] CRRA 2000–2004, ss 193 & 194.

[176] CRRA 2000–2004, s 23(2).

[177] *New York Times Co v Tasini* (00-201) 533 US 48 3 (2001) 206 F3d 161, affirmed.

submitted by freelance journalists and published in the newspapers to searchable databases such as NEXIS. A significant feature of this section is that the authors of computer programs do not benefit from this provision. Programmers hired to write a proprietary program for a newspaper such as that which created the grids of numbers which were the subject of litigation in *Express Newspapers v Liverpool Daily Post and Echo Plc*[178] will not be able to use the program themselves unless permitted by their employer in the normal way. However, there is no equivalent exception for those who create databases on behalf of newspapers, such as searchable archives.

International organisations

[1.61] The author of a work will not be the first owner if it is subject to the copyright of a prescribed international organisation.[179] These organisations may be prescribed by the government pursuant to s 196 of the Act.

Other enactments

[1.62] The author of a work will not be the first owner if the copyright in the work is conferred on some other person, such as his employer, by an enactment.[180]

Dealings: assignments and licences

[1.63] The transfer of copyright in a work must be distinguished from the sale of copies of a work. Buying a copy of a work entitles the purchaser to do no more than use the work as the owner intended. These uses will usually be set out in the contract of sale or licence agreement and often are quite restrictive. Although, copies of works may be sold frequently, assignments of the copyright or a partial copyright in a work are more infrequent. It should be kept in mind that the authors' moral rights cannot be alienated or assigned,[181] although, some can be transmitted on death.[182] The CRRA 2000–2004 provide 'The copyright in a work is transmissible by assignment, by testamentary disposition or by operation of law, as personal or moveable property.'[183]

[1.64] Assignment is a transmission of ownership by a contract or other agreement. A testamentary disposition is a will and operation of law might encompass the transfer of title from a bankrupt to his trustee. Not all the copyright in a work must be transferred at the same time. The CRRA 2000–2004 provide that:

> 'A transmission of the copyright in a work by assignment, by testamentary disposition or by operation of law may be partial, so as to apply—
>
>   (a)   to one or more but not all of the acts[184] the copyright owner has the right to undertake or authorise, and

---

[178] *Express Newspapers v Liverpool Daily Post and Echo Plc* [1985] 3 All ER 680.

[179] CRRA 2000–2004, s 23(1)(c).

[180] CRRA 2000–2004, s 23(1)(d).

[181] CRRA 2000–2004, s 118.

[182] CRRA 2000–2004, s 119.

[183] CRRA 2000–2004, s 120(1).

[184] Unlike the UK CDPA 1988, the Act refers to the transmission of 'the acts, the copyright owner has the right to undertake', (contd/)

(b) to part but not the whole of the period for which the copyright in the work is to subsist'.[185]

[1.65] A typical example of a partial transmission would be to assign the rights to adapt a novel as a film while retaining the right to reproduce the novel itself. Rights so assigned include the right to perform a work professionally[186] and to publish a work in volumes.[187] The New Zealand courts have held that 'the combination of ways in which [an author] may assign his rights is almost endless' and may include the assignment of rights in geographical areas.[188]

Transmission by assignment

[1.66] The difference between assignments and the other forms of transmission is that an assignment must be in writing. The CRRA 2000–2004 state that 'An assignment of the copyright in a work, whether in whole or in part, is not effective unless it is in writing and signed by or on behalf of the assignor'.[189]

Although the assignment must be in writing, it would appear that there is no particular need to mention the transfer of copyright specifically. This is a question of construction and will depend upon the facts in any particular case. In *Murray v King*,[190] the sale of 'all the right, title and interest' in a magazine publisher was held to be sufficient to assign the copyright. In contrast in *Wilden Pump Engineering v Fusfeld*[191] the sale of all the assets on a balance sheet was not sufficient to assign copyrights which did not appear on that balance sheet. The motivation for an assignment would appear to be unimportant. It was held in *Beloff v Pressdram*,[192] that the fact that an assignment was made purely to enable an action for infringement to be brought did not mean that it should be set aside.

[1.67] The Electronic Commerce Act 2000 makes it clear that electronic writing is to be legally recognised. It provides that 'If by law or otherwise a person … is required … to give information in writing … then … the person … may give the information in electronic form, whether as an electronic communication or otherwise.'[193]

The CRRA 2000–2004 define information as including 'all forms of writing and other text'.[194] Although it is not necessary for an assignment to be an actual contract, the Electronic Commerce Act 2000 provides that electronic contracts cannot be denied

---

[184] (\contd) in the UK, the equivalent and similar section refers to the transmission of 'the things, the copyright owner has the exclusive right to do When the UK CDPA 1988 was passing through Parliament the reference to 'things' was included to as to make it clear that classes of rights such as hardback and paperback rights could be assigned separately. The UK legislature feared that use of the term 'acts' would not make this clear.

[185] CRRA 2000–2004, s 120(2).

[186] *British Actors Film Co v Glover* [1918] 1KB 299.

[187] *Johnathan Cape v Consolidated Press* [1954] 1 WLR 1313.

[188] *J Albert & Sons Pty Ltd v Fletcher Construction* [1976] RPC 615.

[189] CRRA 2000–2004, s 120(3).

[190] *Murray v King* [1983-85] 3 IPR 525.

[191] *Wilden Pump Engineering v Fusfeld* [1985-87] 8 IPR 250.

[192] *Beloff v Pressdram* [1973] 1 All ER 241.

[193] The Electronic Commerce Act 2000, s 12.

[194] The Electronic Commerce Act 2000, s 2(1).

solely because they have been concluded by way of an electronic communication[195] and 'Information ... shall not be denied legal effect, validity or enforceability solely on the grounds that it is wholly or partly in electronic form, whether as an electronic communication or otherwise'.[196]

Therefore an email that accompanies[197] the submission of a manuscript or other work may well fulfil the requirement of writing under the CRRA 2000–2004.[198] The remaining question is whether an email can be said to be signed by the author. Most emails will contain the author's name and this may be sufficient for the Act. The courts do not insist that a signature should be in copper plate handwriting and have interpreted the word 'signature' very loosely. Again the Electronic Commerce Act 2000 has clarified the position as it provides that if 'by law or otherwise the signature of a person ... is required ... then ... an electronic signature may be used'.[199]

This is subject to the proviso that the author should consent to the use of an electronic signature.[200] An electronic signature is defined by the Electronic Commerce Act 2000[201] as meaning 'data in electronic form attached to, incorporated in or logically associated with other electronic data and which serves as a method of authenticating the purported originator.'[202]

Assignments of the rental right

[1.68] The term of copyright is quite lengthy. On average a 30-year old author can anticipate that copyright in his work will endure for at least a century assuming he lives to age 60 (of course he may live a lot longer than that). During this period, technological changes may render copyrights that were previously inconsequential, very valuable. In *Peggy Lee v Disney Corporation*[203] the plaintiff had performed and written certain songs for the defendant's film, *Lady and the Tramp*, in the mid-1950s and assigned her copyright to the defendants. Several decades later the film became a huge success when it was released on video. The court accepted that the singer could not and had not assigned her rights in these video sales and awarded her several million dollars.

Future copyright

[1.69] It is not uncommon for an agreement to be made for the commissioning or creation of a new copyright work. Such an agreement will have to deal with a copyright

---

[195] The Electronic Commerce Act 2000, s 19.

[196] The Electronic Commerce Act 2000, s 9.

[197] The Electronic Commerce Act 2000 came into force on the 10 July 2000.

[198] CRRA 2000–2004, s 120.

[199] Electronic Commerce Act 2000, s 13(2)(b).

[200] These provisions clearly apply to copyright property which is defined by the CRRA 2000–2004 as personal and moveable property as s 10(1)(b) states that ss 12–23 of the Electronic Commerce Act 2000 are without prejudice to the laws governing real property. Therefore, it would seem that the Oireachtas intended these provisions to apply to personal and moveable property such as copyright.

[201] Electronic Commerce Act 2000, s 2(1).

[202] The Electronic Commerce Act 2000, s 2(1).

[203] Sakkers, *Licensing and Exploiting Right in Multimedia Products* 11 CLSR 1995.

which has yet to be created and this is termed 'future copyright'.[204] The Act provides for agreements made in relation to future copyright and signed by or on behalf of the prospective owner[205] of the copyright where the prospective owner purports to assign the future copyright, whether in whole or in part, to another person. Where this is done then when copyright comes into existence, the assignee or his or her successor in title, or another person claiming under him or her would be entitled as against all other persons to require the copyright to be vested in him or her. The copyright will therefore vest in the assignee or his or her successor in title and any other person claiming under him or her.[206] This means that the Act recognises the validity of assignments of future copyright. The Act also makes provision for the situation where the person who would be entitled to the copyright dies before it comes into existence. Here the copyright will devolve as if it had subsisted immediately before death and that person had then been the owner of the copyright.[207] If no such agreement is signed, it may still be the case that the equitable ownership of future copyright may be transferred.

Equitable ownership

[1.70] As is made clear by the CRRA 2000–2004, copyright is a form of personal or moveable property. As such, the legal and beneficial ownership of it can vest separately in different people. Typically this happens when a purchaser has paid for the property but the vendor has yet to assign it. So in *Richardson v Flanders*,[208] a computer programmer was paid by the plaintiff to rewrite and improve the plaintiff's computer program. Ferris J, in the English High Court, held that the copyright in any work carried out by the programmer was held on trust by the programmer, for the plaintiff.[209] Ferris J relied on the dicta of the Court of Appeal in *Massine v De Basil*[210] in which the plaintiff had choreographed a ballet for the defendant while in their employment:

> 'the court was of the opinion that it ought to be implied as a term of the agreement that any work done by the plaintiff would be done on the basis that the defendant who had paid for the work should be entitled to such rights as might arise from that payment, and he should not be deprived of the benefit merely on the ground that the person whom he paid was an independent contractor.'

---

[204] "future copyright" is defined by the act as meaning copyright which will or may come into existence in respect of a future work or class of works or on the occurrence of a future event; CRRA 2000–2004, s 121(4).

[205] "prospective owner" is defined as including 'a person who is prospectively entitled to copyright by virtue of an agreement made in relation to future copyright CRRA 2000–2004, s 121(4).

[206] CRRA 2000–2004, s 121(1).

[207] Copyright and Related Rights Acts 2000 – 2004, s 121(2).

[208] *Richardson v Flanders* [1993] FSR 497.

[209] See the unreported judgment of Morris J in *Inter Finance Group Ltd v KPMG Peat Marwick t/a KPMG Management Consulting* [1998] IEHC 217 (29 June, 1998).

[210] *Massine v De Basil* [1936] 45 MCC 223.

Where a work is commissioned, the equitable title may be transferred from the author to the person who commissions the work even though the legal title in the copyright will not have been assigned.

[1.71] Where a work is created in breach of some fiduciary duty, then it may be argued that the fiduciary holds it on trust for the party to whom he owes the duty. This is termed a constructive trust. So, in some limited circumstances it may be argued that beneficial title in a work created by an employee but outside the scope of his employment, will be held on trust by the employee for his employer. In *Missing Link Software v Magee*[211] it was held to be arguable that the defendant had breached his fiduciary duty to the plaintiffs by writing a program to compete with their principle product while he was employed by them. It was suggested that if this were so, two conclusions might be drawn as to the copyright. Firstly, it might be argued that the copyright in the program written by the defendant while in the employment of the plaintiffs was held on constructive trust on behalf of the plaintiffs or secondly, it could be held that the defendant should not be able to assert his own breach of fiduciary duty to deny that the program was written within the course of his employment. This judgement should be treated with caution as it was decided at the interlocutory stage and there was good evidence that the defendant had copied at least some sections of his employer's product.[212] In other circumstances where the employer was acting in an unsavoury manner, the English courts have been unwilling to consider that equitable ownership might arise. In *Service Corporation International v Channel 4 Television*,[213] a reporter for the defendants worked undercover as a trainee in the plaintiff's funeral home. He covertly filmed events at the home including disrespectful and abusive treatment of corpses, such as coffins with corpses in them being used as rubbish bins. The plaintiffs tried to restrain the defendants from showing the film; one of their claims was that they were entitled to the equitable ownership of the copyright in the film. This claim relied on the allegation that the trainee was the maker of the film which he had created in his working hours and in breach of his duty to the defendant. However, Lightman J could see no breach of fiduciary duty in this case and he felt it was clear that the trainee was not a trustee for the plaintiffs of his account of what happened in the funeral home regardless of whether that account was written during the hours of his employment by the plaintiffs or later. Similarly, he did not hold the film on trust for the plaintiffs regardless of when that film was made.

[1.72] Comparisons between copyright cases elsewhere and Irish equity cases are easier to make in this situation than with regard to resulting trusts. As was stated in the old Irish case of *Gabett v Lawder*[214]: 'The fundamental principle upon which the doctrine of constructive trusts proceeds is, that no person in a fiduciary capacity shall be allowed to retain any advantage gained by him in his character as trustee.' Whether such trusts should be constructed in relation to all work created by all employees is very doubtful.

---

[211] *Missing Link Software v Magee* (9 August 1998, unreported) HC.

[212] Such as evidence given at an interlocutory hearing that during his farewell party, the defendant was overheard to say that he had taken all the software he needed before he left the plaintiffs employment.

[213] *Service Corporation International v Channel 4 Television* [1999] EMLR 83.

[214] *Gabett v Lawder* (1883) 11 LR Ir 295 (Chancery Division).

Section 15 of the Organisation of Working Time Act 1997 provides that an employee cannot be permitted to work more than an average of 48 hours a week.[215] So, an employer might find it difficult to assert that works created outside these 48 hours could be created in the course of employment. In *Missing Link Software v Magee*[216] much of the evidence turned on whether the defendant could have in fact produced the offending computer program in his own time. The employer failed in the American case of *Avtec Systems v Peiffer*.[217] The plaintiff supplied computer services to the USA's space programme and the defendant was employed by it as a computer programmer. The plaintiff independently wrote a program to control orbiting satellites, which he demonstrated to his employers and NASA. However, the employee continued to develop it on his own and the program was successfully marketed commercially. The employer sued but its action failed as it was unable to prove that the program was written 'within Avtec authorized time and space limits.'

The duration of copyright

[1.73] The CRRA 2000–2004 implement The Term of Protection of Copyright Directive.[218] The term of protection for a work is dependant upon what category a particular work falls into. Deciding whether a work is a sound recording or a musical work will determine whether it has a protection lasting 50 years or 70 years. This is important for deciding when a work has entered the public domain and for how long it will be necessary to pay the author's descendant's royalties.[219] The term of copyright is calculated from the first day of January of the year following the event that gives rise to that term.[220] So if the author of a literary work died on 21 July 2007, the term of his copyright would be calculated from 1 January 2008 and would therefore expire on 1 January 2078.

Literary, dramatic, musical or artistic works and original databases

[1.74] The copyright in a literary, dramatic, musical or artistic work or an original database will expire 70 years after the death of the author. This is irrespective of the date

---

[215] Organisation of Working Time Act, 1997, s 15 provides: '…An employer shall not permit an employee to work, in each period of 7 days, more than an average of 48 hours, that is to say an average of 48 hours calculated over a period (hereafter in this section referred to as a 'reference period') that does not exceed…4 months, or…6 months…

[216] *Missing Link Software v Magee* (9 August 1998, unreported).

[217] *Avtec Systems v Peiffer* 805 F Supp 1312.

[218] EC Directive no. 93/98/EEC of 29 October 1993 OJ L 248 6/10/1993 p 13.

[219] Cynics might attribute Hollywood's fondness for long dead authors such as Jane Austen or William Shakespeare, not to Hollywood's anglophilia but rather to its phobia of paying these royalties, see the discussion of *It's a wonderful life* above. *Gowers Review of Intellectual Property* also cites the following example: 'The book *The Secret Garden*, since copyright has expired, has been made into a movie, a musical, a cookbook, a CD-ROM version, and two sequels', *Gowers Review of Intellectual Property*, HM Treasury, December 2006, p 70, para 4.95

[220] CRRA 2000–2004, s 35.

on which the work is first lawfully made available to the public.[221] If the work is anonymous or pseudonymous, copyright will expire 70 years after the date on which the work is first lawfully made available to the public. In relation to works of joint authorship, the death of the author will be construed as a reference to the death of the last of the joint authors where the identity of all of the authors is known.[222] Copyright will not subsist in an anonymous or pseudonymous literary, dramatic, musical or artistic work, or original database where it is reasonable to presume that the author has been dead for 70 years or more.[223]

Films

[1.75] The copyright in a film expires 70 years after the last of the directors or authors of the film dies.[224]

Sound recordings, broadcasts and cable programmes

[1.76] The copyright in a sound recording will expire 50 years after the sound recording is made, or if it is first lawfully made available to the public during that period, then copyright will expire 50 years after the date on which it is made available.[225] The copyright in a broadcast will expire 50 years after the broadcast is first lawfully transmitted.[226] Similarly, the copyright in a cable programme will expire 50 years after the cable programme is first lawfully included in a cable programme service.[227] The repeat of a broadcast or cable programme[228] is irrelevant for the purposes of copyright.[229]

Computer generated works

[1.77] The copyright in a computer-generated work will expire 70 years after the date on which the work is first lawfully made available to the public.[230]

Towards eternal copyright?

[1.78] At least one American author has advocated an eternal copyright term, arguing that it would be 'just and fair for those who try to extract a living from the uncertain arts of writing and composing to be freed from a form of confiscation not visited upon anyone else'.[231]

---

[221] CRRA 2000–2004, s 24(1).

[222] CRRA 2000–2004, s 31(4).

[223] CRRA 2000–2004, s 32(2).

[224] CRRA 2000–2004, s 25(1) and s 31(3).

[225] CRRA 2000–2004, s 26.

[226] CRRA 2000–2004, s 27(1).

[227] CRRA 2000–2004, s 28(1).

[228] A repeat broadcast is defined as 'a repeat of a broadcast which has been previously transmitted' and a repeat cable program means 'a repeat of a cable programme which has been previously included in a cable programme service Copyright and Related Rights Acts 2000 – 2004, s 2(1).

[229] Copyright and Related Rights Acts 2000-2004, s 27(2) and s 28(2).

[230] Copyright and Related Rights Acts 2000-2004, s 30.

[231] Helprin, 'A Great Idea Lives Forever. Shouldn't Its Copyright?' (2007) New York Times, 20 May 2007.

The expiry of copyright 70 years after the death of the author is not actually that unfair on authors. This can be shown through a straightforward calculation.[232] At one extreme, assuming that an author lives for 40 years after the publication of his work, copyright would expire 110 years after publication. The author and his estate would then receive 99.997% of what it would have received if the term was unlimited.[233] If copyright terms were to be drastically restricted, to 25 years after publication, an author would still receive almost 92% of what he would receive if his copyright endured for all eternity. There are disadvantages to lengthy copyright terms, not least the problem of orphan works discussed below. Given these problems, and the relatively small benefits that accrue to author's estates, further extension of copyright terms would not seem to be beneficial.

Orphan works

[1.79] As works fall out of print and cease to generate income, their owners may lose interest in them but will still retain copyright. If somebody new wishes to utilise the work, say by incorporating it in a database, they may find identifying the owner very difficult. The problem was explained by *Gowers Review of Intellectual Property* 'The term "orphan work" is used to describe a situation where the owner of a copyright work cannot be identified by someone else who wishes to use the work'.[234]

The British library estimates that about 40% of all works fall into this category.[235] *Gowers Review of Intellectual Property* recommended that an amendment should be made to the Directive on the Harmonisation of Copyright to deal with this problem.[236]

---

[232] 'Suppose a copyright on a particular work would yield $1 per year in perpetuity at a discount rate of 10 percent. Under a system of perpetual copyright, the present value of this infinite stream of income would equal 10 (=1/r). Under a limited copyright term (=t) the present value would be $(1-e^n)/r$ Landes & Posner, *The Economic Structure of Intellectual Property Law* (The Belkamp Press of Harvard Universtity Press, 2003) p 214 fn 12.

[233] Landes & Posner, *The Economic Structure of Intellectual Property Law* (The Belkamp Press of Harvard Universtity Press, 2003), p 296.

[234] *Gowers Review of Intellectual Property* HM Treasury, December 2006, p 69, para 4.91.

[235] The US Copyright Office has also issued a report on this problem: http://www.copyright.gov/orphan/orphan-report-full.pdf.

[236] *Gowers Review of Intellectual Property* HM Treasury, December 2006, p 69, para 4.91, Recommendation 13, p 6.

Chapter 2

Exclusive Rights, Infringement and Enforcement of Copyright Law

Introduction

[2.01] Copyright confers certain exclusive rights on copyright owner. In general the CRRA 2000–2004 do not confer 'positive' rights on right-holders. They do not confer any right upon authors or owners to do anything that they could not already do. Instead, the CRRAs confers 'negative' rights, which are the rights to prevent others from doing certain things such as copying or translating the works. This conferral of 'negative' rights is typical of intellectual property[1] law in general. This marks a fundamental point of difference between intellectual and other forms of property, which generally confer both positive rights (such as the right to live in a house) together with negative rights (such as the right to exclude trespassers).

The rights conferred by copyright

[2.02] Copyright is a self-explanatory term; it gives the owner the right to control copying. Over time the acts controlled by copying have expanded considerably. The CRRA 2000–2004 provide that:

> 'the owner of the copyright in a work has the exclusive right to undertake or authorise others to undertake all or any of the following acts, namely:
>
> ... to copy the work;
>
> ... to make available to the public the work;
>
> ... to make an adaptation of the work'.[2]

The Acts also gives rights to performers, who have the right to authorise or prohibit:

(a) 'the making of a recording of the whole or any substantial part of a qualifying performance directly from the live performance ...

(b) ... the broadcasting live, or including live in a cable programme service, of the whole or any substantial part of a qualifying performance ...

(c) ... the making of a recording of the whole or any substantial part of a qualifying performance directly from a broadcast of, or cable programme including, the live performance'.[3]

---

[1]   'The phrase "intellectual property" is fairly young ... the earliest use of the phrase occurs in the title of the United Nations' World Intellectual Property Organisation, first assembled in 1967', Vaidhyanathan, *Copyrights and Copywrongs* (New York University Press, 2001), p 12.

[2]   CRRA 2000–2004, s 37(1).

[3]   CRRA 2000–2004, s 203(1).

Rights will be 'infringed by a person who, without the consent of the performer, undertakes or authorises another to undertake any of the (above) acts'[4] but an exemption is provided for someone who records a broadcast 'for his or her private and domestic use'.[5]

The reproduction right

[2.03] The CRRA 2000–2004 confer a right to control copying upon the owner of copyright which the Acts refer to as 'the reproduction right'. This is the right to control copying.[6] Information technology makes it easy to copy works by 'ripping' them from CDs. In *Apple Corps Ltd v Apple Computers Inc*[7] Mann J in the English High Court found that music would arrive on an iPod: 'from a potential variety of sources – 'ripping' tracks from CDs, recording from other analogue devices (which might require some intermediate software), downloading from a music site and probably other sources.'[8]

[2.04] In the Australian case of *Universal Music Australia Pty Ltd v Cooper*[9] the plaintiffs executed Anton Piller orders on the defendant's premises. In the course of the search that followed 'a number of MP3 files constituting copies of the applicants' copyright sound recordings were located on the hard drive of Cooper's computer'.[10] The defendant did not give evidence or offer an alternative explanation. As a result Tamberlin J was:

'satisfied that the available inference that Cooper made these copies of the copyright sound recordings on the hard drive himself, most likely by downloading them from his website, can more safely and confidently be drawn. Accordingly, I find that Cooper has infringed the applicants' copyright by making copies of the music sound recordings'.[11]

Transient or incidental copies of a work

[2.05] At one time issues such as whether the copying of a computer program to the RAM of a computer amounted to copying caused the courts some difficulty.[12] The CRRAs deal with this potential difficulty by providing that copying of any work is defined as including: 'storing the work in any medium'[13] and 'the making of copies which are transient or incidental to some other use of the work'.[14] Transient and incidental copies may be permitted in some circumstances.

---

4   CRRA 2000–2004, s 203(2).
5   CRRA 2000–2004, s 203(3).
6   'There shall be a right of the owner of copyright to copy a work or to authorise others to do so which shall be known and in this Part referred to as the "reproduction right". CRRA 2000–2004, s 39(2).
7   *Apple Corps Ltd v Apple Computers Inc* [2006] EWHC 996 (Ch).
8   [2006] EWHC 996 (Ch), para 16.
9   *Universal Music Australia Pty Ltd v Cooper* [2005] FCA 972.
10 [2005] FCA 972, para 55.
11 [2005] FCA 972, para 55.
12 *MAI Sys Corp v Peak Computer, Inc* 991 F 2d 511 (9th Cir 1993).
13 CRRA 2000–2004, s 39(1)(a)(i).
14 CRRA 2000–2004, s 39(1)(a)(ii).

The Acts also provide that:

> 'The copyright in a work is not infringed by the making of a transient and incidental copy of that work which is technically required for the viewing of or listening to the work by a member of the public to whom a copy of the work is lawfully made available.'[15]

But if a copy is made pursuant to this provision and 'subsequently sold, rented or lent, or offered or exposed for sale, rental or loan, or otherwise made available to the public, it shall be deemed to be an infringing copy for those purposes and for all subsequent purposes.'[16]

[2.06] The providers of Internet services and search engines may utilise the 'caching' of incidental copies in the course of their business. It is clear that the caching of legitimate copies of material will not amount to infringement as these copies will have been 'lawfully made available'. However, websites may also contain infringing material and the exemption provided for transient and incidental copies by the CRRA 2000–2004 will not apply to these as they will not have been 'lawfully made available.' In this situation a service or search engine provider may be able to rely upon the Directive on e-Commerce[17] which provides in relation to caching that:

> 'Where an information society service is provided that consists of the transmission in a communication network of information provided by a recipient of the service ... the service provider is not liable for the automatic, intermediate and temporary storage of that information, performed for the sole purpose of making more efficient the information's onward transmission to other recipients of the service upon their request'.

[2.07] This is a very limited exemption, effectively applying only to services provided over electronic communications networks. The exemption will only apply if the following conditions are met:

    (a)   'the provider does not modify the information ...;

    (b)   the provider complies with conditions on access to the information;

    (c)   the provider complies with rules regarding the updating of the information, specified in a manner widely recognised and used by industry;

    (d)   the provider does not interfere with the lawful use of technology, widely recognised and used by industry, to obtain data on the use of the information;

    (e)   the provider acts expeditiously to remove or to disable access to the information it has stored upon obtaining actual knowledge of the fact that the information at the initial source of the transmission has been removed from the network, or access to it has been disabled, or that a court or an administrative authority has ordered such removal or disablement'.[18]

[2.08] Differences may emerge about the interpretation of the above. For example the Directive refers to rules relating to technology and information which are 'widely

---

[15] CRRA 2000–2004, s 87(1).

[16] CRRA 2000–2004, s 87(2).

[17] Directive 2000/31/EC of the European Parliament and of the Council of 8 June 2000 on certain legal aspects of information society services, in particular electronic commerce, in the Internal Market (Directive on electronic commerce).

[18] Directive 2000/31/EC, art 13(1).

recognised and used by industry'. Unfortunately the Directive does not specify which industry. It would not be surprising if information and communication technology industries have quite different interpretations of what is widely recognised and used in comparison with the recording or film industries.[19] The caching exemption will not 'affect the possibility for a court ... of requiring the service provider to terminate or prevent an infringement'.[20]

Alternatively, an Internet service or search provider might rely on the Directive on the harmonisation of copyright,[21] which provides that:

> 'Temporary acts of reproduction ... which are transient or incidental [and] an integral and essential part of a technological process and whose sole purpose is to enable:
>
> (a)   a transmission in a network between third parties by an intermediary, or
>
> (b)   a lawful use
>
> of a work or other subject-matter to be made, and which have no independent economic significance, shall be exempted from the reproduction right ...'[22]

Physical copies of a work

[2.09] The CRRA 2000–2004 provide that the copying of an artistic work will include 'the making of a copy in three dimensions of a two dimensional work and the making of a copy in two dimensions of a three dimensional work'.[23] So using a computer-aided manufacturing tool to create a finished product from a digital image will be infringement.[24]

Copying a photograph from a film

[2.10] The CRRA 2000–2004 provides that copying may result from: 'making a photograph of the whole or a substantial part of any image forming part of the film, broadcast or programme'.[25] This would appear to mean that copying even a small part of a film, television broadcast or cable programme may amount to infringement. The 'jerkiness' of old silent films stems from the fact that they only projected 18 frames per second, modern conventional films project around 24/25 frames per second, and digital

---

[19]   Morrison, 'Silicon Valley duels with Hollywood over piracy law: The technology sector is flexing its muscles to shelve a US crackdown against file-sharing on the internet' (2004) The Financial Times, 13 October.

[20]   Directive 2000/31/EC, art 13(2). See the US case of *Parker v Google, Inc* No. 04-CV-3918, 2006 US Dist LEXIS 9860 (ED Pa Mar 10, 2006) in which it was held that caching by a search engine of Internet postings did not amount to infringement under the USA's Digital Millennium Copyright Act (DMCA) which is similar, but not identical, to the Directive on e-Commerce.

[21]   Directive 2001/29/EC of the European Parliament and of the Council of 22 May 2001 on the harmonisation of certain aspects of copyright and related rights in the information society, OJ L 167, 22/06/2001, p 10–19.

[22]   Directive 2001/29/EC, art 5(1).

[23]   CRRA 2000–2004, s 39(1)(b).

[24]   Cane, 'Designs are flying off the drawing board' (2007) The Financial Times, 28 February.

[25]   CRRA 2000–2004, s 39(1)(c).

systems project between 60 and 70 frames per second.[26] So a modern, but not digital, film that was 90 minutes long would contain about 13,000 frames. Each of those frames amounts to 0.01% of the total film. What the Acts appear to provide is that the copying of a substantial part of just one frame, or not even 0.01% of the film, can amount to infringement.

Transfer of copies in electronic form

[2.11] The CRRA 2000–2004 provide in relation to the transfer of copies in electronic form that:

> 'where there are no express terms … prohibiting the transfer of the copy by the purchaser, imposing obligations which continue after a transfer, prohibiting the assignment of any licence or terminating any licence on a transfer, or … providing for the conditions on which a transferee may undertake the acts which the purchaser was permitted to undertake, then, any acts which the purchaser was permitted to undertake may also be undertaken by a transferee without infringement of the copyright, but any copy or adaptation or copy of an adaptation made by the purchaser which is not also transferred shall be treated as an infringing copy for those purposes and for all subsequent purposes.'[27]

This section will apply where 'a copy of a work in electronic form has been purchased on terms which expressly or impliedly allow the purchaser to copy the work, or to adapt it or make copies of an adaptation, in connection with his or her use of the work'.[28] In particular this provision will apply where 'the original purchased copy is no longer usable and that which is transferred is a further copy used in its place'.[29] And it will apply where the copy is transferred to a third party[30] and a similar provision will apply to recordings of performances in electronic form.[31]

The making available right

[2.12] All forms of making a work available to the public are publication in one form or another. A good argument could be made that the various categories of the 'making available right' are redundant and could simply be replaced by a single right, that of controlling publication. However, the CRRA 2000–2004 do not take this course, and instead provide that that owners of copyright may control the 'making available' of their work through a variety of different channels. Some of these channels are very specific to particular technologies, which may become obsolete. The CRRA 2000–2004 provide that the making available right will include all or any of the following activities:

(a) 'making available to the public of copies of the work, by wire or wireless means, in such a way that members of the public may access the work from a place and at a time chosen by them (including the making available of copies of works through the Internet);

---

[26] Grossman, 'The Last Spin Of The Reel' (2005) The Independent (UK), 11 April.
[27] CRRA 2000–2004, s 86(2).
[28] CRRA 2000–2004, s 86(1).
[29] CRRA 2000–2004, s 86(3).
[30] CRRA 2000–2004, s 86(4).
[31] CRRA 2000–2004, s 242.

(b)   performing, showing or playing a copy of the work in public;

(c)   broadcasting a copy of the work;

(d)   including a copy of the work in a cable programme service;

(e)   issuing copies of the work to the public;

(f)   renting copies of the work;

(g)   lending copies of the work without the payment of remuneration to the owner of the copyright in the work.'

[2.13] Some of the channels are specific to a particular technology, this is true of the regimes for broadcasts, cable programs and Internet downloads. The difficulty with such categories is that they face obsolescence through the phenomenon of convergence, whereby the differences between different forms of electronic communications disappear, at least so far as consumers are concerned. The development of a converged electronic communications sector would have been clear well before the introduction of the Copyright and Related Rights Bill 1999.[32] The EC Commission had previously described the phenomenon of convergence, in which digital technology 'allows both traditional and new communication services – whether voice, data, sound or pictures to be provided over many different networks'.[33]

However, it would be unfair to read too much into the Acts differentiation between broadcasts, cable transmission and Internet uploads. To a great extent this differentiation would have been forced on the Oireachtas by EC legislation such as the European Directive on Satellite broadcasting and cable retransmission[34] and the Directive on the harmonisation of certain aspects of copyright and related rights in the information society.[35]

[2.14] The CRRA 2000–2004 specify that a broadcast is one that is transmitted by wireless means whereas a cable programme is transmitted by means of a wire, beam or other conducting device. But the Act does not specify how these services may be distinguished from the Internet. Convergence is supposed to mean that this sort of distinction is irrelevant. Suppose a consumer is connected to the Internet via the same cable system as that which provides his cable TV service. If he downloads a film from a site such as YouTube[36] is that download a cable programme? If a consumer downloads a film from an Internet site through a wireless modem[37] does this constitute a broadcast? There is no doubt that RTÉ broadcasts its radio programmes on 567 KHz (medium wave) and 252 KHz (long wave), but it also streams them over the Internet. Are those

---

[32] The Bill was moved in the Seanad on 6 May 1999. *Copyright and Related Rights Bill, 1999: Order for Second Stage*, Seanad Éireann, Vol 159, 6 May 1999.

[33] *The Green Paper on the convergence of the telecommunications, media and information technology sectors and the implications for regulation: towards an information society approach,* EC, Brussels, 3 December 1997. See Kelleher and Murray, *IT Law in the European Union,* (Sweet & Maxwell, 1999), p 90.

[34] 1993 OJ L248.

[35] Directive 2001/29/EC of the European Parliament and of the Council of 22 May 2001 on the harmonisation of certain aspects of copyright and related rights in the information society.

[36] http://www.youtube.com.

[37] See eg Comreg, *ComReg increases the availability of wireless broadband,* 15 May 2007.

streams broadcasts, are they cable programmes or are they something else? These issues may come to a head as 'next generation networks' are built in Ireland. These are networks which 'are capable of providing multiple high-bandwidth services, including multimedia services'.[38]

[2.15] Technologies such as these render irrelevant the careful distinctions drawn by the CRRA 2000–2004. For example, NTL uses fibre optic cables to deliver cable programmes, Internet and phone services. Eircom has also 'announced plans to migrate to a Next Generation IP core network and to deploy fibre in its access network in selected urban areas'.[39] Distinguishing between cable programmes, broadcasts and Internet uploads on networks such as these will be very difficult, but it is a distinction that the Acts seek to make.[40] But it is possible that the courts will be able to interpret the Acts so as to make this distinction irrelevant. *Mandarim Records Ltd v Mechanical Copyright Protection Society (Ireland) Ltd*[41] concerned the production of what was termed a 'power CD', which was described to the court as follows:

> 'Power CD's ... combin(e) visual imagery and conventional reproductions of sound recordings made by selected artists or other musicians. In appearance and dimensions Power CD's are identical to the ordinary type which comprises sound reproductions only. Essentially, Power CD's contain not only sound recordings but also text, graphics and visual images which can be availed of when the CD is placed in a computer with a CD-ROM drive'.[42]

The defendant's claimed to be able to do so pursuant to a provision of the Copyright Act 1963. The availability of this defence turned on the definition of 'record' in the Copyright Act 1963. Barr J held that:

> 'There is no doubt that the wonders of contemporary computer technology and in particular the concept of adding a visual dimension to a disc of sound recordings would not have been contemplated by the drafter of the ... (Copyright Act 1963) ... or by the legislators who brought it into law. However, that is not per se a bar to the inclusion of new technology within an existing statutory framework. On the contrary, it is patently desirable that, where possible, advances in technology, even those which could not have been envisaged by the framers of an Act, should be accommodated in statutory interpretation by the court, but only where that can be done without straining the words used beyond their ordinary meaning and having paid due regard to the structure and intent of the statute'.[43]

---

[38] Comreg, *Regulatory Aspects of Next Generation Networks*, Doc. No. 07/40, 8 July 2007, p 6.

[39] Comreg, *Regulatory Aspects of Next Generation Networks*, Doc. No. 07/40, 8 July 2007, p 4.

[40] In particular see *Union des Association Europeenes de Football and others v Briscomb and others* [2006] EWHC 1268 (Ch).

[41] *Mandarim Records Ltd v Mechanical Copyright Protection Society (Ireland) Ltd* [1998] IEHC 146; [1999] 1 ILRM 154.

[42] [1998] IEHC 146; [1999] 1 ILRM 154, para 3.

[43] [1998] IEHC 146; [1999] 1 ILRM 154, para 6.

The decision in *Mandarim Records Ltd v Mechanical Copyright Protection Society (Ireland) Ltd* suggests that the courts will endeavour to interpret the CRRA 2000–2004 to ensure that their provisions apply to new technologies.[44]

Broadcast and cable programme

[2.16] The term 'broadcast' is defined as:

> 'a transmission by wireless means, including by terrestrial or satellite means, for direct public reception or for presentation to members of the public of sounds, images or data or any combination of sounds, images or data, or the representations thereof, but does not include MMDS service'.[45]

'Cable programme' means any item included in a cable programme service[46] which is defined as:

> 'a service, including MMDS, which consists wholly or mainly of sending sounds, images or data or any combination of sounds, images or data, or the representations thereof, by means of a telecommunications system ... for reception at 2 or more places (whether for

---

44 For a discussion of the principles of statutory interpretation see: Bennion, *Statutory Interpretation* (Butterworths, 2002); Langan, *Maxwell on the interpretation of Statutes* (NM Tripathi, 1976); Sullivan, *Driedger on the Construction of Statutes* (3rd edn, Butterworths, 1994); Bell and Engle, *Cross on Statutory Interpretation* (3rd edn, Butterworths, 1995). The leading Irish case on the application of old legislation to new technologies is the decision of the Supreme Court in *Keane and Naughton v An Bord Pleanála and the Commissioners of Irish Lights* [1997] 1 IR 184. The commissioners wished to erect a Loran-C mast at Feeard Cross in the County of Clare. The Commissioners of Irish Lights were charged by the Merchant Shipping Act 1894 with 'the superintendence and management of all lighthouses, buoys, and beacons ... throughout Ireland and the adjacent seas and islands' The commissioners were given the power 'to erect or place any buoy or beacon': Merchant Shipping Act 1894, s 634. The issue before the court was whether this provision gave the commissioners the power to erect a Loran-C mast. The issue before the court was summarised by Denham J (dissenting) in the following terms: 'Loran-C was not invented in 1894 when the Act was passed into law. It is a matter of construction of the statute as to whether the term 'beacon' includes the Loran-C mast ([1997] 1 IR 184 at 225)'. Hamilton CJ took the view that: '(i)t is fundamental to the construction or interpretation of a Statute to ascertain the true original intention of the legislature ([1997] 1 IR 184 at 215)'. Two facts were pertinent in this regard. Firstly, '(a)t the time of the enactment of the Act, "buoys" and "beacons" were regarded as visual aids to navigation'. Secondly:
'(t)he Loran-C system provides an aid to navigation both to ships and aircraft and extends far beyond the area of responsibility of the Commissioners as provided for and envisaged by the legislature and there does not appear to me to be anything contained in the Act and, in particular ... to show that it was the intention of the legislature that the Commissioners be either required or empowered to participate in such a system'.
This led him to the conclusion that:
'(t)he Loran-C system is clearly a system which is altogether beyond the scope of the Act. It is a system designed to enable ships and aircraft to pin-point their position at sea or in the air and not for the purpose of providing guidance to mariners approaching land or providing warning to them of the vicinity of land as was the purpose of ... the Act'. ([1997] 1 IR 184 at 216.)

45 CRRA 2000–2004, s 2(1).

46 CRRA 2000–2004, s 2(1).

simultaneous reception or at different times in response to requests by different users), or ... for presentation to members of the public'.[47]

A 'telecommunications system' is defined as:

'a system for conveying sounds, images or data or any combination of sounds, images or information, or the representations thereof, by means of a wire, beam or any other conducting device through which electronically generated programme-carrying signals are guided over a distance'.[48]

[2.17] The delivery of most, if not all, Internet content may fall within the definition of cable programme. All websites will contain data, many will contain sounds and many more will contain images. Transmitting the content of these sites over the Internet may fall within the Copyright and Related Rights Act's definition of a telecommunications system. RTÉ's website makes content available in different formats. Viewers can watch the RTÉ news on the Internet at the same time as it is broadcast to TV viewers.[49] Suppose a viewer usually watches the RTÉ news on television, which is 'guided' to his home through a fiber optic cable. If he should be late coming home he can download it over the Internet and watch it on his computer[50], the programme being 'guided' to his home through the same fiber-optic cable. It would seem illogical to say that when he watches the news on his television he is watching 'electronically generated programme-carrying signals' but that when he watches it on his computer he is not. However, this is a distinction that the Copyright and Related Rights Acts seek to make. The Acts provide that a cable programme does not include what might be termed interactive services:

'a service or part of a service of which it is an essential feature that while sounds, images or data or any combination of sounds, images or data, or the representations thereof, are being conveyed by the person providing the service, there may be sent from each place of reception, by means of the same system or, as the case may be, the same part of it, data (other than signals sent for the operation or control of the service) for reception by the person providing the service or other persons receiving the service.'

Older, analogue, cable programming systems might fall outside this definition, but newer services and in particular the digital television services[51] that may be introduced on foot of the Broadcasting (Amendment) Act 2007 will almost certainly qualify as interactive services for the purposes of the CRRA 2000–2004. Hence the difficulty with the Acts' definition of cable programmes may not be that it excludes the Internet, but rather that it excludes some forms of cable TV.

[2.18] The fact of being excluded from protection as a cable programme will have varying consequences for the owner of a work in question. The fact that a programme is transmitted will not necessarily create any rights in the programme. The CRRA 2000–

---

[47] CRRA 2000–2004, s 2(1).

[48] CRRA 2000–2004, s 2(1).

[49] http://www.rte.ie/live/.

[50] http://www.rte.ie/news/6news/.

[51] *Dempsey Launches Second Phase of Digital Terrestrial Television (DTT) Pilot* Press Release, Department Communications, Marine and Natural Resources, http://www.dcmnr.ie, 5 March 2007.

2004 provide that: 'copyright shall not subsist in the transmission of a broadcast or other material in a cable programme service unless the transmission alters the content of the broadcast or other materials'.[52] So if a broadcast by RTÉ is received by a cable operator and transmitted by means of a cable programme service, copyright will not subsist in that transmission of that broadcast unless the content is altered by, for example, inserting sub-titles. Even if this were to be done, the copyright so arising could be quite limited as the CRRA 2000–2004 provide that nothing in the above will 'affect the copyright subsisting in the broadcast or other material arising other than by virtue of the transmission'.[53] This would seem to be no more than a restatement of the existing law; it is hard to see how simply transmitting a work could have the necessary quality of originality to result in the subsistence of any copyright.

Are Hypertext links Cable programmes?

[2.19] The difficulties caused by the definition of 'cable programme' are best illustrated by the cases in which Hypertext links have been identified as cable programmes for the purposes of copyright law. This was held by the Scottish Courts in *Shetland Times Ltd v Wills*.[54] In *Sony Music Entertainment (UK) Ltd v Easyinternetcafe Ltd*,[55] Smith J suggested that this decision was correct.[56] In the Australian case of *Universal Music Australia Pty Ltd v Cooper*[57] the defendant operated a website at mp3s4free.net which contained Hypertext links to infringing copies of the plaintiffs' songs, which were accessible on other websites. The defendants alleged that this was in breach of a provision of the Australian Copyright Act, which gave the owner of copyright the exclusive right to communicate a work to the public, 'communicate' being defined as 'to make available online or electronically transmit'.

This may be compared with the CRRA 2000–2004 which gives, as part of the making available right, the owner the right to control 'making available to the public of copies of the work, by wire or wireless means'.

[2.20] In *Universal Music Australia Pty Ltd v Cooper* the plaintiffs submitted that:

> 'the sound recordings have been made available by Cooper through the displaying of hyperlinks on the website, which, when activated by a user clicking an electronic mouse, produce the result that there is an automatic direct downloading of the sound recording to the user's computer from the remote computer of a third party on which the recording is stored. The evidence indicates that for present purposes there are no sound recordings located on the Cooper website. Therefore, there is not, and cannot, be any downloading or transmission of the recordings from the Cooper website'[58]

---

52 CRRA 2000–2004, s 20(1).
53 CRRA 2000–2004, s 20(1).
54 *Shetland Times Ltd v Wills*
55 *Sony Music Entertainment (UK) Ltd v Easyinternetcafe Ltd* [2003] FSR 48.
56 [2003] FSR 48 at para 47, citing in support Laddie, para 8.18.
57 *Universal Music Australia Pty Ltd v Cooper* [2005] FCA 972.
58 [2005] FCA 972, para 60.

Because the defendant's website did not store the infringing copies in question, Tamberlin J was:

> 'not satisfied that the Cooper website has 'made available' the music sound recordings within the meaning of that expression. It is the remote websites which make available the sound recordings and from which the digital music files are downloaded as a result of a request transmitted to the remote website'.[59]

Tamberlin J based his decision that the defendant was not making the infringing copies in question available on two grounds. First of all:

> 'the digital music files to which links were provided on the Cooper website were also available to users through the internet generally. That is, internet users can access the music sound recordings via an alternative route by directly accessing the remote websites, either by typing that website's URL address into the address bar on the user's internet browser or by using a search engine such as Google or Yahoo, rather than by visiting the Cooper website'.[60]

[2.21] Secondly, the defendant's website had no direct involvement in the transmission of the infringing copy to the user:

> '[the Cooper website] contains hyperlinks to thousands of sound recordings which are located on remote websites and are downloaded directly from those websites to the computer of the internet user. When a visitor to the Cooper website clicked on a link on the website to an MP3 file hosted on another server, this caused the user's browser to send a 'GET' request to that server, resulting in the MP3 file being transmitted directly across the internet from the host server to the user's computer. The MP3 file does not pass through or via or across the Cooper website. The Cooper website facilitates the easier location and selection of digital music files and specification to the remote website, from which the user can then download the files by clicking on the hyperlink on the Cooper website. However, the downloaded subject matter is not transmitted or made available from the Cooper website and nor does the downloading take place through the Cooper website. While the request that triggers the downloading is made from the Cooper website, it is the remote website which makes the music file available and not the Cooper website.'[61]

The plaintiffs argued that by creating hyperlinks on his website the defendant was 'transmitting' infringing copies of the works. Again this submission was rejected by Tamberlin J, who found that:

> 'the actual transmission of the music sound recording begins with the commencement of the downloading of the recording from the remote website on which the recording is located to the end user. I accept that the electronic transmission of the sound recording to a user who triggers the hyperlink on the Cooper website is a communication to a member of the public from the remote website, however, it is not a transmission from the Cooper website'.[62]

---

[59] [2005] FCA 972, para 63.
[60] [2005] FCA 972, para 64.
[61] [2005] FCA 972, para 65.
[62] [2005] FCA 972, para 66.

On this basis Tamberlin J did not:

> 'consider that Cooper has 'communicated' the sound recording to the public. That is, Cooper has not made the sound recording available to the public or electronically transmitted it to the public'.[63]

In contrast he did consider that 'the remote websites have made available online and electronically transmitted the music sound recordings to the public.'[64]

[2.22] The view of hypertext links as cable programmes or a cable service would appear to overstretch the language of the CRRA 2000–2004. There is good reason to believe that the Oireachtas was not contemplating hypertext links when they inserted a provision such as this into the Acts. It is more likely that the Oireachtas was contemplating cable TV services like those that were the subject matter of *Paramount Pictures Corporation v Cablelink Ltd.*[65] Instead Tamberlin J determined that the defendant had 'authorised' the infringements in question. The CRRA 2000–2004 do provide that the owner of copyright has the exclusive right to authorise the making available of the work in question. But it is hard to see how creating a hypertext link to an infringing copy amounts to authorising the making of the copy. The whole point of the plaintiffs' action in *Universal Music Australia Pty Ltd v Cooper* was that the making of these infringing copies was unauthorised. The plaintiffs were able to make this argument because the Australian Copyright Act[66] was amended in 2000 to include a definition of authorisation that can best be described as idiosyncratic in that it extends its meaning to failing to prevent. In deciding whether a person has authorised an infringing act, the Australian courts may take the following factors into account:

(a) 'the extent (if any) of the person's power to prevent the doing of the act concerned;

(b) the nature of any relationship existing between the person and the person who did the act concerned;

(c) whether the person took any other reasonable steps to prevent or avoid the doing of the act, including whether the person complied with any relevant industry codes of practice'.[67]

[2.23] Tamberlin J found that the defendant's website did 'facilitate and enable … infringing downloading' and thus permitted or authorised the infringement.[68] This decision is not necessarily preferable to that taken by the Scottish courts in *Shetland Times v Wills.*[69] In any event the current wording of the Irish CRRA 2000–2004 would seem to prevent the Irish Courts following Tamberlin J's decision. Furthermore, the Irish

---

63 [2005] FCA 972, para 67.
64 [2005] FCA 972, para 68.
65 *Paramount Pictures Corporation v Cablelink Ltd* [1991] 1 IR 521.
66 Australia, Copyright Act 1968, as amended.
67 Australian Copyright Act, s 101A.
68 *Universal Music Australia Pty Ltd v Cooper* [2005] FCA 972, para 84.
69 *Shetland Times v Wills.*

courts may attach more weight to the decision of the House of Lords in *CBS Songs v Amstrad*.[70] In that case the plaintiffs submitted that:

> 'by selling a model which incorporates a double-speed twin-tape recorder Amstrad 'authorise' the purchaser of the model to copy a record in which copyright subsists and therefore Amstrad infringe the exclusive right of the copyright owner.'

This argument was rejected by Templeman LJ:

> 'twin-tape recorders, fast or slow, and single-tape recorders, in addition to their recording and playing functions, are capable of copying on to blank tape, directly or indirectly, records which are broadcast, records on discs and records on tape. Blank tapes are capable of being employed for recording or copying. Copying may be lawful or unlawful. Every tape recorder confers on the operator who acquires a blank tape the facility of copying; the double-speed twin-tape recorder provides a modern and efficient facility for continuous playing and continuous recording and for copying. No manufacturer and no machine confers on the purchaser authority to copy unlawfully. The purchaser or other operator of the recorder determines whether he shall copy and what he shall copy. By selling the recorder Amstrad may facilitate copying in breach of copyright but do not authorise it.'

[2.24] Following this judgment, it is submitted that a website which contained hypertext links to infringing copies could be regarded as facilitating the downloading of those infringing copies, but not authorising it. Websites make a great number of hypertext links available, some of those links will connect to infringing content, most of them will not. The operator of a website such as that involved in *Universal Music Australia Pty Ltd v Cooper* might be liable for secondary infringement, but he could not be regarded as authorising the downloading of infringing copies, because he had no authority to do so. The difficulty caused by the Australian interpretation of the word 'authorise' were exposed on appeal. The defendant, Cooper, appealed unsuccessfully. One of the employees of his service provider, a Mr Takoushis, had also been found to have infringed the plaintiff's copyright by authorising the making of infringing copies.[71] This judgment was overturned on appeal on the basis that Mr Takoushis was a 'mere functionary.' The Appeal Court was willing to accept that 'be accepted that Mr Takoushis knew the contents of the website operated by Mr Cooper and that it was likely to give rise to infringements of copyright in the recordings to which it was providing links', but went on to hold that: 'there was no ... reasonable step that he could take to prevent the infringements'.[72] This logic is not easily followed: the Australian courts had found that the proprietor of the mp3s4free.net website which facilitated the downloading of infringing copies by one set of third-parties from other websites run by a separate set of third-parties was liable for the resulting infringement. But the Australian courts were not willing to find that the person who was actually responsible for connecting the mp3s4free.net website to the Internet was liable for that connection. The difficulty here is that both the courts and the legislature of Australia have become confused between the meaning of 'facilitate' and 'authorise'. A proper interpretation of these terms would find that the defendant in *Cooper v Universal Music Australia Pty Ltd*, and the employee of

---

[70] *CBS Songs v Amstrad* [1988] AC 1013.
[71] *Cooper v Universal Music Australia Pty Ltd* [2006] FCAFC 187, para 67.
[72] [2006] FCAFC 187, Para 167.

his Internet service provider had both 'facilitated' the downloading of infringing copies, but neither could really be said to have authorised it.

[2.25] One reason why the Irish courts may find it difficult to extend the definition of programme service to hypertext link is that doing so would make it a criminal offence to knowingly link to infringing material. The CRRA 2000–2004 provide that a criminal offence will be committed where a work is included in a cable programme service if the person who included the work knew or had reason to believe that the copyright in the work would be infringed.[73] Ignorance of the criminal law is no defence, but the corollary of this provision is that the criminal law must be clear and comprehensible.

Are CCTV and other feeds cable programmes?

[2.26] One form of cable programming to which the CRRA 2000–2004 will definitely not apply is pictures provided by means of a closed circuit television systems such as security cameras which are used as part of:

'a service operated for the purposes of a business, trade or profession where—

... no person except that person carrying on the business, trade or profession is concerned in the control of the apparatus comprised in the system,

... sounds, images or data or any combination of sounds, images or data, or the representations thereof, are conveyed by the system exclusively for the purposes of the internal management of that business, trade or profession and not for the purpose of rendering a service or providing amenities for others, and

... the system is not connected to any other telecommunications system'.[74]

[2.27] Similar systems used by private individuals would also be covered:

'a service operated by an individual where—

... all the apparatus comprised in the system is under his or her control,

... sounds, images or data or any combination of sounds, images or data, or the representations thereof, conveyed by the system are conveyed solely for his or her private and domestic use by that individual, and

... the system is not connected to any other telecommunications system'.[75]

[2.28] Services such as the transmission of a lecture or conference in one room to students in another will not be included as the following category of service is excluded from protection:

'services, other than services operated as part of the amenities provided for residents or occupants of premises operated as a business, trade or profession, where—

... all the apparatus comprised in the system is situated in, or connects, premises which are in single occupation, and

... the system is not connected to any other telecommunications system'.[76]

---

[73] CRRA 2000–2004, s 140(5)(c).
[74] CRRA 2000–2004, s 2(1).
[75] CRRA 2000–2004, s 2(1).
[76] CRRA 2000–2004, s 2(1).

Finally, 'services which are, or to the extent that they are, operated for persons providing broadcasting or cable programme services or providing programmes for such services'[77] will be excluded from protection. So a feed from a camera to a screen in front of the producer of a programme would not be covered by the Act, but arguably a similar feed to the producer of a film would be protected.

Internet uploading

[2.29] The CRRA 2000–2004 specify that the owner of copyright has the exclusive right to control the uploading of content to the Internet, providing that the owner may control:

> 'making available to the public of copies of the work, by wire or wireless means, in such a way that members of the public may access the work from a place and at a time chosen by them (including the making available of copies of works through the Internet)'.

This explicitly applies to the Internet; it would also apply to proprietary intranets. Uploading a work to the internal systems of a company or institution might be contrary to the making available right; it all depends on how the term 'public' is defined.

Publication

[2.30] It would seem clear that publication on the Internet can infringe copyright. In *Imutran v Uncaged Campaigns*[78] the plaintiffs ran a research laboratory which undertook experiments on animals. The defendant organisation campaigned against the plaintiff; it received copies of documentation outlining the process of 'an account of pig-to-primate organ transplants'. The defendant published this online and the English High Court injuncted this activity, commenting that 'given the wholesale reproduction of them, can it be doubted that Imutran's copyright ... has been infringed'.[79]

Rental and lending of the work

[2.31] The CRRA 2000–2004 provide for a rental and lending right.[80] This must be considered together with the Directive on the Rental and Lending Right.[81] In Commission v Ireland[82] Ireland was found to have failed to implement this Directive, – steps are currently being taken to appropriately harmonise Irish law.

Infringement

[2.32] To a great extent the music, film and publishing industries exist in a symbiotic relationship with the industries that supply information technology products and other electronic goods. The distribution of electronic content is a case in point. The development of compact disc (CD) players, video cassette recorders (VCRs) and digital video disks (DVDs) have all created fresh markets for electronic content. But the

---

[77] CRRA 2000–2004, s 2(1).
[78] *Imutran v Uncaged Campaigns* [2001] 2 All ER 385.
[79] [2001] 2 All ER 385, para 28.
[80] CRRA 2000–2004, s 42.
[81] Council Directive 92/100/EEC of 19 November 1992 on rental right and lending right and on certain rights related to copyright in the field of intellectual property, OJ L 346, 27.11.1992, p 61–66.
[82] *Commission v Ireland* C-175/05.

information technology and electronic goods that create these new markets for legitimate electronic content may also facilitate the production of infringing copies of those works. The conflict between these two industries was set out by Templeman LJ giving judgment for the House of Lords in *CBS v Amstrad*[83]:

> 'My Lords, during the past half-century there have been continuous improvements in sciences and techniques concerned with the transmission, reception, recording and reproduction of sounds and signals. These developments were required for serious purposes such as war, espionage, safety and communications. The benefits of advances made for serious purposes have been employed for purposes of leisure and pleasure and have spawned two flourishing industries, the electronic equipment industry and the entertainment industry. The electronic equipment industry manufactures and sells sophisticated machines which enable individual members of the public to transmit, receive, record and reproduce sounds and signals in their own homes. The entertainment industry transmits and records entertainment on an enormous scale. Each industry is dependent on the other. Without the public demand for entertainment, the electronic equipment industry would not be able to sell its machines to the public. Without the facilities provided by the electronic equipment industry, the entertainment industry could not provide entertainment in the home and could not, for example, maintain orchestras which fill the air with 20th century cacophony or make gratifying profit from a recording of a group without a voice singing a song without a tune. Although the two industries are interdependent and flourish to their mutual satisfaction there is one area in which their interests conflict. It is in the interests of the electronic equipment industry to put on the market every facility which is likely to induce customers to purchase new machines made by the industry. It is in the interests of the entertainment industry to maintain a monopoly in the reproduction of entertainment. Facilities for recording and reproducing incorporated in machines sold to the public by the electronic equipment industry are capable of being utilised by members of the public to copy the published works of the entertainment industry, thus reducing the public demand for the original works and recordings of the entertainment industry itself. The electronic equipment industry invents and markets new and improved facilities which enable records to be made and copied. The public make use of those facilities to copy the recordings issued by recording companies and thus infringe the copyrights of the recording companies and of the composers, lyricists and others engaged in the entertainment industry. Hence arises the conflict between the electronic equipment industry and the entertainment industry.'[84]

Primary infringement

[2.33] Internet downloads, MP3 players and websites have now replaced the twin-deck tape recorders that were the subject of *CBS v Amstrad*. The infringements that are caused by these new devices and systems are divided by the law into two categories: primary infringement and secondary infringement. Primary infringement of copyright will occur when one of the acts above is undertaken without the permission of the owner of copyright. As the Acts state that the 'copyright in a work is infringed by a person who without the licence of the copyright owner undertakes, or authorises another to undertake, any of the acts restricted by copyright.'[85]

---

[83] *CBS v Amstrad* [1988] AC 1013.
[84] Per Tempelman L, judgment 2.
[85] CRRA 2000–2004, s 37(2).

[2.34] As regards the meaning of infringement, the CRRA 2000 gives statutory effect to the principle that for infringement to occur it is not necessary to copy, make available or adapt an entire work. All that need be shown is that these acts were undertaken in relation to 'a substantial part'. of the work. As the CRRA 2000 states:

> 'References to the undertaking of an act restricted by the copyright in a work shall relate to the work as a whole or to any substantial part of the work and to whether the act is undertaken directly or indirectly'.[86]

The Acts do not just give the owner of copyright the right to control the wholesale copying of an entire work, they also allow him control the copying of a 'substantial part' of that work. The corollary of this view is that the CRRA 2000–2004 provide that the 'incidental' inclusion of copyright material in a work will not amount to infringement. The Acts provide that the 'copyright in a work is not infringed by its inclusion in an incidental manner in another work'.[87]

[2.35] By way of definition, the CRRA 2000–2004 set out what will not be regarded as incidental: 'A work shall not be regarded as included in an incidental manner in another work where it is included in a manner where the interests of the owner of the copyright are unreasonably prejudiced'.[88] The CRRA 2000–2004 also provides that:

> 'The copyright in a work which has been lawfully made available to the public is not infringed by the use of quotations or extracts from the work, where such use does not prejudice the interests of the owner of the copyright in that work and such use is accompanied by a sufficient acknowledgement'.[89]

[2.36] It is notable that this provision only applies where a work 'has been lawfully made available to the public'. This deals with the situation that arose most recently in *Prince of Wales v Associated Newspapers Ltd.*[90] The plaintiff was the UK's Prince of Wales and the defendant a newspaper. At issue between them was the plaintiff's journal of his trip to Hong Kong to mark the transfer of the former UK colony to the People's Republic of China. The plaintiff argued that this were confidential, and the defendant sought to rely upon a similar defence of fair dealing under the UK Copyright Act. The English court held that the defendant could not so rely as 'it is plain that the Hong Kong journal has not been made available to the public'.[91]

The test for determining whether or not infringement has occurred was set out by Costello J in *House of Spring Gardens v Point Blank*[92] where he approved of the following principles set out by Diplock LJ in *Francis Day and Hunter Ltd v Bron*[93]:

---

[86] CRRA 2000–2004, s 37(3). This provision is not an innovation and is similar to the Copyright Act 1963, s 3.
[87] CRRA 2000–2004, s 52(1).
[88] CRRA 2000–2004, s 52(3).
[89] CRRA 2000–2004, s 52(4).
[90] *Prince of Wales v Associated Newspapers Ltd* [2006] EWHC 522 (Ch).
[91] [2006] EWHC 522 (Ch), para 177.
[92] *House of Spring Gardens v Point Blank* [1984] IR 611.
[93] *Francis Day and Hunter Ltd v Bron* [1963] Ch 587.

'(1) In order to constitute reproduction within the meaning of the Act, there must be (a) a sufficient degree of objective similarity between the two works, and (b) some causal connection between the plaintiffs' and the defendants' work.

(2) It is quite irrelevant to enquire whether the defendant was or was not consciously aware of such causal connection.

(3) Where there is a substantial degree of objective similarity, this of itself will afford prima facie evidence to show that there is a causal connection between the plaintiffs' and the defendants' work; at least it is a circumstance from which the inference may be drawn.

(4) The fact that the defendant denies that he consciously copied affords some evidence to rebut the inference of causal connection arising from the objective similarity, but is in no way conclusive'.[94]

[2.37] It is not enough to show that two works are substantially similar; there must also be a causal connection. The reason why the courts insist upon a causal connection were set out by Mummery J in *Sawkins v Hyperion Records Ltd*:[95]

'The general policy of copyright is to prevent the unauthorised copying of certain material forms of expression (literary, dramatic, artistic and musical, for example) resulting from intellectual exertions of the human mind ... The important point is that copyright can be used to prevent copying of a substantial part of the relevant form of expression, but it does not prevent use of the information, thoughts or emotions expressed in the copyright work. It does not prevent another person from coincidentally creating a similar work by his own independent efforts. It is not an intellectual property monopoly in the same sense as a patent or a registered design. There is no infringement of copyright in the absence of a direct or indirect causal link between the copyright work and the alleged copy'.[96]

[2.38] Liability for primary infringement is strict; the question of whether the defendant knew he was infringing copyright is irrelevant. In *Sony v Easyinternetcafe*[97] the plaintiffs alleged that the defendant was providing the following service to their customers:

'Upon payment of a fee, a customer is provided with access to the Internet via a PC. Those PCs are connected into a central server, and there are no copying or other facilities that can be utilised by the customer at the screen. Upon payment of the fee the customer is given a user ID. Files downloaded by a customer can be stored by the customer on a private directory on the Café's server identified by reference to the personal ID.

After the termination of a session a customer can ask the staff to download on to a CD-R the material in his private file area. That area can include sound recordings downloaded from the Internet. If the option is taken up, the customer presents his user ID to the staff member, who has access to the relevant customer's allocated area, and downloads the relevant files on to the CD-R using the CD writer programme.'[98]

The defendant did not dispute that if infringing copies were made through this process, then that would be a breach of the UK's copyright laws. But the defendant disputed its liability. In particular the defendant argued that in creating these CDs its employees were

---

[94] [1984] IR 611 at 670.
[95] *Sawkins v Hyperion Records Ltd* [2005] 1 WLR 3281.
[96] [2005] 1 WLR 3281 at 3289.
[97] *Sony v Easyinternetcafe* [2003] EWHC 62 (Ch).
[98] [2003] EWHC 62 (Ch), para 6–7.

essentially acting as 'automatons',[99] fulfilling the instructions of the plaintiff. This argument was rejected by Smith J who noted that:

> 'liability for (primary) infringement under ... is strict. It is no defence for a person copying an item to assert that he did not know he was infringing a copyright ... Obviously when strict liability is pushed to its boundaries absurd results can arise. It would be absurd if the recipient of a fax over which he has no control could be said to be infringing it merely because his machine is the one that prints the transmission. Generally, the owner of a fax machine cannot stop material being sent. He is an involuntary copier. The same occurs in relation to the Internet Service Provider.

> ... In the present case the only material which is available for this defence is the fact that the Defendant chooses to keep the files of an individual customer confidential allegedly by directing that the employees cannot see them unless the customer consents.

> ... This is not involuntary; it is voluntary. The difficulty only arises because of the terms upon which the Defendant chooses to allow customers to copy information. Further the Defendant is doing this for a profit. I do not see it is any different to a high street printer that is asked to copy material. If the high street printer copies material, which contains infringing copyright material (for example a pirated PhD Thesis) the printer will be liable. He will not know that the material is infringing for obvious reasons. Nevertheless, he is liable. I do not see how it can be said to be different because he *chooses* not to know. This to my mind is to introduce a *mens rea* defence when none is available'.[100]

Secondary infringement

[2.39] Primary infringement can be viewed as prohibiting acts that directly infringe rights in the works in question. Secondary infringement prohibits acts in relation to infringing copies derived from that initial infringement. The difference is significant. On the one hand, it may be more difficult to prove secondary, as opposed to primary, infringement. This is because proving secondary infringement requires proving the motivation of the alleged infringer. On the other hand, if secondary infringement can be proven beyond a reasonable doubt, then criminal penalties may be imposed. The CRRA 2000–2004 define an infringing copy as being a copy where:

(a)   'the making of it constitutes an infringement of the copyright in the work concerned; or

(b)   where it has been or is to be imported into the State, and its making in the State would have constituted an infringement of the copyright in the work concerned, or a breach of an exclusive licence agreement relating to that work'.[101]

The CRRA 2000–2004 create a presumption that where it can be shown that copy right subsists or has subsisted in a work that has been copied, then it will be presumed that the copy was made at a time when copyright subsisted in the work.[102] In addition to the two forms of secondary infringement discussed below, the Acts make permitting premises to

---

[99] [2003] EWHC 62 (Ch), para 32.
[100] [2003] EWHC 62 (Ch), para 33–35.
[101] CRRA 2000–2004, s 44(2).
[102] CRRA 2000–2004, s 44(4).

be used for infringing performances[103] and providing the means for infringing performances secondary infringements.[104]

Dealing in infringing copies

[2.40] The CRRA 2000–2004 provide that 'dealing' in infringing copies will be secondary infringement. The Acts provide that a person will infringe copyright where he or she does any of the following acts in respect of a copy of a work which he 'knows or has reason to believe is, an infringing copy'.[105] For infringement to occur the acts must be done 'without licence'. The acts take place where a person:

(a)   'sells, rents or lends, or offers or exposes for sale, rental or loan;

(b)   imports into the State, otherwise than for his or her private and domestic use;[106]

(c)   in the course of a business, trade or profession, has in his or her possession, custody or control, or makes available to the public; or

(d)   otherwise than in the course of a business, trade or profession, makes available to the public to such an extent as to prejudice the interests of the owner of the copyright.'[107]

[2.41] The question of what might amount to reasonable knowledge that copies of a song were infringing copies was reviewed by Jacob J in the English High Court in *Banks v EMI Songs Ltd and others*.[108] This concerned the lyrics to a hit song by the band UB40 called 'Don't Break My Heart'. In a separate action the plaintiff had succeeded in showing that she had in fact written the lyrics in question, the facts were that:

'the plaintiff was a friend of a Mr Javed Khan who himself was a friend of Mr Campbell of the defendant group. Mr Campbell had asked Mr Khan to write a lyric ... Mr Khan had in fact taken the lyric from his friend, the plaintiff. The judge held that Mr Khan had deceived Mr Campbell and the group in claiming that he had written the whole of the lyric himself'.

The plaintiff sued the defendants alleging that they had distributed infringing copies of her work. In deciding whether or not the defendants had reasonable grounds for believing that they were dealing with infringing copies, Jacob J held that:

'This is the sort of question where one must take all the circumstances into account. I think that there was enough here for the defendants reasonably to have believed that the copies were not infringing copies. This is not a case where they had been assured of the matter by a perfect stranger. The key figure ... had been assured by a very longstanding friend that he had done the job. There was every indication that he had done the job ... not only were the lyrics written in his hand but in his style.'

---

[103] CRRA 2000–2004, s 47.

[104] CRRA 2000–2004, s 48.

[105] On the precise knowledge required see *ZYX Music GmbH v King and others* [1997] 2 All ER 129, [1997] EMLR 319.

[106] But see the community exhaustion principle, eg, Directive 250/91 on the Legal Protection of Computer Programs, art 4(c).

[107] CRRA 2000–2004, s 45.

[108] *Banks v EMI Songs Ltd and others* (13 May 1996) Jacobs J.

Providing means for making infringing copies

[2.42] Providing the means or assistance to make an infringing copy may amount to secondary infringement. The CRRA 2000–2004 provide that:

'A person infringes the copyright in a work where he or she … makes … sells, rents or lends, or offers or exposes for sale, rental or loan … imports … or has in his or her possession, custody or control, of an article specifically designed or adapted for making copies of that work, knowing or having reason to believe that it has been or is to be used to make infringing copies.'[109]

In the US case of *Perfect 10 v Visa* the US Court of Appeals for the Ninth Circuit refused to take the 'radical' step of finding a credit card company liable for processing payments from a website which carried infringing copies.

Fair use

[2.43] The CRRA 2000–2004 allow for a variety of fair uses of copyright works. For example, they provide that:

'Fair dealing with a literary, dramatic, musical or artistic work, sound recording, film, broadcast, cable programme, or non-electronic original database, for the purposes of research or private study, shall not infringe any copyright in the work …'.[110]

The Acts define 'fair dealing' as meaning:

'the making use of a literary, dramatic, musical or artistic work, film, sound recording, broadcast, cable programme, non-electronic original database or typographical arrangement of a published edition which has already been lawfully made available to the public, for a purpose and to an extent which will not unreasonably prejudice the interests of the owner of the copyright.'[111]

[2.44] The CRRA 2000–2004 specifically provide that the fair dealing will not occur where:

'the person copying knows or has reason to believe that the copying will result in copies of substantially the same material being provided to more than one person at approximately the same time and for substantially the same purpose.'[112]

The CRRA 2000–2004 provide that 'the purposes of criticism or review of that or another work or of a performance of a work shall not infringe any copyright in the work where the criticism or review is accompanied by a sufficient acknowledgement'[113] and 'the purpose of reporting current events shall not infringe copyright in that work, where the report is accompanied by a sufficient acknowledgement'.[114] The Acts also contain an

---

[109] CRRA 2000–2004, s 45(1).

[110] CRRA 2000–2004, s 50(1).

[111] CRRA 2000–2004, s 50(3)(b).

[112] CRRA 2000–2004, s 50(4).

[113] CRRA 2000–2004, s 51(1).

[114] CRRA 2000–2004, s 51(2), the term 'sufficient acknowledgement is defined as meaning: 'an acknowledgement identifying the work concerned by its title or other description and identifying the author unless…in the case of a work which has been lawfully made available to the public, it was so made available anonymously, or…in the case of a work which has not been made available to the public, it is not possible for a person without previous knowledge of the facts to ascertain the identity of the author of the work by reasonable enquiry' s 51(3).

exception for the 'making for private and domestic use of a fixation of a broadcast or cable programme solely for the purpose of enabling it to be viewed or listened to at another time or place'.[115]

[2.45] The CRRA 2000–2004 provide for a variety of other fair uses, including uses for the purposes of:

(a)   education;[116]

(b)   libraries and archives;[117] and

(c)   public administration.[118]

Copyright will not be infringed by judicial or parliamentary proceedings. When discussing fair use in the context of information technology it is important to realise that US copyright law provides a general fair use exception which is not available in European and Irish copyright law.[119] Given the European[120] and Irish[121] desire to develop a knowledge society it may seem surprising that a similar measure has not been introduced here. Instead the Directive on the Harmonisation of Copyright provides a list of the specific exceptions or limitations which member states may make to the reproduction right[122] and the making available right.[123]

Enforcement

[2.46] Copyright is only effective if it is enforced. Therefore the CRRA 2000–2004 provide for a variety of different enforcement measures, procedures and remedies. These must all be read in the context of the Directive on the enforcement of intellectual property rights[124], which was enacted 'to approximate legislative systems so as to ensure a high, equivalent and homogeneous level of protection in the internal market.'[125]

Presumptions and procedures

[2.47] The CRRA 2000–2004 provide for a number of presumptions, which will apply in criminal and civil proceedings relating to alleged infringement in a work.[126] The first

---

[115] CRRA 2000–2004, s 101(1).

[116] CRRA 2000–2004, ss 53–58.

[117] CRRA 2000–2004, ss 59–70.

[118] CRRA 2000–2004, ss 71–77.

[119] 'the fair use of a copyrighted work ... is not an infringement of copyright. In determining whether the use made of a work in any particular case is a fair use the factors to be considered shall include ... the purpose and character of the use, including whether such use is of a commercial nature or is for non-profit educational purposes; ... the nature of the copyrighted work ... the amount and substantiality of the portion used in relation to the copyrighted work as a whole; and ... the effect of the use upon the potential market for or value of the copyrighted work' Title 17 US Code § 107.

[120] See '*Presidency conclusion of the Lisbon European summit*' (2000).

[121] Information Society Commission, *Building the Knowledge Society*, December 2002.

[122] Directive 2001/29/EC, art 5(2).

[123] Directive 2001/29/EC, art 5(3).

[124] Directive 2004/48/EC of the European Parliament and of the Council of 29 April 2004 on the enforcement of intellectual property rights.

[125] Directive 2004/48, Recital 10.

[126] CRRA 2000–2004, s 139(1).

presumption is that 'Copyright shall be presumed to subsist in a work until the contrary is proved.'[127]

The Acts also provide that:

'where the subsistence of the copyright in a work is proved or admitted, or is presumed ... the plaintiff shall be presumed to be the owner or ... the exclusive licensee of the copyright, until the contrary is proved'.[128]

[2.48] These presumptions would deal with the situation that arose in *Universal City Studios Incorporated v Mulligan (No 2)*[129] in which the defendant queried whether Disney actually did own the copyright in the film *Pocahontas*. The Acts also provide that where the name of the purported author, owner or licensee of a work appears on a work then that person will be presumed to be the author, owner or licensee:

'Where ... a name purporting to be that of the author of a work or of the owner or exclusive licensee of the copyright, as the case may be, appears on copies of the work, or ... a copy of a work bears or incorporates a statement, label or other mark indicating that a person is the author of the work or the owner or exclusive licensee of the copyright, as the case may be, that name, statement, label or mark shall be admissible as evidence of the fact stated or indicated which shall be presumed to be correct, unless the contrary is proved'.[130]

[2.49] If a person is named as an author in a 'statement, label or other mark' that appears on the work, then it will be presumed that that person did not make that work whilst in the course of employment.[131] Similar provisions will apply in respect of references to joint authors.[132] Other presumptions apply in respect of works of anonymous or dead authors[133] and where the names of the person who first made the work available to the public appear.[134] If the ownership of copyright should be disputed then the CRRA 2000–2004 provides that hearsay evidence may be accepted[135] and that:

'the court may direct that evidence in relation to ownership of the copyright be given on affidavit and the court may decide the issue having considered any affidavit presented to it unless it is satisfied that any conflict of evidence between the affidavits may not be resolved other than by hearing oral testimony in which case the court may order that oral evidence may be adduced.'[136]

The Acts also provide for a variety of search and seizure procedures.[137]

---

[127] CRRA 2000–2004, s 139(2).
[128] CRRA 2000–2004, s 139(3).
[129] *Universal City Studios Incorporated v Mulligan (No 2)* [1999] 3 IR 392.
[130] CRRA 2000–2004, s 139(4).
[131] CRRA 2000–2004, s 139(5).
[132] CRRA 2000–2004, s 139(6).
[133] CRRA 2000–2004, s 139(8).
[134] CRRA 2000–2004, s 139(7).
[135] CRRA 2000–2004, s 127(1).
[136] CRRA 2000–2004, s 127(2).
[137] CRRA 2000–2004, ss 131–134.

Civil remedies

[2.50] The CRRA 2000–2004 provide that 'infringement of the copyright in a work is actionable by the copyright owner.'[138]

As regards the reliefs that will be available to the copyright owner, the Acts provide that 'all relief by way of damages, injunction, account of profits or otherwise is available to the plaintiff as it is available in respect of the infringement of any other property right.'

As regards damages, a court may award 'such damages as, having regard to all the circumstances of the case, it considers just'.[139] A court may award damages under a variety of headings:

'in addition to or as an alternative to compensating the plaintiff for financial loss, the court may award aggravated[140] or exemplary damages[141] or both aggravated and exemplary damages.'[142]

[2.51] However, if the defendant can show that at the time the infringement occurred he 'did not know and had no reason to believe that copyright subsisted in the work to which the action relates' then the plaintiff will not be entitled to damages against him.[143] In *Universal City Studios Incorporated v Mulligan (No 3)*[144] Barr J found that it was:

'impossible to measure the loss of the plaintiffs … in consequence of the defendant's activities … The only evidence before the Court of the defendant's trading activity is that on twenty-two different occasions at different locations over five years, the defendant was in possession for sale of various quantities of pirated video cassettes which included various titles. It is impossible to deduce from the evidence what volume of sales of pirated

---

138 CRRA 2000–2004, s 127(3).

139 CRRA 2000–2004, s 128(1).

140 In *Conway v Irish National Teachers Organisation* [1991] 2 IR 305 Finlay CJ defined these as: 'being compensatory damages increased by reason of … the manner in which the wrong was committed, involving such elements as oppressiveness, arrogance or outrage, or … the conduct of the wrongdoer after the commission of the wrong, such as a refusal to apologise or to ameliorate the harm done or the making of threats to repeat the wrong, or … conduct of the wrongdoer and/or his representatives in the defence of the claim of the wronged plaintiff, up to and including the trial of the action' [1991] 2 IR 305 at 317. See also *Philip v Ryan* [2004] 4 IR 241.

141 In *Conway v Irish National Teachers Organisation* [1991] 2 IR 305 Finlay CJ defined these as 'damages arising from the nature of the wrong which has been committed and/or the manner of its commission which are intended to mark the court's particular disapproval of the defendant's conduct in all the circumstances of the case and its decision that it should publicly be seen to have punished the defendant for such conduct by awarding such damages, quite apart from its obligation, where it may exist in the same case, to compensate the plaintiff for the damage which he or she has suffered. I have purposely used the above phrase "punitive *or* exemplary damages" because I am forced to the conclusion that, notwithstanding relatively cogent reasons to the contrary, in our law punitive and exemplary damages must be recognised as constituting the same element' [1991] 2 IR 305 at 317. See also *Crofter Properties Ltd v Genport Ltd (No 2)* [2005] 4 IR 28.

142 CRRA 2000–2004, s 128(3).

143 CRRA 2000–2004, s 128(2).

144 *Universal City Studios Incorporated v Mulligan (No 3)* [1999] 3 IR 407.

copies of the plaintiffs' titles the defendant achieved, thus inflicting loss on the plaintiffs
... there is no evidence from which one could deduce that the activities of the defendant
affected the commercial success of any title of any plaintiff.'[145]

The defendant had been 'selling pirated videos from market stalls in local markets'. The
plaintiff estimated that this activity was costing it some £2 million a year. Barr J
considered that this estimate defied 'reason and common sense'.[146] Barr J awarded the
plaintiffs £75,000 to include £50,000 penal damages pursuant to the Copyright Act
1963.[147] *Columbia v Robinson*[148] concerned the amount of damages that should be
awarded in respect of an infringing copy of a video cassette. Scott J concluded that the
proper amount of damages would be somewhere between the minimum numbers of
pirated copies sold and the maximum number of copies that the defendant estimated
might have been sold. The difficulty with estimates of this kind is that as *Universal City
Studios Incorporated v Mulligan (No 3)* shows, those who sell infringing copies do not
tend to keep accurate records. This is a particular problem with online infringement,
where it is never clear how many of those who download an infringing copy would have
gone on to buy a legitimate copy if the infringing version were not available.[149]

Offences

[2.52] Section 140 of the CRRA 2000–2004 creates a number of criminal offences.
Firstly, it provides that an offence will be committed by a person who, without the
consent of the owner, does any of the following acts in respect of 'a copy of a work
which is, and which he or she knows or has reason to believe is, an infringing copy of the
work':

    (a)   'makes for sale, rental or loan;

    (b)   ... sells, rents or lends, or offers or exposes for sale, rental or loan[150] ...

    (c)   ... imports into the State, otherwise than for his or her private and domestic use
        ...

    (d)   ... in the course of a business, trade or profession, has in his or her possession,
        custody or control, or makes available to the public ...

    (e)   ... otherwise than in the course of a business, trade or profession, makes available
        to the public to such an extent as to prejudice the interests of the owner of the
        copyright'.[151]

[2.53] An offence will not be committed where the act in question may be 'undertaken
without infringing the copyright in a work'.[152] The maximum penalty that can be

---

[145] [1999] 3 IR407 at 410–411.

[146] [1999] 3 IR407 at 411.

[147] Copyright Act 1963, s 22(4).

[148] *Colombia v Robinson* [1988] FSR 531.

[149] Peitz and Waelbroeck, 'The Effect of Internet Piracy on Music Sales: Cross-Section Evidence'
[2004] Review of Economic Research on Copyright Issues, vol 1(2), pp 71–79.

[150] It should be noted that loaning an infringing copy to a friend or family member will not be a
criminal offence. Instead loan means 'a loan for reward':CRRA 2000–2004, s 140(2).

[151] CRRA 2000–2004, s 140(1).

[152] CRRA 2000–2004, s 140(6).

imposed upon conviction for infringement is a find of €127,500 together with a five-year term of imprisonment.[153] In terms of sentencing, notice might be taken of the English case of *R v Holborough*[154] which was an appeal against sentence by an appellant convicted of supplying thousands of decoders which allowed users to watch encrypted TV signals without a subscription. The victims of the appellant were cable TV companies; by selling decoders to their potential clients, the appellant deprived the cable TV companies of subscription income. In considering sentence the English Court of Appeal held that:

> 'some distinction may be made between those (cases) in which the victim, whether individuals or the public purse in the form of a government department, are defrauded of sums of money or property which pass to the fraudulent party and those where the loss to the victim is indirect, as here. The former category will generally attract a higher sentence.'[155]

[2.54] Mere possession of infringing copies would not appear to be an offence. It must be shown that the copies were made or imported for a commercial purpose. This caused a difficulty for the Irish and Hungarian authorities in *Minister for Justice v Hogyi*.[156] This case concerned a Hungarian whose apartment had been searched by the local police and 'computer programmes (software) and films which had been illegally copied were found on his personal computer and on CD and DVD disc'.[157] Mr Hogyi made his way to Ireland, where the Hungarian authorities applied for a European arrest warrant (EAW) in respect of him. To succeed in the EAW application, it had to be shown that Mr Hogyi's Hungarian activities would have amounted to an offence in Irish law. The Irish authorities argued that Mr Hogyi had not committed the equivalent of the Irish offence of dealing in infringing copies either. The issue then arose of whether Mr Hogyi could have committed an offence under the Copyright and Related Rights Act 2000–2004. Mr Hogyi's counsel submitted that he could not have and 'financial gain cannot arise from the mere possession of the material'.[158] Peart J agreed, holding that the application disclosed:

> 'simply that a large quantity of material illegally copied was found in the respondent's apartment and on his personal computer. While it is stated also that as a result he caused financial injury to the listed commercial entities, that is not the same as stating that he was engaged in a business or that he made illegal copies for sale, rental or loan. In my view there is insufficient factual material alleged in the warrant to go further than to say that he had possession of illegally copied material.'

[2.55] In general secondary or criminal infringement requires that the infringer has a commercial motivation. The exception to this is where the infringer 'otherwise than in the course of a business, trade or profession, makes available to the public to such an extent as to prejudice the interests of the owner of the copyright'. Defining what is

---

[153] CRRA 2000–2004, s 140(8).
[154] *R v Holborough* [2002] EWCA Crim 2631.
[155] [2002] EWCA Crim 2631, para 18.
[156] *Minister for Justice v Hogyi* [2006] IEHC 373.
[157] [2006] IEHC 373.
[158] [2006] IEHC 373.

meant by 'to such an extent as to prejudice the interests of the owner of the copyright' may not be easy. Essentially the courts may view this in two ways: they may examine the damage done to the right-holder in respect of each individual work uploaded to the Internet or they may examine the damage done by the alleged infringer as a whole.[159] Whichever view the court takes it will have to assess the prejudice caused to the right-holder in respect of a simple fact: there is a huge number of infringing works available online. To take an example, connect to a site such as http://www.piratebay.org, enter the name of any popular recording artist, the site will respond with a list of scores of bit-torrent downloads. Not all of them will contain what they promise, but many will contain infringing copies by the gigabyte. If there are hundreds and thousands of infringing copies available online, then it may be difficult to argue that the addition of one more will make that work available to the public 'to such an extent as to prejudice the interests of the owner of the copyright'. Arguably the unfortunate right-holder's interests have already been prejudiced.

Technological protection measures

[2.56] Technological protection measures such as digital rights management (DRM) software, devices and articles may allow the owner of copyright to directly control how their works are accessed and used by consumers and businesses. Most rights technological protection measures rely upon encryption to control access to content. Essentially the program will refuse access until a code or other input is entered; control the code and you control access to the software. Successfully building a system of this sort may prove problematic, as rights management software has an Achilles heal:

> 'in order to produce music or display a motion picture, a recording must at some point generate an unencrypted stream of data that can be interpreted by a sound screen or system. It is hard to prevent the possessor of the recording from capturing that stream in a new, unencrypted recording'.[160]

[2.57] Technological protection measures may be effective in limiting the ability of the average consumer to infringe copyright, but experts will be able to overcome them in time. As a result, much of the focus of litigation on technological protection measures focuses on controlling the distribution of the codes or articles that may be used to overcome them.

---

[159] The latter approach may be preferable, in *R v Holborough* [2002] EWCA Crim 2631 the appellant was a legitimate business man who had diversified his 'business into the dishonest development, manufacture and sale on a wholesale basis of various devices ... which allowed television programmes and films broadcast by cable companies to be received and viewed without appropriate payment to the cable companies' (para 4). The appellant was arrested but released, he went back to his dishonest business was arrested charged and ultimately convicted on two counts of conspiracy to defraud. One count relating to his conduct before his arrest, the other to his conduct after his initial arrest. He appealed his sentence on the grounds *inter alia* that his activities 'represented one continuous episode' (para 14). And this was accepted by the English Court of Appeal.

[160] Fisher, *Promises to Keep* (Stanford Law and Politics, 2004), p 87.

[2.58] Technological protection measures create a serious difficulty for the law of copyright, as they can continue to protect content indefinitely, without regard to the expiry of the term of copyright and may disregard fair use provisions.[161] Whether these difficulties become practical or remain simply conceptual remains to be seen. The term of copyright is very long, typically the life of the author plus 70 years. So if a new work is created today, assuming its author lives for 30 more years, the work will pass into the public domain a century from now. If anyone is still interested in the work then, it may be hoped that technology and society will have continued their advance and developed systems easily able to overcome what will then be antique technological protection measures. European and Irish legislatures may also have dealt with the second point by providing for fair uses so limited that difficulties caused by technological protection measures to those who wish to avail of fair use provisions are likely to be far less of an issue here than in the USA. The CRRA 2000–2004 makes a weak attempt to limit the adverse effects of rights management software on the Act's fair use provisions. The CRRA 2000–2004 provide for the 'non-interference of rights protection measures with permitted acts' and states that the controls that are imposed by Chapter 1 of Part VII of the Act should not be construed as 'as operating to prevent any person from undertaking the acts permitted ... or from undertaking any act of circumvention required to effect such permitted act'.[162]

[2.59] The flaws in this provision are immediately obvious. Firstly, the Act does not require that right-holders enable the removal of rights protection measures so that fair use may be made of the work in question. Secondly, the exemption only applies to Chapter 1 of Part VII, which primarily deals with encrypted broadcasts or programmes. It does not apply to rights protection measures in general, which are protected by Chapter 2 of Part VII. Even if it wanted to the Irish Oireachtas would find it difficult to construct a compromise between the interests of copyright owners and fair use rights in regard to this issue. The Directive on the Harmonisation of Copyright provides that member states should:

> 'promote voluntary measures taken by right-holders ... to accommodate achieving the objectives of certain exceptions or limitations provided for in national law in accordance with this Directive. In the absence of such voluntary measures ... Member States should take appropriate measures to ensure that right-holders provide beneficiaries of such exceptions or limitations with appropriate means of benefiting from them, by modifying an implemented technological measure or by other means ... in order to prevent abuse of such measures taken by right-holders, including within the framework of agreements, or taken by a Member State, any technological measures applied in implementation of such measures should enjoy legal protection'.[163]

The stage at which the provision of 'voluntary measures' would be so unsatisfactory that the Oireachtas could legislate to compel access is unclear. But the Directive on the Harmonisation of Copyright consistently speaks of 'voluntary measures' to be taken by right-holders. It is only in the absence of such 'voluntary measures' that right-holders

---

[161] Lessig, *Code and other laws of Cyberspace.*
[162] CRRA 2000–2004, s 374.
[163] Directive 2001/29/EC, Recital 51 and see also art 6(4).

may be compelled to vary their rights protection measure. Obviously even the suggestion of the introduction of compulsory measures might vitiate the voluntary nature of anything done by the right-holders. So it is likely that right-holders could hold out for quite some time before they could be compelled to vary their rights protection measures to permit fair use.

Encrypted broadcasts

[2.60] The seminal Irish case on technological protection measures is *News Datacom Ltd v Lyons*.[164] The plaintiffs transmitted television signals by satellite in an encrypted format. This system was designed so that viewers could only watch these programmes if they used a set-top decoder. This decoder would be activated by the insertion of a 'smart card', which was available to the plaintiffs' subscribers. The information contained in a computer program on the smart card would enable the decryption of the encoded television signal. As a security measure the plaintiffs changed the smart cards from time to time, which entailed issuing a new smart card to each customer. The defendants started producing and selling smart cards which worked in the plaintiffs' set-top decoders. Whenever the plaintiffs changed smart cards, the defendants would follow suit. The defendants' activities enabled members of the public to view the plaintiffs' programmes without a subscription. The plaintiffs applied for an injunction to restrain the defendants' activities. Flood J refused the injunction on the basis that the plaintiffs were unable to prove that the defendants' activities were the result of copying and the plaintiffs had not offered any scientific basis for their claim that, given the complicated nature of their algorithm, the only explanation for the identical result achieved by the defendants' card was copying. The fact that the defendants' computer program could perform the same function as the plaintiffs' did not constitute direct evidence that there was a similarity in the programs themselves. The fact that the plaintiffs changed their algorithms on a regular basis and that the defendants were able to produce a card capable of decrypting the defendants' signal within a relatively short time made the plaintiffs' claim that the only explanation for such functional similarity was copying highly improbable and gave weight to the defendants' claim that they had not infringed the plaintiffs' copyright.

[2.61] Although the references to source and object codes on the decoder card suggest some confusion on the facts, the decision in *News Datacom Ltd v Lyons* was undoubtedly correct on the law. The decision in *News Datacom Ltd v Lyons* made it clear that merely because something is encrypted does not confer copyright or any other form of legal protection upon it. This was subsequently acknowledged by Jacob J in the English High Court in *Mars UK Ltd v Teknowledge Ltd*.[165] In this case, the plaintiff

---

[164] *News Datacom Ltd v Lyons* [1994] 1 ILRM 450. On the use of decoder cards to control geographical access to content see: *Investors Overseas Services SA v The Home Video Channel (trading as the Adult Channel)* [1997] EMLR 347, (1996) The Times, 2 December.

[165] *Mars UK Ltd v Teknowledge Ltd* [2000] FSR 138, (1999) The Times, 8 July. See also the decision of the US Court of Appeals for the Federal Circuit in *Chamberlain v Skylark* (31 August 2004), which related to the use of encryption in remote control devices for garage doors. The US Court of Appeal ruled that the protections provided by the US copyright act for encrypted systems 'prohibits only forms of access that bear a reasonable relationship to the protections that the Copyright Act otherwise affords copyright owners': at p 40.

encrypted the software for its coin discriminators but the defendant was able to reverse-engineer the program. The plaintiff put forward the proposition that:

'if the reverse engineer, working on an article which he has come by lawfully, discovers that the maker put in some form of encryption, then he is put on notice that the maker regards what is encrypted is confidential. So the encrypted information is to be regarded in law as a trade secret and treated as such. It is unlawful, being a breach of confidence, for anyone, without lawful excuse, to de-cipher the code. So far as I can see the contention must equally apply if the reverse engineer discovers a physical lock in the device and decides to pick that lock – anything which the maker obviously and deliberately put in the way of discovering how the thing works is enough to give rise to an obligation of confidence. Mere difficulty in doing the job is not enough – there must be some element of deliberate difficulty put in the way. Mars make no bones about the far-reaching nature of their case. In the words of their closing submissions 'the issue is whether it is possible to impose confidentiality upon someone who receives information by purchasing an article in the open market.'[166]

[2.62] Jacob J rejected this proposition, holding that the plaintiff's machine was:

'on the market. Anyone can buy it. And anyone with the skills to de-encrypt has access to the information. The fact that only a few have those skills is, as it seems to me, neither here nor there. Anyone can acquire the skills and anyway, a buyer is free to go to a man who has them. Mars suggest that the owner, although he owns the machine, does not own the information within it. That is too glib. What the owner has is the full right of ownership. With that goes an entitlement "to dismantle the machine to find out how it works and tell anyone he pleases".'[167]

The plaintiff argued that the use of encryption was 'equivalent to a notice saying "confidential – you may not de-encrypt"' Jacob J thought this to be incorrect:

'As pure matter of common sense I cannot see why the mere fact of encryption makes that which is encrypted confidential or why anyone who de-encrypts something in code should necessarily be taken to be receiving information in confidence. He will appreciate that the source of the information did not want him to have access, but that is all. He has no other relationship with that source. Nor do the circumstances have an analogy with eavesdropping or secret long-lens photography … .or telephone tapping. In that sort of case the snooper not only knows he is prying into other people's business but he has used some surreptitious means to do so. There is nothing surreptitious in taking a thing apart to find out how it is made.'[168]

[2.63] As the courts were unwilling to protect technological protection measures, the Oireachtas decided to do so. The CRRA 2000–2004 makes it an offence to receive encrypted broadcasts or programmes without a subscription:

'A person who receives a broadcast or cable programme to which rights protection measures have been applied, knowing or having reason to believe that it is being received unlawfully with the intent to avoid payment of any charge applied by the rightsowner for the reception of that broadcast or cable programme shall be guilty of an offence and shall be liable on summary conviction to a fine not exceeding £1,500 (€1,905)'.[169]

---

166 [2000] FSR 138, (1999) The Times, 8 July, para 29.
167 [2000] FSR 138, (1999) The Times, 8 July, para 31.
168 [2000] FSR 138, (1999) The Times, 8 July, para 33.
169 CRRA 2000–2004, s 371.

The Acts recognise that someone who applies technological protection measures will have certain rights. Where a person is authorised by a rights-holder 'to make charges for the reception of programmes included in a broadcast or cable programme service', or 'to send encrypted transmissions of any other description' then that person will have the rights and remedies against any person who:

> 'makes ... sells, rents or lends, or offers or exposes for sale, rental or loan ... imports into the State, or ... has in his or her possession, custody or control, any apparatus or protection-defeating device, knowing or having reason to believe that the apparatus or device is to be used to enable or assist persons to receive those programmes or transmissions when those persons are not so entitled, or ... provides information, or offers or performs any service, intended to enable or assist persons to receive those programmes or transmissions when those persons are not so entitled.'[170]

However, 'in cases of innocent infringement' the court may award damages which 'it considers appropriate in the circumstances, and such damages shall not exceed a reasonable payment in respect of the act complained of'.[171] To avail of these provisions a broadcast must be effectively protected. If the Minister for Enterprise Trade and Employment decides that broadcasts 'are not adequately protected in a country, territory, state or area' then the Minister may restrict the application of these rights by order.

Technological protection measures under the CRRA 2000–2004

[2.64] The Acts protect technological protection measures in a number of ways. Firstly, they provide that an offence will be committed by a person who:

> 'makes ... sells, rents or lends, or offers or exposes for sale, rental or loan ... imports into the State ... or ... has in his or her possession, custody or control, an article specifically designed or adapted for making copies of a work, knowing or having reason to believe that it has been or is to be used to make infringing copies.'[172]

This provision is directed at the protection of 'plates' or 'engravings' for the purpose of making infringing copies. Hence the reference to 'an article specifically designed or adapted for making copies of a work'. Obviously there would be some difficulty in applying this provision to digital technologies which are more flexible. Digital infringement tools are prohibited by the following provision, which states that an offence will be committed by a person, who:

> 'makes ... sells, rents or lends, or offers or exposes for sale, rental or loan ... imports into the State, or ... has in his or her possession, custody or control, a protection-defeating device, knowing or having reason to believe that it has been or is to be used to circumvent rights protection measures, or provides information, or offers or performs any service, intended to enable or assist a person to circumvent rights protection measures.'

The Acts define a 'rights protection measure' as 'any process, treatment, mechanism or system which is designed to prevent or inhibit the unauthorised exercise of any of the rights conferred by this Act.'[173]

---

[170] CRRA 2000–2004, s 372(1).

[171] CRRA 2000–2004, s 372(2).

[172] CRRA 2000–2004, s 140(3).

[2.65] As well as the protections provided for encrypted broadcasts and discussed above, the Acts create specific protections for rights protection measures, devices and information by providing that a person who makes rights protected works available to the public[174] has the same rights and remedies against a person who

'makes ... sells, rents or lends, or offers or exposes for sale, rental or loan ... imports into the State, or ... has in his or her possession, custody or control, a protection-defeating device, knowing or having reason to believe that it has been or is to be used to circumvent rights protection measures, or ... provides information, or offers or performs any service, intended to enable or assist persons to circumvent rights protection measures ...'[175]

[2.66] The equivalent provision of the UK's Copyright, Designs and Patents Act 1988 was considered by Laddie J in *Kabushiki Kaisha Sony Computer Entertainment Inc and others v Ball and others*.[176] In this case the plaintiff was the manufacturer of the PS2 games console and owned the copyright in various PS2 games. The console and games were designed:

'to work together ... they also contain a two part copy protection system ... in which one part is embedded in the console and one part in the CD or DVD carrying the PS2 game. The two parts co-operate together rather like a lock and key enabling the PS2 game to be played on the type of PS2 console for which it is designed ... .the system works as follows. The CD or DVD contains, in digital form, the programs and other creative works needed to play the game. This material is capable of being copied by readily available CD and DVD copying equipment. However the authentic CDs and DVDs also have other codes embedded on the discs which are not recorded by standard copying equipment. An unauthorised copy of the CD or DVD made on such equipment will not contain copies of these other codes. The PS2 console (unlike standard copying equipment) can read the embedded codes and requires those codes to be present before it will allow the game on the CD or DVD to be played. This means that any copy of the PS2 game made on standard copying equipment will not be playable on the PS2 console'.[177]

The system did not just prevent the use of infringing copies; it also controlled the geographical market for PS2 consoles and games:

'Sony have designed their copy protection system in such a way that the embedded codes result in PS2 games designed, say, for Europe being playable only on PS2 consoles destined for the European market. Thus a European PS2 game will not be playable on an American or Japanese console. Japanese and American PS2 games will not be playable on a European console. By this means, parallel importation of PS2 games into Europe from abroad can be frustrated.'[178]

---

[173] CRRA 2000–2004, s 2(1).
[174] CRRA 2000–2004, s 270(1).
[175] CRRA 2000–2004, s 270(2).
[176] *Kabushiki Kaisha Sony Computer Entertainment Inc and others v Ball and others* [2004] All ER (D) 334 (Jul), [2004] EWHC 1738 (Ch).
[177] [2004] All ER (D) 334 (Jul), [2004] EWHC 1738 (Ch), para 4.
[178] [2004] All ER (D) 334 (Jul), [2004] EWHC 1738 (Ch), para 5.

The defendant had designed and marketed a chip, called the Messiah2 chip, which could be:

'fitted into a PS2 console and works so as to trick the console into believing that the CD or DVD being played has the necessary embedded codes. By this means, the modified PS2 console can be made to play not only authentic PS2 games designed for the geographical area for which the console was intended, but also unauthorised copies and also games from either of the two regions which are 'foreign' to the console.'[179]

[2.67] Sony brought proceedings under the UK's Copyright, Designs and Patents Act 1988, relying on a provision similar in wording to the Copyright and Related Rights Act 2000–2004's prohibition on dealing with 'a protection-defeating device'.[180] The defence asserted that it could not be liable under this provision as it was not dealing with an 'article', specifically the defence asserted that it would have to be shown that the defendant:

'knew or had reason to believe that the Messiah2 chip would be used to make articles which are infringing copies. He says that no such articles exist here. The Messiah2 chip is not used for making unauthorised copies of the CD or DVD on which the PS2 game is supplied by Sony. Nor is it argued that an imported authentic, but 'foreign', PS2 game is either an infringing copy or made by use of the Messiah2 chip. If there is to be an infringing copy, it has to be created by the unlocked use of either ... the unlicensed copy CD or DVD or ... the imported foreign game'.[181]

The defendant argued that the brief storage of data in the RAM of the PS2 consol was two short to amount to an infringement of copyright and to make the chip in question an 'infringing article' for the purposes of UK Copyright legislation, counsel for the defendant argued 'that the RAM containing the copy of Sony's digital data is too short lived to be regarded as tangible'.[182]

[2.68] This was rejected by Laddie J who held that:

'The silicon RAM chip is an article. When it contains the copy data, it is also an article. The fact that it did not contain the copy before and will not contain the copy later does not alter its physical characteristics while it does contain a copy. It is always an article but it is only an infringing article for a short time. There is nothing in the legislation which suggests that an object containing a copy of a copyright work, even if only ephemerally, is for that reason to be treated as not an article ... An article becomes an infringing article because of the manner in which it is made. Whether it is an infringing article within the meaning of the legislation must be determined by reference to that moment. It matters not whether it is remains in that state, since retention as a copy is no part of the definition'.[183]

---

[179] [2004] All ER (D) 334 (Jul), [2004] EWHC 1738 (Ch), para 6.

[180] Specifically s 296(2) of the UK's Copyright, Designs and Patents Act 1988 provides that a copyright owner will be able to bring an action for infringement against any person who deals in 'any device or means specifically designed or adapted to circumvent the form of copy-protection employed, or... publishes information intended to enable or assist persons to circumvent that form of copy-protection'.

[181] *Kabushiki Kaisha Sony Computer Entertainment Inc and others v Ball and others* [2004] All ER (D) 334 (Jul), [2004] EWHC 1738 (Ch), para 12.

[182] [2004] All ER (D) 334 (Jul), [2004] EWHC 1738 (Ch), para 13.

[183] [2004] All ER (D) 334 (Jul), [2004] EWHC 1738 (Ch), para 14.

The second argument made by the defendant was that 90% of its chips were exported out of the UK, which was not prohibited by the UK's Copyright, Designs and Patents Act 1988. Laddie J doubted that this point would ultimately succeed, pointing to changes in the UK law and the EC's Directive on the Harmonisation of Copyright. But he also concluded that this was 'not a matter which can be resolved on a summary application'.[184]

[2.69] The CRRA 2000–2004 provide protections for what it terms 'Rights Management Information'. This is defined as including information or any representation thereof which:

    (a)   'Identifies a copyright work, recording of a performance or database';

    (b)   ... identifies the author in relation to a copyright work, the performer in relation to a recording of a performance or the maker in respect of a database'; and

    (c)   ... identifies the owner of any right in a copyright work, recording of a performance or database.'

[2.70] Rights management information can also be information:

'about the terms and conditions of use of a copyright work, recording of a performance or database, where any of these items of information, or any representations thereof, are attached to or appear in connection with a copy of a copyright work or a copy of a recording of a performance, which is lawfully made available to the public, or a copy of a database which is lawfully re-utilised'.[185]

The Acts provide that a person who provides rights management information has the same rights and remedies as a right-holder against a person who:

    (a)   'removes or alters rights management information from copies of copyright works, copies of recordings of performances or copies of databases knowing or having reason to believe that the primary purpose or effect of such removal or alteration is to induce, enable, facilitate or conceal an infringement of any right, conferred by this Act ...'

    (b)   ... makes available to the public copies of copyright works or copies of recordings of performances or re-utilises copies of databases ... knowing or having reason to believe that rights management information has been removed or altered from those copies, or ...

    (c)   ... sells, rents or lends, or offers or exposes for sale, rental or loan ... imports into the State, or ... in the course of a business, trade or profession, has in his or her possession, custody or control, copies of copyright works, copies of recordings of performances or copies of databases ... knowing or having reason to believe that rights management information has been removed or altered from those copies'.[186]

[2.71] The CRRA 2000–2004 also provide for a criminal offence in relation to the removal of rights management information and the making available of infringing copies

---

[184] [2004] All ER (D) 334 (Jul), [2004] EWHC 1738 (Ch), para 22.
[185] CRRA 2000–2004, s 375(2).
[186] CRRA 2000–2004, s 375(1).

of works from which the rights management information has been removed. The Acts provide that an offence will be committed by a person who:

'removes or alters rights management information from copies of copyright works, copies of recordings of performances or copies of databases knowing or having reason to believe that the primary purpose or effect of such removal or alteration is to induce, enable, facilitate or conceal an infringement of any right conferred by this Act ...

... makes available to the public copies of copyright works or copies of recordings of performances or re-utilises copies of databases .... knowing or having reason to believe that rights management information has been removed or altered from those copies, or

... sells, rents or lends, or offers or exposes for sale, rental or loan ... imports into the State, or ... in the course of a business, trade or profession, has in his or her possession, custody or control, copies of copyright works, copies of recordings of performances or copies of databases ... knowing or having reason to believe that rights management information has been removed or altered from those copies.'[187]

The maximum penalty that can be imposed upon conviction for such an offence is a fine of just under €127,000 and a five-year term of imprisonment.[188]

Technological protection measures under the Directive on the harmonisation of copyright

[2.72] The Directive on the Harmonisation of Copyright requires that member states must:

'provide adequate legal protection against the circumvention of any effective technological measures, which the person concerned carries out in the knowledge, or with reasonable grounds to know, that he or she is pursuing that objective'.[189]

'Technological measures' are defined as meaning:

'any technology, device or component that, in the normal course of its operation, is designed to prevent or restrict acts, in respect of works or other subject-matter, which are not authorised by the right-holder of any copyright or any right related to copyright.'

Such a measure will be regarded as 'effective':

'where the use of a protected work or other subject-matter is controlled by the right-holders through application of an access control or protection process, such as encryption, scrambling or other transformation of the work or other subject-matter or a copy control mechanism, which achieves the protection objective.'[190]

[2.73] The Directive on the Harmonisation of Copyright justifies the European harmonisation of these protections on the basis that:

'Technological development will allow right-holders to make use of technological measures designed to prevent or restrict acts not authorised by the right-holders of any copyright, rights related to copyright or the sui generis right in databases. The danger, however, exists that illegal activities might be carried out in order to enable or facilitate the

---

[187] CRRA 2000–2004, s 376(1).
[188] CRRA 2000–2004, s 376(2).
[189] Directive 2001/29/EC, art 6(1).
[190] Directive 2001/29/EC, art 6(3).

circumvention of the technical protection provided by these measures. In order to avoid fragmented legal approaches that could potentially hinder the functioning of the internal market, there is a need to provide for harmonised legal protection against circumvention of effective technological measures and against provision of devices and products or services to this effect'.[191]

Member states must provide adequate legal protection against the distribution of 'devices, products or components or the provision of services' which are designed to circumvent rights protection measures'.[192] In relation to rights management information member states must:

'provide for adequate legal protection against any person knowingly performing without authority any of the following acts:

... the removal or alteration of any electronic rights-management information;

... the distribution, importation for distribution, broadcasting, communication or making available to the public of works ... from which electronic rights-management information has been removed or altered without authority,

if such person knows, or has reasonable grounds to know, that by so doing he is inducing, enabling, facilitating or concealing an infringement of any copyright or any rights related to copyright'.[193]

The Directive defines 'rights-management information' as meaning:

'any information provided by right-holders which identifies the work ... the author or any other right-holder, or information about the terms and conditions of use of the work or other subject-matter, and any numbers or codes that represent such information'.[194]

---

[191] Directive 2001/29/EC, Recital 47.
[192] Directive 2001/29/EC, art 6(2).
[193] Directive 2001/29/EC, art 7(1).
[194] Directive 2001/29/EC, art 7(2).

Chapter 3

Moral Rights

Introduction

[3.01] The protection of moral rights, such as the rights of paternity and integrity, is a requirement of the Berne Convention, and the inclusion of these rights in the CRRA 2000–2004 was a significant change from pre-existing Irish law. Prior to the 2000 Act, it had been argued that the moral rights of the author were protected by existing laws, so the paternity right could be protected by the law of passing off and the reputation of an author might have been protected by the laws of defamation and the constitutional protections for an individual's reputation. In reality, the protection of moral rights contained in these laws was doubtful. The CRRA 2000–2004[1] only carry out the minimum required by the Berne Convention, which specifically art 6(1) Bis requires that signatories:

> 'Independently of the Author's economic rights, and even after the transfer of the said rights, the author shall have the right to claim authorship of the work, and to object to any distortion, mutilation or other modification of, or other derogatory action in relation to, the said work, which would be prejudicial to his honour or reputation'.

The paternity right

[3.02] The 'paternity right'[2] gives the author of a work the right to have his contribution identified:

> 'the author of a work shall have the right to be identified as the author and that right shall also apply in relation to an adaptation of the work'.[3]

The author of a novel, which is used for the inspiration of a computer game or film, has the right to insist that their contribution be acknowledged. The identification does not have to be the author's name: where an author uses a pseudonym, initials or other form of identification, that form can be used to identify his or her work.[4] However, it is not enough to simply mention the author's name, it must also 'identify his authorship'.[5] The paternity right may be important online where sections of email are cut and pasted without their headers (which identify the author) and posted to newsgroups and so

---

[1]   Performers are also entitled to moral rights: Pt IV of the CRRA 2000–2004.

[2]   CRRA 2000–2004, s 107(3): the right conferred by this section shall be known and in this part referred to as the 'paternity right'.

[3]   CRRA 2000–2004, s 107(1). Art 6bis of the Berne Convention provides that: 'the author shall have the right to claim authorship of the work'.

[4]   CRRA 2000–2004, s 107(2).

[5]   *Sawkins v Hyperion Records Ltd* [2005] EWCA Civ 565, [2005] 3 All ER 636, at para 69.

forth.[6] The paternity right may to some extent confer a right of anonymity on the authors of an email since the author has the right to insist on how he is identified. If he insists that his identification be a single letter or a handle such as *The Mad Hacker*,[7] that is his right.[8]

Integrity right

[3.03] The 'integrity right'[9] gives the author of a work the right to object to:

> 'any distortion, mutilation or other modification of, or other derogatory action in relation to, the work which would prejudice his or her reputation and that right shall also apply in relation to an adaptation of the work'.[10]

The right conferred by this section applies to any addition to, deletion from or alteration to or adaptation of parts of a work resulting from any previous addition to, deletion from or alteration to or adaptation of a work or parts of a work by a person other than the author, where those parts are attributed to, or are likely to be regarded as the work of, the author.[11]

[3.04] The French courts have held that the translation and performance of a play, which significantly distorted the original meaning was a breach of the author's moral rights.[12] Similarly, in a decision of the French Supreme Court, *Huston v Turner Entertainment,*[13] it was held that colourising John Huston's black and white film *The Asphalt Jungle* was a breach of the author's *droit moral*.[14] This decision received *obiter* support from Overend J in the English High Court decision of *Pasterfield v Denham and another*.[15] The first-named defendant had been employed to update leaflets, which had been originally designed by the plaintiff.[16] It was alleged that the first-named defendant had subjected the plaintiff's designs to derogatory treatment, in that they were distorted or mutilated and colours changed. Overend J rejected this submission holding that the

---

6   See, generally, Lea, 'Moral rights and the Internet: Some thoughts from a common law perspective' in *The Internet and Authors' Rights* Pollaud-Dulian (ed.), (Sweet & Maxwell, 1999) ch 4.
7   *R v Whitley* [1991] 93 Cr App Rep 25 and also Clough and Mongo, *Approaching Zero* (Faber & Faber, 1992), p 56.
8   CRRA 2000–2004, s 108 sets out the exceptions to the paternity right.
9   CRRA 2000–2004, s 109(3): The right conferred by this section shall be known and in this part referred to as the 'integrity right'.
10 CRRA 2000–2004, s 109(1). Article 6 bis of the Berne Convention provides: '... the author shall have the right...to object to any distortion, mutilation or other modification of, or other derogratory action in relation to, the said work, which would be prejudical to his honour or reputation'.
11 CRRA 2000–2004, s 109(2).
12 *Leonide Zorine v Le Lucernaire* [1987] ECC 54. See also *Rowe v Walt Disney Productions* [1987] FSR 36.
13 *Huston v Turner Entertainment* (28 May 1991), 23 IIC 702.
14 See also *Snow v The Eaton Centre* 70 CPR (2d) 105.
15 *Pasterfield v Denham and another* [1999] FSR 168.
16 The court held that the equitable interest in the copyright had passed from the first- to the second-named defendant.

plaintiff had failed to establish that 'the treatment accorded to his work is ether a distortion or mutilation that prejudices his honour or reputation as an artist. It is not sufficient that the author is himself aggrieved by what has occurred'. This is an 'objective' test for integrity, and Overend J rejected the suggestion that variations in shading and colour could 'come anywhere near what I perceive to be the gross differences between a black and white and a colourised version of the same film'. The integrity right may be significant where works are 'mixed' or altered to create new works; this is particularly significant with digital technology, which allows works to be altered in a host of ways. In *Morrison v Lightbond*[17] it was held to be at least arguable that a medley of five different tunes or 'Megamix' was derogatory treatment. Yet if the *dicta* of Overend J that the test for derogatory treatment is the objective view of the court and not the subjective view of the author, then the interpretation of this section may be interesting and it may be more limited than at first seems. To avail of this right, the author must show that his work is being treated in a manner, that would prejudice the author's reputation. It might be argued that by 'colourising' a black and white film, the owners of copyright were simply making that film accessible to a wider modern audience and so enhancing the author's reputation. The courts would also have to keep in mind that the economic rights in a film will have been willingly assigned, often at not inconsiderable return to the author. On the other hand it may be broader: if the owner of a famous or infamous artistic work were to commence the destruction of that work, he might be prevented on the basis that this was a distortion or mutilation of the author's work.[18]

False attribution

[3.05] This is the moral right, that most closely parallels existing rights under the law of passing off. The Acts provide that '(a) person has the right not to have a work falsely attributed to him or her as author.'[19] Attribution is defined as being a statement, express or implied, as to who is the author of the work.[20] The right can be infringed in two specific ways: firstly, the author has the right to object to the sale and distribution of works which contain a false attribution; secondly, there is the right to object to altered works being sold or distributed as being the unaltered work of the author. The right will be infringed by a person who:

'(a) sells, rents or lends, or offers or exposes for sale, rental or loan,

(b) imports into the State, otherwise than for his or her private and domestic use,

(c) in the course of a business, trade or profession, has in his or her possession, custody or control, or

(d) makes available to the public,

---

[17] *Morrison v Lightbond* [1993] EMLR 144.

[18] CRRA 2000–2004, s 110 of the sets out the exceptions to this right. The right of integrity will not be breached by authorised broadcasters or authorised cable programme service providers, avoiding the inclusion in a programme of anything which is likely to offend public morality or which is likely to encourage or incite to crime or to lead to public disorder.

[19] CRRA 2000–2004, s 113(1).

[20] CRRA 2000–2004, s 113(5).

a work, or a copy of a work, in or on which there is a false attribution, knowing or having reason to believe that the attribution is false'[21]

or 'a work which has been altered as being the unaltered work of the author, or a copy of such a work as being a copy of the unaltered work of the author, knowing or having reason to believe that the work or the copy of the work has been altered'.[22]

Duration

[3.06] The paternity and integrity rights will subsist for the same period of time as the copyright in the work subsists.[23] The right conferred by s 113 in relation to a false attribution of a work will subsist for 20 years after the death of the person on whom the right is conferred.

Waiver

[3.07] Section 116(1) of the Acts provides that moral rights can be waived.[24] A waiver must be in writing and must be signed by the person waiving the right concerned.[25] A waiver made may relate to a specific work, to works of a specified description or to works generally, and may relate to existing or future works.

Joint authors

[3.08] Joint authors also have moral rights, and the Acts provide that the paternity right or the integrity right is, in the case of a work of joint authorship, a right of each joint author.[26] The right to object to false attribution[27] is infringed by: (a) any false statement as to the authorship of a work of joint authorship, or (b) the false attribution of joint authorship in relation to a work of sole authorship, and such a false attribution infringes the right of every person to whom authorship of any description is attributed.[28]

Remedies

[3.09] An infringement of a moral right is actionable as a breach of statutory duty owed to the person entitled to the right concerned.[29] A person may apply to the appropriate court for damages or other relief in respect of an infringement of their moral rights.[30] In proceedings for infringement of the integrity right, the appropriate court may grant an injunction prohibiting any act unless a sufficient disclaimer is made, on such terms and in such a manner as is approved of by the court, dissociating the person entitled to the right from the treatment of the work.[31]

---

[21] CRRA 2000–2004, s 113.
[22] CRRA 2000–2004, s 113(3)(d).
[23] CRRA 2000–2004, s 115(1). Typically, the life of the author in addition to 70 years.
[24] CRRA 2000–2004, s 116(1).
[25] CRRA 2000–2004, s 116(2).
[26] CRRA 2000–2004, s 117(1).
[27] CRRA 2000–2004, s 113.
[28] CRRA 2000–2004, s 117(3).
[29] CRRA 2000–2004, s 137(1).
[30] CRRA 2000–2004, s 137(2).
[31] CRRA 2000–2004, s 137(3).

Chapter 4

The Copyright Protection of Computer Programs

Introduction

[4.01] There is no question that computer programs are protected by the law of copyright. The Copyright and Related Rights Act 2000–2004 makes this explicitly clear. The Act states that 'Copyright subsists ... in ... original literary ... works ... '[1]
The CRRA 2000–2004 then defines the term 'literary work' as follows 'literary work ... means a work, including a computer program.'[2]
In so doing, the CRRA 2000–2004 implements the Directive on the Legal Protection of Computer Programs[3] which provides 'Member States shall protect computer programs, by copyright, as literary works'.[4]
Essentially the Directive on the Legal Protection of computer programs requires that the law of copyright protects computer programs in the same fashion as it protects novels and works of historical fiction. This protection may not be as all-encompassing as the owners of some computer programs would like. If one copies a sufficiently substantial chunk of the text of a book such as the Da Vinci Code, one will be liable for copyright infringement. Similarly, if one copies a sufficiently substantial chunk of a computer program, one will be liable for copyright infringement. But what if you don't copy the text of a book, but only its 'central theme'? That is what was alleged to have occurred in *Baigent and another v Random House Group Ltd.*[5] In this case it was alleged that Dan Brown, author of the best-selling *Da Vinci Code,* had copied the 'central themes' of a previous work: *The Holy Blood and the Holy Grail.* The claim was rejected by the English Court of Appeal as the plaintiffs were unable to establish that their central themes were 'sufficient to qualify as a substantial part of the work.'[6] The problem for the owners of copyright in computer programs is that the 'central theme' of a computer program, such as its unique purpose or capability, may be the part of the program that is of the greatest value. The Directive on the Legal Protection of Computer Programs and the CRRA 2000–2004 will prevent the unauthorised copying of the code in which the computer program is written. But programming skills may be more easily available now than in 1991, as a result of outsourcing[7] abroad and education at home. This means that

---

[1] CRRA 2000–2004, s 17(1)(a).

[2] CRRA 2000–2004, s 2(1).

[3] Council Directive (91/250/EEC) of 14 May 1991 on the legal protection of computer programs, OJ L 122, 17.5.1991, p. 42), amended by Directive 93/98/EEC, OJ L 290 9 24.11.1993.

[4] Directive 91/250, art 1(1).

[5] *Baigent and another v Random House Group Ltd* [2007] EWCA Civ 247.

[6] [2007] EWCA Civ 247, para 99.

[7] 'computer programming can be described in math-based rules that are then sent over the Internet to anywhere there are skilled workers ... a significant amount of basic computer programming work has gone offshore to fast-growing Indian outsourcing companies' Lohr, 'At IBM, a Smarter Way to Outsource' (2007) The New York Times, 5 July.

it may be economical to replicate the look, feel and functioning of another's computer program without infringing copyright in the program.

[4.02] The Directive on the Legal Protection of Computer Programs may impose a different (and not necessarily superior) standard for the protection of software programs than applies to other forms of literary work. The Directive makes the limitations of its protection clear:

> 'Protection in accordance with this Directive shall apply to the expression in any form of a computer program. Ideas and principles which underlie any element of a computer program, including those which underlie its interfaces, are not protected by copyright under this Directive'.[8]

This provision is reinforced by the recitals which state that:

> 'for the avoidance of doubt, it has to be made clear that only the expression of a computer program is protected and that ideas and principles which underlie any element of a program ... are not protected.'

[4.03] Similarly, the CRRA 2000–2004 provides:

> 'Copyright protection shall not extend to the ideas and principles which underlie any element of a work, procedures, methods of operation or mathematical concepts ...'[9]

The principle that copyright law protects the expression of ideas, but not the ideas themselves is well established. In *University of London Press v University Tutorial Press*[10] Peterson J stated that:

> 'Copyright Acts are not concerned with the originality of ideas, but with the expression of thought, and, in the case of 'literary work', with the expression of thought in print or writing'.[11]

The absence of protection for an individual idea was clear from cases such as *Kenrick v Lawrence*[12] in which protection was claimed for an illustration of a hand placing a cross on a square. This was to explain to illiterate voters how to use a ballot paper. The claim was rejected by Wills J who stated that:

> 'I cannot see how ... [the plaintiffs].. can possibly make a higher claim or say that because they have registered a drawing of a hand penciling a cross within a square that no other person in the UK is at liberty to draw a hand penciling a cross with a square for perhaps the next half century.

[4.04] Similarly the Privy Council held that the idea for the talent show, *Opportunity Knocks* was not protected by copyright in *Green v Broadcasting Corpn of New Zealand*.[13] The plaintiff had developed the various elements used in *Opportunity Knocks*

---

8   Directive 91/250, art 1(2).
9   CRRA 2000–2004, s 17(3).
10   *University of London Press v University Tutorial Press* [1916] 2 Ch. 601.
11   More recently, in *Ray v Classic FM* [1998] FSR 622, Lightman J stated 'copyright exists, not in ideas, but in the written expression of ideas' (Quoted by Park J in *Hadley v Kemp* [1999] EMLR 589).
12   *Kenrick v Lawrence* [1890] Ch QBD 99.
13   *Green v Broadcasting Corpn of New Zealand* [1989] RPC 700. See further para **[4.46]**.

such as its title and the use of a clapometer. The defendants had produced their own show which had the same name and contained other similar elements. But as this was no more than the general idea of a talent quest, they were not the subject of copyright. A particular difficulty for the plaintiff was that he did not produce his scripts, which limited the extent to which the Privy Council could assess the possible infringement. In contrast in *Holland v Vivian Van Damm Productions Ltd*,[14] the reproduction of an Oscar Wilde short story as a ballet (where no words are spoken) infringed the copyright in the short story. The CRRA 2000–2004 does not refer to the protection of compilations, which may mean that it is no longer possible to argue that the plot of a book can be protected as a compilation of ideas.[15] A considerable debate has developed in the USA as to what precise elements of a computer program are protected by copyright law, leading to the so called idea/expression dichotomy. However, the Directive appears clear on this point: the expression of an idea in the form of a computer program will be protected; the ideas and principles that underlie that program will not. In *Ibcos Computers Ltd v Barclays Merchantile Highland Finance*[16] Jacob J suggested that:

> 'It should be noted that the aphorism 'there is no copyright in an idea' is likely to lead to confusion of thought. Sometimes it is applied to the question of subsistence of copyright (is there a 'work' and if there is, is it 'original') Sometimes it is applied to the different question of infringement (has a substantial part been taken?) That is not to say that the expression has no use: for instance if all a defendant has done is to copy a general idea then it does not matter whether there is copyright in the plaintiff's work, or whether the plaintiff owns that copyright.'

[4.05] Jacob J rejected appeals to US law on copyright noting that: 'The fact that United States copyright law is not the same as ours, particularly in the area of copyright works concerned with functionality and of compilations. The Americans (many would say sensibly) never developed copyright so that functional things like exhaust pipes could not be copied'.[17] Jacob J was of the view that:

> 'United Kingdom copyright cannot prevent the copying of a mere general idea but can protect copying of a detailed 'idea'. It is a question of skill where a good guide is the notion of overborrowing[18] of skill, labour and judgment that went into the copyright work.'

The idea/expression dichotomy had its most recent outing in the USA in *Aharonian v Gonzales*[19] in which the plaintiff sought a 'prescriptive declaration that software is made

---

[14] *Holland v Vivian Van Damm Productions Ltd* [1935–45] MCC 69.

[15] *Corelli v Gray* [1911–16] MCC 107.

[16] *Ibcos Computers Ltd v Barclays Merchantile Highland Finance* [1994] FSR 275.

[17] [1994] FSR 275 at 292.

[18] In *Cantor Fitzgerald v Tradition* (2000) RPC 95, at para 79, p 135 Pumfrey J stated in relation to the term 'overborrowing': '(the defendant) submitted … that the concept of 'overborrowing', a word used by Jacob J in *Ibcos Computers Ltd v Barclays Merchantile Highland Finance*, was of assistance in forming a view as to substantiality. I do not think it is, and I certainly do not think that Jacob J was using it in that way. This is merely to substitute another term for the statutory concept of substantiality without providing any useful criterion in the process. I have preferred to consider merely how much skill and labour went into the code copied'.

[19] *Aharonian v Gonzales* (3 January 2003) US District Court for the Northern District of California.

up entirely of ... 'ideas' that are beyond the scope of copyright protection'. The court considered that the making of this claim appeared to:

> 'betray a misunderstanding of the differences between copyright and patent law. A declaration that software consists entirely of "ideas" ... has no bearing on the applicability of copyright law to software source code, which ... is a particular written expression of ideas.'

What is a computer program?

[4.06] Computer programs are complex structures of commands which are not comprehensible to the average person in the same way as a novel, a play or a film. As Pumfrey J noted in *Cantor Fitzgerald International v Tradition (UK) Ltd*[20] 'Computers are intrinsically complex, and a coherent explanation of many of the concepts with which the programmers need to be familiar in order to program effectively is difficult'.[21] Pumfrey J described the working of a computer as follows:

> 'A digital computer consists in essence of a memory and a Central Processing Unit ('CPU') The memory consists of storage elements each capable of holding a number of some prescribed length. This number is represented in binary form, that is, consisting of a string of 0's and 1's. Each storage element of the memory has a unique address, and may be selected by the CPU for the purpose either of copying the number stored at a particular address in to the CPU, or for transferring a number in the CPU to the selected storage element.
>
> The numbers stored in the memory of a computer may either be codes for operations to be carried out by the computer (instructions) or may be operands which the CPU is to manipulate (data).'[22]

These codes are a sequence of numbers, known as machine code. Machine code is typically a string of 1's and 0's. The problem is that the machine code that can be used by a machine is not easily comprehensible to a human. Therefore computers are usually programmed in what is known as source code. Laddie J explained what was meant by source code in *Psychometric Services Ltd v Merant International Ltd*[23]:

> 'A computer functions in response to a set of electronic signals supplied to it. The software is the combination of data and instructions which controls the computer. The software which directly controls a computer is written in a language which computers understand but which is incomprehensible to humans. It is said to be a low-level language. It is called object code ... However, computer programs are, in large part, written by or under the control of humans. The authors, that is to say the computer programmers, have to understand what they are doing in order to refine any software and to correct any defects in it. A computer programmer must be able to understand the program, appreciate which parts control which functions and so on. For these reasons the software will be created in a form known as source code. It is a high-level language which is comprehensible to humans (or at least a group of suitably trained ones)'.[24]

---

[20] *Cantor Fitzgerald International v Tradition (UK) Ltd* [2000] RPC 95.
[21] [2000] RPC 95 at Appendix A, para 2, p 145.
[22] [2000] RPC 95 Appendix A, para 3–5, p 145.
[23] *Psychometric Services Ltd v Merant International Ltd* (8 March 2001).
[24] *Psychometric Services Ltd v Merant International Ltd* (8 March 2001), para 18–19.

Own Intellectual creation

[4.07] The Directive on the Legal Protection of Computer Programs provides that a computer program will only be protected if it is the author's own intellectual creation:

> 'A computer program shall be protected if it is original in the sense that it is the author's own intellectual creation. No other criteria shall be applied to determine its eligibility for protection.

This criterion is repeated by the CRRA 2000–2004, which defines a computer program as 'a program which is original in that it is the author's own intellectual creation'.[25]

The inclusion of this criterion may raise the standard of originality required before a computer program will be protected as compared to other literary works. In general all that is required for copyright protection is that substantive skill or labour is expended on its creation. There is a view that the provision contained in the Directive and the Act is substantially different,[26] and for a program to constitute its programmer's own intellectual creation and so qualify for protection there must be some subjective, that is intellectual or creative, contribution. This difference is significant, particularly as a valuable computer program will be continuously updated in different editions. A meticulous revision of a computer program updating and fixing flaws may not receive any new protection as it will lack the creative element. Protection will be based upon the original computer program. This might have implications for the open source movement, where programs are continuously updated by group effort. Normally the application of sufficient 'skill and care' or labour will be enough for copyright to subsist in a work. In *Cantor Fitzgerald International v Tradition (UK) Ltd*[27] Pumfrey J stated:

> 'it is possible that entirely mechanical labour may be saved by copying something produced by entirely mechanical labour, involving no skill. The only question is whether the entirely mechanical labour which went into the earlier work is relevant labour for the purpose of conferring originality in the copyright sense'.[28]

[4.08] In *Ibcos Computers Ltd v Barclays Mercantile Highland* Finance Jacob J stated that

> 'The amount of skill, labour and judgment which went into the (plaintiff's software) package as a whole is very substantial, well above the threshold of originality acceptable in other fields of copyright'.[29]

But contrary to these precedents, the reference in the Directive on the Legal Protection of Computer Programs to a program being 'original in the sense that it is the author's own intellectual creation' may have dispensed with the use of skill and care for deciding eligibility:

---

25 CRRA 2000–2004, s 2(1).
26 Laddie, Prescott and Vitoria, *Modern Law of Copyright and Designs* (3rd edn, LexisNexis, 2000), para 34.27.
27 In *Cantor Fitzgerald International v Tradition* (UK) Ltd [2000] RPC 95.
28 [2000] RPC 95, para 76, p 133. Similarly at para 86: '(the defendant's employee) had still appropriated a substantial part of the skill and labour ... and so infringed copyright'.
29 *Ibcos Computers Ltd v Barclays Merchantile Highland Finance* [1994] FSR 275at 289.

'The requirement that the computer program be the author's own intellectual creation is, it is submitted, fundamentally different in kind to the skill and labour test ... It is not just a revising of the threshold of the amount of skill and labour required to qualify for protection. To constitute the author's own intellectual creation there must, it is submitted, be some subjective contribution. This difference in approach between the (UK's Copyright Act 1988) and the Directive on the Legal Protection of Computer Programs is most important when considering modifications to computer programs. A painstaking and thorough exercise in updating a computer program in accordance with an obvious or predetermined agenda is unlikely to result in something which is the updater's own intellectual creation. This is so regardless of the amount of labour involved. If the proper test is merely a requirement for substantial skill or labour such an exercise would result in a new copyright work.'[30]

[4.09] This view, and it is submitted that it is the correct view, may be contrasted with the finding of Jacob J in *Ibcos Computers Ltd v Barclays Merchantile Highland Finance* that: 'the putting together of the various programs in (the plaintiff's software package) by a kind of organic growth over the years, did result in a copyright work'.[31] If Jacob J is wrong, then an Irish judge would have to ignore this portion of his judgment and construe a different test of originality for computer software than for other forms of literary work.[32]

Design materials

[4.10] The CRRA 2000–2004 defines the term computer program as including 'any design materials used for the preparation of the program'.[33]

Similarly, the Directive on the Legal Protection of Computer Programs states that 'the term 'computer programs' shall include their preparatory design material'.[34]

This provision is expanded upon by the recitals to the Directive which provide that:

'for the purpose of this Directive, the term 'computer program' shall include programs in any form, including those which are incorporated into hardware; ... this term also includes preparatory design work leading to the development of a computer program provided that the nature of the preparatory work is such that a computer program can result from it at a later stage.'

[4.11] So it appears clear that preparatory materials used in the design of a computer program, such as charts, diagrams, plans and other documents are all protected. But it is hard to see how they would not be protected by copyright law anyway as literary or other works in their own right. In any event this provision of the Directive is consistent with

---

[30] Laddie, Prescott and Vitoria, *Modern Law of Copyright and Designs* (3rd edn, LexisNexis, 2000), para 34.27.

[31] [1994] FSR 275 at 304.

[32] As would the English courts: 'The courts may be able (and indeed obliged ...) to overcome the deficiency by construing 'original' in s 1(1) of the (UK's Copyright Act 1988) differently in relation to computer programs so as to comply with the directive. Laddie, Prescott and Vitoria, *Modern Law of Copyright and Designs* (3rd edn, LexisNexis, 2000), para 34.28.

[33] CRRA 2000–2004, s 2(1).

[34] Directive 91/250, art 1(1).

the view of Jacob J in *Ibcos Computers Ltd v Barclays Merchantile Highland Finance* and *Cantor Fitzgerald* that:

> 'Very often the working out of a reasonably detailed arrangement of topics, sub-topics and sub-sub-topics is the key to a successful work of non-fiction. I see no reason why the taking of that could not amount to an infringement. Likewise there may be a considerable amount of skill involved in setting up the division of a program. In practice this is done with the operating division in mind and its construction may well involve enough skill, labour and, I add, judgment, for it to be considered a substantial part of the program as a whole'.[35]

Harmonised protection

[4.12] The purpose of the Directive on the Legal Protection of Computer Programs[36] was to harmonise European laws on the copyright protection of computer programs. As the recitals to Directive 91/250 note 'computer programs are at present not clearly protected in all Member States by existing legislation and such protection, where it exists, has different attributes'.

The reality is that European copyright law continues to vary from state to state, as was noted by Pumfrey J in *Navitaire v Easyjet Airline*[37]:

> 'the law is everywhere in a state of development, and the results differ from jurisdiction to jurisdiction. Within Europe, the German approach appears to be that identity of interface is not objectionable in itself, but may point to copying of the underlying code. In France, the user interface may be protectable'.[38]

Authorship

[4.13] The Directive on the Legal Protection of Computer Programs provides that:

> 'The author of a computer program shall be the natural person or group of natural persons who has created the program or, where the legislation of the Member State permits, the legal person designated as the rightholder by that legislation. Where collective works are recognized by the legislation of a Member State, the person considered by the legislation of the Member State to have created the work shall be deemed to be its author'.[39]

Given the size of most modern computer programs, a great many people may be involved in its creation. As preparatory material is protected, the designer or architect of a program should be regarded as an author. Such an architect might create the various routes by which a program was to be created and then assign the more mundane tasks of actually writing the code to others. The writing of this code may not have the element of originality required by the Directive and given that it is only the 'intellectual creation' of a programmer which is protected then it is arguable that the true author of such a computer program was the architect and that the programmers who actually wrote the

---

35 *Ibcos Computers Ltd v Barclays Merchantile Highland Finance* [1994] FSR 275 at 303.
36 Council Directive (91/250/EEC) of 14 May 1991 on the legal protection of computer programs, OJ L 122, 17.5.1991, p. 42), amended by Directive 93/98/EEC, OJ L 290 9 24.11.1993
37 *Navitaire v Easyjet Airline* [2004] EWHC 1725 (Ch), [2006] RPC 111.
38 [2004] EWHC 1725 (Ch), para 93.
39 Directive 91/250, art 2(1). Article 3 provides that: 'Protection shall be granted to all natural or legal persons eligible under national copyright legislation as applied to literary works'.

code do not qualify. This would be consistent with the provisions of the Directive on the Protection of Computer Programs which provides that:

'Where a computer program is created by an employee in the execution of his duties or following the instructions given by his employer, the employer exclusively shall be entitled to exercise all economic rights in the program so created, unless otherwise provided by contract.'[40]

[4.14] Similarly, the CRRA 2000–2004 provides:

'The author of a work shall be the first owner of the copyright unless ... the work is made by an employee in the course of employment, in which case the employer is the first owner of any copyright in the work, subject to any agreement to the contrary.'[41]

Alternatively, computer programs may be created by two or more individuals working together as joint authors. The CRRA 2000–2004 defines 'a work of joint authorship' as meaning:

'a work produced by the collaboration of two or more authors in which the contribution of each author is not distinct from that of the other author or authors'.[42]

[4.15] Merely testing a computer program and advising upon its functionality will be insufficient to confer the rights of an author upon the tester or advisor, even though the testing and advising may utilise considerable expertise. In *Flyde Microsystems Limited v Key Radio Systems Ltd*[43] the plaintiffs were experts in the production of software, whilst the defendant's expertise lay in the field of radios. They co-operated in 'the design of software to be used in a new generation of radios to be sold by the defendant'.[44] The plaintiff's case was that it wrote the software and that the defendant was selling unlicensed copies of this software. Initially the plaintiff provided chips with the software embedded in them to the defendant. But it was more convenient for the plaintiff to supply the defendant with chips and then allow the defendant install the software itself. This relationship worked until the plaintiff discovered that the defendant was installing its own software on chips that it had not supplied. The plaintiff sued and the defendant asserted that it was a joint author of the software. In his judgment Laddie J ruled that a beta tester could not be regarded as the author of a computer program, stating that:

'It is common for new software to be issued to third parties for testing (so-called 'beta testers'). They are asked to report back to the programmer any faults which they detect. A

---

40 Directive 91/250, art 2(3). Article 2(2) provides that: 'In respect of a computer program created by a group of natural persons jointly, the exclusive rights shall be owned jointly'.

41 CRRA 2000–2004, s 23 (1)(a). The rights of employees of newspapers or periodicals are more limited in respect of computer programs than other works:' Where a work, other than a computer program, is made by an author in the course of employment by the proprietor of a newspaper or periodical, the author may use the work for any purpose, other than for the purposes of making available that work to newspapers or periodicals, without infringing the copyright in the work. CRRA 2000–2004, s 23(2).

42 CRRA 2000–2004, s 22 (1).

43 *Flyde Microsystems Limited v Key Radio Systems Ltd* [1998] EWHC Patents 340. For further discussion, see paras **[4.51]**, **[4.54]** and **[4.76]**.

44 [1998] EWHC Patents 340, para 2.

good beta tester may well spend hours in thinking of ways of testing the software and then carrying out those tests. He may find many bugs, some of them significant. He relieves the programmer of the task of carrying out all the tests on the software and he may save the programmer a lot of time as a consequence. In many cases beta testers can be said to be part of the team who are responsible for the finished software being as good as it is.

... The fact that the programmer is saved time by reason of the beta tester's efforts does not mean that the latter is an author. Although the beta tester may expend skill, time and effort on testing the software, it is not authorship skill ..., it can be likened to the skill of a proof-reader. In all cases it is necessary to have regard to what the time and skill was expended on.'[45]

Laddie J went on to find that the defendant had made a contribution to the software that was 'extensive and technically sophisticated'.[46] But although these contributions 'took a lot of time and were very valuable they did not amount to contributions to the authoring'. of the software.[47]

Infringement of copyright: copying

[4.16] The Directive on the Legal Protection of Computer Programs explicitly includes in the rights of the rightholder in a computer program several exclusive rights. The first of these is the right to do or to authorise:

'the permanent or temporary reproduction of a computer program by any means and in any form, in part or in whole. Insofar as loading, displaying, running, transmission or storage of the computer program necessitate such reproduction, such acts shall be subject to authorization by the rightholder'.[48]

The right to control the reproduction of a literary work is generally provided by the CRRA 2000–2004 which provides that 'the owner of copyright in a work has the exclusive right to undertake or authorise others to undertake ... to copy the work'.[49] Copying is defined as including references to 'storing the work in any medium ... the making of copies which are transient or incidental to some other use of the work'.[50] Copying of a computer program can occur in different ways. Legislative changes mean that the debate about whether copying a program from the hard-drive to RAM can amount to infringement would no longer seem relevant.[51] Software-copying disputes would now appear to fall into two main categories: one invokes the literal copying of the program's code, the other the non-literal copying of elements of the program such as icons or graphical user interfaces.

Literal copying of a computer program

[4.17] Deciding whether there has been infringement of a computer program is extremely difficult, particularly proving that there is a 'substantial similarity' between

---

[45]   [1998] EWHC Patents 340, para 29–30.
[46]   [1998] EWHC Patents 340, para 39.
[47]   [1998] EWHC Patents 340, para 40.
[48]   Directive 91/250, art 4(a).
[49]   CRRA 2000–2004, s 37(1)(a).
[50]   CRRA 2000–2004, s 39(1).
[51]   *MAI Sys Corp v Peak Computer, Inc* 991 F 2d 511 (9th Cir 1993).

two different programs. In earlier cases such as *John Richardson v Flanders*[52] and *Ibcos Computers Ltd v Barclays Mercantile Highland Finance Computers*[53] the evidence of copying was considerable and detailed under a number of headings. In contrast in the more recent case of *Cantor Fitzgerald v Tradition*[54] the defendants appeared to have gone to considerable trouble to disguise their copying.[55] It would appear that existing Irish or English principles, developed for identifying what is substantial similarity between poems, novels or plays, may be of limited and questionable utility in identifying similarities between computer programs. Given the unique basis of protection contained in the EU Directive, decisions from other jurisdictions, notably the USA are of even less use. *Ibcos Computers Ltd v Barclays Mercantile Highland Finance and Cantor Fitzgerald* are interesting examples of how an English court with a sufficient understanding of the law and the technology came to a decision that there was copying in a particular case. But an Irish court would have to approach a case in which copying of software was alleged with an open mind.

Total Information Processing Systems v Daman[56] and *John Richardson v Flanders*[57]

[4.18] The 'somewhat startling propositions'[58] enunciated by Baker QC[59] in *Total Information Processing Systems v Daman*[60] were subsequently rejected by Jacob J in *John Richardson v Flanders.*[61] In *John Richardson v Flanders* the plaintiff was engaged in the production and marketing of computer programs for stock control in pharmacies in the UK. The first-named defendant adapted the plaintiff's program for an IBM-compatible system for the plaintiff's Irish distributor and when he had done this work he started selling the program in the UK in competition with the plaintiff. The particular significance of this case is the reliance placed upon US case law, a reliance which was viewed as incorrect by Jacob J in *Ibcos Computers Ltd v Barclays Mercantile Highland Finance* and elsewhere referred to as 'irrelevant or exotic'.[62] There are a number of

---

[52] *John Richardson v Flanders* [1993] FSR 497.
[53] *Ibcos Computers Ltd v Barclays Merchantile Highland Finance Computers* [1994] FSR 275 at 303.
[54] *Cantor Fitzgerald v Tradition* [2000] RPC 95.
[55] [2000] RPC 95, para 45, p 113 and para 84, p 137.
[56] *Total Information Processing Systems v Daman* [1992] FSR 171.
[57] *John Richardson v Flanders* [1993] FSR 497.
[58] Laddie, Prescott and Vitoria, *Modern Law of Copyright and Designs* (3rd edn, LexisNexis, 2000), para 34.65, fn 12. In *Total Information Processing Systems v Daman* [1992] FSR 171, Barker QC refused to find that a computer program was protected by copyright as to do so would lead to 'great inconvenience. He also suggested that a detailed file structure could not be protected by copyright. Both findings would seem erroneous. Copyright law will apply regardless of the inconvenience it causes, and it is well established that a sufficiently detailed structure of a work may be regarded as a substantial part of the work and thus protected by copyright.
[59] Sitting as a Deputy Judge of the English High Court.
[60] *Total Information Processing Systems v Daman* [1992] FSR 171.
[61] *John Richardson v Flanders* [1993] FSR 497.
[62] Laddie, Prescott & Vitoria, *Modern Law of Copyright and Designs* (3rd edn, LexisNexis, 2000), para 34, 65–66.

decisions on issues such as whether computer programs are protected by copyright[63] that may now be regarded as irrelevant.

Ibcos Computers Ltd v Barclays Merchantile Highland Finance

[4.19] In *Ibcos Computers Ltd v Barclays Merchantile Highland Finance* Poole, a programmer, wrote a general accounting software program and licensed it to Clayton, an agricultural machinery dealer. This program was not suitable for Clayton's purposes, so the two began to discuss how the program might be modified and ultimately went into business together publishing a program called ADS. This business became involved in negotiations with the defendant, which subsequently broke down. The defendant then contacted Poole and offered him a consultancy writing a finance program called POST. Poole commenced work with the defendant, but then had the idea of writing an improved version of ADS called Unicorn. When the plaintiff heard that the defendant was marketing the Unicorn program it became suspicious and sued. At trial Jacob J reviewed the relevant provisions of the UK's Copyright Patents and Designs Act 1988[64] and held that:

'Logically ... the claim in copyright calls to be tested in the following order:

(a)   What are the work or works in which the plaintiff claims copyright?

(b)   Is each such work 'original'?

(c)   Was there copying from that work?

(d)   If there was copying, has a substantial part of that work been reproduced[65]?'

Jacob J stated that he wished to set out the above tests because he wished to avoid using aphorisms such as 'there is no copyright in an idea' or 'prima facie what is worth copying is worth protecting'.[66] In deciding whether there had been infringement, in this case Jacob J set out the following test:

> 'For infringement there must be copying. Whether there was or not is a question of fact. To prove copying the plaintiff can normally do no more than point to bits of his work and the defendant's work which are the same and prove an opportunity of access to his work. If the resemblance is sufficiently great then the court will draw an inference of copying. It may be possible for the defendant to rebut the inference – to explain the similarities in some other way. For instance he may be able to show both parties derived the similar bits from some third party or material in the public domain. Or he may be able to show that the similarity arises out of a functional necessity – that anyone doing this particular job would be likely to come up with similar bits ... The concept of sufficient similarities shifting the onus onto the defendant to prove non-copying is well recognised in copyright law.'[67]

---

[63]   Notably *Computer Edge Pty Ltd v Apple Computers Ltd* [1986] FSR 537 in which the majority of the High Court of Australia got themselves into 'a considerable conceptual misunderstanding. Laddie, Prescott and Vitoria, *Modern Law of Copyright and Designs* (3rd edn, LexisNexis, 2000), para 34.18.

[64]   UK's Copyright Patents and Designs Act 1988, ss 1,3, 165 and 17.

[65]   In*Cantor Fitzgerald v Tradition* [2000] RPC 95, Pumfrey J commented that: 'I am certain that this is right', para 73, p 130.

[66]   *Ibcos Computers Ltd v Barclays Merchantile Highland Finance* [1994] FSR 275 at 289.

[67]   [1994] FSR 275 at 296–297.

[4.20] Jacob J noted that at the stage of deciding whether copying had occurred 'both the important and the unimportant bits of the work being compared count. Indeed it is often identity of trivial matter which traps a copyist'.[68] In this case he found that there was an overwhelming inference of copying. He did not set out all the similarities as to do so would be burdensome, but he set out some of the key items:

(a) *Common spelling mistakes*: there were significant common spelling mistakes in the two programs, including 'Channal', 'shedule' and 'detatched'.

(b) *Headings*: there were identical comment headings, for example the words International Harvester were presented with 21 hyphens to the left and 13 to the right in both programs. In *Cantor Fitzgerald v Tradition* Pumfrey J suggested that 'Experience has shown that copying of comments often betrays the copyist of computer source code'.[69]

(c) *The presence of a sub-program*: this program was a part of the ADS program but not Unicorn, however there were references to it in the Unicorn source code but this had been commented out.

(d) *The presence of file records*: these were virtually identical in the two programs and the plaintiff's explanation that this was the result of copying was preferred by the court.

(e) *Redundant and unexplained code in both programs*: as Jacob J stated:

'It would technically not matter if they were redundant codes or if they had a purpose in ADS and were redundant in Unicorn. But their presence would betray copying. The difficulty from (the defendant's) point of view is that those portions of code are in Unicorn at all. For if he were genuinely writing it from scratch one would not expect redundant code at all ... One would certainly not at all expect identical pieces of redundant code in Unicorn and ADS or bits of redundant code in Unicorn which had a function in ADS. Yet that is what we find here.'[70]

(f) *Other matter*: There were references to the ADS printer test in Unicorn, use of the word OUST for identical purposes, and a very odd definition of zero in both programs.

All of the above similarities led Jacob J to the conclusion that:

'The upshot of these is that the similarities between the two programs can only have resulted from disk to disk copying. The statistical chance of these resemblances occurring twice in the two programs must be infinitesimal.'[71]

The defence offered a number of possible explanations for the copying. Firstly, it was suggested that Poole might have had some sort of memory of how he came to write the

---

[68] Citing Hoffman J in *Billhofer Maschinenfabrik GmbH v Dixon & Co Ltd* [1990] FSR 105 at 123: 'It is the resemblances in inessentials, the small, redundant, even mistaken elements of the copyright work which carry the greatest weight. This is because they are least likely to have been the result of independent design.

[69] *Ibcos Computers Ltd v Barclays Merchantile Highland Finance* [1994] FSR 275 appendix A, para 16.

[70] [1994] FSR 275 at 299–300.

[71] [1994] FSR 275 at 300.

ADS program and that when he came to write Unicorn he was merely going through the same motions. Jacob J rejected this as 'wholly fantastic'. Secondly, there was the 'baseline' argument that an author would have a particular style which would lead him to use words and phrases in a particular way; Jacob J was willing to concede that there might be something to this argument in principle, but it could not begin to explain the similarities in this case. Thirdly, there was the 'toolkit' defence, that some subroutines were available as free shareware but again this could not account for the exact identities of immaterial detail that Jacob J found in this case.

[4.21] Having decided that copying had occurred, Jacob J then had to decide whether or not that copying had taken a 'substantial part' of the ADS program. He rejected reliance on US authorities and held that this was a matter which had to be left to the value judgment of the court. In making this judgment he agreed with Ferris J in *John Richardson* that 'consideration is not to be restricted to the text of the code',[72] so he decided to review not just 'literal similarities' between the two programs but also 'program structure'[73] and 'design features'. Jacob J found that there had been copying at the program structure level but he rejected the suggestion that he should access copying at the design feature level. Both programs had identical features such as nine levels of security, twelve labour rates and a holiday stamp facility. Jacob J felt that these were probably in the Unicorn program as a result of copying, but:

> 'They are features of the package of interest to the customers and no more. We are here at a level of generality where there is little of the programmer's skill, labour and judgment ... the mere taking of those functions would not be an infringement – it would be the taking of a mere general idea or scheme.'[74]

[4.22] Some of the similarities between the different programs related to the data division of the programs. Jacob J held that it would be appropriate to look at this as:[75]

> 'Very often the working out of a reasonably detailed arrangement of topics, sub-topics and sub-sub-topics is the key to a successful work of non-fiction. I see no reason why the taking of that could not amount to an infringement. Likewise there may be a considerable amount of skill involved in setting up the division of a program. In practice this is done with the operating division in mind and its construction may well involve enough skill, labour and, I add, judgment, for it to be considered a substantial part of the program as a whole'.[76]

Jacob J viewed the compilation of the different ADS sub-programs as amounting to a program in itself, and held that the defendant had infringed upon the plaintiff's copyright in this program. He further held that the plaintiff's copyright in the different sub-programs had also been infringed. One approach which Jacob J refused to take was that of viewing the programs from the perspective of a user, commenting that: 'Unicorn is

---

72 *John Richardson v Flanders* [1993] FSR 497 at 526.
73 In *Cantor Fitzgerald v Tradition* [2000] RPC 95 at 134 Pumfrey J suggested that: 'The term 'architecture' may also be used to describe what Jacob J in *Ibcos* ... called program structure'.
74 *Ibcos Computers Ltd v Barclays Merchantile Highland Finance* [1994] FSR 275 at 305.
75 In doing this Jacob J rejected the suggestion of Baker J in *Total* at p 180 that 'It would be very unusual that (the table of contents) of a book could be described as a substantial part of a book'
76 *Ibcos Computers Ltd v Barclays Merchantile Highland Finance* [1994] FSR 275 at 303.

undoubtedly to the user a much friendlier program than ADS was ... it has got convenient cursor movements, colour, error correction and so on, all absent from ADS ... users doubtless think of the programs as very different because they present differently'.[77] However this did not prevent Jacob J from forming the conclusion that Poole had copied ADS while writing Unicorn.

Cantor Fitzgerald International v Tradition (UK) Ltd

[4.23] In *Cantor Fitzgerald International v Tradition (UK) Ltd*[78] the fourth-named defendant had been the plaintiff's managing director. After he was fired he went to work with the first-named defendant and set up a bond-broking business in competition with them. He recruited members of the plaintiff's staff to write a suitable bond-broking computer program. The defendants were extremely successful at this, writing a working program within three months. What had occurred was that when the employees recruited from the plaintiff had left work, one of them had copied the plaintiff's source code and uploaded it onto the defendant's computers. Some elements of the code were missing so one of the plaintiff's former employees dialed into the plaintiff's computer and retrieved this data. The defendant's programmers then used the plaintiff's system for reference while writing the defendant's system and for testing the defendant's system.

[4.24] At trial Pumfrey J held that the loading of the whole of the plaintiff's source code onto the defendant's computer was in itself an infringement of the plaintiff's copyright. In relation to the taking of a substantial part, Pumfrey J attempted to explain how an expression of thought in a human language (as, for example, an essay, a novel or a poem) differs from a program for a computer written in a programming language.

> 'I think that there is a real risk of making an error if one adapts well-known principles which have been developed in the context of literary works addressed to humans and applies them uncritically to literary works whose only purpose is to make a machine operate in such and such a manner. A program expressed in a computer language must not contain any errors of syntax (or it will not compile) and it must contain no semantic errors. Computers do not have the capacity to deduce what the author meant when they encounter errors ... If the software contains semantic errors it will produce the wrong answer or no answer at all: it may merely fail to run. The only opportunity that the programmer gets to express himself in a more relaxed way is provided by the comments in the code which are for the benefit of the human reader only and are ignored when the code comes to be compiled. These considerations might suggest that every part of computer program is essential to its performance and so every part, however, small, is a 'substantial part' of the program'.[79]

Pumfrey J referred to the Australian case of *Autodesk Inc v Dyason*[80] which concerned the copying of a 'dongle' or lock, which was sold as part of a software package. A user would attach it to the back of his computer, and if he failed to do so the software would not run. The dongle contained a code which consisted of 126 bits and corresponded to 16 alphabetic characters in conventional notation. The Australian Court held that

---

[77] See also the judgment of Ferris J in *John Richardson v Flanders* [1993] FSR 497.

[78] *Cantor Fitzgerald International v Tradition (UK) Ltd* [2000] RPC 95.

[79] [2000] RPC 95, para 74, p 130.

[80] *AutodeskInc v Dyason* [1992] RPC 575.

copying these 16 letters amounted to substantial copying, a view which Pumfrey J criticised as 'simplistic'. He expressed the view that:

> 'as far as English law is concerned the correct approach to substantiality is straightforward. It is the function of copyright to protect the relevant skill and labour expended by the author on the work.'[81]

However, Pumfrey J was critical of the proposition that 'a useful test of substantiality is to be found in the maxim 'what is worth copying is worth protecting'. This maxim is open to criticism that it proves too much. So, it is possible that entirely mechanical labour may be saved by copying something produced by entirely mechanical labour, involving no skill. The only question is whether the entirely mechanical labour which went into the earlier work is relevant labour for the purpose of conferring originality in the copyright sense'.[82]

.... it is well established that a substantial part of the author's skill and labour may reside in the plot of a novel or play: and to take that plot without taking any part of the particular manner of its expression may be sufficient to amount to copyright infringement.[83]

... The closest analogy to a plot in a computer program lies perhaps in the algorithms or sequences of operations decided on by the programmer to achieve his object. But it goes wider. It seems to be generally accepted that the 'architecture' of a computer program is capable of protection if a substantial part of the programmer's skill, labour and judgment went into it. In this context, 'architecture' is a vague and ambiguous term. It may be used to refer to the overall structure of the system at a very high level of abstraction'.[84]

[4.25] Pumfrey J considered that in this case he was being asked to assess copying in relation to a number of:

> 'modules ... which ... are individually compiled and thereafter linked into a small number of programs (there are some small stand-alone modules which are not very significant). These programs could each have been compiled from a single source file, but what happened was that the source was distributed into a number of modules. Such a subdivision is essential for ease or organisation, writing and debugging and to enable the code to be used in more than one program. The contents of each module is largely arbitrary: but a successful project depends upon the proper division of labour represented by well-organised division into modules. Here, the division appears to have been generally, but not always, one subroutine per module. Some of the 35 Tradition modules ultimately complained of were directly comparable with Cantor modules in terms of content, and some were not ... .It seems to me on the evidence that the choice of module content, if not arbitrary, is based on an assessment of considerations which have nothing to do with the computer program as a functional unit but relate to extraneous matters such as availability and skill of programmers, convenience of debugging and maintenance and so on. It is not possible to say that the skill and labour involved in making such a choice could never

---

[81]　*Cantor Fitzgerald International v Tradition (UK) Ltd* [2000] RPC 95, para 76 p 131.

[82]　[2000] RPC 95, para 76, p 133, citing in support: *Warwick Films v Eisinger* (1969) 1 Ch 508; *Ladbroke (Football) Ltd v William Hill* [1964] 1 WLR 273; *Macmillan v Cooper 19213* 40 TLR 186 (PC).

[83]　*Cantor Fitzgerald International v Tradition (UK) Ltd* [2000] RPC 95, para 77, p 134, citing *Harman Pictures v Osbourne* (1967) 1 WLR 723; *Rees v Melville* [1911–1916] Mac CC 168.

[84]　*Cantor Fitzgerald International v Tradition (UK) Ltd* [2000] RPC 95, p 134, para 77.

amount to a substantial part of the copyright subsisting in the various modules, but it seems to me to be unlikely'.

This led him to make the judgment that:

'the substantiality of what is taken has to be judged against the collection of modules viewed as a whole. Substantiality is to be judged in the light of the skill and labour in design and coding which went into the piece of code which is alleged to be copied. It is not determined by whether the system would work without the code; or by the amount of use the system makes of the code.'

Application to Irish cases

[4.26] Applying the above cases in Ireland may be difficult. Firstly it is clear that both Jacob J in *Ibcos Computers Ltd v Barclays Mercantile Highland* Finance and Pumfrey J in *Cantor Fitzgerald International v Tradition (UK) Ltd* treated the computer programs which were the subject matter of the cases before them as being 'compilations'. In *Ibcos Computers Ltd v Barclays Mercantile Highland* Jacob J thought that the compilation of various sub-programs resulted in a copyright work; in *Cantor Fitzgerald* Pumfrey J made reference to the 'compilation cases'.[85] However, although compilations were protected as copyright works in the Copyright Act 1963, this provision does not appear in the CRRA 2000–2004. Instead the Act appears to rely upon the protection of databases, but s 1(6) provides that 'A computer program used in the making or operation of data-bases shall not be regarded as a database'. A database is defined as: 'a collection of independent works, data or other materials, arranged in a systematic or methodical way and individually accessible by any means but excludes computer programs used in the making or operation of a database'.[86] A computer program used to make a database may not be protected as a database, but if a database is itself a computer program, is that database/computer program protected? The question is particularly relevant as if a computer program can be a database then it may have further protection under the Database Directive which is implemented by Part V of the Act.

[4.27] The cases detailed above may be seen in a clear succession, with the later decisions of *Ibcos Computers Ltd v Barclays Mercantile Highland* and *Cantor Fitzgerald International v Tradition (UK) Ltd* clearly preferable. But while these cases are an interesting example of how English judges have come to a decision which was substantially correct, and while they can contain important principles such as the essential irrelevance of US case law in this area, it is submitted that these cases do not contain the sort of broad, general principles which might be usefully applied in an Irish case. The following conclusions may be of interest, but an Irish Court approaching an Irish case, will have to use its own judgment in deciding the law.

(a)   US copyright law is different from the English, and so of limited relevance (*Ibcos Computers Ltd v Barclays Mercantile Highland*);

---

[85] [2000] RPC 95, para 76, p 131: 'The closest analogy in the field of literary copyright is to be found in the so-called compilation cases', citing *Warwick Films v Eisinger* (1969) 1 Ch 508; *Ladbroke (Football) Ltd v William Hill* (1964) 1 WLR 273; *Macmillan v Cooper* 19213 40 TLR 186 (PC).

[86] CRRA 2000–2004, s 2(1).

(b)   the fact that two programs generate similar or dissimilar screen displays is irrelevant in deciding whether or not there has been copying of the code that generates those displays (*Ibcos Computers Ltd v Barclays Mercantile Highland*);[87]

(c)   good expert witnesses are vital to the success of a case, in both *Ibcos Computers Ltd v Barclays Mercantile Highland* and *Cantor Fitzgerald International v Tradition (UK) Ltd* the court made it clear that it found the evidence of the successful parties much more credible than that of the unsuccessful side.

Back-up copies

[4.28] The CRRA 2000–2004 provides that:

> 'It is not an infringement of the copyright in a computer program for a lawful user of a copy of the computer program to make a back-up copy of it which it is necessary for him or her to have for the purposes of his or her lawful use'.[88]

This implements Article 5(2) of the Directive on the Legal Protection of Computer Programs, which provides that 'The making of a back-up copy by a person having a right to use a computer program may not be prevented by contract insofar as it is necessary for that use'.

Coppinger comments on the identical UK provision that:

> 'It is not entirely clear, however, when the making of a back up copy will be "necessary". While the making of a back-up copy is no doubt highly desirable, it seems arguable that it will not usually be necessary. It would seem particularly difficult to argue that an additional copy was 'necessary' if, as is normally the case, the program was supplied on CD-ROM or floppy disk with the intention that it should be copied onto the hard drive. Yet where a program is supplied on floppy disk it is widely seen as good practice always to copy the original disks and to use the copies to install the program onto the hard drive, and user manuals frequently provide instructions to this effect. Even in the absence of such specific instructions it might be possible to imply a licence to make such copies by virtue of custom in the trade. It would seem that unless a wide construction is given to this provision, so that ordinary and prudent making of a back up copy is protected, this section will be of virtually no application, but the purchaser will have the benefit of an express or implied licence.[89]

[4.29] The Act does not define what a back-up copy is and how many back-ups are permissible. Electronic storage is far cheaper and more easily available now than it was in 1991. This means that it is far easier to back-up data and program files. So more than one back-up copy of a program is possible and indeed desirable. The noun 'back-up' is defined by the Oxford English Dictionary as a support or a reserve. Where a copy of

---

[87]   See also *John Richardson v Flanders* [1993] FSR 497.

[88]   CRRA 2000–2004, s 80(1).

[89]   *Coppinger on copyright*, para 9-60, pp 532–533. Similarly Laddie, Prescott and Vitoria, *Modern Law of Copyright and Designs* (3rd edn, LexisNexis, 2000), states: 'it is submitted that even in the absence of express authority a right to make back up copies would probably be implied, if not to give business efficiency to the transaction, then by virtue of a well understood industry custom'. At para 34.54.

data is held as a reserve or support for the primary copy then this is 'back-up data'. For example, some users may employ RAID113[90] technology which uses 'two or more drives in combination to reduce the risks from disk failure'. The RAID 1 system is sometimes called mirroring, and it is easy to identify what is 'backup' data in such systems. The computer 'simply takes everything that gets written to the primary hard drive and creates a copy of it on the second drive'. However, RAID 0 systems do not work like this. A RAID 0 system 'divides a data stream and write bits of it to both drives at once in a process called striping'.[91] Arguably, neither drive qualifies as a back-up under RAID 0. If the original copy is lost or destroyed, at least one back-up copy will cease to be a back-up and will become the primary copy of the program. This must be distinguished from the situation where the program licence is sold and transferred to a third party, in which case the back-up copies will become infringing copies. A very good argument can be made that the distinguishing feature of a back-up copy is not the medium in which it is held or the number of such copies. The distinguishing feature of a back-up copy is its purpose or use. To be a back-up copy, the copy must be stored and not in regular use.

Non-literal copying of a computer program

[4.30] Many computer programs are functional tools; they are designed to be discrete and to have only very limited interactions with the humans who rely upon them. Modern car engines are packed with computer programs that monitor and control various functions, but these systems operate without the conscious knowledge of drivers. So someone who learnt to drive a car half a century ago will still be able to drive a car built last week. But other functions of computer programs require that users interact with the software. A program with an easier or more familiar format for interaction with users will have a significant advantage over a program that is harder to use or less familiar. This means that the most valuable parts of a computer program may no longer be the code but instead much of a program's value may reside in the screens and icons which users are most familiar with. As a result case-law has begun to develop in relation to the 'non-literal' copying of computer programs, where there is no allegation that the code of a program has been copied. For example, in the US case of *Lotus Dev Corp v Borland Int'l, Inc*[92] the US Court of Appeals for the First Circuit ruled that the defendant had not infringed copyright by copying the menu hierarchy of the plaintiff's program. In his concurring opinion, Boudin J set out the dilemma that courts may face in this regard:

> 'The menu commands (eg, 'print,' 'quit') are largely for standard procedures that Lotus did not invent and are common words that Lotus cannot monopolize. What is left is the particular combination and sub-grouping of commands in a pattern devised by Lotus. This arrangement may have a more appealing logic and ease of use than some other configurations; but there is certain arbitrariness to many of the choices.
>
> If Lotus is granted a monopoly on this pattern, users who have learned the command structure of Lotus 1-2-3 or devised their own macros are locked into Lotus, just as a typist who has learned the QWERTY keyboard would be the captive of anyone who had a

---

[90] RAID is an acronym for 'Redundant Array of Independent Disks'.
[91] Taylor, 'Hard drives are made easy' (2005) The Financial Times, 28 October.
[92] *Lotus Dev Corp v Borland Int'l, Inc* 516 US 233 (1995).

monopoly on the production of such a keyboard. Apparently, for a period Lotus 1-2-3 has had such sway in the market that it has represented the de facto standard for electronic spreadsheet commands. So long as Lotus is the superior spreadsheet – either in quality or in price – there may be nothing wrong with this advantage.

But if a better spreadsheet comes along, it is hard to see why customers who have learned the Lotus menu and devised macros for it should remain captives of Lotus because of an investment in learning made by the users and not by Lotus. Lotus has already reaped a substantial reward for being first; assuming that the Borland program is now better, good reasons exist for freeing it to attract old Lotus customers: to enable the old customers to take advantage of a new advance, and to reward Borland in turn for making a better product. If Borland has not made a better product, then customers will remain with Lotus anyway.'

Can copyright subsist in a command?

[4.31] The copying of the 'look and feel' of a computer program was assessed by Pumfrey J in *Navitaire v Easyjet Airline*.[93] The case concerned a booking reservation system for a low cost airline, which permitted ticketless booking. The claimant's system was called openers. The respondent's system was called eRes. The claimant's action had what Pumfrey J termed a 'striking feature':

> 'Navitaire does not suggest that easyJet ever had access to the source code of the OpenRes system. What is alleged, and not disputed, is that easyJet wanted a new system that was substantially indistinguishable from the OpenRes system, as easyJet used it, in respect of its 'user interface'. This term is used to denote the appearance the running software presents to the user, who may be an agent in a call centre or a private individual seeking to make a booking by use of the World Wide Web. It substantially achieved this far from simple goal. It is not in dispute that none of the underlying software in any way resembles that of OpenRes, save that it acts upon identical or very similar inputs and produces very similar results, but it is said that the copyright in OpenRes is infringed by what was called 'non-textual copying.'[94]

In other words, what the claimant was alleging was that easyJet had built a system that looked and performed like the claimant's system, without actually copying the code of the claimant's system. Pumfrey J began his judgment by noting that 'non-textual' copying had three elements:

(a)   the copying of the 'look and feel' of the plaintiff's software;

(b)   the detailed copying of many of the individual commands entered by a user to obtain a particular result; and

(c)   the copying of the results of certain commands such as screen displays.

Pumfrey J summarised the claimant's case in the following terms:

> 'the systems are very similar in use. Internally, it is correct to say that they are completely different, subject to a point on the names used to identify certain data in the databases in eRes. Given that near-identity in appearance and function could not have been achieved without a close analysis of the OpenRes system in action, Navitaire say that there is here

---

[93]   *Navitaire v Easyjet Airline* [2004] EWHC 1725 (Ch), [2006] RPC 111.

[94]   [2004] EWHC 1725 (Ch), para 2.

'non-textual' reproduction of either the whole of the OpenRes software considered as a single copyright work or alternatively of the various copyrights subsisting in 'modules' going to make up the system'.[95]

[4.32] The first issue examined by Pumfrey J was that of copying of commands in the claimant's software. These commands came in different forms. There were simple commands which might give access to a sub-program such as the notepad sub-system. There were also complex commands that might generate information relating to availability which would process data including departure and destination locations, dates, flights and fares. The claimant alleged that the respondent had copied these commands without copying the source code and that copyright subsisted in these command sets separately from the source code. Pumfrey J applied *Exxon Corp v Exxon Insurance*[96] and rejected this argument in respect of the simple one word commands, stating that 'it is clear that single words in isolation are not to be considered as literary works. The individual command words and letters do not qualify'.

[4.33] Pumfrey J went on to hold that copyright did not subsist in the more complex commands, holding that the commands were part of a computer programming language, not a program in themselves.[97] He was persuaded by Laddie, Prescott and Victoria[98] and the recitals to Directive 91/250 that computer programming languages are not included in the protection afforded computer programs. Pumfrey J went on to reject the claim that the commands were protected by copyright on the basis that they were compilations. Pumfrey J agreed with counsel for the defendant that:

'there is no overall compilation, but merely an accretion of commands. The only influence that one command or set of commands has on the others is that the others must, by definition, have a different name. It is possible for a work that grows over time (say successive editions of Palgrave) to have a single compiler's copyright, but there must be an overall design. I distinguish between the collection of commands needed for the system, upon each of which skill and labour was expended and the collection of their names, which was never part of the endeavour of the designers. The collection of command names and syntax was never designed as such. It did not have an author, and it did not have joint authors, since it is perfectly possible to distinguish the contributions of the various authors. On this ground also, I think that there is here no compilation.'[99]

[4.34] Pumfrey J went on to reject the suggestion that copyright could subsist in the functional elements of a computer program:

'There is a respectable case for saying that copyright is not, in general, concerned with functional effects, and there is some advantage in a bright line rule protecting only the claimant's embodiment of the function in software and not some superset of that software'.[100]

---

[95] [2004] EWHC 1725 (Ch), para 3.

[96] *Exxon Corp v Exxon Insurance* [1982] Ch 119 in which it was held that copyright could not subsist in the word 'Exxon'.

[97] [2004] EWHC 1725 (Ch), para 84.

[98] Laddie, Prescott and Vitoria, *Modern Law of Copyright and Designs* (3rd edn, LexisNexis, 2000), para 34.19.

[99] *Navitaire v Easyjet Airline* [2004] EWHC 1725 (Ch), para 92.

[100] [2004] EWHC 1725 (Ch), para 94.

Computer programs as artistic works

[4.35] Copyright may subsist in visual images generated by computer programs such as screen icons or graphical user interfaces (GUIs). Such visual images may be protected as an artistic work, and the Directive on the Legal Protection of Computer Programs will not apply to such images. In *Navitaire v Easyjet Airline* Pumfrey J noted that the Directive was:

> 'concerned only with the protection of computer programs as literary works, and I do not read it as having any impact on relevant artistic copyrights'.[101]

The CRRA 2000–2004 defines 'artistic work' as including:

> 'a work of any of the following descriptions, irrespective of their artistic quality—
>
> (a) photographs, paintings, drawings, diagrams, maps, charts, plans, engravings, etchings, lithographs, woodcuts, prints or similar works, collages or sculptures (including any cast or model made for the purposes of a sculpture),
>
> (b) works of architecture, being either buildings or models for buildings, and
>
> (c) works of artistic craftsmanship'.[102]

Images generated by computer programs may be utilitarian and functional and lack the qualitative elements that one might expect to find in an artistic work. But this is irrelevant. As with literary works, protection is conferred regardless of quality, as was stated by Stewart J in *Hay v Sloan*:[103]

> 'I think it unlikely that any legislature would be so addled as to appoint the judiciary to decide whether Frank Lloyd Wright, Palladio, Pheidias, Corbusier or the plaintiff had produced buildings of artistic character or design in the sense that they are artistically good or artistically bad.

[4.36] In a similar vein Walker LJ stated in the Irish case of *Green v Independent Newspapers & Freemans Journal*[104] that a drawing of Santa Clause is protected by copyright 'as if the original drawing was by Millais and its copying by an engraving in the Art Journal'. There is no requirement of fixation in relation to artistic works.[105]

Character-based displays

[4.37] In *Navitaire v Easyjet Airline* Pumfrey J refused to protect a screen that simply displayed printable characters in 80 columns and 24 rows, ruling ruled that:

> 'character-based displays are properly to be viewed as tables and so literary in character for the purposes of copyright ... .They are, in my view, "ideas which underlie its interfaces" in the sense used in art 1(2) of the Directive: they provide the static framework for the display of the dynamic data which it is the task of the software to produce'.[106]

---

[101] [2004] EWHC 1725 (Ch), para 97.

[102] CRRA 2000–2004, s 2(1).

[103] *Hay v Sloan* (1957) 16 Fox Pat C 185, (1957) OWN 445, 27 CPR 132.

[104] *Green v Independent Newspapers & Freemans Journal* [1899] 1 IR 386.

[105] CRRA 2000–2004, s 18.

[106] *Navitaire v Easyjet Airline* [2004] EWHC 1725 (Ch), para 96.

Graphical user interface

[4.38] In *Navitaire v Easyjet Airline* Pumfrey J was asked whether a GUI could amount to an artistic work. Pumfrey J held that it could, stating that:

> 'In my judgment … . GUI screens are artistic works. They are recorded as such only in the complex code that displays them, but I think that this is strictly analogous to more simple digital representations of graphic works. The code constructs the screen from basic elements, and is so arranged to give a consistent appearance to the individual elements. I think, nonetheless, that to arrange a screen certainly affords the opportunity for the exercise of sufficient skill and labour for the result to amount to an artistic work. I consider that the GUI screens satisfy this requirement. There is force in the suggestion that they present a uniform appearance in layout of the elements, and so contribute to a uniformity of interface. On the whole this is sufficient skill and labour to entitle the screens sued on to artistic copyright'.[107]

Graphic images on a screen

[4.39] *Nova Productions v Mazooma Games*[108] concerned the copying of computer games for coin operated arcade machines. The plaintiffs did not contend:

> 'that the defendants ever had access to or copied the code itself. Rather, it is contended that the defendants have infringed the copyright in the program by copying the outputs which appear on the screen'.[109]

The facts were that UK law imposed different regulatory regimes for different games, imposing a stricter regime on 'Amusement with Prizes' games, which require that the player exercise no skill, than on 'Skill with Prizes' games, which require that the player exercise at least some skill. The plaintiffs were innovators in this field and had developed games that rewarded player's hand-eye co-ordination instead of requiring that they answer a question. Initially the plaintiffs developed a game that required a player to aim an arrow at a target, and then they moved onto games that imitated the playing of pool. The defendants then brought out games that shared certain similarities with these latter games. The plaintiff claimed that the defendant's pool-playing games infringed upon its. A major part of the plaintiff's claim was 'founded upon the artistic copyright subsisting in the graphic images appearing on the screen'.[110] The plaintiffs pointed to similarities in the display of pool tables with distorted sides, pockets and balls, the display of 'power meters' and the manner in which players took shots.

[4.40] The plaintiff's claim failed. In his judgment Kitchin J derived the following propositions from the judgment of the House of Lords in *Designers Guild Ltd v Russell Williams (Textiles) Ltd*:[111]

(a)   In an action for infringement of artistic copyright the complaint will be that:
        'the defendant has copied all or a substantial part of the copyright work. It is

---

[107] [2004] EWHC 1725 (Ch), para 98.
[108] *Nova Productions v Mazooma Games* [2006] EWHC 24 (Ch), [2006] All ER (D) 131 (Jan).
[109] [2006] EWHC 24 (Ch), [2006] All ER (D) 131 (Jan), para 129.
[110] [2006] EWHC 24 (Ch), [2006] All ER (D) 131 (Jan), para 121.
[111] *Designers Guild Ltd v Russell Williams (Textiles) Ltd* [2000] UKHL 58; [2001] 1 All ER 700; [2000] 1 WLR 2416, [2001] FSR 11.

important to note, however, that while the copied features must be a substantial part of the copyright work, they need not form a substantial part of the defendant's work. The overall appearance of the defendant's work may therefore be very different from the copyright work while nevertheless infringing'.[112]

(b)   The first step in deciding an action for infringement of artistic copyright will be 'to identify those features of the defendant's design which the claimant alleges have been copied from the copyright work ... the court will consider the similarities and differences between the works and whether or not the particular similarities relied on are sufficiently close, numerous or extensive to be more likely to be the result of copying than coincidence. Similarities may be disregarded because they are commonplace, unoriginal, or consist of general ideas. If the similarities are such as to raise an inference of copying the burden passes to the defendant to establish that, despite the similarities, they did not result from copying'.[113]

(c)   The second step follows from a finding that copying has taken place, the court must then decide 'whether what has been taken constitutes all or a substantial part of the copyright work ... the only issue is whether or not the features which have been taken represent a substantial part of the copyright work. A visual comparison of the two designs to see the extent to which they may differ in appearance is unnecessary and liable to mislead'.[114] In making this assessment 'it is important not to deal with the copied features piece-meal. Rather, it is the cumulative effect of the copied features which is important. The court must consider whether, taken as a whole, they constitute a substantial part of the copyright work'.[115]

[4.41] Kitchin J also derived a number of important propositions[116] from the speech of Hoffman LJ in *Designers Guild Ltd v Russell Williams (Textiles) Ltd*:

(a)   'a copyright work may express certain ideas which are not protected because they have no connection with the literary, dramatic, musical or artistic nature of the work. It is on this ground that, for example, a literary work which describes a system or invention does not entitle the author to claim protection for his system or invention as such. The same is true of an inventive concept expressed in an artistic work. However striking or original it may be, others are (in the absence of patent protection) free to express it in works of their own.

(b)   ... certain ideas expressed by a copyright work may not be protected because, although they are ideas of a literary, dramatic or artistic nature, they are not original, or so commonplace as not to form a substantial part of the work.'[117]

---

[112] *Nova Productions v Mazooma Games* [2006] EWHC 24 (Ch), [2006] All ER (D) 131 (Jan), para 122.

[113] [2006] EWHC 24 (Ch), [2006] All ER (D) 131 (Jan), para 123.

[114] [2006] EWHC 24 (Ch), [2006] All ER (D) 131 (Jan), para 124.

[115] [2006] EWHC 24 (Ch), [2006] All ER (D) 131 (Jan), para 125.

[116] [2006] EWHC 24 (Ch), [2006] All ER (D) 131 (Jan), para 126.

[117] *Designers Guild Ltd v Russell Williams (Textiles) Ltd* [2000] UKHL 58; [2001] 1 All ER 700; [2000] 1 WLR 2416 [2001] FSR 11 at para 24.

(c) ... in cases of artistic copyright, the more abstract and simple the copied idea, the less likely it is to constitute a substantial part. Originality, in the sense of the contribution of the author's skill and labour, tends to lie in the detail with which the basic idea is presented'.[118]

[4.42] Finally, Kitchin J offered a principle of his own:

'The issue of infringement must be considered in relation to each separate copyright work relied upon by the claimant. Copyright protects the skill and labour expended by the author in producing a particular work ... .In the case of each of the games of which complaint is made (the plaintiff) has identified a series of alleged similarities. All of these similarities do not, however, appear in each of the works relied upon. Indeed some do not appear in any of the artistic works relied on at all and are included to assist (the plaintiff) to make good its case on copying. Particular care is therefore needed to assess whether or not, in so far as there has been copying, a substantial part of any particular work has been taken'.[119]

[4.43] Kitchin J formed the overall impression that the visual appearance of the games in question were very different[120] and that there had been no reproduction of any of the plaintiff's artistic copyright material in the defendant's games. Where similar features did appear they were implemented differently and 'expressed at a very high level of generality or abstraction'.[121] Other features did not 'amount to a substantial part of any artistic work. They are ideas at a high level of abstraction and have no meaningful connection with the graphic works relied upon'.[122]

Protection of a sound effect in a computer program

[4.44] Sound effects can be used by computer programs to signify certain events most Mocrosoft Windows users will be familiar with the tune that plays when Windows starts up, for example. Musical compositions can be protected by copyright, but might prove problematic in such a case. A musical composition that is sufficiently substantive to be protected by copyright may be too intrusive to work as a signifier in this way.[123] A better way of protecting such a signifier may be by means of a trademark. Sounds can be registered as a trademark. In the ECJ decision of *Shield Mark BV v Kist*[124] the applicant had registered a trademark with the Dutch Trademark Office consisting of '"Kukelekuuuuu" (an onomatopoeia suggesting, in Dutch, a cockcrow)'.[125] The respondent 'sold a computer program which, when starting up, emits a cockcrow'.[126] The applicant sued and the question of whether a sound could be registered as a trademark

---

[118] [2000] UKHL 58; [2001] 1 All ER 700; [2000] 1 WLR 2416 [2001] FSR 11 at para 25.
[119] [2006] EWHC 24 (Ch), [2006] All ER (D) 131 (Jan), para 127.
[120] [2006] EWHC 24 (Ch), [2006] All ER (D) 131 (Jan), para 136.
[121] [2006] EWHC 24 (Ch), [2006] All ER (D) 131 (Jan), para 245.
[122] [2006] EWHC 24 (Ch), [2006] All ER (D) 131 (Jan), para 252.
[123] *Exxon Corp v Exxon Insurance* (1982) Ch 119.
[124] *Shield Mark BV v Kist* Case C-283/01, [2004] Ch 97, [2004] All ER (EC) 277.
[125] Case C-283/01, para 18.
[126] Case C-283/01, para 22.

reached the ECJ, which held a sound could be registered as a trademark provided that the sound could be:

'represented graphically, particularly by means of images, lines or characters, and that its representation is clear, precise, self-contained, easily accessible, intelligible, durable and objective ... those requirements are satisfied where the sign is represented by a stave divided into measures and showing, in particular, a clef, musical notes and rests whose form indicates the relative value and, where necessary, accidentals'.[127]

Can a computer program be a dramatic work?

[4.45] In *Nova Productions v Mazooma Games*[128] the plaintiffs advanced the argument that the visual experience generated by their computer game was a dramatic work as it generated 'an ordered sequence of events within an overall framework'.[129] This argument was rejected by Kitchin J in the English High Court who noted that a work could not be both a dramatic and a literary work. Kitchin J rejected this argument on four grounds:

(a)   The plaintiff's game was 'not a work of action which is intended to be or is capable of being performed before an audience. On the contrary, it is a game. Although the game has a set of rules, the particular sequence of images displayed on the screen will depend in very large part on the manner in which it is played. That sequence of images will not be the same from one game to another, even if the game is played by the same individual. There is simply no sufficient unity within the game for it to be capable of performance.'[130]

(b)   The plaintiffs claimed that there were various particulars of similarity, but Kitchin J ruled that these could not be features of a dramatic work as they were not capable of performance.[131]

(c)   The plaintiffs contended that their game was a dramatic work and it was recorded in the original development notes for the writing of the program. But Kitchin J had already accepted that these notes amounted to a literary work, so they could not be a dramatic work.[132] Furthermore, these notes contained a sequence of ideas, not all of which would have made it into the finished game.[133]

(d)   Finally, the plaintiff:

'sought to contend that the literary copyright subsists in the source code and the dramatic work is recorded in the object code. Nevertheless (the plaintiff) has not explained how the dramatic work upon which it relies is recorded in the code. It has given no evidence about the code and indeed the source code was not provided to the defendants until shortly before the trial. As I explain below in

---

[127] Case C-283/01, para 64.

[128] *Nova Productions v Mazooma Games* [2006] EWHC 24 (Ch), [2006] All ER (D) 131 (Jan).

[129] [2006] EWHC 24 (Ch), [2006] All ER (D) 131 (Jan), para 110.

[130] [2006] EWHC 24 (Ch), [2006] All ER (D) 131 (Jan), para 116.

[131] [2006] EWHC 24 (Ch), [2006] All ER (D) 131 (Jan), para 117.

[132] According to the UK Copyright Act 1988 and the CRRA 2000–2004.

[133] *Nova Productions v Mazooma Games* [2006] EWHC 24 (Ch), [2006] All ER (D) 131 (Jan), para 118.

considering the issue of infringement of the code as a literary work, it seems to me inevitable that the code contains not a record of any dramatic work but rather a set of instructions which dictates the way in which the game may be played and what will appear on the screen in response to the various inputs made by the person playing the game'.[134]

[4.46] In coming to his decision Kitchin J relied upon the decision of the Privy Council in *Green v Broadcasting Corporation of New Zealand*.[135] The plaintiff had developed a successful show *Opportunity Knocks*. The defendant had produced a show with certain similarities, most notably the same name. The plaintiff claimed that the 'dramatic format' of his show had been copied by the defendant. By this the plaintiff meant elements such as the title, various catch phrases, a 'clapometer' and the use of sponsors to introduce competitors. Bridge LJ commented:

'It is stretching the original use of the word 'format' a long way to use it metaphorically to describe the features of a television series such as a talent, quiz or game show which is presented in a particular way, with repeated but unconnected use of set phrases and with the aid of particular accessories. Alternative terms suggested in the course of argument were 'structure' or 'package'. This difficulty in finding an appropriate term to describe the nature of the 'work' in which the copyright subsists reflects the difficulty of the concept that a number of allegedly distinctive features of a television series can be isolated from the changing material presented in each separate performance ... and identified as an 'original dramatic work' ...

The protection which copyright gives creates a monopoly and "there must be certainty in the subject matter of such monopoly in order to avoid injustice to the rest of the world"[136] ... the subject matter of the copyright claimed for the "dramatic format" of "Opportunity Knocks" is conspicuously lacking in certainty. Moreover, it seems to their Lordships that a dramatic work must have sufficient unity to be capable of performance and that the features claimed as constituting the 'format' of a television show, being unrelated to each other except as accessories to be used in the presentation of some other dramatic or musical performance, lack that essential characteristic'.[137]

Can a computer program be a film?

[4.47] In *Norowzian v Arks (No 1)*[138] it was held that film copyright can only be infringed by photographic copying from the film. In *Nova Productions v Mazooma Games*[139] the plaintiffs conceded that the defendants could not be held at first instance to have infringed any film copyright because the plaintiffs did 'not allege that the defendants copied Pocket Money by photographic means'. However, the plaintiffs formally maintained their 'allegation of infringement of film copyright and reserve(d) it for argument in a higher court'.[140]

---

[134] [2006] EWHC 24 (Ch), [2006] All ER (D) 131 (Jan), para 119.
[135] *Green v Broadcasting Corporation of New Zealand* [1989] RPC 700. See also para **[4.03]**.
[136] Citing *Tate v Fulbrook* [1908] 1 KB 821 at 832, per Farwell J.
[137] *Green v Broadcasting Corporation of New Zealand* [1989] RPC 700 at 702.
[138] *Norowzian v Arks (No 1)* [1998] FSR 394.
[139] *Nova Productions v Mazooma Games* [2006] EWHC 24 (Ch), [2006] All ER (D) 131 (Jan).
[140] [2006] EWHC 24 (Ch), [2006] All ER (D) 131 (Jan) para 120.

Infringement of copyright: adaptation

[4.48] The second right is the right to do copying,[141] is the right to do or to authorise:

'the translation, adaptation, arrangement and any other alteration of a computer program and the reproduction of the results thereof, without prejudice to the rights of the person who alters the program.'[142]

Section 37 of the Act restricts the copying or making available of adaptations of a work, while s 43 provides that the term 'adaptation' in relation to a computer program, includes a translation, arrangement or other alteration of the computer program. The section further continues to the effect that 'In this section "translation", in relation to a computer program, includes the making of a version of the computer program in which it is converted into or out of a computer language or code or into a different computer language or code'.[143]

[4.49] One restriction placed upon the exercise of these two exclusive rights is in s 82 which provides that:

'It is not an infringement of the copyright in a computer program for a lawful user of a copy of the computer program to make a permanent or temporary copy of the whole or a part of the program by any means and in any form or to translate, adapt or arrange or in any other way alter the computer program where such actions are necessary for the use of the program by the lawful user in accordance with its intended purpose, including error correction'.[144]

This provision implements art 5(1) which provides that: 'In the absence of specific contractual provisions, the acts ... shall not require authorization by the rightholder where they are necessary for the use of the computer program by the lawful acquirer in accordance with its intended purpose, including for error correction'. This makes the definition of 'lawful purpose' in relation to a software program particularly important.

The right to translate or adapt a computer program

[4.50] The CRRA 2000–2004 provides that:

'the owner of the copyright in a work has the exclusive right to undertake or authorise others to ... undertake all or any of the following acts, namely:

(a)   to copy the work;

(b)   to make available to the public the work;

(c)   to make an adaptation of the work or to undertake either of the acts referred to in paragraph (a) or (b) in relation to an adaptation'.[145]

The Act goes on to provide that 'an adaptation is made when it is recorded in writing or otherwise'.[146] Computer programs are literary works, and adaptation of a literary work means the 'translation, arrangement or other alteration of the work'.[147] The Act goes on to provide that 'translation' will include:

---

141 See para **[4.10]**.
142 Directive 91/250, art 4(b).
143 CRRA 2000–2004, s 43(3).
144 CRRA 2000–2004, s 81(1).
145 CRRA 2000–2004, s 37(1).

'the making of a version of the computer program in which it is converted into or out of a computer language or code or into a different computer language or code'.[148]

[4.51] This refers to the decompilation of software. In general humans can only read computer programs which are represented by 'source code', whereas computers can only read 'machine' or 'object' code. The relationship between the two forms of code was explained by Laddie J in *Flyde Microsystems Limited v Key Radio Systems Ltd*:

'When a programmer writes a piece of sophisticated software he is writing instructions which the computer processor will understand. The software will contain numerous routines which interact with each other. When he is writing the program he will start by writing it in a way which makes it easy to understand. To do this he will use a language, which is called a 'high level' language, that is to say a language which is based on English (for an English programmer) but is very condensed. It will include within it numerous short explanations, also written in truncated English, explaining what each part of the program is supposed to be doing. This means that the author of the program or any other programmer can readily understand the logical steps by which the program is supposed to work. It facilitates the tracking down of errors and the modification or refinement of the software. This combination of instructions and explanations in high level language is called the source code. It is highly valuable because it contains not just the program but, as explained above, an explanatory manual. The written explanations contained within the source code are neither understood by nor of relevance to the microprocessor. To enable the program to function, the source code is turned into a form which is understood by the microprocessor. The latter does not understand even simple English. It responds to a 'low level' language, called machine code, which is simply a series of numbers. There are programs which will convert source code into machine code. They are called compilers. When the source code is compiled all the explanatory notes are removed ... The machine code for any sizeable program will be unintelligible to any normal human'.[149]

[4.52] The Directive on the Legal Protection of Computer Programs allows for the decompilation of computer programs in certain circumstances. Specifically, it provides that:

'The authorization of the rightholder shall not be required where reproduction of the code and translation of its form ... are indispensable to obtain the information necessary to achieve the interoperability of an independently created computer program with other programs, provided that the following conditions are met:

(a) these acts are performed by the licensee or by another person having a right to use a copy of a program, or on their behalf by a person authorized to so;

(b) the information necessary to achieve interoperability has not previously been readily available to the persons referred to in subparagraph (a); and

---

[146] CRRA 2000–2004, s 43(1)(a). Although it will be 'immaterial to the interpretation of this section whether the adaptation has been recorded in writing or otherwise at the time an act restricted by copyright is undertaken', CRRA 2000–2004, s 43(1)(b).

[147] CRRA 2000–2004 s 43(2)(a)(i).

[148] CRRA 2000–2004, s 43(3).

[149] *Flyde Microsystems Limited v Key Radio Systems Ltd* [1998] EWHC Patents 340 (11 February, 1998), paras 32–33.

(c)   these acts are confined to the parts of the original program which are necessary to achieve interoperability'.[150]

[4.53] This provision is implemented by the CRRA 2000–2004 which provides that it is not an infringement of the copyright in a computer program:

'for a lawful user to make a translation, adaptation, arrangement or any other alteration of the computer program and to copy the results thereof, to achieve the interoperability of an independently created computer program with other programs where the following conditions are complied with:

(i)   those acts are performed by the lawful user or on his or her behalf by a person authorised to do so;

(ii)   the information necessary to achieve interoperability has not previously been available to the person referred to in subparagraph (i); and

(iii)   those acts are confined to the parts of the original program which are necessary to achieve interoperability'.[151]

[4.54] The Directive justified the introduction of this right on the basis that:

'circumstances may exist when such a reproduction of the code and translation of its form … are indispensable to obtain the necessary information to achieve the interoperability of an independently created program with other programs; … it has therefore to be considered that in these limited circumstances only, performance of the acts of reproduction and translation by or on behalf of a person having a right to use a copy of the program is legitimate and compatible with fair practice and must therefore be deemed not to require the authorization of the rightholder; … an objective of this exception is to make it possible to connect all components of a computer system, including those of different manufacturers, so that they can work together; … .such an exception to the author's exclusive rights may not be used in a way which prejudices the legitimate interests of the rightholder or which conflicts with a normal exploitation of the program'.

Few legal reports of decompilation exist.[152] This may reflect the fact that decompilation would be hard to prove, but it may also reflect the reality that it is hard to do and may not result in the generation of usable information.

As Laddie J pointed out in *Flyde Microsystems Ltd v Key Radio Systems Ltd:*

'Programs do exist, called de-compilers, which to a limited extent are able to turn machine code back into something like source code. But even if this is done, all the explanatory notes have been lost. Therefore a decompiled program is likely to be very difficult to understand. This again reinforces the importance of the source code to the programmer or to anyone helping the programmer to write the program.'[153]

---

[150] Directive 91/250, art 6(1).

[151] CRRA 2000–2004, s 81(1)(b).

[152] But see *Audi Performance Racing v Revo Technick*: 'the claimant arranged to make a trap purchase of the first defendant's software. Having acquired it in that way, it was de-compiled and it was sent to an expert … for comparison with the claimant's own software. … (the expert) made a witness statement … in which he expressed the opinion that the first defendant's Flash programme shares the same computer code as the claimant's Flash programme and was copied from it … [2003] EWHC 1668 (Ch) para 11.

[153] *Flyde Microsystems Ltd v Key Radio Systems Ltd* [1998] EWHC Patents 340 (11 February, 1998), paras 32–33.

[4.55] Decompilation was supposed to allow for the interoperability of computer programs. If the EC legislature had not believed that it could provide the necessary information, then other means might have been used to provide for this information. Different computer programs have different functions and so must 'inter-operate' with each other. A computer contains a number of physical components: screen, keyboard, mouse, hard-drive and CPU which must interact if the computer is to work. The software that ensures that these different components can interact is known as the operating system. Such a system was described by Pumfrey J in *Cantor Fitzgerald International v Tradition (UK) Ltd* as follows:

> 'Any electronic computer is a complex piece of equipment. Quite apart from the memory and the CPU ... there has to be some way of getting the data in (a keyboard) and out again (a screen) and of providing more permanent storage for programs and data (one or more disks of various types). Each of these components contains its own processing ability, and must be programmed to operate correctly. To have to program the keyboard controller to scan the keys waiting for one to be pressed, read the key pressed and so on when all the programmer wants to do is to input a number would be immensely wasteful of effort. So all computers have available large programs called operating systems which start automatically when the computer is turned on. Operating systems provide a multitude of services which absolve the programmer from worrying about how to open a file, lay out files on a hard disk, label his files, read his keyboard, output data to the screen and so on. They also come with a number of programs sometimes called utilities. Anyone who has used an Intel-based personal computer will be familiar with the Microsoft Windows family of operating systems: Windows 3.1, Windows 95, Windows 98, Windows NT and so on.'[154]

[4.56] Application programs such as Microsoft Word, Mozilla Firefox or Adobe Photoshop will run on top of the operating system. An application program will not be able to work independently, rather it will rely upon and interact or interoperate with the operating system. The drafters of the Directive on the Legal Protection of Computer Programs had hoped that the threat of decompilation would encourage the owners of operating systems to share this interoperability information. This threat would not appeared to have had the desired effect. In March 2004, the EC Commission issued a decision[155] that Microsoft:

> 'has refused to provide Sun with information enabling Sun to design work group server operating systems that can seamlessly integrate in the 'Active Directory domain architecture', a web of interrelated client PC-to-server and server-to-server protocols that organise Windows work group networks. It is noteworthy that, in order to allow Sun to provide for such seamless integration, Microsoft only had to provide specifications of the relevant protocols, that is to say, technical documentation, and not to give access to the software code of Windows, let alone to allow its reproduction by Sun'.[156]

---

[154] *Cantor Fitzgerald International v Tradition (UK) Ltd* [2000] RPC 95 as appendix C, para 1, p 157.

[155] Commission Decision of 24 May 2004 relating to a proceeding pursuant to art 82 of the EC Treaty and art 54 of the EEA Agreement against Microsoft Corporation (Case COMP/C-3/37.792 – Microsoft), OJ L 32, 6.2.2007, pp 23–28.

[156] Commission Decision of 24 May 2004, para 18.

[4.57] The European Commission held that Microsoft was in a dominant position[157] and had abused this position by refusing to provide the information in question.[158] The Commission's decision is being challenged by Microsoft and at the time of writing the judgment of the Court of First Instance is awaited.[159] The recitals to the Directive on the Legal Protection of Computer Programs did anticipate that such a decision might be made. They provide that 'the provisions of this Directive are without prejudice to the application of the competition rules under Articles ... (81 and 82) ... of the Treaty if a dominant supplier refuses to make information available which is necessary for interoperability as defined in this Directive'. However, there is no sign that the Commission intends to amend these provisions of the Directive on the Legal Protection of Computer Programs to take account of what it clearly views as an inadequacy.

Hence any analysis of the decompilation provisions must take account of the reality that they do not appear to actually confer any practical rights. Decompilation may only be undertaken by a lawful user, this means that the copy of the program which is to be decompiled must have been bought or acquired legally. The CRRA 2000–2004 provides that:

> 'a person is a "lawful user" of a computer program where, whether under a licence to undertake any act restricted by the copyright in the program or otherwise, he or she has a right to use the program, and "lawful use" shall be construed accordingly.'[160]

The above amounts to statutory support for the process of licensing software, as licences enable software publishers to limit the situations in which a use will be lawful. So if software is sold subject to an educational licence, its use may not be lawful if it is used by a commercial company. Unusually the Irish statute departs quite significantly from the right of decompilation as provided for in the European Directive; in particular it appears to limit the 'test of necessity' contained in the European legislation. Article 6 states that decompilation can take place where:

> 'the reproduction of the code and translation of its form are indispensable to obtain the information necessary'.

[4.58] Provisions such as the one above have been criticised for placing a decompiler under a burden which is 'onerous indeed'.[161] It need not be necessary or even desirable to decompile a program, it must be indispensable, so if there is any alternative to decompilation that alternative must be used regardless of how expensive or arduous it is. What is indispensable will vary from case to case, 'causing the supposed right to be shrouded in uncertainty'.[162] In contrast the Irish provision would appear to be clearer and

---

[157] 'Microsoft has acknowledged that it holds a dominant position in the PC operating system market', Commission Decision of 24 May 2004, para 15.

[158] Commission Decision of 24 May 2004, para 19.

[159] *Microsoft Corporation v Commission of the European Communities* (Case T-201/04), OJ C 179, 10.07.2004, p 18.

[160] CRRA 2000–2004, s 80(2).

[161] Laddie, Prescott and Vitoria, *Modern Law of Copyright and Designs* (3rd edn, LexisNexis, 2000), para 34.49.

[162] Laddie, Prescott and Vitoria, *Modern Law of Copyright and Designs* (3rd edn, LexisNexis, 2000), para 34.49.

more favourable to the decompiler. There is no mention of the words indispensable or necessary in the Irish CRRA 2000–2004. The Act simply requires that a lawful user decompile a program in order to achieve the goal of interoperability. This might suggest that any analysis of the actions of a decompiler under Irish law should focus on his motives and objectives, as opposed to the European requirement that his actions be 'indispensable' and 'necessary'. However, the reality is that this provision was only enacted as part of the CRRA 2000 in order to implement the Directive on the Legal Protection of Computer Programs. Thus any interpretation of this provision will have to take the provisions of the Directive into account; otherwise Ireland would be in breach of its obligations under EC Law. This approach to interpretation is known as the 'teleological' approach. The nature of the teleological approach was explained by Denning MR in *Buchanan and Co v Babco Ltd*.[163] Denning MR discussed the rules of interpretation applied by Justices of the ECJ:[164]

> 'They adopt a method which they call in English by strange words – at any rate they were strange to me – the 'schematic and teleological' method of interpretation. It is not really so alarming as it sounds. All it means is that the judges do not go by the literal meaning of the words or by the grammatical structure of the sentence. They go by the design or purpose which lies behind it. When they come upon a situation which is to their minds within the spirit – but not the letter – of the legislation, they solve the problem by looking at the design and purpose of the legislature – at the effect which it was sought to achieve. They then interpret the legislation so as to produce the desired effect. This means that they fill in gaps, quite unashamedly, without hesitation. They ask simply: what is the sensible way of dealing with this situation so as to give effect to the presumed purpose of the legislation?'[165]

[4.59] The above analysis was quoted by Murphy J when he adopted the teleological approach in *Lawlor v Minister for Agriculture*,[166] commenting that:

> 'it does seem to me that the teleological and schematic approach has for many years been adopted in this country ... though not necessarily under that description – in the interpretation of the Constitution. The innumerable occasions in which the preamble to the Constitution has been invoked ... in seeking to 'fill the gaps' in the Constitution is itself an obvious example of the teleological appro ach'.[167]

---

[163] *Buchanan and Co v Babco Ltd* [1977] QB 208.

[164] He was referring in particular to an Article written by the President of the Court, Judge H Kutscher, 'Methods of interpretation as seen by a judge at the Court of Justice', Luxembourg, 1976.

[165] *Buchanan and Co v Babco Ltd* [1977] QB 208 at 213.

[166] *Lawlor v Minister for Agriculture* [1990] 1 IR 356.

[167] *Lawlor v Minister for Agriculture* [1990] 1 IR 356 at 375–376. See also: *Nestor v Murphy* [1979] IR 326; *O'Brien v Ireland* [1991] 2 IR 387; *Bosphorus v Minister for Transport, Energy and Communications* [1994] 2 ILRM 551; *Ailish Young, Plaintiff v The Pharmaceutical Society of Ireland* [1995] 2 IR 91; *DPP v Best* [2000] 2 IR 17; *Coastal Line Container Terminal Ltd v Services Industrial Professional Technical Union* [2000] 1 IR 549; *Marleasing SA v La Comercial International de Alimentacion SA* (Case C–106/89), [1990] ECR 1–4135; *Von Colson and Kamann v Land Nordrhein-Westfalen* (Case 14/83), [1984] ECR 1891; *Coastal Line Container Terminal Ltd v Services Industrial Professional Technical Union* [2000] 1 IR 549 at 559. *Telecom Éireann v Brendan O'Grady* [1998] 3 IR 432.

Therefore the differences between the CRRA 2000–2004 and the Directive on the Legal Protection of Computer Programs may be irrelevant. If the decompilation is necessary, then the decompiler may only proceed if 'the information necessary to achieve interoperability has not previously been available to the (decompiler)'.

[4.60] Arguably this is somewhat less favourable to the decompiler than the Directive, which requires that the information should not have been 'readily' available. This provision has been criticised as unnecessary since 'one would suppose that if the information was readily available anyway, no sensible person would waste his time in decompiling; and, even if he did, it is hard to see why the proprietor of the program would be any the worse off as a result'.[168] One reason for including this provision might be to encourage the making available of the relevant information, a publisher who does not want his program decompiled can avoid this by making this information 'readily available'. A prudent decompiler should undertake an preliminary research to see whether the information is available, and might be well advised to write a letter to the publisher or rightholder of the program which is to be decompiled seeking the relevant information or some direction to where it may be found. Finally there is the requirement that the decompilation be confined to 'the parts of the original program which are necessary to achieve interoperability'.[169]

[4.61] The Directive places limitation on how information acquired through decompilation may be used. It provides that such information may not be used 'for goals other than to achieve the interoperability of the independently created computer program'.[170] The information may not 'be given to others, except when necessary for the interoperability of the independently created computer program'.[171] And the information may be 'used for the development, production or marketing of a computer program substantially similar in its expression, or for any other act which infringes copyright'.[172] Similar limitations are to be found in the Copyright and Related Rights Act 2000 which provides that it is not permissible for information obtained though decompilation:

   (a)   'to be used other than to achieve the interoperability of the independently created computer program;

   (b)   … to be given to persons other than those referred to in that subsection, except where necessary for the interoperability of the independently created computer program; or

   (c)   … to be used for the development, production or marketing of a computer program substantially similar in its expression, or for any other act which infringes copyright.'[173]

[4.62] The first restriction is one of use: decompilation information can only be used to achieve interoperability. This has a number of consequences, decompiling a program

---

[168] Laddie, Prescott and Vitoria, *Modern Law of Copyright and Designs* (3rd edn, LexisNexis, 2000), para 34.49.

[169] Directive91/250, art 6(1)(b).

[170] Directive 91/250, art 6(2)(a).

[171] Directive 91/250, art 6(2)(b).

[172] Directive 91/250, art 6(2)(c).

[173] This provision is virtually identical to art 6(2) of the Directive.

may give access to a variety of interesting information relating to the design, architecture and function of the decompiled program but information other than that used to achieve interoperability should presumably be ignored or destroyed. The second is one of disclosure: the decompilation information may only be given to the lawful user or a person authorised by the lawful user to carry out the decompilation, except where such a disclosure is necessary for interoperability. There is a clear parallel between this provision and that of the law of confidence. Finally this requirement of confidence is reinforced by the provision that the information cannot be used for the development, production or marketing of a program which essentially infringes copyright in the decompiled program. Arguably this last provision is simply there to prevent an infringer arguing that his infringement was in some way authorised by this section.

[4.63] Article 6(3) of the Directive is not explicitly replicated in the Irish Act. This provides that:

> 'In accordance with the provisions of the Berne Convention for the protection of Literary and Artistic Works, the provisions of this Article may not be interpreted in such a way as to allow its application to be used in a manner which unreasonably prejudices the right holder's legitimate interests or conflicts with a normal exploitation of the computer program.

Given how difficult it may be to comply with the other provisions relating to decompilation, it may well be that the omission of this provision will not have greatly prejudiced the rights of software proprietors.

[4.64] It has been suggested that this is an attempt to keep EU Law compatible with art 9(2) of the Berne Convention[174] which provides that:

> 'It shall be a matter for legislation in the Countries of the Union to permit the reproduction of (literary and artistic) works in certain special cases, provided that such reproduction does not conflict with a normal exploitation of the work and does not unreasonably prejudice the legitimate interests of the author.

This article of the Berne Convention mandated the introduction of the Irish provisions on fair dealing. Section 50(1) provides that 'Fair dealing[175] with a literary, dramatic, musical or artistic work, sound recording, film, broadcast, cable programme, or non electronic original database, for the purposes of research or private study, shall not infringe any copyright in the work'. One provisions specific to computer programs is section 50(5) which provides that:

> 'the following acts are not fair dealing—
>
> (a) converting a computer program expressed in a low level computer language into a version expressed in a higher level computer language, or

---

174 Laddie, Prescott and Vitoria, *Modern Law of Copyright and Designs* (3rd edn, LexisNexis, 2000), para 39.50.

175 Where '"fair dealing" means the making use of a literary, dramatic, musical or artistic work, film, sound recording, broadcast, cable programme, non-electronic original database or typographical arrangement of a published edition which has already been lawfully made available to the public, for a purpose and to an extent which will not unreasonably prejudice the interests of the owner of the copyright". CRRA 2000–2004, s 50(4).

(b)   copying a computer program in an incidental manner in the course of converting that program.'

Reverse engineering and the right of repair

[4.65] The Directive on the Copyright protection of Computer Programs provides that:

> 'The person having a right to use a copy of a computer program shall be entitled, without the authorization of the rightholder, to observe, study or test the functioning of the program in order to determine the ideas and principles which underlie any element of the program if he does so while performing any of the acts of loading, displaying, running, transmitting or storing the program which he is entitled to do'.[176]

This is implemented by the CRRA 2000–2004 in near identical form:

> 'It is not an infringement of the copyright in a computer program for a lawful user of a copy of the computer program to observe, study or test the functioning of the program in order to determine the ideas and principles which underlie any element of the program, where he or she does so while performing any of the acts of loading, displaying, running, transmitting or storing the program which he or she is authorised to do'.[177]

[4.66] In *Mars UK Ltd v Teknowledge Ltd*[178] the plaintiffs were 'leaders in the design and manufacture of coin receiving and changing mechanisms.' These mechanisms are 'sensors consisting of coils which take a series of electrical measurements of a coin as it passes through the discriminator. There are sensors which measure the thickness, diameter, electrical resistivity and, most recently, inductance. The signals from the coils are compared with pre-determined sets of data for valid coins. This data is recorded in an electronic memory on a chip'.[179] The plaintiffs had taken steps to make their chips difficult to reverse engineer, but the defendants succeeded in doing so. The plaintiffs sued in respect of the replication of their software, unsuccessfully alleging that their proprietary rights in confidential information had been infringed. However, the plaintiffs made no complaint about the reverse engineering itself.

[4.67] In *Mars UK Ltd v Teknowledge Ltd* the defendants raised the common law right of repair that had been identified by the House of Lords in *British Leyland v Armstrong Patents*.[180] Computer chips are commonplace in modern cars, as is illustrated by the facts of *Audi Performance Racing v Revo Technick*.[181] In this case the repair of cars was not at issue, but rather the alteration of their performance. The defendant was involved in:

> 'a business known as the chipping of motor cars … .this business consists of replacing a computer programme stored on a chip in the engine control unit of the car with a different programme, which provides custom made engine management routines and may enhance the functioning of the engine. The replacement may involve the physical substitution of a new chip, or the old data can be erased and new data installed on the original chip'.[182]

---

[176] Directive 91/250, art 5(2).

[177] CRRA 2000–2004, s 82(2).

[178] *Mars UK Ltd v Teknowledge Ltd* [1999] EWHC 226 (Pat) (11 June 1999).

[179] [1999] EWHC 226 (Pat), para 1.

[180] *British Leyland v Armstrong Patents* [1986] AC 577.

[181] *Audi Performance Racing v Revo Technick* [2003] EWHC 1668 (Ch).

[182] [2003] EWHC 1668 (Ch), para 1. In this case there does not seem to have been any real question that what the defendants were doing was an infringement of copyright.

[4.68] In *British Leyland v Armstrong Patents* plaintiffs produced spare parts for their cars including replacement exhausts; the defendants produced their own replacement exhausts without a licence from the plaintiff and in competition with it. The plaintiffs sued. The car exhausts were purely functional items and could not be protected by the copyright or patents law, so the plaintiff argued that it had created drawings which set out the design of the car exhaust and that the copying of the exhaust amounted to indirect copying of the drawings. The House of Lords upheld this view, but found that there was a 'spare-parts' exception that could be relied upon to permit the manufacture of spare parts in breach of copyright. Lord Templeman based this right on the principle of non-derogation from grant which he imported from land law, this is the principle that: 'a grantor having given a thing with one hand is not to take away the means of enjoying it with the other'.[183] Templeman LJ concluded with the comment that:

> 'The exploitation of copyright laws for purposes which were not intended has gone far enough. I see no reason to confer on a manufacturer the right in effect to dictate the terms on which an article sold by him is to be kept in repair and working order (the lower courts) might have been prepared to come to the same conclusion but balked at extending the rights of an owner of a car to keep it in repair to a manufacturer who makes parts solely for repair. I see no difficulty in such an extension, otherwise the right to repair would be useless'.[184]

[4.69] Templeman LJ rejected the view that a right of repair might arise as some form of implied licence; this is significant as an implied licence could be easily revoked by an appropriate contractual term. However, this would also be the case with non-derogation from grant, as the Privy Council commented in *Canon KK v Green Cartridge Co*,[185] as the:

> 'concept of non-derogation from grant would also suggest that if it were made clear to the purchaser that he was buying the motor car subject to the manufacturer's continuing copyright in the drawings of the parts, no question of non-derogation could arise'.[186]

[4.70] There is a strong argument to be made that the judgment in *British Leyland* is specific to its facts. In *Canon KK v Green Cartridge Co* the Privy Council found that identifying the principle in *British Leyland* was 'no easy matter'[187] and it concluded that:

> 'The basis of the decision in *British Leyland* appears to their Lordships to rest upon two features. First, a compelling analogy with the kind of repair which the ordinary man who bought an article would unquestionably assume that he could do for himself (or commission someone else to do) without infringing any rights of the manufacturer. This is the rhetorical force of Lord Bridge's reference at page 625 to the blacksmith. Secondly, an assumption that the exercise of monopoly power in the aftermarket by means of copyright would unquestionably operate against the interests of consumers. This appears from Lord Templeman's references at pages 628–629 to the customer selling his soul, the tentacles of

---

[183] per Bowen, Birmingham, *Dudley and District Banking Co v Ross* (1888) 38 Ch D 295 at 313, cited by Templeman LJ [1986] AC 577 at 641.
[184] [1986] AC 577 at 644.
[185] *Canon KK v Green Cartridge Co* [1997] AC 729.
[186] [1997] AC 729 at 737.
[187] [1997] AC 729 at 735.

copyright and his mention at page 641 of the Report of the Monopolies and Mergers Commission on the refusal of the Ford Motor Company Limited to grant licences for the manufacture of certain replacement body parts (Cmnd 9437, February 1985), which he said had 'stigmatised' the company's conduct as anticompetitive.

It would appear that the Privy Council considered that the judgment did not really give rise to any general principle that could be applied elsewhere:[188]

'Their Lordships consider that once one departs from the case in which the unfairness to the customer and the anticompetitive nature of the monopoly is as plain and obvious as it appeared to the House of Lords in *British Leyland*, the jurisprudential and economic basis for the doctrine becomes extremely fragile.

[4.71] In *Canon KK v Green Cartridge Co*,[189] the Privy Council expressed serious doubts about the validity of the decision in British Leyland, commenting that its:

'reasoning involves a somewhat unorthodox extension of what would normally be understood by the inherent right to repair one's motor car. Of course one has a right to repair one's car, as one has a right to cultivate one's garden and indulge in all kinds of harmless activities. But such a right is not usually treated as entitling one to invade the property rights of others; for example, by taking a neighbour's dahlias on the ground that this is the most economical way of going about it. It is hard to see why the appropriation of intellectual property rights should be any different ... Indeed so much is in principle acknowledged by Lord Bridge of Harwich[190] ... when he says that the right to repair would not justify the infringement of patents or registered designs. He distinguished these forms of intellectual property as 'truly and expressly monopolistic.'[191]

[4.72] The plaintiff in *Canon KK v Green Cartridge Co* was the manufacturer of photocopiers and printers; it incorporated the parts which might need replacing during the lifetime of a machine in a disposable ink cartridge which would be inserted in the machine by its owner. The defendant manufactured and sold ink cartridges in competition with the plaintiff; the Privy Council refused to allow the defendant rely upon the spare parts principle. This principle was reviewed again by Jacob J in *Mars v Teknowledge* in which he summarised the House of Lords and Privy Council judgments as:

'In broad terms, *Leyland* recognised a 'spare parts' defence to copyright infringement and *Canon* held that any such defence should not be extended and in particular should not be extended to 'consumables' such as copier cartridges'.[192]

[4.73] In *Mars v Teknowledge* the defence of the spare parts exception as set out in *British Leyland* was raised. However, Jacob J refused to extend the spare parts exception to computer programs and databases as he agreed with counsel for the plaintiff that:

---

[188] 'These unusual features of the reasoning in *British Leyland* make it difficult to pick out any particular phrase in the judgments as encapsulating a general principle', [1997] AC 729 at 735, 738.
[189] [1997] AC 729.
[190] [1986] AC 577 at 628.
[191] [1997] AC 729 at 736.
[192] *Mars v Teknowledge* [1999] EWHC 226 (Pat), para 13.

'there was no room for a spare parts or like exception in relation to computer programs and database rights because Parliament and the European Community had clearly considered the position as to defences and had provided a complete statutory code'.[193]

The extension of the rule in *British Leyland* is even more doubtful in Ireland than it is in England and Wales. The judgment in *British Leyland* was reviewed by the Privy Council in *Canon KK v Green Cartridge Co*[194] which commented that:

'It is hard to escape the conclusion that although Lord Bridge of Harwich felt driven to accept that Parliament had created intellectual property rights which covered the manufacture of three-dimensional parts by reverse engineering, he felt free to remedy what he saw as a legislative error by treating such rights as an inferior species of property which could be subordinated to the right to repairs one's motor car. Such pre-potency over statute has not yet been accorded in this country to human rights even such as free speech'.[195]

[4.74] It came to the conclusion that:

'it is of course a strong thing (not to say constitutionally questionable) for a judicially-declared head of public policy to be treated as overriding or qualifying an express statutory right. Their Lordships therefore think that the prospect of any extension of the *British Leyland* should be treated with some caution'.[196]

It does not appear that the right of repair has ever been raised in an Irish court; this last passage may suggest that if it were it could encounter significant difficulties. The Irish Parliament and Judiciary have clearly defined roles, and it may be that faced with a similar controversy the Irish courts will be inclined to follow the lead of Griffith LJ's dissent.

Infringement of copyright: distribution

[4.75] The third exclusive right provided by the Directive on the Legal Protection of Computer Programs is the right to do or to authorise:

'any form of distribution to the public, including the rental, of the original computer program or of copies thereof. The first sale in the Community of a copy of a program by the rightholder or with his consent shall exhaust the distribution right within the

---

[193] [1999] EWHC 226 (Pat), para 17. Noting that in relation to computer programs: 'It is not for national judge-made laws (which may vary from country to country) to override or add to what are clearly intended to be Community wide rules. Were that not so, then there would be little point in having Directives requiring Member-States to align their laws in a specific area'. At para 18 and in relation to databases that: 'It can hardly be for the judges of a particular Member State of their own to act as though they are exercising the option on behalf of that State. If Parliament had wanted to adopt an option in relation to the use of database rights for updating equipment that is a matter for it, not the judges. At para 18. See also: *Dyson Ltd v Qualtex (UK) Ltd* [2004] EWHC 2981 (CH), [2005] RPC 395, [2004] All ER (D) 375 (Dec). An Attempt to extend the right of repair to patents was made in *United Wire Ltd v Screen Repair Services (Scotland) Ltd and others* [2000] FSR 204, (1999) The Times, 18 August.
[194] *Canon KK v Green Cartridge Co* [1997] AC 729.
[195] *Canon KK v Green Cartridge Co* [1997] AC 729 at 736.
[196] *Canon KK v Green Cartridge Co* [1997] AC 729 at 737.

Community of that copy, with the exception of the right to control further rental of the program or a copy thereof'.[197]

[4.76] This distribution right is the same as the right conferred on the owners of trademarks, which allows them to control the importation of products bearing their marks into the EU.[198] This right is replicated by the CRRA 2000–2004, which confers a distribution right upon the owner of copyright.[199] The CRRA 2000–2004 also gives the owner of software the right to control how their products are made available to the public: 'the owner of the copyright in a work has the exclusive right to undertake or authorise others to … make available to the public the work'.[200]

This making available right includes the 'making available to the public of copies of the work, by wire or wireless means, in such a way that members of the public may access the work from a place and at a time chosen by them (including the making available of copies of works through the Internet)'[201] and 'issuing copies of the work to the public'.[202] This provision effectively anticipated the need to implement the Directive on the harmonisation of certain aspects of copyright and related rights in the information society[203] and in particular art 3 thereof. The importance of controlling the distribution of computer software is illustrated in *Flyde Microsystems v Key Radio Systems Ltd*.[204] The plaintiff was a developer of telecommunications software and the defendant manufactured and imported mobile radios. The plaintiff developed software which allowed radios to use radio channels more efficiently and intelligently. The defendant needed this software to enter the substantial market for these sorts of radios. It was able to buy actual radios abroad and import them into the UK but it needed the semi-conductor chips loaded with the plaintiff's software to make those radios work intelligently. Initially, the defendant bought the chips directly from the plaintiff with the program already loaded onto the chips; however, it was more efficient for the defendant to simply load the plaintiffs program onto completed radios which contained chips bought from the plaintiff. The difficulty for the plaintiff was that there was no contract or licence for this agreement, they relied on trust. In particular, the plaintiff did not receive any payment per computer program used, but rather it was paid per chip sold. The defendant began loading the plaintiff's program on to chips which it had not bought from the plaintiff, so avoiding payment. The plaintiff succeeded at trial, however, the absence of a written contract or licence between the parties meant that the defendant was able to claim, firstly, to be a joint author of the software and, secondly, to hold an implied

---

[197] Directive 91/250, art 4.
[198] See *Zino Davidoff v A&G Imports Ltd/ Levi Strauss v Tesco Stores Ltd and Costco (Wholesale) Ltd* [2002] Ch 109, [2002] Ch 109, [2001] ECR I-8691, [2002] RPC 403.
[199] CRRA 2000–2004, s 41.
[200] CRRA 2000–2004, s 37(1)(b).
[201] CRRA 2000–2004, s 40(1)(a).
[202] CRRA 2000–2004, s 40(1)(e).
[203] Directive 2001/29/EC of the European Parliament and of the Council of 22 May 2001 on the harmonisation of certain aspects of copyright and related rights in the information society.
[204] *Flyde Microsystems v Key Radio Systems Ltd* [1998] FSR 449. For further discussion, see paras **[4.15]**, **[4.51]** and **[4.54]**.

licence to use the software as they saw fit. In contrast, companies such as Microsoft sell all their software subject to stringent written end-user licence agreements. As a result they are able to protect their intellectual property very swiftly.

[4.77] The facts in *Microsoft v Electro-Wide Ltd & Another*[205] were broadly similar to *Flyde,* the difference in this case being that the defendants were Original Equipment Manufacturers (OEMs) of personal computers as opposed to radios. In both cases, the fact that the defendant had sold the plaintiff's software without the plaintiff's consent was not in serious dispute. However, it was the clear policy of Microsoft not to allow its software to be sold without an end-user licence agreement (EULA). Since the defendants were doing so, Laddie J came to '... the clear conclusion that the defendants' explanations are not believable and that there is not a fair or reasonable probability of the defendants having a real or *bona fide* defence in relation to these issues'[206] and he granted an interlocutory injunction restraining the defendants from selling copies of the plaintiffs software in the future.

[4.78] Since a lot of software is now sold over the Internet and by means other than by selling boxed sets of software in a shop, the term 'shrink-wrap' licence is falling out of use. Instead, the term 'end user licence agreement (EULA)' is used. Doubts had been expressed about the enforceability of these licences in the past, but the manner in which these licences are proferred to the user has changed. Typically, when a user installs new software, they will be presented with a screen which displays the EULA, tells the user to read it and requires the user to indicate his or her acceptance of the EULA before the installation is initiated. If the user does not indicate his or her acceptance, the installation will be discontinued. An advantage of the software licence system is that it allows publishers to sell the same product at different prices to different users. A spreadsheet program is worth a lot more to an accountancy practice than to someone who wants to keep track of their family budget. Software licences allow these two users to have the benefit of the same program while paying very different prices. However, if the family user decides that they want to run a business they will have to purchase a new commercial licence agreement to use the same program.

[4.79] This occurred in the American case of *ProCD, Inc v Zeidenburg & Silken Mountain Web Services, Inc*[207] where the plaintiff had compiled information from more than 3,000 phone directories into a computer database at a cost of more that $10m. This database was marketed in a number of different ways:

- the database was available on the Internet to users of the America online service but it had been adapted so that it would not be of any use to commercial users;

---

[205]*Microsoft v Electro-Wide Ltd & Another* [1997] FSR 580.

[206] [1997] FSR 580 at 594.

[207] *ProCD, Inc v Zeidenburg & Silken Mountain Web Services, Inc* United States Court of Appeals for the seventh Circuit, 86 F 3d 1447; 1996 US App. LEXIS 14951; 39 USPQ 2D (BNA) 1161; Copy L Rep (CCH) P27, 529; 29 UCCR Serv. See also the Scottish case of *Beta Computers (Europe) Ltd v Adobe Systems (Europe) Ltd* [1996] FSR 367, (1995) IP & T Digest 28.

- it was sold by the plaintiffs on CD-ROM to the general public who could purchase it for $150; and

- commercial users could purchase a CD-ROM for considerably higher price.

The defendant bought a consumer copy of the database in 1994 on a CD-ROM which was contained in a shrink-wrapped box. He ignored the licence and began reselling its contents on the Internet. The plaintiffs sought an injunction enforcing the terms of these licences. The defendant agreed that the transaction was subject to a licence, his argument was that, because the licence was not printed in full on the outside of the box, he could not be bound by it. The court pointed out that it was impractical to put the entire licence on the outside of the box, this could only be done by using microscopic type and by removing other useful information such as the purpose of the software. The court noted that insurance policies, airline and theatre tickets are all sold subject to complex terms which will not be explained to the purchaser when they buy the goods over the phone or through an agent but will instead be sent out later.

[4.80] The court noted that this was not a case where the defendant had opened the box to see a note stating that he owed the plaintiffs an extra $10,000.[208] It pointed out that the law does allow contracts to be accepted in a variety of ways, not just by 'paying the price and walking out of the store'. The vendor may also stipulate that an offer can be accepted by the performance of certain acts and that was what happened here. The plaintiffs proposed a contract that the buyer would accept by using the software after having an opportunity to read the licence at leisure. This is what the defendant did; indeed he was left with no choice as the software placed the licence on the screen of his computer and would not allow him to proceed until he indicated his acceptance. He could have rejected the contract by returning the software and receiving a refund. This case was recently followed in *Adobe Sys Inc v Stargate Software*,[209] *Adobe Sys Inc v One Stop Micro, Inc*[210]and *Meridian Project Systems v Hardin Construction.*[211] The US courts also held that so-called 'browse-wrap' licences may be valid in *Pollstar v Gigimania.*[212] However, the enforceability of 'shrink-wrap' licences remains 'a much-disputed question'.[213]

[4.81] Doubts about the enforceability of shrink-wrap licences turn on the question that if a contract is made at the point of sale (as was held in *Pharmaceutical Society of Great Britain v Boots Cash Chemists*[214]), how can the owner of copyright unilaterally insert a complex licence into the agreement which the purchaser cannot read until he opens the

---

[208] The English law on this sort of condition is given in *Interfoto Picture Library Ltd v Stiletto Visual Programmes Ltd* [1988] 1 All ER 348.

[209] *Adobe Sys Inc v Stargate Software Inc* 216 F Supp 2d 1051 (ND Cal 2002).

[210] *Adobe Sys Inc v One Stop Micro* 84 F Supp 2d 1086 (ND Cal 2000).

[211] *Meridian Project Systems v Hardin Construction* No S-04-4278, 2006 US Dist LEXIS 16751 (ED Cal 6 April, 2006).

[212] *Pollstar v Gigimania* 170 F Supp 2d 974, 980-81 (ED Cal 2000).

[213] *Meridian Project Systems v Hardin Construction* No S-04-4278, 2006 US Dist LEXIS 16751 (ED Cal 6 April, 2006, p 8.

[214] *Pharmaceutical Society of Great Britain v Boots Cash Chemists* (1953) 1 QB 410.

box after he bought it? But computer software is a very different product from the pharmaceuticals which were the subject of *Pharmaceutical Society of Great Britain v Boots Cash Chemists.*[215] When pills are bought from a pharmacy, the goods are assigned from the pharmacy to the customer, and although the customer will acquire the pills he will not learn any of the pharmaceutical company's trade secrets. If he likes the pills or finds them effective, he cannot replicate them and give them to all his friends. The correct view of this contractual arrangement may be that the software is purchased in the knowledge that it is subject to a licence agreement and that if the customer is unhappy with the terms of that licence, then the software should be returned for a refund. It could be argued that this is a condition of the contract of sale which binds the purchaser. The purchaser will make an offer at the cash register and this may be accepted by the vendor, but it will be a condition of the contract of sale so made that the purchaser will be bound by the terms of the licence. The use of the software without acceptance of the licence terms would be a fundamental breach of the contract which would result in the contract being rescinded. This would mean that the purchaser was no longer entitled to use the software and continued use of it would be a breach of copyright.

[4.82] Any software licence will have to comply with the Directive on the Legal Protection of Computer Programs and the CRRA 2000–2004. A software licence cannot limit a user's right to create back-up copies,[216] observe the functioning of a program[217] or decompile a program as permitted by the Directive.[218] Although a licence may limit the user's ability to reproduce or translate a program,[219] the Directive creates the assumption that in the absence of any specific provisions to the contrary, a user may carry out these acts where they are necessary for the 'intended purpose' of the program.[220]

Shareware

[4.83] Simply because a licence is gratuitous does not mean that it cannot be binding. A licence can be given gratuitously to everybody in the world,[221] but anybody who avails of that licence will still be bound by its terms. Computer software is frequently gratuitously distributed as 'shareware'. This is because once a program has become accepted as a standard its sales will often increase as users want to use the program which is most compatible with that used by others. This has led to claims that a 'law of increasing returns' applies to sales of software as opposed to the 'law of diminishing returns' which applies to most other products.[222] In order to acquire market share, smaller companies will often give away free samples of their software, in the hope that some users will be sufficiently impressed with the software to buy it. In order to encourage this, the software will often be sold with a time-lock which will prevent the software from

---

[215] (1953) 1 QB 410.
[216] Directive 91/250, art 5(2).
[217] Directive 91/250, art 5(3).
[218] Directive 91/250, art 6.
[219] Directive 91/250, art 4(a).
[220] Directive 91/250, art 5(1).
[221] See *Mellor v Australian Broadcasting Commission* [1940] AC 491.
[222] See Arthur, 'Increasing Returns and the New World of Business' (1996) Harvard Business Review, July-August, p 100; for criticism see (1996) The Economist, 28 September.

working after a set period, say 30 days, or after a set number of uses. There is nothing unusual in giving away free samples of a product, or in allowing potential customers to test drive software in the same fashion as they might test drive a car. But just because the owner of software is not receiving any payment for his software it does not mean that he or she has renounced all rights in it. The validity of such shareware licences was examined in *Trumpet Software v Ozemail*[223] where the Australian courts held that a licence to use software in limited circumstances would not permit the modification or adaptation of the software. The fact that a licence permits gratuitous use does not mean that reproduction or adaptation is also permitted:

'Copyright law forbids duplication, public performance and so on, unless the person wishing to copy or perform the work gets permission; silence means a ban on copying. A copyright is a right against the world. Contracts by contrast, generally affect only their parties; strangers may do so as they please, so contracts do not create "exclusive rights". Someone who found a copy of (the plaintiff's database) on the street would not be affected by the shrink-wrap licence – though the federal copyright laws of their own force would limit the finder's ability to copy or transmit the application program.'[224]

[4.84] The granting of a gratuitous licence has to be distinguished from the abandonment of copyright. There does not appear to be any decision which directly recognises the abandonment of copyright and the CRRA 2000–2004 makes no provision for this.[225] In *Trumpet Software v Ozemail*[226] the plaintiffs had written a program, 'Trumpet Winsock', which enabled users to connect onto the Internet and in 1994 the defendants offered to distribute the Trumpet Winsock program. This was to be done in two ways: first, by distribution in a forthcoming edition of the magazine *Australian Personal Computer*; and second, in a software package disk which would be sold through retail outlets. After some inconclusive negotiations, the defendants were told that the plaintiff did not want them to go ahead with the distribution as the software did not have a time lock. As time passed, the plaintiffs did not give the defendants the time locked version of the software and the court held that it had been made clear to the defendants that the plaintiff did not wish them to distribute the program without the time lock. However, while this was going on the defendants had agreed with *Australian Personal Computer* magazine that they would supply the program for distribution. Heerey J found that the defendants had got themselves into a position where they 'were determined to go ahead with the distribution regardless of what (the plaintiffs) said.'

[4.85] The plaintiffs sent the defendant a letter refusing to allow the defendants to distribute the software. However, at this stage the defendants had already gone ahead with the distribution of the software through the *Australian Personal Computer* magazine. In spite of considerable correspondence between solicitors, the defendants

[223] *Trumpet Software v Ozemail* (1996) Aust Fedct LEXIS 463; BC 9602953.
[224] Easterbrook J in *ProCD, Inc v Zeidenburg & Silken Mountain Web Services, Inc* United States Court of Appeals for the seventh Circuit, 86 F 3d 1447; 1996 US App. LEXIS 14951; 39 USPQ 2D (BNA) 1161; Copy. L Rep (CCH) P27, 529; 29 UCCR Serv.
[225] There was a suggestion to this effect in the English High Court in *Catnic Components Ltd v Hill & Smith* [1978] FSR 405 but this was not dealt with by the Court of Appeal.
[226] *Trumpet Software v Ozemail* (1996) Aust Fedct LEXIS 463; BC 9602953.

then repeated this with a distribution through Australian PC World. The defendants also altered the software so that it would direct users to connect to their Internet access service. Furthermore they removed files which would inform users that the software was shareware, that it was the property of the plaintiffs and which directed users to register with the plaintiffs.

[4.86] The Australian court found that the defendants had breached the plaintiffs' copyright by reproducing their software on the Internet, and by reproducing it for *Australian Personal Computer* and the Australian PC World distribution. The court found that there was no contract between the parties for the supply of the software as the defendant did not supply any consideration. It was held that the purpose of shareware is to allow evaluation by potential users and that the defendants had sought to adapt the program in the hope of encouraging subscribers to its Internet access service. The plaintiffs suggested that if the licence conferred any rights of distribution on third parties then such licence was subject to conditions that the distribution should be without other software; without modification, addition or deletion; in its entirety; and without charge and not for commercial gain to enable such third parties to use the software for a period of 30 days for the purpose of the evaluation. Although Heerey J had already found that the agreement was not contractual, he felt that the licence must have had some contractual terms and, using the analogy of contract law, he felt that it was an implied term of the licence that it would have to be distributed in its entirety and without modification, alteration or deletion.[227] He also felt that a condition could not be imposed denying the distributor the right to make any commercial gain from the distribution but that the defendant had breached the licence by altering and modifying the software.

---

[227] Where there is no clear agreement on a licence, the courts may be willing to imply one. In *Redwood v Chappell & Co* [1982] RPC 109 at 128, Goff J considered the test for an implied licence to be 'The test to be applied ... (is) an objective one: viz. whether, viewing the facts objectively, the words and conduct of the alleged licensor, as made known to the alleged licensee, in fact indicated that the licensor consented to what the licensee was doing.

Chapter 5

Copyright Protection of Internet Content

Introduction

[5.01] The function of both the World Wide Web and the Internet is to make information and content available as widely as possible. This means that all forms of electronic data can be easily transmitted and exchanged, but it also means that where copyright works are stored as electronic data then those works can be copied, distributed and made available without regard to the rights of the copyright owner. The Internet makes it easy to distribute copyright works that can be reproduced electronically. Easier distribution should mean larger audiences for those works, but copyright owners will only benefit if they can charge for the works in question. By making the distribution of infringing copies easier, the Internet challenges the ability of copyright owners to exploit their work. It is still too early to say whether this will ultimately seriously damage or destroy the basis upon which the modern copyright system exists, but it has certainly seriously damaged some industries, such as the record shops which used to sell music CDs.[1]

Websites

[5.02] Websites can contain just about any data that is capable of being processed electronically. This data may contain works protected by copyright such as literary works, artistic works or recordings of performances. Copyright will subsist in each of these works separately; copyright law may be invoked to restrain the copying of any of these individual elements. A more difficult situation will arise where the 'look-and-feel' of a website is copied.

Structure and layout of websites

[5.03] A website will consist of elements that may be structural, aesthetic or both. The structural elements will be determined by protocols with which the website must comply, such as http, and the program that is used to build the site. It is inevitable that two separate web-sites which were built using the same program, say Dreamweaver or Microsoft Access, will share structural similarities. Alternatively, the purpose of a website may determine its appearance. For example, the US case of *Ross Brovins & Oehmke v LexisNexis Group*[2] concerned the production of legal forms used in the US State of Michigan. Initially these forms were supplied by the plaintiffs to the defendants, but the defendants terminated this relationship and began to produce its own forms. The

---

[1] Braithwaite and Edgecliffe-Johnson, 'Crisis flips Fopp off high street' (2007) Financial Times, 29 June: 'Analysts ... predict() that global music sales by 2009 will be half their level at the peak of the CD boom, down from Dollars 45bn in 1997 to Dollars 23bn in 2009'.

[2] *Ross Brovins & Oehmke v Lexis Nexis Group* US Ct of Apps (6th Cir), Case No 05-1513, 15 September 2006.

plaintiffs sued. One of the difficulties faced by the plaintiffs was that where there were similarities between the two sets of forms, this similarity might be accounted for by the fact that both sets of forms were based on pre-existing legislation. So similarities in the structure of both parties' index of forms stemmed 'from both parties' copying the public Michigan forms index'.³ Similarly, the plaintiff could not claim copyright in its electronic forms as 'programming choices that merely follow the instructions on the underlying form are not creative expression protected by copyright'.⁴ Copyright cannot subsist in something that is not original. As was stated by Pearce J in *Ladbroke (Football) Ltd v William Hill (Football) Ltd:*⁵

> 'The reproduction of a part which by itself has no originality will not normally be a substantial part of the copyright and therefore will not be protected. For that which would not attract copyright except by reason of its collocation will, when robbed of that collocation, not be a substantial part of the copyright and therefore the courts will not hold its reproduction to be an infringement. It is this, I think, which is meant by one or two judicial observations that "there is no copyright" in some unoriginal part of a whole that is copyright'.⁶

[5.04] A website will also contain aesthetic elements such as colour choices, type-faces and pictures in which copyright may subsist, and distinguishing functional from aesthetic elements may not be easy. Laddie J considered that the above quotation was of particular significance in *IPC Media v Highbury-SPL Publishing.*⁷ The applicant was the publisher of a magazine titled *IDEAL HOME*; the respondent published a magazine called *HOME*. The applicant alleged that: 'the outer covers and certain parts of the internal sections of the May, June, July and August 2002 issues of *HOME* are infringements of the copyright in certain earlier issues of *IDEAL HOME*'.⁸

> 'where the author's artistic work was created by blending together known design features … (i)t may well be that the skill and effort involved in that blending operation is sufficient to justify copyright protection. But in such a case, copying one or two of the individual features may not amount to the taking of a substantial part of the copyright work. Each case will depend on its own facts'.⁹

[5.05] One of the great advantages of a website is that it can be updated and amended continuously. This creates a difficulty for the copyright owner of such a site, however: if a site is continuously changing it then it may be difficult to prove which, if any, elements of the site have been copied. In *IPC Media v Highbury-SPL Publishing*¹⁰ the applicant's

---

3   *Ross Brovins & Oehmke v Lexis Nexis Group* US Ct of Apps (6th Cir), Case No 05-1513, 15 September 2006 at p 5.
4   *Ross Brovins & Oehmke v Lexis Nexis Group* US Ct of Apps (6th Cir), Case No 05-1513, 15 September 2006 at p 7.
5   *Ladbroke (Football) Ltd v William Hill (Football) Ltd* [1964] 1 WLR 273.
6   *Ladbroke (Football) Ltd v William Hill (Football) Ltd* [1964] 1 WLR 273 at 293.
7   *IPC Media Ltd v Highbury-SPL Publishing Ltd* [2004] EWHC 2985 (Ch), [2004] All ER (D) 342 (Dec).
8   *IPC Media Ltd v Highbury-SPL Publishing Ltd* [2004] EWHC 2985 (Ch), para 3.
9   *IPC Media Ltd v Highbury-SPL Publishing Ltd* [2004] EWHC 2985 (Ch), para 13.
10   *IPC Media Ltd v Highbury-SPL Publishing Ltd* [2004] EWHC 2985 (Ch), [2004] All ER (D) 342 (Dec).

magazine changed every month. This caused difficulties for both the applicant and the respondent's lawyers. Laddie J held that:

> 'the fact that there are numerous similar works produced by the author does not mean that he does not have to prove that one or more discrete copyright works have been copied. Rather, the court may be persuaded that the specific copyright works relied upon in the action are either the precise ones copied, directly or indirectly, by the defendant or that they substantially reproduce the earliest copyright work which was copied and therefore amount to evidence of what that earliest copyright work was like'.[11]

[5.06] The claimant faced a similar difficulty in *Baigent and another v Random House Group Ltd*[12] which concerned an allegation of non-textual copying. The allegation was that the defendant had published a work of fiction[13] which copied the 'central theme' but not the text of a work previously published by the plaintiffs. However, the claimant could not overcome:

> 'the uncertainty created by the Claimants' own inability clearly to state what the Central Theme is by reason of their changes of the Central Theme. The point is that if the Claimants do not know with certainty what their Central Theme is how can anybody else possibly know'.[14]

[5.07] In *IPC Media v Highbury-SPL Publishing* it was held that the layout of the applicant's magazine had not been copied. An attempt to assert copyright in the layout of a chain of shops was made in *Gadget Shop v Bug Com*.[15] The applicants claimed that 'its shops all enjoy a unique type of design and layout which makes them instantly recognisable'. The applicant made claims of 'infringement of copyright or design right in relation to its shop fitting plans'.[16] The applicant sought interim injunctive relief in relation to certain information about these plans. Rimer J felt that the applicant's claim was 'a somewhat weak one'[17] in relation to breach of confidence, but he noted that the respondent's shop was 'apparently a close and deliberate copy'[18] of the applicant's premises. *IPC Media v Highbury-SPL Publishing and Gadget Shop v Bug Com* suggest that copyright may subsist in the layout of a physical publication or shop. Hence copyright may similarly subsist in the layout of an Internet publication or shop. But proving infringement of such copyright may be problematic.

---

[11] *IPC Media Ltd v Highbury-SPL Publishing Ltd* [2004] EWHC 2985 (Ch), para 6. Laddie J cited his own judgment in *Cala Homes (South) Ltd and Others v Alfred McAlpine Homes East Ltd* [1995] FSR 818 at 872. See also *King Features Syndicate Inc v O & M Kleeman Ltd* [1940] Ch 523.

[12] *Baigent and another v Random House Group Ltd* [2006] EWHC 719 (Ch), [2006] All ER (D) 113.

[13] Dan Brown, *The Da Vinci Code* (Random House, 2003).

[14] *Baigent and another v Random House Group Ltd* [2006] EWHC 719 (Ch), [2006] All ER (D) 113 at para 156.

[15] *Gadget Shop v Bug Com* (2000) The Times, 28 March.

[16] *Gadget Shop v Bug Com* (2000) The Times, 28 March, para 3.

[17] *Gadget Shop v Bug Com* (2000) The Times, 28 March, para 119.

[18] *Gadget Shop v Bug Com* (2000) The Times, 28 March, para 121.

Photographs and collages

[5.08] Photographs are protected as artistic works. The CRRA 2000–2004 states that copyright subsists in artistic works,[19] which it defines as including:

'a work of any of the following descriptions, irrespective of their artistic quality … photographs, paintings, drawings, diagrams, maps, charts, plans, engravings, etchings, lithographs, woodcuts, prints or similar works, collages or sculptures'.[20]

[5.09] Copyright in a photograph can be infringed by recreating the scene photographed and taking a fresh photograph as well as by simply reproducing the original.[21] Where a photograph is recreated in this way, the US Federal Courts have held that while objective elements of an original photograph such as the selection of lighting, shading, timing, angle and film are protected by copyright, the 'relatively amorphous characterstics' of the work such as its conveyance of an 'eerie' mood were not protected. This was held in *Leigh v Warner Brothers, Inc*[22] which related to a photograph of a famous statue of a girl used on the cover of a novel *Midnight in the Garden of Good and Evil*. The film of the book was produced by the defendants who built a replica of the statute and used images of this replica in promotional materials and in the movie itself. The definition of photograph in the Act must be broader than just cameras which contain chemical film and would encompass digital cameras and holograms. X-Rays would be included in this definition which would be consistent with the finding of the Supreme Court in *McCarthy v O'Flynn*[23] that an X-Ray was a document for the purposes of discovery.[24] Although, whether an X-Ray has the necessary originality is very much open to doubt.[25]

[5.10] The subsistence of copyright in a photograph was examined by Neuberger J in the English High Court in *Antiquesportfolio.com v Rodney Fitch*.[26] This was a dispute between a website, which was to sell antiques online, and a company contracted to create its site. The plaintiff refused to pay certain invoices of the defendant, alleging that the defendant had used 'photographs of individual antiques such as items of furniture, glasswear, metal-work, sculpture and the like'. These photographs had been taken from Millers Antiques Encyclopaedia. Neuberger J found that:

'Some of these photographs were effectively reproduced on the website prepared by the defendant. First, four of the seven icons in a pale blue banner across the top of the first page, and of many of the other pages of the website, contain a smaller version of one of the photographs of an antique in the Encyclopaedia. Secondly, the first page of the website includes a box consisting of 25 navigation buttons, arranged five by five. On pressing a particular button one is taken to a page, where goods of the type shown on the button are

---

19 CRRA 2000–2004, s 17(2).
20 CRRA 2000–2004, s 2(1).
21 *Creation Records v News Group Newspapers* [1997] EMLR 444.
22 *Leigh v Warner Brothers, Inc* No 99-10087, 2000 WL 679162 (11th Cir, 25 May 2000).
23 *McCarthy v O'Flynn* [1979] IR 127.
24 Under RSC 1986, ord 31.
25 Photographic processes are used in the manufacture of semi-conductor chips which are also protected separately by the European Communities (Protection of Topographies of Semi-Conductor Products) Regulation 1988 (SI 101/1988).
26 *Antiquesportfolio.com v Rodney Fitch* (2000) The Times, 21 July.

advertised. Each of the items shown on the buttons in the box was a very small-scale version of a photograph of an article in the Encyclopaedia'.[27]

Neuberger J had to decide whether or not copyright subsisted in the original photograph. To assist himself, Neuberger J quoted the following passage from *Copinger and Skone James on Copyright*:

'In terms of what is original, for the purpose of determining whether copyright subsists in a photograph, the requirement of originality is low, and may be satisfied by little more than the opportunistic pointing of the camera and the pressing of the shutter button. There seems no reason of principle why there should be any distinction between the photograph which is the result of such a process and a photograph which is intended to reproduce a work of art, such as a painting or another photograph. Provided that the author can demonstrate that he expended some small degree of time, skill and labour in producing the photograph, (which may be demonstrated by the exercise of judgment as to such matters as the angle from which to take the photograph, the lighting, the correct film speed, what filter to use, et cetera) the photograph ought to be entitled to copyright protection, irrespective of its subject matter. What is the extent of protection afforded by the copyright in a photograph is a different matter.'[28]

Neuberger J also quoted from an American text, *Nimmo on Copyright*:

'Any, or (as will be indicated below) almost any, photograph may claim the necessary originality to support a copyright merely by virtue of the photographer's personal choice of subject matter, angle of photograph, lighting and determination of the precise time when the photograph is to be taken.'[29]

[5.11] Neuberger J considered that these views represented the law of England, holding that:

'In the case of photographs of a three-dimensional object, with which I am concerned in the present case, it can be said that the positioning of the object (unless it is a sphere), the angle at which it is taken, the lighting and the focus, and matters such as that, could all be matters of aesthetic or even commercial judgment, albeit in most cases at a very basic level.

Further, the instant photographs appear to have been taken with a view to exhibiting particular qualities, including the colour (in the case of some items), their features (eg the

---

[27] *Antiquesportfolio.com v Rodney Fitch* (2000) The Times, 21 July.

[28] *Copinger and Skone James on Copyright* (14th, edn, Sweet & Maxwell, 1999), para 3.104.

[29] *Nimmo on Copyright*, para 2.130. Neuberger J noted that Nimmo went on to set out two exceptions to this proposition: 'The first such situation will arise where a photograph or other printed matter is made that amounts to nothing more than a slavish copying. If no originality can be claimed in making an additional print from a photographic negative, there should be no finding of a greater originality where the same effect is achieved by photographing a print rather than printing a negative. In neither case is a distinguishable variation reproduced ... The other situation in which copyright may be denied to a photograph of lack of originality arises where the photographer in choosing a subject matter, camera angle, lighting, et cetera, copies and attempts to duplicate all of such elements as contained in a prior photograph. Here the second photographer has been photographing a live subject rather than the first photograph; but, in so far as the original elements contained in the first photograph are concerned, there is no meaningful distinction.'

glaze in pottery) and, in the case of almost all the items, the details. It may well be that, in those circumstances, some degree of skill was involved in the lighting, angling and judging the positioning.

It may also be relevant that the photographer chose the particular item in order to find a typical example of a certain type of artefact, or a particularly fine example of a certain type of artefact, and that may be a relevant factor.'

[5.12] On the above basis Neuberger J concluded that copyright did subsist in the photographs in question. He then went on to consider whether the reproduction of those photographs in the banner of the site or in navigation boxes could amount to infringement. It seemed to Neuberger J that:

'a very small representation of the photograph on a computer screen does not infringe, on the basis that it does not benefit from any of the originality involved in making the photograph ... Nonetheless, it seems to me that where the whole of the photograph is reproduced, as in the present case, it would be an infringement'.

However, Neuberger J went on to find that the creation of logos by tracing the outline of objects in photographs could not amount to an infringement of copyright in the photograph as if one considered:

'the originality said to be involved in the photographs, namely, focusing, lighting, choice of object and camera angle, it seems to me that really nothing remains in the logos. Obviously, focusing and lighting do not carry through to the logos, although, in a sense, the selection of the particular object does translate in the logos; the logos are gross, as opposed to refined, and the nature of the particular object dictates the shape. Further, the precise angle of the object, although possibly a subtle matter in a photograph, cannot really be said to be reflected to any significant extent in the logos'.

[5.13] A digital image may also be a collage, the 'cut and paste' function to be found in a wide variety of software, such as Adobe Photoshop, enables the easy creation of digital collages. The CRRA 2000–2004 defines artistic work as including a collage[30] but does not offer any further definition of the term. A collage generally means a form of art in which various materials such as pieces of paper or photographs are arranged and glued to a backing.[31] Another definition includes 'a collection of unrelated things'.[32] The definition of collage was examined by Lloyd J in *Creation Records v News Group Newspapers*[33]; it was argued that a scene for a photograph was a collage for the purposes of the Act. His view was that a collage should have more than a temporary existence, stating that the scene was:

'put together solely to be the subject matter of a number of photographs and disassembled as soon as those were taken. This composition was intrinsically ephemeral, or indeed less than ephemeral, the original sense of that word of only living for one day. This existed for a few hours on the ground. Its continued existence was to be in the form of a photographic image.'

---

[30] CRRA 2000–2004, s 2(1).
[31] *The Concise Oxford English Dictionary* (8th edn, OUP, 1990).
[32] *The Concise Oxford English Dictionary* (8th edn, OUP, 1990).
[33] *Creation Records v News Group Newspapers* [1997] EMLR 444.

Collages can be created by a computer as well by arranging physical objects. For example in *Charleston v News Group Newspapers Ltd*[34] a computer game was developed where images of the plaintiffs faces were superimposed onto the bodies of models. Arguably images created in this way could be viewed as collages, particularly as the Act does not specifically protect compilations; they could also be protected as computer-generated works. Other legal issues such as libel which formed the basis of this case would still exist.

Hypertext links to text

[5.14] In the Scottish case of *Shetland Times Ltd v Wills*[35] the plaintiff or 'pursuer' owned and published a newspaper. The defendant was the managing director of a company that provided a news reporting service. The plaintiff established an Internet website which made articles from the newspaper available electronically by clicking on the headline of the desired article from the newspaper. The defendants also ran a website which contained verbatim reproductions of some of the plaintiff's headlines. These headlines linked directly to articles on the plaintiff's site, by-passing the pursuer's front page and thus missing any advertising material placed on it. The plaintiff successfully sought an injunction. The plaintiff successfully made the rather unusual argument that the links embodied in the headlines were cable programmes and that the inclusion of those items in that service constituted an infringement of copyright. The argument that linking to a page is a breach of copyright would seem questionable. It is true that one of the exclusive rights of a copyright owner is to control the distribution of their work or the 'making available' right. And that is precisely what a copyright owner is doing when he uploads his work to a page on the World Wide Web. The entire purpose of such a page is to make the material available worldwide. If the owner of the work is unhappy about how the world makes use of his page, he has a wide variety of options: he can take the page down entirely, he can redesign it, or he can hide the page behind a firewall and charge for access. Once a copyright owner makes material openly available on the World Wide Web it would seem to follow that he is in effect granting others a licence to link to his material at will. However, a different situation will arise where material is placed on the World Wide Web in breach of the owner's copyright and this situation is discussed below.

Hypertext links to pictures

[5.15] *Perfect 10 v Google*[36] is a decision of the US Federal Court of Appeals for the Ninth Circuit. It concerned Google Image Search, which provides responses to search queries in the form of images. The court described the functioning of this system in the following way:

> 'In response to a search query, Google Image Search identifies text in its database responsive to the query and then communicates to users the images associated with the relevant text. Google's software cannot recognize and index the images themselves. Google Image Search provides search results as a webpage of small images called

---

[34] *Charleston v News Group Newspapers* Ltd [1995] 2 All ER 313.
[35] *Shetland Times Ltd v Wills* [1997] FSR 604.
[36] *Perfect 10 v Google* US Ct of Apps (9th Cir) 16 May 2007.

'thumbnails,' which are stored in Google's servers. The thumbnail images are reduced, lower resolution versions of full-sized images stored on third-party computers.

If the user should click on a thumbnail, then:

'the user's browser connects to the website publisher's computer, downloads the full-size image, and makes the image appear at the bottom of the window on the user's screen. Google does not store the images that fill this lower part of the window and does not communicate the images to the user; Google simply provides HTML instructions directing a user's browser to access a third-party website'.

The plaintiff operated a subscription service which provided access to pornographic images for a fee. Google's search engine did not access these images directly. However, third parties were in the habit of copying the plaintiff's images and uploading them to websites in breach of the plaintiff's copyright. Once uploaded to a third party web-site, Google's search engine might 'automatically index the webpages containing these images and provide thumbnail versions of images in response to user inquiries'. The plaintiff objected and sued Google for breach of copyright. The plaintiff alleged that Google was breaching its copyright by displaying its work. Under US law, as under Irish law, the copyright owner has the exclusive right to display his or her copyright work.

[5.16] However, the US court held that by providing thumbnail images Google was not displaying the plaintiff's work. The court held that:

'Google does not, however, display a copy of full-size infringing photographic images for purposes of the Copyright Act when Google frames in-line linked images that appear on a user's computer screen. Because Google's computers do not store the photographic images, Google does not have a copy of the images ... and thus cannot communicate a copy.

... Instead of communicating a copy of the image, Google provides HTML instructions that direct a user's browser to a website publisher's computer that stores the full-size photographic image. Providing these HTML instructions is not equivalent to showing a copy. First, the HTML instructions are lines of text, not a photographic image. Second, HTML instructions do not themselves cause infringing images to appear on the user's computer screen. The HTML merely gives the address of the image to the user's browser. The browser then interacts with the computer that stores the infringing image. It is this interaction that causes an infringing image to appear on the user's computer screen. Google may facilitate the user's access to infringing images. However, such assistance raises only contributory liability issues ... .and does not constitute direct infringement of the copyright owner's display rights'.[37]

The applicant had also argued that the respondent had breached its distribution right. The US court rejected this claim. The Court found that Google's system worked as follows:

'Google's search engine communicates HTML instructions that tell a user's browser where to find full-size images on a website publisher's computer, but Google does not itself distribute copies of the infringing photographs. It is the website publisher's computer that distributes copies of the images by transmitting the photographic image electronically to

---

[37] *Perfect 10 v Google* US Ct of Apps (9th Cir) 16 May 2007 at 5771–5772.

the user's computer ... the user can then obtain copies by downloading the photo or printing it'.[38]

The Court held that:

'Google does not own a collection of Perfect 10's full-size images and does not communicate these images to the computers of people using Google's search engine. Though Google indexes these images, it does not have a collection of stored full-size images it makes available to the public. Google therefore cannot be deemed to distribute copies of these images'.[39]

[5.17] If an equivalent case were to be brought before the Irish courts, it is quite possible that Google would be similarly successful in defending the claim in respect of the display of full-sized images. In particular, the e-Commerce Directive[40] provides that:

'Where an information society service[41] is provided that consists of the transmission in a communication network of information provided by a recipient of the service, or the provision of access to a communication network, Member States shall ensure that the service provider is not liable for the information transmitted, on condition that the provider:

(a)   does not initiate the transmission;

(b)   does not select the receiver of the transmission; and

(c)   does not select or modify the information contained in the transmission'.[42]

Arguably, Google would be able to avail of this provision as all it would be providing was a link to the page in question; it would be for the individual user in question to decide whether or not he would actually click on the particular link. Google would neither initiate the downloading of the image, select the recipient nor select or modify the information. Google's function might instead be categorised as providing access to the communication network in question.

[5.18] The 'mere conduit' defence provided by the e-Commerce Directive is similar to that provided by the US Digital Millennium Copyright Act or DMCA.[43] The application of the US provision to the display of pictures was examined by the same US court in *Perfect 10 v CC Bill*.[44] The US DMCA provides a defence to service providers defined

---

[38]   *Perfect 10 v Google* US Ct of Apps (9th Cir) 16 May 2007 at 5774.

[39]   *Perfect 10 v Google* US Ct of Apps (9th Cir) 16 May 2007 at 5775.

[40]   Directive 2000/31/EC of the European Parliament and of the Council of 8 June 2000 on certain legal aspects of information society services, in particular electronic commerce, in the Internal Market ('Directive on electronic commerce'), OJ L 178, 17/07/2000 P. 1–16, implemented in Ireland as the European Communities (Directive 2000/31/EC) Regulations 2003 (SI 68/2003).

[41]   Directive 2000/31/EC, recital 18 provides that: 'information society services are not solely restricted to services giving rise to online contracting but also, in so far as they represent an economic activity, extend to services which are not remunerated by those who receive them, such as those offering online information or commercial communications, or those providing tools allowing for search, access and retrieval of data'.

[42]   Directive 2000/31/EC, art 12(1).

[43]   US Digital Millennium Copyright Act 17 USC § 512.

[44]   *Perfect 10 v CCBill* No 04-57143.

as: 'an entity offering the transmission, routing, or providing of connections for digital online communications, between or among points specified by a user, of material of the user's choosing, without modification to the content of the material as sent or received'. As with the e-Commerce Directive there is a requirement that the user specify the transmission in question and that the service provider cannot modify the transmission. In *Perfect 10 v CC Bill* the defendant provided billing services to sites that the plaintiff alleged contained infringing copies of its works. The plaintiff argued that the defendant could not avail of the 'mere conduit' defence as it was not actually transmitting infringing images. This argument was rejected by the US Court of Appeals for the Ninth Circuit, which held that the US provision:

> 'provides a broad grant of immunity to service providers whose connection with the material is transient. When an individual clicks on an Internet link, his computer sends a request for the information. The company receiving that request sends that request on to another computer, which sends it on to another. After a series of such transmissions, the request arrives at the computer that stores the information. The requested information is then returned in milliseconds, not necessarily along the same path. In passing the information along, each intervening computer makes a short-lived copy of the data. A short time later, the information is displayed on the user's computer.
>
> … Those intervening computers provide transient connections among users. The Internet as we know it simply cannot exist if those intervening computers must block indirectly infringing content'.[45]

[5.19] The plaintiff in *Perfect 10 v Google* did succeed in showing that 'it would prevail in its prima facie case that Google's thumbnail images infringe Perfect 10's display rights'.[46]

But the US court held that Google would probably be able to successfully avail of the fair use defences provided by US law. However, Irish laws on fair use do not equate to those in the USA and thus it is likely that the provision of thumbnail images would amount to an infringement of copyright in Ireland. If a similar case were to come before the Irish courts, then Google would not be able to rely upon the e-Commerce Directive. This is because Google would not be acting as a mere conduit to the full-sized image. There was no question that Google was displaying a thumb-nail sized version of the plaintiff's image on its search page. Google could not argue that it was acting as a 'mere conduit' in doing so as Google was actually providing the thumb-nail, not providing access to it.

Piracy and counterfeit goods

Internet supply of physical goods: the CD-WOW case

[5.20] Parallel imports, whether of jeans, CDs, DVDs or medicines are a contentious issue. Since the EC's consumers are relatively richer than those in Asia or Africa, identical goods may cost far more here than there. This difference creates potentially lucrative arbitrage opportunities, but EC trademark and copyright laws give the owners of such rights the power to control the importation of such products into the EU.[47] In *KK*

---

[45] *Perfect 10 v CCBill* No 04-57143, 6558.
[46] *Perfect 10 v CCBill* No. 04-57143, 6558 at 5775.

Sony Computer Entertainment v Pacific Game Technology (Holding) Ltd[48] the defendant was a company registered in Hong Kong and carrying on business there. The defendant set up a website 'to offer for sale a variety of commercial video-games, consoles and accessories for playing music, video-games and suchlike'. Fysh QC[49] had to decide whether 'the target of such solicitation is customers in the EEA[50] and in the UK in particular'.[51] Fysh QC held that it was. Fysh QC adopted the pragmatic approach of plaintiff's counsel, holding that:

> 'One had to visit the website with an intelligent and discriminating attitude … and then decide whether on a fair reading, the information it contained would convey to a reasonable person (or an average consumer), an offer for sale within the UK (or the EEA). In the context of websites, the contrast between commercial information of a general kind and information which has been specifically targeted was well brought out in a summary judgment case, *Euromarket Designs Inc v Peters and Crate & Barrel Ltd*[52] … .The learned judge made it clear that the owner of a website who used a sign (ie a trade mark) on that website should not be regarded as having thereby used it in every country of the world. In that case he likened the Defendants' website as an invitation to visit its shop in Dublin 'Via the web you can look into the Defendant's shop in Dublin.'

[5.21] Fysh QC followed this approach when examining the defendant's website, and found the following important features:

(i)   the website was in English and English was its default language, user guides being additionally available in French and Spanish;

(ii)   prices were quoted in pounds sterling and sterling was the default currency when the site was accessed from England;

(iii) manuals were available in English and other European languages;

(iv)   a number of testimonials were available on the website from UK purchasers;

(v)   the defendant's ran a free shipping promotion until the very day before the plaintiff's Console was launched in Europe;

(vi)   A spurious EC Certificate of Conformity was included with the product shipped to Europe.[53]

[5.22] Fysh QC regarded as irrelevant the defendant's assertions that they were a Hong Kong company with no trading presence in the UK and that the name of their site was

---

[47]   See *Zino Davidoff v A&G Imports Ltd/ Levi Strauss v Tesco Stores Ltd and Costco (Wholesale) Ltd* [2002] Ch 109, [2002] Ch 109, [2001] ECR I-8691, [2002] RPC 403.

[48]   *KK Sony Computer Entertainment v Pacific Game Technology (Holding) Ltd* [2006] EWHC 2509 (Ch).

[49]   Sitting as a Deputy Judge of the English High Court.

[50]   European Economic Area.

[51]   *KK Sony Computer Entertainment v Pacific Game Technology (Holding) Ltd* [2006] EWHC 2509, para 3.

[52]   *Euromarket Designs Inc v Peters and Crate & Barrel Ltd* [2001] FSR 288, [2000] IP & T 1290.

[53]   *KK Sony Computer Entertainment v Pacific Game Technology (Holding) Ltd* [2006] EWHC 2509, para 24.

meaningless in English but meant strong or energetic in Chinese. This led Fysh QC to the conclusion that:

> 'The acts of which complaint is made have in my view been perpetrated not in Hong Kong but here in the EEA, and without Sony's consent. Moreover, it would make no sense if intellectual property rights in the EEA could be avoided merely by setting up a website outside the EEA crafted to sell within it. Were the acts of which complaint is made to have been committed physically within the EEA they would unarguably have been infringing acts. I cannot see how the electronic intermediary of a website which focussed at least in part on the EEA would make them any less so. In my judgment, Sony are entitled to relief in this action.'[54]

[5.23] This judgment was followed by Evans-Lombe J in the *CD-WOW*[55] case. The defendant ran a website in Hong Kong which supplied product, principally CDs and DVDs, to consumers in Europe. The defendant agreed that it would only supply to European consumers product which had previously been made available in Europe. The operation of the CD-WOW business was described as follows:

> 'A customer is able to order a CD or DVD from CD-WOW by accessing its web site and clicking on the appropriate icon. Thereafter the customer, having chosen the Product which he or she wishes to acquire, indicates that choice and types in credit card details and the required delivery address. The customer will then receive, by email, a confirmation of the order. Customer's orders are serviced from CD-WOW's warehouse in Hong Kong where stocks of Products, available for sale and advertised on CD-WOW's web site, are maintained'.[56]

Unfortunately the plaintiff found that the defendant was continuing to dispatch non-compliant product to Europe and the plaintiff responded by initiating an action for contempt in respect of some 33 test purchases which had resulted in the receipt by the plaintiffs in the UK of non-compliant product sent by the defendant in Hong Kong. Evans-Lombe J found that there had been infringement of copyright in the UK and that damages were payable in respect of that infringement. The defendant submitted that damages should only be payable in respect of the 33 test purchases, but Evans-Lombe J rejected that submission, holding that:

> 'I have found that the 33 test purchases are evidence of substantial breach of the Claimants' rights continuing after the issue of the Contempt Application. In my judgment the Claimants, and those they represent, are entitled to damages in respect of any breaches of their copyright disclosed by an enquiry which result from the importation into the United Kingdom by CD-WOW of any Product to which that copyright extends'.[57]

---

[54] *KK Sony Computer Entertainment v Pacific Game Technology (Holding) Ltd* [2006] EWHC 2509, para 25. See also the decision of Lawrence Collins J in *Kabushiki Kaisha Sony Computer Entertainment (t/a Sony Computer Entertainment Inc) v Nuplayer Ltd* [2005] EWHC 1522 (Ch). The defendants offered to permanently remove the plaintiff's trademarks from the goods in question and to inform consumers that they were doing so, something that Lawrence Collins J adjudged to be itself 'an offending use of the marks' [2005] EWHC 1522 (Ch), para 97.

[55] *Independiente Ltd and others v Music Trading online* [2007] EWHC 533 (Ch).

[56] [2007] EWHC 533 (Ch), para 5.

[57] [2007] EWHC 533 (Ch), para 54

Internet supply of electronic goods: websites

[5.24] Websites can be used to make infringing copies available electronically. In the English case of *Union des Association Europeenes de Football and others v Briscomb and others*[58] the plaintiffs (UEFA) owned the copyright in certain football matches. The defendants were alleged to have infringed this copyright 'by way of the deployment on the internet of those broadcasts'.[59] Lindsay J held that to do so was a breach of UK copyright legislation as it amounted to the communication of the broadcasts in question. The UK's Copyright Designs and Patents Act 1988[60] provides that the 'broadcasting of the work or its inclusion in a cable programme service' is an act restricted by copyright.[61] It is very likely that an Irish court would find on similar facts that a breach of the CRRA 2000–2004 had occurred. There are a number of provisions that might apply. The making available of a work is one of the acts restricted by copyright.[62] The Act goes on to define the making available of a work as:

> 'making available to the public of copies of the work[63], by wire or wireless means, in such a way that members of the public may access the work from a place and at a time chosen by them (including the making available of copies of works through the Internet).'[64]

It should be noted that the CRRA 2000–2004 does exempt service providers from some liabilities. The Act provides that 'the provision of facilities for enabling the making available to the public of copies of a work shall not of itself constitute an act of making available to the public of copies of the work.'[65]

[5.25] However, this exemption is not total. The Act goes on to provide that:

> 'where a person who provides facilities referred to in that subsection is notified[66] by the owner of the copyright in the work concerned that those facilities are being used to infringe the copyright in that work and that person fails to remove that infringing material as soon as practicable thereafter that person shall also be liable for the infringement'.[67]

---

58 *Union des Association Europeenes de Football and others v Briscomb and others* [2006] EWHC 1268 (Ch).

59 [2006] EWHC 1268 (Ch), para 5.

60 UK's Copyright Designs and Patents Act 1988, s 20.

61 See similarly the US case of *Live Nation Motor Sports v Robert Davis* United States District Court Northern District of Texas Dallas Division, Civil Action No 3:06-CV-276-L, 11 December 2006, in which the plaintiff was the promoter of motorcycle races known as 'Supercross'. Coverage of these events was broadcast via television, radio and the Internet. The defendant copied these broadcasts and made them available at his own website. The plaintiff successfully applied for an injunction enjoining the defendant from continuing to do so. It is likely that a similar action would succeed in Ireland.

62 CRRA 2000–2004, ss 17(b) and 40(8).

63 Or indeed the original, CRRA 2000, s 40(2).

64 CRRA 2000–2004, s 40(1)(a).

65 CRRA 2000–2004, s 40(3).

66 The Minister for Enterprise, Trade and Employment may specify the form and content of such a notification, CRRA 2000–2004, s 40(4).

67 CRRA 2000–2004, s 40(4).

The making available right is a primary right of copyright. It is possible that secondary infringement could occur on a website. For example a website might provide the means for making infringing copies. This will be secondary infringement, and the CRRA 2000–2004 specifically provides that:

> 'A person infringes the copyright in a work where he or she, without the licence of the copyright owner, transmits the work by means of a telecommunications system (otherwise than by broadcasting or inclusion in a cable programme service) knowing or having reason to believe that infringing copies of the work may be made by means of the reception of the transmission in the State or elsewhere'.[68]

Finally, making a work available on a website in this way may amount to a criminal offence. The CRRA 2000–2004 provides that an offence will be committed by a person who:

> 'without the consent of the copyright owner … in the course of a business, trade or profession, has in his or her possession, custody or control, or makes available to the public, or … otherwise than in the course of a business, trade or profession, makes available to the public to such an extent as to prejudice the interests of the owner of the copyright, a copy of a work which is, and which he or she knows or has reason to believe is, an infringing copy of the work, shall be guilty of an offence'.[69]

Internet supply of electronic goods: P2P

[5.26] Websites allow the distribution of electronic goods and a website such as i-tunes allows anyone with the time, money and equipment to download music, films and other media. Websites allow the distribution of electronic material from a centralised point. Websites have many obvious advantages for commercial business, and some such as amazon.com are very successful commercially. The creation of a website posits centralised control over the distribution of content and centralised control is not without its disadvantages. Someone has to be responsible for setting up the website, connecting it to the Internet, ensuring that connection has the capacity to deal with all the potential users, ensuring that users can download the content they want and being liable if unwanted or illegal content appears on their site. Peer-to-peer (P2P) networks offer a different model of distribution; essentially the distribution network becomes distributed amongst all users. There is no hub at the centre of the network, there are just links between each of the nodes that make up the network. A P2P system is not necessarily superior or inferior to a centralised system, it is just different. The fact that a P2P network is being used should not be taken as a prima facie indication that a network is being used for illegal or infringing purposes. P2P networks offer users a host of advantages, such as cost-effectiveness, speed, scalability and adaptability[70] which legal

---

[68] CRRA 2000–2004, s 46(2).

[69] CRRA 2000–2004, s 140(1).

[70] See, Rodriguez, Tan and Gkantsidis, 'On the feasibility of Commercial, Legal P2P Content Distribution', paper delivered to the 10th International Web Caching and Content Distribution workshop on the future of P2P in content distribution, http://research.microsoft.com/~pablo/papers/CCR.pdf.

and legitimate companies, organisations and groups take advantage of.[71] The advantages of P2P systems were set out by the US Supreme Court in *MGM Studios v Grokster*:[72]

'The advantage of peer-to-peer networks over information networks of other types shows up in their substantial and growing popularity. Because they need no central computer server to mediate the exchange of information or files among users, the high bandwidth communications capacity for a server may be dispensed with, and the need for costly server storage space is eliminated. Since copies of a file (particularly a popular one) are available on many users' computers, file requests and retrievals may be faster than on other types of networks, and since file exchanges do not travel through a server, communications can take place between any computers that remain connected to the network without risk that a glitch in the server will disable the network in its entirety. Given these benefits in security, cost, and efficiency, peer-to-peer networks are employed to store and distribute electronic files by universities, government agencies, corporations, and libraries, among others'.[73]

P2P networks: infringement by operators

[5.27] It is undeniable that P2P offers a potent tool for the distribution of illegal or infringing material. Since P2P systems dispense with a decentralised hub, there is nobody who can be centrally liable for the distribution of illegal and infringing content.

Australia: Universal Music Australia Pty Ltd v Sharman License Holdings[74]

[5.28] The Australian High Court decision in *Universal Music Australia Pty Ltd v Sharman License Holdings* concerned the KaZaA system, which was described by Wilcox J as allowing:

'one user to share with other users any material the first user wishes to share, whether or not that material is subject to copyright, simply by placing that material in a file called 'My Shared Folder'. A user who is interested in obtaining a copy of a particular work, such as a musical item, can instantaneously search the 'My Shared Folder' files of other users, worldwide. If the file is located, the title will be displayed against a blue icon on the first user's computer'.

Wilcox J held that the applicants had overstated their case and that the operators of the KaZaA system could not be said to have communicated the works in question. But he did hold that defendants had infringed the Australian Copyright Act by authorising an infringement.[75] Wilcox J found the following evidence of this authorisation:

---

[71] For example EMI makes its music available over QTRAX a 'legitimate' P2P network, see, EMI, Press Release, 5 June 2006, http://www.emigroup.com/Press/2006/press25.htm.

[72] *MGM Studios, Inc v Grokster Ltd* 545 US, 125 SCt 2764 (2005).

[73] 125 SCt 2764 (2005), pp 1–2.

[74] *Universal Music Australia Pty Ltd v Sharman License Holdings Ltd* [2005] FCA 1242. See Ginsburg and Ricketson, 'Inducers and Authorisers: A Comparison of the US Supreme Court's Grokster Decision and the Australian Federal Court's KaZaA Ruling' Media and Arts Law Review, Vol 11, No. 1, 2006.

[75] Section 101 of the Australian Copyright Act provides that copyright is infringed by a person who, not being the owner of the copyright and without the licence of the copyright owner, authorises another person to do in Australia an infringing act.

(i) Although the KaZaA website contained warnings against infringements of copyright, it was obvious that those warnings were not discouraging infringements and the defendants were well aware that their system was being used for this purpose.

(ii) The defendants could have taken technical measures, such as filtering searches, to curtail infringement but had failed to do so. Wilcox J noted that it was in the defendants' interests to maximise the number of files shared on their site, as they relied upon advertising for their revenue.

(iii) The defendants extorted the sharing of files in defiance of the record industry and other copyright owners, whilst not explicitly seeking the sharing of copyrighted material.

[5.29] The judgment was appealed but the action was then settled.[76] It is probable that an Irish Court would come to a similar conclusion but might have to rely upon similar reasoning. Somewhat surprisingly the provisions of the CRRA 2000–2004 on secondary infringement might not apply. The CRRA 2000 provides that copyright will be infringed by a person who 'sells, rents or lends, or offers or exposes for sale, rental or loan … an infringing copy'.[77]

However, the operator of the KaZaA type system would not be involved in placing an individual copy of a song in the file of material that a user was willing to share online. Furthermore that material was being offered or exposed for permanent copying. This would not necessarily fall into any of the categories of 'sale, rental or loan. Similarly, the CRRA 2000–2004 provides that secondary infringement may occur where a person 'in the course of a business, trade or profession, has in his or her possession, custody or control, or makes available to the public … an infringing copy'.[78]

[5.30] Again the operators of the system would have neither possession, custody nor control of the infringing copy in question. Nor would they be making it available to the public. The person who would be doing this would be the person who placed an infringing copy in their 'shared' folder. The CRRA 2000–2004 does contain a provision that was designed to apply to the transmissions of infringing copies:

> 'A person infringes the copyright in a work where he or she, without the licence of the copyright owner, transmits the work by means of a telecommunications system (otherwise than by broadcasting or inclusion in a cable programme service) knowing or having reason to believe that infringing copies of the work may be made by means of the reception of the transmission in the State or elsewhere.

The difficulty with applying this provision to a KaZaA type system is that Wilcox J specifically found that the operators of the system could not be held to be communicating the works in question. In addition, it is quite possible that an Irish court would be forced to follow a line of reasoning similar to that of Wilcox J if faced with a similar case. The CRRA 2000–2004 provides that the exclusive rights of the copyright owner include the rights to copy a work, make that work available to the public and to

---

[76] Sainsbury, 'Internet Piracy lawsuit settled' (2006) *The Australian*, 28 July.

[77] CRRA 2000–2004, s 45(a).

[78] CRRA 2000–2004, s 45(d).

authorise these acts. In particular the making available right includes the right to undertake or authorise the following acts:

'making available to the public of copies of the work, by wire or wireless means, in such a way that members of the public may access the work from a place and at a time chosen by them (including the making available of copies of works through the Internet)'.[79]

The operators of a KaZaA-type system could not be said to be making individual copies available; they would simply be providing the means by which such works were made available. Instead the argument would have to be made that the operators were authorising this infringement. As with the other cases discussed below, such a finding would be very much determined by its facts. Such facts might relate to the design of an individual system, but also to the business model developed to take advantage of it.

USA: A & M v Napster and MGM Studios v Grokster

[5.31] In *A & M Records v Napster*[80] the defendant's system used some elements of a P2P system; primarily material located on each member's hard drive could be shared with others. Napster made software available to do this, but it also maintained servers and software. The system was reviewed by the US Court of Appeals for the Ninth Circuit and found to infringe.[81] The difficulty for Napster was that it relied upon a centralised index. The Court of Appeal held that the Napster system was not infringing of itself: 'The mere existence of the Napster system, absent actual notice and Napster's demonstrated failure to remove the offending material is insufficient to impose contributory liability'. But that did not mean that Napster could completely escape liability. In particular it would be 'vicariously liable when it fails to affirmatively use its ability to patrol its system and preclude access to potentially infringing files listed in its search index'.[82]

[5.32] Whilst the judgment of the Ninth Circuit would ultimately prove fatal to this particular Napster system,[83] it created two potential loopholes in the law. The first was that the operators might avoid knowledge of infringing activity on their system by failing to record any activity at all. This approach was disposed of by the US Court of Appeals for the Seventh Circuit in *Re Aimster Copyright Litigation*[84] which noted that the operators had: 'failed to produce any evidence that its service [had] ever been used for a noninfringing use, let alone evidence concerning the frequency of such uses'.[85] The second potential loophole was the use of decentralised software to ensure that there was no centralised file-sharing network to supply the knowledge necessary for contributory

---

[79] CRRA 2000–2004, s 40(1)(a).

[80] *A & M Records v Napster* US Ct of Apps (9rh Cir), 239 F.3d 1004.

[81] Discussion primarily focused on whether Napster could avail of the US fair use defence, which is not available in Ireland.

[82] At 48.

[83] Napster.com has since been relaunced as a legitimate system, see http://www.napster.com

[84] *Re Aimster Copyright Litigation* 334 F 3d 643.

[85] 334 F 3d 643 at 653.

infringement or the control necessary for vicarious infringement.[86] This latter approach was taken by the defendants in *MGM Studios v Grokster*.[87]

[5.33] The US Supreme Court decision of *MGM Studios v Grokster* concerned two networks: FastTrack operated by Grokster and Gnutella operated by Streamcast. These networks, particularly the Gnutella network, were designed to dispense with centralised nodes of control. The process of sharing information without a centralised control was described as follows by the US Supreme Court:

> 'peer computers using the protocol communicate directly with each other. When a user enters a search request into the Morpheus software, it sends the request to computers connected with it, which in turn pass the request along to other connected peers. The search results are communicated to the requesting computer, and the user can download desired files directly from peers' computers. As this description indicates, Grokster and StreamCast use no servers to intercept the content of the search requests or to mediate the file transfers conducted by users of the software, there being no central point through which the substance of the communications passes in either direction'.[88]

Of course not every file downloaded from these networks contained material that infringed another's copyright. The plaintiffs claimed that about 90% of the material available infringed copyright, a fact disputed by the defendants. The US Supreme Court considered that the plaintiff's evidence gave it reason to think that:

> 'the vast majority of users' downloads are acts of infringement, and because well over 100 million copies of the software in question are known to have been downloaded, and billions of files are shared across the FastTrack and Gnutella networks each month, the probable scope of copyright infringement is staggering'.[89]

[5.34] The defendants conceded that most of the material downloaded from their networks did infringe copyright. The Court accepted that whilst the defendants could not control the material on their network, they were certainly aware of it. There was also evidence before the court that both Streamcast and, to a lesser effect, Grokster had set out to capture the market of users of the 'notorious file sharing service',[90] Napster. The court held that:

> 'the business models employed by Grokster and StreamCast confirm that their principal object was use of their software to download copyrighted works ... both companies generate income by selling advertising space, and they stream the advertising to ... users .... As the number of users of each program increases, advertising opportunities become worth more ... .While there is doubtless some demand for free Shakespeare, the evidence shows that substantive volume is a function of free access to copyrighted work. Users seeking Top 40 songs ... are certain to be far more numerous than those seeking a free Decameron, and Grokster and StreamCast translated that demand into dollars.[91]

---

86 See Choi, 'The Grokster Dead-End' Harvard Journal of Law and Technology, Vol 19, 2006 p 393, 396–397.

87 *MGM Studios v Grokster* 125 SCt 2764 (2005).

88 125 SCt 2764 (2005), pp 3–4.

89 125 SCt 2764 (2005), p 5.

90 125 SCt 2764 (2005), p 6.

91 125 SCt 2764 (2005), p 8.

Although Grokster had sent emails to users requesting that they desist from sharing copyrighted material, neither defendant had ever actually done anything to prevent the sharing of copyrighted material on their system. Thus the US Supreme Court found that there was 'evidence of infringement on a gigantic scale'.[92] This created a problem for the defendants. The defendants had argued that they should be treated the same as the appellant in *Sony Corp of America v Universal City Studios, Inc.*[93] This case concerned the sale of Video Cassette Recorders or VCRs. Sony had been sued by copyright owners who claimed that Sony 'was contributorily liable for infringement that occurred when VCR owners taped copyrighted programs because it supplied the means used to infringe, and it had constructive knowledge that infringement would occur'. However, Sony was able to show at trial that 'the principal use of the VCR was for 'time-shifting' or taping a program for later viewing at a more convenient time'.[94] In *Sony Corp of America v Universal City Studios, Inc* the court held that this was not an infringing use. The US Supreme Court went on to hold that 'because the VCR was capable of commercially significant noninfringing uses … the manufacturer could not be faulted solely on the basis of its distribution.'[95]

[5.35] In *MGM Studios v Grokster* the US Supreme Court adopted the inducement rule, which provides that:

> 'one who distributes a device with the object of promoting its use to infringe copyright, as shown by clear expression or other affirmative steps taken to foster infringement, is liable for the resulting acts of infringement by third parties.'[96]

This adoption of this rule by the US Supreme Court does not mean that every distribution system which might be used for an illegitimate purpose will be illegal under US law. The court went on to limit the application of this doctrine as the court was 'mindful of the need to keep from trenching on regular commerce or discouraging the development of technologies with lawful and unlawful potential'. The court held that:

> 'mere knowledge of infringing potential or of actual infringing uses would not be enough here to subject a distributor to liability. Nor would ordinary acts incident to product distribution, such as offering customers technical support or product updates, support liability in themselves. The inducement rule, instead, premises liability on purposeful, culpable expression and conduct, and thus does nothing to compromise legitimate commerce or discourage innovation having a lawful promise.'[97]

[5.36] The US Supreme Court held that the inducement rule contained three elements:

(i)   'intent to bring about infringement …

(ii)   … distribution of a device suitable for infringing use …

(iii)   … actual infringement by recipients of the device'.[98]

---

[92]   125 SCt 2764 (2005), p 23.

[93]   *Sony Corp of America v Universal City Studios, Inc* 464 US 417 (1984).

[94]   125 SCt 2764 (2005), p 13.

[95]   *Sony Corp of America v Universal City Studios, Inc* 464 US 417 (1984), cited at 125 SCt 2764 (2005), p 14.

[96]   *MGM Studios v Grokster* 125 SCt 2764 (2005), p19.

[97]   125 SCt 2764 (2005), pp 19–20.

[98]   125 SCt 2764 (2005), p 23.

The court found that the defendants had been communicating an inducing message to their users in a number of different ways. Firstly, the defendants, and Streamcast in particular, had advertised their systems to Napster users as an alternative to that system. The court held that the defendants':

> 'efforts to supply services to former Napster users, deprived of a mechanism to copy and distribute what were overwhelmingly infringing files, indicate a principal, if not exclusive, intent on the part of each to bring about infringement'.[99]

[5.37] Secondly, neither defendant 'attempted to develop filtering tools or other mechanisms to diminish the infringing activity using their software'. The US Court of Appeals for the Ninth Circuit had considered that 'the defendant's failure to develop such tools as irrelevant because they lacked an independent duty to monitor their user's activity. However, the US Supreme Court thought that this evidence underscored the defendants' 'intentional facilitation of their users' infringement'.[100] Finally, both defendants had made money by selling advertisements, which required high volume use of the defendants' systems. The Court felt that this evidence alone 'would not justify an inference of unlawful intent, but viewed in the context of the entire record its import is clear'. This led the US Supreme Court to conclude that: 'the unlawful objective is unmistakeable'.[101]

[5.38] The US Supreme Court concluded that *MGM Studios v Grokster* was significantly different from *Sony Corp of America v Universal City Studios, Inc* as:

> '*Sony* dealt with a claim of liability based solely on distributing a product with alternative lawful and unlawful uses, with knowledge that some users would follow the unlawful course. The case struck a balance between the interests of protection and innovation by holding that the product's capability of substantial lawful employment should bar the imputation of fault and consequent secondary liability for the unlawful acts of others'.[102]

In contrast in *MGM Studios v Grokster* the evidence showed:

> 'a purpose to cause and profit from third-party acts of copyright infringement. If liability for inducing infringement is ultimately found, it will not be on the basis of presuming or imputing fault, but from inferring a patently illegal objective from statements and actions showing what that objective was'.[103]

The US Supreme Court therefore found in favour of the MGM and its co-plaintiffs and remanded the case back to the lower court for reconsideration. As noted above the US Supreme Court distinguished its previous decision in *Sony Corp of America v Universal City Studios, Inc.* This decision equates to that of the House of Lords in *CBS Songs Ltd v Amstrad Consumer Electronics PLC*.[104] This was a claim by a copyright owner against the manufacturer of tape machines which contained a high speed dubbing function. The

---

[99] 125 SCt 2764 (2005), p 22.
[100] 125 SCt 2764 (2005), p 22.
[101] 125 SCt 2764 (2005), p 23.
[102] 125 SCt 2764 (2005), pp 23–24.
[103] 125 SCt 2764 (2005), p 24.
[104] *CBS Songs Ltd v Amstrad Consumer Electronics PLC* [1988] 1 AC 1013.

House was unanimous in finding that the claim should be dismissed, Templeman LJ holding that:

> 'Amstrad do not procure infringement by offering for sale a machine which may be used for lawful or unlawful copying and they do not procure infringement by advertising the attractions of their machine to any purchaser who may decide to copy unlawfully. Amstrad are not concerned to procure and cannot procure unlawful copying. The purchaser will not make unlawful copies because he has been induced or incited or persuaded to do so by Amstrad. The purchaser will make unlawful copies for his own use because he chooses to do so. Amstrad's advertisements may persuade the purchaser to buy an Amstrad machine but will not influence the purchaser's later decision to infringe copyright'.[105]

[5.39] The decision of the US Supreme Court in *MGM v Grokster* has been criticised for focusing upon the specific inducements offered by the defendants to infringe copyright. The US Supreme Court focused upon this issue instead of seeking to resolve the question of 'whether P2P technology is sufficiently valuable to society to merit immunity at the expense of artistic copyright'.[106] Such criticism may be unfair; arguably the resolution of such an issue is a matter for the legislature not the judiciary. In any event P2P systems are continuing to evolve into new products to which the judgment of the US Supreme Court in *MGM v Grokster* may not be easily applied. It is clear from the judgments of the diverse courts in *Sony Corp of America v Universal City Studios, Inc; CBS Songs Ltd v Amstrad Consumer Electronics PLC* and *MGM v Grokster* that a prudent approach to advertising the benefits of one's service will be crucial in ensuring the legal compliance of that service.

The future: new systems, new laws

[5.40] One defect with the *Grokster* and *Streamcast* system was that they combined both delivery and search functions. A person who wanted to find a song online would search for it on one part of the system (the search function); once the song was located it would be delivered by another part of the same system (the delivery function). New P2P networks are being developed that combine these search and delivery functions into a single system. For example *yousendit.com* allows users to upload files to a centralised server, other users can then download those files – and they download a lot of files, around 30,000 gigabytes per day:

> 'YouSendIt is merely an online file storage service and chooses not to publish a central directory anywhere on its site, links to shared files must be posted in other locations, usually in public, thirdparty web forums, but sometimes also on private email lists. While this increases the difficulty for downloaders to discover files, it is equally difficult for copyright owners to track and take down any infringing files'.[107]

Yousendit differs from Grokster in that it splits the discovery function from the delivery function, it disregards the search function, but completely centralises the delivery

---

[105] [1988] 1 AC 1013 at 1058
[106] Choi, 'The Grokster Dead-End' Harvard Journal of Law and Technology, Vol. 19, 2006 p 393 at 398.
[107] Choi, 'The Grokster Dead-End' Harvard Journal of Law and Technology, Vol. 19, 2006 p 393 at 402.

function. BitTorrent also differs from Grokster, but it is a completely decentralised system:

> 'BitTorrent is ... merely a delivery mechanism. The original host makes a file available by placing a "torrent" file on the Internet ... This is a tiny file that only contains information about the original file's name, its length, and the URL of a "tracker", which tells your computer where to download the original file ... There is no central directory of files; rather, users depend upon a wide variety of search engines (like the one on BitTorrent.com itself) to locate these trackers. Each search engine is maintained independently, and many even operate like private forums, requiring a login and password, and creating communities around specific genres ... .While trackers can be shut down and removed from the Internet, this process is about as tedious as shutting down individual direct infringers'.[108]

[5.41] These new systems succeed by dispensing with centralised search mechanisms. This makes searching for illegal downloads harder for both users and copyright owners. Under the e-Commerce Directive a service provider that hosts or stores data will not be liable for the contents of that data. The e-Commerce Directive provides:

> 'Where an information society service is provided that consists of the storage of information provided by a recipient of the service, Member States shall ensure that the service provider is not liable for the information stored at the request of a recipient of the service ... '

This exemption form liability is conditional, the service provider cannot have 'actual knowledge of illegal activity or information and ... .is not aware of facts or circumstances from which the illegal activity or information is apparent'. Alternatively, the service provider must 'upon obtaining such knowledge or awareness, act (...) expeditiously to remove or to disable access to the information'.[109] The e-Commerce Directive states, however, that this exemption does 'not affect the possibility for a court or administrative authority, in accordance with Member States' legal systems, of requiring the service provider to terminate or prevent an infringement, nor does it affect the possibility for Member States of establishing procedures governing the removal or disabling of access to information'.[110] A copyright owner who can show that a service provider is hosting his material will still have ready access to a remedy. But the copyright owner will find it much harder to identify the location of infringing material that is hosted by a site such as yousendit.com than it would have on napster.com.

[5.42] Similarly, a service provider who unknowingly transmits or distributes infringing material may benefit from the 'mere conduit' defence provided by the e-Commerce Directive.

As noted above the e-Commerce Directive states that the provider of an information society service will not be liable for a transmission where he:

(a)   does not initiate the transmission;

---

[108] Choi, 'The Grokster Dead-End' Harvard Journal of Law and Technology, Vol. 19, 2006 p 393 at 403.

[109] Directive 2000/31/EC, Art 14(1).

[110] Directive 2000/31/EC, Art 14(1).

(b)   does not select the receiver of the transmission; and

(c)   does not select or modify the information contained in the transmission.[111]

It is of particular significance that the e-Commerce Directive provides that service providers cannot be made subject to a general obligation to monitor, providing that:

> 'Member States shall not impose a general obligation on providers … .to monitor the information which they transmit or store, nor a general obligation actively to seek facts or circumstances indicating illegal activity'.[112]

P2P networks: infringement by users

[5.43] Litigation substantially lowers the attractiveness of creating a Napster or Grokster type system with centralised or reasonably centralised indexes of material. Litigation has made decentralised systems much more attractive. It is harder to find infringing material on a decentralised system, but there is no longer someone in control who can be conveniently held liable for the infringement:

> 'As the pipeline disperses … there will no longer be a convenient Napster or Grokster to sue. Instead, copyright owners will have to go after smaller and smaller fish … . It will be difficult to establish that a party who only provides some minor functionality of the pipeline has sufficient knowledge, control, or even intent to merit liability for the entire operation. More likely, the balance of interests will shift in favor of protecting these neutral technological innovations and courts will be disinclined to assign liability'.[113]

[5.44] This means that copyright owners may have no choice but to pursue individual downloaders as opposed to the operators of the systems that they use. There would not seem to be any question that someone who makes copyright works available on a P2P system without the express permission of the copyright owner will be liable for breach of copyright. In *Polydor v Brown*[114] the evidence before the English High Court was as follows:

> 'the shared directory of a computer connected to the Internet … .was making available more than 400 audio files to all other users of the Nutella P2P network … .A sample of files was downloaded … from the computer … (the defendant) … admitted that he had used P2P software, but was unaware that by doing so, he said, he was distributing music, and he said that he had had the software on his computer for about a year, and that his children had used it for downloading music'.[115]

Lawrence-Collins J held that the defendant had become an infringer by 'making the recording available to the public, and authorising the performance of the infringement'. The defendant did submit that: 'he did not know that he was doing anything wrong or

---

[111] Directive 2000/31/EC, Art 14(3).

[112] Directive 2000/31/EC, Art 15(1).

[113] Choi, 'The Grokster Dead-End' Harvard Journal of Law and Technology, Vol. 19, 2006 p 393 at 405–406.

[114] *Polydor v Brown* [2005] EWHC 3191 (Ch).

[115] [2005] EWHC 3191 (Ch), para 3–4.

illegal, and only let his children download music for themselves ... and he has not made anything in monetary terms from downloading the music'. Lawrence-Collins J ruled that these submissions were 'not defences, because ignorance is not a defence and he has accepted that he himself was a user ... which gives rise to direct liability'.[116] Lawrence-Collins J ruled that connecting 'a computer to the Internet, where the computer is running P2P software, and in which music files containing copies of the claimant's copyright works are placed in a shared directory[117] ... was an act of primary copyright infringement. This finding was significant as 'it does not matter whether the person knows, or has reason to believe, that what they are doing is an infringement, because innocence or ignorance is no defence. The mere fact that the files were present and were made available is sufficient for the infringement ... to have been committed'.[118]

[5.45] In Ireland copyright infringement might occur before a song is made available to a P2P network. A work might be initially copied from one medium, say a CD, to another. This process, known as 'ripping' is copying and is one of the acts that the copyright owner has the exclusive right to do or authorise.[119] Making a work available to a P2P network may be in breach of the making available right, which includes 'making available to the public of copies of the work, by wire or wireless means, in such a way that members of the public may access the work from a place and at a time chosen by them (including the making available of copies of works through the Internet)'.[120]

[5.46] Secondary infringement might also occur. The CRRA 2000 provides that copyright will be infringed by a person who:

> 'otherwise than in the course of a business, trade or profession, makes available to the public to such an extent as to prejudice the interests of the owner of the copyright, a copy of the work which is, and which he or she knows or has reason to believe is, an infringing copy of the work'.[121]

Secondary infringement may also occur where a person:

> 'transmits the work by means of a telecommunications system (otherwise than by broadcasting or inclusion in a cable programme service) knowing or having reason to believe that infringing copies of the work may be made by means of the reception of the transmission in the State or elsewhere.'[122]

---

[116] Choi, 'The Grokster Dead-End' Harvard Journal of Law and Technology, Vol. 19, 2006 p 393 at 398.

[117] [2005] EWHC 3191 (Ch), para 7.

[118] [2005] EWHC 3191 (Ch), para 8. See also *Warner Bros Records v Payne*, No W-06-CA-051, slip op at 2 (WD Tex 17 July 2006).

[119] CRRA 2000–2004, ss 37(1)(a) and 39.

[120] CRRA 2000–2004, s 40(1)(a).

[121] CRRA 2000–2004, s 45(d).

[122] CRRA 2000–2004, s 46(2).

Finally, making a copyright work available to a P2P network may be a criminal offence contrary to the CRRA 2000–2004 which provides that an offence will be committed by a person who without the consent of the copyright owner:

> 'otherwise than in the course of a business, trade or profession, makes available to the public to such an extent as to prejudice the interests of the owner of the copyright, a copy of a work which is, and which he or she knows or has reason to believe is, an infringing copy of the work'.[123]

Upon conviction upon indictment a maximum penalty may be imposed of 'a fine not exceeding £100,000, or imprisonment for a term not exceeding 5 years, or both'.[124]

---

[123] CRRA 2000–2004, s 140(1)(e).
[124] CRRA 2000–2004, s 140(7)(b).

Chapter 6

The Protection of Designs

Introduction

[6.01] As the information technology industry has matured, many of its products have become commodities. A good example of this is the personal computer. Consumers may compare specific attributes such as memory, RAM, CPU and screen-size, but most computers are treated as substitutable products much like shovels or toasters. One consequence of the comodification of personal computers is this sector of industry has become an arena of crushing competition,[1] where prices and profit margins are driven ever lower. Design, and design that is linked to branding in particular, offers an alternative business model,[2] and this is a business model that is becoming increasingly significant in markets for electronic goods such as the mobile phone market.[3] Hence the significance of the Industrial Designs Act 2001. Unregistered designs may be protected by the Community Design Regulation[4] or possibly as an artistic work under the Copyright and Related Rights Acts 2000–2004.

The Industrial Designs Act 2001

[6.02] The Industrial Designs Act 2001[5] provides for the registration of designs that are 'new' and have 'registrable character'.[6] A design will be ' considered to be new where no design identical[7] to it has been previously made available to the public'.[8] Designs

---

1   Kessler, 'Computer industry sits at critical crossroads; Changing market, stingy profits force tough choices', (2007) USA Today, 5 March.
2   'For decades computer and consumer electronics companies sold products based on superior functions and capabilities. But the emphasis in consumer markets has now shifted from performance to consumer aspiration, which means that design is becoming more emotive across a wide range of products' O'Shaughnessy, 'Getting a good look' (2007) The Irish Times, 11 July.
3   'if you do not provide ... design-led newness, you risk losing significant market share. Motorola discovered this ... when profits fell – partly ... because of the company's inability to capitalise upon and renew its design-led Razr. 'We started thinking about the Razr as a product...Now we know it is a franchise and brand.' Friedman, 'The handbag effect: Why companies are reaching out to talent from the fashion industry' (2007) Financial Times, 7 May 2007.
4   Council Regulation (EC) No 6/2002 of 12 December 2001 on Community designs, OJ L 3, 5.1.2002, p 1–24.
5   As amended by Patents Act 2006.
6   Industrial Designs Act 2001, s 11.
7   'A design shall be deemed to be identical to a design which has been previously made available to the public where its features differ only in immaterial details': Industrial Designs Act 2001, s 12(2).
8   Industrial Designs Act 2001, s 12(1).

which are in conflict with prior designs will not be registrable.[9] The individual character of a design is assessed in terms of the 'overall impression it produces on the informed user' and whether that differs from the overall impression produced by previous designs.[10] Designs that are applied to components of complex products will only be protected if the design is visible during normal use.[11] Significantly, the Act provides that functional designs are not registrable, providing the 'features of appearance of a product which are solely dictated by its technical function shall not be registrable'.[12]

This means that spare parts are not registrable. This exclusion is made clear by the Act, which provides:

> 'The features of appearance of a product which are necessarily reproduced in their exact form and dimensions in order to permit the product in which the design is incorporated or to which it is applied to be mechanically connected to or placed in, around or against another product so that either product may perform its function shall not be registrable under this Act'.[13]

The Act provides for the authorship and ownership of designs,[14] as well as their registration[15] and the management of the Register of Designs.[16] Registration of a design creates a property right in that design.[17] This Right will confer on its owner the 'exclusive right to use the design and to authorise others to use it, including the right to make, offer, put on the market, import, export or use a product in which the design is incorporated or to which it is applied, or to stock such a product for those purposes'.[18]

[6.03] Primary infringement will occur when a person undertakes any of the above acts without licence from the licensed proprietor of the right.[19] The Act also provides for secondary infringement[20] and infringement by providing the means to enable infringement to occur.[21] The Act provides for remedies,[22] a defence of innocent

---

9   Industrial Designs Act 2001, s 15.
10 Industrial Designs Act 2001, s 13.
11 Industrial Designs Act 2001, s 14.
12 Industrial Designs Act 2001, s 16(1).
13 Industrial Designs Act 2001, s 16(2). However, certain products such as Lego bricks can be registered. The Act specifically provides that 'a design serving the purpose of allowing multiple assembly or connection of mutually interchangeable products within a modular system shall be registrable under this Act', s 16(3).
14 Industrial Designs Act 2001, Pt I, Ch 2.
15 Industrial Designs Act 2001, Pt I, Ch 3. Under Regulation 6/2002 designs may also be made for a Community Design to the Office for Harmonisation in the Internal Market. This allows one application to be made to register a design throughout the EU, Regulation 6/2002, Title IV.
16 Industrial Designs Act 2001, Pt I, Ch 4.
17 Industrial Designs Act 2001, s 42(1).
18 Industrial Designs Act 2001, s 42(4).
19 Industrial Designs Act 2001, s 51.
20 Industrial Designs Act 2001, s 52.
21 Industrial Designs Act 2001, s 53.
22 Industrial Designs Act 2001, Pt I, Ch 8.

infringement[23] and a cause of action in respect of groundless threats.[24] Damages may be awarded for financial loss, together with aggravated and/or exemplary damages. Rights in a registered design will expire five years after registration,[25] but may be renewed for up to five terms of five years each, for a total of 25 years.[26] A right-holder who fails to renew on time may have the right restored on payment of an increased, if he applies within 6 months of the lapse,[27] or else he will have to show that he took reasonable care and apply within 12 months of the lapse.[28] The Act also provides a procedure for the invalidation of design rights.[29]

Unregistered designs

[6.04] The enactment of the Community Design Regulation means that unregistered designs will be protected in Ireland. The regulation created a regime for unregistered designs to meet the needs of different sectors of industry:

> 'Some … sectors produce large numbers of designs for products frequently having a short market life where protection without the burden of registration formalities is an advantage and the duration of protection is of lesser significance. On the other hand, there are sectors of industry which value the advantages of registration for the greater legal certainty it provides and which require the possibility of a longer term of protection corresponding to the foreseeable market life of their products'.[30]

The protection available to unregistered designs is more limited than that available to those designs that are registered. Rights in unregistered designs will only endure for three years[31] and infringement proceedings may only be taken where the infringement in question is alleged to result from the copying of the protected design.[32]

---

23 Industrial Designs Act 2001, s 58.
24 Industrial Designs Act 2001, s 56.
25 Industrial Designs Act 2001, s 43(1).
26 Industrial Designs Act 2001, s 43(3).
27 Industrial Designs Act 2001, s 44(4).
28 Industrial Designs Act 2001, s 44 and SI 280/2002.
29 Industrial Designs Act 2001, s 47.
30 Regulation 6/2002, recital 16.
31 Regulation 6/2002, art 11(1).
32 Regulation 6/2002, art 19(2).

Chapter 7

The Protection of Semiconductor Chip Topographies

Introduction

[7.01] Semiconductor chips are valuable products, as evidenced by the contribution made by Intel to Ireland's prosperity. The primary market for the chips created by Intel is as central processing unit (CPUs) in personal computers. This is just one use for semiconductor chips, which are also used to 'operate microwave ovens, televisions, computers, robots, X-ray machines, and countless other now indispensable apparatuses'.[1] Many of the processes that are used to create a semiconductor chip will be protected by patent. The software programs that are processed by the chip will be protected by copyright law. In the early 1980s concerns developed that the topography of semiconductor chips lacked adequate protection. In simple terms the topography of a semiconductor chip is 'the physical arrangement of the components on the chip' or 'a block diagram showing the basic arrangement of the chip'.[2] The process of creating a semiconductor chip is as follows:

> 'chip design starts with a high level idea and moves toward the placement of individual transistors on a chip in several layers. Ultimately, the schematics and floor plans are used to develop the specific placement of every transistor that will eventually go on the chip. Glass disks are etched with the pattern for each layer of the chip, and these glass disks, called masks, are printed onto the semiconductor chip, one layer at a time, by photolithography ... Generally, there are eight to twelve layers to the chip, each of which requires a separate mask ... The series of all of the masks is the mask work'.[3]

[7.02] In order to function each semiconductor chip will contain a copy of its topography; this makes reverse engineering easy for those with the right skills and equipment:

> 'Reverse engineering has long been an accepted practice in the semiconductor chip industry. By photographing and chemically dissolving each layer of the chip, a second company can recreate the entire mask work for any chip. The process allows legitimate analysis of chips to spur innovation and improvement on existing designs, but also makes direct copying of chips feasible.'[4]

[7.03] The European Communities (Protection of Topographies of Semiconductor Products) Regulations 1988[5] (Semiconductor Regulations) implement the EC's Directive

---

[1]   *Altera v Clear Logic* (15 September 2005), 424 F 3d 1079 (9th Cir 2005), 13308.
[2]   424 F 3d 1079 (9th Cir 2005), 13311.
[3]   424 F 3d 1079 (9th Cir 2005), 13312.
[4]   424 F 3d 1079 (9th Cir 2005), 13312.
[5]   SI 101/1988.

on the legal protection of topographies of semiconductor products[6] (Semiconductor Directive). The EC justified the need for the Semiconductor Directive on the ground that:

> 'semiconductor products are playing an increasingly important role in a broad range of industries and semiconductor technology can accordingly be considered as being of fundamental importance for the Community's industrial development'.

The EC noted that:

> 'the functions of semiconductor products depend in large part on the topographies of such products and whereas the development of such topographies requires the investment of considerable resources, human, technical and financial, while topographies of such products can be copied at a fraction of the cost needed to develop them independently'.

[7.04] The recitals go on to discuss possible divergences between the protections provided by different Member States for the topographies of semiconductor chips[7] and the danger that:

> 'certain existing differences in the legal protection of semiconductor products offered by the laws of the Member States have direct and negative effects on the functioning of the common market as regards semiconductor products and such differences could well become greater as Member States introduce new legislation on this subject.'

Relationship to copyright and patent law

[7.05] The Semiconductor Regulations specify that topography rights 'apply without prejudice' to rights provided by the Copyright or Patent Acts.[8] Topography rights may be viewed as filling 'the gap between copyright law and patent law'.[9] Europe, and Ireland's semiconductor chip topography legislation is based upon the USA's Semiconductor Chip Protection Act. This law 'borrows heavily from copyright law, and was initially proposed as an extension of existing copyright protection'.[10] In *Brooktree Corp v Advanced Micro Devices, Inc*[11] the US Federal Circuit sanctioned the use of concepts derived from copyright law to determine whether infringement had occurred contrary to the US Act.[12] Similarly in *Altera v Clear Logic* the plaintiff sued for breach of its rights under both the USA's Semiconductor Chip Protection Act and its Copyright Act.[13]

---

[6]   Directive 87/54/EEC of 16 December 1986 on the legal protection of topographies of semiconductor products OJ L 024, 27/01/1987 P. 0036–0040.

[7]   'topographies of semiconductor products are at present not clearly protected in all Member States by existing legislation and such protection, where it exists, has different attributes'.

[8]   SI 101/1988, reg 8.

[9]   *Altera v Clear Logic* (15 September 2005), 424 F 3d 1079 (9th Cir 2005), 13308.

[10] 424 F 3d 1079 (9th Cir 2005), 13313.

[11] *Brooktree Corp v Advanced Micro Devices, Inc* 977 F 2d 1555 (Fed Cir 1992).

[12] See Kasch, 'The Semiconductor Chip Protection Act: Past, Present, and Future' Berkley Technology Law Journal, Vol 7, Issue 1 (Spring 1992).

[13] See Smith, 'Ninth Circuit Report: Semiconductor Chip Protection Act Case Reveals Scope of Act and Enforcement of Internet Software License Agreement' New Matter, Vol. 31, No. 3, 49.

Legal base

[7.06] This apparent danger means that the Semicondutor Directive has its legal base in the Internal Market Provisions of the EC Treaties.[14] This creates an interesting legal defence for the defendant should an action ever be brought under the Semiconductor Regulations. It would appear that the Semiconductor Directive was not enacted in response to perceived European divergences in the protection of European semiconductor chip topographies, but rather as a response to the USA's Semiconductor Chip Protection Act of 1984. This limits protection to US citizens and 'a national, domiciliary, or sovereign authority of a foreign nation that is a party to a treaty affording protection to mask works to which the United States is also a party'.[15]

So if Europe had not introduced protections similar to those provided by the USA, the topographies of European semiconductor chips would not have been protected under the USA's Semiconductor Chip Protection Act. The reasoning behind Europe's motivations for enacting the Semiconductor Directive would normally be irrelevant, but for the fact that these will affect the legal base upon which the Directive was enacted. A defendant to an action brought under the Semiconductor Regulations could argue that the European instrument implemented by this SI lacked a legal base and so was *ultra vires* the EC.[16]

Definitions

[7.07] The Semiconductor Regulations contain the following definitions: a 'topography' is defined as a 'topography of a semiconductor product'; and a 'topography right' is defined as meaning 'an exclusive right conferred by ... these Regulations'.[17] The Semiconductor Regulations also provide that:

> 'A word or expression that is used in these Regulations and is also used in the Council Directive shall, unless the contrary intention appears, have in these Regulations the same meaning that it has in the Council Directive'.[18]

The Semiconductor Directive contains three definitions. Firstly the Semiconductor Directive defines a 'semiconductor product' as:

> 'the final or an intermediate form of any product: ... consisting of a body of material which includes a layer of semiconducting material; and ... having one or more other layers composed of conducting, insulating or semiconducting material, the layers being arranged in accordance with a predetermined three-dimensional pattern; and ... intended to perform, exclusively or together with other functions, an electronic function'.[19]

---

[14] What was Article 100 TEC and is now art 95.

[15] (US), Semiconductor Chip Protection Act, 1984, s 902(a)(1)(A)(ii).

[16] On the inappropriate reliance upon the internal market provisions of the EC Treaty to ensure European compliance with non-European trading partners, see the judgments of the ECJ in c-317/04 and c-318/04. This case concerned the European Commission's use of an internal market instrument (the Data Protection Directive, 95/46) to implement an agreement on the transfer of passenger data to the USA.

[17] SI 101/1988, reg 2(1).

[18] SI 101/1988, reg 2(2).

[19] Directive 87/54, art 1(a).

[7.08] Secondly, the Semiconductor Directive defines the 'topography' of a semiconductor product as:

> 'a series of related images, however fixed or encoded; ... representing the three-dimensional pattern of the layers of which a semiconductor product is composed; and ... in which series, each image has the pattern or part of the pattern of a surface of the semiconductor product at any stage of its manufacture.'[20]

Finally, 'commercial exploitation' is defined as 'the sale, rental, leasing or any other method of commercial distribution, or an offer for these purposes.'

But in certain circumstances 'exploitation under conditions of confidentiality' where 'no further distribution to third parties occurs' may not amount to commercial exploitation.[21]

The subsistence of the right

[7.09] The Semiconductor Regulations provide that 'A topography right shall subsist ... in favour of its creator where that topography ... is the result of the creator's own intellectual effort, and ... is not commonplace in the semiconductor industry'.[22]

If a topography 'consists of elements that are commonplace in the semiconductor industry' then that topography will only be protected by the Semiconductor Regulations 'only to the extent that the combination of such elements' is not commonplace in the semiconductor industry. In other words the Semiconductor Regulations will protect novel combinations of elements even though the elements themselves are commonplace. The originality requirements of the USA's Semiconductor Chip Protection Act were reviewed by the US Federal Circuit in *Brooktree Corp v Advanced Micro Devices, Inc.* The defendants asserted that the topography in question had been reverse-engineered and that this reverse engineering was substantiated by a voluminous paper trail.[23] The US Federal Circuit held that 'the paper trail is evidence of independent effort, but it is not conclusive or incontrovertible proof of originality'.[24] The US Court of Appeal for the Ninth District held that the judge in a lower court was correct to instruct a jury that 'only minimal ingenuity is necessary for a second chip to qualify as original'.[25]

[7.10] Since 1 January 1996, this right has extended to anyone from a member state of the WTO. The right extends to all those:

(a)   'natural persons who are nationals of, or are domiciled in the territory of, a Member of the WTO Agreement, shall be treated as nationals of a Member State' and,

(b)   'legal entities which or natural persons who have a real and effective establishment for the creation of topographies or the production of integrated circuits in the territory of a Member of the WTO Agreement shall be treated as

---

[20]   Directive 87/54, art 1(b).
[21]   Directive 87/54, art 1(c).
[22]   SI 101/1988, reg 3(1).
[23]   *Brooktree Corp v Advanced Micro Devices, Inc* 977 F 2d 1555 (Fed Cir 1992), at 1569.
[24]   977 F 2d 1555 (Fed Cir 1992), at 1570.
[25]   *Altera v Clear Logic* 424 F 3d 1079 (9th Cir 2005), 13321 at para 7.

legal entities or natural persons having a real and effective industrial or commercial establishment in the territory of a Member State'.[26]

Where a topography is created in the course of employment or pursuant to a commission, the topography right will apply in favour of the employer or the person commissioning the topography. However, the creator's contract of employment or commission may stipulate that this provision does not apply.[27] The right to protection may be availed of by the persons:

'who first exploit commercially a topography in a Member State which has not yet been exploited anywhere in the world ... and ... who have been exclusively authorised to exploit commercially the topography throughout the territories of the Member States by the person entitled to dispose of the rights in that topography'.[28]

The right to protection conferred by these regulations will apply to successors in title.[29] This means that the right may be transferred or assigned.

The rights conferred

[7.11] The topography right is similar to copyright and patents in that it is a 'negative' right. It does not confer a right on its owner to exploit the topography; rather it gives the owner the exclusive right to prevent others exploiting the topography. This means that the value of a topography will very much depend upon the owner's willingness to exploit it. Specifically, the Regulations provide that the topography right confers on its owner the right to 'authorise or prohibit' the following acts 'the reproduction of a topography' and 'the commercial exploitation or the importation for that purpose of a topography or of a semiconductor product manufactured by using the topography'.[30]

[7.12] In *Brooktree Corp v Advanced Micro Devices, Inc* the defendant claimed that it had copied no more than 80% of the plaintiff's topography. The defendant asserted that under the US Act the entirety of a topography would have to be copied for infringement to occur. This assertion was rejected by the US Federal Circuit, which held that substantial similarity could be found from less than wholesale copying.

[7.13] Infringements of topography rights 'shall be actionable at the suit of the owner of that topography right'.[31] The Semiconductor Regulations also provide for a right analogous to the distribution right provided by EC trademarks and copyright enactments. It states that:

---

26 94/824/EC: Council Decision of 22 December 1994 on the extension of the legal protection of topographies of semiconductor products to persons from a Member of the World Trade Organization OJ L 349, 31/12/1994 p 0201 – 0202, art 1. Regulation 6 of the European Communities (Protection of Topographies of Semiconductor Products) (Amendment) Regulations, 1993 (SI 310/1993) inserts the following reg 12 into the Semiconductor Regulations: 'The right to protection...shall extent to natural persons, companies or other legal persons ... to the extent that future Decisions of the Council may so provide...'.

27 SI 101/1988, reg 3(4).

28 SI 101/1988, reg 3(5).

29 SI 101/1988, reg 3(6).

30 SI 101/1988, reg 4(1).

31 SI 101/1988, reg 6(1).

'The exclusive rights to authorise or prohibit the ... (commercial exploitation or the importation for that purpose of a topography) ... .shall not apply to any such act committed after the topography or the semiconductor product has been put on the market in a Member State by the person entitled to authorise its marketing or with his consent'.[32]

A broad range of remedies will be available. The Semiconductor Regulations provide that:

'in an action by the owner of a topography right for an infringement thereof all such relief, by way of damages, injunction, account of profits or otherwise shall be available to the plaintiff as is available in any corresponding proceedings in respect of infringement of other proprietary rights'.[33]

[7.14] However, the remedies available will be limited to the damages that would equate to 'a reasonable royalty payment' where it is proven or admitted that:

(a)   'an infringement was committed by reproducing, importing, distributing or dealing in a topography or a semiconductor product incorporating an infringing topography', and'

(b)   'at the time of the acquisition of a topography or a semiconductor product incorporating an infringing topography, the defendant did not know and had no reasonable grounds to believe, that the topography or the semiconductor product was protected by law'.[34]

The owners of topography rights may indicate the existence of their right by placing a mark in the form of a T* on their products.[35]

Reverse engineering

[7.15] The Semiconductor Regulations provide that others may reverse engineer semiconductor topographies in certain circumstances. The Regulations provide that a person may 'reproduce a topography privately for non commercial aims' and 'reproduce a topography for the purpose of analysis or evaluation or teaching of the concepts, processes, systems or techniques embodied in a topography.'[36]

The Regulations provide that it is not an infringement to undertake any of the acts restricted by the Regulations in respect of a topography created on the basis of an analysis and evaluation of another topography for the purpose of analysis or evaluation or teaching. However, such a topography must be original or composed of elements that are not commonplace in the industry.[37]

[7.16] The reverse engineering provisions of the equivalent US Act were reviewed by the US Court of Appeals for the Ninth Circuit in *Altera v Clear Logic*.[38] The plaintiffs were competitors in the semiconductor chip sector. The plaintiff manufactured programmable

---

[32]   SI 101/1988, reg 4(4).
[33]   SI 101/1988, reg 6(2).
[34]   SI 101/1988, reg 6(3).
[35]   SI 101/1988, reg 7.
[36]   SI 101/1988, reg 4(2).
[37]   That is, comply with the provisions of reg 3(1) of SI 101/1988, reg 4(3).
[38]   *Altera v Clear Logic* 424 F 3d 1079 (9th Cir 2005), 13309.

semiconductor chips. The plaintiff also supplied software, which its customers would use to route the functions of thousands of transistors on the programmable chips. The plaintiff would work with its customers programming and reprogramming the plaintiff's chips, until the performance of that chip had been optimised. The plaintiff might spend months working with a customer before this optimal performance had been achieved. The defendant manufactured a different sort of chip, one that was not programmable. Sometimes customers who had started with a programmable chip would decide to use non-programmable chips. Non-programmable chips are smaller and less power-intensive than the programmable kind; they can also be cheaper, especially when they are bought in bulk. The disadvantage of moving from a programmable chip to the non-programmable kind is that the entire product development process must restart.

> 'This can take a few months and there is a substantial risk that even after the initial attempt, the first chip will not work and more time and money will have to be invested in perfecting the product.'[39]

The defendant dispensed with this business model. Instead:

> 'When customers program Altera devices, using the Altera software, a file called a bitstream is generated. Clear Logic asks customers to send the bitstream to Clear Logic, and Clear Logic uses the bitstream to create a ... (non-programmable chip) ... for the customer. Clear Logic only produces ... (non-programmable chips) ... that are compatible with Altera chips. The laser process Clear Logic uses to create chips with the bitstream allows for a turnaround time of just a few weeks, and rarely produces an incompatible chip.'[40]

The plaintiff sued, alleging that the defendant 'infringed its rights ... by copying the layout design of its registered mask works for three families of chip products'.[41] The plaintiff succeeded at trial and was awarded $36m in damages. The defendant appealed, asserting the 'reverse engineering' defence which is provided by the US Act and equates to that in the Irish and European legislation. The US Court of Appeals for the Ninth Circuit ruled that:

> 'The SCPA's reverse engineering provision allows copying the entire mask work. It does not distinguish between the protectable and non-protectable elements of the chip as long as the copying is for the purpose of teaching, evaluating, or analyzing the chip. Although the product created from that analysis must be original, the process of studying the chip is not limited to copying ideas or concepts.'[42]

Commencement and duration of the right

[7.17] The topography right will commence 'when the topography is first fixed or encoded'.[43]

---

[39] 424 F 3d 1079 (9th Cir 2005), 13309.

[40] 424 F 3d 1079 (9th Cir 2005), 13309.

[41] 424 F 3d 1079 (9th Cir 2005), 13309.

[42] 424 F 3d 1079 (9th Cir 2005), 13321 at para 6.

[43] SI 101/1988, reg 5(1)(a).

Where a topography right vests in a person on the basis that they were the first person to commercially exploit that topography in the EU,[44] then that right will commence on 'the date of first commercial exploitation anywhere in the world.'[45] The topography right will:

> 'come to an end 10 years from the end of the calendar year in which the topography is first commercially exploited anywhere in the world, or, where it has not been commercially exploited anywhere in the world, within a period of 15 years from its first fixation or encoding.'[46]

---

[44] That is under reg 3(5) of SI 101/1988.

[45] SI 101/1988, reg 5(1)(b).

[46] SI 101/1988, reg 5(2).

PART II: PATENTS

Chapter 8

Patents

Introduction

[8.01] Patents are commonly thought of as intellectual property, but the property analogy is not necessarily helpful. Patents are not a form of property like your car or your house. It is immediately obvious that you will be disadvantaged if a stranger started driving one or living in the other. But it is not so immediately obvious that the Irish health system will be disadvantaged if African AIDS victims get access to cheap medication in defiance of international patent treaties. Patents are better understood as statutory monopolies. A patent owner is given a monopoly on the exploitation of an invention for a set period of time. During this period only he can exploit the process or method set out in his patent. Like copyright a patent is a negative right. The grant of a patent does not give the grantee the right to do something, all it does is confer on the grantee the right to prevent others doing something. The justification for conferring such a monopoly on a patent owner is the incentive that this monopoly provides for invention and innovation. The justification for the patent system is therefore comparable to that provided by the copyright system, but with a 'twist':

> 'A twist not present in the copyright area ... is that in the absence of legal protection for an invention, the inventor will try to keep the invention secret, thus reducing the stock of knowledge available to society as a whole. Patent law combats this incentive by requiring ... that the patent application ... disclose the steps constituting the invention in sufficient detail to enable readers of the application ... to manufacture the patented product themselves'.[1]

[8.02] The number of patents issued is now taken as an important indicator of the health of individual companies, nations and continents.[2] The European Commission in particular obsesses about divergences in the number of patents lodged in European, American and Japanese patent offices. Europeans are not just applying for fewer patents, they may also be applying for less valuable patents:

> 'The fragmented single market for patents has serious consequences for the competitiveness of Europe ... Even in Europe, the US and Japan patent more than the EU: at the EPO 137 patents per million population are from the EU versus 143 patents from the US and 174 from Japan. The lack of critical patent mass at home translates in less patents that are filed in both the US, the EU and Japan, the so called triadic patents. Whereas Europe has 33 triadic patents per million population, the US has 48 and Japan has 102.

---

[1] Landes and Posner, *The Economic Structure of Intellectual Property Law* (Harvard University Press, 2003), p 294.

[2] 'But garnering a plethora of patents does not necessarily mean that a firm is hugely innovative: the brute number says nothing about the value of the inventions': 'Innovation and its enemies' (2006) The Economist, 12 January.

Therefore, the US and Japan have respectively 45% and 209% more triadic patents than the EU. This is of particular concern since triadic patents are the most valuable ones and are considered the best patent indicator for innovation.[3]

There can be no doubt that the larger number of patent applications made in the USA reflects the reality that research and development budgets are far higher in the USA and may also be more productively used. However, the numbers of US patents also reflects the unfortunate habit of the US Patent and Trademark Office (USPTO) granting 'poor quality' or 'junk' patents,[4] a habit which may reflect resource and staff retention failures in the USPTO.[5] It is probably incorrect to think that Europe needs more patents. What Europe needs is more patents that are valuable. In patents as in many other things, quality not quantity is important.

Difficulties with the patent system

[8.03] In the USA the debate about patents appears to focus upon the possibility that the US patent provides strong protections for patent owners too easily. One focus of this debate is the activity of so-called patent trolls,[6] described by the European Commission as:

> 'patent owners (often investors who buy patents cheaply from failed companies) who use these rights to threaten companies with infringement actions and interlocutory injunctions,

---

[3] EC Commission, *Communication from the Commission to the European Parliament and the Council, Enhancing the patent system in Europe*, COM/2007/0165 final, Brussels, 3 April 2007, p 2.

[4] From 1930 until 1982 the number of patent applications to the USPTO rose by about 1% a year. In 1982 the US Court of Appeals for the Federal Circuit was created, after which point the number of patents rose at a rate of 5.7% a year. Jaffe and Lerner comment: 'If this increase in patenting reflected an explosion in US inventiveness, it would be a cause for celebration. But unfortunately it is clear that the rapid rise in the rate of patenting has been accompanied by a proliferation of patent awards of dubious merit.': *Innovation and its Discontents* (Princeton University Press, 2004), pp 11–12. For a counter to Jaffe and Lerner's argument, see Field, 'Patent Systems: More Easily Faulted Than Fixed' Journal of Intellectual Property Rights, Vol 12, p 123, 2007.

[5] The USPTO has issued a wide variety of dubious patents. Jaffe and Lerner cite the example of US Patent No 6004596, *Sealed Crustless Sandwich:* see *Innovation and its Discontents*. These authors prefer the example of US Patent No 6,368,227, *Method of Swinging on a Swing*, granted to the five-year-old son of a patent agent, see Noah, *How to Swing*, http://www.slate.com, 28 June 2006: 'read it and weep. But see also US Patent No 5443036, *Method of Exercising a Cat:* 'A method for inducing cats to exercise consists of directing a beam of invisible light produced by a hand-held laser apparatus onto the floor or wall or other opaque surface in the vicinity of the cat, then moving the laser so as to cause the bright pattern of light to move in an irregular way fascinating to cats'. US Patent No D384595, *Snowman Decorating Kit*, has to be seen to be believed. Fortunately, the comb-over patent has expired: see US Patent No 4022227: 'A method of styling hair to cover partial baldness using only the hair on a person's head'.

[6] Patent trolling isn't even innovative in itself; the activity dates back to the nineteenth century when they were known as 'patent sharks': Magliocca, 'Blackberries and Barnyards: Patent Trolls and the Perils of Innovation' Notre Dame Law Review, Forthcoming Available at SSRN: http://ssrn.com/abstract=921252.

forcing them into financial settlements to avoid expensive litigation. Such threats can potentially affect an entire industry sector'.[7]

The activities of patent trolls have been widely condemned, and a range of solutions to this problem have been proposed, ranging from legislation to simply suing them.[8] The argument can be made that patent trolls actually benefit society by acting 'as a market intermediary in the patent market. Patent trolls provide liquidity, market clearing, and increased efficiency to the patent markets—the same benefits securities dealers supply capital markets'.[9] But others would argue that patent trolls have an adverse effect because they may seek to 'trap' technology users and 'extort' payment from them. Interestingly, some of those who produced the latter analysis suggest that changes in the law cannot provide a solution, which can only be provided by managerial changes.[10] The US Supreme Court may have gone some way towards offering its own solution when it issued judgment in *eBay Inc v MercExchange*.[11] That judgment made it harder for a patent holder to get a permanent injunction against an infringer in the US courts and since that judgment 'district courts appear to have consistently denied permanent injunctions in cases where an infringer has contested the patent holder's request for such relief and the infringer and patent holder were not competitors'.[12]

[8.04] The activities of patent trolls have yet to attain the same significance in Europe as they do in the USA. This may be because the USA is perceived as having too many patents, Europe is perceived as having too few:

'concerns have been raised that a spiraling demand for patents could result in increased granting of low quality patents. This is one of the reasons that could lead to the emergence of "patent thickets"[13] and "patent trolls" in Europe. A high quality patent regime in the EU

---

[7] EC Commission, *Communication from the Commission to the European Parliament and the Council, Enhancing the patent system in Europe*, COM/2007/0165 final, Brussels, 3 April 2007, p 12, n 31. See also 'eBay's bid to stop the injunctions' (2006) The Economist, 30 May.

[8] Rantanen, 'Slaying the Troll: Litigation as an Effective Strategy Against Patent Threats', Santa Clara Computer and High Technology Law Journal, Vol 23, No 1, 2006, pp 159–210.

[9] McDonough, 'The Myth of the Patent Troll: An Alternative View of the Function of Patent Dealers in an Idea Economy' Emory Law Journal, Vol 56, 2006, 189 at 190.

[10] Henkel, and Reitzig, 'Patent Sharks and the Sustainability of Value Destruction Strategies' (May 2007). Available at SSRN: http://ssrn.com/abstract=985602.

[11] *eBay Inc v MercExchange* 126 S Ct 1839.

[12] Golden, 'Patent Trolls' and Patent Remedies' Texas Law Review, Vol 85, 2007, 2111 at 2113.

[13] A patent thicket is described by the EC Commission as: 'the potential problem that in view of the high number of patents necessary to produce a product innovatation in the sector is slowed down because of fear of hold-up and patent infringement litigation': EC Commission, *Communication from the Commission to the European Parliament and the Council, Enhancing the patent system in Europe*, COM/2007/0165 final, Brussels, 3 April 2007, p 12, n 30. 'The patent thickets problem, a form of a "tragedy of the anticommons", is a phenomenon by which people underuse scarce resources because of overlapping ownership. In the patent thickets, a technology is prone to underuse because of the high costs of licensing resulting from multiple ownership stakes in the same technology. (contd/)

is an essential instrument to prevent such innovation hampering and destructive behaviour in Europe'.[14]

[8.05] The European Commission is concerned that Europeans are not applying for sufficient patents in general, but particularly in the field of computer-implemented inventions. There seems no question that applying and protecting is a far more expensive process in Europe than in the USA or elsewhere:

> 'Recent studies have also shown that a European patent designating 13 countries is about 11 times more expensive than a US patent and 13 times more expensive then a Japanese patent if processing and translation costs are considered. For the total costs with up to 20 years of protection, European patents are nearly nine times more expensive then Japanese and US patents. If the analysis focuses on patent claims, the cost differences increase further'.[15]

Europe's problem is that, for all its faults, the USPTO has the great advantage of being a single office what works through a single language. In contrast, each of the 27 EU member states has its own patent office, which together with the European Patent Office (EPO) in Munich gives 28. Very considerable energy has been expended in trying to reduce these costs, but to date no solution has been found. Europe's failure to agree stems from a variety of sources, most notably the issue of linguistic rights. And in spite of the emergence of English as the global language of commerce and science, many European countries refuse to countenance similarly limiting the translation of patents.[16]

[8.06] The European Commission has become particularly concerned that Europe is granting patents for computer-implemented inventions in insufficient numbers. In Europe a 'technical contribution' must be provided by an invention before it can be patented. In contrast in the US, the requirement is simply that the invention must be within the technological arts and, if this is so, then no technological contribution is needed. The mere fact that the invention uses a computer or software makes it become part of the technological arts if it also provides a 'useful, concrete and tangible result'. As the US does not require the invention to provide a technical contribution, this means

---

[13] (\contd) The patent thicket problem is at the forefront in corporate settings, as evidenced by the defensive use of patent portfolios. Patent portfolios are being used defensively in efforts to alleviate the patent thicket problem, encourage cross-licensing, and create leverage in infringement lawsuits. Essentially, if a company is threatened with a suit, it can threaten to countersue with patents from their own patent portfolio, thereby encouraging a more favourable settlement. Commentators deem the defensive use of patent portfolios necessary to balance competition in this patent-rich environment': McDonough, 'The Myth of the Patent Troll: An Alternative View of the Function of Patent Dealers in an Idea Economy' Emory Law Journal, Vol 56, 2006, 189 at 203.

[14] EC Commission, *Communication from the Commission to the European Parliament and the Council, Enhancing the patent system in Europe*, COM/2007/0165 final, Brussels, 3 April 2007, p 12.

[15] EC Commission, *Communication from the Commission to the European Parliament and the Council, Enhancing the patent system in Europe*, COM/2007/0165 final, Brussels, 3 April 2007, citing Van Pottelsberghe de la Potterie & François, *The Cost Factor in Patent Systems*, Université Libre de Bruxelles Working Paper WP-CEB 06-002, Brussels 2006.

[16] Dombey, 'A deal that never came to pass' (2004) The Financial Times, 30 April.

that the restrictions on patenting of business methods (apart from the requirements of novelty and an inventive step) are negligible.[17] A study commissioned by the EU identified three separate concerns relating to the granting of patents for computer-implemented inventions in the US. Firstly, there was the grant of allegedly 'clearly invalid patents' (in particular for ecommerce); that is patents which are granted for inventions that are either not new or where inventive step is, on the face of it, lacking. Secondly, there was the granting of patents for computer-implemented inventions that might strengthen big players' market positions. Finally, it identified the grant of patents for incremental innovations. These are typical of the software industry and granting patents for them imposes economic costs such as figuring out the patent holders and negotiating the necessary licences. The response of the European Commission was the publication of its 'Proposal for a Directive of the European Parliament and of the Council on the Patentability of Computer-implemented Inventions'.[18] The EC legislature was unable to agree to this legislation and the proposal has now lapsed.

[8.07] At a global level, issues relating to the international recognition of patents would appear to have been largely solved by the international agreement on Trade Related Aspects of International Property Rights (TRIPS). Unfortunately, enforcement of patent rights in poorer countries may mean that vital drugs are too expensive for indigent victims to purchase. Following considerable public pressure[19] and agreement in the WTO,[20] the EC enacted a Regulation on compulsory licensing of patents relating to the manufacture of pharmaceutical products for export to countries with public health problems.[21] This allows applications to be made for the import of pharmaceutical products into developing countries. An application for such a licence may be made by 'any person … '[22] but the licence will come with strict conditions attached such as the 'amount of product … manufactured under the licence shall not exceed what is necessary to meet the needs of the importing country or countries cited in the application'.[23]

Do patents work?

[8.08] There seems little question that patents offer an imperfect mechanism for encouraging industrial innovation. But whilst the mechanism may be imperfect, it would

---

[17] *Proposal for a Directive of the European Parliament and of the Council on the Patentability of Computer-implemented Inventions, Brussels*, 20.02.2002 COM(2002) 92 final, p 5.

[18] *Proposal for a Directive of the European Parliament and of the Council on the Patentability of Computer-implemented Inventions* OJ C 151E, 25.6.2002, p 129–131.

[19] Unfortunately the controversy is not ended, see: Jack, 'A new mood of co-operation' (2006) Financial Times, 1 December and 'A gathering storm' (2007) The Economist, 7 June.

[20] Regulation (EC) No 816/2006, Recital 2.

[21] Regulation (EC) No 816/2006 of the European Parliament and of the Council of 17 May 2006 on compulsory licensing of patents relating to the manufacture of pharmaceutical products for export to countries with public health problems.

[22] Regulation (EC) No 816/2006, art 6(1).

[23] Regulation (EC) No 816/2006, art 10(2).

also appear to be highly effective. The European Commission does not doubt the importance of the patents:

'The Commission believes that in today's increasingly competitive global economy, it is not sustainable for the EU to lose ground in an area as crucial for innovation as patent policy … If Europe wants to be at the forefront of innovation, an improved patent strategy is indispensable.'[24]

The Commission has done far more than just talk about patents. It has also persistently pursued the enactment of legislation that would harmonise the Community's patent and patent litigation systems. The Commission's own research confirms that simply counting the number of patents granted to an individual company, country or continent is a poor guide to the level of innovation therein. A study into the value of European patents found that 'the value of patents is very skewed, that is few patents are worth large amounts of money, while most patents have no or very small monetary values'.[25]

[8.09] The survey found that the average European patent was worth about €3m, but the median patent was only worth about a tenth as much.[26] This finding is consistent with a study of 772 patents granted by the German Patent Office, which found that 54% of the total value of all the patents was accounted for by just 5 patents.[27] So a patent can be very valuable, but the value of the patent depends upon the subject matter and how that subject matter is exploited. Patents may promote the growth of industry. One survey of the biotechnology industry found that small firms would avoid competing in areas that were heavily patented by larger firms.[28] In contrast a survey of anti-spam software patents in the USA found that:

'it is actually the start-up firms that are licensing technology to the incumbents; this suggests that the patent system may well be serving to protect start-up firms from having their technology appropriated by cloning or reverse engineering'.[29]

[8.10] However, a market failure may better illustrate the benefits of patents. One of the world's most serious diseases is malaria, which: 'kills more than 1m people a year, and perhaps as many as 2.5m. The disease is so heavily concentrated in the poorest tropical

---

24 EC Commission, *Communication from the Commission to the European Parliament and the Council, Enhancing the patent system in Europe*, COM/2007/0165 final, Brussels, 3 April 2007.

25 Study on evaluating the knowledge economy what are patents actually worth? The value of patents for today's economy and society, Tender n° MARKT/2004/09/E, Lot 2, 23 July 2006, p 2.

26 Study on evaluating the knowledge economy what are patents actually worth? The value of patents for today's economy and society, Tender n° MARKT/2004/09/E, Lot 2, 23 July 2006, pp 5–6.

27 Scherer, FM, Harhoff D (2000), 'Policy Implications for a World with Skew-Distributed Returns to Innovation,' *Research Policy,* Vol 29, pp 559–566.

28 Lerner, 'Patenting in the Shadow of Competitors' 38 JL & ECON 463, 463 (1995).

29 Campbell-Kelly and Valduriez, 'An Empirical Study of the Patent Prospect Theory: An Evaluation of Antispam Patents' 1 September 2005, p 38. Available at SSRN: http://ssrn.com/abstract=796289. See also: Mann *Do Patents Facilitate Financing in the Software Industry?* . Texas Law Review, Vol 83, p 961, 2005; Bessen, and Hunt, 'An Empirical Look at Software Patents' Journal of Economics and Management Strategy, Vol 16, No 1, pp 157–189, Spring 2007.

countries, and overwhelmingly in sub-Saharan Africa, that nobody even bothers to keep an accurate count of clinical cases or deaths. Providing a cure should be possible, but little research is being done as pharmaceutical companies:

> 'believe that there is no market in malaria. Even if they spend the hundreds of millions, or perhaps billions, of dollars to do the R&D and come up with an effective vaccine, they believe, with reason, that their product would just be grabbed by international agencies or private-sector copycats. The hijackers will argue, plausibly, that the poor deserve to have the vaccine at low prices—enough to cover production costs but not the preceding R&D expenditures'.[30]

The future of patents

[8.11] The patent system is built around innovation and the system must itself inevitably innovate if patents are to continue to service the needs of society. In April 2007 the EPO published a discussion document called 'Scenarios for the Future'. This paper asked two questions:

(i) How might intellectual property regimes evolve by 2025?

(ii) What global legitimacy might such regimes have?[31]

[8.12] The paper sets out four possible scenarios for the future development of patent law:

(i) *Market Rules*: where the 'balance of power is held by multinational corporations with the resources to build powerful patent portfolios, enforce their rights in an increasingly litigious world and drive the patent agenda'.

(ii) *Whose Game?*: in which the 'developed world increasingly fails to use IP to maintain technological superiority; new entrants try to catch up so they can improve their citizens' living standards'.

(iii) *Trees of Knowledge*: where 'diminishing societal trust and growing criticism of the IP system result in its gradual erosion.

(iv) *Blue Skies*: in which 'Complex new technologies based on a highly cumulative innovation process are seen as the key to solving systemic problems such as climate change, and diffusion of technology in these fields is of paramount importance. The IP needs of these new technologies come increasingly into conflict with the needs of classic, discrete technologies'.[32]

[8.13] The patent system is already being challenged or at least is perceived being challenged, by the development of open-source systems such as those that created the LINUX and Firefox software programs.[33] At the same time, advanced encryption systems may make it more attractive for some developers to rely upon trade secrets

---

30 Sachs, 'Helping the world's poorest' (1999) The Economist, 12 August.
31 EPO, 'Scenarios for the Future' April 2007, p 9.
32 EPO, 'Scenarios for the Future' April 2007, pp 10–11.
33 'Open, but not as usual' (2006) The Economist, 16 May. See Feldman, 'The Open Source Biotechnology Movement: Is it Patent Misuse?' Minnesota Journal of Law, Science and Technology, Vol 6, 2004; Evans and Layne-Farrar, 'Software Patents and Open Source: The Battle Over Intellectual Property Rights' 9 Va JL and Tech 10 (2004); (contd/)

instead of patent law.[34] Finally, where the patent system fails then there may be some merit in creating a system of 'prizes' for producing inventions that are publicly beneficial but unsuitable for private exploitation. Prizes, if sufficiently valuable, have proven a potent tool for generating innovation. Most famously in 1714 the British Admiralty offered a £20,000 prize for a navigational device that would allow sailors to determine their longitude at sea.[35] More recently, concerns about the pharmaceutical industry's failure to develop treatments that disproportionately affect poor countries has led to the mooting of the 'Advanced Purchase Commitment'. This is:

> 'a legally binding commitment to buy a vaccine, if and when one is invented. If credible, such a promise would create an incentive for profit-seeking companies to find, test and make life-saving jabs or pills'.[36]

The sources of patent law

[8.14] Patent law in Ireland comes from three separate but interlinked sources[37]:

(i) Domestic legislation, such as the Patents Act 1992–2006.[38] Prior to the enactment of the Industrial and Commercial Property (Protection) Act 1927 there was a single patents office for England, Wales, Scotland and Ireland, which had been established under the Patents Amendment Act 1852. The Industrial and Commercial Property (Protection) Act 1927 established the Irish Patents Office and was amended in 1929 and 1957. It was replaced by the Patents Act 1964, which was substantially similar to the UK's Patent Act 1949.

(ii) EC law, principally the Directive on the legal protection of biotechnological inventions.[39] The ability of the EC to legislate for patents was endorsed by the ECJ in *Netherlands v Parliament and Council*.[40] The EC has made sterling efforts to legislate for patents over the decades but has found it difficult to reach agreement on much.

---

33 (\contd) Mann, 'The Commercialization of Open Source Software: Do Property Rights Still Matter?' Harvard Journal of Law and Technology, Vol 20, No1, Fall 2006; and McJohn, 'The Paradoxes Of Free Software' George Mason Law Review, Vol 9, p 25, Fall 2000.

34 Lipton, 'IP's Problem Child: Shifting the Paradigms for Software Protection' Hastings Law Journal, Fall 2006.

35 Sobel, *Longitude* (Penguin), 1995.

36 'Push and pull' (2006) The Economist, 23 March.

37 For a comprehensive and incisive review of Irish patent law, see Clark and Smyth, *Intellectual Property Law in Ireland* (2nd edn, Tottel Publishing, 2005).

38 The Patents (Amendment) Act 2006 gives effect to certain provisions of the Agreement on trade-related aspects of Intellectual Property rights annexed to the agreement establishing the world trade organisation done at Marrakesh on 15 April 1994, it gives further effect to the European Patent Convention signed at Munich on 5 October 1973 and it gives effect to the Patent Law Treaty adopted at Geneva on 1 June 2000. The Patents (Amendment) Act 2006, s 51, does not provide for the citation of the 2006 Act together with the principle Act from 1992, so this chapter and the following simply refer to the Patents Act 1992.

39 Directive 98/44/EC of the European Parliament and of the Council of 6 July 1998 on the legal protection of biotechnological inventions OJ 1998 L 213, p 13.

40 *Netherlands v Parliament and Council* Case C-377/98, 9 October 2001.

(iii)   International treaties, most notably the European Patents Convention (EPC), which is implemented by the Patents Act 1992. Ireland signed the Paris Convention or International Convention for the Protection of Industrial Property in 1925, the Strasbourg Convention on the Unification of Certain Points of Substantive Law on Patents for Inventions in 1980 and the European Patents Convention in 1973. The EC, Ireland and other members of the EU are bound by the International agreement on Trade-Related Aspects of Intellectual Property Rights (TRIPS). TRIPs provides that: 'patents shall be available for any inventions … in all fields of technology … patents shall be available and patent rights enjoyable without discrimination as to … the field of technology'.[41] The European Commission took the view that these principles 'should accordingly apply to computer- implemented inventions'[42] and used this as a justification for the introduction of its Proposal for a Directive of the European Parliament and of the Council on the Patentability of Computer-implemented Inventions.[43] As noted above, this proposal was rejected by the EC's legislature in 2005. The applicability of the TRIPS principles to the EPC was considered by the Technical Board of Appeal of the EPC in *IBM's Application*.[44] The board was not convinced that TRIPS could be applied directly to the EPC, as the EPO was not a member of the WTO and did not sign TRIPs. The Board did express its opinion that 'it is the clear intention of TRIPS not to exclude from patentability any inventions, whatever field of technology they belong to, and therefore, in particular, not to exclude programs for computers'.[45]

[8.15] Of all the above sources of law, the EPC has by far the most practical significance at present. Virtually every European State is either a Member of the EPC or else recognises patents issued pursuant to it.[46] The Patent Act 1992 closely follows its provisions, and the activities of the EPO have long eclipsed the work of our own Controller of Patents. The Controller of Patents, Designs and Trade Marks received 864 patent applications in 2005, a rise of 19 since the previous year. As the Office points out 'Following Ireland's ratification of the European Patent Convention in 1992, there was a

---

[41]   TRIPs, art 27(1).
[42]   Recital 6. Proposal for a Directive of the European Parliament and of the Council on the Patentability of Computer-implemented Inventions, Brussels, 20.02.2002 COM(2002) 92.
[43]   20.02.2002 COM(2002) 92.
[44]   *IBM's Application* [1999] RPC 861.
[45]   [1999] RPC 861 at 868 at para 2.3.
[46]   As of June 2007 Member States of the EPC were: Austria, Belgium, Bulgaria, Switzerland, Cyprus, Czech Republic, Germany, Denmark, Estonia, Spain, Finland, France, United Kingdom, Greece, Hungary, Ireland, Iceland, Italy, Liechtenstein, Lithuania, Luxembourg, Latvia, Monaco, Malta, Netherlands, Poland, Portugal, Romania, Sweden, Slovenia, Slovakia, Turkey. Norway is set to become a member as of 1st January 2008. Albania, Bosnia and Herzegovina, Croatia, the former Yugoslav Republic of Macedonia and Serbia all recognise EPC patents. Of these Croatia and the former Yugoslav Republic of Macedonia have been invited to join the EPC. See EPO, *Member states of the European Patent Organisation*, http://www.epo.org/about-us/epo/member-states.html.

substantial drop in the annual volume of patent applications being filed at the Office'.[47] The Controller estimates that only about one-quarter as many patent applications are being made as previously. In comparison, almost 194,000 European Patent Applications were filed with the EPC in 2005, a rise of 7.2% on the previous year.[48] The EPC granted 26,866 patents in 2005 which were designated as applying in Ireland; the Irish Controller of Patents, Designs and Trade Marks granted 349 patents in the same year.

Applications

[8.16] Anyone can apply for a patent either alone or jointly with another.[49] The right to a patent belongs to the inventor or his successor in title. The Patents Act 1992 defines 'inventor' as meaning the actual deviser of an invention and the term 'joint inventor' must be construed accordingly.[50] If the inventor is an employee, the right to a patent shall be determined in accordance with the law of the state in which the employee is wholly or mainly employed or, if the identity of such state cannot be determined, in accordance with the law of the state in which the employer has his place of business to which the employee is attached.[51] Patents are granted on a priority basis; if two or more persons have made an invention independently of each other, the right to a patent for the invention will vest in the first person to file an application, but this will apply only if the earliest or earlier application has been duly published under this Act.[52] The 'Priority Right' is further set out by the Patents Act 1992, which provides that:

> 'A person who has duly filed in or for the State, or in or for any other state party to the Paris Convention for the Protection of Industrial Property, an application for a patent or for the registration of a utility model or for a utility certificate or for an inventor's certificate, or his successors in title, shall enjoy, for the purpose of filing a subsequent patent application under this Act in respect of the same invention, a right of priority during such period as may be prescribed, subject to compliance with any prescribed conditions and the payment of any prescribed fee.'[53]

    i.   Someone who wishes to take advantage of the priority afforded by a previous application must file a declaration of priority.[54] The inventor has the right to be mentioned in the specification of a patent granted for his or her invention.[55] A patent application must be accompanied by the appropriate fee and contain the following:

    ii.   a request for the grant of a patent;

---

[47] Controller of Patents, Designs and Trade Marks, *Seventy Eighth Annual Report of the Controller of Patents, Designs and Trade Marks*, 19 May 2006, p8.
[48] EPC, *Annual Report 2005*, p 15.
[49] Patents Act 1992, s 15.
[50] Patents Act 1992, s 2.
[51] Patents Act 1992, s 16(1).
[52] Patents Act 1992, s 16(2).
[53] Patents Act 1992, s 25(1).
[54] Patents Act 1992, s 26(1).
[55] Patents Act 1992, s 17.

iii.   a specification containing a description of the invention to which the application relates, one or more claims and any drawing referred to in the description or the claim or claims; and

iv.   an abstract.[56]

[8.17] Patent law confers a monopoly upon the successful patent applicant, but in return the inventor must fully disclose his or her invention. Section 19 of the Patents Act 1992 provides that a patent application must disclose the invention to which it relates in a manner sufficiently clear and complete for it to be carried out by a person skilled in the art. Similarly the claim or claims shall define the matter for which protection is sought, must be clear and concise and must be supported by the description given. The claims are very important; s 45 of the 1992 Act provides that the extent of the protection conferred by a patent will be determined by the terms of the claims, although the description and drawings may also be used. An application must be published 18 months after the date of filing.[57] An application can be made to the Irish Controller of Patents for a patent which will apply in Ireland alone, but most applicants will seek broader rights by bringing an application in the EPO or by availing of the provisions of the Patent Co-operation Treaty (PCT).[58] Where an application is brought in the Irish Patents Office and the EPO, the courts may be willing to stay the Irish proceedings.[59]

[8.18] The interpretation of patents was discussed by the Supreme Court in *Ranbaxy Laboratories v Warner Lambert.*[60] McCracken J cited the following passage from Diplock LJ in *Catnic Components v Hill & Smith*:[61]

> 'A patent specification should be given a purposive construction rather than a purely literal one derived from applying to it the kind of meticulous verbal analysis in which lawyers are too often tempted by their training to indulge. The question in each case is: whether persons with practical knowledge and experience of the kind of work in which the invention was intended to be used, would understand that strict compliance with a particular descriptive word or phrase appearing in a claim was intended by the patentee to be an essential requirement of the invention so that *any* variant would fall outside the monopoly claimed, even though it could have no material effect upon the way the invention worked.'[62]

---

[56]   Patents Act 1992, s 18.

[57]   Patents Act 1992, s 28.

[58]   Ireland is a member of an international system for the award of patents. An application can be made in Ireland for a patent from the EPO which will apply in all countries of the European Patent Convention. Similarly applications can be made in other countries such as Germany, Spain or France for patents which will apply in Ireland. An application for protection in more than one state can also be brought under the Patent Co-operation Treaty (PCT).

[59]   *Merck and Co v GD Searle & Co* [2002] 2 ILRM 363.

[60]   *Ranbaxy Laboratories, Ranbaxy Europe and Ranbaxy Ireland v Warner Lambert* [2006] 1 IR 193.

[61]   *Catnic Components v Hill & Smith* [1982] RPC 183.

[62]   [1982] RPC 183 at 243.

McCracken J commented on the above that:

'The relevance of this passage … is the emphasis on the understanding of persons with practical knowledge and experience rather than being on the actual intention of the patentee. Frequently … .claims in a patent are of a very technical nature and the nuances of such claims would not be understood by the ordinary man in the street. The test therefore is not what the claim would mean to the man in the street but rather what it would mean to an expert in the field to which it relates, or what has been expressed in a number of cases as a person skilled in the art. A patent is addressed to and intended to be read and understood by such persons. It may well be that the understanding of such persons may not be a meaning which was actually intended by the patentee or the inventor, but as the purpose of a claim in a patent is to provide certainty as to the extent of the monopoly granted, the relevant test is the understanding of the persons to whom it was addressed rather than the understanding of the patentee or inventor'.[63]

The effect of a patent

[8.19] Once a patent is granted it will stay in effect for 20 years from the date of its grant,[64] although it may lapse if the owner fails to pay the relevant renewal fees.[65] Short-term patents can also be granted;[66] these last for only ten years. While in force, a patent gives its owner the right:

'to prevent all third parties not having his consent from doing in the State all or any of the things following:

(a) making, offering, putting on the market or using a product which is the subject-matter of the patent, or importing or stocking the product for those purposes;

(b) using a process which is the subject-matter of the patent, or, when the third party knows, or it is obvious to a reasonable person in the circumstances, that the use of the process is prohibited without the consent of the proprietor of the patent, offering the process for use in the State;

(c) offering, putting on the market, using or importing, or stocking for those purposes, the product obtained directly by a process which is the subject-matter of the patent.[67]

---

[63] *Ranbaxy Laboratories, Ranbaxy Europe and Ranbaxy Ireland v Warner Lambert* [2006] 1 IR 193 at 197.

[64] Patents have a shorter duration than copyrights, but that reflects the reality that patents offer better protection and are generally more valuable. In any event patent owners are not particularly prejudiced by a shorter term of protection: 'At a discount rate of 10% the present value of a constant stream of income to be received for twenty years is 85 percent of the same stream received in perpetuity': Landes and Posner, *The Economic Structure of Intellectual Property Law* (Harvard University Press, 2003), p 296. Landes and Posner note that 'At a discount rate of 5 percent the percentage figure() (will) fall() to 62.3 percent … But the higher discount rate seems more appropriate in light of the uncertainty associated with income from intellectual property. Landes & Posner, p 296, n 2.

[65] Patents Act 1992, s 36.

[66] Patents Act 1992, Pt III.

[67] Patents Act 1992, s 40.

[8.20] A patent owner can also prevent indirect use of the invention. A patent owner has the right to prevent all third parties from supplying the means, relating to an essential element of that invention, for putting the invention into effect, where the third party knows, or it is obvious, that those means are suitable and intended for putting the invention into effect.[68] However the rights conferred by a patent do not extend to:

'(a)   acts done privately for non-commercial purposes;

(b)   acts done for experimental purposes relating to the subject-matter of the relevant patented invention;

(c)   the extemporaneous preparation for individual cases in a pharmacy of a medicine in accordance with a medical prescription issued by a registered medical practitioner or acts concerning the medicine so prepared;

(d)   the use on board vessels registered in any of the countries of the Union of Paris for the Protection of Industrial Property, other than the State, of the invention which is the subject of the patent, in the body of the vessel, in the machinery, tackle, gear and other accessories, when such vessels temporarily or accidentally enter the territorial waters of the State, provided that the invention is used in such waters exclusively for the needs of the vessel;

(e)   the use of the invention which is the subject of the patent in the construction or operation of aircraft or land vehicles of countries of the Union of Paris for the Protection of Industrial Property, other than the State, or of such aircraft or land vehicle accessories when such aircraft or land vehicles temporarily or accidentally enter the State;

(f)   the acts specified in Article 27 of the Convention on International Civil Aviation, where those acts concern the aircraft of countries, other than the State, benefiting from the provisions of that Article'.[69]

However, the rights conferred by a patent will not extend to any act that cannot be prevented by the proprietor of the patent, pursuant to any obligations imposed by the law of the treaties establishing the European Communities.[70]

Infringement

[8.21] The owner of a patent may sue for infringement and where he or she does so, he may seek the following orders:

'(a)   for an injunction restraining the defendant from any apprehended act of such infringement;

(b)   for an order requiring the defendant to deliver up or destroy any product covered by the patent in relation to which the patent is alleged to have been infringed or any article in which the product is inextricably comprised;

(c)   for damages in respect of the alleged infringement;

(d)   for an account of the profits derived by the defendant from the alleged infringement;

---

[68]   Patents Act 1992, s 41.
[69]   Patents Act 1992, s 42.
[70]   Patents Act 1992, s 43.

(e)   for a declaration that the patent is valid and has been infringed by the defendant'.[71]

There are limitations on what damages can be awarded. The owner cannot be awarded both damages and an account of profits in respect of the same infringement.[72] Damages or an account of profits cannot be awarded against a defendant who proves that at the date of the infringement he was not aware, and had no reasonable grounds for supposing, that that patent existed. Merely printing the words 'patented' or 'patent' on a product is insufficient to create awareness, the number of the patent concerned must also be attached.[73] The court may issue a declaration of non-infringement[74] or a certificate of validity.[75]

[8.22] The Act imposes limitations on those who might falsely claim to hold a patent or that their patent was being infringed. If a person threatens court proceedings for patent infringement then the recipient of those threats may go to court himself and seek the following reliefs:

(a)   a declaration to the effect that the threats complained of were unjustifiable;

(b)   an injunction against the continuance of the threats; and

(c)   such damages, if any, as have been sustained by him by reason of the threats.[76]

However, the mere notification of the existence of a patent will not of itself constitute a threat of proceedings for the purposes of this provision. [77]

[8.23] More potently, section 112 provides that 'If any person falsely represents that any product sold by him is patented, he shall be guilty of an offence and shall be liable on summary conviction to a fine not exceeding £1,000'. Simply stamping, engraving or impressing the words 'patent' or 'patented' or any other word implying that a product is patented is sufficient to amount to a representation that the product is patented.

Property in a patent

[8.24] Patents are personal property, as is stated in s 79 'the rules of law applicable to the ownership and devolution of personal property shall apply in relation to patent applications and patents as they apply in relation to other choses in action.

Section 80 provides that where a patent is granted to two or more persons, each of them will be entitled to an equal undivided share in common in the patent unless they agree otherwise. Applications may be made to the High Court to determine the ownership of a patent.[78] If a patent is assigned to a person or they acquire an interest in a patent by other

---

[71]   Patents Act 1992, s 47(1).
[72]   Patents Act 1992, s 47(2).
[73]   Patents Act 1992, s 49.
[74]   Patents Act 1992, s 54.
[75]   Patents Act 1992, s 52.
[76]   See *Kenburn Waste Management v Heinz Bergman* [2002] FSR 456 at 711.
[77]   Patents Act 1992, s 53. See *Easycare Inc v Bryan Lawrence & Co* [1995] FSR 597: 'the world of commerce has never been a place for the mealy mouthed' at p 604. See also *Unilever PLC v Proctor and Gamble* [2000] FSR 344.
[78]   Patents Act 1992, s 81.

means, then that assignment or interest must be recorded in the register of patents.[79] Any person aggrieved by an omission from the register may apply to the Courts for redress.[80] If a court orders that a patent be transferred, then all licences which were in force prior to the transfer will lapse once the transfer has taken place.[81]

Revocation

[8.25] Section 58 sets out the grounds upon which a patent may be revoked, which include the following:

(i) the subject-matter of the patent is not patentable;

(ii) the specification of the patent does not disclose the invention in a manner sufficiently clear and complete for it to be carried out by a person skilled in the art;

(iii) the matter disclosed in the specification of the patent extends beyond that disclosed in the application as filed;

(iv) the protection conferred by the patent has been extended by an amendment of the application or the specification of the patent; and

(v) the proprietor of the patent is not the inventor or otherwise entitled thereto under s 16(1).

[8.26] Any person may apply to have a patent revoked[82] and the application can be brought in the High Court or before the Controller of Patents,[83] although the controller has the power to revoke a patent on his own initiative.[84] The validity of a patent can only be questioned on one of the above grounds and also in circumstances limited to the following:

(i) by way of defence in proceedings for infringement;

(ii) in revocation proceedings;

(iii) in proceedings claiming relief in relating to groundless threats patent infringement proceedings; or

(iv) where the patent is sought for use in the service of the state.[85]

---

[79] Patents Act 1992, s 85(1).

[80] Patents Act 1992, s 86, see *Beecham Group v Controller of Patents* [1979] IR 330.

[81] Patents Act 1992, s 82.

[82] See *Cairnstores Ltd v Aktiebolaget Hassle* [2002] FSR 35 in which the defendant was the proprietor of two European patents. The plaintiff applied for revocation, and the defendant objected on the grounds that the plaintiff was only a 'straw' applicant, being an off-the-shelf company. The defendant sought to have the application dismissed or alternatively to identify the person behind the plaintiff. Both applications were dismissed but an order for security for costs was made.

[83] Patents Act 1992, s 57.

[84] Patents Act 1992, s 60.

[85] Patents Act 1992, s 61.

The Controller of Patents must be notified in writing of any infringement proceedings in which it is intended to question the validity of a patent and he must also be informed of the courts decision.[86] It is possible to surrender a patent.[87]

The Controller of Patents

[8.27] The Controller of Patents is appointed by the state, is a civil servant[88] and has the power to appoint officers[89] and charge fees.[90] He may get advice from the Attorney General[91] and must publish an annual report.[92] He has, of course, the power to grant patents,[93] and his office is responsible for maintaining the register of patents.[94] If the Controller has a discretionary power then he cannot exercise that power without giving a person who is adversely affected an opportunity to be heard.[95] The Controller can impose costs[96] and receive evidence by way of statutory declaration or, if necessary, *viva voce*.[97] There is a right of audience before the Controller[98] and appeals from decisions of the Controller may be taken to the High Court.[99]

Proposals to harmonise EC patent law

[8.28] There is no question of whether the EC has the right to reform EC patent law. The question was raised before the ECJ in *Netherlands v Parliament and Council*[100] in relation to the Directive on the legal protection of biotechnological inventions. The Netherlands challenged the ability of the EC to enact this legislation, but the ECJ held:

> 'The legal basis on which an act must be adopted should be determined according to its main object ... the aim of the Directive is to promote research and development in the field of genetic engineering in the European Community, the way in which it does so is to remove the legal obstacles within the single market that are brought about by differences in national legislation and case-law and are likely to impede and disrupt research and development activity in that field.
>
> ... Approximation of the legislation of the Member States is therefore not an incidental or subsidiary objective of the Directive but is its essential purpose ...
>
> ... It follows that the Directive was correctly adopted on the basis of Article ... (95) ... of the Treaty.'[101]

---

86 Patents Act 1992, s 62.
87 Patents Act 1992, s 39.
88 Patents Act 1992, s 97.
89 Patents Act 1992, s 98.
90 Patents Act 1992, s 99.
91 Patents Act 1992, s 102.
92 Patents Act 1992, s 103.
93 Patents Act 1992, s 7.
94 Patents Act 1992, s 84.
95 Patents Act 1992, s 90.
96 Patents Act 1992, s 91.
97 Patents Act 1992, s 92.
98 Patents Act 1992, s 93.
99 Patents Act 1992, s 96.
100 *Netherlands v Parliament and Council*, Case C-377/98, (9 October 2001) ECJ.
101 Case C-377/98, para 27–29.

[8.29] Over the years, the EC has repeatedly attempted to harmonise EC patent laws in different ways. The Luxembourg Convention on the Community Patent (The Luxembourg Convention) was signed in 1975, and amended in 1989, but did not enter into force as it was never ratified by a sufficient number of member states. Its failure was attributed by the EU to the costs of the Community Patent, and the system of enforcement which would have allowed the courts of member states to make declarations that patents were invalid – declarations which would have been effective throughout the EU. This latter provision 'aroused the distrust of interested parties, who considered it to be a major element of legal uncertainty'.[102] In spite of this failure, the EC has remained committed to patent harmonisation. In the Lisbon Strategy the EU noted that if Europe was to succeed in attaining its objective of becoming 'the most competitive and dynamic knowledge-based economy in the world'[103] by 2010 then 'innovation and ideas must be adequately rewarded within the new knowledge-based economy, particularly through patent protection.'[104]

However, in spite of this commitment, the European Commission has failed to get the community to commit to a harmonised patent system. In April 2007, the Commission was still stating that:

> 'the creation of a single Community patent continues to be a key objective for Europe. The Community patent remains the solution which would be both the most affordable and legally secure answer to the challenges with which Europe is confronted in the field of patents and innovation. Statistics show that in the context of overall costs … the Community patent is far more attractive than models under the present system of European patents.'[105]

[8.30] At present there are basically two separate sets of proposals being negotiated at EC and International levels. These proposals are aimed at solving two different problems:

(i) Firstly, there is the need to reform the process by which patents are granted. The EC proposal is the proposal for a Community Patent Regulation.[106] The International proposal is the London Agreement.

(ii) Secondly, there is the need to reform the procedure by which patents may be enforced. The EC has proposed creating a new jurisdiction for the ECJ. The International Proposal is the European Patent Litigation Agreement (EPLA).

Each of the above issues is considered in turn below.

---

[102] *Proposal for a Council Regulation on the Community Patent*, Explanatory Memorandum, para 1.1.

[103] EU Council, *Presidency Conclusions*, Lisbon, 24 March 2000, para 5

[104] EU Council, *Presidency Conclusions*, Lisbon, 24 March 2000, para 12

[105] EC Commission, *Communication from the Commission to the European Parliament and the Council, Enhancing the patent system in Europe*, COM/2007/0165 final, Brussels, 3 April 2007, p 4.

[106] *Proposal for a Council Regulation on the Community patent* OJ C 337E, 28.11.2000, p 278. A common political approach was developed in March 2003 but as of the time of writing no consensus has developed about the enactment of this proposal.

Reforms to the grant of patents

[8.31] One solution to this problem proposed by the European Commission is the Proposal for a Community Patents Regulation. However this proposal was criticised on two grounds:

(i)   the high costs of translation arrangements, which would have involved translation into all the official languages of the EU; and

(ii)   excessive centralisation of the proposed jurisdictional system. This issue was closely tied to the court jurisdiction issue discussed below.

Whilst the EC is continuing to pursue its own proposal, some Members of the EPC have proposed the so-called London Agreement on translation, which would reduce translation costs within the framework of the EPC.[107]

Reforms to the patent enforcement process

[8.32] Although the EPC gives Europe a common system for the grant of patents, it does not provide a common system for the enforcement or interpretation of patents. This is a serious defect, as the EC Commission has commented:

'once a European Patent has been granted it becomes a national patent and is subject to the national rules of the contracting EPO states designated in the application. The European patent is not a unitary title; it is a bundle of national patents. There is at present no single jurisdiction for disputes on European Patents which raise issues which go beyond the borders of one state …

Consequently, claimants and defendants bear the risk of multiple litigation in a number of Member States on the same patent issue …

The existing system with the danger of multiple patent litigation has several consequences which weaken the patent system in Europe and make patents less attractive.'[108]

[8.33] The cost implications of this for individual litigants is obviously significant. But an even greater problem is that the Courts of different countries can give different interpretations of what their EPC patents mean. And the Commission notes:

'the possibility of different application and interpretation of substantive patent law, enshrined in the EPC, relating to crucial items such as patentable subject-matter and scope of protection conferred by a European patent.

Divergent decisions on the substance of the cases cause lack of legal certainty for all involved in patent proceedings. This uncertainty has an impact on crucial business decisions relating to investments, production and marketing of patented products which

---

[107] 'Ten EPC contracting states (Denmark, France, Germany, Liechtenstein, Luxembourg, Monaco, Netherlands, Sweden, Switzerland and United Kingdom) signed the Agreement dated 17 October 2000': EC Commission, *Communication from the Commission to the European Parliament and the Council, Enhancing the patent system in Europe*, COM/2007/0165 final, Brussels, 3 April 2007, p 3, n 10.

[108] EC Commission, *Communication from the Commission to the European Parliament and the Council, Enhancing the patent system in Europe*, COM/2007/0165 final, Brussels, 3 April 2007, p 5.

must often be made on the basis of complicated assessments regarding the likely outcome of a number of cases dealt with in various jurisdictions'.[109]

[8.34] However, the Commission weakens its case for harmonising patent litigation law by noting that: 'more than 90% of current patent litigation in the Community takes place before the tribunals of just four Member States (Germany, France, UK and the Netherlands).'[110] The Commission has found that there are substantial variations in the cost of going to court in these four member states.

'In Germany, the overall cost for each party of a patent case with an average sum in dispute of around €250,000 is estimated to lie at around €50,000 at first instance and €90,000 at second instance for both validity and infringement. In France, the cost of an average patent litigation case in the above-mentioned range lies between €50,000 and €200,000 at first instance and between €40,000 and €150,000 at second instance. In the Netherlands, the estimated cost of an average patent case varies between €60,000 and 200,000 at first instance and between €40,000 and €150,000 at second instance. In the UK the cost of a similar case is assessed to range from €150,000 (fast-track procedure) to €1,500,000 at first instance and from €150,000 to €1,000,000 at second instance. This means that the accumulated costs of parallel litigation in these four Member States would vary between €310,000 and €1,950,000 at first instance and €320,000 and €1,390,000 at second instance.

The European Commission compares the above costs with what it says would be the cost of going to its proposed European Patent Court: 'between €97,000 and €415,000 at first instance and between €83,000 and €220,000 at second instance.

The International Proposal: The European Patent Litigation Agreement (EPLA)

[8.35] The European Patent Litigation Agreement (EPLA) is currently being discussed by a working party of the contracting states of the EPC. If agreed and implemented, it would result in the creation of an entirely new European Patent Judiciary.

'The European Patent Judiciary would comprise a Court of First Instance, a Court of Appeal and a Registry. The Court of First Instance would comprise a Central Division set up at the seat of the European Patent Court. However, Regional Divisions of the Court of First Instance would be set up in Contracting States. EPLA Contracting States could file a request for setting up a Regional Division that should ensure the local presence in the first instance of the European Patent Court (with a maximum of three first instance courts per country), mainly financed by the Contracting States in question. The decisions of the Court of First Instance would be appealed to the Court of Appeal. The Register of the EPC would be responsible for co-ordinating the division of work in cases allocated to the Regional Divisions'.[111]

---

[109] EC Commission, *Communication from the Commission to the European Parliament and the Council, Enhancing the patent system in Europe*, COM/2007/0165 final, Brussels, 3 April 2007, p 5.

[110] EC Commission, *Communication from the Commission to the European Parliament and the Council, Enhancing the patent system in Europe*, COM/2007/0165 final, Brussels, 3 April 2007, p 6.

[111] EC Commission, *Communication from the Commission to the European Parliament and the Council, Enhancing the patent system in Europe*, COM/2007/0165 final, Brussels, 3 April 2007, p 9.

The European Proposal: Proposal for Council Decisions establishing a Community Patent Court

[8.36] In 2003 the European Commission proposed a couple of decisions, which, if enacted, would create a patent court as a part of the existing European Court of Justice. These proposals were:

(i) Proposal for a Council Decision establishing the Community Patent Court and concerning appeals before the Court of First Instance; and[112]

(ii) Proposal for a Council Decision conferring jurisdiction on the Court of Justice in disputes relating to the Community patent.[113]

However these proposals did not meet with approval from some member states and other interested parties as:

'A number of Member States, supported by some stakeholders, seem to have the view that a EU-wide patent court established within the Community framework would not be workable in practice. It is feared that procedures would turn out to be inefficient and inadequate and it is furthermore doubted whether it would be possible to appoint technically educated judges with no full legal qualifications'.[114]

[8.37] However, the Commission believed that 'consensus could be built on the basis of an … integrated approach which combines features of both EPLA and a Community jurisdiction as initially proposed by the Commission'.[115] At the time of writing, the Commission was advocating:

'a unified and specialised patent judiciary with competence for litigation on European patents and future Community patents. … It should comprise a limited number of first instance chambers as well as a fully centralised appeal court which would ensure uniformity of interpretation. The chambers, which could make use of existing national structures, should form an integral part of the single jurisdictional system.

The jurisdiction would have competence for infringement and validity actions as well as for related claims such as damages and for specific proceedings responding to the needs of stakeholders.

---

[112] *Proposal for a Council Decision establishing the Community Patent Court and concerning appeals before the Court of First Instance,* Brussels, 23.12.2003COM(2003) 828 final.

[113] *Proposal for a Council Decision conferring jurisdiction on the Court of Justice in disputes relating to the Community patent,* Brussels, 23.12.2003, COM(2003) 827 final.

[114] EC Commission, *Communication from the Commission to the European Parliament and the Council, Enhancing the patent system in Europe,* COM/2007/0165 final, Brussels, 3 April 2007, p 10.

[115] EC Commission, *Communication from the Commission to the European Parliament and the Council, Enhancing the patent system in Europe,* COM/2007/0165 final, Brussels, 3 April 2007, p 10.

The appeal court and the first instance chambers should work under common rules of procedure based on best practices in the Member States. This would be by using the knowledge and experience of specialised patent tribunals within the EU ... The patent jurisdiction should comprise both legally and technically qualified judges ...

Finally, the patent jurisdiction must respect the European Court of Justice as the final arbiter in matters of EU law, including questions related to the ... validity of future Community patents.'[116]

---

[116] EC Commission, *Communication from the Commission to the European Parliament and the Council, Enhancing the patent system in Europe*, COM/2007/0165 final, Brussels, 3 April 2007, p 11.

Chapter 9

Patenting Software, Business Methods, Games and Presentations of Information

Introduction

[9.01] Article 52(1) of the European Patent Convention (EPC) provides 'European patents shall be granted for any inventions which are susceptible of industrial application, which are new and which involve an inventive step.

This is replicated by s 9(1) of the Patents Act 1992, which provides 'An invention in all fields of technology[1] shall be patentable ... if it is susceptible of industrial application, is new and involves an inventive step.

Therefore, to get a patent, a number of the following criteria must be satisfied. The invention must:

   (i)   be an invention;

  (ii)   be novel or new;

 (iii)   must involve an inventive step;

 (iv)   be susceptible of industrial application.

Each of these criteria is discussed below.

Invention

[9.02] Article 52(2) of the EPC provides that the

   'following in particular shall not be regarded as inventions within the meaning of paragraph 1:

   (a)   discoveries, scientific theories and mathematical methods;

   (b)   aesthetic creations;

   (c)   schemes, rules and methods for performing mental acts, playing games or doing business, and programs for computers;

   (d)   presentations of information.

Again this provision is replicated in the Patents Act 1992.[2] The EPC goes on to provide that the above provisions 'shall exclude patentability of the subject-matter or activities referred to in that provision only to the extent to which a European patent application or European patent relates to such subject-matter or activities as such'.[3]

[9.03] This chapter focuses on those of the above exclusions that most affect information technologies: namely computer programs; business methods, games and presentations of

---

[1]   As inserted by the Patents (Amendment) Act 2006, s 3(a).

[2]   Patents Act 1992, s 9(2).

[3]   EPC, art 52(3).

information. Deciding what is and is not an invention raises complex questions. The term is not defined by the EPC or the Patent Act 1992. The EPO considers that an invention must have a technical character in order to be patentable.[4] In recent years the view of the EPO's Technical Boards of Appeal of what amounts to technical character has evolved. Earlier decisions adopted the 'contribution approach'. This held that an invention would have the requisite technical character if it contributed something to state of the art in a field not excluded from patentability.[5] Subsequent decisions then criticised this approach. In Decision T-931/95 the EPO Board held that there was no basis in the EPC for distinguishing between new features of an invention and features of that invention which were known from the prior art when examining whether the invention concerned could be considered to be an invention within the meaning of art 52(1) of the EPC. The Board criticised the contribution approach as confusing the requirement of 'invention' with the requirements of 'novelty' and 'inventive step'. Subsequently, in Decision T748/03 the EPO Board held that:

> 'the technical character of an invention was closely linked with the requirement of reproducibility under Art 83 EPC. A person skilled in the art had to be able, using the means proposed, to achieve repeatedly the result specified as the aim of the disclosed teaching. Reproducibility of an invention required, first of all, a causal link between the technical instructions and the desired result. R 27(1)(c) EPC gave form to that condition by requiring that the claimed invention be disclosed in such terms that the technical problem and its solution could be understood. However, the requirement of a causal link did not mean that the inventor had to grasp the scientific basis for the teaching according to the invention. Rather, it sufficed that the outwardly apparent link between cause and effect was recognised and disclosed'.[6]

[9.04] Interpretation the EPC is further complicated by the reality that whilst signatories of the EPC are bound to implement its provisions they are not bound by the EPO's interpretation of the Convention. So different states may interpret the EPC differently. In *Aerotel/Macrossan*[7] the English Court of Appeal noted the EPO Boards had adopted these different approaches, but suggested that the 'contribution approach' had a lot to be said for it:

> 'Patents are essentially about information as to what to make or do. If all the patentee has taught new is something about an excluded category, then it makes sense for the exclusion to apply. If he has taught more, then it does not'.[8]

---

4   See EPO Board decisions: T 931/95, OJ 2001, 441; T 258/03, OJ 2004, 575; T 619/02, OJ 2007.
5   See EPO Board decisions: T 121/85, T 38/86, OJ 1990, 384; T 95/86, T 603/89, OJ 1992, 230; T 71/91, T 236/91, T 833/91, T 77/92.
6   EPO, *Legal Research Service for the Boards of Appeal, Case Law of the Boards of Appeal of the European Patent Office* (5th edn, December 2006), pp 2–3.
7   *Aerotel/Macrossan* [2006] EWCA Civ 1371. Mann J held in the lower court that that merely because an activity is 'is carried out for remuneration by solicitors' would not exclude that activity from patentability (*Re Macrossan's Application* [2006] EWHC 705 (Pat), para 30).
8   [2006] EWCA Civ 1371, para 32.

[9.05] The court questioned the validity of criticisms of the contribution approach, but also noted that it was bound by precedent, namely *Merrill Lynch*,[9] *Gale*[10] and *Fujitsu Ltd.*[11] The court then set out what it termed the 'technical effect approach'.[12] This is a structured approach involving four steps, which are set out below.

(i)   'No-one could quarrel with the first step – construction. You first have to decide what the monopoly is before going on to the question of whether it is excluded. Any test must involve this first step'.[13]

(ii)   'The second step – identify the contribution … is an exercise in judgment probably involving the problem said to be solved, how the invention works, what its advantages are. What has the inventor really added to human knowledge perhaps best sums up the exercise. The formulation involves looking at substance not form – which is surely what the legislator intended … .[14] If an inventor claims a computer when programmed with his new program, it will not assist him if he alleges wrongly that he has invented the computer itself, even if he specifies all the detailed elements of a computer in his claim. In the end the test must be what contribution has actually been made, not what the inventor says he has made'.[15]

(iii)   'The third step – is the contribution solely of excluded matter?... Ask whether the contribution thus identified consists of excluded subject matter as such?'.[16]

(iv)   'The fourth step – check whether the contribution is 'technical' – may not be necessary because the third step should have covered that. It is a necessary check however if one is to follow Merrill Lynch[17]'.[18]

Computer programs

[9.06] The EPC excludes 'programs for computers' from patentability,[19] and this exclusion is replicated by section of the Irish Patents Act 1992. Yet the reality is that approximately 20,000 patents for computer programs have been issued by the EPO.[20]

---

9   *Merrill Lynch* [1989] RPC 561 (CA).

10   *Gale* [1991] RPC 305.

11   *Fujitsu* [1996] RPC 511 (Laddie J) and [1997]RPC 608 (CA).

12   *Aerotel/Macrossan* [2006] EWCA Civ 1371, para 38.

13   [2006] EWCA Civ 1371, para 42.

14   [2006] EWCA Civ 1371, para 43.

15   [2006] EWCA Civ 1371, para 44.

16   [2006] EWCA Civ 1371, para 45.

17   *Merrill Lynch* [1989] RPC 561.

18   [2006] EWCA Civ 1371, para 46.

19   EPC, art 52(2).

20   Explanatory Memorandum Proposal for a Directive of the European Parliament and of the Council on the Patentability of Computer-implemented Inventions, Brussels, 20.02.2002 COM(2002) 92 final, p 2.

As Pumfrey J noted in *Research in Motion UK v Inpro Licensing*[21]:

> 'All modern industry depends upon programmed computers, and one must be astute not to defeat patents on the ground that the subject matter is excluded ... unless the invention lies in excluded subject matter as such.'[22]

This made Pumfrey J anxious that exclusions from patentability should not be given too wide a scope; it is only computer programs 'as such' that are excluded from patentability. In Decision T1173/97[23] the Technical Board of Appeal of the EPO took the view that the exclusion of computer programs 'as such' from patentability indicated that the framers of the convention did not want to exclude all computer programs. It took the view that the exclusion of computer programs 'as such' could be construed to mean that such programs are considered to be mere abstract creations, lacking in technical character. This meant that the main problem for interpretation was to define the meaning of 'technical character'. The Board held that:

> 'technical character ... could be found in the further effects deriving from the execution (by the hardware) of the instructions given by the computer program. Where said further effects have a technical character or where they cause the software to solve a technical problem, an invention which brings about such an effect may be considered an invention, which can, in principle, be the subject matter of a patent.
>
> Consequently a patent may be granted not only in the case of an invention where a piece of software manages, by means of a computer, an industrial process or the working of a piece of machinery, but in every case where a program for a computer is the only means, or one of the necessary means, of obtaining a technical effect within the meaning specified above, where for instance, a technical effect of that kind is achieved by the internal functioning of a computer itself under the influence of the said program.'[24]

[9.07] The Board reviewed the case law and concluded that it allowed an invention to be patentable when the basic idea underlying the invention resides in the computer program itself.[25] It noted that to its knowledge there was no decision in which a board of appeal has attributed a technical character to a computer program for the sole reason that the program is destined to be used in a technical apparatus, such as a computer.[26] The Board continued:

> 'Every computer program product produces an effect when the program concerned is made to run on a computer. The effect only shows in physical reality when the program is being run. Thus the computer program product itself does not directly disclose the said effect in physical reality. It only discloses the effect when being run and consequently only possesses the 'potential' to produce said effect.
>
> ... a computer program product may possess the potential to produce a 'further' technical effect.

---

[21] *Research in Motion UK v Inpro Licensing* [2006] EWHC 70 (Pat), [2006] RPC 517.
[22] [2006] EWHC 70 (Pat), [2006] RPC 517 para 187.
[23] *IBM's Application* [1999] RPC 861.
[24] [1999] RPC 861 at 871 at para 6.4.
[25] [1999] RPC 861 at 871 at para 7.4.
[26] [1999] RPC 861 at 871 at para 7.1.

... Once it has been clearly established that a specific computer program product, when run on a computer, brings about a technical effect in the above sense, the Board sees no good reason for distinguishing between a direct technical effect on the one hand and the potential to produce a technical effect, which may be considered as an indirect technical effect, on the other hand.

A computer program product may therefore possess a technical character because it has the potential to cause a predetermined further technical effect ...

This means that a computer program product having the potential to cause a predetermined further technical effect is, in principle, not excluded from Patentability ... Consequently computer program products are not excluded from Patentability under all circumstances'.[27]

In conclusion the Board stated:

'a computer program claimed by itself is not excluded from Patentability if the program when running on a computer or loaded into a computer, brings about, or is capable of bringing about, a technical effect which goes beyond the 'normal' physical interactions between the program (software) and the computer (hardware) on which it is run.

[9.08] The European Commission considers that this case 'has been interpreted as meaning that it should be allowable to claim such a program by itself or as a record on a carrier or in the form of a signal (eg stored as a file on a disk or transmitted across the internet)'.[28] This decision was refined further in *Controlling Pension Benefits system*[29] in which it was held that all programs when run in a computer are by definition technical because a computer is a machine. The EPO Guidelines for Substantive Examination state that:

'if a computer program is capable of bringing about, when running on a computer, a further technical effect going beyond these ... physical effects, it is not excluded from patentability, irrespective of whether it is claimed by itself or as a record on a carrier'.[30]

The Guidelines go on to recommend that the following should be kept in mind when considering whether a computer-implemented invention is patentable:

'In the case of a method, specifying technical means for a purely non-technical purpose and/or for processing purely non-technical information does not necessarily confer technical character on any such individual step of use or on the method as a whole. On the other hand, a computer system suitably programmed for use in a particular field, even if that is, for example, the field of business and economy, has the character of a concrete apparatus, in the sense of a physical entity or product, and thus is an invention'[31]

The EPO Guidelines note that if a claimed invention does not have a *prima facie* technical character, then it will not be patentable under art 52 of the EPC. As Pumfrey J

---

[27] [1999] RPC 861 at 872 at para 9.4.
[28] Explanatory Memorandum on Proposal for a Directive of the European Parliament and of the Council on the Patentability of Computer-implemented Inventions, Brussels, 20.02.2002 COM(2002) 92 final, p 7.
[29] T-0931/1995 decision dated 8.09.2000.
[30] EPO, Guidelines for Substantive Examination, Part C, June 2005, section C-IV 2.3.6.
[31] Citing EPO Decision T 931/95, OJ 10/2001, 441).

stated in *Cappellini v Comptroller of Patents; Bloomberg LP v Comptroller of Patents*,[32] the technical effect to be identified had to be a technical effect over and above that to be expected from the mere loading of a program into a computer.'[33]

[9.09] Pumfrey J had previously explained the distinction between an invention and a computer program as follows:

> 'An invention may be viewed as a solution to a concrete technical problem. Merely to program a computer so that it operates in a new way is not a solution to any technical problem, although the result may be considered to be a new machine.'[34]

In *Aerotel/Macrossan* the English Court of Appeal suggested that the question to be asked was as follows:

> 'is it (the artifact or process) new and non-obvious merely because there is a computer program? Or would it still be new and non-obvious in principle even if the same decisions and commands could somehow be taken and issued by a little man at a control panel, operating under the same rules? For if the answer to the latter question is 'Yes' it becomes apparent that the computer program is merely a tool, and the invention is not about computer programming at all. It is about better rules for governing an automatic pilot or better rules for conducting the manufacture of canned soup'.[35]

[9.10] Decision T-424/03 of the EPO Board concerned a patent application for a 'method in a computer system having a clipboard for performing data transfer of data in a clipboard format'. The EPO Board held that:

> 'a method implemented in a computer system represents a sequence of steps actually performed and achieving an effect, and not a sequence of computer-executable instructions (ie a computer program) which just have the potential of achieving such an effect when loaded into, and run on, a computer. Thus, the Board holds that the claim category of a computer-implemented method is distinguished from that of a computer program. Even though a method, in particular a method of operating a computer, may be put into practice with the help of a computer program, a claim relating to such a method does not claim a computer program in the category of a computer program. Hence, (the) present claim cannot relate to a computer program as such.'

---

[32] *Cappellini v Comptroller of Patents; Bloomberg LP v Comptroller of Patents* [2007] EWHC 476 (Pat), [2007] All ER (D) 200 (Mar).

[33] [2007] EWHC 476 (Pat), [2007] All ER (D) 200 (Mar), para 5. In doing so he was summarizing his view in *Shoppalotto's Application* [2005] EWHC 2416: 'Suppose a program written for a computer that enables an existing computer to process data in a new way and so to produce a beneficial effect, such as increased speed, or more rapid display of information. It is difficult to say these are not technical effects. The real question is whether this is a relevant technical effect, or, more crudely, whether there is enough technical effect: is there a technical effect over and above the fact that it covers a programmed computer. If there is a contribution outside the list of excluded matter, then the invention is patentable, but if the only contribution to the art lies in excluded matter, it is not patentable' [2005] EWHC 2416 at para 9.

[34] [2005] EWHC 2416 at para 11.

[35] *Aerotel/Macrossan* [2006] EWCA Civ 1371, para 104.

In the view of the EPO, having a technical character is a 'necessary but not sufficient' criterion for patentability of a computer-implemented invention. As the EPO's Technical Board of Appeal noted in T-931/95:

> 'the mere occurrence of technical features in a claim does thus not turn the subject-matter of the claim into an invention ... Such an approach would be too formalistic and would not take due account of the term "invention".'

[9.11] Therefore, the EPO Guidelines suggest that an examiner may wish 'to proceed directly to the questions of novelty and inventive step, without considering beforehand the question of technical character'. The EPO Guidelines recommend that:

> 'In assessing whether there is an inventive step, the examiner must establish an objective technical problem which has been overcome ... The solution of that problem constitutes the invention's technical contribution to the art. The presence of such a technical contribution establishes that the claimed subject-matter has a technical character and therefore is indeed an invention ... If no such objective technical problem is found, the claimed subject matter does not satisfy at least the requirement for an inventive step because there can be no technical contribution to the art, and the claim is to be rejected on this ground.'

The EPO is almost certainly correct that the inventive step and novelty issues are of greater real importance in assessing patents for software rather than the issue of technical implementation. A failure to properly assess novelty and inventiveness has greatly contributed to the growth in US 'junk' patents.

The Proposed Directive on Computer-Implemented Inventions

[9.12] In Europe a 'technical contribution' must be provided by an invention before it can be patented. In contrast in the US, the requirement is simply that the invention must be within the technological arts and, if this is so, then no technological contribution is needed. The mere fact that the invention uses a computer or software makes it become part of the technological arts if it also provides a 'useful, concrete and tangible result'. As the US does not require the invention to provide a technical contribution, this means that the restrictions on patenting of business methods (apart from the requirements of novelty and inventive step) are negligible.[36] A study commissioned by the EU identified three separate concerns relating to the granting of patents for computer-implemented inventions in the US. Firstly there was the grant of allegedly 'clearly invalid patents' (in particular for ecommerce), that is patents which are granted for inventions that are either not new or where the inventive step is, on the face of it, lacking. Secondly there was the granting of patents for computer-implemented inventions which might strengthen big players' market positions. Finally it identified the grant of patents for incremental innovations, these are typical of the software industry; granting patents for them imposes economic costs such as figuring out the patent holders and negotiating the necessary licences.

[9.13] The response of the European Commission was the publication of its Proposal for a Directive of the European Parliament and of the Council on the Patentability of

---

[36] Proposal for a Directive of the European Parliament and of the Council on the Patentability of Computer-implemented Inventions, Brussels, 20.02.2002 COM(2002) 92 final, p 5.

Computer-implemented Inventions[37] in February 2002. The scope of the proposed Directive was defined as being to lay 'down rules for the patentability of computer-implemented inventions'.[38] The objective of the Proposal is to ensure that:

'the legal rules as interpreted by Member States' courts should be harmonised and the law governing the patentability of computer-implemented inventions should be made transparent. The resulting legal certainty should enable enterprises to derive the maximum advantage from patents for computer-implemented inventions and provide an incentive for investment and innovation'.[39]

To this end the Proposal contained two clear definitions. The first definition was of 'computer-implemented invention' which it defined as:

'any invention the performance of which involves the use of a computer, computer network or other programmable apparatus and having one or more *prima facie* novel features which are realised wholly or partly by means of a computer program or computer programs'.[40]

The second was the definition of 'technical contribution' which the proposal defined as 'a contribution to the state of the art in a technical field which is not obvious to a person skilled in the art'.[41]

[9.14] The proposal then sets out different requirements that would have had to be complied with by member states. Member States would have had to ensure that a computer-implemented invention is considered to belong to a field of technology.[42] The proposal would also have imposed certain 'conditions for patentability' that member states would have had to comply with before issuing a patent for a computer-implemented invention. These were:

'1.   Member States shall ensure that a computer-implemented invention is patentable on the condition that it is susceptible of industrial application, is new, and involves an inventive step.

2.   Member States shall ensure that it is a condition of involving an inventive step that a computer-implemented invention must make a technical contribution.

3.   The technical contribution shall be assessed by consideration of the difference between the scope of the patent claim considered as a whole, elements of which may comprise both technical and non-technical features and the state of the art'.[43]

Member States would have to ensure that a computer-implemented invention may be claimed as a product, that is as a programmed computer, a programmed computer network or other programmed apparatus, or as a process carried out by such a computer,

---

37   Proposal for a Directive of the European Parliament and of the Council on the Patentability of Computer-implemented Inventions OJ C 151E, 25.6.2002, pp 129–131.

38   Article 1.

39   Recital 5.

40   Article 2(a).

41   Article 2(b).

42   Article 3.

43   Article 4.

computer network or apparatus through the execution of software.[44] Whether the proposal would actually have resulted in enhanced growth in the European software industry will never be known as it was rejected by the European Parliament, and the legislative process concluded in July 2005.[45]

Business methods

[9.15] In *State Street Bank v Signature Financial Group*[46] the US Federal Circuit endorsed the grant of business method patents. The case concerned a 'hub and spoke' investment structure for mutual funds, and fuelled interest in the patenting of business methods.[47] The patentability of similar methods was examined by the EPO's Technical Board of Appeal in T 931/95.[48] At issue was an application for a patent for a 'method of controlling a pension benefits program by administering at least one subscriber employer account on behalf of each subscriber employer's enrolled employees each of whom is to receive periodic benefits payments.'

In its appeal the applicant pointed out that it had been granted a patent by the USPTO in respect of an identical application. However, the EPO Technical Board of Appeal rejected the application. The Board held that the system had a technical character and so was not excluded from patentability on this ground. In particular the board held that 'a computer system suitably programmed for use in a particular field, even if that is the field of business and economy, has the character of a concrete apparatus in the sense of a physical entity, manmade for a utilitarian purpose and is thus an invention.'

However, the Board went on to find that the system in question was not patentable on the basis that it was a business method as 'the improvement envisaged by the invention according to the application is an essentially economic one, ie lies in the field of economy, which, therefore, cannot contribute to inventive step. The Board noted that the:

'feature of using technical means for a purely non-technical purpose and/or for processing purely non-technical information does not necessarily confer technical character to any such individual steps of use or to the method as a whole: in fact, any activity in the non-technical branches of human culture involves physical entities and uses, to a greater or lesser extent, technical means.'

The Board went on to conclude that:

'Methods only involving economic concepts and practices of doing business are not inventions ...

A feature of a method which concerns the use of technical means for a purely non-technical purpose and/or for processing purely non-technical information does not necessarily confer a technical character to such a method'.[49]

---

[44] Article 5.
[45] See statement of Commissioner Benita Ferrero-Waldner to the European Parliament, 6 July 2005.
[46] State *Street Bank v Signature Financial Group* 149 F 3d 1368 (Fed Cir 1998).
[47] *Aerotel/Macrossan* [2006] EWCA Civ 1371, para 104.
[48] EPO Board Decision: T 931/95, OJ 2001, 441.

[9.16] In *Cappellini v Comptroller of Patents; Bloomberg LP v Comptroller of Patents*[50] Pumfrey J expressed his opinion that whilst this decision was 'correct in the result' it was 'incorrectly reasoned.' He justified his opinion on the following basis:

'This was a case of a computer program to perform a particular business method, the business method itself being held to be excluded subject matter, but the computer so programmed held to be patentable subject matter but to be obvious. The basic reasoning appears to have been that the Technical Board of Appeal considered that contributions to inventive step lying in excluded matter should not be taken into account in considering the obviousness of the claim. I really cannot see how this is permissible reasoning, if only because a vast class of inventions depend for their non-obviousness on a new discovery of some property of nature – such a discovery being excluded subject matter. I prefer to approach this problem from the direction indicated by the Court of Appeal in Aerotel: what is the claimed invention as a matter of substance? A claim to a programmed computer as a matter of substance is just a claim to the program on a kind of carrier. A program on a kind of carrier which, if run, performs a business method adds nothing to the art that does not lie in excluded subject matter.'[51]

[9.17] *Re Oneida Indian Nation*[52] concerned the following invention:

'In the prior art, a wager is placed followed by the generation and display of results by the apparatus in one sequence of operations. In contrast, [in] the present invention, apparatus pre-generates and stores the results following the wager, but the player must make a separate request to display the results. The separate request may be made on- or off-site and may be time shifted from the time of the wager, eg to comply with local gaming laws.'[53]

In making his decision Floyd QC noted that there was 'no dispute between the parties that gaming is a business and that therefore a "gaming apparatus" is an apparatus for performing the specific business of gaming'.[54] He went on to hold that:

'The applicant has contributed an apparatus for performing a new method of conducting business (gaming) transactions. The advantages relied ... are advantages of the new method of doing business and so fall wholly within the exclusion. Although they can be described as 'technical', they do not count as such: they are not a relevant technical effect. They are merely the consequence of putting the new business method into effect. The hardware involved is standard and forms no part of the contribution'.[55]

---

[49] See also the Board's decision in T 27/99 which concerned a method for use in electronic systems of encrypting or decrypting a message which would be represented in the form of a digital word encrypted using RSA-type public key algorithms. The Board ruled that the invention was a method in the computer and telecommunications field and thus not excluded from patentability even if it was based on an abstract algorithm or mathematical method.

[50] *Cappellini v Comptroller of Patents; Bloomberg LP v Comptroller of Patents* [2007] EWHC 476 (Pat), [2007] All ER (D) 200 (Mar).

[51] [2007] EWHC 476 (Pat), [2007] All ER (D) 200 (Mar), para 9.

[52] *Re Oneida Indian Nation* [2007] EWHC 954 (Pat), [2007] All ER (D) 23.

[53] [2007] EWHC 954 (Pat), [2007] All ER (D) 23, para 14.

[54] [2007] EWHC 954 (Pat), [2007] All ER (D) 23, para 27.

[55] [2007] EWHC 954 (Pat), [2007] All ER (D) 23, para 28.

[9.18] *Bloomberg LP v Comptroller of Patents*[56] concerned an application for a patent for the following:

> 'a method of distributing data in which the data transmitted to a user is mapped (using a record relating to the applications that that user has access to) to a form suitable for the application to be used by the user in question. As a matter of substance, such a method is to be performed in software only. The data is put into a form ('mapped') that is suitable for the specific application which the particular user wishes or is authorised to use. The result is said to be improved interoperability, in the sense that the application at the user's terminal is not called upon further to map the raw data: rather, it is processed on the server side before transmission'.[57]

Pumfrey J was unable to identify any technical effect over and above that of a computer program as such and so rejected the application. *Cappellini v Comptroller of Patents* concerned an application which Pumfrey J described as 'a remarkable piece of work'. The application consisted of 'some 214 pages of text and 127 pages of diagrams.' and it related to 'what must be assumed to be a novel algorithm for determining the routes to be taken by a carrier when delivering packages'.[58] Pumfrey J upheld the Comptroller's rejection of this application as 'There is, in my judgment, no relevant technical effect in merely moving vehicles and their cargos around according to a routing algorithm.'[59]

[9.19] The leading UK decision on patenting a business method remains *Merrill Lynch's Application*[60] which concerned an invention that related:

> 'to business systems and, more specifically, to an improved data processing based system for implementing an automated trading market for one or more securities. The system retrieves and stores the best current bid and asked prices; qualifies customers buy/sell orders for execution; executes the orders; and reports the trade particulars to customers and to national stock price reporting systems. The system apparatus also determines and monitors stock inventory and profit for the market maker.'[61]

The English Court of Appeal held that this was not patentable as:

> 'The end result ... is simply 'a method . . . of doing business', and is excluded ... The fact that the method of doing business may be an improvement on previous methods of doing business does not seem to me to be material. The prohibition ... is generic; qualitative considerations do not enter into the matter. The section draws no distinction between the method by which the mode of doing business is achieved'.[62]

[9.20] In *Aerotel/Macrossan* the English Court of Appeal noted that whilst business methods *per se* might be excluded from patentability, that did not mean that the commercial context of an invention was irrelevant.

---

[56] *Cappellini v Comptroller of Patents; Bloomberg LP v Comptroller of Patents* [2007] EWHC 476 (Pat), [2007] All ER (D) 200 (Mar).
[57] [2007] EWHC 476 (Pat), [2007] All ER (D) 200 (Mar), para 11.
[58] [2007] EWHC 476 (Pat), [2007] All ER (D) 200 (Mar), para 15.
[59] [2007] EWHC 476 (Pat), [2007] All ER (D) 200 (Mar), para 21.
[60] *Merrill Lynch's Application* [1989] RPC 561.
[61] [1989] RPC 561.
[62] [1989] RPC 561.

'A new advance in business methods, of itself, cannot supply that element of novelty and non-obviousness that is required to support a patent claim. However, if it is possible that the claim is capable of being supported on other grounds, the business context is not irrelevant. It may well be relevant background on obviousness. As Sedley LJ noted in *Dyson Appliances Ltd v Hoover*[63] ... people do not make inventions in a vacuum ... Thus the commercial background may help to show that a certain technical advance ... or was not obvious. The EPO cases on the topic are open to the danger of being interpreted otherwise. They should not be interpreted otherwise'.[64]

Games

[9.21] Information technology has permitted the development of a host of different games, ranging from role-playing to gambling games. Games 'as such' are excluded from patentability by art 52 of the EPC and this exclusion is repeated by the Irish Patents Act 1992. Decision T-951/02 of the EPO Board of Appeal concerned a combined games and gambling device. The Board found that the aim of the invention was to provide a games device offering a player particular inducements to play, thus preventing the player from starting to become bored. The board rejected the application as the requisite modifications to the gambling device were therefore limited to the adaptation of the control program to the new games system. Such modifications to the control program of the device were within the scope of normal practice for an expert.

[9.22] In the English decision of *IGT v Comptroller General of Patents*[65] Warren J distinguished between games in the physical and virtual worlds, commenting that:

'One needs to consider to some extent what is meant by a 'game' in this context. In the physical world, it is (usually) possible to describe a game in words and to set out its rules in writing ... it is straightforward to identify the rules of the game, for the game is really defined by its rules. And, once the rules of the game have been set, players may be able to develop successful stratagems – methods of play – for playing the game better than others.[66]

... in the virtual world, things may be different. It is possible to emulate existing games and it is possible to invent new games. In the case of an emulated game, it might be possible ... that the rules of the game are the same as the rules of the real game and that the computer program, insofar as it reflects those rules but no further, falls within the excluded area'.[67]

[9.23] Thus a computerised version of poker, tennis or golf will not be a patentable invention. *IGT v Comptroller General of Patents* concerned four separate applications which had 'a common thread running through them ... that they all relate(d) to systems for playing gambling games of the type in which there is a "main game" and a "bonus game".[68] Warren J agreed with the patent examiner that all of these games were excluded from patentability and dismissed the applicant's appeals. *Shopalotto.Com v Comptroller*

---

63 *Dyson Appliances v Hoover* [2001] EWCA Civ 1440, [2002] RPC 22.
64 *Aerotel/Macrossan* [2006] EWCA Civ 1371, para 101.
65 *IGT v Comptroller General of Patents* [2007] EWHC 1341 (Ch), [2007] All ER (D) 39 (Jun).
66 [2007] EWHC 1341 (Ch), [2007] All ER (D) 39 (Jun), para 22.
67 [2007] EWHC 1341 (Ch), [2007] All ER (D) 39 (Jun), para 23.
68 [2007] EWHC 1341 (Ch), [2007] All ER (D) 39 (Jun), para 48.

General of Patents, Designs and Trade Marks[69] concerned 'a computer operating in a new way, to permit a user to play in a lottery'.[70] Pumfrey J held that this was a method of doing business and so excluded from patentability.

Presentations of information

[9.24] The EPO Guidelines for Substantive Examination note that:

> 'A representation of information defined solely by the content of the information is not patentable. This applies whether the claim is directed to the presentation of the information per se[71] ... or to processes and apparatus for presenting information[72] ... If, however, the presentation of information has new technical features, there could be patentable subject-matter in the information carrier or in the process or apparatus for presenting the information'.[73]

For example, the EPO Board of Appeal granted a patent for:

> 'a two-part picture retrieval system comprising a record carrier and a read device, ie two separate but co-operative articles which may be sold separately, but each of which is specially adapted to implement complementary aspects of the same inventive idea'.[74]

[9.25] Laddie J considered the meaning of the phrase the 'presentation of information' in *Re Townsend's Patent Application*.[75] He set out his understanding of its meaning as follows:

> 'To mark an advent calendar door with the words 'only three more shopping days to Christmas' is the provision of information. To require those words to be printed in Times Roman font is to stipulate the expression of the information carried by the words. (Counsel for the applicant) argues that the latter, but not the former, is excluded from protection ...[76]

> ... In my view, this is a simple point with a simple answer. 'Presentation of information' ... does encompass providing information. It is the natural and primary meaning of those words. As ... (Counsel for the Comptroller of Patents) ... argues, the provision consists of ordinary English words. They are not ambiguous. If the indicium on the advent calendar door consists of the words 'this is for Paul' or 'don't be greedy, it's your sister's turn', it is conveying or presenting information'.[77]

---

[69] *Shopalotto.Com v Comptroller General of Patents, Designs and Trade Marks* [2005] EWHC 2416 (Pat).

[70] [2005] EWHC 2416 (Pat), para 2.

[71] Such as by 'acoustical signals, spoken words, visual displays, books defined by their subject, gramophone records defined by the musical piece recorded, traffic signs defined by the warning thereon.'

[72] Such as by 'indicators or recorders defined solely by the information indicated or recorded.'

[73] EPO, Guidelines for Substantive Examination, Part C, June 2005, s 2.3.7.

[74] See similarly, EPO Board of Appeal Decision T 163/85, OJ 1990, 379, which concerned a signal for colour television.

[75] *Re Townsend's Patent Application* [2004] EWHC 482 (Pat).

[76] [2004] EWHC 482 (Pat), para 9.

[77] [2004] EWHC 482 (Pat), para 10.

[9.26] *Raytheon Company v Comptroller General of Patents, Designs and Trade Marks*[78] was an appeal from a refusal to grant a patent for an invention which related to a method of inventory management. The invention contained databases which in turn contained 'both textual and pictorial information about the facility and all the items it contains which can be displayed on, for example, a web browser. The system provides an interactive graphical map of the facility and its layout from which the user can select a particular equipment rack and view a more detailed representation of it'.[79] Kitchin J upheld a refusal to grant a patent on the following grounds:

> 'is the idea of presenting inventory information in pictorial form a method of doing business? I think it is. It is a convenient way of displaying inventory information needed in the conduct of the business, just as it might be convenient on occasion to present it in numerical or text only form. For the same reason it seems to me to be no more than the presentation of information'.[80]

[9.27] In *Crawford v Jones*[81] a patent was applied for 'a display system for buses. The display may be used to indicate in which of two modes the bus is operating. If the bus is operating in boarding mode then it will both pick up and drop off passengers. If the bus is operating only in exit mode then it will only drop off passengers'.[82] Kitchin J rejected an appeal against a refusal to grant a patent for this system on the basis that it was both a method for doing business and of presenting information.

Novelty

[9.28] Article 54(1) of the EPC provides that 'An invention shall be considered to be new if it does not form part of the state of the art'.
The EPO explains that the purpose of this article 'is to prevent the state of the art being patented again'.[83] The EPC goes on to define the state of the art as:

> 'The state of the art shall be held to comprise everything made available to the public by means of a written or oral description, by use, or in any other way, before the date of filing of the European patent application'.[84]

In *Wavin Pipes Ltd v The Hepworth Iron Co Ltd*[85] Costello J held that prior art was not limited to material that had been published in Ireland.

---

[78] *Raytheon Company v Comptroller General of Patents, Designs and Trade Marks* [2007] EWHC 1230 (Pat), [2007] All ER (D) 360 (May).
[79] [2007] EWHC 1230 (Pat), [2007] All ER (D) 360 (May), para 6.
[80] [2007] EWHC 1230 (Pat), [2007] All ER (D) 360 (May), para 40.
[81] *Crawford v Jones* [2005] EWHC 2417 (Pat).
[82] [2005] EWHC 2417 (Pat), para 2.
[83] EPO, *Legal Research Service for the Boards of Appeal, Case Law of the Boards of Appeal of the European Patent Office*, Fifth edn, December 2006, p 46–47.
[84] EPC, Article 54(2).
[85] *Wavin Pipes Ltd v The Hepworth Iron Co Ltd* [1982] FSR 32.

Inventive step

[9.29] Article 56 of the EPC provides 'An invention shall be considered as involving an inventive step if, having regard to the state of the art, it is not obvious to a person skilled in the art.

This provision is implemented in Irish law by the Patents Act 1992, s 13. In *Rawls v Irish Tyre and Rubber Services Ltd*[86] Budd J held that 'It is apparent that the mere simplicity of the device is no objection and that a very slight advance, something approaching a scintilla, will suffice to support the invention'.[87] *Rocky Mountain Traders v Hewlett Packard*[88] concerned a patent for a device for sticking a concentric label on a compact disc. Aldous LJ noted that 'Any member of the public is entitled without fear of patent infringement, to take a prior art device and improve upon it in an obvious way'.[89] The EPO explains that:

'To assess inventive step, the boards normally apply the 'problem and solution approach'. This consists essentially of (a) identifying the 'closest prior art', (b) assessing the technical results (or effects) achieved by the claimed invention when compared with the 'closest state of the art' established, (c) defining the technical problem to be solved as the object of the invention to achieve these results, and (d) examining whether or not a skilled person, having regard to the state of the art ... would have suggested the claimed technical features in order to obtain the results achieved by the claimed invention.'[90]

Industrial application

[9.30] Article 57 of the EPC provides that 'An invention shall be considered as susceptible of industrial application if it can be made or used in any kind of industry, including agriculture'

Again this is implemented in the Patents Act 1992.[91] The requirement of an inventive step means that an invention should have some useful purpose;[92] what this might amount to was examined by the EPO Boards in T 870/04. This concerned a patent for the manufacture of a polypeptide. The Board noted that:

'No doubt exists that a BDP1 polypeptide could be 'made and used' as a further tool ... in the regulation of cellular processes and, possibly, disease states. But the whole burden is left to the reader to guess or find a way to exploit it in industry by carrying out work in search for some practical application geared to financial gain, without any confidence that any practical application exists.'[93]

---

[86] *Rawls v Irish Tyre and Rubber Services Ltd* [1960] IR 11.
[87] [1960] IR 11 at 30.
[88] *Rocky Mountain Traders v Hewlett Packard* [2002] FSR 1.
[89] [2002] FSR 1 at para 48.
[90] EPO, *Legal Research Service for the Boards of Appeal, Case Law of the Boards of Appeal of the European Patent Office*, Fifth edn, December 2006, p 120.
[91] Patents Act 1992, s 14.
[92] *Chiron Corporation v Murex Diagnostics* [1996] RPC 535.
[93] EPO Board Decision: T 870/04, para 19.

The Board continued:

'although the present application describes a product (a polypeptide), means and methods for making it, and its prospective use thereof for basic science activities, it identifies no practical way of exploiting it in at least one field of industrial activity. In this respect, it is considered that a vague and speculative indication of possible objectives that might or might not be achievable by carrying out further research with the tool as described is not sufficient for fulfillment of the requirement of industrial applicability.'[94]

The Board concluded its discussion with the admonition that:

'The purpose of granting a patent is not to reserve an unexplored field of research for an applicant[95] ... the only practicable use suggested is to use what is claimed to find out more about the natural functions of what is claimed itself. This is not in itself an industrial application, but rather research undertaken either for its own sake or with the mere hope that some useful application will be identified.'[96]

Exclusions to patentability

[9.31] Article 53(1) of the EPC provides that the following inventions are excluded from patentability:

'inventions the publication or exploitation of which would be contrary to 'order public' or morality, provided that the exploitation shall not be deemed to be so contrary merely because it is prohibited by law or regulation in some or all of the Contracting States.

Again this provision is replicated by the Patents Act 1992 which provides:

'A patent shall not be granted in respect of ... an invention the publication or exploitation of which would be contrary to public order or morality, provided that the exploitation shall not be deemed to be so contrary only because it is prohibited by law.'[97]

---

94 EPO Board Decision: T 870/04, para 21.
95 EPO Board Decision: T 870/04, para 21.
96 EPO Board Decision: T 870/04, para 22.
97 Patents Act 1992, s 10(a).

PART III: TRADEMARKS, PASSING OFF AND DOMAIN NAMES

Chapter 10

Trade Marks

Introduction

[10.01] Trade marks and domain names can appear similar. Both require registration with a centralised authority. But they are not the same. Trade marks are intellectual property; domain names are not. Domain names can be used to exploit intellectual property, which may exist in the form of a registered trade mark or as the goodwill that has developed in a particular name, but they are not intellectual property in themselves. Trade marks are registered in accordance with legislation, whether Irish or European. Domain names are not registered in accordance with any statutory authority.

Trade Marks Act 1996

[10.02] The Trade Marks Act 1996 defines a trade mark as 'any sign capable of being represented graphically which is capable of distinguishing goods or services of one undertaking from those of other undertakings'.[1] If a mark does not come within this definition, then it cannot be registered as a trade mark. A trade mark might consist in particular of 'words (including personal names), designs, letters, numerals or the shape of goods or of their packaging'.[2] A registered trade mark is personal property.[3] The Act defines a registered trade mark as a property right obtained by the registration of the trade mark. If a trade mark is not registered, then no proceedings will lie to prevent or recover damages for the infringement of an unregistered trade mark as such.[4] The registration of a trade mark is therefore essential to acquiring the protection of the Act. A trade mark will be registered for a period of ten years and it may be renewed for further periods of ten years.[5] The Act sets out things that cannot be registered as trade marks. These are:

    (i)   'trade marks which are devoid of any distinctive character', a single colour or combination of colours can be registered[6] but the ECJ upheld a refusal[7] to register a round tablet comprising two layers, one red and one white, for a

---

[1] Trade Marks Act 1996, s 6(1).
[2] Trade Marks Act 1996, s 6(2).
[3] Trade Marks Act 1996, s 26.
[4] Trade Marks Act 1996, s 7. Nothing in the Act affects the law relating to passing off.
[5] Trade Marks Act 1996, s 47.
[6] *BP Amoco v John Kelly* [2002] FSR 5; *Orange Personal Communications Services Application* [1998] ETMR 337; *Wm Wrigley Jr Company's Application* [1999] ETMR 214.
[7] Trade Marks Act 1996, s 8(1)(b).

washing product.[8] The Dutch courts have asked the ECJ to rule on whether Sounds can be registered as trade marks[9]

(ii)   'trade marks which consist exclusively of signs or indications which may serve, in trade, to designate the kind, quality, quantity, intended purpose, value, geographical origin, the time of production of goods or of rendering of services, or other characteristics of goods or services'.[10] In *Fry-Cadbury v Synott*[11] the Irish courts held that the term 'crunch' was essentially descriptive.

(iii)   'trade marks which consist exclusively of signs or indications which have become customary in the current language or in the bona fide and established practices of the trade'.[12]

[10.03] However a trade mark cannot be refused by reason of the above if, before the date of application for registration, it has in fact acquired a distinctive character as a result of the use made of it.[13] Failure to acquire a trade mark can be costly[14], as is illustrated by the English case of *Reality Group v Chance*.[15] One of the plaintiffs provided web design services under or by reference to the mark 'Reality'. It was acquired by one of the other plaintiffs and on 17 May 2000 an announcement was made, attended by considerable publicity, of the launch of business solution services under the mark 'Reality'. A couple of days later an application was made by the defendants to register the mark 'Reality' as a community trade mark. The plaintiff sought injunctive relief from the English courts, but it would have been far cheaper and easier for it to have simply registered its mark before it launched its product.

[10.04] Section 8 sets out the absolute grounds upon which a trade mark can be refused registration. The first of these relates to the qualities that are inherent in the sign itself. A sign cannot be registered as a trade mark if it consists exclusively of the shape which results from the nature of the goods themselves or the shape of goods which is necessary to obtain a technical result, the shape which gives substantial value to the goods.[16] However, it might be possible to register such a shape under the Industrial Designs Act. A trade mark should not be registered if it is contrary to public policy or to accepted principles of morality,[17] or it is of such a nature as to deceive the public, for instance as

---

8   See *Henkel v Office for Harmonisation in the Internal Market*, T337/99, (19 September 2001) ECJ.
9   See [2002] EIPR N-7.
10   Trade Marks Act 1996, s 8(1)(c).
11   *Fry-Cadbury v Synott* [1936] IR 700.
12   Trade Marks Act 1996, s 8(1)(d).
13   Trade Marks Act 1996, s 8(1).
14   One of the best examples is New Zealand's failure to protect the name 'Kiwi Fruit' with a trademark: 'the Kiwis relaunched the chinese gooseberry as kiwi fruit. It was an outstanding success but they failed to protect the name and soon kiwi fruit were being grown all over the world, with not a dollar going back to NZ'. Bennet, 'Oh Deer, Change The Name' (1999) Daily Telegraph (Australia), 10 March.
15   *Reality Group v Chance* [2002] FSR 13.
16   Trade Marks Act 1996, s 8(2).
17   See *French Connection Ltd v Sutton (t/a Teleconexus Email)* (2 December 1999) HC (Eng).

to the nature, quality or geographical origin of the goods or service.[18] Finally, a trade mark will not be registered if or to the extent that its use is prohibited in the State by any enactment or rule of law or by any provision of Community law, or if the application for registration is made in bad faith by the applicant.[19] Section 8 protects State emblems and symbols of authority from being registered as trade marks without the appropriate consent and the controller can refuse to register a mark that includes the national flag.[20]

[10.05] Section 10 sets out the 'relative' grounds for refusing to register a trade mark. A trade mark cannot be registered if it is identical to an earlier trade mark and the goods or services for which the trade mark is applied for are identical to the goods or services for which an earlier trade mark is protected. A trade mark cannot be registered if it is identical or similar to an earlier registered mark and there exists a likelihood of confusion on the part of the public, which includes the likelihood of association of the later trade mark with the earlier trade mark. If a mark that is identical to an earlier mark is to be registered but for different goods or services that registration may not take place if the earlier trade mark has a reputation in the state and the use of the later trade mark without due cause would take unfair advantage of, or be detrimental to, the distinctive character or reputation of the earlier trade mark. A trade mark which is identical to or similar to an earlier trade mark, and is to be registered for goods or services which are not similar to those for which the earlier trade mark is protected, cannot be registered if the earlier trade mark has a reputation and the use of the later trade mark without due cause would take unfair advantage of, or be detrimental to, the distinctive character or reputation of the earlier trade mark. In *General Motors v Yploon SA*[21] it was held by the ECJ that for an earlier trade mark to be protected by this provision it would have to be known by a significant part of the public concerned by the products or services covered by the mark. The ECJ held that this decision would have to be made taking into account all the relevant facts in the case, in particular the market share held by the trade mark, the intensity, geographical extent and duration of its use, and the size of the investment made by the undertaking promoting it.

[10.06] A trade mark cannot be registered if its use is liable to be prevented by virtue of any rule of law (in particular, the law of passing off) protecting an unregistered trade mark or other sign used in the course of trade or by virtue of an earlier right, other than those referred to above, in particular by virtue of the law of copyright, registered designs or any other law relating to a right to a name, a right of personal portrayal or an industrial property right. A trade mark can be revoked on grounds including the failure to use the mark for a period of five years, or that 'in consequence of acts or inactivity of the proprietor, it has become the common name in the trade for a product or service for which it is registered'.[22] The registration of a trade mark can also be declared invalid.

---

[18] Trade Marks Act 1996, s 8(3).
[19] Trade Marks Act 1996, s 8(4).
[20] Trade Marks Act 1996, s 9.
[21] *General Motors v Yploon SA* [1999] ECR I-5421, 2000 RPC 572, 1999 ETMR 122.
[22] Trade Marks Act 1996, s 51(1)(c).

[10.07] Trade marks can be assigned[23] and such transactions should be registered.[24] Licences may also be given.[25] Once a trade mark is registered its proprietor will have exclusive rights in it and his rights will be infringed by the use of that trade mark in the State without the proprietor's consent.[26] An action for infringement can be brought by the owner of the trade mark[27], and he or she will be entitled to all forms of relief by way of damages, injunctions, accounts or otherwise as are available to the proprietor in respect of the infringement of any other property right.[28] Delivery up orders may also be sought[29], but the statute also contains remedies for groundless threats of infringement proceedings.[30] Certain actions will particularly infringe upon the rights of a trade mark proprietor, such as using in the course of trade a sign which is identical to a trade mark in relation to goods or services which are identical to those for which it is registered. Another such infringing anchor involves using a sign where there exists a likelihood that the public would associate that sign with a registered trade mark. Infringement may result from using a sign which is identical to a trade mark which has a reputation in Ireland and the use of the sign, being without due cause, takes unfair advantage of, or is detrimental to, the distinctive character or the reputation of the trade mark. Use of a sign will include: affixing it to goods or packaging; offering or exposing goods for sale, marketing or stocking goods under the sign, or offering or supplying services under the sign; importing or exporting goods under the sign; or using the sign on business papers or in advertising.[31] The Act also specifies acts that will not infringe a trade mark; in particular one registered trade mark shall not be infringed by the use of another registered trade mark in relation to goods or services for which the latter is registered.[32] A registered trade mark will not be infringed by:

'(a) the use by a person of his own name or address;

(b) the use of indications concerning the kind, quality, quantity, intended purpose, value, geographical origin, the time of production of goods or of rendering of the service or other characteristics of goods or services; or

(c) the use of the trade mark where it is necessary to indicate the intended purpose of a product or service, in particular, as accessories or spare parts'.[33]

---

[23] Trade Marks Act 1996, s 28.

[24] Trade Marks Act 1996, s 29.

[25] Trade Marks Act 1996, s 32.

[26] Trade Marks Act 1996, s 13.

[27] Such actions should be brought promptly: 'It was in 1879 that James LJ observed that 'the very life of a trade mark depends on the promptitude with which it is vindicated', *Johnston v Orr-Ewing* (1879) 13 Ch D 434 at 464. Nothing has changed. Like gardens, trade mark cases always get worse with neglect – even if rights are not actually lost, delay is apt to turn what would be over in a few weeks by a quick application into a mini State Trial' per Jacob J in *Phones4u v Phone4u.co.uk Internet* [2006] EWCA Civ 244.

[28] Trade Marks Act 1996, s 18.

[29] Trade Marks Act 1996, s 20.

[30] Trade Marks Act 1996, s 24. The remedies are similar to those available under section – of the Patents Act 1992 and the Copyright and Related Rights Act 2000.

[31] Trade Marks Act 1996, s 14.

[32] Unless the latter mark is found to be invalid pursuant to s 52.

[33] Trade Marks Act 1996, s 15(2).

The Act does include the proviso that such use must be in accordance with honest practices in industrial and commercial matters.

The Community Trade mark

[10.08] The First Trade Mark Directive was adopted on 21 December 1988, and implemented belatedly in Ireland in the Trade Marks Act 1996. The Council Regulation on the Community Trade Mark[34] provides for the registration of Community trade marks: a community trade mark has a unitary character. It shall have equal effect throughout the Community: it shall not be registered, transferred or surrendered or be the subject of a decision revoking the rights of the proprietor or declaring it invalid, nor shall its use be prohibited, save in respect of the whole Community'.[35] The regulation provides for the registration and use of Community trade marks under conditions similar to those provided for in the 1989 Directive. The Community Trade Mark Office is located in Alicante in Spain.

Use of a trade mark on the Internet

[10.09] In *1-800 Flowers Incorporated v Phonenames Ltd*[36] the applicant argued that 'any use of a trade mark on any website, wherever the owner of the site was, was potentially a trade mark infringement anywhere in the world because website use is in an omnipresent cyberspace; that placing a mark on a web was "putting a tentacle" into the computer user's premises. However, Jacob J rejected this argument as 'absurd'.[37] This argument was briefly reviewed on appeal by Parker LJ who commented:

> 'There is something inherently unrealistic in saying that A 'uses' his mark in the United Kingdom when all that he does is to place the mark on the internet, from a location outside the United Kingdom, and simply wait in the hope that someone from the United Kingdom will download it and thereby create use on the part of A. By contrast, I can see that it might be more easily arguable that if A places on the internet a mark that is confusingly similar to a mark protected in another jurisdiction, he may do so at his peril that someone from that other jurisdiction may download it; though that approach conjured up in argument before us the potentially disturbing prospect that a shop in Arizona or Brazil that happens to bear the same name as a trademarked store in England or Australia will have to act with caution in answering telephone calls from those latter jurisdictions.'

[10.10] This judgment and that of Jacob J in *Euromarket Designs Inc v Peters and Crate & Barrel Ltd*[38] were subsequently reviewed by the English High Court in *Dearlove (t/a 'Diddy') v Combs (t/a 'Sean 'Puffy' Combs', 'Puffy' and 'PDiddy')*.[39] *Euromarket Designs Inc v Peters and Crate & Barrel Ltd* concerned a shop in Dun Laoghaire,

---

[34] Council Regulation on the Community Trade Mark (EC) No 40/94 of 20 December 1993, OJ NO. L 011, 14/01/1994 P. 0001–0032, amended by 394R3288 (OJ L 349 31.12.94, p 83) and Implemented by 395R2868 (OJ L 303 15.12.95, p 1).

[35] Council Regulation on the Community Trade Mark, art 1(2).

[36] *1-800 Flowers Incorporated v Phonenames Ltd* [2001] EWCA Civ 721.

[37] [2001] EWCA Civ 721, para 134.

[38] *Euromarket Designs Inc v Peters and Crate & Barrel Ltd* [2001] FSR 288, [2000] IP & T 1290.

[39] *Dearlove v Combs* [2007] EWHC 375 (Ch).

Ireland. It also ran an internet site under the domain name crateandbarrell.ie. The question before Jacob J was 'is it rational to say that the Defendants are using the words 'Crate & Barrel' in the United Kingdom in the course of trade in goods?'[40] Jacob J held that it was and endorsed Counsel's analogy that:

> 'the Internet was more like the user focusing a super-telescope into the site concerned; he asked me to imagine such a telescope set up on the Welsh hills overlooking the Irish Sea...Via the web you can look into the Defendant's shop in Dublin. Indeed the very language and the Internet conveys the idea of the user going to the site - 'visit' is the word.'

[10.11] In *Dearlove (t/a 'Diddy') v Combs (t/a 'Sean 'Puffy' Combs', 'Puffy' and 'PDiddy')*[41] Kitchen J reviewed these authorities and concluded that it could, stating that:

> 'placing a mark on the Internet from a location outside the UK can constitute use of that mark in the UK. The Internet is now a powerful means of advertising and promoting goods and services within the UK even though the provider himself is based abroad. The fundamental question is whether or not the average consumer of the goods or services in issue within the UK would regard the advertisement and site as being aimed and directed at him. All material circumstances must be considered and these will include the nature of the goods or services, the appearance of the website, whether it is possible to buy goods or services from the website, whether or not the advertiser has in fact sold goods or services in the UK through the website or otherwise, and any other evidence of the advertiser's intention'.[42]

So the Irish courts could conclude that placing a trade mark on a website outside Ireland could amount to use of that trade mark within Ireland.

Use of trade marks as domain names

[10.12] In *Fields v Klaus Kobec*[43] Sheldon QC concluded that registering a trade mark as a domain name is identical use of the trade mark in question. He stated that he had 'come to the conclusion that 'klauskobec.com' is identical use of the Mark, the addition of '.com' having no trade mark significance'.[44] The significance of registering a name as a trade mark is illustrated by the English High Court decision of *IBM v Web-Sphere*. In this case there was no allegation that the defendants were using these domain names as 'instruments of fraud', hence the plaintiff was not able to rely on *BT v One-in-a-million*. The plaintiff had a product, a computer program, which it marketed under the trade mark Websphere. This trade mark had been registered as a community trade mark on 6 May 1998. The defendant traded as Web-Sphere and had three domain names: www.web-sphere.com; www.web-sphere.net and www.web-sphere.org. The defendant had changed its name to Web-Sphere on 9 June 1999 and had registered its domain names on 12 May 1999. The defence argued that it was not replicating the plaintiff's mark. Its name

---

[40] *Euromarket Designs Inc v Peters and Crate & Barrel* [2001] FSR 288, [2000] IP & T 1290, para 24.
[41] *Dearlove v Combs* [2007] EWHC 375 (Ch).
[42] [2007] EWHC 375 (Ch), para 25.
[43] *Fields v Klaus Kobec* [2006] EWHC 350 (Ch).
[44] *Fields v Klaus Kobec* [2006] EWHC 350 (Ch), para 71.

contained a hyphen and this was sufficient to distinguish the two. The plaintiff's argument went as follows:

'The average consumer for the goods and services with which this case is concerned is a person who is a sophisticated computer user, and who uses the Internet. In accessing sites on the Internet, he types an address into his computer. What he types is a string of alphanumeric characters. The computer converts what is typed into a string of numbers. The string of numbers is then used by a router to connect the computer to the relevant web site. Each string of numbers is a Uniform (or Unique) Resource Locator ('URL') which is, in effect, a separate address. In converting the typed input into the URL the computer treats the hyphen in exactly the same way as it would treat any other character. Thus the hyphen serves an important function, namely to connect a computer to Web-Sphere, rather than to IBM. Since the average consumer is a sophisticated computer user and a user of the Internet, he will appreciate the necessity of absolute accuracy in typing an Internet address. Consequently the hyphen is not insignificant'.[45]

[10.13] Jacob J rejected this argument. He pointed out that it assumed that communication would only occur online, but both parties in fact promoted their names 'by more conventional visual means'.[46] However, the decision of Jacob J in *Phones4u v Phone4u.co.uk Internet*[47] complicates the position of trade mark owners who wish to allege that their rights are being infringed by the registration or use of a domain name. The plaintiffs, Phones4u, had registered their name as a trade mark and carried on a substantial trade under that mark. However, the plaintiff had limited their mark stating that it was 'limited to the colours red, white and blue'.[48] This was a problem for the plaintiffs: by agreeing to limit their claim to a coloured mark they could only claim an infringement where their mark was used in colour and specifically in the colours red, white and blue.

Use of trade marks on MySpace and YouTube

[10.14] MySpace was described by Kitchin J in *Dearlove (t/a 'Diddy') v Combs (t/a 'Sean 'Puffy' Combs', 'Puffy' and 'PDiddy')*[49] in the following terms:

'MySpace is something of an online cultural phenomenon. It describes itself as a social networking service that allows members to create personal profiles online in order to find and communicate with old and new friends. Members are able to maintain web-pages accessible by members of the public and which contain photographs, music, videos and text. MySpace is now widely used by artists as a way of promoting and marketing their music.'[50]

[10.15] YouTube was described as follows:

'YouTube is in some ways similar to MySpace, but concentrates on allowing users to share and view video footage online. It originally started as a personal video sharing service but, like MySpace, is now used by artists as a way of promoting their recordings and

---

[45] *IBM v Web-Sphere* [2004] EWHC 529, para 57.
[46] [2004] EWHC 529, para 58.
[47] *Phones4u v Phone4u.co.uk Internet* [2006] EWCA Civ 244.
[48] *Phones4u v Phone4u.co.uk Internet* [2006] EWCA Civ 244, para 49.
[49] *Dearlove v Combs* [2007] EWHC 375 (Ch).
[50] [2007] EWHC 375 (Ch), para 27.

performances. As Mr Calvert accepts, YouTube is a valuable promotional and marketing tool for many current music artists. Indeed, it is one of the fastest growing websites on the Internet.'[51]

Kitchen J held that placing a mark on MySpace and YouTube could amount to using that mark in the UK.[52]

Use of trade marks on search engines: Metatags and Adwords

[10.16] The use of trade marks in metatags and Google AdWords was recently reviewed by the US District Court for the Eastern District of Pennsylvania in *Wentworth v Settlement Funding.*[53] Metatags were described by the court thus:

'Meta tags' are pieces of the Hyper Text Markup Language ('HTML') source code which contain keywords used to describe the contents of a web page … Meta tags are invisible to Internet users but are used by search engines to index websites. Upon indexing relevant websites, a search engine uses algorithms to process the keywords in the meta tags to produce a search results page that displays links to relevant websites in a list typically in order of decreasing relevance.'

[10.17] Google Adwords is a commercial service, by which Google matches advertisements to search terms entered by users. The process was set out by the US District Court for the Eastern District of Pennsylvania in *Wentworth v Settlement Funding:*[54]

'Google's AdWords program is the keyword-triggered advertising program that generates the Sponsored Links section on the search-results screen. Advertisers participating in AdWords purchase or bid on certain keywords, paying Google for the right to have links to their websites displayed in the Sponsored Links section whenever an internet user searches for those words. Additionally, each time an internet user clicks on a particular Sponsored Link, Google charges a fee to the AdWords participant associated with that linked website. Businesses often participate in the AdWords program to generate more visits to their websites.'

The plaintiff alleged that the defendant had infringed its rights in its trade marks by purchasing AdWords that corresponded to those marks. Specifically it alleged that 'an internet search for those terms produces a Sponsored Link to defendant's website immediately proximate to the link to plaintiff's website on the search-results screen'. In response to the plaintiff's arguments, the defendant argued that:

'defendant's alleged uses of plaintiff's marks in this case through Google's AdWords program and in keyword meta tags in no way identify the source of the goods and services, as the alleged uses of the plaintiff's marks are confined to source code unpublished to potential consumers.'

[10.18] Ultimately the court held that using trade marks in this way was a breach of US trade marks legislation. But it went on to grant the defendant's motion to dismiss. The court did so because whilst the plaintiff had established that the defendant had

---

[51]   [2007] EWHC 375 (Ch), para 28.
[52]   [2007] EWHC 375 (Ch), para 36.
[53]   *Wentworth v Settlement Funding* [2007] WL 30115.
[54]   [2007] WL 30115.

wrongfully used its marks, this wrongful use had not resulted in a likelihood of confusion sufficient to amount to a breach. To reach this conclusion, the court distinguished the previous decision of the Ninth Circuit Court of Appeals in California in *Brookfield Communications v West Coast Entertainment.*[55] It did so on the basis that the Ninth Circuit's judgment was based upon:

> 'a material mischaracterization of the operation of internet search engines The Ninth Circuit described a process whereby internet users who were searching for the plaintiff's products would be 'taken by a search engine to' the defendant's website. The District Court pointed out that search engine's do not work like this.

> At no point are potential consumers 'taken by a search engine' to defendant's website due to defendant's use of plaintiff's marks in meta tags. Rather, as in the present case, a link to defendant's website appears on the search results page as one of many choices for the potential consumer to investigate. As stated above, the links to defendant's website always appear as independent and distinct links on the search result pages regardless of whether they are generated through Google's AdWords program or search of the keyword meta tags of defendant's website.'

There was no allegation that the defendant's advertisement or links incorporated the plaintiff's trade marks in any discernable way. Therefore the District Court dismissed the plaintiff's claim as it could not establish that the defendant's use of its marks was causing confusion.

[10.19] This approach would appear consistent with that of the English Court of Appeal in *Reed Executive v Reed Business Information.*[56] The judgment of Jacob J first considered the use of the plaintiff's trade mark to trigger banner or pop-up ads which were generated by the Yahoo! search engine. Giving judgment for the Court, Jacob J held that he could not:

> 'see that causing the unarguably inoffensive-in-itself banner to appear on a search under the name 'Reed' or 'Reed jobs' can amount to an … infringement. The web-using member of the public knows that all sorts of banners appear when he or she does a search and they are or may be triggered by something in the search. He or she also knows that searches produce fuzzy results – results with much rubbish thrown in. The idea that a search under the name Reed would make anyone think there was a trade connection between a totaljobs banner making no reference to the word 'Reed' and Reed Employment is fanciful. No likelihood of confusion was established'.[57]

[10.20] Jacob J came to a similar conclusion in relation to meta tags. Jacob J was willing to assume that meta tag use could amount to use of a trade mark, but even if he did 'there

---

[55] *Brookfield Communications, Inc v West Coast Entertainment Corp* 174 F 3d 1036 (9th Cir 1999).

[56] *Reed Executive plc and another v Reed Business Information Ltd and others* [2004] EWCA Civ 159.

[57] [2004] EWCA Civ 159, at para 140. Jacob J went on to note 'That is not to say, of course, that if anyone actually clicked through (and few did) and found an infringing use, there could not be infringement. Whether there was or not would depend solely on the site content, not the banner'. [2004] EWCA Civ 159, at para 141.

is simply no confusion here'.[58] Whilst reserving his opinion on this point, Jacob J pointed out that there were 'several difficult questions' here:

(i) 'does metatag use count as use of a trade mark at all? In this context it must be remembered that use is important not only for infringement but also for saving a mark from non-use. In the latter context it would at least be odd that a wholly invisible use could defeat a non-use attack ... Uses read only by computers may not count – they never convey a message to anyone.'

(ii) 'If metatag use does count as use, is there infringement if the marks and goods or services are identical? This is important: one way of competing with another is to use his trade mark in your metatag – so that a search for him will also produce you in the search results. Some might think this unfair – but others that this is good competition provided that no-one is misled.'

[10.21] The above decisions are both quite specific to the technologies that they discuss. But a couple of conclusions can be drawn from them. First, there is continuing confusion as to whether 'invisible' use of a trade mark as a meta tag or as a term in an advertisement allocation program can amount to infringement. Second, it would seem highly likely that causing individuals to view advertisements that do not directly infringe trade marks cannot create the necessary likelihood of confusion. The fact that those advertisements are generated in response to the entry of a trade mark into a search engine would seem to be irrelevant.

---

[58] [2004] EWCA Civ 159, para 148.

Chapter 11

Domain Names

Introduction

[11.01] The American courts have described domain names in the following terms:

> 'The Internet has been described as 'a vast system of interconnected computers and computer net works' Each computer that is connected to the Internet has a unique Internet Protocol ('IP') number that functions as a kind of Internet address. An IP number consists of four sets of numbers separated by periods. Early Internet innovators created the Domain Name System ('DNS'), a system designed to relate easily-remembered domain names with difficult-to-remember IP numbers. Domain names are comprised of alphanumeric fields separated by dots — eg, <www.courtinfo.ca.gov> — where the field farthest to the right ('gov' in the example) is the Top Level Domain ('TLD'). The field second from the TLD is the Second Level Domain; and the field third from the TLD is the Third Level Domain.'[1]

[11.02] Every site on the Internet will have an IP address, which is a sequence of numbers. Names are easier to find and remember than numbers and this is the function fulfilled by domain names. Each active domain name should correspond to an IP address, so http://www.ictlaw.com corresponds to the IP address 81.17.252.40. Domain names were particularly significant before the development of modern search engines such as Google. In the late 1990s, typing a domain name into the address bar of a computer was the easiest way of finding a site. As search engines improved, the importance of having an obvious domain name has declined. Whilst their relative importance may have declined, domain names remain valuable commodities. Domain names can be divided into two separate categories: generic domain names (gTLD) and country domain names (ccTLD.) At the time of writing the following gTLDs were recognised:

   (i)   the .aero domain, which is reserved for members of the air-transport industry and is sponsored by Société Internationale de Télécommunications Aéronautiques (SITA);

   (ii)   the .asia domain, which is restricted to the Pan-Asia and Asia Pacific community and is operated by DotAsia Organisation;

---

[1] See *Kramer v Network Solutions (NSI)* (January 2003) US Ct of Apps (9th Cir), No 01-15899 DC No CV-98-20718-JW, Northern District of California, San Jose. See also the description given by Aldous LJ in *BT v One in a Million* [1998] 4 All ER 476, [1999] 1 WLR 903, [1999] RPC 1: 'A domain name comprises groups of alphanumeric characters separated by dots. A first group commonly comprises the name of the enterprise or a brand name or trading name associated with it, followed by a "top level" name identifying the nature and sometimes the location of the organisation.'

(iii)   the .biz domain, which is restricted to businesses and is operated by NeuLevel, Inc;

(iv)   the .cat domain, which is reserved for the Catalan linguistic and cultural community and is sponsored by Fundació puntCat;

(v)   the .com domain, which is operated by VeriSign Global Registry Services;

(vi)   the .coop domain, which is reserved for cooperative associations and is sponsored by Dot Cooperation LLC;

(vii)   the .info domain, which is operated by Afilias Limited;

(viii)   the .jobs domain, which is reserved for human resource managers and is sponsored by Employ Media LLC;

(ix)   the .mobi domain, which is reserved for consumers and providers of mobile products and services and is sponsored by mTLD Top Level Domain, Ltd;

(x)   the .museum domain, which is reserved for museums and is sponsored by the Museum Domain Management Association;

(xi)   the .name domain, which is reserved for individuals and is operated by Global Name Registry;

(xii)   the .net domain, which is operated by VeriSign Global Registry Services;

(xiii)   the .org domain, which is operated by Public Interest Registry. It is intended to serve the non commercial community, but all are eligible to register within .org;

(xiv)   the .pro domain is restricted to credentialed professionals and related entities and is operated by RegistryPro;

(xv)   the .tel domain is reserved for businesses and individuals to publish their contact data and is sponsored by Telnic Ltd;

(xvi)   the .travel domain, which is reserved for entities whose primary area of activity is in the travel industry and is sponsored by Tralliance Corporation.

A number of other gTLD domains also exist, such as .gov (reserved for the US government); .mil (reserved for the US military) and, .int (reserved for recognised public international organisations). The country domain assigned to Ireland is .ie, which is currently administered by IEDR and subject to regulation by ComReg.

[11.03] The precise nature of a domain name was analysed by the US Court of Appeals for the Ninth Circuit in *Kremen v Online Classifieds Inc.*[2] The US court held that a publicly-funded company which provided gratuitous registration of Internet domain names could be liable in conversion, on a footing of strict liability, for transferring a registered name to a third party, having acted in good faith on the authority of a forged letter. The US court held that the domain name was intangible property which could be converted in the same way as a chattel and that the registration company could be liable for its value. This decision was described as 'remarkable' by Hoffman LJ in *Douglas v Hello!*.[3] Hoffman LJ went on to comment that whilst he had 'no difficulty with the proposition that a domain name may be intangible property, like a copyright or trade

---

[2]   *Kremen v Online Classifieds Inc* (2003) 337 F 3rd 1024.
[3]   *Douglas v Hello!* [2007] UKHL 21.

mark, but the notion that a registrar of such property can be strictly liable for the common law tort of conversion is, I think, foreign to English law'.[4]

[11.04] As they are key elements of the Internet, domain names are both relatively recent and controversial. The controversies that have surrounded the registration and administration of domain names have included the following issues:

(i)   The global domain name system is administered by ICANN in the USA. Whilst this reflects the history of the Internet, retaining control of ICANN in the USA had been perceived as giving the USA a significant advantage in controlling how the Internet develops.[5]

(ii)   The management of individual domain name registries and registrars. Examples of such controversies include: the pacific state of Tuvalu – making its country domain .tv available on a global basis[6]; the fraudulent transfer of the domain name sex.com[7]; or the failure of domain name administrator registryfly.com.[8]

(iii)   Most prominently, the infringement of intellectual property through the registration of domain names. In large part it is this latter controversy that is the subject of the subsequent chapter.

The administration of the .ie domain

[11.05] The Irish domain suffix is .ie. At the time of writing this is administered by the IEDR, a private limited company.[9] Historically the .ie domain was administered by UCD, which transferred this function to IEDR, an 'independent not for profit organisation'.[10] A Ministerial power to regulate the .ie domain was created by Part 4 of the Electronic Commerce Act 2000. This power has now been transferred to ComReg by the Communications Regulation (Amendment) Act 2007. Under this legislation the purpose of regulating the '.ie' domain is 'to facilitate easy comprehension, fairness, transparency, avoidance of deception, promotion of fair competition and public confidence with respect to the use of '.ie' domain names.'[11]

---

4   [2007] UKHL 21, para 101.

5   The administration of the domain names has provoked continuous controversy, see Crampton, 'Adult Web site suffix rejected by regulator' (2007) International Herald Tribune, 31 March: 'Supporters of the .xxx proposal on the ICANN board argued that the agency's proper role is to serve as a technical arbiter about the feasibility of new domain names, not to discriminate on the basis of content'.

6   Baram, 'Drowning in money' (2005) The Guardian, 25 March.

7   *Kremen v Online Classifieds Inc* (2003) 337 F 3rd 1024, for an account of the facts behind this case, see McCarthy, 'Sex.com' Quercus, 2007.

8   'ICANN Welcomes GoDaddy.com Takeover of RegisterFly Data' (2007) ICANN, Press Release, 29 May. See 'Domain review' (2007) The Advertiser (Australia), 28 May.

9   Previously the domain had been administered by UCD: Costello, 'Domain Registry to be privatised' (2007) The Irish Times, 18 February; Lyons, 'UCD to shed role in Internet domain' (1997) The Irish Times, 19 December.

10   http://www.iedr.ie/AboutUs.php.

11   Electronic Commerce Act 2000, s 32(1).

[11.06] Prior to regulating, ComReg must consult with the Minister for Enterprise, Trade and Employment and such other persons as it feels are appropriate.[12] It is an offence to use an .ie domain name that has not been registered in accordance with such regulations.[13] First, ComReg has the power to 'specify an entity as the authority authorised to register ".ie" domain names'.[14] ComReg also has the power to designate an interim authority.[15] This interim designation will be for a period that cannot exceed 12 months and may be on such terms as are specified by ComReg.[16] It may then be renewed for a further period of 12 months.[17] Second, ComReg may prescribe the 'circumstances and manner' under which an application for registration or renewal of an ".ie" domain name may be made or refused. ComReg may also specify the fees to be paid in respect of such applications. Third, ComReg may empower the registering authority to revoke registrations 'in specified circumstances'. Fourth, ComReg may confer a right of appeal against these decisions and provide procedures for such appeals. Finally, ComReg gives the general power to create regulations which are necessary or desirable for the purposes set out above. However, this last general power is of limited consequence in the light of the decision of the Supreme Court in *Mulcreevy v Minister for the Environment*.[18] Contravention of such regulations is an offence, punishable on summary conviction to a fine not exceeding €5,000. ComReg may impose a levy on the entity authorised to register domain names to meet the expenses incurred in performing the functions set out above.[19] Finally, ComReg has at all times a statutory power to 'access … all internet ".ie" domain name databases and any associated records'.[20]

[11.07] At the time of writing, ComReg has yet to implement these new powers and the IEDR is still administered in accordance with its own internal procedures. It would seem highly likely that the allocation of domain names by the IEDR and the general administration of the registry can be judicially reviewed. Certainly in *Zockoll v Telecom Éireann*[21] the High Court took the view that the administration of alpha-numeric phone numbers by Telecom Éireann could be subject to a judicial review. Kelly J took the view that the defendant was placed in the same position as the VHI in *Callanan v VHI*,[22] in which case Keane J held that the defendant as 'a public body established by the Oireachtas with statutorily defined objects and powers...must use the powers entrusted to it fairly and reasonably'. Keane J went on to state that while the actions of the VHI

> 'might have been unexceptional in legal terms in the case of a private commercial firm vigorously defending its own interests, they were not however, a fair and reasonable use of

---

[12] Electronic Commerce Act 2000, s 32(3).
[13] Electronic Commerce Act 2000, s 32(2).
[14] Electronic Commerce Act 2000, s 32(4)(a).
[15] Electronic Commerce Act 2000, s 35(1).
[16] Electronic Commerce Act 2000, s 35(2).
[17] Electronic Commerce Act 2000, s 35(3).
[18] *Mulcreevy v Minister for the Environment* [2004] 1 IR 72.
[19] Electronic Commerce Act 2000, s 33(1).
[20] Electronic Commerce Act 2000, s 34(1).
[21] *Zockoll v Telecom Éireann* [1997] IEHC 178, [1998] 3 IR 287.
[22] *Callanan v VHI* (22 April 1993, unreported) HC (Keane J).

the powers entrusted expressly and by implication to the VHI by the Oireachtas for the common good and I am, accordingly, satisfied that the plaintiffs are entitled to appropriate relief in respect of those actions'.

In Kelly J's opinion this judgment had equal application to the *Zockoll* case and he took the view that 'in exercising such discretion as it has in relation to the withdrawal of telephone numbers which have been allocated to a customer, the defendant must use the powers entrusted to it fairly and reasonably'.[23]

[11.08] However, Kelly J was not satisfied that public law principles would apply to the commercial relationship which exists between the defendant and its customers. The IEDR is not established under statute and whilst its functions may be regulated by ComReg pursuant to a statutory function, such regulations have yet to be made. But a good argument can be made that the relationship between the IEDR and those who wish to register domain names is a public one, and therefore subject to judicial review. As Denham J stated in *Beirne v Commissioner of An Garda Síochána*:[24]

'The principle which, in general, excludes from the ambit of judicial review decisions made in the realm of private law by persons or tribunals whose authority derives from contract is … confined to cases or instances where the duty being performed by the decision making authority is manifestly a private duty and where his right to make it derives solely from contract or solely from consent or the agreement of the parties affected. Where the duty being carried out by a decision-making authority … is of a nature which might ordinarily be seen as coming within the public domain, that decision can only be excluded from the reach of the jurisdiction in judicial review if it can be shown that it solely and exclusively derived from an individual contract made in private law'.[25]

---

[23] Kelly J found support for this view in the judgment of the English Court of Appeal in *Timeload Ltd v British Telecom Plc* [1995] EMLR 459. In this case the plaintiff had acquired the number 0800-192 192, but in the UK 192 is the number for directory enquiries. The plaintiff was using this number to supply a commercial directory enquiry service to the public. The defendants withdrew the number from the plaintiff on the basis that it had been acquired through misrepresentation and the defendant was concerned that the public would be confused by the number and would assume that there was some connection between the plaintiff and the defendant. On appeal, Bingham MR stated: 'It is therefore correct, speaking very generally, to regard BT as a privatised company, no longer a monopoly but still a very dominant supplier closely regulated to ensure that it operates in the interests of the public ... I can see strong grounds for the view that in the circumstances of this contract BT should not be permitted to exercise a potentially drastic power of termination without demonstrable reason or cause for doing so.'

[24] *Beirne v Commissioner of An Garda Síochána* [1993] ILRM 1.

[25] [1993] ILRM 1 at 2. For a more pragmatic approach, see the dicta of O'Flaherty J in *Geoghegan v Institute of Chartered Accountants in Ireland* [1995] 3 IR 86: 'in my judgment the actual *form* of procedure used to judicially review an action by a body entrusted with great powers which can effect the livelihood of persons is of secondary importance. It may be that the most appropriate procedure in any given case is the one that gets the case on quickest'. As Walsh J observed in *The State (Lynch) v Cooney* [1982] IR 337 at p 373: 'the quicker the procedure available the better for everyone' [1995] 3 IR 86 at 121.

[11.09] Although the IEDR is a private limited company, it could probably be regarded as a public body as the register that it administers may be regulated under Part 4 of the Electronic Commerce Act 2000. The public nature of this register was acknowledged by the Minister who introduced the Act, who stated 'The 'ie' domain name is a national resource which should be managed in the public interest and in the interests of the Internet community'.[26]

Therefore, it may be possible to judicially review decisions of the IEDR.[27] Judicial review of decisions of a public registry does offer significant advantages to applicants: a broad range of remedies are available, the process may be quicker and evidence will usually be provided on affidavit. A judicial review will assess the fairness and appropriateness of the procedures followed in taking a decision and thus might be appropriate for some cases. But in other cases framing what is essentially a claim for the tort of passing off or a trade mark infringement action as an administrative law matter may prove cumbersome.

Zockoll v Telecom Éireann

[11.10] *Zockoll v Telecom Éireann*[28] concerned the allocation of alpha-numeric telephone numbers[29], which may be compared to domain names. The plaintiffs in this case owned the trade marks 'Dyno' and 'Dyna'. The second-named plaintiff was a subsidiary of the first and ran a drain-cleaning franchise business in the UK and Ireland. The third plaintiff was also a subsidiary of the first and it had been set up to promote the concept of alpha-numeric marketing. This company would lease telephone numbers from telephone companies and then licence them to third parties through Phone Names. The example of its *modus operandi* given by Kelly J was that it would identify a business sector such as building societies. It would then identify the generic words used everyday in that business, such as 'mortgage' or 'home loans'. It would then request from a service provider like Telecom Éireann the telephone number that would correspond to the letters making up 'mortgage' or 'home loans'. Once that was done, it would create service marks and marketing slogans (known as 'strap lines') allied to the business of building societies which would then be marketed to the industry.

---

26 The Minister for Public Enterprise, Mary O'Rourke TD, Seanad Éireann – Volume 162 – 14 April, 2000, Electronic Commerce Bill 2000: Second Stage.

27 An attempt to review Nominet, the UK domain name administrator failed before the English High Court in *CyberBritain Group Ltd v Nominet UK* (2005) The Times, 16 June. But, the failure apparently related to the applicant's failure to adhere to time limits. See Richardson, 'What's in a name?' (2006) New Law Journal, 28 April and Ellison, 'Nominet faces High Court over iTunes row' (2005) Timesonline, 16 June.

28 *Zockoll v Telecom Éireann* [1997] IEHC 178, [1998] 3 IR 287.

29 Alpha-numeric numbers are common in the USA although they have never come into use in Ireland. In this system, eight of the numbers on a telephones key-pad have letters assigned to them. So ABC is assigned to 2, DEF is assigned to 3 and so on. The system works by allowing people to remember words instead of numbers so somebody who wants to ring a doctor will dial 1-800-DOCTOR instead of 1800362867. This is not dissimilar to the domain name system where the IP address 81.17.252.40 corresponds to the domain name http://www.ictlaw.com.

[11.11] The defendant, Telecom Éireann, supplied and serviced various freephone (1-800) numbers, which were issued as standard numbers and not generic phone names or alpha-numeric numbers. A customer could request either a random 1-800 number or a choice 1-800 number. If the customer choose a random number, then he or she would pay less than if they chose a choice number. These numbers would be supplied on a first-come, first-served basis and Kelly J and all expert witnesses in the case agreed that this was the best method of allocation. At the time, Kelly J was satisfied that there was little awareness in Ireland of the fact that an easily remembered alpha numeric sequence such as 1-800-FLOWERS might ultimately be of more value than an easily remembered number sequence such as 1-800-123 456. In May 1995 the plaintiff applied for eight 1-800 numbers in Ireland which would correspond to numbers they already held in the UK. These numbers were available from Telecom Éireann and were supplied to the plaintiffs. An application form was filled out in respect of each of the eight numbers. The plaintiff described its business as 'property services' and the reason for using the service was described as 'marketing'. The numbers requested from the defendant included numbers which correspond to words such as 'florist', 'service' and 'insure'. The plaintiffs agreed to pay connection charges and so forth in respect of these numbers and they carried out their obligations in this regard.

[11.12] In November of 1995 the defendant wrote a letter to the plaintiffs, which noted that under art 51 of the Telecommunications Scheme 1994, subscribers to Telecom Éireann's services did not have any proprietary right in their numbers. Furthermore, Telecom Éireann pointed out that it had reserved to itself the right to alter or replace a subscriber's telephone number at any time. The plaintiffs were given notice that with effect from the end of November it would be withdrawing service on the plaintiffs' numbers. The parties entered into a correspondence and, one of the demands of the plaintiff was that they should be given an explanation from the defendant for taking away the numbers. The defendant's representative, Ms O'Byrne, gave four reasons: 'operational reasons', the numbers were seldom used, the numbers were useful vanity numbers and, finally, the defendant believed that the plaintiff was brokering the numbers. The parties corresponded vigorously during the start of December 1995 during which the plaintiff requested that a further 270 choice numbers be assigned to them. These would have covered 1-800 numbers such as the equivalent of 1-800-SOLICITOR and 1-800-LEGAL AID.

[11.13] The plaintiffs initiated a legal action against the defendants, which was heard over some 20 days and judgment was given by Kelly J on 28 November 1997. The plaintiffs sought to prevent the defendants from withdrawing the remaining six of the original eight numbers which were allocated to them and to have the further 270 numbers which they sought allocated to them. The plaintiff claimed that they were entitled to these numbers under contract law and furthermore that the defendant was abusing its dominant position contrary to art 86 of the Treaty of Rome. The defendant contested all these allegations.

The decision to withdraw the numbers

[11.14] Kelly J was satisfied that there was only one reason why the defendant decided to withdraw the telephone numbers and this was that the defendant feared that the plaintiff was going to engage in 'brokering' these numbers. This was the process by which, in the words of one of the defendant's witnesses 'a number will be rented from us for onward sale or rent to another customer'.[30] This witness was a Mr Donnelly, who took the decision to withdraw the numbers. Kelly J was critical of the decision-making process within Telecom Éireann. Mr Donnelly was told by his staff that the plaintiffs were engaged in brokering in the UK. However, this was never written down, Mr Donnelly never saw any of the relevant documentation but he trusted what he was told by his colleagues and subordinates. Kelly J was satisfied that Mr Donnelly did not have a proper understanding of the plaintiff's business practices at the time that he made this decision and that the defendant's thinking on this matter was 'confused'.

[11.15] The brokering allegations against the defendant appear to have arisen from a conference on telemarketing organised by the defendant towards the end of 1995. Ms O'Byrne approached a Mr McCann to speak at the conference; Mr McCann is the owner of the 1-800-FLOWERS business in the USA. Mr McCann spoke at the conference and his appearance was very successful. Prior to his appearance at the conference he had expressed an interest in obtaining the 1-800-FLOWERS number for himself in Ireland but this had already been allocated to the plaintiffs. In October 1995 Ms O'Byrne wrote to Mr McCann to tell him that they had written to the defendants informing them that the relevant number was being retrieved. Further to this on 30 November 1995, Mr McCann wrote to Ms Byrne, informing her that he had been engaged in negotiations to try and buy the 1-800-FLOWERS number from the plaintiffs in the UK. Mr McCann also held out the prospect that once the plaintiff's claim on these numbers in Ireland and the UK had been removed, he would then contemplate setting up a small telecentre in Ireland. This letter enclosed copies of correspondence which had been entered into between the plaintiffs and Mr McCann; one letter in particular set out a draft contract which had been sent to Mr McCann by the plaintiffs. When this was put to Mr Donnelly in cross-examination he could not recall reading it and he agreed that it put a construction on the relationship between Mr McCann and the plaintiffs that was different to the understanding which he had at the time that he made the decision to withdraw these numbers from the plaintiffs. He confirmed in cross-examination that the sole and exclusive legal reason he withdrew the numbers was that he believed that they were being brokered. The sole and exclusive commercial reason was because he wanted to give the 1-800-FLOWERS number to Mr McCann.

[11.16] Kelly J was satisfied that the defendant had an incorrect understanding of the relationship between the plaintiffs and Mr McCann. The real position was that the plaintiffs were attempting to set up a number of franchises in the UK based on the alpha-numeric system, and were endeavouring to create brand-value in these numbers. They approached British Telecom and made presentations to 30 major companies with a view to trying to get them to advertise on the 1-800 system. One number that they were particularly interested in exploiting was 1-800-FLOWERS and they applied for the trade mark in 1-800-FLOWERS in the UK, prior to Mr McCann doing so. None of this was known to Mr Donnelly at the time when he decided to deprive the plaintiffs of the numbers. In Kelly J's view the decision to remove the original eight numbers was based

---

[30] p 35 of Kelly's J judgment.

on a misunderstanding of the plaintiff's method of trade together with a desire to accommodate the commercial concerns of Mr McCann. This was not sufficient to justify the decisions taken. Furthermore, any doubts which the defendants might have had with regard to the plaintiffs should have been assuaged by the fact that the plaintiffs were willing to give undertakings relating to their future conduct. [31]

The exercise of the defendant's powers

[11.17] Kelly J considered that Telecom Éireann could only withdraw telephone numbers in very limited circumstances:

'the "absolute discretion" given to the defendant to alter the subscriber's telephone number may only be exercised if it can be shown

(a) that the subscriber is in breach of his contract with the defendant, or

(b) circumstances exist which in the interest of some revision of the Telecommunications Service it is necessary to change the subscriber's telephone number'. [32]

Kelly J was satisfied that there were no such reasons in this case, hence the defendant was not entitled to take the action which it did take. The plaintiffs took issue with the procedures followed by the defendant and Kelly J was satisfied that if the rules of natural justice applied in this situation, then the defendant's procedures would not comply with the *audi alteram partem* rule. However, he was not satisfied that public law principles would apply to the commercial relationship which exist between the defendant and its customers. But, Kelly J was

'quite satisfied that the procedure adopted by the defendant in this case could not be regarded as a fair and reasonable use of the powers entrusted to it. As I have already held that such powers must be exercised fairly and reasonably, it follows that the procedure adopted by the defendant in the instant case was fatally flawed. In my view there was no entitlement to serve the notice in question without at least affording the plaintiffs an opportunity to explain their position in the light of the information that the defendant had in its possession.'

Therefore, Kelly J found that the plaintiffs were entitled to have the original eight numbers restored.

[11.18] Kelly J also found that the plaintiff was entitled to the remaining 270 numbers. He was satisfied that in common with practically every service provider in the US and the UK, the defendant operates a policy of allocating numbers on a first-come, first-served basis. There was no evidence that any of these numbers had been allocated to a party other than the plaintiff. Kelly J held that:

'In my opinion the defendant is under a statutory duty to allocate the numbers to the plaintiffs save and except where such numbers might already have been allocated to another person or where there are other good and objectively justifiable reasons present.

---

[31] See also the decision of the High Court in *Zockoll Group Ltd [Formerly Phonenames Ltd] v Controller of Patents Designs & Trade Marks* [2006] IEHC 300; and the English decision of the Court of Appeal in *1-800 Flowers Incorporated v Phonenames Ltd* [2001] EWCA Civ 721.

[32] *Zockoll v Telecom Éireann* [1997] IEHC 178, [1998] 3 IR 287, para 95.

> The defendant, in my view, is in breach of its statutory obligation by failing to allocate the numbers to the Plaintiffs and continuing to maintain that it will not do so.'

Kelly J suggested that this approach to the matter was but another aspect of the application of the obligation which had been placed upon the defendant to exercise its powers and entitlements in a fair and reasonable way. He suggested that there might be one exception to this; the defendant could refuse to allocate a number which was of national importance, such as an emergency number.

The significance of Zockall v Telecom Éireann[33]

[11.19] The decision of Kelly J in *Zockall v Telecom Éireann* is significant for a number of reasons.

(i)   Kelly J endorsed the use of a first-come, first-served method of allocating phone numbers in this case. Whether this endorsement can be applied as a precedent in other cases is very much open to question. However, Kelly J's finding may have some influence when deciding on a policy for allocating domain names.

(ii)   The defendant in *Zockall v Telecom Éireann* alleged that the plaintiffs were brokering the names. Kelly J held the defendant's allegations of brokering had been based on the following facts: 'they had accumulated numbers which … (the defendant) thought did not relate to the Zockoll business … they had made little use of the numbers and … they had accumulated numbers in other countries'.[34] So merely accumulating a large number of domain names which are unused may not be, of itself, sufficient to establish that an individual is attempting to broker those names. But Kelly J made this decision on the basis that the plaintiff was genuinely in the process of establishing a franchise business.

(iii) Kelly J held that the plaintiff was able to assuage the defendant's suspicions and establish its bona fides before Kelly J by offering the defendant: 'undertakings concerning their future conduct which are capable of being summarily enforced'.[35] These undertakings required that the plaintiffs actually establish their franchise business, and each undertaking was: 'capable of being enforced in a summary way and, if breached, would have very serious consequences for the plaintiffs'.[36]

(iv)   Most significantly, although Kelly J was not convinced that public law would apply to Telecom Éireann's allocation of phone numbers, he did hold that Telecom Éireann had to discharge these functions 'fairly and reasonably Telecom Éireann should have afforded the plaintiffs an opportunity to be heard before considering whether to transfer the numbers in question'.[37] Telecom

---

[33]   *Zockoll v Telecom Éireann* [1997] IEHC 178, [1998] 3 IR 287.

[34]   [1997] IEHC 178, [1998] 3 IR 287, para 64–65.

[35]   [1997] IEHC 178, [1998] 3 IR 287, para 89.

[36]   [1997] IEHC 178, [1998] 3 IR 287, para 90.

[37]   [1997] IEHC 178, [1998] 3 IR 287, para 99.

Éireann could not arbitrarily take numbers away from one client and give them to another simply because it wanted to.

The assignment of domain names by the IEDR

[11.20] At the time of writing registration for a domain name is subject to IEDR's rules. These rules attempt to impose restrictions upon those who apply for domain names. The first restriction is geographic.

(i)   To apply for an '.ie' domain name an applicant must be a resident within the 32 Counties of Ireland' or else be able to 'demonstrate a Real and Substantive Connection with Ireland Such a connection may be demonstrated by the production of documents such as 'High-quality brochures.'

(ii) The second restriction might be described as a limited form of qualitative restriction. IEDR restricts the registration of domain name to those who can establish some form of entitlement to the name. This restriction would not seem insurmountable for individuals or businesses who wish to register their own name.

(iii) Previously individuals could register only their initials followed by a two digit number so Denis Kelleher could register dk01.ie or Karen Murray could register km07.ie. Following a consultation process to relax this policy, any individual resident on the island of Ireland is now entitled to register their full name or slight variations of their name (eg karenmurray.ie, kmurray.ie, k-murray.ie). Individuals must produce documentary evidence of their name, such as a passport or a birth certificate. The IEDR also provides for a 'discretionary name'.

(iv) Registered companies can register their company name; this must be proven by reference to their company's office registration number. So too can holders of registered business names, state agencies, publications, educational institutions and unincorporated associations such as clubs or societies.

(v)   Trade mark owners can register their trademark as a domain name and they may also register domains that are similar to their trademark but contain 'plurals, descriptors, or non-descriptive elements such as numbers or letters and may also differ in respect of signs, symbols or punctuation'.

[11.21] Registering a generic domain name under these seeming restrictive rules may be inconvenient, but it can be done. A review of the IEDR WHOIS register would suggest that first registering a name under the Register of Business Names Act 1963 and then registering that name as a domain name is a proven method of registering generic domain names. And this impression is reinforced by a review of rulings under the IEDR dispute resolution policy. The 'managed' policy of IEDR may be contrasted with that of the EC which explicitly endorsed the first-come, first-served principle when it established the .eu domain.[38] Such a managed policy is not unique: for example the .asia domain restricts registrations to 'Legal entities within the Pan-Asia and Asia-Pacific region'.[39]

---

[38]   Commission Regulation 874/2004, art 2.

[39]   http://www.dotasia.org/about/faq.html#q21.

The IEDR policy on disputes

[11.22] Innumerable domain names are possible, but only some domain names will be valuable. Given this reality, disputes about the limited number of valuable domain names are inevitable. To deal with these disputes, the IEDR utilises an arbitration process provided by the WIPO Arbitration and Mediation Centre. Anyone who registers with IEDR must agree to 'submit to a mandatory administrative proceeding before an independent and impartial panel'. Paragraph 1 of the IEDR policy places on the complainant the obligation to establish a *prima facie* case that:

(i)   the domain name at issue is identical or misleadingly similar to a protected identifier in which the complainant has rights; and

(ii)   the registrants have no rights in law or legitimate interests in respect of the domain name at issue; and

(iii)   the domain name at issue has been registered or is being used in bad faith.[40]

[11.23] The policy sets out what can be considered as evidence of registration in bad faith[41] or evidence of legitimate rights.[42] The policy is very similar, although not identical, to the standard unified dispute resolution procedure used by ICANN,[43] and this similarity has been invoked by WIPO panellists when arbitrating disputes.[44] Some would say that the WIPO arbitration process is biased in favour of trade mark owners,[45] although others say that any apparent bias is an advantage.[46] However, it would not seem that trade mark holders can be compelled to invoke the ADR process. In *Tesco v*

---

40   IEDR, Mandatory Administrative Proceeding, para 1.

41   IEDR, Mandatory Administrative Proceeding, para 2.

42   IEDR, Mandatory Administrative Proceeding, para 3.

43   *Uniform Domain Name Dispute Resolution Policy* Adopted by ICANN on August 26, 1999, http://www.icann.org/udrp/udrp-policy-24oct99.htm

44   See: *Department of Arts, Sport and Tourism v Odyssey Internet Portal Ltd*, WIPO Arbitration and Mediation Centre Case No DIE2005-0002, para 6; and, *Eoin Murphy and Ciaran Murphy trading as Wise Owl v Paul Baird* WIPO Arbitration and Mediation Center Case No DIE2006-0002, para 6.

45   See Geist, 'Fair.com?: An Examination of the Allegations of Systemic Unfairness' in the ICANN UDRP which: '...provides compelling evidence that forum shopping has become an integral part of the UDRP and that the system may indeed be biased in favor of trademark holders. Both WIPO and the NAF, the two dominant ICANN-accredited arbitration providers, feature case allocation data that suggests that the panelist selection process is not random. Rather, it appears to be heavily biased toward ensuring that a majority of cases are steered toward complainant-friendly panelists'. The study found that complainants won in 82% of cases heard before WIPO panels. The author reviewed his study a year later and found that the: 'updated data provides compelling evidence that forum shopping and suspect case allocation concerns continue to taint the fairness of the ICANN UDRP'. See http://www.udrpinfo.com/.

46   'In 2006, a total of 1,823 complaints alleging cybersquatting were filed with WIPO's arbitration and mediation department. If those cases are similar to previous years, roughly 85% of brand owners will succeed against the domain name holder. These are not great odds if your business is established to profit from domain names'. Gingras, 'Expensive typos' (2007) New Law Journal, 11 May.

Elogicom[47] the defendant argued that the plaintiff should have invoked the dispute resolution process offered by Nominet, the UK domain name registrar.

This argument was rejected by Sales who stated:

> 'the defendants maintain that Tesco should have used available internet domain name dispute resolution procedures rather than issuing proceedings. However, Tesco and the Defendants are not party to any agreement between themselves which would make use of such procedures mandatory in preference to court proceedings. In any event, the internet dispute resolution procedures to which the Defendants make reference make it clear on their face that they are provided as a possible alternative to court proceedings, and not with a view to excluding recourse to the courts. Nor do I consider that there was anything unreasonable in Tesco deciding to have recourse to the courts to protect its rights in the circumstances of this case. Use of the internet dispute resolution procedures would not have provided Tesco with access to injunctive relief of the sort which it seeks in these proceedings, to protect its position for the future. Nor would they have provided Tesco with protection in respect of costs'.[48]

[11.24] In *B & S Ltd v Varga and Petho*[49] and *Adidas v Varga and Petho*[50] a WIPO panel ordered the transfer of the domain names adidas.ie and buy-sell.ie, respectively.[51] In these cases the respondents were alleged to be 'engaged in a pattern of registering Internet domain names that are identical or confusingly similar to well known trade marks'. However they also had 'an official valid Irish Registered Business Name and a copy of the Certificate of Registration of Business Name issued by the Companies Registration Office ... (was) ... annexed to the Response'. The IEDR has clear rules for registering, stating that 'A Sole Trader, Company or Unincorporated Association who hold a registered business name can apply for a domain name under this category.'

[11.25] Unfortunately the Registration of Business Names Act 1963 does not provide for challenges to entries made in the register. Unlike the IEDR, the Register of Business Names does not check that those who register names are entitled to do so. This creates a problem for the IEDR which 'has always prided itself on being a managed domain'.[52] The solution that the IEDR has developed is to register domain names that correspond to entries in the Register of Business Names and to provide an arbitration process. If the arbitration process rules that the domain name in question is to be transferred, then the

---

[47] *Tesco v Elogicom* [2006] EWHC 403.

[48] [2006] EWHC 403 (Ch) at para 40.

[49] *B & s Ltd v Varga and Petho* WIPO Arbitration and Mediation Center Case No DIE2006-0005.

[50] *Adidas v Varga and Petho* WIPO Arbitration and Mediation Center Case No DIE2006-0004.

[51] Other WIPO Arbitration center decisions on the Irish ccTLDs have included: *Palmerston Ltd v Alan Mahon* WIPO Arbitration and Mediation Center Case No DIE2005-0001 which concerned the domain name http://www.three.ie; *Travel Counsellors plc and Travel Counsellors (Ireland) Ltd v Portlaoise Travel Ltd* WIPO Arbitration and Mediation Center Case No DIE2006-0001; *Eoin Murphy and Ciaran Murphy trading as Wise Owl v Paul Baird* Arbitration and Mediation Center Case No DIE2006-0002; *Electricity Supply Board v Lislyn Retail Ltd and Northern Retail Ltd* WIPO Arbitration and Mediation Center Case No DIE2003-0001; and *Department of Arts, Sport and Tourism v Odyssey Internet Portal Ltd* WIPO Arbitration and Mediation Center Case No DIE2005-0002.

[52] 'Personal .ie addresses on way' (2007) The Irish Times, 1 June.

IEDR will presumably comply with that ruling. There is no difficulty with the arbitration process as such. Where a difficulty arises is where the IEDR transfers a domain name on foot of such a ruling. What the IEDR appears to be doing is, in effect, reviewing the appropriateness of entries in the Register of Business Names. It does so without any statutory authority. The IEDR is doing this because there is no extra-judicial process by which entries in the Register of Business Names can be reviewed.[53] Review of entries in the Register of Business Names should be done by amending the Registration of Business Names Act 1963. A good argument can be made that the IEDR cannot review the validity of entries in the Register in the absence of such an amendment. The only route by which entries in the Register of Business Names may be properly queried is through the courts. Arguably, the IEDR should either recognise the validity of all entries in the register or none.

The administration of the .eu domain

[11.26] The .eu domain is administered pursuant to a number of EC Regulations. The following persons or entitities can apply to register a domain name in the '.eu' registry:

(i)   Any undertaking having its registered office, central administration or principal place of business within the Community;

(ii)   Any organisation established within the Community without prejudice to the application of national law; and

(iii)   Any natural person resident within the Community.[54]

Whilst endorsing the first-come, first-served principle, the EC sought to avoid abusive registrations of domain names in a number of ways. Firstly, the EC introduced a sequence of phased registrations which allowed those with 'prior rights' to register their names before others.[55] Secondly, the EC provided for a revocation procedure for 'speculative and abusive registrations'. In effect this procedure may be invoked by initiating an ADR procedure[56], although the possibility of invoking other extra-judicial or judicial procedures would seem to be left open.[57] The .eu Registry may select providers of ADR services, these must be 'reputable bodies with appropriate expertise in an objective, transparent and non-discriminatory manner'.[58]

[11.27] This procedure may be invoked 'where that name is identical or confusingly similar to a name in respect of which a right is recognised or established by national and/or Community law'.

---

53   And it would not seem possible to introduce such a process without a statutory amendment. The Registration of Business Names Act 1963 gives the Minster the power to regulate 'generally the conduct and regulation of registration under this Act'. However, following the decision in *Mulcreevy v Minister for the Environment* [2004] 1 ILRM 419, the Minister would almost certainly not be able to regulate for such a review process.

54   Commission Regulation 733/2002, art 4(2)(b).

55   Commission Regulation 874/2004, arts 10 and 12.

56   Commission Regulation 874/2004, art 22.

57   Commission Regulation 874/2004, art 21(1).

58   Commission Regulation 874/2004, art 23(1).

Such rights would include:

> 'registered national and community trademarks, geographical indications or designations of origin, and, in as far as they are protected under national law in the Member-State where they are held: unregistered trademarks, trade names, business identifiers, company names, family names, and distinctive titles of protected literary and artistic works'.[59]

For this revocation procedure to be invoked, the domain name in question must have been 'registered by its holder without rights or legitimate interest in the name'. In addition, it may be that it has been 'registered or is being used in bad faith'.

[11.28] To establish a legitimate interest a party may establish the following:

(i) 'prior to any notice of an alternative dispute resolution (ADR) procedure, the holder of a domain name has used the domain name or a name corresponding to the domain name in connection with the offering of goods or services or has made demonstrable preparation to do so';

(ii) 'the holder of a domain name, being an undertaking, organisation or natural person, has been commonly known by the domain name, even in the absence of a right recognized or established by national and/or Community law'; or

(iii) 'the holder of a domain name is making a legitimate and non-commercial or fair use of the domain name, without intent to mislead consumers or harm the reputation of a name on which a right is recognised or established by national and/or Community law'.[60]

[11.29] Bad faith may be demonstrated by the following:

(i) 'circumstances indicate that the domain name was registered or acquired primarily for the purpose of selling, renting, or otherwise transferring the domain name to the holder of a name in respect of which a right is recognised or established by national and/or Community law or to a public body;'

(ii) 'the domain name has been registered in order to prevent the holder of such a name in respect of which a right is recognised or established by national and/or Community law, or a public body, from reflecting this name in a corresponding domain name, provided that:

- ... a pattern of such conduct by the registrant can be demonstrated; or
- ... the domain name has not been used in a relevant way for at least two years from the date of registration; or
- ... in circumstances where, at the time the ADR procedure was initiated, the holder of a domain name in respect of which a right is recognised or established by national and/or Community law or the holder of a domain name of a public body has declared his/its intention to use the domain name in a relevant way but fails to do so within six months of the day on which the ADR procedure was initiated;'

(iii) 'the domain name was registered primarily for the purpose of disrupting the professional activities of a competitor;'

---

[59] Commission Regulation 874/2004, art 10(1).
[60] Commission Regulation 874/2004, art 21(2).

(iv) 'the domain name was intentionally used to attract Internet users, for commercial gain, to the holder of a domain name website or other online location, by creating a likelihood of confusion with a name on which a right is recognised or established by national and/or Community law or a name of a public body, such likelihood arising as to the source, sponsorship, affiliation or endorsement of the website or location or of a product or service on the website or location of the holder of a domain name;'

(v) 'the domain name registered is a personal name for which no demonstrable link exists between the domain name holder and the domain name registered.'

WHOIS data

[11.30] Domain name registries such as the IEDR publicly provide data relating to registrants through their WHOIS database. This has proven controversial and was criticised by Europe's Data Protection Commissioners:

'where an individual registers a domain name ... there is no legal ground justifying the mandatory publication of personal data referring to this person ... The ... purpose of the WHOIS directories can ... be served as the details of the person are known to the ISP that can, in case of problems related to the site, contact the individual.'[61]

Privacy issues relating to WHOIS databases are not merely theoretical as the data contained in them may be gathered by spammers. Privacy and other issues relating to WHOIS databases are currently being examined by ICANN.[62] The .eu domain established by the EU limits access to personal data on the WHOIS database in two ways firstly, it restricts the contact information published to that of a single email address; and secondly, it provides a service whereby registrants can create a specific email address for use in the WHOIS database.[63]

Protected designations of origin

[11.31] The Council Regulation on the protection of geographical indications and designations of origin for agricultural products and foodstuffs[64] creates Protected Geographic Indications and Protected Designations of origin.[65] Registration of names under this regulation would create rights that might be exploited or infringed by the registration of a domain.

---

[61] Article 29 – Data Protection Working Party, 'Opinion 2/2003 on the application of the data protection principles to the Whois directories' 10972/03/EN final, 13 June 2003.

[62] http://gnso.icann.org/issues/whois-privacy/whois-services-final-tf-report-12mar07.htm.

[63] EURID, '.eu Domain Name WHOIS Policy': http://www.eurid.eu/images/Documents/WHOIS_Policy/whois_en.pdf.

[64] Council Regulation (EEC) No 2081/92 of 14 July 1992 on the protection of geographical indications and designations of origin for agricultural products and foodstuffs, OJ L 208, 24/07/1992, P 1–8.

[65] For a general discussion of these indications and appellations, see Clark and Smith, *Intellectual Property Law in Ireland* (2nd edn, Tottel Publishing 2005), ch 37.

Chapter 12

Cybersquatting

Introduction

[12.01] It is true that a near infinite number of domain names are possible, but unfortunately this fact is irrelevant. Only a limited number of domain names are valuable. In any given domain only 17576 three letter names can be made available, but again not all of these will be valuable. The domain name sun.ie is registered by Sun Microsystems, but a range of other businesses could validly claim the name from, The Sun newspaper to Sun Life Assurance. It is important to keep in mind that just because someone is accused of having invalidly registered a domain name does not mean that he or she has done anything wrong. Unlike trade mark, it is impossible to categorise the purposes for which a domain name can be registered. Offline, Sun Microsystems, The Sun Newspaper and Sun Life Assurance can all co-exist without interfering with each others, businesses. This is because it is easy to distinguish between a vendor of IT goods and services, a newspaper and an insurance provider. Unfortunately it is not possible to distinguish between domain names in this way. There can only be one domain 'sun.ie' and only one registrant of that domain. Disputes about domain names are therefore inevitable.

[12.02] In *MBNA v Freeman*[1] the plaintiffs were a credit card issuer and the defendant was an advertising executive who had registered the domain name mbna.co.uk. The defendant was endeavouring to establish a 'banner-exchange business', which basically sold Internet advertisements. He claimed to have chosen the name 'Marketing Banners for Net Advertisers' as the name for his business. The defendant gave evidence that 'it was now impossible to find a three letter acronym which has not already been registered … and very difficult to find a four letter acronym; 'MBNA.co.uk' was the nearest he could find which was descriptive of the proposed businesss'.[2] The plaintiff sought injunctive relief arguing that if some potential customers would search for their credit card business at http://www.mbna.co.uk, when they encountered the defendant's website they might conclude that the plaintiff did not have a presence on the web and stop searching. Strauss QC pointed out the flaw in this argument:

> 'if one assumes an internet user who cannot be bothered to conduct a search when he comes up against a brick wall, then it is difficult to see why the result would not be the same if Mr Freeman's website were not there; having tried MBNA.co.uk and drawn a blank, he would give up.'

---

[1]   *MBNA v Freeman* (17 July 2000, unreported) HC.
[2]   (17 July 2000, unreported) HC, para 10.

Strauss QC therefore refused the interlocutory injunction sought by the plaintiffs restraining the defendant from commencing business using the mbna.co.uk domain name before hearing.

[12.03] In any domain name dispute, the claimant will be in the strongest position if he or she has already registered the name or a variant of it as a trade mark, whilst the registrant has not. However, this does not always happen as many businesses do not register their names as trade marks. In this situation the business or individual must rely upon the tort of passing off and show that the use of a domain name will damage the goodwill in their business.

Passing off

[12.04] In *O'Neills Irish International Sports Co Ltd v O'Neills Footwear Dryer Co Ltd*[3] Barron J stated the law as follows:

> 'The nature of the tort is to be found in its name. The wrong is that of passing off ones goods as those of another. This can be done by similarity of name, appearance, get-up or any other similarity which achieves the same purpose. How it is done is immaterial so long as the similarity is calculated to deceive those who might buy or otherwise deal in the goods. Deliberate intention is not necessary.'[4]

Although deliberate intention is not necessary, it is very useful if it can be shown at trial[5] and this issue may influence the award of damages or grant of an injunction. In *D & S Ltd v The Irish Auto Trader Ltd*[6] McCracken J adopted the view that the following are the characteristics that identify passing off:

> '(1) a misrepresentaion;
>
> (2) made by a trader in the course of his trade;
>
> (3) to perspective customers of his or ultimate customers of goods or services supplied by him;
>
> (4) which is calculated to injure the business or good will of another trader (in the sense that it is a reasonably foreseeable consequence);
>
> (5) which causes actual damage to a business or goodwill of the trader by whom the action is brought or (in a quia timet action) would probably do so'.[7]

[12.05] In *DSG Retail v PCWorld*[8] Laffoy J adopted the following passage as setting out the essential elements of the tort of passing off:

> '(the plaintiff) must establish a goodwill or reputation attached to the goods or services which he supplies in the minds of the purchasing public by association with the identifying

---

3   *O'Neills Irish International Sports Co Ltd v O'Neills Footwear Dryer Co Ltd* (30 April 1997, unreported) HC (Barron J).

4   (30 April 1997, unreported) HC at p 4–5.

5   See *C & A Modes v C & A (Waterford) Ltd* [1976] IR 198 and *Grange Marketing v M&Q Plastics* (17 June 1976, unreported) HC (McWilliam J).

6   *D & S Ltd v The Irish Auto Trader Ltd* [1995] 2 IR 142.

7   [1995] 2 IR 142 at 144, adopting a passage from the speech of Lord Diplock in *Erven Warnick BV v J Townend and Sons* [1979] AC 731 at 742.

8   *DSG Retail v PCWorld* (13 January 1998, unreported) HC (Laffoy J).

get-up (whether that consists simply of a brand name or trade description or the individual features of labelling or packaging) under which its particular goods or services are offered to the public, such that the get-up is recognised by the public as distinctive, specifically as the plaintiff's goods or services. Second, he must demonstrate a misrepresentation by the defendant to the public (whether or not intentional) leading or likely to lead the public to believe the goods or services offered by him are the goods or services of the plaintiff ... Third he must demonstrate that he suffers or in a quia timet action that he is likely to suffer damage by reason of her erroneous belief engendered by the defendant's misrepresentation that the sources of the defendant's goods or services is the same as those offered by the plaintiff'.

[12.06] In *Muckross Park Hotel Ltd v Randles*[9] Barron J held that 'the matter which has to be established is whether or not persons are likely to be deceived and it is not necessary that an actual instance of deception should be established in the case'.[10] So the High Court refused an injunction in *An Bord Trachtala v Waterford Foods Plc*[11] where the 'possibility of any significant confusion ... is remote'.[12] In *DGS Retail Limited v PCWorld Ltd*[13] the plaintiff had been trading under the name PCWorld in the UK since October 1991 whereas the defendant had been using the same name since January 1997 in the Dublin region. Laffoy J held that given the disproportionate market strengths of the parties, and the defendant's assertion that it had acted bona fide, an interlocutory injunction would not be granted, although she did impose other conditions on the defendant.

[12.07] Companies and businesses are not the only bodies that can build up goodwill; individuals can also do so, and a photograph of a well-known celebrity using or wearing a product can be very valuable. Celebrities can charge considerable sums for agreeing to be seen in such a context. However, digital technology allows the manipulation of images so that a celebrity may appear with a branded product. This occurred in *Irvine v Talksport*.[14] The plaintiff was a well-known Formula 1 racing driver. The defendant was a radio broadcaster, which had published promotional material including a brochure with a picture of the plaintiff on the front. This picture had been digitally manipulated: the original showed him speaking on a mobile phone, whilst the manipulated image showed him listening intently to a radio bearing the defendant's name. The use of the photograph had not been sanctioned by the plaintiff, who brought an action for passing off. Laddie J held that the law would vindicate the claimant's exclusive right to his reputation or goodwill; it would not allow the defendant to so use the goodwill as to reduce, blur or diminish its exclusivity.

---

[9]   *Muckross Park Hotel Ltd v Randles* [1995] 1 IR 130.

[10] [1995] 1 IR 130 at 135, citing *Worcester Royal Porcelain Company v Locke & Co* [1902] 19 RPC 479.

[11] *An Bord Trachtála v Waterford Foods Plc* [1994] FSR 316.

[12] [1994] FSR 316 at 324 per Keane J.

[13] *DGS Retail Ltd v PC World Ltd* (13 January 1998, unreported) HC (Laffoy J).

[14] *Irvine v Talksport* [2002] EMLR 32. See also *BBC v Talksport* [2001] FSR 6 at 53.

It was therefore possible for a claim of passing off to succeed in a false endorsement case but the plaintiff would have to prove that:

(a) at the time of the acts complained of the plaintiff had a significant reputation or goodwill; and

(b) the actions of the defendant gave rise to a false message which would be understood by a not insignificant section of his market that his goods had been endorsed, recommended or approved by the claimant.[15]

Laddie J held that both elements had been proven in this case and found in favour of the plaintiff.

[12.08] Because the Internet is an international medium, assessing the value and importance of goodwill can be difficult. If an Irish company registers the name of a domestic rival which has considerable goodwill in Ireland in a foreign domain such as .co.uk, is that registration, or indeed use, actionable in the Irish courts? An analogous dispute occurred in *An Bord Trachtála v Waterford Foods Plc*[16], and here Keane J refused to entertain the plaintiff's application for an injunction as there was no evidence to establish that the plaintiff had any goodwill in the UK in the name that it sought to protect. In *C & A Modes v C & A (Waterford) Ltd*[17] it was established that it was not necessary for a business to be established in the state for it to sustain an action for passing off here.[18]

[12.09] The Internet creates a global market, but a brand that is globally prominent may have difficulty in establishing that it has the local goodwill needed to pursue a passing off action in any particular market. For example, *Euromarket Designs Incorportated v Peters*[19] concerned the website crateandbarrell.ie. The plaintiff was a successful American company with a chain of stores under the name Crate and Barrell, and it had registered its name as a trade mark in the UK and European Trademark Offices. The defendant ran one shop and a website in Ireland and was sued in the English courts, which, given that neither party traded in the UK led, Jacob J to comment that 'No-one but a lawyer could call this rational'.[20] Jacob J went on to dismiss the plaintiff's application as the plaintiff was unable to establish that it had any goodwill or trade in the UK or indeed in Europe. In *Dearlove (t/a 'Diddy') v Combs (t/a 'Sean 'Puffy' Combs',*

---

[15] For an opinion on the legal and ethical implication of 'ambush' or 'parasitic' marketing, where a company seeks to have itself associated with an event such as the Olympic games without paying the sponsorship fees, see Garrigues, 'Ambush Marketing: Robbery or Smart Advertising' (2002) 11 EIPR 505.

[16] *An Bord Trachtála v Waterford Foods Plc* [1994] FSR 316.

[17] *C & A Modes v C & A (Waterford) Ltd* [1976] IR 198.

[18] *C & A Modes v C & A (Waterford) Ltd* [1976] IR 198 at 212: 'If there are in the State sufficient customers of a plaintiff's business to justify his claim to have a vested right to retain and expand that custom, then there is ample authority in principle and in the decided cases for the conclusion that, no matter where the plaintiff's business is based, he is entitled to be protected against it being taken away or dissipated by someone whose deceptive conduct is calculated to create a confusion of identity in the minds of existing potential customers.'

[19] *Euromarket Designs Incorportated v Peters* (25 July 2000, unreported) HC (Jacob J).

[20] (25 July 2000, unreported) HC at para. 8.

'*Puffy*' and '*PDiddy*')²¹ the defendant had pages on myspace.com, youtube.com and another site. These pages were outside the UK, but Kitchen J held that they were directed at the UK on the basis that: the defendant was an international celebrity whose music was sold in the UK, he was undertaking a UK music tour and the defendant's agents pretty much admitted that they were using these pages to promote the defendant internationally.²²

[12.10] The situation may become more complex where a distributor is appointed within a country to market and promote a foreign product. In *Medgen Inc v Passion for Life Products*²³ the plaintiff was the USA-based manufacturer of a product called 'Snorenz', it appointed the plaintiff distributor in the UK and subsequently trade marked the name. A dispute arose between the parties and the defendant ceased to receive supplies from the plaintiff so it sourced a new product and started marketing it under identical packaging under the name 'Snoreeze'. The plaintiff failed in its action for passing off, it being held that in a dispute between a foreign manufacturer and a domestic distributor there was no rule of law or presumption of fact that the goodwill in a product would belong to the foreign manufacturer.²⁴

[12.11] These cases may be contrasted with the earlier decision of *Jian Tools for Sale Ltd v Roderick Manhattan Group Ltd*²⁵ where the plaintiff had established goodwill and reputation in its product 'BizPlan Builder' in the USA. The plaintiff had no business or employees in the UK. The defendant had negotiated with the plaintiff to sell its product in the UK but after negotiations broke down, the defendant launched its own similar product in the UK called 'BusinessPlan Builder'. The plaintiff sued and the defendant argued that there was insufficient goodwill in the UK to support an action for passing off. Knox J in the English High Court held that in order to succeed in a passing off action a foreign plaintiff who had no place of business in the UK had to at least show that it had customers there. The plaintiff had sold 127 units in the UK in the seven years prior to trial. Its product had been extensively advertised in US magazines, some of which circulated in the UK and these advertisements were shown to have generated UK sales in a few instances. Given that the defendant had adopted a name that could cause confusion between the two products, particularly the use of a capital 'P' in the defendant's product name and that the plaintiff had adopted the name in the face of clear and explicit opposition from the plaintiff, an injunction was granted restraining the defendant's use of the name.

[12.12] Section 7(2) of the Trade Marks Act 1996 states that 'nothing in this Act shall affect the law relating to passing off', but by allowing the registration of service marks and reforming the law on trade marks in the state, the 1996 Act has inevitably impacted on the significance of the law of passing off. A business which builds up significant goodwill in a name, symbol or other mark will be very unwise if it does not register that

---

²¹ *Dearlove v Combs* [2007] EWHC 375 (Ch).
²² [2007] EWHC 375 (Ch), at para 35.
²³ *Medgen Inc v Passion for Life Products* [2001] FSR 30.
²⁴ *Dearlove v Combs* [2007] EWHC 375 (Ch) at 510, para 49.
²⁵ *Jian Tools for Sale Ltd v Roderick Manhattan Group Ltd* [1995] FSR 924.

mark to protect it. The law of passing off will continue but it may become more common to see actions for passing off taken in addition to actions for breach of trade mark. However, the law of passing off may still confer some advantage on litigants, in that it may allow for the protection of descriptive terms such as 'savings certificates', which might not necessarily be trade marked. [26]

Local Ireland Ltd and Nua Ltd v Local Ireland online Ltd

[12.13] The leading Irish case on disputes is *Local Ireland Ltd and Nua Ltd v Local Ireland online Ltd*.[27] The second-named plaintiff had developed a website which provided information about Ireland under the name 'localireland' or 'Local ireland', sometimes written as a single word, sometimes as two words, but always with the first letter a distinctive form of capital and the remaining eleven letters lower case. A number of domain names which were variants of this name were then registered in 1997: local.ie; localireland.com; local-ireland.org; and local-ireland.net. In 2000 the plaintiffs became aware that the defendants were establishing a business trading under the name 'Local Ireland-Online' which would also trade online using the domain name 'localireland-online.com'. The plaintiffs issued proceedings and the defendant then decided to change its name to 'Locally Irish' and register a new domain name 'locallyirish.com'. The plaintiff then sued in respect of this name also claiming that the similarity of the business names and associated domain names, the similarity of get-up, the similarity of the logos and the similarity of services provided by the parties would:

> 'as a reasonable probability, result in customers and prospective customers of the first named Plaintiff being mislead into thinking that the services offered by the Defendants … was as a Branch or licensee of the first named plaintiff.'

[12.14] The defendants argued that they were using words in common use and that the plaintiffs were not entitled to an unfair monopoly in those words as the differences between the different names and logos were sufficient to distinguish the different businesses.[28] The issue of descriptive terms is a significant one: the plaintiff was not just seeking to establish a monopoly in the combination of two words 'local' and 'Ireland' but also in derivatives of those words such as 'locally' and 'Irish'[29]. The word 'local' is descriptive in its normal use, but it can have other functions, so in *Jian Tools for Sale Ltd v Roderick Manhattan Group Ltd*[30] it was held that the name 'Bizplan Builder' was largely but not entirely descriptive, there being a metaphorical use of the word

---

[26] See *An Post v The Irish Permanent Plc* [1995] 1 IR 140, but see also*Radio Limerick One Ltd v Treaty Radio Ltd* (13 November 1997, unreported) HC (Costello J).

[27] *Local Ireland Ltd and Nua Ltd v Local Ireland online Ltd* (2 October 2000, unreported) HC (Herbert J).

[28] Relying upon the cases of *Reddaway v Banham* [1896] AC 199; *Office Cleaning Services v Westminster Office Cleaning Association* [1946] 1 All ER 320; and *BS v Irish Auto Trader* [1995] 2 ILRM 252.

[29] There is one precedent for registering an Irish place name as a trade mark; see the judgment of the Supreme Court in *Waterford Glass Ltd v Controller of Patents, Designs and Trade Marks* [1984] ILRM 565.

[30] *Jian Tools for Sale Ltd v Roderick Manhattan Group Ltd* [1995] FSR 924.

'Builder'.[31] It might be argued here that the word local has a similar metaphorical function in the name Localireland. The law of passing off can protect descriptive terms. In *An Post v The Irish Permanent Plc*[32] the High Court prevented the use of the title 'Savings Certificates' by the defendants although it has been argued that if the plaintiff ceased to be a State body, then a court might decide otherwise.[33]

[12.15] Herbert J was satisfied that the plaintiffs had established a strong *prima facie* case that in respect of the name 'Local Ireland' there existed a 'large body of the public which in the words of Barron J in the case of *Muckross Park Hotel Ltd v Randles and Others*[34] "know it and what it stands for" namely the Internet Information Service' of the plaintiffs. He was also satisfied that the plaintiffs had made out a strong *prima facie* case that they had a very valuable reputation in the name 'Localireland' or 'Local Ireland' and its associated domain names. This was based upon the evidence of the plaintiff that it had spent £594,000 (€754,224) on advertising its business name and services in Ireland and abroad, employed programmers and concluded agreements with local partners or franchises. Elsewhere in his judgment Herbert J refers to the assertion by the plaintiff that its site was the second busiest site in the state with 205,000 separate visits per month. This evidence did not appear to be queried by the defendant, and Herbert J found it 'very significant' that the defendant was not able to call any similar evidence in respect of its own website.

[12.16] This led Herbert J to the conclusion that the plaintiffs had made out a *bona fide* case that the use by the defendants 'of the business name "Local Ireland-Online" and its associated domain name 'localireland.com' which takes over and incorporates the name of the first named plaintiff as a whole, would result in a very high probability of deception as amounting to 'a misrepresentaion by the defendants to the public (whether or not intentional) leading or likely to lead the public to believe that the services offered by (them) are the services of the plaintiff(s) see *Reckitt and Coleman Products limited v Borden*'[35] or that the defendants in providing such services are in some way associated with the plaintiff's business, for example as a branch or licensee of the plaintiff's'. Herbert J was further satisfied that the plaintiffs had made out a fair *bona fide* case that the use by the defendants of the business name 'Locally Irish' and its associated domain name 'locallyirish.com' are so close to the business name and domain name of the first-named plaintiff that no sufficient or real distinction could reasonably be said to exist between them, particularly having regard to the similarity of the relevant service, that is, 'the subscription listing of commercial undertakings accessible through the central web of the provider', carried on by the first named plaintiff and the first named defendant and that as a matter of reasonable probability the public are likely to be similarly misled'. Herbert J did not consider the fact that the plaintiffs also provided other services under the same business name and associated domain name lessened the force of this argument.

---

[31] [1995] FSR 924 at 938.

[32] *An Post v The Irish Permanent Plc* [1995] 1 IR 140.

[33] See McMahon and Binchy *Law of Torts* (3rd edn, Tottel Publishing, 2000), ch 31.

[34] *Muckross Park Hotel Ltd v Randles and Others* [1995] 1 IR 130.

[35] *Reckitt and Coleman Products limited v Borden* [1990] I All ER 873 at 880.

[12.17] *Local Ireland Ltd and Nua Ltd v Local Ireland online Ltd* was decided at the interlocutory stage the refusal of the parties to treat this hearing as the trial of the action was described by Herbert J as 'somewhat regrettable'. As an interlocutory hearing, Herbert J was required only to be satisfied that in the case of the business name 'Locally Irish', and the business name, 'Local Ireland-Online' and their associated domain names the plaintiffs had established a fair *bona fide* case to be tried that the getup and logo of the defendants is in the case of each business name so similar to their getup and logo as to lead to similar public confusion to the detriment of the plaintiffs, or, in the alternative that there was insufficient difference between each getup and logo. Having considered the adequacy of damages and the balance of convenience, Herbert J made an order in the following terms:

   (i)   restraining the defendants from commencing or carrying on business under the name: 'Local Ireland-Online Limited', 'localireland-online.com', 'Locally Irish Limited' or 'locallyirish.com' or any other name in which the words 'local' and 'Ireland' or their cognates appear sequentially in either order; and

   (ii) restraining the defendants from possessing, holding, operating, managing or controlling an Internet address or domain name under the name 'localireland-online.com' or 'locallyirish.com'.

Although the second part of the order is framed as being propitiatory, its effects would have been the same as a mandatory order requiring the defendant to transfer the domain names. However mandatory orders are not usually available at the interlocutory stage[36], hence Herbert J made an order prohibiting the defendant from holding the name as opposed to transferring it to the plaintiff.

Cybersquatting

[12.18] Cybersquatting was described as follows by Park J in *Global Projects Management v Citigroup:*[37]

   'Persons with no connection with a well-known business name would find some permutation containing the name and a suffix, but where that particular permutation had not been registered by the real owner of the business. The person concerned would then register that permutation himself and try to make money through being bought out by the true owner'.[38]

The effect of the above was analysed by the English Court of Appeal in *WH Smith v Peter Colman*[39] where Walker J concluded that:

---

[36] A fact acknowledged by the plaintiff in *MBNA America Bank NA and another v Freeman* (17 July 2000) HC (Eng).

[37] *Global Projects Management Ltd v Citigroup Inc and others* [2005] EWHC 2663.

[38] [2005] EWHC 2663, para 12. See also the view of Laddie J who described cybersquatters as: 'individuals who search the commercial world for valuable trademarks, register domain names which incorporate those trademarks for themselves, and then use what are best described as blackmail techniques to extract a high price for the domain names from the proprietors of the trademarks': *Renault UK Ltd v Derivatives Risk Evaluation and Management* (22 October 2001) HC (Eng).

[39] *WH Smith v Peter Colman* [2001] FSR 9 at 91.

'The general effect of those decisions is that the opportunistic registration and subsequent offer for sale of domain names, reflecting the goodwill of other traders' businesses and trademarks, is an unlawful activity liable to attract strict and summary sanctions'.[40]

BT v One in a Million

[12.19] In *BT v One in a Million*[41] Sumption QC sitting as a deputy Judge of the English High Court set out the possible purposes for which a dealer might register a domain name:

'For a dealer in Internet domain names there are in principle only four uses to which the names can be put. The first and most obvious is that it may be sold to the enterprise whose name or trade mark has been used, which may be prepared to pay a high price to avoid the inconvenience of there being a domain name comprising its own name or trade mark which is not under its control. Secondly, it may be sold to a third party unconnected with the name, so that he may try to sell it to the company whose name is being used, or else use it for purposes of deception. Thirdly, it may be sold to someone with a distinct interest of his own in the name, for example a solicitor by the name of John Sainsbury or the Government of the British Virgin Islands, with a view to its use by him. Fourthly, it may be retained by the dealer unused and unsold, in which case it serves only to block the use of that name as a registered domain name by others, including those whose name or trade mark it comprises.'

[12.20] Sumption QC granted a *quia timet* order to the respondents, which was then appealed. The facts were that the appellants 'made a speciality of registering domain names for use on the Internet comprising well-known names and trade marks without the consent of the person or company owning the goodwill in the name or trade mark'. The respondents were owners of the trade marks Marks & Spencer, Ladbroke, Sainsbury, Virgin, BT and Cellnet. This fact was accepted by the appellants, as was the fact that the respondents used these trade marks in the course of their business. Aldous LJ in the English Court of Appeal held that 'substantial goodwill' had been built up in these names. The English Court of Appeal held that there was:

'clear evidence of systematic registration by the appellants of well-known trade names as blocking registrations and a threat to sell them to others. No doubt the primary purpose of registration was to block registration by the owner of the goodwill. There was, according to Mr Wilson nothing unlawful in doing that. The truth is different. The registration only blocks registration of the identical domain name and therefore does not act as a block to registration of a domain name that can be used by the owner of the goodwill in the name. The purpose of the so-called blocking registration was to extract money from the owners of the goodwill in the name chosen. Its ability to do so was in the main dependent upon the threat, expressed or implied that the appellants would exploit the goodwill by either trading under the name or equipping another with the name so he could do so.'

The appellants submitted 'that mere registration did not amount to passing-off'. Further, Marks & Spencer Plc had not established any damage or likelihood of damage.

---

[40] [2001] FSR 9 at 93.
[41] *BT v One in a Million* [1998] 4 All ER 476, [1999] 1 WLR 903, [1999] RPC 1.

Aldous LJ rejected this submission:

> 'The placing on a register of a distinctive name such as marksandspencer makes a representation to persons who consult the register that the registrant is connected or associated with the name registered and thus the owner of the goodwill in the name ... registration of the domain name including the words Marks & Spencer is an erosion of the exclusive goodwill in the name which damages or is likely to damage Marks & Spencer Plc

Aldous LJ went on to conclude that:

> 'domain names comprising the name Marks & Spencer are instruments of fraud. Any realistic use of them as domain names would result in passing-off and there was ample evidence to justify the injunctive relief granted by the judge to prevent them being used for a fraudulent purpose and to prevent them being transferred to others.'

[12.21] The judgment of Aldous LJ in *BT v One in a Million* makes it clear that one of the key factors in deciding whether to grant relief is the intent of the alleged cybersquatter. In *BT v One in a Million* the intent of the defendants was apparent, both from their correspondence with the plaintiffs and the 'clear evidence of systematic registration'. that was found to exist. Similar clear evidence was not available in *Global Projects Management v Citigroup*[42] where the plaintiffs had registered the domain name citigroup.co.uk. They did not use this domain name and anyone who tried to log onto the site would get an error message. Anyone who mistakenly sent an email to an address such as someone@citigroup.co.uk would receive a polite email by return telling them that their email had been 'wrongly addressed and needs to be re-submitted'. The plaintiffs never tried to sell the domain name to the defendants or third parties. When the defendants sought to invoke the UK's domain name arbitration service, the plaintiffs initially co-operated, but then initiated an action seeking declaratory relief that the defendant's claims of trademark infringement and passing off were unfounded. The defendant counter-claimed for an injunction similar to that which had been granted in *BT v One in a Million* and sought summary judgment.

[12.22] Park J applied the decision of Aldous J in *BT v One in a Million*. Park J considered that:

> 'A key strand in Aldous's LJ reasoning was that the main names which One in a Million succeeded in having registered to it were "instruments of fraud". I do not think that he meant fraud in the criminal and most pejorative sense of the term. The directors of One in a Million no doubt thought that they were entitled to do what they had done and that they were not in breach of any legal rules. Nevertheless 'instruments of fraud' was the expression which Aldous LJ used.'[43]

Park J noted that:

> 'The mere registration and maintenance in force of a domain name which leads, or may lead, people to believe that the holder of the domain is linked with a person (e.g. Marks & Spencer or British Telecom, or, I would add, Citigroup) is enough to make the domain a potential 'instrument of fraud', and it is passing off'.[44]

---

[42] *Global Projects Management v Citigroup* [2005] EWHC 2663.
[43] [2005] EWHC 2663, para 39.
[44] [2005] EWHC 2663, para 40.

[12.23] Park J also noted that the plaintiffs did not have a cybersquatting track record, but there was other evidence that showed:

> 'irrefutably that their object was to obtain a domain name which carried the potential threat of deception harmful to Citigroup Inc. That evidence is the timing of the application to Nominet for the domain name citigroup.co.uk. The application was made later in the very day on which the agreement to form Citigroup had been announced with high publicity. Add to that that the next day ... (the defendants) ... tried to register citigroup.com as well, and the conclusion is even more irresistible'.[45]

Furthermore, whilst the defendants indicated that they had no intention of using the name, they were unwilling to transfer it the defendants, without offering a satisfactory explanation for this refusal. One of the defendants claimed that he wished to continue to receive mail that was intended for the defendant so that he could 'look out for improprieties'. Park J noted that this carried 'the unacceptable connotation that he intends to snoop on ... emails, including confidential emails'.[46] Park J therefore granted the defendant the orders it sought and summarily dismissed the plaintiff's claim.

Typosquatters

[12.24] The judgment in *BT v One in a Million* is very much a product of its facts and its time. The appellants were quite open about what they were doing. For example in response to a query from lawyers for J Sainsbury PLC, they replied:

> 'We are not trading under the name Sainsbury nor do we intend to trade under the name Sainsbury. We have merely purchased the Internet domain names j-sainsbury.com, sainsbury.com and sainsburys.com as part of our personal collection.'

Communications such as these, together with other evidence, made it possible for judges in both the English High Court and Court of Appeal to conclude that the purpose of registering these domain names was:

> 'to extract money from the owners of the goodwill in the name chosen. Its ability to do so was in the main dependent upon the threat, expressed or implied, that the appellants would exploit the goodwill by either trading under the name or equipping another with the name so he could do so.'

[12.25] Cybersquatters have since learnt to be more circumspect. Gringras suggests that there are three reasons for this: firstly, the unsympathetic response of the courts to their claims; secondly, the establishment of ADR systems such as those provided by WIPO; and, finally, 'cybersquatters can make more money by keeping the domain name and by, in effect, renting it to advertisers, than by selling it to its rightful owner'. For example, a lucrative alternative to registering a domain name that corresponds to a brand name is to register a domain that corresponds to a misspelt brand name.[47] This mechanism has been described in the following terms:

> 'Cybersquatters ... purchase domain names on a systematic basis. They usually use software specially designed to throw up the most common typographical errors in a

---

[45] [2005] EWHC 2663, para 43.
[46] [2005] EWHC 2663, para 45.
[47] See *Toys R Us, Inc v Abir* USSPQ 2d (BNA) SDNY [1997].

domain name ... .Only those domain names generating significant traffic are permanently registered ... they are then 'parked' or hosted with companies specifically set up for carrying paid advertisements under domain names ... The cybersquatters then sit back and watch pennies turn into pounds in their online accounts as tricked users click on advertising hyperlinks. The advertising links provided can range from the brand owner's competitors to pornographic websites'.[48]

[12.26] In effect the domain name owners in this case rent it to advertisers. This occurred in the English case of *Tesco v Elogicom*.[49] The plaintiff is the well-known UK-based store, which had entered into an agreement with a company named Tradedoubler to boost traffic on Tesco's website. Tradedoubler operated:

'a system whereby a provider of another website can become an 'affiliate' of one of its clients such as Tesco. The affiliate provides on the face of its website an advert or panel which, when clicked with a mouse by the individual who is visiting that website, takes the individual to the website of TradeDoubler's client. TradeDoubler runs software which tracks this process occurring, and which detects any sales made by its client from its website to the individual directed there from the affiliate's website. The client then pays commission via TradeDoubler to the affiliate in relation to the sales generated in this way'.[50]

The defendant was one such affiliate who sought to take advantage of this system by registering a number of domain names such as www.tesco2u.co.uk; www.tesco2u.com; www.tesco2you.co.uk; and www.tesco2you.com. The system as operated by the defendants was very well designed. Someone who entered www.tesco2u.co.uk into the address bar of their Internet browser would be taken directly to a legitimate Tesco website. Hence the possibility of passing off was not immediately apparent, but that did not mean that the defendant was not benefiting from this process:

'the TradeDoubler software system picked up and recorded traffic to Tesco's websites generated by persons entering any of these Tesco related domain names which had been registered by Elogicom ... The effect was that if any individual consumer entered one of these domain names in his computer, was taken directly to a Tesco website and then made purchases on that website, TradeDoubler would charge Tesco commission on those sales under the client agreement, and would pay Elogicom that commission under the affiliate agreement'.[51]

[12.27] In May 2005 the defendant benefited to the tune of £26,688, after it registered domain names such as www.tesco-diets.com. Attracting attention in this way was a mistake, as Tesco personnel made enquiries and subsequently instructed their solicitor. Tesco instituted proceedings under the UK Trade Marks Act, submitting that:

'the registration and use of the 'tesco' related domain names ... involved use of a sign in the course of trade where because the sign is in each case similar to the trade marks registered by Tesco ... and was used in relation to services identical with or similar to

---

[48] Gringras, 'Expensive Typos' (2007) New Law Journal, 11 May.
[49] *Tesco v Elogicom* [2006] EWHC 403 (Ch).
[50] *Tesco v Elogicom* [2006] EWHC 403 (Ch), para 6.
[51] [2006] EWHC 403 (Ch), para 17.

those for which the trade mark is registered, there existed a likelihood of confusion on the part of the public, including the likelihood of association with the trade mark'.[52]

Sales, who sat as a Deputy Judge of the English High Court, considered that this submission would have to be carefully considered as Elogicom, the defendant:

'did not use the 'tesco' related domain names which it registered in order to direct consumers to any website which it operated. Instead, where individuals browsing on the net entered those domain names in the address bars on their computers, they would be taken direct to a Tesco website. Elogicom did not use those domain names in order to sell any goods or services of its own'.[53]

[12.28] Sales considered that Elogicom was seeking to benefit from the plaintiff's trademark as it was:

'seeking to benefit from use of domain names which incorporated the word 'tesco' by 'fishing' for persons browsing the internet who might be searching for goods or services provided by Tesco and, being unsure of the precise address for a Tesco website, might by guesswork enter in the address bars on their computers names closely associated with Tesco in the hope that those addresses would take them to the Tesco website they were searching for. To the extent that Elogicom could capture some internet traffic represented by consumers who entered the 'tesco' related domain names it had registered, and direct that traffic to Tesco websites under the auspices of the TradeDoubler affiliate system, it sought to be able to reap commissions for itself from Tesco.'[54]

Sales considered that using a domain was of itself a service to the public; this led him to decide that:

'by registering and making its 'tesco' related domain names available as pathways on the internet to Tesco websites with a view to generating income for itself in the form of commission, Elogicom did use in the course of trade a series of signs (those domain names) which were each similar to the trade marks registered by Tesco and were each used in relation to services (the provision of internet access to Tesco websites) identical with or similar to those for which the trade marks were registered, and in circumstances where there existed a likelihood of confusion on the part of the public.'[55]

[12.29] This led Sales to the conclusion that Elogicom had infringed Tesco's trade marks. Whilst Sales noted that there were significant differences between the facts of this case and those of *BT v One in a Million,* the principles enunciated by Aldous LJ in that case applied in this:

'Elogicom did not register the 'tesco' related domain names with a view to selling them to Tesco or third parties, but with a view to using them itself in order to generate commission from Tesco ... the 'tesco' related domain names which Elogicom registered all fell into the category of names which were inherently misleading, as with the 'Marksandspencer' related domain names in the One in a Million case ... the only use of the domain name by someone other than Tesco would, realistically, have to involve infringement of Tesco's trade mark ... I consider that Tesco has, like Marks & Spencer Plc in the One in a Million

---

[52]   [2006] EWHC 403 (Ch), para 30.
[53]   [2006] EWHC 403 (Ch), para 31.
[54]   [2006] EWHC 403 (Ch), para 32.
[55]   [2006] EWHC 403 (Ch), para 33.

decision, made out its case that there is a sufficient threat of future use of the names that quia timet injunctive relief should be granted. In addition, I consider that the very maintenance by Elogicom of those domain names on the register itself involves a continuing use by Elogicom of Tesco's name for Elogicom's own business purposes, which represents a continuing infringement of Tesco's registered trade marks ... which is itself sufficient to warrant injunctive relief'.[56]

Sales similarly came to the conclusion that Elogicom had sought to benefit from Tesco's goodwill and so the case for passing-off had been made out. Finally, Sales summarily dismissed Elogicom's claim for outstanding commission. He did this on the basis that 'the affiliate agreement should be interpreted in the light of Tesco's own entitlements under the general law not to have its trade marks infringed and not to suffer from passing off by affiliates'.[57]

Honest dispute

[12.30] Disputes between two persons or entities which have a legitimate entitlement to a domain name can and do occur. The decision of Laddie J in *Renault v Derivatives Risk Evaluation and Management*[58] provides an interesting contrast to that of Aldous LJ in *BT v One in a Million*. This decision concerned the domain name vavavoom.co.uk. The plaintiffs did not claim to have invented the phrase 'va va voom' but they were intensively advertising their cars with a campaign that used the phrase. The defendants had registered the domain name to be used by the fashion business that was run by one of them. Having registered the domain name, that defendant decided that it was unsuitable and registered other names which they subsequently used. Thus the domain name vavavoom.co.uk was unused when the plaintiff sought to purchase it. The plaintiff initially offered £1,500 without disclosing its identity, but when the defendant realised who they were dealing with, they sought £15,000. The plaintiff was unhappy about this, but as Laddie J noted 'That is what happens in a seller's market'.[59] Laddie went on to refuse the plaintiff's application for summary judgment on a number of grounds. Firstly the plaintiff accepted that the defendants were 'not cyber-squatters and that this is not a simple blackmailing operation but, at least on the present evidence, simply a clash of two enterprises who happen to have chosen a similar domain name'.[60] Secondly, he noted that:

> 'The law of passing off does not give traders monopolies in words or get-ups. Just because a company has used one or more words in the course of trade does not give that company per se a monopoly in those words against all other people. The requirement that the Claimants show a relevant goodwill is important'.[61]

---

[56] [2006] EWHC 403 (Ch), para 49.
[57] [2006] EWHC 403 (Ch), para 59.
[58] *Renault v Derivatives Risk Evaluation and Management* (22 October 2001) EWHC (Ch).
[59] (22 October 2001) EWHC (Ch), para 11.
[60] (22 October 2001) EWHC (Ch), para 21.
[61] (22 October 2001) EWHC (Ch), para 22.

Thirdly, Laddie J found that it was at least arguable that the plaintiff would not be able to establish that misrepresentation had occurred. This was significant as the plaintiff was seeking summary judgment, and Laddie J therefore refused the order sought.

[12.31] Another examples of a High Court decision involving two companies who could legitimately claim the same domain name is *Pitman Training v Nominet UK & Pitman Publishing* [62] Pitman Publishing had initially registered the domain name pitman.co.uk; however, a franchisee of Pitman Training (the plaintiff) later successfully registered the same name. How this occurred mystified the technical experts who gave evidence in the case. When Pitman Publishing realised what had happened, they notified their solicitors who were ultimately successful in persuading *Nominet UK* to transfer the domain name pitman.co.uk back to the publishing house. The plaintiff then initiated legal proceedings. *Pitman Training v Nominet UK & Pitman Publishing* is unusual as the second-named defendant and the plaintiff had originally been part of the same business, established in 1849, which had been broken up and sold off in 1985. This made it difficult (if not impossible) to raise a claim that one party or the other was engaging in passing off, furthermore contracts entered into in 1985 limited the plaintiff's use of the name 'Pitman' to situations in which it was accompanied by the word 'training'. When the matter came before Scott VC, he rejected the plaintiff's application for an interlocutory injunction as the plaintiff was unable to show any viable or reasonably arguable cause of action against the defendants.

Own name defences

[12.32] The Trade Marks Act 1996 expressly provides that a trade mark may include personal names,[63] but this is limited by s 15(2) which provides that a registered trade mark will not be infringed by 'the use by a person of his own name or address'. The Act does include the proviso that such use must be in accordance with honest practices in industrial and commercial matters. This defence attaches to the name by which a person is commonly known or called. The defence of use of one's own personal name can be invoked by a natural person, but a company may also be able to rely upon this defence. [64] The defence will apply to the business names by which the public know both legal and natural persons. [65] However the defence is limited, as a name cannot be adopted for the purposes of availing of another's good name or reputation since this would infringe against the rule that the name must be used in accordance with honest practices. This test

---

[62] *Pitman Trainingv Nominet UK & Pitman Publishing* [1997] FSR 797; see also *Prince PLC v Prince Sports Group* [1998] FSR 21.

[63] 'a trade mark may, in particular, consist of words (including personal names), designs, letters, numerals or the shape of goods or of their packaging': Trade Marks Act 1996, s 6(2).

[64] See *Scandecor Development v Scandecor Marketing* [1998] FSR 500. This issue was not dealt with on appeal. See [1999] FSR 26. See also *Euromarket Designs v Peters* (25 July 2000, unreported) Jacob J. However, see the judgment of Ferris J in *AD Electronics v NAD Computer Systems* [1997] FSR 380.

[65] See*Mercury Communications v Mercury Interactive* [1995] FSR 850.

is an objective one and was set out in the case of *Volvo v Heritage*[66] as being: if members of the trade concerned knew all the relevant facts known to the defendant, would they say that the use complained of was honest? The ease with which this decision can be made will depend upon the facts in the individual case, and in some cases this will be very difficult indeed.

[12.33] It would be open to a court to decide that once an electronic address or domain name is allocated to an individual or family then an action by a business with a similar name could not succeed. However, the fact that one is trading under one's own name may not be sufficient to establish a defence to an action for passing off. In *O'Neills Irish International Sports Company Ltd v O'Neills Footwear Dryer Co Ltd*[67] Barron J was satisfied that the plaintiffs had built up a considerable reputation in the name O'Neills, which was associated with sports goods. The defendant was set up by a Mr John O'Neill who had patented a footwear dryer, which he was marketing as the 'O'Neill's Footwear Dryer' and selling through stores, particularly sporting goods shops in Ireland. Barron J was satisfied that the defendant's product was being marketed in a manner 'which ... is calculated to lead persons seeing that product ... to believe that the product is the product of the plaintiffs'. An injunction was granted restraining the defendant, Barron J commenting that:

> 'No doubt John O'Neill believed that since his name was O'Neill he could form a company with O'Neill in its name and market his product under that name. In that belief he was wrong. While a person may use his own name in the course of trade and cannot be faulted on that ground alone, that does not entitle him to use his own name in such a way as is calculated to lead others to believe his goods are those of another.'

[12.34] This issue was described as 'a tricky area of passing off law'[68] by Jacob J in n *Asprey and Garrard v WRA (Guns) Ltd.*[69] The claimant was a company known as Asprey Ltd, which dated back to 1781 and it was sold in 1995 to Garrard, which operated it as a supplier of luxury goods under the combined names. The second-named defendant was a member of the Asprey family who used to work for the claimant. After the sale of the business, he set up on his own as 'William R. Asprey, Esquire' and traded through a company called WRA (Guns) Ltd, the first-named defendant. The first-named defendant relied heavily, in its promotional literature and otherwise, on its association with the

[66] In the English case of *Volvo v Heritage* [2000] FSR 253 the defendant ceased to be an approved Volvo dealer, so he began to refer to himself as a Volvo 'specialist' or as being independent, where the words 'independent' and 'specialist' were in much smaller letters than the word Volvo. He was held to be unable to avail of the equivalent of paragraph c above as his use was calculated to cause confusion. In contrast the European Court of Justice held that a garage which specialised in the repair of BMWs could only advertise these services by using the BMW trade mark (*BMW v Deenik* [1999] ETMR 339).
[67] *O'Neills Irish International Sports Co Ltd v O'Neills Footwear Dryer Co Ltd* (30 April 1997, unreported) HC (Barron J).
[68] *Asprey and Garrand v WRA (Guns) Ltd* [2002] FSR 30 at p 482.
[69] [2002] FSR 30.

claimant. Jacob J reviewed the authority of *Joseph Rogers & Sons v WN Rogers & Co*[70] in which Romer J stated:

'no man is entitled to carry on his business in such a way as to represent that it is in the business of another, or is in any way connected with the business of another; that is the first proposition. The second proposition is, that no man is entitled so to describe or mark his goods as to represent that the goods are the goods of another. To the first proposition there is, I myself think, an exception: a man, in my opinion, is entitled to carry on his business in his own name so long as he does not do anything more than that to cause confusion with the business of another and so long as he does it honestly. It is an exception to the rule which has of necessity been established'. [71]

Jacob J took the view that the basis of this exception is necessity and that there was nothing necessary about the way Mr Asprey was trading. On that basis he held that passing off was been carried on.

[12.35] The defendants also relied upon s 11(2) of the UK's CDPA which corresponds to art 6.1 of the Directive and s 15 of the Irish Trade Marks Act 1996. Section 11(2)(a) of the UK Act permits the use by a person of his own name provided the use is in accordance with honest practice in industrial or commercial matters. Jacob J set out his view of the test on this point:

'It is not a subjective test. You look at what they are actually doing and ask whether it is in accordance with honest practice in industrial and commercial matters. The very language suggests that this is so. Honest practice cannot involve causing deception, even if it is unintended and unanticipated.'[72]

Jacob J's ruling was appealed to the Court of Appeal which noted that 'the (own name) defence has never been held to apply to names of new companies as otherwise a route to piracy would be obvious. For the same reason a trade name, other than its own name newly adopted by company cannot avail (of the own name defence)'.[73] The Court of Appeal upheld Jacob J's injunction against the company but it refused to extend that injunction against William Asprey himself, limiting it to restraining Mr Asprey from acting as a joint tortfeasor. The Court of Appeal did note, *obiter*, that 'however honest his subjective intentions may be, any use of his own name which amounts to passing off cannot be in accordance with honest practice in industrial or commercial matters'.[74]

[12.36] The Irish courts reviewed the appropriateness of attaching suffixes to personal names for gain in *Dickson & Sons v Dickson & Sons*.[75] The plaintiff 'Alexander Dickson & Sons' had 'a most valuable tradename'[76] as rose growers. The defendant, Alexander Dickson, entered the rose growing trade and in 1907 started to advertise himself as

---

[70] *Joseph Rogers & Sons v WN Rogers & Co* (1924) 41 RPC 277.
[71] (1924) 41 RPC 277 at 291. It should be noted that doubts were expressed about this decision by the House of Lords in *Parker Knoll Ltd v Knoll International Ltd* [1962] RPC 268.
[72] *Asprey and Garrand v WRA (Guns) Ltd* [2002] FSR 30 at 486.
[73] [2002] FSR 31 at 501, para 43.
[74] [2002] FSR 31 at 502, para 49.
[75] *Dickson & Sons v Dickson & Sons* [1909] 1 IR 194.
[76] [1909] 1 IR 194 at 195.

'Alexander Dickson & Sons'. It was held by the Irish Court of Appeal that the defendant was not entitled to advertise himself as this as he had not taken his sons into partnership at all but had 'put forward a sham partnership, for the dishonest purpose of helping him in the wrongful assumption of the trade name of Alexander Dickson & Sons'.[77] It could be argued that this case is authority for the view that the addition of other suffixes such as .com or .ie will not shield a defendant from an action of passing off, where the suffix is added for the 'dishonest purpose of ... helping ... in the wrongful assumption of ... (a) ... trade name'.

[12.37] In *WH Smith v Peter Colman*[78] the plaintiff was the well known UK retailer and newsagent and the defendant had registered the domain name whsmith.com. The plaintiff sued, seeking injunctive relief against use of the domain name and a mandatory order requiring the defendant to take all steps within his power to transfer the domain name to the claimant. The defendant then claimed to have transferred the domain name to a 'William Harold Smith', who was allegedly a resident of the USA but who had an address in the Bahamas. The plaintiff doubted the existence of this individual and sought summary judgment relying upon a letter written by the defendant to the Chairman of the plaintiff's board which was described as 'disingenuous, rambling, repetitious and unrealistic ... It is basically a plea ... to stop what the defendant regarded as an oppressive action and to settle amicably'.[79] At first instance Hoffman LJ ruled that he was not prepared to treat this letter as a genuine offer to negotiate on the basis that it contained the 'unambiguous impropriety[80] 'required to set aside the protection of the 'without prejudice' rule. However, the Court of Appeal held that in this instance the letter was protected by the rule. A significant reason for overturning Hoffman LJ's decision (while agreeing with his legal reasoning) was that the Court of Appeal had sight of 'without prejudice' communications between the parties' lawyers prior to the sending of the letter, which was not opened to Hoffman LJ .[81]

[12.38] In *BT v One in a Million* the appellants had registered a number of domain names which corresponded to trade marks owned by major companies, Sainsbury,

---

[77]   [1909] 1 IR 194 at 196.

[78]   *WH Smith v Peter Colman* [2001] FSR 9 at 91.

[79]   [2001] FSR 9 at 96.

[80]   [2001] FSR 9 at 96. The Court of Appeal affirmed its previous decision in *Unilever v Proctor and Gamble* [2000] FSR 344 that the protection of the 'without prejudice' rule could be removed by unambiguous impropriety, in which it approved the decision of Hoffman LJ in *Foster v Friedland* (10 November 1992) CAT 1052 and referred to *Finch v Wilson* (8 May 1987) and*Hawick Jersey International v Caplan* (1988) The Times, 11 March.

[81]   [2001] FSR 9 at 96 The Court of Appeal approved of examples given by Hoffman LJ of situations where the courts would remove the protection of the without prejudice rule for 'improper threats'. These were: a Canadian case, *Greenwood v Fitt* [1961] 29 DLR 1 at 260, where the defendant was a blackmailer who told the plaintiffs in the course of without prejudice negotiations that unless their claim was withdrawn he would give perjured evidence and bribe witnesses; in *Hawick Jersey International v Caplan* (1988) The Times, 11 March, the plaintiff was a blackmailer who during the negotiations admitted that his claim was bogus. The defendant said: 'you are not going to force my hand by blackmailing me', to which the plaintiff replied with 'disarming candour', 'But I have got to. What would you do if you had been me?'

Ladbroke, Virgin and British Telecom. The appellants argued that these domain names were not instruments of fraud because 'there are people called Sainsbury and Ladbroke and companies, other than Virgin Enterprises Ltd, who have as part of their name the word Virgin and also people or firms whose initials would be BT.'

This submission was rejected by Aldous LJ in the English Court of Appeal, who noted that the lower court had found that the defendant's activities disclosed 'a deliberate practice followed over a substantial period of time of registering domain names which are chosen to resemble the names and marks of other people and are plainly intended to deceive.'

[12.39] Aldous LJ went on to comment that:

> 'The trade names were well-known 'household names' denoting in ordinary usage the respective respondent. The appellants registered them without any distinguishing word because of the goodwill attaching to those names. It was the value of that goodwill, not the fact that they could perhaps be used in some way by a third party without deception, which caused them to register the names ... The registrations were made with the purpose of appropriating the respondents' property, their goodwill, and with an intention of threatening dishonest use by them or another. The registrations were instruments of fraud and injunctive relief was appropriate. '[82]

Gripe sites

[12.40] It is not unheard of for consumers and others who have issues with branded products and services to start 'gripe sites', where those of a similar mind can discuss the issues that concern them.[83] For example, the late American preacher the Reverend Gerry Falwell was well known for his views about persons of a homosexual orientation.[84] To make his own response to the views of Rev Falwell, Christopher Lamparello registered the domain name fallwell.com. This site contained statements such as 'Jerry Falwell has been bearing false witness (Exodus 20:16) against his gay and lesbian neighbors for a long time' and linked to 'Bible verses that Dr. Falwell chooses to ignore'.[85] The parties

---

[82] See also*Fields v Klaus Kobec* [2006] EWHC 350 (Ch);*Blue IP Inc v KCS Herr Voss UK Ltd* [2004] EWHC 97.

[83] Some trade mark owners exhaustively register domain names in an effort to avoid the registration of such sites. In the USA, Verizon registered some 700 such names, but was stymied by the registration of verizoneatspoop.com. See Robinson, 'Cybersquatters must be punished' http://www.theregister.co.uk, 15 June 2006.

[84] The Rev. Falwell considered that AIDS was 'the wrath of a just God against homosexuals' (Rich, 'The Reverend Falwell's Heavenly Timing' (2007) New York Times, 20 May) and that Tinky Winky of the Tellytubbies was a homosexual ('The Political Preacher Divided America' (2007) Pittsburgh Post-Gazette (Pennsylvania), 17 May). Following the 9/11 attacks he expressed the view that 'I really believe that the pagans and the abortionists and the feminists and the gays and the lesbians ... all of them who have tried to secularize America, I point the finger in their face and say: "You helped this happen".' Stearns, 'Evangelical mainstay dies' (2007) The Kansas City Star, 16 May. This last allegation was so 'unfortunate' ((2007) The New York Post, 16 May) that many of the Rev. Falwell's obituaries could not bear to mention it.

[85] *Christopher Lamparello v Jerry Falwell* US Ct of App (4th Cir), (24 August 2005). See also *TMI, Inc v Maxwell* 368 F 3d 433, 434–35 (5th Cir. 2004) and *Lucas Nursery & Landscaping, Inc v Grosse* 359 F 3d 806, 810 (6th Cir 2004).

agreed that Lamparello had never tried to sell goods or services from fallwell.com and that his site had no discernable impact on the Rev. Falwell's own site falwell.com. The Rev. Falwell sought the closure of the fallwell.com site and brought court proceedings. Initially he succeeded but this ruling was overturned on appeal. The US Court of Appeal held:

'Reverend Falwell and Lamparello do not offer similar goods or services. Rather they offer opposing ideas and commentary. Reverend Falwell's mark identifies his spiritual and political views; the website at www.fallwell.com criticizes those very views. After even a quick glance at the content of the website at www.fallwell.com, no one seeking Reverend Falwell's guidance would be misled by the domain name — www.fallwell.com — into believing Reverend Falwell authorized the content of that website. No one would believe that Reverend Falwell sponsored a site criticizing himself, his positions, and his interpretations of the Bible'.[86]

[12.41] As the court held that there was no possibility of confusion, it overturned the decision of the lower court. It would seem that simply using a domain name can amount to a 'use' of a trade mark relating to that domain name. In *Tesco v Elgiocom*:

'the use of internet domain names is itself a service offered to the public, whereby the entry of such a name in the address bar of the computer of an individual browsing the internet will take them to a website. In my view, by registering and making its 'tesco' related domain names available as pathways on the internet to Tesco websites with a view to generating income for itself in the form of commission, Elogicom did use in the course of trade a series of signs (those domain names) which were each similar to the trade marks registered by Tesco and were each used in relation to services (the provision of internet access to Tesco websites) identical with or similar to those for which the trade marks were registered, and in circumstances where there existed a likelihood of confusion on the part of the public, including the likelihood of association of Elogicom's service (the provision of internet access to Tesco websites) with the trade marks'.[87]

[12.42] What Elgiocom were doing was somewhat similar to what a legitimate gripe site might do. Elgiocom had registered and was using a number of domain names such as tesco2u.co.uk which were similar to the Tesco trade mark. But Elgiocom were using these domain names for a commercial purpose and in this they would differ from a legitimate gripe site. Certainly the US courts have taken a very strong view that whilst registering and using a domain name similar to a trade mark as a gripe site may be permitted under US trade mark legislation, this exception will only be permitted where the gripe site has no commercial purpose. [88] Irish courts may come to a similar conclusion. Under the Trade Marks Act 1996 infringement will occur where a sign, identical or similar to a trade mark, is used 'in the course of trade'.[89] But it is also likely that an Irish court would only come to this conclusion if it were convinced that the gripe site was genuine. And in assessing the bona fides of a site's owner a court might have

---

[86] *Christopher Lamparello v Jerry Falwell* US Ct of App (4th Cir), (24 August 2005), p 9.

[87] *Tesco v Elogicom* [2006] EWHC 403 (Ch), para 33.

[88] In *Taubman Co* 319 F 3d at 775 the court found a commercial purpose in respect of a gripe site that had two links to commercial sites.

[89] Trade Marks Act 1996, s 14.

regard to the number of domain names that had been registered by the owner. [90] Anyone considering setting up a gripe site should also consider that even if trade mark law permits the registration and use of a suitable domain name, it will not confer any immunity from the tort of defamation.

[90] The fact that the operator of what he claimed was a parody site had registered 50–60 domain names was a significant factor that led to a finding of cybersquatting in the US case of*People for the Ethical Treatment of Animals v Doughney* 263 F 3d 359, 364 (4th Cir 2001). The fact that the operator of a site had only registered one domain name was held to be equally significant in deciding that they were not a cyber-squatter in*Lucas Nursery & Landscaping, Inc v Grosse* 359 F 3d 806, 810 (6th Cir 2004) and *Christopher Lamparello v Jerry Falwell* US Ct of Apps (4th Cir) (24 August 2005).

PART IV: DATA, DATABASES AND DATA PROTECTION

Chapter 13

Data

Introduction

[13.01] As a general rule information or data cannot be 'owned' or 'controlled' by an individual. That is not to say that certain controls cannot be imposed upon the use or extraction of certain forms of information in certain circumstances. One option is to compile information into a database and then rely upon the database right. This option is discussed in the following chapter. Alternatively, one may assert rights in confidential information, but the assertion of such rights can be problematic. The discussion of the legal base of confidence is not one of sterile academic interest. An individual who wishes to make a claim of confidence must establish a legal basis upon which to make the claim, whether contract, equity, property, statute or otherwise. The importance of doing so is clear from the decision in *Mahon v Post Publications*[1] in which the plaintiff's appeal to the Supreme Court failed because it was unable to establish 'any legal justification for its claim of confidentiality'.[2]

Jurisdictional basis

[13.02] There is a continuing controversy as to what jurisdiction or category of law confidential information falls into: it may be equity, tort,[3] some variant of property law[4] or bailment.[5] On the one hand, the courts may ground an injunction [6] to protect confidential information in equity, as occurred in *House of Spring Gardens v Point Blank Ltd*[7] in which there is little question that Costello J viewed confidentiality as being an equitable doctrine, referring to 'equitable principles'[8] and 'what is essentially a moral

---

[1]   *Mahon v Post Publications* [2007] IESC 15.

[2]   [2007] IESC 15, para 87.

[3]   See Lavery, *Commercial Secrets* (Sweet and Maxwell, 1996) pp 38–42.

[4]   See Lavery, *Commercial Secrets* (Sweet and Maxwell, 1996) pp 42–50; Toulson & Phipps, *Confidentiality* (Sweet and Maxwell, 1996), ch 2; Palmer and Kohler, *Information as Property* (Palmer and McKendrick, eds) (Interests in Goods Lloyds Press, 1993) ch 7.

[5]   8(1) *Halsbury's Laws of England* (4th edn) (1996 reissue) para 408: 'An entrustment of confidential and intangible material may, however, be treated as a bailment of information, creating rights and duties akin to those which arise under a true bailment; this is on the basis that confidential information can be property'. See also Palmer and Kohler, *Information as Property* (Palmer and McKendrick, eds) (Interests in Goods Lloyds Press, 1993) pp 199–201; *Palmer on Bailment* (2nd edn, Sweet and Maxwell, 1991) pp 13–15.

[6]   On the application of the American Cyanmide principles for the grant of interlocutory relief to the protection of breach of confidence, see Series 5, *Software v Philip Clarke* [1996] FSR 273. See also *CMI Centers v Phytopharm* [1999] FSR 235.

[7]   *House of Spring Gardens v Point Blank Ltd* [1984] IR 611.

[8]   [1984] IR 611 at 658.

obligation'.[9] This view was echoed by Fennelly J in the Supreme Court in *Mahon v Post Publications*. He held that 'The law with regard to confidential information ... was ... developed to regulate the behaviour of private parties and was based on the doctrine of trust'.[10] Fennelly J then proceeded to set out the 'contours of the equitable doctrine of confidence'.[11] On the other hand, in *National Irish Bank Ltd v Radio Telefís Éireann*[12] Shanley J stated 'Where a person in whom confidential information reposes discloses that information to the detriment of the party who has confided in him, he commits the tort of breach of confidence'.[13] A third view is that of Griffin J in *House of Spring Gardens v Point Blank Ltd* in which he refers to the defendants having 'misused confidential information the property of'[14] the plaintiff. This controversy is highly significant as it could determine the remedies that would be available to a complainant. It is entirely normal for damages to be awarded in respect of a tort, but more unusual to see them awarded in a case of equity.[15] An equitable jurisdiction would make it easier for the courts to force third parties (who have not signed any confidentiality clause in any contract) to respect the confidentiality of the information.[16] The issue of whether or not confidential information is property has particular relevance in Ireland given that private property is specifically protected by the Irish Constitution.[17] The general view of the authorities is that treating breach of confidence as an action grounded in tort or property law is dubious if not incorrect.[18] Perhaps the most succinct analysis of this controversy is given by Palmer and Kohler: 'If some aspects of the law's treatment of confidential information display a proprietary parallel, that does not mean that confidential information is property *per se* but that in that regard it displays a proprietary characteristic'.[19]

---

9   [1984] IR 611 at 663.
10 *Mahon v Post Publications* [2007] IESC 15, para 70.
11 [2007] IESC 15, para 74.
12 *National Irish Bank Ltd v Radio Telefís Éireann* [1998] 2 IR 465.
13 [1998] 2 IR 465 at 474.
14 *House of Spring Gardens v Point Blank Ltd* [1984] IR 611 at 702.
15 Although the remedy of tracing might suit (see *Keane on Equity* (Butterworths, 1988), ch 20), there is also an argument to be made that equitable compensation can be awarded as in the case of breach of duty by a fiduciary see: Toulson and Phipps, *Confidentiality* (Sweet and Maxwell, 1996) p 32; *Nocton v Ashburton* [1914] AC 932. See also *Aerospares Ltd v Thompson et al* (13 January 1999, unreported) HC (Kearns J).
16 See *Oblique Financial Services v The Promise Production Co Ltd* [1994] 1 ILRM 74.
17 Article 43.
18 See Lavery, *Commercial Secrets* (Sweet and Maxwell, 1996) p 50; Toulson and Phipps, *Confidentiality* (Sweet and Maxwell, 1996) p 31; Palmer & Kohler, *Information as Property* (Palmer and McKendrick, eds) (Interests in Goods Lloyds Press, 1993), p 205. Although see *Electro Cad Australia v Mejati* [1999] FSR 291 in which the High Court of Malaysia held that 'due to the rapid and highly volatile revolution in technology ... the courts must take a broader view of the meaning of property and include information as such' at p 313.
19 Palmer and Kohler, *Information as Property* (Palmer and McKendrick, eds) (Interests in Goods Lloyds Press, 1993) p 205.

[13.03] These issues were reviewed by the Supreme Court of Canada in *Cadbury Schweppes v FBI Foods*[20] in which the plaintiffs claimed that the defendant's product 'Caesar Cocktail' had been manufactured through misuse of confidential information. The plaintiffs claimed a proprietary remedy, that all the defendant's sales of Caesar Cocktail should be treated as belonging to the plaintiff. The court ruled that its jurisdiction in such a case should be dictated by the facts of the case rather than strict doctrinal or jurisdictional considerations. The court could find authority for the view that breach of confidence actions were *sui generic*; it was satisfied that any analysis of the appropriateness of a remedy would have to start from equitable principles. The court refused to treat the defendant's conduct as a breach of fiduciary duty, noting that fiduciary obligations were rarely present in the dealings of experienced businessmen. The court rejected a remedy based upon property principles, holding that such a remedy would be inappropriate. However, the court did hold that tort principles could have an impact on the assessment of equitable compensation, which in this case would support the restoration of the plaintiff to the position it would have held 'but for' the defendant's breach. This left it to the plaintiff to establish the amount of detriment it did in fact suffer, but the court was happy that the authority to award financial compensation for breach of confidence was inherent in the general equitable jurisdiction. The court did refuse to grant an injunction as the information which was the subject of the action was 'nothing very special'.[21] This judgment is significant, both for its willingness to grant monetary compensation and for the willingness of the court to recognise breach of confidence as a *sui generis* cause of action not tied to any particular jurisdiction.

[13.04] The confidentiality of certain types of information can be protected by statute, for example s 71 of the Credit Union Act 1997[22] or s 20 of the Courts and Court Officers Act 1995.[23] The application of s 7 of the Waiver of Certain Tax, Interest and Penalties Act 1993, which deals with confidentiality was reviewed by the High Court in *The Comptroller and Auditor General v Ireland*[24] and was held not to interfere with the ability of the plaintiff to discharge his constitutional function.

What is confidential information?

[13.05] In *Coco v AN Clark (Engineers) Ltd*[25] Megarry J set out three requirements which should be present if (save in the case of contract) a breach of confidence action is to succeed:

(a)   the information must be of a confidential nature;

---

20   *Cadbury Schweppes v FBI Foods* [2000] FSR 491.
21   [2000] FSR 491 at 520, para 72.
22   '... during his term of office or at any time thereafter, an officer or voluntary assistant of a credit union shall not disclose or permit to be disclosed any information which concerns an account or transaction of a member with, or any other business of, the credit union.'
23   'All proceedings of the (Judicial Appointments Advisory) Board and all communications to the Board shall be confidential and shall not be disclosed except for the purposes of this Act'.
24   *The Comptroller and Auditor General v Ireland* [1997] 1 IR 248.
25   *Coco v AN Clark (Engineers) Ltd* [1969] RPC 41.

(b)   the information must have been communicated in circumstances importing an obligation of confidence; and

(c)   there must be unauthorised use of the information.[26]

The judgment of Megarry J in *Coco v AN Clark (Engineers) Ltd* was followed by the Supreme Court in *Mahon v Post Publications* in which the Supreme Court held that:

'1.   The information must in fact be confidential or secret: it must, to quote Lord Greene, 'have the necessary quality of confidence about it'[27];

2.   It must have been communicated by the possessor of the information in circumstances which impose an obligation of confidence or trust on the person receiving it;

3.   It must be wrongfully communicated by the person receiving it or by another person who is aware of the obligation of confidence'.[28]

[13.06] If information is to be protected by the law of confidentiality, then it must be kept secret, so information which is 'well known in the trade' will not be protected. [29] Identifying whether or not information is confidential is therefore a crucial step. In *Thomas Marshall v Guinle*[30] Megarry J suggested the following principles would assist in the identification of confidential information in a industrial or trade setting:

(a)   the party claiming confidentiality must believe that release of the information would be injurious to him or of advantage to his rivals or others;

(b)   the party claiming confidentiality must believe that the information is confidential, that is it is not already in the public domain;

(c)   the belief under the above two headings must be reasonable; and

(d)   the information must be judged in the light of the usage and practices of the particular industry or trade concerned.

[13.07] In *House of Spring Gardens v Point Blank*[31] the principle plaintiff was the designer of a bullet proof vest which other defendants manufactured and sold with some success. The defendants included an individual who had substantial business interests,

---

[26]   [1969] RPC 41 at 47. In *Dunford and Elliot v Johnson & Firth* [1978] FSR 143 Denning MR approved the above but added a fourth: 'If the stipulation for confidence was unreasonable at the time of making it; or if it was reasonable at the beginning, but afterwards, in the course of subsequent happenings, it becomes unreasonable that it should be enforced: then the courts will decline to enforce it: just as in the case of a covenant in restraint of trade', p 148.

[27]   The Supreme Court was quoting Lord Greene in *Saltman Engineering Co Ltd v Campbell Engineering Co Ltd* (1948) 65 RPC 203 at 215.

[28]   *Mahon v Post Publications* [2007] IESC 15, para 74.

[29]   In *Ryan v Capital Leasing* (2 April 1993, unreported) HC (Lynch J), Lynch J. held against the plaintiff as: 'It was, I am sure, well known in the trade that MVS and the plaintiff were in financial difficulties...', at p 26 of the judgment. Similarly, information published in a patent journal will not be protected by the law of confidence as it is not secret: *Mustad v Dosen* [1963] RPC 41. Although information which is known only to the men folk of an aboriginal tribe may be protected, see *Foster v Mountford* [1978] FSR 582.

[30]   *Thomas Marshall v Guinle* [1979] 1 Ch 227.

[31]   *House of Spring Gardens v Point Blank* [1984] IR 611.

including contacts with Libya. This defendant was able to secure a contract for the supply of vests to the Libyan army. The principle plaintiff and this defendant then formed a joint venture to fulfil this contract, as a result of which valuable commercial information was disclosed to the defendants. However relations between the parties broke down, and the defendants started manufacturing vests on their own account. It was claimed that this vest was designed by the defendants but no credible evidence was produced to back up this claim. The plaintiff sued for breach of contract and misuse of confidential information. Costello J reviewed the authorities and this enabled him to formulate the following principles. Costello J considered that these principles should be applied to a case where the court's equitable jurisdiction is invoked in relation to the law of confidence:

'The Court, it should be borne in mind is being asked to enforce what is essentially a moral obligation. It must firstly decide whether there exists from the relationship between the parties an obligation of confidence regarding the information which has been imparted and it must then decide whether the information which was communicated can properly be regarded as confidential information. In considering both (i) the relationship and (ii) the nature of the information , it is relevant to take into account the degree of skill, time and labour involved in compiling the information. As to (i), if the informant himself has expended skill, time and labour on compiling the information, then he can reasonably regard it as of value and he can reasonably consider that he is conferring on its recipient a benefit. If this benefit is conferred for a specific purpose then an obligation may be imposed to use it for that purpose and for no other purpose. As to (ii), if the information has been compiled by the skill, time and labour by the informant then, although he has obtained it from sources which are public, (in the sense that any member of the public with the same skills could obtain it had he acted like the compiler of the information) the information may still, because of its value, be regarded as 'confidential' information and subject to an obligation of confidence. Furthermore, the court will readily decide that the informant correctly regarded the information he was imparting as confidential information, if although based on material which is accessible to the public it is of an unique nature which has resulted from the skill and labour of the informant. Once it is established that an obligation in confidence exists and that the information is confidential, then the person to whom it is given has a duty to act in good faith, and this means that he must use the information for the purpose for which it has been imparted, and he cannot use it to the detriment of the informant.'[32]

Costello J held that once it was clear that the plaintiff had expended a great deal of skill, time and labour in producing the bullet proof vest which was a valuable commercial product, then the fact that some other person could have travelled to the USA and obtained similar information did not deprive the information given by the plaintiff to the defendants of its confidential nature.[33] The fact that the vest was unique, on the defendant's own evidence, assisted in establishing the confidentiality of that

---

[32] [1984] IR 611 at 663–664. This passage was quoted in full by O'Higgins CJ who stated that he agreed entirely with it: [1984] IR 611 at 696.

[33] [1984] IR 611 at 666.

information, as did the fact that information gleaned in the USA would have to be considerably processed before it was useful in the UK.[34]

[13.08] Merely because information is encrypted does not mean that it will be confidential. In *Mars UK Ltd v Teknowledge Ltd*[35] the plaintiff was a leader in the design and manufacture of coin receiving and changing mechanisms. These machines use coin discriminators to automatically identify coins and these had been reverse engineered by the defendant. The plaintiff sued. Jacob J ruled that the encrypted information held on the plaintiff's machines did not have the necessary quality of confidence as the machine was openly on the market and anyone with the skills to decrypt it would have access to the information. The fact that only a few might have such skills was irrelevant, as the owner of a machine has an entitlement 'to dismantle the machine to find out how it works and tell anyone he pleases'. [36] This did not mean that a person could steal the information from the plaintiffs and dispense with the work of reverse engineering. But in this case the encrypted information did not have 'the necessary quality of confidence about it'. He rejected the notion that merely because information is published in encrypted form, that means that it has been published in circumstances importing an obligation of confidence stating that 'As pure matter of common sense I cannot see why the mere fact of encryption makes that which is encrypted confidential or why anyone who decrypts something in code, should necessarily be taken to be receiving information in confidence'.[37] Jacob J explicitly rejected analogies between decryption and eavesdropping, long lens photography or telephone tapping: 'There is nothing surreptitious about taking a thing apart to find out how it is made'.[38] Although in this case Mars had not placed anything on the machine to indicate its contents were confidential, Jacob J stated *obiter* that 'I do not think that even an express statement would work to override the buyer's entitlement to find out how his machine worked' .[39]

[13.09] As technology changes, it may affect what information may be viewed as confidential. In *Exchange Telegraph Co Ltd v Central News Ltd*[40] the plaintiff was a news service which supplied horse racing results to subscribers, on the basis that this

---

[34] [1984] IR 611 at 667.

[35] *Mars UK Ltd v Teknowledge Ltd* [2000] FSR 138. See para **[2.61]** ff.

[36] [2000] FSR 138 at 149, para 31 citing *Alfa Laval Cheese Systems v Wincanton Engineering* [1990] FSR 583.

[37] [2000] FSR 138 at 150, para 33.

[38] [2000] FSR 138 at 150, para 33

[39] [2000] FSR 138 at 151, para 35. In contrast *Halsbury* states that 'The offering for sale of a product embodying confidential information will not of itself destroy the confidence even though the relevant information could be discovered by analysing the product; if the effort and expense of analysis can be avoided by revealing the information it will retain protection, but in time it may become so generally known that protection will be lost'. Halsbury relies upon the decisions in: *Ackroyds (London) Ltd v Islington Plastics* [1962] RPC 97; *Cranleigh Precision Engineering Ltd v Bryant* [1966] RPC 81; and *Yates Circuit Foil Co v Electrofoils* [1976] FSR 345.

[40] *Exchange Telegraph Co Ltd v Central News Ltd* (1897) 2 Ch 48.

information was for private use only. An injunction was granted preventing the defendant from surreptitiously obtaining these results from the plaintiff's customers. The defendant had argued that members of the public in the area where the races took place would know this information anyway. But the court was still happy to treat the information as confidential as although it was available to a large number of persons, there were a great deal more who were ignorant of it. It is highly questionable that such a view would survive today given the proliferation of news services in all media. [41]

[13.10] In the English case of *De Maudsley v Palumbo*,[42] the plaintiff went to a supper party where he met the defendant to whom he disclosed an idea for a nightclub which had several novel features. The plaintiff claimed that the defendant was so impressed with the possibilities that he offered to fund the nightclub or arrange for its funding. The parties commenced preparations, which the plaintiff alleged ultimately led to the setting up of the Ministry of Sound nightclub. However the plaintiff had no involvement in this venture. The plaintiff sued alleging that he had revealed his ideas to the defendant at the supper party in circumstances which implied confidence. Knox J rejected this contention holding that:

> 'it is not essential in order to constitute confidential information for the material to be in writing or other permanent form....it is essential for the material to have at least some attractiveness to an end user and be capable of being realised 'as an actuality' by which I understand to be meant as a finished product in the relevant medium....It is the...element of being capable of being realised as a finished product which is significant...Before the status of confidential information can be achieved by a concept or an idea it is necessary to have gone far beyond identifying a desirable goal. A considerable degree of particularity in a definite product needs to be shown to be the result of the mental process in question. This does not of course exclude simplicity.' [43]

The plaintiff's action failed. Knox J accepted that the plaintiff had 'sowed the original seed in Mr Palumbo's mind' and had been 'rather shabbily treated' by the defendant.[44] However, the fact that confidential information has been communicated orally may not prejudice its protection.[45] Information which is false will not be protected[46] nor will 'trivial tittle tattle'[47] but the simplicity of information will not necessarily restrict its protection.[48] There would not appear to be any requirement that information be original

[41] See Lavery p 69 and*Attorney General v Guardian Newspapers Ltd and others* (1987) 1 WLR 1248 at 1269: 'The truth of the matter is that in the contemporary world of electronics and jumbo jets news anywhere is news everywhere'.

[42] *De Maudsley v Palumbo* [1996] FSR 447.

[43] [1996] FSR 447 at 456. See also *Fraser v Thames Television* [1983] 2 All ER 101 at 121.

[44] [1996] FSR 447 at 459.

[45] *Fraser v Thames Television* [1984] QB 44, [1983] 2 All ER 101.

[46] Per Sedley J *Financial Times v Interbrew* (8 March 2002, unreported) CA, 'there can be no confidentiality in false information' at para 27.

[47] Per Megarry J in*Coco v An Clark (Engineers) Ltd* [1961] RPC 41 at p 421.

[48] *Coco v AN Clark Engineers* and *Cranleigh Precision Engineering Ltd v Bryant* [1966] RPC 81.

or novel.[49] In *Re Ansbacher*[50] the High Court held that the fact that information had been disclosed in confidence would not inhibit the court's ability to publish a report pursuant to the Companies Act 1990. In *EMI v Eircom*[51] Kelly J was:

> 'satisfied that whether the right to confidentiality arises by statute or by contract or at common law, it cannot be relied on by a wrongdoer or a person against whom there is evidence of wrongdoing to protect his or her identity. The right to privacy or confidentiality of identity must give way where there is *prima facie* evidence of wrongdoing[52]'.

An obligation of confidence

[13.11] The second element required by Megarry J in *Coco v AN Clark* is that the information should be subject to an obligation of confidence. The courts will impose an obligation of confidence where a production company is approached with an idea for a screenplay or film.[53] But they will not imply such an obligation where a prototype steering lock was offered for sale to the Argos chain of stores.[54] A duty of confidentiality can arise by virtue of a person's relationships with others. In *National Irish Bank Ltd v RTÉ*[55] Lynch J stated that:

> 'There is no doubt that there exists a duty and a right of confidentiality between a banker and customer as also exists in many other relationships such as for example doctor and patient and lawyer and client. This duty of confidentiality extends to third parties into whose hands confidential information may come and such third parties can be injuncted to prohibit disclosure of such confidential information. There is a public interest in the maintenance of such confidentiality for the benefit of society at large'.[56]

If Irish law still recognises the privilege of the confessional[57] then it is *sui iuris*[58] and may not necessarily be extended to other organisations.[59] Communications between

---

[49] See *House of Spring Gardens v Point Blank Ltd* [1984] IR 611.

[50] *Re Ansbacher* [2004] 3 IR 194.

[51] *EMI v Eircom* [2005] 4 IR 148.

[52] [2005] 4 IR 148 at 152.

[53] *Fraser v Thames Television Ltd* [1984] QB 44; see particularly the dicta of Hirst J at p 65: 'every witness in the theatre or television business on both sides agreed that if he or she received an idea from another it would be wrong to make use of it without the consent of the communicator'.

[54] *Carflow Products v Linwood Securites* [1996] FSR 424. Contrast with *Indata Equipment Supplies Ltd (t/a Autofleet) v ACL Ltd* (31 July, 1997, unreported) CA. See also *Derek Ryan v Capital Leasing Investments* (2 April 1993, unreported) HC (Lynch J).

[55] *National Irish Bank Ltd v RTÉ* [1998] 2 IR 465.

[56] [1998] 2 IR 465 at 494. See also *Cooper Flynn v RTÉ* [2000] 2 IR 344.

[57] See *Cook v Carroll* [1945] IR 515; where priest acting as marriage guidance counsellor, see *ER v JR* [1981] ILRM 125.

[58] 'I think that the absolute unwaivable privilege which probably does attach in Irish Common law to the priest penitent relationship in the confessional is sui iuris' see *Johnston v Church of Scientology* (30 April 1999, unreported) HC (Geoghan J) at p 6.

[59] *Johnston v Church of Scientology* (30 April 1999, unreported) HC (Geoghan J).

spouses are confidential,[60] as may be communications between lovers[61] and 'friends', particularly friends who have signed confidentiality agreements.[62]

[13.12] In *House of Spring Gardens v Point Blank*, Costello J stated that: 'All the cases show that there is no simple test for deciding what circumstances will give rise to an obligation of confidence'.[63] However, such a test was proposed by Megarry J in *Coco v An Clark (Engineers) Ltd*:

'It may be that the hard-worked creature, the reasonable man, may be pressed into service once more; for I do not see why he cannot labour in equity as well as at law.. It seems to me that if the circumstances as such that any reasonable man standing in the shoes of the recipient would have realised upon reasonable grounds the information was being given to him in confidence, then this should suffice to impose upon him an equitable obligation of confidence'.[64]

[13.13] This test was criticised by the Australian courts in *Smith, Kline and French Laboratories (Aust) Ltd v Secretary, Dept of Community Services and Health:*[65]

'this test does not give guidance as to the scope of an obligation where one exists. Sometimes the obligation imposes no restriction on use of the information, as long as the confidee does not reveal it to third parties. In other circumstances, the confidee may not be entitled to use it except for some limited purpose....there can be no breach of the equitable doctrine unless the court concludes that a confidence reposed has been abused, that unconscientious use has been made of the information'.

The reasonable man test was explicitly applied by Jacob J in *Mars UK v Teknowledge*.[66] An obvious circumstance where an obligation of confidence would arise is where an individual or company will have signed a confidentiality clause in a contract guaranteeing to keep certain information confidential.[67] In *Oblique v The Promise Production Co*[68] the parties had entered into an agreement which bound them to

---

60 See Article 40.3.1°2° of the Constitution; *McGee v Attorney General* [1974] IR 284 at common law, see *Argyll v Argyll* [1967] 1 Ch 227.

61 *Stephans v Avery* [1988] 1 Ch 449; *Barrymore v News Group Newspapers* [1997] FSR 600;*A v B Plc* [2002] EMLR 7 at 125, but visiting a brothel may not be confidential, see *Theakson v MGN Ltd* [2002] EMLR 22 at 398: 'The nature of the relationship, the nature of the activity and all the other circumstances in which that activity takes place affect the attribution by the law of the quality of confidentiality to the acts in questions. Indeed apparently similar circumstances could justifiably lead to different conclusions as to confidentiality depending on the individual personalities engaged', per Ouseley J at p 418.

62 *McKevitt v Ash* [2005] EWHC 3003.

63 *House of Spring Gardens v Point Blank* [1984] IR 611 at 662. Noting that the courts had held that such an obligation arose '... when inventors had communicated information in the course of business negotiations with a view to joint ventures'.

64 *Coco v An Clark (Engineers) Ltd* [1969] RPC 41 at 420–421.

65 *Smith, Kline and French Laboratories (Aust) Ltd v Secretary, Dept of Community Services and Health* (1991) 28 FCR 291 10.32.

66 *Mars UK v Teknowledge* [2000] FSR 138, para 34.

67 For example, see *Oblique Financial Services v The Promise Production Co Ltd* [1994] 1 ILRM 74; *Meadox Medicals Ltd v VPI* (27 April 1982, unreported) HC (Hamilton J).

'absolute and total confidentiality' and Keane J granted an interlocutory injunction restraining the defendants from publishing such confidential information.

Unauthorised use or disclosure of the information

[13.14] It is a basic requirement that for there to have been a breach of confidence then there must have been misuse of the information concerned; *House of Spring Gardens v Pointblank* is a good example of this. There is no requirement that the misuse be intentional,[69] but there is no clear test as to what will and will not amount to misuse. Disclosure of confidential information may be justified by circumstance. In *Tournier v National Provincial and Union Bank*[70] Bankes J in the Court of Appeal suggested that disclosure would be justified in the following circumstances:

(a)   where disclosure is under compulsion by law;

(b)   where there is a duty to the public to disclose;

(c)   where the interests of the defendant require disclosure;

(d)   where the disclosure is made by the express or implied consent of the plaintiff[71]

[13.15] In *National Irish Bank Ltd v RTÉ*[72] the plaintiff was seeking to prevent the publication by the defendant of information which allegedly related to the bank's customers. Keane J in the Supreme Court approved of the following:

'there is no confidence as the disclosure of iniquity. You cannot make me the confidant of a crime or fraud, and be entitled to close up my lips upon any secret which you have the audacity to disclose to me relating to any fraudulent intention of your part: such a confidence cannot exist'.[73]

Keane J also referred Keane J, noting that this right of disclosure may be limited and quoting the following passage from Denning MR[74]:

'The disclosure must, I should think, be to one who has a proper interest to receive the information. Thus it would be proper to disclose a crime to the police; or a breach of the restrictive Trade Practices Act to the Registrar. There may be cases where the misdeed is of such a character that the public interest may demand, or at least excuse, publication to a broader field, even to the press'.[75]

[13.16] These and other authorities led Keane J to the conclusion that:

'where some one is in possession of confidential information establishing that serious misconduct has taken place or is contemplated, the courts should not prevent disclosure to person who have a proper interest in receiving information. The defendant accordingly, should not be restrained in this case from disclosing to the Revenue Commissioners the

---

68   [1994] 1 ILRM 74.

69   *Seager v Copydex* (1967) 1 WLR 923.

70   *Tournier v National Provincial and Union Bank* (1924) 1 KB 461.

71   (1924) 1 KB 461 at 473.

72   *National Irish Bank Ltd v RTÉ* [1998] 2 IR 465.

73   [1998] 2 IR 465 at p 482, quoting from Wood VC in *Gartside v Outram* (1857) 26 LJ Ch 113 at 114.

74   [1998] 2 IR 465 at 483.

75   *Initial Services v Putterill* (1968) 1 QB 396 at 405.

confidential information in its possession which, it says, establishes that this scheme had been availed of in order to evade the payment of tax. Nor should it be restrained form making use of the information in order to pursue an investigation which it has legitimately undertaken'.[76]

However Keane J did make provision to allow customers who might be named by RTÉ time to apply to the court themselves.

Who may sue?

[13.17] A party needs *locus standi* in order to bring a claim for breach of confidence and the courts have rejected claims where no *locus standi* is apparent.[77] This issue brings the question of the jurisdiction of confidential information law into prominence again. If confidential information is not property, the assignor cannot pass to the assignee the personal right to have the information as confidential and therefore the assignee cannot sue to enforce a duty of confidence but can only seek to comply the assignor to do so.[78]

Duration

[13.18] The period for which information will remain confidential may be determined by the terms of the agreement under which the information was acquired.[79] Such terms will be subject to the requirements that they be reasonable having regard to public policy. Information will cease to be confidential once it enters the public domain, so if information is published in a patent application, then it will cease to be confidential.[80] However the English Courts have developed the spring-board doctrine which holds that 'a person who has obtained information in confidence is not allowed to use it as a spring-board for activities detrimental to that person who made the confidential communication, and spring-board it remains even when all the features have been published or can be ascertained by actual inspection by any member of the public'.[81] This was followed in *Cranleigh Precision Engineering v Bryant*.[82] In *Attorney General v Guardian Newspapers (Spycatcher)*[83] the House of Lords held that while confidential information could not be protected once it was in the public domain, the court would act to prevent a wrongdoer profiting from his wrongdoing. Therefore the doctrine of 'springboard' would appear to be alive in the English courts. [84] In *Aksjeselskapet Jotul v Waterford Iron Founders Ltd*[85] this doctrine was raised in the Irish courts and approved

---

76 (1968) 1 QB 396 at 487.
77 *Fraser v Evans* (1969) 1 QB 349; *Ryan v Capital Leasing* (2 April 1993, unreported) HC (Lynch J).
78 See Toulson and Phipps *Confidentiality* (Sweet and Maxwell, 1996) p 54; Hope JA in *Moorgate Tobacco v Philip Morris* (1982) 64 FLR 387 at 404.
79 So in *AG v Baker* [1990] 3 All ER 257, the Court of Appeal held that a lifelong and worldwide restriction was valid where it did not affect future employment.
80 See *O Mustad v Dosen* (1964) 1 WLR 109 or *Prout v British Gas* [1992] FSR 478.
81 *Terrapin Ltd v Builders Supply Co (Hayes) Ltd* [1967] RPC 375 at 391 (the judgment dates back to 1959).
82 *Cranleigh Precision Engineering v Bryant* [1966] RPC 81.
83 *Attorney General v Guardian Newspapers (Spycatcher)* (1990) 1 AC 109.
84 See *PSB International v Whitehouse* [1992] FSR 489, [1992] IRLR 279; and *Sun Valley Foods v John Philip Vincent* [2000] FSR 825.

by McWilliam J. [86] A similar issue was subsequently raised in *House of Spring Gardens v Point Blank* but Costello J held that the information had not entered the public domain.

Liability of third parties

[13.19] Equity allows the courts to grant injunctions which bind third parties who may not have been a party to the original confidentiality agreement. In *Oblique v The Promise Production Co*[87] the first-named defendant entered into an agreement with the plaintiff under conditions of absolute confidence, Keane J was willing to grant an injunction restraining the third- and fourth-named defendants who were not parties to the agreement from publishing that information:

> 'It is obvious from the cases and indeed it is a matter of common sense that the right to confidentiality, which the law recognises in these cases, would be of little value, if the third parties to whom this information has been communicated were at liberty to publish it to another party, or in this case to publish it to the general public, without the court being in a position to intervene. So, that being the statement of the law, both here in Ireland and in the United Kingdom, it is quite clear that the legal position would appear to be that the obligation of confidentiality of a company cannot be enforced against third parties.'[88]

Confidential information and the constitution

[13.20] In *Oblique v The Promise Production Co* the defendants argued that granting an injunction to restrain the defendants from publishing confidential information infringed upon their constitutional right to freedom of expression. Keane J rejected this contention as misconceived, holding that the plaintiff's rights in a case such as this one would flow not from Article 40.6.1°, which deals generally with freedom of expression, but from Article 40.3.1° which guarantees the personal right of the citizen:

> 'Article 40.6.1° is concerned, not with the dissemination of factual information, but the rights of the citizen, in formulating or publishing convictions or opinions, or conveying an opinion; and the rights of all citizens including conveying information, arises in our law, not under Article 40.6.1° but from Article 40.3.1°'.[89]

Keane took the view that it was clear from the judgment of Costello J in *AG v Paperlink* that this right is not absolute but qualified having regard to other legal constraints: 'the respondent's right to communicate information must be subject to other rights and duties, and in particular, to the right of confidentiality enjoyed by ... the plaintiff'.[90] Some clue as to the position of confidentiality in the hierarchy of rights was given in *Re Ansbacher (Cayman) Ltd*[91] where McCracken J in the Supreme Court stated that 'I have

---

[85] *Aksjeselskapet Jotul v Waterford Iron Founders Ltd* (8 November 1977, unreported) HC (McWilliam J). See Lavery, pp 59–63.
[86] Referring to *Terrapin Ltd v Builders Supply Co (Hayes) Ltd* [1967] RPC 375.
[87] *Oblique v The Promise Production Co* [1994] 1 ILRM 74.
[88] [1994] 1 ILRM 74 at 77–78.
[89] [1994] 1 ILRM 74 at 78.
[90] [1994] 1 ILRM 74 at 79.
[91] *Re Ansbacher (Cayman) Ltd* [2002] 2 ILRM 491.

no hesitation whatever in saying that the right to have justice administered in public far exceeds any right to privacy, confidentiality or a good name'.[92]

Confidential information and the ECHR

[13.21] Article 10 of the European Convention on Human Rights (ECHR) provides that:

'Everyone has the right to freedom of expression. This right shall include freedom to hold opinions and to receive and impart information and ideas without interference by public authority and regardless of frontiers. This article shall not prevent States from requiring the licensing of broadcasting, television or cinema enterprises'.[93]

However, the ECHR goes on to provide that:

'The exercise of these freedoms, since it carries with it duties and responsibilities, may be subject to such formalities, conditions, restrictions or penalties as are prescribed by law and are necessary in a democratic society….for preventing the disclosure of information received in confidence…'[94]

[13.22] Following the enactment of the European Convention on Human Rights Act 2003, Irish courts must interpret the law 'in a manner compatible with the State's obligations'[95] under the ECHR. This means that the courts must interpret the law of confidential information in a manner compatible with the State's obligations under the ECHR. So the right to freedom of expression may be balanced against the need to prevent the disclosure of confidential information. In *The Sunday Times v United Kingdom (No 2)*[96] the European Court of Human Rights (ECtHR) expressed doubts about the legitimacy of use of an injunctive remedy to prevent newspapers from exercising their right and duty to purvey information, already available, on a matter of legitimate public concern.[97] The interaction between confidential information and art 10 of the ECHR (freedom of expression) was examined in *Imutran v Uncaged Campaigns*.[98] The plaintiff was engaged in research into xenotransplantation, which is the transplantation of organs from pigs to humans, primarily at Huntington Life Sciences. The defendant received an anonymous package through the post containing a large amount of confidential information relating to this work. The defendant then published these documents on its website. The plaintiff sought an injunction restraining the publication and the defendant argued that publication was justified in the public interest. Morritt VC reviewed the case law on this point and concluded that the public interest in disclosure may outweigh the right of the plaintiff to protect his confidences. He further concluded that the court would have to consider how much disclosure the public interest requires; the fact that some disclosure may be required does not mean that disclosure to the whole world should be permitted.[99] The defendant also argued that it

---

92 [2002] 2 ILRM 491 at 505.
93 ECHR, art 10(1).
94 ECHR, art 10(2).
95 European Convention on Human Rights Act 2003, s 2(1).
96 *The Sunday Times v United Kingdom (No 2)* [1992] 14 EHRR 229.
97 [1992] 14 EHRR 229 at 244.
98 *Imutran v Uncaged Campaigns* [2002] FSR 2.
99 [2002] FSR 2, para 20. (contd/)

was entitled to publish the information by art 10. Morritt VC held that the effect of this article was that the protection of confidential information which is a restriction on the exercise of the right to freedom of expression must be justified as being no more than is necessary in a democratic society.[100]

[13.23] In *Ashworth Hospital Authority v MGN Ltd*[101] the defendant published an article about the Moors murderer Ian Brady which relied upon information taken from a database maintained by the plaintiff. The plaintiff then sought a Norwich Pharmacal order to identify the person who had supplied this information to the defendant. The defendant resisted this application relying upon art 10 to argue that disclosure would restrict freedom of expression as it would interfere with journalistic sources.[102] The ECHR upheld the protection of journalistic sources in *Goodwin v United Kingdom*[103]: 'Protection of journalistic sources is one of the basic conditions for press freedom…without such protection, sources may be deterred from assisting the press in informing the public on matters of public interest…'. The House of Lords drew from this case that the necessity for any restriction of freedom of expression had to be convincingly established and that limitations on the confidentiality of the journalistic sources called for the most careful scrutiny by the court. Therefore, disclosure should only be ordered to meet a pressing social need and if it was proportionate to a legitimate aim.[104] Medical records are always to be confidential[105] but given the difficulty and danger of caring for patients such as Ian Brady the need for protection was particularly great. Given this, it was essential that the source of the information be identified and punished; accordingly an order for disclosure was made.

[13.24] Freedom of expression is a public interest in itself. This is significant as the courts have permitted the publication of confidential information in the public interest.[106] In *Mahon v Post Publications* the defendant argued that publication of certain information would be in the public interest. Fennelly J responded:

> 'The courts do not pass judgment on whether any particular exercise of the right of freedom of expression is in the public interest. The media are not required to justify publication by reference to any public interest other than that of freedom of expression itself. They are free to publish material which is not in the public interest. I have no doubt that much of the material which appears in the news media serves no public interest whatever. I have equally no doubt that much of it is motivated, and perfectly permissibly so, by the pursuit of profit. Publication may indeed be prompted by less noble motives.[107]

---

99   (\contd) See *Initial Public Services v Putterill* (1968) 1 QB 396; *Hubbard v Vosper* (1972) 2 QB 84; *Francome v Mirror Group Newspapers Ltd* (1984) 1 WLR 892; *Lion Laboratories Ltd v Evans* [1985] QB 526; *Re A company's Application* [1989] CH 477 and *Attorney-General v Observer Ltd* (1990) 1 AC 109.

100 [2002] FSR 2, para 21.

101 *Ashworth Hospital Authority v MGN Ltd* [2002] EMLR 36.

102 See also *Mersey Care NHS Trust v Ackroyd* [2007] EWCA Civ 101, 94 BMLR 84.

103 *Goodwin v United Kingdom* [1966] 22 EHRR 123.

104 [1966] 22 EHRR 123, paras 61–62.

105 *Z v Finland* [1998] 25 EHRR 371.

106 *National Irish Bank v RTÉ* [1998] 2 IR 465.

107 *Mahon v Post Publications* [2007] IESC 15, para 42.

… The right of freedom of expression extends the same protection to worthless, prurient and meretricious publication as it does to worthy, serious and socially valuable works. The undoubted fact that news media frequently and implausibly invoke the public interest to cloak worthless and even offensive material does not affect the principle.'[108]

Fennelly J went on to analyse the right to Freedom of Expression under art 10 of the European Convention on Human Rights and its interaction with the constitutional right. He also examined the plaintiff's claim to confidentiality and concluded that:

'The Tribunal seeks an order which will restrict freedom of expression. It claims that the press should be restrained from publishing information which it has designated as confidential. It has not been able to identify any legal power which it possesses to designate information released by it in that way. It seeks an order in very wide terms in respect of unspecified information, which would affect the entire media'.[109]

[13.25] The ECtHR sought to strike a balance between a duty of confidence and the right to freedom of expression in *Editions Plon v France*.[110] The applicant had published a book co-authored by a journalist and President Mitterrand's former physician. The book appears to have been written to rebut allegations that President Mitterrand had not been properly cared for.[111] However, President Mitterrand's surviving children and widow successfully sought an injunction prohibiting the book's publication.[112] The physician was also convicted of breaching professional confidence, fined and given a four month prison sentence, which was suspended.[113] The book was published the day after President Mitterrand's funeral 'which itself had taken place barely ten days after President Mitterrand's death'. The ECtHR was of the opinion that:

'the distribution so soon after the President's death of a book which depicted him as having consciously lied to the French people about the existence and duration of his illness and…constituted a prima facie breach of medical confidentiality could only have intensified the grief of the President's heirs following his very recent and painful death. Moreover, the President's death, after a long fight against his illness and barely a few months after he had left office, certainly aroused strong emotions among politicians and the public, so that the damage caused by the book to the deceased's reputation was particularly serious in the circumstances'.[114]

As regards the status of the French law of confidence, the ECtHR noted that:

'a norm cannot be regarded as a 'law'… unless it is formulated with sufficient precision to enable the citizen to regulate his conduct; he must be able – if need be with appropriate advice – to foresee, to a degree that is reasonable in the circumstances, the consequences which a given action may entail. Those consequences need not be foreseeable with absolute certainty. Whilst certainty is desirable, it may bring in its train excessive rigidity and the law must be able to keep pace with changing circumstances. Accordingly, many

---

108 [2007] IESC 15, para 43.
109 [2007] IESC 15, para 101.
110 *Editions Plon v France* (18 May 2004) ECtHR.
111 (18 May 2004) ECtHR, para 6–8.
112 (18 May 2004) ECtHR, paras 9–11.
113 (18 May 2004) ECtHR, para 12
114 (18 May 2004) ECtHR, para 47.

laws are inevitably couched in terms which, to a greater or lesser extent, are vague and whose interpretation and application are questions of practice.'[115]

[13.26] The court reviewed the French law of medical confidentiality and concluded that 'the applicant company cannot maintain that it was unable to foresee 'to a reasonable degree' the likely legal consequences'[116] of publishing confidential information. The ECtHR held that in the circumstances of this case the grant of an interim injunction 'may be regarded as having been 'necessary in a democratic society' for the protection of the rights of President Mitterrand and his heirs'. And, this interim relief did not violate article 10 of the ECHR. However, the French courts were subsequently determined to 'put an end to the injury suffered by the victim and to prevent the recurrence of the damage that would necessarily result from resumption of the distribution of the piece of writing'.[117]

Therefore, in order to preserve the confidentiality of the deceased's medical records and to prevent further distress, the French courts issued a perpetual injunction. The ECtHR held that the issue of this injunction was not justified. It was issued nine and a half months after the death of President Mitterrand and 'as the President's death became more distant in time … (the legitimate emotions of the deceased's relatives) … became less important'.

Furthermore, some 40,000 copies of the book had been sold, its contents had been disseminated online and discussed in the media. As a result 'the book was to a large extent no longer confidential in practice'.[118] Therefore the ECtHR concluded that there was no 'pressing social need' which justified the issue of the perpetual injunction.[119]

[13.27] In *Stoll v Switzerland*[120] the Swiss Courts had fined the applicant €520 'for having made public "secret official deliberations".'[121] of the Swiss Diplomatic Corps. In finding that there had been a breach of art 10, the ECtHR found 'that the confidentiality of diplomatic reports is justified in principle, but cannot be protected at any price'.[122] Confidential information has been discussed by the ECtHR in relation to rights other than freedom of expression. The ECtHR protected communications of confidential information to and from lawyers in *Istratii v Moldova*[123] where the ECtHR stated that:

'One of the key elements in a lawyer's effective representation of a client's interests is the principle that the confidentiality of information exchanged between them must be protected'.[124]

---

[115] (18 May 2004) ECtHR, para 26.
[116] (18 May 2004) ECtHR, para 31.
[117] (18 May 2004) ECtHR, para 52.
[118] (18 May 2004) ECtHR, para 53.
[119] (18 May 2004) ECtHR, para 55.
[120] *Stoll v Switzerland* (25 April 2005) ECtHR.
[121] (25 April 2005) ECtHR, para 44.
[122] (25 April 2005) ECtHR, para 48.
[123] *Istratii v Moldova* (27 March 2007) ECtHR.
[124] *Istratii v Moldova* (27 March 2007) ECtHR, para 89.

State information

[13.28] In *AG for England and Wales v Brandon Book Publishers*[125] Costello J held that information disclosed by a government to a private individual was protected on a different basis to information disclosed between private individuals, quoting the following passage with approval[126]:

> 'The equitable principle has been fashioned to protect the personal, private and proprietary interests of the executive citizen, not to protect the very different interests of the executive government. It acts or is supposed to act, not according to standards of private interest but in the public interest. This is not to say that equity will not protect information in the hands of the government, but it is to say that when equity protects government information it will look at the matter through different spectacles'.[127]

[13.29] The courts have been willing to impose liability upon the State when public servants wrongfully disclose confidential information. This occurred in the decision of *Hanahoe v Hussey*.[128] The plaintiffs were a law firm of 'the highest reputation'.[129] The gardaí got a warrant to search their offices, but news leaked to the media in advance of the search warrant being executed. Kinlen J held that:

> 'This was a deliberate leaking to the media which caused considerable embarrassment to the applicants. It was intended to embarrass and distress the applicants and it most certainly did. It was an outrageous interference with their privacy and their constitutional rights.'[130]

Kinlen J awarded damages for the 'tort of misfeasance of public office' that resulted in the creation of '"a media circus" ... to highlight the search of the applicants' office'.[131] Kinlen J awarded damages of €127,500 to mark the court's 'strong disapproval'[132] of the State's conduct. This case is *iusdem generic*; by definition the tort of misfeasance of public office can only apply to the State. However, Kinlen J did suggest that 'The court must be ever conscious of the fact that this is a new and serious invasion of constitutional rights including the invasion of privacy and possibly the invasion of confidential relationships'[133]

[13.30] In *Gray v Minister for Justice Equality and Law Reform*[134] Quirke J was satisfied that information relating to a relative of a family had been leaked to journalists by gardaí and awarded the family €70,000 in compensation.

---

[125] *AG for England and Wales v Brandon Book Publishers* [1986] IR 597.
[126] [1986] IR 597 at 601.
[127] *The Commonwealth of Australia v John Fairfax & Sons* [1980] 147 CLR 39 at 51–52.
[128] *Hanahoe v Hussey* [1998] 3 IR 69.
[129] [1998] 3 IR 69 at 72.
[130] [1998] 3 IR 69 at 108.
[131] [1998] 3 IR 69 at 107.
[132] [1998] 3 IR 69 at 109.
[133] [1998] 3 IR 69 at 94.
[134] '€70,000 for family in ruling against Garda' (2007) The Irish Times, 18 January.

Statutory obligations of confidence

[13.31] In *Mahon v Post Publications* the Supreme Court noted that 'It is not unknown for the Oireachtas to enact specific rules ordaining the confidentiality of categories of documents or information under pain of criminal penalty: see for example section 37 of the Commissions of Investigation Act 2004.'[135]

The most obvious example of the state protecting its own confidentiality is the Official Secrets Act 1963. This provides that:

> 'A person shall not communicate any official information to any other person unless he is duly authorised to do so or does so in the course of and in accordance with his duties as the holder of a public office or when it is his duty in the interest of the State to communicate it.' [136]

and that:

> 'A person shall not retain any official document or anything which constitutes or contains official information when he has no right to retain it or when not required by his duty as the holder of a public office to retain it'.[137]

[13.32] The Act also contains provisions relating to the carrying out of 'Acts contrary to safety or preservation of State'[138] and 'Communication with foreign agents or members of unlawful organisations'.[139] The maximum penalty for breach of the Act's provisions is seven years' penal servitude.[140] In contrast, the Freedom of Information Acts create a right of access to public information. The Acts provide that 'Subject to the provisions of this Act, every person has a right to and shall, on request thereof, be offered access to any record held by a public body and the right so conferred is referred to in this Act as the right of access.'[141]

[13.33] This right may be exercised by making a request in writing stating that the request is made under the Act, giving sufficient particulars to enable the identification of the record concerned and specifying the form or manner of access,[142] which may be in the form of 'a computer disk or other electronic device containing the information'.[143] The Act makes no specific provision for access to be granted over the Internet but this might come within the more general provisions of the Act.[144] Records which contain commercially sensitive information may be exempt from requests for access.

---

[135] *Mahon v Post Publications* [2007] IESC 15, para 87.
[136] Official Secrets Act 1963, s 4(1). However legislation has created new exemptions such ass 48 of the Freedom of Information Act 1997;s 16(2) of the Committees of the Houses of the Oireachtas (Compellability, Privileges and Immunities of Witnesses) Act 1997.
[137] Official Secrets Act 1963, s 6(1).
[138] Official Secrets Act 1963, s 9.
[139] Official Secrets Act 1963, s 10.
[140] Official Secrets Act 1963, s 13(3).
[141] Freedom of Information Acts 1997–2003, s 6(1).
[142] Freedom of Information Acts 1997–2003, s 7(1).
[143] Freedom of Information Acts 1997–2003, s 12(1)(c).
[144] Freedom of Information Acts 1997–2003, s 12(1)(g).

Section 27 of the Act requires that a request for access be refused if the record contains:

'(a) trade secrets of a person other than the requester concerned,

(b) financial, commercial, scientific or technical or other information whose disclosure could reasonably be expected to result in a material financial loss or gain to the person to whom the information relates, or could prejudice the competitive position of that person in the conduct of his or her profession or business or otherwise in his or her occupation, or

(c) information whose disclosure could prejudice the conduct or outcome of contractual or other negotiations of the person to whom the information relates'.

[13.34] A request for access to such information may be permitted where: the person to whom the record relates consents in writing or otherwise[145] to the request being granted; the information is in the public domain; the information relates only to the requester; the person to whom the information relates gave it to a public body with an indication that it might be made available to the general public; or disclosure of the information concerned is necessary in order to avoid a serious and imminent danger to the life or health of an individual or to the environment.[146] Similarly a request for information must be refused where:

'the record concerned contains information given to the public body concerned in confidence and on the understanding that it would be treated by it as confidential (including such information as aforesaid that a person was required by law, or could have been required by the body pursuant to law, to give to the body) and, in the opinion of the head (of the public body), its disclosure would be likely to prejudice the giving to the body of further similar information from the same person or other persons and it is of importance to the body that such further similar information as aforesaid should continue to be given to the body.'

The above provision will not apply to a record which is prepared by a person working for a public body in the course of the performance of his or her functions unless disclosure of the information concerned would constitute a breach of a duty of confidence that is provided for by an agreement or statute or otherwise by law and is owed to a person other than a public body or head or a director, or member of the staff of, a public body or a person who is providing or provided a service for a public body under a contract for services.[147] A record will be exempt if disclosure of the information concerned would constitute a breach of a duty of confidence provided for by a provision of an agreement or enactment or otherwise by law.[148] The Act also provides for exemptions for: deliberations of public bodies,[149] functions and negotiations of public bodies,[150]

---

[145] However the identity of the person making the request must be verified in this situation, Freedom of Information Acts 1997–2003, s 27(2).
[146] Freedom of Information Acts 1997–2003, s 27(2).
[147] Section 26(2).
[148] Section 26(1)(b).
[149] Section 20.
[150] Section 21.

parliamentary, court and other matters,[151] law enforcement and public safety,[152] security, defence and international relations,[153] personal information,[154] research and natural resources,[155] and financial and economic interests of the state and public bodies.[156]

---

[151] Section 22.
[152] Section 23.
[153] Section 23.
[154] Section 28.
[155] Section 30.
[156] Section 31.

Chapter 14

Databases

Introduction

[14.01] Traditionally, the creator of a compilation would have to apply a considerable amount of creativity in deciding which works were sufficiently appropriate or relevant to be compiled, using limited storage media such as a book or a paper file. So *The Golden Treasury of the Best Songs and Lyrical Poems in the English Language* was protected by copyright as its compilation required extensive reading and study, together with the exercise of taste and judgment.[1] In contrast, digital media can offer virtually limitless storage at extremely low cost. In this environment it is the comprehensive nature of a database that is important. So the object of the LEXIS database is to provide access to the maximum number of legal judgments. Creativity is more likely to be applied by users of the database, who must decide the best strategy for searching its contents. A major difference between computerised databases and collections of paper documents is the ease with which the entire contents of a database can be extracted and, in effect, stolen. Anyone who decided to copy the Golden Pages would face a long and arduous labour in front of a photocopier; it would be a lot cheaper and easier just to order a legitimate copy. In contrast the contents of a CD-ROM could be copied in one go and connected to the Internet in rivalry with the existing Golden Pages site, which is what occurred in the American case of *Zeidenburg & Silken Mountain Web Services, Inc.*[2] The EC's solution to this perceived problem was the enactment of the Directive on the Legal Protection of Databases[3] or Database Directive, which is implemented in Ireland as Pt V of the CRRA 2000–2004. One of the Directive's key innovations was its creation of the *sui generis* right, which is referred to as the 'database right' in the CRRA 2000.[4] It was hoped that improving rights in this way would encourage the creation of European databases, but it would appear to have had the opposite effect.

[14.02] A database is defined by the CRRA 2000–2004 as:

> 'a collection of independent works, data or other materials, arranged in a systematic or methodical way and individually accessible by any means but excludes computer programs used in the making or operation of a database'.[5]

---

[1]   *Macmillan v Suresh Chunder Deb* [1890] ILR 17.
[2]   *Zeidenburg & Silken Mountain Web Services, Inc* US Ct of Apps (7th Cir), 86 F 3d 1447, 1996 US App. LEXIS 14951; 39 USPQ 2D (BNA) 1161, Copy L Rep (CCH) P27, 529, 29 UCCR Serv.
[3]   908 F Supp 640 (WD Wis 1996).
[4]   CRRA 2000–2004, s 321.
[5]   CRRA 2000–2004, s 2(1).

The Act protects databases in two ways. Firstly, databases are protected as copyright works. Secondly, the Act creates a new 'database right' for the creators of databases. In doing so the Act implements the Directive on the Legal Protection of Databases.[6] The justification for the Directive was based upon the need to harmonise member state's database protection legislation. But, the primary purpose of the Directive was to:

> 'to promote and protect investment in data storage and processing systems which contribute to the development of an information market against a background of exponential growth in the amount of information generated and processed annually in all sectors of activity.'[7]

[14.03] A decade after the enactment of the Directive, it must be concluded that it has failed to obtain these objectives. In particular Europe has continued to fall behind the USA in the production of databases. When the Directive was enacted there were two databases in the USA for every one in Europe. By 2004 this ratio had increased to 3:1 in favour of America.[8] In particular the *sui generis* right provided by the Database Directive would appear to be counterproductive. As was acknowledged in a study published by the EC Commission:

> 'there has been a considerable growth in database production in the US, whereas, in the EU, the introduction of 'sui generis' protection appears to have had the opposite effect ... Introduced to stimulate the growth of databases in Europe, the new instrument has had no proven impact on the production of databases.'[9]

[14.04] The EC protects databases by separating their functions into three separate elements and conferring separate protections on each. These parts are:

(a)   the software used to operated the database, which is protected by copyright and, in particular, the software directive;

(b)   the structure of an original database, which is protected by copyright; and

(c)   the content of the database, which is protected by the database right.

Each of these rights applies to different elements of a database, but the distinctions between these rights may prove difficult to make in practice. And, in practice all elements of a database may be given the same effective protection. This is controversial, as content of databases which is made without any creative input may now receive the same protection as is available under copyright law.

Protection of database software

[14.05] The Database Directive makes it clear that its provisions do not apply to computer programs that may be used to operate databases. It states that 'Protection

---

6   Directive 96/9, OJ L 077 , 27/03/1996, pp 20–28.

7   ECJ (Grand Chamber) in*Fixtures Marketing v Oy Veikkaus* Ab C-46/02 (9 November 2004) ECJ, para 33, citing the 9th, 10th and 12th recitals to the Directive.

8   EC Commission, *DG Internal Market and Services Working Paper, First evaluation of Directive 96/9/EC on the legal protection of databases* (2005) Brussels, 12 December, pp 22–23.

9   EC Commission, *DG Internal Market and Services Working Paper, First evaluation of Directive 96/9/EC on the legal protection of databases* (2005) Brussels, 12 December, p 24.

under this Directive shall not apply to computer programs used in the making or operation of databases accessible by electronic means.'[10] This provision is replicated in the CRRA 2000–2004 which 'excludes computer programs used in the making or operation of a database'[11] from the definition of database. But in practice it may prove difficult to distinguish between a computer program that operates a database and the database itself. In this regard, see the English decision of *Navitaire Inc v Easyjet Airline Co Bulletproof Technologies Inc.*[12]

Protection of database structure

[14.06] The CRRA 2000–2004 provides that copyright will subsist in 'original databases.'[13] An original database is one 'in any form which by reason of the selection or arrangement of its contents constitutes the original intellectual creation of the author'.[14] The protections provided by copyright are limited; in particular that Act provides that copyright protection:

> 'shall not extend to the ideas and principles which underlie any element of a work, procedures, methods of operation or mathematical concepts and, in respect of original databases, shall not extend to their contents and is without prejudice to any rights subsisting in those contents'.

[14.07] Thus the Act makes a clear distinction between the structure of a database and its content. For copyright protection to apply to a database it must be 'recorded in writing or otherwise by or with the consent of the author.'[15] The author of a database will be 'the individual or group of individuals who made the database.'[16] Copyright in an original database will expire some 70 years after the death of the author.[17] The significance of copyright is that it gives the author of a database the exclusive right to undertake or authorise others to undertakes:

> '(a) to copy the work;
>
> (b) to make available to the public the work;
>
> (c) to make an adaptation of the work or to undertake either of the acts referred to in paragraph (a) or (b) in relation to an adaptation.'[18]

Copyright in an original database will be infringed by any person who 'without the licence of the copyright owner undertakes, or authorises another to undertake, any of the acts restricted by copyright.'[19] However, the Act does provide that it:

---

[10] Directive 96/9, art 1(3).

[11] CRRA 2000, s 2(1).

[12] *Navitaire Inc v Easyjet Airline Co Bulletproof Technologies Inc* [2004] EWHC 1725 (Ch), [2006] RPC 111.

[13] CRRA 2000–2004, s 17(2).

[14] CRRA 2000–2004, s 2(1).

[15] CRRA 2000–2004, s 18(1).

[16] CRRA 2000–2004, s 21(g).

[17] CRRA 2000–2004, s 24(1).

[18] CRRA 2000–2004, s 37(1).

[19] CRRA 2000–2004, s 37(2).

'is not an infringement of the copyright in an original database for a person who has the right to use the database or any part thereof, whether under a licence to undertake any of the acts restricted by the copyright in the original database or otherwise, to undertake, in the exercise of that right, anything which is necessary for the purposes of access to or use of the contents of the database or part thereof.'[20]

Whether there is any difference between the rights conferred by copyright and those provided by the database right is doubtful. As one author has commented the database right 'incorporates, and is identical to, the exclusive rights enjoyed by copyright holders ... it is in effect a copyright'.[21]

Protection of database contents: the database or *sui generis* right

[14.08] The Act creates a new property right which is to be known as the 'database right', referred to by the Database Directive as the *sui generis* right. When it was originally proposed this right was to have been minimalist in nature, but the right that appears in the enacted text 'can be categorized as a new form of copyright that applies to databases, covering both sweat of the brow and creative aspects of making a database'. Broadly, the Database Directive seeks to give database owners exclusive rights that are 'in effect a copyright'.[22] The Directive grants only very limited exceptions to this right; exceptions that 'are appropriate to ... copyright systems with relatively high standards of originality.'[23] A study published by the EC Commission suggested that the withdrawal of the *sui generis* right 'would largely be based on a strict application of the 'better regulation' principles. These principles would probably suggest that the 'sui generis' right be withdrawn as it has revealed itself to be an instrument that is ineffective at encouraging growth in the European database industry'.[24] These authors would heartily concur with this assessment.

[14.09] The database right will subsist in a database where there has been 'a substantial investment in obtaining, verifying or presenting the contents of the database'.[25] So there is no requirement of creativity or originality for the subsistence of the database right, rather there is a requirement of 'investment'. The Act defines investment as including any investment, whether of financial, human or technical resources, and cognate words are to be construed accordingly.[26] Therefore investment may be labour such as 'sweat of the brow'[27] or it may be financial investment or the application of technical know-how.[28] The right enables the owner of the database right to undertake or authorise others to

---

20 CRRA 2000–2004, s 83.
21 Davison, *The Legal Protection of Databases, Cambridge Studies in Intellectual Property Rights* (Cambridge University Press, 2003) p 99.
22 Davison, p 99.
23 Davison, p 99.
24 EC Commission, *DG Internal Market and Services Working Paper, First evaluation of Directive 96/9/EC on the legal protection of databases* (2005) Brussels, 12 December, p 24.
25 CRRA 2000–2004, s 321(1).
26 CRRA 2000–2004, s 320(1).
27 *Feist Publications Inc v Rural Telephone Service Co* [1991] 20 IPR 129.
28 See also Recital 7 of the Database Directive.

undertake, certain acts in Ireland in relation to the database which are designated by the 2000 Act as acts restricted by the database right.[29] The database right will not subsist in a database unless the requirements of qualification are complied with.[30] The owner of the database right has the right to undertake or to authorise others to undertake all or any of the following acts in relation to all or a substantial part of the contents of a database: (a) extraction, or (b) re-utilisation.[31]

[14.10] The Act defines 'extraction' as the permanent or temporary transfer of all or a substantial part of the contents of a database to another medium by any means or in any form.[32] The term 'substantial' means substantial in terms of quantity or quality or a combination of both.[33] 'Re-utilisation' is defined as making those contents available to the public by any means.[34] Therefore, the database right allows the maker of a database to control how the contents of his database are removed and how those contents may subsequently be made available to the public. These acts are referred to as acts restricted by the database right'.[35] The database right will be infringed by a person who, without the licence of the owner of the database right, undertakes, or authorises another to undertake, either of these acts.[36] The repeated and systematic extraction or re-utilisation of insubstantial parts of the contents of a database which conflicts with the normal exploitation of the database or which prejudices the interests of the maker of the database will be deemed to be extraction or re-utilisation of a substantial part of those contents.[37] So a user who repeatedly extracts small elements of a database may infringe the database right.

British Horseracing Board v William Hill

[14.11] The extent of the database right was examined by the ECJ in *British Horseracing Board v William Hill*.[38] The British Horse Racing Board (BHB) managed the horse racing industry in Britain. In this capacity it compiled and maintained the BHB database which contained information on the pedigrees of one million horses and pre-race information on races to be held in the UK. This pre-race information was compiled by a data processor which registered information about the entrants, decided on handicapping and compiled a list of the horses running. The final list of runners would be published on the day before the race. Thus the BHB database contained 'essential information, not only for those directly involved in horse racing but also for radio and television broadcasters and for bookmakers and their clients.'[39]

---

[29] CRRA 2000–2004, s 321(2).
[30] CRRA 2000–2004, s 321(4).
[31] Subject to the exceptions specified in Ch 8 (fair use exceptions) and to the provisions relating to licensing in Ch 11 of Part V of the Act.
[32] CRRA 2000–2004, s 320(1).
[33] CRRA 2000–2004, s 320(1).
[34] CRRA 2000–2004, s 320(1).
[35] CRRA 2000–2004, s 324(1).
[36] CRRA 2000–2004, s 324(2).
[37] CRRA 2000–2004, s 324(3).
[38] *British Horseracing Board v William Hill* Case C-203/02 (9 November 2004) ECJ (GC).
[39] Case C-203/02, para 15.

The BHB spent £4m on the database annually, but was only generating fees of around £1m from users. The BHB made its information available on the Internet. William Hill, the defendant, set up rival sites which provided the same race details. However, it was accepted that:

> 'the information displayed on William Hill's internet sites represents a very small proportion of the total amount of data on the BHB database ... .Also ... the horse races and the lists of runners are not arranged on William Hill's internet sites in the same way as in the BHB database.'[40]

The BHB alleged that the extraction of this information from their database was an infringement of their *sui generis* rights and contrary to the database directive. The interpretation of the Database Directive was referred to the ECJ which was asked a number of questions in relation to art 7 of the Database Directive, which provides:

> 'Member States shall provide for a right for the maker of a database which shows that there has been qualitatively and/or quantitatively a substantial investment in either the obtaining, verification or presentation of the contents to prevent extraction and/or re-utilisation of the whole or of a substantial part, evaluated qualitatively and/or quantitatively, of the contents of that database'.

[14.12] The first issue addressed by the ECJ was the 'clarification of the concept of investment in the obtaining and verification of the contents of a database within the meaning of art 7(1) of the Directive.'[41] The ECJ held that the phrase 'be understood to refer to the resources used to seek out existing independent materials and collect them in the database, and not to the resources used for the creation as such of independent materials'. The ECJ made the proper distinction between a database and its contents, stating that:

> 'The purpose of the protection by the *sui generis* right provided for by the directive is to promote the establishment of storage and processing systems for existing information and not the creation of materials capable of being collected subsequently in a database.'[42]

The ECJ noted that just because a person created both the content of a database and the database itself would not prevent that person claiming the protection of the *sui generi* right 'provided that he establishes that the obtaining of those materials, their verification or their presentation ... required substantial investment in quantitative or qualitative terms, which was independent of the resources used to create those materials.'[43] The ECJ was asked whether the investment made by the plaintiff in the creation of the BHB database was sufficient to engage the *sui generis* right. In its argument the plaintiff stressed the substantial nature of its investment. But the ECJ was of the opinion that:

> 'investment in the selection, for the purpose of organising horse racing, of the horses admitted to run in the race concerned relates to the creation of the data which make up the lists for those races which appear in the BHB database. It does not constitute investment in obtaining the contents of the database.'[44]

---

40 Case C-203/02, para 19.
41 Case C-203/02, para 28.
42 Case C-203/02, para 31.
43 Case C-203/02, para 35.
44 Case C-203/02, para 38.

The ECJ similarly concluded that this investment could not amount to the verification of the contents of a database.[45] This led the ECJ to the ultimate conclusion that 'The resources used to draw up a list of horses in a race and to carry out checks in that connection do not constitute investment in the obtaining and verification of the contents of the database in which that list appears.'[46]

[14.13] The ECJ came to similar decisions in *Fixtures Marketing v Oy Veikkaus Ab*[47] and *Fixtures Marketing v Svenska Spel AB*.[48] These cases concerned to the use of data relating to English premier league football. The ECJ was of the view that:

> 'Finding and collecting the data which make up a football fixture list do not require any particular effort on the part of the professional leagues. Those activities are indivisibly linked to the creation of those data, in which the leagues participate directly as those responsible for the organisation of football league fixtures. Obtaining the contents of a football fixture list thus does not require any investment independent of that required for the creation of the data contained in that list.'[49]

Similarly the ECJ concluded that neither the verification nor presentation of that data required a substantial investment on the part of the football league. The ECJ viewed this data as being a by-product of the league itself. The data was generated by the playing, postponement or cancellation of matches. As such, it did not require the substantial investment necessary to engage the *sui generis* right under the database directive.

[14.14] The next question asked of the ECJ was whether the defendant was engaging in the extraction and re-utilisation of the contents of the BHB database. Specifically the ECJ was asked 'whether the protection conferred by the *sui generis* right also covers the use of data which, although derived originally from a protected database, were obtained by the user from sources other than that database.[50]

The ECJ held that objective of the *sui generis* right was 'to protect the maker of the database against "acts by the user which go beyond [the] legitimate rights and thereby harm the investment" of the maker.'[51]

The ECJ considered that 'the Community legislature intended to give the concepts of extraction and re-utilisation a wide definition.'[52] As a result:

> 'the concepts of extraction and re-utilisation cannot be exhaustively defined as instances of extraction and re-utilisation directly from the original database at the risk of leaving the maker of the database without protection from unauthorised copying from a copy of the database.'[53]

---

[45] Case C-203/02, para 40.
[46] Case C-203/02, para 42.
[47] *Fixtures Marketing v Oy Veikkaus Ab* C-46/02 (9 November 2004).
[48] *Fixtures Marketing v Svenska Spel AB* C-338/02 (9 November 2004).
[49] C-46/02, para 44.
[50] *British Horseracing Board v William Hill* Case C-203/02 (9 November 2004) ECJ (Grand Chamber), para 43.
[51] Case C-203/02, para 45, citing recital of the Directive.
[52] Case C-203/02, para 51.
[53] Case C-203/02, para 52.

[14.15] The ECJ analysed what could amount to an act of extraction and re-utilisation and held:

> 'that acts of extraction ... and acts of re-utilisation ... which affect the whole or a substantial part of the contents of a database require the authorisation of the maker of the database, even where he has made his database, as a whole or in part, accessible to the public or authorised a specific third party or specific third parties to distribute it to the public.'[54]

The ECJ noted that art 9 of the Directive:

> 'defines exhaustively three cases in which Member States may stipulate that lawful users of a database which is made available to the public in whatever manner may, without the authorisation of its maker, extract or re-utilise a 'substantial part' of the contents of that database. Those cases are: extraction for private purposes of the contents of a non-electronic database, extraction for the purposes of illustration for teaching or scientific research and extraction and/or re-utilisation for the purposes of public security or an administrative or judicial procedure.'[55]

However, the defendant's activities did not fall within any of these exceptions. The ECJ concluded that:

> 'The terms "extraction" and 're-utilisation' in Article 7 of the directive must be interpreted as referring to any unauthorised act of appropriation and distribution to the public of the whole or a part of the contents of a database. Those terms do not imply direct access to the database concerned.
>
> The fact that the contents of a database were made accessible to the public by its maker or with his consent does not affect the right of the maker to prevent acts of extraction and/or re-utilisation of the whole or a substantial part of the contents of a database.'[56]

[14.16] The next question examined by the ECJ was the meaning of 'substantial part' and 'insubstantial part'. The ECJ noted that 'The expression "substantial part, evaluated quantitatively", of the contents of a database ... refers to the volume of data extracted from the database ... and must be assessed in relation to the volume of the contents of the whole of that database.'[57] The ECJ further noted that 'the materials displayed on William Hill's internet sites, which derive from the BHB database, represent only a very small proportion of the whole of that database[58]'. The BHB argued that this data 'represent a significant investment'.[59] Having noted these facts the ECJ went onto make a number of observations. Firstly the ECJ stated that 'the intrinsic value of the data affected by the act of extraction and/or re-utilisation does not constitute a relevant criterion for assessing whether the part in question is substantial, evaluated qualitatively'.[60] Next the ECJ observed that 'the resources used for the creation as such

---

54 Case C-203/02, para 61.
55 Case C-203/02, para 62.
56 Case C-203/02, para 67.
57 Case C-203/02, para 70.
58 Case C-203/02, para 74.
59 Case C-203/02, para 75.
60 Case C-203/02, para 78.

of the materials included in a database cannot be taken into account in assessing whether the investment in the creation of that database was substantial.'⁶¹ Having made these observations, the ECJ came to the following conclusion:

> 'The resources deployed by BHB to establish, for the purposes of organising horse races, the date, the time, the place and/or name of the race, and the horses running in it, represent an investment in the creation of materials contained in the BHB database. Consequently, and if, as the order for reference appears to indicate, the materials extracted and re-utilised by William Hill did not require BHB and Others to put in investment independent of the resources required for their creation, it must be held that those materials do not represent a substantial part, in qualitative terms, of the BHB database.'⁶²

[14.17] The final substantive question examined by the ECJ concerned art 7(5) of the Database Directive, which provides:

> 'The repeated and systematic extraction and/or re-utilisation of insubstantial parts of the contents of the database implying acts which conflict with a normal exploitation of that database or which unreasonably prejudice the legitimate interests of the maker of the database shall not be permitted'.

The ECJ held that this provision prohibited:

> 'unauthorised actions for the purpose of reconstituting, through the cumulative effect of acts of extraction, the whole or a substantial part of the contents of a database protected by the *sui generis* right and/or of making available to the public, through the cumulative effect of acts of re-utilisation, the whole or a substantial part of the contents of such a database, which thus seriously prejudice the investment made by the maker of the database.'⁶³

In other words the Directive prohibited the recreation of a database by means of a number of repeated but individually insubstantial extractions of the contents of the database. In this case, the ECJ accepted that William Hill was engaging in repeated and systematic extractions from the BHB database. But, the ECJ concluded that:

> 'such acts are not intended to circumvent the prohibition laid down in Article 7(1) of the directive. There is no possibility that, through the cumulative effect of its acts, William Hill might reconstitute and make available to the public the whole or a substantial part of the contents of the BHB database and thereby seriously prejudice the investment made by BHB in the creation of that database.'⁶⁴

Maker and ownership of the databases

[14.18] Since there is no requirement of creativity for protection under the database right, it would be inappropriate to refer to the person who makes the database as an author or creator. The Act refers to the person who makes the database as the 'maker' and defines this person as the person 'who takes the initiative in obtaining, verifying or presenting the contents of a database and assumes the risk of investing in that obtaining, verification or presentation'.⁶⁵ Where a database is made by an employee in the course

---

⁶¹ Case C-203/02, para 79.
⁶² Case C-203/02, para 80.
⁶³ Case C-203/02, para 89.
⁶⁴ Case C-203/02, para 91.
⁶⁵ CRRA 2000–2004, s 322(1).

of employment, his employer will be regarded as the maker of the database, subject to any contract to the contrary.[66] In the English case of *Ray v Classic FM,*[67] the plaintiff was very well known in the UK for his encyclopedic knowledge of classical knowledge. He had been engaged by the defendant as a consultant music advisor. He advised on the categorisation of the defendant's catalogue and database of classical music. At the time of judgment this included some 50,000 tracks. The plaintiff maintained that he was the sole author of the music catalogue, which was then used to create a database. The defendant argued that the creation of the database was a new work in which it was joint author. Lightman J described this 'heresy' as being 'wholly repugnant to the basic principles of the law of copyright'. If a similar case were to be decided now on the basis of the database right, it is not certain that an Irish court would come to a similar conclusion. Such a case might turn on whether the defendant made the necessary 'substantial investment in obtaining, verifying or presenting the contents of the database'. Certainly a contemporary court could not dismiss the assertion of a database right with the same distain as was employed by Lightman J in *Ray v Classic FM.*

[14.19] Where a database is made by an officer or employee of the government in the course of his duties, the government will be considered the maker of the database.[68] Where a database is made by or under the direction or control of either or both of the Houses of the Oireachtas—

(a) the House by whom, or under whose direction or control, the database is made will be regarded as the maker of the database; and

(b) where the database is made by or under the direction or control of both Houses, both Houses will be regarded as the joint makers of the database.[69]

Where a database is made by an international organisation[70] or by an officer or employee of such an organisation in the course of his duties, that organisation will be regarded as the maker of the database.[71] If the database right is conferred on a person by an enactment, that person will be regarded as the maker of the database.[72]

[14.20] A database may be created by joint authors and the Act provides that a database will be made jointly[73] where two or more persons acting together in collaboration take the initiative in obtaining, verifying or presenting the contents of the database and assume the risk of investing in that obtaining, verification or presentation.[74] The requirement of initiative may contrast with the position of an employee, this may suggest that the 'control test' or at least the amount of initiative shown by a person may be

---

[66] CRRA 2000–2004, s 322(2).

[67] *Ray v Classic FM* [1998] FSR 622. See paras **[1.48]–[1.49]**.

[68] CRRA 2000–2004, s 322(3).

[69] CRRA 2000–2004, s 322(4).

[70] As prescribed by the Minister under CRRA 2000–2004, s 196(2).

[71] CRRA 2000–2004, s 322(6).

[72] CRRA 2000–2004, s 322(7).

[73] CRRA 2000–2004, s 320(1) defines 'jointly' in relation to the making of a database which is made jointly as referring to all the makers of the database.

[74] CRRA 2000–2004, s 322(5).

decisive in deciding whether or not a database was created in the course of employment. The Supreme Court has held that 'the degree of control exercised over how the work is to be performed, although a factor to be taken into account, is not decisive'.[75] The identification of the maker of a database is important as the maker of a database will be the first owner of the database right in the database.[76]

Duration of database right

[14.21] The database right will expire 15 years from the end of the calendar year in which the making of the database was completed.[77] So, if a database is completed on the 13 March 2007, the database right will expire on 31 December 2022.[78] However this period can be extended. The Act provides that if a database is lawfully re-utilised before the expiration of the 15-year period, the database right will expire 15 years from the end of the calendar year in which the database was first so re-utilised.[79] So, connecting a database to the Internet for the first time, would give a database maker 15 years of protection from the end of the year on which that first connection was made. To ensure that databases are updated, the Act provides that any substantial change to the contents of a database, including a substantial change resulting from the accumulation of successive additions, deletions or alterations, which would result in the database being considered to be a substantial new investment, will qualify the database for a new term of protection.[80]

Qualification

[14.22] Qualification for the database right is limited. Only the following persons will qualify: citizens or subjects of, or other individuals domiciled or ordinarily resident in, a member state of the European Economic Area (EEA); bodies incorporated under the law of a member state of the EEA; or partnerships or unincorporated bodies formed under the law of a member state of the EEA.[81] Such incorporated or unincorporated bodies will only receive protection if they have their principal place of business or operations within a member state. They must have their registered office within a member state and must operate in a member state and they must also have a genuine link with the economy of the state, at the material time.[82] The material time is defined as being: when the database was made or a substantial part of the period during which the database was made,[83] in the case of a database which has not been lawfully re-utilised. In the case of a database

---

[75] Keane J in *Denny v Minister for Social Welfare* [1998] 1 IR 34.

[76] CRRA 2000–2004, s 323.

[77] CRRA 2000–2004, s 325(1).

[78] Article 10(1) of the Database Directive provides that the *sui generis* (database) right will expire 15 years from the 1 January of the year following the date of completion of the database.

[79] CRRA 2000–2004, s 325(2).

[80] CRRA 2000–2004, s 325(3). This section applies notwithstanding para 45 of the First Schedule which provides for the copyright protection of databases created on or before the 27 March 1996 (s 325(4)).

[81] CRRA 2000–2004, s 326(1).

[82] CRRA 2000–2004, s 326(3).

[83] Where the making of the database extended over a period.

which has been lawfully re-utilised, then the material time is when the database was first lawfully re-utilised or, where the maker had died before that time, immediately before his or her death.[84]

[14.23] The government may by order extend the provisions of this section to countries, territories, states or areas outside the member states of the EEA. Such an order must be made pursuant to or in conformity with an agreement of the Council of the European Communities allowing for such an extension of protection on the basis that comparable protection of databases is available under the law of those countries, territories, states or areas.[85] The Act also provides that where a database is made by the government, the Oireachtas or a prescribed international organisation, the database right will subsist in that database.[86]

Rights and obligations of lawful users

[14.24] A lawful user of a database is entitled to extract or re-utilise insubstantial parts of the contents of the database for any purpose.[87] The term 'lawful user' means 'any person who, whether under a licence to undertake any of the acts restricted by any database right in the database, or otherwise, has a right to use the database'.[88] This provision will inform the interpretation of contracts of licences for the utilisation of databases. However, the term 'any purpose' may be quite limited as s 324(3) makes it clear that repeated and systematic extraction or re-utilisation of insubstantial parts of a database will infringe the re-utilisation right. This will occur where the extraction or re-utilisation of the database is in conflict with the normal exploitation of the database or prejudices the interests of the database maker. So it will be important for contracts or licences for database use to set out clearly what the normal exploitation of that database will be. This provision must be balanced with the Act's stipulation that where a person has a right to use a database, any term or condition in the agreement allowing them to do so will be void in so far as it purports to prevent that person from extracting or re-utilising insubstantial parts of the contents of the database for any purpose.[89] Therefore, it would be important that agreements should set out clearly what rights a user has to extract or re-utilise the contents of that database. If the agreement should limit the rights of the user too severely, it would appear that the entire agreement will not be void, or even the entirety of the particular term, but that it will only be void to the extent that it is too severe. Users will not be able to avail of this right to infringe the copyright of third parties whose works may be contained in the database. A lawful user of a database may not use the right of insubstantial extraction or re-utilisation to prejudice the rights of the owner of any other rights conferred by the Act in respect of works or other subject matter contained in the database.[90]

---

84   CRRA 2000–2004, s 326(5).
85   CRRA 2000–2004, s 326(4).
86   CRRA 2000–2004, s 326(2).
87   CRRA 2000–2004, s 327(1). This is without prejudice to s 324(3).
88   CRRA 2000–2004, s 320(1).
89   CRRA 2000–2004, s 327(2).
90   CRRA 2000–2004, s 327(3).

Fair dealing

[14.25] The Act contains various exemptions from the database right which allow databases to be used for purposes such as education and public administration. The Act states that an act may be exempted under more than one category of exemption and the exemption of an act under one category of exemption will not preclude its exemption under another category.[91] In the case of a non-electronic database which has been re-utilised, the database right is not infringed by fair dealing with a substantial part of its contents by a lawful user of the database where that part is extracted for the purposes of research or private study.[92] Therefore, if a non-electronic or paper database such as logarithmic tables is made available to the public, a substantial part of its contents made be extracted for the purposes of research. But the contents could not be published commercially and this is made clear: while extraction is permitted, re-utilisation is not. Furthermore, 'fair dealing' is defined as 'the extraction of the contents of a database by a lawful user to an extent which will not unreasonably prejudice the interests of the rightsowner'.[93] An action such as this may only be carried out by a lawful user, that is somebody using the database in accordance with a valid licence. Such licences may seek to limit the definition of what is fair dealing.

Education

[14.26] The database right in a database is not infringed by fair educational dealing with a substantial part of its contents. This may only be done by a lawful user which will include an educational establishment.[94] The extraction must be carried out for the purposes of illustration in the course of instruction or preparation for instruction and where:

(a) the extraction is done by or on behalf of a person giving or receiving instruction; and

(b) the source is indicated.[95]

No re-utilisation is permitted, it would not be permitted to place a substantial part of a database on a college's website even if it were done for the purposes of teaching.

Public administration

[14.27] The Act contains various provisions to ensure that the administration of the state is not prejudiced by the database right. The right will not be infringed by anything done for the purposes of parliamentary or judicial proceedings or for the purpose of reporting those proceedings.[96] It will not be infringed by anything done for the purposes of a statutory inquiry or for the purpose of reporting any such inquiry[97] and it will not be

---

91 CRRA 2000–2004, s 328.
92 CRRA 2000–2004, s 329(1).
93 CRRA 2000–2004, s 329(2).
94 CRRA 2000–2004, s 330(2).
95 CRRA 2000–2004, s 330(1).
96 CRRA 2000–2004, s 331.
97 CRRA 2000–2004, s 332(1).

infringed by the publication of copies of a report of a statutory inquiry containing the contents of the database.[98] This is an important provision as tribunals may pay particular attention to bank records and the like, which will usually be held as part of the database. Without this provision, the database right could be asserted in an attempt to frustrate a tribunal investigation.

[**14.28**] All or a substantial part of the contents of a database which are comprises which are open to public inspection may be extracted or re-utilised without infringing the database right.[99] Although this provision appears quite straightforward, s 334, which follows, contains a number of statements which appear quite convoluted. Although the exceptions set out below do permit extractions and re-utilisations of the contents of databases which may be inspected by the public, this permission is subject to the authority of the person maintaining those records. This authority cannot be abused or used arbitrarily, but it may be invoked to prevent such utilisation or extraction as is permitted. In particular, all or a substantial part of the contents of a database may not be provided pursuant to the provisions below, unless the person granting access to the contents of the database has first obtained from the person requesting the contents of the database a declaration, in such form as may be prescribed, indicating that the contents of the database are required for the sole purpose of enabling the contents of the database to be inspected at another time or place or to otherwise facilitate the exercise of the right of public inspection.[100] Where all or a substantial part of the contents of a database are re-utilised pursuant to the provisions below, the person granting access to the contents of the database must ensure that those contents bear a mark clearly indicating that they are provided for the purpose of inspection and that no other use of the contents of the database may be made without the licence of the owner of the database right.[101]

[**14.29**] The Act sets out how the contents of a database that is open to public inspection may be extracted and also may be re-utilised.

(a)   The database right is not infringed by the extraction of all or a substantial part of the contents of a database that are open to public inspection pursuant to a statutory requirement, or are on a statutory register. This is provided that the extraction is not for a purpose which involves re-utilisation of all or a substantial part of the contents as contains factual information of any description. This must be done by or with the authority of the person required to make the contents of the database open to public inspection or, as the case may be, the person maintaining the register.[102]

(b)   Where the contents of a database are open to public inspection pursuant to a statutory requirement, or are on a statutory register, the database right in the database is not infringed by the extraction or re-utilisation of all or a substantial part of the contents for the purpose of enabling the contents of the database to

---

98   CRRA 2000–2004, s 332(2).
99   CRRA 2000–2004, s 333.
100 CRRA 2000–2004, s 334(4).
101 CRRA 2000–2004, s 334(3).
102 CRRA 2000–2004, s 334(1).

be inspected at another time or place, or otherwise facilitating the exercise of any right for the purpose of which the requirement is imposed, by or with the authority of the person required to make the contents of the database open to public inspection or, as the case may be, the person maintaining the register.[103]

(c)   Where the contents of a database which are open to public inspection pursuant to a statutory requirement, or are on a statutory register, contain information about matters of general, scientific, technical, commercial or economic interest, the database right in the database is not infringed by the extraction or re-utilisation of all or a substantial part of the contents for the purpose of disseminating that information, by or with the authority of the person required to make the contents of the database open to public inspection or, as the case may be, the person maintaining the register.[104]

[14.30] The Minister may prescribe the conditions which are to be complied with before the contents of a database are made available to the public.[105] Ministerial orders may be made, stating that the above provisions will apply to the contents of a database made open to public inspection by an international organisation or a person specified in the order who has functions in the state under an international agreement to which the state is a party.[106] He may also make a similar order in relation to a register maintained by an international organisation, in relation to the contents of a database open to public inspection pursuant to a statutory requirement, or on a statutory register.[107]

[14.31] Where the contents of a database have been communicated to the government or to the Houses of the Oireachtas[108] for any purpose, by or with the licence of the owner of the database right, and any fixation or any thing containing the contents of the database is owned by, or is in the custody, possession or control of the government, the government or the Houses of the Oireachtas may extract or re-utilise all or a substantial part of the contents. This may only be done for the purpose for which the contents of the database were communicated to them, or for any related purpose which could reasonably have been anticipated by the owner of the database right, without infringing the database right in the database.[109] The government and the Houses of the Oireachtas are not permitted to re-utilise all or a substantial part of the contents of a database or cause the contents to be extracted or re-utilised of this provision, where the contents have previously been lawfully re-utilised otherwise than under this section.[110] So if a copy of a commercially available database is communicated to the government, the government cannot place this database on the Internet in rivalry with the commercially available version. Subsequent legislation other than copyright law may provide for acts dealing in databases and where the undertaking of a particular act is specifically authorised by such

---

[103] CRRA 2000–2004, s 334(2).

[104] CRRA 2000–2004, s 334(5).

[105] CRRA 2000–2004, s 334(6).

[106] CRRA 2000–2004, s 334(7)(a).

[107] CRRA 2000–2004, s 334(7)(b).

[108] To either or both of the Houses of the Oireachtas.

[109] CRRA 2000–2004, s 335(1).

[110] CRRA 2000–2004, s 335(2).

an enactment then, unless the enactment provides otherwise, the undertaking of that act will not infringe the database right in a database.[111] This provision cannot be construed as excluding any defence available under any enactment.[112]

[14.32] CRRA 2000, s 337(1) provides that:

> 'The database right in a database is not infringed by the extraction or re-utilisation of all or a substantial part of the contents of the database when, or pursuant to arrangements made when—
>
> > (a)   it is not possible by reasonable inquiry to ascertain the identity of the maker of the database; and
> >
> > (b)   it is reasonable to assume that the database right has expired.'[113]

In the case of a database made jointly, the reference here to the possibility of ascertaining the identity of the maker of the database is to be construed as a reference to its being possible to ascertain the identity of any of its makers.[114]

Presumptions

[14.33] The Act sets out presumptions that will apply in either civil or criminal proceedings for infringement of the database right in any database.[115] The database right, in particular, will be presumed to subsist in a database unless the contrary is proved.[116] Therefore, in a dispute relating to a database, the person claiming to be the maker of the database will have to prove that it is in fact a database, but once that fact is proven, the alleged infringer will bear the burden of proving that the database right does not subsist in that particular database. This would be done by showing that the investment in the database was too insubstantial to merit protection. The Act does not expand on what amounts to a substantial investment as discussed above.

[14.34] Where the subsistence of the database right in a database is proved or admitted, or is presumed, the plaintiff will be presumed to be the owner or, as the case may be, the exclusive licensee of the database right, unless the contrary is proved.[117] Where a name purporting to be that of the maker of a database or of the owner or exclusive licensee of the database right appears on copies of the database, that name will be admissible as evidence of the fact stated or indicated which will be presumed to be correct, unless the contrary is proved.[118] Similarly, where a copy of a database bears or incorporates a statement, label or other mark indicating that a person is the maker of the database or the owner or exclusive licensee of the database right, that statement, label or mark will be admissible as evidence of those facts which will be presumed to be correct, unless the contrary is proved.[119] The person named or in respect of whom a statement, label or

---

[111]   CRRA 2000–2004, s 336(1).
[112]   CRRA 2000–2004, s 336(2).
[113]   CRRA 2000–2004, s 337(1).
[114]   CRRA 2000–2004, s 337(2).
[115]   CRRA 2000–2004, s 339(1).
[116]   CRRA 2000–2004, s 339(2)(a).
[117]   CRRA 2000–2004, s 339(2)(b).
[118]   CRRA 2000–2004, s 339(3).
[119]   CRRA 2000–2004, s 339(3).

other mark appears on or is borne on or is incorporated in copies of a database will be presumed not to have made the database:

(a) in the course of employment[120] or in the course of employment as an officer or employee of a prescribed international organisation[121] or in the course of employment as an officer or employee of the government;[122]

(b) under the direction or control of either or both of the Houses of the Oireachtas;[123] or

(c) in circumstances in which the database right is conferred on another person by an enactment.[124]

Where a database purports to be a database made jointly, these presumptions will apply in relation to each person purporting to be one of the makers of the database.[125]

Licensing of databases

[14.35] Chapter II of Pt V of the CRRA 2000 sets out provisions relating to the licensing of databases. The absence of effective licensing arrangements is one of the Directive's most controversial features,[126] and a refusal to license the contents of a database was referred to the ECJ in *IMS Health v NDC Health*.[127]*I* The parties were both engaged in the tracking of pharmaceutical and healthcare products in the German marketplace. IMS provided regional sales data in a format which divided the German marketplace into 2,847 'bricks'. This brick format was widely distributed and the German Court found that it had 'become the normal industry standard to which its clients adapted their information and distribution systems'. The defendant company was established by a former manager of the plaintiff. Initially this company had sought to create its own 'brick' structure, but customer demand forced it to create a structure similar to the plaintiff's. The plaintiff then initiated legal proceedings to prevent the defendant imitating the structure of its database. These succeeded in the German courts. The defendant then sought a licence for the plaintiff's 'brick' structure. This was refused. The defendant argued that this refusal was an abuse of the plaintiff's dominant position and thus contrary to art 82 of the EC Treaty. The ECJ reviewed its previous judgments in *Magill*[128] and *Volvo* [129] and concluded that:

> 'the refusal by an undertaking which holds a dominant position and owns an intellectual property right in a brick structure indispensable to the presentation of regional sales data

---

[120] CRRA 2000–2004, s 322(2).

[121] CRRA 2000–2004, s 322(6).

[122] CRRA 2000–2004, s 322(3).

[123] CRRA 2000–2004, s 322(4) above.

[124] CRRA 2000–2004, ss 322(7) and s 339(4).

[125] CRRA 2000–2004, s 339(5).

[126] 'the (database) right is untrammeled by any system of compulsory licensing': Davison, *The Legal Protection of Databases, Cambridge Studies in Intellectual Property Rights* (Cambridge University Press, 2003), p 99.

[127] *MS Health v NDC Health*, c-418/01 (29 April 2004).

[128] *RTÉ and ITP v Commission ('Magill')* 241/91 P and c-242/91 P [1995] ECR I-743.

[129] *Volvo* c-238/87 [1988] ECR 6211.

on pharmaceutical products in a Member State to grant a licence to use that structure to another undertaking which also wishes to provide such data in the same Member State, constitutes an abuse of a dominant position within the meaning of Article 82 EC where the following conditions are fulfilled:

— the undertaking which requested the licence intends to offer, on the market for the supply of the data in question, new products or services not offered by the owner of the intellectual property right and for which there is a potential consumer demand;

— the refusal is not justified by objective considerations;

— the refusal is such as to reserve to the owner of the intellectual property right the market for the supply of data on sales of pharmaceutical products in the Member State concerned by eliminating all competition on that market.'[130]

[14.36] *IMS Health v NDC Health* dealt with a refusal to licence the structure of a database. A refusal to licence the contents of a database was dealt with by the English Court of Appeal in *Attheraces Ltd and another v British Horseracing Board Ltd*.[131] The subject matter of the case was the terms upon which the defendant supplied pre-race data to the plaintiff. The Court of Appeal agreed that the defendant was in a dominant position, but held that the plaintiff had failed to establish that the defendant had 'abused its market dominance ... by specifying charges that were excessive, unfair or discriminatory or by unreasonably threatening to terminate the supply of pre-race data to ATR.'[132]

---

[130] *IMS Health v NDC Health* C-418/01, para 52.
[131] *Attheraces Ltd and another v British Horseracing Board Ltd* [2007] EWCA Civ 38.
[132] [2007] EWCA Civ 38, para 281.

Chapter 15

Data Protection

Introduction

[15.01] Data protection law is made up of a complex set of rules which control how the personal data of data subjects are processed by data controllers. Germany led in the development of Europe's data protection laws and the first data protection law was enacted in the Germany Lander of Hesse in 1970. Thus Ireland's Data Protection Acts are not the result of any domestic initiative but rather they implement the Data Protection Directive[1] and give effect to the earlier Strasbourg Convention.[2] One difficulty with the Data Protection Directive is that its actual purpose is not the preservation of the individual's privacy. Rather it is the standardisation of data processing controls within Europe to ensure that there are no restrictions on the transfer of personal data between member states of the European Union. Improved privacy standards are a by-product of the EC's desire to build an internal common market. This is clear from the text of the Data Protection Directive itself, which provides:

> 'In accordance with this Directive, Member States shall protect the fundamental rights and freedoms of natural persons, and in particular their right to privacy with respect to the processing of personal data.[3]

> and

> ... Member States shall neither restrict nor prohibit the free flow of personal data between Member States for reasons connected with the protection afforded (above)'.[4]

The legal base of the Directive is in the internal market provisions of the EC Treaty which provide for the issue of directives that affect the functioning of the common market. This choice of legal base makes it clear that the protection of privacy is not and cannot be the primary objective of Europe's data protection laws. The objective of the Data Protection Directive is to ensure that personal data can be transferred from Ireland to any other location in the EU.

[15.02] That is not to suggest that data protection laws are a bad thing. Data protection allows individuals to control how their data is processed by the state and by major Institutions such as banks and insurance companies. Although identity theft is a problem for some Irish people, it is unlikely to become the endemic problem that it has in the

---

[1] Directive 95/46/EC of the European Parliament and of the Council October 1995 on the protection of individuals with regard to the processing of personal data and on the free movement of such data, OJ L 281 , 23/11/1995 pp 31–50.

[2] Council of Europe Convention on the Protection of Individuals with Regard to Automatic Processing of Personal Data, done at Strasbourg on 28 January 1981.

[3] Directive 95/46, art 1(1).

[4] Directive 95/46, art 1(2).

USA. This is because Europe's data protection laws offer two safeguards that are not available to Americans. Firstly, data protection means that banks, telecoms companies and others are under a clear onus to control disclosures of personal data. Secondly, data protection gives individuals the right to check their personal data such as their credit rating and demand the correction of inaccuracies. This means that Europeans who suffer identity theft will find it much easier to rectify their personal data than will Americans.

[15.03] Data protection laws are designed to apply to information technology. Unfortunately, data protection laws were never designed for information technologies such as the laptop computer upon which this book is being written or search engines such as Google that are being used in its research. The impetus for the development of data protection laws was a desire to ensure that Europeans would not repeat data processing operations of the sort undertaken by the Nazis during the holocaust. Prior to World War II, the Netherlands had a highly advanced system for gathering census data about its citizens. The Nazis put this system to use and it enabled them to identify and kill 71% of Dutch Jews. In contrast, an absence of sophisticated data sources and the sabotage of the French data processing system meant that the Nazis found it harder to identify French Jews and could only kill some 25% of them. The infamous numbers tattooed on the forearms of victims in Auschwitz were actually index numbers that were processed by Hollerith card punch machines.[5] Living under totalitarianism made Europeans realise the dangers of data processing. This realisation became the motivation behind the development of data protection laws in countries like Germany. But this development occurred in the 1960s and 1970s, when automated data processing was a rarified activity undertaken by men in white coats on mainframe computers. Mainframes were large, expensive and access to them could be easily controlled. Indeed given their expense and rarity, access had to be carefully controlled. Anyone who wanted to process any sort of data on such a system would typically have to fill out a form stating what they wanted to do and the authority upon which they made their request. Given that a bureaucracy for controlling computerised data processing already existed it seemed sensible to suggest that this bureaucracy should be required to impose some specific controls where personal data was being processed.

[15.04] But data is no longer processed in this way. Information technology is now cheap and widely available. The easiest way to start processing personal data is to connect a computer to the Internet and log on to an Internet search engine such as Google or Yahoo! Search engines such as these create powerful tools for discovering personal information about individuals. Sites such as YouTube, bebo and flickr all make personal information available in moments. Data protection law expects that anyone who wishes to visit a site such as these will carefully assess the purpose of their visit to the site. Initially they must assess if data protection law applies to their visit. If it does, they must then consider questions, such as: does the processing of personal data as a result of the visit comply with the principals of data protection? is that processing legitimate? will the visitor encounter sensitive forms of personal data and, if so, can they process them? Of course it is doubtful that many people, if anyone at all, ever undertake a detailed analysis of this sort. The complex and detailed provisions of the Data Protection Acts may seem

---

[5]   Black, *IBM and the Holocaust* (Three Rivers Presss, 2001), Chapter XI.

disproportionate when it is so easy to process personal data and so much personal data is freely available. But the Data Protection Acts are the law. It may seem unreasonable to expect data protection law to be applied by the proverbial teenager in his bedroom. But the Data Protection Acts definitely apply and will definitely be expected to apply to may of the data processing operations undertaken by the state and institutions such as banks. This may appear to create a double standard. But this reflects the reality that many of the data processing operations that have the greatest impact upon the lives of individuals are those that are undertaken by the state and institutions like banks. Data protection will apply to data processing operations such as those involving an individual's entitlement to benefits such as disability payments or the old-age pension. Data protection law will apply to the analysis that banks undertake when assessing an individual's suitability for receiving a loan. In this way data protection law continues to have positive benefits for individuals, regardless of the difficulties of applying it to modern technology.

Where does data protection law come from?

[15.05] The Data Protection Act 1988 gave effect to the Strasbourg Convention. The Data Protection Act 2003 implemented the Data Protection Directive. Together these enactments are known as the Data Protection Acts (DPA).

Who is protected by data protection law?

[15.06] Data protection is very specific about who it protects: it protects 'data subjects' or rather their personal data. A data subject is 'an individual who is the subject of personal data'.

The definition of personal data is somewhat more detailed 'personal data' means data relating to a living individual who is or can be identified either from the data or from the data in conjunction with other information that is in, or is likely to come into, the possession of the data controller.'[6]

[15.07] So data protection law will protect the personal data of living persons only. This means that the personal data of dead persons will not be protected by the Data Protection Acts, nor will data relates to legal persons such as public limited companies. Data protection law will apply to data that relating to an identifiable living person. So data relating to anonymous persons will not be covered. But data will have to be genuinely anonymous. If a data controller can identify data by using other information that is in his position or is likely to come into his possession, then data protection law will apply. Data protection law will apply to electronic data that is held on computerized databases. It will also apply to manual files and this provision will be completely effective from 24 October 2007. Data protection will not apply to personal information that is held on random bits of paper. It will apply only to personal information that is 'recorded as part of a relevant filing system or with the intention that it should form part of a relevant filing system.'[7] A relevant filing system is:

'any set of information relating to individuals to the extent that, although the information is not processed by means of equipment operating automatically in response to

---

[6] DPA, s 2(1).
[7] DPA, s 2(1).

instructions given for that purpose, the set is structured, either by reference to individuals or by reference to criteria relating to individuals, in such a way that specific information relating to a particular individual is readily accessible.'[8]

The extension of data protection law to such manual filing systems can best be understood as an anti-circumvention measure.[9] Given that the Strasbourg Convention and DPA 1988 only applied to 'automated data processing', anyone who wanted to process personal information that was particularly sensitive would have been well advised to process it by means of manual files to which data protection law did not apply. The Data Protection Directive which was implemented by the DPA 2003 remedied this situation. The Data Protection Directive and DPA 2003 also extended the application of data protection law to the processing of 'sound and image' data. This extension will only apply if the processing of the sound and image data is 'automated or if the data processed are contained or are intended to be contained in a filing system structured according to specific criteria relating to individuals, so as to permit easy access to the personal data in question.'[10]

[15.08] It would appear that data protection law applies to all forms of sound and image data that are generated electronically, such as those created by digital cameras or CCTV systems. Given that most cameras are automated to some extent, only image data that is created manually, by painting or drawing, would seem to be exempt. Given that even the most primitive recording systems must be automated to some extent, it would seem likely that all forms of sound data are covered.

Whose activities are controlled by data protection law?

[15.09] Data protection law controls the activities of data controllers. A data controller is 'a person who, either alone or with others, controls the contents and use of personal data.' In deciding who is the controller of a particular item of data, the key issue will be one of control. Of course it is not necessary that a single individual be identified as a controller; the definition makes it clear that data may be controlled by groups of persons as well as individuals. Where a data controller hires someone else to undertake the work of actually processing personal data this person will be known as a 'data processor'. However, it is not possible for a data controller to avoid his obligations by simply hiring a third party to undertake his processing. Data controllers must ensure that data processors are bound by the Data Protection Acts and data controllers must have a contract in writing with any data processors.[11] This is particularly significant where data is transferred to an offshore location such as India and the Data Protection Acts have specific provisions to deal with this situation.[12]

[15.10] The Data Protection Acts exempt a variety of activities from their provisions. Some of these exemptions are absolute and entirely exempt some activities from data protection law. Other exemptions are partial, where some activities are exempted from

---

8   DPA, s 2(1).
9   Directive 95/46, recital 27.
10 Directive 95/46, recital 15.
11 DPA, s 2C(3)(a).
12 DPA, s 11.

certain obligations such as the right of access or the Data Protection Acts' controls on processing. The first absolute exemption is territorial. The Data Protection Acts only apply to data controllers who are established in the state and who process data in the context of that establishment. The Data Protection Acts will also apply to data processing operations that occur within the state and which are undertaken on behalf of a controller who is established outside the EEA. In general the data protection laws of the country in which a controller is established will apply to that data controller. If someone who is established in Estonia wishes to process data in Enniskerry then they will do so under the Estonian *Isikuandmete kaitse seadus*,[13] not the Irish Data Protection Acts. The second exemption is for personal data that 'in the opinion of the Minister or the Minister for Defence are, or at any time were, kept for the purpose of safeguarding the security of the State'. The third is for 'personal data consisting of information that the person keeping the data is required by law to make available to the public'. A fourth exemption is for 'personal data kept by an individual and concerned only with the management of his personal, family or household affairs or kept by an individual only for recreational purposes.'[14]

[15.11] A rather complicated exemption is provided for journalism, literature and art. This exemption is provided solely for processing that is undertaken with a view to the publication of journalistic, literary or artistic material. The journalist, author or artist must believe that this publication is in the public interest, having regard to the 'public interest in freedom of expression'. The journalist, author or artist must reasonably believe that compliance with the relevant provision of the Data Protection Acts would be incompatible with his purposes. The exemption from the Data Protection Acts, provisions is not total.[15] It extends to most of the principles of data protection[16] except for the obligation to secure.[17] It extends to the data protection criteria[18] and the special controls for data processing.[19] It also extends to the right of information,[20] access,[21] objection[22] and to avoid automated decision making.[23] Certain sections of the Act provide for specific exemptions from provisions such as the right of access, controls on processing and the obligation to register.

---

[13] Estonian Personal Data Protection Act, passed 12 February 2003 (RT1 I 2003, 26, 158), entered into force 1 October 2003.
[14] DPA, s 1(4).
[15] DPA, s 22A(2).
[16] DPA, s 2.
[17] DPA, s 2(1)(d).
[18] DPA, s 2A.
[19] DPA, s 2B.
[20] DPA, s 3.
[21] DPA, s 6.
[22] DPA, s 6A.
[23] DPA, s 6B.

What activites are controlled by data protection Law?

[15.12] Data protection law controls the processing of personal data. The processing of personal data is defined as:

'performing any operation or set of operations on the information or data, whether or not by automatic means, including—

(a) obtaining, recording or keeping the information, or data

(b) collecting, organising, storing, altering or adapting the information or data,

(c) retrieving, consulting or using the information or data,

(d) disclosing the information or data by transmitting, disseminating or otherwise making it available, or

(e) aligning, combining, blocking, erasing or destroying the information or data'.

This is a very comprehensive list and it is likely that processing has a very broad meaning indeed. The Data Protection Acts exempt a variety of activities from the restrictions that it imposes on processing. These activities are processing operations which are:

'(a) in the opinion of a member of the Garda Síochána not below the rank of chief superintendent or an officer of the Permanent Defence Force who holds an army rank not below that of colonel and is designated by the Minister for Defence under this paragraph, required for the purpose of safeguarding the security of the State,

(b) required for the purpose of preventing, detecting or investigating offences, apprehending or prosecuting offenders or assessing or collecting any tax, duty or other moneys owed or payable to the State, a local authority or a health board.

(c) required in the interests of protecting the international relations of the State,

(d) required urgently to prevent injury or other damage to the health of a person or serious loss of or damage to property,

(e) required by or under any enactment or by a rule of law or order of a court,

(f) required for the purposes of obtaining legal advice or for the purposes of, or in the course of, legal proceedings in which the person making the disclosure is a party or a witness,

(h) made at the request or with the consent of the data subject or a person acting on his behalf.'[24]

The controls on data processing imposed by data protection law

[15.13] Chapter II of the Data Protection Acts sets out 'General rules on the lawfulness of the processing of personal data'. These rules can be divided into three categories:

(a) the principles of data protection;

(b) the criteria for making data processing legitimate (section); and

(c) special controls for sensitive data.

---

[24] DPA, s 8.

Whilst each of these categories is discussed separately below, they must all be complied with simultaneously.

The principals of data protection

[15.14] The Principals of data protection are set out in s 2 of the Data Protection Acts, which provide that:

'A data controller shall, as respects personal data kept by him or her, comply with the following provisions:

(a) the data or, as the case may be, the information constituting the data shall have been obtained, and the data shall be processed, fairly

(b) the data shall be accurate and complete and, where necessary, kept up to date,

(c) the data—

> (i) shall have been obtained only for one or more specified, explicit and legitimate purposes,

> (ii) shall not be further processed in a manner incompatible with that purpose or those purposes,

> (iii) shall be adequate, relevant and not excessive in relation to the purpose or purposes for which they were collected or are further processed, and

> (iv) shall not be kept for longer than is necessary for that purpose or those purposes

(d) appropriate security measures shall be taken against unauthorised access to, or unauthorised alteration, disclosure or destruction of, the data, in particular where the processing involves the transmission of data over a network, and against all other unlawful forms of processing.'[25]

[15.15] Even in isolation this provision imposes quite serious limitations on how personal data may be processed. The first principle is that data or the information from which that data has been derived must be fairly obtained. The Act does not define what it means by 'fair'. But it does state that data cannot be regarded as having been obtained fairly unless the following information is supplied or made readily available to the data subject[26]:

(a) the identity of the data controller or the controller's representative;

(b) the purpose of the processing;

(c) any other information that is required to ensure that the data be fairly processed. This information might relate to the identity of who will ultimately receive the information, whether the provision of data is obligatory or voluntary, the consequences of failing to provide the data and the existence of rights of access and rectification.[27]

Where data is obtained otherwise than directly from the data subject, then the categories of data obtained and the identity of the data controller who originally supplied the data

---

[25] DPA, s 2(1).
[26] DPA, s 2D(1).
[27] DPA, s 2D(2).

will also have to be provided.[28] A key feature of the Irish legislation is that this information need not be supplied directly to the data subject but only be made readily available. So it might be sufficient to simply inform a data subject that certain information is available on a website or elsewhere. This divergence from the Directive follows the UK legislation and this divergence has been noted by the European Commission. Once the data has been obtained it will still have to be processed 'fairly'. It is impossible to imagine what might be 'fair' in any given circumstance, but the courts might regard the term 'fair' as being the equivalent of just and equitable.

[15.16] The second principal is that the data must be accurate, complete and up to date. The Data Protection Commissioner has dealt with a great number of complaints relating to inaccurate personal data over the years and has held that data should not be misleading, even where it is factually correct. The third and probably most significant principal is that of purpose. Data can only be obtained for specific, explicit and legitimate purposes and cannot be processed in a manner that is incompatible with those purposes. This places a very serious limitation upon data controllers as they cannot adapt data that has been collected for one purpose to enable it to be processed for new purposes. Thus data controllers must carefully consider the purpose for which they are obtaining data. A data controller who registers with the Data Protection Commissioner must disclose the purpose for which he processes his data. But that disclosure will not be definitive. All factors relating to the processing of the data must be examined when deciding the purpose for which it was obtained. To give an example, the Department of Education obtained information on union membership from teachers to enable it to deduct union subscriptions from their salaries. Then the teachers went on strike. The Department sought to stop the pay of striking teachers, using the subscription data to identify strikers. A complaint was made to the Data Protection Commissioner. The Department argued that its entry in the data protection register described one of the purposes of it holding personal data as being 'Administration of teaching staff for second level schools'. It argued that stopping the pay of striking teachers fell within this purpose. The Data Protection Commissioner disagreed. He was of the view that the purpose of the processing had to be determined from the circumstances in which the data had been obtained. And there was no suggestion that trade union subscription data was ever being obtained for the purpose of enabling the Department to stop the salaries of striking teachers. Therefore the Data Protection Commissioner concluded that using this data to stop pay was an incompatible purpose.[29]

[15.17] Data must be adequate, relevant and not excessive for the purpose for which it was obtained. In many ways this is a reprise of the requirement that data be accurate. What is significant about this provision is that it ties the requirement of accuracy directly to the purpose of the processing. On the one hand data controllers cannot ignore data that is inconvenient for their purposes. On the other hand data controllers cannot gather more data from subjects than they need for the purpose of their initial processing in the anticipation that they may need it subsequently. So a data controller should not gather

---

[28] DPA, s 2D(3).
[29] Data Protection Commission, Case Study 2/2000.

data about the marital status of customers simply because he is concerned that he may be subsequently sued on equality grounds.[30]

[15.18] The data cannot be held for longer than is necessary. Suppose a customer of a data controller pays a bill by credit card.[31] The controller should dispose of the credit card data once payment has been received from the credit card company. The controller cannot retain the credit card data and reuse subsequently whenever the controller feels that the customer owes him money.[32] How long is necessary will depend upon the circumstances of any particular case. Sometimes the necessary period may be imposed by statute, such as the Statute of Limitations. It should be noted that specific obligations may be imposed in relation to the retention of telecommunications data under Part VII of the Criminal Justice (Terrorist Offences) Act 2005.

[15.19] The final principle is that data controllers must keep personal data securely. This is not an absolute obligation. The controller must take 'appropriate' measures against specified threats, namely unauthorised access to, alteration, disclosure or destruction of the data. There is no requirement to preserve the data from the more mundane but more commonplace threats of accidental damage or technological malfunction. The obligation to secure is subject to a further limitation where data is transmitted on a network. When deciding on the security measures that are appropriate for transmitted data, a controller may have regard to 'the state of technological development and the cost of implementing the measures'. The controller must 'ensure that the measures provide a level of security appropriate to ... the harm that might result from unauthorised or unlawful processing, accidental or unlawful destruction or accidental loss of, or damage to, the data concerned, and ... the nature of the data concerned.'[33] Given the growth in computer intranets, extranets and the Internet, a good argument can be made that this distinction between transmitted and non-transmitted data is obsolete and that the same security standards should apply to all forms of personal data and personal data processing.

[15.20] It should be noted that a specific obligation to secure is imposed on telecommunications service providers by SI 535/2003[34] which implements Directive 2002/58. Service providers must secure their services and must also notify users of any specific risks that they may encounter. This duty is linked to that imposed by the Data Protection Acts above. It is clear from SI 535/2003 that service providers must warn users of any risks that they may face from illegal threats, but should they also warn users of legal threats such as the Norwich Pharmacal orders which were obtained in *EMI v Eircom*[35]?

---

[30] Data Protection Commission, Case Study 1/2002.
[31] Data Protection Commission, Case Study 4/2001.
[32] Following the enactment of the Criminal Justice (Theft and Fraud Offences) Act 2001 a complaint to the Data Protection Commissioner might prove to be the least of the controller's worries in this circumstance.
[33] DPA, s 2C(1).
[34] European Communities (Electronic Communications Networks and Services (Data Protection and Privacy) Regulations 2003 (SI 535/2003).
[35] *EMI v Eircom* [2005] IEHC 233.

The criteria for making data processing legitimate

[15.21] The Data Protection Acts require that data may only be processed in accordance with the principles of data protection. In addition data may only be processed where the criteria for making data processing legitimate are complied with. Somewhat redundantly a criterion for legitimate data processing is that it should comply with the principles of data protection. The remaining criteria for making data processing legitimate are:

'(a)   the data subject has given his or her consent to the processing or, if the data subject, by reason of his or her physical or mental incapacity or age, is or is likely to be unable to appreciate the nature and effect of such consent, it is given by a parent or guardian or a grandparent, uncle, aunt, brother or sister of the data subject and the giving of such consent is not prohibited by law,

(b) the processing is necessary—

   (i)   for the performance of a contract to which the data subject is a party,

   (ii)   in order to take steps at the request of the data subject prior to entering into a contract,

   (iii)   for compliance with a legal obligation to which the data controller is subject other than an obligation imposed by contract, or

   (iv)   to prevent—

      (I)   injury or other damage to the health of the data subject, or

      (II)   serious loss or damage to property of the data subject,

   or otherwise to protect his or her vital interests where the seeking of the consent of the data subject or another person referred to in paragraph (a) of this subsection is likely to result in those interests being damaged,

(c)   the processing is necessary—

   (i)   for the administration of justice,

   (ii)   for the performance of a function conferred on a person by or under an enactment,

   (iii)   for the performance of a function of the Government or a Minister of the Government,

   (iv)   for the performance of any other function of a public nature performed in the public interest by a person,

(d)   the processing is necessary for the purposes of the legitimate interests pursued by the data controller or by a third party or parties to whom the data are disclosed, except where the processing is unwarranted in any particular case by reason of prejudice to the   fundamental rights and freedoms or legitimate interests of the data subject'.

[15.22] A controller who wishes to ensure that his processing is legitimate might seek to rely upon the consent of the subject. But this reliance would be unwise. The Data Protection Acts do not define consent and, unlike the Data Protection Directive, do not state that the subject's consent must be 'unambiguous'. The Directive defines the data subject's consent as meaning 'any freely given specific and informed indication of his wishes by which the data subject signifies his agreement to personal data relating to him being processed.'[36]

---

[36]   Directive 95/46, art 2(h).

Therefore it would seem that for a consent to be valid it must be:

(a)   unambiguous;

(b)   freely given;

(c)   specific; and,

(d)   informed.

The concept of consent in the Data Protection Acts differs substantially from the concept of consent used by the laws of nullity and contract. In particular a consent given under the Data Protection Acts will not be binding and may be withdrawn at any time. That at least is the view of Europe's Data Protection Commissioners who have stated in relation to the processing of personal data in the employment context that 'Reliance on consent should be confined to cases where the worker has a genuine free choice and is subsequently able to withdraw the consent without detriment.'[37]

[15.23] Thus a prudent data controller might seek to rely upon a criterion for making his data processing legitimate other than that of consent. The first criterion other than consent is where the processing is necessitated on contractual, pre-contractual or legal grounds or to prevent an injury or other damage to the subject. So an employer might legitimately process personal date about an employee's bank account so that the employee might be paid in accordance with his contract of employment. Legitimate processing of personal data might occur at the pre-contractual stage where an insurance quote was being sought by a customer. Personal data might be processed on legal grounds where a controller owed a duty of care to a subject under the law of torts. Data may be legitimately processed in order to prevent the subject's death or to prevent damage to their health or property. This criterion can only be relied upon where seeking the consent of the subject is likely to result in damage to the subject.

[15.24] The next criterion is that of what might be termed the public interest. This includes the administration of justice such as the processing of pleadings by the courts. It includes the discharge of functions imposed by enactments such as the creation of voter rolls pursuant to the Electoral Acts. It also includes the discharge of functions of government ministers, but this provision was probably nullified by *Mulcreavy v Minister of the Environment*.[38] This criterion includes the discharge of functions of a public nature in the public interest, which would seem to legitimise the disclosure of data in circumstances such as arose in *National Irish Bank v RTÉ*[39] where the disclosure of personal data by RTÉ was held to be in the public interest. The final criterion is that of processing which is in the legitimate interests of the data controller. The legitimate interest of the controller must be balanced with the fundamental rights and freedoms of the subject. This criterion might apply to the activities of credit reference agencies and the use made of those services by banks and building societies.

---

[37] *Article 29 Working Party on Data Protection, Opinion 8/2001 on the processing of personal data in the employment context*, 13 September 2001, p 3.

[38] *Mulcreavy v Minister for the Environment* [2004] 1 IR 72.

[39] *National Irish Bank v RTÉ* [1998] 2 IR 465.

Sensitive data

[15.25] Certain types of data such as data relating to an individuals health, ethnicity or political membership are regarded as being particularly sensitive and thus requiring special standards. This is 'sensitive personal data'. The Data Protection Acts define this as being data that falls into one of the following categories:

'(a)   the racial or ethnic origin, the political opinions or the religious or philosophical beliefs of the data subject,

(b)   whether the data subject is a member of a trade-union,

(c)   the physical or mental health or condition or sexual life of the data subject,

(d)   the commission or alleged commission of any offence by the data subject, or

(e)   any proceedings for an offence committed or alleged to have been committed by the data subject, the disposal of such proceedings or the sentence of any court in such proceedings.'[40]

[15.26] These categories are quite broad. If data does not fall into one of them, then it will not be regarded as being 'sensitive' for the purposes of the Data Protection Acts. The Data Protection Acts set out stricter controls on the processing of these categories of data, but controllers must still comply with the principles and criteria as they would for any other category of data. The Data Protection Acts provide that sensitive personal data may only be processed where at least one of the following conditions has been fulfilled:

(i)   consent to the processing is explicitly given;

(ii)   the processing is in connection with employment;

(iii)   the processing is necessary to prevent injury or other damage where consent to the processing cannot be given or the data controller cannot reasonably be expected to obtain such consent, or such consent has been unreasonably withheld;

(iv)   the processing is carried out in the course of its legitimate activities by any body corporate;

(v)   the processing is undertaken by an unincorporated body of persons whose activities are not carried on for profit, and which exists for political, philosophical, religious or trade-union purposes;

(vi)   the data has been (deliberately) made public by the data subject;

(vii)   processing is necessary for the administration of justice or for the performance of a function conferred on a person by or under an enactment, or for the performance of a function of the government or a minister of the government;

(viii)   processing is required for obtaining legal advice or for legal proceedings or is otherwise necessary for the purposes of establishing, exercising or defending legal rights;

(ix)   processing is necessary for medical purposes and is undertaken by a health professional, or a person who owes a duty of confidentiality to the data subject that is equivalent to that of a health professional;

---

[40]   DPA, s 2(1).

   (x)   processing is in accordance with the Statistics Act 1993;

   (xi)   processing is carried out by political parties, or candidates in the course of electoral activities for the purpose of compiling data on people's political opinions;

   (xii)   processing is authorised by regulations;

   (xiii) processing is necessary for the purpose of the assessment, collection or payment of any tax duty, levy or other moneys owed or payable to the State; or

   (xiv) processing is necessary for the purposes of determining entitlement to any benefit, pension, assistance, allowance, supplement or payment.[41]

[15.27] The processing of sensitive personal data will first be permitted where the subject has given his 'explicit' consent. Doubts may be expressed as to whether there is any difference between the requirement of explicit consent here and simple consent that is required by the criteria for making data processing legitimate above. The second category of permitted processing is that of processing necessitated by employment. This might include the processing of personal data to discharge obligations arising under the Disability Act 2005. The third category is that of processing necessitated to prevent injury or damage. This provision would seem to permit the processing of personal data where consent has been 'unreasonably withheld'. But it is not exactly clear what might amount to the unreasonable withholding of consent.

[15.28] Fourth, there is the processing undertaken by non-profit organisations such as political interest groups, churches or trade unions. Fifth, there is the processing of personal data that has been deliberately made public by an individual. It is not entirely clear what amounts to deliberate conduct, but it is likely to be something that is conscious or intentional. So it might not include information that is made public in a casual conversation. It is also not clear what the meaning of 'public' is. Disclosing information on a freely accessible website might amount to making it public, disclosing it in a private conversation to a confidant would probably not. Sixth, there is processing that is undertaken in the administration of justice. In *McGrory v ESB*[42] the Supreme Court held that if the plaintiff wanted to pursue his claim for damages against the defendant, then he could not withhold his consent to the defendant's doctors discussing his condition with his own. The court upheld the imposition of a stay on the plaintiff's action until he provided the consent sought.

[15.29] Seventh there is processing that is undertaken for 'medical purposes'. The restriction on the disclosure of data about a person's health is not limited to medical records such as those processed by consultants and GPs. In *Bodil Lindqvist v Sweden*[43] the applicant worked for a church. She disclosed on her website that one of her colleagues had hurt her foot and was only working part-time on medical grounds. The ECJ ruled that this amounted to 'personal data concerning health'. Eighth there is the processing of statistics under the Statistics Act 1993, which essentially permits the

---

[41] DPA, s 2B(1)(b).

[42] *McGrory v ESB* [2003] 3 IR 407.

[43] *Bodil Lindqvist v Sweden* C-101/01, 6 November 2003.

processing of data by the Central Statistics Office in the course of its activities, for example, the census.

[15.30] Ninth, there is political processing. One problem with this exemption is that it only applies to 'electoral activities' Irish elections are actually quite short. The Constitution provides that an election must occur within 30 days of the dissolution of the Dáil. Someone cannot become a candidate for political office until they register under the Electoral Acts. But political parties and candidates will be engaged in the processing of data far in advance of elections. It might be assumed that this exemption will apply to any activity undertaken by any political party or prospective political candidate at any time. However it is not clear from the text that this is so. Tenth, there is processing which a Minister deems to be substantially in the public interest. This category is almost certainly defunct following the case of *Mulcreavy v Minister for the Environment*.[44] Finally there is the processing of personal data where it is necessary for the payment or assessment of benefits by the Minister for Social and Family Affairs.

[15.31] A particularly sensitive form of personal data is that relating to criminal convictions. The Data Protection Acts provide for the making of regulations by the Minister for Justice, Equality and Law Reform in relation to the processing of data relating to allegations of criminal conduct and actual convictions. Such regulations have yet to be made. But that is not to say that the gardaí cannot process such data using systems such as PULSE. One particularly sensitive form of conviction data is that relating to convictions for sex offences. A person convicted of such an offence must notify their name and address to the gardaí under the Sex Offenders Act 2001. This information must be kept confidential by the gardaí. This position may be contrasted with the USA where enactments known as 'Megan's Laws' places a positive obligation on police forces to publicly identify individuals who have committed sex offences against children. In *Gray v Minister for Justice Equality and Law Reform*[45] Quirke J awarded €70,000 to a family who had provided accommodation to a nephew who had been released from prison having served a term of imprisonment for rape. Information about this individual was disclosed to the media. As a result the family had to leave their home in Ballybunion, County Kerry and return to Dublin. Quirke J was satisfied that this 'disclosure by a garda or gardaí … to a journalist … .breached the duty of care which the State owed to the Gray family'. The issue of processing data relating to suspected sex offenders remains extremely sensitive, particularly following the infamous Soham murder case in the UK. In that case Ian Huntley was convicted of the murder of two young girls. He was the caretaker in the girls' school and had been previously suspected of serious sex offences when he lived elsewhere in the UK. These suspicions were never disclosed to either Soham's local police force or the management of the school in which he worked. The fact that an individual is suspected of sex offences can be disclosed to a school in which they are studying, but only in accordance with the fair procedure rules set out in *MQ v Gleeson*.[46] To ensure that information relating to individuals who may commit offences against children can be freely exchanged, an

---

[44] *Mulcreavy v Minister for the Environment* [2004] 1 IR 72.
[45] '€70,000 for family in ruling against Garda' (2007) The Irish Times, 18 January.
[46] *MQ v Gleeson* [1998] 4 IR 85.

amendment to the Constitution has been proposed which would insert the following Article 42.5.1° into the Constitution:

'Provision may be made by law for the collection and exchange of information relating to the endangerment, sexual exploitation or sexual abuse, or risk thereof, of children, or other persons of such a class or classes as may be prescribed by law.'[47]

The rights of data subjects

[15.32] Data protection law is designed to be self-regulating. The Data Protection Acts do this by providing data subjects with certain rights. These rights are:

(a)   the right to information;

(b)   the right of access;

(c)   the right to object;

(d)   the right of rectification and erasure; and

(e)   the right not to be subject to automated processing in certain situations.

Each of these rights will be considered in further detail below.

The right to information

[15.33] The right to information may be invoked by any individual who believes that someone else is keeping personal data in relation to him. A request for information must be made in writing. Where a request is received, the recipient must inform the individual 'whether he keeps any such data' If the recipient does keep such data he must give the individual 'a description of the data and the purposes for which they are kept'. This description must be given by the recipient 'as soon as may be and in any event not more than 21 days after the request has been given or sent to him.'[48] The right of information is more limited than the right of access. Unlike an access request, a data controller does not have to provide a subject with a copy of his data in response to a request for information. All that need be provided is a 'description' of the data. However, the right of information does have a couple of advantages. Firstly, no restrictions are placed on its use. A request for information may be made in respect of any data to which the Data Protection Acts apply. Secondly, the responses to a request for information are free of charge. There is no provision in the Data Protection Acts which allows a controller to charge a fee for responding to a request for information.

The right of access

[15.34] The right of access is the core right that is provided by the Data Protection Acts. The right of access gives subjects the right to check their personal data. It ensures that subjects can learn what data is held in relation to them, why it is being processed and how. The Data Protection Acts provide that 'an individual shall, if he or she so requests a data controller by notice in writing ... be informed by the data controller whether the data processed by or on behalf of the data controller include personal data relating to the individual'.[49]

---

[47]   Twenty-Eighth Amendment of the Constitution Bill 2007.

[48]   DPA, s 3.

[49]   DPA, s 4(1)(a)(i).

The subject does not have to make his request in any set form. The Data Protection Acts only require that the access request be made in writing and that the subject 'supply the data controller concerned with such information as he may reasonably require in order to satisfy himself of the identity of the individual and to locate any relevant personal data or information.'[50] If a controller receives an access request from a data subject in respect of whom the controller is processing data, then the controller must supply the subject with a description of the following:

(a)   the categories of data being processed by or on behalf of the data controller;

(b)   the personal data constituting the data of which that individual is the data subject;

(c)   the purpose or purposes of the processing; and

(d)   the recipients or categories of recipients to whom the data are or may be disclosed.

[15.35] The subject must also 'have communicated to him or her in intelligible form' the following:

(a)   'information constituting any personal data of which that individual is the data subject'; and

(b)   'information known or available to the data controller as to the source of those data unless the communication of the information is contrary to the public interest'.[51]

Where processing is undertaken by automatic means and that processing 'has constituted or is likely to constitute the sole basis for any decision significantly affecting him' the subject has the right to 'be informed free of charge by the data controller of the logic involved in the processing'.[52]

[15.36] A response to an access request must be provided 'as soon as may be' or at least within 40 days. However the data protection commissioner has concluded that this period of 40 days will only begin when the controller has completed any preliminary steps that need to be undertaken such as verifying the identity of the requester or receiving all the details necessary to identify the location of the data sought.[53] Finally, a controller must respond to an access request in terms that can be understood by the average person. The Data Protection Acts provide that 'where any of the information is expressed in terms that are not intelligible to the average person without explanation, the information shall be accompanied by an explanation of those terms.'[54]

---

[50] DPA, s 4(3).

[51] This information must be communicated 'in permanent form unless ... the supply of such a copy is not possible or would involve disproportionate effort, or ... the data subject agrees otherwise',DPA, s 4(9).

[52] However this disclosure will not require: '... the provision of information as to the logic involved in the taking of a decision if and to the extent only that such provision would adversely affect trade secrets or intellectual property (in particular any copyright protecting computer software)',DPA, s 4(12).

[53] Data Protection Commission, Case Study 1/2000.

[54] DPA, s 4(1)(a).

[15.37] If a controller refuses an access request, then he must write to the subject informing him of the grounds for his refusal and indicating that if the subject is unhappy with this refusal, then the subject may complain to the Data Protection Commissioner. One ground upon which a controller may refuse an access request is that the controller has previously responded to an access request and the subject has failed to allow a 'reasonable interval' to pass before making a fresh request. [55] Controllers may charge a fee form complying with access requests.[56] At the present time this fee is set at €6.35.[57] If a data controller has multiple entries in the data protection register in respect of data kept for different purposes, then the subject must make separate access requests in respect of each entry and pay a separate fee in respect of each access request.

[15.38] A controller cannot be obliged to disclose information relating to persons other than the subject in response to an access request, unless that other person consents to the disclosure. Alternatively, the controller may omit details of other persons from his response.[58] Controllers should not 'clean' personal data before responding to an access request. The Data Protection Acts provide that:

> 'Information supplied ... may take account of any amendment of the personal data concerned made since the receipt of the request by the data controller (being an amendment that would have been made irrespective of the receipt of the request) but not of any other amendment.'[59]

Expressions of opinion about a data subject, such as employment references or assessments, may be disclosed in response to access requests without obtaining the consent of the person who made the assessment. This will not apply to prison governors or other places of detention. It also will not apply where 'the expression of opinion referred to in that paragraph was given in confidence or on the understanding that it could be treated as confidential.'[60]

[15.39] It should be kept in mind that this exemption only applies to 'expressions of opinion'. If an employment reference contains factual assertions, then these should be disclosed. Differentiating between expressions of opinion and factual assertions may be difficult. A reference that described someone as 'difficult' or 'obnoxious' might not be disclosed with the consent of the author as there are expressions of opinion. But descriptions of a person as a 'thief' or a 'liar' might have to be disclosed without consent of the author as these are assertions of fact: that on a specific occasion the person stole something or told a lie.

[15.40] Where a request is made for an examination result, then that request will be treated as being made upon the first day of publication for the results of the examination

---

[55] DPA, s 4(10). The controller would appear to have a discretion in deciding what is a reasonable interval but must have '... regard ... to the nature of the data, the purpose for which the data are processed and the frequency with which the data are altered', DPA, s 4(11).

[56] DPA, s 4(1)(c).

[57] Or £5.00: Data Protection (Fees) Regulations 1988.

[58] DPA, s 4(4).

[59] DPA, s 4(5).

[60] DPA, s 4(4A).

in question. The time within which a request for an examination result must be complied with is extended to 60 days from the usual 40.[61] Requests for data held on individuals by the Health Service, medical professionals or social workers are regulated[62] by the Data Protection (Access modification) (Health) Regulations 1989[63] and the Data Protection (Access Modification) (Social Work) Regulations 1989.[64]

[15.41] One provision of the Data Protection Acts that has yet to enter into force relates to the seeking of criminal and other records by employers. This practice developed in the UK. An employer will require prospective employees to seek a copy of their criminal record from the police, the offer of employment being dependent upon the prospective employee being able to show that they do not have a criminal record. Obviously, this system is unsatisfactory. On the one hand it is a clear abuse of the employee's rights provided by the Data Protection Acts. On the other hand it offers inadequate protection for employers in sensitive areas such as schools, since responses to access requests may be faked or altered. In response to such concerns, a new offence was created by the Data Protection Act 2003. This provides that:

> 'A person shall not, in connection with ... the recruitment of another person as an employee ... the continued employment of another person, or ... a contract for the provision of services to him or her by another person require that other person ... to make ... (an access) ... request ... or ... to supply him or her with data relating to that other person obtained as a result of such a request.'[65]

However, this provision has yet to be commenced.[66]

Exceptions to the right of access

[15.42] The Data Protection Acts provide for a number of exceptions to the right of access. First, the right of access will not apply to data that is 'kept for the purpose of preventing, detecting or investigating offences, apprehending or prosecuting offenders'. So a criminal cannot avail of the Data Protection Acts to learn what information the gardaí are holding on him. Second, the right of access will not apply to data that is used for 'assessing or collecting any tax, duty or other moneys owed or payable to the State, a local authority or a health board'. So the right of access cannot be used to ascertain what information the Revenue Commissioners are holding in relation to an individual. Third, the right of access will not apply to data whose disclosure 'would be likely to prejudice the security of, or the maintenance of good order and discipline in ... a prison' or another place of detention. Fourth, the right of access will not apply to data that is being kept for the purpose of performing functions that are 'designed to protect members of the public against financial loss occasioned by ... dishonesty, incompetence or malpractice on the part of persons concerned in the provision of banking, insurance, investment or other financial services or in the management of companies or similar

---

[61] DPA, s 4(6).
[62] DPA, s 4(8).
[63] Data Protection (Access modification) (Health) Regulations 1989 (SI 82/1989).
[64] Data Protection (Access Modification) (Social Work) Regulations 1989 (SI 83/1989).
[65] DPA, s 4(13).
[66] Data Protection (Amendment) Act 2003 (Commencement) Order 2003 (SI 207/2003).

organizations ... or ... the conduct of persons who have at any time been adjudicated bankrupt'. Fifth, where permitting access to the data in question 'would be contrary to the interests of protecting the international relations of the State'. Sixth, the right of access will not apply to estimates of liability in compensation cases. Seventh, the right of access will not apply to privileged communications between a client and his professional legal advisers. Eighth, the right of access will not apply to data kept by the Data Protection or Information Commissioners for the purposes of their functions. Ninth, the right of access will not apply to research data or data 'kept only for the purpose of preparing statistics ... (where) ... the resulting statistics or the results of the research are not made available in a form that identifies any of the data subjects'. Finally, the right of access will not apply to back-up data. Identifying what is, or is not, 'back-up data' may be problem. The noun 'back-up' is defined by the *Oxford English Dictionary*[67] as a support or a reserve. Where a copy of data is held as a reserve or support for the primary copy then this is 'back-up data'. For example, some users may employ RAID[68] technology which uses 'two or more drives in combination to reduce the risks from disk failure'. The RAID 1 system is sometimes called mirroring and it is easy to identify what is 'back-up' data in such systems. The computer will 'simply take ... everything that gets written to the primary hard drive and creates a copy of it on the second drive'. The right of access will apply to the primary drive but not the secondary, as this will be 'back-up' data. In contrast a RAID 0 system will 'divide a data stream and write bits of it to both drives at once in a process called striping.'[69] Arguably neither drive qualifies as a back-up under RAID 0.

[15.43] The Data Protection Acts also enable the Minister for Justice to make regulations restricting the right of access.[70] Under the Data Protection Act 1988 (Restriction of Section 4) Regulations 1989 the Minister excluded data under s 22(5) of the Adoption Act 1952 and s 9 of the Ombudsman Act 1980 from the application of the right of access.

The right of objection

[15.44] The Data Protection Acts also provide a right of objection. A subject may write to a controller and request that he either cease or else not commence processing of data that is to be processed in the public interest, pursuant to a public authority or for the purposes of the controller's legitimate interests. The subject may make his objection on the grounds that the processing would cause substantial and unwarranted personal distress to the subject or another person. The subject will not be able to object to processing where he has given his explicit consent or where the processing is undertaken by political parties. The right of objection will not apply where the processing is necessary: for the performance of a contract to which the subject is a party, to take steps at the request of the data subject prior to his or her entering into a contract, for compliance with any legal obligation to which the data controller or data subject is

---

67 *Concise Oxford English Dictionary* (10th edn, OUP, 2002).
68 RAID is an acronym for 'Redundant Array of Independent Disks'.
69 Taylor, 'Hard drives are made easy' (2005) The Financial Times, 28 October.
70 DPA, s 5(3)(a).

subject other than one imposed by contract, or to protect the vital interests of the data subject.[71] The controller must respond to an objection within 20 days. This response must be served on the subject. If the controller regards the request as being unjustified in whole or in part, then the controller should set out the grounds for his belief. If the controller intends to comply with the request in part, then he should specify what parts he will be complying with. The Data Protection Commissioner may investigate a refusal to comply with a notice of objection. If the Data Protection Commissioner upholds the objection, then the controller must comply with the Data Protection Commissioner's direction. If the controller does not comply, then the Data Protection Commissioner may serve a notice of enforcement on the controller.[72]

The right of rectification or erasure

[15.45] Data subjects have the right to demand the rectification, blocking or erasure of any data in respect of which the controller has contravened any of the principles of data protection. This request must be made in writing. The controller must comply with this request within 40 days. Where the data is inaccurate or not up to date, then the controller may supplement the data with an appropriate statement. Where a controller complies with a request for rectification he must notify the subject, he must also notify any person to whom the data has been disclosed within the previous 12 months, unless that is impossible or involves disproportionate effort.[73]

Automated processing

[15.46] The Data Protection Acts restricts the use of automated processing to make certain decisions about individuals. The Data Protection Acts provide that:

> 'a decision which produces legal effects concerning a data subject or otherwise significantly affects a data subject may not be based solely on processing by automatic means of personal data in respect of which he ... is the data subject and which is intended to evaluate certain personal matters ... such as ... .his or her performance at work, creditworthiness, reliability or conduct.'[74]

The restriction will not apply where the processing is undertaken for the purpose of considering whether to enter into a contract with the data subject, with a view to entering into such a contract, or in the course of performing such a contract. Nor will the restriction apply where the processing is authorised or required by any enactment and the data subject has been informed of the proposal to make the decision. In both cases the effect of the automated decision making must be to grant a request of the data subject, or else adequate steps have been taken to safeguard the legitimate interests of the data subject. Finally, the restriction on automated processing will not apply where the subject gives his consent to the decision being made in this way.

---

[71] The DPA purports to confer a power upon the Minister for Justice Equality and Law Reform to pass regulations stipulating other cases where the right of objection will not apply. But it is doubtful if this power has survived the decision in *Mulcreavy v Minister for the Environment* [2004] 1 IR 72.

[72] DPA, s 6A.

[73] DPA, s 6.

[74] DPA, s 6B(1).

The Data Protection Commissioner

[15.47] The Data Protection Commissioner is an independent[75] official who is the Irish supervisory authority for the purposes of the Data Protection Directive.[76] The Commissioner has a number of functions under the Data Protection Acts:

(a) he may investigate contraventions of the Data Protection Acts, using information notices and authorised officers in his investigations[77];

(b) he may enforce the provisions of the Data Protection Acts by way of enforcement notices[78];

(c) he may prohibit the transfer of personal data outside the state[79];

(d) he may engage in prior checking of processing operations likely to cause substantial damage or distress to data subjects[80];

(e) he must encourage the development of codes of practice by trade associations and the like[81];

(f) he must publish an annual report[82];

(g) he must establish and maintain a register of data processing operations and he may refuse to register certain operations, it being illegal to process personal data without having registered it[83];

(h) he must arrange for the dissemination of findings of the EU in relation to transfers of data outside the Union[84];

(i) he must perform such functions in relation to data protection as are conferred upon him by ministerial regulation;[85] and

(j) he may prosecute summary offences under the Data Protection Acts.[86]

[15.48] Arguably the core function discharged by the Data Protection Commissioner is the maintenance of the Data Protection Register. The Data Protection Act 2003 provides that the Data Protection Commissioner must establish and maintain a register and make appropriate entries therein.[87] Members of the public may inspect this register at all times free of charge[88] although the Data Protection Commissioner may charge for copies.[89]

---

[75] DPA, Sch II, para 3.

[76] DPA, s 9(1C).

[77] DPA, s 10(1).

[78] DPA, s 12.

[79] DPA, s 24.

[80] DPA, s 10(2).

[81] DPA, s 11.

[82] DPA, s 12A.

[83] DPA, s 13.

[84] DPA, s 9(1B).

[85] DPA, s 9(1D).

[86] DPA, s 30.

[87] DPA, s 16(2).

[88] DPA, s 16(3)(a).

[89] DPA, s 16(3)(b).

The register is actually available online,[90] the significance of such copies is that they may be used as evidence of the entry in legal proceedings.[91] Anyone who wishes to register with the Data Protection Commissioner must make an application in writing, using the appropriate form.[92] A controller who wishes to process data for two or more unrelated purposes must make separate applications for registration in respect of each.[93] The Data Protection Commissioner must accept such an application, provided the fee has been paid[94] and the appropriate form has been filled out.[95] But the Data Protection Commissioner cannot accept an application if the particulars furnished by the applicant are insufficient or the Data Protection Commissioner is of the opinion that the controller is likely to contravene the Data Protection Acts.[96] Furthermore, the Data Protection Commissioner may not accept an application from someone who keeps sensitive data unless he is satisfied that 'appropriate safeguards for the protection of privacy ... are being, and will continue to be, provided by' the controller.[97] A registration will last for a limited period,[98] currently set at one year.[99] A controller may request that his registration be removed at any stage.[100]

[15.49] Under the Data Protection Act 2003 virtually all data controllers are supposed to register with the Data Protection Commissioner. All data controllers and data processors must register, except those who carry out:

> 'processing whose sole purpose is the keeping in accordance with law of a register that is intended to provide information to the public and is open to consultation either by the public in general or by any person demonstrating a legitimate interest, ... processing of manual data ... or ... any combination of the foregoing.'[101]

[15.50] So the provider of a telephone directory, whether in paper or electronic form or indeed both, would not have to register. A further exemption from the obligation to register is provided for any data controller that is:

> 'a body that is not established or conducted for profit and is carrying out processing for the purposes of establishing or maintaining membership of or support for the body or

---

90 http://www.dataprivacy.ie.
91 DPA, s 16(3)(c).
92 DPA, s 17(1)(a).
93 DPA, s 17(1)(c).
94 Registration fees under the DPA are set at a sliding scale, ranging from €25.37 for a controller with five or fewer employees to €317.43 for a controller with 26 or more employees, see Data Protection (Fees) Regulations 1996.
95 The form is set out in the Data Protection (Registration) Regulations 1988 (SI 351/1988). It requires that the controller disclose details such as the purpose of the processing, a description of the data and the name and address of the controller.
96 DPA, s 17(2).
97 DPA, s 17(3).
98 DPA, s 18(1).
99 Data Protection (Registration Period) Regulations 1988 (SI 350/1988).
100 DPA, s 18(4).
101 DPA, s 16(1)(a).

providing or administering activities for individuals who are either members of the body or have regular contact with it.' [102]

[15.51] This exemption might apply to bodies such as churches, sports clubs or trade unions. Given these very limited exceptions, virtually every data controller will have to register under the Data Protection Act 2003. However this provision has yet to be commenced by the Minister for Justice, Equality and Law Reform.[103] At the time of writing only the more limited categories of data subject set out in the Data Protection Act 1988 are required to register. The Data Protection Act 1988 only requires that the following categories of data controller register:

(a) public authorities;

(b) Financial institutions, insurers, direct marketers, credit reference agencies and debt collectors;

(c) controllers keeping data relating to racial origin, political opinions, religious or other beliefs, physical or mental health, criminal convictions;

(d) data processors; and

(e) prescribed categories of data controllers and data processors.[104]

The data protection register should enable data subjects check what data is being processed. But the real effect of the register is that it is illegal for anyone who should register to process personal data if they are not registered.[105] Where the Data Protection Commissioner refuses an application for registration, he must notify the applicant in writing, giving reasons and informing the applicant that he has a right of appeal to the Circuit Court.[106] Given the consequences of failing to register, one might expect that most, if not all, of those who are required to register would do so. But it would seem that the majority of potential registrants do not register. As of March 2005 there were at least 21,000 institutions, agencies, companies and persons who should have been registered with the Data Protection Commissioner,[107] but there were only 5933 entries on the register.[108] This suggests that at best only 30% of those who are supposed to register were actually doing so.

[15.52] The Data Protection Act 2003 also provides that the Data Protection Commissioner can undertake prior checking.[109] This checking may be undertaken in respect of any processing operation that appears to the Data Protection Commissioner to be particularly likely to cause significant damage or distress to data subjects. A data controller may also request that the Data Protection Commissioner undertake such a check. It is an offence[110] to process personal data that requires prior checking unless the

---

[102] DPA, s 16(1)(b) as inserted by DPA 2003.

[103] Data Protection (Amendment) Act 2003 (Commencement) Order 2003 (SI 207/2003).

[104] DPA 1988, s 16.

[105] DPA, s 18(2).

[106] DPA, s 17(3).

[107] Kelleher, *Privacy and Data Protection Law in Ireland* (Tottel Publishing, 2006) p 354.

[108] Data Protection Commissioner, *Annual Report 2005*, Schedule 2, p 49.

[109] DPA, s 12A(1).

[110] DPA, s 12A(7).

controller is already registered or else if the controller has requested that the Data Protection Commissioner undertake such prior checks and is awaiting the results.[111]

International data transfers

[15.53] As noted above, the primary objective of the Data Protection Directive, and so the Data Protection Act 2003, is ensuring that personal data can be freely exchanged between member states. But the Data Protection Acts impose controls on the transfer of data outside the EEA providing that:

> 'The transfer of personal data by a data controller to a country or territory outside the European Economic Area may not take place unless that country or territory ensures an adequate level of protection for the privacy and the fundamental rights and freedoms of data subjects in relation to the processing of personal data having regard to all the circumstances surrounding the transfer of the data.'

[15.54] A number of factors must be considered in deciding whether a state has an adequate level of protection for privacy, such as the law in force in that country or territory, any codes of conduct or other rules that may apply, the security measures taken and the international obligations of that country.[112] The EC undertakes its own assessments of the data protection standards provided by countries outside the EEA. Where such an EC assessment exists it will bind the Irish authorities.[113] The Data Protection Acts' restrictions on the transfer of data outside the EEA will not apply in certain circumstances. These circumstances may be summarised as follows:

(a)   the transfer is authorised by an enactment or convention or other instrument imposing an international obligation on the State;

(b)   the data subject has given his consent to the transfer;

(c)   the transfer is necessary for the performance of a contract between the data subject and the data controller;

(d)   the transfer is necessary for the taking of steps at the request of the data subject with a view to his or her entering into a contract with the data controller;

(e)   the transfer is necessary for the conclusion of a contract between the data controller and a person other than the data subject that is entered into at the request of the data subject; and is in the interests of the data subject, or for the performance of such a contract;[114]

(f)   the transfer is necessary for reasons of substantial public interest;

(g)   the transfer is necessary for the purposes of obtaining legal advice or in connection with legal proceedings or the establishment or defence of legal rights;

(h)   the transfer is necessary in order to prevent injury or damage to the health or property of the data subject;

---

[111] DPA, s 12A(6).

[112] DPA, s 11(1).

[113] DPA, s 11(2).

[114] This would cover foreign holiday bookings where a travel agent would have separate contractual arrangements with the prospective holiday-maker and a hotel or other service.

(i)   the transfer is of part only of the personal data on a register established by or under an enactment; and

(j)   the transfer has been authorised by the Data Protection Commissioner.[115]

[15.55] One particularly sensible way of ensuring that data protection rights are respected when transferring data outside the EEA is by use of contractual provisions. The EC has approved the use of standard form contractual terms for this purpose.[116] And the Data Protection Acts provide for the enforcement of such contractual provisions.[117] Data transfers to the USA are particularly controversial. The USA and the EU entered into a 'safe harbour' agreement for European personal data, which does offer some protections. However, the European Commission is unable to effectively verify compliance with those protections.[118] The reality is that whilst avoidance of Europe's controls on data transfers outside the EEA might pose an ethical or moral problem, but is unlikely to challenge the legal skills of the average lawyer. In particular the ECJ held in *Bodil Lindqvist v Sweden*[119] that when the EC legislature enacted the Data Protection Directive it had not 'intended the expression transfer (of data) to a third country to cover the loading, by an individual in Mrs Lindqvist's position, of data onto an internet page, even if those data are thereby made accessible to persons in third countries with the technical means to access them.'[120]

[15.56] Thus uploading data to the Internet does not amount to an international data transfer, even if that data can be downloaded by someone in China or the USA.

Offences and enforcement

[15.57] The Data Protection Acts create a number of criminal offences. These are:

(a)   requiring someone to make an access request in connection with recruitment, employment or the provision of services[121];

(b)   failing or refusal to comply with a requirement of an enforcement notice[122];

(c)   failing to comply with a prohibition contained in a prohibition notice[123];

(d)   failure or refusal to provide information as required by an information notice or knowingly providing false information in response to an information notice[124];

(e)   processing in breach of s 12A(6) of the Data Protection Acts[125];

---

[115] DPA, s 11(4)(a).

[116] Commission Decision C-2001/1539 of 15 June 2001 on standard contractual clauses for the transfer of personal data to third countries, OJ L 181/19, 04/07/2001.

[117] DPA, s 11(6).

[118] Commission staff Working Document on the implementation of Commission Decision 520/2000/EC on the Safe Harbour Principals, Brussels, 20 October 2004, SEC 2004 1323.

[119] *Bodil Lindqvist v Sweden* C-101/01, 6 November 2003.

[120] C-101/01, para 68.

[121] DPA, s 4(13).

[122] DPA, s 10(9).

[123] DPA, s 11(15).

[124] DPA, s 12(5).

[125] DPA, s 12A(7).

(f)   keeping personal data without there being an entry in the register in respect of the data controller[126];

(g)   providing information known to be false and misleading in respect of an entry in the register[127];

(h)   disclosure of data by a data processor with the prior authority of the data controller[128];

(i)   obtaining access to personal data with the prior authority of the data controller[129];

(j)   obstructing or impeding an authorised officer of the Data Protection Commissioner[130]; and

(k)   disclosure of confidential information by the Data Protection Commissioner or his staff.[131]

[15.58] The penalty for an offence under the Data Protection Acts is a fine of €3000 on summary conviction[132] or €100,000 on conviction on indictment.[133] Where a person is convicted of an offence under the Data Protection Acts, the court may order '... any data material which appears to the court to be connected with the commission of the offence to be forfeited or destroyed and any relevant data to be erased.'[134] The court cannot make such an order if it considers that the person convicted was not the owner of the data in question, at least until the owner of the data has been given an opportunity to be heard on this point.[135] If the accused should wish to plead guilty in the District Court to an offence under the Data Protection Acts, then s 13 of the Criminal Procedure Act 1967 will apply.[136] The Data Protection Commissioner may bring and summarily prosecute offences under the Data Protection Acts[137] and summary proceedings may be initiated up to one year from the date of the offence.[138] The Data Protection Acts provide for the prosecution of corporate offences.[139]

[15.59] The most potent enforcement tool in the Data Protection Acts may prove to be the ability to sue for damages for breach of the Data Protection Acts' provisions.

---

[126] DPA, s 19(6).

[127] DPA, s 20(2).

[128] DPA, s 21(2).

[129] DPA, s 22(1).

[130] DPA, s 24(6).

[131] DPA, Sch II, para 10(2).

[132] DPA, s 31(1)(a).

[133] DPA, s 31(1)(b).

[134] DPA, s 31(2).

[135] DPA, s 31(3).

[136] DPA, s 31(4).

[137] DPA, s 30(1).

[138] 'Notwithstanding s 10(4) of the Petty Sessions (Ireland) Act 1851', DPA, s 30(2).

[139] DPA, s 29.

The Acts provide that:

'For the purposes of the law of torts and to the extent that that law does not so provide, a person, being a data controller or a data processor, shall, so far as regards the collection by him of personal data or information intended for inclusion in such data or his dealing with such data, owe a duty of care to the data subject concerned.'[140]

A claim for breach of the Data Protection Acts might be ancillary to a claim for breaches of privacy rights under the Constitution and the ECHR.

---

[140] DPA, s 7.

PART V: PRIVACY

Chapter 16

Electronic Privacy

Introduction

[16.01] Privacy is a right, of that there is no question. A right to privacy is implicitly provided by the Irish Constitution, explicitly provided by the European Convention on Human Rights (ECHR), and privacy may also be protected by common law and equity. Although the origins of the right to privacy may be ancient, the case-law on the subject is relatively new. It would appear that everyone has some sort of right to privacy at all times, but privacy is not an unlimited right. At one stage it seemed that privacy was a right which could only be asserted in relation to the most intimate details of one's life,[1] but now the right to privacy has moved out onto the public roadway[2] and into the prison cell.[3] How the right to privacy will transfer to the public and private spaces of the Internet remains to be seen. Many may find it surprising that a public figure, such as a princess, will have a right to privacy when she is eating in a public restaurant. But she does. Will it also seem so surprising that a private individual who sets out details of their private life online, whether on a personal website or a site such as YouTube or Facebook, could argue that they also have a right to privacy in that material? It is quite possible that they do, and it remains to be seen how the courts will analyse issues such as this. It is certainly true that the Courts have expressed concerns about the threat posed by new technologies to the privacy of individuals. In *R v Brown*[4] Hoffman LJ commented that:

> 'one of the less welcome consequences of the information technology revolution has been the ease with which it has become possible to invade the privacy of the individual. No longer is it necessary to peep through keyholes or listen under the eaves. Instead, more reliable information can be obtained in greater comfort and safety by using the concealed surveillance camera, the telephoto lens, the hidden microphone and the telephone bug. No longer is it necessary to open letters, pry into files or conduct elaborate inquiries to discover the intimate details of a person's business or financial affairs, his health, family, leisure interests or dealings with central or local government. Vast amounts of information about everyone are stored on computers, capable of instant transmission anywhere in the world and accessible at the touch of a keyboard. The right to keep oneself to oneself, to tell other people that certain things are none of their business, is under technological threat'.[5]

---

[1]   *McGee v Attorney General* [1974] IR 284, (1975) 109 ILTR 29.
[2]   *Von Hannover v Germany* (24 June 2004) ECtHR.
[3]   *DPP v Kenny* [1992] 2 IR 141.
[4]   *R v Brown* [1996] 2 WLR 203.
[5]   [1996] 2 WLR 203 at 214.

The sources of privacy rights

[16.02] Rights to privacy may be derived from a variety of different sources, which are: the Constitution, the European Convention on Human Rights, equity and statutory provisions. Each of these sources is discussed below.

Privacy as constitutional right[6]

[16.03] The right to privacy was first successfully asserted[7] before the Irish courts in *Kennedy & Arnold v Ireland*[8] where Hamilton P (as he then was) found that:

'Though not specifically guaranteed by the Constitution, the right of privacy is one of the fundamental personal rights of the citizen which flow from the Christian and democratic nature of the State. It is not an unqualified right. Its exercise may be restricted by the constitutional rights of others, by the requirements of the common good and is subject to the requirements of public order and morality.'[9]

[16.04] The facts of *Kennedy & Arnold v Ireland* make it particularly relevant in the context of electronic communications. Two of the plaintiffs were 'distinguished and well known political correspondents with Irish national newspapers with extensive circulation within the state'.[10] Their phones were tapped by the state, and the state admitted that 'the system of safeguards ... was either disregarded in the cases in question or, what amounts to the same thing, was operated in such a way as to be rendered meaningless'. The state admitted that 'the "tapping" of the telephones was improper'. However the state also argued that it was 'not illegal and did not interfere with any constitutional rights of the plaintiffs'. Hamilton P found that this was 'a submission which I cannot accept'.[11] Hamilton P was in no doubt that the right to privacy included:

'the right to privacy in respect of telephonic conversations and the right to hold such conversations without deliberate, conscious and unjustified interference therewith and intrusion thereon by servants of the State, who listen to such conversation, record them, transcribe them and make the transcriptions thereof available to other persons.'[12]

[16.05] There is no doubt that the right to privacy exists, but it is not an unlimited right. As Denham J noted in *Bailey v Flood*[13]:

'That the applicants have a constitutional right to privacy is beyond debate. It is equally well established that this is not an absolute right but one which must in certain circumstances be weighed against or balanced with the exigencies of the common good.'

---

[6]   See Kelleher, *Privacy and Data Protection Law in Ireland* (Tottel Publishing, 2006) ch 2.

[7]   A right to marital privacy had been previously identified in*McGee v Attorney General* [1974] IR 284, (1975) 109 ILTR 29. However, the Supreme Court declined to identify a general right to privacy in *Norris v Attorney General* [1984] IR 36.

[8]   *Kennedy & Arnold v Attorney General* [1987] IR 587.

[9]   [1987] IR 587 at 592. Hamilton CJ's judgment was approved by the Supreme Court in*Re a Ward of Court (No 2)* 1996 2 IR 79.

[10] The third plaintiff was one of their spouses [1987] IR 587 at 588.

[11] [1987] IR 587 at 589.

[12] [1987] IR 587 at 592.

[13] *Bailey v Flood* (14 April 2000, unreported) SC.

Hamilton P pointed out that the plaintiffs 'must accept the risk of accidental interference with his communications and the fact that in certain circumstances the exigencies of the common good may require and justify such intrusion and interference'.[14] The circumstance in which the exigencies of the common good will justify interference with the right to privacy are many and varied. In *AG v Open Door Counselling*[15] Hamilton P held that the right to privacy cannot be invoked to interfere with the right to life of the unborn. In *People (DPP) v McCann*[16] the Court of Criminal Appeal held that the right of privacy would have to yield to 'the most fundamental constitutional right of all ... the right to life.'[17] In *Desmond v Glackin (No 2)*[18] the right had to yield to the needs of intra-governmental communication. It has also had to yield to the exigencies of military law,[19] the requirement that court proceedings be in public[20] and the unique bond of mother and child.[21] Court decisions such as these reflect the reality that people decide to balance their privacy with other interests all the time.

Privacy as a human right[22]

[16.06] The ECHR provides for a right to privacy 'Everyone has the right to respect for his private and family life, his home and his correspondence'.[23] The Convention goes on to provide that there 'shall be no interference by a public authority with the exercise of this right'.[24] Although attempts were made to invoke the ECHR before the Irish courts,[25] the above was not a part of Ireland's domestic law until the commencement of the European Convention on Human Rights Act 2003 on 31 December 2003.[26] The European Convention on Human Rights Act 2003 provides:

> 'In interpreting and applying any statutory provision or rule of law, a court shall, in so far as is possible, subject to the rules of law relating to such interpretation and application, do so in a manner compatible with the State's obligations under the Convention provisions.'[27]

[16.07] In doing so, the courts must 'take due account of the principles laid down'[28] by the European Court of Human Rights. The Act goes on to provide that 'Subject to any

---

[14] *Kennedy & Arnold v Attorney General* [1987] IR 587 at 593.
[15] *AG v Open Door Counselling* [1988] IR 593.
[16] *People (DPP) v McCann* [1998] 4 IR 397.
[17] *People (DPP) v McCann* [1998] 4 IR 397 at 413.
[18] *Desmond v Glackin (No 2)* [1993] 3 IR 67.
[19] *Re C* [1998] 2 IR 447.
[20] *Roe v Blood Transfusion Board* [1996] 3 IR 67; contrast with *The Attorney General v X* [1992] 1 IR 1.
[21] *IO'T v B* [1998] 2 IR 321.
[22] See Kelleher, *Privacy and Data Protection Law in Ireland* (Tottel Publishing, 2006) ch 3.
[23] ECHR, art 8(1).
[24] ECHR, art 8(2).
[25] For example, 'the European Convention on Human Rights is not part of the domestic law of this country', per Barrington J *Barry v Medical Council* [1998] 2 IR 368; see also *Norris v Attorney General* [1984] IR 36 and *Re Ó Laighléis* [1960] IR 93.
[26] See European Convention on Human Rights Act (Commencement) Order 2003 (SI 483/2003).
[27] European Convention on Human Rights Act 2003, s 2(1).
[28] European Convention on Human Rights Act 2003, s 4.

statutory provision (other than this Act) or rule of law, every organ of the State shall perform its functions in a manner compatible with the State's obligations under the Convention provisions'.[29] The Act confers a right of action upon those aggrieved by a failure to abide by this latter provision.[30] The European Court of Human Rights has applied a broad definition to the term 'private life'. In *Pretty v United Kingdom*[31] the court reiterated that:

> 'the concept of 'private life' is a broad term not susceptible to exhaustive definition. It covers the physical and psychological integrity of a person ... It can sometimes embrace aspects of an individual's physical and social identity ... Elements such as, for example, gender identification, name and sexual orientation and sexual life fall within the personal sphere protected by art 8 ... art 8 also protects a right to personal development, and the right to establish and develop relationships with other human beings and the outside world ... Although no previous case has established as such any right to self-determination as being contained in art 8 of the Convention, the Court considers that the notion of personal autonomy is an important principle underlying the interpretation of its guarantees.'[32]

[16.08] The Convention will protect the privacy of an individual's professional life, workplace[33] and telephone conversations.[34] It will also allow an individual to gain access to records such as those held by social workers,[35] army doctors[36] and secret policemen.[37] Like the right provided by the Irish Constitution, the right provided by art 8 of the ECHR is a limited one. The Convention specifically provides that interference in the right may occur where it is:

> 'in accordance with the law and is necessary in a democratic society in the interests of national security, public safety or the economic well-being of the country, for the prevention of disorder or crime, for the protection of health or morals, or for the protection of the rights and freedoms of others.'[38]

[16.09] In other words a public authority may interfere in the privacy rights of an individual if the following two conditions are met:

  (i)   the interference is 'in accordance with the law'; and

  (ii) the interference is 'necessary in a democratic society' in the interests of at least one of the following:

     (a)   national security;

     (b)   public safety, or;

---

[29] European Convention on Human Rights Act 2003, s 3(1).
[30] European Convention on Human Rights Act 2003, s 3(2).
[31] *Pretty v United Kingdom* (29 April 2002) ECtHR.
[32] (29 April 2002) ECtHR, para 61.
[33] *Niemetz v Germany* (16 December 1992) [1993] 16 EHRR 97.
[34] *Klass v Germany* (1979–80) 2 EHRR 214.
[35] *Gaskin v United Kingdom* (1989) 12 EHRR 36.
[36] *McGinley and Egan v The United Kingdom* (1998) 27 EHRR 1.
[37] *Rotaro v Romania* (4 May 2000) ECtHR.
[38] ECHR, art 8(2).

(c)   the economic well-being of the country;

(d)   for the prevention of disorder or crime;

(e)   for the protection of health or morals, or;

(f)   for the protection of the rights and freedoms of others.

[16.10] The fact that the Convention refers to 'interference by a public authority' would not seem to mean that interferences by private individuals will be permissible. For example, in *Von Hannover v Germany* the interference at issue was the publication of photographs in a commercial magazine; there was no suggestion that the German state was publishing the photographs in question. But by failing to provide the plaintiff with a remedy by which she might restrain publication, the state was interfering in her privacy:

'although the object of Article 8 is essentially that of protecting the individual against arbitrary interference by the public authorities, it does not merely compel the State to abstain from such interference: in addition to this primarily negative undertaking, there may be positive obligations inherent in an effective respect for private or family life. These obligations may involve the adoption of measures designed to secure respect for private life even in the sphere of the relations of individuals between themselves.'[39]

Privacy as a common law or equitable right[40]

[16.11] In *Campbell v MGN*[41] the English House of Lords held that details of the plaintiff's attendance at Narcotics Anonymous were 'private information which imported a duty of confidence'.[42] The plaintiff was a 'celebrated fashion model. Hers is a household name, nationally and internationally. Her face is instantly recognisable. Whatever she does and wherever she goes is news'.[43] In February 2001 the *Daily Mirror* newspaper carried a front page story headed: 'Naomi: I am a drug addict'. The story that followed detailed that the plaintiff was attending Narcotics Anonymous. It was illustrated with photographs showing the plaintiff arriving for those meetings. Upon publication of this story, the plaintiff issued legal proceedings; a couple of other stories then followed, one of which was 'offensive and disparaging'.[44] The plaintiff proceeded with her legal action. It ultimately reached the House of Lords, which reiterated that 'there is no general tort of invasion of privacy'.[45] However, the House went on to find that the right to privacy might be protected by other laws:

'the right to privacy is in a general sense one of the values, and sometimes the most important value, which underlies a number of more specific causes of action, both at common law and under various statutes. One of these is the equitable action for breach of confidence, which has long been recognised as capable of being used to protect privacy'.[46]

---

[39] *Von Hannover v Germany* (24 June 2004) ECtHR, para 57.

[40] See Kelleher, *Privacy and Data Protection Law in Ireland* (Tottel Publishing, 2006) ch 4.

[41] *Campbell v MGN* [2004] UKHL 22.

[42] [2004] UKHL 22, para 95, per Hope LJ.

[43] [2004] UKHL 22, para 1, *per* Nicolls LJ. 'Even the Judges know who Naomi Campbell is', per Hale LJ, para 127.

[44] [2004] UKHL 22, per Nicholls LJ at para 9.

[45] [2004] UKHL 22, para 43, per Hoffman LJ.

[46] [2004] UKHL 22, para 43, per Hoffman LJ.

The house unanimously agreed that there was a right to control the dissemination of private information, Nicholls LJ having identified private information as being matter whose disclosure 'would be highly offensive to a reasonable person'.[47] The decision of the House of Lords in *Campbell v MGN* is of great and undoubted significance for English law. The decision gives a clear cause of action – breach of confidence – upon which to ground claims for breach of privacy before the English courts. The decision may have somewhat less significance for Irish law. A claim for breach of privacy has had a clear cause of action – breach of constitutional rights – since the decision of the High Court in *Kennedy and Arnold v Attorney General* in 1986. The House of Lords' decision in *Campbell v MGN* was also significant in that it related to the publication of pictures of the plaintiff taken in a public place. However, this aspect of the decision has been overtaken by the decision of the ECtHR in *Von Hannover v Germany*. The Irish courts are under a statutory obligation to 'take due account of the principles laid down' in judgments of the ECtHR. Although the Irish courts might well be persuaded by a reference to the decision of the House of Lords in *Campbell v MGN*, they will not be bound to take account of that decision in the same way.

Statutory rights to privacy[48]

[16.12] A number of Acts provide for limited and specific rights to privacy. For example, the CRRA 2000 provides for a right to privacy in certain photographs and films.[49]

How valuable are privacy rights?

[16.13] The value of privacy rights is variable; anyone who uses a loyalty card will be selling the aspects of their privacy contained in their shopping list to a supermarket for a 1% discount on their grocery shopping.[50] One can effectively sell one's right to privacy. In *Jane O'Keefe v Ryanair*[51] it was held that the surrender of the plaintiff's privacy was worth €67,500. In *Kennedy and Arnold v Attorney General* the plaintiffs were awarded the sum of €63,486.90 for breach of their privacy. In assessing this amount Hamilton P commented that:

> 'In determining the damages to which the plaintiffs are entitled, I must have regard not only to the distress which was suffered by the plaintiffs as a result of the infringement of their constitutional right to privacy, the implication thereof and the publicity consequent

---

47 [2004] UKHL 22, para 22; citing *Australian Broadcasting v Lenah Game Meats* (2001) 185 ALR 1.

48 See Kelleher, *Privacy and Data Protection Law in Ireland* (Tottel Publishing, 2006) para 2.40.

49 CRRA 2000, s 114. See also, Surveillance chapter.

50 On the one hand Tesco (http://www.tesco.ie/clubcard/) promises that with its ClubCard customers can 'Earn 1 point (1cent) for every EUR 1 you spend' but 'The consumer pays… in the constant stream of information they are supplying about themselves to the company. This begins with the filling in of the application form and continues every time the card is swiped for a transaction. If the company can convince customers to join their loyalty schemes, then every day they can find out more about their customers' likes and dislikes, their family and their lifestyle': 'Shoppers give too much away with loyalty card' (2001) The Irish Times, 1 June.

51 *Jane O'Keefe v Ryanair* [2002] 3 IR 228.

thereto but also to the fact that the infringement was carried out deliberately, consciously and without justification by the executive organ of the State which is under a constitutional obligation to respect, vindicate and defend that right.'[52]

[16.14] In *Aherne v RTÉ*,[53] Clarke J seemed to be willing to contemplate that an individual could compromise their right to privacy in return for compensation, noting the fact that the plaintiffs in the UK case of *Douglas v Hello!*[54] 'had in fact allowed significant publicity to attach to their wedding lessened the right of privacy'. The Data Protection Acts 1988–2003 confer a statutory right to sue for damages where individuals' rights under the Acts are breached, providing that:

> 'For the purposes of the law of torts and to the extent that that law does not so provide, a person, being a data controller or a data processor, shall, so far as regards the collection by him of personal data or information intended for inclusion in such data or his dealing with such data, owe a duty of care to the data subject concerned.'[55]

There would not appear to have been any awards of damages pursuant to this provision in Ireland. Where awards have been made under the UK legislation they have tended to be quite paltry; in *Douglas v Hello!*[56] the plaintiffs were awarded no more than nominal damages for breach of their data protection rights by the English courts.

Not all privacy rights are equal

[16.15] Supermarket loyalty cards may encourage customers to stay loyal to a supermarket, but many customers will have loyalty cards for different chains, earning the benefits of remaining loyal to each. Supermarkets may take a similarly cynical approach to their customers, using the data to differentiate between them.[57] The reality of modern life is that not all privacy rights are equal: some people's privacy is worth more than others.

Politicians v Princesses

[16.16] Election to public office has consequences for politicians that are many and varied; one of the less commonly considered is that politicians effectively renounce their right to privacy. This is clear from the European Court of Human Rights decision in *Karhuvaara and Iltalehti v Finland*.[58] The applicants had been convicted of breaching the privacy of a member of the Finnish Parliament for publishing an article entitled 'Husband of member of Parliament got heavy sentence for violence in restaurant'. The ECtHR ruled that the conviction was contrary to the ECHR, finding that:

---

[52] *Kennedy and Arnold v Attorney General* [1987] IR 587 at 594.

[53] *Aherne v RTÉ* (2005) IEHC 180, Clarke J.

[54] *Douglas v Hello!* [2005] EWCA Civ 595.

[55] Data Protection Acts 1988–2003, s 7.

[56] *Douglas v Hello!* (2001) QB 967, (2001) 2 WLR 992.

[57] This may work out better for some customers than for others: 'Loyalty programmes such as Tesco's ClubCard offer customers benefits in exchange for giving up their personal information, allowing the retailer to make decisions about who the best customers are. Special promotions and lower prices can now be directed at customers a retailer wants to retain'. Birchall, 'Retailers get inside track on your lifestyle', (2006) Financial Times, 11 October.

[58] *Karhuvaara And Iltalehti v Finland* (16 November 2004) ECtHR.

'the public has the right to be informed, which is an essential right in a democratic society that, in certain special circumstances, may even extend to aspects of the private life of public figures, particularly where politicians are concerned.'[59]

In contrast In *Von Hannover v Germany*[60] the applicant was 'the eldest daughter of Prince Rainier III of Monaco'.[61] This gave her the title of Princess and made her of interest to the media, but she did not 'perform any function within or on behalf of the State of Monaco or any of its institutions'.[62] The court considered that:

'a fundamental distinction needs to be made between reporting facts – even controversial ones – capable of contributing to a debate in a democratic society relating to politicians in the exercise of their functions, for example, and reporting details of the private life of an individual who, moreover, as in this case, does not exercise official functions.[63]

... although the public has a right to be informed, which is an essential right in a democratic society that, in certain special circumstances, can even extend to aspects of the private life of public figures, particularly where politicians are concerned.'[64]

Persons with siblings who are criminals v Persons with law-abiding siblings

[16.17] Being born into a criminal family was always bad luck, but the consequences of having criminals for relatives are becoming more serious. A person's DNA is inherited from their parents and is quite unique them. For example, in *DPP v Crerar*[65] the defendant was accused of the murder of Phyllis Murphy in 1979. Her murder had remained unsolved for almost 20 years, when in 1998 Irish and UK laboratories compared blood samples, taken from her corpse by the gardaí, with samples taken from 50 local men during the earlier criminal investigation and retained since then. Evidence of the resulting match between Crerar's DNA and that found on Phyllis Murphy's body led to his conviction for murder. The problem with DNA is that a person's DNA will be less distinct from their siblings than it will be from other persons. This point was successfully argued in *Allen v DPP*.[66] The applicants had been convicted of armed robbery on the basis of DNA analysis of material found on a balaclava allegedly worn by one of the robbers. On appeal the defendant argued that he had three full brothers and two half brothers and that at least one brother had been convicted of a criminal offence. The defendant went on to argue that the probability of DNA matching amongst siblings is one in ten thousand as opposed to on in one thousand million. This was not disputed by the prosecution. The Court of Criminal Appeal overturned the conviction and ordered a retrial.[67]

---

59   (16 November 2004) ECtHR, para 45.
60   *Von Hannover v Germany* (24 June 2004) ECtHR.
61   (24 June 2004) ECtHR, para 8.
62   (24 June 2004) ECtHR, para 9.
63   (24 June 2004) ECtHR, para 63.
64   (24 June 2004) ECtHR, para 64.
65   *DPP v Crerar* (31 October 2002, unreported) CCC.
66   *Allen v DPP* (18 December 2003, unreported) CCA.
67   Kelleher, *Privacy and Data Protection Law in Ireland* (Tottel Publishing, 2006), paras 20.51–20.61.

Patients who are litigants v patients who are not

[16.18] Patients have a particular right to privacy in their medical records. As well as the general right to privacy, information about an individual's medical treatment receives specific protection from medical ethics, the law of confidence and the Data Protection Acts 1988–2003.[68] But if a patient's medical condition is relevant to litigation undertaken by the patient then the patient may have to renounce their right to confidence in that information. In *McGrory v ESB*[69]the defendant sought to have its medical advisors discuss the plaintiff's condition with the plaintiff's medical advisors. The plaintiff refused to consent to this, so the defendant sought to stay the plaintiff's proceedings. The Supreme Court held for the defendant, Keane CJ stating:

> 'The plaintiff who sues for damages for personal injuries by implication necessarily waives the right of privacy which he would otherwise enjoy in relation to his medical condition. The law must be in a position to ensure that he does not unfairly and unreasonably impede the defendant in the preparation of his defence by refusing to consent to a medical examination ... I have no doubt that the courts enjoy an inherent jurisdiction to stay proceedings where justice so requires and that it should be exercised in cases where the plaintiff refuses to submit to a medical examination or to disclose his medical records to the defendant or to permit the defendant to interview his treating doctors.'[70]

[16.19] Similarly, in *Shelly-Morris v Dublin Bus*[71] the plaintiff claimed that she had sustained such serious injuries whilst a passenger on the defendant's bus that 'She ... had to retire from her work on health grounds'.[72] However, she was followed by a private investigator on behalf of the defendant. He videotaped the plaintiff and the tape showed her movements to be 'natural and unhindered'.[73] This led the trial judge to conclude that she was exaggerating her symptoms,[74] a decision upheld by the Supreme Court. With regard to the use of video evidence in such trials, Hardiman J commented in *O'Connor v Dublin Bus*[75] that:

> 'A significant number of personal injury claims feature injuries which are not, or not wholly, capable of being proved or negatived by the normal processes of clinical medicine. The credibility of the plaintiff is central in such cases, some of which are very substantial ones. Video surveillance of the kind featured in this case is often resorted to as a check or control of the plaintiffs' account'.

Nurses v Patients

[16.20] *Aherne v RTÉ* concerned standards of care in a care home; 'an experienced care worker was engaged by RTÉ to seek and take up a job at (the plaintiff's nursing home)'.

---

[68] Kelleher, *Privacy and Data Protection Law in Ireland* (Tottel Publishing, 2006), paras 12.26–12.51.

[69] *McGrory v ESB* [2003] 3 IR 407.

[70] [2003] 3 IR 407 at 414–415.

[71] *Shelly-Morris v Dublin Bus* [2003] 1 IR 232 at 245.

[72] [2003] 1 IR 232 at 251.

[73] [2003] 1 IR 232 at 251.

[74] [2003] 1 IR 232 at 252.

[75] *O'Connor v Dublin Bus* [2003] 4 IR 459.

Ultimately, he was 'equipped by RTÉ with a concealed camera. A significant amount of footage ensued some of which was included in the intended broadcast'. The plaintiff argued that this footage should not be broadcast, as it would breach their right to privacy. Clarke J rejected their application, and permitted the broadcast on the basis that the defendant would 'seek() to protect the privacy interests of patients by obscuring their identities through a technical process known as pixilation, or by obtaining the consent of the patients families to the proposed broadcast, or both'. However, he displayed no such concern for the privacy of the owners and staff of the home against whom serious allegations were being made.

Parents v Children

[16.21] The parental right to privacy is different from that of the child. Article 41.1 of the Constitution provides that 'the State recognises the Family as the natural primary and fundamental unit group of society ...'. In *North Western Health Board v HW*[76] Hardiman J held that:

> 'a child will not himself or herself be capable of making or of acting upon any decision as to its own welfare, these decisions must necessary be made by some person or agency on his or her behalf ... in the choice of decision maker, the Constitution plainly accords a primacy to the parent and this primacy, in my view gives rises to a presumption that the welfare of the child is to be found in the family exercising its authority as such. This reflects the right, both of the parents and of the children, to have the family protected in its Constitution and authority.'[77]

The primacy of the family means that children will not have a right to privacy from their parents. Parents are entitled to get it 'wrong' in relation to their children. Given that parents are entitled to object to the taking of a medical test of their child, which offered benefits to the child with no ill effects, it may be taken that parents will also be able to monitor their children's privacy online. The tracking of children's mobile phones by concerned or curious parents is developing as a niche business in the UK.[78] If this tracking is to be effective, then the child should not know that it is going on. Therefore, the question arises as to whether a parent can give a valid consent to the tracking on behalf of the child. It is certainly true that the law treats children as having a different capacity to consent than adults; a contract will not normally be binding against a child under the age of 18.[79] It is likely that a parent can validly consent to the monitoring of their child for the purposes of the Data Protection Acts 1988–2003. The monitoring in question could be legitimised on the basis that it was being done to prevent the child from injury or in the legitimate interests of the parent.[80]

---

[76] *North Western Health Board v HW* [2001] 3 IR 622.

[77] [2001] 3 IR 622 at 764.

[78] See eg: http://www.kidsok.net; http://www.childlocate.co.uk. Although tracking a child's mobile phone may seem intrusive, it is mild compared to some of the other options open to parents, including inserting a microchip transponder under their skin (Lane, 'Would a microchip keep your child safe?' (2003) BBC News Online Magazine, 18 December, http://news.bbc.co.uk/1/hi/magazine/3307471.stm) or hiring a private detective to infiltrate a child's social circle (Moorhead, 'Would you spy on your child?' (2003) The Guardian, 17 December).

[79] Age of Majority Act 1985, s 18.

Privacy in a public place

[16.22] Nobody should be in any doubt that the Internet is a public place, but that does not mean that just because a person goes online, they renounce all their privacy rights. Both the Irish courts and the European Court of Human Rights (ECtHR) have recognised that an individual may have a right to privacy in a public space. In *Kane v Governor of Mountjoy Prison*.[81] the gardaí placed the applicant under intense and overt surveillance whilst they waited for a District Court Judge to come available who might grant an extradition warrant. The applicant was followed by car and watched whilst he consulted a solicitor. In the Court of Criminal Appeal, Finlay CJ was willing to accept:

'the submission made on behalf of the applicant, that as far as privacy is concerned, overt surveillance may under certain circumstances be more onerous than covert surveillance. This is not always true, and indeed, one can conceive of circumstances in which the reverse would be true. I would be prepared to assume, without deciding, for the purpose of dealing with this submission that a right of privacy may exist in an individual, even while travelling in the public streets and roads.'

Finlay CJ also expressed his agreement with the view that 'if overt surveillance of the general type proved in this case were applied to an individual without a basis to justify it, it would be objectionable, and I would add, would be clearly unlawful'. In *Von Hannover v Germany* the applicant was photographed in a variety of mundane, albeit public situations, such as 'shopping with a bag slung over her shoulder ... in a restaurant ... alone on a bicycle ... doing her shopping at the market ... [82] ... leaving her house[83] ... and ... tripping over an obstacle and falling down'.[84] These photographs were then published in German magazines. The applicant then sued in the German courts, with limited success. The case ultimately reached the ECtHR, where the German State argued that its laws did provide adequate protections for the applicant's privacy. Germany argued that the reason it's courts had not protected the applicant's privacy was that the photographs in question 'had not been taken in a secluded place'.[85]

[16.23] However, the ECtHR held that 'there is no doubt that the publication by various German magazines of photos of the applicant in her daily life either on her own or with other people falls within the scope of her private life'.[86]
The court went on to make the point that the applicant had a right to privacy whilst in a public place explicitly clear:

'the photos of the applicant in the various German magazines show her in scenes from her daily life, thus involving activities of a purely private nature such as engaging in sport, out walking, leaving a restaurant or on holiday'.[87]

---

[80] See Kelleher, *Privacy and Data Protection Law in Ireland* (Tottel Publishing, 2006) paras 17.51–17.52.
[81] *Kane v Governor of Mountjoy Prison* [1988] IR 757.
[82] *Von Hannover v Germany* (24 June 2004) ECtHR, para 14.
[83] (24 June 2004) ECtHR, para 15.
[84] (24 June 2004) ECtHR, para 17.
[85] (24 June 2004) ECtHR, para 45.
[86] (24 June 2004) ECtHR, para 53.
[87] (24 June 2004) ECtHR, para 61.

The court then reiterated:

> 'the fundamental importance of protecting private life from the point of view of the development of every human being's personality. That protection ... extends beyond the private family circle and also includes a social dimension. The Court considers that anyone, even if they are known to the general public, must be able to enjoy a 'legitimate expectation' of protection of and respect for their private life'.[88]

The ECtHR concluded that the applicant's right to privacy had been breached by the publication of photos of her in public places. In its judgment, the ECtHR noted that 'increased vigilance in protecting private life is necessary to contend with new communication technologies which make it possible to store and reproduce personal data'.[89]

[16.24] The Internet is a global network, but the information superhighway is a rather different place from the public road. The ECtHR made it clear in *Von Hannover v Germany* that someone who goes out in public to the shops, the beach or a restaurant will still retain a right to privacy. Can it be argued that someone who goes out in public on a website such as MySpace or Second Life also has a right to privacy? It remains to be seen.

MySpace

[16.25] MySpace was described by Kitchin J in *Dearlove (t/a 'Diddy') v Combs (t/a 'Sean 'Puffy' Combs', 'Puffy' and 'PDiddy')*[90] in the following terms:

> 'MySpace is something of an online cultural phenomenon. It describes itself as a social networking service that allows members to create personal profiles online in order to find and communicate with old and new friends. Members are able to maintain web-pages accessible by members of the public and which contain photographs, music, videos and text. MySpace is now widely used by artists as a way of promoting and marketing their music'.[91]

The entire point of MySpace is to allow people to view the profiles of others; the difficulty with doing this is that material created for one social context, such as college life, may not be helpful to the creator if viewed in another context, such as that of applying for a job. A phenomenon has emerged in the USA where 'some recruiters are looking up applicants on social networking sites like Facebook, MySpace, Xanga and Friendster, where college students often post risque or teasing photographs and provocative comments about drinking, recreational drug use and sexual exploits in what some mistakenly believe is relative privacy.'

[16.26] A person's expectations of privacy on a site will depend upon the restrictions that are placed on accessing their information: 'college students must have a college email address to register. Personal pages on Facebook are restricted to friends and others on the user's campus, leading many students to assume that they are relatively private.'

---

[88] (24 June 2004) ECtHR, para 69.
[89] (24 June 2004) ECtHR, para 70.
[90] *Dearlove v Combs* [2007] EWHC 375 (Ch).
[91] [2007] EWHC 375 (Ch), para 27.

Of course it may be possible to avoid such restrictions: 'companies can gain access to the information in several ways. Employees who are recent graduates often retain their college email addresses, which enables them to see pages. Sometimes, too, companies ask college students working as interns to perform online background checks'.[92] Acquiring information in this way would undoubtedly breach the privacy of the individuals in question.[93] Whether that breach is justified is another matter. Certainly the Employment Appeals Tribunal has been willing to countenance the dismissal of employees on the basis of material posted on social websites. In *Fogarty and O'Connor v IBM*[94] a complaint had been made to the respondent 'about the existence of a particular website'. This website was known as 'Virtual Vengeance' and was 'a chat site where people could access and type statements about employees ... (of the respondent company). The entries were grossly offensive, sexual, racist and deeply offensive about various employees'. The respondent investigated and was satisfied that the claimants had accessed the site in question. The claimants denied having written anything on the site. However, they were dismissed by the respondents and these dismissals were ruled fair by the EAT.

[16.27] Researching the background of potential employees in this way would create a number of potential legal difficulties for employers. One is that an employer might learn something about the sexual life of the applicant and decide to discriminate against them on that basis. For example, one recruiter was curious about an applicant and:

> 'went to her page on Facebook. She found explicit photographs and commentary about the student's sexual escapades, drinking and pot smoking, including testimonials from friends. Among the pictures were shots of the young woman passed out after drinking.'[95]

The recruiter then decided to neither interview nor recruit the applicant. The Employment Equality Acts 1998–2004 make it illegal to discriminate when recruiting employees.[96] One might argue that it is neither abnormal nor unusual for a young, single person to have a lively social life and that to refuse to recruit a person on that basis might amount to discrimination on a number of different grounds: 'the gender ground', 'the marital status ground', 'the family status ground', 'the sexual orientation ground', 'the religion ground', or 'the age ground'.[97] Undertaking such search and making a decision about an applicant on the basis of what was found during such a search is clearly a breach of fair procedures. This would particularly be the case where the applicant is not given the opportunity to answer any allegations being made against her. The other difficulty for an employer undertaking such a search might also be a breach of

---

92 Finder, 'When a Risque Online Persona Undermines a Chance for a Job' (2006) The New York Times, 11 June.
93 Of course the reality is that an unsuccessful applicant who was rejected on the basis of their Internet profile would probably never know that this was why he or she had been rejected, and thus never be able to challenge any such breach to their privacy.
94 *Fogarty and O'Connor v IBM* UD771/2000 UD661/2000, unreported EAT.
95 Finder, 'When a Risque Online Persona Undermines a Chance for a Job' (2006) The New York Times, 11 June.
96 Employment Equality Acts 1998–2004, s 8.
97 Employment Equality Acts 1998–2004, s 6(2).

the Data Protection Acts 1988–2003, if such a search were undertaken without informing the applicant that personal data was being gathered about them in this way.[98] The processing might also be unfair[99] and excessive.[100] However, there may be some doubt as to whether the Data Protection Acts 1988–2003 would apply to Internet sites such as MySpace. This follows from the judgment in *Bodil Lindqvist v Sweden,*[101] wherein the ECJ considered that:

> 'Given ... the state of development of the internet at the time (the Data Protection) Directive ... was drawn up ... one cannot presume that the Community legislature intended the expression transfer [of data] to a third country to cover the loading, by an individual in Mrs Lindqvist's position, of data onto an internet page, even if those data are thereby made accessible to persons in third countries with the technical means to access them.'[102]

[16.28] The ECJ was talking about a quite specific function of the Internet, namely that information uploaded to a website might be downloaded by someone outside Europe.[103] The court felt that the Data Protection Directive could not apply to this activity as it was not within the contemplation of the EC legislature at the time that the Directive was enacted, namely 1995. Neither could MySpace have been within the contemplation of the EC legislature at that time. So the argument could be made that searching MySpace for personal information is a form of data processing to which the Data Protection Acts 1988–2003 do not apply.

Search engines such as Google and Yahoo!

[16.29] 'Googling' an individual, or researching someone online, has become a well established part of modern life:

> 'I was scheduled for a job interview at a university, a member of the search committee Googled me and found my blog, where I refer to him (but not by name) as a belligerent jerk. He canceled the interview.'[104]

Again, undertaking such a search and using the resulting information in the recruitment process would be a breach of fair procedures and probably the Data Protection Acts 1988–2003.[105] Where a person undertakes such a search out of idle curiosity, it will probably not breach the Data Protection Acts 1988–2003 as the data will be 'kept by an individual ... for recreational purposes'.[106] One difficulty with using Googled information is that just because information is returned in an Internet search, does not make it true. Unfortunately, the Internet is host to a wide variety of inaccurate

---

[98]   Data Protection Acts 1988–2003, s 2D.
[99]   Data Protection Acts 1988–2003, s 2(1)(a).
[100] Data Protection Acts 1988-2003, s 2(1)(c)(iii).
[101] *Bodil Lindqvist v Sweden* Case C-101/01, 6 November 2003, ECJ.
[102] Case C-101/01, 6 November 2003, ECJ, para 68.
[103] Specifically countries outside the European Economic Area.
[104] Cohen, 'Google Gotcha' (2006) The New York Times, 26 February.
[105] Again subject to the view of the ECJ in *Bodil Lindqvist v Sweden* Case C-101/01, 6 November 2003, ECJ.
[106] Data Protection Acts 1988-2003, s 1(4).

information. Arguably information that is untrue about a person can be just as harmful to their privacy as information that is true, but it remains to be seen if the publication of such information could amount to a breach of privacy as opposed to straightforward defamation. If privacy were breached as a result of such a search, then the search engine used might not be liable. The e-Commerce Directive[107] provides that:

> 'Where an information society service[108] is provided that consists of the transmission in a communication network of information provided by a recipient of the service, or the provision of access to a communication network, Member States shall ensure that the service provider is not liable for the information transmitted, on condition that the provider:
>
> (a)   does not initiate the transmission;
>
> (b)   does not select the receiver of the transmission; and
>
> (c)   does not select or modify the information contained in the transmission'.[109]

[16.30] Arguably, Google would be able to avail of this provision as all it would be providing was a link to the privacy-invasing information in question; it would be for the individual user to decide whether or not he would actually click on the particular link. Google would neither initiate the downloading of the information, select the recipient nor select or modify the information. Google's function might instead be categorised as providing access to the communication network in question.

YouTube

[16.31] YouTube was described by Kitchin J in *Dearlove (t/a 'Diddy') v Combs (t/a 'Sean 'Puffy' Combs', 'Puffy' and 'PDiddy')* thus:[110]

> 'YouTube is in some ways similar to MySpace, but concentrates on allowing users to share and view video footage online. It originally started as a personal video sharing service but, like MySpace, is now used by artists as a way of promoting their recordings and performances. ... YouTube is a valuable promotional and marketing tool for many current music artists. Indeed, it is one of the fastest growing websites on the Internet'.[111]

[16.32] The posting of videos on YouTube that have been taken on Irish public roads has become controversial in recent years. In 2006 controversy attached to the display of a video on YouTube which:

> 'appears to have been recorded using a camera phone, depicts a teenage boy, dressed in black tracksuit bottoms and an oversized, zipped-up black bomber jacket.

---

[107] Directive 2000/31/EC of the European Parliament and of the Council of 8 June 2000 on certain legal aspects of information society services, in particular electronic commerce, in the Internal Market ('Directive on electronic commerce'), OJ L 178 , 17/07/2000 P. 1–16 implemented in Ireland as the European Communities (Directive 2000/31/EC) Regulations 2003 (SI 68/2003).

[108] Directive 2000/31/EC, recital 18 provides that: 'information society services are not solely restricted to services giving rise to online contracting but also, in so far as they represent an economic activity, extend to services which are not remunerated by those who receive them, such as those offering online information or commercial communications, or those providing tools allowing for search, access and retrieval of data'.

[109] Directive 2000/31/EC, art 12(1).

[110] *Dearlove v Combs* [2007] EWHC 375 (Ch).

[111] [2007] EWHC 375 (Ch), para 28.

The events are outdoors, at night and there appear to be a number of teenage boys and girls gathered outside one of the tower blocks in Ballymun. The boy's face is clearly visible as he takes a number of steps back and then runs towards the girl, jumps in the air and kicks her 'kung fu style' in the side of the face.

The girl, aged 15, with brown hair tied back, staggers to the side and, losing her balance, falls forward, her head hitting the ground by a waist-height bollard. Her father said she broke her arm in the incident.

She is wearing a denim mini-skirt, black tights and a zip-up, quilted jacket, while the boy has black hair and pale skin. There is some whooping and cheering during and after the assault, and someone goes to the girl's assistance.'[112]

The taking of the video would amount to a breach of the victim's right to privacy, as would the posting of the video on the website. The Data Protection Acts 1988–2003 would probably apply; these Acts do not specifically refer to sound and image data, but they implement the Data Protection Directive. The Directive makes it clear that data protection law will apply to data of this type:

'given the importance of the developments under way, in the framework of the information society, of the techniques used to capture, transmit, manipulate, record, store or communicate sound and image data relating to natural persons, this Directive should be applicable to processing involving such data.'[113]

[16.33] Uploading a video of a person to a website such as YouTube may well be a breach of their privacy rights, even if recording the original image is not. In *Peck v United Kingdom*[114] the applicant:

'was suffering from depression as a result of personal and family circumstances ... he walked alone down the high street towards a central junction in the centre of Brentwood with a kitchen knife in his hand and he attempted to commit suicide by cutting his wrists ... unaware that a CCTV camera, mounted on the traffic island in front of the junction, filmed his movements. The police were notified by the CCTV operator.'[115]

[16.34] The council that operated the CCTV system permitted footage of the incident to circulate widely; it was eventually shown on a national TV show with 9.2 million viewers.[116] The applicant ' ... did not complain that the collection of data through the CCTV-camera monitoring of his movements and the creation of a permanent record of itself amounted to an interference with his private life'. He in fact admitted that the system might well have saved his life'.[117] Instead the applicant complained of the disclosure of the CCTV footage to the public. The ECtHR went on to note that the CCTV footage had been broadcast by national audiovisual media and that it was 'commonly acknowledged that the audiovisual media have often a much more

---

[112] Holland, 'Councillor calls for arrest over assault clip on internet' (2006) The Irish Times, 1 November.

[113] Data Protection Directive 95/46, recital 14.

[114] *Peck v United Kingdom* [2003] ECHR 44.

[115] [2003] ECHR 44, paras 10–11.

[116] [2003] ECHR 44, para 20.

[117] [2003] ECHR 44, para 60.

immediate and powerful effect than the print media'. The ECtHR also noted that the applicant's identity 'was not adequately, or in some cases not at all, masked in the photographs and footage so published and broadcast. He was recognised by certain members of his family and by his friends, neighbours and colleagues.'[118] Therefore, the ECtHR concluded that the CCTV footage 'was viewed to an extent which far exceeded any exposure to a passer-by or to security observation ... and to a degree surpassing that which the applicant could possibly have foreseen ...'.[119] Therefore the ECtHR considered that 'the disclosure by the Council of the ... (CCTV) ... footage constituted a serious interference with the applicant's right to respect for his private life'.[120] Posting a video on YouTube may be a breach of the subject's privacy in the same way as making the CCTV images available to TV companies was a breach of the applicant's privacy in *Peck v United Kingdom.*

Remedies for privacy breaches

[16.35] A right to privacy will only have value if individuals have access to remedies where it is breached. Irish law provides for both civil and criminal remedies, but the availability of these remedies is limited. At present there would not appear to be any generally available remedy. For example, the Data Protection Acts 1988–2003 provide for extensive remedies,[121] such as rights of access[122] and erasure,[123] but these remedies will only be available where a privacy breach occurs that is a breach of the Acts, controls on the processing of personal data. If the privacy breach is not contrary to the Data Protection Acts, or it does not involve the processing of personal data, then these remedies will not be available.

Criminal remedies

[16.36] The most powerful remedy provided by Irish law for the protection of privacy is probably the offence of harassment, which is set out by the Non-Fatal Offences Against the Person Act 1997. This provides that the offence of harassment will be committed by a person who 'without lawful authority or reasonable excuse, by any means ... harasses another by persistently following, watching, pestering, besetting or communicating with him or her'.[124]

The Acts defines 'harasses' as occurring where a person 'by his or her acts intentionally or recklessly, seriously interferes with the other's peace and privacy ... and ... his or her acts are such that a reasonable person would realise that the acts would seriously interfere with the other's peace and privacy'.[125] Such an offence is punishable by a fine

---

[118] [2003] ECHR 44, para 62, citing *Jersild v Denmark* (23 September 1994), Series A no 298, pp 23–24, § 31.

[119] *Peck v United Kingdom* [2003] ECHR 44, para 62.

[120] [2003] ECHR 44, para 63.

[121] See Kelleher, *Privacy and Data Protection Law in Ireland* (Tottel Publishing, 2006), Pt IV.

[122] Data Protection Acts 1988–2003, s 4.

[123] Data Protection Acts 1988–2003, s 6.

[124] Non-Fatal Offences Against the Person Act 1997, s 10(1).

[125] Non-Fatal Offences Against the Person Act 1997, s 10(2).

and up to seven years' imprisonment.[126] There have been a number of convictions for offences pursuant to this provision. In *DPP v Ronayne*,[127] a 'mechanic who threatened to distribute explicit photographs of his former girlfriend to her family was found guilty of harassment by a jury'. In April 2003 '(a) A Galway city landlord who hid miniature cameras in the ceilings of his tenant's bedroom and bathroom was sentenced to a total of 16 months in prison at Galway District Court ...'.[128] He had pleaded guilty to offences of harassment. He had:

> 'spied on people he shared his house with over a two to three-year period before he was caught by one observant tenant who noticed the hidden cameras and made a complaint to gardaí. In all, 49 women and 14 men, who had stayed in the rental house over the preceding years, were captured on 19 videos and CDs seized by gardaí.'[129]

[16.37] In the English High Court decision of *Tulley v Microsoft*[130] it was held that litigation could not amount to harassment. The plaintiffs had produced and supplied counterfeit Microsoft products. The plaintiffs brought proceedings under the UK's Protection from Harassment Act 1997 alleging that Microsoft:

> 'had subsequently harassed them in a number of ways including by suborning the police into raiding the home of one of the claimants, by conducting oppressive litigation, by suborning witnesses into lying in the course of that litigation, and by telephoning one of the claimants late at night.'

However, these allegations were rejected by Brown J who refused the plaintiffs injunctive relief on the basis that 'Apart from the telephone call, which was an isolated incident, none of the activities came anywhere near falling under the prohibition of the Act'.

Civil remedies

[16.38] Where the state breaches a citizen's right to privacy, then the courts will provide a remedy. This has been clear since 1987 and the decision of the High Court in *Kennedy & Arnold v Ireland*.[131] The state's obligation to respect the privacy of its citizens was re-examined by the High Court two decades later in *Gray v Minister for Justice*.[132] In this case the plaintiffs were a family who had moved from Dublin to Kerry. Unfortunately a nephew of the family joined them there following his release from prison, where he had served a lengthy sentence for violent rape. The nephew became a suspect in a garda investigation into serious sexual offences and local gardaí sought to interview him at the

---

[126] Non-Fatal Offences Against the Person Act 1997, s 10(3).

[127] 'Mechanic guilty of 'mean, nasty and shabby' offence' (2004) The Irish Times, 23 January. He was given a sentence of 12 months' imprisonment and fined €10,000.

[128] He was sentenced to nine months for harassment and seven months on charges of possessing child pornography.

[129] 'Passing sentence, Judge John Garavan said O'Donnell had engaged in voyeuristic and obsessive behaviour': Healy, 'Landlord who spied on his tenants jailed' (2004) The Irish Times, 8 April.

[130] *Tuppen v Microsoft* Times Law Reports, 15 November 2000.

[131] *Kennedy & Arnold v Attorney General* [1987] IR 587.

[132] *Gray v Minister for Justice* [2007] IEHC 52 (17 January 2007, unreported) HC (Quirke J).

family's home. Subsequently, the fact that a convicted rapist had moved from Dublin to Kerry became local and national news. As a result the family left Kerry and went back to Dublin. They lived in a B&B for six months, spending their days in the family car and eating in fast food restaurants. The mother became significantly depressed and contemplated suicide. The family initiated a claim for damages against the state, alleging that information relating to the nephew had been leaked by the gardaí to the media. Quirke J held that 'a member ... of An Garda Síochána negligently disclosed confidential and sensitive information to an organ of the media.'

[16.39] The difficulty with this judgment from a privacy perspective is that whilst Quirke J referred to the plaintiffs' right to privacy, he would appear to have actually awarded damages against the defendant because of the 'negligence' of the gardaí. Specifically Quirke J stated that:

> 'I am satisfied that the unlawful and negligent disclosure by a member ... of An Garda Síochána of the relevant information ... comprised a violation of the ... right enjoyed by ... the plaintiffs to privacy'.

Quirke J appears to have regarded the breach of the plaintiffs' privacy as being a consequence of the defendant's negligence. One interpretation of this judgment might be that Quirke J did not treat breach of the plaintiffs' privacy as being a cause of action. Quirke J appeared to regard the plaintiffs' cause of action as being primarily one of negligence. Instead Quirke J appeared to treat breach of privacy as being a head for the assessment of damages. The difficulty with this interpretation is that Quirke J did not assess damages for breach of privacy; instead he assessed the plaintiffs' damages purely in terms of the distress, upset and inconvenience that was caused to them, just as he might assess damages in any other negligence case. Unlike *Kennedy & Arnold v Attorney General, Gray v Minister for Justice* was not a decision purely about the right to privacy. In *Gray v Minister for Justice* a number of different causes of action were mixed together: negligence, breach of confidence and breach of privacy. It is clear from the judgment that Quirke J gave the most weight to the defendant's negligence, but it is not clear how much weight he attached to the other causes of action.

[16.40] *Gray v Minister for Justice* undoubtedly extends the ruling of the High Court in *Hanahoe v Hussey.*[133] In that case it was held that the leaking to the media of the news that the gardaí were about to search the offices of a highly reputable solicitor was misfeasance of public office by servants of the state. *Gray v Minister for Justice* means that in future plaintiffs may not have to establish misfeasance in similar cases; they may only have to establish negligence. This may make it much easier to establish similar claims in future. *Gray v Minister for Justice* similarly extended the rule of the High Court in *Kennedy and Arnold v Attorney General.* In the latter case the High Court held that the state's deliberate recording of the plaintiffs' telephone breached their privacy. In *Gray v Minister for Justice* held that the plaintiffs' privacy had been breached by the state's negligence. So future claimants who wish seek damages for breach of their privacy by the state may only need to prove negligence, not that the state deliberately breached their privacy.

---

[133] *Hanahoe v Hussey* [1998] 3 IR 69.

[16.41] *Gray v Minister for Justice* ensures that those who sue the state for breach of their privacy may have a more effective remedy. But the state and its officers are subject to very different duties than private citizens. It may not be possible to stretch the judgment of Quirke J in *Gray v Minister for Justice* far enough to create something analogous to the 'general tort of invasion of privacy' that the European Court of Human Rights appears to expect signatories to the convention to provide. In *Wainwright v Home Office*[134] the applicants had been strip-searched whilst visiting a relative in prison. This left one of them feeling 'upset, angry and dirty'[135] and the other suffering from post traumatic stress disorder.[136] The European Court of Human Rights held that the manner in which the strip-searches were undertaken amounted to a breach of the applicants rights under art 8 of the Convention.[137] Unfortunately English law did not provide the applicants with a remedy in respect of this breach. The applicants sued in the English courts for breach of their right to privacy, but were ultimately refused by the House of Lords, which rejected 'the invitation to declare that since at the latest 1950 there has been a previously unknown tort of invasion of privacy'.[138]

[16.42] In response the applicants took proceedings before the European Court of Human Rights.[139] Article 13 of the ECHR provides that 'Everyone whose rights ... are violated shall have an effective remedy before a national authority'.[140] The ECtHR held that this article had also been breached and:

> 'While it is true that the applicants took domestic proceedings seeking damages for the searches and their effects they had on them, they were unsuccessful ... the Court observes that the House of Lords found that negligent action disclosed by the prison officers did not ground any civil liability, in particular as there was no general tort of invasion of privacy. In these circumstances, the Court finds that the applicants did not have available to them a means of obtaining redress for the interference with their rights under Article 8 of the Convention.'[141]

[16.43] This suggests that English law would have to change to provide a remedy for breaches of privacy. *Gray v Minister for Justice* and *Kennedy & Arnold v Ireland* suggest that Irish law does provide a remedy where the privacy of individuals is breached by servants of the state. But the extent to which this remedy will be available where a breach is caused by private citizens must remain unclear until the appropriate action is adjudged by the Superior Courts. An effort to clarify the remedies available was made with the publication of the Privacy Bill 2006. This would have created a tort of violation of privacy[142] and provided that an individual was entitled to 'the privacy ...

---

134 *Wainwright v Home Office* [2003] 3 WLR 1137.
135 *Wainwright v United Kingdom* (26 September 2006) ECtHR, para 17.
136 (26 September 2006) ECtHR, para 19.
137 (26 September 2006) ECtHR, para 49.
138 *Wainwright v Home Office* [2003] 3 WLR 1137 at 1147.
139 *Wainwright v United Kingdom* (26 September 2006) ECtHR.
140 (26 September 2006) ECtHR, para 50.
141 (26 September 2006) ECtHR, para 55.
142 Privacy Bill 2006, s 2.

which is reasonable in all the circumstances having regard to the rights of others and to the requirements of public order, public morality and the common good'.[143]

[16.44] The Bill went on to provide a number of situations which would amount to breach of privacy, such as 'to subject an individual to surveillance'[144] and 'to disclose information, documentation or material obtained by surveillance whether or not such surveillance was carried out by or on behalf of the person disclosing such information'.[145] The Bill set out a number of circumstances to which a court should have regard[146] and a number of defences which would be available.[147] The Bill would have provided for a variety of remedies including prohibitory injunctive relief, damages and orders for delivery up.[148] It would also have provided for a maximum limitation period of two years.[149]

---

[143] Privacy Bill 2006, s 3(1).
[144] Privacy Bill 2006, s 3(2)(a).
[145] Privacy Bill 2006, s 3(2)(b).
[146] Privacy Bill 2006, s 4.
[147] Privacy Bill 2006, s 5.
[148] Privacy Bill 2006, s 8.
[149] Privacy Bill 2006, s 11.

Chapter 17

Surveillance

Introduction

[17.01] Surveillance has been a part of Irish life for centuries; the *Valley of the Squinting Windows*[1] has long been a reality for many Irish people:

> 'John Brennan ... was an object of curiosity and conjecture. The windows would squint at him as he went past through power of the leering faces behind; men would run to the hedges and gaze after him as he went far down the road.'[2]

Surveillance technologies can provide the tools that may allow everyone, everywhere, to live as John Brennan, constantly watched without regard to his consent, wishes or needs:

> 'One hundred years ago everyone could have personal privacy. You and a friend could walk into an empty field look around to see that no one else was nearby, and have a level of privacy that has forever been lost ... Technology has demolished that world view. Powerful directional microphones can pick up conversations hundreds of yards away ... The ability to trail someone remotely has existed for a while ... The technology to automatically search ... for suspicious behavior in satellite images, or for faces on a 'wanted list' of criminals in on-street cameras isn't commonplace yet, but it's just a matter of time.'[3]

Offline surveillance

[17.02] When discussing surveillance technologies, it is important to keep in mind that just because a technology invades the privacy of individuals, does not mean that the technology is effective at combating crime, terrorism or anything else. To take the example of CCTV, studies have shown that CCTV cameras that are specifically sited at certain locations can be highly effective at combating crime. A CCTV camera that is sited with a clear view of the cash register in a shop may provide valuable evidence where a robbery occurs. The importance of such footage was analysed by Hardiman J in *Braddish v DPP*[4]: 'fundamentally, this is a video tape which purports actually to show the robbery in progress. It is not acceptable, in my view, to excuse the absence of so vital and direct a piece of evidence simply by saying that the prosecution are not relying on it, but prefer to rely on an alleged confession. First, the confession is hotly disputed. Secondly, a confession should if possible be corroborated and relatively recent history both here and in the neighbouring jurisdiction has unfortunate examples of the risks of

---

[1] MacNamara, *The Valley of the Squinting Windows* (Anvil Books Ltd, 1996).
[2] MacNamara, *The Valley of the Squinting Windows* (Anvil Books Ltd, 1996) p 30.
[3] Schneier, *Secrets and Lies* (Wiley Computer Publishing, 2000), pp 20–21.
[4] *Braddish v DPP* [2001] 3 IR 127.

excessive reliance on confession evidence. Thirdly, the video tape has a clear potential to exculpate as well as to inculpate.'[5]

[17.03] Studies have shown that placing a CCTV[6] camera at the exit to a car park can be an extremely effective method of reducing the number of cars stolen from that car park.[7] On occasion, CCTV evidence can prove extremely useful at solving an individual crime.

> 'Barbara Riouall's neck was slashed in the knife attack which occurred just two yards away from the door to her Dublin apartment ... Riouall's male attacker fled ... But he could not escape the ever-present eyes of the hundreds of privately-operated closed circuit television (CCTV) cameras that pan along the streets ... CCTV footage taken in the minutes after the attacker fled the crime scene was central to the garda investigation. Obtaining footage from both private premises and Dublin city council, gardaí quickly amassed over 100 hours worth of evidence. Within a short space of time, garda detectives pinpointed the fleeing assailant. Critically, a number of high-resolution cameras clearly recorded a small logo on the back of his jacket. It was the logo of construction company CLG. A company official matched the print-out of the image with employee Aleksejus Belousovas.'[8]

[17.04] But CCTV appears to be very ineffective at reducing crime on a more general basis. The UK contains an extraordinary number of CCTV systems,[9] even though studies undertaken by the UK Home Office have found that these systems are surprisingly ineffective at reducing crime. This research reviewed the effects of CCTV installation on 13 areas in the UK. Crime rates fell in 6 areas, but rose in 7,[10] and the research concluded that 'CCTV ... produced no overall effect on ... crime.'[11] This

---

5   [2001] 3 IR 127 at 133.

6   For a discussion of the law applying to CCTV systems, see Kelleher, *Privacy and Data Protection Law in Ireland* (Tottel Publishing, 2006), paras 17.70–17.109.

7   Reductions in car crime of up to 75 per cent 'occurred in car parks, which were closed environments with a limited number of entrances and exits, and where CCTV could be trained on these ... Gill, Spriggs, 'Assessing the impact of CCTV' (2005) Home Office Research Study 292, Home Office Research, Development and Statistics Directorate, February, p 59. 'studies ... show that CCTV can be most effective in reducing crime in car parks'; Welsh and Farrington, 'Crime prevention effects of closed circuit television: a systematic review' (2002) Home Office Research Study 252, Home Office Research, Development and Statistics Directorate, August, p 45.

8   Burke, 'HIGH TECH: the invisible witness' (2007) Sunday Business Post' 22 July.

9   'There are four million closed-circuit television cameras in the UK – one for every 14 people. If you live in London you are likely to be on camera 300 times a day. And the police are about to start using a new system that will automatically link an estimated 3,000 CCTV cameras across the country with car registration records and other data'; Duguid, 'Crime Watch' (2006) Financial Times, 28 January.

10 Gill, Spriggs, 'Assessing the impact of CCTV' (2005) Home Office Research Study 292, Home Office Research, Development and Statistics Directorate, February, pvi.

11 'the CCTV schemes that have been assessed had little overall effect on crime levels. Even where changes have been noted ... very few are larger than could be due to chance alone and all could in fact represent either chance variation or confounding factors. Where crime levels went up it is not reasonable to conclude that CCTV had a negative impact'; Gill, Spriggs, pp 33 and 43.

research offers a clue as to why CCTV is so surprisingly ineffective; it only affected premeditated crimes, not 'more spontaneous offences, such as violence against the person and public order offences.'[12] The research came to the conclusion that: 'CCTV is an ineffective tool if the aim is to reduce overall crime rates and make people feel safer[13] ... (and) ...produced few cost-benefits.'[14]

[17.05] Intensive surveillance of small groups of individuals or confined locations can be an effective method of reducing crime in a specific area. The courts consider that the gardaí should undertake surveillance of this type. In Surveillance is undertaken by the gardaí on a routine basis. For example, in *The People (DPP) v Byrne*[15] the Court of Criminal Appeal described a 'very elaborate professionally devised surveillance operation' undertaken by An Garda Síochána as being 'a perfectly proper operation set up on foot of reasonable information and all this was demonstrated by the result.'[16]

[17.06] Similarly, in *The People (DPP) v Bambrick*,[17] Carney J noted that 'the proper methods of preventing crime are the long-established combination of police surveillance, speedy trial and deterrent sentences.'[18] In *Kane v Governor of Mountjoy Prison*[19] McCarthy J expressed the view that 'the gardaí ... may lawfully "stake-out" premises which they believe will be burgled, or ... may lawfully and overtly or otherwise follow a suspect with a view to investigating or detecting crime.'[20]

[17.07] These judicial endorsements of Garda surveillance must be set against the concerns expressed by Finlay CJ in *Kane v Governor of Mountjoy Prison* that:

'Such surveillance is capable of gravely affecting the peace of mind and public reputation of any individual and the courts could not, in my view, accept any general application of such a procedure by the police, but should require where it is put into operation and challenged, a specific adequate justification for it.'[21]

[17.08] The ECtHR expressed concerns about the dangers of cover surveillance in *Klass v Germany*[22]:

'Powers of secret surveillance of citizens, characterising as they do the police state, are tolerable under the Convention only in so far as strictly necessary for safeguarding the democratic institutions[23] ...

the Court being aware of the danger such a (telecoms interception) law poses of undermining or even destroying democracy on the ground of defending it, affirms that the

---

12 Gill, Spriggs, p 59.
13 Gill, Spriggs, p 61.
14 Gill, Spriggs, p 114.
15 *The People (DPP) v Byrne* [2003] 4 IR 423.
16 [2003] 4 IR 423 at 427.
17 *The People (DPP) v Bambrick* [1996] 1 IR 265.
18 [1996] 1 IR 265 at 273.
19 *Kane v Governor of Mountjoy Prison* [1988] IR 757.
20 [1988] IR 757 at 770.
21 [1988] IR 757 at 769.
22 *Klass v Germany* (1979–80) 2 EHRR 214.
23 (1979–80) 2 EHRR 214, para 42.

Contracting States may not, in the name of the struggle against espionage and terrorism, adopt whatever measures they deem appropriate.... The Court must be satisfied that, whatever system of surveillance is adopted, there exist adequate and effective guarantees against abuse. This assessment has only a relative character: it depends on all the circumstances of the case, such as the nature, scope and duration of the possible measures, the grounds required for ordering such measures, the authorities competent to permit, carry out and supervise such measures, and the kind of remedy provided by the national law.'[24]

But in spite of these concerns, the court went on to find that the surveillance undertaken in *Klass v Germany* did not breach art 8 of the European Convention on Human Rights. The court found that the surveillance was justified on the basis of national security:

'The first (justification) consists of the technical advances made in the means of espionage and, correspondingly, of surveillance; the second is the development of terrorism in Europe in recent years. Democratic societies nowadays find themselves threatened by highly sophisticated forms of espionage and by terrorism, with the result that the State must be able, in order effectively to counter such threats, to undertake the secret surveillance of subversive elements operating within its jurisdiction.'[25]

[17.09] Even where it is legal, there are a number of practical difficulties with relying upon surveillance as a crime-prevention or detection tool. Firstly, even intensive surveillance can be extraordinarily ineffective.[26] Secondly, surveillance, particularly electronic surveillance, can generate huge amounts of useless data. The processing of such data may swamp investigators, dispatching them in the pointless pursuit of false leads.[27] Thirdly, the targets of the surveillance, be they Dublin criminal gangs,[28] car

---

[24] (1979–80) 2 EHRR 214, paras 49–50.

[25] (1979–80) 2 EHRR 214, para 48.

[26] The academic and author Timothy Garton-Ash was a student in the DDR in the late 1970s/early 1980s. He was subject to intensive surveillance by the East German secret police, the Stasi. The Stasi observed his movements and ensured that many of his East German acquaintances were actually Stasi informers. In spite of all this, the Stasi never learned that he was writing a book about the DDR until the day Der Spiegel published it. Garton-Ash, *The File* (Vintage Books, 1997), p 159.

[27] Following 9/11, the US authorities intercepted vast quantities of useless electronic data in a process described as 'a tragic waste of the FBI's resources in dangerous times'; 'Spying on Ordinary Americans' (2006) New York Times, 18 January. 'FBI agents repeatedly complained to the spy agency (the USA's National Security Agency or NSA) that the unfiltered information was swamping investigators ... the torrent of tips led (the FBI) to few potential terrorists (the FBI) did not know of from other sources and diverted agents for counterterrorism work they viewed as more productive'. Bergman, Lichtblau, Shane and Vatta, 'Spy agency data after Sept 11 led FBI to dead ends' (2006) New York Times, 17 January

[28] 'sophistication is evident in gang members' ease with technology. Apart from their numerous, disposable mobile phones, coded conversations on Internet chat rooms are also a favoured method of communication', Sheridan 'Not in our neighbourhood?' (2005) The Irish Times, 19 November.

thieves,[29] illegal Internet music downloaders[30] or the head of Hamas,[31] may change their behaviour once they realise that they are being watched. This 'displacement'[32] has been called the 'Achilles' Heal'[33] of any surveillance system. Finally, there is the danger that the proliferation of surveillance systems may mean that juries will come to expect surveillance evidence of crimes in progress and to refuse to convict where such evidence is not available. Some have observed the emergence of the 'CSI effect'[34] in the USA.[35] Jurors 'know' that modern technology exists (at least on TV) that can provide definitive evidence of guilt or innocence. They thus have a 'higher expectation'[36] of the quality of evidence put before them and may refuse to convict on the basis of circumstantial evidence. As of yet, Irish juries have proven quite willing to convict on the basis of evidence derived from electronic surveillance. In *DPP v O'Reilly* the successful prosecution was based upon a variety of circumstantial evidence, including CCTV footage[37] and the location-tracking of mobile phones.[38] It remains to be seen if they will become less willing to convict in the absence of such material.

---

[29] Tilley, 'Understanding Car Parks, Crime and CCTV: Evaluation Lessons from Safer Cities' (Crime Prevention Unit series paper 42) Home Office.

[30] 'Even if the record industry succeeds in scaring downloaders away from the mainstream filesharing networks, they can still get their hands on free music elsewhere ... fear of lawsuits and a flood of low-quality junk files has led many downloaders to turn to so-called 'darknets' – private, invitation-only networks that allow users to trade files anonymously'. Allison, 'The battle for Grokster leaves a war to be won' (2005) Financial Times, 20 December.

[31] 'Abdul-Aziz Rantissi, the Hamas leader ... sits in a Gaza office ... his ... bodyguard ... handing him a big military two-way radio receiver. I think ... that this is to protect the Hamas leader. Mobile phones are traceable to within a few feet. Israel ... (is a) ... master .. of analogue and digital technology ... '. Fisk, *The Great War for Civilization* (Fourth Estate, 2005), p 621.

[32] 'Displacement is often defined as the unintended increase in targeted crimes in other locations following from the introduction of a crime reduction scheme', Welsh and Farrington, 'Crime prevention effects of closed circuit television: a systematic review', Home Office Research Study 252, Home Office Research, Development and Statistics Directorate, August 2002, p 7.

[33] 'Displacement has long been the Achilles' heel of situational measures and CCTV is no exception'. Gill, Spriggs, p 6.

[34] 'Prosecutors claim that the show makes juries less inclined to convict because they have inflated expectations for the comprehensiveness, sophistication and clarity of forensic evidence', Cole and Diso, 'Law and the Lab' (2005) The Wall Street Journal, 13 May.

[35] See Cather, 'The CSI effect: fake TV and its impact on jurors in criminal cases' (2004) The Prosecutor Vol 38 (2), March–April; and Thomas, 'The CSI effect and its real-life impact on justice' (2005) The Prosecutor, Vol 39 (5), September–October. Some doubt its existence: Cole and Diso, 'Law and the Lab' (2005) The Wall Street Journal, 13 May. On the other hand, the effect has also been observed in Canada; see Robertson, 'Courts Feeling CSI effect' (2006) Toronto Sun, 4 January. Wainwright, 'Forensic fans have high hopes for DNA' (2007) Sydney Morning Herald (Australia), 2 June.

[36] The 'CSI effect' sprung into prominence when a Californian jury failed to convict actor Robert Blake for the murder of his wife as it was '..very dismissive of circumstantial evidence ... (and) ... expected so much more ... in terms of evidence' See Blankstein and Buccione, '"CSI" Effect or Just Flimsy Evidence? The Jury Is Out' (2005) Los Angeles Times, 18 March.

Remote sensing and covert listening devices

[17.10] Unlike the interception of telephone calls, there is no Irish enactment or guidelines controlling the remote surveillance of individuals. In *Govell v United Kingdom*:[39]

> 'the police drilled a hole into (the applicant's) living room wall from the adjoining house that would have enabled someone to listen from next door or to attach a listening device. The police also installed camera equipment in the next door property.'[40]

[17.11] The UK government did not dispute that this was an interference with the applicant's rights under art 8(1) of the ECHR, but claimed that the surveillance was 'in accordance with the law'. The European Commission rejected this claim, finding that in the UK 'there is no existing statutory system to regulate the use of covert listening devices'. The existing Home Office guidelines were neither legally binding nor were they publicly accessible.'[41] Therefore, the commission concluded that 'that the interference in the present case cannot be considered to be 'in accordance with the law.'[42] This judgment was then followed by the ECtHR decision of *Khan v United Kingdom*[43] in which a listening device had been installed in the applicant's home. The ECtHR concluded that there had been a breach of art 8(1), which could not be justified within the terms of art 8(2).[44] In contrast to the UK, Irish law gives citizens a clear right to sue gardaí in respect of unjustified interference in the privacy of individuals.[45] This means that a covert surveillance operation could not be challenged on the basis that the state did not provide citizens with an effective remedy as is required by the Convention. But that does not mean that covert surveillance will necessarily be 'in accordance with the law.'

The ability of the gardaí to enter onto a premises and engage in surveillance was reviewed by the Supreme Court in *DPP v McMahon*.[46] The defendants were accused of offences contrary to the Gaming and Lotteries Act 1956. Evidence was given in court that plain clothes gardaí had 'entered each of the ... premises ... for the specific purpose of ascertaining whether offences ... were being committed within them, and made certain observations while present in the premises, leading to further evidence which *prima facie* established the commission of the offences'. The plain clothes gardaí in question did not identify themselves to the occupiers of the premises in question or

---

[37] Sheridan, 'Expert's view on grainy CCTV blobs taxes court' (2007) The Irish Times, 18 July.

[38] 'Calls analysis tallies with colleague's account' (2007) The Irish Times, 11 July.

[39] *Govell v United Kingdom*, Report of European Commission on Human Rights, 14 January 1998.

[40] *Govell v United Kingdom*, para 17

[41] *Govell v United Kingdom*, para 62.

[42] *Govell v United Kingdom*, para 63.

[43] *Khan v United Kingdom* (12 May 2000) ECtHR. See the similar judgments of the ECtHR in *PG and JH v United Kingdom* (25 September 2001) and *Hewitson v United Kingdom* (27 May 2003).

[44] *Khan v United Kingdom* (12 May 2000) ECtHR, para 27.

[45] See *Kennedy & Arnold v Attorney General* [1987] IR 587; *Gray v Minister for Justice* [2007] IEHC 52, (17 January 2007, unreported) HC (Quirke J).

[46] *DPP v McMahon* [1986] IR 393.

procure a search warrant prior to commencing their surveillance.[47] Investigations of breaches of the Gaming and Lotteries Act 1956 were governed by a variety of statutes dating back to the 19th century. Having reviewed these, Finlay CJ was satisfied that:

> 'the Garda Síochána on entering each of the licensed premises involved in this case did not have any statutory authority so to do and were outside, by reason of their intention in so doing, the implied invitation of the owner of the licensed premises. They were, therefore, in my view, in law trespassers, and the evidence which they obtained by inspecting the use of gaming machines within these premises was evidence obtained by unlawful means, though not, of course, by the commission of any offence against the criminal law.'[48]

[17.12] If a similar case were to arise today, the defendants might claim to have an action for damages in respect of an alleged breach of their privacy. It is highly unlikely that such an action would succeed. Since the gardaí had observed activity in the public areas of the premises in question, the expectation of privacy there would have been extremely low, if it existed at all. As Finlay CJ stated in *DPP v MacMahon*:

> 'The act of entering, as a trespasser, the public portion of a licensed premises which is open for trade does not, of course, constitute any invasion or infringement of any constitutional right of the owner of those premises.'[49]

Camera phones

[17.13] Attaching a digital camera to a mobile phone greatly enhances the phone's capabilities. Users may take digital photographs and send them to wherever they want. Concerns about the use of camera phones are not limited to simple breach of privacy issues, for example their use may amount to a contempt of court, for example.[50] This potential abuse of privacy has resulted in a variety of responses. In Ireland, camera phones have been banned by Gaeltacht summer schools[51] and some swimming pools.[52] The USA has gone further, with its Video Voyeurism Prevention Act of 2004, which provides that:

> 'Whoever ... has the intent to capture[53] an image of a private area of an individual[54] without their consent, and knowingly does so under circumstances in which the individual has a

---

[47] [1986] IR 393 at 395. See also *The Minister for Justice v Wang Zhu Jie* [1993] 1 IR 426.

[48] [1986] IR 393 at 398.

[49] [1986] IR 393 at 398.

[50] In November 2004, Shaun Nash was given a six-month custodial sentence by an English Crown Court for using his camera phone to take pictures of a criminal trial, including pictures of the jury. Mr Nash was in court for the trial of a friend and claimed the images were taken as innocent souvenirs. The court did not agree, the trial was abandoned and Mr Nash was convicted of contempt and sentenced. Sherriff, 'Youth jailed for court camera phone pics' 29 November 2004, http://www.theregister.co.uk.

[51] Downes, 'Mobile crackdown in summer schools' (2004) The Irish Times, 2 July.

[52] 'Photo mobile phones have been banned at Nenagh swimming pool and leisure centre in Co Tipperary after a 12-year old girl was caught photographing an undressed woman in a changing room', McCormack, 'Pool bans phones after woman pictured' (2004) The Irish Times, 10 February.

[53] Where capture means 'with respect to an image ... to videotape, photograph, film, record by any means, or broadcast,' 18 USC 1801 (b)(1) and 'broadcast' means to electronically transmit a visual image with the intent that it be viewed by a person or persons' 18 USC 1801(b)(2).

reasonable expectation of privacy, shall be fined ... or imprisoned not more than one year, or both'.

The Act defines the phrase 'under circumstances in which that individual has a reasonable expectation of privacy' as meaning 'circumstances in which a reasonable person would believe that he or she could disrobe in privacy, without being concerned that an image of a private area of the individual was being captured'. This might cover a situation where a person is surreptitiously photographed or filmed whilst changing in their bedroom. The phrase also covers 'circumstances in which a reasonable person would believe that a private area of the individual would not be visible to the public, regardless of whether that person is in a public or private place'.

[17.14] Where a person's privacy is breached by such photography or filming, then a variety of remedies will be available to them. If the breach is a serious one, they might complain to the gardaí, which could result in a prosecution for harassment contrary to s 10 of the Non Fatal Offences against the Person Act 1997. Alternatively, the victim might sue for damages. Such an action was brought before the Australian courts in *Giller v Procopets*,[55] in which the plaintiff claimed 'damages for distress and hurt caused by the defendant showing and threatening to distribute a video of the parties indulging in sexual activities.'[56] The facts of the case were that:

> 'on number of occasions in November 1996 the parties engaged in sexual relations. The defendant secretly filmed their activities. On the sixth occasion the plaintiff became aware of the filming and agreed to it[57] ... the parties fell out[58] ... The defendant threatened the plaintiff that he would show the video to her friends, acquaintances and her employer ... the defendant went to the plaintiff's parents' premises and ... produced a video of the parties engaging in sexual relations ... the defendant attended the residence of ... the mother of a friend of the plaintiff ... (and) produced a video cassette and asked her to view it. When she informed him they had no VCR the defendant returned with a VCR and connected it to the TV and commenced to play the video cassette.'[59]

The Australian court concluded that, although:

> 'the plaintiff has established the elements of the tort of intentionally inflicting mental harm', it also found that ... the harm was annoyance and distress and is not recoverable. It follows that the plaintiff's claim must fail.'[60]

---

54 Where 'the term "a private area of the individual" means the naked or undergarment clad genitals, pubic area, buttocks, or female breast of that individual', 18 USC 1801 (b)(3) and 'the term "female breast" means any portion of the female breast below the top of the areola' 18 USC 1801(b)(4).

55 *Giller v Procopets* [2004] VSC 113.

56 [2004] VSC 113, para 1.

57 [2004] VSC 113, para 268.

58 [2004] VSC 113, para 269.

59 [2004] VSC 113, para 270

60 [2004] VSC 113, para 284.

[17.15] The facts of *Murray v Falcon Holidays*[61] were rather different, but the conclusion was the same. The plaintiff was a schoolgirl whose photograph was taken whilst she was on holiday. The photograph was subsequently used in the defendant's holiday brochure in which the plaintiff 'was pictured lying on an air-bed splashing about in a swimming pool in Greece.'[62] Her claim for damages was dismissed by the Circuit Court. Similarly, the Superior Courts have been quite willing to permit the surveillance of parties in legal actions.[63] Whether this will continue to be the case may be questioned. The ECtHR made it clear in *Von Hannover v Germany* that photographing a person could breach their privacy. The ECtHR suggested that increased vigilance should apply to 'the systematic taking of specific photos and their dissemination to a broad section of the public.'[64] Given that Irish courts must 'take due account of the principles laid down'[65] by judgments of the ECtHR, it may be that this view will have to be reassessed.

Privacy in a photograph

[17.16] The CRRA 2000 provides that a person who, for private and domestic purposes only, commissions the taking of a photograph or the making of a film has, where copyright subsists in the resulting work, the right not to have the work or copies of the work made available to the public. [66] This right will be infringed by the act of making available to the public, or authorising the making available to the public, of a photograph or film without the authority of the person who commissions it.[67] The purpose of this provision would appear to be to deal with the common situation that where photographs, such as wedding photographs, are commissioned from a professional photographer, copyright in the photographs is retained by the photographer. This provision prevents the photographer from selling the photographs to 'anyone whatsoever'. So, where a 'celebrity' organises their own Christmas photographs, the photographer cannot subsequently sell copies of those photos, even if the photographer retains the copyright in them. The English courts have examined this issue, but only in the context of photographs that were commissioned for commercial purposes. In *Creation Records v News Group Newspapers*,[68] the plaintiffs had organised the taking of a photograph for an album that was released by the band known as Oasis. This involved

---

[61] *Murray v Falcon Holidays* (unreported) CC, Linnane J; 'Student sues holiday firm for using photo of her in brochure' (2004) Irish Times, 8 April and 'Student denied damages for photograph' (2005) Irish Times, 7 May.

[62] 'Student denied damages for photograph' (2005) Irish Times, 7 May.

[63] See *Nason v Cork Corporation* (12 April 1991, unreported) (Keane J); *Shelly Morris v Dublin Bus* [2003] 1 IR 232; and *Conor O'Connor v Dublin Bus* [2003] 4 IR 459.

[64] *Von Hannover v Germany* (24 June 2004) ECtHR, para 70.

[65] European Convention on Human Rights Act 2003, s 4.

[66] CRRA 2000, s 114(1). This right will not be infringed by any act which would not infringe the copyright in the work under s 52 of the CRRA 2000 (acts done for the purposes of instruction or examination), s 71 (parliamentary and judicial proceedings), s 72 (statutory inquiries), s 76 (acts done under statutory authority) or s 88 (acts permitted in relation to anonymous or pseudonymous works). CRRA 2000, s 114(2).

[67] CRRA 2000, s 114(3).

[68] *Creation Records v News Group* Newspapers [1997] EMLR 444.

organising the placing of a Rolls Royce in swimming pool at an English hotel. A freelance photographer commissioned by *The Sun* newspaper booked himself into the hotel and took photographs from a hotel window. The defendant then published the photograph. The plaintiff argued that, as a member of the band had organised the setting of the scene that was then photographed by the plaintiff 's photographer, that band member owned the copyright in photographs of that scene taken by the defendant's photographer. Lloyd J rejected this argument, but did hold that there was at least an arguable case that the photographs had been taken in breach of confidence. In *Douglas and Zeta-Jones v Hello!*,[69] the plaintiffs 'were and are very well-known film stars'[70] They had sold the rights to photograph their wedding to OK! magazine. A contract between the parties stipulated that the plaintiffs retained joint ownership of any photographs taken and placed strict controls upon the distribution of such photographs. The plaintiffs also undertook to provide tight security to ensure that no unauthorised photographs were taken. However, 'a paparazzo ... had infiltrated the reception, and surreptitiously taken photographs, including some of the bride and groom.'[71] These photographs were then sold to and published by Hello! magazine. The plaintiffs sued for *inter alia* breach of privacy and confidence. The House of Lords recognised that the plaintiffs 'retained a residual right of privacy, or confidentiality, in those details of their wedding which were not portrayed by those of the official photographs which they released.'[72]

Online surveillance

[17.17] As the lives of Irish people are increasingly undertaken online, surveillance of their online activities will increasingly threaten their privacy. Surveillance can be undertaken in a variety of different ways. Some forms of surveillance will simply focus upon the analysis of the traffic data that is generated by electronic communications networks. More invasive forms of surveillance will focus upon the content of electronic communications. When discussing electronic surveillance, it is important to realise that the Irish law on electronic surveillance and the attitude of the Irish state to that surveillance is utterly different from that of the UK or USA. It is not just that Ireland lacks large, well-funded agencies, such as the USA's National Security Agency (NSA) or the UK's GCHQ in Cheltenham, to undertake such surveillance. Even if Ireland had such an agency, it would lack the legal powers to do very much at all. Essentially the surveillance of electronic communications networks in Ireland appears to be limited to two specific technologies:

- the retention of traffic data; and
- The interception of communications data.

---

[69] *Douglas and Zeta-Jones v Hello!* [2005] EWCA Civ 595.

[70] [2005] EWCA Civ 595, para 3.

[71] [2005] EWCA Civ 595, para 11.

[72] [2005] EWCA Civ 595, para 136.

A key difficulty with such surveillance in Ireland is that not all operators will have the technology to enable the surveillance to occur. The larger operators will, but there is no obligation upon smaller operators to install the necessary equipment.

Surveillance of traffic data

[17.18] A vast amount of traffic data is generated by Irish communication systems. The use of this traffic data has been significant in a number of criminal trials. The use of mobile phone data to secure the conviction of criminals first became prominent, in Ireland at least, in *DPP v Colm Murphy* where it was alleged that the accused had been involved in the bombing of Omagh on 15 August 1998. The court was told of 11 calls made on Mr Murphy's mobile phone:

> 'Six of the calls were routed through mobile phone masts on the Vodafone network in Co Tyrone, including one through a mast sited at the Omagh College of Further Education, Bridge Street, Omagh.'[73]

Although the location data given to the court does not appear to have been particularly detailed or precise, it was sufficient to convict Mr Murphy of his role in the bombing. Murphy appealed successfully on grounds related to the legality of his arrest and the regard taken by the Special Criminal Court of his previous convictions. He also appealed on the ground that 'the Special Criminal Court wrongly admitted telephone records as evidence'. The Court of Criminal Appeal did not agree with him, holding that 'The fact that a recording is produced mechanically without human intervention makes no difference to its general admissibility in evidence.' Mobile phone location data was also used to convict the accused a husband of murdering his wife in *DPP v O'Reilly*. A variety of evidence of mobile phone calls and locations was presented at trial, including that 'on the day his wife was murdered, there were 18 communications between … (the) … accused … and the woman with whom he was having an affair'.[74]

[17.19] Given the value of location data, the state needs to ensure that it is retained. At present the legal basis for data retention is set out by Part VII of the Criminal Justice (Terrorist Offences) Act 2005.[75] This legislation applies to 'data[76] relating to

---

73 The evidence of mobile phone location was not particularly detailed: 'the first call was made at 12:41 pm and was routed through a mast sited in Castleblayney, Co Monaghan. The next nine went through masts at Emyvale, Co Monaghan; Aughnacloy, Co Tyrone; Bridge Street, Omagh; Pigeon Top, Mount Pollnaghunt, Co Tyrone; Ballygawley, Co Tyrone; Cavan Garvan, Stranooden, Co Monaghan; and Castleblayney, Co Monaghan. The final call, at 17:23, was routed through the mobile mast at Clarmont Carns, north of Dundalk', 'Phone may have been used in Omagh, Dundalk' (2001) The Irish Times, 9 November. Murphy did not actually plant the bomb; rather he lent phones to the bombers. The data of the phone calls made to and from the phones was thought to disclose the route taken by the bombers. 'Conviction built on painstaking trace of four mobile phones' (2002) The Irish Times, 23 January.

74 '18 "contacts" between O'Reilly and Pelley' (2007) The Irish Times, 11 July.

75 The introduction of this legislation followed a controversy about the absence of a proper legal base. Initially the Data Protection Commissioner concluded that the retention of such data was illegal, as it was pursuant to a Direction issued under s 110 of the Postal and Telecommunications Services Act 1983, (contd/)

communications transmitted by means of a fixed line or mobile telephone, but it does not apply to the content of such communications.'[77] In broad terms Part VII provides for the retention of such communications data for a three year period, access to that data and safeguards to protect the privacy of persons. It provides that:

> 'the Garda Commissioner may request a service provider[78] to retain, for a period of 3 years, traffic data or location data or both for the purposes of— ... the prevention, detection, investigation or prosecution of crime (including but not limited to terrorist offences), or ... the safeguarding of the security of the State.'[79]

The effect of making such a request is that:

> 'Notwithstanding any other enactment or instrument, a service provider shall retain, for the purposes and the period specified ... the data specified in a data retention request made to the provider.'[80]

[17.20] However, the request cannot 'be taken as requiring a service provider to retain aggregated[81] data or data that have been made anonymous.'[82] This 'data retention request' must be made in writing.[83] Traffic data and location data that are in the possession of a service provider on the passing of the Act and which were retained by the service provider for the purposes specified above will be deemed to have been the subject of a data retention request, but only if the three-year retention period for the data

---

[75] (contd/) see DPC *Annual Report 2002*, Appendix 1, 'Statement by the Data Protection Commissioner at the Forum on the Retention of Communications Traffic Data' on 24 February 2003, p 40. At one stage the DPC threatened to seek judicial review of the Minister for Justice, see Lillington, 'Court threat for State over data privacy' (2003) The Irish Times, 26 May. However, these proceedings were then postponed: DPC, *Annual Report 2003,* p 4. In January 2005 the DPC felt that he had 'no option but to issue enforcement notices in early January 2005 to three telecommunications companies requiring them with effect from 1 May 2005 to hold such data for national security purposes for a maximum period of twelve months'. However, after the publication of the amendments that now form Part VII these enforcement notices were cancelled on 7 February 2005: DPC *Annual Report 2004*, p 4. For journalistic criticism of Part VII see Lillington, 'Data retention slips into Law' (2005) The Irish Times, 19 March and Lillington, 'McDowell's sneaky data law heralds a surveillance State' (2005) The Irish Times, 25 March.

[76] 'Data' is defined as 'communications data', Criminal Justice (Terrorist Offences) Act 2005, s 61(1). Words and expressions used but not defined in Part VII of the Criminal Justice (Terrorist Offences) Act 2005 but defined in Directive 2002/58 have the same meaning in Part VII as they have in Directive 2002/58.

[77] Criminal Justice (Terrorist Offences) Act 2005, s 62.

[78] 'Service provider' is defined as 'a person who is engaged in the provision of a publicly available electronic communications service by means of fixed line or mobile telephones', Criminal Justice (Terrorist Offences) Act 2005, s 61(1).

[79] Justice (Terrorist Offences) Act 2005, s 63(1).

[80] Criminal Justice (Terrorist Offences) Act 2005, s 63(5).

[81] Defined as meaning 'data that cannot be related to individual subscribers or users',Criminal Justice (Terrorist Offences) Act 2005, s 61(1).

[82] Criminal Justice (Terrorist Offences) Act 2005, s 63(6).

[83] Criminal Justice (Terrorist Offences) Act 2005, s 63(2).

has not elapsed before the passing of the Act.[84] The three-year retention period begins on the date upon which the data in question was first processed,[85] regardless of whether that date is before or after the date upon which the Act was passed.[86] Part VII provides that retained data may be accessed at the behest of senior members of the gardaí and the Defence Forces. It provides that:

> 'If a member of the Garda Síochána not below the rank of chief superintendent is satisfied that access to any data retained by a service provider ... is required for the purposes for which the data were retained, that member may request the service provider to disclose the data to the member.'[87],

[17.21] Such a disclosure request must be made in writing. However, 'in cases of exceptional urgency the request may be made orally (whether by telephone or otherwise)' by a member of the gardaí or Permanent Defence Forces of the requisite rank.[88] Where a request is made orally, it must be confirmed in writing within 24 hours.[89] Other than in accordance with a disclosure request, retained data may only be accessed by the service provider save in the following circumstances:

(a)   'at the request and with the consent of the person to whom the data relate',

(b)   for the purpose of complying with a disclosure request ...,

(c)   in accordance with a court order',

(d)   for the purpose of civil proceedings in any court',

(e)   as may be authorised by the Data Protection Commissioner'.[90]

[17.22] However, the section concludes with the statement that:

> 'Where all or part of the period specified in a data retention request coincides with the period during which any of the data specified in the request may, in accordance with law, be processed for purposes other than those specified in the request, this section does not prevent that data from being processed for those other purposes.'[91]

A number of safeguards are provided by Part VII of the Criminal Justice (Terrorist Offences) Act 2005. These are primarily taken from the Interception of Postal Packets and Telecommunications Messages (Regulation) Act 1993.[92]

---

[84] Criminal Justice (Terrorist Offences) Act 2005, s 63(3).

[85] 'Processing' is stated to have '... the same meaning as in the Data Protection Acts 1988 and 2003'Criminal Justice (Terrorist Offences) Act 2005, s 61(1).

[86] Criminal Justice (Terrorist Offences) Act 2005, s 63(4).

[87] Criminal Justice (Terrorist Offences) Act 2005, s 64(1). Similarly, s 64(2) provides: 'If an officer of the Permanent Defence Force not below the rank of colonel is satisfied that access to any data retained by a service provider ... is required for the purpose of safeguarding the security of the State, that officer may request the service provider to disclose the data to the officer'.

[88] Criminal Justice (Terrorist Offences) Act 2005, s 64(4).

[89] Criminal Justice (Terrorist Offences) Act 2005, s 64(5).

[90] Criminal Justice (Terrorist Offences) Act 2005, s 64(1).

[91] Criminal Justice (Terrorist Offences) Act 2005, s 64(7).

[92] These safeguards are reviewed in Kelleher, *Privacy and Data Protection Law in Ireland* (Tottel Publishing, 2006), paras 9.63–9.64.

European developments

[17.23] At a European level the retention data produced by electronic communications networks is regulated by Directive 2006/24/EC of the European Parliament and of the Council of 15 March 2006 on the retention of data generated or processed in connection with the provision of publicly available electronic communications services or of public communications networks and amending Directive 2002/58/EC.[93] This Directive provides that such data must be: 'retained for periods of not less than six months and not more than two years from the date of the communication'.[94]

Tracking the location of mobile phones and other devices

[17.24] Virtually every Irish person now has a mobile phone and so carries around their own personal electronic tagging and tracking device. Mobile phone networks must be able to identify the location of each phone on the system, so that the network can forward calls to and from the phones. A mobile phone network will be made up of a series of cells; these cells are the areas of coverage surrounding each mobile phone mast. If a switched-on mobile phone user is within range of one of the network masts, or within the cell, then the system will automatically identify the location of the phone as being within that cell. The system will also identify when a phone moves from one cell to another. Cells vary in size, depending on environmental conditions and the population of users in a particular location. They will be small in cities; one's phone might pass through several different cells whilst walking down Grafton Street in Dublin. They will be large in rural areas, where one might have to travel many kilometres before changing cell. Other technologies can enhance such location data[95]: a technique called triangulation, comparing signals from several different mobile phone masts, allows a location to be refined to within 300 metres; Third Generation (3G) mobile phones can refine locations down to a few metres and phones with global positioning system receivers are accurate to within a single metre.[96] The Directive on Privacy on Electronic Communications Networks provides:

> "(w)here location data other than traffic data, relating to users or subscribers of public communications networks or publicly available electronic communications services, can be processed, such data may only be processed when they are made anonymous, or with the consent of the users or subscribers to the extent and for the duration necessary for the provision of a value added service. The service provider must inform the users or subscribers, prior to obtaining their consent, of the type of location data other than traffic data which will be processed, of the purposes and duration of the processing and whether the data will be transmitted to a third party for the purpose of providing the value added

---

[93] OJ L 105 , 13/04/2006 P. 0054–0063. This Directive is currently being challenged by Ireland, see case C-301/06, *Ireland v Council of the European Union*, European Parliament.

[94] Directive 2006/24/EC, art 6.

[95] Location data is defined by Directive 2002/58, art 1 as meaning 'any data processed in an electronic communications network, indicating the geographic position of the terminal equipment of a user of a publicly available electronic communications service'. This definition is reproduced in SI 535/2003, reg 2(1).

[96] Butcher, 'New mobile services are all about location, location, location' (2003) The Irish *Times*, 16 May.

service. Users or subscribers shall be given the possibility to withdraw their consent for the processing of location data other than traffic data at any time.'[97]

[17.25] Using mobile phones to track users has many different applications. They may be used, for example, by trucking and logistics companies who want to know where their employees are of for the creation of 'friendster' type networks of mobile phone users who wish to let others know where they are. These different uses will have different data protection implications. Anyone who logs on to a 'friendster' type network will be consenting to the use of their data; their data should only be used in accordance with the purpose which they understood their data was to be used for, and should they leave the network, then so should their data. Different uses of mobile phones will have different implications for privacy; some of these uses are: companies tracking their customers,[98] parents tracking their children,[99] criminal investigations,[100] rescue services[101] and Radio Frequency Identification ('RFID') tags.[102]

Tracking Online locations

[17.26] Although the Internet was once viewed as being borderless, the reality is that:

'(a) number of companies ... offer 'geolocation services' that enable websites to determine the physical locations of individual users. This is done using a database that links internet protocol (IP) addresses of users' computers to specific countries, cities or even postcodes. Groups of IP addresses are assigned to particular universities, companies or other organisations, which often have known locations; providers of internet access allocate specific IP addresses to customers in particular regions. When you visit a website that uses geolocation technology, your IP address is relayed to the geolocation provider's server. It looks up where you are and passes the information back to the website, which can then modify its content accordingly.[103]

Unless users take measures to hide it, their location may be identified by websites, service providers and others. It is important to keep in mind that all forms of 'location data' are covered by Directive 2002/58 on privacy on electronic communications networks and not just mobile phone location data.

[17.27] Article 9(1) of Directive 2002/58 makes a number of provisions regarding location data:

(a)   Location data other that traffic data can only be processed where it is made anonymous. This seems to suggest that art 9(1) applies to any data about a phone's location that is more detailed than the bare minimum required to

---

[97] Directive 2002/58 on privacy on electronic communications Networks, art 9(1).

[98] See Kelleher, *Privacy and Data Protection Law in Ireland* (Tottel Publishing, 2006), para 17.50.

[99] Kelleher, paras 17.51–17.52.

[100] Kelleher, paras 17.53–17.55.

[101] Kelleher, paras 17.56–17.59.

[102] Kelleher, paras 17.61–17.69. But 'RFID has not lived up to expectations' (2007) The Economist, 7 June.

[103] 'The revenge of geography' (2003) The Economist, 13 March.

connect the phone to the service. It may be questioned whether this distinction means anything in practice.

(b)   If 'value added services' are provided, then this must be done with the consent of the users or subscribers. Article 9(1) appears to leave open the possibility that user and subscriber could be different persons. It does not really clarify what will occur in the not untypical situation where an employer (the subscriber) gives a mobile phone to an employee (the user) and then uses that phone to track the employee's movements whilst he is going about his work.

(c)   The service provider must supply users or subscribers with certain information before getting their consent:

    (i)   'the type of location data other than traffic data which will be processed';

    (ii)   'the purposes and duration of the processing'; and

    (iii)   'whether the data will be transmitted to a third party for the purpose of providing the value added service'.

(d)   Finally, users or subscribers must 'be given the possibility to withdraw their consent ... at any time'.

[17.28] Article 9(1) of Directive 2002/58 refers to the consent of users or subscribers. This may be read as suggesting that the consent of the subscriber alone will be sufficient for the purposes of art 9(1). Such a reading may be significant, as the typical situation where a subscriber and user of a mobile phone will be separate people is where an employee is given a mobile phone in the course of their employment. What art 9(1) states is that the service provider must at least get the consent of the subscriber. The processing of the data which will be supplied to the subscriber will still have to conform to the DPA. Arguably, in this situation the subscriber is the data controller, the service provider is the data processor and the user is the data subject. Even if art 9(1) does provide that service providers need only get the consent of subscribers, and not users, and it would take a decision of the Irish or European courts to be certain of this, the reality is that the subscriber will still have to process the data in accordance with the DPA. Article 9(1) may permit service providers to provide location data to subscribers without getting the consent of each user. It does not alter the duty of subscribers to process that data fairly and lawfully.

[17.29] Article 9(2) provides:

'Where consent of the users or subscribers has been obtained for the processing of location data other than traffic data, the user or subscriber must continue to have the possibility, using a simple means and free of charge, of temporarily refusing the processing of such data for each connection to the network or for each transmission of a communication'.

In other words, the user or the subscriber must have the ability to 'switchoff' the location data sent from their phone. Again, the ability to do this must be given to the 'subscriber or the user', not the subscriber and the user. So, arguably, this provision may not prevent a subscriber, such as an employer, denying a user, such as one of its employees, access to this 'switchoff' function. But again, it must be emphasised that the employer will have to process any data that results in accordance with the DPA and with respect to the employee's right to privacy. Even where location data is supplied, the uses to which it may be put are limited. Article 9(3) states that:

'processing of location data other than traffic data in accordance with paragraphs 1 and 2 must be restricted to persons acting under the authority of the provider of the public communications network or publicly available communications service or of the third party providing the value added service, and must be restricted to what is necessary for the purposes of providing the value added service'.

This appears to mean that raw location data can only be provided to the service provider; it cannot be sent onwards to the subscriber himself. The subject's location must be extracted by processing the raw data. This activity must be undertaken by 'the provider of the public communications network or publicly available communications service or of the third party providing the value added service'. The use to which that location data is then put will depend upon the service being provided. If the service is some form of advertising then only the advertiser knows the location of those who receive the adverts that its processes. The customer, whose adverts are being processed by the advertisers, will not have access to the location data. On the other hand, if the service being provided is one of specifically identifying the location of a mobile phone, then the customer for that service will have access to the processed, not the raw, location data.

Implementation in SI 535/2003

[17.30] The European Communities (Electronic Communications Networks and Services) (Data Protection and Privacy Regulations give effect to Directive 2002/58/EC. Regulation 9(1) provides that location data other than traffic data relating to users or subscribers cannot be processed unless the data is made anonymous or the consent of the users or subscribers has been obtained 'to the extent and for the duration necessary for the provision of a value added service'. Undertakings are obliged to inform their users or subscribers 'of the type of location data other than traffic data which will be processed, of the purposes and duration of the processing and whether the data will be transmitted to a third party for the purpose of providing the value added service'. This information must be provided before consent is obtained.[104] Users or subscribers have the right to withdraw their consent to the processing of location data other than traffic data at any time.[105] The user or subscriber must also have the ability to temporarily refuse the processing of location data 'for each connection to the public communications network or for each transmission of a communication'.[106] Finally, the processing of location data must be restricted to the telecoms undertaking or a third party providing a value added service based upon data provided by the undertaking and such processing must be restricted to what is necessary for the purposes of providing the value added service.[107]

---

[104] SI 535/2003, reg 9(2).
[105] SI 535/2003, reg 9(3).
[106] SI 535/2003, reg 9(4).
[107] SI 535/2003, reg 9(5).

Interception of telecommunications data

[17.31] As noted above, in *Kennedy and Arnold v Ireland and the Attorney General* the state admitted that it had intercepted or 'tapped' the phones of two journalists, which Hamilton P held to be:

> 'a deliberate, conscious and unjustifiable interference by the State through its executive organ with the telephonic communications of the plaintiffs and such interference constitutes an infringement of the constitutional rights to privacy of the three plaintiffs.'[108]

Some six years after the *Kennedy and Arnold v Ireland and the Attorney General* judgment, the interception of telecommunications was regularised by the Interception of Postal Packets and Telecommunications Messages Act 1993. This Act set in place a structure of ministerial authorisation and review by a judge of the High Court. The years since 1993 have seen rapid, significant and pervasive developments in both the capabilities and use of communications technology. Directive 2002/58 on privacy on Electronic Communications Networks is the EU's reaction to these developments, the Directive notes that:

> 'The Internet is overturning traditional market structures by providing a common, global infrastructure for the delivery of a wide range of electronic communications services. Publicly available electronic communications services over the Internet open new possibilities for users but also new risks for their personal data and privacy.'[109]

[17.32] The Irish law on interception of communications is spread across a variety of legislation, which must be read, together with the Irish Constitution and the European Convention on Human Rights. This legislative framework[110] comprises:

(a) Postal and Telecommunications Services Act 1983;

(b) Interception of Postal Packets and Telecommunications Messages Act 1993;

(c) Directive 2002/58 on Privacy on Electronic Communication Networks, implemented by SI 535/2003; and,

(d) The Data Protection Directive implemented by the Data Protection Acts 1988-2003.[111]

---

[108] *Kennedy and Arnold v Ireland and the Attorney General* [1987] IR 587 at 593.

[109] Directive 2002/58, Recital 6.

[110] In *The People (DPP) v Dillon* [2002] 4 IR 501 Hardiman J had to interpret s 98 of the Postal and Telecommunications Services Act 1983. He noted the decision of Hamilton CJ in *Lawlor v Flood* [1999] 3 IR 107, in which it was particularly 'emphasised that in interpreting a particular section or subsection, it must be construed in the light of the entirety of the section or Act of which it forms part and also of the 'legislative framework' of which it forms part. This framework may include other statutes, whether passed before or after the provision being construed. In this case, the whole of s 98 of the Act of 1983 is relevant as is the Interception of Postal Packets and Telecommunications Messages (Regulation) Act 1993' [2002] 4 IR 501 at 505–506.

[111] These are all comprehensively reviewed in Kelleher, *Privacy and Data Protection Law in Ireland* (Tottel Publishing, 2006), ch 18.

[17.33] Section 98(1) of the Postal and Telecommunications Services Act 1983 provides that a:

'(1) person who—

    (a)   intercepts or attempts to intercept, or

    (b)   authorises, suffers or permits another person to intercept, or

    (c)   does anything that will enable him or another person to intercept, telecommunications messages being transmitted by ... (authorised undertaking) ... or who discloses the existence, substance or purport of any such message which has been intercepted or uses for any purpose any information obtained from any such message shall be guilty of an offence'.

[17.34] An offence may be committed under s 98(1) of the Postal and Telecommunications Services Act 1983 in a wide variety of ways:

    (a)   intercepting telecommunications messages;

    (b)   attempting to intercept telecommunications messages;

    (c)   authorising or permitting the interception;

    (d)   enabling the interception;

    (e)   disclosing the existence or content of an intercepted message; and

    (f)   using information from an intercepted message.

[17.35] The meaning of 'interception' was discussed by the Court of Criminal Appeal in *DPP v Dillon*.[112] A member of the gardaí had taken possession of a mobile phone from two men. They were suspected by the gardaí of involvement in illegal drugs. The garda answered a number of calls on the phone and this evidence was sought to be admitted into evidence at trial. 'Interception' is defined by the Postal and Telecommunications Services Act 1983 as meaning:

'listening to, or recording by any means, or acquiring the substance or purport of any telecommunications message without the agreement of the person on whose behalf that message is transmitted ... And of the person intended by him to receive that message.'[113]

Giving judgment in the Court of Criminal Appeal, Hardiman J held that the above subsection defined:

'"nterception" in relation to a relevant call as covering the following activities:

    (a)   listening to it;

    (b)   recording it by any means; and

    (c)   acquiring the substance or purport of it.

These activities are within the definition of 'interception (which is criminalised by the earlier provisions of s 98) if they are done without the agreement' of each of two persons, viz the person making the call and "the person intended by him to receive that message"'.[114]

---

[112] *DPP v Dillon* [2002] 4 IR 501.
[113] Postal and Telecommunications Services Act 1983, s 98(5).
[114] *DPP v Dillon* [2002] 4 IR 501 at 508.

This led him to the clear conclusion that:

> 'the recording of a telephone conversation by one party to it without the consent of the other is an "interception". It also appears clear that the phrase "the agreement of the person intended by him to receive that message" is intended to capture a situation where a person becomes privy to a telephone call by misrepresenting his identity to the caller.'[115]

[17.36] The court went on to consider the meaning of the word 'agreement' and held that '(i)t seems to us ... that the Inspector by adopting a false name shows that he knew (as is only common sense) that (the caller) would not have spoken to him had he known his true identity'. The court then held that the interception was illegal as:

> 'The Inspector acted in this way to facilitate the detection of a serious crime. Apart from the provisions of the Act, this seems an intelligent and indeed a natural way for a detective to behave. But the Act makes no distinction between calls made for criminal purposes and other calls and creates no general exception in favour of members of An Garda Síochána other than those contained in sub-s (2) of s 98, which does not extend to the present circumstances.'[116]

Counsel for the DPP did submit that:

> 'the right to privacy in a telephone conversation is restricted to a conversation which is in some sense personal to one or both of the parties. In this case, (counsel for the DPP) submits, the message from 'Joe' was not personal to anyone but directed to a person, no matter who they might be, who might supply with him drugs. It was also submitted, briefly, that the protection of privacy in telephone conversations, considered as a constitutional right, could not apply to a conversation which, it turns out, was for the purpose of furthering the commission of a crime.'[117]

[17.37] Hardiman rejected these arguments stating that '(t)he effect of these submissions, if accepted would be to establish that the actions of the gardaí trenched upon a purely legal, as opposed to constitutional, right of the defendant.'[118] He went on to state that:

> 'It seems to us that the status of the interception must be determined as of the time of its commencement, and cannot change on the basis of what develops during the conversation intercepted. An interception which is unlawful cannot become lawful on the basis of what is heard during it. Nor can an accused person be estopped from raising a question of admissibility of evidence based on unlawful interception on the basis of the illegal purport of the conversation intercepted. If that were permissible it would set at nought the detailed and specific statutory provisions relating to interception because it is only where a conversation evidences unlawful activity that it will be sought to introduce it in evidence. If a Defendant could be so estopped, unlawful interception could take place within impunity so long as it yielded useful evidence, and there would be no practical restriction on unlawful interception which did not yield such evidence because its occurrence would not become known.'[119]

---

[115] [2002] 4 IR 501 at 508.
[116] [2002] 4 IR 501 at 511.
[117] [2002] 4 IR 501 at 513.
[118] [2002] 4 IR 501 at 513.
[119] [2002] 4 IR 501 at 513.

Finally Hardiman J examined whether the evidence of the call could be admissible on the basis of 'extraordinary extenuating circumstances' as set out in *DPP v Kenny*. He held that no such circumstances were set out in this case. Finally, Hardiman J addressed the following rhetorical question raised by counsel for the DPP: 'what was the Inspector to do? Ignore the ringing telephone[120]?' It was the view of the Court of Criminal Appeal that he should have.

Confidentiality of communications under Directive 2002/58/EC

[17.38] Directive 2002/58 concerning privacy on electronic communications networks places member states under the obligation to ensure the confidentiality of their citizens' communications. This obligation is not directly imposed upon service providers. Instead, it is for the legislatures of individual member states to provide the requisite protections.[121] This requires that member states:

> 'ensure the confidentiality of communications and the related traffic data by means of a public communications network and publicly available electronic communications services, through national legislation. In particular, they shall prohibit listening, tapping, storage or other kinds of interception or surveillance of communications and the related traffic data by persons other than users, without the consent of the users concerned.'[122]

[17.39] Two comments should be made about the above. Firstly, the obligation of confidentiality is imposed in relation to 'traffic data' as well as communications. This would seem to be a greater obligation than that imposed by the ECtHR in the *Malone v United Kingdom*[123] case. If art 5(1) is read in conjunction with recital 21 of Directive 2002/58, then it seems clear that all forms of unauthorised access to telecommunications are to be prohibited and not just unauthorised access that is unintentional:

> 'Measures should be taken to prevent unauthorised access to communications in order to protect the confidentiality of communications, including both the contents and any data related to such communications, by means of public communications networks and publicly available electronic communications services. National legislation in some Member States only prohibits intentional unauthorised access to communications.'[124]

[17.40] Secondly, art 5(1) explicitly states that this obligation of confidence does not prevent service providers storing communications during transmission for technical

---

[120] [2002] 4 IR 501 at 513.

[121] It should always be kept in mind, however, that the primary obligation in the European law of privacy is that imposed by art 8 of the ECHR. This obligation is acknowledged by recital 5 of Directive 2002/58, which states that: 'Confidentiality of communications is guaranteed in accordance with the international instruments relating to human rights, in particular the European Convention for the Protection of Human Rights and Fundamental Freedoms, and the constitutions of the Member States'.

[122] Directive 2002/58, art 5(1). The text of art 5(1) provides for two exceptions: first, where they are provided by Directive 2002/58, art 15(1); and second, in the case of 'technical storage which is necessary for the conveyance of a communication without prejudice to the principle of confidentiality'.

[123] *Malone v United Kingdom* (27 June 1984) ECtHR.

[124] Directive 2002/58, recital 24.

reasons. [125] Article 5(3) expands upon this, providing that unless communications are being stored or accessed for technical reasons or on request of the user, then the service provider must get the user's informed consent before accessing them.[126] This provision is implemented by reg 5(1) of the European Communities (Electronic Communications Networks and Services) (Data Protection and Privacy) Regulations 2003.[127]

Confidentiality of Internet transmissions

[17.41] Does s 98 of the Postal and Telecommunications Services Act 1983 apply to the Internet? The answer to this question is both yes and no. Section 98 applies to the interception of 'telecommunications messages being transmitted by an authorised undertaking'. The term 'telecommunications messages' is not defined by the Postal and Telecommunications Services Act 1983. However, the term 'intercept' is. It is defined as:

> 'listen to, or record by any means, in the course of its transmission, a telecommunications message but does not include such listening or recording where either the person on whose behalf the message is transmitted or the person intended to receive the message has consented to the listening or recording, and cognate words shall be construed accordingly.[128] Neither does it include any filtering mechanisms or processes utilised by undertakings for the purposes of preventing unsolicited commercial emails where such a service has been requested or accepted by a subscriber or user, having first been provided with clear and comprehensive information about the purposes of such filtering.'[129]

---

[125] This is implemented in two successive paragraphs of SI 535/2003. Regulation 5(2) provides that reg 5(1) which implements art 5(1) of Directive 2002/58, 'does not prevent any technical storage of or access to information for the sole purpose of carrying out or facilitating the transmission of a communication over an electronic communications network or which is strictly necessary in order to provide an information society service explicitly requested by the subscriber or user'.Regulation 5(3) provides that the Post and Telecommunications Act 1983, s 98 does not apply to 'technical storage of communications and the related traffic data which is necessary for the conveyance of a communication without prejudice to the principle of confidentiality'.

[126] 'Member States shall ensure that the use of electronic communications networks to store information or to gain access to information stored in the terminal equipment of a subscriber or user is only allowed on condition that the subscriber or user concerned is provided with clear and comprehensive information in accordance with Directive 95/46/EC, inter alia about the purposes of the processing, and is offered the right to refuse such processing by the data controller. This shall not prevent any technical storage or access for the sole purpose of carrying out or facilitating the transmission of a communication over an electronic communications network, or as strictly necessary in order to provide an information society service explicitly requested by the subscriber or user'. See also recital 22.

[127] SI 535/2003. For an analysis of the implementation of this provision and its application to employee communications, see Kelleher, *Privacy and Data Protection Law in Ireland* (Tottel Publishing, 2006), paras 18.14–18.18.

[128] Section 98(5) as inserted by Interception of Postal Packets and Telecommunications Messages (Regulation) Act 1993, s 13(2).

[129] As inserted by the European Communities (Electronic Communications Networks And Services) (Data Protection And Privacy) Regulations 2003 (SI 535/2003), reg 23(2).

[17.42] The final portion of the above definition, inserted by SI 535/2003, clearly anticipates, referring as it does to the filtering of emails, that s 98 will apply to the Internet. And although the term 'telecommunications messages' is not defined by the 1983 Act, it is likely that the courts would interpret that the term has quite a broad meaning. The *Oxford English Dictionary* defines 'message' as meaning 'a verbal, written or recorded communication sent by one person to another'. Although email would not have been commonplace in Ireland in 1983, the Oireachtas clearly contemplated its existence and concerns were expressed during the debate about the 1983 Act as to how this new technology would affect the telecommunications market in Ireland. During the second reading of the Bill in the Dáil, Mr Barry Desmond TD stated that he had:

> 'maintained very strongly that the communications scene will in the nineties and up to the year 2000 show quite dramatic changes from the current system of communication by means of the letter, telephone and telex services of today. With the introduction of computer based message systems, the development of electronic mail and television systems of communication, the revolution in communications which we are now witnessing.'[130]

[17.43] Therefore, s 98 does apply to the Internet. Or to be precise, it applies to those portions of the Internet that are controlled by authorised undertakings. So if an email is being transmitted by someone other than an authorised undertaking, intercepting it will not be an offence. Such a situation arose in the US Federal Court of Appeal decision of *USA v Councilman*.[131] The defendant was a vice-president of a company called Interloc. Interloc's primary business was as an online rare book and out-of-print book listing service and the defendant was employed to manage this service. The defendant instructed some junior employees to write a computer program that would intercept and copy all incoming communications from Amazon.com to third party book-dealers. This program was designed to work only within the confines of Interloc's computer. What Interloc appears to have been doing was providing a service that matched up buyers with sellers of books. The defendant intercepted communications between buyers and sellers to develop a list of desirable books, learn about competitors and attain a commercial advantage for Interloc. The defendant was ultimately charged with conspiracy to intercept electronic communications under US Federal wiretapping laws.

---

[130] Dáil Éireann Debates – Volume 336 – 23 June 1982, Estimates 1982 – Postal and Telecommunications Services Bill 1982: Second Stage (Resumed). Of equal significance is the fact that in enacting the Post and Telecommunications Services Act 1983, the Oireachtas adopted what would be termed 'technology neutral' language. For example, it replaces the offence of sending an obscene message 'by telephone' in the Post Office Amendment Act 1951, s 13(1) with one of sending a message 'by means of the telecommunications system'. See the Post and Telecommunications Services Act 1983, s 8 and Sch IV.

[131] *USA v Councilman* (29 June 2004), US Ct of App, 1st Cir. Other decisions of the US courts that may be of interest, although not directly relevant, are *Konop v Hawaian Airlines Inc* 302 F 3d 868 (9th Cir 2002), cert. denied 537 US 1193 (2003) and *United States v Smith* 156 F 3d 1051 (9th Cir 1998).

He moved to have these charges dismissed, arguing that:

> 'the emails at issue were stored communications when they were being processed for delivery in his company's computers, and, therefore, they were not the type of 'evanescent' transmissions i.e. telephone calls travelling through a wire, that the Wiretap Act addresses.'[132]

[17.44] This approach was characterised in the dissenting judgment of the court as being that 'an email would only be subject to the Wiretap Act when it is travelling through cables and not when it is being processed by electronic switches and computers during transit and delivery.'[133] The US government's counterargument focused on 'the temporal nature of (the defendant)'s actions and argue(d) that he violated the Wiretap Act because he copied the emails 'contemporaneously with their transmission'. This argument failed and so the US Federal Court of Appeal concluded that 'no intercept had occurred in this case.'[134]

[17.45] It is submitted that an Irish court would have to give serious consideration to a similar argument made on behalf of a similar defendant who had intercepted communications that were being processed by his own terminal equipment and not that of authorised undertakings. Section 98 of the Postal and Telecommunications Services Act 1983 applies only to authorised undertakings. It clearly does not apply to the processing of communications that is being undertaken by third parties who are not authorised undertakings. ComReg has held that authorisations are not required for the following activities: 'Electronic communications networks and electronic communications services which are wholly for own use including use by connected entities.'[135] Since authorisation is not required for such activities, those who undertake them will not be authorised undertakings and therefore may not be subject to the protection provided by s 98 of the Postal and Telecommunications Services Act 1983. Thus it is important to be able to identify when a communication is in transmission and when it is not. This difference may depend upon the technology used to communicate over those circuits. When a message is communicated using Internet Protocol (IP), it is broken into different packets of data by the sender's system. These packets are then sent over the Internet. When they reach the recipient's computer, they are automatically reassembled. The messages may contain anything – emails; video, or the sound of a person's voice. The content of the data packets does not matter to the Internet; it just moves the packet along. Deciding where the recipient's computer begins and the Internet ends is extremely difficult. Obviously, data packets flitting across the Internet will be in transmission, but will they still be in transmission when the recipient's computer is reassembling them into a coherent message for the user to read, view or listen to? It may be argued that the making of such distinctions is no longer relevant on modern converged communications systems.

---

[132] (29 June 2004), US Ct of Apps, 1st Cir, p 24.

[133] (29 June 2004), US Ct of Apps, 1st Cir, p 25.

[134] (29 June 2004), US Ct of Apps, 1st Cir, p 15.

[135] ComReg Determination: Exemption of Certain Electronic Communications Networks and Services under reg 4(6) of the European Communities (Electronic Communications Networks and Services) (Authorisation) Regulations, 2003 (SI 306/2003), Doc No 03/90, 25 July 2003.

[17.46] However, with the Electronic Commerce Act 2000, the Oireachtas did try to make such distinctions. Section 21(1) provides that:

> 'Where an electronic communication[136] enters an information system, or the first information system, outside the control of the originator,[137] then, unless otherwise agreed between the originator and the addressee,[138] it is taken to have been sent when it enters such information system or first information system'.

In other words, an email will be deemed to be sent from a computer as soon as it enters the system of the sender's ISP or the Internet itself. Section 21(2) of the Electronic Commerce Act 2000 provides that:

> 'Where the addressee of an electronic communication has designated an information system for the purpose of receiving electronic communications, then, unless otherwise agreed between the originator and the addressee or the law otherwise provides, the electronic communication is taken to have been received when it enters that information system'.

[17.47] So if a user should designated an Internet-based account, say one on http:// www.ireland.com, then the email would be deemed to be received when it entered that account. If this rule were to be applied to the interception of data, then the email would no longer be in transit once it reached the account on http://www.ireland.com. Instead, it would be stored on 'a computer-data storage medium'. Section 21(3) provides that:

> 'Where the addressee of an electronic communication has not designated an information system for the purpose of receiving electronic communications, then, unless otherwise agreed between the originator and the addressee, the electronic communication is taken to have been received when it comes to the attention of the addressee'.

Where an email address is listed in a directory, such as the Law Society Directory or the Bar Council Diary, a message will no longer be in transit once it reaches that email address, as the recipient (or addressee) will have designated that information system 'for the purpose of receiving electronic communications'. However, if the recipient has not designated his email address in this or a similar way, then the message will remain in

---

[136] Where 'electronic communication' is defined s 2(1) of the Electronic Commerce Act 2000 as 'information communicated or intended to be communicated to a person or public body, other than its originator, that is generated, communicated, processed, sent, received, recorded, stored or displayed by electronic means or in electronic form, but does not include information communicated in the form of speech unless the speech is processed at its destination by an automatic voice recognition system'.

[137] Where 'originator' is defined by the Electronic Commerce Act 2000, s 2(1) as 'the person or public body by whom or on whose behalf the electronic communication purports to have been sent or generated before storage, as the case may be, but does not include a person or public body acting as a service provider in relation to the generation, processing, sending or storing of that electronic communication or providing other services in relation to it'.

[138] Where 'addressee' is defined by the Electronic Commerce Act 2000, s 2(1) as 'in relation to an electronic communication, ... a person or public body intended by the originator to receive the electronic communication, but (this) does not include a person or public body acting as a service provider in relation to the processing, receiving or storing of the electronic communication or the provision of other services in relation to it'.

transit until the recipient views it; hence, the argument that such distinctions are artificial and of no real relevance.

[17.48] It remains to be seen whether the courts will apply the definitions of 'dispatch' and 'receipt of electronic communications' contained in the Electronic Commerce Act 2000 to the interception of communications. There is an argument that they should not, that the Electronic Commerce Act 2000 is plainly directed at the 'legal recognition of electronic contracts, electronic writing, electronic signatures and original information in electronic form in relation to commercial and non-commercial transactions and dealings and other matters'[139] and that s 21 must be read in this context. On the other hand, deciding when or where a communication is dispatched or addressed is a complex issue and one upon which the courts may be happy to defer to the Oireachtas.

[17.49] In deciding the meaning of 'transmission' in s 98 of the Postal and Telecommunications Services Act 1983, the courts might also have regard to Directive 2002/58. Recital 24 of this provides that:

> 'Terminal equipment of users of electronic communications networks and any information stored on such equipment are part of the private sphere of the users requiring protection under the European Convention for the Protection of Human Rights and Fundamental Freedoms'.

However, this provision does not appear to be going so far as to provide that information stored on a computer can be regarded as being in transmission. Directive 2002/58 does provide specific protections for what it terms 'traffic data'. Furthermore, electronic communications networks are defined as including 'switching or routing equipment' by Directive 2002/21.[140] However, the reference in recital 24 of Directive 2002/58 to the 'private sphere of users' would appear to suggest that terminal equipment is outside such networks.

[17.50] The significance of deciding whether or not a message is in transit is twofold. This will determine the offence that may be committed by someone who intercepts such a message. If the material is in transit, then an offence under s 98 of the Postal and Telecommunications Services Act 1983 may be committed. If it is not, an offence under s 9(1) of the Criminal Justice (Theft and Fraud Offences) Act 2001 might be committed. This provides that:

> 'A person who dishonestly, whether within or outside the State, operates or causes to be operated a computer within the State with the intention of making a gain for himself or herself or another, or of causing loss to another, is guilty of an offence'.

If a computer was 'hacked' into for the purpose of accessing the message, then the offence of 'unauthorised access' under s 5 of the Criminal Damage Act 1991 might also be committed. Identifying whether or not a communication is in transit will also determine the legislation under which the authorities may proceed to access the contents of that communication. If a communication is in transit, then the authorities will have to proceed in accordance with the Interception of Postal Packets and Telecommunications

---

[139] The Preamble to the Electronic Commerce Act 2000.
[140] Directive 2002/21, art 2(a).

Messages (Regulation) Act 1993, as set out above. However, if a communication is considered to have been received or to be awaiting dispatch, then it may be necessary to apply for a search warrant. The difference is that of applying to the Minister for Justice or applying to the District Court. Most, if not all, modern criminal statutes and other statutes that provide for criminal offences will provide for the grant of search warrants.

Voice over Internet Protocol

[17.51] The technology of Voice over Internet Telephony (VoIP)[141] is now well established and it is anticipated that this technology may replace the existing telecommunications system in the long term.[142] VoIP[143] is described by ComReg as:

> 'a technology that allows users to make and receive calls over an Internet Protocol (IP) transmission network (including the Internet) rather than the public switched telephone network.[144] IP is the shorthand term for a group of communications standards that enable information to be sent over most packet networks, including the Internet.'[145]

In other words, VoIP allows users to speak to friends and family over the Internet rather than over the conventional phone network. A VoIP call may well use the same phone line as a conventional call; the difference is in the technology used to process the data.[146] As with other forms of Internet communication, s 98 of the Postal and Telecommunications Services Act 1983 will apply to the call, at least so long as the message is being communicated over the network of an authorised undertaking. Again, reg 5 of SI 535/2003 will probably apply to VoIP and, where it does not, the DPA will.

---

[141] VoIP is defined by ComReg as 'the generic name for the transport of voice traffic using Internet Protocol (IP) technology. The VoIP traffic can be carried on a private managed network or the public Internet (see Internet telephony) or a combination of both. Some organisations use the term 'IP telephony' interchangeably with "VoIP". http://www.comreg.ie/sections/common.asp?ctype=3&nid=100006&navid=19#73. VoIP is sometimes referred to as 'Voice over Broadband'.

[142] ComReg, *Consultation Paper Numbering for VoIP services* Doc No 04-72, 17 June 2004, p 4.

[143] See: ComReg, *Briefing Note: Voice over Internet Protocol*, Doc No 03/21, 18 February 2003; 'From pipes to services: Telecoms and computing are converging' (2003) The Economist, 9 October; 'If you can't beat 'em, join 'em' (2003) The Economist, 18 December.

[144] The Public Switched Telephone Network is the existing fixed Irish telephone system and is commonly referred to by the acronym PSTN.

[145] ComReg, *Voice over Internet Protocol (VoIP): A Guide*, ComReg Doc No 04/103a, 14 October 2004, p 2.

[146] ComReg describes the process in the following terms: 'Using a personal computer or by an adaptor on your telephone, you can contact someone using a standard phone or another VoIP user, using your high speed broadband connection over the Internet and/or a managed IP network. The quality levels of this service are heavily influenced by the amount of bandwidth available. Broadband would clearly provide for a higher quality of service. Narrow-band connections can also be used, although it is generally accepted that unless a broadband connection is used the phone quality may suffer'. Com Reg, *Voice over Internet Protocol (VoIP): A Guide*, ComReg Doc No 04/103a, 14 October 2004, p 2.

Interception of telecommunications messages by the State

[17.52] The granting of authorisations for the interception of telecommunications messages is subject to the Interception of Postal Packets and Telecommunications Messages (Regulation) Act 1993. The provisions of this legislation are comprehensively discussed in Chapter 18 of Kelleher, *Privacy and Data Protection Law in Ireland*.[147] All of the Irish case law and legislation on the interception of telecommunications must be read in the context of judgments of the European Court of Human Rights, of which there are quite a number.[148]

Interception by other means

[17.53] Irish law provides different protections for different technologies. The technologically naïve or simply honest will speak openly on PTSN circuits where the gardaí may listen in, provided they get the authorisation of the Minister for Justice. The technologically savvy or criminally inclined may use Internet protocols and encryption to place themselves beyond the reach of authorisations issued under the Interception of Postal Packets and Telecommunications Messages Act 1993. The privacy of the latter group will be protected by superior technology. It will also be protected by superior legal rights. As Ireland's telecommunications infrastructure becomes more sophisticated, it is arguable that this variance in protection will be unsustainable in the longer term. Because more and more communications are formulated on computers prior to being sent the current, artificial, distinction between messages that are sent over telecommunications networks and so are subject to the Interception of Postal Packets and Telecommunications Messages Act 1993 and those that are not will break down. There is now a host of different technologies and programs which allow for the interception of messages and the violation of privacy without ever intruding upon the telecommunications networks of authorised undertakings. The use of such technologies is illustrated by the US case of mobster Nicodemo Scarfo Jr, who in 2002 pleaded guilty to a bookmaking charge.[149] Previously, the FBI had relied heavily upon wiretaps but Scarfo was able to use PGP to keep his most sensitive data secret. In response, the FBI installed a keylogger program upon Scarfo's PC. This program recorded every keystroke Scarfo entered. Since the keystrokes were not encrypted, the FBI was able to harvest Scarfo's passwords and use the passwords to access his data.[150] The privacy implications of keyloggers and other such technologies are discussed below.

Keyloggers or keyboard sniffer programs

[17.54] A keylogger or a keyboard sniffer is a program that monitors the keystrokes entered on keyboard, thus enabling the monitoring of much of what a user enters into a computer. Once installed, these programs may be used by computer hackers to 'discover passwords, bank details and other sensitive information' although use by parents

---

[147] See Kelleher, *Privacy and Data Protection Law in Ireland* (Tottel Publishing, 2006), paras 18.36–18.48.

[148] See Kelleher, *Privacy and Data Protection Law in Ireland* (Tottel Publishing, 2006), paras 18.49–18.56.

[149] McCullagh, 'Scarfo update', http//www.wired.com, 2 March 2002.

[150] 'Judge orders FBI to reveal surveillance methods' (2001) The Guardian, 8 August.

concerned about their children's online activities is cited as a legitimate use.[151] In *USA v Ropp*,[152] charges were dismissed against a Larry Ropp who had installed a program called 'KEYKatcher' on a computer used by a secretary to compose *inter alia* email messages. This program 'attaches inline with a keyboard connector, and stores every keystroke in an internal memory for later retrieval'.[153] The charges were dismissed on the basis that the interception of keystrokes between the keyboard and the computer's CPU did not fall within the remit of the US Federal Wiretap Act.[154] The English case of *Ashton Investments Ltd v OJSC Russian Aluminium*[155] concerned a bitter dispute between parties with interests in Russia. The applicant employed IT staff who routinely scanned their systems, one such scan:

'revealed a hidden software product often called 'spyware'. Further investigation showed that it was a product called 'Perfect Keylogger' produced by a software company called Blazing Tools. The program was designed to be installed surreptitiously on a computer – often via an innocent-looking email sent from a remote computer. The software manufacturers claim that the software is 'absolutely undetectable' [3]. Having been installed, the spyware makes a log of everything typed on the computer. It can also carry out 'visual surveillance' by taking a snapshot of the computer screen and any information saved on file. This information can then be secretly transmitted to the person who installed it.'[156]

[17.55] The plaintiffs alleged that following the installation of the keylogger program, it gathered the administrative account name and password. The defendants were then alleged able to use this to gather 'secret and privileged information' from the plaintiff's server.[157]

---

[151] 'Keylogger programs may be installed by viruses such as Bugbear' (2004) The Guardian, 22 April. Millar, 'Email Virus strikes in New Form' (2003) The Guardian, 6 June.
[152] *United States v Larry Lee Ropp* (6 October 2004), US District Court for the Central District of California, Judge Garry Allan Feess. It was agreed between the parties that '... Ropp placed the KeyKcatcher on the cable that connects (the secretary)'s keyboard to her computer's central processing unit (CPU). As Mrs Beck composed emails and other messages by depressing keys on the keyboard (an act known to some of use as 'typing') the KeyKatcher recorded and stored the electronic impulses travelling down the cable between her keyboard and the computer to which it was attached. The KeyKatcher in this way, 'eavesdrops' on the person typing messages into the computer'.
[153] Poulsen, 'Judge dismisses keylogger case' http://www.theregister.co.uk, 20 November 2004.
[154] A judgment based, in part, upon the earlier decision in *United States v Councilman* 373 F 3d, 197 (1st Cir 2004). In July 2003 a New Yorker pleaded guilty on charges of computer fraud. He had installed 'the commercial keyboard sniffer program Invisible Keylogger Stealth' on computers in Manhattan Internet cafés. He used this program to gather some 250 passwords, which he subsequently used to access at least one victim's home computer. Poulsen, 'Guilty plea in kinko's keystroke caper', http://www.theregiser.co.uk, 19 July 2003.
[155] *Ashton Investments Ltd v OJSC Russian Aluminium* [2006] EWHC 2545 (Comm), [2007] 1 All ER (Comm) 857.
[156] [2006] EWHC 2545 (Comm), para 16.
[157] [2006] EWHC 2545 (Comm), para 30.

[17.56] Keyloggers have also shown up in Irish litigation. In the Employment Appeals Tribunal (EAT) decision of *Scally v First Class Productions Ltd T/A Storm Cinemas*[158] the applicant was dismissed from his job after he installed a keylogger program on his employer's computers without authorisation. The EAT ruled that the dismissal was fair, as the employee did not install the program on his employer's behalf. The applicant's actions were detected when the employer installed its own keylogger program. Although the EAT described a keylogger program as an 'intrusive device ... effectively, a piece of spy software', the EAT discussion and decision focused only on the disciplinary implications of the employee's actions, and did not examine the privacy implications of either the applicant's or his employer's actions.

[17.57] It might be argued that the installation and use of a keyboard logger on an Irish PC without the consent of the user will be contrary to reg 5 of SI 535/2003 since it will 'use an electronic communications network to store information'. The term 'electronic communications network is defined by reg 2(1) of SI 307/2003 as:

> 'transmission systems and, where applicable, switching or routing equipment and other resources which permit the conveyance of signals by wire, by radio, by optical or by other electromagnetic means, including satellite networks, fixed (circuit- and packet-switched, including Internet) and mobile terrestrial networks, electricity cable systems, to the extent that they are used for the purpose of transmitting signals, networks used for radio and television broadcasting, and cable television networks, irrespective of the type of information conveyed'.

Furthermore, recital 24 of Directive 2002/58 provides that:

> 'Terminal equipment of users of electronic communications networks and any information stored on such equipment are part of the private sphere of the users requiring protection under the European Convention for the Protection of Human Rights and Fundamental Freedoms. So-called spyware, web bugs, hidden identifiers and other similar devices can enter the user's terminal without their knowledge in order to gain access to information, to store hidden information or to trace the activities of the user and may seriously intrude upon the privacy of these users. The use of such devices should be allowed only for legitimate purposes, with the knowledge of the users concerned'.

[17.58] Keylogger programs are probably spyware of this type and so should only be employed with the consent of the user. The installation of a keylogger program without the consent of the user might amount to an offence under s 9(1) of the Criminal Justice (Theft and Fraud Offences) Act 2001, which provides that '(a) person who dishonestly ... operates or causes to be operated a computer within the State with the intention of making a gain for himself or herself or another, or of causing loss to another, is guilty of an offence'. The loss in question might be the user's loss of privacy. However, keylogger programs of this type are being increasingly used to commit financial and other crimes.[159] The installation of a keylogger by the gardaí would not be dishonest, but

---

[158] *Scally v First Class Productions Ltd T/A Storm Cinemas*, Employment Appeals Tribunal 20/ 07/2006 UD 1231/2004, RP656/2004, MN960/2004, FL12789.

[159] 'Joe Lopez, the owner of a small computer supply company in Miami, sued Bank of America after cybercrooks were able to use a keylogging Trojan planted on his business computers to swipe bank account information and transfer $90,000 to Latvia'. Zeller, 'Cyberthieves Silently Copy Your Passwords as You Type' (2006) New York Times, 27 February.

in the absence of statutory power to do so such an installation would not be 'in accordance with the law' and so would fall foul of art 8(2) of the ECHR.

[17.59] If a keylogger program cannot be installed on a computer, then acoustic keyboard eavesdropping might be employed. This involves monitoring the 'acoustic emanations of a PC keyboard, the clicks, to eavesdrop upon what is being typed'. This form of monitoring was characterised by two IBM researchers as being 'inexpensive and non-invasive'.[160] The technique may be as effective as installing a keylogger program within a machine, but, being non-invasive, will not fall foul of legislation such as the Criminal Damage Act 1991. If premises were entered illegally to place a microphone adjacent to the targeted keyboard, a criminal offence might be committed. However, entering a premises may not be necessary if a sufficiently sophisticated and sensitive microphone is used. The use of such monitoring may infringe upon the victim's rights under the DPA, Constitution and ECHR and be actionable as such. However, it may not necessarily be a criminal offence. Nevertheless, the admissibility of evidence so gathered may be questioned.

Spyware

[17.60] Spyware has been described by the US Federal Trade Commission in the following terms:

> '(i)nstalled on your computer without your consent, spyware software monitors or controls your computer use. It may be used to send you pop-up ads, redirect your computer to websites, monitor your Internet surfing, or record your keystrokes, which, in turn, could lead to identity theft.'[161]

Spyware is becoming an endemic problem. A survey of Internet users undertaken by AOL in the USA found an average of 93 spyware programs on each machine surveyed, with one machine having 1059 such programs.[162] Although spyware is becoming an endemic feature of the Internet, it should be pointed out that many users do not mind it,

---

[160] 'It is inexpensive because in addition to a computer, the only other hardware required is a parabolic microphone. It is non-invasive because it does not require physical intrusion into the system; the sound can be recorded from a substantial distance'. Asonov, R Agrawal, 'Keyboard Acoustic Emanations', in Proc of IEEE Symposium on Security and Privacy, pp 3–11, May 2004. See also Mihm, 'Acoustic keyboard eavesdropping' (2004) New York Times, 12 December.

[161] http://www.ftc.gov/bcp/conline/pubs/alerts/spywarealrt.htm. A less dramatic (perhaps obsolete or naïve) definition is given by US-CERT, the US Computer Emergency Readiness Team: 'Despite its name, the term "spyware" doesn't refer to something used by undercover operatives, but rather by the advertising industry. In fact, spyware is also known as "adware". It refers to a category of software that, when installed on your computer, may send you pop-up ads, redirect your browser to certain web sites, or monitor the web sites that you visit. Some extreme, invasive versions of spyware may track exactly what keys you type', http://www.uscert.gov/cas/tips/ST04-016.html.

[162] AOL/NCSA Online Safety Study, October 2004, http://www.staysafeonline.info/.

since if they did they wouldn't put up with so much of the stuff.[163] In the Canadian case of *Desjean v Intermix Media*,[164] the plaintiff made three substantive allegations against the defendant. Firstly, he alleged that the defendant:

> 'offers ostensibly free software programs, such as screensavers and games, that anyone can download. Without disclosure to consumers, however, Intermix surreptitiously tacks onto these programs one or more additional programs that deliver ads and other invasive content. Thus, when Mr. Desjean installed a 'free' Intermix screensaver or game on his computer, he also unwittingly installed one or more spyware programs. In this manner, known as 'bundling', Intermix has spread its advertising programs onto Mr Desjean's hard drive.'[165]

[17.61] Secondly, the plaintiff alleged that the defendant did not:

> 'adequately inform consumers that its software has been installed on their computers. The only hint of disclosure that additional software was bundled with the screensaver is the vague statement in very tiny font on a single web page, telling users that 'by downloading this screensaver, [they] agree to our Terms of Service.' This 'Terms of Service' page, in turn, apparently addresses primarily legal issues and does not adequately warn users of what they will be receiving.'[166]

Finally, the plaintiff alleged that the defendant was exacerbating the harm from its installation of hidden spyware programs by:

> 'Exacerbating the harm from its installation of hidden spyware programs, Intermix is alleged to employ deceptive methods to prevent users from detecting and removing its software. For example, Mr Desjean contends that Intermix designs its spyware programs so that when users uninstall the program with which the spyware was bundled (for example, a screensaver), Intermix's spyware products remain behind, installed and fully operational. Intermix also prevents its spyware programs from being listed in the commonly accessed 'Add/Remove Programs' utility in the Microsoft Windows operating system, making removal yet more difficult. Additionally, it fails to provide its own 'uninstall' utility within many of its spyware programs' files or folders.'[167]

The plaintiff submitted that taken together these activities amounted to 'deceptive, fraudulent and illegal practices, and false advertising'.[168] However the Canadian courts dismissed the case at a preliminary stage they lacked the requisite jurisdiction to try the matter.

---

[163] Users are not completely irrational in this: often spyware is bundled with other forms of software and users may accept a reduction in their privacy in return for software they like. 'I think some users are exhausted by security threats and privacy leaks ... If your personal information isn't private anyway...then why not give a little more away and get some free software too?' Delio, 'Spyware on my machine? So what?' http://www.wired.com, 6 December 2004.

[164] *Desjean V Intermix Media*, Federal Court of Canada, 2006 FC 1395, 17 November 2006.

[165] 2006 FC 1395, para 6.

[166] 2006 FC 1395, para 8.

[167] 2006 FC 1395, para 9.

[168] 2006 FC 1395, para 10.

Spyware, cookies and Directive 2002/58

[17.62] Article 5 of Directive 2002/58 provides that member states must ensure the confidentiality of communications. Recital 24 of Directive 2002/58 makes it clear that this provision extends to spyware, stating that:

> 'So-called spyware, web bugs, hidden identifiers and other similar devices can enter the user's terminal without their knowledge in order to gain access to information, to store hidden information or to trace the activities of the user and may seriously intrude upon the privacy of these users. The use of such devices should be allowed only for legitimate purposes, with the knowledge of the users concerned.'[169]

This provision places the providers of spyware under two obligations: firstly, their products may only be used for legitimate purposes; secondly, they may only be used with the knowledge of the users concerned. This provision does place a quite considerable limitation on the use of spyware. The *Concise Oxford English Dictionary*[170] defines 'legitimate' as 'conforming to the law or to rules' or 'able to be defended by law or justification'. This would seem to allow for two different interpretations of the term. Legitimate may mean 'lawful' or it may have the slightly broader meaning of 'justified'. The courts generally appear to prefer the former meaning. [171] Jowitt suggests that the word legitimate 'signifies lawful,'[172] a view which it is submitted is correct. Lawful would then have to be construed in accordance with the DPA, the constitutional right to privacy and the ECHR. Discharging such a burden would not be easy, especially as the most obvious method, getting the subject's consent, must be dependent upon users having 'knowledge' of the use of the spyware. Many users inadvertently give their consent to the installation of spyware on their machines.[173] However, compliance with

---

[169] The recital begins with the statement that: 'Terminal equipment of users of electronic communications networks and any information stored on such equipment are part of the private sphere of the users requiring protection under the European Convention for the Protection of Human Rights and Fundamental Freedoms'.

[170] *Concise Oxford English Dictionary* (10th edn, OUP, 2002).

[171] For example, the doctrine of legitimate expectation. The use of the word 'legitimate' is deliberate, carrying with it an expectation of legal, as opposed to practical, consequences. As set out by Diplock LJ in *Council of Civil Service Unions v Minister for the Civil Service* [1985] AC 374, quoted by McCracken J in *Abrahamson v Law Society* [1996] 1 IR 403 at 417: 'I prefer to continue to call the kind of expectation that qualifies ... a "legitimate expectation" rather than "a reasonable expectation", in order thereby to indicate that it has some consequences to which effect will be given in public law, whereas an expectation or hope that some benefit or advantage would continue to be enjoyed, although it might well be entertained by a "reasonable" man, would not necessarily have such consequences'. See also the judgement of the Australian courts in *Salemi v Minister for Immigration and Ethnic Affairs (No 2)* (1977) 14 ALR 1 at 7, in which Barwick CJ stated: 'I cannot attribute any other meaning in the language of a lawyer to the word "legitimate" than a meaning which expressed the concept of entitlement or recognition by law'.

[172] *Jowitt's Dictionary of English Law* (2nd edn, Sweet and Maxwell, 1977), J Burke ed, p 1081.

[173] See: Leyden, 'Insecurity begins at home', http://www.theregister.co.uk, 26 October 2004; 'Spyware: users say yes to it' (2004) Wired, 31 October.

Directive 2002/58[174] would appear to require that users be informed of exactly what spyware they were installing on their machines and what that spyware would do with their personal data once it was installed.[175] Of course, if users did receive such information, none of them would consent to the installation of the spyware in question.[176] The AOL survey quoted above found that 90 per cent of users did not know what the spyware programs were doing on their computers and that 95 per cent of users believed that they had not given permission for the installation of spyware on their machines.

Implementation in SI 535/2003

[17.63] Regulation 5(1) of SI 535/2003 provides that '(n)o person shall use an electronic communications network to store information or to gain access to information stored in the terminal equipment of a subscriber or user ...' unless the user is offered a right of refusal.

Back-door programs

[17.64] A precursor to spyware that is commonly distributed over the Internet is the 'back-door'. This is an adaptation made to commercially available encryption software to allow the authorities to gain access to communications. In the 1990s a Swiss manufacturer of cryptography products was revealed to have installed such back-doors into its products. These back-doors were used to decrypt messages sent by using the Swiss technology and the technique was used to capture the murderers of an exiled Iranian politician.[177] A proposal from the US government to formalise the installation of such back-doors into encryption products, the 'Clipper Chip', failed.[178] The surreptitious installation of a back-door into software, particularly encryption software upon which users rely to protect their privacy or digital rights management systems that controlled the use of copyrighted material,[179] might well be contrary to the DPA. However, it is most likely that such back-doors would be installed for the purpose of state security or for preventing, investigating or prosecuting offences. As such, the installation would be

---

[174] And in particular the requirement of disclosure of information to the data subject set out in arts 10 and 11 of Directive 95/46.

[175] See also *The People (DPP) v Dillon* [2002] 4 IR 501.

[176] So called 'driveby downloads', where the user's consent is not sought, would still remain a problem, however. A variety of products are now available, both free and for purchase, which remove spyware or prevent its infestation in the first place. The GetNetWise site at http://getnetwise.org/, which is backed by companies such as Dell and IBM, is as good a place to start as any.

[177] Singh, *The Code Book* (Fourth Estate, 1999) p 319.

[178] See Levy, *Crypto* (Allen Lane, The Penguin Press, 2000).

[179] For example, 'Sony BMG's music CDs ... installed a 'rootkit' program that buried its DRM software deep on consumers' hard drives when they were played on a PC', Taylor and Van Duyn, 'Music industry asks whether fair use is fair play' (2005) The Financial Times, 28 November. Sony subsequently settled a number of class action law suits and 'agreed to bring in an independent auditor to confirm to customers it has not and will not use their personal data'. Edgecliffe-Johnson, 'Sony BMG settles suits over "flawed" music CDs' (2006) Financial Times, 2 January.

beyond the scope of the DPA. However, it would still be subject to review under the Constitution and ECHR.

Cookies

[17.65] Cookies are small bits of code that are placed on users' computers, usually when they visit a website, so that the website can monitor their use. Microsoft defines a cookie as '(a) very small text file placed on your hard drive by a Web Page server. It is essentially your identification card, and cannot be executed as code or deliver viruses. It is uniquely yours and can only be read by the server that gave it to you.'[180] Microsoft defines the purpose of a cookie as '(t)o tell the server that you returned to that Web page.'[181] Similarly, the Irish communications regulator ComReg suggests that 'cookies provide important functionality for Internet websites and are used for legitimate marketing purposes.'[182] Others do not have such a benign view.[183]

[17.66] At one stage during the passage of the Directive on Privacy and Electronic Communications,[184] the European Parliament accepted an amendment to the Directive that would have outlawed cookies altogether. However, this amendment was subsequently dropped. Recital 25 of the Directive distinguishes cookies from other forms of 'spyware, web bugs, hidden identifiers and other similar devices' and provides that:

---

[180] A more detailed description of what cookies do is offered by the UK's Department of Trade and Industry: '(c)ookies are normally defined as software sent to and stored in the terminal of an internal user by a service provider: the device then acts as a marker or identifier that can be recognised automatically by the service provider. They may be used for a wide range of purposes: some operators use them, for example, to log how many visits a particular website, or page of a website, is getting, or the order in which visitors navigate around a site; they can therefore be used to monitor how attractive a site is, for design or advertising purposes. Cookies can be used to monitor repeat visits from the same terminal, enabling site providers to record their language preferences, or vary the banner adverts sent to that visitor. They may be used in conjunction with other information provided by the visitor to provide a picture of what a web-visitor has previously bought or expressed an interest in, or to facilitate online purchasing procedures or security/identity checks. They may be used to send a return message – to prompt the visitor to buy from the site, for instance'. UK Department of Trade and Industry 'Consultation Document Implementation of the Directive on Privacy and Electronic Communications' March 2003, p 23. See also the Article 29 working group's description of how a cookie works in its 'Working document on determining the international application of EU data protection law to personal data processing on the Internet by non-EU based web sites' 30 May 2002, p 10.

[181] http://www.microsoft.com/info/cookies.mspx.

[182] ComReg, 'Security Implications for New and Emerging Telecommunications Technologies', 04/29, 12 March 2004, p 15.

[183] See Cohen, 'Be Sure you never take a cookie from strangers' (2000) The Guardian, 1 April; 'EU wages war on Cookie Monster', http://www.theregister.co.uk, 14 November 2001.

[184] Directive 2002/58/EC of the European Parliament and of the Council of 12 July 2002 concerning the processing of personal data and the protection of privacy in the electronic communications sector (Directive on Privacy and Electronic Communications) OJ L 201/37, 31 July 2002.

'"cookies", can be a legitimate and useful tool, for example, in analysing the effectiveness of website design and advertising, and in verifying the identity of users engaged in online transactions. Where such devices, for instance cookies, are intended for a legitimate purpose, such as to facilitate the provision of information society services, their use should be allowed on condition that users are provided with clear and precise information in accordance with Directive 95/46/EC about the purposes of cookies or similar devices so as to ensure that users are made aware of information being placed on the terminal equipment they are using. Users should have the opportunity to refuse to have a cookie or similar device stored on their terminal equipment. This is particularly important where users other than the original user have access to the terminal equipment and thereby to any data containing privacy-sensitive information stored on such equipment. Information and the right to refuse may be offered once for the use of various devices to be installed on the user's terminal equipment during the same connection and also covering any further use that may be made of those devices during subsequent connections. The methods for giving information, offering a right to refuse or requesting consent should be made as user-friendly as possible. Access to specific website content may still be made conditional on the well-informed acceptance of a cookie or similar device, if it is used for a legitimate purpose'.

[17.67] Thus recital 25 makes it absolutely clear that a user must be informed that a cookie is being installed and be offered the opportunity to refuse the installation. However, Directive 2002/58's provisions themselves are not technology specific; they do not apply simply to cookies as the term was understood on 12 July 2002.[185] Article 5's provisions apply to any use of an electronic communication network to 'store information or to gain access to information stored in the terminal equipment of a subscriber or user'. Therefore, any form of monitoring device placed on the terminal equipment of a subscriber or user would be covered by this provision.

Implementation in SI 535/2003

[17.68] Regulation 5(1) of SI 535/2003 provides that 'No person shall use an electronic communications network to store information or to gain access to information stored in the terminal equipment of a subscriber or user' unless the user is offered a right of refusal.

Surveillance in an international context

[17.69] The Internet is an international network, so to be effective, the state's powers of surveillance must be capable of international application. In this context, the Criminal Justice (Mutual Assistance) Bill 2005 should be noted, which would have implemented a variety of European legislation and international agreements.[186] Given its manifold security concerns, the USA is particularly active in relation to the interception of international communications and data transfers. The European Union has negotiated a number of agreements with the USA in relation to the surveillance of passenger name record (PNR) data relating to the records of passengers travelling on aircraft to the

---

[185] UK Department of Trade and Industry Consultation Document 'Implementation of the Directive on Privacy and Electronic Communications' March 2003, p 23.

[186] The relevant provisions of this Bill are analysed in Kelleher, *Privacy and Data Protection Law in Ireland* (Tottel Publishing, 2006), paras 18.88–18.90.

USA.[187] These agreements were made in the context of the USA's very large-scale interception operations. Previously much attention had been focused on the ECHELON system. On 5 July 2000 the European Parliament decided to set up a temporary committee on this system.[188] The resulting report found that:

> 'the existence of a global system for intercepting communications, operating by means of cooperation proportionate to their capabilities among the USA, the UK, Canada, Australia and New Zealand under the UKUSA Agreement, is no longer in doubt; ... it seems likely ... that its name is in fact ECHELON ... there can now be no doubt that the purpose of the system is to intercept, at the very least, private and commercial communications, and not military communications.'[189]

[17.70] The report went on to resolve that 'the surveillance system depends, in particular, upon worldwide interception of satellite communications'. However, it concluded that the effect of this system was limited, as:

> 'in areas characterised by a high volume of communications only a very small proportion of those communications are transmitted by satellite; ... this means that the majority of communications cannot be intercepted by earth stations, but only by tapping cables and intercepting radio signals, something which ... is possible only to a limited extent'.

The interception of large volumes of communications has practical consequences, as the report noted:

> 'the numbers of personnel required for the final analysis of intercepted communications imposes further restrictions; ... therefore, the UKUSA states have access to only a very limited proportion of cable and radio communications and can analyse an even more limited proportion of those communications, and ... further, however extensive the resources and capabilities for the interception of communications may be, the extremely high volume of traffic makes exhaustive, detailed monitoring of all communications impossible in practice'.

[17.71] Following the publication of the report, the Economic and Social Committee of the European Parliament[190] asked that 'the Council of Ministers ... take firm action on this matter.'[191] Given that these activities are outside the scope of European law[192] and

---

[187] Agreement between the European Union and the United States of America on the processing and transfer of passenger name record (PNR) data by air carriers to the United States Department of Homeland Security, OJ L 298, 27.10.2006, pp 29–31.

[188] OJ C 121, 24.4.2001, p 36.

[189] OJ C 121, 24.4.2001, p 36.

[190] Opinion of the Economic and Social Committee on the 'Communication from the Commission to the Council, the European Parliament, the Economic and Social Committee and the Committee of the Regions – Creating a safer Information Society by Improving the Security of Information Infrastructures and Combating Computer-related Crime', OJ C 311, 2001, Item 4 (2001/C 311/04). See, generally, Radden-Keefe, *Chatter: Dispatches from the Secret World of Global Eavesdropping* (Random House, 2005) and Bamford, *Body of Secrets* (Arrow, 2002).

[191] Opinion of the Economic and Social Committee on the 'Communication from the Commission to the Council, the European Parliament, the Economic and Social Committee and the Committee of the Regions – Creating a safer Information Society by Improving the Security of Information Infrastructures and Combating Computer-related Crime' OJ C 311, 2001, Item 4 (2001/C 311/04) para 5.2.6.

[192] Title V of the European Treaties.

the new priorities that have been imposed upon a post-9/11 world, it is unsurprising that the Council of Ministers has not responded to the committee's request. When this request was repeated by an MEP in 2002 the council responded by referring to existing European legislation, none of which is properly applicable to ECELON, and promised that: '(i)f further provisions are necessary, the Council will examine any initiative coming from the Commission or a Member State.'[193] Since the 9/11 attacks the indications are that the USA and other western states have ramped up their electronic surveillance efforts, which has required the development of new technologies:

> 'Despite the popular image of spies operating undercover, most of the West's intelligence efforts against potential terrorist threats rely on electronic eavesdropping technology which generates mind-boggling quantities of data. Faced with mountains of recordings from satellite interception of telephone taps various agencies in the US and UK have turned to the new generation of storage technologies to manage their information haul.'[194]

[17.72] The significance of ECHELON may be that its existence has been documented; it may be assumed that this is just one element in a number of interception operations. French security services have banned the cabinet of the French government from using BlackBerries because 'the BlackBerry system is based on servers located in the US and the UK, and that highly sensitive strategic information being passed between French ministers could fall into foreign hands.'[195] In August 2007 the USA amended its Foreign Intelligence Surveillance Act (FISA) to enable the interception of communications on fibre-optic cables that pass in and out of the USA:

> 'most international telephone conversations to and from the United States are conducted over fiber-optic cables, and the most efficient way for the government to eavesdrop on them is to latch on to giant telecommunications switches located in the United States. By changing the legal definition of what is considered "electronic surveillance," the new law allows the government to eavesdrop on those conversations without warrants -- latching on to those giant switches – as long as the target of the government's surveillance is "reasonably believed" to be overseas.'[196]

---

[193] Question asked by Brice Hortefeux (PPE-DE), OJ C 92E, 2003, Item 215 (2003/C 92E/215).

[194] For example 'solid-state storage disks, essentially a giant version of the solid state memory sticks that are increasingly popular for random back-up of PC data. Because these contain no moving parts they can analyse and retrieve data much more quickly than conventional spinning storage disks'. Dempsey, 'Smarter software shows the way forward' (2004) Financial Times, 17 November.

[195] Solomans, 'BlackBerry ban for French cabinet' (2007) Financial Times, 20 June.

[196] Risen, 'Bush signs law to widen reach for wiretapping' (2007) New York Times, 6 August.

Chapter 18

Anonymity

Introduction

[18.01] A now famous cartoon shows two dogs staring at a computer screen, one turned to the other, saying 'On the Internet, nobody knows you're a dog'.[1] This assertion is easy to make, and if users take precautions that are inconvenient, and possibly illegal,[2] then they can stay anonymous online. But if precautions are not taken, then users may be surprised at how easy IP addresses and Norwich Pharmacal orders make it to uncover their identity.[3] As the ability to stay anonymous has declined online, the Internet has helped strip away the vestiges of offline anonymity. There was a time when sperm donors could donate, secure in the expectation that the anonymity of their parenthood would be forever inviolate. If that were ever true, it is not so now. In 2005 a teenager learned an approximate spelling of the surname of the sperm donor used to sire him. Armed with this knowledge, together with the man's date of birth, place of birth and his college degree, he was able to go online and identify his biological father.[4] It is certainly true that Irish law recognises that individuals have a right to anonymity, albeit a limited one. The law was held to be so in the Supreme Court decision in *IO'T v B and The Rotunda Girls Aid Society*.[5] This case concerned an adult woman, adopted as a child, who sought an order from the Circuit Court to force the defendant to disclose the identity of her birth mother. Hamilton CJ considered that the mother of an adopted girl had legal and constitutional rights (such as those arising from the rights of privacy and confidentiality[6]), which might permit her to maintain her anonymity.

---

1. The cartoon was by Peter Steiner and was published in the New Yorker magazine Vol 69, 5 July 1993, p 61.
2. For example, a basic method of retaining one's online anonymity would be to connect to a wi-fi network that has been improperly secured. Doing so is hardly practical and possibly illegal.
3. Norwich Pharmacal orders are not always necessary. For example, *McGuire v Gill* concerned the website http://www.rate-your-solicitor.com. The plaintiff alleged that defamatory material that breached her privacy was hosted on the site. She applied for injunctive relief requiring the defendant remove this material. The defendant denied having control of the site, but the High Court granted the plaintiff injunctive relief requiring that he remove the offending material. See Collins, 'When online gets out of line' (2006) The Irish Times, 25 November; Carolyn, 'Man avoids jail after material about barrister removed from website' (2006) The Irish Times, 24 November.
4. Motluck, 'Anonymous sperm donor traced on internet' (2005) New Scientist, 3 November.
5. *O'T v B and The Rotunda Girls Aid Society* [1998] 2 IR 321.
6. [1998] 2 IR 321 at 349.

He therefore found that the Circuit Court was correct:

> 'in holding that the natural mothers should be given an opportunity of asserting a claim of privilege and any other claim to privacy which the Constitution or law would leave open to them, without having their identities disclosed to the ... plaintiff.'[7]

The courts attached a quite considerable value to anonymity and treated it as real consideration for the purposes of the law of contract in *Jane O'Keefe v Ryanair*.[8] The plaintiff was identified by the defendant as its millionth passenger and assented to engaging in publicity. Kearns J held that:

> 'The surrender by the plaintiff of her anonymity and privacy and her active participation in the generation of the publicity that was created on the day in question in my view amounted to a real consideration and is sufficient to support a valid contract.'[9]

Kearns J assessed Ryanair's consideration, free flights for life, as being worth €67,500.[10] Of course identifying the location of a computer is not the same as asserting definitive proof that a particular individual sent a message or downloaded something from the Internet. For example, in *R v Stubbs*,[11] a fraudster confessed that he had 'made ... password changes on colleagues' computers when they were left unattended.'[12]

[18.02] In *R (on the application of C) v Chief Constable of 'A' Police*[13] the applicant was accused of downloading child pornography, his home was searched and he was arrested. He unsuccessfully sought an injunction preventing the police from continuing their investigation on the grounds, *inter alia,* that it was more likely that the material had been sent 'to his son, P, who was ... a teenager living at home'.[14] In *BMG Canada Inc v John Doe*[15] the Canadian Federal Court of Appeals cautioned that:

> 'If there is a lengthy delay between the time the request for the identities is made by the plaintiffs and the time the plaintiffs collect their information, there is a risk that the information as to identity may be inaccurate. Apparently this is because an IP address may not be associated with the same individual for long periods of time. Therefore it is possible that the privacy rights of innocent persons would be infringed and legal proceedings against such persons would be without justification. Thus the greatest care should be taken to avoid delay between the investigation and the request for information. Failure to take such care might well justify a court in refusing to make a disclosure order.'[16]

---

[7]   [1998] 2 IR 321 at 353.

[8]   *Jane O'Keefe v Ryanair* [2002] 3 IR 228.

[9]   [2002] 3 IR 228 at 231.

[10] Similarly, the US Supreme Court has upheld the right to anonymity, finding *inter alia* that to require that persons identify themselves before they are entitled to a free speech right would have the effect of negating that right, see *NAACP v Alabama* 357 US 449; also *Talley v California* 362 US 60; also *McIntyre v Ohio Elections Commission* 514 US 334; and *Watchtower Bible and Tract Society v Village of Stratton* 240 F 3d 553.

[11] *R v Stubbs* [2006] EWCA Crim 2312.

[12] [2006] EWCA Crim 2312, para 37.

[13] *R (on the application of C) v Chief Constable of 'A' Police* [2006] EWHC 2352 (Admin), [2006] All ER (D) 124 (Sep).

[14] [2006] EWHC 2352 (Admin), [2006] All ER (D) 124 (Sep), para 3.

[15] *BMG Canada Inc v John Doe (FCA)* 2005 FCA 193, [2005] 4 FCR 81.

[16] 2005 FCA 193, [2005] 4 FCR 81 at para 43.

A number of services exist which offer the prospect of anonymous internet use. For example, relakks.com is a Swedish service which works by directing users internet usage through a Swedish Internet service provider. The connection between the users' own service and that of the ISP is encrypted. This offers limited anonymity, but that anonymity would be stripped away if a user should commit a criminal offence, which might necessitate the service of a European Evidence Warrant on the Swedish authorities or commit tortuous or other wrongful acts which would result in the victim getting Norwich Pharmacal relief[17] and enforcing the order through the Swedish courts.

Norwich Pharmacal relief

[18.03] Norwich Pharmacal relief, sometimes referred to as the 'action for discovery', is an order which requires that the defendant reveal the identity of a person who has wronged the plaintiff. The modern doctrine[18] was established by the House of Lords in *Norwich Pharmacal v Customs and Excise Commissioners*.[19] The principle upon which it was based was set out by Reid LJ in the following terms:

> 'If through no fault of his own a person gets mixed up in the tortuous acts of others so as to facilitate their wrongdoing, he may incur no personal liability, but he comes under a duty to assist the person who has been wronged by giving him full information and disclosing the identity of the wrongdoers.'[20]

Norwich Pharmacal orders will not be available where the information may be obtained by other means.[21]

[18.04] In Irish law the order can be sought against a third party who has no involvement in the wrongdoing in question,[22] but the position would appear to be different in the

---

[17] For a discussion of the legal vulnerability of this service, see Comber and Staple, 'Internet Anonymity: Limits of Identity Masking Services' (2007) e-Commerce Law & Policy, Vol 9, Issue 7, July.

[18] 'The action for discovery is of ancient origin' per O'Flaherty J in *Megaleasing UK Ltd v Barrett* [1993] ILRM 497 at 507. See *Orr v Diaper* [1876] 4 Ch D 92.

[19] *Norwich Pharmacal v Customs and Excise Commissioners* [1974] AC 133.

[20] [1974] AC 133 at 175.

[21] *Mitsui & Co Ltd v Nexen Petroleum UK Ltd* [2005] EWHC 625 (Ch), [2005] 3 All ER 511.

[22] See the judgment of the Supreme Court in *L(A) v N(M) and G(D)* (4 March 2002, unreported) SC. The plaintiff alleged that he had been sexually assaulted by a Catholic priest. The High Court made an order of discovery requiring that the defendants make available to the plaintiff 'all documents which are or have been in their power possession or procurement relating to the identity and attendance of persons in Holy Orders engaged in the administration of sacraments and other rites of the Roman Catholic Church including Confession at Knock in the County of Mayo on the 1 day of September 1991'. On appeal to the Supreme Court, the parties' submissions 'included references to *Norwich Pharmacal Co and Ors v Commissioners of Customs and Excise* ... and *Doyle v Commissioners of An Garda Síochána.*' Murphy J commented that 'These are cases ... dealing with an action which is brought solely for the purpose of obtaining discovery. Accordingly they have no relevance to the present case which is brought as an action against the defendants for wrongs allegedly committed by them, their servants or agents. (contd/)

UK.[23] It is no longer necessary to show that the wrongdoing in question was a tort. This issue was reviewed by the House of Lords in *Ashworth Hospital Authority v MGN*[24] in which Woolf LJ stated 'Whether the ... wrongdoing was tortious or in breach of contract in my judgment matters not.'[25] However, prior to this judgment, the Supreme Court had extended the use of the order even further in *IO'T v B and the Rotunda*,[26] in which Hamilton CJ stated:

> 'If the action for discovery is available to a litigant who simply seeks to assert a legal right to redress against wrongdoing, as in *Megaleasing UK Ltd*, a remedy must equally be available to a person in the position of the plaintiff who seeks to assert a constitutional right.'[27]

Where justice cannot otherwise be done, a plaintiff is entitled to discovery against a defendant in order to obtain information for use in bringing proceedings against a third party, even though it cannot be ascertained, without the information sought, that the third party has committed a tort against the plaintiff.[28]

[18.05] In the English case of *Ashworth Hospital Authority v MGN*[29] the fact that the wrongdoing at issue amounted to a criminal offence did not bar relief. This may be contrasted with the Australian Federal Court decision in *GSM (Trademarks) Pty Ltd v Shao (No 2)*[30] which concerned the importation of goods into Australia that infringed the plaintiff's trade mark rights. This was a criminal offence under Australian law. The court rejected as 'entirely inappropriate'[31] an application for an order requiring that the defendant swear an affidavit setting out 'the names and all known current contact details'[32] of everyone involved in this activity. Given that the privilege against self-incrimination is a Constitutional right,[33] it is likely that the Irish courts will have to come to their own judgment on this point.

[18.06] The validity of Norwich Pharmacal orders was recognised by the Irish Supreme Court in *Megaleasing UK Ltd v Barrett*.[34] The circumstances in which the remedy can be sought are quite limited. Finlay CJ stated that 'the granting of an order for discovery in

---

[22] (\contd) The significance of the Pharmacal and other cases is that they contain an analysis of particular circumstances and in particular cases in which knowledge of the 'innocent' defendant of an actual wrongdoer might be an appropriate justification for instituting proceedings for discovery only. That debate and analysis may have misled both parties into believing that this line of authority has some relevance to the present case. It has not'.

[23] *Arsenal Football Club Plc v Elite Sports Distribution Ltd* [2002] EWHC 3057 (Ch).

[24] *Ashworth Hospital Authority v MGN* [2002] 1 WLR 2033.

[25] [2002] 1 WLR 2033 at 2041.

[26] *IO'T v B and the Rotunda* [1998] 2 IR 321.

[27] [1998] 2 IR 321 at 352.

[28] See *P v T Ltd* [1997] 1 WLR 1309.

[29] See *Ashworth Hospital Authority v MGN* [2002] 1 WLR 2033.

[30] *GSM (Trademarks) Pty Ltd v Shao (No 2)* [2006] FCA 1393 (12 October 2006).

[31] [2006] FCA 1393 (12 October 2006), para 13.

[32] [2006] FCA 1393 (12 October 2006), para 4.

[33] *Heaney v Ireland* [1996] 1 IR 580.

[34] *Megaleasing UK Ltd v Barrett* [1993] ILRM 497.

an action of sole discovery prior to the institution of proceedings against any defendant is a power which for good reasons must be sparingly used.'[35] He went on to state that:

'The remedy should be confined to cases where very clear proof of wrongdoing exists and possibly, so far as it applies to an action for discovery alone prior to the institution of any other proceedings, to cases where what is really being sought is the names and identity of wrongdoers rather than the factual information concerning the commission of the wrong.'[36]

[18.07] An order was refused in this case as the plaintiff failed in the 'very clear and unambiguous establishment of a wrongdoing.'[37] Similarly in *Ryanair v Ryanair European Pilots' Association (Repa)* the plaintiff was refused relief because 'no actionable wrong' was disclosed by its application.[38] In *Doyle v The Commissioner of An Garda Síochána*[39] the plaintiff 's daughter had been murdered in the Dublin and Monaghan bombings of 1974. The plaintiff sought Norwich Pharmacal relief. Barrington J, giving judgment for the Supreme Court, stated that:

'There is no doubt that the High Court has jurisdiction at common law to entertain an action for sole discovery such as the present one. But the authorities establish that this is a jurisdiction to be exercised sparingly and it has been exercised only in cases where the plaintiff was in the position to prove that he had suffered a wrong but he was not, and the defendant was, in a position to establish the identity of the wrong doer.'[40]

[18.08] It is not necessary to show that the respondent to a Norwich Pharmacal order has done anything wrong, only that the respondent has been involved or participated in the wrongful actions of the respondent[41]:

'this requirement of involvement or participation on the part of the party from whom discovery is sought is not a stringent requirement; it is still a significant requirement. It distinguishes that party from a mere onlooker or witness. The need for involvement (the reference to participation can be dispensed with because it adds nothing to the requirement of involvement) is a significant requirement because it ensures that the mere onlooker cannot be subjected to the requirement to give disclosure. Such a requirement is an intrusion upon a third party to the wrongdoing and the need for involvement provides justification for this intrusion.'[42]

Norwich Pharmacal Orders are a discretionary remedy, as was stated by the House of Lords:

'this is a discretionary jurisdiction which enables the court to be astute to avoid a third party who has become involved innocently in wrongdoing by another from being

---

[35] [1993] ILRM 497 at 503.
[36] [1993] ILRM 497 at 504.
[37] [1993] ILRM 497 at 503, although see *IO'T v B and the Rotunda Girls Aid Society* in which Hamilton CJ emphasised that it is 'not a precondition to the granting of the relief that the persons against whom it is sought should themselves have been guilty of any wrongdoing'.
[38] 'High Court rejects Ryanair bullying claim' (2006) The Irish Times, 13 July.
[39] *Doyle v The Commissioner of An Garda Síochána* [1999] 1 IR 249.
[40] [1999] 1 IR 249 at 266.
[41] See *Ashworth Hospital Authority v MGN* [2002] 1 WLR 2033 at 2041.
[42] [2002] 1 WLR 2033 at 2042.

subjected to a requirement to give disclosure unless this is established to be a necessary and proportionate response in all the circumstances ... The need for involvement can therefore be described as a threshold requirement. The fact that there is involvement enables a court to consider whether it is appropriate to make the order which is sought. In exercising its discretion the court will take into account the fact that innocent third parties can be indemnified for their costs while at the same time recognising that this does not mean there is no inconvenience to third parties as a result of becoming embroiled in proceedings through no fault on their part.'[43]

[18.09] The award of costs following the grant of a Norwich Pharmacal relief was examined by the English courts in *Totalise PLC v The Motley Fool.*[44] Aldous LJ, giving judgment for the court, set out the following principles that would apply:

'The Court when considering its order as to costs, after a successful *Norwich Pharmacal* application should consider all the circumstances. In a normal case the applicant should be ordered to pay the costs of the party making the disclosure including the costs of making the disclosure. There may be cases where the circumstances require a different order, but we do not believe they include cases where:

(a)   the party required to make the disclosure had a genuine doubt that the person seeking the disclosure was entitled to it;

(b)   the party was under an appropriate legal obligation not to reveal the information, or where the legal position was not clear, or the party had a reasonable doubt as to the obligations; or

(c)   the party could be subject to proceedings if disclosure was voluntary; or

(d)   the party would or might suffer damage by voluntarily giving the disclosure; or

(e)   the disclosure would or might infringe a legitimate interest of another. That does not mean that a party who supports or is implicated in a crime or tort or seeks to obstruct justice being done should believe that the Court will do other than require that party to bear its costs and, if appropriate, pay the other party's costs.'[45]

Norwich Pharmacal Orders and the Internet

[18.10] Online anonymity has been an issue before the Irish courts on a number of occasions. As well as the unreported decisions of *McGuire v Gill* and *Ryanair v Ryanair European Pilots' Association (Repa)* discussed above, there is also the reported decision of *EMI Records (Ireland) Ltd. v Eircom Ltd.*[46]

Totalise PLC v The Motley Fool

[18.11] Norwich Pharmacal type relief was granted by the English courts to force the identification of a person who was using a website to publish defamatory statements about the plaintiff in *Totalise PLC v The Motley Fool.*[47] The plaintiff was an Internet service provider. The defendants operated websites which contained discussion boards on which members of the public were able to post material. An individual who used the

---

[43]   [2002] 1 WLR 2033 at 2042.
[44]   x*Totalise PLC v The Motley Fool* [2001] EWCA Civ 1897, 19 December 2001.
[45]   [2001] EWCA Civ 1897, (19 December 2001), para 30.
[46]   *EMI Records (Ireland) Ltd v Eircom Ltd* [2005] 4 IR 148.
[47]   *Totalise PLC v The Motley Fool* [2001] EMLR 750.

'nom de web'[48] 'Z Dust' used this facility to publish defamatory statements making allegations *inter alia* that the plaintiff's competence and integrity were questionable and that the plaintiff was on the brink of collapse. Owen J held that these statements were 'plainly defamatory'.[49] He was asked to make an order in the following terms:

'The defendants do forthwith disclose to the claimant ... (a) the full name and address of Z Dust, the author of defamatory postings on the defendant's websites, and (b) all documents which are or have been in their possession custody or power relating to the identity of Z Dust.'[50]

Owen J held that it was not necessary for the plaintiff to establish that it intended to take any further legal action against Z Dust, once the poster's true identity was revealed. [51] The defendants also invited the court to consider whether or not it was appropriate to make a Norwich Pharmacal order in the light of the duty imposed upon data controllers by the Data Protection Principles and, in particular, the restrictions placed on the disclosure of data. Owen J referred to s 35 of the UK's Data Protection Act 1998:

'(1) Personal data are exempt from the non-disclosure provisions where the disclosure is required by or under any enactment by any rule of law or by order of a court;

(2) Personal data are exempt from the non-disclosure provisions where the disclosure is necessary:

(a) for the purpose of connection with any legal proceedings including prospective legal proceedings; or

(b) for the purpose of obtaining legal advice or as otherwise necessary for the purposes of establishing, exercising or defending legal rights.'

[18.12] It was held by Owen J that the above preserved and did not restrict the Norwich Pharmacal principles. It is submitted that the position is even clearer in Ireland, where the Irish equivalent of the above provides that:

'Any restrictions in this Act on the disclosure of personal data do not apply if the disclosure is ... required by or under any enactment or by a rule of law or order of a court ... (or) ... required for the purposes of obtaining legal advice or for the purposes of, or in the course of, legal proceedings in which the person making the disclosure is a party or a witness.'[52]

The extension of the exemption to 'legal proceedings in which the person making the disclosure is a party or a witness' would appear to create an explicit exemption for orders such as Norwich Pharmacal. In conclusion, Owen J had to decide how to exercise his discretion. In doing so, he was satisfied on five points: (1) much of Z Dust's content was defamatory and the plaintiff had demonstrated a strong prima facie case against Z Dust; (2) the defamatory material was of a very serious nature; (3) the concerted campaign waged by Z Dust, which had a vast potential audience and no geographical

---

48 [2001] EMLR 750 at 753.
49 [2001] EMLR 750 at 753.
50 [2001] EMLR 750 at 752.
51 Citing *X Ltd v Morgan Grampian* [1991] 1 AC 3.
52 Data Protection Acts 1988–2003, s 8.

limit, was a very considerable threat to the plaintiff; (4) Z Dust was hiding behind the anonymity afforded to them by the defendants; and, (5) the plaintiff had no means other than a Norwich Pharmacal order of identifying Z Dust. In balance, Owen J stated that:

'I am mindful of the fact that both defendants have a policy of confidentiality with regard to personal information relating to those using its websites and do not wish to deviate from that policy. But the claimant argues that it simply wants the author of the Z Dust postings to take responsibility for his actions, and that, when balancing the interests of those parties, the respect for and protection of privacy of those who choose to air their views in the most public of for a must take second place to the obligation imposed upon those who become involved in the tortuous acts of others to assist the party injured by those acts.'[53]

Owen J therefore found in favour of the plaintiff and granted the order sought stating that:

'I have no hesitation in finding that the balance weighs heavily in favour of granting the relief sought. To find otherwise would be to give the clearest indication to those who wish to defame that they can do so with impunity behind the screen of anonymity made possible by the use of websites on the Internet.'[54]

John v Express Newspapers

[18.13] In *Elton John and others v Express Newspapers*,[55] a well known singer was involved in a legal dispute. He sought legal advice, Counsel was instructed, and advices sought. A copy of the draft advices was supplied to a journalist from within Counsel's chambers, and an injunction was then granted restraining publication. The copy of the advices was subsequently posted on the Internet. Although the chambers were concerned about this security breach, no investigation was undertaken. So, the plaintiff sought an injunction seeking to force the defendant to identify the person who had disclosed the advices to the journalist. An injunction was granted at trial on the grounds *inter alia* that 'there could be within the chambers a sense of mistrust if the perpetrator was not detected.'[56] The injunction was overturned on appeal, Woolf MR stating that:

'(t)he disclosure was not established to be necessary in the interests of justice and, even if it had been, the judge should have exercised his discretion to refuse disclosure. In our view it is important that, when orders are made requiring journalists to depart from their normal professional standards, the merits of their doing so in the public interest are clearly demonstrated. If the judge's order were to be allowed to stand, there would be a real danger that this would not be the position here. The decision would be wrongly interpreted as an example of lawyers attaching a disproportionate significance to the danger to their professional privilege while undervaluing the interests of journalists and thus the public. ... Although there has now been a publication on the Internet of the contents of the advice, which suggests that there is an individual at some stage of the chain who is motivated to cause mischief to the claimants, this is still a one-off infringement of professional legal

---

53 *Totalise PLC v The Motley Fool* [2001] EMLR 750 at 757.
54 At 757–758.
55 *Elton John and others v Express Newspapers* (2000) 1 WLR 1931.
56 (2000) 1 WLR 1931 at 1939.

confidentiality which does not justify making an inroad on the other privilege, the privilege of the journalist.'[57]

Takenaka (UK) v Frankl[58]

[18.14] An example of how Norwich Pharmacal relief can enable the identification of even a wrongdoer who has gone to considerable lengths to hide their identity is given by the English Court of Appeal decision in *Takenaka (UK) v Frankl*. The defendant denied sending three defamatory emails to the plaintiff, but '(w)ith considerable effort and a series of Norwich Pharmacal proceedings against various internet service providers including HotMail and I think also Compuserve, the claimants came to the conclusion that the emails emanated from a computer located in Turkey'.[59] The plaintiffs were able to link this computer to the defendant. When the computer was examined it was found that that the 'hard disk ... had been subjected ... to the most extensive corruption'. The plaintiff 's expert concluded that there had been 'a deliberate attempt ... to destroy material and that the operator on that date had intended to create the impression of enthusiastic and uninformed searching, browsing and copying.'[60] The plaintiff 's expert 'found that what was left on the hard disk was quite sufficient, when viewed in conjunction with the information obtained from the Norwich Pharmacal proceedings to enable him to conclude that the three relevant emails had emanated from the computer examined by him and that the author was the defendant.'[61] In contrast, the defendant claimed that 'somebody else was setting him up and interfering with his computer in order to make it appear as if he had sent three defamatory emails.'[62] Ultimately, the Court of Appeal held in favour of the plaintiff and the defendant's attempt to overturn an award of damages for defamation, made against him, failed.

Grant v Google UK

[18.15] In *Grant v Google UK*[63] the plaintiff owned the copyright in a book, which appeared on the Internet prior to publication. The book could be downloaded for free from a website, which was publicised by adverts provided by the defendant. This website 'had been registered through a company called Domains By Proxy, which is said to specialise in the cloaking of the identity of domain owners. Requests ... have failed to reveal the identity of the owners of the website.'[64] Instead the plaintiff applied for Norwich Pharmacal relief against the defendant, and was granted such an order by Rimer J in the Chancery Division of the English High Court.

---

[57] Leave to appeal to the House of Lords was refused. See [2000] I WLR 2039.
[58] *Takenaka (UK) v Frankl* [2001] EWCA Civ 348.
[59] [2001] EWCA Civ 348, para 3.
[60] [2001] EWCA Civ 348, para 9.
[61] [2001] EWCA Civ 348, para 10.
[62] [2001] EWCA Civ 348, para 17.
[63] *Grant v Google UK* [2005] EWHC 3444 (Ch).
[64] [2005] EWHC 3444 (Ch), para 2.

EMI Records v Eircom and BT Communications

[18.16] In *EMI Records v Eircom and BT Communications*, the plaintiffs sought Norwich Pharmacal orders 'requiring the defendants to make disclosure of the names and addresses of 17 of their subscribers'. These subscribers were 'internet subscribers who are designated by what is called an Internet Protocol Address'. The plaintiffs had been 'assigned the copyright in a large number of sound recordings' and belonged to the Irish Recorded Music Association (IRMA). IRMA employed experts to 'investigate and gather evidence of what were perceived as activities which infringed the plaintiff's copyright'. Kelly J was satisfied 'that there is prima facie demonstration of a wrongful activity'[65] in that:

> 'certain computers connected to the Internet via the Defendant's facilities have been used to make available to the public a significant volume of sound recordings, the copyright in which has been exclusively licensed to the plaintiffs'.

In other words, Kelly J was satisfied that the plaintiffs had discharged their burden under *Megaleasing UK Ltd v Barrett* of establishing 'very clear evidence of wrongdoing,'[66] the wrongdoing in question being 'infringement of the plaintiff's copyright'. Kelly J was satisfied that the defendants could identify the wrongdoers in question:

> '(i)t has been possible to download from these computers sample recordings and so to identify the internet protocol addresses which have been allocated by the Defendants to the computers in question'.

[18.17] Kelly J then set out how the alleged wrongdoers might be identified from the protocol addresses:

> '(w)hen the computer of a subscriber connects from time to time to one of the Defendant internet service providers it allocates a unique number which is this Internet Protocol Address. When downloading the sample recordings in these proceedings that address allocated to the computer for which the sample recording and other recordings were being made was recorded. It is the names and addresses of the subscribers to whom these Internet protocol addresses were allocated that is now being sought'.

Kelly J noted that the defendants accepted that the only way that the plaintiffs could acquire the names and addresses of the subscribers in question was by bringing the action before him. Kelly J considered the obligation of confidentiality owed by the defendants to their subscribers, but, given the evidence of wrongdoing before him, he concluded that:

> 'whether the right to confidentiality arises by statute or by contract or at common law, it cannot be relied on by a wrongdoer or a person against whom there is evidence of wrongdoing to protect his identity. The right to privacy or confidentiality of identity must

---

[65] *EMI Records v Eircom and BT Communications* [2005] 4 IR 148 at 151. Kelly J added 'that there is neither a suggestion nor evidence of any wrongdoing on the part of the individual Defendants'.

[66] *Megaleasing UK Ltd v Barrett* [1993] ILRM 497 at 504.

give way where there is prima facie evidence of wrongdoing.[67] There is such evidence here.'

[18.18] Kelly J inserted two safeguards into the order that he made. Firstly, he required that the plaintiffs give an undertaking to the effect that information disclosed pursuant to the order would only be used for the purpose of seeking redress in respect of copyright infringements in sound recordings for which the plaintiffs held exclusive licences. Secondly, the plaintiffs were required to undertake:

'not to disclose to the general public, by making or issuing a statement to the media, the names and addresses of any person or persons whose identity is made known to the(m) ... as a result of the grant of the relief ordered ... until after the (plaintiffs) have begun the process of enforcing their copyright ... against such person.'

Kelly J thought that this latter undertaking was probably unnecessary. However, he made his order conditional upon the giving of such an undertaking stating that:

'this is being done in protection of the rights and entitlements of the subscribers because it may turn out that they were not in fact guilty of any wrongdoing ... Therefore, their identity ought to be protected so as to ensure that it does not come into the public domain, save in circumstances where it arises in the context of infringement proceedings.'

Kelly J ordered that the defendants disclose the following information in respect of each subscriber:

(a) name;

(b) postal address; and

(c) telephone number.[68]

---

[67] In addition to *Norwich Pharmacal* there is another relevant line of case law where the courts have permitted the breach of individuals' privacy: that is where the defendant in personal injury action has sought to verify the details of the plaintiff's claim. There are a number of cases where the courts have sanctioned the monitoring or other invasion of the plaintiff 's privacy (See *Nason v Cork Corporation* (12 April 1991, unreported), HC (Keane J); *Shelly Morris v Dublin Bus* [2003] 1 IR 232; and *Conor O'Connor v Dublin Bus* [2003] 4 IR 459). However, these cases can be distinguished from *EMI Records v Eircom and BT Communications*, as in these cases the plaintiff had initiated the litigation in question and should have been aware when he initiated his claim that the defendant would be entitled to take such steps as were necessary to verify the details of his claim. In effect, his consent to such breaches of privacy might be implied from the initiation of his claim. And it is clear from the judgment of the Supreme Court in *McGrory v ESB* ([2003] 3 IR 407) that should the plaintiff become unhappy with the nature of the breaches being taken, then the plaintiff would always have the option of staying or discontinuing their claim.

[68] Following the disclosure of this information, IRMA 'took cases against 17 individuals and companies. Of these, 12 settled out of court at an average of €2,500 each. IRMA is suing a further three and is considering its legal options in the two remaining cases'. (2005) The Irish Times, 16 November. In June 2007 another order was granted by the High Court 'requiring seven internet service providers (ISPs) to release the names and addresses of 23 people involved in sharing copyrighted music online', Collins, 'Irma to get web users' details' (2007) The Irish Times, 8 June.

[18.19] In *EMI Records v Eircom and BT Communications*, Kelly J was bound, by two separate decisions of the Supreme Court[69] to apply the judgment of the House of Lords in *Norwich Pharmacal v Customs and Excise Commissioners*. Unfortunately, that judgment long predates the domestic recognition of the European Convention on Human Rights by both Irish and English law. As a result, it fails to afford the persons whose identity was to be disclosed on foot of the order 'an opportunity of asserting a claim of privilege and any other claim to privacy which the Constitution or law would leave open to them, without having their identities disclosed to the … plaintiff.'[70] As a consequence, 'the person most concerned' with the preservation of their anonymity is not present in court. These authors would argue that the Norwich Pharmacal order should be adapted to allow the person who is to be identified to appear without losing their anonymity. And, if they did appear, they might well argue in a similar case that the evidence by which they had been identified would have been inadmissible. Each of these arguments will be considered in turn below.

Claims of privilege and privacy

[18.20] It can be argued that the procedure set out in *Norwich Pharmacal v Customs and Excise Commissioners* should not be rigidly applied in Ireland. Under the Norwich Pharmacal procedure, the third party whose identity is sought has no effective right of audience. As Kelly J pointed out in *EMI Records v Eircom*, the defendants were 'concerned because they owe duties of confidentiality to their subscribers.'[71] And, Kelly J made his decision by:

> 'balancing the rights of the plaintiffs with the obligations of the defendants towards their subscribers and the rights of those subscribers. These obligations are obligations of confidentiality or privacy. These duties of confidentiality owed by the defendants to their subscribers and the subscribers entitlements may arise under statute, by contract or at common law.'[72]

It would appear from the above passage that Kelly J made his decision by balancing the obligation of confidentiality owed by the defendants to their subscribers with the rights of the plaintiff. Kelly J does not refer to the guarantee owed by the state, under the Constitution and the European Convention on Human Rights, to preserve the confidentiality and privacy of the subscribers in question. And, the reason why he did not consider those guarantees may be that the Norwich Pharmacal procedure does not contain any mechanism by which the subscribers to whom that guarantee has been given could seek to enforce them in the Norwich Pharmacal proceedings. There is a good

---

[69]   *Megaleasing UK Ltd v Barrett* [1993] ILRM 497 and *Doyle v The Commissioner of An Garda Síochána* [1999] 1 IR 249.

[70]   *IO'T v The Rotunda Girls Aid Society* [1998] 2 IR 321 at 353.

[71]   *EMI Records v Eircom and BT Communications* [2005] 4 IR 148 at 152.

[72]   Similarly in *Totalise PLC v The Motley Fool*, the Court of Appeal commented that: 'We … believe that it is legitimate for a party, such as Interactive, who reasonably agrees to keep information confidential and private to refuse to voluntarily hand over such information… we are not convinced that Interactive were free to hand over the material without coming to a view on the merits. That was not their task. The position could have been different, if they were in some way implicated or involved in the wrongful act' [2001] EWCA Civ 1897, para 28.

reason why such mechanism is not provided by the Norwich Pharmacal procedure: such guarantees were not offered to citizens of the UK in 1973 when the House of Lords heard the case of *Norwich Pharmacal v Customs and Excise Commissioners*. Even now, there is good reason to believe that the right to privacy granted by the House of Lords' decision in *Campbell v MGN* is far inferior to that afforded to Irish citizens. The argument can be made that a mechanism, similar to that approved by the Supreme Court in *IO'T v B and The Rotunda Girls Aid Society,* should be provided to those who are the subject of a Norwich Pharmacal order. Arguably, the subjects of Norwich Pharmacal orders should be afforded 'an opportunity of asserting a claim of privilege and any other claim to privacy which the Constitution or law would leave open to them, without having their identities disclosed to the … plaintiff.'[73]

[18.21] Such an approach would appear to have the endorsement of the English Court of Appeal. In *Totalise PLC v The Motley Fool*, the award of costs was appealed by one of the defendants. Giving judgment for the court, Aldous LJ made the following *obiter* comments:

'(i)n a case such as the present, and particularly since the coming into force on 2 October 2000 of the Human Rights Act 1998, the court must be careful not to make an order which unjustifiably invades the right of an individual to respect for his private life, especially when that individual is in the nature of things not before the court: see the Human Rights Act 1998, s 6, and the European Convention on Human Rights, arts 10 and (arguably at least) 6(1). There is nothing in art 10 … (to support the) … contention that it protects the named but not the anonymous, and there are many situations in which … the protection of a person's identity from disclosure may be legitimate.'

It is difficult to see how the court can carry out this task if what it is refereeing is a contest between two parties, neither of whom is the person most concerned, the data subject; one of whom is the data subject's prospective antagonist; and the other of whom knows the data subject's identity, has undertaken to keep it confidential so far as the law permits, and would like to get out of the cross-fire as rapidly and as cheaply as possible. However the website operator can, where appropriate, tell the user what is going on and to offer to pass on in writing to the claimant and the court any worthwhile reason the user wants to put forward for not having his or her identity disclosed. Further, the Court could require that to be done before making an order. Doing so will enable the court to do what is required of it with slightly more confidence that it is respecting the law laid down in more than one statute by Parliament and doing no injustice to a third party, in particular not violating his convention rights.'[74]

---

[73] *IO'T v B and The Rotunda Girls Aid Society* [1998] 2 IR 321 at 353. Although it could be argued that the decision in *IO'T v B and The Rotunda Girls Aid Society* can be distinguished from the decision in *EMI Records v Eircom and BT Communications*. There was not allegation in *IO'T v B and The Rotunda Girls Aid Society* that the applicant's birth mother, whose identity was sought by the applicant, was guilty of any wrongdoing [1998] 2 IR 321 at 351. However, Kelly J was satisfied that there was prima facie evidence of wrongdoing in *EMI Records v Eircom and BT Communications*.

[74] *Totalise PLC v The Motley Fool* [2001] EWCA Civ 1897 (19 December 2001), paras 25–26.

[18.22] The argument can be made that the courts have not permitted the bringing of actions anonymously in other cases[75]and so should not permit a third party to make anonymous submissions in a Norwich Pharmacal application. However, the position of an applicant who sought to bring an action anonymously in *Re Ansbacher (Cayman) Ltd*[76] would seem rather different to the position of a person whose identity is being sought by way of a Norwich Pharmacal order. Furthermore, the provision of a mechanism by which the subject of a Norwich Pharmacal order could make submissions to the court would seem to be in accordance with the judgment of the European Court of Human Rights (ECtHR) in *Matheron v France*.[77] The applicant had been prosecuted for international drug trafficking. Evidence gathered from phone taps which had been admitted in the trial of a co-defendant was used in his trial. The applicant argued that this evidence was inadmissible, but the trial court ruled that it had no jurisdiction as the material had already been deemed admissible elsewhere. The applicant complained to the ECtHR. He argued that evidence against him had been obtained from telephone tapping in separate proceedings. Not being a party to those proceedings, he had been unable to contest their validity. The ECtHR examined whether or not an 'effective control' had been available to the applicant to challenge the evidence derived from the monitoring of telephone calls. It was clear to the ECtHR that the applicant had been unable to intervene in the proceedings in which the order to monitor telephone calls had been made. The ECtHR was of the view that the reasoning followed by the French courts could lead to decisions that would deprive a number of people, namely those against whom evidence obtained from telephone tapping in separate proceedings was used, of the protection afforded by French law. Therefore, the ECtHR found that the applicant had not had access to 'effective control' allowing him to contest the validity of the evidence obtained through telephone tapping. The ECtHR therefore concluded that there had been a violation of art 8 of the European Convention on Human Rights. Of course, it could be argued that any person who is the subject of a Norwich Pharmacal order will have an opportunity to contest the gathering of evidence against them when they are served with separate proceedings by the plaintiff. However, such an argument disregards the reality that the loss of anonymity that follows from the making of a Norwich Pharmacal order is itself a substantial interference in the subject's right to privacy.

[18.23] Should a court decide to adopt such a mechanism, then the decision of the Supreme Court decision in *IO'T v B and The Rotunda Girls Aid Society* suggests the following procedure. First to be decided is the issue between the plaintiff who seeks the identity of the subject and the defendant who is obliged to keep the subject's identity confidential. Then, if the court decides that the defendant should reveal the subject's identity, prior to doing so, the court should afford the subject an opportunity to be heard.

---

[75] See *Re Ansbacher (Cayman) Ltd* [2002] 2 IR 517 and *Roe v The Blood Transfusion Service Board* [1996] 3 IR 67.

[76] [2002] 2 IR 517.

[77] *Matheron v France* (29 March 2005) ECtHR.

Admissibility of evidence[78]

[18.24] Unfortunately, the judgment in *EMI Records v Eircom and BT Communications* does not give a detailed account as to how the plaintiffs came by the Internet protocol addresses, the names and addresses of whose subscribers were sought. Kelly J states that:

'It is not necessary for me to set out in any detail the way in which (the plaintiffs') investigation was carried out and the various technical matters that are addressed in some detail in the affidavit evidence which has been placed before the court'.

The only details given into how the plaintiffs' evidence obtained the Internet protocol addresses of the defendant's subscribers in *EMI Records v Eircom and BT Communications* are set out as follows:

'It has been possible to download from these computers sample recordings and so to identify the internet protocol addresses which have been allocated by the defendants to the computers in question ... When the computer of a subscriber connects from time to time to one of the defendant Internet service providers it allocates a unique number which is this Internet Protocol Address. When downloading the sample recordings in these proceedings th(e) address allocated to the computer for which the sample recording and other recordings were being made was recorded'.

[18.25] It is not clear from the above whether the downloading of the sample recordings and the identification or recording of the Internet protocol address is a single process or two separate, albeit integrated, processes. There are a number of statutory provisions that might apply to a process such as that set out in the judgment of Kelly J. The first of these is the Postal and Telecommunications Services Act 1983, which provides that a:

'person who ... intercepts ... telecommunications messages being transmitted ... or who discloses the existence, substance or purport of any such message which has been intercepted or uses for any purpose any information obtained from any such message shall be guilty of an offence.'[79]

[18.26] So, could the downloading of a sound recording over the Internet amount to interception? Probably not. However, in *EMI Records v Eircom and BT Communications* the sound recording downloaded appears to have been irrelevant to the identification of the subscribers in question. What was of significance was the Internet protocol addresses which the plaintiff's experts recorded at the time of downloading. The key questions are where was the Internet protocol address recorded from and how was it recorded? If the address was downloaded together with the sound recording, then

---

[78] Other criticisms have been made of cases such as this. It has been noted that BREIN, the Dutch equivalent of IRMA, lost a similar case based upon evidence gathered by the same company as was used by the plaintiffs in *EMI Records v Eircom and BT Communications:* '(p)rivacy concerns underpinned much of the decision and, although BREIN is unlikely to give up the fight, it was significant that the court was not satisfied that the internet addresses submitted by BREIN were connected to the individuals whose details were sought. In fact, the Dutch ISPs demonstrated that the US company and BREIN had made numerous errors in making these connections. It is not unheard of for technical investigations to identify 'false positives'. Nolan, 'IRMA legal case not open and shut' (2005) The Irish Times, 19 August.

[79] Postal and Telecommunications Services Act 1983, s 98(1).

it could not be said to be intercepted.[80] Or rather it could be said that the sender of the sound recording had consented to the downloading of both the sound recording and the recording of the Internet protocol address simultaneously. [81] However, if the Internet protocol address was recorded in a process which was separate from the downloading of the sound recording, it could certainly be argued that this was an interception for the purposes of the Postal and Telecommunications Services Act 1983. Section 98(1) requires that both the recipient and the sender of a message must consent to the recording or interception of that message. If the sound recording and the Internet protocol addresses were transmitted separately, then the person who initiated the transmission could argue that whilst he consented to the downloading of the sample recording, he did not consent to the recording of his Internet protocol address. Section 98(1) cannot be interpreted in isolation. It must be interpreted in accordance with Directive 2002/58, which imposes an obligation on member states to ensure the confidentiality of communications. Directive 2002/58 provides that:

> '(m)ember States shall ensure the confidentiality of communications and the related traffic data by means of a public communications network and publicly available electronic communications services, through national legislation. In particular, they shall prohibit listening, tapping, storage or other kinds of interception or surveillance of communications and the related traffic data by persons other than users, without the consent of the users concerned.'[82]

[18.27] This provision protects the confidentiality of both communications and traffic data. Both terms have very broad meaning. 'Communication' is defined as 'any information exchanged or conveyed between a finite number of parties by means of a publicly available electronic communications service.'[83] 'Traffic data' is defined as 'any data processed for the purpose of the conveyance of a communication on an electronic communications network or for the billing thereof.'[84] The recitals explain the link between communications and traffic data in the following terms:

> 'communication may include any naming, numbering or addressing information provided by the sender of a communication or the user of a connection to carry out the communication. Traffic data may include any translation of this information by the network over which the communication is transmitted for the purpose of carrying out the transmission.[85]'

---

[80] However, if this were so, then it could be argued that the Internet protocol address was 'calling line data' and that art 8 of Directive 2002/58 would then apply. If this were so, then the defendants should have offered their subscribers 'the possibility, using a simple means and free of charge, of preventing the presentation of the calling line identification on a per-call basis' (Directive 2002/58, art 8(1)).

[81] However, unless the plaintiffs' expert openly identified himself on the network as working for IRMA, the validity of that consent would be very much open to question, see *DPP v Dillon* [2002] 4 IR 501.

[82] Directive 2002/58, art 5(1).

[83] Directive 2002/58, art 2(d).

[84] Directive 2002/58, art 2(b).

[85] Directive 2002/58, recital 15.

[18.28] It is clear from Directive 2002/58 on Privacy on Electronic Communication Networks that both communications and traffic data that are related to those communications must be kept confidential. It would therefore seem quite possible that an Internet protocol address could be either communication or traffic data or, indeed, both. The recitals to Directive 2002/58 suggest that an Internet protocol address may well be traffic data providing that:

> '(t)raffic data may, *inter alia*, consist of data referring to the routing, duration, time or volume of a communication, to the protocol used, to the location of the terminal equipment of the sender or recipient, to the network on which the communication originates or terminates, to the beginning, end or duration of a connection'

It would not seem unreasonable to suggest that an Internet protocol address could be data referring to 'the routing ... of a communication'; 'the location of the terminal equipment of the sender'; or 'to the network to which the communication originates'. If s 98(1) of the Postal and Telecommunications Act 1983 is interpreted in accordance with Directive 2002/58, it is quite possible that a court would find that an Internet protocol address is a 'telecommunications message' for the purposes of that section. For a breach of s 98(1) to occur, the interception of such a message would have to occur. 'Interception' is defined as:

> 'to listen to, or record by any means, in the course of its transmission, a telecommunications message[86]but does not include such listening or recording where either the person on whose behalf the message is transmitted or the person intended to receive the message has consented to the listening or recording, and cognate words shall be construed accordingly.'[87]

[18.29] Clearly, nobody can 'listen to' an Internet protocol address. However, such an address can be recorded. In *EMI Records v Eircom and BT Communications* the plaintiff's experts obtained Internet protocol addresses in question by the following method: 'th(e) (internet prorocol) address allocated to the computer for which the sample recording and other recordings were being made was recorded'. Compliance with the Data Protection Acts 1988–2003 raises a separate set of issues. Unfortunately, the judgment does not explain how the plaintiffs' experts complied with the Data Protection Acts 1988–2003, but it must be assumed that they did. Again, it is not possible to ascertain exactly how the plaintiffs' experts went about gathering the evidence in question. It may well be that they accessed some form of peer-to-peer network, such as Grokster, and commenced sharing files.[88] However, the experts in

---

[86] The argument could be made that an Internet protocol address was not a 'telecommunications message' for the purposes of s 98. This term is not defined by Irish law. However, it has to be interpreted in accordance with Directive 2002/58, which protects the confidentiality of both telecommunications messages and 'traffic data'. Section 98(1) of the Post and Telecommunications Act 1983.

[87] Section 98(5) of the Postal and Telecommunications Act 1983 as inserted by the Ireland Interception of Postal Packets and Telecommunications Messages (Regulation) Act 1993, s 13(2).

[88] An entrapment argument, that the plaintiffs' experts were acting as *agents provocateurs* might be made. However, even if they were (and they probably weren't) this would not necessarily render their evidence inadmissible: see *Dental Board v O'Callaghan* [1969] IR 181, but contrast this with the decision of *DPP v Dillon* [2002] 4 IR 501.

question would still have to comply with the Data Protection Acts 1988–2003, which require that data be fairly obtained. In particular, the Data Protection Acts 1988–2003 provides that personal data cannot be fairly obtained unless the following information is disclosed to the data subject from whom it is obtained[89]:

(a)   'the identity of the data controller';

(b)   'the purpose or purposes for which the data are intended to be processed';

(c)   'and any other information which is necessary, having regard to the specific circumstances in which the data are or are to be processed, to enable processing in respect of the data to be fair to the data subject'.[90]

[18.30] The argument could be made that when logging on to a peer-to-peer network, experts in a case such as this should disclose to other users that the purpose of them logging onto the network was to gather personal data.[91] They should state that this data would be controlled by their employer and that the purpose of their gathering this data was to enable their employer to initiate court proceedings against alleged wrongdoers. The Data Protection Acts 1988–2003 exempt from its restrictions data processing that is 'required for the purpose of preventing, detecting or investigating offences (or) apprehending or prosecuting offenders.'[92] What was alleged by the plaintiffs in *EMI Records v Eircom and BT Communications* could certainly amount to a criminal offence.[93] The difficulty which the plaintiffs would have encountered in availing of this exemption was that a Norwich Pharmacal order is civil relief and there was no suggestion that they intended to prosecute the subscribers for any offence. Had a prosecution been in prospect, then it is suggested that the appropriate procedure would be that of seeking an order pursuant to s 52 of the Criminal Justice (Theft and Fraud Offences) Act 2001. The argument could also be made that s 8(b) of the Data Protection Acts 1988–2003 only applies to activities of the state, as it implements art 3(2) of the Data Protection Directive, which exempts only 'the activities of the State in areas of criminal law'

[18.31] The judgment does not provide any detailed information as to how the Internet protocol addresses in question were obtained, but Kelly J was satisfied that:

> 'Each of the statutory entitlements, whether they arise under the Data Protection legislation or the Postal and Telecommunications legislation, are subject to a provision which permits of the confidentiality to be legitimately breached by an order of the Court'.

---

[89]   Data Protection Acts 1988–2003, s 2D(1).

[90]   Data Protection Acts 1988–2003, s 2D(2).

[91]   Personal data is defined as 'data relating to a living individual who is or can be identified either from the data or from the data in conjunction with other information that is in, or is likely to come into, the possession of the data controller' (Data Protection Acts 1988–2003, s 1(1)). The Internet protocol addresses obtained in *EMI Records v Eircom and BT Communications* would seem to fall within this definition, as it was ultimately possible to identify the data subjects from it. Indeed identification of those subjects was the entire purpose of the proceedings in question.

[92]   Data Protection Acts 1988–2003, s 8(b).

[93]   For example, CRRA 2000–2004, s 140(1)(e) makes it an offence to make a work 'available to the public to such an extent as to prejudice the interests of the owner of the copyright'.

Kelly J did not identify which provisions of that legislation he is referring. It is certainly true that the Data Protection Acts 1988–2003 will allow the breach of confidential information pursuant to a court order[94] as will the Postal and Telecommunications Services Act 1983.[95] And, this may well be what Kelly J was referring to: should he order the disclosure of the information sought by the plaintiffs, then neither enactment could prevent that order being enforced. However, if in a subsequent case it were to be shown that evidence had been obtained contrary to either the Postal and Telecommunications Services Act 1983 or the Data Protection Acts 1988–2003, then a future court might hesitate before issuing a Norwich Pharmacal order on the basis of that information. The gathering of evidence in a manner contrary to law would be a breach of the privacy of the individual in question. The Constitution guarantees that the State will use 'its laws to respect, and, as far as practicable ... defend and vindicate the personal rights of citizens'.[96] One of those rights is the right to privacy. And, it is clear from the decision of Hamilton P in *Kennedy and Arnold v Ireland*[97] that monitoring the communications of citizens is an 'interference ... with the telephonic communications of the plaintiffs and such interference constitutes an infringement of the constitutional rights to privacy of the three plaintiffs.'[98]

[18.32] Article 8 of the European Convention on Human Rights has a similar effect, providing that rights under that article can only be interfered with 'in accordance with the law'.[99] Under the exclusionary rule, evidence obtained by unconstitutional means is usually inadmissible before the courts.[100]

---

94 Data Protection Acts 1988–2003, s 8(e).
95 Postal and Telecommunications Services Act 1983, s 98(2A)(d), inserted by the Interception of Postal Packets and Telecommunications Messages Act 1993, s 13(2) provides: that '(a) person ... who discloses to any person an y in formation concerning the use made of telecommunications services provided for any other person by the company shall be guilty of an offence unless the disclosure is made ... in pursuance of an order of a court'.
96 Bunreacht na hÉireann, Article 40.3.1°.
97 Bunreacht na hÉireann, Article 40.3.1°.
   Kennedy and Arnold v Ireland [1987] IR 587.
98 [1987] IR 587 at 593.
99 ECHR, art 8(2).
100 'I am satisfied that the correct principle is that evidence obtained by the invasion of the constitutional personal rights of the citizen must be excluded unless a court is satisfied that either the act constituting the breach of constitutional rights was committed unintentionally or accidentally, or is satisfied that there are extraordinary excusing circumstances' per Finlay CJ, *The People (DPP) v Kenny* [1990] 2 IR 110. In *Universal City Studios v Mulligan (No 2)* [1999] 3 IR 392, Laffoy J applied the exclusionary rule in a case of copyright infringement stating that: '(a)lthough this is a civil action, I am satisfied that as a matter of principle the exclusionary rule laid down by the Supreme Court in *The People (DPP) v Kenny* ... in relation to the admissibility in criminal trials of evidence obtained by invasion of the constitutional rights of a citizen is applicable': at 404.

PART VI: ECOMMERCE

Chapter 19

Electronic Contracts, Signatures and Documents

Introduction

[19.01] The Internet is a global market, which is what really makes e-commerce different from traditional forms of business. Anyone who establishes a website can sell anything to anywhere in the world. This is particularly significant in Europe, where the EC has long struggled to make the internal market a reality. The Internet allows goods and services to flow seamlessly and electronically across internal borders. The creation an internal market is more than a legal obligation for the EC; it is one of the EC's fundamental principles:

> 'the activities of the Community shall include ... an internal market characterised by the abolition, as between Member States, of obstacles to the free movement of goods, persons, services and capital.'[1]

This obligation must be read together with others such as the obligation to develop a '... common commercial policy.'[2] and the obligation to ensure 'the approximation of the laws of Member States to the extent required for the functioning of the common market.'[3] The Treaty on the European Community (TEC) defines the internal market in the following terms:

> 'The internal market shall comprise an area without internal frontiers in which the free movement of goods, persons, services and capital is ensured in accordance with the provisions of this Treaty.'[4]

[19.02] The TEC then goes on to state:

> 'The Council shall ... adopt the measures for the approximation of the provisions laid down by law, regulation or administrative action in Member States which have as their object the establishment and functioning of the internal market.'[5]

These provisions give the EC the ability to introduce the legislation that is being used to create the internal market. Europe is now a union of 459 million people, 4.29 million (or a little less than 1%) of whom reside in Ireland. Given this disparity, it is inevitable that much of Ireland's ecommerce activity is focused on the wider European market. So when one is discussing Ireland's ecommerce laws, one is really discussing the implementation of European ecommerce laws in Ireland. It should also be kept in mind that the internal market and other provisions of the TEC make it illegal for Ireland to

---

[1] TEC, art 3(1)(c).
[2] TEC, art 3(1)(b).
[3] TEC, art 3(1)(h).
[4] TEC, art 14(2).
[5] TEC, art 95.

attempt to shield its domestic market from that of the wider European one. It should be noted that in recent years the EC has encountered some resistance from its member states in its efforts to build an internal market. This resistance was evident in the debate about the Services Directive[6] and also in relation to the enforcement of wage agreements that have been collectively negotiated by trade unions.[7] It should be noted that the European Commission is currently implementing its 2010 strategy which has the following priorities:

(i)   'the completion of a Single European Information Space which promotes an open and competitive internal market for information society and media';

(ii) 'strengthening Innovation and Investment in ICT research to promote growth and more and better jobs';

(iii) 'achieving an Inclusive European Information Society that promotes growth and jobs in a manner that is consistent with sustainable development and that prioritises better public services and quality of life.'[8]

[19.03] If objectives such as these are to be achieved, it would seem important to ensure that the information, documents and contracts generated by electronic services should have legal recognition. The Electronic Commerce Act 2000 provides this recognition, setting out a framework for the recognition of electronic contracts, signatures and documents. However, it does not force people to move from existing formats to electronic formats. The Act states that its provisions may not be construed as:

(a)   'requiring a person or public body to generate, communicate, produce, process, send, receive, record, retain, store or display any information, document or signature by or in electronic form, or ...

(b)   prohibiting a person or public body engaging in an electronic transaction from establishing reasonable requirements about the manner in which the person will accept electronic communications, electronic signatures or electronic forms of documents.'[9]

Electronic contracts

[19.04] A contract is a legally binding agreement between two or more people that must contain three essential elements:

(i)   the agreement is made by offer and acceptance of that offer;

(ii) there is a bargain, supported by consideration; and

(iii) the parties must have an intention to create legal relations.[10]

---

6   Minder, 'Services Bill' (2006) Financial Times, 15 February.

7   *Laval un Partneri Ltd v Svenska Byggnadsarbetareförbundet and Others* c-341/05, ECJ.

8   EC Commission, i2010 – A European Information Society for growth and employment, Brussels, 1 June 2005, COM(2005) 229 final.

9   Electronic Commerce Act 2000, s 24.

10 For a full discussion on the law of contract, see the following texts: Friel, *Law of Contract* (2nd edn, Round Hall Press, 2000); Clark, *Contract Law* (4th edn, Round Hall Sweet and Maxwell, 1998). See also Haigh, *Contract Law in an E-Commerce Age* (Round Hall, 2001).

The terms of the contract must be clear and complete, although terms may be implied into the contract from other sources including legislation. Some contracts must be a particular form; some must be supported by written evidence. For example, contracts for the sale of land or copyrights must be in writing. A mistake or misrepresentation may affect the validity of the contract and a consent obtained through duress or undue influence may also affect the enforceability of the contract. Electronic commerce could not function – would not exist – if consumers and businesses could not enter into legally enforceable contracts online. Legislation has been enacted to ensure that this does occur. Arguably such enactments were unnecessary in Ireland as the common law of contract could easily have adapted to the Internet in much the same way as it had previously adapted to the telephone and the telex machine. However, these enactments were in large part implementations of EC law and thus Ireland had no choice but to enact them.

Admissibility of electronic contracts

[19.05] The Directive on e-commerce requires that member states must recognise the validity of electronic contracts. They must:

> 'ensure that their legal system allows contracts to be concluded by electronic means. Member States shall in particular ensure that the legal requirements applicable to the contractual process neither create obstacles for the use of electronic contracts nor result in such contracts being deprived of legal effectiveness and validity on account of their having been made by electronic means.'[11]

The recitals make clear that member states are obliged to remove only 'obstacles resulting from legal requirements and not practical obstacles resulting from the impossibility of using electronic means in certain cases.'[12] These provisions are implemented in Ireland by the Electronic Commerce Act 2000 which provides that:

> 'In any legal proceedings, nothing in the application of the rules of evidence shall apply so as to deny the admissibility in evidence of ... an electronic contract ... on the sole ground that it is ... an electronic contract ... or ... if it is the best evidence that the person or public body adducing it could reasonably be expected to obtain, on the grounds that it is not in its original form.'[13]

[19.06] The Act defines an electronic contract as being one that is 'concluded wholly or partly by means of an electronic communication.[14]

Scope of the Electronic Commerce Act 2000

[19.07] The Directive on e-Commerce provides that member states are not obliged to remove obstacles to the recognition of electronic contracts in relation to those contracts that fall into one of the following categories:

(a)   contracts that create or transfer rights in real estate, except for rental rights;

(b)   contracts requiring by law the involvement of courts, public authorities or professions exercising public authority;

---

[11]   Directive on e-Commerce, art 9(1).
[12]   Directive on e-Commerce, Recital 37.
[13]   Electronic Commerce Act 2000, s 22(a).
[14]   Electronic Commerce Act 2000, s 2(1).

(c)   contracts of suretyship granted and on collateral securities furnished by persons acting for purposes outside their trade, business or profession; and

(d)   contracts governed by family law or by the law of succession.[15]

[19.08] Member states utilise one of the above exceptions, then they must inform the Commission, and submit a report every five years explaining why they are continuing to apply the exception.[16] The Directive on Electronic Signatures provides that it does not apply to:

> 'aspects related to the conclusion and validity of contracts or other legal obligations where there are requirements as regards form prescribed by national or Community law nor does it affect rules and limits, contained in national or Community law, governing the use of documents.'[17]

The Electronic Commerce Act 2000 states that its provisions do not prejudice the following laws and legislation:

(a)   the law governing the creation, execution, amendment, variation or revocation of—

>   (i)   a will, codicil or any other testamentary instrument to which the Succession Act, 1965, applies,
>
>   (ii)   a trust, or
>
>   (iii)   an enduring power of attorney,

(b)   the law governing the manner in which an interest in real property (including a leasehold interest in such property) may be created, acquired, disposed of or registered, other than contracts (whether or not under seal) for the creation, acquisition or disposal of such interests,

(c)   the law governing the making of an affidavit or a statutory or sworn declaration, or requiring or permitting the use of one for any purpose, or

(d)   the rules, practices or procedures of a court or tribunal, except to the extent that regulations … may from time to time prescribe.[18]

[19.09] The Act provides for the removal of items from this list by regulation where the Minister for Communications is of the opinion that:

(a)   technology has advanced to such an extent, and access to it is so widely available, or

(b)   … adequate procedures and practices have developed in public registration or other services, so as to warrant such action, or …

(c)   … the public interest so requires.

Then the Minister may 'after consultation with such Minister or Ministers as in the Minister's opinion has or have a sufficient interest or responsibility in relation to the matter' create regulations.[19]

---

[15]   Directive on e-Commerce, art 9(2).

[16]   Directive on e-Commerce, art 9(3).

[17]   Directive on Electronic Signatures, art 1.

[18]   Electronic Commerce Act 2000, s 10(1).

[19]   The regulation-making power is provided by the Electronic Commerce Act 2000, s 3.

This regulation must be:

> 'for the purpose of encouraging the efficient use of electronic communication facilities and services in commerce and the community generally while at the same time protecting the public interest, extend the application of this Act or a provision of this Act to or in relation to a matter specified ... (above) ... . subject to such conditions as he or she thinks fit, and the Act as so extended shall apply accordingly.'[20]

[19.10] This extension does not have to be permanent; it may be made on a trial basis[21] In addition, the Electronic Commerce Act 2000 states that it does not affect the following legislation:

(a) any law relating to the imposition, collection or recovery of taxation or other Government imposts, including fees, fines and penalties,

(b) the Companies Act, 1990 (Uncertificated Securities) Regulations, 1996 (S.I. No. 68 of 1996) or any regulations made in substitution for those regulations,

(c) the Criminal Evidence Act, 1992,

(d) the Consumer Credit Act, 1995, or any regulations made thereunder and the European Communities (Unfair Terms in Consumer Contracts) Regulations, 1995 (S.I. No. 27 of 1995).[22]

Formation of an electronic contract

[19.11] In general terms, a contract will be formed when an offer is accepted by another. The jurisdiction of the state where the contract is formed may have jurisdiction over any disputes relating to that Contract. There is some case law that tries to identify the location where a contract may be said to have been formed. In *Entores v Miles Far East Corporation*[23] the plaintiffs were an English company and the defendant was an American company that used a Dutch agent. The plaintiffs claimed that a contract had been made between them by means of a telex machine. This technology was described by Denning LJ (as he then was) in the following terms:

> 'Communications by Telex are comparatively new. Each company has a teleprinter machine in its office; and each has a Telex number like a telephone number. When one company wishes to send a message to the other, it gets the Post Office to connect up the machines. Then a clerk at one end taps the message on to his machine just as if it were a typewriter, and it is instantaneously passed to the machine at the other end, which automatically types the message onto paper at that end.'[24]

The plaintiffs argued that the contract was made in England from where the offer was sent and the acceptance was received; the defendants argued that the contract was made in the Netherlands where the offer was received and from where the acceptance was sent. The question that fell to be decided by the English Court of Appeal was the location

---

[20] Electronic Commerce Act 2000, s 10(2).

[21] Electronic Commerce Act 2000, s 10(3).

[22] Electronic Commerce Act 2000, s 11.

[23] *Entores v Miles Far East Corporation* [1955] 2 QB 327, [1955] 2 All ER 493, [1955] 3 WLR 48, [1955] 1 Lloyd's Rep 511, 17 May 1955.

[24] [1955] 3 WLR 48 at 49.

where the contract was made. Denning LJ began by distinguishing the position of electronic communications from that which had subsisted with regard to postal communications:

'When a contract is made by post it is clear law throughout the common law countries that the acceptance is complete as soon as the letter is put into the post box, and that is the place where the contract is made. But there is no clear rule about contracts made by telephone or by Telex. Communications by these means are virtually instantaneous and stand on a different footing.'[25]

[19.12] Denning LJ explained the law by setting out the following situations where contracts might be formed at a distance. The first related to a contract formed by shouting across a river:

'Suppose, for instance, that I shout an offer to a man across a river or a courtyard but I do not hear his reply because it is drowned by an aircraft flying overhead. There is no contract at that moment. If he wishes to make a contract, he must wait till the aircraft is gone and then shout back his acceptance so that I can hear what he says. Not until I have his answer am I bound.'[26]

The second situation concerned a contract formed by means of a telephone conversation:

'Suppose, for instance, that I make an offer to a man by telephone and, in the middle of his reply, the line goes 'dead' so that I do not hear his words of acceptance. There is no contract at that moment. The other man may not know the precise moment when the line failed. But he will know that the telephone conversation was abruptly broken off: because people usually say something to signify the end of the conversation. If he wishes to make a contract, he must therefore get through again so as to make sure that I heard. Suppose next, that the line does not go dead, but it is nevertheless so indistinct that I do not catch what he says and I ask him to repeat it. He then repeats it and I hear his acceptance. The contract is made, not on the first time when I do not hear, but only the second time when I do hear. If he does not repeat it, there is no contract. The contract is only complete when I have his answer accepting the offer.'[27]

[19.13] The final situation concerned a contract formed by means of an exchange of telexes:

'Suppose a clerk in a London office taps out on the teleprinter an offer which is immediately recorded on a teleprinter in a Manchester office, and a clerk at that end taps out an acceptance. If the line goes dead in the middle of the sentence of acceptance, the teleprinter motor will stop. There is then obviously no contract. The clerk at Manchester must get through again and send his complete sentence. But it may happen that the line does not go dead, yet the message does not get through to London. Thus the clerk at Manchester may tap out his message of acceptance and it will not be recorded in London because the ink at the London end fails, or something of that kind. In that case, the Manchester clerk will not know of the failure but the London clerk will know of it and will immediately send back a message 'not receiving.' Then, when the fault is rectified, the Manchester clerk will repeat his message. Only then is there a contract. If he does not

---

[25] [1955] 3 WLR 48 at 50.
[26] [1955] 3 WLR 48 at 50.
[27] [1955] 3 WLR 48 at 50–51.

repeat it, there is no contract. It is not until his message is received that the contract is complete.'[28]

[19.14] The common thread through all of these examples was that the man who sent the message of acceptance knew that it had not been received and so knew to repeat it. But Denning LJ then wondered what would happen if the sender did not know that the message had not been received. Denning LJ thought that:

'if there should be a case where the offeror without any fault on his part does not receive the message of acceptance – yet the sender of it reasonably believes it has got home when it has not – then I think there is no contract.'[29]

This led Denning LJ to conclude that:

'the rule about instantaneous communications between the parties is different from the rule about the post. The contract is only complete when the acceptance is received by the offeror: and the contract is made at the place where the acceptance is received.'[30]

[19.15] The House of Lords was asked to review the application of the rule in *Entores v Miles Far East* in *Brinkibon Ltd v Stahag Stahl*.[31] The House held that no such review was necessary, Wilberfoce LJ noting that:

'The general rule, it is hardly necessary to state, is that a contract is formed when acceptance of an offer is communicated by the offeror. And if it is necessary to determine where a contract is formed (as to which I have already commented) it appears logical that this should be at the place where acceptance is communicated to the offeror. In the common case of contracts, whether oral or in writing inter praesentes, there is no difficulty; and again logic demands that even where there is not mutual presence at the same place and at the same time, if communication is instantaneous, for example by telephone or radio communication, the same result should follow.'[32]

The relevance of this case-law issue is very much open to question in the electronic context. The Brussels Convention provides that 'A person domiciled in a Contracting State may, in another Contracting State, be sued … in matters relating to a contract, in the courts for the place of performance of the obligation in question.'[33]

[19.16] Following the enactment of the Jurisdiction of Courts and Enforcement of Judgments Act 1998 this provision and other provisions of the Brussels Convention will be binding upon the Irish courts when deciding whether the Irish courts or those of another contracting state to the Brussels Convention should have jurisdiction in relation to a contract case.[34] Where a jurisdictional dispute arises with the courts of a non-contracting state, the Irish courts may have to decide whether they offer a *forum conveniens* to hear the dispute in accordance with the decision of the Supreme Court in

---

[28] [1955] 3 WLR 48 at 51.
[29] [1955] 3 WLR 48 at 51.
[30] [1955] 3 WLR 48 at 51.
[31] *Brinkibon Ltd v Stahag Stahl* [1982] 2 WLR 264.
[32] [1982] 2 WLR 264 at 266.
[33] Brussels Convention, art 5(1).
[34] Jurisdiction of Courts and Enforcement of Judgments Act 1998, s 5.

Analog Devices BV v Zurich Insurance Co.[35] In addition, the continuing application of *Entores v Miles Far East* and *Brinkibon Ltd v Stahag Stahl* in an age of instantaneous communications was reconsidered by the English High Court in *Apple Corps Ltd v Apple Computer Inc.*[36] The facts were that the two companies – one, the record label that is primarily famous for publishing the Beatles; the other, the computer company – were locked in a trademark dispute. This dispute was initially settled; the question then arose of which country had jurisdiction over the settlement. The plaintiff argued in favour of England; the defendant preferred California. The defendant based its argument on the then accepted principle enunciated in *Entores v Miles Far East*. The plaintiff argued that the court should take a more novel approach, inviting Mann J to:

> 'find that in the context of this case, and taking due account of the different ways in which contracts might now be concluded which did not exist when the traditional rules were laid down, it would be right to find in principle that a contract can be made in two places at once, and that this was such a contract.'[37]

[19.17] In considering this argument, Mann J confessed that he could:

> 'detect no conceptual barriers to the notion of a contract being treated as having been made in two places, and some not inconsiderable attractions. In a case where the two parties to a contract are not in the same location at the time of contracting, the notion of where the contract is made is essentially a lawyer's construct. It seldom matters of course, but where it does matter (principally for the purposes of jurisdiction under English law) the law has to provide some answers where an application of the experience of everyday life does not enable one to provide them. Hence the rule in Entores and Brinkibon ... That form of approach assumes that one can analyse the formation of a contract in offer and acceptance terms ... in the post-Brinkibon world, where oral telephone communications are even more common, and where such communications can involve three or more participants in three or more different jurisdictions, and where parties might even conclude a written contract by each signing, and observing each other signing, over a video link, the law may have to move on and to recognise that there is nothing inherently wrong or heretical in allowing the notion of a contract made in two (or more) jurisdictions at the same time. This is not merely a way of avoiding an unfortunate, and perhaps difficult, evidential enquiry. It may well reflect the reality of the situation. Take the case of three parties who each agree to complete a written agreement by signing simultaneously over a three-way video link – where is that contract made? The natural answer is that it is made in all three jurisdictions. Such a conclusion does not necessarily create practical difficulties. If one of those jurisdictions is England, then one of the foundations for the English courts to assume jurisdiction is present, but it does not necessarily follow that jurisdiction will be assumed; because a claimant who seeks to sue here would still have to establish that it is the most appropriate jurisdiction in which to sue. Jurisdiction would then dealt with on the basis of a mature forum conveniens doctrine rather than what might otherwise be a very forced and artificial analysis of trying to establish in which single jurisdiction the contract was made.'[38]

---

[35] *Analog Devices BV v Zurich Insurance Co* [2002] 1 IR 272.
[36] *Apple Corps Ltd v Apple Computer Inc* [2004] EWHC 768 (Ch).
[37] [2004] EWHC 768 (Ch), para 9.
[38] [2004] EWHC 768 (Ch), para 37.

[19.18] Mann J acknowledged that no authority supported the plaintiff's proposition. However, Mann J considered that in the case before him:

'The parties had, by a long process of negotiation, arrived at agreed forms of agreement which were not to be made binding until both parties indicated that they were. If both parties had met in order to sign and complete in the same place, it might well have been extremely difficult to find anything amounting to an offer and acceptance. Where completion takes place at a distance over the telephone, it might well be possible to construct an offer and acceptance analysis (indeed, each party has sought to do so in this case) but it might equally be thought that that analysis is extremely forced and introduces a highly random element. The offer and acceptance may well depend on who speaks first and who speaks second, which is likely to be largely a matter of chance in closing an agreement of this sort. It is very arguably a much more satisfactory analysis to say that the contract was made in both places at the same time.'[39]

[19.19] What the above means is that identifying where and when a communication was sent may not have the significance that it once had for contract law and the jurisdiction of the Irish courts. In any event the parties may by an express term set out the place where the contract is made. However, the Electronic Commerce Act 2000 does contain complex provisions setting out the time and place where an electronic communication may be deemed to have been dispatched and received. The Act provides that:

'Where an electronic communication enters an information system, or the first information system, outside the control of the originator, then, unless otherwise agreed between the originator and the addressee, it is taken to have been sent when it enters such information system or first information system.'[40]

So if someone sends an email from their workplace computer it will most likely enter their office *intranet* initially. The message will not be deemed to be sent at this stage. It is only when the message enters the *Internet*, or more likely the network of the service provider who connects the person's workplace to the Internet, that the message will be deemed to be sent. The reverse will also be true when the message is received.

'Where the addressee of an electronic communication has designated an information system for the purpose of receiving electronic communications, then, unless otherwise agreed between the originator and the addressee or the law otherwise provides, the electronic communication is taken to have been received when it enters that information system.'[41]

[19.20] The above two provisions apply where the parties have agreed to use specific systems to send and receive electronic communications. The Electronic Commerce Act 2000 also provides for the situation where no such system has been designated:

'Where the addressee of an electronic communication has not designated an information system for the purpose of receiving electronic communications, then, unless otherwise agreed between the originator and the addressee, the electronic communication is taken to have been received when it comes to the attention of the addressee.'[42]

---

[39] [2004] EWHC 768 (Ch), para 42.
[40] Electronic Commerce Act 2000, s 21(1).
[41] Electronic Commerce Act 2000, s 21(2).
[42] Electronic Commerce Act 2000, s 21(3).

The geographical location of the system that sends or receives an email or other electronic communication would seem to be irrelevant. The Act provides that the above provisions will:

> 'apply notwithstanding that the place where the relevant information system is located may be different from the place where the electronic communication is taken to have been sent or received, as the case may be, under those subsections.'[43]

[19.21] In addition, the Act provides that:

> 'Unless otherwise agreed between the originator and the addressee of an electronic communication, the electronic communication is taken to have been sent from and received at, respectively, the place where the originator and the addressee have their places of business.'[44]

The Act also allows for the situation where an individual may have more than one place of business, providing that:

> 'if the originator or addressee has more than one place of business, the place of business is the place that has the closest relationship to the underlying transaction or, if there is no underlying transaction, the principal place of business.'[45]

The Act also allows for the situation where an individual does not have a place of business, providing that 'if the originator or addressee does not have a place of business, the place of business is taken to be the place where he or she ordinarily resides.'[46]

[19.22] Finally, the Act allows for the situation where a message is being sent to a company, providing that:

> 'If an electronic communication is or is in connection with a notification or other communication required or permitted by or under an Act to be sent or given to, or served on, a company at its registered office, the registered office is taken to be the place of business of the company in connection with that electronic communication.'[47]

Acknowledgement of a communication

[19.23] The Electronic Commerce Act 2000 also provides for the situation where an acknowledgement of the receipt of a communication is sought or provided. The Act states that:

> 'Subject to any other law, where the originator of an electronic communication indicates that receipt of the electronic communication is required to be acknowledged but does not indicate a particular form or method of acknowledgement, then, unless the originator and the addressee of the electronic communication agree otherwise, the acknowledgement shall be given by way of an electronic communication or any other communication (including any conduct of the addressee) sufficient to indicate to the originator that the electronic communication has been received.'[48]

---

43 Electronic Commerce Act 2000, s 21(4).
44 Electronic Commerce Act 2000, s 21(5).
45 Electronic Commerce Act 2000, s 21(6)(a).
46 Electronic Commerce Act 2000, s 21(6)(b).
47 Electronic Commerce Act 2000, s 21(7).
48 Electronic Commerce Act 2000, s 20(1).

The Act also deals with the situation where an acknowledgement is sought, but not sent:

> 'Where the originator of an electronic communication indicates that receipt of the electronic communication is required to be acknowledged, the electronic communication, in relation to the establishing of legal rights and obligations between parties, shall, until the acknowledgement is received by the originator and unless the parties otherwise agree, be treated as if it had never been sent.'[49]

[19.24] In addition, the Act provides that:

> 'Where the originator of an electronic communication has indicated that receipt of the electronic communication is required to be acknowledged but has not stated that the electronic communication is conditional on the receipt of acknowledgement and the acknowledgement has not been received by the originator within the time specified or agreed or, if no time has been specified or agreed, within a reasonable time, then the electronic communication, in relation to the establishing of legal rights and obligations between parties, shall, unless the parties otherwise agree, be treated as if it had never been sent.'[50]

This rule may lead to rather harsh consequences, as it would appear to mean that the sender of a communication, who quite legitimately sought an acknowledgement but failed to get one, would have their communication disregarded. Suppose you wish to complain about the provision of a service or apply for a job by sending an email. You might well request that your communication be acknowledged upon receipt. But, if the recipient fails to respond, then it will be as if your message was never sent. This might lead to quite pernicious consequences in respect of job applications. Suppose you send an application for a position in the public service to the Public Appointments Commission, requesting a receipt. Suppose you request acknowledgement of your application, but instead of sending it right away, the Commission stores all the applications in an electronic folder and does not examine the contents until after the application deadline has passed. It is only then that the Commission responds to your initial communication. In that circumstance, it might be argued that your communication was not effectively sent by you until the acknowledgment was sent after the application deadline had passed. It may be anticipated that, given the ridiculous nature of such a result, a court would quickly deal with such an argument. But this illustrates that deciding when and where a communication is received is an issue perhaps better dealt with on a case-by-case basis, rather than by legislating with general effect.

The validity of electronic signatures

[19.25] The Directive on Electronic Signatures[51] is implemented in Ireland by the Electronic Commerce Act 2000. The Directive states that its purpose is:

> 'to facilitate the use of electronic signatures and to contribute to their legal recognition. It establishes a legal framework for electronic signatures and certain certification-services in order to ensure the proper functioning of the internal market.'[52]

---

[49] Electronic Commerce Act 2000, s 20(2).
[50] Electronic Commerce Act 2000, s 20(3).
[51] Directive 1999/93/EC of the European Parliament and of the Council of 13 December 1999 on a Community framework for electronic signatures OJ L 013 , 19/01/2000 P 12–20.
[52] Directive on Electronic Signatures, art 1.

The Directive on Electronic Signatures was enacted in 1999 in the anticipation that there would soon be a thriving European market for electronic signature services:

'Electronic signatures will be used in a large variety of circumstances and applications, resulting in a wide range of new services and products related to or using electronic signatures; the definition of such products and services should not be limited to the issuance and management of certificates, but should also encompass any other service and product using, or ancillary to, electronic signatures, such as registration services, time-stamping services, directory services, computing services or consultancy services related to electronic signatures.'[53]

[19.26] Unfortunately this was not to be and in its 2006 report on the implementation of the Directive[54] the EC Commission noted that:

'The two dominating electronic signature applications are related to e-government and personal e-banking services. Many Member States and several other European countries have launched e-government applications or are planning to do so. A number of these e-government applications are based on the use of electronic ID cards. The electronic ID card can be used both as an identification document and to provide online access to public services for the citizens. In most cases these ID cards will contain the three functionalities: identification, authentication and signing.

The other major application for electronic signatures – personal e-banking – is now taking off in most EU countries. Most of the authentication systems for personal e-banking services are relying on one-time passwords (OTP) and tokens, which means the simplest form of electronic signature according to the Directive. Many e-banking applications are only using these technologies for authentication of the user but electronic signing of transactions is increasing. For corporate e-banking (business-to-business) and inter-bank clearing, it is more common to use smart cards which are considered to provide a higher level of security.'[55]

[19.27] The Commission is dubious about the success of this Directive and notes that:

'The use of qualified electronic signatures has been much less than expected and the market is not very well developed today. Today, users do not have a single electronic certificate to sign documents or transactions in the digital environment in the same way as on paper. Therefore, the internal market objective of the Directive, the free circulation of qualified electronic signatures, cannot be assessed comprehensively at this stage.'[56]

The Commission suggests that there are two possible reasons for this failure, one economic, the other technical. The Commission attributes most of the blame to economic reasons, stating that:

'The main reason for the slow take-off of the market is economic: service providers have little incentive to develop multi-application electronic signature and prefer to offer solutions for their own services, for instance, solutions developed by the banking sector.

---

[53] Directive on Electronic Signatures, Recital 9.
[54] Report from the Commission to the European Parliament and the Council – *Report on the operation of Directive 1999/93/EC on a Community framework for electronic signatures*, 15 March 2006.
[55] 15 March 2006, para 3.2.
[56] 15 March 2006, para 5.2.

This slows down the process of developing interoperable solutions. The lack of applications, such as comprehensive solutions for electronic archives, might also prevent the development of a multi-purpose e-signature, which requires reaching a critical mass of users and usage.'[57]

[19.28] The second reason for this failure suggested by the Commission is technical:

'There is no simple answer to why the market for electronic signatures has not developed faster, but the market is facing a number of technical challenges ... The lack of technical interoperability at national and at cross-border level causes another obstacle for the market acceptance of e-signatures. It has resulted in many isolated islands of e-signature applications, where certificates can only be used for one single application ... most of the Member states have specified national standards in order to promote interoperability.'[58]

In particular, the Commission blames the use of public key infrastructure (PKI) systems for the purposes of providing advanced electronic signatures. The Commission appears to regard this system as being overly complex. One reason not advanced by the Commission is legal: there may never have been an overriding need for the Directive on this point in the first place. As a matter of law, the physical or electronic act of signing a contract is of no great significance. It is well established that the illiterate may sign a contract by means of a tick or a mark and that the blind or disabled may have another person sign a document on their behalf. The law has tended to regard the intention of the person signing the document as significant, not the physical act itself. The Commission does appear to recognise that one of the reasons why electronic signatures have not been widely adopted is an absence of need. In order to provide this need the Commission has required that electronic signatures be used in the public procurement process. And the Commission communication concludes with a promise that the Commission will continue to seek to create a need for electronic signatures in future.[59] The electronic signatures regime created by the EC may be a good idea whose time has yet to come, but it remains to be seen if it ever will.

What is an electronic signature?

[19.29] The Directive on Electronic Signatures defines an electronic signature as 'data in electronic form which are attached to or logically associated with other electronic data and which serve as a method of authentication.'[60]

The Electronic Commerce Act 2000 implements this definition in slightly different form. It defines electronic signature as 'data in electronic form attached to, incorporated in or logically associated with other electronic data and which serves as a method of authenticating the purported originator, and includes an advanced electronic signature.'[61]

---

[57]   15 March 2006, para 5.2.
[58]   15 March 2006, para 3.3.2.
[59]   15 March 2006, para 5.2.
[60]   Directive on Electronic Signatures, art 2(1).
[61]   Electronic Commerce Act 2000, s 2(1).

[19.30] The Electronic Commerce Act 2000 defines the term 'originator' as:

'the person or public body by whom or on whose behalf the electronic communication purports to have been sent or generated before storage, as the case may be, but does not include a person or public body acting as a service provider in relation to the generation, processing, sending or storing of that electronic communication or providing other services in relation to it.'[62]

The definition of electronic signature would appear to be so broad as to be almost meaningless. An email will contain a variety of information which may be used to authenticate it, such as the sender's address in the header. If such information were to be treated as being the same as the physical signature of an individual, anyone who sends an email to another could find themselves contractually bound by the contents of that email, regardless of their actual intent. However, in *J Pereira Fernandes SA v Mehta*[63] the English High Court held that this interpretation was fallacious. In *J Pereira Fernandes SA v Mehta* the defendant was a director of a company that owed the plaintiff a sum of money. The plaintiff brought a petition to wind up the company; in response an email was sent to the plaintiff which purported to promise that in return for a stay in the proceedings, the defendant would personally guarantee the debt. The email was not signed by the defendant but was 'described in the header as having come from nelmehta@aol.com.'[64]

[19.31] The question of whether this email amounted to a signed document was of great significance for the defendant as s 4 of the Statute of Frauds provides that:

'no action shall be brought ... whereby to charge the defendant upon any special promise to answer for the debt default or miscarriages of another person ... unless the agreement upon which such action shall be brought or some memorandum or note thereof shall be in writing and signed by the party to be charged therewith or some other person thereunto by him lawfully authorised.'

Pelling QC[65] noted that:

'The purpose of the statute of frauds is to protect people from being held liable on informal communications because they may be made without sufficient consideration or expressed ambiguously or because such a communication might be fraudulently alleged against the party to be charged.'[66]

Pelling QC began his discussion of whether the email in question could have been said to be signed by the defendant by noting that it was:

'not signed by anyone in a conventional sense. Mr Mehta's name or initials do not appear at the end of the email or, indeed, anywhere else in the body of the email. Inevitably, therefore ... (the plaintiff) ... must contend that the presence of the email address at the top of the email constitutes a signature sufficient to satisfy the requirements of s 4.'[67]

---

[62] Electronic Commerce Act 2000, s 2(1).
[63] *J Pereira Fernandes SA v Mehta* [2006] EWHC 813 (Ch), [2006] 2 All ER 891, [2006] 1 All ER (Comm) 885, [2006] 2 Lloyd's Rep 244.
[64] [2006] EWHC 813 (Ch), para 3.
[65] Sitting as a Deputy Judge of the English High Court.
[66] [2006] EWHC 813 (Ch), para 16.
[67] [2006] EWHC 813 (Ch), para 18.

[19.32] Pelling QC went on to point out that this email address was 'not inserted by the sender of the email in any active sense. It is inserted automatically.'[68] Counsel for the plaintiff submitted that:

> 'the appearance of the sender's address at the top of the document constitutes a signature either by the sender or by 'some other person thereunto by him lawfully authorised' because it is well known to all users of email that the recipient of the email will always be told the email address of the email account from which the email is sent in the form it appears on the email … above. That being so, it is submitted that by authorising an agent to send an email using the sender's email account, to a third party the sender knows that his, her or its email address will appear on the recipient's copy and that is sufficient for it to be held to be a signature for the purposes of s 4.'[69]

This submission was rejected by Pelling QC who held that:

> 'What is relied upon is an email address. It is the email equivalent of a fax or telex number. It is well known that the recipient of a fax will usually receive a copy that has the name and/or number of the sender automatically printed at the top together with a transmission time. Can it sensibly be suggested that the automatically generated name and fax number of the sender of a fax on a faxed document that is otherwise a s 4 note or memorandum would constitute a signature for these purposes?'[70]

Pelling QC reviewed the case law and concluded that:

> 'it seems to me that a party can sign a document for the purposes of s 4 by using his full name or his last name prefixed by some or all of his initials or using his initials, and possibly by using a pseudonym or a combination of letters and numbers (as can happen for example with a Lloyds slip scratch), providing always that whatever was used was inserted into the document in order to give, and with the intention of giving, authenticity to it. Its inclusion must have been intended as a signature for these purposes.'[71]

[19.33] Pelling QC noted that in this case 'the issue is whether the automatic insertion of a person's email address after the document has been transmitted by either the sending and/or receiving ISP constitutes a signature for the purposes of s 4.'[72] Pelling QC went on to conclude that:

> 'In my judgment the inclusion of an email address in such circumstances is a clear example of the inclusion of a name which is incidental … in the absence of evidence of a contrary intention. Its appearance divorced from the main body of the text of the message emphasises this to be so. Absent evidence to the contrary, in my view it is not possible to hold that the automatic insertion of an email address is … 'intended for a signature'. To conclude that the automatic insertion of an email address in the circumstances I have described constituted a signature for the purposes of s 4 would I think undermine or potentially undermine what I understand to be the Statute's purpose, would be contrary to the underlying principle to be derived from the cases to which I have referred and would have widespread and wholly unintended legal and commercial effects.'[73]

---

68 [2006] EWHC 813 (Ch), para 19.
69 [2006] EWHC 813 (Ch), para 20.
70 [2006] EWHC 813 (Ch), para 23.
71 [2006] EWHC 813 (Ch), para 26.
72 [2006] EWHC 813 (Ch), para 28.
73 [2006] EWHC 813 (Ch), para 29.

[19.34] Pelling QC was careful to distinguish the situation where an email address is automatically inserted by an ISP and that where an individual deliberately types their name in the body of an email.

> 'I have no doubt that if a party creates and sends an electronically created document then he will be treated as having signed it to the same extent that he would in law be treated as having signed a hard copy of the same document. The fact that the document is created electronically as opposed to as a hard copy can make no difference[74] ... . if a party or a party's agent sending an email types his or her or his or her principal's name to the extent required or permitted by existing case law in the body of an email, then in my view that would be a sufficient signature for the purposes of s 4.'[75]

What is an advanced electronic signature?

[19.35] An advanced electronic signature is defined by the Electronic Commerce Act 2000 as:

> 'an electronic signature ... uniquely linked to the signatory ... capable of identifying the signatory ... created using means that are capable of being maintained by the signatory under his, her or its sole control, and ... linked to the data to which it relates in such a manner that any subsequent change of the data is detectable.'[76]

It should be noted that the Act defines 'electronic' as 'electrical, digital, magnetic, optical, electromagnetic, biometric, photonic and any other form of related Technology'.

This very broad definition, which extends electronic to include both biological features and light, would seem to go far beyond the normal understanding of what is and is not electronic. The breadth of this definition would seem to have been an expression of the Commission's desire to use 'technology-neutral' definitions. It might perhaps be easier to conceive of the advanced electronic signatures as being signatures created or verified by advanced technology. However, such conception is unnecessary; the Commission has acknowledged that in practice advanced electronic signatures use a single, electronic, system. The Commission's 2006 report on the implementation of the Directive on Electronic Signatures notes that with regard to the definition of advanced electronic signatures:

> 'The Directive is technology neutral but in practice, this definition refers mainly to electronic signatures based on a public key infrastructure (PKI). This technology uses encryption technology to sign data, which requires a public and a private key[77] ... One frequently highlighted problem that could contribute to the slow take up of advanced or qualified electronic signatures in Europe is the complexity of the PKI technology. The often stressed advantage of PKI is that this technology uses the system of the trusted third party which allows parties that have never met to trust each other on the internet. In many of the current applications there seems, however, to be little interest from the service

---

[74] [2006] EWHC 813 (Ch), para 28.
[75] [2006] EWHC 813 (Ch), para 28.
[76] Electronic Commerce Act 2000, s 2(1).
[77] *Report from the Commission to the European Parliament and the Council - Report on the operation of Directive 1999/93/EC on a Community framework for electronic signatures*, 15 March 2006, para 2.3.2.

providers, essentially for liability reasons, to allow their customers to use their authentication device for other services ... national standards in order to promote interoperability ... Today, in the PKI environment, the smart card is the mostly used signature-creation-device because the smart card provides a means to store the private key securely. This technology is expensive and requires physical infrastructure investments (distribution of cards and card readers etc).'[78]

The role of certification service providers

[19.36] The drafters of the Directive on Electronic Signatures and the Electronic Commerce Act 2000 regarded certification service providers as being integral to the system of electronic signatures that they were seeking to create. The Electronic Commerce Act 2000 provides that 'A person or public body is not required to obtain the prior authority of any other person or public body to provide certification or other services relating to electronic signatures.'[79]

A 'scheme of voluntary accreditation of certification service providers for the purpose of the Directive and to enhance levels of certification service provision in the State, and [that] may designate accreditation authorities and prescribe such matters relating to their designation as the Minister thinks appropriate for the purpose' may be established by Ministerial regulation. A person that provides certification services may apply to this accreditation authority to participate in any such scheme.[80] Ministerial regulation may prescribe 'a scheme of supervision of certification service providers established in the State who issue qualified certificates to the public.'[81] The Minister may designate by order 'persons or public bodies for the purposes of determining whether secure signature creation devices conform with the requirements of Annex III.'[82] Annex III of the Act provides the requirements for secure signature-creation devices such as 'the signature-creation-data used for signature generation can practically occur only once, and that their secrecy is reasonably assured.'[83] This provision concludes with an exemption from liability for such designated public bodies in respect of 'any determination made or thing done by the person or public body, in good faith, in the performance or purported performance of a function under a scheme referred to.'[84]

Liability of certification service providers

[19.37] One of the key ideas behind the Electronic Commerce Act 2000 was that 'certification service provider(s)' would develop a business that would issue certificates, which were defined as:

' an electronic attestation which links signature verification data to a person or public body, and confirms the identity of the person or public body.'[85]

---

[78] 15 March 2006, para 3.3.2.
[79] Electronic Commerce Act 2000, s 29(1).
[80] Electronic Commerce Act 2000, s 29(2).
[81] Electronic Commerce Act 2000, s 29(3).
[82] Electronic Commerce Act 2000, s 29(4).
[83] Electronic Commerce Act 2000, Annex III, para 1(a).
[84] Electronic Commerce Act 2000, s 29(4).
[85] Electronic Commerce Act 2000, s 2(1).

The Directive on Electronic Signatures requires that member states must:

> 'ensure that by issuing a certificate as a qualified certificate to the public or by guaranteeing such a certificate to the public a certification-service-provider is liable for damage caused to any entity or legal or natural person who reasonably relies on that certificate:
>
> (a)   as regards the accuracy at the time of issuance of all information contained in the qualified certificate and as regards the fact that the certificate contains all the details prescribed for a qualified certificate;
>
> (b)   for assurance that at the time of the issuance of the certificate, the signatory identified in the qualified certificate held the signature-creation data corresponding to the signature-verification data given or identified in the certificate;
>
> (c)   for assurance that the signature-creation data and the signature-verification data can be used in a complementary manner in cases where the certification-service-provider generates them both.'

However, the certification service provider will be able to avoid liability if he can show that 'he has not acted negligently.'[86] The Directive goes on to provide that at a minimum:

> 'Member States shall ensure that a certification-service-provider who has issued a certificate as a qualified certificate to the public is liable for damage caused to any entity or legal or natural person who reasonably relies on the certificate for failure to register revocation of the certificate unless the certification-service-provider proves that he has not acted negligently.'[87]

[19.38] Member states may allow certificate service providers to limit the uses to which a certificate may be put[88] and the value of transactions for which it may be used,[89] provided such limitations are clearly indicated. As regards the liability of service providers, the Electronic Commerce Act 2000 provides that:

> 'A certification service provider who provides a service to the public of issuing certificates and who as a part of that service issues a certificate as a qualified certificate or guarantees such a certificate, shall be liable for any damage caused to a person who, or public body which, reasonably relies on the certificate unless the certification service provider proves that he, she or it has not acted negligently.'[90]

The Act imposes a number of duties upon certification service providers,[91] who must take reasonable steps to ensure that:

> (a)   'the accuracy of all information in the qualified certificate as at the time of issue and that the certificate contains all the details required by Annex I to be so contained in a qualified certificate,

---

[86]   Directive on Electronic Signatures, art 6(1).

[87]   Directive on Electronic Signatures, art 6(2).

[88]   Directive on Electronic Signatures, art 6(3).

[89]   Directive on Electronic Signatures, art 6(4).

[90]   Electronic Commerce Act 2000, s 30(1).

[91]   'who provides to the public a service of issuing certificates and who issues a certificate as a qualified certificate or guarantees such a certificate': Electronic Commerce Act 2000, s 30(2).

(b) that, at the time of the issue of the certificate, the signatory identified in the certificate held the signature creation device corresponding to the signature verification device given or identified in the certificate, and

(c) that the signature creation device and the signature verification device act together in a complementary manner, in cases where the certification service provider generates both.'[92]

Certification service providers will also be liable if they fail to register or publish notice that the certificate has been revoked.[93] However, if the certification service provider clearly indicates that a certificate is limited, then he will not be liable if those limitations are exceeded or ignored.[94]

The validity of an electronic signature

[19.39] The Electronic Commerce Act 2000 provides that:

'If by law or otherwise the signature of a person or public body is required (whether the requirement is in the form of an obligation or consequences flow from there being no signature) or permitted, then ... an electronic signature may be used.'[95]

An electronic signature may only be used in respect of a public body where it:

'is required or permitted to be given to a public body or to a person acting on behalf of a public body and the public body consents to the use of an electronic signature but requires that it be in accordance with particular information technology and procedural requirements ... .if the public body's requirements have been met and those requirements have been made public and are objective, transparent, proportionate and non-discriminatory, and ... where the signature is required or permitted to be given to a person who is neither a public body nor acting on behalf of a public body— if the person to whom the signature is required or permitted to be given consents to the use of an electronic signature.'[96]

[19.40] In other words, the Electronic Commerce Act 2000 cannot be used to force someone to accept a document that has been electronically signed. These provisions are stated to be:

'without prejudice to any other provision of this Act or law requiring or permitting an electronic communication to contain an electronic signature, an advanced electronic signature, an electronic signature based on a qualified certificate, an electronic signature created by a secure signature creation device or other technological requirements relating to an electronic signature.'[97]

---

92 Electronic Commerce Act 2000, s 30(2).
93 Electronic Commerce Act 2000, s 30(3).
94 Electronic Commerce Act 2000, s 30(4).
95 Electronic Commerce Act 2000, s 13(1).
96 Electronic Commerce Act 2000, s 13(2).
97 Electronic Commerce Act 2000, s 13(3).

Documents required to be witnessed

[19.41] If a document is required to be witnessed, then this requirement may be fulfilled electronically. The Electronic Commerce Act 2000 provides that such requirements may be:

'taken to have been met if ... the signature to be witnessed is an advanced electronic signature, based on a qualified certificate, of the person or public body by whom the document is required to be signed ... the document contains an indication that the signature of that person or public body is required to be witnessed, and ... the signature of the person purporting to witness the signature to be witnessed is an advanced electronic signature, based on a qualified certificate.'[98]

[19.42] The Electronic Commerce Act 2000 goes on to provide the following requirement:

'An advanced electronic signature based on a qualified certificate may be ... only ... where the signature required or permitted to be witnessed is on a document to be given to a public body or to a person acting on behalf of a public body and the public body consents to the use of an electronic signature of both the person attesting the document and witnessing the signature but requires that the document and signatures be in accordance with particular information technology and procedural requirements (including that a qualified certificate on which the signature or signatures are based be issued by an accredited certification service provider)— if the public body's requirements are met and those requirements have been made public and are objective, transparent, proportionate and non-discriminatory, and ... where the document on or in respect of which the signature is to be witnessed is required or permitted to be given to a person who is neither a public body nor acting on behalf of a public body— if the person to whom it is required or permitted to be given consents to the use of an advanced electronic signature based on a qualified certificate for that purpose.'[99]

Using electronic signatures to create documents under seal

[19.43] The law may require that certain documents be authenticated by a seal. For example, the Ministers and Secretaries Act 1924, provides that:

'The seal of each Minister who is a head of a Department of State established under this Act shall, when affixed to any instrument or document, be authenticated by the signature of such Minister, or of some person authorised by that Minister to act in that behalf.'[100]

Such seals may be affixed electronically. The Electronic Commerce Act 2000 provides that:

'If by law or otherwise a seal is required to be affixed to a document ... then ... that requirement is taken to have been met if the document indicates that it is required to be under seal and it includes an advanced electronic signature, based on a qualified certificate, of the person or public body by whom it is required to be sealed.'[101]

---

[98] Electronic Commerce Act 2000, s 14(1).
[99] Electronic Commerce Act 2000, s 14(2).
[100] Ministers and Secretaries Act 1924, s 15.
[101] Electronic Commerce Act 2000, s 16(1).

[19.44] The Electronic Commerce Act 2000 goes on to provide that an advanced electronic signature may only be so used where:

'the document to be under seal is required or permitted to be given to a public body or to a person acting on behalf of a public body and the public body consents to the use of an electronic signature but requires that it be in accordance with particular information technology and procedural requirements ... if the public body's requirements have been met and those requirements have been made public and are objective, transparent, proportionate and non-discriminatory, and ... where the document to be under seal is required or permitted to be given to a person who is neither a public body nor acting on behalf of a public body— if the person to whom it is required or permitted to be given consents to the use of an advanced electronic signature based on a qualified certificate.'[102]

Admissibility of electronic signatures

[19.45] The Electronic Commerce Act 2000 provides for the admissibility of electronic signatures into evidence, stating that:

'In any legal proceedings, nothing in the application of the rules of evidence shall apply so as to deny the admissibility in evidence of ... an electronic signature ... on the sole ground that the signature is in electronic form, or is not an advanced electronic signature, or is not based on a qualified certificate, or is not based on a qualified certificate issued by an accredited certification service provider, or is not created by a secure signature creation device, or ... if it is the best evidence that the person or public body adducing it could reasonably be expected to obtain on the grounds that it is not in its original form.'[103]

Misuse of electronic signatures

[19.46] The Directive on Electronic Signatures provides a number of criminal offences which may be committed by those who misuse electronic signatures. The Act provides that these offences may be committed by persons or by public bodies. The Act provides that an offence will be committed by any such person or public body which:

'(a) knowingly accesses, copies or otherwise obtains possession of, or recreates, the signature creation device[104] of another person or a public body, without the authorisation of that other person or public body, for the purpose of creating or allowing, or causing another person or public body to create, an unauthorised electronic signature using the signature creation device,

(b) knowingly alters, discloses or uses the signature creation device of another person or a public body, without the authorisation of that other person or public body or in excess of lawful authorisation, for the purpose of creating or allowing, or causing another person or public body to create, an unauthorised electronic signature using the signature creation device,

---

[102] Electronic Commerce Act 2000, s 16(2).

[103] Electronic Commerce Act 2000, s 22(b).

[104] 'signature creation device' is defined as a 'device, such as configured software or hardware used to generate signature creation data'; 'signature creation data' is defined as: 'unique data, such as codes, passwords, algorithms or private cryptographic keys, used by a signatory or other source of the data in generating an electronic signature': Electronic Commerce Act 2000, s 2(1).

(c)   knowingly creates, publishes, alters or otherwise uses a certificate or an electronic signature for a fraudulent or other unlawful purpose,

(d)   knowingly misrepresents the person's or public body's identity or authorisation in requesting or accepting a certificate or in requesting suspension or revocation of a certificate,

(e)   knowingly accesses, alters, discloses or uses the signature creation device of a certification service provider used to issue certificates, without the authorisation of the certification service provider or in excess of lawful authorisation, for the purpose of creating, or allowing or causing another person or a public body to create, an unauthorized electronic signature using the signature creation device, or

(f)   knowingly publishes a certificate, or otherwise knowingly makes it available to anyone likely to rely on the certificate or on an electronic signature that is verifiable with reference to data such as codes, passwords, algorithms, public cryptographic keys or other data which are used for the purposes of verifying an electronic signature, listed in the certificate, if the person or public body knows that—

    (i)   the certification service provider listed in the certificate has not issued it,

    (ii)   the subscriber listed in the certificate has not accepted it, or

    (iii)   the certificate has been revoked or suspended, unless its publication is for the purpose of verifying an electronic signature created before such revocation or suspension, or giving notice of revocation or suspension.'[105]

The above offences will be committed even where the acts in question 'took place partly outside the State.[106] The Act also provides for the investigation[107] and prosecution[108] of such offences, as well as the criminal liability of bodies corporate.[109] Where a conviction is obtained on indictment in respect of such an offence, then maximum penalties of a fine not exceeding €634,869 (£500,000) and a term of imprisonment not exceeding 5 years may be imposed.[110]

Confidentiality of electronic signatures

[19.47] In practice the use of advanced electronic signatures involves the use of encryption technology. A document will be encrypted with a key that is specific to an individual user; the encryption and the signature are in effect the same thing. By making it an offence to access, copy, obtain possession of or recreate the signature creation device of another, the Electronic Commerce Act 2000 may make it very difficult for the Irish authorities to attempt to decrypt such messages. Of course some would argue that doing so is impossible technically anyway, but by making it illegal to attempt to decrypt messages by recreating the signature creation device of a suspect, the Electronic

---

[105] Electronic Commerce Act 2000, s 25.
[106] Electronic Commerce Act 2000, s 26.
[107] Electronic Commerce Act 2000, s 27.
[108] Electronic Commerce Act 2000, s 6.
[109] Electronic Commerce Act 2000, s 7.
[110] Electronic Commerce Act 2000, s 8.

Commerce Act 2000 protects all such devices, regardless of the strength of the encryption that they use. The Electronic Commerce Act 2000 does not provide any power that may be invoked to force a suspect to provide his encryption keys or to decrypt the data in question himself. Indeed the Electronic Commerce Act 2000 takes the opposite approach, providing that none of its provisions:

> 'shall be construed as requiring the disclosure or enabling the seizure of unique data, such as codes, passwords, algorithms, private cryptographic keys, or other data, that may be necessary to render information or an electronic communication intelligible.'[111]

For those who can configure their systems to fit within the parameters of the Electronic Commerce Act 2000 it offers a very good and entirely legal method of ensuring that their data can be kept confidential, even from An Garda Síochána. Of course the gardaí might be able to apply to access such data under other provisions, such as those provided by the Criminal Justice (Theft and Fraud Offences) Act 2001. But those provisions only apply to offences that are committed under that Act.

Electronic documents

[19.48] There can never have been much question as to whether or not documents were invalid simply because they were stored electronically. The Irish courts have been willing to interpret the meaning of document quite broadly, in *McCarthy v O'Flynn*[112] the defendant sought discovery of an X-ray plate of the plaintiff's injuries. The Supreme Court granted discovery, Keane J holding that:

> 'an X-ray plate and photograph are documents … Etymologically the word 'document' is derived from the Latin word 'documentum' which in turn comes from the verb 'docere.' Therefore, it is something which teaches or gives information or a lesson or an example for instruction. The main characteristic of a document is that it is something which gives information. An X-ray plate or photograph gives information and so it is a document and the defendant is entitled to discovery of it. All the better authorities support this view.'[113]

It would not require a very great extension of Keane J's judgment in *McCarthy v O'Flynn* to similarly rule that computer print-outs and electronic documents are documents for legal purposes. Certainly, if the Irish courts had ever had to address this issue there is plenty of precedent from the English courts to support such a view. In *Glencore International AG and Another v Bank of China*,[114] which predated the Electronic Commerce Act 2000 by about 5 years, the English Court of Appeal ruled that a computer print-out was a document for the purposes of the Uniform Customs and Practice Code, which was used to regulate practice in relation to payment under documentary credits in international sales transactions. This code provided that: 'banks would accept as an original document a document produced or appearing to have been produced by reprographic, automated or computerised systems, provided it was marked

---

[111] Electronic Commerce Act 2000, s 26.
[112] *McCarthy v O'Flynn* [1979] IR 127.
[113] [1979] IR 127 at 130–131.
[114] *Glencore International AG and Another v Bank of China* (1995) Times Law Reports 27 November.

as original and, where necessary, appeared to be signed.' The documents at issue were printed out from a computer and then photocopied. The English Court of Appeal was willing to accept that original documents could be 'produced by word processor and laser printer' and even photocopied. However the code required that originals be marked as such, and the failure to so mark the documents in this case was fatal to the plaintiff's claim.

[19.49] In *Hastie and Jenkerson v. McMahon*[115] the Master of the English High Court ordered that certain documents be served on the defendant. The defendant served them by fax. Defendant's counsel argued that: 'what was transmitted by fax was not the document but an electronic message'. Woolf LJ, in the English Court of Appeal disagreed, holding that a fax was a document for the purposes of the English Rules of Court. In *Victor Chandler International v Commissioners of Customs and Exci*[116]*se* the English Court of Appeal held that a teletext advertisement transmitted on teletext could be a document for the purposes of the UK's Betting and Gaming Duties Act 1981. Regardless of whether it was necessary to do so, the Electronic Commerce Act 2000 provides, in some considerable detail, that electronic documents are to be treated as indistinguishable from their paper counterparts.

Information to be provided in writing

[19.50] The Electronic Commerce Act 2000 provides that:

> 'If by law or otherwise a person or public body is required ... or permitted to give information in writing ... then ... the person or public body may give the information in electronic form, whether as an electronic communication or otherwise.[117]

This will apply whether the words 'give', 'send', 'forward', 'deliver', 'serve' or a similar word or expression is used in a particular enactment.[118] The phrase 'give information' is stated to include, but not to be limited to, the making of an application, making or lodging of a claim; return or a request; the making of an unsworn declaration; the making or issuing of a certificate; the making, variation or canceling of an election; the lodgment of an objection; the giving of a statement of reasons; the recording and dissemination of a court order or the giving, sending or service of a notification.[119] Information may be given in such an electronic format:

> 'only ... if at the time the information was given it was reasonable to expect that it would be readily accessible to the person or public body to whom it was directed, for subsequent reference ... where the information is required or permitted to be given to a public body or to a person acting on behalf of a public body and the public body consents to the giving of the information in electronic form, whether as an electronic communication or otherwise, but requires ... the information to be given in accordance with particular information technology and procedural requirements, or ... that a particular action be taken by way of verifying the receipt of the information, if the public body's requirements have been met

---

[115] *Hastie and Jenkerson v McMahon* (1990) Times Law Reports, 3 April.

[116] *Victor Chandler International v Commissioners of Customs and Excise* [2000] 1 WLR 1296.

[117] Electronic Commerce Act 2000, s 12(1).

[118] Electronic Commerce Act 2000, s 12(4).

[119] Electronic Commerce Act 2000, s 12(5).

and those requirements have been made public and are objective, transparent, proportionate and non-discriminatory ... and ... where the information is required or permitted to be given to a person who is neither a public body nor acting on behalf of a public body— if the person to whom the information is required or permitted to be given consents to the information being given in that form.'[120]

The above provisions are stated not to prejudice 'any other law requiring or permitting information to be given ... in accordance with particular information technology and procedural requirements ... on a particular kind of data storage device, or ... by means of a particular kind of electronic communication.'[121]

Electronic originals

[19.51] As noted above, in 1995 the English Court of Appeal had held that original documents could be created electronically in *Glencore International AG and Another v Bank of China*. Similarly the Electronic Commerce Act 2000 provides that:

'If by law or otherwise a person or public body is required ... or permitted to present or retain information in its original form, then ... the information may be presented or retained, as the case may be, in electronic form, whether as an electronic communication or otherwise.'[122]

Electronic originals may only be used:

'(a) if there exists a reliable assurance as to the integrity of the information from the time when it was first generated in its final form, whether as an electronic communication or otherwise,

(b) where it is required or permitted that the information be presented— if the information is capable of being displayed in intelligible form to a person or public body to whom it is to be presented,

(c) if, at the time the information was generated in its final form, it was reasonable to expect that it would be readily accessible so as to be useable for subsequent reference,

(d) where the information is required or permitted to be presented to or retained for a public body or for a person acting on behalf of a public body, and the public body consents to the information being presented or retained in electronic form, whether as an electronic communication or otherwise, but requires that it be presented or retained in accordance with particular information technology and procedural requirements— if the public body's requirements have been met and those requirements have been made public and are objective, transparent, proportionate and non-discriminatory, and,

(e) where the information is required or permitted to be presented to or retained for a person who is neither a public body nor acting on behalf of a public body— if the person to whom the information is required or permitted to be presented or for whom it is required or permitted to be retained consents to the information being presented or retained in that form.'[123]

---

[120] Electronic Commerce Act 2000, s 12(2).
[121] Electronic Commerce Act 2000, s 12(3).
[122] Electronic Commerce Act 2000, s 17(1).
[123] Electronic Commerce Act 2000, s 17(2).

[19.52] The Electronic Commerce Act 2000 sets out the criteria by which integrity and reliability may be measured. The criteria for measuring integrity are:

'whether the information has remained complete and unaltered, apart from the addition of any endorsement or change which arises in the normal course of generating, communicating, processing, sending, receiving, recording, storing or displaying.'[124]

Reliability is to be assessed 'in the light of the purpose for which and the circumstances in which the information was generated.'[125]

These provisions are stated to be 'without prejudice to any other law requiring or permitting information to be presented or retained ... in accordance with particular information technology and procedural requirements ... on a particular kind of data storage device, or ... by means of a particular kind of electronic communication.'[126]

Retention and production of electronic documents

[19.53] The law requires the retention of various documents for a variety of purposes. However, the European Commission has noted a reluctance to rely upon electronic archiving:

'the archiving of electronically signed documents is considered too complex and uncertain. Legal obligations to keep documents for as long as over 30 years require costly and cumbersome technology and procedures to ensure readability and verification of such period of time.'[127]

The problem, as anyone who has replaced a VHS camcorder system with a digital one knows, is that as technologies change, data stored on an obsolete technology may not easily be read by its replacement. So a family's VHS recording of holidays, birthdays and the like cannot be read on their new digital system. The old data must be transferred to the new. This may be a straightforward process now, as the old technology is still being phased out and a variety of systems and services are available to ease the transition, but if the transfer is not made, then it may be far harder in a decade or two's time to access and use the older data. Furthermore, as current digital recording formats themselves become obsolete, data will have to be transferred from old to new. This all costs money and takes time. The Electronic Commerce Act 2000 provides for the retention of such documents electronically. The Act provides that:

'If by law or otherwise a person or public body is required ... or permitted to retain for a particular period or produce a document that is in the form of paper or other material on which information may be recorded in written form, then ... the person or public body may retain throughout the relevant period or, as the case may be, produce, the document in electronic form, whether as an electronic communication or otherwise.'[128]

---

[124] Electronic Commerce Act 2000, s 17(4)(a).

[125] Electronic Commerce Act 2000, s 17(4)(b).

[126] Electronic Commerce Act 2000, s 17(3).

[127] *Report from the Commission to the European Parliament and the Council – Report on the operation of Directive 1999/93/EC on a Community framework for electronic signatures*, 15 March 2006, para 3.3.2.

[128] Electronic Commerce Act 2000, s 18(1).

[19.54] Such documents may only be retained electronically:

'(a)   if there exists a reliable assurance as to the integrity of the information from the time when it was first generated in its final form as an electronic communication,

(b)   in the case of a document to be produced— if the information is capable of being displayed in intelligible form to the person or public body to whom it is to be produced,

(c)   in the case of a document to be retained— if, at the time of the generation of the final electronic form of the document, it was reasonable to expect that the information contained in the electronic form of the document would be readily accessible so as to be useable for subsequent reference,

(d)   where the document is required or permitted to be retained for or produced to a public body or for or to a person acting on behalf of a public body, and the public body consents to the document being retained or produced in electronic form, whether as an electronic communication or otherwise, but requires that the electronic form of the document be retained or produced in accordance with particular information technology and procedural requirements— if the public body's requirements have been met and those requirements have been made public and are objective, transparent, proportionate and nondiscriminatory, and,

(e)   where the document is required or permitted to be retained for or produced to a person who is neither a public body nor acting on behalf of a public body— if the person for or to whom the document is required or permitted to be retained or produced consents to it being retained or produced in that form.'[129]

[19.55] The Electronic Commerce Act 2000 sets out the criteria by which integrity and reliability may be measured. The criteria for measuring integrity are:

'whether the information has remained complete and unaltered, apart from the addition of any endorsement or change which arises in the normal course of generating, communicating, processing, sending, receiving, recording, storing or displaying.'[130]

Reliability is to be assessed 'in the light of the purpose for which and the circumstances in which the information was generated.'[131]

These provisions are stated to be 'without prejudice to any other law requiring or permitting information to be presented or retained ... in accordance with particular information technology and procedural requirements ... on a particular kind of data storage device, or ... by means of a particular kind of electronic communication.'[132]

Admissibility of electronic documents

[19.56] The Electronic Commerce Act 2000 provides for the admissibility of electronic signatures into evidence, stating that:

'In any legal proceedings, nothing in the application of the rules of evidence shall apply so as to deny the admissibility in evidence of ... an electronic communication, an electronic

---

[129] Electronic Commerce Act 2000, s 18(2).
[130] Electronic Commerce Act 2000, s 18(4)(a).
[131] Electronic Commerce Act 2000, s 18(4)(b).
[132] Electronic Commerce Act 2000, s 18(3).

form of a document ... or writing in electronic form ... on the sole ground that it is an electronic communication, an electronic form of a document, an electronic contract, or writing in electronic form, or ... if it is the best evidence that the person or public body adducing it could reasonably be expected to obtain, on the grounds that it is not in its original form.'[133]

The validity of electronic information

[19.57] The Electronic Commerce Act 2000 provides that:

'Information (including information incorporated by reference) shall not be denied legal effect, validity or enforceability solely on the grounds that it is wholly or partly in electronic form, whether as an electronic communication or otherwise.'[134]

---

[133] Electronic Commerce Act 2000, s 22(a).
[134] Electronic Commerce Act 2000, s 9.

Chapter 20

Marketing and Selling Goods and Services Online

Introduction

[20.01] Electronic commerce, or 'e-Commerce', is a somewhat abused term for the sale of goods and services over the Internet. The business has undergone a revolution since the glory days of the dot-com boom, when everything including petfood was being sold online.[1] Many goods are services are now sold online: there are entertainment services providing music and games, banking services, insurance services, gambling, auctioning and a whole range of advertising services. Consumers will expect the same rights online as they receive offline. To this end the Electronic Commerce Act 2000 provides that:

> 'All electronic contracts within the State shall be subject to all existing consumer law and the role of the Director of Consumer Affairs in such legislation shall apply equally to consumer transactions, whether conducted electronically or non-electronically.'[2]

But as consumers move online, by definition they will take their trade away from physical shops. This process may challenge member states, but it will also encourage the growth of the EC's internal market. The resulting tensions can probably only be resolved at EC level, whether by the institutions of the EC or by the ECJ.

Selling goods and services online in Europe

[20.02] EC law on selling goods online is spread across a number of Directives. Some of these apply to particular areas of the economy, such as the Directive on the Distance Selling of Financial Services. Others are of more general application such as the Directive on e-Commerce and the Distance Selling Directive. Inevitably these different enactments overlap. The Directive on e-Commerce and the Distance Selling Directive both apply to the sale of goods and services over the Internet and both provide a list of the information that must be provided to consumers. Unfortunately, they are different lists, with the one provided by the latter being longer than that of the former. The two lists are not incompatible, but providing two of them imposes an unnecessary compliance cost on consumers. To this list must also be added the list of information that must be provided to consumers, in their role as data subjects, pursuant to the Data Protection Directive. Again, this list is not incompatible with the other two, but a compliance cost must be imposed upon businesses. Finally, deciding whether or not a service is provided online or offline may prove to be a key issue for many businesses. The EC facilitates the provision of offline services throughout the EU in the form of the Services Directive.[3] But the regime created for offline services is not as easy as that

---

[1] See Cassidy, *Dot-Con* (Penguin, 2005).

[2] Electronic Commerce Act 2000, s 15.

[3] Directive 2006/123/EC of the European Parliament and of the Council of 12 December 2006 on services in the internal market, OJ L 376 , 27/12/2006 P. 36–68.

created for online services by the Directive on e-Commerce and the Distance Selling Directive. This regulatory structure creates significant incentives for anyone who wants to sell services throughout the EU to structure their business as an online entity and not an offline one. Of course, if a business is configured in such a way and if it is successful, then the owner may find it even more attractive to out-source many of the functions off-shore[4]

The Services Directive

[20.03] The Services Directive[5] creates a regulatory regime for the offline supply of services. This regime allows member states to assert far more control over services provided from other member states than the equivalent regime for online services. The Services Directive requires that member states must:

> 'examine the procedures and formalities applicable to access to a service activity and to the exercise thereof. Where procedures and formalities examined ... are not sufficiently simple, Member States shall simplify them.'[6]

Unfortunately, the Directive does not really explain what 'simplify' means, although the recitals suggest that in deciding when examining regulations with a view to deciding what needs to be simplified, national authorities should have regard to those regulations 'necessity, number, possible duplication, cost, clarity and accessibility, as well as the delay and practical difficulties to which they could give rise for the provider concerned.'[7] The difference between the regimes for online and offline service provision is most clearly evident with regard to authorisations. No authorisation requirement may be imposed before the provision of an online service is commenced. In contrast, the Services Directive does allow for the imposition of authorisation conditions, stating that:

> 'Member States shall not make access to a service activity or the exercise thereof subject to an authorisation scheme unless the following conditions are satisfied ... the authorisation scheme does not discriminate against the provider in question ... the need for an authorisation scheme is justified by an overriding reason relating to the public interest ... the objective pursued cannot be attained by means of a less restrictive measure, in particular because an a posteriori inspection would take place too late to be genuinely effective.'[8]

The Services Directive makes it explicitly clear that this provision will not apply to 'those aspects of authorisation schemes which are governed directly or indirectly by other Community instruments.' Of course, the provision of a service may be split into two parts: one offline that may require authorisation and one online that will not. Hence there may be significant advantages to configuring a service in such a way that it will fall under the online regime.

---

4   Friedman, *The World is Flat* (Penguin, 2006).
5   Directive 2006/123/EC of the European Parliament and of the Council of 12 December 2006 on services in the internal market OJ L 376 , 27/12/2006 P. 36–68.
6   Services Directive, art 4(2).
7   Services Directive, recital 45.
8   Services Directive, art 9(1).

The Directive on e-Commerce

[20.04] The Directive on e-Commerce[9] (implemented as European Communities (Directive 2000/31/EC) Regulations 2003) is stated to seek 'to contribute to the proper functioning of the internal market by ensuring the free movement of information society services between the Member States.'[10] The purpose of the Directive is to approximate:

> 'certain national provisions on information society services relating to the internal market, the establishment of service providers, commercial communications, electronic contracts, the liability of intermediaries, codes of conduct, out-of-court dispute settlements, court actions and cooperation between Member States.'[11]

The Directive does not apply to taxation, data protection or competition law issues. It does not apply to the activities of notaries, lawyers, gamblers and bookies.[12] The exclusion of gambling from the scope of the Directive is not absolute. The Directive will not apply to 'games of chance, lotteries and betting transactions, which involve wagering a stake with monetary value'. However, the Directive will apply to 'promotional competitions or games where the purpose is to encourage the sale of goods or services and where payments, if they arise, serve only to acquire the promoted goods or services'.[13] The Directive does not affect actions undertaken by the EC to 'promote cultural and linguistic diversity and to ensure the defence of pluralism'.[14]

The co-ordinated field

[20.05] The Directive on e-Commerce applies to what it terms the 'co-ordinated field', this is defined as:

> 'requirements laid down in Member States' legal systems applicable to information society service providers or information society services, regardless of whether they are of a general nature or specifically designed for them.'[15]

The Directive goes on to explain that the 'co-ordinated field' concerns:

> 'requirements with which the service provider has to comply in respect of ... the taking up of the activity of an information society service, such as requirements concerning qualifications, authorisation or notification ... the pursuit of the activity of an information society service, such as requirements concerning the behaviour of the service provider, requirements regarding the quality or content of the service including those applicable to advertising and contracts, or requirements concerning the liability of the service provider.'[16]

---

[9] Directive 2000/31/EC of the European Parliament and of the Council of 8 June 2000 on certain legal aspects of information society services, in particular electronic commerce, in the Internal Market ('Directive on electronic commerce').

[10] Directive on e-Commerce, art 1(1).

[11] Directive on e-Commerce, art 1(2).

[12] Directive on e-Commerce, art 1(5).

[13] Directive on e-Commerce, recital 16.

[14] Directive on e-Commerce, art 1(6).

[15] Directive on e-Commerce, art 2(h).

[16] Directive on e-Commerce, art 2(i).

However, the co-ordinated field will not cover requirements such as 'requirements applicable to goods as such'; 'requirements applicable to the delivery of goods' or 'requirements applicable to services not provided by electronic means.'[17] The recitals note that 'The scope of the coordinated field is without prejudice to future Community harmonisation relating to information society services and to future legislation adopted at national level in accordance with Community law'. The recitals go on to note that the co-ordinated field will only cover 'requirements relating to online activities such as online information, online advertising, online shopping, online contracting'. The recitals make it clear that the co-ordinated field:

> 'does not concern Member States' legal requirements relating to goods such as safety standards, labelling obligations, or liability for goods, or Member States' requirements relating to the delivery or the transport of goods, including the distribution of medicinal products.'[18]

Information society services

[20.06] The definition of 'information society services' is a key provision of the Directive on e-Commerce. The recitals to the Directive note that 'Information society services span a wide range of economic activities which take place online'. The Directive defines 'information society services' by cross-referring to Directive 98/34/EC laying down a procedure for the provision of information in the field of technical standards and regulations.[19] This directive defines 'information technology services' as 'any service normally provided for remuneration, at a distance, by electronic means and at the individual request of a recipient of services'. The Directive laying down a procedure for the provision of information in the field of technical standards and regulations goes on to explain a number of terms used in this definition in greater detail. For the purposes of the definition, 'at a distance' is defined as meaning that 'the service is provided without the parties being simultaneously present'. Examples of services that are not provided at a distance include:

> 'Services provided in the physical presence of the provider and the recipient, even if they involve the use of electronic devices:
>
> (a)	medical examinations or treatment at a doctor's surgery using electronic equipment where the patient is physically present;
>
> (b)	consultation of an electronic catalogue in a shop with the customer on site;
>
> (c)	plane ticket reservation at a travel agency in the physical presence of the customer by means of a network of computers;

17	Directive on e-Commerce, art 2(j).

18	And the co-ordinated field will not 'cover the exercise of rights of pre-emption by public authorities concerning certain goods such as works of art'. Directive on e-Commerce, recital 21.

19	Directive 98/34/EC laying down a procedure for the provision of information in the field of technical standards and regulations (OJ L 204, 21. 7. 1998 p 37) as amended by Directive 98/48/EC of the European Parliament and of the Council (O J L 217, 05/08/1998 p 18).

(d) electronic games made available in a video-arcade where the customer is physically present.'[20]

[20.07] Similarly 'by electronic means' is defined as:

'that the service is sent initially and received at its destination by means of electronic equipment for the processing (including digital compression) and storage of data, and entirely transmitted, conveyed and received by wire, by radio, by optical means or by other electromagnetic means'.

The definition does not apply to radio or broadcasting services. The following are 'indicative' examples of services that are not provided by electronic means:

1. 'Services having material content even though provided via electronic devices ... (such as) ... automatic cash or ticket dispensing machines ... (or) ... access to road networks, car parks, etc., charging for use, even if there are electronic devices at the entrance/exit controlling access and/or ensuring correct payment is made.'

2. 'offline services: distribution of CD roms or software on diskettes.'

3. 'Services which are not provided via electronic processing/inventory systems ... (such as) ... voice telephony services ... telefax/telex services ... services provided via voice telephony or fax ... telephone/telefax consultation of a doctor ... telephone/telefax consultation of a lawyer ... telephone/telefax direct marketing'[21]

[20.08] Finally, the Directive laying down a procedure for the provision of information in the field of technical standards and regulations defines 'at the individual request of a recipient of services' as: 'the service is provided through the transmission of data on individual request'. Again, 'indicative examples' of what this means are given by the Directive:

'Services provided by transmitting data without individual demand for simultaneous reception by an unlimited number of individual receivers ... (such as) ... television broadcasting services ... including near-video on-demand services ... radio broadcasting services ... teletext.'[22]

The recitals to the Directive on e-Commerce provide further explanations of what is or is not an information society service. They explain that:

'television broadcasting ... and radio broadcasting are not information society services because they are not provided at individual request; by contrast, services which are transmitted point to point, such as video-on-demand or the provision of commercial communications by electronic mail are information society services'.[23]

---

[20] Directive 98/34/EC laying down a procedure for the provision of information in the field of technical standards and regulations (OJ L 204, 21. 7. 1998 p 37) as amended by Directive 98/48/EC of the European Parliament and of the Council (O J L 217, 05/08/1998 p 18), Sch V, para 1.

[21] Directive 98/34/EC, Sch V, para 2.

[22] Directive 98/34/EC, Sch V, para 3.

[23] Directive 98/34/EC, recital 18.

The recitals to the Directive on e-Commerce further explain that whilst the sale of goods online will be covered by the Directive, the delivery of those goods or the provision of offline services will not be covered. online services are increasingly provided for free or, to be more precise, are funded by the provision of advertising to people who use or view online content. The recitals make it clear that the Directive will apply to such activities:

> 'information society services are not solely restricted to services giving rise to online contracting but also, in so far as they represent an economic activity, extend to services which are not remunerated by those who receive them, such as those offering online information or commercial communications, or those providing tools allowing for search, access and retrieval of data.'

So it would seem that the provision of ads by Google on its search page is covered by the Directive. The Directive will also apply to 'services consisting of the transmission of information via a communication network, in providing access to a communication network or in hosting information provided by a recipient of the service.'

[20.09] Finally, the use of email will not, of itself, amount to an information society service:

> 'the use of electronic mail or equivalent individual communications for instance by natural persons acting outside their trade, business or profession including their use for the conclusion of contracts between such persons is not an information society service; the contractual relationship between an employee and his employer is not an information society service; activities which by their very nature cannot be carried out at a distance and by electronic means, such as the statutory auditing of company accounts or medical advice requiring the physical examination of a patient are not information society services.'[24]

Member states and the Commission are expected to encourage the drawing up of codes of conduct for information society service providers[25] and to co-operate with each other more generally.[26]

The internal market

[20.10] As noted above, the legal base of the Directive on e-Commerce lies in the internal market provisions of the TEC.[27] The Directive provides that, in general, information society service providers will be regulated by the Member State where they are based. The Directive does this in two ways. Firstly, it provides that:

> 'Each Member State shall ensure that the information society services provided by a service provider established on its territory comply with the national provisions applicable in the Member State in question which fall within the coordinated field.'[28]

In other words, Ireland has a duty to ensure that information society providers who are established in Ireland, such as Google or Microsoft, comply with Irish law. Secondly,

---

[24] Directive 98/34/EC, recital 18.
[25] Directive on e-Commerce, art 16.
[26] Directive on e-Commerce, art 17.
[27] Specifically arts 47(2), 55 and 95, Directive on e-Commerce, Preamble.
[28] Directive 98/34/EC, art 3(1).

the Directive provides that 'Member States may not, for reasons falling within the coordinated field, restrict the freedom to provide information society services from another Member State.'[29]

[20.11] These two provisions do not apply in the following fields:

(i)   copyright, neighbouring rights, semiconductor chip topography and database rights as well as industrial property rights;

(ii) the emission of electronic money by institutions in respect of which member states have applied one of the derogations provided for by the Directive on e-Money;[30]

(iii) the marketing of undertakings for collective investment in transferable securities;[31]

(iv) the provision of non-life insurance[32] and life assurance;[33]

(v)   the freedom of the parties to choose the law applicable to their contract;

(vi) contractual obligations concerning consumer contacts;

(vii) formal validity of contracts creating or transferring rights in real estate where such contracts are subject to mandatory formal requirements of the law of the member state where the real estate is situated;

(viii) the permissibility of unsolicited commercial communications by electronic mail.[34]

[20.12] The above list primarily consists of fields where the EC is already providing regulation; hence the EC would be anxious to ensure that the Directive on e-Commerce would not overlap with other regulations. The Directive on e-Commerce also provides that individual member states may regulate 'a given information society service' which is based in another member state in the following circumstances. Firstly, the measures taken must be:

'necessary for one of the following reasons':

–   public policy, in particular the prevention, investigation, detection and prosecution of criminal offences, including the protection of minors and the fight

---

[29]   Directive 98/34/EC, art 3(2).

[30]   Directive 2000/46/EC of the European Parliament and of the Council of 18 September 2000 on the taking up, pursuit of and prudential supervision of the business of electronic money institutions OJ L 275 , 27 October 2000, p 39, art 8(1).

[31]   Council Directive 85/611/EEC of 20 December 1985 on the coordination of laws, regulations and administrative provisions relating to undertakings for collective investment in transferable securities (UCITS) OJ L 375, 31 December 1985, p 3, art 44(2).

[32]   Council Directive 92/49/EEC of 18 June 1992 on the coordination of laws, regulations and administrative provisions relating to direct insurance other than life assurance and amending Directives 73/239/EEC and 88/357/EEC (third non-life insurance Directive) OJ L 228, 11 August 1992, p 1, art 30 and Title IV.

[33]   Council Directive 92/96/EEC of 10 November 1992 on the coordination of laws, regulations and administrative provisions relating to direct life assurance and amending Directives 79/267/EEC and 90/619/EEC (third life assurance Directive), Title IV.

[34]   Directive on e-Commerce, art 3(3), Annex.

> against any incitement to hatred on grounds of race, sex, religion or nationality, and violations of human dignity concerning individual persons,
>
> – the protection of public health,
> – public security, including the safeguarding of national security and defence,
> – the protection of consumers, including investors.

[20.13] Secondly, the measures must be taken against 'a given information society service' which prejudices any of the above objectives or which 'presents a serious and grave risk of prejudice to those objectives'. Thirdly, the measures must be proportionate to the objective which is prejudiced by the service in question. Finally, before it can impose the measures in question, the member state that intends taking the measure must have received an inadequate response to a request to that member state where the service provider is based take action. Furthermore, a notification that it is intended to impose such measures must have been sent to the Commission and the member state where the service is based.[35] This last requirement of notification may be dispensed with in an emergency.[36] Where the Commission is notified that a member state intends to take such measures, then:

> 'Without prejudice to the Member State's possibility of proceeding with the measures in question, the Commission shall examine the compatibility of the notified measures with Community law in the shortest possible time; where it comes to the conclusion that the measure is incompatible with Community law, the Commission shall ask the Member State in question to refrain from taking any proposed measures or urgently to put an end to the measures in question.'[37]

In a sense, this last provision is just a restatement of the existing law. The European Commission is not given any new power to force an individual member state to comply with the Directive on e-Commerce, but that is as it should be. Under the EC Treaty, the Commission is required to 'ensure that the provisions of this Treaty and the measures taken ... are applied' in order to 'ensure the proper functioning and development of the common market.'[38]

Ban on the authorisation requirement

[20.14] The Directive ensures that member states cannot impose an obligation on service providers to apply for authorisation to the State before commencing service. The Directive provides that:

> 'Member States shall ensure that the taking up and pursuit of the activity of an information society service provider may not be made subject to prior authorisation or any other requirement having equivalent effect.'[39]

The Directive specifies that this provision will not prejudice 'authorisation schemes which are not specifically and exclusively targeted at information society services'.[40]

---

35 Directive on e-Commerce, art 3(4).
36 Directive on e-Commerce, art 3(5).
37 Directive on e-Commerce, art 3(6).
38 TEC, art 211.
39 Directive on e-Commerce, art 4(1).
40 Directive on e-Commerce, art 4(2).

However, service providers must set out certain information. This information must be 'easily, directly and permanently accessible to the recipients of the service and competent authorities'. The information in question is:

    (i)   the name of the service provider, together with his physical and electronic addresses;

    (ii)   where the service provider is registered in a trade or similar public register, the trade register in which the service provider is entered and his registration number, or equivalent means of identification in that register;

    (iii) where the activity is subject to an authorisation scheme, the particulars of the relevant supervisory authority;

    (iv) where the service is provided by a member of a regulated profession, then the details of 'any professional body or similar institution with which the service provider is registered' must be provided, together with 'the professional title and the Member State where it has been granted' and 'a reference to the applicable professional rules in the Member State of establishment and the means to access them;

    (v)   the service providers VAT number, where services are provided that are subject to VAT.[41]

Where a service provider sets out details of prices charged, then:

'In addition to other information requirements established by Community law, Member States shall at least ensure that, where information society services refer to prices, these are to be indicated clearly and unambiguously and, in particular, must indicate whether they are inclusive of tax and delivery costs.'[42]

[20.15] The Directive on e-Commerce provides that where a contract is being concluded with a consumer,[43] then, in addition to any other requirements of EC law such as the Data Protection Directive, member states must ensure that:

'at least the following information is given by the service provider clearly, comprehensibly and unambiguously and prior to the order being placed by the recipient of the service:

    (a)   the different technical steps to follow to conclude the contract;

    (b)   whether or not the concluded contract will be filed by the service provider and whether it will be accessible;

    (c)   the technical means for identifying and correcting input errors prior to the placing of the order;

    (d)   the languages offered for the conclusion of the contract.'[44]

---

[41] Directive on e-Commerce, art 5(1).

[42] Directive on e-Commerce, art 5(2).

[43] The Directive on e-Commerce uses the formulation 'except when otherwise agreed by parties who are not consumers'. Strictly speaking, this is broader than just consumers, businesses can still be bound by such provisions if they do not agree to avoid them.

[44] Directive on e-Commerce, art 10(1).

When dealing with a consumer, the service provider must indicate whether he is bound by any codes of conduct.[45] This requirement to provide information does not apply 'to contracts concluded exclusively by exchange of electronic mail or by equivalent individual communications.'[46]

[20.16] However, the recitals to the Directive make it clear that this provision 'should not enable ... the by-passing of those provisions by providers of information society services'.[47] The drafters of the Directive may have been seeking to distinguish between large scale suppliers of information society services, such as i-Tunes, and contracts made between individuals. Contractual terms and other information cannot be simply shown on a pop-up; the consumer must be able to store them permanently 'Contract terms and general conditions provided to the recipient must be made available in a way that allows him to store and reproduce them.'[48] When consumers order goods online, the following principles apply:

(i)   the service provider has to acknowledge the receipt of the recipient's order without undue delay and by electronic means; and

(ii)   the order and the acknowledgement of receipt are deemed to be received when the parties to whom they are addressed are able to access them.[49]

The following must be available to the consumer: 'appropriate, effective and accessible technical means allowing him to identify and correct input errors, prior to the placing of the order'.

The Distance Selling Directive

[20.17] The European Directive on Distance Selling (Directive 97/7EC) was implemented into Irish Law by the EC (Protection of Consumers in respect of contracts made by means of distance communication) Regulations 2001.[50] The Directive notes that for consumers, cross-border distance selling could be one of the main tangible results of the completion of the internal market and it is essential to the smooth operation of the internal market that consumers are able to have dealings with a business outside their country, even if it has a subsidiary in the consumer's country of residence.[51] New technologies increase the number of ways for consumers to obtain information about offers anywhere in the Community and to place orders.[52] The objective of the Directive is to approximate the laws, regulations and administrative provisions of the member states concerning distance contracts between consumers and suppliers. A distance contract means:

---

45   Directive on e-Commerce, art 10(2).
46   Directive on e-Commerce, art 10(4).
47   Directive on e-Commerce, recital 39.
48   Directive on e-Commerce, art 10(3).
49   Directive on e-Commerce, art 11(1).
50   SI 207/2001.
51   Directive on Distance Selling, recital 3.
52   Directive on Distance Selling, recital 4.

'any contract concerning goods or services concluded between a supplier and a consumer under an organized distance sales or service-provision scheme run by the supplier, who, for the purpose of the contract, makes exclusive use of one or more means of distance communication up to and including the moment at which the contract is concluded'.[53]

A 'consumer' means any natural person who contracts at a distance and is acting for purposes that are outside his trade, business or profession.[54] A 'supplier' is any natural or legal person who is acting in his commercial or professional capacity.[55] An 'operator of a means of communication' means any public or private natural or legal person whose trade, business or profession involves making one or more means of distance communication available to suppliers.[56] The Directive has no application to the following contracts: financial services[57], contracts concluded by means of automatic vending machines or automated commercial premises, contracts concluded with telecommunications operators through the use of public payphones, contracts concluded for the construction and sale of immovable property or relating to other immovable property rights, except for rental, and contracts concluded at an auction.[58]

Right to prior information

[20.18] Prior to the conclusion of any distance contract, the consumer must be provided with the following information:

'(a)   the identity of the supplier and, in the case of contracts requiring payment in advance, his address;

(b)   the main characteristics of the goods or services;

(c)   the price of the goods or services including all taxes;

(d)   delivery costs, where appropriate;

(e)   the arrangements for payment, delivery or performance;

(f)   the existence of a right of withdrawal, except in the cases referred to in Article 6(3);

(g)   the cost of using the means of distance communication, where it is calculated other than at the basic rate;

(h)   the period for which the offer or the price remains valid;

(i)   where appropriate, the minimum duration of the contract in the case of contracts for the supply of products or services to be performed permanently or recurrently.[59]'

---

[53]   Directive on Distance Selling, art 1(1).
[54]   Directive on Distance Selling, art 2(2).
[55]   Directive on Distance Selling, art 2(3).
[56]   Directive on Distance Selling, art 2(5).
[57]   Annex II lists a non-exhaustive list. It includes investment services, insurance, reinsurance operations, banking services and operations relating to dealings in futures or options.
[58]   Directive on Distance Selling, art 3. Restated in reg 3.
[59]   Directive on Distance Selling, art 4(1). Set out in Sch 3 in the regulations.

The information must be provided in a clear and comprehensible manner in any way appropriate to the means of distance communication used.[60] Article 2(4) defines 'means of distance communication' as 'any means which, without the simultaneous physical presence of the supplier and the consumer, may be used for the conclusion of a contract between those parties. Annex 1 lists the following: unaddressed printed matter; addressed printed matter; standard letter; press advertising with order form; catalogue; telephone with human intervention; telephone without human intervention (automatic calling machine, audiotext); radio; videophone; telephone with screen); videotex (microcomputer and television screen) with keyboard or touch screen; email; fax; and television (teleshopping).[61] Due regard must be taken, in particular, to the principles of good faith in commercial transactions and the principles governing the protection of those who are unable to give their consent, such as minors.[62] In the case of telephone communications, the identity of the supplier and the commercial purpose of the call must be made explicitly clear at the beginning of any conversation with the consumer. A person who fails to comply with this is guilty of an offence.[63]

Right to written confirmation of information

[20.19] The consumer is entitled to receive written confirmation, by email for example, or confirmation in another durable medium available and accessible to him, of the information set out above in good time. This means that the information should be provided during the performance of the contract, and, at the latest, at the time of delivery where goods not for delivery to third parties are concerned, unless the information has already been given to the consumer prior to conclusion of the contract in writing or in another durable medium available and accessible to him. In any event the following must be provided:

'– written information on the conditions and procedures for exercising the right of withdrawal,

– the geographical address of the place of business of the supplier to which the consumer may address any complaints,

– information on after-sales services and guarantees which exist,

– the conclusion for cancelling the contract, where it is of unspecified duration or a duration exceeding one year'.[64]

This does not apply to services that are performed using a means of distance communication, where they are supplied on only one occasion and are invoiced by the operator of the means of distance communication. Nevertheless, the consumer must in all cases be able to obtain the geographical address of the place of business of the

---

[60] Directive on Distance Selling, Recital 8 notes that the languages used for distance contracts are a matter for member states.

[61] Directive on Distance Selling, art 10 provides that member states must ensure that the means of distance communication, other than those referred to above, which allow individual communications may only be used where there is no clear objection from the consumer.

[62] Directive on Distance Selling, art 4(2).

[63] SI 207/2001, reg 4(3).

[64] Directive on Distance Selling, art 5(1).

supplier to which he may address any complaints.[65] A person who fails to comply with this is guilty of an offence.[66]

Right of withdrawal

[20.20] Consumers are given a right to withdraw from the contract where they buy online or from a catalogue, because they are not able to see the product or ascertain the nature of the service provided before concluding the contract.[67] The consumer is entitled to at least seven working days in which to withdraw from the contract without penalty and without giving any reason. The only charge that may be made to the consumer because of the exercise of his right of withdrawal is the direct cost of returning the goods. The seven days begin:

'–   in the case of goods, from the day of receipt by the consumer where the obligations laid down in Article 5 have been fulfilled

–   in the case of services, from the day of conclusion of the contract or from the day on which the obligations laid down in Article 5 were fulfilled if they are fulfilled after conclusion of the contract, provided that this period does not exceed the three-month period referred to in the following subparagraph. If the supplier has failed to fulfil the obligations laid down in Article 5, the period shall be three months. The period shall begin:

–   in the case of goods, from the day of receipt by the consumer,

–   in the case of services, from the day of conclusion of the contract.

If the information referred to in Article 5 is supplied within this three-month period, the seven working day period referred to in the first subparagraph shall begin as from that moment'.[68]

Where a consumer exercises his rights, the supplier is obliged to reimburse the sums paid by the consumer free of charge. The only charge that may be made is the direct cost of returning the goods. Such reimbursement must be carried out as soon as possible and in any case within 30 days.[69]

[20.21] Unless the parties have agreed otherwise, the consumer may not exercise the right of withdrawal in respect of contracts:

'–   for the provision of services if performance has begun, with the consumer's agreement, before the end of the seven working day period ...

–   for the supply of goods or services the price of which is dependent on fluctuations in the financial market which cannot be controlled by the supplier,

–   for the supply of goods made to the consumer's specifications or clearly personalized or which, by reason of their nature, cannot be returned or are liable to deteriorate or expire rapidly,

---

[65]   Directive on Distance Selling, art 5(2).
[66]   SI 207/2001, reg 5(5).
[67]   Directive on Distance Selling, Recital 14.
[68]   Directive on Distance Selling, art 6(1).
[69]   Directive on Distance Selling, art 6(2).

- for the supply of audio or video recordings or computer software which were unsealed by the consumer,
- for the supply of newspapers, periodicals and magazines,
- for gaming and lottery services'.[70]

If the price of goods or services is fully or partly covered by credit granted by the supplier, or if that price is fully or partly covered by credit granted to the consumer by a third party on the basis of an agreement between the third party and the supplier, the credit agreement must be cancelled, without any penalty, if the consumer exercises his right to withdraw from the contract.[71]

Performance

[20.22] Unless the parties have agreed otherwise, the supplier must execute the order within a maximum of 30 days from the day following that on which the consumer forwarded his order to the supplier.[72] Where a supplier fails to perform his side of the contract on the grounds that the goods or services ordered are unavailable, the consumer must be informed of this situation and must be able to obtain a refund of any sums he has paid as soon as possible and in any case within 30 days.[73] The supplier may provide the consumer with goods or services of equivalent quality and price provided that this possibility was provided for prior to the conclusion of the contract or in the contract. He should be informed of this in a clear and comprehensible manner. The cost of returning the goods should be borne by the supplier and the consumer must be informed of this.[74] Failure to comply with this provision is an offence.[75]

[20.23] The rights to prior information (Article 4), written confirmation (Article 5), withdrawal (Article 6) and requirements regarding performance (Article 7) do not apply to contracts for the supply of foodstuffs, beverages or other goods intended for everyday consumption supplied to the home of the consumer, to his residence or to his workplace by regular roundsmen or contracts for the provision of accommodation, transport, catering or leisure services, where the supplier undertakes, when the contract is concluded, to provide these services on a specific date or within a specific period.[76] A consumer has the right to cancel a payment where fraudulent use has been made of his payment card[77] in connection with a distance contract and, where a fraudulent use has been made, to be recredited with the sums paid or have them returned.[78] Failure to comply with this is an offence.[79]

---

[70] Directive on Distance Selling, art 6(3).
[71] Directive on Distance Selling, art 6(4).
[72] Directive on Distance Selling, art 7(1).
[73] Directive on Distance Selling, art 7(2).
[74] Directive on Distance Selling, art 7(3).
[75] Under SI 207/2001, reg 9(6).
[76] Exceptionally, in the case of outdoor leisure events, the supplier can reserve the right not to apply art 7(2) in specific circumstances.
[77] SI 207/2001, reg 10(4) defines this as including store cards, credit cards, debit cards and charge cards.
[78] Directive on Distance Selling, art 8. SI 207/2001, reg 10.
[79] Under SI 207/2001, reg 10(3).

Inertia selling

[20.24] Inertia selling is prohibited; that is the supply of goods or services to a consumer without their being ordered by the consumer beforehand, where such supply involves a demand for payment. The absence of a response does not constitute consent.[80] Automatic calling machines and fax may only be used where the consumer gives his consent in advance.[81] The use of these without the consumer's consent is also an offence.[82]

Enforcement

[20.25] Regulation 17 provides that offences are prosecuted by the Director of Consumer Affairs and any person guilty of an offence will be liable on summary conviction to a fine not exceeding €3,000.

Distance Selling of Financial Services

[20.26] The Directive on the Distance Selling of Financial Services[83] has as its object the approximation of 'the laws, regulations and administrative provisions of the Member States concerning the distance marketing of consumer financial services.'[84] Where a financial service is initially sold at a distance, but is then followed by a number of steps that are not undertaken at a distance, this directive will only apply to the initial sale and not the subsequent steps. The Directive provides that:

> 'In the case of contracts for financial services comprising an initial service agreement followed by successive operations or a series of separate operations of the same nature performed over time, the provisions of this Directive shall apply only to the initial agreement.'[85]

The recitals of the Directive explain this provision by means of examples suggesting that an initial service agreement:

> 'may be considered to be for example the opening of a bank account, acquiring a credit card, concluding a portfolio management contract, and 'operations' may be considered to be for example the deposit or withdrawal of funds to or from the bank account, payment by credit card, transactions made within the framework of a portfolio management contract. Adding new elements to an initial service agreement, such as a possibility to use an electronic payment instrument together with one's existing bank account, does not constitute an 'operation' but an additional contract to which this Directive applies. The subscription to new units of the same collective investment fund is considered to be one of 'successive operations of the same nature.'[86]

---

[80] Directive on Distance Selling, art 9.
[81] Directive on Distance Selling, art 10.
[82] SI 207/2001, reg 12(2).
[83] Directive 2002/65/EC of the European Parliament and of the Council of 23 September 2002 concerning the distance marketing of consumer financial services and amending Council Directive 90/619/EEC and Directives 97/7/EC and 98/27/EC, OJ L 271, 09/10/2002 P. 16–24.
[84] Directive 2002/65/EC, art 1(1).
[85] Directive 2002/65/EC, art 1(2).
[86] Directive 2002/65/EC, recital 17.

[20.27] The scope of the Directive is effectively set out by the definition of 'financial service', which is defined as 'any service of a banking, credit, insurance, personal pension, investment or payment nature.'[87] The primary purpose of the Directive is to set out the information that must be supplied to consumers prior to the conclusion of a 'distance contract' for financial services. A 'distance contract' is defined as meaning:

> 'any contract concerning financial services concluded between a supplier and a consumer under an organised distance sales or service-provision scheme run by the supplier, who, for the purpose of that contract, makes exclusive use of one or more means of distance communication up to and including the time at which the contract is concluded.'[88]

The information that is to be supplied to such consumers[89] must be supplied in 'good time before the consumer is bound by any distance contract or offer'.[90] The 'commercial purpose … must be made clear' and it must be:

> 'provided in a clear and comprehensible manner in any way appropriate to the means of distance communication used, with due regard, in particular, to the principles of good faith in commercial transactions, and the principles governing the protection of those who are unable, pursuant to the legislation of the Member States, to give their consent, such as minors.'[91]

[20.28] The information falls into four categories. As regards the supplier, the consumer must be supplied with the following information:

'(a) 'the identity and the main business of the supplier, the geographical address at which the supplier is established and any other geographical address relevant for the customer's relations with the supplier;

(b) the identity of the representative of the supplier established in the consumer's Member State of residence and the geographical address relevant for the customer's relations with the representative, if such a representative exists;

(c) when the consumer's dealings are with any professional other than the supplier, the identity of this professional, the capacity in which he is acting vis-à-vis the consumer, and the geographical address relevant for the customer's relations with this professional;

(d) where the supplier is registered in a trade or similar public register, the trade register in which the supplier is entered and his registration number or an equivalent means of identification in that register;

(e) where the supplier's activity is subject to an authorisation scheme, the particulars of the relevant supervisory authority.'[92]

---

87 Directive 2002/65/EC, art 2(b).
88 Directive 2002/65/EC, art 2(a).
89 It should be noted that reduced amounts of information only need be given where the transaction is conducted by means of 'voice telephony' Directive 2002/65/EC, art 3(3).
90 Directive 2002/65/EC, art 3(1).
91 Directive 2002/65/EC, art 3(2).
92 Directive 2002/65/EC, art 3(1)(1).

[20.29] As regards the financial service itself, the consumer must be supplied with the following information:

'(a) a description of the main characteristics of the financial service;

(b) the total price to be paid by the consumer to the supplier for the financial service, including all related fees, charges and expenses, and all taxes paid via the supplier or, when an exact price cannot be indicated, the basis for the calculation of the price enabling the consumer to verify it;

(c) where relevant notice indicating that the financial service is related to instruments involving special risks related to their specific features or the operations to be executed or whose price depends on fluctuations in the financial markets outside the supplier's control and that historical performances are no indicators for future performances;

(d) notice of the possibility that other taxes and/or costs may exist that are not paid via the supplier or imposed by him;

(e) any limitations of the period for which the information provided is valid;

(f) the arrangements for payment and for performance;

(g) any specific additional cost for the consumer of using the means of distance communication, if such additional cost is charged.'[93]

[20.30] As regards the distance contract, the consumer must be informed of:

'(a) the existence or absence of a right of withdrawal ... and, where the right of withdrawal exists, its duration and the conditions for exercising it, including information on the amount which the consumer may be required to pay ... .as well as the consequences of non-exercise of that right;

(b) the minimum duration of the distance contract in the case of financial services to be performed permanently or recurrently;

(c) information on any rights the parties may have to terminate the contract early or unilaterally by virtue of the terms of the distance contract, including any penalties imposed by the contract in such cases;

(d) practical instructions for exercising the right of withdrawal indicating, inter alia, the address to which the notification of a withdrawal should be sent;

(e) the Member State or States whose laws are taken by the supplier as a basis for the establishment of relations with the consumer prior to the conclusion of the distance contract;

(f) any contractual clause on law applicable to the distance contract and/or on competent court;

(g) in which language, or languages, the contractual terms and conditions, and the prior information referred to in this Article are supplied, and furthermore in which language, or languages, the supplier, with the agreement of the consumer, undertakes to communicate during the duration of this distance contract'.[94]

---

[93] Directive 2002/65/EC, art 3(1)(2).
[94] Directive 2002/65/EC, art 3(1)(3).

[20.31] As regards the consumer's right of redress, he must be supplied with the following information:

'(a) whether or not there is an out-of-court complaint and redress mechanism for the consumer that is party to the distance contract and, if so, the methods for having access to it;

(b) the existence of guarantee funds or other compensation arrangements, not covered by Directive 94/19/EC of the European Parliament and of the Council of 30 May 1994 on deposit guarantee schemes[95] and Directive 97/9/EC of the European Parliament and of the Council of 3 March 1997 on investor compensation schemes.'[96]

This list is not exclusive; if other laws require that further information be given, then that information should be given.[97] Where a transaction would result in contractual obligations, then the information to be given during the pre-contractual negotiations must 'be in conformity with the contractual obligations which would result from the law presumed to be applicable to the distance contract if the latter were concluded.'[98]

[20.32] All of the above information must be supplied 'on paper' or 'on another durable medium available and accessible to the consumer in good time before the consumer is bound by any distance contract or offer'.[99] The term 'durable medium' is defined as:

'any instrument which enables the consumer to store information addressed personally to him in a way accessible for future reference for a period of time adequate for the purposes of the information and which allows the unchanged reproduction of the information stored.'[100]

In addition, the consumer is entitled at any time 'to receive the contractual terms and conditions on paper ... (and) ... to change the means of distance communication used, unless this is incompatible with the contract concluded or the nature of the financial service provided'.[101] Consumers may have a right of withdrawal,[102] but they may need to pay for any services that they receive before they exercise their right.[103] The Directive also deals with the situation where contracts for services allow for the tacit renewal of such services; it provides that Member States must:

'prohibit the supply of financial services to a consumer without a prior request on his part, when this supply includes a request for immediate or deferred payment ... (and) ...

---

95 OJ L 135, 31.5.1994, p 5.
96 OJ L 84, 26.3.1997, p 22.
97 Directive 2002/65/EC, art 3(4).
98 Directive 2002/65/EC, art 4.
99 Directive 2002/65/EC, art 5(1).
100 Directive 2002/65/EC, art 2(f).
101 Directive 2002/65/EC, art 4.
     Directive 2002/65/EC, art 5(3).
102 Directive 2002/65/EC, art 6.
103 Directive 2002/65/EC, art 7.

exempt the consumer from any obligation in the event of unsolicited supplies, the absence of a reply not constituting consent.'[104]

[20.33] This Directive is implemented in Ireland by the European Communities (Distance Marketing of Consumer Financial Services) Regulations 2004.[105] The Irish regulations are stated to apply to: 'every distance contract for the supply of a financial service'. However, the regulations will not apply to such a contract:

'if it is entered into between a consumer in the State and a supplier who is carrying on business from within another Member State to the extent that ... the other State has implemented the Distance Marketing Directive, or ... a law of the other State imposes obligations corresponding to those provided for by these Regulations.'[106]

[20.34] The Irish regulations are more specific than the European Directive about the format in which information is to be given to consumers. The regulations require that the supplier must:

'(a)   make known to the consumer the commercial purpose of the contract, and

(b)   give that information in a way that is clear and comprehensible, taking into account the means of communication used, and

(c)   in giving that information, comply with all enactments and rules of law that—

    (i)   require good faith in commercial transactions, or

    (ii)   provide protection to those who are unable to give their consent, such as minors.'[107]

[20.35] The regulations go on to provide that information will be deemed to be given in a clear way only if it 'is easily, directly and at all times accessible to the consumer of the financial service concerned, and ... can be stored by the consumer in a durable medium'.[108] The Irish regulations also provide that a consumer will not have a right to withdraw from such a service where:

'(a)   the price payable for the service depends on fluctuations that may occur in the financial market during the cancellation period and such fluctuations are outside the supplier's control, or

(b)   the service supplied is or relates to a travel or baggage insurance policy or an insurance policy under which insurance cover is provided for less than 1 month, or

(c)   the contract under which the service is supplied was entered into at the consumer's request and has been fully performed by both parties before the consumer gave notice of cancellation, or

(d)   the service is or relates to the provision of a housing loan.'[109]

---

[104] Directive 2002/65/EC, art 9.

[105] European Communities (Distance Marketing of Consumer Financial Services) Regulations 2004 (SI 853/2004).

[106] SI 853/2004, reg 4(1).

[107] SI 853/2004, reg 6(2).

[108] SI 853/2004, reg 6(3).

[109] SI 853/2004, reg 12(1).

[20.36] As regards the supply of unsolicited financial services,[110] the Regulations make it an offence to demand payment for such services:

'having no reasonable cause to believe that there is a right to payment, in the course of carrying on a business makes a demand for payment, or asserts a present or prospective right to payment, for what the supplier knows to be an unsolicited financial service supplied to a consumer commits an offence.'[111]

The regulations go on to provide that an offence will be committed by a supplier who:

'A supplier who, having no reasonable cause to believe there is a right to payment, in the course of any business and with a view to obtaining payment for what the supplier knows to be an unsolicited financial service supplied to a consumer ... threatens to bring legal proceedings, or ... places, or causes to be placed, the name of the consumer on a list of defaulters or debtors, or threatens to do so, or ... invokes, or causes to be invoked, any other collection procedure, or threatens to do so.'[112]

The regulations also provide that:

'A consumer to whom an unsolicited financial service is supplied is under no obligation to pay for the service, unless the consumer has, either in writing or in some other durable medium, notified the supplier that the consumer is willing to be supplied with the service.'[113]

Penalties of a fine not exceeding €3,000 or to imprisonment for a term of not more than 12 months may be imposed on natural persons convicted of such an offence. Where the offender is a body corporate, then a fine of up to €5,000 may be imposed.[114]

online pharmacies in the internal market

[20.37] The sale of prescribed medicines is tightly regulated in Ireland; the Pharmacy Act 2007 provides that it is an offence to carry on the business of a pharmacy unless the pharmacist is registered and the business of the pharmacy is conducted in accordance with the Act.[115] However, as anyone with an email account knows it is possible to sell medicines over the Internet, and a considerable amount of spam contains advertisements for such products. Medicines are well suited to online distribution. Obviously the actual medicines will have to be physically transported to their customer, but as they tend to be low-weight, high-value goods, doing so is an economical proposition. As noted earlier, the EC is supposed to be creating an internal market and there are obvious discrepancies between the prices charged for medicines in some EC states and those charged in

---

[110] Which SI 853/2004, reg 19(4) defines as: 'a financial service supplied otherwise than at the request of the consumer, but does not include a financial service so supplied if the service is supplied under a renewal of an existing contract that is in the economic interests of the consumer.'

[111] SI 853/2004, reg 19(1).

[112] SI 853/2004, reg 19(2).

[113] SI 853/2004, reg 19(3).

[114] SI 853/2004, reg 22.

[115] Pharmacy Act 2007, s 26.

others.[116] So it is hardly surprising that attempts have been made to establish online pharmacies to take advantage of such price discrepancies. In *Deutscher Apothekerverband eV v 0800 DocMorris*[117] the ECJ assessed the legal regime for online pharmacies in Europe. The case concerned:

> 'Internet pharmacies and the question whether the member states may restrict the supply of medicinal products by a pharmacy established in another member state on the basis of individual orders placed by consumers on the Internet'.

In particular, the case concerned 'the interpretation of the principle of free movement of goods'.[118] The applicant was an association of German pharmacists. The respondent was a Dutch pharmacy which had been:

> 'offering for sale, at the Internet address 'www.0800DocMorris.com', prescription and non-prescription medicinal products for human use, in languages including German, for end users in Germany. Some of the medicinal products in question are authorised in Germany and most of them are authorised in another member state.'[119]

[20.38] This site advertised pharmaceuticals for sale in the following way:

> 'The individual medicines are divided into product groups under headings such as 'Painkillers', 'Blood-pressure reducers', 'Cancer therapy', 'Immunostimulants', 'Cholesterol reduction', 'Urologics/potency', 'Detoxification', etc. Each heading first contains an introduction of a few sentences. The medicines are then listed alphabetically under their product name, the contents of the package are described and the price is stated in Euro. Beside the indication as to any prescription requirement, there is a box. By clicking on that box, the medicine in question is ordered. Further information about the product itself may be obtained by clicking on the product name. The consumer also has the opportunity, by clicking on the appropriate icon, to search for a particular product from the range. The defendants also offer services via the Internet (doctor search, personal health service, book tips, etc). A given medicine is classified by DocMorris ... as available only on prescription where it is classified as such in the Netherlands or in the member state in which the consumer resides. Medicines of this type are supplied only on production of the original prescription.'[120]

[20.39] A number of delivery options were offered by the site:

> 'The customer may collect the order in person from DocMorris. Alternatively, they may, at no additional cost, use a courier service recommended by DocMorris to collect the order and take it to the address given by the recipient. Finally, the customer can use another courier service at their own expense.'[121]

---

[116] A survey undertaken by the UK's Office of Fair Trading found that prices for pharmaceutical drugs in Ireland were 103% of those in the UK, whilst prices in Spain and Italy were 84% of those in the UK: Office of Fair Trading, *The Pharmaceutical Price Regulation Scheme*, 20 February 2007, Annex F, http://www.oft.gov.uk/advice_and_resources/resource_base/market-studies/price-regulation.

[117] *Deutscher Apothekerverband eV v 0800 DocMorris* (Case C-322/01); 81 BMLR 33.

[118] (Case C-322/01), opinion of Advocate General Stix-Hackl, para 1.

[119] (Case C-322/01), opinion of Advocate General Stix-Hackl, para 31.

[120] (Case C-322/01), opinion of Advocate General Stix-Hackl, para 31.

[121] (Case C-322/01), opinion of Advocate General Stix-Hackl, para 32.

The applicants challenged the right of the respondent to supply medicines in this way by bringing proceedings in the German courts.[122] The German court then referred the following questions to the ECJ:

1. Are the principles of the free movement of goods under ... (the EC Treaty) ... infringed by national legislation which prohibits human medicines, which are required to be handled only through pharmacies, from being imported commercially from other EU Member States in mail-order business through authorised pharmacies on the basis of individual orders placed by consumers over the Internet?'

2. 'Is it compatible with ... (the EC Treaty) ... for a national prohibition on advertising medicines by mail order, prescription medicines and medicines available only through pharmacies that are authorised in the State of origin but not the importing State to be interpreted so broadly that the Internet presentation of a pharmacy of an EU Member State, which in addition to presentation of its business describes individual medicines with their product name, prescription status, package size and price and at the same time offers the possibility of ordering those medicines by means of an online order form, is classified as prohibited advertising, with the result that cross-border orders of medicines by Internet including delivery of those orders is at the very least made substantially more difficult.[123]

[20.40] The ECJ began its judgment by noting that:

'national rules or practices likely to have a restrictive effect, or having such an effect, on the importation of pharmaceutical products are compatible with the Treaty only to the extent that they are necessary for the effective protection of health and life of humans ... no doubt is cast on the fact that the 'virtual pharmacy' is subject to supervision by the Netherlands authorities, with the result that the arguments put forward by the Apothekerverband to assert generally that the supervision to which such a pharmacy is subject is inadequate, in comparison with that to which a traditional pharmacy is subject, cannot be accepted.'[124]

The court considered that:

'The only arguments which are capable of providing adequate reasons for prohibiting the mail-order trade in medicinal products are those relating to the need to provide individual advice to the customer and to ensure his protection when he is supplied with medicines and to the need to check that prescriptions are genuine and to guarantee that medicinal products are widely available and sufficient to meet requirements.'[125]

---

[122] Selling to Germany from Holland would likely have been profitable for the respondent. The UK's Office of Fair Trading's analysis of prices for medicines in Europe, which was subsequent to the *Deutscher Apothekerverband eV v 0800 DocMorris* case, found a considerable discrepancy between Dutch (95% of the UK) and German (108% of the UK) prices for medicines: Office of Fair Trading, *The Pharmaceutical Price Regulation Scheme*, 20 February 2007, Annex F.

[123] (Case C-322/01), opinion of Advocate General Stix-Hackl, para 38.

[124] (Case C-322/01), paras 104–105.

[125] (Case C-322/01), para 106.

In other words, Internet pharmacies are perfectly legal, so long as the pharmacy is able to verify the accuracy and authenticate the provenance of prescriptions. The ECJ went on to note that no arguments had been made before it which could 'provide a valid basis for the absolute prohibition on the sale by mail order of non-prescription medicines.'[126]

[20.41] In particular, the ECJ noted that as regards non-prescription medicines 'considerations relating to their delivery do not justify an absolute prohibition on their sale by mail order'.[127] However, the ECJ noted that 'The supply to the general public of prescription medicines needs to be more strictly controlled'.[128] The key difficulty with the supply of prescription medicines online is the need to verify the accuracy and providence of prescriptions. The ECJ noted that:

> 'Given that there may be risks attaching to the use of these medicinal products, the need to be able to check effectively and responsibly the authenticity of doctors' prescriptions and to ensure that the medicine is handed over either to the customer himself, or to a person to whom its collection has been entrusted by the customer, is such as to justify a prohibition on mail-order sales. As the Irish government has observed, allowing prescription medicines to be supplied on receipt of a prescription and without any other control could increase the risk of prescriptions being abused or inappropriately used. Furthermore, the real possibility of the labelling of a medicinal product bought in a member state other than the one in which the buyer resides being in a language other than the buyer's may have more harmful consequences in the case of prescription medicines.'[129]

[20.42] The ECJ went on to rule that the sale of prescription medicines online could be prohibited under EC law, but not that of non-prescription medicines. Many of the respondent's arguments relating to the structure and practices of pharmacies were rejected by the ECJ. For example, it found that:

> 'Community law does not preclude a prohibition on mail-order selling of prescription medicines, which means that a prohibition on advertising the sale by mail order sale of that class of medicinal products cannot be found to prevent a lawful method of selling medicinal products.'[130]

If a secure system of inputting and verifying prescriptions could be developed, then it would probably be possible to sell medicines online in Europe. But developing such as system would pose quite a technical challenge, as it would have to 'check effectively and responsibly the authenticity of doctors' prescriptions' and also ensure that the person to whom the medicines were ultimately dispensed was the person to whom the prescription was issued. Arguably the sending of the medicines by registered post to the name and address of the person to whom the prescription was issued would be sufficient to meet the latter of these challenges. But it is very hard to see how the authenticity of prescriptions could be validated without involving the doctor who originally issued the script.

---

[126] (Case C-322/01), para 112.
[127] (Case C-322/01), para 115.
[128] (Case C-322/01), para 117.
[129] (Case C-322/01), para 119.
[130] (Case C-322/01), para 147.

Online gambling in the internal market

[20.43] Gambling in Ireland is subject to a variety of laws and legislation. In particular the Betting Act 1931 provides that bookmakers must be licenced:

'No person shall carry on business or act as a bookmaker or hold himself out or represent himself to be a bookmaker or a licensed bookmaker unless he holds a bookmaker's licence granted to him under this Act and for the time being in force.'[131]

[20.44] Contravention of this provision is an offence.[132] The Revenue Commissioners must keep a list of premises 'in which the business of bookmaking is carried on'.[133] and these premises must have a certificate of suitability.[134] The paying of betting duty is subject to the Greyhound Industry Act, 1958 and the Irish Horseracing Industry Act 1994 as amended by the Horse and Greyhound Racing (Betting Charges and Levies) Act 1999. Whether one regards bookmaking as a product, a service or a vice, it is clear that it is highly regulated in Ireland. Other EU member states have regulatory regimes that are more or less restrictive. The USA has gone further than this and has prohibited US gamblers from using credit cards, cheques and electronic fund transfers to settle online bets.[135] The virtual world of Second Life has also banned virtual gambling, rather than try to comply with real world laws.[136]

[20.45] Differences in betting duty and regulation may make it attractive to establish sites that enable citizens of one member state to gamble online in another. Of course, the resulting loss of revenue and control will not be to the liking of the state whose citizens are targeted and that state may attempt to restrict the activities of the site in question. This was at issue in the ECJ decision of *Italy v Gambelli*[137] in which the respondents were accused of 'having unlawfully organised clandestine bets and of being the proprietors of centres carrying on the activity of collecting and transmitting betting data, which constitutes an offence of fraud against the state.'[138]

[20.46] The facts were that the Italian authorities had identified:

'the operation of a widespread and complex organisation of Italian agencies, linked via the internet to the British bookmaker Stanley International Betting Ltd ... which is involved in the collection in Italy of bets reserved by law to the State. It does this as follows: the bettor notifies the person in charge of the agency of the games on which he wishes to bet and how much he intends to bet. The person in charge of the agency forwards a request for acceptance of the bet via the internet to the British bookmaker and indicates the football matches in question and the bets placed. The bookmaker forwards confirmation of the acceptance of the bet via the internet immediately (literally: in real time). That

---

[131] Betting Act 1931, s 2(1). The holder of a licence or permit for a lottery is not be required to hold a bookmaker's licence under s 35 of the Gaming and Lotteries Act 1956–1986.

[132] Betting Act 1931, s 2(2) as amended.

[133] Betting Act 1931, s 8(1).

[134] Betting Act 1931, s 10.

[135] Ward, 'Legislation gives US a stronger hand' (2006) Financial Times, 2 October.

[136] Nutall, 'Virtual casino falls foul of ban on gambling' (2007) Financial Times, 27 July.

[137] *Italy v Gambelli* (Case C-243/01) ECJ; see similarly, *Criminal proceedings against Placanica*, ECJ, (Joined cases C-338/04, C-359/04 and C-360/04); [2007] All ER (EC) 827.

[138] Case C-243/01) ECJ, para 5.

confirmation is forwarded to the bettor, whereupon he pays the amount owed which is then forwarded to the British bookmaker and paid into a special foreign account.'[139]

[20.47] The Italian authorities considered that this system breached the Italian state monopoly on such betting. The English operation was not unregulated; the ECJ noted that it was:

> 'authorised to carry on its activity in the UK and abroad. It organises and manages bets under a UK licence, identifying the events, setting the stakes and assuming the economic risk. Stanley pays the winnings and the various duties payable in the UK, as well as taxes on salaries and so on. It is subject to rigorous controls in relation to the legality of its activities, which are carried out by a private audit company and by the Inland Revenue and Customs and Excise.
>
> ... Stanley offers an extensive range of fixed sports bets on national, European and world sporting events. Individuals may participate from their own home, using various methods such as the internet, fax or telephone, in the betting organised and marketed by it.
>
> ... Stanley's presence as an undertaking in Italy is consolidated by commercial agreements with Italian operators or intermediaries relating to the creation of data transmission centres. Those centres make electronic means of communication available to users, collect and register the intentions to bet and forward them to Stanley.'[140]

The respondents were Stanley's Italian agents, who argued that:

> 'by prohibiting Italian citizens from linking up with foreign companies in order to place bets and thus to receive the services offered by those companies by internet, by prohibiting Italian intermediaries from offering the bets managed by Stanley, by preventing Stanley from establishing itself in Italy with the assistance of those intermediaries and thus offering its services in Italy from another Member State and, in sum, by creating and maintaining a monopoly in the betting and gaming sector, the legislation at issue in the main proceedings amounts to a restriction on both freedom of establishment and freedom to provide services.'[141]

The respondents went on to argue that:

> 'The purpose of the Italian legislation is also to protect licensees under the national monopoly by making that monopoly impenetrable for operators from other Member States, since the invitations to tender contain criteria relating to ownership structures which cannot be met by a capital company quoted on the stock exchange but only by natural persons, and since they require applicants to own premises and to have been a licence-holder over a substantial period.'[142]

[20.48] The ECJ considered that:

> 'Where a company established in a Member State (such as Stanley) pursues the activity of collecting bets through the intermediary of an organisation of agencies established in

---

[139] (Case C-243/01) ECJ, Opinion of Advocate General Abler, para 8.
[140] (Case C-243/01) ECJ, paras 12–14.
[141] (Case C-243/01) ECJ, para 25.
[142] (Case C-243/01) ECJ, para 27.

another Member State (such as the defendants in the main proceedings), any restrictions on the activities of those agencies constitute obstacles to the freedom of establishment.'[143]

The ECJ went on to note that:

'the freedom to provide services involves not only the freedom of the provider to offer and supply services to recipients in a Member State other than that in which the supplier is located but also the freedom to receive or to benefit as recipient from the services offered by a supplier established in another Member State without being hampered by restrictions.'[144]

It was clear that Italians who gambled online in another member state were committing an offence under Italian law. The Italian government having confirmed to the court that:

'an individual in Italy who from his home connects by internet to a bookmaker established in another Member State using his credit card to pay is committing an offence.'[145]

The court ruled that:

'Such a prohibition, enforced by criminal penalties, on participating in betting games organised in Member States other than in the country where the bettor is established constitutes a restriction on the freedom to provide services ... .The same applies to a prohibition, also enforced by criminal penalties, for intermediaries such as the defendants in the main proceedings on facilitating the provision of betting services on sporting events organised by a supplier such as Stanley, established in a Member State other than that in which the intermediaries pursue their activity, since the prohibition constitutes a restriction on the right of the bookmaker freely to provide services, even if the intermediaries are established in the same Member State as the recipients of the services.'[146]

This led the court to the conclusion that the Italian laws constituted 'a restriction on the freedom of establishment and on the freedom to provide services'.[147] Italy claimed that these restrictions were justified on public interest grounds, the ECJ having previously accepted that:

'restrictions on gaming activities may be justified by imperative requirements in the general interest, such as consumer protection and the prevention of both fraud and incitement to squander on gaming, restrictions based on such grounds and on the need to preserve public order must also be suitable for achieving those objectives, inasmuch as they must serve to limit betting activities in a consistent and systematic manner.'[148]

[20.49] However, in this case it had been pointed out by the referring court that 'the Italian state is pursuing a policy of substantially expanding betting and gaming at national level with a view to obtaining funds'.[149]

---

[143] (Case C-243/01) ECJ, para 46.
[144] (Case C-243/01) ECJ, para 55.
[145] (Case C-243/01) ECJ, para 56.
[146] (Case C-243/01) ECJ, paras 57–58.
[147] (Case C-243/01) ECJ, para 59.
[148] (Case C-243/01) ECJ, para 67.
[149] (Case C-243/01) ECJ, para 67.

The ECJ therefore held that:

> 'Insofar as the authorities of a Member State incite and encourage consumers to participate in lotteries, games of chance and betting to the financial benefit of the public purse, the authorities of that State cannot invoke public order concerns relating to the need to reduce opportunities for betting in order to justify measures such as those at issue.'[150]

This led the ECJ to the conclusion that:

> 'national legislation which prohibits on pain of criminal penalties the pursuit of the activities of collecting, taking, booking and forwarding offers of bets, in particular bets on sporting events, without a licence or authorisation from the Member State concerned constitutes a restriction on the freedom of establishment and the freedom to provide services provided for ... (by the EC Treaty)'.[151]

The ECJ also considered that it was for the Italian courts to decide:

> 'whether the criminal penalty imposed on any person who from his home connects by internet to a bookmaker established in another Member State is not disproportionate in the light of the court's case-law ... especially where involvement in betting is encouraged in the context of games organised by licensed national bodies.'[152]

Whilst stating that this was a matter for the Italian courts, the ECJ gave a quite broad hint as to what it thought the position should be:

> 'The national court will ... need to determine whether the imposition of restrictions, accompanied by criminal penalties of up to 1 year's imprisonment, on intermediaries who facilitate the provision of services by a bookmaker in a Member State other than that in which those services are offered by making an internet connection to that bookmaker available to bettors at their premises is a restriction that goes beyond what is necessary to combat fraud, especially where the supplier of the service is subject in his Member State of establishment to a regulation entailing controls and penalties, where the intermediaries are lawfully constituted ... As to the proportionality of the Italian legislation in regard to the freedom of establishment, even if the objective of the authorities of a Member State is to avoid the risk of gaming licensees being involved in criminal or fraudulent activities, to prevent capital companies quoted on regulated markets of other Member States from obtaining licences to organise sporting bets, especially where there are other means of checking the accounts and activities of such companies, may be considered to be a measure which goes beyond what is necessary to check fraud ... It is for the national court to determine whether the national legislation, taking account of the detailed rules for its application, actually serves the aims which might justify it, and whether the restrictions it imposes are disproportionate in the light of those aims.'[153]

Online advertising

[20.50] Advertising in Ireland is regulated by a variety of different laws, primarily the Consumer Information Act 1978 and the European Communities (Misleading

---

[150] (Case C-243/01) ECJ, para 68.
[151] (Case C-243/01) ECJ, para 76.
[152] (Case C-243/01) ECJ, para 72.
[153] (Case C-243/01) ECJ, paras 73–75.

Advertising) Regulations 1988.[154] There is also a variety of sectoral regulation, which regulates the advertising of goods such as tobacco products and services such as those provided by solicitors. Advertising online has many different features from more traditional forms and it is far more pervasive and largely unregulated. The most prominent form of advertising is that of unsolicited communications such as spam. The sending of spam is illegal, and its content is invariably misleading and often criminal. Other forms of advertising litter the Internet; websites in themselves are often a form of advertising. Indeed there is a good case to be made that a website dedicated to a commercial product is, in reality, one big advertisement. However, the Internet makes it difficult to distinguish what is advertising and what is editorial content. It should be obvious in a newspaper where the advertising begins and ends; it may not be so obvious online.

[20.51] The Consumer Information Act (CIA) 1978 provides that an offence will be committed by a person who:

> 'in the course or for the purposes of a trade, business or profession ... makes a statement which he knows to be false, or ... recklessly makes a statement which is false as to any of the following matters ...

> (i) the provision in the course of the trade, business or profession of any services, accommodation or facilities,

> (ii) the nature, effect or fitness for purpose of any services, accommodation or facilities provided in the course of the trade, business or profession,

> (iii) the time at which, manner in which or persons by whom any services, accommodation or facilities are so provided,

> (iv) the examination, approval, use or evaluation by any person of any services accommodation or facilities so provided, or

> (v) the place where any service, facility or accommodation is so provided or the amenities of any such accommodation.'[155]

Ambiguity will not necessarily help the maker of the statement. The Act goes on to provide that 'anything ... likely to be taken for such a statement as to any of those matters as would be false shall be deemed to be a false statement as to that matter.'[156]

[20.52] The Act defines 'reckless' in the following terms 'a statement made regardless of whether it is true or false shall be deemed to be made recklessly, unless the person making it had adequate reasons for believing that it was true.'[157] 'False' means 'false to a material degree'.[158] As regards advertising for services such as the application of a treatment or a process or the making of repairs, then the Act will also apply to 'the effect of the treatment, process or repair'.[159] An offence will also be committed by one who

---

[154] The European Communities (Misleading Advertising) Regulations 1988 (SI 134/1988).
[155] CIA 1978, s 6(1).
[156] CIA 1978, s 6(2)(a).
[157] CIA 1978, s 6(2)(b).
[158] CIA 1978, s 6(4).
[159] CIA 1978, s 6(3).

gives a misleading statement of prices or cost. The Act provides that such an offence will be committed where:

> 'a person offering to supply goods of any description or provide any services or accommodation gives by any means a false or misleading indication of ... the price or charge for the goods, services or accommodation ... the price or charge at or for which the goods or goods of the same description or the services or accommodation were or was previously offered ... a recommended price for the goods, or ... any charge for installation of or servicing of the goods or any price for ancillary equipment reasonably required for the purpose of the use or enjoyment of the goods.'[160]

One exception to this is that it will not be an offence for a credit institution to provide credit at a lower rate of interest than had been advertised.[161] Finally, in respect of misleading advertisements, the Act provides that:

> 'A person shall not publish, or cause to be published, an advertisement in relation to the supply or provision in the course or for the purposes of a trade, business or profession, of goods, services or facilities if it is likely to mislead, and thereby cause loss, damage or injury to members of the public to a material degree.'[162]

Contravention of the above will amount to an offence.[163] Where convictions are obtained in respect of any offences contrary to the CIA 1978 they will be punishable by the imposition of a fine not exceeding €12,967 (£10,000) and a term of imprisonment of up to two years.[164]

Advertisements for consumer credit

[20.53] The Consumer Credit (CCA) 1995 defines 'advertisement' as including:

> 'every form of advertising, whether in a publication, by television or radio, by display of notices, signs, labels, showcards or goods, by distribution of samples, circulars, catalogues, price lists or other material, by exhibition of pictures, models or films, or in any other way, and references to the publishing of advertisements shall be construed accordingly.'[165]

Although quite comprehensive, as of 1995, this list does not mention the Internet or other forms of electronic advertising. It would be a matter for a court to decide whether the definition would extend to the Internet. Whilst the definition does not explicitly refer to the Internet, there is nothing in the definition to suggest that it does not. The definition does state that advertising includes 'every form of advertising'. It is highly likely that the courts would hold that every form of advertising would include that provided online. The issue that is more likely to trouble a court in the online context is deciding what is an online advertisement for consumer credit subject to the CCA 1995 and what amounts to the distance marketing of consumer financial services, which would be subject to the

---

[160] CIA 1978, s 7(1).
[161] CCA 1995, s 21(1).
[162] CIA 1978, s 8(1).
[163] CIA 1978, s 8(1).
[164] CIA 1978, s 21.
[165] CCA 1995, s 2(1).

Distance Selling of Financial Services Directive. It is likely that every case will depend on its individual facts. The courts might regard as an advertisement a screen that pops-up when a user accesses a website and which indicates that consumer credit may be available elsewhere. It will depend upon the content of the screen, whether any hypertext links are supplied in the screen and what they link to. If the screen links to a page that contains the information required by the Distance Selling of Financial Services Directive, then such a screen might be regarded as an advertisement. On the other hand, if the screen links directly to an application form for financial services, then it might be considered that the screen should have provided the information required by the Distance Selling of Financial Services Directive.

[20.54] As regards the information that must be provided in advertising material for consumer credit, the CCA 1995 provides that:

> 'An advertisement in which a person offers to provide or arrange the provision of credit shall, if mentioning a rate of interest or making any claim in relation to the cost of credit, contain a clear and prominent statement of the APR, using a representative example if no other means is practicable, provided it is indicated that this is only a representative example, and no other rate of interest shall be included in the advertisement.'[166]

This statement must be afforded no less prominence than other information such as the payment period, number of payments required and details of advance payments.[167] Conditions must be stated,[168] as well as requirements for the provision of security[169] and any other restrictions.[170] In relation to the advertising of 'a financial accommodation in relation to the acquisition of goods or the provision of a service', an advertisement must provide the following information:

> 'the nature of the financial accommodation ... the cash price of the goods or service ... . the APR and the total cost of credit or the hire-purchase price ... the number and amount of instalments ... the duration of the intervals between instalment payments ... . the number of any instalments which have to be paid before delivery of the goods, and ... . details of any deposit payable.'[171]

Advertisements for package holidays and airline tickets

[20.55] The Package Holiday Directive[172] provides that certain information must be provided to consumers, such as passport and visa information, but the Directive also provides that:

---

[166] CCA 1995, s 21(1), as substituted by SI 245/1996.
[167] CCA 1995, s 21(2), as substituted by SI 245/1996.
[168] CCA 1995, s 21(3), as substituted by SI 245/1996.
[169] CCA 1995, s 21(4), as substituted by SI 245/1996.
[170] CCA 1995, s 21(6), as substituted by SI 245/1996.
[171] CCA 1995, s 22, as substituted by SI 245/1996.
[172] Council Directive 90/314/EEC of 13 June 1990 on package travel, package holidays and package tours OJ L 158, 23/06/1990 P. 0059–0064. See Buttimore, *Holiday Law in Ireland* (Blackhall Publishing, 1998).

'Any descriptive matter concerning a package and supplied by the organizer or the retailer to the consumer, the price of the package and any other conditions applying to the contract must not contain any misleading information.'[173]

The Directive also provides that brochures must contain certain content, including the price and 'adequate information' concerning:

'(a) the destination and the means, characteristics and categories of transport used;

(b) the type of accommodation, its location, category or degree of comfort and its main features, its approval and tourist classification under the rules of the host Member State concerned;

(c) the meal plan;

(d) the itinerary;

(e) general information on passport and visa requirements for nationals of the Member State or States concerned and health formalities required for the journey and the stay;

(f) either the monetary amount or the percentage of the price which is to be paid on account, and the timetable for payment of the balance;

(g) whether a minimum number of persons is required for the package to take place and, if so, the deadline for informing the consumer in the event of cancellation'[174]

[20.56] The Directive does not define the term 'brochure', but it is likely that it does extend to Internet sites. The Directive was implemented in Ireland by the Package Holidays and Travel Trade Act 1995. This does not explicitly define a brochure as something that may be supplied electronically, but the possibility that documents might be saved electronically was clearly within the contemplation of the Oireachtas when it enacted the legislation. The Package Holidays and Travel Trade Act 1995 defines a record as:

'any book, document or any other written or printed material in any form including any information stored, maintained or preserved by means of any mechanical or electronic device, whether or not stored, maintained or preserved in a legible form.'[175]

Again this definition is not tied to references to the content of brochures; it is actually relevant to the execution of powers of authorised officers under the Act.[176] However, it does show that electronic methods of storage were being considered at the time of enactment. The argument might be made that as the Oireachtas clearly thought that documents in general might be stored electronically, it might also have thought that documents that were travel brochures might be similarly stored.

[20.57] The Consumer Information (Advertisements for Airfares) Order 2000[177] provides that advertisements for airfares must be clear. The regulations provide that every advertisement for an airfare must comply with the following provisions:

---

[173] Directive 90/314/EEC, art 3(1).

[174] Directive 90/314/EEC, art 3(2).

[175] Package Holidays and Travel Trade Act 1995, s 2(1).

[176] Package Holidays and Travel Trade Act 1995, s 21.

[177] Consumer Information (Advertisements for Airfares) Order 2000 (SI 468/2000).

'(i)   the total price payable for the airfare[178] by the purchaser shall be clearly stated as one single amount and in the currency in which it is payable;

(ii) where applicable, and separately, the monetary amount of any charge to be imposed in respect of the method of payment of the airfare shall be clearly stated.'[179]

The term 'advertisement' is stated to include 'every form of advertising' and the term 'charge' is defined as including 'a fee or a tax by whichever source imposed or levied'.[180] Whilst an airfare must be stated as a single amount, 'a statement of the individual amounts which constitute the total price payable for the airfare may be included in such an advertisement and where such a statement is included it shall specify every such amount together with the item in respect of which it is payable'.[181]

[20.58] The Consumer Information (Advertisements for Airfares) Order 2000 defines a restriction on an airfare as including:

'restrictions on ... flight times; ... the number of seats or the percentage of total aircraft capacity on specific routes; ... specific days of the week or months of the year; ... specific airports in relation to arrival or departure; ... specific source or method of booking; and ... method of payment.'[182]

Where restrictions are placed on an advertised fare, then those restrictions must be disclosed on any advertisement:

'where an advertisement for an airfare contains a statement about the method of booking or the method of payment for the airfare and there are restrictions with respect to the use of either such method applicable, the existence of those restrictions shall be clearly stated in the advertisement.'[183]

Where restrictions are imposed on an airfare, then:

a.   'in the case of a written advertisement for the airfare, every such restriction shall be clearly specified in the advertisement'

b.   ... in the case of an advertisement for the airfare, other than a written such advertisement, the existence of every such restriction shall be clearly stated in the advertisement'.

[20.59] The regulations state that the term 'written' is to be 'construed as including electronic modes of representing or reproducing words in visible form.' The regulation goes on to define the term 'electronic' as including 'electrical, digital, magnetic, optical, electromagnetic, biometric, photonic and any other form of related technology.'[184] So the requirement that the restrictions on an airfare must be disclosed would clearly apply to

---

[178] "total price payable for the airfare" means the total price of the airfare payable by the purchaser of the airfare, and includes all charges payable by him or her other than any charges imposed in respect of the method of payment' SI 468/2000, reg 3.

[179] SI 468/2000, reg 4(1).

[180] SI 468/2000, reg 3.

[181] SI 468/2000, reg 4(2).

[182] SI 468/2000, reg 3.

[183] SI 468/2000, reg 5.

[184] SI 468/2000, reg 3.

an online advertisement. However, the regulations go on to provide that this requirement:

> 'shall not be construed as requiring the specification of such a restriction to have the same degree of prominence in the advertisement concerned as the statement in the advertisement of the total price payable for the airfare has.'[185]

Legal services

[20.60] Pursuant to the Solicitors (Advertising) Regulations 2002[186] it is lawful for solicitors to advertise,[187] where an advertisement is defined as:

> 'any communication (whether oral or in written or other visual form and whether produced by electronic or other means) which is intended to publicise or otherwise promote a solicitor in relation to the solicitor's practice, including ... any electronic address or any information provided by the solicitor that is accessible electronically.'[188]

Such an advertisement may be published by:

> 'claiming in public (whether orally, in written form or electronically) the superiority of the legal services offered by the solicitor over those of, or offered by, other persons who are not solicitors.'[189]

The regulations impose limitations on the contents[190] and locations of advertisements.[191] As regards barristers' the Code of Conduct of the Bar of Ireland provides that:

> 'Barristers may advertise by placing prescribed information concerning themselves on the website of the Bar Council and subject to such rules and regulations as may be promulgated from time to time by the Bar Council in respect of the content of such an entry. Barristers may advertise by such other means as the Bar Council may prescribe by way of regulations promulgated from time to time, which regulations shall be promulgated for the purposes of protecting the public interest, facilitating competition and maintaining proper professional standards.'[192]

Tobacco products

[20.61] The Public Health (Tobacco) Act 2002 makes it an offence to advertise tobacco, providing that 'a person who advertises, or causes the advertisement of, a tobacco product shall be guilty of an offence.'[193]

---

[185] SI 468/2000, reg 6(2).
[186] Solicitors (Advertising) Regulations 2002 (SI 518/2002).
[187] SI 518/2002, reg 3.
[188] SI 518/2002, reg 2(a).
[189] SI 518/2002, reg 6(iv).
[190] SI 518/2002, regs 4 and 5.
[191] SI 518/2002, reg 6.
[192] Bar Council of Ireland, *Code of Conduct for the Bar of Ireland*, Adopted on 13 March 2006, para 6.1
[193] Public Health (Tobacco) Act 2002, s 33(1).

Online auctions

[20.62] The Internet offers a novel environment in which to hold auctions and sites such as http://www.ebay.ie/ cater to this market. Whilst the marketplace for auctions may be new, the law is well established. For example *Harris v Nickerson*[194] is authority for the proposition that if an auction is advertised for a specified time and place, then that will amount to a declaration of intent alone, not an offer to hold the auction in question. Deciding whether to place a reserve on the bids that will be accepted is a significant step. If a reserve is not placed, the courts will interpret this as an offer to sell to the highest bidder.[195] It remains to be seen how the courts will apply contract law to online auctions, but is likely that the existing case law will transfer easily enough. That is not to say that auction sites cannot give rise to interesting legal issues. For example, some auction sites have been used to sell stolen goods,[196] which can give rise to criminal charges. Ratings given to buyers and sellers may also prove contentious.[197] The Distance Selling Directive does not apply to auction sales, stating that 'This Directive shall not apply to contracts ... concluded at an auction.'[198]

Payments online

[20.63] Given that the Internet is a global network, paying for goods is always going to be a problem. There is no straightforward way for an Irish person to buy goods from an American site such as http://www.amazon.com. The solution that has been adopted by the industry is the use of credit cards. Alternative solutions such as electronic money are also being adopted, but the prime instance of this is a niche market that nobody would have predicted back in 2000 when the EC was enacting its e-Money Directive.

Credit cards

[20.64] Irish law provides that consumers will not be liable for fraudulent payments online on their credit card under the EC(Protection of Consumers in Respect of Contracts made by means of Distance Communication) Regulations, 2001[199] and the EC (Distance Marketing of consumer financial services) Regulations 2004.[200] Proving that a credit card purchase was fraudulently made can be very difficult. Of course, sometimes it will be obvious. On one occasion, a Dublin schoolboy logged onto the website of a

---

[194] *Harris v Nickerson* (1873) LR 8 QB 286.
[195] *Tully v Land Commission* (1961) 97 ILTR 174. See Ryan, *Contract Law* (Roundhall, 2006).
[196] 'End of road for gang that sold lorry loot' (2006) Yorkshire Evening Post, 10 May.
[197] Morgan and Brown, 'Reputation in Online Auctions: The Market for Trust' California Management Review, Vol 49/1 (Fall 2006): 61–81.
[198] Distance Selling Directive, art 3(1). It is worth noting that http://www.ebay.ie states: 'The Regulations apply to sales made by a seller acting in the course of business to a consumer which have been concluded at a distance. In other words, where there is no face to face contact between the seller and the consumer. This would cover sales over the internet. Business sellers need to comply with a certain number of obligations such as providing clear information about themselves and providing the consumer with certain rights such as a cooling off/cancellation period', http://pages.ebay.ie/help/policies/listing-distance.html.
[199] SI 207/2001.
[200] SI 853/2004.

major chocolate manufacturer, ordered a large amount of chocolate and 'paid' for it all with the credit card number of a South American. Although the schoolboy did get his chocolate, he also got a visit from gardaí.[201] Proving that the credit card in question was wrongfully used would not have been difficult in this circumstance. But proving fraudulent use may be far more difficult in other cases. In *R (on the application of O) v Coventry Justices*[202] the defendant was accused of having used his credit card to purchase access to online child pornography, a charge that he denied. The charges related to the use of credit card numbers on the infamous Landslide website in the USA; similar evidence was to give rise to the Gardaí's Operation Amethyst.[203] At trial the court heard evidence that:

> 'The person accessing the Landslide website was invited by the pre-programmed content to complete a form, entering certain personal data. That data consisted of their name, address and email address, and also financial information such as credit card details. In that way, the person was able to select which hyperlinked websites could be accessed and could access those websites for a pre-set time, and a predetermined price would then be debited against the nominated credit card.'[204]

[20.65] The court then heard evidence that:

> 'a credit card number is given which on five of the occasions is the same as that of the Claimant's credit card number. There is then in one column a code in which it appears that the credit card was accepted on four occasions and rejected on three occasions ... there is a computer printout produced by the Alliance and Leicester witness which shows that ... the Claimant's credit card was debited with sums which were payable or paid to Landslide Productions at Fort Worth.'[205]

The claimant was convicted. He appealed and on appeal questioned 'whether there was a sufficiency of information to connect the Claimant with the computer printout'.[206] The English High Court held that there was, finding that:

> 'the evidence that is admitted, namely the details of his address, email and credit card, is sufficient for a jury to draw the conclusion, if so minded, that the person with that identity was the person who had keyed the information into the computer. (The) submission that the one does not follow the other in my judgment puts the cart before the horse. Once there is evidence to show that the credit card details are those of the Claimant, it seems to me it is sufficient to show that an inference is capable of being drawn that it was him who keyed the information into the computer.'[207]

Distance Selling Directive

[20.66] The Distance Selling Directive provides that Member States must ensure that consumers can 'request cancellation of a payment where fraudulent use has been made

---

[201] Kelleher, 'E-commerce law to affect us all' (1999) The Irish Times, 13 September.

[202] *R (on the application of O) v Coventry Justices* [2004] EWHC 905 (Admin), CO/6342/2003, [2004] Crim LR 948.

[203] Downes, 'Numbers investigated on child porn in decline' (2006) The Irish Times, 23 October.

[204] *R (on the application of O) v Coventry Justices* [2004] EWHC 905 (Admin), para 10.

[205] [2004] EWHC 905 (Admin), paras 18–19.

[206] [2004] EWHC 905 (Admin), para 26.

[207] [2004] EWHC 905 (Admin), para 27.

of his payment card in connection with distance contracts covered by this Directive ... (and) 'in the event of fraudulent use, to be recredited with the sums paid or have them returned.'[208] This provision is implemented by the European Communities (Protection Of Consumers in Respect of Contracts made by Means of Distance Communication) Regulations 2001:[209]

> 'The consumer may request cancellation of any payment made under a distance contract or, as appropriate, the recredit or return of such a payment, where fraudulent use had been made of his or her payment card.'[210]

Such a request must be complied with immediately;[211] failure to immediately comply will be an offence.[212] Where a conviction is obtained in respect of such an offence, then a fine not exceeding €3,000 (£2,362.69) may be imposed.[213]

Directive on Distance Selling of Financial Services

[20.67] The Directive on Distance Selling of Financial Services provides in relation to 'payment by card' that member states must ensure that consumers can 'request cancellation of a payment where fraudulent use has been made of his payment card in connection with distance contracts ... (and) '... in the event of such fraudulent use, to be re-credited with the sum paid or have them returned'.[214] This provision is now implemented by the European Communities (Distance Marketing of Consumer Financial Services) Regulations 2004,[215] which provides that certain clauses will be implied into the contract between the supplier of a credit card and the user of that card. The first of these is that:

> 'The contract between the provider of a payment card and the consumer relating to the payment card shall be deemed to provide ... for relevant payments to be recredited or returned to the consumer whenever the card is used fraudulently in connection with a distance contract for the supply of a financial service.' [216]

The second is that the consumer will not be liable for any such payment 'after the consumer has informed the card provider of the loss, theft or misappropriation of the card.'[217]

---

[208] Directive 97/7/EC, art 8.

[209] European Communities (Protection Of Consumers in Respect of Contracts made by Means of Distance Communication) Regulations 2001 (SI 207/2001).

[210] SI 207/2001, reg 10(1) where the term '"payment card" includes credit cards, charge cards, debit cards and store cards', reg 10(4).

[211] SI 207/2001, reg 10(2).

[212] SI 207/2001, reg 10(3).

[213] SI 207/2001, reg 17(2).

[214] Directive 2002/65/EC, art 8.

[215] European Communities (Distance Marketing of Consumer Financial Services) Regulations 2004 (SI 853/2004).

[216] SI 853/2004, reg 29(1)(a), as substituted by SI 63/2005.

[217] SI 853/2004, reg 29(1)(b), as substituted by SI 63/2005.

The provider of a credit or other payment card must:

'ensure that facilities are available to enable the consumer ... to request cancellation of (such) a payment ... and ... .to immediately notify the provider if the card is lost, stolen or misappropriated.'[218]

Where the provider of a card fails to comply with this last provision, then 'the consumer is not liable for the financial consequences resulting from the loss, theft or misappropriation of the card.'[219] Finally, the regulations provide that in any proceedings relating to a fraudulent payment for Financial Services provided at a distance, if :

'the consumer alleges that the consumer's payment card has been used without the consumer's authorisation, the onus is on the provider of the card to prove that the consumer authorised its use.'[220]

eMoney

[20.68] Electronic money has never really taken off online; most users continue to rely upon credit cards. There are alternatives, of course; for example PayPal offers a method of paying for goods by creating an account with them. This limits consumers' exposure online, but placing funds in a PayPal account is still typically done by credit card. However, there is one forum where electronic money appears to have taken off and it is that of online games such as Second Life:

'The Second Life economy has its own currency, Linden dollars, which can be bought and sold on LindeX, the currency exchange, for real-world currency. More than Dollars 1m in real-world dollars are spent on Second Life assets every day.'[221]

The existence of these funds has led to calls for states to tax virtual incomes[222] and Second Life's financial system is quite sophisticated with 'Banks and stock exchanges ... housed in huge, formal structures draped in marble and glass'.[223] The EC has developed a regulatory regime for electronic money systems in the form of the e-Money Directive.[224] But the EC would have had real world activities in mind when it did so. The European Commission has reviewed the operation of the e-Money Directive and concluded that:

'There is widespread agreement among stakeholders that the e-money market has developed more slowly than expected, and is far from reaching its full potential. However, while no e-money product has gained widespread acceptance as a general means of payment, some products(in particular server-based ones) have found relative success in niche markets and for very specific uses. New products are also emerging, or are expected

---

[218] SI 853/2004, reg 29(2), as substituted by SI 63/2005.

[219] SI 853/2004, reg 29(3).

[220] SI 853/2004, reg 29(4), as substituted by SI 63/2005.

[221] 'Increased appetite for networking feeds virtual world' (2007) Financial Times, 23 August.

[222] Holder, 'Treasury urged to collect "virtual" revenues' (2007) Financial Times, 29 May.

[223] Boss, 'Even in a Virtual World, "Stuff" Matters' (2007) New York Times, 9 September.

[224] Directive 2000/46/EC of the European Parliament and of the Council of 18 September2000 on the taking up, pursuit of and prudential supervision of the business of electronic money institutions, OJ L 275/39, 27 October 2000. These are implemented in Ireland by the European Communities (Electronic Money) Regulations 2002 (SI 221/2002).

to emerge shortly. The number of issuers making use of the instruments of the Directive (electronic money institution (ELMI) status, waiver) is still low, and limited to a few Member States.'[225]

[20.69] The e-Money Directive defines electronic money as:

'monetary value as represented by a claim on the issuer which is: ... stored on an electronic device; ... issued on receipt of funds of an amount not less in value than the monetary value issued ... accepted as means of payment by undertakings other than the issuer.'[226]

It goes on to provide that 'Member States shall prohibit persons or undertakings that are not credit institutions ... from carrying on the business of issuing electronic money.'[227] The Irish Financial Services Regulatory Authority has interpreted the e-Money Directive to mean that 'the regulated activity of issuing e-money is restricted to banks, building societies and (Electronic Money Institutions).'[228] This means that if a virtual world were to be hosted on an Irish site, then if it established the equivalent of the Linden Dollar, it might have to create an electronic money institution to do so. Of course, it could avoid this by providing that its virtual currency was not convertible into euros or other real world currencies, but that might make its virtual world less attractive to users and less profitable for the host. The e-Money Directive defines an Electronic Money Institution as 'an undertaking or any other legal person, other than a credit institution ... which issues means of payment in the form of electronic money.'[229]

The activities of Electronic Money Institutions are limited by the Directive to:

'(a) the provision of closely related financial and non-financial services such as the administering of electronic money by the performance of operational and other ancillary functions related to its issuance, and the issuing and administering of other means of payment but excluding the granting of any form of credit; and

(b) the storing of data on the electronic device on behalf of other undertakings or public institutions.'[230]

[20.70] So whilst it would be possible for the host of an Irish virtual world to issue the equivalent of Linden Dollars, they could not loan them. However, there is no real regulation of such virtual world's virtual currencies and financial systems. This may become a problem in future:

'The stock exchanges and banks in (Second Life) are imposing, but they are unregulated and unmonitored. Investors fed Linden dollars into savings accounts at Ginko Financial bank, hoping to earn the promised double-digit interest. Some did, but in July there was a run on the bank and panic spread as Ginko A.T.M.'s eventually stopped giving depositors

---

[225] DG Market, Evaluation of the E-Money Directive, 17 February 2006, p 2, http://ec.europa.eu/internal_market/bank/docs/e-money/evaluation_en.pdf.

[226] Directive 2000/46/EC, art 1(3)(b).

[227] Directive 2000/46/EC, art 1(4).

[228] IFSRA, Guidance Notes on the Submission of Applications and on going Supervisory Requirements of Electronic Money Institutions, February 2003, p 3.

[229] Directive 2000/46/EC, art 1(3)(a).

[230] Directive 2000/46/EC, art 1(5).

their money back. The bank has since vanished. With no official law and order in Second Life, investors have little recourse ... Some Second Life residents are calling for in-world regulatory agencies — the user-run Second Life Exchange Commission has just begun operating — and some expect real-world institutions to become involved as the Second Life population and economy expands.'[231]

Unfortunately the losses that stemmed from the collapse of Second Life's bank were not virtual and have been put at $750,000.[232] Were a similar virtual world to be established in Ireland, it would certainly be possible for it to be regulated. IFSRA takes the view that:

'(Electronic Money Institution)s are required to comply with the Authority's supervision requirements at all times. Compliance with the requirements and standards however, does not relieve the boards and management of (Electronic Money Institution)s of the fundamental responsibility to conduct the operations of their institutions in accordance with the relevant laws and in a prudent manner with full and primary regard for the safety of a customer's e-money.'[233]

Online taxes

[20.71] The application of tax law to ecommerce and the gathering of revenue online was considered by the Revenue Commissioners in some detail back in 1999.[234] The Commissioners stated that:

'The fundamental issues for the taxation of e-commerce are ... Identification of a transaction ... _ Identification of the parties to a transaction, in particular the taxpayer ... Verification of the details of a transaction (for example, the item traded, its price, the taxing jurisdiction, etc.) ... In the case of VAT, application of the correct taxing rules and rates and the calculation and remittance of any tax due to the correct taxing authority ... Generation of an audit trail.'[235]

The Revenue Commissioners considered that:

'there is a need to ensure that the practical application of these principles results in the neutral tax treatment of e-commerce transactions. Where a product can be delivered in a physical and a digitized form the neutrality principle strictly applied demands that the tax treatment should be similar. However, in applying the principles already agreed at international level, different tax treatments could conceivably emerge depending on the product and whether it is subject to tax in its physical manifestation. For example, the purchase of a book online in a digitized form may be treated as a service and under current rules subject to VAT at the standard rate of 21 per cent. In contrast, the same book ordered online but delivered physically would be zero rated for VAT. The issue is not, however, black and white. The price of a digitized book may include a license authorising the purchaser to use the information in the book for various purposes.'[236]

---

[231] Boss, 'Even in a Virtual World, "Stuff" Matters' (2007) New York Times, 9 September.

[232] Adler and Hopkins, 'Washington People, The American Banker' (2007) 27 August.

[233] IFSRA, Guidance Notes on the Submission of Applications and on going Supervisory Requirements of Electronic Money Institutions, February 2003, p 4.

[234] Revenue Commissioners, *Electronic Commerce and the Irish Tax System*, 1999, http://www.revenue.ie/pdf/e_commerce/e_commerce.pdf.

[235] Revenue Commissioners, para 5.1.

[236] Revenue Commissioners, para 5.2–5.3.

The Revenue Commissioners also expressed concerns about the effects of disintermediation:

'Obviously, as consumers deal direct with producers ordering and receiving online products in a digital form the business of traditional Irish based intermediaries such as shipping companies, customs agents, distribution and transportation companies, wholesalers and retailers could decline. The use of the internet to order goods for subsequent physical delivery will lead to a reduction in the need for wholesalers and retailers, although this development will, of course, increase the business of the international parcel carriers. These processes may result in a reduction in the tax base as profits which would normally have accrued to such traders will no longer arise in this jurisdiction. It is likely that this reduction in the tax base will be accompanied by factors which will tend to compensate for the decline.'[237]

[20.72] VAT may be chargeable on goods and services bought and sold online. The Revenue Commissioners have analysed this issue and concluded that:

'VAT affects three broad categories of e-commerce transactions ... supplies of physical goods, ordered over the internet, to both business and private consumers ... online supplies of digitized goods and services from business to business; and ... online supplies of digitized goods and services from business to private customers.'[238]

VAT invoices may be processed electronically,[239] as may returns for capital gains[240], betting duty,[241] corporation[242] and income tax.[243] As regards services provided electronically from outside the EU, the EC has provided that:

'electronically supplied services provided from third countries to persons established in the Community or from the Community to recipients established in third countries should be taxed at the place of the recipient of the services.'[244]

---

[237] Revenue Commissioners, para 5.9.

[238] Revenue Commissioners, para 7.3.

[239] Value-added Tax (Electronic Invoicing and Storage) Regulations 2002 (SI 504/2002).

[240] SI 443/2003.

[241] SI 803/2004.

[242] SI 522/2001.

[243] SI 441/2001.

[244] Council Directive 2002/38/EC of 7 May 2002 amending and amending temporarily Directive 77/388/EEC as regards the value added tax arrangements applicable to radio and television broadcasting services, OJ L128/41, 15 May 2002, Recital 3.

Chapter 21

Spam, Spit, Spim and Splogs

Introduction

[21.01] As anyone with an email account knows, unsolicited commercial email is a serious inconvenience and it is one that is getting worse.[1] Irish inboxes are getting more spams than ever before; at the time of writing, in or around 65% of email received in Ireland was spam.[2] This suggests that Ireland is escaping the worst of the problem, as spam makes up to 95% of global email traffic.[3] At the same time, the content of this email is changing. As well as the old reliables, such as pornography, drug and 419 scams, 'Pump-and-dump' stock market frauds are becoming increasingly commonplace. Spam can be sent on pretty much any electronic communications system spam sent via SMS texts to mobile phones is already a problem in Ireland.[4] In the summer of 2007 the DPC raided 'a number of companies engaged in the mobile phone text marketing sector'. These raids were in response to a 'large number of complaints'.[5] As VoIP (Voice-over-Internet-Protocol) lowers the cost of making a phone call to almost nothing, spam will be joined by spit (Spam over Internet Telephony). Research has commenced into defence mechanisms, but spit is likely to be even more inconvenient to deal with than email spam.[6] And, spam has already been joined by spim[7] and splog. Splog, that is spam placed in blogs, is becoming an increasing problem.[8] A splog is a 'is blog-style site consisting of nonsense words, cribbed content or a mixture of both'. The creators of such sites aim to make money by selling advertising and tens of thousands of such

---

[1] For a review of why the problem is getting worse, see Arthur, 'Why spam is out of control' (2006) The Guardian, 9 November.

[2] In July 2007 about 63% of all email received in Ireland were spam. This figure is actually lower than normal, reflecting a seasonal variation is the habits of spam senders. See 'IE Internet, Spam and Virus rates low in July' (2007) Press Release, 1 August.

[3] 'Drowning in Numbers' (2007) Financial Times, 11 July.

[4] In DPC Case Study 5/2004, the DPC 'received a number of complaints from people who had received unsolicited mobile phone text messages from Realm Communications offering a free stay in one of 30 Irish Hotels'. DPC, *Annual Report 2003*, p 34. The DPC investigated and concluded that Realm Communications was in breach of SI 192/2002, which has now been superseded by SI 535/2003.

[5] 'Office of the Data Protection Commissioner' (2007) Press Release, 20 July.

[6] Leyden, 'Spam gets vocal with VoIP' http://www.theregister.co.uk, 17 February 2005.

[7] SPIM are unsolicited instant messages. See Delio, 'Spam monster eyes another target', http://www.wired.com, 26 March 2004.

[8] A survey undertaken in the summer of 2007 found some 300 Irish websites whose message boards contained links to pornographic sites Ryan, 'Irish web forums riddled with porn links', http://www.enn.ie, 10 July 2007.

splogs can be created by a single person. Of the 120,000 blogs created every day,[9] about 90% may be splogs.[10]

[21.02] A primary reason why spam is a problem is that email is free;[11] the endemic nature of spam reflects the 'Tragedy of the Commons'.[12] The fact that spam will be disregarded by 99% of recipients is irrelevant; the fact that email is free makes it possible to deluge inboxes with a 'Tsunami'[13] of spam so that the responsive 1% is profitable.[14] Although sending a spam may be free to the sender, it imposes substantial costs on users and infrastructure. Professional services firms may find that spam is their primary client;[15] the use of filtering software can reduce the amount of time wasted on spam, but it would be a foolish solicitor who automatically deleted spam without having someone check the content. Spam creates serious difficulties for the development of systems for serving by email. In *Bernuth Lines Ltd v High Seas Shipping Ltd*[16] the respondent attempted to serve a document by email, but as the applicant's solicitor explained:

> 'the persons who received the emails did not know what to do with them and ignored them ... as 'spam' ... the address receives hundreds of spam and unsolicited emails every day and that 'the Customer Service Representative took the view that no serious legal matter would be sent to the Applicant using that address' and 'that the email was not serious and that serious legal correspondence would go through appropriate channels ... One has in mind the frequency with which junk email is received containing apparently legitimate legal email correspondence which is in fact spurious.'[17]

This has led to calls to charge for email;[18] many users also filter their emails. Some will use filtering software; others simply ignore email from unfamiliar addresses.

---

[9]   Technorati, 'The State of the Blogosphere' 5 April 2005.

[10] Rigby, 'Splogging is clogging up the blogosphere' (2006) Financial Times, 31 October. However, technorati estimate that only about 6000–7000 splogs are created every day; in other words, less than 10% of the total number of blogs.

[11] 'The minimal marginal cost of sending emails has enabled spam to flourish', Drowning in Numbers, (2007) Financial Times, 23 January.

[12] Hardin, 'The Tragedy of the Commons', (1968) *Science* (162)3859, pp 1243–1248.

[13] Taylor, 'Networks under threat from "tsunami" of spam' (2006) The Financial Times, 9 November.

[14] 'People who undertake spam attacks assume that you send out 100 emails and get one reply – that's the rate of return they're looking at ....'. 'The assumption is if they send out a million or tens of millions, that 1 per cent becomes thousands of people'; Thomson, You've got mail: junk messages that will never self-destruct', (2007) Sun Herald (Australia), 11 February.

[15] Suppose such a firm has 200 fee-earning partners and associates, suppose each of them spends half an hour a day dealing with spam, and that is 100 hours every day.

[16] *Bernuth Lines Ltd v High Seas Shipping Ltd* [2005] EWHC 3020 (Comm).

[17] [2005] EWHC 3020 (Comm), para 27.

[18] Kraut et al, 'Markets for Attention: Will Postage for Email Help?' (2002) *Yale ICF Working Paper No 02-28.*

The nature of the spam problem

[21.03] 'Spam' has been described by the English High Court as 'an unwanted nuisance.'[19] It has been defined by the European Commission as 'a term ... commonly used to describe unsolicited, often bulk emails ... (it) ... is ... a shortcut for unsolicited commercial electronic mail'.[20] The origins of the term spam were set out by Arnold QC[21] in *Hormel Foods v Antilles Landscape Investments*[22]:

> 'By December 1997 the word SPAM had acquired a meaning of 'unsolicited commercial electronic messages comprising either postings to USENET newsgroups (i.e. discussion groups) or email'. This meaning would have been known to many users of the Internet and to the majority of those in the field of computer programming services by that date, although it does not appear to have entered any dictionary by then. This use of the word SPAM appears to derive from a sketch in the popular BBC television programme Monty Python 's Flying Circus in which repetitive singing of the word SPAM (used to denote the Claimant's product) drowns out other conversation. Although the word SPAM had been used in nuisance messages sent on electronic messaging systems in the 1980s, the use of the word to mean unsolicited commercial electronic messages appears to date from about 1994.'[23]

[21.04] It is the unsolicited nature of spam that causes so many problems for users. Spam has to be distinguished from legitimate marketing emails that are sent with the consent of the recipients or otherwise in accordance with the law.[24] The commission suggests a number of reasons why spam is a problem.[25]

(a)   Spam is an invasion of the privacy of individuals. It can be misleading, deceptive or pornographic, and it is frequently all three.[26]

---

[19] *Microsoft Corporation v McDonald* [2006] EWHC 3410 (Ch), para 1.

[20] EU Commission, Communication from the Commission to the European Parliament, the Council, the European Economic and Social Committee and the Committee of the Regions on Unsolicited Commercial Communications or 'spam', Brussels, 22.01.2004 COM(2004) 28 final, p 5. The UK All Party Internet Group defined spam as '... meaning any email that was not requested by its recipient and has clearly been sent out en masse'. UK All Party Parliamentary Internet Group, 'Spam: Report of an Inquiry by the All Party Internet Group', October 2003, p 5.

[21] Sitting as a Deputy Judge of the English High Court.

[22] *Hormel Foods v Antilles Landscape Investments* [2005] EWHC 13 (CH), [2005] All ER (D) 206 (Jan).

[23] [2005] EWHC 13 (CH), [2005] All ER (D) 206 (Jan), Para 128(i).

[24] For example, Tesco sends around 16 to 20 million marketing emails each month to the email addresses of some 4 million customers. In October 2005, UK supermarkets sent out 76 different mass marketing emails, of which 44 came from Tesco. Brook, 'Tesco unleashes email marketing blitz', (2005) The Guardian, 11 November.

[25] Of course, some spammers do sell products that people actually buy 'the pernicious root of the spam crisis does not appear to be legislative or technological. It is human – in particular, the humans who buy from spammers'. McWilliams, *Spam Kings* (O'Reilly, 2005) p 296.

[26] In 2004 a spam-filtering company revealed that, of spam messages sent to London school children, 'half are pushing drugs, a fifth promote porn and another fifth promote cheap software'. Sherriff, 'London schoolkids drown in spam tsunami', http:// www.theregister.co.uk 11 August 2004.

(b)   Removing spam from inboxes wastes time and money. Spam creates considerable costs for businesses, both directly, in the form of time wasted by employees dealing with it, and indirectly, where legitimate commercial or business emails are excluded by anti-spam filters.[27]

(c)   Spam creates costs for the society in general in the form of lost productivity,[28] undermining consumer confidence[29]and discouraging the development of services such as 'always on' wireless access, which may result in receiving large amounts of spam.[30]

[21.05] The nature of the spam problem was analysed by the Dutch Presidency of the Council of the European Union in the following terms:

'Spam is an increasing problem, both in number and in the criminal nature of it. The methods of spammers get more and more sophisticated and due to more and more illegal applications the business case gets increasingly interesting to spammers. Worldwide there is agreement amongst countries that the battle against spam and its malicious practices is to be fought actively. Within the EU, member states also agree on the urgency of this problem. The Presidency sees spam as a priority issue in the internet security field and stresses the need for short term actions ... the problem is very complex, multifaceted, and moreover worldwide (no geographical boundaries) and growing rapidly'.[31]

[21.06] The roots of the email spamming problem lie in the origins of the Internet.[32] Email was invented in 1971, when only a tiny number of people used the Internet and all

---

[27]   In 2004 a survey of 83 major US corporations found that the average employee received nearly 7500 spam messages per year; 3.1% of his productivity lost to dealing with spam and the cost of this was some $1934 per hour, see 'Nucleus Research, Spam: The Serial ROI Killer' Research Note e50, June 2004, http://www.nucleusresearch.com. See also the German neo-nazi emails that started bombarding Irish Government systems on the 60th anniversary of WWII: Reid, 'Neo Nazi spam emails bombard Government Department Network', (2005) The Irish Times, 20 May.

[28]   A survey published by the University of Maryland estimates that in 2004 Americans spent 422.9 million hours a week deleting spam, which is the equivalent of 573,000 people working a 40-hour week. This time is estimated to cost the American economy $21.6 billion a year. University of Maryland, Smith, 'School of Business, 2004 National Technology Readiness Survey' 3 February 2005. Research produced by Ferris Research (http:// www.ferris.com) suggests that spam's worldwide cost in 2005 will be $50 billion.

[29]   For example, 'phishing' typically involves 'email spam that appears to come from a trusted brand name such as a bank. This email usually urges recipients to clik on an embedded link that takes them to a fraudulent website where they are duped into entering personal, financial and other confidential information'. Taylor, 'Phishy business of net security', http//:www.ft.com, 22 September 2005.

[30]   COM(2004) 28 final, pp 8–9.

[31]   Council of the European Union, Unsolicited communications for direct marketing purposes or spam – Presidency Paper, Brussels, 24 November 2004, 5691/04 TELECOM 11, p 1.

[32]   Electronic spam is distinguished from SPAM, the luncheon meat, by keeping 'spam' lower case. The owner of the trade mark SPAM, Hormel Meats, gave up trying to control the use of its name several years ago. See Glasner, 'A Brief History of SPAM, and Spam', http:// www.wired.com 26 May 2001.

of them knew each other. No security measures were included in email protocols for the very good reason that none were necessary.[33] Although spam could have been a problem from the very inception of email, for almost a quarter of a century informal controls ensured that spam remained socially unacceptable. Then two American lawyers, Laurence Canter and Martha Siegel, placed an advertisement on 6000 Usenet news groups advertising legal services. The Internet community mobilised to bombard Canter and Siegel with emails. As a result Canter and Siegel were disconnected by their ISP. However, they were inspired by their experience to write *How to make a Fortune on the Information Superhighway,*[34] which was read by Jeff Slaton, the 'Spam King'.[35] The Internet community attempted to impose social controls on Slaton, not least by publishing his home address and photograph online. Slaton achieved some success. He became 'the Internet's public enemy number one … ' and was sued repeatedly. Court actions and community opprobrium had a considerable effect and by 2001 it seemed 'safe to say that (the) spam phenomenon as it existed in the US in the mid-1990's is now in decline'.[36]

[21.07] This prediction was to prove regretfully false, as Slaton's successors took 'spam into the industrial age'.[37] It would appear that most email traffic is now spam; estimates of the precise percentage can vary from 75 to 88 per cent.[38] As the European Commission acknowledged in early 2004, when the figure was 'only' 50 per cent, 'Unsolicited commercial communications by email, otherwise known as 'spam' have reached worrying proportions'.[39] In spite of a variety of legal and practical initiatives, spam has continued to develop as a serious problem. The US Federal Trade Commission ('US FTC') has suggested a number of reasons for this.[40] The US FTC believes that spammers exploit the anonymity provided by email protocols. They use 'spoofing' to falsify email headers or even the originating IP address. This 'allows spammers to send email without accountability, often disguised as personal email'.[41] A number of consequences flow from this lack of accountability:

> 'A spammer can send out millions of spoofed messages, but any bounced messages – messages returned as undeliverable – or complaints stemming from the spoofed emails will only go to the person whose address was spoofed. The spammer never has to deal with them. As a result, an innocent email user's inbox may become flooded with

---

[33] Granneman, 'Exploring the law of unintended consequences' http:// www.theregister.co.uk 21 January 2005.

[34] Cantor and Siegel, *How to make a Fortune on the Information Superhighway* (Harper-Collins, 1994).

[35] Jeff Slaton is described in research published by the EU Commission as 'a true pioneer: it was he who invented the fake email address and the forged domain name to avoid detection: Gauthronet and Drouard, 'Unsolicited Commercial Communications and Data Protection' EU Commission, January 2001, p 15.

[36] Gauthronet and Drouard, p 17.

[37] Gauthronet and Drouard, p 16.

[38] Gross, 'CAN-SPAM not seen to be effective' (2004) Infoworld, 26 December.

[39] COM(2004) 28 final, p 3.

[40] US FTC, 'National Do Not Email Registry: A Report to Congress' June 2004.

[41] US FTC, p 8.

undeliverable messages and angry, reactive email, and the innocent user's Internet service may be shut off due to the volume of complaints'.[42]

[21.08] Spammers may also relay their spam across different servers, obscuring their tracks and 'making it difficult to trace the path their message takes from sender to recipient'.[43] They also use 'proxies' for the same purpose.[44] Perhaps the most serious escalation has occurred recently, involving 'the exploitation of millions of home computers, using malicious viruses, worms, or "Trojans".[45] The consequence of this is that these 'infections, often sent via spam, turn any computer into an open or compromised proxy called a "zombie drone" … Once a computer is infected with one of these programs, a spammer can remotely hijack and send spam from it'.[46] 'Zombies' or 'bots' are an increasing problem. As of March 2005, there were estimated to be about 1 million such machines under the control of spammers, hackers and other miscreants.[47] By the autumn of 2005, Dutch Authorities had uncovered a 'botnet' of 1.5 million machines.[48] The European Commission has suggested that '(a) number of factors seem to influence the effectiveness of enforcement mechanisms'. These factors are:

(a)   'the possibility to enforce legislation with effective fines or other penalties. Some regulatory authorities apparently still lack (effective) enforcement powers;

(b)   the nature of complaints mechanisms and remedies available to individuals and companies;

(c)   the need for clarity and co-ordination among national authorities in view of their sometimes overlapping duties in this area;

(d)   the level of awareness among users about their rights and how to enforce them. Users need to be given information on where to complain, what will be investigated or not, what types of enforcement action may be taken, and what information they need to provide for the authorities to launch an investigation;

(e)   co-ordination and co-operation among Member States and between Member States and third countries on the national law applicable to given cases;

(f)   the resources available to track down 'spammers' operating within the EU or off shore and hiding their identity including by using others' identity, addresses or servers'.[49]

[21.09] Over the years, Europe has embraced a variety of different initiatives, both legislative and otherwise. But, as the European Commission has acknowledged '(t)here

---

[42]   US FTC,, p 8–9.

[43]   US FTC, p 9.

[44]   US FTC, pp 9–10.

[45]   US FTC, p 10.

[46]   US FTC, p 10.

[47]   The Honeynet Project and Research Alliance, 'Know your enemy: tracking botnets' 13 March 2005. See also Leyden, 'Rise of the botnets' http://theregister.co.uk, 15 March 2005.

[48]   Ilett, 'The crime gangs that covert your computer network' (2005) The Financial Times, 8 November.

[49]   COM(2004) 28 final, pp 12–13.

is … no "silver bullet" for addressing spam'.[50] The European Commission has identified the following factors as being critical to the success of Europe's fight against spam:

'–   A strong commitment by central government to fight online malpractices

–   Clear organisational responsibility for enforcement activities

–   Adequate resources for the enforcement authority.'

The Commission notes that: 'these factors are not present in all Member States'.[51]

European anti-spam legislation

[21.10] In addition to legislative initiatives, both the EC and the EU have sought to encourage member states and stakeholders to engage in the fight against spam. The Council of the EU has invited member states 'to commit to fighting spam … in particular through improved cooperation between competent authorities at national and international level.'[52] The European Commission has reported that 'protection against spyware and … malware..is gaining in importance. As spam and malware are increasingly used in combination for criminal profit, enforcement action in these two fields is becoming linked.[53] Given the serious nature of the spam problem, Europe has responded with a number of legislative initiatives. There are now three separate items of European legislation that have attempted to deal with spam or, to use the EC's preferred term, 'unsolicited commercial electronic mail'. These laws are to be found in:

(1)   Directive 95/46;

(2)   Directive 2002/58; and

(3)   the e-Commerce Directive.

The fact that the EC has tried three[54] times to legislate to prohibit spam reflects both the extent of the problem posed by spam and the impotence of the legislation introduced. These measures and their relevant provisions are discussed below.

Directive 95/46

[21.11] Directive 95/46 requires that member states provides a data subject with the right:

'to object, on request and free of charge, to the processing of personal data relating to him which the controller anticipates being processed for the purposes of direct marketing, or to be informed before personal data are disclosed for the first time to third parties or used on

---

[50]   COM(2004) 28 final, p 3.

[51]   Communication from the Commission to the European Parliament, the Council, the European Economic and Social Committee and the Committee of the Regions on fighting spam, spyware and malicious software, Brussels, 15 November 2006, COM(2006)688 final, para 4.1.1.

[52]   Council Resolution of 22 March 2007 on a Strategy for a Secure Information Society in Europe, OJ C 68, 24.3.2007, p. 1–4.

[53]   Communication from the Commission to the European Parliament, the Council, the European Economic and Social Committee and the Committee of the Regions - European electronic communications regulation and markets 2006, Brussels, 29 March 2007, COM(2007) 155 final.

[54]   Four, if one counts Directive 97/66/EC, which was replaced by Directive 2002/58.

their behalf for the purposes of direct marketing, and to be expressly offered the right to object free of charge to such disclosures or uses'.[55]

Member states must take the 'necessary measures' to ensure that data subjects are aware of the existence of this right. Of course, the impact of Directive 95/46 should be much broader than simply providing subjects with a right of objection. Directive 95/46 should work to ensure that subjects have control over how their personal information and data is collected and used by marketing companies. Directive 95/46 provides that member states may 'specify the conditions under which personal data may be disclosed to a third party for the purposes of marketing'.[56] The Article 29 Working Party has adopted an opinion on Unsolicited communications for marketing purposes.[57] Unfortunately, this focuses on a number of technical points, which might be relevant to a discussion of how a legitimate business might go about sending emails to its customers. However, it does not discuss the difficulties posed by spammers who do not even pretend to be legitimate businesses and who engage in legal and technological subterfuge in order to spam.

Implementation in the DPA

[21.12] Direct marketing is defined by the Data Protection Acts 1988–2003 as including:

> 'direct mailing other than direct mailing carried out in the course of political activities by a political party or its members, or a body established by or under statute or a candidate for election to, or a holder of, elective political office.'[58]

The DPA 1988–2003 impose a number of controls on direct marketing. First, it provides that where data is kept for the purposes of direct marketing, then the subject may request in writing that the controller not process the data for that purpose. In this case, the controller must erase the data not more than 40 days after the request was received, where the data is only processed for the purposes of direct marketing. If the data is processed for a number of purposes, then it must not be processed for direct marketing purposes after the expiration of the same period. Secondly, the DPA provides that where data is kept for the purposes of direct marketing, then the subject may request in writing that the controller cease processing the data for that purpose. In this case, the controller must erase the data after not more than 40 days, if it is only used for the purpose of direct marketing. If the data is used for a number of different purposes, then the controller must cease processing it for the purposes of direct marketing within the same period. The controller must then notify the subject in writing. If the data is still to be processed for purposes other than direct marketing, then the controller must inform the subject of what those purposes are.[59] Finally, the DPA 1988–2003 provide that:

> 'Where a data controller anticipates that personal data, including personal data that is required by law to be made available to the public, kept by him or her will be processed

---

[55] Directive 95/46, art 14(b).
[56] Directive 95/46, recital 30.
[57] Article 29 Working Party, Opinion 5/2004 on unsolicited communications for marketing purposes under art 13 of Directive 2002/58/EC, 27 February 2004.
[58] DPA 1988–2003, s 1(1).
[59] DPA 1988–2003, s 2(7).

for the purposes of direct marketing, the data controller shall inform the persons to whom the data relates that they may object, by means of a request in writing to the data controller and free of charge, to such processing.'[60]

[21.13] Clearly, the sending of unsolicited spam will give rise to a number of data protection problems. Firstly, when the spammer gathers or harvests the email addresses of potential recipients he is under an obligation to inform those who are data subjects of how they intend to process the subject's data.[61] Emails and other electronic addresses may be acquired by spammers by a variety of means. For example, the DPC received a complaint from an individual who had received an unsolicitated text message. The Commissioner investigated and found that:

> 'the complainant had attended a major music concert ... During the concert, those attending were encouraged to text support for the Global Call Against Poverty Campaign. The complainant did so. The information collected from these texts was stored in a database held by Opera Telecom and was subsequently used by the company for the purpose of sending unsolicited direct marketing SMS messages'.[62]

The misuse of this database concerned the DPC and he issued an enforcement notice directing that it be deleted.

[21.14] Secondly, the spammer must bring himself into compliance with the criteria for making data processing legitimate.[63] Thirdly, he should comply with the principles[64] by avoiding excessive or unfair processing. And, finally, he should register with the DPC.[65] Few spammers comply with such provisions. In contrast, older forms of direct mail are relatively well regulated.[66] The DPC has prosecuted at least one spammer, but this prosecution was brought pursuant to SI 535/2003.

Directive 2002/58

[21.15] Directive 2002/58 acknowledges that:

> 'unsolicited commercial communications may on the one hand be relatively easy and cheap to send and on the other may impose a burden and/or cost on the recipient ... in some cases their volume may also cause difficulties for electronic communications networks and terminal equipment.'[67]

Therefore, Directive 2002/58 bans spam, stating that:

> 'the practice of sending electronic mail for purposes of direct marketing, disguising or concealing the identity of the sender on whose behalf the communication is made, or

---

[60] DPA 1988–2003, s 2(8).
[61] DPA 1988–2003, s 2D.
[62] Data Protection Commissioner, Case Study 5/06.
[63] DPA 1988–2003, s.2A.
[64] DPA 1988–2003, s 2.
[65] DPA 1988–2003, s 16.
[66] For example, the Irish Direct Marketing Association runs a mail preference service. See DPC, 'A consumer guide to dealing with unsolicited direct marketing', 28 October 2005.
[67] Directive 2002/58, Recital 40.

without a valid address to which the recipient may send a request that such communications cease, shall be prohibited.'[68]

[21.16] Directive 95/46 does allow for the electronic sending of direct marketing to consumers, but only to those who have given their prior consent.[69] Where a business obtains a customer's email address whilst making a sale to that consumer, then the business may send marketing material to that email address. This can only be done if the consumer is given the option of refusing this material.[70] The Directive also gives member states the option of setting up either an 'opt-in' or an 'opt-out' register for direct mail.[71]

Implementation in SI 535/2003

[21.17] SI 535/2003 bans a variety of direct marketing activities in a variety of ways. However, it also contains an absolute ban on the sending of spam:

> 'A person shall not send electronic mail for the purposes of direct marketing, which disguises or conceals the identity of the sender on whose behalf the communication was made, or without a valid address to which the recipient may send a request that such communication shall cease.'[72]

Breach of this provision is an offence and 'the sending of each unsolicited communication or making of each unsolicited call constitutes a separate offence'.[73] Offences may be prosecuted by the DPC[74] and where 'a person is convicted of an offence ... the court may order any data material, which appears to the court to be connected with the offence to be forfeited or destroyed and any relevant data to be erased'.[75] For what is presumed to be the avoidance of doubt, this regulation concludes with the statement that 'personal data shall be deemed to include a phone number or an email address of a subscriber'.[76]

[21.18] SI 535/2003 goes on to ban a variety of specific forms of unsolicited communications. First, it bans the use of electronic communications services for sending 'an unsolicited communication for the purpose of direct marketing' to subscribers who are natural persons, unless the recipient has consented to receiving such

---

[68] Directive 2002/58, art 13(4).

[69] 'The use of automated calling systems without human intervention (automatic calling machines), facsimile machines (fax) or electronic mail for the purposes of direct marketing may only be allowed in respect of subscribers who have given their prior consent'. Directive 2002/58, art 13(1). This right applies only to natural persons, Directive 2002/58, art 13(4).

[70] Directive 2002/58, art 13(2).

[71] Directive 2002/58, art 13(3). This right applies only to natural persons: Directive 2002/58, art 13(4).

[72] SI 535/2003, reg 13(8).

[73] SI 535/2003, reg 13(9).

[74] SI 535/2003, reg 13(10).

[75] SI 535/2003, reg 13(11). Although, if a person other than the person convicted owns the data in question, the court must give them an opportunity to be heard, SI 535/2003, reg 13(12).

[76] SI 535/2003, reg 13(12).

communications. This ban applies to automated calling machines, faxes and emails.[77] The DPC successfully prosecuted an offence under this provision in September 2005. The defendant employed staff to ring mobile phones and hang up, leaving a 'missed call' notification on the phone. When some recipients returned the call they were directed to call a premium rate line. The defendant pleaded guilty and was fined €300 for each of the five calls in respect of which a complaint had been made.[78] The DPC dealt with a complaint about political spam in *Case Study 5/2004*. The facts were that the DPC received a complaint 'about an unsolicited email of a political nature'. It was alleged that this sender of this email 'had "harvested" email addresses from the address line of an email sent by a third party – who was also a County Councillor but of another party'. The DPC investigated and received confirmation that the email addresses in question had been deleted.

[21.19] A second provision of SI 535/2003 bans the 'use' of 'any publicly available electronic communications service to make an unsolicited call for the purpose of direct marketing' to subscribers who are legal persons such as companies or state institutions, where the sender has been notified that the subscriber does not consent to the receipt of such calls and the relevant information is recorded in the National Directory Database.[79] Unsolicited communications cannot be sent electronically by any person who has been notified that the recipient does not wish to receive such communications.[80] Unsolicited phone calls should not be made to subscribers who have notified the person who is making the call that they do not wish to receive such calls or who has made an entry in the National Directory Database to that effect.[81] Where unsolicited calls are made, or faxes are sent, for the purposes of direct marketing, then such calls or faxes must include the name of the person making the call together with other details. Where an email or other electronic message is sent, then the name of the sender and their contact details must be included.[82] Where contact details are provided by customers in the context of the sale of a product or service, then these details may be used by the vendor 'for direct marketing of only its own similar products or services'. Customers must be 'clearly and distinctly given the opportunity to object' to such marketing.[83] Breach of any of these provisions will be an offence and may be prosecuted in the same manner as discussed above.[84] The DPC has published a guide, 'Dealing with unsolicited commercial communications',[85] which sets out the situations in which the DPC believes that they may be able to bring a prosecution.

---

77 SI 535/2003, reg 13(1).
78 Kelly, 'Premium rate phone firm fined for spam' (2005) The Irish Times, 2 September.
79 SI 535/2003, reg 13(2).
80 SI 535/2003, reg 13(3).
81 SI 535/2003, reg 13(4), subject to a 28-day time limit imposed by SI 535/2003, reg 13(5).
82 SI 535/2003, reg 13(6).
83 SI 535/2003, reg 13(7).
84 SI 535/2003, reg 13(8).
85 DPC, 'Dealing with unsolicited commercial communications', http://www.dataprivacy.ie/ viewdoc.asp?DocID=289, 24 November 2005.

The e-Commerce Directive

[21.20] The e-Commerce Directive[86] provides that:

'Member States which permit unsolicited commercial communication by electronic mail shall ensure that such commercial communication by a service provider established in their territory shall be identifiable clearly and unambiguously as such as soon as it is received by the recipient'.

This is stated to be 'In addition to other requirements established by Community law'.[87] The Directive goes on to require that:

'Member States shall take measures to ensure that service providers undertaking unsolicited commercial communications by electronic mail consult regularly and respect the opt-out registers in which natural persons not wishing to receive such commercial communications can register themselves.'[88]

Implementation in SI 68/2003

[21.21] SI 68/2003 attempts to control spam by requiring that:

'An unsolicited commercial communication by a relevant service provider established within the State shall be identified clearly and unambiguously as such as soon as it is received by the recipient by stating that it is an unsolicited commercial communication.'[89]

Non-compliance with this provision is an offence,[90] which may be prosecuted by the DPC.[91] If a person is convicted under this provision, then 'the court may order any data material which appears to the court to be connected with the offence to be forfeited or destroyed and any relevant data to be erased'.[92] Certain provisions of the DPA apply to the regulations. These are provisions relating to definitions and scope,[93] investigations by the DPC and enforcement notices,[94] information notices,[95] authorised officers,[96] service of notices,[97] appeals to the Circuit Court,[98] evidence in proceedings,[99] court

---

[86] Directive 2000/31/EC of the European Parliament and of the Council of 8 June 2000 on certain legal aspects of information society services, in particular electronic commerce, in the Internal Market, OJ L 178, 17/07/2000, pp 1–16.

[87] Directive 2000/31/EC, art 7(1).

[88] Directive 2000/31/EC, art 7(2).

[89] SI 68/2003, reg 9(1).

[90] SI 68/2003, reg 9(2).

[91] SI 68/2003, reg 9(3).

[92] SI 68/2003, reg 9(4). Although the owner of the data will have a right of audience: SI 68/2003, reg 9(5).

[93] DPA 1988–2003, s 1.

[94] DPA 1988–2003, s 10.

[95] DPA 1988–2003, s 12.

[96] DPA 1988–2003, s 24.

[97] DPA 1988–2003, s 25.

[98] DPA 1988–2003, s 26.

[99] DPA 1988–2003, s 27.

proceedings other than in public,[100] offences by bodies corporate,[101] and summary proceedings.[102]

[21.22] SI 68/2003 also applies a number of rules to communications that are 'part of a relevant service'. A relevant service is defined as 'any service normally provided for remuneration, at a distance, by electronic means and at the individual request of a recipient of the service'.[103] Such a communication must comply with the following conditions:

(a)   it must be identified as a 'communication that is part of a relevant service';

(b)   the person on whose behalf the communication is sent must be 'clearly identifiable';

(c)   the service provider must prominently display on their website and places, such as registration forms, 'details of how natural persons can register their choice regarding unsolicited commercial communications';

(d)   promotional offers must be clearly identified as what they are and 'the conditions which must be satisfied in order to qualify for them shall be easily accessible and be presented clearly and unambiguously'; and

(e)   promotional competitions and games must be clearly identified and the conditions for participation must be clearly and unambiguously set out.[104]

Failure to comply with this provision will be an offence,[105] which may be prosecuted by the Director of Consumer Affairs.[106] Specific rules may also be made by 'the designated authority for a regulated profession' in relation to commercial communications.[107]

Opting out of spam?

[21.23] One seemingly attractive option is that of creating an 'opt-out' register. This would allow subscribers and other persons to indicate whether or not they wished to receive spam or other forms of direct mail. Such registries have been quite successful in dealing with older forms of direct marketing, such as material sent through the post[108] or phone calls.[109] SI 535/2003 provides that the National Directory Database may state that 'the subscriber does not consent to unsolicited telephone calls for the purpose of direct marketing or to such calls by means of automated calling machines or facsimile

---

[100] DPA 1988–2003, s 28.

[101] DPA 1988–2003, s 29.

[102] DPA 1988–2003, s 30.

[103] SI 68/2003, reg 1(1). This definition is explicitly tied to that which appears in Directive 98/34/EC, art 1.2 as amended by Directive 98/48/EC and is subject to the exceptions that appear in schedule I of the Regulations.

[104] SI 68/2003, reg 8(1).

[105] SI 68/2003, reg 8(2).

[106] SI 68/2003, reg 8(3).

[107] SI 68/2003, reg 9.

[108] See the Mailing Preference Service provided by the Irish Direct Marketing Association.

[109] See, for example, the USA's National Do Not Call Registry at http://www.donotcall.gov.

machines'.[110] Following the implementation of this provision, the DPC received a number of complaints relating to unsolicited calls from a telecommunications company, which resulted from a failure by the company to match its database with that of the opt-out register.[111]

[21.24] As of January 2004, the European Commission retained at least some faith in the concept of an 'opt-in' regime, suggesting that 'adaptation of direct marketers' practices to the opt-in regime may be necessary. Direct marketers could in particular agree on specific, legally compliant methods to collect personal data.'[112] However, there are good technical reasons for believing that an opt-in or opt-out register would fail to work. These reasons were outlined by the US FTC in its June 2004 report, which examined whether a 'National Do Not Email Registry' would work. The US FTC concluded that it would not and would in fact 'pose substantial security risks because a list of valid email addresses is extremely valuable – far more valuable than a list of working telephone numbers'.[113] An opt-out registry would in fact 'be a gold mine' to spammers, as one of the main difficulties spammers have is identifying the email addresses of 'live' people. Much spam is sent to email addresses that either do not exist or have been abandoned by their users. Only someone who was actually using an address would bother to register it in an 'opt-out' registry. The US FTC concluded that:

> 'Knowing that they will be reaching millions of people, spammers very likely would pay a premium for a list of active email addresses. Because a Registry likely would be so valuable to spammers, many sources we spoke with expressed serious concern. They are convinced that spammers would stop at nothing to obtain this list and misuse it to the detriment of consumers. The [US Federal Trade] Commission agrees with their assessment.'[114]

The US FTC went on to consider whether any security measures could be employed to secure the list, but concluded that such measures were 'inadequate'.[115]

Other relevant Irish legislation

[21.25] As discussed above, in 2003[116] Ireland implemented three separate items of EU legislation that attempt to deal with spam. The continued existence, and indeed increase, of the spamming problem in Ireland strongly suggests that this is a problem of enforcement, not one that can be solved by the enactment of fresh legislation. However, there are a number of provisions that might be relied upon should an Irish spammer be

---

[110] SI 535/2003, reg 14(3). On 21 July 2005 ComReg and the DPC announced 'the launch of the NDD opt out register for direct marketing'. See 'New cold calling opt-out register unveiled', http://www.ireland.com, 21 July 2005. Smyth, 'New phone rules to curtail "cold calling" by sales firms' (2005) The Irish Times, 10 June.

[111] Data Protection Commissioner, Case Study 2/06.

[112] COM(2004) 28 final P 22.

[113] US FTC, 'National Do Not Email Registry: A Report to Congress' June 2004 p 16. US FTC, p 17.

[114] US FTC, p 18.

[115] US FTC, pp 18–23.

[116] DPA 1988–2003, SI 535/2003 and SI 68/2003.

prosecuted before the Irish courts. Once potential offence is to be found in the Criminal Justice (Theft and Fraud Offences) Act 2001, which provides that:

> 'A person who dishonestly, whether within or outside the State, operates or causes to be operated a computer within the State with the intention of making a gain for himself or herself or another, or of causing loss to another, is guilty of an offence'.[117]

[21.26] A couple of difficulties might be encountered in seeking a conviction under this provision. As discussed above, spammers will go to exceptional lengths to retain their anonymity. So, proving beyond a reasonable doubt that a spammer had operated a computer that sent a spam could be very difficult. Furthermore, proving that the intent of the spammer was to cause a gain to themselves or a loss to another could be problematic. As the US FTC has found ' ... spammers ... often use novel payment methods, offshore banks, stolen credit card accounts, and other techniques that make tracing the flow of money a painstaking, and often futile, endeavor'.[118] The Criminal Justice (Theft and Fraud Offences) Act 2001 will be particularly applicable to the 'pump and dump' schemes now commonplace online. On Thursday, 9 August 2007 'inboxes around the world were flooded with crude PDF documents promoting the stock of the Prime Time Group'. The documents advised buying the stock of the company as it was about to 'move like a commet ... The wave of spam email peaked at 9:33 a.m. on Thursday. By 12:30 p.m., the stock price had hit 11 cents, up 25 percent from its close on Wednesday, and 84 percent from the start of trading on Monday.' The price of the stock then collapsed on the Friday of that week.[119] Regulatory authorities in the USA have taken action against such schemes. In July 2007 the US Securities and Exchange Commission (SEC) charged two men, alleging that they had swindled investors out of $4.6 million 'by obtaining shares from at least 13 penny stock companies and selling those shares into an artificially active market they created through manipulative trading, spam email campaigns, direct mailers, and Internet-based promotional activities.'[120] The operation of such a scheme in Ireland might commit a number of offences contrary to the Criminal Justice (Theft and Fraud Offences) Act 2001, in particular making a gain or causing a loss by deception.[121] Where spam is 'grossly offensive or of an indecent, obscene or menacing character', then an offence may be committed under the Post Office (Amendment) Act 1951.[122] Finally, where spam is sent so repeatedly that it amounts to harassment, an offence might be committed under the Non-Fatal Offences against the Person Act 1997.[123]

---

[117] Criminal Justice (Theft and Fraud Offences) Act 2001, s 9(1).

[118] US FTC, 'National Do Not Email Registry: A Report to Congress' June 2004 p 24.

[119] Mindlin, 'A Stock Soars After a Spam Swarm' (2007) The New York Times, 13 August.

[120] SEC, 'SEC Charges Two Texas Swindlers In Penny Stock Spam Scam Involving Computer Botnets' (2007) Press Release, 9 July.

[121] Criminal Justice (Theft and Fraud Offences) Act 2001, s 6.

[122] Post Office Amendment Act 1951, s 13, as inserted by the Postal and Telecommunications Services Act 1983, s 8 and Sch IV.

[123] Non-Fatal Offences against the Person Act 1997, s 10.

Civil remedies

[21.27] If it were possible to identify an Irish spammer, then it might be tempting to seek a civil remedy against them. Civil remedies have been successfully sought against individual spammers in the USA.[124] One of the attractions of seeking a civil remedy is the much lower standard of proof that must be discharged in the civil, as opposed to the criminal, courts. It is likely that a spammer would have interfered with the data protection rights of many people, not least by processing their personal data unfairly and unlawfully. In such a situation, a spammer might be sued for damages in accordance with s 7 of the DPA. Other claims, such as one for trespass to goods,[125] might also be pleaded, but might prove more difficult to set out. In *Microsoft Corporation v McDonald*[126] an action seeking damages and injunctive relief was successfully brought against the defendant who sold databases of email addresses. The action was brought on the basis of a breach of the UK implementation of the EC's Directive on privacy on Electronic Communications Networks. This provided that any person who suffered damage as a result of non-compliance with the UK regulations could sue for damages. [127] The equivalent provision in the Irish regulations states:

> 'A person who suffers loss and damage as a result of a contravention of any of the requirements of these Regulations by any other person shall be entitled to damages from that other person for that loss and damage.'

So a similar action might be brought against an Irish spammer or spam enabler under the Irish regulations. Microsoft claimed damages in respect of:

> 'considerable damage to its goodwill. If subscribers are not effectively protected by Microsoft against SPAM they are less willing to continue as subscribers of MSN or to subscribe to its paying services. In addition, Microsoft itself spends a large amount of money in fighting SPAM and it has had to invest in additional servers in order to cope with the sheer volume of SPAM which is transmitted across the networks.'[128]

Lewison J was 'satisfied that Microsoft has suffered a loss as a result of the breach of the Regulations and ... entitled to compensation'.[129] Lewison J granted an injunction 'restraining the defendant from transmitting or instigating the transmission of unsolicited commercial emails to hotmail accounts.'[130] It should be noted that the DPA

---

[124] For example, in August 2005, Scott Ritter, a one-time pretender to the tarnished crown of 'Spam King' agreed to pay Microsoft $7m to settle a case that alleged that he had sent some 8,000 emails containing 40,000 fraudulent statements. Wilson and Johnson, 'He sent 38 billion emails and called himself the spam king' (2005) The Guardian, 11 August.

[125] See McMahon and Binchy, *Law of Torts* (Tottel Publishing, 2000) ch 28.

[126] *Microsoft Corporation v McDonald* [2006] EWHC 3410 (Ch).

[127] 'A person who suffers damage by reason of any contravention of any of the requirements of these Regulations by any other person shall be entitled to bring proceedings for compensation from that other person for that damage' Privacy and Electronic Communications (EC Directive) Regulations 2003 (UK), reg 30.

[128] *Microsoft Corporation v McDonald* [2006] EWHC 3410 (Ch), para 30.

[129] [2006] EWHC 3410 (Ch), para 31.

[130] [2006] EWHC 3410 (Ch), para 32.

1988–2003 also allow a data subject to sue for damages,[131] but that would not allow a company such as Microsoft to sue in respect of the losses it had suffered.

Spam filtering

[21.28] One solution that is being eagerly embraced by the US FTC is that of spam filtering. This follows the publication of a study[132] that found that spam filters were able to exclude up to 96 per cent of spam sent to accounts at ISP.[133] The US FTC therefore concluded that '(t)his encouraging result suggests that anti-spam technologies may be dramatically reducing the burden of spam on consumers'.[134] The process of filtering email messages is defined in the following terms:

> 'A mail filter is a piece of software which takes an input of an email message. For its output, it might pass the message through unchanged for delivery to the user's mailbox, it might redirect the message for delivery elsewhere, or it might even throw the message away. Some mail filters are able to edit messages during processing.'[135]

[21.29] Spam filtering involves the interception of communications and such interference can give rise to legal complications. In January 2005, a German court held that it was illegal for a German university to filter out emails sent by a former employee to recipients at the university.[136] However, no such complications would seem to arise in Ireland. Section 98(5) of the Postal and Telecommunications Services Act 1983 provides that the definition of interception does not:

> 'include any filtering mechanisms or processes utilised by undertakings for the purposes of preventing unsolicited commercial emails where such a service has been requested or accepted by a subscriber or user, having first been provided with clear and comprehensive information about the purposes of such filtering.'[137]

---

[131] DPA 1988–2003, s 7: 'For the purposes of the law of torts and to the extent that that law does not so provide, a person, being a data controller or a data processor, shall, so far as regards the collection by him of personal data or information intended for inclusion in such data or his dealing with such data, owe a duty of care to the data subject concerned'

[132] US FTC, 'Email Address Harvesting and the Effectiveness of Anti-spam Filters' November 2005.

[133] The methodology was that 50 email addresses were at an ISP that had no spam filter, 50 were at filtered ISP I and 50 at filtered ISP II. In a two week period, the 50 unfiltered addresses received some 2,129 spams. Filtered ISP I excluded 78 per cent of spam, whilst Filtered ISP II excluded 96 per cent of spam. US FTC, 'Email Address Harvesting and the Effectiveness of Anti-spam Filters' November 2005, pp 5–6.

[134] US FTC 'Email Address Harvesting and the Effectiveness of Anti-spam Filters' November 2005, p 6. In contrast, others have suggested that '… all (the study) … really shows is that spam filtering is better than leaving email accounts exposed to the elements …'. Leyden, 'Spam filters thwart junk mail menace' http://www.theregister.co.uk, 29 November 2005.

[135] http://en.wikipedia.org/wiki/Spam_filtering.

[136] Libbenga, 'German Court Rules email blocking illegal' http://www.theregister.co.uk, 18 January 2005. See also the interim decision in the Canadian case of *CT Comm Edmonton Ltd v Shaw Communications Inc* 2007 ABQB 473.

[137] Section 98(5) of the Postal and Telecommunications Services Act 1983 as inserted by the European Communities (Electronic Communications Networks And Services) (Data Protection And Privacy) Regulations 2003 (SI 535/2003), reg 23(2).

[21.30] The Article 29 Working Party issued an opinion on email filtering in early 2006. It considered that filtering emails to detect viruses might be justified for safeguarding the security of services, but that service providers should ensure the following: the content of filtered emails would have to be kept secret; if a virus is found then the installed software should offer guarantees regarding confidentiality; and, if the filtering is done automatically, then the system should be set up for this purpose only and should not scan the emails for any other purpose.[138] Filtering emails to eliminate spam is slightly more problematic. Where spam filtering is used, the Working Party wants users to be able to easily opt in and out of having their emails filtered. To avoid the problem of false positives, the Working Party would like to see users given a list of filtered emails so that users may identify those that are not spam. Ultimately, the Article 29 Working Party would like to see users empowered to control the spam that they receive, not system administrators.[139] The Working Party also considers the filtering of emails for the purposes of detecting content, that might contravene a usage policy. The Working Party is of the view that 'the screening of emails for detecting predetermined content, even if considered as alleged unlawful material, cannot be considered as necessary technical and organisational measures to safeguard security of email services'. The Working Party concludes that:

> 'email providers are prohibited from engaging in filtering, storage or any other kinds of interception of communications and the related traffic data for the purposes of detecting any predetermined content without the consent of the users of the services or they must be legally authorised to engage in such screening.'[140]

The Working Party notes that service providers who engage in filtering are bound by the obligation to inform.[141] Finally, the Working Party examines the issue of:

> 'Did they read it services', which allow senders of emails and text messages to be informed of when the recipients have read the message. The Working Party 'expresses the strongest opposition to this processing because personal data about addressees' behaviour are recorded and transmitted without an unambiguous consent of a relevant addressee ... to carry out the data processing activity consisting in retrieving from the recipient of an email, whether the recipient has read it ... unambiguous consent from the recipient of the email is necessary. No other legal grounds justify this processing'.[142]

Is a solution possible?

[21.31] In December 2004, the Council of the European Union invited all market players to 'continue to cooperate strongly among themselves and with public authorities in the fight against "spam".' It invited the Commission to 'evaluate whether differences in the national laws on privacy and electronic communications, including those implementing Directives ... 2002/58/EC1 and 95/46/EC2 might represent an obstacle to effective

---

[138] Article 29 Working Party, *Opinion 2/2006 on privacy issues related to the provision of email screening services*, WP 118, 21 February 2006, p 6.

[139] Article 29 Working Party, p 7.

[140] Article 29 Working Party, p 8.

[141] Article 29 Working Party, pp 7–9.

[142] Article 29 Working Party, p 9.

cross-border enforcement'.[143] The Dutch Presidency of the Council of the European Union suggested that '(f)or a large part, spam is a security problem. If all end-users would properly secure their systems, it would be much more difficult for spammers to reach their goals'.[144] The EU Commission has invited member states to 'assess the effectiveness of their system of remedies and penalties for infringements and create adequate possibilities for victims to claim damages'.[145] In February 2005:

> '"Anti-spam" enforcement authorities in 13 European countries ... agreed to share information and pursue complaints across borders in a pan-European drive to combat 'spam' electronic mail. They will cooperate in investigating complaints about cross-border spam from anywhere within the EU, so as to make it easier to identify and prosecute spammers anywhere in Europe.'[146]

There is no doubt that enforcing the law against spammers is likely to prove highly problematic. The experience of the US FTC is that 'the primary law enforcement challenge is identifying and locating the targeted spammer'. There are technical reasons why it is difficult to identify spammers:

> 'The ability of spammers to hide their identities by using false headers, open relays, open proxies, zombie drones, and foreign servers makes tracing an email's path an often fruitless task. Tracing an email almost always leads to a dead end because spammers rarely send messages from their own email accounts'.

[21.32] The US FTC cites a couple of examples that illustrate the difficulty of pursuing spammers: '(a) prosecutor in Washington State spent four months and sent out 14 pre-suit civil investigative demands ... just to identify the spammer in one lawsuit'. Likewise 'it took the Virginia Attorney General, over the course of four months, multiple subpoenas to domain registrars, credit card companies, and Internet providers, and the execution of a search warrant, before having enough information to file a case against a spammer'.[147] The difficulties encountered by ISPs that sought to identify spammers are illustrated by the following example:

> 'One major ISP reports that after collecting and analyzing over 45 million spam messages received by its 'honeypot' email accounts during 2003, it linked only about 2.6 million to a person responsible for them. In all, this ISP identified 271 parties responsible for these 2.6 million spam messages, but acquired sufficient information to file a lawsuit or send a warning letter to only 91 of the parties. To identify these 91 parties, the ISP estimates that its internal and outside legal teams expended approximately 12,100 hours – an average of 133 hours per spammer.'[148]

---

[143] Council of the European Union, 2629th Council Meeting, Brussels, 9–10 December 2004, Press Release, p 9.

[144] Council of the European Union, 'Unsolicited communications for direct marketing purposes or spam' Presidency Paper, Brussels, 24 November 2004, 5691/04 TELECOM 11, p 4.

[145] COM(2004) 28 final, p 15.

[146] European Commission, Press Release, IP/05/146, Brussels, 7 February 2005.

[147] US FTC, pp 24–25.

[148] US FTC, p 25.

That said, the US Authorities have had some success in recent years. In April 2005, one spammer was jailed by the Courts of Virginia for nine years.[149] However, in spite of these enforcement efforts, the USA remains the world's leading source of spam.

An international problem

[21.33] One particularly difficult issue faced by the EU is that much of the spam that clogs European inboxes comes from outside the EU. In 2004, the UK's All Party Parliamentary Internet Group was 'presented with compelling evidence that although national initiatives on spam do have some value, the problem cannot be fully dealt with except at the international level'.[150] The figures given by UK-based organisation, Spamhaus,[151] as of 30 November 2005, for the '10 Worst Spam Countries'[152]are set out in the table below. Beside these figures are those given by Sophos,[153] a security consultancy firm for the period April 2005 to September 2005.[154] Only one EU member state, the United Kingdom, appears in the Spamhaus list. However, in the Sophos list, it is joined by France, Spain and Germany. However, it would appear that in both lists most spam is coming from outside the EU, principally from the United States, South Korea and China. However, it should be kept in mind that whilst spam may originate from a country such as China or South Korea, the spammer may reside elsewhere.

Ranking	IE Internet[155] Country	Percentage of spam	Spamhaus[156] Country	Percentage of spam
1	USA	30.34	USA	53.41
2	France	24.99	China	11.6
3	China	17.25	Russia	6.41
4	Germany	9.69	South Korea	4.69
5	UK	9.65	Japan	4.67
6			UK	4.59
7			Germany	4.53
8			Canada	3.74
9			France	3.38
10			Italy	2.97

---

[149] Orlowski, 'Nine years in slammer for US spammer', http://www.theregister.co.uk, 8 April 2005.

[150] UK All Party Parliamentary Internet Group, 'Spam': Report of an Inquiry by the All Party Internet Group, October 2003, p 4.

[151] http://www.spamhaus.org.

[152] Defined as 'Countries with ISPs currently providing connectivity and hosting to spam gangs directly responsible for the World's spam problem'.

[153] http://www.sophos.com.

[154] Differences between the figures probably reflect the reality that Spamhaus lists the countries with the highest number of 'known spam issues', as of 30 November 2005. The Sophos list is based upon figures for a six-month period from April to September 2005.

[155] IE Internet, 'Spam and Virus rates low in July' (2007) Press Release, 1 August.

[156] http://www.spamhaus.org/statistics/countries.lasso.

[21.34] One response to the international nature of the spam problem has been to encourage countries outside the EU to deal with the sources of spam within their borders. In February 2005:

'A joint drive to combat 'spam' email from Europe and Asia was agreed by Government participants attending an Asia-Europe (ASEM) conference ... 25 European and 13 Asian member countries agree(d) to take action to fight spam nationally and to promote anti-spam efforts in international organisations and by industry.'[157]

Although encouraging, such an agreement would seem to fall far short of a treaty whose obligations are enforceable at international law. However, efforts are continuing and:

'The Commission is also active bilaterally not least with the USA, another important source of spam, and in multilateral discussions ongoing in the Inter national Telecommunications Union and in the OECD Task Force on spam'.

Conclusion: towards a 'Balkanized' Internet?

[21.35] Whilst efforts at enforcing the law continue, others are continuing to seek other practical solutions. In November 2004, Internet search engine Lycos started distributing a program that could be used to bombard spam sites with messages; in effect a denial-of-service attack.[158] However, this was highly controversial (and possibly a criminal offence)[159] and was discontinued a week later.[160] One cause for concern is that the Internet may divide into discrete blocks of users who only communicate with one another; as one expert has commented: 'The 'Net is balkanizing, ... There are communities of trust forming in which traffic is accepted only from known friends'.[161]

[21.36] In February 2005, Verizon, a US-based ISP with three million customers, started blocking email from Europe 'in a misguided attempt to reduce spam'.[162] Another concern is that spammers plainly profit from the anonymity that the Internet offers. The problem of spam is already giving rise to calls for the introduction of better authentication procedures for email users, and the US FTC has concluded that 'It is clear, based on spammers' abilities to exploit the structure of the email system, that the development of a practical and effective means of authentication is a necessary tool to fight spam'.[163]

---

[157] European Commission Press Release, IP/05/210, Brussels, 24 February 2005.

[158] Libbenga, 'Lycos screensaver to blitz spam servers', http://www.theregister.co.uk, 26 November 2004,.

[159] Rasch, 'Lycos goes straight', http://www.theregister.co.uk, 6 December 2005.

[160] Libbenga 'Lycos antispam site taken offline' http://www.theregister.co.uk, 3 December 2004.

[161] Karl Auerbach, an elected director of ICANN, the Internet policy board, and a veteran Internet engineer, quoted in 'Do I Know You? Email Barricades' http://www.wired.com, 8 June 2003.

[162] Leyden 'Verizon persists with European email blockade' http:// www.theregister.co.uk, 14 January 2005.

[163] US Federal Trade Commission 'National Do Not Email Registry A Report to Congress' June 2004 p 37.

Such 'means of authentication' will enable and ease the identification of email senders.[164] Thus, the ultimate impact of spam upon the individual may not be the annoyance of dealing with it but rather the loss of anonymity and concomitant reduction in privacy that dealing with the spam problem may entail.

---

[164] 'Even though domain-level authentication cannot necessarily authenticate the particular person who sent an email, it does authenticate the domain from which the email originated. Law enforcement can then contact the domain to obtain information that could identify the individual sender of the email'. US Federal Trade Commission 'National Do Not Email Registry A Report to Congress' June 2004, p 35.

Chapter 22

Defects, Jurisdiction and Dispute Resolution

Introduction

[22.01] Information, software and physical products can all be defective in different ways. Where such defects arise, they may cause dispute. Such disputes may be resolved in courts or by means of procedures such as alternative dispute resolution. Disputes will typically give rise to issues relating to the laws of tort and contract, the principles of which are both very well established by the common law.[1]

Defective information

[22.02] Unfortunately there is a lot of inaccurate information on the Internet and, where such information has a defamatory effect, it may be actionable. In one notorious case an individual posted information on http://www.wikipedia.org that John Seigenthaler Sr a former editor of The Tennessean in Nashville, Tennessee, USA, had been involved in the assassination of John F. Kennedy, the American President, and his brother Robert. The posting was meant as a prank but resulted in the poster losing his job.[2] Where inaccurate information is relied upon to the detriment of an individual, it is conceivable that an action for damages could result, but such a claim would have to overcome significant hurdles to be successful as it would be difficult to prove that the parties were sufficiently proximate for the requisite duty of care to result.[3] In *Mebrom NV v European Commission*[4] the plaintiff was engaged in the importation of Methyl Bromide into the EU. The plaintiff was told in December 2004 that from the following month it would have to apply for permits to do so on the defendant's website. However, the defendant was unable to get its website started in time and permits were not issued until February 2005. As a result, the plaintiff missed out on two months' worth of permits. The plaintiff sued. The Court of First Instance noted that for the Commission to be liable in such circumstances, three conditions would have to be met:

> 'the conduct of which the institutions are accused must have been unlawful, there must be actual damage and a causal link must exist between the conduct and the damage alleged.'[5]

As the plaintiff was unable to establish that it had suffered damage, the claim failed.

---

[1]   For an introductory guide to contract law, see Ryan, *Contract Law* (Thomson Round Hall, 2006); Robert Clark, *Contract Law* (4th edn, Round Hall Sweet and Maxwell, 1998) and McDermott, *Contract Law* (Tottel Publishing, 2001). For a text book on the Law of Torts, see Healy, *Principles of Irish Tort* (Clarus Press, 2006) and McMahon and Binchy *Law of Torts* (3rd edn, Tottel Publishing, 2000).

[2]   Seelye, 'A Little Sleuthing Unmasks Writer of Wikipedia Prank' (2005) The New York Times, 11 December.

[3]   *Glencar Exploration v Mayo County Council* [2002] ILRM 481.

[4]   *Mebrom NV v European Commission* (Case T-198/05).

[5]   (Case T-198/05), para 33.

Defective products

[22.03] Information technology devices can be defective, and where a producer supplies a defective product, then he may be liable for any damage that results form the product's use. The Liability for Defective Products (LDPA) Act 1991[6] gives effect to Council Directive 85/374 concerning liability for defective products.[7] The Act provides that 'The producer shall be liable in damages in tort for damage caused wholly or partly by a defect in his product.'[8] The Act defines 'producer' as:

> 'the manufacturer or producer of a finished product, or … the manufacturer or producer of any raw material or the manufacturer or producer of a component part of a product, or … in the case of the products of the soil, of stock-farming and of fisheries and game, which have undergone initial processing, the person who carried out such processing, or … any person who, by putting his name, trade mark or other distinguishing feature on the product or using his name or any such mark or feature in relation to the product, has held himself out to be the producer of the product, or … any person who has imported the product into a Member State from a place outside the European Communities in order, in the course of any business of his, to supply it to another.'[9]

In addition, a supplier may be deemed to be a producer in certain circumstances.[10] A product will be deemed to be defective where:

> 'it fails to provide the safety which a person is entitled to expect, taking all circumstances into account, including … the presentation of the product … the use to which it could reasonably be expected that the product would be put, and … the time when the product was put into circulation.'[11]

But a product will not 'be considered defective for the sole reason that a better product is subsequently put into circulation.'[12] The Act confers a number of advantages upon plaintiffs, whilst attempting to limit the impact on producers. In particular, the Act creates a strict liability for producers whose defective products injure people. In *Henderson v AEI Inc*[13] the Master of the High Court refused discovery of certain documentation on the basis that it was unnecessary for the plaintiff's claim as she did not need to prove the negligence of the defendant 'the liability is in no way contingent upon proof of any want of care. It is a strict liability. There is no standard of care. There is no need to prove carelessness.'

[22.04] The Act places a number of limitations upon who can claim for such damages, what they can claim for and how their claim will be processed. The onus of proving that a product is defective is placed upon the person claiming to have been injured by the

---

6   As amended by EC (Liability for Defective Products) Regulations 2000 (SI 401/2000).
7   Council Directive 85/374/EEC of 25 July 1985 on the approximation of the laws, regulations and administrative provisions of the Member States concerning liability for defective products, OJ L 210 , 07/08/1985, pp 29–33.
8   LDPA 1991, s 2(1).
9   LDPA 1991, s 2(2).
10 LDPA 1991, s 2(3).
11 LDPA 1991, s 5(1).
12 LDPA 1991, s 5(2).
13 *Henderson v AEI Inc* 12/05/2005 2002 No 9004P [FL11922].

product.[14] The Act requires that persons injured or damaged by a defective purpose must pay an 'excess'.[15] The chief limitation on the Act's operation is its limitation of the word 'damage', which is defined as 'death or personal injury, or ... loss of, damage to, or destruction of, any item of property other than the defective product itself.' Furthermore, the defective product that has caused the damage must be one that is 'of a type ordinarily intended for private use or consumption, and ... was used by the injured person mainly for his own private use or consumption'.[16] In *Delahunty v Player & Wills*[17] the plaintiff was a smoker for 57 years who became ill suffering from coughing, including coughing blood, recurrent chest infections, weight loss and shortness of breath'.[18] The plaintiff then sued a number of tobacco companies claiming that the cigarettes she had smoked:

> 'were defective in that they ... were and are addictive and did at all material times hereto contain and produce substances and additives which were inherently dangerous to the health and welfare of all those who consumed the said cigarettes, including the plaintiff'.[19]

The defendants sought to have the plaintiff's action struck out at the interlocutory stage. The Supreme Court refused to do so, Fennelly J noting that it would 'require a great deal of evidence to be given at the trial' before a court could find that the cigerettes smoked by the plaintiff had failed 'to provide the safety which a person is entitled to expect'.[20]

Defective software

[22.05] Modern computer programs are enormous and complex constructions made up of millions of lines of code, thousands of different functions and algorithms. Some regard computer programs as the most complex devices ever created by man. Given this complexity, it is inevitable that programs will fail from time to time. Examples of such failure abound:

- In August 2007 Skype was forced to shut down its Internet phone system for 24 hours by 'a deficiency in an algorithm within Skype networking software. This controls the interaction between the user's own Skype client and the rest of the Skype network';[21]

- In April 2007 the Blackberry system failed leaving North American 'crackberry' addicts bereft of their email fix for up to 12 hours; and[22]

- 'a software failure near Toledo, Ohio ... cause(d) a blackout in eight Northeastern and Midwestern states and Ontario. The cost of that blackout ... was estimated at $4 billion to $10 billion.'[23]

---

[14] Liability For Defective Products Act 1991, s 4.
[15] Liability For Defective Products Act 1991, s 3.
[16] Liability For Defective Products Act 1991, s 1(1).
[17] *Delahunty v Player and Wills* [2006] 1 IR 304.
[18] [2006] 1 IR 304 at 307.
[19] [2006] 1 IR 304 at 306.
[20] [2006] 1 IR 304 at 311.
[21] Taylor, 'Skype moves to calm clients after service failure' (2007) The Financial Times, 18 August.
[22] Sorensen, 'BlackBerry blackout' (2007) Toronto Star, 19 April.
[23] Perrow, 'The Government's Con Ed Bill' (2007) The New York Times, 8 July.

Software bugs or glitches that cause incidents such as the above are regrettably commonplace. What makes the above examples exceptional is that their consequences were particularly noticeable: it is difficult to ignore a software glitch that knocks out a region's power grid or cuts the communications of millions of people. The difficulty of writing sufficiently robust code can lead to the cancellation of entire software systems. In July 2007:

> 'the Health Service Executive finally gave up on PPARS, its computerised payroll and human resources system. Originally intended to serve 17 agencies in the health system, it was expected to cost €9 million, but by late 2005, €130 million had been spent and PPARS was still only operating in three health service regions. There were also technical problems with the system; one employee in the northwest was paid €1 million in error. The HSE is now looking at a new computer system.'[24]

Previously the Irish League of Credit Unions 'spent €34 million on a new IT system before having to abandon the project'.[25] It is important to keep in mind that often it is not the unfortunate programmer's fault that many of these systems fail.[26] The failure of the PPARS system may have had more to do with poor management and implementation of the system rather than actual code.[27] Problems may arise at any stage – failure to clearly specify the object or purpose of a system at an early stage would seem to be a particularly dangerous way of risking project failure.[28] Complex computer programs make for attractive scape goats, and what may be described as a software failure, may really be a failure of management or design.

[22.06] The failure of a computer program or a project to develop such a program will not uncommonly lead to a dispute between the customer and vendor or creator of the program. This is what occurred in *Pegler Ltd v Wang (UK) Ltd*[29] where the defendant's performance was described as 'disastrous'[30]; the defendant 'did little to make progress with the contract and then abandoned the job entirely when it was far from complete'.[31]

---

[24] 'Spending: where the money went' (2007) The Irish Times, 31 July.

[25] Keena, 'Credit union league in fresh bid to develop IT platform' (2004) The Irish Times, 12 March.

[26] The dangers that such projects pose has spawned a minor sub-genre of computer manuals, see: Yourdan, *Death March* (Prentice Hall, 2003), 'The #1 guide to surviving "doomed" projects' and DeMarco, *Waltzing With Bears: Managing Risk on Software Projects* (Dorset Publishing, 2003).

[27] 'It appears that the project governance from the start has not been strong ... overall project governance appears to have gone'. Hennessy, 'Managers have no confidence in PPARS, says report' (2006) The Irish Times, 26 October.

[28] 'The objectives and scope for PPARS have not been sufficiently clear from the start, and this lack of clarity is still an issue.' Hennessy, 'Managers have no confidence in PPARS, says report' (2006) The Irish Times, 26 October.

[29] *Pegler Ltd v Wang (UK) Ltd* 70 ConLR 68. See also *Intelligente Systemen, Database toepassingen, Elektronische diensten BV (IDE) v Commission of the European Communities* Case no c-114/94, ECJ.

[30] 70 ConLR 68, para 20.

[31] 70 ConLR 68, para 90.

The plaintiff sued, seeking damages of around £22m. In response, the defendant argued that it could rely upon the following terms in the contract between the parties:

> 'Wang shall not in any event be liable for any indirect, special or consequential loss, howsoever arising (including but not limited to loss of anticipated profits or of data) in connection with or arising out of the supply, functioning or use of the Hardware, the Software or the Services even if Wang shall have been advised of the possibility of such potential loss and shall not be liable for any loss except as provided for in this Contract.

> ... Except in respect of the liability of Wang for death or personal injury resulting from the negligence of Wang or its employees or in respect of a claim for non-payment of monies due under this Contract, no action, regardless of form, arising out of the transactions in relation to this Contract may be brought by either party more than two years after the cause of action has occurred.'[32]

The defence failed. The plaintiff argued that the above clauses only applied after the software was supplied: as the defendant had abandoned the project before completion, the above clauses never applied. In particular, the defendant argued that the plaintiff's claim was barred by the second clause. Counsel for the defendant argued that 'a cause of action which arises in respect of late delivery of a module arises when the failure or delay first occurs ... the two-year period begins to run from the first day of delay.'

[22.07] However, Bowsher QC rejected this submission, citing *Johnson v Agnew*[33] and *Segal Securities Ltd v Thoseby*[34] in support of his view that 'delay in delivery is a continuing breach and there is a fresh cause of action every day until the duty to perform ceases by acceptance of repudiation or in some other way.' Bowsher QC was of the opinion that the courts should take a pragmatic approach to the interpretation of such provisions. Although the contract imposed a two-year limitation period, it was envisaged that it would run over a number of years and the parties were 'commercial men':

> 'Where late delivery is complained of, the damage arising from the first day alone is likely to be so small that it would be disregarded if delivery were effected on the next day ... It cannot have been intended that a party should be forced to begin proceedings to preserve its rights at a time when performance was still due and being offered. Legal refinements should be overlooked in the construction of this clause, and a continuing breach should be regarded as one cause of action with the two-year period beginning when the duty to perform ceases either by performance or termination of the contractual duty to perform.'[35]

Bowsher QC held that the plaintiff's cause of action had arisen in December 1995 when both parties accepted that the defendant had ceased to perform any functions in relation to the contract. The plaintiff had issued its first writ in February 1996, which meant that the plaintiff's case was not barred by the contractual term.[36]

---

[32]　70 ConLR 68, para 44.
[33]　*Johnson v Agnew* 1 All ER 883 at 894–895, [1980] AC 367 at 398–399.
[34]　*Segal Securities Ltd v Thoseby* 1 All ER 500 at 507–508, [1963] 1 QB 887 at 901–902.
[35]　70 ConLR 68, para 52.
[36]　70 ConLR 68, para 53.

[22.08] Exclusionary clauses such as those that were sought to be enforced in *Pegler Ltd v Wang (UK) Ltd* are a normal feature of computer licences. For example, the laptop upon which this book is being written runs on Microsoft Windows XP, the End User Licence Agreement (EULA) provides for the following (which is set out entirely in capitals in the original):

> 'To the maximum extent permitted by applicable law, in no event shall manufacturer or its suppliers ... be liable for any special, incidental, punitive, indirect, or consequential damages whatsoever (including, but not limited to, damages for loss of profits or confidential or other information, for business interruption, for personal injury, for loss of privacy, for failure to meet any duty of good faith or of reasonable care, for negligence, and for any other pecuniary or other loss whatsoever) arising out of or in any way related to the use of or inability to use the software, the provision of or failure to provide support or other services, information, software, and related content through the software, or otherwise arising out of the use of the software, or otherwise under or in connection with any provision of this EULA, even in the event of the fault, tort (including negligence), misrepresentation, strict liability, breach of contract or breach of warranty of manufacturer or any supplier ... and even if manufacturer or any supplier ... has been advised of the possibility of such damages.'[37]

[22.09] Exemption clauses such as the above are invariably feature in software contracts. Typically a consumer will not view such a clause until after he has paid for the software in question and is installing it on a computer. Invariably, the installation module for a computer program will present the user with a copy of the licence and require that the user indicate his acceptance of the terms. The user will usually be offered the option of returning the software for a refund if he does not agree. Of course, few, if any, users ever read such terms. At one stage, a practice arose of forcing users to scroll down through the license before indicating acceptance, but this practice appears to have been dispensed with. Regardless of whether users actually read such contracts, it is well established that a person who signs a contract will be bound by it, even if they have not read it.[38] Whether clicking a box to indicate that a user accepts the terms of a contract could amount to a signature is one issue; the user would certainly seem to have the requisite intent.[39] But whatever about treating something like an email address as being a signature, some may feel that regarding right-clicking a mouse as going too far. It is most likely that the contract for purchase of software would have been made when the user paid the vendor for it and received a copy of the software, whether over the Internet or on a disk. It would seem more difficult to argue that the contract was not made until the user had commenced the installation process. The courts might regard the advertisement of software as being an invitation to treat,[40] but it is difficult to see why they would regard the purchase of the software in the same light.

---

[37] Microsoft, EULA for Microsoft XP, clause 25.
[38] *L'estrange v Graucob* (1934) 2 KB 394.
[39] *J Pereira Fernandes SA v Mehta* [2006] EWHC 813 (Ch), [2006] 2 All ER 891, [2006] 1 All ER (Comm) 885, [2006] 2 Lloyd's Rep 244.
[40] *Pharmaceutical Society of Great Britain v Boots Cash Chemists* [1953] 1 All ER 482; *Minister for Industry and Commerce v Pim* [1966] IR 154.

[22.10] Instead, it is more likely that the vendor would argue that the purchaser had notice of the clause prior to purchase. So in *Parker v SE Railway*[41] a passenger left a bag in a railway cloakroom and was issued with a ticket at that time. There was a notice on the front of the clause referring the customer to the back of the ticket. On the back there was an exemption clause, which stated that the defendant's liability was limited to £10. The English Court of Appeal ruled that the passenger's claim for compensation could be denied as the defendant had taken reasonable steps to bring the clause to the passenger's attention. Whilst software vendors do not typically require that purchasers read through detailed contracts before they buy, at least in the case of 'off-the-shelf' software, they will typically include a notice referring the customer to those conditions before purchase.[42]

[22.11] In addition to the requirement that the purchaser be put on notice of it before purchase, an exclusion clause must be carefully drafted to be effective. In *Tektrol v International Insurance Co*[43] the plaintiffs had an 'all risks' policy with the defendant. This policy excluded a number of such risks including:

> 'DAMAGE caused by or consisting of or CONSEQUENTIAL LOSS arising directly or indirectly from ... erasure loss distortion or corruption of information on computer systems or other records programmes or software caused deliberately by ... malicious persons ... other erasure loss distortion or corruption of information on computer systems or other records programmes or software.'[44]

[22.12] The plaintiff's business was the supply of energy-saving devices, for which the plaintiffs created software. The plaintiffs lost all their copies of the source code for this software by a 'very unusual series of unrelated incidents'.[45] These incidents were as follows:

> 'The source code was held in five ways: on two computers located at Tektrol's business premises; on a laptop of the managing director ... on a computer at a remote site operated by an independent company ... ; and on a hard copy print-out ... Tektrol received an e-mail with an attachment apparently consisting of a Christmas card from a firm of solicitors ... (the Managing Director) realised what had happened, believed that the remote site had not been corrupted, and repaired and reloaded the laptop from the remote site ... Tektrol's business premises were (then) burgled. The burglars stole various items including the two computers and the hard copy print-out ... The burglary was discovered ... and it was then found that the virus had also deleted the source code held at the remote site and thus it had not been restored on the laptop ... All copies of the source code had therefore been lost. The virus had erased the copies on the laptop and at the remote site and about a fortnight later the burglars had stolen the two computers which held the other copies and the only hard copy.'[46]

---

41 *Parker v SE Railway* (1877) 2 CPD 416.
42 *Olley v Marlborough Court* [1949] KB 532; *Thornton v Shoe Lane Parking* [1971] 1 All ER 686.
43 *Tektrol V International Insurance Co* [2005] EWCA Civ 845, [2005] 2 Lloyd's Rep 701, [2006] Lloyd's Rep IR 38.
44 [2005] EWCA Civ 845, para 5.
45 [2005] EWCA Civ 845, para 1.
46 [2005] EWCA Civ 845, para 1.

[22.13] The English Court of Appeal ruled that the plaintiffs were entitled to succeed under the policy. The defendant argued that the claim was excluded as the loss caused by the virus was 'caused deliberately by … malicious persons'. The Court of Appeal disagreed. Buxton LJ commented that:

> 'A hacker's interest is to cause as much disruption as possible, wherever possible. It is a matter of indifference to him whether Tektrol is amongst his victims, but it is not a matter of indifference whether persons falling into the same category as Tektrol, computer users susceptible to viruses, should be injured. Injury to that category of persons, where it occurs, is thought-out and intended. The injury is caused deliberately because it is the aim and object of the hacker's actions, as opposed to occurring casually or accidentally in the course of some other operation. The latter would not be the case with any hacker, whose whole object is to damage the system; but the requirement for deliberate causation of the damage would exclude other persons who simply sought to use the system, whether with permission or not, and by carelessness, accident or incompetence in doing so damaged its workings.'[47]

The problem for the insurer was that its exclusion of the deliberate acts of malicious persons was part of a list of individuals who might seek to damage the plaintiff's premises such as rioters and locked-out strikers. Buxton LJ considered that since the reference to malicious persons was part of such a list it: 'suggests strongly that the context envisaged by the draftsman is of interferences directed specifically at those computers and committed on or near the insured's premises'.[48] As regards the theft of the computers, Buxton J ruled that the physical theft of the computers containing the software source codes was not covered by the exemption clause either.

[22.14] Even if a clause such as this appears in the standard licence agreement proffered by a software vendor, the vendor can contract out of it. In *Watford Electronics Ltd v Sanderson CFL*[49] the standard terms subject to which the software was supplied provided that 'Neither the Company nor the Customer shall be liable to the other for any claims for indirect or consequential losses whether arising from negligence or otherwise.'[50] However, an addendum had been added to the contract between the parties, which provided that the vendors would 'commit to their best endeavours in allocating appropriate resources to the project to minimise any losses that may arise from the Contract.'[51] The Court of Appeal ruled that the vendor could not rely upon the exclusion clause in the standard licence unless it could:

> 'show that it did use its best endeavours to allocate appropriate resources to ensure that the Software performs the specified functions, it cannot rely on the provision … excluding claims for indirect or consequential losses'.[52]

---

[47] [2005] EWCA Civ 845, para 10.
[48] [2005] EWCA Civ 845, para 11.
[49] *Watford Electronics Ltd v Sanderson CFL Ltd* (2001) The Times 9 March, [2001] EWCA Civ 317, [2001] BLR 143.
[50] [2001] EWCA Civ 317, para 32.
[51] [2001] EWCA Civ 317, para 8.
[52] [2001] EWCA Civ 317, para 46.

[22.15] Finally, it should be noted that a clause or condition that imposes a particularly unusual or onerous term on another party should be fairly brought to their attention.[53] The problem is that in the industry the existence of bugs or other defects in software is not considered either unusual or onerous. Although this may be true, it is not hard to agree with the view of Bowsher QC[54] in *SAM Business Systems Ltd v Hedley & Co*[55] that:

'I cannot see that it is right that (the defendant software supplier) should be paid for putting right a defect in respect of which they have excluded liability to pay damages. Of course, any product, whether it be a motor car, or a washing machine, or computer software, may, after working well to start with, then develop faults and faults arising in that way, provided they did not exist in a hidden form on delivery, would be the proper subject of a maintenance agreement. But no consumer would or should accept liability to pay for rectification of defects existing in goods on delivery even if there was no contractual liability on the part of the supplier to pay damages arising out of those defects. If a company supplies to a factory a power unit that from the outset does not work, the supplier may be able to sustain a case that he cannot be sued because of his exclusion clauses, but he could not conceivably charge for making it work under a maintenance contract. Exclusion clauses exclude liability for breach of contract: they do not amount to an agreement that performance has been given by providing equipment that is fit to be maintained: nor do they amount to an agreement that the purchaser should pay for any efforts made by the supplier to put right the defects.'[56]

Exclusion of implied terms and conditions under the Sale of Goods Acts

[22.16] The Sale of Goods Acts (SGA) 1893–1980 limits the effectiveness of such clauses where software is sold to consumers and others. Before discussing the application of the SGA 1893–1980 to the licencing of computer programs, it should be noted that in *St Albans City and District Council v International Computers* Glidewell LJ in the English Court of Appeal queried whether the licencing of a computer program could amount to the sale of a good for the purposes of the UK's sale of goods legislation:

'it is clear that the defective program … was not sold, and it seems probable that it was not hired. The evidence is that, in relation to many of the program releases, an employee of ICL went to St Albans' premises where the computer was installed taking with him a disk on which the new program was encoded, and himself performed the exercise of transferring the program into the computer … the program itself is not "goods" within the statutory definition.'[57]

---

[53] See *Interfoto Picture Library v Stiletto Visual Programmes* [1988] 1 All ER 348 where the clause which was 'unusual' should have been 'fairly brought to the attention of the other party'.

[54] Sitting as a Deputy Judge of the English High Court.

[55] *SAM Business Systems Ltd v Hedley & Co* [2002] EWHC 2733 (TCC), [2003] 1 All ER (Comm) 465.

[56] [2002] EWHC 2733 (TCC), para 79.

[57] *St Albans City and District Council v International Computers* [1995] FSR 686, (1994) IP&T Digest 26.

[22.17] However, Glidewell's doubts did not appear to be shared by his fellow judges on the Court of Appeal. The Acts provide that a condition will be implied into all commercial sales that the goods supplied must be of merchantable quality. This condition will not be implied into a private sale, such as one between friends or neighbours. The Acts provide that where a seller sells goods in the course of a business

> 'there is an implied condition that the goods supplied under the contract are of merchantable quality, except that there is no such condition—
>
> (a) as regards defects specifically drawn to the buyer's attention before the contract is made, or
>
> (b) if the buyer examines the goods before the contract is made, as regards defects which that examination ought to have revealed.'[58]

[22.18] Goods are of merchantable quality where they are 'as fit for the purpose or purposes for which goods of that kind are commonly bought and as durable as it is reasonable to expect having regard to any description applied to them, the price (if relevant) and all the other relevant circumstances'.[59] One of the unusual features of the software is that manufacturers openly acknowledge that their systems may fail to function on occasion, and this reality is accepted by users. For example, the EULA for Microsoft Windows XP provides: 'Manufacturer warrants that the SOFTWARE will perform substantially in accordance with the accompanying materials for a period of ninety (90) days from the date of receipt.'[60] The licence goes on to acknowledge that in countries where the law provides for longer periods, those periods will apply. The brevity of the period for which Microsoft is willing to stand over its product is notable, as is the fact that Mircrosoft is only warranting that its product will work 'substantially' as described. As regards sales by description such as this, the SGA 1893–1980 provide that the goods must correspond with the description as set out in for example, the label, advertisement, catalogue or photograph. Section 13, as amended, provides where there is a contract for the sale of goods by description that:

> 'there is an implied condition that the goods shall correspond with the description; and if the sale be by sample as well as by description, it is not sufficient that the bulk of the goods corresponds with the sample if the goods do not also correspond with the description'.

[22.19] A sale of goods is a sale by description, even where the buyer selects them.[61] A reference to goods on a label or other descriptive matter accompanying goods exposed for sale may constitute or form part of the description.[62] Limitation of liability clauses will typically be contained in licences that will only be read by purchasers after they have paid for the product in question, whether this is after they open the 'shrinkwrap' in which the software is packaged or after they download software online. The

---

58 SGA 1893–1980, s 14(2). Section 14(5) provides that an implied condition or warranty as to quality or fitness for a particular purpose may be annexed to a contract of sale by usage.
59 SGA 1893–1980, s 14(3).
60 Microsoft, EULA Windows XP, para 23.
61 SGA 1893–1980, s 13(2).
62 SGA 1893–1980, s 13(3).

enforceability of such licences has given rise to case law in relation to their intellectual property rights. The enforceability of limitation of liability clauses as a matter of contract law is another measure. On the face of it, an obscure clause deep in the text of a licensing agreement that will only be viewed after purchase should not be able to bind the purchaser. But the reality is that software is notoriously unreliable. Anyone who buys a software product will do so in the knowledge that the product may 'crash' on occasion and in the hope that it will not do so so frequently that the product becomes unusable. A good argument can be made that describing something as software is to describe it as an inherently unreliable good. And anyone who uses such a good must take precautions, such as frequently and securely backing up data to protect against the failures that will inevitably follow from the software's use. Goods will be of merchantable quality where they are fit for the purpose for which they are commonly bought.[63] The unfortunate reality of the modern software industry is that reliability is often questionable and whilst one might hope that software will not malfunction, one should also anticipate this occurrence. What this means in practice is that users of software must live with a level of error and failure that would be unacceptable with the products of other industries such as motor vehicles. As a matter of reality, it is only where a product becomes exceptionally error-prone that a purchaser could realistically claim that the product was not fit for the purpose for which it was bought. In this regard, the SGA 1893–1980 provide that where the seller sells goods in the course of a business and the buyer:

> 'expressly or by implication, makes known to the seller any particular purpose for which the goods are being bought, there is an implied condition that the goods supplied under the contract are reasonably fit for that purpose, whether or not that is a purpose for which such goods are commonly supplied, except where the circumstances show that the buyer does not rely, or that it is unreasonable for him to rely, on the seller's skill or judgement'.[64]

[22.20] Section 55, as amended by s 22 of the 1980 Act, sets out the rules governing exclusion clauses where the buyer deals as a consumer and otherwise. Any term in a contract that excludes s 12 (title to goods) is void.[65] Any contractual term that excludes ss 13 (sale by description), 14 (merchantable quality) or 15 (sale by sample) is also void where the buyer is a consumer. In a contract where the buyer is a not a consumer, any term that restricts ss 13, 14 or 15 will not be enforceable unless it is shown that it is 'fair and reasonable'.[66] A court cannot be prevented from holding that a term that purports to exclude or restrict any of the provisions of ss 13, 14 or 15 of the Act is not a term of the contract.[67]

---

[63] See *Wallis v Russell* [1902] 2 IR 585.

[64] SGA 1893–1980, s 14(4).

[65] SGA 1893–1980, s 55(3).

[66] SGA 1893–1980, s 55(4).

[67] SGA 1893–1980, s 55(5). Any reference in s 55 to a term of a contract includes a reference to a term which although not contained in a contract, is incorporated in the contract by another term of the contract, s 55(7).

Who is a consumer?

[22.21] Section 3 of the Sale of Goods and Supply of Services Act 1980 provides that a party to a contract deals as a consumer in relation to another party if:

'(a) he neither makes the contract in the course of a business nor holds himself out as doing so, and

(b) the other party does make the contract in the course of a business, and

(c) the goods or services supplied under or in pursuance of the contract are of a type ordinarily supplied for private use or consumption'.

Where a buyer deals as a consumer he will always be entitled to the conditions implied by ss 12, 13, 14 and 15 and any term restricting this will be void. Whether a person may be regarded as a consumer depends to a great extent on the transaction itself. He must buy from a person selling in the course of a business and the goods must be supplied for private use or consumption. So if a person were to buy 300 i-Pods, he could not be considered a consumer because they could not be considered to be for his own private use. The onus is on those claiming that a party does not deal as consumer to show that he does not.[68] Importantly, on a sale by competitive tender or a sale by auction (i) of goods of a type, or (ii) by or on behalf of a person of a class defined by the Minister by order, the buyer is not in any circumstances to be regarded as dealing as consumer.[69] So a person who buys goods from Internet auction sites should be aware that the law cannot regard him as a consumer, and so he loses the protections provided by the SGA 1893–1980.

'Fair and reasonable'

[22.22] Where the buyer is not a consumer, a term excluding the provisions of ss 13, 14 and 15 will only be valid where it is fair and reasonable. The test for deciding what is fair and reasonable under the Act is that:

'it shall be a fair and reasonable one to be included having regard to the circumstances which were, or ought reasonably to have been, known to or in contemplation of the parties when the contract was made'.[70]

The schedule to the Act lists the following relevant facts to be considered in determining this:

(a) the strength of the bargaining positions of the parties relative to each other, taking into account (among other things) alternative means by which the customer's requirements could have been met;

(b) whether the customer received an inducement to agree to the term, or in accepting it had an opportunity of entering into a similar contract with other persons, but without having to accept a similar term;

(c) whether the customer knew or ought reasonably to have known of the existence and extent of the term (having regard, among other things, to any custom of the trade and any previous course of dealing between the parties);

---

[68] Sale of Goods and Supply of Services Act 1980, s 3(3).
[69] Sale of Goods and Supply of Services Act 1980, s 3(2).
[70] Sale of Goods and Supply of Services Act 1980, Sch.

(d) where the term excludes or restricts any relevant liability if some condition is not complied with, whether it was reasonable at the time of the contract to expect that compliance with that condition would be practicable; and

(e) whether any goods involved were manufactured, processed or adapted to the special order of the customer.

[22.23] In *St Albans City and District Council v International Computers Ltd*[71] the plaintiffs had acquired a computer system from the defendants for the purposes of estimating the local taxes, then called the community charge, which it had to raise from local residents. The software used in the system was defective and underestimated the amount of charge that had to be levied on each resident. As a result, the plaintiff suffered a variety of serious financial consequences, which it sued to recover. Its action was met with a limitation of liability clause, which provided that the defendant's liability was limited to stg£100,000. Scott-Baker J held that the limitation clause was not reasonable because:

(i) The parties were of unequal bargaining power;

(ii) The defendants had not justified the figure of £100,000, which was small both in relation to the potential risk and the actual loss;

(iii) The defendants were insured in an aggregate sum of £50m worldwide.

(iv) The practical consequences favoured holding an international computer company liable instead of requiring that the loss in question be bourne by the plaintiff's charge-payers.

This judgment was upheld on appeal, but the award of damages was reduced as the Court of Appeal ruled that it could be recovered from the plaintiff's charge-payers.

Performance bonds

[22.24] Given the difficulty encountered in the supply of computer systems, some commercial contracts require that parties provide bonds to guarantee their performance. The execution of such a bond was the subject of *TTI Team Telecom International Ltd and another v Hutchison 3G UK Ltd (H3G)*.[72] Contractual relations between the parties created a number of provisions that were designed to ensure performance. For example, the contract required that the price to be paid by the defendant to the plaintiff was:

'payable against the achievement of defined milestones, being the staged delivery and the successful acceptance testing of a defined part of the overall functionality to be provided by the MOM. A first or advance payment ... had to be paid by H3G ... before TTI had performed any services or delivered any of the software. The next five Milestones provided for the five stages of delivery ... The contract programme schedule identified the Milestone dates for the completion of each Milestone and the lump-sum Milestone

---

[71] *St Albans City and District Council v International Computers Ltd* [1995] FSR 686, (1994) IP & T Digest 26. See also *The Salvage Association v CAP Financial Services Ltd* [1995] FSR 654, (1992) IP & T Digest 56 and *SAM Business Systems Ltd v Hedley & Co* [2002] EWHC 2733 (TCC), [2003] 1 All ER (Comm) 465.

[72] *TTI Team Telecom International Ltd and another v Hutchison 3G UK Ltd* [2003] EWHC 762 (TCC), [2003] 1 All ER (Comm) 914.

payments to be paid on each of these dates. Each of the first four Functionality Milestone payments was for the same lump sum ... and that for the fifth was for twice that sum.'[73]

[22.25] In addition, the plaintiff software supplier TTI was required to procure an 'advance payment bond' from its bank. The parties fell into dispute and the customer H3G sought to draw down the bond. The plaintiff disputed the defendant's right to do so and sought injunctive relief from the English courts. This dispute arose because of 'significant delays in progress and in the provision, testing and bringing into service of the programmed functionality and the relevant Milestone dates were not achieved as programmed'.[74] The plaintiff claimed that these delays were caused by the defendant's 'inability to provide the information and data storage facilities required'. The defendant took the view that the delays 'were caused by TTI's failure to mobilise sufficient resources or to plan the works properly'.[75] Thornton QC reviewed the case law that dealt with the circumstances under which the English courts would contemplate restraining a beneficiary such as H3G from calling on a bond.

'1.   A third party seeking to restrain a beneficiary from calling a bond must initially show that such an application is supporting an underlying entitlement or claim based on a breach by the beneficiary of the underlying contract or on some other cause of action or basis for injunctive relief such as fraud, restitution or a breach of faith.

2.   When a third party seeks to restrain a beneficiary from calling a bond, or from receiving the product of a call, the court's starting point is that a call will ordinarily only be restrained where there has been fraud in setting up or calling the bond or where there is a lack of a breach of faith by the beneficiary in threatening a call.

3.   The basis for a contention of a breach of faith must be established by clear evidence even for the purposes of interim relief.

4.   In addition, where it appears that the call would be a nullity, a court will intervene to restrain that invalid call.'

[22.26] However, the above were the only circumstances in which the courts would intervene to restrain a call on a performance bond. Thornton QC went on to note that:

'an allegedly incorrect calling of a performance bond will not be restrained merely because the factual basis of the call arising out of the underlying contract is disputed. Thus disputes as to whether a breach of contract, a determination of a contract for cause, a repudiation of a contract or the incurring of loss have occurred, where these are events covered by the performance guarantee, will not be allowed to found an application to restrain a call unless these disputes reveal a breach of faith by the beneficiary. Any consequent payment under the bond to the beneficiary which over-compensates the beneficiary may be recouped in the 'accounting' exercise that the third party may claim in subsequent litigation against the beneficiary under the underlying contract.'

Furthermore, Thornton QC expressed the view that the courts would not grant interim relief 'unless a third party has a real prospect of succeeding in both the entitlement to

---

[73]   [2003] EWHC 762 (TCC), para 3.

[74]   [2003] EWHC 762 (TCC), para 10.

[75]   [2003] EWHC 762 (TCC), para 13.

restrain the call and in its underlying claim which ought to be tried out before a call is made'.[76] The courts would also have to consider the Balance of Convenience before granting interim relief. Thornton QC went on to apply his analysis of the law to the case before him, and concluded that the plaintiff's were not entitled to an interim injunction restraining the defendant from enforcing the bond.

Title

[22.27] Software is easily replicated, but software licences are expensive. Some unscrupulous suppliers may be tempted to supply the former and infringe the latter. In the process they may make money, but they may cause their customers serious embarrassment.[77] Section 12 of the 1893 Act, as amended by the Sale of Goods and Supply of Services Act 1980, implies three terms in every contract for the sale of goods:

(1) there is an implied condition[78] on the part of the seller that, in the case of a sale, he has a right to sell the goods and, in the case of an agreement to sell, he will have a right to sell the goods at the time when the property is to pass;

(2) there is an implied warranty[79] that the goods are free, and will remain free until the time when the property is to pass, from any charge or encumbrance not disclosed to the buyer before the contract is made; and

(3) there is an implied warranty that the buyer will enjoy quiet possession of the goods.[80]

Section 2(2) sets out an exception to the above. Where it appears from the contract, or is to be inferred from the circumstances of the contract, that there is an intention that the seller should transfer only such title as he or a third person may have, there is (a) an implied warranty that all charges or encumbrances known to the seller have been disclosed to the buyer before the contract is made, and (b) an implied warranty that neither (i) the seller, nor (ii) in a case where the parties to the contract intend that the seller should transfer only such title as a third person may have, that person, nor (iii) anyone claiming through or under the seller or that third person otherwise than under a charge or encumbrance disclosed to the buyer before the contract is made, will disturb the buyer's quiet possession of the goods.

Escrow

[22.28] The use of computer software will be integral to the operation of any modern company. That software may be in form of off-the-shelf programs such as those provided by the Microsoft Office. But some users may have more idiosyncratic needs. If they have the resources and the software is particularly important for their operations, a user may produce it in-house, retaining full control of the process and full ownership of any and all intellectual property rights. Alternatively, a company or institution may hire

---

[76] [2003] EWHC 762 (TCC), para 46.
[77] See, for example, *Microsoft Corporation v Ling* [2006] EWHC 1619 (Ch).
[78] A breach of a condition entitles the innocent party to terminate the contract and claim damages.
[79] A breach of a warranty entitles the innocent party to damages only. The contract will not come to an end.
[80] Except so far as it may be disturbed by the owner or other person entitled to the benefit of any charge or encumbrance so disclosed.

a third party supplier to create appropriate bespoke software for it. The ownership of the intellectual property in the software and the source codes for it, may be retained by the supplier indefinitely or until the contract is completed and the final payment made. This process will work well enough, so long as the supplier remains solvent or the parties don't become embroiled in a dispute with each other. But if something should happen, such as the supplier going into liquidation, then the customer will not be able to access the source code so that it may maintain the software. In the English case of *Psychometric Services v Merant International*[81] the plaintiffs had commissioned software from the defendant. Unfortunately, the software produced proved to be unsatisfactory. Facing serious difficulties, the plaintiff went to court and was granted an order requiring that the defendant hand over the source codes to the software in question.

[22.29] In an effort to avoid situations such as this, the contract between the parties may provide for the source codes to be held in escrow by a trusted third party. The interpretation of an escrow agreement was the subject of *CardBASE Technologies (CBT) v ValuCard Nigeria.*[82] The facts were that:

> 'Valucard is a company set up by a consortium of Nigerian banks to operate an electronic card payment system … Valucard entered into an agreement … with CBT, under which CBT granted Valucard a non-exclusive licence to use certain 'smart card' computer software. The products licensed included the computer programme in object code, defined in the Licence Agreement as 'computer executable embodiment of the computer code derived from the source code', but not the source code material.'[83]

The licencing agreement between the parties provided that 'CBT would enter into a source code escrow agreement with Valucard and an independent third party'. The source codes were then deposited with a UK provider of such services, NCC. The escrow agreement between the parties provided that the source codes would be released to the defendants if it:

> 'enters into any competition or arrangement with its creditors or being a company enters into liquidation . . . or has a receiver or administrative receiver appointed . . . or a petition is presented for an administration order.'[84]

Following the appointment of an examiner to the plaintiff by the High Court in Dublin where the plaintiff was based, the defendant sought the release of the source codes in question from NCC. The plaintiff applied to the English courts for an order restraining the release of the codes to the defendant. However, the plaintiff's application failed.

Unfair terms in consumer contracts

[22.30] European Communities (Unfair Terms in Consumer Contracts) Regulations 1995 and 2000[85] implement Council Directive 93/13/EEC on unfair terms in consumer

---

[81] *Psychometric Services v Merant International* (8 March 2001) HC (England and Wales) Laddie J.
[82] *CardBASE Technologies v ValuCard Nigeria* [2002] EWHC 991 (Ch).
[83] [2002] EWHC 991 (Ch), para 3.
[84] [2002] EWHC 991 (Ch), para 9.
[85] SI 27/1995.

contracts into Irish law. A contractual term that has not been individually negotiated is unfair if, contrary to the requirement of good faith, it causes a significant imbalance in the parties' rights and obligations arising under the contract, to the detriment of the consumer, taking into account the nature of the goods or services for which the contract was concluded and all circumstances attending the conclusion of the contract and all other terms of the contract or of another contract on which it is dependent.[86] Under the Directive a 'consumer' means 'any natural person who, in contracts covered by this Directive, is acting for purposes which are outside his trade, business or profession.'[87]

In making an assessment of what constitutes 'good faith', the Regulations provide the following guidelines: regard should be had to the strength of the bargaining positions of the parties; whether the consumer had an inducement to agree to the term; whether the goods or services were sold or supplied to the special order of the consumer, and the extent to which the seller or supplier has dealt fairly and equitably with the consumer whose legitimate interests he has to take into account.[88] A term will always be regarded as not being individually negotiated where it has been drafted in advance and the consumer has therefore not been able to influence the substance of the term, particularly in the context of a pre-formulated standard contract. The fact that certain aspects of a term or one specific term have been individually negotiated will not exclude the application of the Regulations to the rest of a contract if an overall assessment of the contract indicates that it is nevertheless a pre-formulated standard contract.[89] Where any seller or supplier claims that a standard term has been individually negotiated, the burden of proof is on him to show that it was.[90] A 'seller or supplier' means 'any natural or legal person who, in contracts covered by this Directive, is acting for purposes relating to his trade, business or profession, whether publicly owned or privately owned'.[91]

[22.31] The following is an indicative and non-exhaustive list of the terms that may be regarded as unfair.[92] These are terms which have the object or effect of:

> '(a) excluding or limiting the legal liability of a seller or supplier in the event of the death of a consumer or personal injury to the latter resulting from an act or omission of that seller or supplier;

---

[86] SI 27/1995, reg 3(2). The regulations do not apply to the following: contracts of employment; contracts relating to succession rights; any contract relating to rights under family law; any contract relating to the incorporation and organisation of companies or partnerships; any terms which reflect— (i) mandatory, statutory or regulatory provisions of Ireland, or (ii) the provisions or principles of international conventions to which the member states or the Community are party.

[87] Council Directive 93/13/EEC, art 2(b). The regulations define a 'consumer' as a natural person who is acting for purposes that are outside his business.

[88] SI 27/1995, Sch 2, Guidelines for Application of the Test of Good Faith.

[89] SI 27/1995, reg 3(5).

[90] SI 27/1995, reg 3(6).

[91] Council Directive 93/13/EEC, art 2(c).

[92] Council Directive 93/13/EEC, art 3(3).

(b) inappropriately excluding or limiting the legal rights of the consumer vis-à-vis the seller or supplier or another party in the event of total or partial non-performance or inadequate performance by the seller or supplier of any of the contractual obligations, including the option of offsetting a debt owed to the seller or supplier against any claim which the consumer may have against him;

(c) making an agreement binding on the consumer whereas provision of services by the seller or supplier is subject to a condition whose realization depends on his own will alone;

(d) permitting the seller or supplier to retain sums paid by the consumer where the latter decides not to conclude or perform the contract, without providing for the consumer to receive compensation of an equivalent amount from the seller or supplier where the latter is the party cancelling the contract;

(e) requiring any consumer who fails to fulfil his obligation to pay a disproportionately high sum in compensation;

(f) authorizing the seller or supplier to dissolve the contract on a discretionary basis where the same facility is not granted to the consumer, or permitting the seller or supplier to retain the sums paid for services not yet supplied by him where it is the seller or supplier himself who dissolves the contract;

(g) enabling the seller or supplier to terminate a contract of indeterminate duration without reasonable notice except where there are serious grounds for doing so[93];.

(h) automatically extending a contract of fixed duration where the consumer does not indicate otherwise, when the deadline fixed for the consumer to express this desire not to extend the contract is unreasonably early;

(i) irrevocably binding the consumer to terms with which he had no real opportunity of becoming acquainted before the conclusion of the contract;

(j) enabling the seller or supplier to alter the terms of the contract unilaterally without a valid reason which is specified in the contract[94];

(k) enabling the seller or supplier to alter unilaterally without a valid reason any characteristics of the product or service to be provided;

(l) providing for the price of goods to be determined at the time of delivery or allowing a seller of goods or supplier of services to increase their price without in both cases giving the consumer the corresponding right to cancel the contract if

---

[93] This is without hindrance to terms by which a supplier of financial services reserves the right to terminate unilaterally a contract of indeterminate duration without notice where there is a valid reason, provided that the supplier is required to inform the other contracting party or parties thereof immediately, SI 27/1995, Sch 3(2).

[94] This is without hindrance to terms under which a supplier of financial services reserves the right to alter the rate of interest payable by the consumer or due to the latter, or the amount of other charges for financial services without notice where there is a valid reason, provided that the supplier is required to inform the other contracting party or parties thereof at the earliest opportunity and that the latter are free to dissolve the contract immediately. This is also without hindrance to terms under which a seller or supplier reserves the right to alter unilaterally the conditions of a contract of indeterminate duration, provided that he is required to inform the consumer with reasonable notice and that the consumer is free to dissolve the contract, SI 27/1995, Sch 3(2).

the final price is too high in relation to the price agreed when the contract was concluded[95];

(m) giving the seller or supplier the right to determine whether the goods or services supplied are in conformity with the contract, or giving him the exclusive right to interpret any term of the contract;

(n) limiting the seller's or supplier's obligation to respect commitments undertaken by his agents or making his commitments subject to compliance with a particular formality;

(o) obliging the consumer to fulfil all his obligations where the seller or supplier does not perform his;

(p) giving the seller or supplier the possibility of transferring his rights and obligations under the contract, where this may serve to reduce the guarantees for the consumer, without the latter's agreement;

(q) excluding or hindering the consumer's right to take legal action or exercise any other legal remedy, particularly by requiring the consumer to take disputes exclusively to arbitration not covered by legal provisions, unduly restricting the evidence available to him or imposing on him a burden of proof which, according to the applicable law, should lie with another party to the contract'.[96]

[22.32] Where a term is considered an unfair term, it will not be binding on a consumer[97] but the contract will continue to bind the parties if it is capable of continuing in existence without the unfair term.[98] In a written contract with a consumer, the seller or supplier must ensure that the terms are drafted in plain, intelligible language[99] and if there is any doubt over the meaning of a term, it will always be interpreted in favour of the consumer.[100]

Jurisdiction

[22.33] The Jurisdiction of Courts and Enforcement of Judgments Act 1998 provides that 'The Conventions shall have the force of law in the State and judicial notice shall be taken of them.'[101] The Conventions in question are the Brussels Convention, the Accession Conventions to the Brussels Convention and the 1971 protocol on the

---

[95] This is without hindrance to price-indexation clauses, where lawful, provided that the method by which prices vary is explicitly described. Paragraphs (g), (j) and (l) do not apply to transactions in transferable securities, financial instruments and other products or services where the price is linked to fluctuations in a stock exchange quotation or index or a financial market rate that the seller or supplier does not control. They do not apply to contracts for the purchase or sale of foreign currency, traveller's cheques or international money orders denominated in foreign currency, SI 27/1995, Sch 3(2).

[96] SI 27/1995, Sch 3(1).

[97] SI 27/1995, reg 6(1).

[98] SI 27/1995, reg 6(2).

[99] SI 27/1995, reg 5(1).

[100] SI 27/1995, reg 5(2).

[101] Jurisdiction of Courts and Enforcement of Judgments Act 1998, s 5.

interpretation of the Conventions by the ECJ. In general, the Brussels Convention provides that 'persons domiciled in a Contracting State shall, whatever their nationality, be sued in the courts of that State.'[102] The Brussels Convention provides special rules for contracts in general and consumer contracts in particular. It provides that 'A person domiciled in a Contracting State may, in another Contracting State, be sued ... in matters relating to a contract, in the courts for the place of performance of the obligation in question.'[103] As regards consumers, the Brussels Convention provides that:

> 'A consumer may bring proceedings against the other party to a contract either in the courts of the Contracting State in which that party is domiciled or in the courts of the Contracting State in which he is himself domiciled.

> Proceedings may be brought against a consumer by the other party to the contract only in the courts of the Contracting State in which the consumer is domiciled.

> These provisions shall not affect the right to bring a counter-claim in the court in which, in accordance with this Section, the original claim is pending.'[104]

Consumers may contract out of this provision, but only where the departure from the provision is agreed after the dispute has arisen[105] or the agreement allows the dispute to be heard in courts other than those mentioned above[106] or the agreement:

> 'is entered into by the consumer and the other party to the contract, both of whom are at the time of conclusion of the contract domiciled or habitually resident in the same Contracting State, and which confers jurisdiction on the courts of that State, provided that such an agreement is not contrary to the law of that State.'[107]

The Convention also provides a special rule in the case of torts, stating that 'A person domiciled in a Contracting State may, in another Contracting State, be sued ... in matters relating to tort ... in the courts for the place where the harmful event occurred.'[108] The Directive on e-Commerce also provides that:

> 'Member States shall ensure that court actions available under national law concerning information society services' activities allow for the rapid adoption of measures, including interim measures, designed to terminate any alleged infringement and to prevent any further impairment of the interests involved.'[109]

Alternative dispute resolution

[22.34] Given the Internet's global reach, the cost of bringing a dispute to court will be prohibitive in many cross-border cases. Alternative dispute resolution may offer a

---

[102] Brussels Convention, art 2.
[103] Brussels Convention, art 5(1).
[104] Brussels Convention, art 14.
[105] Brussels Convention, art 15(1).
[106] Brussels Convention, art 15(2).
[107] Brussels Convention, art 15(3).
[108] Brussels Convention, art 5(3).
[109] Directive on e-Commerce, art 18.

mechanism for dealing with such disputes quickly, cheaply and effectively.[110] To encourage this process, the Directive on e-Commerce provides, in respect of out of court dispute settlement that member states must:

'shall ensure that, in the event of disagreement between an information society service provider and the recipient of the service, their legislation does not hamper the use of out-of-court schemes, available under national law, for dispute settlement, including appropriate electronic means.'[111]

Member States are expected to:

'encourage bodies responsible for the out-of-court settlement of, in particular, consumer disputes to operate in a way which provides adequate procedural guarantees for the parties concerned.'[112]

And, finally, Member States must:

'encourage bodies responsible for out-of-court dispute settlement to inform the Commission of the significant decisions they take regarding information society services and to transmit any other information on the practices, usages or customs relating to electronic commerce.'[113]

---

[110] Arbitration is a voluntary process where parties refer their dispute to an impartial third party known as an arbitrator. Arbitration Acts 1954–1998, s 2 defines an arbitration agreement as 'a written agreement to refer present or future differences to arbitration, whether an arbitrator is named therein or not'. For further reading, see Stewart, *Arbitration Commentary and Sources* (FirstLaw, 2004).

[111] Directive on e-Commerce, art 17(1).

[112] Directive on e-Commerce, art 17(2).

[113] Directive on e-Commerce, art 17(3).

Chapter 23

Competition

Introduction

[23.01] The Treaty Establishing the European Communities (TEC) provides that 'the activities of the community ... include ... the strengthening of the competitiveness of community industry ... (and) the promotion of research and technological development'.[1] In pursuit of these objectives, the TEC imposes a number of specific conditions on how business is conducted in the EU. In particular, the TEC prohibits anti-competitive agreements between undertakings and the abuse of dominant positions; and it restricts on the extent to which the state can provide aid to undertakings. The TEC's prohibitions on anti-competitive agreements and abuse of dominant position are implemented in Ireland by the Competition Acts 2002 and 2006; the restrictions on state aid are in the form of EC regulations and so have direct effect upon the state. Each of these prohibitions and restrictions has implications for information technology law and these implications are discussed below.

[23.02] The Competition Acts 2002 and 2006[2] provide for the enforcement of EC competition law in Ireland. The Acts enact the relevant provisions of the TEC as Irish law. The Acts then provide that breaches of both Irish and European competition law will be criminal offences.[3] These offences are punishable by fines of up to €4,000,000 or 10 per cent of the turnover of the individual or undertaking in the financial year ending in the 12 months prior to the conviction or to imprisonment for a term not exceeding 5 years where a person is convicted.[4] The Acts provide for the provision of information to juries,[5] expert evidence [6]and the application of certain presumptions to the consideration of criminal guilt.[7] They also provide for the establishment of the Competition Authority and the exercise of various functions conferred upon it.[8] The Competition Acts also provide that private individuals may sue in respect of losses that they have suffered as a result of anti-competitive abuses or practices. They provide that:

> 'Any person who is aggrieved in consequence of any agreement, decision, concerted practice or abuse which is prohibited ... shall have a right of action ... for relief against either or both of the following, namely ... any undertaking which is or has at any material time been a party to such an agreement, decision or concerted practice or has done any act

---

[1] Consolidated Version of the Treaty Establishing the European Community, art 3(1)(m) & (n).
[2] Referred to as the Competition Acts.
[3] Competition Acts, ss 6 and 7.
[4] Competition Acts, s 8(1)(b)(ii).
[5] Competition Acts, s 10.
[6] Competition Acts, s 9.
[7] Competition Acts, s 12.
[8] Competition Acts, Part 4.

that constituted such an abuse ... any director, manager or other officer of such an undertaking, or a person who purported to act in any such capacity, who authorised or consented to, as the case may be, the entry by the undertaking into, or the implementation by it of, the agreement or decision, the engaging by it in the concerted practice or the doing by it of the act that constituted the abuse.'[9]

Abuse of dominant position

[23.03] The TEC provides that:

'Any abuse by one or more undertakings of a dominant position within the common market or in a substantial part of it shall be prohibited as incompatible with the common market in so far as it may affect trade between Member States.'[10]

The TEC goes on to provide that the following activities may constitute such abuse:

(a) 'directly or indirectly imposing unfair purchase or selling prices or other unfair trading conditions;

(b) limiting production, markets or technical development to the prejudice of consumers;

(c) applying dissimilar conditions to equivalent transactions with other trading parties, thereby placing them at a competitive disadvantage;

(d) making the conclusion of contracts subject to acceptance by the other parties of supplementary obligations which, by their nature or according to commercial usage, have no connection with the subject of such contracts.'[11]

[23.04] Before a case for abuse of dominant abuse can be established, two facts must be proven: firstly, that the alleged abuser was in a dominant position at the time, and secondly, that the alleged abuser's conduct amounted to abuse. The definition of the market in which the abuse is alleged to have been committed will probably be the most important decisions taken in any such exercise. For example, in the *Microsoft v Commission*[12] decision discussed below the Commission examined the activities of Microsoft in three separate product markets: PC operating systems,[13] servers[14] and media players.[15] The Commission also examined the activities across a geographic market, namely that of the entire world.[16] No statutory definition of dominant position exists, but the ECJ suggested that it was:

'A position of Economic strength enjoyed by an undertaking which enables it to hinder the maintenance of effective competition on the relevant market by allowing it to behave to an appreciable extent independently of its competitors'. [17]

---

[9] Competition Acts, s 14(1).

[10] TEC, art 82.

[11] TEC, art 82.

[12] *Microsoft v Commission* Case No T-201/04, (17 September 2007) Court of First Instance.

[13] T-201/04, para 24.

[14] T-201/04, para 25.

[15] T-201/04, para 28.

[16] T-201/04, para 29.

[17] *Michelin v Commission* Case C-322/81. See also *United Brands v Commission* Case 27/76, *Hoffman La Roche* Case c-86/76 and *Eurpemballage v Commission* Case C-6/72.

Microsoft v Commission

[23.05] It should be noted that initially this investigation had been conducted in parallel with one undertaken by the US authorities. In *United States v Microsoft*[18] US District Court Judge Penfield Jackson held that:

> 'Viewed together, three main facts indicate that Microsoft enjoys monopoly power. First, Microsoft's share of the market for Intel-compatible PC operating systems is extremely large and stable. Second, Microsoft's dominant market share is protected by a high barrier to entry. Third, and largely as a result of that barrier, Microsoft's customers lack a commercially viable alternative to Windows.'[19]

Judge Penfield Jackson's findings of fact examined a variety of evidence which notably related to the manner in which Microsoft competed with Netscape Navigator in the mid-to-late nineties. His findings concluded with the following comment:

> 'Most harmful of all is the message that Microsoft's actions have conveyed to every enterprise with the potential to innovate in the computer industry. Through its conduct toward Netscape, IBM, Compaq, Intel, and others, Microsoft has demonstrated that it will use its prodigious market power and immense profits to harm any firm that insists on pursuing initiatives that could intensify competition against one of Microsoft's core products. Microsoft's past success in hurting such companies and stifling innovation deters investment in technologies and businesses that exhibit the potential to threaten Microsoft. The ultimate result is that some innovations that would truly benefit consumers never occur for the sole reason that they do not coincide with Microsoft's self-interest'.[20]

Judge Penfield Jackson's decision was appealed, initially an attempt was made to put the case directly into the Supreme Court, but this was rejected. Instead, the decision was reviewed by the US Court of Appeals. Whilst Judge Penfield Jackson had displayed an impressive grasp of detail and an ability to marshal facts and legal opinion into well written judgments, he unfortunately displayed remarkably poor judgment in other ways. In public he made a number of pejorative comments regarding Microsoft, notably comparing it to a drug gang. Unsurprisingly he was roundly and rightly condemned for this conduct by the US Court of Appeal.[21] The court threw out Judge Penfield Jackson's order, which would have broken up Microsoft;[22] ultimately settlement on a final judgment was reached.[23] Legal policy and anti-competition policy has changed significantly in the USA since then, but more significantly technology has also changed. These changes have had the effect of reducing the importance of Microsoft's monopoly:

---

[18]   *United States v Microsoft* 87 F Supp 2d 30 (DDC 2000).

[19]   87 F Supp 2d 30 (DDC 2000), para 34.

[20]   87 F Supp 2d 30 (DDC 2000), para 412.

[21]   Labaton, 'Judges Voice Doubt On Order Last Year To Split Microsoft' (2001) New York Times, 28 February.

[22]   Labaton, 'US VS Microsoft: Appeals Court voids order for breaking up Microsoft but finds it abused power' (2001) The New York Times, 29 June.

[23]   Harmon, 'US VS Microsoft: Judge backs terms of US settlement in Microsoft case' (2002) The New York Times, 2 November.

'The battlefront among technology companies has shifted from computer desktop software, a category that Microsoft dominates, to Internet search and Web-based software programs that allow users to bypass products made by Microsoft.'[24]

[23.06] The changes in technology are important. The facts that underlie the judgment of *Microsoft v Commission*[25] were about nine years old when the Court of First Instance gave judgment. In 1998 the Commission received a complaint from Sun Microsystems requesting that Microsoft provide it with certain information necessary to ensure that Sun's products could interoperate with Microsoft's. The Commission commenced an investigation and ultimately decided that Microsoft held a dominant position in the PC operating systems market[26] and the market for server software.[27] The Commission went on to find that Microsoft had abused its dominant position in these markets in two ways: firstly, by refusing to supply and authorise the use of interoperability information and, secondly, by tying the Windows client PC operating system to the Windows Media Player.[28] In response to this decision, Microsoft applied to the Court of First Instance for an order annulling the Commission decision.[29] The Court of First Instance refused Microsoft the relief sought, although it did refuse to impose a monitoring trustee on the company. The judgment in *Microsoft v Commission* is lengthy and detailed, but the sum of its parts are perhaps more significant than any individual finding made by the Court of First Instance. The Commission had undertaken an extensive and detailed investigation before coming to its decision and all aspects of this were approved by the court. This is a significant endorsement of the Commission's procedures. The court also approved the Commission's decision to regulate industry in this way.

Interoperability information

[23.07] The Court began by noting that the following facts were accepted by the parties:

'the function of a computer program is to communicate and work together with other components of a computer system and with users and, for this purpose a logical and, where appropriate, physical interconnection and interaction is required to permit all elements of software and hardware to work with other software and hardware and with users in all the ways in which they are intended to function ... the parts of the program which provide for such interconnection and interaction between elements of software and hardware are generally known as 'interfaces' ... this functional interconnection and interaction is generally known as 'interoperability' ... such interoperability can be defined as the ability to exchange information and mutually to use the information which has been exchanged.'[30]

The Court reviewed the technological background and concluded that the Commission was correct to assert that 'the common ability to be part of [the Windows domain architecture] is a feature of compatibility between Windows client PCs and Windows

---

[24] Labaton, 'Microsoft finds legal defender in justice dept' (2007) The New York Times, 10 June.
[25] *Microsoft v Commission* T-201/04 (17 September 2007) Court of First Instance.
[26] T-201/04, para 31.
[27] T-201/04, para 33.
[28] Case COMP/C-3.37.792 – Microsoft, OJ 2007 L 32, p 23.
[29] T-201/04, para 76.
[30] T-201/04, para 157.

work group servers'.[31] Microsoft was accused of withholding indispensable information necessary to ensure this compatibility. The Commission then split the decision as to whether this information was indispensable into two parts:

> 'Firstly it ... examined the degree of interoperability with the Windows domain architecture that the work group server operating systems supplied by Microsoft's competitors must achieve in order for those competitors to be able to remain viably on the market'.

Secondly, the Commission 'proceeded to determine whether the interoperability information to which Microsoft refused access was indispensable to the attainment of that degree of interoperability'.[32] The court rejected an assertion by Microsoft that the Commission was trying to force it to enable its competitors to clone or reproduce parts of its products.[33]

Compulsory licensing of intellectual property

[23.08] The Court then went on to consider Microsoft's claims that its interoperability information was protected by intellectual property laws. Mircosoft put forward a series of arguments:

> 'designed to demonstrate that its communication protocols are technologically innovative. Communication protocols are often developed in connection with the performance of specific tasks by server operating systems and are intimately linked with the way in which those tasks are performed. Licensing those communication protocols therefore necessarily means providing competitors with information about the internal features of the server operating systems with which those communication protocols are used. In addition, a large number of engineers and significant financial resources are used in developing and improving communication protocols.'[34]

Microsoft asserted that these innovations were patentable and their specifications were protected by copyright. These assertions were extensively discussed at hearing and in written submissions by all parties. However, the court held that it was not necessary to consider them as the Commission 'adopted the decision on the assumption that Microsoft was able to rely on such rights'.[35] The decision then moved on to discuss the circumstances under which an intellectual property owner can be compelled to license its intellectual property. The ECJ reviewed the case law and concluded that:

> 'the refusal by an undertaking holding a dominant position to license a third party to use a product covered by an intellectual property right cannot in itself constitute an abuse of a dominant position ... It is only in exceptional circumstances that the exercise of the exclusive right by the owner of the intellectual property right may give rise to such an abuse.'[36]

[23.09] The Court held the following circumstances would 'in particular' be exceptional:

---

[31] T-201/04, para 189.
[32] T-201/04, para 207.
[33] T-201/04, para 234.
[34] T-201/04, para 267.
[35] T-201/04, para 284.
[36] T-201/04, para 331.

— in the first place, the refusal relates to a product or service indispensable to the exercise of a particular activity on a neighbouring market;

— in the second place, the refusal is of such a kind as to exclude any effective competition on that neighbouring market;

— in the third place, the refusal prevents the appearance of a new product for which there is potential consumer demand.[37]

The Court went on to find that:

'Once it is established that such circumstances are present, the refusal by the holder of a dominant position to grant a licence may infringe Article 82 EC unless the refusal is objectively justified.'[38]

Finally, the Court noted that:

'it is appropriate to add that, in order that a refusal to give access to a product or service indispensable to the exercise of a particular activity may be considered abusive, it is necessary to distinguish two markets, namely, a market constituted by that product or service and on which the undertaking refusing to supply holds a dominant position and a neighbouring market on which the product or service is used in the manufacture of another product or for the supply of another service. The fact that the indispensable product or service is not marketed separately does not exclude from the outset the possibility of identifying a separate market.'[39]

[23.10] The Court then went on to consider whether the interoperability information was 'indispensable'. The court noted the Commission's finding that Microsoft's dominant position in the PC operating systems market exhibited 'extraordinary features' as it's had 90% of the market and its systems were a 'quasi-standard' for those operating systems.[40] The court went on to find that Microsoft failed to show that the interoperability information was not indispensable.[41] Microsoft had also submitted that its refusal to licence was 'not such as to exclude all competition on a secondary market'.[42] Microsoft challenged the Commission's definition of the relevant product market. In this case the Commission had restricted the market to 'the work group server operating systems market'.[43] In making this decision, the court noted that the Commission had undertaken a complex economic analysis of the market, which could not be reviewed by the court. The Court ruled that the decision that it had to make was:

'whether the Commission based its assessment on accurate, reliable and coherent evidence which contains all the relevant data that must be taken into consideration in appraising a complex situation and whether it is capable of substantiating the conclusions drawn from it.'[44]

---

37 T-201/04, para 332.
38 T-201/04, para 333.
39 T-201/04, para 335.
40 T-201/04, para 337.
41 T-201/04, para 436.
42 T-201/04, para 437.
43 T-201/04, para 480.
44 T-201/04, para 482.

[23.11] The Court undertook this analysis and concluded that the Commission's market analysis was correct.[45] The Court agreed that the Commission was correct to conclude that there was a risk of competition elimination given that Microsoft had a market share of about 60% of the server market at that time. This share was combined with other advantages such as the proven record of Microsoft's established product and the existing skill-base of persons expert in that products use: 'Microsoft's very high market share on the work group server operating system market has the consequence that a very large number of technicians possess skills which are specific to Windows operating systems'.[46]

The Court then dealt with Microsoft's argument that its actions had not prevented the emergence of a new product for which there was unsatisfied customer demand.[47] The court that this issue related to TEC, art 82(b) which prohibits practices that limit production, markets or technical developments to the detriment of consumers. The Court considered that the Commission's decision rested upon:

> 'the concept that, once the obstacle represented for Microsoft's competitors by the insufficient degree of interoperability with the Windows domain architecture has been removed, those competitors will be able to offer work group server operating systems which, far from merely reproducing the Windows systems already on the market, will be distinguished from those systems with respect to parameters which consumers consider important.'[48]

[23.12] The Court considered that a number of points had to be borne in mind. Firstly:

> 'Microsoft's competitors would not be able to clone or reproduce its products solely by having access to the interoperability information covered by the contested decision ….the information at issue does not extend to implementation details or to other features of Microsoft's source code.'[49]

Secondly, the Court thought that Microsoft's competitors would not have any interest:

> 'in merely reproducing Windows work group server operating systems. Once they are able to use the information communicated to them to develop systems that are sufficiently interoperable with the Windows domain architecture, they will have no other choice if they wish to take advantage of a competitive advantage over Microsoft and maintain a profitable presence on the market, than to differentiate their products from Microsoft's products with respect to certain parameters and certain features'.[50]

Finally, Microsoft argued that 'it will have less incentive to develop a given technology if it is required to make that technology available to its competitors.'[51] The Court held that this was irrelevant to the issue of whether Microsoft had limited the production of new products by others as at this stage the court was examining 'the impact of the

---

[45] T-201/04, para 531.
[46] T-201/04, para 619.
[47] T-201/04, para 621.
[48] T-201/04, para 656.
[49] T-201/04, para 657.
[50] T-201/04, para 658.
[51] T-201/04, para 659.

refusal to supply on the incentive for Microsoft's competitors to innovate and not on Microsoft's incentives to innovate.'[52]

The Court went on to find that Microsoft had failed to show that the Commission was incorrect when it concluded that: 'Microsoft's refusal limits technical development to the prejudice of consumers'.[53] The Court separately considered the impact of the Commission's decisions on Microsoft's innovation incentives; in this regard, Microsoft argued that its information was secret, of great value, and contained important innovations. In response, the court noted that: 'the fact that the technology concerned is secret is the consequence of a unilateral business decision on Microsoft's part'.[54] The court agreed that the information was of great value, noting that:

> 'from the moment at which it is established that ... the interoperability information is indispensable, that information is necessarily of great value to the competitors who wish to have access to it.'[55]

[23.13] Finally, the Court noted that: 'it is inherent in the fact that the undertaking concerned holds an intellectual property right that the subject-matter of that right is innovative or original. There can be no patent without an invention and no copyright without an original work'.[56] The Court commented that it 'did not sufficiently establish that if it were required to disclose the interoperability information that would have a significant negative impact on its incentives to innovate'.[57] The court considered that Microsoft had only 'put forward vague, general and theoretical arguments' in relation to this issue. The Court cited the Microsoft statement that: 'disclosure would ... eliminate future incentives to invest in the creation of more intellectual property'. The Court responded that Microsoft had failed to specify 'the technologies or products to which it thus referred'.[58] It concluded that 'it has not been demonstrated that the disclosure of the information to which that remedy relates will significantly reduce – still less eliminate – Microsoft's incentives to innovate.'[59] In addition, the court observed that:

> 'it is normal practice for operators in the industry to disclose to third parties the information which will facilitate interoperability with their products and Microsoft itself had followed that practice until it was sufficiently established on the work group server operating systems market. Such disclosure allows the operators concerned to make their own products more attractive and therefore more valuable. In fact, none of the parties has claimed in the present case that such disclosure had had any negative impact on those operators' incentives to innovate.'[60]

---

[52] T-201/04, para 659.
[53] T-201/04, para 665.
[54] T-201/04, para 693.
[55] T-201/04, para 694.
[56] T-201/04, para 695.
[57] T-201/04, para 697.
[58] T-201/04, para 698.
[59] T-201/04, para 701.
[60] T-201/04, para 702.

The Court, therefore, concluded that the exceptional factors, which its analysis of the case law had indicated had to be present before a refusal to licence could be regarded as an abuse of a dominant position, were not present in this case.[61]

The Court then went on to consider an issue of fact: whether Sun's rather ambiguous letter from 1998 had actually amounted to a request for interoperability information.[62] The Court held that it had.[63]

The bundling of Windows Media Player with the Windows PC operating system

[23.14] The Court began its analysis by repeating relevant portions of the original Commission Decision. The court noted that the Commission had defined:

> 'media players as software products that are able to 'play back' audio and video content, that is to say, to decode the corresponding data and translate them into instructions for the hardware, such as loudspeakers or a display.'[64]

The Commission went on to explain:

> 'that the audio and video content is arranged in digital media files according to certain specific formats and that compression and decompression algorithms have been developed in order to reduce the storage space required by that content without any loss of audio or video quality. Those algorithms are implemented in media players and in encoding software which make it possible to generate compressed files. The piece of code in a media player that implements a compression/decompression algorithm is called a "codec" and, in order to be able to act correctly with a compressed media content in a specific format using a specific compression/decompression algorithm, a media player needs to understand that format and that compression/decompression algorithm, that is to say, it needs to implement the corresponding codec.'[65]

The Court noted that the Commission had identified two situations where such content could be received from the Internet. The first was where:

> 'the end user is able to access audio and video content via the Internet by downloading the relevant file to his client PC, that is to say, by copying the file and transferring it to his client PC. Once it has been downloaded, the file may be "played back" by a media player compatible with the file's format'.[66]

The second was where:

> 'the end user ... receive(d) audio and video content streamed over the Internet. Where that method is used, there is no longer any need to wait for an entire file to be downloaded, as the file is sent to the client PC in the form of a sequence of small pieces, that is to say, as a "stream" of data which the media player plays as it goes along. Streaming requires the presence of a streaming media player on the client PC'.[67]

---

[61] T-201/04, para 712.
[62] T-201/04, para 713.
[63] T-201/04, para 776.
[64] T-201/04, para 817.
[65] T-201/04, para 818.
[66] T-201/04, para 819.
[67] T-201/04, para 820.

The significance of streaming was that:

'the streaming of audio and video content to an end user often entails specific streaming protocols which govern communications between the media player and the software server which distributes the content over the Internet. In order to access sound and video content streamed using a given protocol, the user must have a media player that 'understands' that protocol.'[68]

[23.15] Finally, the Court adopted the Commission's explanation that:

'by using encoding software streaming servers and media players which are compatible in terms of codec, format and streaming protocol support, it is possible to build a software infrastructure for delivery and consumption of streamed digital audio or video content over IT networks. Such an infrastructure will also be able to provide a platform for the development of other applications, which will use the services provided by it. In particular, media players may exhibit APIs which other applications will call in order, for example, to trigger the playback of a file by the player.'[69]

[23.16] The Court referred to the Commission's analysis of the market for media players and the media players on the market. The Commission's analysis focused on the impact of Microsoft's activities on just one of these products, RealNetworks. The Commission set out how Microsoft had moved from partnering RealNetworks to bundling its own media player with the Windows operating system, which then ceased to provide native support for RealNetworks' formats. Microsoft challenged the Commission's findings on a variety of grounds; in considering those grounds, the court first turned to consider the necessary conditions for a finding of abusive tying. The Commission had decided that the bundling or tying of Windows Media Player with the Windows operating system amounted to an abuse on the following grounds:

— first, the tying and tied products are two separate products;

— second, the undertaking concerned is dominant in the market for the tying product;

— third, the undertaking concerned does not give customers a choice to obtain the tying product without the tied product; and

— fourth, the practice in question forecloses competition.'[70]

For its part, Microsoft challenged the above criteria on the basis that they were incompatible with Article 82 TEC. These arguments were rejected by the court as being 'purely semantic and cannot be accepted'.[71] The Court began its detailed analysis by indicating that the second condition was satisfied as 'it is common ground that Microsoft has a dominant position on the market for what is alleged to be the tying product, namely client PC operating systems'.[72] The Court then went on to consider Microsoft's claim that Windows and Windows Media Player were not separate products, but rather one single one. It noted that:

---

[68] T-201/04, para 821.
[69] T-201/04, para 822.
[70] T-201/04, para 842.
[71] T-201/04, para 850.
[72] T-201/04, para 870.

'the IT and communications industry is an industry in constant and rapid evolution, so that what initially appear to be separate products may subsequently be regarded as forming a single product, both from the technological aspect and from the aspect of the competition rules.'[73]

[23.17] The issue before the Court was whether these were two separate products as of May 1999, when Microsoft released a version of Windows incorporating Windows Media Player. The court considered that the Commission had correctly explained that:

'the argument which Microsoft puts forward in connection with the bundling of Windows and Windows Media Player relies to a large extent on the vague concept of media functionality. In that regard, it must be emphasised that it is clear from the contested decision that, so far as that issue is concerned, the impugned conduct concerns only the application software that is Windows Media Player, to the exclusion of any other media technology included in the Windows client PC operating system ... Microsoft itself differentiates, in its technical documentation, the files which constitute Windows Media Player from the other media files, in particular those relating to the basic media infrastructure of the operating system. It is also appropriate to mention the example of the Microsoft product called Windows XP Embedded ... From the technical aspect, that product is a genuine client PC operating system, but Microsoft's licensing conditions limit its use to certain specialised machines, such as bank automatic teller machines and decoders. The particular feature of that product is that it enables IT engineers to select the components of the operating system. In order to do so, they use a tool called 'Target Designer' to access a menu of the components which they can include in, or exclude from, their operating systems. Those components specifically include Windows Media Player. Furthermore, the menu contains separate entries for the media infrastructure and for the media applications, and Windows Media Player is expressly included among the latter applications.'[74]

The Court approved the Commission's view that 'the distinctness of products for the purpose of an analysis under Article 82 EC has to be assessed by reference to customer demand'.[75] The Court also approved the view of the Commission that 'in the absence of independent demand for the allegedly tied product, there can be no question of separate products and no abusive tying'.[76] The Court also pointed to the role of Original Equipment Manufacturers (OEMs), which it felt Microsoft's arguments ignored. The Court noted that:

'if OEMs and consumers were able to obtain Windows without Windows Media Player, that would not mean that they would choose to obtain Windows without a streaming media player. OEMs follow consumer demand for a pre-installed media player on the operating system and offer a software package including a streaming media player that works with Windows, the difference being that that player would not necessarily be Windows Media Player.'[77]

---

[73] T-201/04, para 913.
[74] T-201/04, para 916.
[75] T-201/04, para 917.
[76] T-201/04, para 918.
[77] T-201/04, para 923.

[23.18] The Court referred to a variety of other evidence that Media Player was a separate product from the Windows operating system:

(i)   Windows was system software whilst Media Player was application software;[78]

(ii) media players were produced independently of operating systems by companies such as Apple and RealNetworks;[79]

(iii) Microsoft supplied editions of its Media Player that were designed to work with operating systems other than Windows, such as Apple's Mac OS X and Sun's Solaris;[80]

(iv) Windows Media Player could be downloaded separately from the Windows operating system;[81]

(v)   it advertised[82] and licensed Windows Media Player independently of the Operating system;[83]

(vi) consumers were continuing to use media players other than that supplied with their Windows operating system.[84]

All of this led the Court to agree with the Commission's assessment that: 'client PC operating systems and streaming media players constituted separate products'.[85] The Court then moved on to consider if consumers were able to chose to buy windows without also buying Windows Media Player. The court concluded that they could not. The Court noted that the Commission was correct in its view that:

> 'coercion is applied primarily to OEMs, and is then passed on to consumers. OEMs, who assemble client PCs, install on those PCs a client PC operating system provided by a software producer or developed by themselves. OEMs who wish to install a Windows operating system on the client PCs which they assemble must obtain a licence from Microsoft in order to do so. Under Microsoft's licensing system, it is not possible to obtain a licence on the Windows operating system without Windows Media Player. The Court notes, in that regard, that it is common ground that the vast majority of sales of Windows client PC operating systems are made through OEMs, that is to say, by means of licences purchased when a client PC is purchased, while only 10% of sales of those systems are generated by the sale of individual Windows licences[86] .... it is common ground that it was not technically possible to uninstall Windows Media Player[87] ... As OEMs act in their relationships with software producers as intermediaries on behalf of end users, and as they supply end users with an 'out-of-the-box' PC, the impossibility of acquiring the Windows client PC operating system without simultaneously acquiring Windows Media Player applies ultimately to those users.'[88]

---

78 T-201/04, para 926.
79 T-201/04, para 927.
80 T-201/04, para 928.
81 T-201/04, para 929.
82 T-201/04, para 930.
83 T-201/04, para 931.
84 T-201/04, para 932.
85 T-201/04, para 944.
86 T-201/04, para 962.
87 T-201/04, para 963.
88 T-201/04, paras 962–964.

[23.19] Microsoft argued that customers were not charged extra for Media Player, but the court responded that 'the price of Windows Media Player is included in the total price of the Windows client PC operating system'.[89] The Court, therefore, concluded that the Commission was correct in its finding that: 'the condition relating to the imposition of supplementary obligations was satisfied in the present case'.[90]

[23.20] Next the Court moved on to consider whether Microsoft's actions foreclosed competition. The Commission's analysis took three steps.

1. The Commission established that 'the Windows client PC operating system is pre-installed on more than 90% of client PCs shipped worldwide, so that, by bundling Windows Media Player with Windows, Microsoft ensures that its media player is as ubiquitous as Windows on client PCs. Users who find Windows Media Player pre-installed on their client PCs are generally less inclined to use another media player'.[91]

2. Then the Commission considered that 'the option of entering into distribution agreements with OEMs constitutes a less efficient means of obtaining media player distribution than Microsoft's bundling.'[92]

3. Finally the Commission asserted that 'neither the downloading of media players from the Internet nor other distribution channels, including the tied sale of a media player with other software or Internet access services and retail sale of media players, can offset Windows Media Player's ubiquity.'[93]

The Court also noted that the Commission had emphasised that:

'it is on the basis of the percentages of installation and use of media players that content providers and software developers choose the technology for which they will develop their complementary software. Those operators tend to develop their solutions on the basis of Windows Media Player, since that enables them to reach all users of Windows, that is, more than 90% of client PC users. Furthermore, once complementary software is encoded in the proprietary Windows media formats, it will work with competitors' media players only if Microsoft licenses the relevant technology.'[94]

This led the Commission to find that:

'since supporting many different technologies generates additional development, infrastructure and administration costs, content providers tend to give priority to a single set of technologies. Furthermore, the fact that a given media player incorporating a number of media technologies is widely installed is an important factor likely to convince content providers to create media content for the technologies used by that player. By supporting the most widely-disseminated media player, content providers maximise the potential reach of their own products. The Commission concludes that the ubiquity of

---

89 T-201/04, para 968.
90 T-201/04, para 975.
91 T-201/04, para 980.
92 T-201/04, para 981.
93 T-201/04, para 982.
94 T-201/04, para 984.

Windows Media Player on Windows client PCs therefore gives Microsoft a competitive advantage unrelated to the intrinsic qualities of its product.'[95]

[23.21] Microsoft made a number of counter-arguments. Firstly, it argued that 'the inclusion of media functionality does not interfere with the functioning of third-party media players'.[96] Secondly, it claimed that 'in its agreements with Windows distributors – that is, essentially, OEMs – it ensures that vendors of competing media players retain the possibility of distributing their own products'.[97] Thirdly, Microsoft stated that 'in its contracts with software developers, content providers or anyone else, it never requires them to distribute or otherwise promote Windows Media Player either exclusively or as a fixed percentage of their total distribution of media software'.[98] Fourthly it contended that 'the integration of media functionality into Windows does not prevent the use of third-party media players on Windows or their "widespread distribution".'[99] The Court rejected Microsoft's arguments, holding that these arguments were 'unfounded and that they are based on a selective and inaccurate reading of the contested decision.'[100]

[23.22] The court was of the view that the Commission's decision was based upon its finding that:

> 'the bundling of Windows Media Player with the Windows client PC operating system – the operating system pre-installed on the great majority of client PCs sold throughout the world – without the possibility of removing that media player from the operating system, allows Windows Media Player to benefit from the ubiquity of that operating system on client PCs, which cannot be counterbalanced by the other methods of distributing media players'.[101]

The Court went found it clear that:

> 'owing to the bundling, Windows Media Player enjoyed an unparalleled presence on client PCs throughout the world, because it thereby automatically achieved a level of market penetration corresponding to that of the Windows client PC operating system and did so without having to compete on the merits with competing products ... in 2002 Microsoft had a market share of 93.8% by units shipped on the client PC operating systems market (see also recital 431 to the contested decision) and that Windows – and, as a result, Windows Media Player – was pre-installed on 196 million of the 207 million client PCs shipped in the world between October 2001 and March 2003.'[102]

The Court explained that:

> 'no third-party media player could achieve such a level of market penetration without having the advantage in terms of distribution that Windows Media Player enjoys as a result of Microsoft's use of its Windows client PC operating system.'[103]

---

95 T-201/04, para 985.
96 T-201/04, para 993.
97 T-201/04, para 994.
98 T-201/04, para 995.
99 T-201/04, para 996.
100 T-201/04, para 1033.
101 T-201/04, para 1036.
102 T-201/04, para 1038.
103 T-201/04, para 1039.

The Court then looked at the Commission's analysis of how consumers bought, set-up and used PCs. The Court pointed out that:

'the release of the bundled version of Windows and Windows Media Player as the only version of the Windows operating system capable of being pre-installed by OEMs on new client PCs had the direct and immediate consequence of depriving OEMs of the possibility previously open to them of assembling the products which they deemed most attractive for consumers and, more particularly, of preventing them from choosing one of Windows Media Player's competitors as the only media player. On this last point, it must be borne in mind that at the time RealPlayer had a significant commercial advantage as market leader. As Microsoft itself acknowledges, it was only in 1999 that it succeeded in developing a streaming media player that performed well enough, given that its previous player, NetShow, 'was unpopular with customers because it did not work very well' (recital 819 to the contested decision). It must also be borne in mind that between August 1995 and July 1998 it was RealNetworks' products – first RealAudio Player, then RealPlayer – that were distributed with Windows. There is therefore good reason to conclude that if Microsoft had not adopted the impugned conduct competition between RealPlayer and Windows Media Player would have been decided on the basis of the intrinsic merits of the two products.'[104]

[23.23] The Court did not think that it would have been sufficient for third party developers of media-player products to reach agreements with OEMs to pre-install their products with PCs, even if that were possible. The developers would 'still be in a disadvantageous competitive position by comparison with Microsoft'. There were a number of reasons for this.

'First, as Windows Media Player cannot be removed by OEMs or by users from the package consisting of Windows and Windows Media Player, the third-party media player could never be the only media player on the client PC. In particular, the bundling prevents developers of third-party media players from competing with Microsoft for that purpose on the intrinsic merits of the products. Second, as the number of media players that OEMs are prepared to pre-install on client PCs is limited, developers of third-party media players compete with each other in order to have their products pre-installed, while, owing to the bundling, Microsoft evades that competition and the significant additional costs which it entails.'[105]

The Court went on to find that the Commission had been correct to find that methods of distributing media-players other than having them pre-installed by OEMs 'could not offset Windows Media Player's ubiquity'.[106] The Court cited the following evidence in support of this finding:

'First, while it is true that downloading via the Internet enables suppliers to reach a large number of users, it is less effective than pre-installation by OEMs. First, downloading does not guarantee competing media players distribution equivalent to Windows Media Player's ... Second, downloading, unlike using a pre-installed product, is seen as complicated by a significant number of users. Third ... a significant number of download attempts ... are not successfully concluded ... Fourth, users will probably tend to consider

---

[104] T-201/04, para 1046.
[105] T-201/04, para 1047.
[106] T-201/04, para 1049.

that a media player integrated in the client PC which they have bought will work better than a product which they install themselves ... Fifth and last, in most undertakings employees cannot download software from the Internet as that complicates the work of the network administrators.'[107]

[23.24] Furthermore, the Court noted that:

'Microsoft has put forward no argument capable of calling in question the Commission's finding that the other methods of distributing streaming media players mentioned in the contested decision, namely bundling the media player with other software or Internet access services, and retail sale, are only a 'second-best solution and [do] not rival the efficiency and effectiveness of distributing software pre-installed'.[108]

Having considered all of the Commission's findings and Microsoft's counter-arguments the Court concluded that:

'In the light of all the foregoing considerations, the Court concludes that the Commission's findings in the first stage of its reasoning are in themselves sufficient to establish that the fourth constituent element of abusive bundling is present in this case. Those findings are not based on any new or speculative theory, but on the nature of the impugned conduct, on the conditions of the market and on the essential features of the relevant products. They are based on accurate, reliable and consistent evidence which Microsoft, by merely contending that it is pure conjecture, has not succeeded in showing to be incorrect.'[109]

[23.25] This finding meant that the court did not have to consider a number of other challenges made by Microsoft to other elements of the reasoning behind its decision and in particular the Commission's analysis of the impact of bundling Media Player with Windows upon content providers and software designers. The Court noted that:

'The Commission's theory is based on the fact that the market for streaming media players is characterised by significant indirect network effects or, to use the expression employed by Mr Gates, on the existence of a 'positive feedback loop' (recital 882 to the contested decision). That expression describes the phenomenon where, the greater the number of users of a given software platform, the more there will be invested in developing products compatible with that platform, which, in turn reinforces the popularity of that platform with users.'[110]

The Court considered that the Commission was correct to find that such a phenomenon existed in this case. The Court also approved the Commission's method of making this finding.

'The Court considers that the Commission was correct to find that such a phenomenon existed in the present case and to find that it was on the basis of the percentages of installation and use of media players that content providers and software developers chose the technology for which they would develop their own products ... The Commission correctly stated, first, that those operators tended primarily to use Windows Media Player as that allowed them to reach the very large majority of client PC users in the world and,

---

[107] T-201/04, para 1050.

[108] T-201/04, para 1053.

[109] T-201/04, para 1058.

[110] T-201/04, para 1061.

second, that the transmission of content and applications compatible with a given media player was in itself a significant competitive factor, since it increased the popularity of that media player, and, in turn, favoured the use of the underlying media technology, including codecs, formats (including DRM) and server software ... [111]

... the Commission was quite correct to find that the provision of several different technologies gave rise to additional development, infrastructure and administrative costs for content providers, who were therefore inclined to use only one technology for their products if that allowed them to reach a wide audience ... [112]

... it follows from the evidence gathered by the Commission ... that encoding streamed content in several formats is expensive and time-consuming.' [113]

[23.26] The Court held that it was apparent from the evidence that 'the more widely distributed a media player is, the more content providers are inclined to create content for the technology implemented in that media player ... by supporting the widely disseminated media player, developers maximise the potential reach of their own products'. [114] The Court found that similar incentives existed for software developers, finding that:

'software developers were inclined to create applications for a single platform if that enabled them to reach virtually all potential users of their products, whereas porting, marketing and supporting other platforms gave rise to additional costs.' [115]

[23.27] All of the above evidence led the Commission to the following conclusions, which were approved by the Court:

— Microsoft uses Windows as a distribution channel to ensure for itself a significant competitive advantage on the media players market ...

— because of the bundling, Microsoft's competitors are a priori at a disadvantage even if their products are inherently better than Windows Media Player ...

— Microsoft interferes with the normal competitive process which would benefit users by ensuring quicker cycles of innovation as a consequence of unfettered competition on the merits ...

— the bundling increases the content and applications barriers to entry, which protect Windows, and facilitates the erection of such barriers for Windows Media Player ...

— Microsoft shields itself from effective competition from vendors of potentially more efficient media players who could challenge its position, and thus reduces the talent and capital invested in innovation of media players ...

— by means of the bundling, Microsoft may expand its position in adjacent media-related software markets and weaken effective competition, to the detriment of consumers ...

---

[111] T-201/04, para 1062.
[112] T-201/04, para 1064.
[113] T-201/04, para 1065.
[114] T-201/04, para 1067.
[115] T-201/04, para 1072.

— by means of the bundling, Microsoft sends signals which deter innovation in any technologies in which it might conceivably take an interest and which it might tie with Windows in the future.'[116]

The Court considered that the above findings gave the Commission grounds to state that:

'that there was a reasonable likelihood that tying Windows and Windows Media Player would lead to a lessening of competition so that the maintenance of an effective competition structure would not be ensured in the foreseeable future. It must be made clear that the Commission did not state that the tying would lead to the elimination of all competition on the market for streaming media players.'[117]

[23.28] Microsoft had also argued that the Commission's decision lacked any objective justification. The Court considered that this broke down into two separate arguments. The first was that:

'Microsoft takes issue with the Commission for having ignored the benefits flowing from its business model, which entails the ongoing integration of new functionality into Windows ... it claims ... that the integration of media functionality in Windows is indispensable in order for software developers and Internet site creators to be able to continue to benefit from the significant advantages offered by the 'stable and well-defined' Windows platform.'[118]

This argument was rejected by the Court, which first noted that:

'The circumstance to which the Commission takes exception in the contested decision is not that Microsoft integrates Windows Media Player in Windows, but that it offers on the market only a version of Windows in which Windows Media Player is integrated, that is to say, that it does not allow OEMs or consumers to obtain Windows without Windows Media Player or, at least, to remove Windows Media Player from the system consisting of Windows and Windows Media Player.'[119]

The Court considered that this meant that:

'the Commission does not interfere with Microsoft's business model in so far as that model includes the integration of a streaming media player in its client PC operating system or the possibility for that operating system to allow software developers and Internet site creators to take advantage of the benefits offered by the 'stable and well-defined' Windows platform. The Commission takes issue with the fact that Microsoft does not market the version of Windows that corresponds to its business model and at the same time a version of that system without Windows Media Player, thus permitting OEMs or end users wishing to do so to install the product of their choice on their client PC as the first streaming media player.'[120]

In addition, the Court did not think that Microsoft could rely upon the fact that:

'the bundling ensures the uniform presence of media functionality in Windows, which enables software developers and Internet site creators to avoid the need to include in their

---

[116] T-201/04, para 1088.
[117] T-201/04, para 1089.
[118] T-201/04, para 1146.
[119] T-201/04, para 1149.
[120] T-201/04, para 1150.

products mechanisms which make it possible to ascertain what media player is present on a particular client PC and where necessary to install the necessary functionality ... The fact that that tying enables software developers and Internet site creators to be sure that Windows Media Player is present on virtually all client PCs in the world is precisely one of the main reasons why the Commission correctly took the view that the bundling led to the foreclosure of competing media players from the market. Although the uniform presence to which Microsoft refers may have advantages for those operators that cannot suffice to offset the anti-competitive effects of the tying at issue'.[121]

[23.29] The Court and the Commission were willing to acknowledge that what Microsoft was doing would impose a standard on the market and that there were advantages to standardization, but 'standardization ... cannot be allowed to be imposed unilaterally by an undertaking in a dominant position by means of tying.'[122] The second argument, which was also rejected by the Court, was that:

'Microsoft claims that the removal of media functionality from the system consisting of Windows and Windows Media Player would create a series of problems to the detriment of consumers, software developers and Internet site creators. It refers, in particular, to the fact that its Windows operating system relies on the method know as 'componentisation' ... and that the withdrawal of media functionality would result in the degrading and 'fragmentation' of that system.'[123]

The Court pointed out that Microsoft had not actually identified any real loss of functionality[124] or degradation of the Windows operating system.[125] The Court described Microsoft's argument that unbundling Windows Media Player would lead to the 'fragmentation' of its operating system as: 'hypothetical and speculative'.[126] The last substantive argument made by Microsoft was that the Commission's decision was disproportionate. This argument was rejected by the Court.[127] Microsoft unsuccessfully challenged both the imposition of a fine on it by the Commission[128] and the amount of that fine.[129]

[23.30] However, Microsoft did succeed on one point. The Commission decision had sought to impose a monitoring trustee upon Microsoft. This trustee would have had the primary function of issuing 'opinions on whether Microsoft has, in a specific instance, failed to comply with the (Commission's) decision'. These opinions would have been given on the application of a third party or the Commission, or could be unilaterally issued by the trustee. Thus the trustee would have had both a proactive and a reactive role. The trustee would have had the functions of deciding whether or not Microsoft had released complete and accurate interoperability information, whether that information

---

[121] T-201/04, para 1151.
[122] T-201/04, para 1152.
[123] T-201/04, para 1147.
[124] T-201/04, para 1164.
[125] T-201/04, para 1165.
[126] T-201/04, para 1166.
[127] T-201/04, para 1228.
[128] T-201/04, para 1330.
[129] T-201/04, para 1366.

had been released on reasonable and non-discriminatory terms and whether it had been released in a timely manner. In relation to the tying of product, the trustee would have advised the Commission whether substantiated complaints by third parties about Microsoft's compliance were well founded from a technical point of view. The Trustee would also have had to advise the Commission whether the version of Windows without Windows Media Player was performing less well than any bundled version of Windows that Microsoft would continue to market and whether Microsoft was hindering the performance of rival media players.[130] As regards the appointment of the Trustee: he would have been appointed by the Commission from a list submitted by the Commission; he would have been independent of Microsoft; had reasonable access to information, documents, premises, employees and relevant source codes; and his salary and other costs would have been paid by Microsoft.[131] The Court summarised his position as follows:

> 'the Commission sees the monitoring trustee's role as being to evaluate and monitor the implementation of the remedies ... while acting independently and, indeed, on his own initiative.'[132]

But the independence of the trustee meant that his appointment was illegal, as it would not have been permissible for the Commission to delegate its functions in this way.[133] The Court referred to the case law and stated that 'The case-law shows, moreover, that the Commission does not have unlimited discretion when formulating remedies to be imposed on undertakings for the purpose of putting an end to an infringement.'[134]

The order

[23.31] Although Microsoft had lost the fundamental parts of its action, it had succeeded in relation to the trustee. Therefore, the court directed that Microsoft should pay 80% of its own costs and 80% of the Commission's costs the Commission was ordered to pay 20% of both. The court annulled those parts of the Commission's decision[135] that related to the monitoring trustee, but upheld the rest. The Commission had provided for the following remedies in respect of the provision of interoperability information, and these remedies were upheld. The remedies were, firstly, that Microsoft had to 'disclose the information that it has refused to supply and to allow its use for the development of compatible products. The disclosure order is limited to protocol specifications and to ensuring interoperability with the essential features that define a typical work group network'. The order specifically provided that Microsoft would not be able to assert its intellectual property rights in respect of such information.[136] The disclosure would have

---

130 T-201/04, para 1261.

131 T-201/04, para 1262.

132 T-201/04, para 1263.

133 T-201/04, para 1271.

134 T-201/04, para 1276.

135 Commission Decision of 24 May 2004 relating to a proceeding pursuant to Article 82 of the EC Treaty and Article 54 of the EEA Agreement against Microsoft Corporation, OJ L 32, 6 February 2007, p 23–28.

136 OJ L 32, 6 February 2007, pp 23–28, para 30.

to be made in a timely manner.[137] The right to seek such disclosure could be invoked by anyone as it applied 'not only to Sun, but to any undertaking that has an interest in developing products that constitute a competitive constraint to Microsoft in the work group server operating system market'. The conditions, including remuneration, under which Microsoft made this information available would have to be reasonable, non-discriminatory and predictable. Any remuneration charged 'should not reflect the strategic value stemming from Microsoft's market power in the PC operating system market or in the work group server operating system market'. In addition, Microsoft would not be able to 'impose restrictions as to the type of products in which the specifications may be implemented, if such restrictions create disincentives to compete with Microsoft, or unnecessarily restrain the ability of the beneficiaries to innovate.'[138]

[23.32] In relation to tying, the decision ordered Microsoft 'to offer to end users and OEMs for sale in the EEA a full-functioning version of Windows which does not incorporate WMP (Windows Media Player)'.[139] In addition, Microsoft will have to:

> 'refrain from using any means which would have the equivalent effect of tying WMP to Windows, for example by reserving privileged interoperability with Windows to WMP, by providing selective access to Windows APIs, or by promoting WMP over competitors' products through Windows. Microsoft is also prevented from giving OEMs or users a discount conditional on their obtaining Windows together with WMP, or de facto, financially or otherwise, removing or restricting OEMs' or users' freedom to choose the version of Windows without WMP. The unbundled version of Windows must not be less performing than the version of Windows which comes bundled with WMP, regard being had to WMP's functionality which, by definition, will not be part of the unbundled version of Windows.'[140]

In addition, fines totaling €497,196,304 were imposed. Although a fine of almost half-a-billion euro may seem large, it must be put in context. Microsoft is an astonishingly wealthy and successful company; in early 2007 it was sitting on cash reserves of $30bn.[141]

Anti-competitive agreements

[23.33] Article 81 of the TEC provides that certain agreements are prohibited as being incompatible with the Common Market, that is:

> 'all agreements between undertakings, decisions by associations of undertakings and concerted practices which may affect trade between Member States and which have as their object or effect the prevention, restriction or distortion of competition within the common market.'

---

[137] OJ L 32, 6 February 2007, pp 23–28, para 32.

[138] OJ L 32, 6 February 2007, pp 23–28, para 31.

[139] OJ L 32, 6 February 2007, pp 23–28, para 33.

[140] OJ L 32, 6 February 2007, pp 23–28, para 34.

[141] McKenna, 'Fat on profits, firms hoarding oodles of cash' (2007) The Globe and Mail (Canada), 29 January.

In particular, the TEC prohibits any agreements that:

(a) directly or indirectly fix purchase or selling prices or any other trading conditions;

(b) limit or control production, markets, technical development, or investment;

(c) share markets or sources of supply;

(d) apply dissimilar conditions to equivalent transactions with other trading parties, thereby placing them at a competitive disadvantage;

(e) make the conclusion of contracts subject to acceptance by the other parties of supplementary obligations which, by their nature or according to commercial usage, have no connection with the subject of such contracts.[142]

[23.34] If such agreements are made, then they will be 'automatically void'.[143] However, these rules are not absolute and the TEC does provide for exceptions. The TEC states that any agreement or concerted practice which 'contributes to improving the production or distribution of goods or to promoting technical or economic progress, while allowing consumers a fair share of the resulting benefit' may be legal. This possibility of legality will depend upon the agreement or practice not imposing on undertakings 'restrictions which are not indispensable to the attainment of these objectives' and the agreement or practice cannot 'afford such undertakings the possibility of eliminating competition in respect of a substantial part of the products in question'.[144] This provision is implemented in Irish law by the Competition Acts, which enact it as Irish law. Although the Competition Acts provide that such provisions are prohibited and void,[145] they also provide that such provisions may be severed from the rest of an agreement.[146]

Competition law and intellectual property

[23.35] The term 'intellectual property' is a misnomer. Copyright patents and trademarks legislation do not create property as such. What they create are time-limited statutory monopolies. The rights to these monopolies may be traded as property, but they are not property rights as such. Intellectual property rights, as opposed to intellectual property remedies, are best analysed as a sub-set of competition law, because that is what they are. On occasion, intellectual property law and competition law intersect. One intersection will occur where a company tries to buttress its market position with intellectual property rights. If that company should be in a dominant position in that market, then legitimate protection of intellectual property rights may be difficult to disentangle from illegal abuse of a dominant position. This issue has been reviewed by the ECJ on a number of occasions and the resulting case law is discussed below. Another intersection will occur where licences are provided for the transfer of intellectual property rights; the obligations imposed by those licences may appear indistinguishable from restrictions prohibited by the TEC. The Commission has dealt with this issue by providing a block exemption for technology transfers and this exemption is discussed below.

---

[142] TEC, art 81(1).

[143] TEC, art 81(2).

[144] TEC, art 81(3).

[145] Competition Acts, s 4(1).

[146] Competition Acts, s 4(6).

Abusive use of intellectual property rights by dominant undertaking

[23.36] The ECJ has analysed such cases on a number of occasions. In *Magill v RTÉ*[147] the respondents refused to provide TV schedule information so that the applicant might develop a TV and Radio listings magazine. The court ruled that the applicant should receive the information as there was consumer demand for the product and no objective reason why it should not be provided. In *IMS Health v NDC*[148] the applicant was a successful supplier of pharmaceutical sales data in Germany. As part of its business the applicant had developed a 'brick structure' which divided Germany into 1860 zones or bricks for the purposes of data analysis. This structure had become a national standard in Germany for the processing of such data. The respondent was a competitor which wished to licence the 'brick structure' so that it could compete with the applicant in the pharmaceutical data market. The applicant refused to provide a licence and the respondent appealed to the Commission, which ruled in its favour. The applicant then appealed and the case reached the European Court of Justice, which ruled:

> 'The refusal by an undertaking which holds a dominant position and owns an intellectual property right in a brick structure indispensable to the presentation of regional sales data on pharmaceutical products in a Member State to grant a licence to use that structure to another undertaking which also wishes to provide such data in the same Member State, constitutes an abuse of a dominant position within the meaning of Article 82 EC where the following conditions are fulfilled:
>
>> the undertaking which requested the licence intends to offer, on the market for the supply of the data in question, new products or services not offered by the owner of the intellectual property right and for which there is a potential consumer demand;
>>
>> – the refusal is not justified by objective considerations;
>>
>> – the refusal is such as to reserve to the owner of the intellectual property right the market for the supply of data on sales of pharmaceutical products in the Member State concerned by eliminating all competition on that market.'

The above principles were then applied by the Court of First Instance in *Microsoft v Commission*, which ultimately concluded that Microsoft should grant the licence sought.

The Technology Transfer Block Exemption

[23.37] The Commission Regulation on the application of Article 81(3) of the Treaty to categories of technology transfer agreements gives technology licensing agreements an exemption from EC competition law. The regulation explains that such an exemption is justified as these agreements:[149]

> 'will usually improve economic efficiency and be pro-competitive as they can reduce duplication of research and development, strengthen the incentive for the initial research

---

147 *Magill v RTÉ* OJ 1989 L78/ 43, [1989] 4 CMLR 749; appeal to Court of First Instance Case T-69/ 89 *RTÉ v Commission* [1991] 4 CMLR 586; appeal to ECJ C-241 and 242/ 91.

148 *IMS Health v NDC* C-418/01.

149 Commission Regulation (EC) No 772/2004 of 27 April 2004 on the application of Article 81(3) of the Treaty to categories of technology transfer agreements, OJ L 123, 27 April 2004 pp 11–17.

and development, spur incremental innovation, facilitate diffusion and generate product market competition.'[150]

However, the regulation goes on to note that:

'The likelihood that such efficiency-enhancing and pro-competitive effects will outweigh any anti-competitive effects due to restrictions contained in technology transfer agreements depends on the degree of market power of the undertakings concerned and, therefore, on the extent to which those undertakings face competition from undertakings owning substitute technologies or undertakings producing substitute products.'[151]

As it is a regulation, the Block Exemption has direct effect in Ireland.[152] The regulation will expire 10 years after its adoption, on 30 April 2014.[153]

The exemption

[23.38] What the regulation actually does is declare that 'Article 81(1) of the Treaty shall not apply to technology transfer agreements entered into between two undertakings permitting the production of contract products.' The exemption will apply where such agreements contain restrictions of competition that actually fall within the scope of art 81(1). The exemption will 'apply for as long as the intellectual property right in the licensed technology has not expired, lapsed or been declared invalid or, in the case of know-how, for as long as the know-how remains secret'.[154] A technology transfer agreement is defined as:

'a patent[155] licensing agreement, a know-how licensing agreement, a software copyright licensing agreement or a mixed patent, know-how[156] or software copyright licensing agreement, including any such agreement containing provisions which relate to the sale and purchase of products or which relate to the licensing of other intellectual property rights or the assignment of intellectual property rights, provided that those provisions do not constitute the primary object of the agreement and are directly related to the production of the contract products; assignments of patents, know-how, software copyright or a combination thereof where part of the risk associated with the exploitation

---

[150] Technology Transfer Block Exemption, recital 5.

[151] Technology Transfer Block Exemption, recital 6.

[152] 'A regulation shall have general application. It shall be binding in its entirety and directly applicable in all Member States', TEC, art 249. See also Technology Transfer Block Exemption, art 11: 'This Regulation shall be binding in its entirety and directly applicable in all Member States'.

[153] Technology Transfer Block Exemption, art 11.

[154] Technology Transfer Block Exemption, art 2.

[155] The regulation defines patent as: 'patents, patent applications, utility models, applications for registration of utility models, designs, topographies of semiconductor products, supplementary protection certificates for medicinal products or other products for which such supplementary protection certificates may be obtained and plant breeder's certificates'. Technology Transfer Block Exemption, art 1(1)(h).

[156] The regulation defines know-how as: 'a package of non-patented practical information, resulting from experience and testing, which is ... secret, that is to say, not generally known or easily accessible...substantial, that is to say, significant and useful for the production of the contract products, and ... identified, that is to say, described in a sufficiently comprehensive manner so as to make it possible to verify that it fulfils the criteria of secrecy and substantiality'. Technology Transfer Block Exemption, art 1(1)(i).

of the technology remains with the assignor, in particular where the sum payable in consideration of the assignment is dependent on the turnover obtained by the assignee in respect of products produced with the assigned technology, the quantity of such products produced or the number of operations carried out employing the technology, shall also be deemed to be technology transfer agreements.'[157]

The exemption provided by the regulation is far from absolute. The regulation provides a number of quite substantive restrictions upon its application. The first of these restrictions relates to market share. The regulation provides that:

'Where the undertakings party to the agreement are competing undertakings, the exemption ... shall apply on condition that the combined market share of the parties does not exceed 20 % on the affected relevant technology and product market.'[158]

[23.39] The regulation defines 'competing undertakings' as 'undertakings which compete on the relevant technology market and/or the relevant product market'. The regulation stipulates that the following will be competing undertakings:

(i)   competing undertakings on the relevant technology market, being undertakings which license out competing technologies without infringing each others' intellectual property rights (actual competitors on the technology market); the relevant technology market includes technologies which are regarded by the licensees as interchangeable with or substitutable for the licensed technology, by reason of the technologies' characteristics, their royalties and their intended use,

(ii)   competing undertakings on the relevant product market, being undertakings which, in the absence of the technology transfer agreement, are both active on the relevant product and geographic market ... on which the contract products are sold without infringing each others' intellectual property rights (actual competitors on the product market) or would, on realistic grounds, undertake the necessary additional investments or other necessary switching costs so that they could timely enter, without infringing each others' intellectual property rights, the(se) relevant product and geographic market ... in response to a small and permanent increase in relative prices (potential competitors on the product market); the relevant product market comprises products which are regarded by the buyers as interchangeable with or substitutable for the contract products, by reason of the products' characteristics, their prices and their intended use.'[159]

Where the undertakings which are party to the agreement then the exemption will apply: 'on condition that the market share of each of the parties does not exceed 30% on the affected relevant technology and product market'.[160] The regulation defines market share:

'in terms of the presence of the licensed technology on the relevant product market ... A licensor's market share on the relevant technology market shall be the combined market share on the relevant product market of the contract products produced by the licensor and its licensees.'[161]

---

[157] Technology Transfer Block Exemption, art 1(1)(b).
[158] Technology Transfer Block Exemption, art 3(1).
[159] Technology Transfer Block Exemption, art 1(j)(i).
[160] Technology Transfer Block Exemption, art 3(2).
[161] Technology Transfer Block Exemption, art 3(3).

The regulation also sets out how market share is to be calculated. The regulation states that market share will be calculated:

> 'on the basis of market sales value data. If market sales value data are not available, estimates based on other reliable market information, including market sales volumes, may be used to establish the market share of the undertaking concerned … The market share shall be calculated on the basis of data relating to the preceding calendar year.'[162]

[23.40] If the market share of an undertaking or undertakings is not initially greater than 20% or 30% respectively but subsequently rises above those levels, then the exemption will continue to apply for a period of two consecutive calendar years following the year in which the threshold was first exceeded.[163] As regards market definition, the Commission Guidelines on the regulations[164] state that:

> 'Technology is an input, which is integrated either into a product or a production process. Technology licensing can therefore affect competition both in input markets and in output markets. For instance, an agreement between two parties which sell competing products and which cross license technologies relating to the production of these products may restrict competition on the product market concerned. It may also restrict competition on the market for technology and possibly also on other input markets. For the purposes of assessing the competitive effects of licence agreements it may therefore be necessary to define relevant goods and service markets … as well as technology markets …
>
> The (Regulations) and these guidelines are concerned with effects both on product markets for final products and on product markets for intermediate products. The relevant product market includes products which are regarded by the buyers as interchangeable with or substitutable for the contract products incorporating the licensed technology, by reason of the products' characteristics, their prices and their intended use.
>
> Technology markets consist of the licensed technology and its substitutes … Starting from the technology which is marketed by the licensor, one needs to identify those other technologies to which licensees could switch in response to a small but permanent increase in relative prices.'[165]

Hardcore restrictions

[23.41] The regulation then provides what it titles 'hardcore' restrictions. These are restrictions that will apply to agreements made between competing undertakings. The exemption will not apply to 'agreements which, directly or indirectly, in isolation or in combination with other factors under the control of the parties' have as their object:

    (a)   the restriction of a party's ability to determine its prices when selling products to third parties;

---

[162] Technology Transfer Block Exemption, art 8(1).
[163] Technology Transfer Block Exemption, art 8(2).
[164] Commission Notice – Guidelines on the application of Article 81 of the EC Treaty to technology transfer agreements OJ C 101, 27/04/2004, pp 2–42.
[165] Guidelines, paras 20–22.

(b) the limitation of output, except limitations on the output of contract products imposed on the licensee in a non-reciprocal[166] agreement or imposed on only one of the licensees in a reciprocal[167] agreement;

(c) the allocation of markets or customers except:

    (ii) the obligation on the licensee(s) to produce with the licensed technology only within one or more technical fields of use or one or more product markets,

    (ii) the obligation on the licensor and/or the licensee, in a non-reciprocal agreement, not to produce with the licensed technology within one or more technical fields of use or one or more product markets or one or more exclusive territories reserved for the other party,

    (iii) the obligation on the licensor not to license the technology to another licensee in a particular territory,

    (iv) the restriction, in a non-reciprocal agreement, of active and/or passive sales by the licensee and/or the licensor into the exclusive territory or to the exclusive customer group reserved for the other party,

    (v) the restriction, in a non-reciprocal agreement, of active sales by the licensee into the exclusive territory or to the exclusive customer group allocated by the licensor to another licensee provided the latter was not a competing undertaking of the licensor at the time of the conclusion of its own licence,

    (vi) the obligation on the licensee to produce the contract products only for its own use provided that the licensee is not restricted in selling the contract products actively and passively as spare parts for its own products,

    (vii) the obligation on the licensee, in a non-reciprocal agreement, to produce the contract products only for a particular customer, where the licence was granted in order to create an alternative source of supply for that customer,

(d) the restriction of the licensee's ability to exploit its own technology or the restriction of the ability of any of the parties to the agreement to carry out research and development, unless such latter restriction is indispensable to prevent the disclosure of the licensed know-how to third parties.'[168]

---

[166] The Regulations define 'non-reciprocal agreement' as: 'a technology transfer agreement where one undertaking grants another undertaking a patent licence, a know-how licence, a software copyright licence or a mixed patent, know-how or software copyright licence, or where two undertakings grant each other such a licence but where these licences do not concern competing technologies and cannot be used for the production of competing products', Technology Transfer Block Exemption, art 1(1)(d).

[167] The Regulations define 'reciprocal agreement' as: 'a technology transfer agreement where two undertakings grant each other, in the same or separate contracts, a patent licence, a know-how licence, a software copyright licence or a mixed patent, know-how or software copyright licence and where these licences concern competing technologies or can be used for the production of competing products', Technology Transfer Block Exemption, art 1(1)(c).

[168] Technology Transfer Block Exemption, art 4(1).

[23.42] Where the undertakings to the agreement are not in competition, then the exemption will not apply 'to agreements which, directly or indirectly, in isolation or in combination with other factors under the control of the parties' have the following as their object:

(a) the restriction of a party's ability to determine its prices when selling products to third parties, without prejudice to the possibility of imposing a maximum sale price or recommending a sale price, provided that it does not amount to a fixed or minimum sale price as a result of pressure from, or incentives offered by, any of the parties;

(b) the restriction of the territory into which, or of the customers to whom, the licensee may passively sell the contract products, except:

   (i) the restriction of passive sales into an exclusive territory or to an exclusive customer group reserved for the licensor,

   (ii) the restriction of passive sales into an exclusive territory or to an exclusive customer group allocated by the licensor to another licensee during the first two years that this other licensee is selling the contract products in that territory or to that customer group,

   (iii) the obligation to produce the contract products only for its own use provided that the licensee is not restricted in selling the contract products actively and passively as spare parts for its own products,

   (iv) the obligation to produce the contract products only for a particular customer, where the licence was granted in order to create an alternative source of supply for that customer,

   (v) the restriction of sales to end-users by a licensee operating at the wholesale level of trade,

   (vi) the restriction of sales to unauthorised distributors by the members of a selective distribution system,

(c) the restriction of active or passive sales to end-users by a licensee which is a member of a selective distribution system[169] and which operates at the retail level, without prejudice to the possibility of prohibiting a member of the system from operating out of an unauthorised place of establishment'.[170]

Both of the above 'hardcore' restrictions will apply if 'the undertakings party to the agreement are not competing undertakings at the time of the conclusion of the agreement but become competing undertakings afterwards ... unless the agreement is subsequently amended in any material respect'.[171]

---

[169] 'Selective Distribution' system is defined as: 'a territory in which only one undertaking is allowed to produce the contract products with the licensed technology, without prejudice to the possibility of allowing within that territory another licensee to produce the contract products only for a particular customer where this second licence was granted in order to create an alternative source of supply for that customer', Technology Transfer Block Exemption, art 1(1)(l).

[170] Technology Transfer Block Exemption, art 4(2).

[171] Technology Transfer Block Exemption, art 4(3).

Excluded restrictions

[23.43] The regulation will not exempt certain obligations that may be included in technology transfer agreements:

(a) any direct or indirect obligation on the licensee to grant an exclusive licence to the licensor or to a third party designated by the licensor in respect of its own severable improvements to or its own new applications of the licensed technology;

(b) any direct or indirect obligation on the licensee to assign, in whole or in part, to the licensor or to a third party designated by the licensor, rights to its own severable improvements to or its own new applications of the licensed technology;

(c) any direct or indirect obligation on the licensee not to challenge the validity of intellectual property rights which the licensor holds in the common market, without prejudice to the possibility of providing for termination of the technology transfer agreement in the event that the licensee challenges the validity of one or more of the licensed intellectual property rights.[172]

If the undertakings that are party to the agreement are not competing undertakings, then the exemption provided by the regulation will not:

'apply to any direct or indirect obligation limiting the licensee's ability to exploit its own technology or limiting the ability of any of the parties to the agreement to carry out research and development, unless such latter restriction is indispensable to prevent the disclosure of the licensed know-how to third parties.'[173]

The Commission guidelines on the regulation state that the purpose of this Article is to 'avoid block exemption of agreements that may reduce the incentive of licensees to innovate'.[174]

Powers of the European Commission

[23.44] The Commission is provided with a couple of powers by the regulation. The first is to that of withdrawing the benefit of the regulation. The regulation provides that:

'The Commission may withdraw the benefit of this Regulation[175] ... where it finds in any particular case that a technology transfer agreement to which the exemption ... applies nevertheless has effects which are incompatible with Article 81(3) of the Treaty'.

The regulation goes on to set out a number of situations where its benefit may be withdrawn, 'in particular' where:

(a) access of third parties' technologies to the market is restricted, for instance by the cumulative effect of parallel networks of similar restrictive agreements prohibiting licensees from using third parties' technologies;

---

[172] Technology Transfer Block Exemption, art 5(1).
[173] Technology Transfer Block Exemption, art 5(2).
[174] Guidelines, para 109.
[175] In doing so, the Commission will be acting 'pursuant to Article 29(1) of Regulation (EC) No 1/2003'.

(b)   access of potential licensees to the market is restricted, for instance by the cumulative effect of parallel networks of similar restrictive agreements prohibiting licensors from licensing to other licensees;

(c)   without any objectively valid reason, the parties do not exploit the licensed technology.[176]

[23.45] The Competition Authority of a member state may withdraw the benefit of the regulation where, 'in particular':

'a technology transfer agreement to which the exemption ... applies has effects which are incompatible with Article 81(3) of the Treaty in the territory of a Member State, or in a part thereof, which has all the characteristics of a distinct geographic market, the competition authority of that Member State may withdraw the benefit of this Regulation[177] ... in respect of that territory, under the same circumstances as those set out (above).'[178]

The guidelines explain that the Commission is granted these powers as 'the list of hardcore restrictions and the list of excluded restrictions do not take into account all the possible impacts of licence agreements. In particular, the block exemption does not take account of any cumulative effect of similar restrictions contained in networks of licence agreements'.[179] In addition, the Commission may also declare by means of a regulation[180] that:

'where parallel networks of similar technology transfer agreements cover more than 50% of a relevant market, this Regulation is not to apply to technology transfer agreements containing specific restraints relating to that market. '[181]

In relation to this power, the Commission guidelines point out that 'there is no presumption of illegality of agreements that fall outside the scope of the block exemption provided that they do not contain hardcore restrictions of competition. In particular, there is no presumption that Article 81(1) applies merely because the market share thresholds are exceeded. Individual assessment based on the principles described in these guidelines is required.'[182]

The Regulation of Electronic Communications Networks

[23.46] At one stage, all phones in Ireland were provided by a single supplier: the Post Office. The parts of the Post Office were spun off into the telecommunications operator Telecom Éireann in 1983. This company ultimately became Eircom, having been privatised in 1999. All European countries have similar histories of state-run monopoly providers being privatized. The problem is that whilst Eircom is now in private hands, it still retains large segments of infrastructure which it acquired when it was a monopoly.

---

[176] Technology Transfer Block Exemption, art 6(1).
[177] Made 'pursuant to Article 29(2) of Regulation (EC) No 1/2003'.
[178] Technology Transfer Block Exemption, art 6(2).
[179] Guidelines, para 121.
[180] Made pursuant to 'Article 1a of Regulation No 19/65/EEC'.
[181] Technology Transfer Block Exemption, art 7(1). A regulation made pursuant to this provision: 'shall not become applicable earlier than six months following its adoption', art 7(2).
[182] Guidelines, para 130.

This infrastructure is primarily the copper-wire networks which still connect most Irish homes and businesses to the national and international telecommunications infrastructure. Since Eircom and other former incumbents retain large segments of their former monopolies, they have tended to remain the dominant undertakings in their respective national markets. As of the second quarter of 2007, Eircom was still the supplier of some 68% of telecommunications services in Ireland, although its share is slowly declining, being down from 74% a year earlier.[183] The EC has responded to this dominance with a framework of legislation, in addition to the Directive on Privacy on Electronic Communications Networks.[184] This Framework is made up of four Directives:

1. Directive 2002/21/EC on a common regulatory framework;[185]

2. Directive 2002/19/EC on access and interconnection;[186]

3. Directive 2002/20/EC on the authorisation of electronic communications networks and services;[187]

4. Directive 2002/22/EC on universal service and users' rights relating to electronic communications networks and services.[188]

[23.47] In addition, there is also a regulation on unbundled access to the local loop[189] as well as a range of relevant decisions. This legislation is implemented in Ireland by both statutory instruments and primary legislation. Directive 2002/21/EC on a common regulatory framework requires the establishment of a National Regulatory Authority,[190] which was done by the Communications Regulation Act 2002.[191] The independence of

---

[183] Comreg, Quaterly Key Data Report, 9 December 2007, p 11.

[184] Directive 2002/58, implemented in Ireland by the European Communities (Electronic Communications Networks and Services)(Data Protection and Privacy) Regulations 2003 (SI 535/2003).

[185] Directive 2002/21/EC on a common regulatory framework, OJ L 108, 24.4.2002, p 33, implemented in Ireland by the European Communities (Electronic Communications Networks and Services) (Market Definition and Analysis) Regulations 2003 (SI 80/2003).

[186] Directive 2002/19/EC on access and interconnection, OJ L 108, 24.4.2002, p 7, implemented in Ireland by the European Communities (Electronic Communications Networks and Services) (Access) Regulations 2003 (SI 305/2003).

[187] Directive 2002/20/EC on the authorisation of electronic communications networks and services OJ L 108, 24.4.2002, p 21, implemented in Ireland by the European Communities (Electronic Communications Networks and Services)(Authorisation) Regulations 2003 (SI 306/2003).

[188] Directive 2002/22/EC on universal service and users' rights relating to electronic communications networks and services OJ L 108, 24.4.2002, p 51 implemented in Ireland by the European Communities (Electronic Communications Networks and Services) (Universal Service and Users' Rights) Regulations 2003 (SI 308/2003).

[189] Regulation 2000/2887/EC on unbundled access to the local loop, OJ L 336, 30.12.2000, p 4.

[190] Directive 2002/21, art 3(1).

[191] Communications Regulation Act 2002, s 6.

Commission for Communications Regulation, or ComReg is ensured by Directive 2002/21/EC.[192] A number of functions are conferred on ComReg by the 2002 Act, such as:

> 'to ensure compliance by undertakings with obligations in relation to the supply of and access to electronic communications services, electronic communications networks and associated facilities and the transmission of such services on such networks.'[193]

ComReg is also given a number of objects that it is to obtain such as:

> 'in relation to the provision of electronic communications networks, electronic communications services and associated facilities ... to promote competition ... to contribute to the development of the internal market, and ... to promote the interests of users within the Community.'[194]

ComReg's powers have been considerably increased by the Communications Regulation (Amendment) Act 2007, which gives ComReg the power to force persons to give it information or documents[195] and ensures the protection of whistle-blowers.[196] Anyone who wishes to provide an electronic communications service in Ireland can do so, all that they need do is 'notify the Regulator of his or her intention to provide such a network or service'.[197] This notification must contain the following information:

> '(a) the name of the person concerned including, in the case of a body corporate, the company registration number,
>
> (b) the names, addresses and contact numbers of relevant contact persons,
>
> (c) the business address of the person concerned and, in the case of a body corporate, where that address differs from the address of its registered office, the address of its registered office,
>
> (d) a short description of the network or service the subject matter of the notification, including a statement as to whether the relevant network or service is to be publicly available, and
>
> (e) the estimated date of commencement for the relevant activity.'[198]

[23.48] But other than the provision of this notification and the required information, nothing further needs be done. This is clear from Directive 2002/20/EC on the authorisation of electronic communications networks and services, which provides that 'Member States shall ensure the freedom to provide electronic communications networks and services.'[199] The Directive goes on to provide that 'The provision of electronic communications networks or the provision of electronic communications services may ... only be subject to a general authorization.' This is a remarkable change from the Postal and Telecommunications Services Act 1983, which conferred on Eircom's predecessor:

---

[192] Directive 2002/21, art 3(2).
[193] Communications Regulation Act 2002, s 10(1)(a).
[194] Communications Regulation Act 2002, s 12(1)(a).
[195] Communications Regulation (Amendment) Act 2007, s 10.
[196] Communications Regulation (Amendment) Act 2007, s 7.
[197] European Communities (Electronic Communications Networks and Services)(Authorisation) Regulations 2003 (SI 306/2003), reg 4(1).
[198] SI 306/2003, reg 4(2).
[199] Directive 2002/20/EC, art 3(1).

'the exclusive privilege of offering, providing and maintaining telecommunications services for transmitting, receiving, collecting and delivering telecommunications messages within the State up to (and including) a connection point in the premises of a subscriber for any such service.'[200]

As of the second quarter of 2007, there were 392 authorised operators in the state, although this number 'does not necessarily reflect the total number of commercially active organisations or entities currently operating in the market'.[201]

Digital spectrum

[23.49] Radio spectrum is a valuable resource. If you use a mobile phone to talk, give yourself interoperability by using a Bluetooth device or Internet access by means of a wi-fi connection then you are using the digital spectrum. The value of the digital spectrum delivered some spectacular benefits to the UK government in 2000 when bidders paid the UK government £22.5bn for digital spectrum rights, in history's largest auction.[202] In Ireland the function of regulating the digital spectrum is split between ComReg and the Minister for Communications. The Communications Regulation Act 2002 provides that the functions of ComReg include managing the radio frequency spectrum[203] in accordance with Directions issued by the Minister.[204] At a European level the EC is seeking to become more involved in the management of radio spectrum (see the *Radio Spectrum Decision*).[205] Radio spectrum is a finite resource; there are only so many radio or televisions that can broadcast at any one time. Hence some limitations have to be placed on who broadcasts where, but the EC has sought to ensure that those limitations are restricted. The Directive 2002/20/EC on the authorisation of electronic communications networks and services provide that:

'Member States shall, where possible, in particular where the risk of harmful interference is negligible, not make the use of radio frequencies subject to the grant of individual rights of use but shall include the conditions for usage of such radio frequencies in the general authorization.'[206]

Broadcasting

[23.50] For a long time Ireland had only one broadcaster: Radio Telefís Éireann or RTÉ. Liberalisation of the market however, has created many more entrants and the Broadcasting Commission of Ireland (BCI) currently licences 58 independent radio stations and 1 independent terrestrial television station. In many ways, this structure is archaic. If you watch TV3 on the television, the broadcast will be licensed and regulated by the BCI; if you watch the same programme on http://www.youtube.com it will not.

---

[200] Postal and Telecommunications Services Act 1983, s 87(1).

[201] ComReg, *Quaterly Key Data Report*, 9 December 2007, p 5.

[202] Harford, *The Undercover Economist* (Oxford, 2006) p 173.

[203] Communications Regulation Act 2002, s 10(1)(b).

[204] Communications Regulation Act 2002, s 13.

[205] Decision No 676/2002/EC of the European Parliament and of the Council of 7 March 2002 on a regulatory framework for radio spectrum policy in the European Community, OJ L 108/1, 24 April 2002.

[206] Directive 2002/20/EC, art 5(1).

The EC is conscious of this problem and is working to update the Television without Frontiers Directive to take account of recent developments. As it currently stands, the amended Directive will provide that:

> 'Each Member State shall ensure that all audiovisual media services transmitted by media service providers under its jurisdiction comply with the rules of the system of law applicable to audiovisual media services intended for the public in that Member State.[207]

'Audiovisual media services' are defined as:

> 'a service ... which is under the editorial responsibility of a media service provider and the principal purpose of which is the provision of programmes in order to inform, entertain or educate, to the general public by electronic communications networks'.[208]

[23.51] Electronic communications networks are defined by Directive 2002/21/EC on a common regulatory framework as:

> 'resources which permit the conveyance of signals by wire, by radio, by optical or by other electromagnetic means, including satellite networks, fixed (circuit- and packet-switched, including Internet) and mobile terrestrial networks, electricity cable systems, to the extent that they are used for the purpose of transmitting signals, networks used for radio and television broadcasting, and cable television networks, irrespective of the type of information conveyed.'[209]

Television programmes can be on-demand services, which are defined as:

> 'audiovisual media service provided by a media service provider for the viewing of programmes at the moment chosen by the user and at his/her individual request on the basis of a catalogue of programmes selected by the media service provider.'[210]

It is not hard to see how this definition could encompass a service such as http://www.youtube.com. This presents users with a catalogue of programmes, which they can view as they chose. Of course http://www.youtube.com does not actually select the files that are uploaded to it; the whole point of the site is that anyone who wants to upload a clip to the site can do so. So the Television without Frontiers Directive might not apply to http://www.youtube.com. But the amended Directive may apply to any site which does select the programmes that it makes available for download. The definitions that are proposed may mean that some broadcasts over the Internet will be regulated under the Television without Frontiers Directive, whilst others will not. This is significant as the Directive imposes obligations upon member states to prohibit product placement[211] and as regards on-demand services:

> 'Member States shall take appropriate measures to ensure that on-demand services provided by media service providers under their jurisdiction which might seriously impair

---

[207] Draft Amended Television Without Frontiers Directive, 24 May 2007, art 2(1). Whilst the text of this draft is unlikely to change before it is finally published, unfortunately the numbering of the individual articles will.

[208] Draft Amended Television Without Frontiers Directive, 24 May 2007, art 1(a).

[209] Directive 2002/21/EC, art 2(a).

[210] Draft Amended Television without Frontiers Directive, 24 May 2007, art 1(e).

[211] Draft Amended Television without Frontiers Directive, 24 May 2007, art 3f.

the physical, mental or moral development of minors are only made available in such a way that ensures that minors will not normally hear or see such on-demand services.'[212]

Furthermore, member states must:

'ensure that on-demand services provided by media service providers under their jurisdiction promote, where practicable and by appropriate means, production of and access to European works. Such promotion could relate, inter alia, to the financial contribution made by such services to the production and rights acquisition of European works or to the share and/or prominence of European works in the catalogue of programmes proposed by the service.'[213]

[23.52] The convergence of telecommunications and broadcasting sectors will further complicate the funding of public broadcasting in Ireland. At present, this is funded by means of a television licence. Pursuant to the Wireless Telegraphy Acts, everyone who owns a television set needs a televison licence. The Wireless Telegraphy Act 1972 defines 'television set' as:

'any apparatus for wireless telegraphy capable of receiving and exhibiting television programmes broadcast for general reception (whether or not its use for that purpose is dependent on the use of anything else in conjunction therewith) and any assembly comprising such apparatus and other apparatus.'[214]

It is not hard to see how this definition could apply to mobile phones or computers. The Joint Oireachtas Committee on Communications acknowledged this fact in its review of proposals to reform Ireland's broadcasting laws:

'As the definition of a 'television set', in the context of modern digital methods of viewing and broadcasting moving pictures, is next to impossible the licensing mechanism should be scrapped in favour of one that acknowledges, embraces and utilises new emerging and converging technologies ... all computers are capable of receiving and exhibiting television programs albeit that most PCs would require a special television receiving card. Accordingly, any business/individual with a computer is arguably already required to have a television licence regardless of what they use the computer for. Clearly this is an additional cost burden on business.'[215]

State aid

[23.53] If Ireland is to become a part of the information society, then investment in communications and broadband structure must be a priority. Ireland is not highly placed in international comparison tables on the provision of broadband infrastructure.[216]

---

[212] Draft Amended Television without Frontiers Directive, 24 May 2007, art 3g.

[213] Draft Amended Television without Frontiers Directive, 24 May 2007, art 3h(1).

[214] Wireless Telegraphy Act 1972, s 1 as amended by Broadcasting and Wireless Telegraphy Act 1988, s 2(2).

[215] Joint Oireachtas Committee on Communications, Marine and Natural Resources, Considerations, recommendations and conclusions on the Joint Committee's consultation on the draft General Scheme of the Broadcasting Bill, April 2007, p 59.

[216] 'It gives me, as Chairman, and the members of the Joint Committee no satisfaction to reflect on how over the lifetime of this Dáil Ireland has fallen from the top of the league to where the latest EU report highlighted a "two-speed" Europe and noted that ... Ireland remains near the bottom of the pile in terms of penetration. (contd/)

Private investment can provide this infrastructure, provided that there is a market for the product. But building broadband networks is not cheap. If Ireland wants to develop the infrastructure it needs, it must provided incentives for investors. One type of incentive is to provide the builders of such infrastructure with a monopoly on the supply of such services in a set area. This was the model pursued by the state over many years through the provision of telephone services by the Post Office. Nowadays, EC law complicates the provision of such services by the State. The TEC contains a variety of restrictions on the ability of Member States to intervene directly in markets. In particular, the TEC provides that:

> 'In the case of public undertakings and undertakings to which Member States grant special or exclusive rights, Member States shall neither enact nor maintain in force any measure contrary to the rules contained in this Treaty'.[217]

The *Telemarketing*[218] decision concerned the Luxembourg Radio and Television station RTL, upon which exclusive broadcasting rights had been conferred by the Luxembourg state. RTL then extended those rights to telemarketing, showing adverts which displayed phone numbers, but requiring that advertisers use a particular telemarketer to take the call. The ECJ held that:

> 'an abuse within the meaning of Article 86 is committed where, without any objective necessity, an undertaking holding a dominant position on a particular market reserves to itself, or to an undertaking belonging to the same group an ancillary activity which might be carried out by another undertaking as part of its activities on a neighbouring but separate market, with the possibility of eliminating all competition from such undertaking.'[219]

[23.54] The TEC does contain an absolute prohibition upon the state supporting public undertakings. It goes on to provide that:

> 'Undertakings entrusted with the operation of services of general economic interest or having the character of a revenue-producing monopoly shall be subject to the rules contained in this Treaty, in particular to the rules on competition, in so far as the application of such rules does not obstruct the performance, in law or in fact, of the particular tasks assigned to them. The development of trade must not be affected to such an extent as would be contrary to the interests of the Community.'[220]

The TEC confers upon the Commission the role of policing member state's compliance with this provision: 'The Commission shall ensure the application of the provisions of

---

[216] (\contd) This is unsustainable and the issue must be addressed'. Joint Oireachtas Committee on Communications, Marine and Natural Resources, Review of progress on broadband rollout, April 2007, p 3.

[217] TEC, art 86(1).

[218] *Telemarketing* (3rd October 1985) ECJ.

[219] *Telemarketing*, para 27.

[220] TEC, art 86(2).

this Article and shall, where necessary, address appropriate directives or decisions to Member States'.[221]

[23.55] If the State wants to ensure the provision of infrastructure such as broadband it might want to provide aid to ensure that it gets built. The National Development Plan anticipates the spending of €435 on 'Communications and Broadband' over the years 2007–2013.[222] Using state moneys in this way has proved controversial in the past. For example, the Commission ruled that a €9bn credit line provided by the French State to France Telecom was illegal state aid.[223] The Commission has permitted the provision of state aid by Ireland in relation to projects such as the Regional Broadband Programme: Metropolitan Area Networks.[224] If the Irish state wishes to provide aid as part of such telecoms investment, then the provision of that aid will have to comply with the TEC, which provides that:

> 'any aid granted by a Member State or through State resources in any form whatsoever which distorts or threatens to distort competition by favouring certain undertakings or the production of certain goods shall, in so far as it affects trade between Member States, be incompatible with the common market.'[225]

The TEC goes on to provide that 'The following may be considered to be compatible with the common market … aid to facilitate the development of certain economic activities or of certain economic areas, where such aid does not adversely affect trading conditions to an extent contrary to the common interest'.[226] Again, the role of ensuring compliance with the TEC's rules on state aid is conferred upon the Commission:

> 'The Commission shall, in cooperation with Member States, keep under constant review all systems of aid existing in those States. It shall propose to the latter any appropriate measures required by the progressive development or by the functioning of the common market.'[227]

The Commission has the power to require that where state aid is being misused, it must be abolished or altered.[228] A key requirement is that the Commission must be informed of any proposal to grant state aid 'in sufficient time to enable it to submit its comments, of any plans to grant or alter aid'.[229] The Commission must review the proposal in question. Whilst it is doing so the member state in question may not 'put its proposed measures into effect'. The Commission's procedures for dealing with state aid are set

---

[221] TEC, art 86(3).

[222] National Development Plan 2007–2013, Government Publications, p 14.

[223] 2006/621/EC: Commission Decision of 2 August 2004 on the State Aid implemented by France for France Télécom (notified under document number C(2004) 3060), OJ L 257, 20.9.2006, pp 11–67.

[224] State aid No 284/2005 – Ireland, Regional Broadband Programme: Metropolitan Area Networks OJ C 207/2006

[225] TEC, art 87(1).

[226] TEC, art 87(3)(c).

[227] TEC, art 88(1).

[228] TEC, art 88(2).

[229] TEC, art 88(3).

out in various regulations.[230] The Commission provides block exemptions for certain forms of state aid such as that which is provided for research and development,[231] risk capital[232] and public service broadcasting.[233]

---

[230] See Council Regulation (EC) No 659/1999 of 22 March 1999 laying down detailed rules for the application of Article 93 of the EC Treaty, OJ L 83, 27 March 1999, pp 1–9 which is implemented by Commission Regulation (EC) No 794/2004 of 21 April 2004 implementing Council Regulation (EC)No 659/1999 laying down detailed rules for the application of Article 93 of the EC Treaty, OJ L 140, 30.4.2004, pp 1–134.

[231] Community Framework for State Aid for Research and Development and Innovation, OJ C 323/1, 30 December 2006.

[232] Community guidelines on state aid to promote risk capital investments in small and medium-sized enterprises, OJ C 194, 18 August 2006, pp 2–21.

[233] Communication from the Commission on the application of State aid rules to public service broadcasting, OJ C 320, 15 November 2001, pp 5–11.

PART VII: CONTENT

Chapter 24

The Child Trafficking and Pornography Acts 1998 and 2004

Introduction

[24.01] Child pornography has been described as 'the work of the devil'.[1] It has existed in its modern form since shortly after the invention of photography.[2] Child pornography was openly produced and sold in Europe and America until the latter part of the 1970s.[3] Whilst the child pornography then produced still circulates online, attitudes towards its production, distribution and use have changed dramatically. In part, this change in attitude reflects a realisation of the prevalence and severity of the phenomenon of child abuse.[4] However, it also reflects a realisation that a very unhealthy sub-culture of child pornography has developed online.[5] This sub-culture thrives upon the production and circulation of images of child abuse. It normalises and facilitates the production of images which are the product of the rape, trauma and humiliation of children. The primary function of the Child Trafficking and Pornography Act 1998 (CTPA)[6] is the

---

[1] District Judge Sean McBride quoted in Donnellan, 'Some are jailed and some walk free over child porn' (2003) The Irish Times, 18 January.

[2] 'Not long after photography became well known, it was used to exploit children'. Investigating Child Exploitation and Pornography: The Internet, the law and Forensic Science (Elsevier Academic Press, 2004) p 10.

[3] For a discussion of the development of the modern culture of child pornography see Jenkins 'Beyond Tolerance: child pornography online' (2001) New York University Press.

[4] 'On behalf of the State and of all citizens of the State, the Government wishes to make a sincere and long overdue apology to the victims of childhood abuse for our collective failure to intervene, to detect their pain, to come to their rescue,' apology given by An Taoiseach to victims of child abuse. Tynan, 'Inquiry into child sex abuse to start in September' (1999) The Irish Times, 12 May. The Sexual Abuse and Violence in Ireland (SAVI) report found that 'One in five women (20.4 per cent) reported experiencing contact sexual abuse in childhood and one in 10 reported non-contact sexual abuse ... One in six men (16.2 per cent) reported experiencing sexual abuse in childhood, with one in 14 reporting non-contact abuse'. Browne, 'No strategy to deal with child abuse' (2004) The Irish Times, 11 August.

[5] 'By its very nature, the internet cultivates special interests however dark and sinister, encourages voyeurism and unaccountable viewing and in itself can be addictive'. Sharry, 'The dark side of the Net' (2004) The Irish Times, 13 July. 'If the coming of the Internet has not exactly legalised child pornography of the most worrisome kind, then it has made such material extraordinarily accessible and almost risk free to those viewing it', Jenkins, 'Beyond Tolerance: child pornography online', (2001) New York University Press.

[6] The Child Trafficking and Pornography Act 2004 inserts section 13 which enables the Committees of the Houses of the Oireachtas to give directions in relation to child pornography and to possess, distribute, print, publish or show child pornography in accordance with its Constitutional and legal functions.

prohibition of the production, distribution, publication, sale and possession of such material. Child pornography is more than just a law enforcement issue. If any solution can be found to this problem, and it must be doubted that a complete solution can ever be found, then it will have to involve a broad segment of society. As Irish psychologists, who are Europe's leading experts in the field, comment 'we need to move understanding out of narrow law enforcement and social welfare arenas, and to develop a more systematic understanding of both child pornography, and the principle means of distribution, the Internet'.[7]

[24.02] Whilst the growth of the Internet has brought many benefits, unfortunately it has also fuelled '…an explosion in the availability of high-quality child pornography in digital form'[8]. Research for the UK children's charity NCH concluded that '(t)he Internet has facilitated a huge increase in the volume of child abuse images that are being viewed and collected'.[9] Others are of the view that:

> 'The Internet revolutionized the child pornography industry. Illicit materials that in the 1970s and 1980s cost hundreds of dollars to buy and required traveling to an unsavory neighborhood and risking all of a sudden could be accessed easily over the Internet, viewed immediately, and downloaded for later viewing'[10].

Digital cameras have eliminated one risk factor for child pornographers – that getting their films developed would result in their arrest and conviction.[11] However, this has now been replaced by the danger that they may be identified by services that they use to repair their computer.[12] It would seem that the problem posed by child pornography can only get worse, as one Irish academic has commented:

> 'The introduction of the internet has made child pornography easily available on a global scale. Images of the most horrendous abuse are only a few keystrokes away. As computer use becomes more widespread, the number of broadband connections increases, and users become more sophisticated at covering their tracks, it is likely that this type of criminal activity will become both more prevalent and more difficult to eradicate'[13].

However, the number of persons investigated for child pornography offences has actually fallen in recent years and this led the authors of a report for the Department of Justice to warn 'that as offenders have become more sophisticated at covering their tracks, such offences are becoming increasingly difficult for the gardaí to detect.'[14]

---

[7] Taylor and Quayle, *Child Pornography: an Internet Crime* (Brunner-Routledge, 2003) p 20.

[8] Ferraro, Casey, *Investigating Child Exploitation and Pornography: The Internet, the law and Forensic Science* (Elsevier Academic Press, 2004), p11.

[9] NCH, *Child pornography, child abuse and the Internet*, 12 January 2004, executive summary, p i.

[10] Ferraro, Casey & McGrath, *Investigating Child Exploitation and Pornography: The Internet, the law and Forensic Science* (2005) Elsevier Academic Press, p11.

[11] *State v Zarick* 227 Conn 207; 630 A 2d 565 (1993).

[12] *R v Bowden* 2001 QB 88.

[13] O'Donnell, 'Facing the challenge of child porn's growth' (2006) The Irish Times, 23 October.

[14] Downes, 'Numbers investigated on child porn in decline' (2006) The Irish Times, 23 October.

The CTPA and 2004

[24.03] The CTPA was introduced as one of a series of enactments to update the law on sexual offences and it must be seen in the context of those other enactments. At the second reading of the Bill, the Minister for Justice commented that:

> 'The Child Trafficking and Pornography Bill, 1997, is the latest legislation that offers protection against sexual abuse ... in the recent past we have passed the Criminal Law (Incest Proceedings) Act, 1995 ... the Sexual Offences (Jurisdiction) Act, 1996 ... and the Non-Fatal Offences Against the Person Act, 1997.'[15]

The Minister went on to describe the Bill as:

> '...an important and integral part of the ongoing programme of legislation aimed at providing comprehensive protection against sexual abuse or exploitation. Child sexual exploitation can take many forms, ranging from direct physical sexual assaults to the depiction of children in pornographic materials. The making of child pornography constitutes child sexual abuse and can often involve the most horrendous violation and abuse of children. With increasing globalisation and greater movement between countries, new forms of child sexual exploitation have begun to emerge. To deal with the continuing and changing nature of the problem, imaginative and novel responses by both law enforcement agencies and legislators are required.'[16]

A key justification for the Bill was the Belgian *Dutrox* case[17] and the resulting EU Joint Council Action on trafficking in human beings and sexual exploitation of children. [18] This Action required member states to take action to prevent 'the exploitative use of children in pornographic performances and materials, including the production, sale and distribution or other forms of trafficking in such materials, and the possession of such materials.'[19] The Acts have been described as representing the response of the 'the Oireachtas to widespread concern, not confined to Ireland, concerning the scandal of the abuse and exploitation of children for the sexual gratification of evilly disposed persons'.[20]

---

[15] Dáil Éireann – Volume 489 – 02 April 1998, Child Trafficking and Pornography Bill 1997: Second Stage.

[16] Dáil Éireann – Volume 489 – 02 April 1998, Child Trafficking and Pornography Bill 1997: Second Stage.

[17] 'The Bill ... represents a response to the horrific events surrounding the Belgian paedophile ring which was uncovered in 1996. The tragic fate of the young Belgian children who fell victim to that paedophile ring galvanised the EU into immediate action', the Minister for Justice, Dáil Éireann – Volume 489 – 02 April 1998, Child Trafficking and Pornography Bill 1997: Second Stage. 'Dutrox and his accomplices ... were responsible ... for the kidnapping, rape and murder of six girls, two of them starved to death in a cellar under Dutroux's house' Barnard et al, *How Can One not be Interested in Belgian History* (Academia Press, 2002) p 28.

[18] Joint Action 97/154/JHA of 24 February 1997 adopted by the Council on the basis of art K.3 of the Treaty on European Union concerning action to combat trafficking in human beings and sexual exploitation of children, OJ L 63 of 04.03.1997.

[19] Joint Action 97/154/JHA of 24 February 1997 adopted by the Council on the basis of art K.3 of the Treaty on European Union concerning action to combat trafficking in human beings and sexual exploitation of children, OJ L 63 of 04.03.1997, Title II.

[20] *DPP v Loving* [2006] IECCA 28.

Justifications for the CTPA 1998 and 2004

[24.04] Child pornography has to be distinguished from adult pornography. There is a strong argument to be made that the term 'child pornography' is inappropriate and that the more accurate 'child abuse images' is to be preferred. Child pornography does not just require the abuse of children in its production, it also corrupts and depraves those who view it, encouraging the subsequent abuse of children and functioning as a tool in that abuse. As the Minister for Justice commented:

> 'One ... form of temptation (to paedophiles) is child pornography. Possessing and looking at child pornography by paedophiles poses a real threat to children by reinforcing cognitive distortions and fuelling fantasies. Child pornography can also be used in grooming or conditioning possible child victims into believing that what they are watching constitutes normal behaviour. There can be no comparison in this context between the possession of child pornography and the possession of other forms of pornography for personal use. This is why it is necessary to specifically outlaw child pornography in all its manifestations. The making and use of child pornography by paedophiles is frightening. Most of us will never see it unless we come upon it accidentally, because it tends to circulate among paedophile rings and not otherwise.'[21]

[24.05] *Taylor and Quayle*[22] suggest that the following are some of the reasons for being concerned about the viewing of child pornography.

(a) Child pornography requires the abuse of a child to produce it. The viewer is in a sense aiding and abetting that abuse by providing a demand and a market for the pornography.

(b) Child pornography is preserved as a photographic record of the abuse. The distribution of that pornography increases the availability of that record and can have very severe and traumatic implications for the victim as well as violating their privacy.

(c) Child pornography generates inappropriate sexual fantasies in individuals; there must then be a concern that these fantasies will become real, that 'watching a sexual assault ... normalises the activity and encourages the viewer subsequently to commit such an assault'. Taylor and Quayle point out that although this concern seems reasonable, there is no evidence of this link with adult pornography, but they suggest that such a link may exist for Child molesters. Furthermore, they suggest that child pornography may become the model that encourages viewers to take photographs themselves as they quote one perpetrator: 'When I made this video tape I was copying these ... movie clips ... I'd downloaded ... I wanted to be ... doing what they were doing'.

(d) Child pornography can act as a learning tool in the grooming process, whereby a child is desensitised to sexual demands and encouraged to normalise inappropriate activities.

(d) Child pornography may sexualise other aspects of childhood and family life.[23]

---

21 Dáil Éireann – Volume 489 – 02 April 1998, Child Trafficking and Pornography Bill 1997: Second Stage.

22 Taylor and Qualye, *Child Pornography: An Internet Crime* (Brunner-Routledge 2003).

23 Taylor and Qualye, *Child Pornography: An Internet Crime* (Brunner-Routledge 2003) pp 24–26

[24.06] One of the key justifications for the CTPA is the apparent link between child pornography and the molestation of children. This link must exist at the most basic level since, unless sophisticated digital technology is used, it is impossible to produce child pornography without molesting children. As the US Supreme Court commented: '(t)he distribution of photographs and films depicting sexual activity by juveniles is intrinsically related to the sexual abuse of children'.[24] One organisation that has identified such a link is the US Postal Service. Its Postal Inspectors:

> 'have long seen a correlation between child molester and those who sell, purchase, and trade child pornography. In 1997 Postal Inspectors first began compiling statistics in these areas: ... Postal inspectors have stopped 476 Child Molesters (roughly 36% of 1327 arrests) ... Inspectors rescued 530 child victims from further abuse ... in ... 2002 ... (a)s a result of Inspectors work ... 93 child molesters were identified and 96 victims saved from further abuse.'[25]

The link between paedophile and pornographer in Ireland is illustrated by the case of *DPP v McC*.[26] The defendant in that case raped and otherwise abused a number of boys; he also used them for the production of child pornography. One boy's mother was a friend of the defendant. She told him that her son was interested in computers and the defendant then offered to help the boy with his computer skills. During the 'lesson' the defendant showed pornographic material on the computer and persuaded the boy to let him take photographs of the boy undressing. The defendant used similar methods to involve other boys in the production of child pornography; his most serious offence was the rape of another boy whilst recording the scene on a camcorder.

Child pornography and child abuse

[24.07] Much research needs to be done into the existence of a link between the possession or viewing of child pornography and the carrying out of actual offences of child abuse:

> 'The function of child pornography and its relationship to contact offences remains unclear ... there are people involved in both accessing and distributing child pornography who have no apparent history of child molestation ... Whether paedophiles use pornography more than the general population, how this relates to contact offenses and the role that the Internet may play in this remains unclear'.[27]

---

24 New York v Ferber 458 US 747, 1982.
25 US Postal Inspection Service *Annual Report of Investigations*, December 2002, pp 23–24. This trend has continued: '(i) n ... 2004, Inspectors arrested 338 suspects for child sexual exploitation and obscenity related to the mail, stopped 97 child molesters, and rescued 158 children from sexual abuse'. US Postal Inspection Service, *Annual Report of Investigations*, April 2005, p 1. A survey of arrests for possession of child pornography in the USA in 2000–2001 found that '40% of arrested C(hild) P(ornography) possessors were "dual offenders", who sexually victimized children and possessed child pornography, with both crimes discovered in the same investigation', Wolak, Finkelhor and Mitchell, *Child-Pornography Possessors Arrested in Internet-Related Crimes* (National Center for Missing & Exploited Children (USA). 2005) p viii.
26 *DPP v McC* (31 October 2003, unreported) CCA.
27 Quayle and Taylor 'Child pornography and the Internet: Perpetuating a cycle of abuse' (2002) Deviant Behaviour 23 (4), 331–362.

Whilst a link between the use of child pornography and the actual abuse of children has yet to be conclusively defined, there is some evidence that the use of child pornography encourages the subsequent abuse of children. As the Minster for Justice commented:

> 'Not all persons who possess child pornography are necessarily paedophiles. However, all paedophiles will probably possess child pornography; it could almost be described as a necessary accessory to their activities. It is this connection between paedophilia and child pornography which this Bill targets'.[28]

The link between child pornography and offending was apparent to District Judge Frank O'Donnell when sentencing a Garda Sergeant to three years' imprisonment on conviction for attempting to procure a child for the purposes of her sexual exploitation and possessing child pornography. Judge O'Donnell stated:

> 'This case may appear to be less serious than others because there may be no victims but there are parents on the streets of Dublin who would be only too willing to offer their children for sexual exploitation and it is on this basis that I cannot ignore the link between the possession of child pornography and the solicitation.'[29]

[24.08] Others would go further. In a report published in 2004, the English Charity NCH concluded that:

> 'Several studies appear to support the idea that there is a definite link between possessing and collecting child abuse images and being involved in abusing children. The largest study suggests that one in three of those arrested solely for possessing child abuse images is likely to be involved, or to have been involved, in hands-on abuse. Others think that the proportion is much higher and that, in any event, everyone found in possession of child abuse images should be investigated and assessed on that basis.'[30]

The NCH suggests that as the Internet has increased the availability of child pornography, it is having the effect of causing greater numbers of children to be abused.

> 'Many paedophiles acknowledge that exposure to child abuse images fuels their sexual fantasies and plays an important part in leading them to commit hands-on sexual offences against children ... the internet is facilitating larger number of individuals becoming involved in collecting and possessing child abuse images ... it is highly likely that more children are therefore now being abused than would otherwise have been the case'.[31]

A controversial and as yet unpublished study of American prisoners suggests that 85% of those convicted of possession of child pornography will also abuse children in ways ranging from inappropriate touching to rape.[32]

---

[28] Dáil Éireann – Volume 489 – 02 April 1998, Child Trafficking and Pornography Bill, 1997: Second Stage

[29] 'Three years' jail for seeking child for sex' (2003) The Irish Times, 8 February.

[30] NCH, 'Child pornography, child abuse and the Internet',12 January 2004, executive summary, p i.

[31] NCH, 'Child pornography, child abuse and the Internet', 12 January 2004, executive summary, p i.

[32] Sher and Carey, 'Federal Study Stirs Debate on Child Pornography's Link to Molesting' (2007) The New York Times, 19 July.

Child pornographers as paedophiles

[24.09] Although the link between paedophiles and pornography is significant, the link should not be over-emphasised. As the Minister for Justice told the Dáil 'Not all persons who possess child pornography are necessarily paedophiles'.[33] Although possession of child pornography is a serious offence, it does not of itself mean that the possessor is a paedophile. The dangers of making this assumption are illustrated by *DPP v Ferris*.[34] The defendant was accused of indecent assault on a male, contrary to the Offences against the Person Act 1861. The defendant called two aunts to give evidence as to his character. Having put his character at issue the defendant was recalled to give evidence. Under cross-examination he admitted that the gardaí had obtained a search warrant under the customs acts, searched his flat and found child pornography. The trial judge summed up this evidence to the jury as follows:

> 'the fact that he was someone who was or had a disposition to employ pornographic and paedophilic material for his entertainment might well be something that would assist you in assessing his credit in regards to his testimony and very, very definite denial of any wrongdoing on his part.'

He was convicted and appealed. The Court of Appeal ordered a retrial on the ground that the applicant should not have been cross-examined with regard to the material found at his flat.

CTPA 1998 and 2004: Definitions

[24.10] The CTPA was enacted on 29 June 1998 and was commenced one month later.[35] It describes itself as: '(a)n Act to prohibit trafficking in, or the use of, children for the purposes of their sexual exploitation and the production, dissemination, handling or possession of child pornography'.[36] This Act is probably superior to its equivalents in the UK and the USA. Its offences are flexible and are not tied to a particular technology[37] or to a particular definition of what is and is not child pornography.[38] The Minister for Justice described to the Dáil the offenders against whom the Bill was directed in the following terms:

> 'There may still be some people who think of paedophiles as pathetic old men,[39] as much to be pitied as feared. Nothing could be further from the truth. Paedophiles may appear to

---

[33] Dáil Éireann – Volume 489 – 02 April 1998m Child Trafficking and Pornography Bill 1997: Second Stage.

[34] *DPP v Ferris* (10 June 2002, unreported) CCA.

[35] CTPA, s 1(2).

[36] CTPA, Preamble.

[37] As in the UK's Protection of Children Act 1978.

[38] As in the US Federal Child Pornography Prevention Act 1996.

[39] A survey of arrests for possession of child pornography in the USA in 2000-2001 found that 52% of those arrested were aged 18–39. It also found that: 'Virtually all of the arrested C(hild) P(ornography) possessors were men … They were predominantly white (91%) and older than 25 (86%). Only 3% were younger than 18. Most were unmarried at the time of their crime, either because they had never married (41%) or because they were separated, divorced, or widowed (21%). (contd/)

be ordinary people who live apparently ordinary lives but they can be highly manipulative and seductive, often charming themselves into people's confidences so that they can insinuate themselves into a position where they have unsupervised access to children. They are capable of taking the long view, even spending years to get themselves into positions of trust with the parents of their targeted victim. They will similarly use the devious side of their characters to obtain positions of trust, power and responsibility directly over children'[40].

Child pornography?

[24.11] Taylor and Quayle suggest that 'at its worst, child pornography is a picture of a sexual assault on a child … (t)o produce it someone has to assault a child, or pose a child in a sexualised way, and to make a photographic record of it.'[41] It is clear that child pornography is highly unpleasant and very disturbing. This is apparent from the statements of members of the judiciary who have viewed such material when sentencing offenders. Judge O'Donnell described child pornographic images as being 'very offensive'.[42] In one case Judge Groarke described child pornography as being 'a gross obscenity to any right thinking person' and 'the basest form of abuse'.[43] In another he described child pornography as 'a heinous trade, as every photograph describes a crime against those most in need of protection'.[44] In *DPP v McC*[45] Carney J opened his sentencing with the following statement:

> 'The facts of this case have been fully given in evidence and I don't intend to repeat them. The video evidence produced has been so disgusting that I, as the judge of this court who handles up to a 140 cases of this nature every year; couldn't go through with watching ten minutes of it.

[24.12] The English judiciary have reached similar conclusions. In *Atkins v DPP*[46] Simon Brown LJ in the English Court of Appeal described child pornography as being 'unpleasant'.[47] In *R v Richard Haynes*[48] Kennedy LJ described how the Court of Appeal assessed the child pornography a father created using his daughter:

---

[39] (\contd) Thirty-eight percent were either married or living with partners...few … possessors had histories of problem or criminal behavior. Few had been diagnosed with mental or sexual disorders … Not many had been violent to any extent known to law enforcement (11%) or had prior arrests for nonsexual offending (22%). Eleven percent had been previously arrested for sex offenses committed against minors'. Wolak, Finkelhor and Mitchell, *Child-Pornography Possessors Arrested in Internet-Related Crimes* National Center for Missing & Exploited Children (USA) 2005), pp 1–2.

[40] Dáil Éireann – Volume 489 – 02 April 1998, Child Trafficking and Pornography Bill 1997: Second Stage.

[41] Taylor and Quayle, *Child Pornography: An Internet Crime* (Brunner-Routledge 2003) p 21.

[42] 'Three years' jail for seeking child for sex' (2003) The Irish Times, 8 February.

[43] 'Man jailed for having 500 images of child porn' (2003) The Irish Times, 31 July.

[44] 'Convicted man appalled by his actions' (2003) The Irish Times, 3 December.

[45] *DPP v McC* [2003] 3 IR 609.

[46] *Atkins v DPP* (2000) Cr App R 248.

[47] *Atkins v DPP* (2000) Cr App R 248 at 257.

[48] *R v Richard Haynes* [1998] EWCA Crim 1475 (5 May 1998).

'We have ... see(n) ... the photographs which were taken by this man of his daughter. They are distressing. They show that he had no real conception of her as an individual, simply as an object through which he could take pleasure as he chose'.

[24.13] In *R v Thompson*[49] the trial judge described the child pornography in question as follows:

'in very unpleasant focus and close up, young girls engaging in sexual activity – intercourse – with other people (some adult, certainly). It is gross behaviour to be adopted towards any young child. In this case, two of the children were aged between five and six. It really does not bear thinking about as to what those little girls are going to make of their lives in later years, because each of them is a victim. Whether they will ever be able to recover from this is something that none of us will know.[50]

[24.14] In *R v Oliver and Others*[51] the Court of Appeal promulgated sentencing guidelines for offences under the UK's Protection of Children Act 1978. The court set out a hierarchy of seriousness of child pornographic images:

(a)   images depicting erotic posing with no sexual activity;

(b)   sexual activity between children or solo masturbation by a child;

(c)   non-penetrative sexual activity between adults or children;

(d)   penetrative sexual activity between adults and children; and

(e)   sadism or bestiality.

This hierarchy was utilised in Ireland by the Court of Criminal Appeal in *DPP v McC*. At the lower end of the scale might be the video taken by the defendant in *R v Fuller*.[52] The defendant had gone into the male changing room at a public swimming baths and used a video camera hidden in a bag to video men, and more particularly boys, changing. The video taken in *R v Watkins*[53] might be towards the higher end of the scale, in that case the victim's:

'mother had tied her to a bed, used a vibrator on her vagina, put pegs on her nipples, and beaten her with a stick. Her mother had then sat on her chest and urinated in her mouth. These events were recorded on a video by the father.'

A search of the family home revealed other videos 'depicting horrific attacks' on the victim, and the judgment in this case is deeply disturbing by itself. The pornography produced by the defendant in *DPP v McC* would appear to fall between these two extremes.

Child

[24.15] 'Child' is defined by the CTPA as being 'a person under the age of 17 years'.[54] During the debate on the Bill, the then Minister for Justice commented that:

---

[49] *R v Thompson* [2004] EWCA Crim 669.
[50] [2004] EWCA Crim 669, para 5.
[51] *R v Oliver and Others* (2003) Crim LR 127.
[52] *R v Fuller* [1997] EWCA Crim 2136 (20 August 1997). See para **[24.28]** below.
[53] *R v Watkins* [1998] EWCA Crim 2058 (23 June, 1998).

'The other important definition in section 2 is that of a 'child'. There are several different ages for which one could make a case. I have decided that the most logical and appropriate age is 17 years, that is, the age of consent to a sexual relationship in this jurisdiction.'[55]

One difficulty that might be encountered in prosecuting an offence of child pornography is of proving the age of the children in pornographic representations. So the CTPA provides:

'In any proceedings for an offence under section 3 (Child trafficking), 4 (Allowing child to be used for child pornography), 5 (Producing, distributing, etc., child pornography) or 6 (Possession of child pornography) a person shall be deemed, unless the contrary is proved, to be or have been a child, or to be or have been depicted or represented as a child, at any time if the person appears to the court to be or have been a child, or to be or have been so depicted or represented, at that time'[56].

So the fact that an individual actor or actress was in fact over 17 is irrelevant, if they appear to be a child, then the court will presume that they are a child, until the contrary is proven. This provision may be compared to the Sexual Offences (Jurisdiction) Act 1996.[57]

'In proceedings for an offence, which is an offence under or by virtue of section 2 or 3 of this Act, the court may have regard to a person's physical appearance or attributes for the purpose of determining whether that person is under the age of 17 years or was, at the time of the alleged commission of the offence to which the proceedings relate, under the age of 17 years.'[58]

[24.16] The CTPA presumes that a person is a child if they are depicted or represented as one, or if they appear to the court to be one. This requires a court to make a subjective finding as to how old the court thinks the individual depicted is. If the court decides that an individual appears to be a child or to be represented or depicted as one, then it is for the defendant to disprove this finding. Similarly, the CTPA defines child pornography not as being a representation of a child, but rather as being a representation of someone who 'is depicted as being a child'.[59] The definition is subjective or objective it is irrelevant if the person engaged in the sexual activity is over 17 or even 21. what matters is that they are depicted as being a child. This makes the offence easier to prosecute as in cases of doubt it is not necessary to find the person involved in the making of the child pornography and prove that at the time the pornography was made they were under 17 years of age.

---

[54] CTPA, s 2(1). Article 9 of The Cybercrime Convention requires that a child pornography law prohibits pornography involving 'all persons under 18 years of age'. However, the Convention does allow parties to it to require a lower age-limit, not less than 16 years. Therefore, Ireland's age limit of 17 years would appear to comply with the Convention.

[55] Dáil Éireann – Volume 489 – 02 April 1998, Child Trafficking and Pornography Bill 1997: Second Stage.

[56] CTPA, s 2(3).

[57] Sexual Offences (Jurisdiction) Act 1996, s 8. See Charlton, McDermott and Bolger, *Criminal Law* (Tottel Publishing, 1999), para 8.95.

[58] Sexual Offences (Jurisdiction) Act 1996, s 8.

[59] CTPA, s 2(3).

[24.17] The definition of child in CTPA can be compared to the definition used in the equivalent UK legislation. The English Protection of Children Act 1978 provides 'a person is to be taken as having been a child at any material time if it appears from the evidence as a whole that he was then under the age of 16.'[60] A defendant before the Irish courts may find it harder to disprove the presumption under the CTPA than a defendant before the English courts charged under that jurisdiction's legislation. The Irish Act allows for a finding to be made where the victim is depicted or represented as being under 17, whereas the English Act only allows a finding to be made where 'it appears from the evidence as a whole' that the victim was under 18. The argument has been made that the English Act requires the making of an objective finding as to the age of the victim. However, this argument was rejected by the English Court of Appeal in *R v Land*.[61] The defendant was convicted of possessing indecent photographs of a child. He appealed on the basis that the trial judge incorrectly charged the jury by telling them that in the absence of evidence as to the age of the persons depicted in the photographs, they could use their own experience to decide whether it was proved that the photographs depicted children. His counsel argued before the Court of Appeal that this presumption could lead to some alarming results:

'a man might buy and keep an indecent magazine believing that the photographs contained in it depicted adults, and subsequently find himself convicted of possession of an indecent photograph of a child if, without his knowledge, it emerged that the person he believed was an adult was only 15 years old. In the absence of unequivocal language in the statute such an individual should not be subject to the rigours of law'.[62]

In essence, the defendant's argument was that the jury should have been required to find that he knew that the photographs concerned were of children and not adults. This argument was rejected by Judge LJ:

'An offence ... (under the English Protection of Children Act 1978) ... may be committed in a variety of ways which include possession of an indecent photograph of a child with a view to distribution. The object is to protect children from exploitation and degradation. Potential damage to the child occurs when he or she is posed or pictured indecently and whenever such an event occurs the child is being exploited. It is the demand for such material which leads to the exploitation of children and the purpose of the 1978 Act is to reduce, indeed as far as possible to eliminate, trade in or possession of it ...

Accordingly ... (o)nce it is or should be appreciated that ... material is indecent then its continued retention or distribution is subject to the risk of prosecution if the source of the material should prove to be a child or children. The anxiety expressed ... (by Counsel for the defendant) ... who does not know that the material depicts someone who in fact a child is misplaced. Ignoring members of the child's own family, who will know his or her age, it will be rare in the extreme for a complete stranger to be in possession of indecent photographs of someone who although appearing to be mature could nevertheless be proved by the prosecution to be a child. A glance will quickly show whether the material

---

[60] Protection of Children Act 1978 (UK), s 2(3).
[61] *R v Land* [1998] WLR 323.
[62] [1998] WLR 323 at 326.

is or may be depicting someone who is under the age of 16 and if it is or may be then prosecution may be avoided by destroying or having nothing further to do with it'.[63]

The decision of the Court of Appeal in *Land* is particularly pertinent in relation to the charge to be given to the jury.

'The judge directed the jury that in deciding whether or not it was proved that the photographs were of a child:

'You can do no more than use your own experience, your judgment and your critical faculties in deciding this issue. It is simply an issue of fact for you, the jury, to decide what you have seen with your own eyes.'

In our judgment this direction is not open to question. In any event such expert evidence rendered by either side would be inadmissible. The purpose of expert evidence is to assist the court with information which is outside the normal experience and knowledge of the judge or jury. Perhaps the only certainty which applies to the problem in this case is that each individual reaches puberty in his or her own time. For each the process is unique and the jury is as well placed as an expert to assess any argument addressed to the question whether the prosecution has established, as it must before there can be a conviction, that the person depicted in the photograph is under 16 years'.[64]

So the decision as to whether or not an individual, depicted in an item of pornography, is a child is clearly a matter of fact to be decided by the jury without the assistance of expert witnesses. However, even if the defendant could prove that the person depicted pornographically were over the age of 17 that might be irrelevant as the Irish Act defines child pornography as being something in which an individual is 'depicted as being a child'.

Virtual child pornography

[24.18] Given the harm that must be caused to the children who are victimised in the production of child pornography, it would seem impossible not to argue for its prohibition. However, what if child pornography could be produced using sophisticated digital techniques so that no children would be involved in its production at all? Technology exists that 'makes it possible to create realistic images of children who do not exist'. As was noted by the US Supreme Court in 'Virtual child pornography is not 'intrinsically related' to the sexual abuse of children'.

[24.19] Should the production, distribution and possession of virtual child pornography be permitted in those circumstances? Probably not. This issue was debated by the US Federal Legislature when enacting the Child Pornography Prevention Act 1996.

---

[63] [1998] WLR 323 at 326–327.

[64] [1998] WLR 323 at 327–328. It should be kept in mind that 'reasonable belief' as to the age of a child was subsequently re-examined by the House of Lords in *B v DPP* [2000] UKHL 13, [2000] 2 AC 428, [2000] 2 WLR 452, [2000] 1 All ER 833, [2000] Crim LR 403 and *R v K* [2001] UKHL 41 (25 July 2001).

Wasserman[65] analysed the Federal debates and suggests that the US Congress had no less than five justifications for banning virtual child pornography.

1. *Virtual child pornography can be used to seduce children.* The US Congress heard from psychologists who attested that paedophiles used child pornography in this way.

2. *New technology allows child pornographers to evade prosecution.* It was argued that computer generated child pornography supplied a 'built-in reasonable doubt standard in every child exploitation/pornography prosecution' as a defendant could argue that the prosecution would have to prove that the pornography was real and not virtual. Given the advances in modern technology, proof of this point would be difficult.

3. *Banning virtual child pornography will encourage paedophiles to destroy all child pornography and help close the child pornography market.* Banning virtual child pornography eliminates a potential defense and encourages the material's destruction.

4. *Virtual child pornography incites paedophiles to abuse children.* The US Congress found that 'child pornography is often used by pedophiles and child sexual abusers to stimulate and whet their own sexual appetites and as a model for sexual acting out with children; such use of child pornography can desensitize the viewer to the pathology of sexual abuse'.[66]

5. *Virtual child pornography leads to the sexualisation of minors.* The US Congress concluded that 'the erotixcation of children through child pornography, virtual or real, 'has a deleterious effect on all children by encouraging a societal perception of children as sexual objects and leading to further sexual abuse and exploitation of them'. The sexualisation of minors creates an unwholesome environment that negatively impact juvenile development and threatens parental efforts to ensure the sound mental and moral growth of children.'[67]

[24.20] The Child Pornography Prevention Act 1996 was challenged in *Ashcroft v Free Speech Coalition*.[68] The US Attorney General argued that virtual child pornography should be banned, as it is interchangeable with images created through the use of real children. The US Supreme Court rejected this argument, Justice Kennedy stating that:

---

[65] Wasserman, 'Virtual.child.porn.com: Defending the Constitutionality of the criminalization of Computer-Generated Child Pornography' (1998) Harvard Journal on Legislation, Vol 35, p 245.

[66] Omnibus Consolidated Appropriations Act of 1997, Pub L No 104-208, SS121(1)(4), 1996 USCCAN. (110 Stat. 3009) 3009–26.

[67] Wasserman, 'Virtual.child.porn.com: Defending the Constitutionality of the criminalization of Computer-Generated Chld Pornography' (1998) Harvard Journal on Legislation, Vol 35 p 273–274

[68] *Ashcroft v Free Speech Coalition* US LEXIS 2789, 122 SC 1389 (2002) Pub L No 100-690 (1988).

'Virtual images, the Government contends, are indistinguishable from real ones; they are part of the same market and are often exchanged. In this way, it is said, virtual images promote the trafficking in works produced through the exploitation of real children. The hypothesis is somewhat implausible. If virtual images were identical to illegal child pornography, the illegal images would be driven from the market by the indistinguishable substitutes. Few pornographers would risk prosecution by abusing real children if fictional, computerized images would suffice'.[69]

[24.21] As is noted above, the protections for free speech provided by the Irish Constitution and the ECHR are far more limited than those provided by the US Constitution. The Irish Constitution specifically allows for the limitation of free speech to preserve 'public order and morality'[70]. This allows the Irish Oireachtas to ban virtual pornography in circumstances where the US Houses of Congress cannot. Furthermore, the US Supreme Court was persuaded that virtual child pornography could still be distinguished from that produced using real children. Justice Thomas, concurring, commented that:

'technology may evolve to the point where it becomes impossible to enforce actual child pornography laws because the Government cannot prove that certain pornographic images are of real children. In the event this occurs, the Government should not be foreclosed from enacting a regulation of virtual child pornography that contains an appropriate affirmative defense or some other narrowly drawn restriction.'[71]

[24.22] A person charged with an offence under the CTPA might claim that the images in question were entirely digitally created and, as such, did not depict persons. This possibility was 'the Government's most persuasive asserted interest'[72] in *Ashcroft v Free Speech Coalition*. But the US Government was unable to point to a case 'in which a defendant has been acquitted based on a "computer-generated images" defense'[73]. In the subsequent case of *United States v Deaton*[74] the appellant had been convicted of possession of child pornography. He appealed, arguing that the prosecution should have proven that the images in respect of which he was convicted depicted actual children. His appeal failed. CTPA would seem to prohibit the making of a similar argument in Ireland. It provides that references to 'person' in the definition of child pornography:

'shall be construed as including a reference to a figure resembling a person that has been generated or modified by computer-graphics or otherwise, and in such a case the fact, if it is a fact, that some of the principal characteristics shown are those of an adult shall be disregarded if the predominant impression conveyed is that the figure shown is a child.'[75]

---

[69]   US LEXIS 2789, 122 SC 1389 (2002) Pub L No 100-690 (1988). Justice Kennedy delivering the opinion of the court.

[70]   Bunreacht na hÉireann, Article 40.6.1°.

[71]   US LEXIS 2789, 122 SC 1389 (2002) Pub L No 100-690 (1988), concurring opinion of Justice Thomas.

[72]   US LEXIS 2789, 122 SC 1389 (2002) Pub L No 100-690 (1988), concurring opinion of Justice Thomas.

[73]   US LEXIS 2789, 122 SC 1389 (2002) Pub L No 100-690 (1988), concurring opinion of Justice Thomas.

[74]   *United States v Deaton* 328 F 3d 454, 2003 US App LEXIS 8751 (8th Cir 2003).

[75]   CTPA, s 2(2).

Child pornography

[24.23] The definition of 'child pornography' in section 2 of the Act is complex. Child pornography is not just visual or audio representations of depictions of children being involved in explicit sexual activity. It is also anything that 'advocates, encourages or counsels' the committing of such activity. There is an argument to be made that using the Internet to 'groom' a child would be an offence under this section. Child pornography is also anything that advertises a child as being available for sexual exploitation.

"child pornography' means—

    (a)   any visual representation—

        (i)   that shows or, in the case of a document, relates to a person who is or is depicted as being a child and who is engaged in or is depicted as being engaged in explicit sexual activity,

        (ii)   that shows or, in the case of a document, relates to a person who is or is depicted as being a child and who is or is depicted as witnessing any such activity by any person or persons, or

        (iii)   whose dominant characteristic is the depiction, for a sexual purpose, of the genital or anal region of a child

Sexual purpose

[24.24] The definition of child pornography relies upon the term 'sexual', but does not define it. The *Oxford English Dictionary* defines 'sexual' as 'relating to the instincts, physiological processes, and activities connected with the physical attraction or intimate physical contact between individuals'.

[24.25] The definition of child pornography is three-fold: it is a depiction of a child engaged in sexual activity, witnessing sexual activity or the display of a child's genital or anal regions 'for a sexual purpose'. The first two parts of the definition are relatively straightforward and require an objective assessment of whether what is occurring is sexual activity. The use of the term 'for a sexual purpose', however, appears to require an assessment of the dominant characteristic of purpose of the work in question. This assessment may require a subjective assessment of the motivations of whoever produced, distributed or published the material in question. This subjective assessment is to be contrasted with the use of the term 'indecent' in the UK's Child Protection Act. The test for deciding what is and is not indecent was set out by the English Court of Appeal in *R v Stamford*;[76] a decision of what is indecent depends upon its 'impropriety'.[77] Since 'the standards of impropriety vary from age to age'.[78] what is

---

[76] *R v Stamford* [1972] 2 WLR 1055.

[77] 'one way of expressing the test of indecency or obscenity which are at either end of the scale common to both, was that a matter is obscene if it is one that offends against recognised standards of propriety, and it may be that the same test applies to a matter alleged to be indecent, bearing in mind, as the courts have said, that those are different concepts, different steps on the scale of impropriety, obscenity being the graver of the two'. *R v Stamford* [1972] 2 WLR 1055 at 1060.

[78] Ibid p 1060.

improper now, may not be improper in ten years time or vice versa. The English law is that:

> 'The circumstances and motivation of a the taker of a photograph might be relevant to his *mens rea* as to whether his taking was intentional or accidental – they are not relevant to whether the photograph is indecent.'[79]

[24.26] It is unclear whether 'sexual purpose' for the purposes of the CTPA is to be assessed by reference to standards of propriety and decency prevalent in society or whether 'sexual purpose' is assessed by reference to the specific individual charged before a court. A straightforward reading of the text definition suggests that the latter interpretation is to be preferred. It defines child pornography as:

> 'any visual representation…whose dominant characteristic is the depiction, for a sexual purpose, of the genital or anal region of a child.'

[24.27] The above definition does not require a court to inquire as to whether the depiction in question is indecent or obscene. All it requires the court do is assess what the dominant characteristic of the visual representation is. It is not clear from the Act whether this is to be done by reference to society's standards of sexual interest in general, or those of the specific individual before the court. Assessing the dominant characteristic of a visual depiction by reference to a specific individual may prove problematic, however. This is because persons who produce or possess child pornography may have very different sexual purposes to persons who are judges or members of a jury and those purposes may be difficult to discern. As Taylor and Quayle state:

> 'What we can say is that the dynamic processes associated with child pornography are at the moment complex and obscure, and it seems likely that not all individuals who collect child pornography do so for the same reasons, or indeed have the same degree of sexual interest in children.'[80]

[24.28] A depiction that would seem innocent and mundane to most people, such as children changing their clothes on a beach, can have a sexual purpose for some. It would appear the 'sexual purpose' is that of the person who produces or possesses child pornography. A paedophile who surreptitiously films children changing their clothes may have a sexual purpose. That purpose will not be affected by the purpose of the children, who are simply changing their clothes. This issue came before the English Court of Appeal in *R v Fuller*.[81] The defendant had gone into a male changing room at a public swimming baths and used a video camera hidden in a bag to video men, and more particularly boys, changing. The defendant's intent was evidenced by the fact that he altered 'the direction of the camera…in order to take advantage (if such be the appropriate expression) of the fact that another child was obviously about to remove his swimming trunks'.

---

[79] Archbold 2004, 31–108 citing *R v Graham-Kerr* 88 Cr App R 302 and *R v Smethurst* 2002 1 Cr App R 6.

[80] Taylor and Quayle, *Child Pornography: An Internet Crime* (Brunner-Routledge 2003) p 196.

[81] *R v Fuller* [1997] EWCA Crim 2136 (20 August 1997).

[24.29] On the following day the defendant took video footage openly on a beach of children changing into swimming costumes. A school teacher became suspicious and she in turn photographed the appellant taking that film and in consequence the appellant was arrested. The appellant was convicted at trial in respect of the offence which he was alleged to have committed in the changing rooms and acquitted in respect of the offence that he was alleged to have committed on the beach. He appealed to the Court of Appeal on the basis that the video taken in the changing rooms was not indecent, but his appeal failed. It is arguable that the appellant's conviction for the beach filming would have been upheld in Ireland, if he had filmed the genital or anal regions of the children in question. He plainly had a sexual purpose in undertaking the filming. It is true that a parent of one of the children might innocently have filmed the same scene, without committing a criminal offence, but their purpose in doing so would not have been sexual.

Visual and audio representations

[24.30] One of the main challenges for the CTPA was to develop a definition of pornography itself that would be flexible enough to apply to a broad variety of technologies, not all of which would be sophisticated. It would appear that the Act successfully overcomes this challenge. The term 'visual representation' used by the CTPA is not tied to any particular technology, and can be very favourably compared to the use of the term 'photographs' and 'pseudo-photographs' in the UK Protection of Children Act 1978. In *R v Goodland*[82] the defendant had sellotaped two separate photographs together, one an image of a girl aged 10, the other a pornographic image of an older girl or young woman. The question before the court was whether two photographs sellotaped together could form a photograph for the purposes of the English Act. A divisional sitting of the English High Court held that it did not, although it recognised *obiter* that if the two photographs had been photocopied, the resulting single photocopy could well be said to constitute a photograph for the purposes of the English Act. In contrast, two photographs sellotaped together would probably form a 'visual representation' for the purposes of the CTPA. Of course, far more sophisticated technology is now available to cut and paste or 'morph' children's faces onto adult's bodies and vice versa.[83]

[24.31] It is important to recognise the breadth of the above definition in the Irish Act. Child pornography is defined as including a document that 'relates to a person who is or is depicted as a child'. So a literary work, of fact or fiction, which depicts a child or a person pretending to be a child, engaging in or witnessing sexual activities will fall

---

82 *R v Goodland* [2000] EWHC Admin 302 (8 March 2000).

83 'Products such as Photoshop or some other software can be employed to take part of a digitized picture and past it together with another, and the software user can blend the images together and add to it'. Ferraro and Casey, *Investigating Child Exploitation and Pornography: The Internet, the law and Forensic Science* (Elsevier Academic Press, 2004) p 237. At the time of writing US Authorities had initiated a prosecution against one Karen Fletcher who is accused of distributing child pornography on-line which was 'composed entirely of text without any images'. Lewis, 'A Prosecution Tests the Definition of Obscenity' (2007) The New York Times, 28 September.

within the definition of child pornography.[84] The Act may also apply to databases. Photographs of naked children are not uncommon; nappy and children's wear advertisements may depict children in varying states of undress and nudity. These photographs are not child pornography as their purpose is commercial and illustrative, not sexual. However, if such photographs are cut out of their surrounding material, their purpose may be changed. A picture of a naked child, together with an advertising blurb such as 'Buy Nappies' will not be child pornography. But once devoid of its advertising context, the same picture may be child pornography. If such pictures were to be collected into a database for the purpose of an individual's sexual gratification, that database or collection would then be child pornography. Context may be key in deciding what is and is not child pornography. The Irish courts may wish to adopt the views of Justice Potter Stewart of the US Supreme Court, who declined to define what was or was not hard-core pornography, but commented that 'I know it when I see it'.[85]

[24.32] A Visual representation is broadly defined as including:

'(a) any photographic,[86] film or video representation, any accompanying sound or any document,[87]

(b) any copy of any such representation or document, and

(c) any tape, computer disk or other thing on which the visual representation and any accompanying sound are recorded.'

Child pornography is also 'any audio representation of a person who is or is represented as being a child and who is engaged in or is represented as being engaged in explicit sexual activity'. This definition would extend to a recording of the sounds of a child being abused, but it would also apply to an oral description of how abuse took place. The term 'audio representation' is defined as including 'any such representation by means of tape, computer disk or other thing from which such a representation can be produced, and…any tape, computer disk or other thing on which any such representation is recorded'. This is similar to the definition of visual representation.

[24.33] The definitions in CTPA are broadened by not particularly defining the medium in which the representation is saved. There is a reference to 'photographic, film or video', but it is clearly intended that the definition should be wider than these particular technologies. First of all, the definition extends to any copy of any photograph, film or video and, secondly, it extends to 'any tape, computer disk or other thing'. The inclusion of the word 'thing' suggests that this definition is as broad as is possible. The breadth of

---

[84] A view that is bolstered by the fact that the definition of child pornography is explicitly stated not to include 'any book or periodical publication' examined by the Censorship of Publications Board. CTPA, s 2(1).

[85] *Jacobellis v Ohio* 378 US 184, 197 (1964).

[86] Where photographic is defined as including 'the negative as well as the positive version', CTPA, s 2(1).

[87] Document is defined as including 'any book, periodical or pamphlet, and … where appropriate, any tape, computer disk or other thing on which data capable of conversion into any such document is stored', CTPA, s 2(1).

the definition of child pornography is ensured by the conclusion of the definition, which provides:

'irrespective of how or through what medium the representation, description or information has been produced, transmitted or conveyed and, without prejudice to the generality of the foregoing, includes any representation, description or information produced by or from computer-graphics or by any other electronic or mechanical means.'

So in the case of child pornography, the medium does not matter. What matters is what is represented. The definition further extends to child pornography that it manufactured using computer graphics. This makes it clear that child pornography is seen as being criminal in itself; it is not just criminalised because it is made by abusing children. Even when no children are used, child pornography is illegal, which is consistent with the definition of child pornography as being something that depicts the sexual abuse of children.

Advocates, encourages or counsels

[24.34] The definition of child pornography also extends to anything that advocates or advertises the sexual abuse of children and extends to:

'any visual or audio representation that advocates, encourages or counsels any sexual activity with children which is an offence under any enactment, or

… any visual representation or description of, or information relating to, a child that indicates or implies that the child is available to be used for the purpose of sexual exploitation.'

This provision is discussed in the following chapter.

Chapter 25

Offences and Defences

Introduction

[25.01] The Child Trafficking and Pornography Act 1998 (CTPA 1998) seeks to criminalise both child pornography and the activities that are ancillary to its production and distribution. Therefore, it makes it an offence to produce, market, distribute and possess child pornography. It also criminalises the use of children in the production of child pornography. One of the key features of CTPA 1998 is that it criminalises not just child pornographers, but anyone who knowingly facilitates its production, possession or distribution. What this means is that employers, supervisors and system administrators may themselves become criminally liable if they should 'turn a blind eye' in situations where it is suspected that child pornography is being produced or distributed.[1]

The abuse of children in the production of child pornography

[25.02] The CTPA 1998 makes it a specific offence to use children in the production of child pornography. It provides that:

'Any person who—

    (a)   takes, detains, or restricts the personal liberty of, a child for the purpose of his or her sexual exploitation,

    (b)   uses a child for such a purpose, or

    (c)   organises or knowingly facilitates such taking, detaining, restricting or use'.[2]

The CTPA 1998 clearly extends this offence to the use of a child in the making of child pornography by defining 'sexual exploitations' as:

'inducing or coercing the child to engage ... in the production of child pornography ... using the child for ... the production of child pornography ... inducing or coercing[3] the child to participate in any sexual activity which is an offence under any enactment, or ... the commission of any such offence against the child'.[4]

---

[1]   A criticism frequently made of the Catholic Church and other institutions of the state is that they did turn a blind eye to child abuse. For example, see O'Toole, 'The strut of power gave them a sense they could do whatever they liked, wherever they liked' (2005) The Irish Times, 29 October.

[2]   CTPA 1998, s 3(2).

[3]   Regarding the inducements and coercion used in the production of videos of child pornography *Taylor and Quayle* say 'the bribes and threats made by the photographer to induce the child to do what is required can ... be heard ...'. Taylor and Quayle, *Child Pornography: an Internet Crime* (Brunner-Routledge, 2003), p 22.

[4]   CTPA 1998, s 3(3).

[25.03] A person convicted of such an offence will be liable on conviction on indictment to imprisonment for a term not exceeding 14 years.[5] The production of child pornography will often cause direct harm to the the children involved. Taylor and Quayle note that 'often sexual assault(s) ... lie at the very heart of the production of child pornography'.[6] Obviously, this offence might be committed by a person who arranged for or actually made child pornography initially. It is highly likely that whenever child pornography is initially produced, it is be produced 'knowingly'. Taylor and Quayle comment that:

> 'We can reasonably assert ... that the production of child pornography is never accidental. It is a construction and its content is both deliberate and stylised to meet certain implicit and explicit requirements ... .there are two broad kinds of context ... in which child pornography is produced. The first relates to private production for the use of the producer ... The second relates to production, with a view to further distribution, either between a small circle of likeminded people, or perhaps with reference to some commercial context ... the photographer is most likely to be someone from the child's immediate circle of family or friends.'[7]

The initial production of the more extreme forms of child pornography, depictions of sexual assaults would be an offence anyway, whether under The Punishment of Incest Act 1908, The Criminal Law Amendment Act 1935, The Criminal Law (Rape) (Amendment) Act 1990 or otherwise. But merely because the production of child pornography does not involve the assault of children does not mean that it will not be child pornography. The fact that child pornography is produced openly, in public, is irrelevant. In *R v Jacques Henry Resse*[8] the facts were as follows:

> 'At Brighton there is a nudist beach, and on 10th May 1995 Charlene came to the nudist beach following an earlier meeting with the appellant and brought with her the other 14 year old Emma. The appellant had a video camcorder, and the two girls took up various modelling poses on the beach and were filmed by the appellant'.

The English Court of Appeal upheld the defendant's conviction for taking indecent photographs of a child, but reduced his sentence from four months to two.

Allowing a child to be used for the production of child pornography

[25.04] The CTPA 1998 makes it an offence to 'organise() or knowingly facilitate()' the sexual exploitation of a child. The CTPA 1998 also makes it an offence for any person who 'having the custody, charge or care of a child, allows the child to be used for the production of child pornography'.[9]

[25.05] A person convicted upon indictment of such an offence will liable on conviction on indictment to a fine not exceeding £25,000 or to imprisonment for a term not

---

5   CTPA 1998, s 3(2).
6   Taylor and Quayle, p 22.
7   Taylor and Quayle, pp 22–23.
8   *R v Jacques Henry Resse* [1997] EWCA Crim 694 (11 March 1997).
9   CTPA 1998, s 4(1).

exceeding 14 years or both.[10] The responsibility of parents, guardians and those *in loco parentis* is broadly defined under this section. It provides that:

'(a) any person who is the parent or guardian of a child or who is liable to maintain a child shall be presumed to have the custody of the child and, as between parents, one parent shall not be deemed to have ceased to have the custody of the child by reason only that he or she has deserted, or does not reside with, the other parent and child,

(b) any person to whose charge a child is committed by any person who has the custody of the child shall be presumed to have charge of the child, and

(c) any person exercising authority over or having actual control of a child shall be presumed to have care of the child'.[11]

Allowing a child to be used for the purposes of child pornography can be compared with being an accomplice and this provision must be read in addition to the Criminal Law Act 1997, which provides for the complicity of third parties, stating 'Any person who aids, abets, counsels or procures the commission of an indictable offence shall be liable to be indicted, tried and punished as a principal offender'.[12]

Trafficking in children

[25.06] Research would suggest that the social support that may be provided to paedophiles by Internet-based communities, may be as important to them as the child pornography that they may find online.[13] There is a real danger that the Internet supplies both encouragement and social support to paedophiles:

'Prior to the Internet, paedophiles remained a relatively isolated group, but through this new technology they have been able to form much larger social networks that have been referred to as 'virtual communities' ... Such communities can contact each other, and also potential victims, through the Internet in a way that is subject to few external controls ... paedophiles who have never felt able to function at an optimal level in the 'real world' may feel that they have the chance to do so through the Internet, where conventional structures have broken down.

In allowing paedophiles to communicate so freely with each other, the Internet reinforces the belief that such behaviour is valid and normal activity, and is an expression of 'love' for children rather than abuse'.[14]

---

[10] CTPA 1998, s 4(1).

[11] CTPA 1998, s 4(2).

[12] Criminal Law Act 1997, s 7.

[13] 'th(e) social aspect of the Internet appears to be as important as the collectible material itself' Quayle and Taylor, 'Paedophiles, Pornography and the Internet' (2002) British Journal of Social Work 32, 863–875, 867.

[14] Quayle and Taylor, 'Paedophiles, Pornography and the Internet' (2002) British Journal of Social 32, 863–875, 867.

The likelihood that Internet-based communities may encourage the abuse of children should cause great concern:

'Through the Internet we see a potential change in the offenders' beliefs, values, and cognitive styles, as they act and interact outside of the confines of a conventional hierarchy. One consequence of this (and also a contributory factor) may be increased risktaking behavior. It is possible that such experiences may empower sex offenders, who have otherwise felt marginalized within a conventional society'.[15]

[25.07] The CTPA 1998 makes it an offence to traffic in children. It does this by extending the definition of 'child pornography' to include 'any visual representation or description of, or information relating to, a child that indicates or implies that the child is available to be used for the purpose of sexual exploitation'.[16] This means that anyone who produces, prints, publishes, distributes or otherwise commits any of the offences under ss 3, 4, 5 and 6 of CTPA 1998 in relation to anything that may indicate or imply that a child is available for sexual exploitation will commit an offence. This offence should be seen in the context of The Sexual Offences (Jurisdiction) Act 1996. This is 'An Act to extend ... (Irish) ... criminal law ... to sexual acts involving children done outside the state by ... (Irish Citizens)'.[17] A person who 'aids, abets, counsels or procures'.[18] or 'conspires with, or incites'.[19] another person to do such acts will be guilty of an offence. Section 4 provides that:

'A person who publishes information which is intended to or, having regard to all the circumstances, is likely to promote, advocate or incite the commission of an offence, which is an offence by virtue of section 2 (1) of this Act, shall be guilty of an offence'.

One of the functions of The Sexual Offences (Jurisdiction) Act 1996 was to prohibit the advertisement of the sexual availability of children outside the state. The definition of child pornography in CTPA 1998 creates a similar prohibition on advertisements relating to children within the state.

Offences

[25.08] The CTPA 1998 broadly criminalises the production, distribution, importation and possession of child pornography. The breadth of this offence is limited only by the requirement that it must be committed 'knowingly'. This requirement serves may have the effect of encouraging those who comes into contact with child pornography to contact the gardaí as soon as possible. Once a service provider learns that one of its customers is using its systems to distribute child pornography or an employer learns that one of its employees is storing child pornography on his company laptop, the gardaí must be informed. To do otherwise would mean that the service provider or employer was 'knowingly' facilitating the distribution or possession of child pornography.

---

[15] Quayle and Taylor, 'Model of Problematic Internet Use in People with a Sexual Interest in Children' (2003) Cyberpsychology and Behavior, Vol 6, Number 1, 93, 104.

[16] CTPA 1998, s 2(1).

[17] CTPA 1998, Long Title.

[18] CTPA 1998, s 2(3).

[19] CTPA 1998, s 2(5).

The CTPA provides that:

'any person who—

(a)   knowingly produces, distributes[20], prints or publishes any child pornography,

(b)   knowingly imports, exports, sells or shows any child pornography,

(c)   knowingly publishes or distributes any advertisement likely to be understood as conveying that the advertiser or any other person produces, distributes, prints, publishes, imports, exports, sells or shows any child pornography,

(d)   encourages or knowingly causes or facilitates any activity mentioned in paragraph (a), (b) or (c), or

(e)   knowingly possesses any child pornography for the purpose of distributing, publishing, exporting, selling or showing it,

shall be guilty of an offence'.[21]

This is an extremely broad offence; it criminalises the production and distribution of child pornography at almost every stage. As well as criminalising production in (a) above, pre-production – the encouragement 'or' facilitation of production – is also criminalised at (d). The advertisement of child pornography is criminalised at (c) and its distribution is criminalised by (a), (b), (d) and (e). Offences under this section are punishable by 'a fine not exceeding £1,500 or ... imprisonment for a term not exceeding 12 months or both' on summary conviction and 'a fine or ... imprisonment for a term not exceeding 14 years or both' on conviction on indictment. It would appear that 'knowingly' does not necessarily mean absolute knowledge; recklessness or suspicion as to the nature of certain images may be sufficient.

Section 5(1)(a): Knowingly produces, distributes, prints or publishes

[25.09] Arguably this subsection is most applicable to more traditional media such as books or magazines; however, it clearly applies to digital and Internet media as well.

Produce

[25.10] Section 3 of the Act is primarily aimed at the initial production of child pornography. However, in the leading Irish case on the production of child pornography, *DPP v McC*,[22] charges were brought pursuant to s 5(1), not s 3. In this case the defendant pleaded guilty to offences in relation to a number of male children, including filming one boy masturbating and photographing the anal and genital regions of others, including filming them in the shower on a camera connected to the Internet.

[25.11] Section 5(1)(a) clearly criminalises the initial production of pornography. However, the English Court of Appeal decision in *R v Bowden*[23] suggests that 'produce' may have a meaning that is broader than this initial production. In *R v Bowden* the issue

---

[20] CTPA 1998, s 5(2) provides that 'In this section "distributes", in relation to child pornography, includes parting with possession of it to, or exposing or offering it for acquisition by, another person, and the reference to "distributing" in that context shall be construed accordingly'.

[21] CTPA 1998, s 5(1).

[22] *DPP v McC* [2003] 3 IR 609.

[23] *R v Bowden* [2001] QB 88.

before the English Court of Appeal was whether downloading and/or printing out of computer data of indecent images of children is capable of amounting to an offence contrary to s 1(1)(a) of the English Protection of Children Act 1978 which provides 'It is an offence for a person ... to take, or permit to be taken, or to make any indecent photograph or pseudo-photograph of a child'.

In *R v Bowden* the defendant took his computer hard drive to a computer firm for repair. While examining the computer, the repairer found indecent material on the hard drive. As a result of a subsequent investigation, police seized a computer and equipment including hard drive and floppy disks from the defendant. They examined the discs which contained indecent images of young boys. The defendant had downloaded the photographs from the Internet and either printed them out himself, or stored them on his computer disks. It was not contested that all the photographs were indecent and involved children under 16 years of age. When arrested and interviewed, the defendant accepted that he had obtained the indecent material from the Internet and downloaded it onto his hard drive in his computer for his own personal use. The defendant did not know that this was illegal. It was not part of the prosecution's case that the defendant created for the first time any image that did not already exist in a visually identical form.[24]

[25.12] The defendant appealed, his counsel submitting that he 'was not guilty of making photographs'. His appeal failed. The Court of Appeal noted that no definition of the words 'to make' is provided by the Protection of Children Act 1978. In this circumstance the court had to give those words their natural and ordinary meaning, which the court held to be 'to cause to exist; to produce by action, to bring about', quoting from the *Oxford English Dictionary*. The court did not accept that these words were 'ambiguous, obscure or illogical' or that their interpretation would lead to an absurdity. The court preferred the submission of the prosecution that:

> 'A person who either downloads images on to disc or who prints them off is making them. The Act is not only concerned with the original creation of images, but also their proliferation. Photographs ... found on the Internet may have originated from outside the United Kingdom; to download or print within the jurisdiction is to create new material which hitherto may not have existed therein'.[25]

[25.13] It is submitted that the words 'to make' used in the English Act have the same meaning as the word 'produces' used in s 5(1)(a) of the CTPA 1998. The Court of Appeal defined 'to make' as *inter alia* ' to produce by action'. Section 5(1)(a) specifically criminalises any person who 'prints' child pornography. It is submitted that in this context, any person who similarly 'produces' child pornography by reproducing on a computer screen will have committed a similar offence. It remains to be seen whether the Irish courts would consider that the term 'produce' used in s 5(1)(a) of the 1998 has the same meaning as 'make' in the English Act. The initial production of child pornography is criminalised in s 3(1), so if s 5(1)(a) is limited to the initial production of child pornography, it is irrelevant. This may be seen as supporting the view that s 5(1)(a) applies to something other than the initial production of child pornography and, in fact, refers to the production of child pornography by someone who downloads it to their

---

[24]   [2001] QB 88 at 92.
[25]   [2001] QB 88 at 95.

computer screen or prints it out of their printer. In *R v Hamilton*[26] the defendant was a practising barrister who was in the habit of surreptitiously filming up the skirts of women. In order to make these films he would stand in the queues at supermarkets:

> 'Before entering the supermarket he placed his Sony digital camera in a rucksack with the lens hidden and pointing upwards and wedged in position; he disabled the indicator light that would have flashed when he was filming. He manoeuvred the rucksack into a position whereby it was pointed up the inside of a woman's skirt to film her underclothes in the area of her crotch; the camera would automatically focus on what was in the centre of the lens. This was a random method of filming, but he found that one of the best points at which to film was at check out queues where the woman up whose skirt he was filming was more likely to be stationary. This practice is known as "up-skirting".'[27]

Ultimately the police searched the defendant's home and found a large quantity of video material. They were unable to identify the women concerned, but the one of his subjects was:

> 'a schoolgirl who had been filmed wearing a school uniform in the Westgate Leisure Centre in Chichester. She was at the time 14 years and 5 months. The appellant had been confident that she was ... at least 16 years old and had expressed surprise to hear that she was only 14'.[28]

The defendant was also found to have downloaded child pornography from the Internet, which he claimed was accidental. The defendant was tried on charges of both outraging public decency contrary to common law and making indecent photographs of children contrary to the UK's child pornography legislation. The defendant argued that the charges should have been severed as 'there was severe prejudice to the appellant in defending both in the same trial[29]... (and) ... the fact that he had filmed up women's skirts was relevant only to an interest in adult pornography and not to child pornography'.[30] This argument was rejected by the English Court of Appeal, which held that:

> 'In our view the evidence was admissible as it was relevant to the issue of accidental download; as to the difference between an interest in adult and child pornography, that was for the jury to consider when deciding the weight to be attached to the evidence. Furthermore count 10 of the indictment related to filming up the skirt of a schoolgirl and the retention of that film. Although the appellant had denied knowing she was under 16, it was a further common link which enabled the prosecution to contend that the retention of this film was evidence that the jury could use in deciding if the child pornography downloaded from the internet was accidental.'[31]

---

[26]   *R v Hamilton* [2007] EWCA Crim 2026, [2007] All ER (D) 99 (Aug).
[27]   [2007] EWCA Crim 2026, para 5.
[28]   [2007] EWCA Crim 2026, para 7.
[29]   [2007] EWCA Crim 2026, para 45.
[30]   [2007] EWCA Crim 2026, para 47.
[31]   [2007] EWCA Crim 2026, para 48.

Distribute

[25.14] Section 5(2) provides that:

> 'In this section 'distributes', in relation to child pornography, includes parting with possession of it to, or exposing or offering it for acquisition by, another person, and the reference to 'distributing' in that context shall be construed accordingly'.

Given the ease with which electronic material can be copied, it may be unlikely that an individual who willingly possessed child pornography would ever need to part with the electronic possession of it. It is much more likely that child pornography would be distributed by making it available for copying. Child pornography might be exposed or offered for acquisition by others by placing it on a website or making it available through peer-to-peer networks. It is submitted that such activities would fall within the definition of distribution in sub-s 5(2).

[25.15] The reality is that any number of methods can be used to distribute child pornography; it might be offered for rental or sale through a shop or uploaded to an Internet website. In *R v Fellows and Arnold*[32] the first-named defendant, Fellows, was an employee of Birmingham University. He used his employer's computer to store some 1,875 images of child pornography. He made the material available online, using a password system to control access. Only those who provided fresh material to the first-named defendant would get a password; the second-named defendant, Arnold, was one of those who did so. The facts were summarised by the Court of Appeal as follows:

> 'the first appellant created an archive of data stored in the hard disc of the Birmingham computer which was derived from pornographic photographs of children which could be down-loaded by other computers whose operators knew the correct password. The data could be used to create either screen images or documentary print outs which were indistinguishable from the photograph from which it was derived. The second appellant up loaded the computer with data relating to a relatively small number of photographs so that he could obtain the password from the first appellant. He said in his statement that he was not interested in child pornography and had only done this in order to gain access to the rest of the archive'.

[25.16] The Court of Appeal rejected an appeal that 'the data was not ... distributed ... merely by reason of its being made available for what is called down-loading by other computer users'. Anyone who undertook activities similar to Fellows and Arnold could be similarly convicted under the 1998 Act, as anyone who uploads child pornography to an Internet website or other resource could probably be convicted of a like offence.

[25.17] Fellows accumulated his archive of child pornography in the 12 months up to April 1994. The child pornographer's need for anonymity and advances in technology have changed the means of distributing child pornography. Changes in technology and increased surveillance and enforcement of the law have changed how pornography is distributed. Jenkins[33] describes a 'typical' example of distributing child pornography as of 2001, which involves a number of steps:

---

[32] *R v Fellows and Arnold* [1996] EWCA Crim 825.

[33] Jenkins, 'Beyond tolerance: child pornography online' (2001) New York University Press.

'First, he obtains a proxy that contains his name and location and acquires a new email account under a false name from an anonymous provider, likely in a third world nation ... With these bogus credentials, he opens an account that permits him to set up a home page on an innocent and aboveboard public server ... Unknown to the provider ... (he) ... now loads ... photographs or videos featuring illegal child porn materials ... .Still the site is of no use to anyone as yet, in that nobody is likely to stumble across it by accident.'[34]

What Jenkins suggests would then happen is that the distributor would place a link to his site on one of the BBS boards frequented by those interested in child pornography.

'The hypothetical individual now announces the posting of the series on the ... board ... where the message is read and acknowledged gratefully ... consumers then flock to the site advertised ... and they download the pictures. The images exist at that site only for a few hours before they are removed and the site ceases to exist'.[35]

[25.18] This is a much more complex process than the one described in *R v Fellows and Arnold*. The material in question will criss-cross different jurisdictions, complicating any possible prosecution. However, the above description may well be out of date as child pornographers embrace newer forms of communication such as file-sharing software and P2P networks. As Jenkins states:

'In addition to ... (existing) ... methods of clandestine distribution, the ... (child pornography) ... subculture watches keenly for new technologies that might enhance security and secrecy ... A file-sharing system, Freenet represents a sizable advance over existing technologies ... The total anonymity of distributed or peer-to-peer system offers the prospect of "near-perfect anarchy" .'[36]

Peer-to-peer networks pose a very serious challenge for enforcement of the 1998 Act and may require the gardaí to adopt new investigative techniques. Other technologies, such as Internet Relay Chat, may also pose a problem. However, it remains to be seen whether new distribution technologies will force the revision of the 1998 Act itself. The question must remain open at present. Distribution is distribution, however it is done. There may be a substantial technological difference between posting child pornography on a website and making it available over a peer-to-peer network, but legally both are forms of distribution.

[25.19] In *R v Dooley*[37] the appellant's home had been searched by the police. His computer had been seized and 'many thousands of indecent photographs of children'.[38] were found to be on it. Many of these photographs had been downloaded using the KaZaA file-sharing program (see para **5.22**). The English Court of Appeal described the functioning of this program as follows:

'KaZaA is a peer-to-peer file-sharing network that enables Internet users to share any type of computer file. Users become part of a network of other KaZaA members worldwide by downloading the necessary software from the Internet. All members have a 'My shared

---

[34] Jenkins, pp 68–69.

[35] Jenkins, pp 68–69.

[36] Jenkins, pp 79–80.

[37] *R v Dooley* (2006) 1 WLR 775.

[38] (2006) 1 WLR 775 at 777.

folder' which contains files which, when the computer is connected to the Internet, can be accessed by any KaZaA member. At any one time, there may be in excess of four million KaZaA members connected to the system.

KaZaA effectively functions as an enormous 'library' with its contents stored on the computers of all its active members at any one time. A member wishing to find a particular type of file will enter a term into a search engine, which is part of the software. KaZaA will then search the 'My shared folders' of all members currently connected to the Internet and provide a list of matching files. The person searching can then select a file and download to his 'My shared folder'. Unless it is moved from their 'My shared folder' it becomes part of the 'stock' of the 'library' and can in turn be accessed by the other members. There is a facility for making the 'My shared folder' inaccessible to others, but the defendant appears to have been unaware of it'.[39]

[25.20] The appellant's argument was that the downloading of material by KaZaA would have taken many days. The appellant argued that he only intended to download the photographs in question, not to make them available to others and that 'it was his "specific intention" to remove the photograph or image from the 'My shared folder' to some other part of his computer, where it could not be seen by others'.[40] However, the appellant did not get around to doing so. It would seem that the facts in *R v Dooley* would amount to an offence under the CTPA 1998. CTPA 1998 makes it an offence to distribute child pornography. It defines distributing as including 'exposing or offering it for acquisition by, another person'.

Leaving an item of child pornography in a shared folder, where it could be accessed and shared on a network such as KaZaA would seem to fall within this definition. The child pornography would be distributed simply by leaving it in a shared folder where other persons on that particular KaZaA network could access it. This is illustrated by the facts in *R v Humphreys*[41] where 'someone using the name 'A-Z-Z-Y' was monitored on the internet using the KaZaa peer-to-peer file sharing network'.[42] The defendant's home was searched and it was found that the defendant had downloaded and stored two images of child pornography on the hard drives of two computers. He pleaded guilty, but entered the following plea in mitigation:

> 'The Defendant accepts that he downloaded large quantities of material from the internet, including pornography and that included amongst the pornography downloaded there were unlawful child images. However these images were not what he was seeking to download/obtain/view … He deleted some such images when he encountered them but accepted that some … were not deleted … Although it was not the subject of a count or a charge he denied that he had visited specifically child pornography websites … He believes that the traces of these found on his computer are unsolicited pop-ups that may have appeared when visiting other websites whether pornographic, music or software related.'[43]

---

[39]   2006) 1 WLR 775 at 776–777.
[40]   (2006) 1 WLR 775 at 777.
[41]   *R v Humphreys* [2006] EWCA Crim 640. See also *R v Murphy* [2007] EWCA Crim 1609.
[42]   [2006] EWCA Crim 640, para 5.
[43]   [2006] EWCA Crim 640, para 7.

The defendant's guilty plea was accepted by the Court. He appealed against sentence and his appeal was partially successful. What makes P2P networks different from more conventional forms of distribution is that every user of the network becomes involved in the distribution of the material. That is how the software works; all data on the P2P network is available to all. Where a request is made for a particular piece of data, such as an image of child pornography, the software will distribute that data from the most convenient location. So a person who joins a P2P network to download pornography will also become a distributor as well as a possessor of child pornography. P2P networks will make them commit two offences instead of one. In the English case of *R v Rooke*[44] the UK police were alerted by their UK counterparts that a UK resident had published the following advertisement on the Internet:

'I have a young daughter available for your pleasure. I'm only interested in a swop for somebody else's daughter, niece or granddaughter. Please send me a pic of your girl and brief description of her experiences. I will reply with photo and description too.'[45]

In response the UK police 'searched the Appellant's home and recovered a computer ... also discovered two photographic images which had been printed off the computer and which showed sexual abuse of young girls'.[46] The contents of the appellant's computer were analysed and a large amount of child pornography was recovered including two images and two video files of the most serious kind. The appellant was interviewed and he:

'admitted downloading indecent photographs of children and that the material was automatically available for distribution.'

The appellant pleaded guilty to charges including those of 'distributing indecent photographs of a child'. He was sentenced to a total of 15 months imprisonment, which was upheld on appeal. The English Court of Appeal noted that the appellant:

'had distributed the material to other users. He had software on his computer called peer to peer, which automatically exchanged the images with others without having to surf the net to look for the material and he used this automatic software to exchange images.'[47]

The English Court of Appeal noted that the appellant's behaviour exhibited a number of aggravating features. One was the age of the children depicted in the material recovered, another was:

'the sophisticated means of collection and distribution of the images by the Appellant's participation in internet paedophile newsgroups to advertise his wares and access those of others and by the use of peer to peer software which amounted to a form of trading.'[48]

Similarly in the decision of the US Court of Appeal for the 10th Circuit in *US v Robinson*[49] the defendant 'used a computer file-sharing program called "KaZaA" to

---

[44] *R v Rooke* [2005] EWCA Crim 832.
[45] [2005] EWCA Crim 832, para 2.
[46] [2005] EWCA Crim 832, para 3.
[47] [2005] EWCA Crim 832, para 5.
[48] [2005] EWCA Crim 832, para 11.
[49] *US v Robinson* (8th February 2006) US Ct of Apps (10th Cir).

download graphic image files 'by searching the Internet to find other "KaZaA" users who had graphic image files depicting minors engaged in sexually explicit conduct'. These images were downloaded to the defendant's folder of files that were available to be shared on KaZaA: 'immediately ... available to any individual who was using the "KaZaA" program on a computer and who searched the Internet using certain search terms associated with the graphic image files contained in [his] "KaZaA" shared folder'. The defendant pleaded guilty, was convicted and sentenced on the basis that he had engaged in the trafficking of these images'. A sentence of almost 7 years (80 months) was imposed. The defendant sought to challenge this sentence. He argued that he should have been sentenced on the basis that he possessed the images not that he was trafficking them. However, his appeal failed.

Print

[25.21] The inclusion of print in s 5(1)(a) explicitly applies to the printing of child pornography. This may not have been strictly necessary[50], but does ensure clarity.

Publish

[25.22] There is a constitutional right to publish information. In *AG v Brandon Book Publishers*[51] Carroll J held that:

> 'Article 40, s 6, sub-s. 1 guarantees liberty for the exercise of the right of citizens to express freely their convictions and opinions subject to public order and morality. In the expansion of that, the Article refers to the organs of public opinion *preserving their rightful liberty of expression* provided it is not used to undermine public order or morality or the authority of the State. There is no question of public order or morality or the authority of the State being undermined here. Therefore in my opinion there is *prima facie* a constitutional right to publish information'.[52]

Clearly child pornography will raise issues of both pubic order and morality, so it is unlikely that any constitutional right to publish could be successfully invoked to protect it.

[25.23] Unlike 'distribute', the term 'publish' is not defined by CTPA 1998. The term 'publishing' did appear in s 8 of the Copyright Act 1963, however, the Copyright Act 2000 replaced this right with new rights such as the distribution right and the making available right. There is an argument to be made that, taken together, the effect of 'publish' and 'distribute' in s 5(1)(a) of the 1998 Act is to create an offence of making child pornography available, whether to individual third parties or the public in general. Section 23(5) of the Criminal Justice (Public Order) Act 1994 defines 'publish' as meaning 'publish to the public or a section of the public'.

---

[50] As mentioned above, in *R v Bowden* the defendant admitted that he 'printed out photographs from the images he had downloaded' from the Internet and the English Court of Appeal held that in doing so he made child pornography.

[51] *AG v Brandon Book Publishers* [1986] IR 597.

[52] [1986] IR 597 at 600.

[25.24] In the English case *R v Perrin*[53] the defendant appealed a conviction for publication of an obscene article. The publication was a webpage, the contents of which were described by the Court of Appeal as follows:

> 'The obscene article in question was a web page on the internet ... an officer with the Obscene Publications Unit, in the course of his duties ... used a computer to access the web page which he found at an identified site. ... That web page ... was in the form of a trailer, a preview, available free of charge to any one with access to the internet. Any one wanting more of the type of material which it displayed could click on to a link marked 'subscription to our best filthy sites.' The officer did that, and provided his name, address and credit card details. He was then given access to a further web page.'

The defendant appealed against his conviction for publishing an obscene article on the basis that 'the preview page would not be visited by accident. To reach it a viewer would have to type in the name of the site, or conduct a search for material of the kind displayed'.[54] The Court of Appeal rejected this argument commenting that 'The publication relied on in this case is the making available of preview material to any viewer who may choose to access it (including of course vulnerable young people)'.[55]

[25.25] The defendant's appeal against both conviction and sentence was dismissed. The Court of Appeal had reference to its previous judgment in *R v Waddon.*[56] In that case the police accessed a website entitled 'xtreme-perversion'. The defendant conceded that he was involved both in the transmission of material to a website in the USA and its transmission back to England. The Court of Appeal held that it was not the case that there could only be publication once, but that numerous publications could take place. There may be publication on a web site abroad when images are uploaded and there can be further publication when the images are downloaded elsewhere. As Kennedy LJ commented in *R v Perrin* 'it is clear from the decision of this court in *Waddon* ... that there is publication ... both when images are uploaded and when they are downloaded'.[57]

[25.26] So the publication takes place in the jurisdiction where the images are downloaded or uploaded. In *R v Perrin* it was submitted by the defendant that 'an Internet publisher should only be prosecuted, if at all, in the country where the major steps in relation to publication could be shown by the prosecution to have taken place'. The defendant was relying upon a judgment of the US Third District Court of Appeal in *ACLU v Reno (No 3).*[58] He submitted that this judgment was to the effect that:

> 'any court or jury asked to consider whether there has been publication by a defendant of a web page which is obscene should be instructed to consider first where the major steps in relation to publication took place, and only to convict if satisfied that those steps took place within the jurisdiction of the court'.[59]

---

[53] *R v Perrin* [2002] EWCA Crim 747.
[54] [2002] EWCA Crim 747, para 17.
[55] [2002] EWCA Crim 747, para 22.
[56] *R v Waddon* (6 April 2000, unreported) CA (Eng), see Masons CLR, October 2000, p 38.
[57] *R v Perrin* [2002] EWCA Crim 747, para 20.
[58] *ACLU v Reno (No 3)* [2000] 217 F 3d 162 at 168–169.
[59] Per Kennedy LJ in *R v Perrin* [2002] EWCA Crim 747 at para 33.

The prosecution argued that to adopt the defendant's view would 'lead to publishers taking their major steps in countries with the most relaxed laws, but such countries might also have little interest in prosecuting, especially if the offensive material was targetted elsewhere'.[60] The Court of Appeal did not consider this argument, but the finding in *Waddon* that there can be multiple publications when uploading and downloading material would seem to be an implicit rejection of the 'major steps of publication' argument.

[25.27] The one difficulty with referencing *Perrin* and *Waddon* in an Irish context is that they were decided in relation to the UK's Obscene Publications Act 1959. Unlike the CTPA 1998 Act, s 1(3) of this defines publish in the following terms: 'a person publishes an article who ... in the case of an article containing or embodying matter to be looked at ... where the matter is data stored electronically, transmits that data'. This definition should not prevent Irish courts referencing *Perrin* and *Waddon,* unless it were to be archaicly and incorrectly suggested that 'publish' in 1998 did not include Internet or electronic publication, which must involve the electronic storage and transmission of data.

Section 5(1)(b): Knowingly imports, exports, sells or shows

[25.28] Given the realities of the Internet, it may be difficult to distinguish this offence from that contained in s 5(1)(a) above. Once child pornography is made available online it is quite likely to be exported or imported. If there is a distinction to be made between sub-s 5(1)(a) and 5(1)(b) it may be that this subsection appears to be focused more upon commercial exploitation of child pornography, such as its import, export or sale.

Import

[25.29] Ireland is, of course, a member of the European Union and it is very important that any restriction on child pornographers should be as rigorously enforced against domestic producers as it is against importers. In *Conegate v Her Majesty's Customs and Excise*[61] consignments of erotic dolls being imported from Germany were seized and forfeiture subsequently ordered. However, the manufacture of such goods was not restricted in the UK. The European Court of Justice ruled that:

> 'although Community law leaves the member-States free to make their own assessments of the indecent or obscene character of certain articles, it must be pointed out that the fact that goods cause offence cannot be regarded as sufficiently serious to justify restrictions on the free movement of goods where the member-State concerned does not adopt, with respect to the same goods manufactured or marketed within its territory, penal measures or other serious and effective measures intended to prevent the distribution of such goods in its territory ... It follows that a member-State may not rely on grounds of public morality in order to prohibit the importation of goods from other member-States when its legislation contains no prohibition on the manufacture or marketing of the same goods on its territory'.[62]

---

[60] [2002] EWCA Crim 747, para 51.
[61] *Conegate v Her Majesty's Customs and Excise* (1986) 1 CMLR 739.
[62] (1986) 1 CMLR 739 at 753 at para 15. The judgment was subsequently applied in the English courts in *R v Bow Street Magistrate* (1990) 1 QB 123.

[25.30] So Ireland can restrict the importation of child pornographic materials, but only to the extent that the production, publication and distribution of those materials is restricted domestically. The offence of knowingly importing child pornography under s 5(1)(a) of the 1998 Act can be compared to s 186 of the Customs Consolidation Act 1866 which provides that an offence will be committed by 'Every person who shall ... be ... in any way knowingly concerned in any fraudulent evasion or attempt at evasion ... of the laws and restrictions ... relating to the importation ... and delivery of goods'.

A somewhat similarly worded UK provision[63] was recently reviewed by the House of Lords In *R v Forbes*.[64] The defendant was stopped at Heathrow Airport in possession of two video films falsely labelled as 'Spartacus' and 'The Godfather Part 2'. Upon investigation these videos were found to in fact, contain child pornography. The appellant claimed that he had gone to Amsterdam for a break and he met a man in a bar who asked him to bring two videos into the UK. The appellant thought that the videos were prohibited in the UK, but did not think that they were child pornography. He was charged with fraudulent evasion of the prohibition on the importation of indecent photographic material of children and was convicted. He appealed unsuccessfully to the House of Lords where Hope LJ stated:

'For over 30 years it has been the law in this country that, if the defendant knows that what is on foot is the evasion of a prohibition or restriction and he knowingly takes part in that operation, that is sufficient to justify his conviction even if he does not know precisely what sort of goods are being imported'.

So it may be that a person who smuggles child pornography into the state under the misapprehension that it is, say, videos that do not have a certificate under The Video Recordings Act 1989 might be committing an offence under s 186.

Export

[25.31] In the English case of *Gold Star Publications v DPP*[65] it was suggested that a pornography business that catered exclusively to the export market was not subject to England's Obscene Publications Act 1959. The police raided a warehouse containing magazines which were undoubtedly obscene. The defendant claimed that the articles (150,000 in all) were bound for Europe and the USA. This gave rise to a question of law as to whether the Act applied only to material published in England or whether it also applied to material destined for publication abroad. There were two objections to the view that the Act did apply. The first was that of 'moral imperialism or paternalism'. This was rejected by Wilberforce LJ in the House of Lords. He took the view that 'parliament may not want England to become a "flourishing export trade in pornography" and may have thought that profits made by export could help to sustain

---

[63] The UK Customs and Excise Management Act 1979, s 170(2) as amended by the Police and Criminal Evidence Act 1984, s 114(1), which provides 'if any person is, in relation to any goods, in any way knowingly concerned in any fraudulent evasion or attempt at evasion ... of any prohibition or restriction for the time being in force with respect to the goods under or by virtue of any enactment ... he shall be guilty of an offence'.

[64] *R v Forbes* (2002) 2 AC 512.

[65] *Gold Star Publications v DPP* [1981] 2 All ER 257.

the domestic trade'.[66] Furthermore, this objection would prevent the authorities in England from dealing with pornography bound for Scotland and Northern Ireland. Wilberforce LJ considered that this was unlikely to have been the intention of Parliament. The second objection was that if the Act was applied to goods for export, this would make the Act unworkable as English magistrates would be required to assess the likely effect of pornography on foreigners of different attitudes and mores. Wilberforce LJ rejected these arguments and held that a magistrate could so adjudicate on this case and the UK Act did apply to publication outside the jurisdiction of the English courts.

Sell

[25.32] It is a grim reality that child pornography is a profitable part of the $70bn pornography industry, as research undertaken by one UK children's charity concluded:

> 'online child pornography is now big business and the involvement of organised crime in producing and distributing child pornography through the Internet means that yet more children will be abused to create new images for them to sell'.[67]

It would appear that the production and distribution of child pornography is becoming increasingly commercialised. In 2001 Jenkins described what he termed the subculture of child porn in the following terms:

> 'this is a society of deviants united by a common passion, rather than any commercial nexus. There are instance in which money changes hands and videos are sold, but many Web sites that demand payment for access are bogus ... The non-commercial nature of the trade deserves emphasis because so many writers on the topic still make highly inaccurate remarks about the supposedly profitable nature of the trade and its organised crime ties'.[68]

[25.33] By 2003 Taylor and Quayle were becoming less sanguine:

> 'for the moment, we can say that child pornography distribution, and in most cases production, remains a complex international conspiracy not primarily driven by money; but alarmingly it is one in which money seems increasingly to be a factor ... this emphasises the fact that the child involved in this transaction was essentially a commodity ... As far as the distributors are concerned the pornographic material produced is simply a product.'[69]

When child pornography is sold online, it can generate large sums of cash. One child pornogrpahy provider, Landslide Productions, grossed $1.4m in just one month. This company was investigated and taken over by the FBI who identified 35,000 individual subscribers in the USA and 7,200 in the UK.[70] The information passed to the gardaí led to operation Amethyst in which around 80 raids were carried out throughout Ireland. The contrast between these figures and those generated by magazine publishers gives an

---

66 [1981] 2 All ER 257 at 259.
67 NCH, 'Child pornography, child abuse and the Internet' press release, 12 January 2004.
68 Jenkins, 'Beyond Tolerance: child pornography online' (2001) New York University Press, pp 90–91.
69 Taylor and Quayle, *Child Pornography: an Internet Crime* (Brunner-Routledge 2003), p 8.
70 'Calm the witch-hunt' (2004) The Guardian, 18 January.

impression of how the Internet has allowed the upscaling of the commercial child pornography industry. In the 1970s, the 'longest lasting, biggest-selling underground child pornography magazine of the 1970s ... never sold to more than 800 individuals, nor grossed more than $30,000 in a year'.[71]

[25.34] Anyone who purchases child pornography from such a website could be convicted of importing, producing or possessing child pornography. Obviously, if the vendor were within the Irish jurisdiction, they could be convicted of selling child pornography as well as publishing, distributing and showing it. The possible criminal liability of the credit card company which allowed a child pornographer to become an accredited merchant may also be questioned. The reality is that credit card companies such as Visa or Mastercard and the banks that approve merchants and provide them with card facilities are never told that they are working with a child pornographer. One credit card company, for example, employs contractors and software to identify child pornography sites that use its trade mark.[72] If it were not so careful, it might be liable for knowing facilitation of the sale of child pornography pursuant to s 5(1)(d).

[25.35] It would appear to still be more usual for child pornography to be swapped or exchanged without any money changing hands. It is not clear if this amounts to selling the pornography, at first glance it cannot. However, s 3 of the Video Recordings Act 1998 exempts a supply of a video from its provisions that is: 'neither a supply for reward nor a supply in the course or furtherance of a business'. If 'sells' can be defined is including a 'supply for reward', then there is an argument to be made that a person who swaps child pornography with a third party in anticipation of getting child pornography or other services in return, sells that child pornography.

Show

[25.36] In the English case of *R v Fellows and Arnold* it was argued that the first-named defendant was not 'showing' child pornography as it was held on his employer's mainframe computer, that 'showing' is active rather than passive, and that the first appellant did nothing more than permit others, including the second appellant, to have access to his archive'. The Court of Appeal rejected this argument stating that:

> 'As regards the first submission, even if it is accepted, as we are prepared to do for present purposes, that some active conduct on the first appellant's part was necessary, it seems to us that there was ample evidence of such conduct on his part. He took whatever steps were necessary not merely to store the data on his computer but also to make it available world-wide to other computers via the internet. He corresponded by email with those who sought

---

[71] Figure derived from 1980 study, 'Sexual exploitation of children' presented by a special investigative committee of the Illionois State Legislature and quoted in Jenkins, 'Beyond Tolerance: child pornography online' (2001) New York University Press, p 35. By enabling discrete publication to a global audience, the Internet and other technologies have increased the profits of publishers, whilst reducing the cost to the individual purchaser. The contents of a magazine that retailed at $108 in the 1970s and a video that retailed at $215 might be downloaded at no financial cost today, although the user might be expected to barter other material in return. See Ferraro and Casey, *Investigating Child Exploitation and Pornography: The Internet, the law and Forensic Science* (Elsevier Academic Press, 2004) p 11.

[72] (2003) The Guardian, 18 October.

to have access to it and he imposed certain conditions before they were permitted to do so. He gave permission by giving them the password. He did all of this with the sole object of allowing others, as well as himself, to view exact reproductions of the photographs stored in his archive'.

It was further argued that 'where transmission takes place the recipient does not view the material held in the first appellant's archive, but rather a fresh reproduction of new data which is held in the recipient's computer after transmission takes place'. Again this argument was rejected by the Court of Appeal, Evans LJ stating that:

> 'The fact that the recipient obtains an exact reproduction of the photograph contained in the archive in digital form does not mean, in our judgment, that the (copy) photographs in the archive are not held in the first appellant's possession with a view to those same photographs being shown to others. The same data is transmitted to the recipient so that he shall see the same visual reproduction as is available to the sender whenever he has access to the archive himself'.

Therefore *R v Fellows and Arnold* is authority for the proposition that where an image is transmitted over the Internet, that to 'show' the image for the purposes of the 1998 Act.

Section 5(1)(c): Publishes or distributes any advertisement

[25.37] Section 5(1)(c) provides that an offence will be committed by any person who:

> 'knowingly publishes or distributes any advertisement likely to be understood as conveying that the advertiser or any other person produces, distributes, prints, publishes, imports, exports, sells or shows any child pornography'.

In essence this subsection serves to criminalise the advertising of child pornography. Advertisement is not defined by CTPA 1998, so it is not clear whether advertisement refers exclusively to commercial advertising. Where advertising is defined in other legislation, that definition seems dependent upon context. The Planning and Development Act 2000 defines advertisement as: 'any word, letter, model, balloon, inflatable structure, kite, poster, notice, device or representation employed for the purpose of advertisement, announcement or direction'. According to the Medical Preparations (Advertising) Regulations 1993,[73] it is 'the sponsorship of scientific congresses'. There are similar, context-specific, definitions of advertisements and advertising in other legislation. Therefore, it may well be that 'advertisement' in the CTPA 1998 should be interpreted in a similarly context-specific manner. Where child pornography is advertised on the Internet, it will typically take the form of a single line on a BBS telling users that material is available at a specific website. Although highly effective within the sub-culture of child pornographers, this is very different from conventional advertising. However, in the context of child pornogrpahy, it can be argued that it is advertising.

Section 5(1)(d): Encourages, causes or facilitates

[25.38] This provides that an offence will be committed by any person who 'encourages or knowingly causes or facilitates any activity' mentioned in the preceding paragraphs. This sub-section would appear to be effective against two groups: firstly, those who

---

[73]   SI 76/1993.

would actively encourage the production and dissemination of child pornography; and, secondly, those who may facilitate that activity. This subsection could be compared to a statutory offence of conspiracy: anyone who encourages or knowingly facilitates another's production, publication or distribution of child pornography is arguably conspiring to produce child pornography. It would be advantageous to prosecutors to construe this offence as being one of conspiracy, as the actions and statements of a conspirator done or made in pursuance of a conspiracy are admissable against his co-conspirators. In contrast, the general rule is that an act or statement of an accused is only admissable against a co-accused if done or said in his presence.[74] Construing encouragement and facilitation as being part of a conspiracy would clearly benefit the prosecutors of Internet child pornography offences. The Internet child pornography sub-culture allows its members to develop online relationships that are enduring and close without ever being in each other's presence.[75]

Encourages

[25.39] Child pornography is defined as meaning *inter alia* 'any visual or audio representation that advocates, encourages or counsels any sexual activity with children which is an offence under any enactment'.

The sub-culture of child pornographers that has formed on the Internet is described by Jenkins and Taylor and Quayle. There is a not inconsiderable danger that this sub-culture is, by itself, encouraging the production of child pornography. For example, Jenkins quotes a senior member of the sub-culture upbraiding newer members for failing to provide their own material 'its time for all the ... (new members) ... to learn to get some new material, pics, vids, whatever, buy a digital camera or a camcorder do some home-mades and post to some site ... don't be shy, get snapping and contributing'.[76]

Overt encouragement such as the above will plainly be an offence under this provision. However, more subtle forms of encouragement may also offend. Taylor and Quayle express the concern that:

> 'child pornography on the Internet has important functions other than simply sexual arousal. It is at the center of the sexual exploitation of children on the Internet, and it facilitates a number of important social processes. Perhaps the greatest source of concern is that the social engagement on the Internet around and with child pornography both de-sensitises and normalises adult sexual issues in children. What might have been a personal fantasy becomes less fantastic and more real through social engagement around these issues ...
>
> The Internet ... seems to serve for some people as a stepping-stone to other forms of abuse. Normalisation processes, which allow of open discussion of kinds and methods of sexual exploitation of children, for example, presumably contribute to this'.[77]

---

[74] Charleton, McDermott, and Bolger, *Criminal Law* (Tottel Publishing, 1999) para 4.122, p 323.

[75] 'Not only do participants never meet, but the mere suggestion that they ever could (outside a police cell) is greeted with derision', in Jenkins, 'Beyond Tolerance: child pornography online' (2001) New York University Press, p 89.

[76] Jenkins, p 95.

[77] Jenkins, p 200.

Anything that normalises child pornography may subtly encourage offences under s 5(a), (b) and (c) and as such may be an offence under (d). It should be noted that there is no requirement under section 5(1)(d) that the encouragement be given 'knowingly'.

[25.40] The prohibition on encouraging the production, publication or distribution of child pornography contained in s 5(1)(d) reinforces the definition of child pornography in s 2 of CTPA 1998. This defines child pornography as meaning 'any visual or audio representation that advocates, encourages or counsels any sexual activity with children'. So any individual who advocates, encourages or counsels sexual activity with children could be charged under any of the offences under CTPA 1998. However, it is suggested that the offence contained in s 5(1)(d) of encouraging 'any activity' mentioned in subsections (a),(b) and (c) of s 5(1), is the most appropriate offence under which to charge an individual who encourages the abuse of a child for the purpose of producing child pornography.

Facilitates

[25.41] Section 5(1)(d) provides that an offence will be committed by any person who 'knowingly causes or facilitates any activity mentioned' in subsections (a),(b) and (c) of s 5(1). This sub-section has the effect of greatly expanding the pool of persons who may be liable pursuant to CTPA 1998. It has the effect of requiring any person who comes into knowledge that another is engaging in any of the activities prohibited by those subsections to contact the gardaí. If they fail to do so, then the argument can be made that they are knowing, causing or facilitating the illegal conduct. This places employers and service providers under not inconsiderable pressure to contact the gardaí in the event that they come into the knowledge that one of their employees or customers is using their systems to produce, publish or distribute child pornography. Arguably, CTPA 1998 does not require employers or ISPs to take reasonable steps upon making such a discovery. They either disconnect the person they suspect has committed an offence and contact the gardaí or they commit an offence themselves. Given the extraordinary opprobrium within which child pornographers are held, particularly in Ireland, it is unlikely that many will be willing to take a chance.

[25.42] It remains for the courts to decide the extent to which employers or others must act reasonably if they are to avoid liability under this section. This is a particularly pertinent question for one group of service providers: the credit card companies who enable commercial child pornographers to generate their profits.

> 'the creation of an offence under which a bank or card organisation and their director are liable if involved in such a transaction, with a burden on them to show that they had taken reasonable steps to prevent it, would virtually destroy one of the world's most deplored industries.'[78]

Arguably, s 5(1)(d) of the CTPA 1998 is such an offence. To suggest a hypothetical example: imagine that a commercial child pornography site were discovered operating within the jurisdiction; once the prosecution could establish that the site was using credit

---

[78] (2003) The Guardian, 18 October.

cards to process payments, it would then fall to the credit card companies in question to prove that they had no knowledge that their systems were being used in this way.

Section 5(1)(e): Possesses for purposes of distributing, publishing, exporting, selling or showing

[25.43] Section 5(1)(e) provides that a person will commit an offence who 'knowingly possesses any child pornography for the purpose of distributing, publishing, exporting, selling or showing it'.

So while mere possession of child pornography is punishable by a maximum sentence of five years' imprisonment, possession for the purpose of distributing, publishing, exporting, selling or showing child pornography is punishable by a maximum term of 14 years. However, the imposition of this lengthier sentence is dependent upon the purpose or intent of a defendant being proven. Charleton has suggested that:

> 'Intent necessarily involves a conscious child to bring about a particular state of affairs ... Intent is not recklessness ... Intent is present where the purpose of the accused is to engage in conduct ... or to achieve a result'.[79]

Smith and Hogan summarise the English case law as meaning that: a result is intended when it is the defendant's purpose; a court may also infer that a result is intended, though it is not desired, when the result is a virtually certain consequence of the act and the defendant knows that it is a virtually certain consequence.[80] So a person who possesses child pornography for the purposes of uploading it to the Internet may fall foul of this provision. A virtually certain consequence of uploading child pornography to the Internet is that others will download it, so distributing, publishing and exporting it.

Section 6: Possession

[25.44] Section 6(1) provides that 'any person who knowingly possesses any child pornography shall be guilty of an offence'.

A person convicted of possessing child pornography is liable on summary conviction to a fine not exceeding £1,500 (€1,905) or to imprisonment for a term not exceeding 12 months or both, or on conviction on indictment to a fine not exceeding £5,000 (€6,349) or to imprisonment for a term not exceeding 5 years or both. This offence is stated to be without prejudice to the offence created by s 5(1)(e) which criminalises possession of child pornography for what might be termed commercial purposes: 'distributing, publishing, exporting, selling or showing it'. The difference between the two offences is the penalty, possession for commercial purposes carries a maximum prison sentence almost three times the length of that under this section together with an unlimited fine.

[25.45] In one Irish case it was suggested at a procedural hearing that the child pornography in question was downloaded in clusters and that 'There was no evidence that all the images were actually seen by the defendant'.[81] However, the question of whether or not an image is actually viewed by a defendant may be irrelevant since it is

---

[79] Charleton, *Offences Against the Person* (The Round Hall Press, 1992), quoted in Charleton, McDermott and Bolger, *Criminal Law* (Tottel Publishing, 1999) para 1.73.

[80] Smith and Hogan, *Criminal Law* (8th edn, LexisNexis Butterworths, 1996), p 58.

[81] (2003) The Irish Times 9 April.

possession, and not the viewing or hearing of child pornography, that is criminalised. In the same way, viewing or hearing child pornography is not an offence.

[25.46] It would appear that possession of a single item of child pornography is sufficient for a conviction on a charge of possession, even where that single item is held in a shop full of legal pornography. In *R v Matrix*[82] the defendant worked in a sex shop in Soho, London. The shop specialised in the sale and rental of video cassettes for those of 'different sexual orientations'. The police raided the shop and found three copies of a video, that showed young boys engaged in sexual activities. The defendant was convicted of possession and appealed to the English Court of Appeal. Swinton-Thomas LJ distilled the following propositions relating to possession from a review of the case law, particularly that relating to the possession of drugs[83]:

> 'First of all a man does not have possession of something which has been put into his pocket or into his house without his knowledge: in other words something which is 'planted' on him, to use the current vulgarism. Secondly, a mere mistake as to the quality of a thing under the defendant's control is not enough to prevent him being in possession. For instance, if a man in possession of heroin, believing it to be cannabis or believing it perhaps to be aspirin'.

[25.47] Swinton-Thomas LJ held that the second proposition was particularly relevant to the case before him as:

> 'There is no suggestion in this case that the videos had been planted on this appellant. There was no question, for instance, of them being hidden in a safe unknown to him. They were behind the counter, and the appellant knew they were there. One had been sold that day.
>
> The position ... is much more akin, in our judgment, to the person who has in his possession heroin believing it, for example, to be aspirin'.

He noted that 'each case depends very much upon its own facts' and went on to conclude that:

> 'the appellant was in sole charge of this shop, taking on the role of the manager. It was conceded that he had taken possession of stock in the shop. He did not suggest that he was unaware of the presence of these videos in the shop or that the offending video had in any way been planted on him in the way in which it is sometimes alleged in cases concerning drugs. His contention was that he was unaware that the offending video contained explicit sexual material relating to underage boys. It was, as we have indicated, a shop selling explicit material ... .In our judgment ... . this video was plainly in his possession.'

[25.48] A few months before its decision in *R v Matrix* the Court of Appeal abruptly dismissed an appeal partially grounded on a claim that the defendant, the 'front-man' for an illegal hardcore video store, 'could not be said to be aware that he was dealing with obscene videos' in *R v Pace*.[84] Like *Matrix,* although the appellant was in control of a shop full of hardcore videos, he was only convicted in respect of a single item of child

---

[82] *R v Matrix* [1997] EWCA Crim 2058 (4 August 1997).
[83] *Warner* (1968) 52 Cr App R 373; *James McNamara* (1988) 87 Cr App R 246.
[84] *R v Pace* [1997] EWCA Crim 1279 (20 May 1997).

pornography. More recently, in *R v Collier,*[85] the appellant's home was raided and searched by the police, who seized a number of video tapes, which:

'contained films of homosexual adult pornography which ran for between one hour 18 and one hour 49 minutes each. Following the films there were trailers of a duration between two minutes to ten minutes advertising films involving young boys. Those trailers showed male children engaging in sexually explicit acts whilst naked'.[86]

At trial the appellant conceded that he was in possession of the tapes and that he knew them to contain indecent material.[87] However, the English Court of Appeal ruled that the appellant should have been allowed to assert the defence 'that he had not seen the indecent photograph of a child alleged in the charge against him and nor had he any cause to suspect it to be an indecent photograph of a child'.[88]

[25.49] There are no decisions in Ireland, that are equivalent to those in *Matrix* and *Pace* in respect of child pornography, or the other decisions of the English Courts in respect of possession of drugs. However, Charleton does suggest that:

'With most articles and substances their nature is apparent from their appearance. A gun looks like a gun. On occasion, however, substances such as controlled drugs may resemble innocent household items. Whilst this issue has never been directly dealt with by the Irish Courts, it seems consistent with the approach in *The People (DPP) v Murray*[89] that before guilt can be established in respect of an illicit substance or outlawed thing, the prosecution should be able to infer recklessness or knowledge as to the nature of the substance from the facts. However, where a person has no knowledge or suspicion of the nature of the object in their possession, it is, it is submitted, contrary to constitutional principles of fairness to render them criminally liable'.[90]

If a case with facts equivalent to those in *Matrix* should come before the Irish courts, it is quite possible that a decision would be reached that would be similar to those of the English Court of Appeal. In *Matrix* the defendant was managing video shops that contained explicit sexual video cassettes. The fact that the video in respect of which he was convicted was held behind the counter might well be enough to enable the prosecution to infer recklessness or even knowledge of the nature of the contents of that video, as Charleton suggests is required. The decisions in *Matrix* and *Pace* make clear that possession of even a single item of child pornography amongst a host of other material may be sufficient to ensure conviction.

[25.50] The meaning of possession was examined by the English Court of Appeal in *R v Porter.*[91] The facts were that:

'the police raided the appellant's house and seized some hard drives and two computers ... which were linked to the internet almost permanently. The appellant worked in the field of

---

[85] *R v Collier* (2005) 1 WLR 843.
[86] (2005) 1 WLR 843 at 844.
[87] (2005) 1 WLR 843 at 846.
[88] (2005) 1 WLR 843 at 846.
[89] *The People (DPP) v Murray* [1977] IR 360.
[90] Charleton, McDermott and Bolger, *Criminal Law* (Tottel Publishing, 1999), para 5.27, p 360.
[91] *R v Porter* [2006] EWCA 560.

information technology and had built two computers. 3575 still images and 40 movie files of child pornography were recovered from the hard disk drives of the two computers'[92].

None of this material was readily available. Some of it was retrieved from the computers' recycle bins, other material was retrieved from temporary Internet files.[93] The defendant argued that:

> 'a person does not commit the offence of possession of indecent photographs or pseudo-photographs on the hard disk drive of his computer unless the images are 'readily accessible to the accused for viewing at the time when they are said to be possessed, or capable of being made so accessible without the need to obtain additional specialist software.'[94]

[25.51] The English Court of Appeal considered that it offended common sense to say that the appellant was in possession of some 2700 thumbnail images, which the police had only been able to recover using specialist equipment supplied by the US Government.[95] The prosecution conceded this point. As regards the other deleted images, the Trial Judge had summed up the law as follows:

> 'the mere fact that an image is on a deleted file, rather than an active file, does not mean that the user is not in possession, because the file deleted or not, is one of the files he had on a hard disk which was in his possession, was his computer and his hard disk.'[96]

The English Court of Appeal was unhappy with such an approach and felt that it was appropriate to import the concept of 'custody or control' of the images in question. In the specific context of deleted images, the court suggested that:

> 'if a person cannot retrieve or gain access to an image, in our view he no longer has custody or control of it. He has put it beyond his reach just as does a person who destroys or otherwise gets rid of a hard copy photograph. For this reason, it is not appropriate to say that a person who cannot retrieve an image from the hard disk drive is in possession of the image because he is in possession of the hard disk drive and the computer'[97].

[25.52] It is possible that child pornography may be placed in the computer of an individual without their knowledge. One such circumstance is where a malicious computer program sometimes referred to as a Trojan has placed the information on their system. This defence was successfully raised in the English case of *Julian Greene*.[98] The defendant was arrested after his home was searched and 172 images of child pornography were found on his hard drive. His solicitor engaged a computer forensics expert, who found 11 Trojan horse type programs on this computer. These programs were set to log onto 'inappropriate sites' without the defendant's permission. The prosecution was dropped once the expert's report was produced. A similar defence

---

92 [2006] EWCA 560, para 3.
93 [2006] EWCA 560, para 4-6.
94 [2006] EWCA 560, para 9.
95 [2006] EWCA 560, para 17.
96 [2006] EWCA 560, para 8.
97 [2006] EWCA 560, para 21.
98 See http//www.theregister.co.uk: 'Suspected Paedophile cleared by computer forensics' 28 October 2003.

succeeded at trial in the case of *Karl Schofield.*[99] It would seem that there are a number of malicious programs in existence that will download images of child pornography, without the knowledge or consent of the user. One such program is CWS, of a type known as a Browser hijacker. Programs such as these will change browser settings, altering designated default start and search pages. They will also produce pop-up adverts for pornography and add bookmarks, some of which may link to child pornography. Removing such programs can prove extremely difficult, and even if the program is removed, the child pornography it has downloaded may remain.[100] So it is quite possible that child pornography can be downloaded without the knowledge or consent of the user. However, every case will depend upon its facts, and much may depend upon the quality of the expert evidence that is furnished to the court.

[25.53] In *People (DPP) v Byrne*[101] the considered that the Oireachtas would intend, at least with regard to the possession of drugs contrary to The Misuse of Drugs Act 1977,[102] to:

'avoid the injustice of a person being convicted solely because he is in possession of the drugs, where it is clear that he did not know and had not any reason to suspect that he had drugs in his possessi[103]on'.

[25.54] In *R v Porter* the Court of Appeal suggested the following:

'Suppose that a person receives unsolicited images of child pornography as an attachment to an email. He is shocked by what he sees and immediately deletes the attachment and deletes it from the recycle bin. Suppose further that he knows that the images are retrievable from the hard disk drive, but he believes that they can only be retrieved and removed by specialists who have software and equipment which he does not have. It does not occur to him to seek to acquire the software or engage a specialist for this purpose. So far as he is concerned, he has no intention of ever seeking to retrieve the images and he has done all that is reasonably necessary to make them irretrievable. We think that it would be surprising if Parliament had intended that such a person should be guilty of an offence.'[104]

It should be noted that there is no offence of facilitating the production of child pornography. An employer who discovered that one of his employees was storing child pornography on the employer's computer system could not be guilty of knowing facilitation. The employer could only be liable if he knew that his employee was using the employer's system to produce, publish or distribute child pornography and did nothing about it.

---

[99] See http//www.theregister.co.uk: 'Trojan Defence clears man on child porn charges' 24 April 2003.

[100] See http//www.wired.com: 'Nasty malware fouls PCs with Porn' 30 April 2004 and 'Browser hijackings ruining lives' 11 May 2004.

[101] *People (DPP) v Byrne* [1998] 2 IR 417.

[102] Misuse of Drugs Act 1977, s 29.

[103] *People (DPP) v Byrne* [1998] 2 IR 417 at 434.

[104] *R v Porter* [2006] EWCA 560, para 18.

Defences

[25.55] Section 6 provides a small number of limited exceptions to offences relating to the production, possession and distribution of child pornography:

'(2) Section 5(1) and subsection (1) shall not apply to a person who possesses child pornography—

(a) in the exercise of functions under the Censorship of Films Acts 1923 to 1992, the Censorship of Publications Acts, 1929 to 1967, or the Video Recordings Acts, 1989 and 1992, or

(b) for the purpose of the prevention, investigation or prosecution of offences under this Act.

(3) Without prejudice to subsection (2), it shall be a defence in a prosecution for an offence under section 5(1) or subsection (1) for the accused to prove that he or she possessed the child pornography concerned for the purposes of bona fide research'.

No statutory exceptions are provided in CTPA 1998 to offences relating to the taking and use of children in the production of child pornography under s 3 or allowing a child to be used for the purposes of producing child pornography under s 4.

[25.56] Only a very limited number of persons will be able to benefit from the exception contained in s 6(2). This section provides for two exceptions, the first of which relates to those who may possess pornography as part of their jobs. Specifically possession 'in the exercise of functions under the Censorship of Films Acts, 1923 to 1992, the Censorship of Publications Acts, 1929 to 1967, or the Video Recordings Acts, 1989 and 1992' or possession 'for the purpose of the prevention, investigation or prosecution of offences under this Act'.[105] Clearly only a very limited number of persons will be able to benefit from this provision. Merely because a person is a member of one of the Censorship Boards or a member of An Garda Síochána will not give them *carte blanche* to possess child pornography at will. In 2002 a former garda sergeant was sentenced to three years imprisonment.[106] The sergeant had paid a prostitute to find a seven-year old child for sex, however the prostitute herself contacted the gardaí. Once the sergeant was identified, his home was raided where two computers were seized, one of which contained images of child pornography. The other had a number of images deleted but investigating gardaí were able to access various child pornography websites that the accused had visited. The fact that he was a garda did not afford him any excuse when the case came to trial, as he was not in possession of the material for the purpose of preventing, investigating or prosecuting any offences.

Bona fide research

[25.57] At first glance a broader defence is created by s 6(3), which provides that 'it shall be a defence in a prosecution for an offence under s 5(1) or subsection (1) for the accused to prove that he or she possessed the child pornography concerned for the purposes of bona fide research'. However, the key phrase in the above exemption is 'bona fide research'. Only a very limited number of persons will be able to rely on this

---

[105] CTPA 1998, s 6(2).
[106] http://www.rte.ie/news/2003/0207/ohallorank.html.

exemption. There are circumstances where the viewing of child pornography will be necessary for the purposes of *bona fide* research. But, any researcher about to undertake such research must be very careful to establish their bona fides. The English decision in *Atkins v DPP*[107] is of some assistance here. Although it examines the meaning of the term 'a legitimate reason' for the purposes of the UK Protection of Children Act 1978, it is submitted that in this context this term has a meaning similar to that of '*bona fide*' used in s 5(3) of the 1998 Act.[108]

[25.58] In *Atkins v DPP* the defendant was a lecturer in English at the University of Bristol who was found to have child pornography stored on his office computer. His defence that he was conducting 'honest and straightforward research into child pornography' was rejected at trial. However, a case was stated to the English divisional High Court where this point was considered so that the Courts might have some guidance. Simon Brown LJ stated that:

> 'The question of what constitutes 'a legitimate reason' ... is a pure question of fact ... in each case. The central question, where the defence is legitimate research, will be whether the defendant is essentially a person of unhealthy interests in possession of indecent photographs in the pretence of undertaking research or by contrast a genuine researcher with no alternative but to have this sort of unpleasant material in his possession.'[109]

A few months after the decision in *Atkins* the English Court of Appeal considered a similar defence in *R v Wrigley*.[110] The defendant had just completed a four-year undergraduate degree in Keele University. On 25 July 1995 the police searched the defendant's room and found a large amount of child pornography. There was evidence before the court that the defendant was using the Internet to communicate, swap and discuss these images with two paedophiles based in the USA. The defendant admitted possession of the pornography but again raised the 'legitimate reason' defence. Henry LJ stating that:

> 'The issue here was whether the (defendant) could prove on the balance of probabilities that he had a legitimate reason for possessing the indecent material, namely genuine academic research. His defence was that he was conducting an informal pilot study as to whether there was material for a PhD. This required him to pose as a paedophile while he evaluated the different responses to specific indecent pictures of ... different sorts of paedophile ... The Crown's response to this was that his own reason was to satisfy his own interest in indecent material featuring young boys: in his own words (but, he would say, while posing as a paedophile) 'I love young boys'.[111]

[25.59] The defendant had evidential difficulties: firstly, he had not discussed his proposed research with his University tutors; secondly, he realised that it would be difficult to get permission to use pornographic pictures and, thirdly, after his arrest his

---

[107] *Atkins v DPP* (2000) Cr App R 248.
[108] The UK Protection of Children Act 1978, s 1(4) provides that 'Where a person is charged with an offence ... it shall be a defence for him to prove ... that he had a legitimate for distributing or showing the photographs ... or ... having them in his possession'.
[109] *Atkins v DPP* (2000) Cr App R 248 at 257.
[110] *R v Wrigley* [2000] EWCA Crim 44 (26 May 2000).
[111] [2000] EWCA Crim 44 (26 May 2000), para 9.

tutors advised him to take his research material to the police, but he did not do so. The appellant claimed to have destroyed this material, claiming that he did not want it to fall into the wrong hands. Henry LJ noted that he was referring to the police as 'the wrong hands'. It was the prosecution's case that there was no such research material and that what documents there were had been created after the appellants arrest. Finally, when the appellant was originally arrested he told a totally different story. He had claimed to have been looking at the photographs 'to find out about myself'.[112] When given a chance to say he needed the material for research, he did not say so, subsequently claiming that he did not trust the police.

[25.60] Henry LJ did note that:

> 'there is no doubting (the appellant's) interest in children, nor his academic abilities, nor his interest in the Internet and human response to questions from computers. His suggested PhD study was not strictly speaking relevant to his undergraduate course work, but sufficiently close for academics to take it seriously. The (prosecution's) case was, of course, that this was just a smoke screen to conceal his real prurient interest in young boys'.[113]

The defendant was convicted at trial and an appeal was taken on the basis of an incorrect summing up to the jury. This was rejected by the Court of Appeal, which held that:

> 'the judge made the proper analysis of the statutory defence – namely that the appellant had to prove that his academic reason was his legitimate reason. The crown met that by contending that his sexual interest in small boys was his reason. That was the proper and the clearest way to put the real issue before the jury'.[114]

[25.61] So any student, academic or other person intending to undertake bona fide research that will involve the possession of child pornography should do so in the full realisation that the may face the burden of proving the bona fides of their research. This is likely to prove extremely difficult. Wrigley suggests that anyone intending to undertake bona fide research should put proper protocols in place prior to commencement. The sanction of any relevant University or other institution should be got and it would be a good idea to talk to legitimate interested parties such as An Garda Síochána or fellow academics in advance. It would also seem advisable to keep very complete records of all research undertaken and to make this material available if requested by the gardaí or other legitimate interested parties such as the authorities of the institution to which the researcher is attached. *Atkins* is authority for the view that a bona fide researcher will be someone 'who has no alternative but to have this sort of unpleasant material in his possession'. In considering the alternatives to possessing child pornography, one might consider that Jenkins was required by US law to write a book about the activities of Internet child pornographers without ever viewing child pornography itself.[115]

---

[112] [2000] EWCA Crim 44 (26 May 2000), para 12.

[113] [2000] EWCA Crim 44 (26 May 2000), para 11.

[114] [2000] EWCA Crim 44 (26 May 2000), para 28.

[115] Jenkins, 'Beyond Tolerance: child pornography online' (2001) New York University Press, p 20.

[25.62] In reality only very few academics will have no alternative but to possess child pornography. Some undoubtedly have no alternative, such as the researches working on the COPINE research project at University College Cork. As is made clear in *R v Smehurst*[116] the decision as to what and what is not child pornography is an issue of fact for the judge or jury in a case. As such it is irrelevant to the law. Obviously there are aspects of child pornography that do have relevance to the law, such as its effect on its victims or its tendency to corrupt and deprave its users. However, there is a strong argument to be made that these aspects are best researched by a review of academic literature that analyses those effects without requiring the actual sight or possession of child pornography.[117] That is not to say that there will never be circumstances where a lawyer might legitimately need to view child pornography for the purposes of bona fide research, but any lawyer doing so should be aware that the burden of proving their bona fides is likely to be a heavy one.

'Good Samaritans'

[25.63] The revulsion with which child abusers and pornographers are regarded has meant that individual citizens are willing to take extraordinary steps to identify and expose such activities. In one case, discussed at para **[24.97]** above, a prostitute contacted Bridewell Garda Station to report the suspicious activities of a garda sergeant. The facts in *Atkins* display similar standards of public spirited determination to expose those who use child pornography. The defendant was a lecturer at Bristol University, when child pornography was found on his department's computer. He was then investigated by a fellow staff member and her husband. Anyone who has good reason to suspect that someone they know is producing, publishing or possessing child pornography should report their suspicions to the gardaí. It would be very unwise for an individual to attempt their own investigation. In *R v Calley*[118] the following defence was raised:

> 'the appellant explained how, having acquired a home computer, he had subscribed to the Internet, and it was in those circumstances that he literally came across these various sources of child pornography. During the course of the next six to eight weeks he had – to use the jargon – "downloaded" the images on to the floppy disks which the police had found. He accepted that the material was pornographic, but then went on to explain that he worked as a private investigator – and, indeed, he had done – and that, in an attempt to establish a reputation for himself in that capacity he had proposed to infiltrate a paedophile ring on the pretext of supplying them with material. Having decided that Mr Corble was or may have been a paedophile, he had approached him and invited him to assist him, in the hope that, by that means, he (the appellant) could infiltrate such a ring in the Frinton area. His plan then, given the success he hoped for, was to report the matter to the police, thereby establishing a reputation for himself in his chosen field and further, thereby, creating the possibility of being able to sell his story to the press'.

The defendant's claim to have been investigating child pornography was open to question. The investigation into his own activities commenced after he approached

---

[116] *R v Smehurst* (2002) Cr App R 6.
[117] Such as Taylor and Quayle, *Child Pornography: an Internet Crime* (Brunner-Routledge, 2003).
[118] *R v Calley* [1998] EWCA Crim 3501 (10 December 1998).

another man with child pornography and suggested the possibility of using the child pornography to publish a magazine that would sell for £50 a copy. The defendant was sentenced to 30 months imprisonment.

[25.64] It is submitted that anyone attempting to infiltrate the child pornography sub-culture is taking a serious risk. In order to pose as a paedophile online they may have to make highly incriminating statements such as those made by *Wrigley*: 'I love young boys'.[119] They will also have to swap and possess child pornography. The 1998 Act does contain a clear exception for investigations and prosecutions, but given the nature of the material in question, it is likely that this exception is limited to members of the An Garda Síochána engaged in the discharge of their official duties.

Journalists

[25.65] In *USA v Matthews*[120] the defendant was an award-winning journalist who was convicted for sending and receiving child pornography over the Internet. He admitted trading pornography but claimed that he did so only to research a news story. The defendant had previously run stories on pornography and had contacted the FBI in relation to what he had found. He stated that he was trying to discover whether child prostitution was real or just something people talked about. Matthews set up his own chatroom, but AOL shut it down. Afterwards he logged onto other chatrooms and initiated conversations with persons who identified themselves as minor females. It was somewhat ironic that Matthews was actually talking to FBI Agents at the time. The FBI identified approximately 160 photographs depicting child pornography sent or received by Matthews in or around that time.

[25.66] Several months later the FBI searched Matthew's home. They did not find any child pornography, but nor did they find any of the notes that Matthews might have been expected to retain for his journalistic work. However, Matthews did admit to the FBI that he had traded child pornography over the Internet and he had done so as part of his legitimate journalistic work. He was tried and convicted of offences under the US Protection of Children Against Sexual Exploitation Act. The US 4th District Court of Appeals rejected an appeal based, *inter alia,* on Matthews First Amendment rights as a journalist. As in the UK, the American court concluded that in the absence of a specific exception in the legislation, the defendant's conviction would stand. The 1998 Act contains no exception for journalists, so it must be assumed that any Irish journalist in a similar position to Matthews will be similarly convicted.

Works of art

[25.67] One difficulty with the Act is that it may clash with the legitimate needs of artists. It is not unheard of for legitimate works of art to depict 'the genital or anal region of a child'. However the dominant characteristic of those paintings is not the depiction of those regions for a sexual purpose. A similar issue came before the English Court of Appeal in *R v Smehurst.*[121] The appellant admitted that he had 'made' a set of

---

[119] *R v Wrigley* [2000] EWCA Crim 44 (26 May 2000), para 9.
[120] *USA v Matthews* US 4th CA (13 April 2000).
[121] *R v Smehurst* (2002) Cr App R 6.

photographs of naked young girls which had been downloaded from the Internet and printed as stills. Woolf LJ had regard to the previous decision of the Court of Appeal in *Graham-Kerr* in which the court came to the conclusion that 'if someone deliberately made a photograph ... of a subject, which was considered to be indecent by right-thinking people'[122](then an offence under the Protection of Children Act 1978 was made out. Woolf went on to comment that:

> 'the fact that what is or what is not indecent very much depends upon the judgment of the individual. There can be conduct which some would regard as highly indecent, which others would regard as acceptable ... what is or what is not indecent must be objectively assessed'.

As Woolf rather drily commented 'The difficulty that this appellant is in is that Parliament did not make an exception for his desire to study the female form'.[123]

Family photos

[25.68] The above leaves a large number of situations where visual or aural depictions, which are produced for innocent purposes, will fall within the remit of CTPA 1998. This difficulty was considered by Woolf CJ in *R v Smehurst,* where he discussed the example of a family taking photographs of their children unclothed:

> 'No one could possibly suggest that a family taking photographs of their own children in the ordinary way would be a situation where it would be appropriate to prosecute. However, the difficulty is that the Act is designed to protect children from being exploited. Unless there is a prohibition against the taking of indecent photographs, then there is no way in which children can be protected from being exploited. The balance has been drawn by Parliament ... that balance has the consequence indicated to the appellant, who says that he was acting perfectly innocently in his situation.'[124]

[25.69] Article 41 of the Constitution 'recognises the Family as the natural primary and fundamental unit group of Society'.[125] In *North Western Health Board v HW*[126] it was held that the courts would only intervene 'contrary to the parents' decisions, and consent to procedures for the child, in exceptional circumstances'.[127] The Supreme Court suggested an example of where the courts would intervene as being 'a surgical or medical procedure in relation to an imminent threat to life or serious injury'. Obviously, intervention is permissible where a child is being used in the overt production of child pornography. However, Article 41 means that parents may be allowed greater leeway in the types of photographs that they take of their children than they might be in the UK or elsewhere. Whether this will make any real difference in practice is open to question. As outlined above, the appropriate manner of assessing whether or not an item is

---

[122] (2002) Cr App R 6 at 15.

[123] (2002) Cr App R 6 at 21.

[124] (2002) Cr App R 6 at 21.

[125] Bunreacht na hÉireann, Article 41 provides that the State 'recognises the Family as the natural primary and fundamental unit group of Society, and as a moral institution possessing inalienable and imprescriptible rights, antecedent and superior to all positivelaw'.

[126] *North Western Health Board v HW* [2001] 3 IR 622.

[127] [2001] 3 IR 622 at 727.

pornographic may be to assess whether it was produced or distributed for a sexual purpose. *Fuller* is authority for the view that the purpose is that of the producer or possessor, the child need not know that he or she is being photographed or filmed for a sexual purpose for an offence to be committed. The context within which a photograph is possessed or produced may be important. If the parent or sibling of a child filmed them in the bath (albeit without focusing on their genitalia) in the context of keeping a record of their child similar to filming a birthday party, this might not be an offence. The court might consider that the film was innocent if it were displayed to relatives and grandparents at family functions. The court might take an adverse view if the film were stored on an Internet website and swapped with strangers. Each case will depend upon its facts.

[25.70] Furthermore, the courts may treat an offence as being much more serious if it is perpetrated by a parent or relative upon a child. This would appear to be the intention of the Minister for Justice who introduced the Bill, who rhetorically asked the Dáil the following question 'Is there a worse breach of trust than parents allowing their children to be sexually exploited by others[128]?'

The severity with which the Oireachtas views offences by family members against children is perhaps best illustrated by the statutory prohibition against incest to be found in the Punishment of Incest Act 1908, recently updated by the Criminal Law (Incest Proceedings) Act 1995.

Houses of the Oireachtas

[25.71] The Child Trafficking and Pornography (Amendment) Act 2004 is a companion to the Committees of the Houses of the Oireachtas (Compellability, Privileges and Immunities of Witnesses) (Amendment) Act 2004. The Child Trafficking and Pornography (Amendment) Act 2004 was described as being an Act that 'will permit the Members of the Houses of the Oireachtas, together with any appropriate officials and advisers, to carry out their appropriate functions in circumstances where issues relating to child pornography might be involved'.[129] Section 1 of the Act inserts a new s 13 in CTPA 1998:

'Nothing in this Act prevents—

(a) the giving of or compliance with a direction under s 3 of the Committees of the Houses of the Oireachtas (Compellability, Privileges and Immunities of Witnesses) Act 1997, or

(b) the possession, distribution, printing, publication or showing by either House of the Oireachtas, a committee (within the meaning of that Act) or any person of child pornography for the purposes of, or in connection with, the performance of any function conferred by the Constitution or by law on those Houses or conferred by a resolution of either of those Houses or resolutions of both of them in such a committee.'

---

[128] Dáil Éireann – Volume 489 – 02 April 1998, Child Trafficking and Pornography Bill 1997: Second Stage.

[129] Seanad Éireann debates, 27 May 2004.

Again s 13 should not be seen as conferring a carte blanche on members of the Oireachtas to possesses, distribute, print, publish or show child pornography. The immunity conferred by the section is limited to the discharge of functions conferred by the Constitution or by law.[130]

[130] See the judgment of the Supreme Court in *Curtin v Dáil Éireann* [2006] IESC 14, 9 March 2006.

Chapter 26

Procedure, Evidence and Sentencing

Introduction

[26.01] Child pornography cases are unique. The offence itself is a quite recent creation and it is only very recently that a significant number of child pornography offences have come before the courts. This novelty meant that there are many legal points that have yet to be considered by the courts. The extreme nature of the material that must be at the core of any child pornography prosecution creates its own problems; by its nature it may unfairly prejudice the courts against the accused and disturb those who view it. Therefore, particular care needs to be taken when handling such evidence and when sentencing offenders.

The presentation of evidence

[26.02] Child pornography trials can require judges and juries to examine images of often incomprehensible abuse of small children. Such examination can expose the defendant to a risk of prejudice that is unacceptable in the Irish courts. In *DPP v McC*,[1] Carney J opened his sentencing with the following statement:

> 'The facts of this case have been fully given in evidence and I don't intend to repeat them. The video evidence produced has been so disgusting that I, as the judge of this court who handles up to a 140 cases of this nature every year; couldn't go through with watching ten minutes of it.'

What the judge saw on that video clearly influenced him. He gave the defendant the maximum sentence available to him, which was overturned by the Court of Criminal Appeal. Geoghan J commented that:

> 'It would seem reasonably clear from this introduction that in imposing maximum sentences the judge was influenced by what he actually saw on the video. No view had been expressed by either side at the hearing as to whether the judge should or should not look at the video evidence, the parties leaving it to the judge to decide. In the event, the judge decided that he would look at it but 'after a few minutes indicated that he found it so disgusting that he could look at it no more … the judge was clearly influenced by the part of the video evidence which he did see.'

Given the substantial prejudical effect of viewing child pornography, it would seem prudent to limit that prejudice. Given that child pornography can 'corrupt and deprave' those who view it, it would be naïve to assume that judges, lawyers and jurors will be immune from that corruption and depravity. It is therefore submitted that child pornography evidence must be carefully managed before the Irish courts to avoid these adverse effects.

---

[1]   *DPP v McC* [2003] 3 IR 609.

Categorisation

[26.03] One method of managing child pornography evidence is to categorise it. In *DPP v McC*.[2] Geoghan J noted that the English Court of Appeal in *R v Oliver*[3] had provided five categories of pornographic images based on the 'level of seriousness' involved (see para **[23.09]** for further details).

The decision in *DPP v McC* may be taken as some support for the categorisation of child pornography evidence before it is presented to an Irish court. However, the actual categories set out in *R v Oliver* are open to criticism. The purpose of these categories is to facilitate the imposition of consistent sentencing throughout England and Wales. For example, the English Sentencing Advisory Panel advises that a custody threshold in child pornography cases would be crossed where a person is found in possession of a large amount of level 2 material or a small amount of level 3. This standardised approach to sentencing was rejected by the Irish Supreme Court in *DPP v Tiernan*.[4] Although the *R v Oliver* criteria are useful, the fact that they are used to standardise sentencing means that the criteria are necessarily vague and broad. This standardisation may limit their utility in the Irish courts.

[26.04] Professor Max Taylor and Ethel Quayle of the COPINE foundation, run through UCC, suggest a more sophisticated and useful categorisation in their 'Taxonomy of different kinds of Child pornography':

Level	Name	Description of Picture Qualities
1	Indicative	Non-erotic and non-sexualised pictures showing children in their underwear, swimming costumes, etc. from either commercial sources or family albums; pictures of children playing in normal settings, in which the context or organisation of the pictures by the collector indicates inappropriateness.
2	Nudist	Pictures of naked or semi-naked children in appropriate nudist settings, and from legitimate sources.
3	Erotica	Surreptitiously taken photographs of children in play areas or other safe environments showing either underwear or varying degrees of nakedness.
4	Posing	Deliberately posed pictures of children fully, partially clothed or naked (where the amount, context and organisation suggests sexual interest).
5	Erotic Posing	Deliberately posed pictures of fully, partially clothed or naked children in sexualised or provocative poses.
6	Explicit Erotic Posing	Emphasising gential areas where the child is either naked, patially or fully clothed.

---

2 *DPP v McC* [2002] 3 IR 609.
3 *R v Oliver* [2003] 2 Cr App 15.
4 *DPP v Tiernan* [1988] IR 250.

7	Explicit Sexual Activity	Involves touching, mutual and self masturbation, oral sex and intercourse by child not involving an adult.
8	Assault	Pictures of children being subject to a sexual assault, involving digital touching, involving an adult.
9	Gross Assault	Grossly obscene pictures of sexual assault, involving penetrative sex, masturbation or oral sex involving adult.
10	Sadistic/ Bestiality	a. Pictures showing child being tied, bound, beaten, whipped or otherwise subject to something that implies pain. b. Pictures where an animal is involved in some form of sexual behaviour with a child.

It is submitted that the above categorisation is superior to that provided by the English Court of Appeal in a number of aspects. It is far more detailed, it is more sensitive, having more categories, and allows for clearer differentiation between different categories. It is also supported by substantial academic research and is used as a tool in that research.[5] Taylor and Quayle suggest that:

'victimisation is the central topic to focus on when analysing picture content, and when attempting to develop descriptive categories'.

Taylor and Quayle's focus upon the victim is consistent with that preferred by the Irish courts[6] and the Oireachtas;[7] their taxonomy is also consistent with that established by the English courts in *R v Oliver.* It is simply more detailed and so more useful.

Sampling

[26.05] In *DPP v McC* the accused was found in possession of 'ten CD ROMs, one hard drive disc and three floppy discs as well as videos and stories. In total there were 200,000 images on the various CDs. Out of 200,000 images 783 were images of child pornography'. In a case that came before the District Court in Letterkenny, the accused pleaded guilty to possessing over 3000 such images. It is impractical, and probably prejudicial, to expect a judge to view every one of those images. So the judge will probably engage in some form of sampling. That is what Carney J did in effect when he turned the video that was at the core of the case off after 10 minutes. The danger with

---

[5] *Taylor and Quayle's* taxonomy is based upon: 'a descriptive analysis of the extensive collection of images in the COPINE database, and the experiences of the COPINE Project team in reviewing and categorising the material. This database contains examples of most of the material publicly available, and represents a very large sample of the total amount of material in public circulation at the moment, with a particular focus on newer material. It is wholly based on Internet sources. From, this analysis ... (the) ... ten levels of severity of photographs can be discerned based upon increasing sexual victimisation', p 31.

[6] Eg In *DPP v Tiernan* Finlay CJ set out the reasons why rape was 'one of the most serious offences contained in our criminal law'. These reasons focused upon the impact of rape on its victims, such as its 'gross attack upon the human dignity and bodily integrity of a woman'. See also *The People (DPP) v JT* 3 Frewen 141.

[7] Criminal Justice Act 1993, s 5(3).

sampling undertaken by a judge is that there is a significant danger that the judge's sample will be biased as he may select images that are untypically serious or benign. It is submitted that a better approach would be for the prosecution, in agreement with the defence, to submit the images to the judge, divided into categories. It should be a decision for the defence in any particular case whether they want the images categorised; however, a failure to categorise the images may irredeemably prejudice the trial judge by requiring him to view the whole.

[26.06] In *Thompson v R*[8] Thomas LJ in the English Court of Appeal set out how this categorisation should take place in a case involving a large number of photographs. The trial judge was presented with 11 photographs that related to 11 specific counts before him and 3,735 cases that related to a general count. These photographs were of varying seriousness, with some of them falling into the fourth of the above categories, and the children were of different ages. The Court of Appeal considered that 'the judge allowed himself to be placed in a very difficult position in this case by not requiring to be told of the approximate number of images at each level contained in the count relating the 3,736 images'.[9]

Given the difficulties in this and other cases within the experience of the Court of Appeal, the Court suggested that the following practices should be followed in future:

(i)   In cases where there are significant numbers of photographs, in addition to the specific counts, the inclusion of a comprehensive count covering the remainder is a practice that should be followed.

(ii)   The photographs used in the specific counts, should, if it is practicable, be selected so as to be broadly representative of the images in the comprehensive count. If agreement can then be reached between the parties that (say) five images at level 2, ten at level 3 and two at level 4 represent 500 level 2, 100 level 3 and 200 level 4 images in the comprehensive count of 800 images, the need of the judge to view the entirety of the offending material may be avoided.

(iii)   Where it is impractical to present the court with specific counts, that have been agreed to be representative of the comprehensive count, an approximate breakdown of the number of images at each of the levels must be available to the court. This may best be achieved by the prosecution providing the defence with a schedule setting out the information and ensuring that the defence have an opportunity, well in advance of the sentencing hearing, of viewing the images and checking the accuracy of the schedule.[10]

(iv)   Each image charged in a specific case should be identified by reference to its 'jpg' or other reference so that it is clear with which image the specific count is dealing.

---

[8]   *Thompson v R* (17 March 2004, unreported) CA (Eng).

[9]   (17 March 2004, unreported) CA (Eng) at para 10.

[10] The court also suggested that the charge should make clear whether or not an image was a 'photograph' or a 'pseudo-photograph'. It is submitted that such distinction is irrelevant at Irish law.

(v)   The estimated age range of the child shown in each of the images should, where possible, be provided to the court.

The procedure in Bristol Crown Court

[26.07] Concerns with the number of disturbing images being generated in such cases before Bristol Crown Court, and inconsistencies that were emerging in the handling of cases, led to the establishment of a protocol for the handling of such images.[11] This protocol requires that all parties have an acceptable understanding of the technical aspects of the issues, particularly the downloading and saving of images. A full report on the contents of the hard disk or disk containing the material in question must be served as part of the prosecution evidence, and agreement should be reached between counsel as to its accuracy and admissability. The statement will detail the number of images and the ratio of photographs to films. It should also indicate where the images were found on the drive, and how the accused may have acquired them, whether through peer-to-peer groups, websites or email. It should detail any attempts to frustrate a forensic examination, such as the use of encryption technology or evidence-eliminator software and set out any proof that the images were distributed to third parties.

[26.08] Given the disturbing nature of the material itself, the object of the protocol is to minimise the need for discussion of that material. In cases where there are a large number of images, Bristol Crown Court requires that the indictment should be drawn up to include the most serious images.

'The Officer in charge of the particular investigation should prepare (or arrange to have prepared) a statement setting out in detail the content of the indicted images. This should be checked by Prosecution Counsel. Necessarily, to avoid repeated viewing of these images by others, the description of each image will have to be in some depth. The estimated age of the child or children should be included, together with a description of the image. If a film clip, the length of the clip should be included, together with a sufficiently detailed summary of the contents of the clip to make further viewing by others unnecessary. If there is a sound track with the clip this should be stated.'

Less severe images are to be classified in accordance with *R v Oliver.* This

'statement should be prepared conservatively, the Court is not likely to be assisted by marginal differences in opinion as to the classification of images. It will not usually be necessary or desirable therefore for the Defence to view all the images to satisfy themselves as to the precise accuracy of the classification evidence relating to images that have not been indicted'.

Obviously, the above procedure is very much dependent upon agreement being reached between defence and prosecution counsel, particularly with regard to the indicative specific counts. If no such agreement is reached then 'this should be specifically stated at the plea and directions hearing, together with the evidential and/or legal basis for this contention. The Court will then decide on appropriate steps to resolve the issue'.

[26.09] At trial or sentence a Police Officer is required to attend court with the images in question saved on CD and a suitably equipped laptop, so that the judge can view the

---

[11]   Davies, *Indecent Exposure* 2004 SJ (06.02.04), p 130.

images. The judge should view the images before sentencing and the procedures anticipate that this will take 20 minutes or so.

Sentencing

[26.10] The authors of a report undertaken for the Department of Justice interviewed twelve judges involved in the sentencing of offenders under the CTPA 1998. Analysis of their responses suggested that the judges:

> 'attach particular weight to the seriousness of the crime when determining punishment. Imprisonment was the only penalty handed out by the courts for the production or distribution of child pornography. But for simple possession, the full range of sentencing options – from the maximum of five years imprisonment to 12 months probation – was used.'[12]

According to new research 'The vast majority of the cases studied related to simple possession of child pornography material, with sentences ranging from five years imprisonment with the last two years suspended, to a €600 fine'.[13]

Any court imposing a sentence for 'possession of child pornography will have regard to two of the basic mitigating factors in sentencing. They are: firstly whether the accused accepts responsibility for the offence, including his plea of guilty. Secondly, the previous character of the accused with particular reference to the offence in question'.[14] In the DPP v Loving, the Court of Appeal stated the issues to be considered included

> 'how serious and numerous were the actual pornographic images...[A] court should consider the circumstances and the duration of the activity leading to the possession of the images. In the present case, the garda evidence was that they were downloaded during a comparatively short period from December 2002 to January 2003, when the applicant accessed the sites in question a maximum of fifteen times. He did not subscribe to these sites. Most significantly, it seems clear that he ceased using them after that time. When his house was searched in September 2003, it seems clear that he had not accessed any of them since January of that year. There is no reason to dispute his own statement that he had lost interest and had left the material unused in a box over that time ... [I]t is fully accepted that the applicant had never shared the material with any other person or otherwise circulated or distributed it in any way.'[15]

Sentences upon conviction for possession of child pornography can certainly vary. In one case arising from the gardaí's 'Operation Amythyst', a former teacher was jailed for nine months, with three suspended, for possession of child pornography. In contrast, a Cork-based restaurteur had to pay a €40,000 to a Calcutta charity and spend 240 hours on community service.[16] The six-month suspended sentence and €1,500 fine imposed upon a Galwegian electrician, arrested in the same operation, would seem to fall

---

[12] Downes, 'Numbers investigated on child porn in decline' (2006) The Irish Times, 23 October.

[13] Downes, 'Sentences vary greatly for child sex offences – study' (2007) The Irish Times, 24 September. See O'Donnell & Milner, *Child Pornography, Crime, Computers and Society* (Willan Publishing, 2007).

[14] *DPP v Loving* [2006] IECCA 28.

[15] *DPP v Loving* [2006] IECCA 28.

[16] (2003) The Irish Times, 18 January.

between these two extremes.[17] A South Korean student arrested before Operation Amethyst was sentenced to two years in jail, suspended for five years, on condition that he return to South Korea and not revisit Ireland for five years.[18] Serious public disquiet was expressed on foot of the apparent discrepancy in these sentences and in a subsequent case the former owner of a children's fun park was sentenced to six months' imprisonment for possession of child pornography.[19] A former priest who pleaded guilty to having over 3000 child pornographic images in his possession was sentenced to two years' imprisonment, with the last six months suspended.[20] However, such reports have to be treated with serious caution, as *Charleton* comments 'The only current source of ... material is media memory, a less than wholly reliable foundation for informed discussion'.

In *DPP v Loving* the Court of Appeal noted that:

'Counsel for the applicant has provided the Court with a very helpful list of fourteen cases reported in the Irish Times from 1st January 2003 to 1st February 2006. Counsel for the prosecution did not dispute the accuracy of this material. In every case, there was a guilty plea. In seven cases, heard in the Circuit Court, the court imposed a suspended sentence of two or three years, in three of those cases accompanied by a fine. In one case, a term of nine months (not suspended) was imposed. In one, involving a very large number of images, many of extremely young children, the court imposed a sentence of two years, with the last six months suspended. Both these cases were Circuit Court cases based on Operation Amethyst. That meant that the culprits had been traced as a result of investigations in the United States, where credit cards had been used to purchase child pornography. In the remaining three cases, heard in the District Court, the sentences were respectively, six months suspended, six months (not suspended) and a fine of €1,000 and 240 hours Community Service'.[21]

[26.11] The variation in sentences before the Irish courts is a result of a deliberate policy on the part of the Irish courts, which have never countenanced the introduction of definite sentencing guidelines. The Supreme Court declined to set out guidelines for the sentencing of rapists when asked to do so in *The People (DPP) v Tiernan*,[22] Finlay CJ stating:

'having regard to the fundamental necessity for judges in sentencing in any form of criminal case to impose a sentence which in their discretion appropriately meets all the particular circumstances of the case (and very few criminal cases are particularly similar), and the particular circumstances of the accused, I would doubt that it is appropriate for an appellate court to appear to be laying down any standardisaton of tariff of penalty for cases.'[23]

---

[17] (2003) The Irish Times, 29 April.
[18] (2003) The Irish Times, 18 January.
[19] The Irish Times, 3 December.
[20] (2003) The Irish Times, 16 October.
[21] *DPP v Loving* [2006] IECCA 28.
[22] *The People (DPP) v Tiernan* [1988] IR 250.
[23] [1988] IR 250 at 254.

This principle was restated by Flood J in *The People (DPP) v WC*[24]: 'the Irish Courts, unlike the position of the English Court of Appeal, do not adopt a formulaic or tariff approach to sentencing'.[25] Instead, the Irish courts take a variety of different factors into account, as Denham J stated in *The People (DPP) v MS*[26]:

> 'Sentencing is a complex decision. It may involve aspects of retribribution, deterrence, protection, reparation and rehabilitation. In cases relating to sexual offences there are important aspects relating to protection of society and rehabilitation of the defendant.' [27]

[26.12] One of the most important mitigating factors in deciding sentence is the making of an admission of guilt, as was stated by Egan J in the Supreme Court in *The People (DPP) v M*[28] 'To my mind the most important mitigating factor in this case is the fact that the appellant admitted his guilt promptly and has pleaded guilty at his trial.'[29] Egan J cited *The People (DPP) v Tiernan* to the effect that 'This Court recognised that this was an important mitigating factor in cases of rape'. In *The People (DPP) v Tiernan* the Supreme Court clearly considered that another important factor was the effect of a sexual crime upon its victim, Finlay CJ stating:

> 'The Act of forciable rape not only causes bodily harm but is also inevitably to be followed by emotional, psychological and psychiatric damage to the victim which can often be of long term, and sometimes of lifelong duration.
>
> In addition to those damaging consequences, rape can distort the victim's approach to her own sexuality.[30]'

[26.13] Child pornography cases are different from rape cases in that often the only evidence that can be taken from the frequently unidentified victims is the gleaned about the crimes directly perpetrated upon the victims and recorded in the pornographic images themselves. These images are deeply disturbing. In addition the offences may be committed using information technology with which the Court is relatively unfamiliar. It is clear that the Irish Courts will have no regard to decisions of the English Court of Appeal on the precise tariff that should be imposed in any particular case. As was stated by Geoghan J in *DPP v McC*[31] in the Court of Criminal Appeal:

> 'English precedents can only be of very limited value but it is probably fair to say that the level of public disapproval of and revulsion against computer offences relating to children is much the same in both jurisdictions'.

However, Geogahan J did suggest that English decisions could be of some assistance and he averred to the English case of *R v Oliver and Others*. In *R v Oliver*[32] the Court of

---

[24] *The People (DPP) v WC* [1994] ILRM 321.

[25] [1994] ILRM 321 at 329.

[26] 2000] 2 IR 592.

[27] [2000] 2 IR 592 at 600, cited by the Court of Criminal Appeal in *The People (DPP) v R O'D* [2000] 4 IR 361 at 367.

[28] *The People (DPP) v M* [1994] 3 IR 306.

[29] [1994] 3 IR 306 at 313.

[30] *The People (DPP) v Tiernan* [1988] IR 250 at 253.

[31] *DPP v McC* (31 October 2003, unreported) CA.

[32] *R v Oliver, Hartrey and Brown* [2003] Crim LR 127.

Appeal promulgated sentencing guidelines for offences under the UK's Protection of Children Act 1978. The Court set out a hierarchy of seriousness of child pornographic images:

1.   Images depicting erotic posing with no sexual activity;

2.   Sexual activity between children solo or masturbation as a child;

3.   Non-penetrative sexual activity between adults and children;

4.   Penetrative sexual activity between children and adults;

5.   Sadism or bestiality.

[26.14] The court commented that the seriousness of an individual offence increased with the offender's proximity to and responsibility for the original abuse. In the court's view any element of commercial gain would place an offence at a high level of seriousness. Swapping of images could properly be regarded as commercial activity, albeit without financial gain, because it fuelled demand for such material. Widespread distribution, even without financial profit, was intrinsically more harmful that a transaction limited to two or three individuals, both by reference to the potential use of the material by active paedophiles and by reference to the shame and degradation to the original victims. Merely locating an image on the Internet would generally be less serious than downloading it. Downloading such an image would generally be less serious that taking an original film or photography of indecent posing or activity. The court suggested that the choice between a custodial or non-custodial sentence was particularly difficult and acknowledged the pressure exerted by public opinion and Parliament for the imposition of custodial sentences. However, it also acknowledged that sex offender treatment programmes could be effective in preventing future offending and that in any case where the court was deliberating over whether to impose a custodial sentence, the offender's suitability for such treatment should be assessed. Similarly, in *The People (DPP) v R O'D* the Court of Criminal Appeal acknowledged that in that case there was 'a strong public interest in not sending this appellant to jail but strictly on condition that he completes his … (treatment) … and participates in … aftercare'.[33]

[26.15] The dangers of relying upon media reports in relation to sentence length should be reiterated. However, it would appear that the not uncommon sanction in this jurisdiction of a six-month jail sentence upon receipt of a guilty plea on a charge of possession of child pornography, is considerably more than that contemplated by the English Court of Appeal. In *R v Oliver* the Court of Appeal considered that a fine would normally be appropriate in a case where the offender was merely in possession of material solely for his own use. This would include cases where the material was downloaded from the Internet but not further distributed and either the material consisted entirely of 'pseudo-photographs', the making of which had involved no abuse or exploitation of children, or there was no more than a small amount of material at the lowest level in the hierarchy of severity set out above. The Court of Appeal suggested that a conditional discharge might be appropriate in such a case if the defendant pleaded guilty and had no previous convictions.

---

[33]   *The People (DPP) v R O'D* [2000] 4 IR 361 at 368.

[26.16] A key difference between Irish and English Law is the distinction made between 'pseudo-photographs' and photographs of 'real' children in English Law. Section 7 of the UK Protection of Children Act 1978 defines 'pseudo-photograph' as 'an image, whether made by computer graphics or otherwise howsoever, which appears to be a photograph'. The Irish CTPA 1998 allows for no such distinction. However, it may be of interest to note that the Court of Appeal suggested that possession, including downloading of artificially created pseudo-photographs and the making of such images, should generally be treated as being at a lower level of seriousness than the making and possessing or making of photographic images of real children. It is submitted that following this approach incorrect as modern technologies are so sophisticated that it is easily possible to generate 'pseudo-photographs' that are indistinguishable from 'real' photographs. Allowing for such a distincition would place Irish courts under the impossible burden of having to identify which photographs were 'real' and which were 'pseudo'. Of course there may be some cases where such a distinction could be easily made, but allowing for the making of such a distinction injects a large measure of arbitrariness into the sentencing process. What would occur is that those who were in possession of poorly made 'pseudo' photographs would receive lower sentences than those in possession of well made 'pseudo' photographs that could not be distinguished from 'real'. This would create a situation where individuals were being sentenced not on the basis of their own actions or circumstances, but rather on the basis of the dexterity and skill of the third party who made the pseudo-photograph. It is submitted that if any such a distinction is to be made, then it is a matter for the court in any particular case. It is further submitted that this is a good illustration of the difficulty that can arise when a higher court imposes clear guidelines on sentencing and a good illustration of why the higher Irish courts have shied away from doing so. Finally, making a distinction between 'real' and 'pseudo' images of child abuse would be to arguably frustrate the will of the Oireachtas, which rejected the making of such a distinction and adopted to treat all depictions of child abuse identically, however they were created. In *R v Fuller*[34] the defendant had been sentenced to 12 months' imprisonment and he appealed against his sentence on the basis *inter alia* that 'there was no corruption of any of these children in that, in particular, they were no doubt wholly unaware that they were being photographed'. His appeal against sentence failed.

The decision in DPP v McC

[26.17] The defendant in *DPP v McC* used a number of young boys in the production of child pornography. He was found in possession of 783 images of child pornography. In the Court of Criminal Appeal Geoghan J made specific reference to the judgment of the Court of Appeal in *R v Oliver and Others*[35] and commented that:

> 'Although the English legislative scheme is different, the court in arriving, at a proper sentence can gain some assistance from the recent judgment of the Criminal Division of the English Court of Appeal comprising the Vice-President (Rose LJ), Gibbs J and Davis J in *R v Oliver and Others* … The court took the view that in relation to offences involving indecent photographs or pseudo photographs of children the two primary factors

---

34   *R v Fuller* [1997] EWCA Crim 2136 (20 August 1997).
35   *R v Oliver and Others* [2003] 1 Cr App 28.

determining the seriousness of a particular offence were the nature of the indecent material and the extent of the offender's involvement in it.'

Geoghan J noted the hierarchy of seriousness developed by the Court of Appeal in that case and commented that 'In relation to the offender's involvement, the seriousness of the offence increased with the offender's proximity to and responsibility for the original abuse'. He then quoted Rose LJ:

'Any element of commercial gain will place an offence at a high level of seriousness. In our judgment, swapping of images can properly be regarded as a commercial activity, albeit without financial gain, because it fuels demand for such material. Widescale distribution, even without financial profit is intrinsically more harmful than a transaction limited to two or three individuals, both by reference to the potential use of the images by active paedophiles and by reference to the shame and degradation to the original victims.

Merely locating an image on the internet will generally be less serious than downloading it. Downloading will generally be less serious than taking an original film or photograph of indecent posing or activity'.[36]

[26.18] Geoghan J noted that the English judgment went on to suggest different levels of sentence for different degrees of seriousness of the offences. He noted that under the relevant English Act 'ten years and not fourteen years, as in our-jurisdiction, is the maximum'. Geoghan J considered this to be relevant when considering the following sentence:

'Sentences approaching the ten year maximum will be appropriate in very serious cases where the defendant has a previous conviction either for dealing in child pornography or for abusing children sexually or with violence. Previous such convictions in less serious cases may result in the custody threshold being passed and will be likely to give rise to a higher sentence where the custody threshold has been passed.'[37]

Geoghan J considered that in *DPP v McC*:

'A serious aspect of this case is that in each instance the pornographic pictures were produced in relation to children over which the applicant was in a position of trust. In the case of three of the victims the applicant used alcohol to further his desires. On the other hand, as has already been pointed out, it is not suggested that the images were used or intended to be used for anything other than the applicant's own sexual gratification. There was no commercial or quasi-commercial user. Nor is there any evidence of the applicant using these images for the purpose of swapping with others and still less in connection with any paedophile ring. The offences in relation to the different victims all came to light at more or less the same time and were included in the same indictment. A higher sentence has to be imposed than would be imposed if there was simply one individual child involved, but that does not mean that the sentence should be the maximum sentence and certainly, not on the basis that the overall sentence would be more than fourteen years if consecutive sentences were imposed. There were undoubtedly aggravating factors here not merely in relation to the position of trust – but there was also a strong element of depravity in the surrounding circumstances in which the photographs were taken. Nevertheless credit must be given for the plea of guilty, the absence of previous

---

[36] At p 619.
[37] ibid at p 620.

convictions and the cooperation with the gardaí. In all the circumstances and taking into account that there were five children involved and not merely one, the appropriate sentence would seem to be eight years'.

[26.19] Geoghan J then turned to consider the sentence that should be imposed on the charges of possession of pornography:

'The count of possession of child pornography contrary to s 6(1) of the 1998 Act was a count of possession only. There was a plea of guilty and no previous convictions. The applicant cooperated in relation to the investigation of that offence. It is of some interest to note how the Criminal Division of the English Court of Appeal approached a somewhat similar situation in the *Oliver* case cited above. A search warrant had been executed at the offender's home and his computer and some floppy discs were seized. They were found to contain approximately 20,000 images of children some as young as six or seven performing oral sex on adult males in some instances and in others being anally raped. The accused pleaded guilty to six offences of making indecent photographs or pseudo photographs of children and was sentenced to eight months imprisonment with an extended licence period of twenty-eight months. It was ordered that he be registered under the English Sex Offenders Act; 1997. In the second case which was before the Criminal Division the accused had made and distributed indecent photographs of children. When his computer system was seized and analysed there were a total of 20,000 indecent images and 500 computer files of child abuse identified with images of naked children of both sexes aged from six upwards performing sexual acts on other children and adults. Some of the children were clearly distressed. There was a plea of guilty to one charge of distributing an indecent photograph or pseudo photograph of a child and one charge of making such a photograph and there was a sentence of three years imprisonment. In the third case before the court the accused had pleaded guilty to four counts of indecent assault on a female, four counts of taking indecent photographs of a child and two counts of distributing the photographs. The victim in each case was the daughter aged eight or nine of a family friend. The sentence in that case was three years imprisonment.

In relation to the first case the Criminal Division of the English Court of Appeal held that the sentence passed 'was entirely appropriate'. In the second case there was evidence of distress on the faces of some of the children and there appeared to be also an element of a paedophile ring. The three years sentence was upheld as being 'the minimum appropriate in accordance with the guidelines which we have indicated.'

As noted above, Geoghan J went onto comment that:

'English precedents can only be of very limited value but it is probably fair to say that the level of public disapproval of and revulsion against computer offences relating to children is much the same in both jurisdictions. Although there is no evidence that the *'possession'* of the child pornography was for any commercial use or for the purpose of any swapping of pictures etc. there is certainly evidence that the collection was being used to show to others when it suited the applicant for his own sexual gratification. In these circumstances a custodial sentence is appropriate and given the surrounding circumstances in this case as to how this collection was put to use this court considers that the correct sentence is three years notwithstanding the mitigating factors. In respect of count number 1 therefore a sentence of three years will be substituted for the sentence of five years. All sentences shall run concurrently'.

[26.20] The use of English precedents with regard to sentencing must remain in dispute in Ireland, a dispute well illustrated by *DPP v McC*. Given the very substantial differences in sentencing practice between the two jurisdictions, the ideal situation would be to be able to ignore the English decisions. However, the English courts have developed a highly structured method of both presenting evidence and sentencing in such cases. Given the emotive nature of these cases, and the entirely understandable reactions of disgust and horror with which members of the judiciary react when presented with the subject matter, it would appear that the Irish courts must have reference to those structures when sentencing here.

[26.21] The Irish and English decisions can finally be compared to those of the US courts. Thomas Reedy, whose website was used to gather the information that led to Amethyst, was sentenced at trial to 89 consecutive 15-year sentences or 1,355 years in jail, a sentences subsequently reduced on appeal.[38] In *DPP v McC* Geoghan J commented that: 'The learned sentencing judge is quite right in rejecting what he calls "American type sentences of hundreds of years". Such sentences would be alien to our jurisprudence'.

Aggravation

[26.22] The Irish courts will have regard to whether or not an offence has been aggravated in any way, as occurred for example in *The People (DPP) v Tiernan* where 'very many though not all of the most serious aggravating circumstances which can be attached to the crime of rape were present.'[39] In *DPP v McC* Geoghan J commented that:

> 'It is not in dispute that there was no evidence to suggest any passing on of these images via the computer either for commercial gain or otherwise it appears to be accepted that the images were produced and availed of solely for the sexual gratification of the applicant. While this is not a mitigating factor, if the evidence had been to the opposite effect it would certainly have been an aggravating factor'.

[26.23] In *Toomer* the English Court of Appeal held that the following specific factors were capable of aggravating the seriousness of a particular offence:

   (i)   The images had been shown or distributed to a child.

   (ii)   There were a large number of images.

   (iii)   The way in which a collection of images was organised on a computer might indicate a more or less sophisticated approach on the part of an offender to trading, or a higher level of personal interest in the material. An offence would be less serious if images had been viewed but not stored.

   (iv)   Images posed on a public area of the Internet, or distributed in a way making it more likely that they would be found accidentally by computer users not looking for pornographic material, would aggravate the seriousness of the offence.

   (v)   The offence would be aggravated if the offender was responsible for the original production of the images, particularly if the child or children involved

---

38   (2004) The Examiner, 13 April.
39   *The People (DPP) v Tiernan* [1988] IR 250 at 254.

were members of the offender's own family, or were drawn from vulnerable groups, such as those who had left or been taken from their home, or if the offender had abused a position of trust, as in the case of a teacher, friend of the family, social worker, or youth leader.

(vi) the age of the children might be an aggravating feature. In many cases it would be difficult to quantify the effect of the age by reference to the impact of the child. Assaults on babies or very young children attracted particular repugnance and might by the conduct depicted in the image indicate a likelihood of physical injury to the private parts of the victim. Such conduct might manifestly have induced fear or distress in the victim, and some conduct which might not cause distress to an adolescent child might cause fear or distress tO a child of six or seven.

The utility of some of the above may be questioned.

Old images

[26.24] Once an image of child abuse is distributed in digital form, it has the potential to remain in circulation forever. In *R v Fellows and Arnold* the fact that an image was 'old' was raised by the defendant before the Court of Appeal, Evans LJ commenting that:

> 'photographs or some of them were taken as long ago as the early 1970's, and ... (the defendant's counsel) ... emphasised that data stored in the first appellant's archive was 'old material' both in terms of its age and because it was some distance from its original source. We must confess, however, that we do not understand why this should affect the issue of guilt or be relevant as mitigation if the offences were committed'.

The fact that an image of this type can remain in circulation for so long can be deeply traumatic for the victim and his or her family. So there is an argument to be made that the possession of 'old' images is an aggravating factor, as opposed to a mitigating one. On the other hand, the possession of new images may be a cause for concern. Taylor and Quayle comment that the possession of new or private material 'may also relate to the extent to which the collector has access to producers, or to the circle around which new and valued material circulates ... it may be indicative of the degree of involvement in the child pornography world.'[40]

It is submitted that the age of images is irrelevant. It would be improper for a court to assume that a defendant is more deeply involved in the child pornography world solely because he has been found in possession of 'new' images of child pornography. It would be incorrect for a court to treat possession or distribution of 'old' images of child pornography as being less serious than possession of more recently produced material. If the age of images is relevant at all it may be relevant to the issue of aggravation as child pornography is 'a permanent record of the children's participation and the harm to the children is exacerbated by their circulation'.[41]

---

[40] *Taylor and Quayle Child Pronography: an Internet Crime* (Brunner-Routledge, 2003), p 40.
[41] *New York v Ferber* 458 US 754, 1982.

The Sex Offenders Act 2001

[26.25] A conviction under the 1998 Act will have important consequences for the Sex Offenders Act 2001. In particular s 26 of the 2001 Act makes it an offence for a person convicted under CTPA 1998 to apply for a job that would give them 'unsupervised access to ... children or ... mentally impaired ... persons'. Although not every person who is found in possession of child pornography will be a paedophile, the fact that a person has been found in possession of child pornography does greatly increase the likelihood that they will go on to sexually abuse children. Convicting a person under CTPA 1998 will ensure that they are monitored under the provisions of the Sex Offenders Act 2001. So in *Smethurst*[42] the defendant was conditionally discharged and ordered to pay £600 costs. This seemingly light sentence contained a 'sting'[43]: the requirement to register with the police under the English Sexual Offenders Act 1997. In *Mark McQuaid v Secretary of State for Education and Skills*[44] the plaintiff was employed as a social worker in a sex offenders programme. Shortly after he commenced work he began to access child pornography, not, he said out of any sexual interest, but rather out of morbid curiosity. He was arrested and convicted in the Scottish counterpart of the Irish Operation Amethyst. Following his conviction, he was included on a list of persons deemed unsuitable to work with children. He appealed against his inclusion, arguing that the material for which he received a conviction was at the low end of the scale of child pornography. His appeal failed, the Tribunal holding that it 'wishes to make it quite clear that it is not branding the appellant a paedophile, nor is it saying that the appellant represents a risk, per se, to children. However ... it is satisfied, on the balance of probabilities that he is unsuitable to work with children'.

[26.26] In the USA, legislation known as Megan's Law requires public notification of the presence of convicted sex offenders in a neighbourhood. In contrast the Sex Offenders Act 2001 requires only that sex offenders register at their local garda station and inform potential employers of their conviction before applying for a job that involves working with children. The difficulties of monitoring sex offenders post-release from prison is illustrated by the case of *R v The Chief Constable for the North Wales Police Area*.[45] This concerned offenders who were believed by Northumbria Police to be: "extremely dangerous people who will pose a considerable risk to children and vulnerable adults in the community where they settle and they will target and procure such people for sexual abuse'. The offenders were forced to move repeatedly by both media attention and local police forces. As a result they went to ground 'and their whereabouts ... (were) ... not known to the authorities'. The offenders had ceased to co-operate with the authorities and were no longer receiving counseling from a forensic psychologist.

---

[42] *Smethurst* 2002 Cr App R 6.
[43] Per Simon Brown LJ in *Goodland* at 2000 2 Cr App R 264.
[44] *Mark McQuaid v Secretary of State for Education and Skills* (2003) 206 PC 2, March 2004 at Leeds Combined Court.
[45] *R v The Chief Constable for the North Wales Police Area* (18 March 1998).

Entry search and seizure

[26.27] Section 7 of the CTPA 1998 provides that:

'Where, on the sworn information of a member of the Garda Síochána not below the rank of sergeant, a judge of the District Court is satisfied that there are reasonable grounds for suspecting that evidence of or relating to an offence ... (under the Act) ... is to be found at a place[46] specified in the information, the judge may issue a warrant for the search of that place and any persons found at that place.

'Operation Amethyst' was a major operation launched by the gardaí on 27 May 2002, in which some 500 gardaí raided 80 premises.[47] Gathering and correctly processing so many warrants is a complex task and sub-s 2 sets out how the warrant is to be used:

'A warrant issued under this section shall authorise a named member of the Garda Síochána, alone or accompanied by such other members of the Garda Síochána and such other persons as may be necessary—

    (a)   to enter, within 7 days from the date of the warrant, and if necessary by the use of reasonable force, the place named in the warrant,

    (b)   to search it and any persons found there, and

    (c)   to seize anything found there, or anything found in the possession of a person present there at the time of the search, which that member reasonably believes to be evidence of or relating to an offence under ... (this Act).'

[26.28] In *DPP v Curtain*[48] it was held by Judge Carroll Moran that:

'there is no doubt that ... the day on which the search warrant was issued has to be included in the reckoning and since the warrant was issued on 20 May, 2002, it was spent when the Garda Síochána purported to rely on it in their search of the accused's home on 27 May 2002'.

Subsection 3 provides that 'A member of the Garda Síochána acting in accordance with a warrant issued under this section may require any person found at the place where the search is carried out to give the member his or her name and address'. Subsection 4 provides that:

'Any person who—

    (a) obstructs or attempts to obstruct any member of the Garda Síochána acting in accordance with a warrant issued under subsection (1),

    (b) fails or refuses to comply with a requirement under this section, or

    (c) gives a name or address which is false or misleading,

shall be guilty of an offence and shall be liable on summary conviction to a fine not exceeding £1,500 or to imprisonment for a term not exceeding 12 months or both.'

The gardaí may arrest, without warrant, any person whom they suspect of having committed an offence under this subsection.

---

[46] Where place is defined as 'any dwelling, any building or part of a building and any vehicle, vessel or structure'.

[47] (2002) The Irish Times, 27 May.

[48] (2004) The Irish Times, 24 April.

Forfeiture

[26.29] Section 8 of the CTPA 1998 provides that, upon conviction, anything seized pursuant to a search under section 7 of the Act or 'anything shown to the satisfaction of the court to relate to the offence', may be ordered forfeit or destroyed by the Court. Provision is made for the owner of the thing in question to apply to the court to show cause why the order should not be made.

Offences by bodies corporate

[26.30] Section 9(1) of the CTPA 1998 provides that:

> 'Where an offence under section 3, 4, 5 or 6 is committed by a body corporate and is proved to have been committed with the consent or connivance of, or to be attributable to any neglect on the part of, any person, being a director, manager, secretary or other similar officer of such body or a person who was purporting to act in any such capacity, that person as well as the body corporate shall be guilty of an offence and shall be liable to be proceeded against and punished as if he or she were guilty of the first-mentioned offence'.

This has particular application to the situation where employees of a company are producing, distributing or possessing child pornography on their workplace systems. Section 9(2) provides that: 'Where the affairs of a body corporate are managed by its members, subsection (1) shall apply in relation to the acts and defaults of a member of that body in connection with the member's functions of management as if he or she were a director or manager of it'.

The Criminal Evidence Act 1992

[26.31] Part III of the Criminal Evidence Act 1992 provides *inter alia* for the giving of evidence through a television link. Section 10 of the CTPA 1998 amends s 12 of the Criminal Evidence Act 1992 to include the offence of child trafficking under s 3 of the CTPA 1998 in the list to which Part III of the Criminal Evidence Act 1992 applies.

Section 3(1) of the 1998 Act and the Sexual Offences (Jurisdiction) Act 1996

[26.32] Section 3(1) of the 1998 Act provides that:

> 'Any person who organises or knowingly facilitates—
>
> (a) the entry into, transit through or exit from the State of a child for the purpose of his or her sexual exploitation, or
>
> (b) the provision of accommodation for a child for such a purpose while in the State,
>
> shall be guilty of an offence and shall be liable on conviction on indictment to imprisonment for life'.

[26.33] This provides that an Irish citizen or Irish resident who commits a sexual offence outside the state will be guilty of an offence. Section 11 includes offences of child trafficking contrary to s 3 and allowing a child to be used for child pornography contrary to s 4 in the schedule of offences to which the Sexual Offences (Jurisdiction) Act 1996 applies.

The Bail Act 1997

[26.34] Section 12 of the CTPA 1998 includes offences of child trafficking contrary to s 3 and producing and distributing child pornography contrary to section 4 in the schedule of serious offences in the Bail Act 1997. This means that a person accused of such 'serious offences' can be refused bail in accordance with s 2 of the Bail Act 1997.

Chapter 27

Freedoms of Expression and Communication

Introduction

[27.01] The Irish Constitution and the European Convention on Human Rights (ECHR) both provide rights to freedom of expression. However, neither of these rights is absolute. Both rights have to be balanced with the rights of others and the duties of the state. European law will also play a role. Firstly, freedom of expression is one of the fundamental rights that the EU has to uphold. Secondly, content can be regarded as a commodity or good like coal or cars. Hence the free movement of goods and internal market provisions of the EC Treaty may be invoked where regulation may impose restrictions on the movement of that content. This is particularly true of electronic content, which can be made available to all the citizens of the EU as easily as it can be made available to the citizens of a single member state.

The constitutional rights

[27.02] Article 40.6.1°(i) provides that 'The State guarantees liberty for the exercise of ... (t)he right of the citizens to express freely their convictions and opinions'. It would appear that this right 'protects the dissemination of information as well as the expression of convictions and opinions'.[1] This view is based upon the judgment of Barrington J in *The Irish Times v Ireland*:[2]

> 'These rights must include the right to report the news as well as the right to comment on it. A constitutional right which protected the right to comment on the news but not the right to report it would appear to me to be a nonsense. It therefore appears to me that the right of the citizens 'to express freely their convictions and opinions' guaranteed by Article 40 of the Constitution is a right to communicate facts as well as a right to comment on them. It appears to me also that when the European Convention on Human Rights states that the right to freedom of expression is to include 'freedom . . . to receive and impart information' it is merely making explicit something which is already implicit in Article 40.6.1° of our Constitution'.[3]

Barrington J's dictum was subsequently endorsed by the Supreme Court in *Murphy v Independent Radio and Television Commission*.[4] However, this does not mean that the right to freedom of expression is far from being absolute or untrammelled. The Constitution places a number of explicit limitations upon the right. Firstly, the guarantee is stated to be 'subject to public order and morality'.[5]

---

[1]   Hogan and Whyte, *Kelly: The Irish Constitution* (4th edn, Tottel Publishing, 2003) para 7.5.08.
[2]   *The Irish Times v Ireland* [1998] 1 IR 359.
[3]   [1998] 1 IR 359 at 405.
[4]   *Murphy v Independent Radio and Television Commission* [1999] 1 IR 12.
[5]   Bunreacht na hÉireann, Article 40.6.1°.

Secondly, the Constitution expressly allows for state control of the media, stating that:

> 'The education of public opinion being, however, a matter of such grave import to the common good, the State shall endeavour to ensure that organs of public opinion, such as the radio, the press, the cinema, while preserving their rightful liberty of expression, including criticism of public policy, shall not be used to undermine public order or morality, or the authority of the State'.[6]

[27.03] Thirdly, the Constitution expressly allows for the criminalisation of certain forms of speech. 'The publication or utterance of blasphemous, seditious or indecent matter is an offence which shall be punishable in accordance with law'.[7]

Fourthly, it may be argued that the speech in question must be related to 'public activities' if the Constitutional protection is to be engaged.[8] This argument is based upon another dictum of Barrington J, this time in *Murphy v Independent Radio and Television Commission:*

> 'Article 40.6.1° ... .is concerned with the public activities of the citizen in a democratic society. That is why, the Court suggests, the framers of the Constitution grouped the right to freedom of expression, the right to free assembly and the right to form associations and unions in the one sub-section. All three rights relate to the practical running of a democratic society'.[9]

Hogan and Whyte suggest that '(t)his passage appears to draw a distinction between speech directed at the public or a section thereof and private speech, the guarantee of freedom of expression applying only to the former'.[10]

[27.04] Finally, the right to freedom of expression must be balanced with other rights. In particular, freedom of expression must be balanced with the right of individuals to their own good name. In *Hunter v Duckworth*[11] O'Caoimh was of the view that:

> 'This court must recognise the fact that the Constitution gives recognition and expression both to the freedom of expression and to the right to a person's good name. It is accordingly necessary that the law should balance these rights in an appropriate manner ...
>
> It is clear that in the context of Ireland being a democratic state, clear recognition has to be given to the right to freedom of expression. I believe that this right should not be undermined by the provisions of the Constitution relating to the protection of one's reputation. It is clear that the rights have to be construed on a harmonious basis. Nevertheless, it is clear that in certain cases, in the context of the democratic nature of the State, primacy may have to be given to freedom of expression'.

---

6   Bunreacht na hÉireann, Article 40.6.1° (i).
7   Bunreacht na hÉireann, Article 40.6.1°(i).
8   Hogan and Whyte, *Kelly: The Irish Constitution* (4th edn, Tottel Publishing, 2003) para 7.5.10
9   *Murphy v Independent Radio and Television Commission* [1999] 1 IR 12 at 24.
10 Hogan and Whyte, *Kelly: The Irish Constitution* (4th edn, Tottel Publishing, 2003) para 7.5.11. The authors of *Kelly on the Constitution* are referring to a more extensive quotation from *Murphy v Independent Radio and Television Commission* than that used by these authors.
11 *Hunter v Gerald Duckworth & Co Ltd & Anor* [2003] IEHC 81 (31 July 2003).

[27.05] In *O'Brien v Mirror Group Newspapers*[12] Denham J expressed the opinion that:

'The rights guaranteed in the Irish Constitution are not absolute, neither are the rights of the European Convention. Both documents require that a balance be achieved and that balance going to matters of reputation, information, communication and the freedom of expression is a matter of importance in a democracy and is of public interest'.[13]

[27.06] Similarly, in *Foley v Sunday Newspapers,*[14] Kelly J stated that:

'The right to freedom of expression is ... an important right and one which the courts must be extremely circumspect about curtailing particularly at the interlocutory stage of a proceeding. Important as it is, however, it cannot equal or be more important than the right to life[15]'

The limitations on the right are the subject matter of the chapters that follow. In being so limited the Irish Constitutional right is similar to the right provided by art 10 of the European Convention on Human Rights (ECHR). The Irish and ECHR rights must be compared with the relatively untrammeled right provided by the First Amendment of the US Constitution[16]: 'Congress shall make no law ... abridging the freedom of speech or of the press'. Whilst the Irish and ECHR provisions explicitly require that freedom of expression be balanced with the rights of others and the duties of the State, similar explicit limitations are not provided by the US Constitution. This means that US law on free speech is fundamentally incompatible with that of Ireland and Europe. This means that US discussions about Internet speech will be of limited relevance in a European context. Much as they might want to, American authorities simply cannot restrict free speech as easily as do Irish and European legislatures.[17]

[27.07] The Constitution also provides a right of communication. In *Murphy v Independent Radio and Television Commission*[18] Barrington J expressed the view that 'the right to communicate must be one of the most basic rights of man. Next to the right to nurture it is hard to imagine any right more important to man's survival'.[19]

---

[12] *O'Brien v Mirror Group Newspapers* [2001] 1 IR 1.

[13] [2001] 1 IR 1 at 32–33.

[14] *Foley v Sunday Newspapers* [2005] 1 IR 88.

[15] [2005] 1 IR 88 at 101.

[16] Amendments 1–10 of the US Constitution are more commonly known as the 'Bill of Rights'.

[17] See the US Federal Communications Decency Act of 1996, two provisions of which sought 'to protect minors from harmful material on the Internet'. The US Supreme Court struck these down as unconstitutional, commenting that: 'As a matter of constitutional tradition, in the absence of evidence to the contrary, we presume that governmental regulation of the content of speech is more likely to interfere with the free exchange of ideas than to encourage it. The interest in encouraging freedom of expression in a democratic society outweighs any theoretical but unproven benefit of censorship'. See: *Reno, Attorney General of the United States, et al v American Civil Liberties Union et al*, No 96–511, 26 June 1997.

[18] *Murphy v Independent Radio and Television Commission* [1999] 1 IR 12.

[19] [1999] 1 IR 12 at 24.

Perhaps the clearest statement of the right to communicate was made by Costello J in *Attorney General v Paperlink*,[20] wherein he stated that:

> 'As the act of communication is the exercise of such a basic human facility ... a right to communicate must inhere in the citizen by virtue of his human personality and must be guaranteed by the Constitution ... the very general and basic right to communicate ... must be one of those personal unspecified rights of the citizen protected by Article 40.3.1°'.[21]

[27.08] As with freedom of expression, the right to communicate is not an absolute right.[22] The relationship between the right to communicate and to freedom of expression was analysed by Barrington J in *The Irish Times v Ireland:*

> 'In some respects the two rights may overlap and may be complimentary. But the right of freedom of expression is primarily concerned with the public statements of the citizen. When the Constitution guarantees the citizen liberty for the exercise of this right it is guaranteeing to him that he will not be punished by the criminal law or placed under any unconstitutional restriction for freely stating in public his convictions and opinions, be they right or wrong. A *fortiori* it guarantees him, but again subject to the same constitutional restrictions, the right to state the facts on which these convictions and opinions are based. The Constitution guarantees to the organs of public opinion liberty for the criticism of government policy. But it would be absurd to suggest that the press enjoys constitutional protection under Article 40.6.1° (i) when criticising government policy but not when reporting the facts on which its criticism is based'.[23]

The ECHR right

[27.09] On the face of it, the ECHR confers a clear and explicit right to freedom of expression upon Europeans. Article 10(1) of the ECHR states that:

> 'Everyone has the right to freedom of expression. This right shall include freedom to hold opinions and to receive and impart information and ideas without interference by public authority and regardless of frontiers.'

The ECHR may be relied upon before the Irish courts[24] following the enactment of the European Convention on Human Rights Act 2003, which was commenced on 31 December 2003.[25]

---

[20] *Attorney General v Paperlink* [1984] ILRM 343. The right has been invoked by prisoners on a number of occasions, see: *Murray v Governor of Limerick Prison* (23 August 1978, unreported) HC; *Kearney v Minister for Justice* [1986] IR 116; and *Holland v Governor of Portlaoise Prison* [2004] 2 IR 573.

[21] [1984] ILRM 343 at 381.

[22] Hogan and Whyte, *Kelly: The Irish Constitution* (4th edn, Tottel Publishing, 2003) para 7.3.205.

[23] *The Irish Times v Ireland* [1998] 1 IR 359 at 406.

[24] Prior to the enactment of the European Convention on Human Rights Act 2003, Articles 15.2.1 and 29.6 had posed an insurmountable obstacle to invoking the ECHR before the Irish Courts: see *Re O'Laighlieis* [1960] IR 93; *Norris v Attorney General* [1984] IR 36; and *Kavanagh v Governor of Mountjoy Prison* [2002] 3 IR 97.

[25] European Convention on Human Rights Act 2003 (Commencement) Order 2003 (SI 483/2003).

This provides that:

> 'In interpreting and applying any statutory provision or rule of law, a court shall, in so far as is possible, subject to the rules of law relating to such interpretation and application, do so in a manner compatible with the State's obligations under the Convention provisions'.[26]

The Act goes on to provide that 'every organ of the State shall perform its functions in a manner compatible with the State's obligations under the Convention provisions'.[27] And it provides a cause of action for any person who has suffered an injury as a result of a failure by the State to perform its functions in a compatible manner.[28] Judicial notice must be taken of the ECHR's provisions, together with judgments of the ECtHR and decisions of the Committee of Ministers. The courts must 'take due account of the principles laid down by those declarations, decisions, advisory opinions, opinions and judgments'.[29] It remains to be seen how the Irish courts will integrate the Irish and ECHR rights. Judicial opinions would appear to differ on the compatibility of these rights. In *The Irish Times v Ireland* Barrington J was of the view that:

> 'if one compares Article 40.6.1° ... of the Irish Constitution with art. 10 of the European Convention on Human Rights (which deals with freedom of expression) one finds significant similarities as well as important differences'.[30]

[27.10] This view may be contrasted to that of Denham J in *O'Brien v Mirror Group Newspapers*:[31]

> 'The right to communicate, the right to information and the right to freedom of expression, guaranteed by Article 40.3.1° and 40.6.1°(i) of the Constitution of Ireland, are similar to the right of freedom of expression guaranteed by art 10 of the European Convention on Human Rights.'[32]

So, too, in *Hunter v Duckworth*[33] O'Caoimh stated that:

> 'I am satisfied that no essential difference exists between the provisions of the Convention and the provisions of Article 40.6.1° of the Constitution. What is relevant is how they should be interpreted ... However, Article 10 recognises that the protection given to freedom of expression may be curtailed and may be subject to restrictions as a prescribed by law and as are necessary in a democratic society for a variety of interests including the protection of the reputation or rights of others. It is, however, necessary to assess whether the common law of defamation as traditionally interpreted in this jurisdiction meets the requirements of the Constitution. In interpreting the Constitution this Court can have regard to the interpretation of the Convention insofar as it indicates how Article 40.6.1° may be interpreted'.

---

[26] European Convention on Human Rights Act 2003, s 2(1).
[27] European Convention on Human Rights Act 2003, s 3(1).
[28] European Convention on Human Rights Act 2003, s 3(2).
[29] European Convention on Human Rights Act 2003, s 4.
[30] *The Irish Times v Ireland* [1998] 1 IR 359 at 404.
[31] *O'Brien v Mirror Group Newspapers* [2001] 1 IR 1.
[32] [2001] 1 IR 1 at 33.
[33] *Hunter v Gerald Duckworth & Co Ltd & Anor* [2003] IEHC 81 (31 July 2003).

[27.11] The differences between the views of Barrington J, Denham J and O'Caoimh J should not be overstated. Barrington J notes that there are differences as well as similarities between the Constitution and the ECHR. Barrington J has to be correct in his view, given that the text of Article 40.6.1° of the Constitution and Article 10 of the ECHR are in fact different. What Barrington J does not suggest is that the Article 10 right may be incompatible with that provided by Article 40.6.1°. The judgment of O'Caoimh J suggests that compatibility may be ensured by interpreting Article 40.6.1° having regard to Article 10. The apparent difference in these opinions probably stems from the time at which the judgments were given. Barrington J. was giving judgment at a time when a comparison between Irish Constitutional and ECHR rights was an abstract question. Until the enactment of the European Convention on Human Rights Act 2003, ECHR rights could not be enforced in the Irish courts. In contrast, O'Caoimh J's judgment was given after this enactment.[34] Hence, O'Caoimh J was not discussing an abstract issue, but rather focusing on the practicalities of how the Constitutional and ECHR rights were to be integrated.

[27.12] As with the Irish Constitutional right, the ECHR right is limited. The right to freedom of expression cannot 'prevent States from requiring the licensing of broadcasting, television or cinema enterprises'.[35] Article 10(2) goes on to explicitly state that the exercise of freedom of expression 'carries with it duties and responsibilities'. Such freedom of expression may be subject to 'formalities, conditions, restrictions or penalties', which must be 'prescribed by law'; and 'necessary in a democratic society, in the interests of national security, territorial integrity or public safety, for the prevention of disorder or crime, for the protection of health or morals, for the protection of the reputation or rights of others, for preventing the disclosure of information received in confidence, or for maintaining the authority and impartiality of the judiciary'. Each of these limitations will be discussed in further detail in the chapters that follow.

European law

[27.13] Pending ratification of the European Constitution, European Union law is to be found in two basic texts: the Treaty on European Union (TEU) and the Treaty Establishing the European Community (TEC).

The Treaty on European Union (TEU)

[27.14] The European Union is bound to respect Article 10 of the ECHR, as the TEU provides that:

> 'The Union is founded on the principles of liberty, democracy, respect for human rights and fundamental freedoms, and the rule of law, principles which are common to the Member States.[36]

---

[34] Albeit prior to the commencement of the Act. The European Convention on Human Rights Act 2003 was enacted on 30 June 2003. O'Caoimh J gave judgment in *Hunter v Duckworth* on 31 July 2003.

[35] ECHR, art 10(1).

[36] Treaty on European Union (Nice consolidated version) EU Treaty (Maastricht 1992) OJ C 325, 24/12/2002 p 0005–0032, art 6(1). The signatories having confirmed their 'attachment to the principles of liberty, democracy and respect for human rights and fundamental freedoms and of the rule of law' in the preamble to the Treaty.

... The Union shall respect fundamental rights, as guaranteed by the European Convention for the Protection of Human Rights and Fundamental Freedoms signed in Rome on 4 November 1950 and as they result from the constitutional traditions common to the Member States, as general principles of Community law'.[37]

[27.15] So, for example, the Council Decision on the execution in the European Union of orders freezing property or evidence[38] 'does not prevent any Member State from applying its constitutional rules relating to ... freedom of the press and freedom of expression in other media,'[39] Further, one of the priorities listed in the Council Decision on the principles, priorities and conditions contained in the Accession Partnership with Turkey[40] is that Turkey should: 'Ensure the exercise of freedom of expression, including freedom of the press, in line with the European Convention on Human Rights and in accordance with the case law of the European Court of Human Rights.'[41]

Treaty Establishing the European Community (TEC)

[27.16] It may seem cynical, but expressions and opinion can be viewed as economic goods or commodities that can be traded in the form of books, websites and magazines.[42] The trade in expressions and opinions is a part of the internal market of the EC, and as such can only be restricted in accordance with EC Law. The European Community is tasked with:

'establishing a common market ... to promote ... a harmonious, balanced and sustainable development of economic activities, a high level of employment and of social protection, equality between men and women, sustainable and non-inflationary growth, a high degree of competitiveness and convergence of economic performance ... the raising of the standard of living and quality of life, and economic and social cohesion and solidarity among Member States'.[43]

To this end, the EC includes 'an internal market[44] characterised by the abolition, as between Member States, of obstacles to the free movement of goods, persons, services and capital.'[45]

---

[37] TEU, art 6(2).

[38] Council Framework Decision 2003/577/JHA of 22 July 2003 on the execution in the European Union of orders freezing property or evidence, OJ L 196 , 02/08/2003 p 0045–0055.

[39] Council Framework Decision 2003/577/JHA, preamble.

[40] 2006/35/EC: Council Decision of 23 January 2006 on the principles, priorities and conditions contained in the Accession Partnership with Turkey, OJ L 022 , 26/01/2006 p 0034–0050.

[41] 2006/35/EC, art 3.1.

[42] In 2001 the artistic exemption granted pursuant to section – of the Tax Acts was worth €23.5 million. Some 1,300 Irish residents benefited from this exemption, with 80% of the benefit going to 10% of the recipients. See Brian Cowen TD, Minister for Finance, Written Answers. – Tax Code, Dáil Éireann – Volume 604 – 16 June, 2005.

[43] Consolidated version of the Treaty Establishing the European Community OJ C 325, 24.12.2002, 33–184.

[44] The internal market is defined as comprising 'an area without internal frontiers in which the free movement of goods, persons, services and capital is ensured in accordance with the provisions of this Treaty', Article 14(2).

[45] Article 3(1)(c).

[27.17] The right to free movement of goods is provided by Part 3, Title 1 of the TEC. This provides for a customs union 'which shall cover all trade in goods and which shall involve the prohibition between Member States of customs duties on imports and exports and of all charges having equivalent effect'.[46] Quantative restrictions on imports[47] and exports[48] between member states are also prohibited. However the TEC provides that this prohibition on quantative restrictions:

> 'shall not preclude prohibitions or restrictions on imports, exports or goods in transit justified on grounds of public morality, public policy or public security; the protection of health and life of humans ... or the protection of industrial and commercial property. Such prohibitions or restrictions shall not, however, constitute a means of arbitrary discrimination or a disguised restriction on trade between Member States'.[49]

This provision clearly provides for restrictions on the grounds of 'public morality'. The impact of such restrictions was discussed by the ECJ in *Quietlynn Ltd v Southend Borough Council*.[50] The applicants claimed that the Borough Council's refusal to give them a licence to run a sex shop amounted to 'a measure having an effect equivalent to a quantitative restriction on imports'.[51] In essence, the refusal to give the applicants a licence stopped them selling goods to the public and so importing them wholesale from other member states. The application failed.

[27.18] To ensure the creation of the internal market, Article 95 of the TEC provides that the EC may:

> 'adopt ... measures for the approximation of the provisions laid down by law, regulation or administrative action in Member States which have as their object the establishment and functioning of the internal market'.[52]

A number of measures adopted pursuant to Article 95 have implications for freedom of expression. The e-Commerce Directive[53] provides that 'Member States may not ... restrict the freedom to provide information society services from another Member State'.[54] This provision only applies to 'reasons falling within the coordinated field',[55] which in effect means that it only applies to what the e-Commerce Directive terms

---

[46] TEC, art 23(1).

[47] TEC, art 28.

[48] TEC, art 29.

[49] TEC, art 30.

[50] *Quietlynn Ltd v Southend Borough Council* C-23/89, 11 July 1990, ECR 1990, p I-03059.

[51] C-23/89, para 12.

[52] Article 95(1).

[53] Directive 2000/31/EC of the European Parliament and of the Council of 8 June 2000 on certain legal aspects of information society services, in particular electronic commerce, in the Internal Market ('Directive on electronic commerce'), OJ L 178 , 17/07/2000 p 0001–0016.

[54] Directive 2000/31/EC, art 3(2).

[55] The 'coordinated field' of Directive 2000/31/EC means 'requirements laid down in Member States' legal systems applicable to information society service providers or information society services, regardless of whether they are of a general nature or specifically designed for them'. (contd/)

'Information society services'. Of course, such services are increasingly used to circulate content and opinion throughout the EC. Member states may 'take measures to derogate' from this provision 'in respect of a given information society service', but only if certain specific conditions are fulfilled. Firstly, the measure in question must be necessary for obtaining one of the following objectives:

- public policy, in particular the prevention, investigation, detection and prosecution of criminal offences, including the protection of minors and the fight against any incitement to hatred on grounds of race, sex, religion or nationality, and violations of human dignity concerning individual persons;

- the protection of public health; or,

- public security, including the safeguarding of national security and defence.

[27.19] Secondly, the measure must be taken against an information society service that prejudices one of the above objectives or that presents a serious and grave risk of prejudice to those objectives. Thirdly, the measure taken must be proportionate to the above objectives. Finally, the member state that takes the measure in question must have asked the member state that hosts the information society service in question to take the measures, and that member state must have failed to do so. The Commission and the host member state must also have been notified of the intentions of member state that is to take the measure.[56]

The e-Commerce Directive also limits the ability of member states to place controls upon who provides information society services. This means that member states cannot impose the licensing schemes on websites, similar to the licences that member states may require for theatres or dance halls. The e-Commerce Directive provides that:

'Member States shall ensure that the taking up and pursuit of the activity of an information society service[57] provider may not be made subject to prior authorisation or any other requirement having equivalent effect'.[58]

---

[55] (\contd) It concerns requirements with which the service provider had to comply in respect of 'the taking up of the activity of an information society service, such as requirements concerning qualifications, authorisation or notification', and 'the pursuit of the activity of an information society service, such as requirements concerning the behaviour of the service provider, requirements regarding the quality or content of the service including those applicable to advertising and contracts, or requirements concerning the liability of the service provider'. The 'coordinated field' does not include requirements applicable to: 'goods as such'; 'the delivery of goods'; and 'services not provided by electronic means'. Directive 2000/31/EC, art 2.

[56] Directive 2000/31/EC, art 3(4).

[57] 'Information society service' is defined as 'any service normally provided for remuneration, at a distance, by electronic means and at the individual request of a recipient of services' by Directive 98/48/EC of the European Parliament and of the Council of 20 July 1998 amending Directive 98/34/EC laying down a procedure for the provision of information in the field of technical standards and regulations, OJ L 217 , 05/08/1998 p 0018–0026, art 1(2).

[58] Directive 2000/31/EC, art 4(1).

[27.20] Similarly, the Authorisation Directive[59] provides that:

'Member States shall ensure the freedom to provide electronic communications networks and services ... To this end, Member States shall not prevent an undertaking from providing electronic communications networks or services'.[60]

The Authorisation Directive goes on to provide that:

'The provision of electronic communications networks or the provision of electronic communications services may ... only be subject to a general authorisation. The undertaking concerned may be required to submit a notification but may not be required to obtain an explicit decision or any other administrative act by the national regulatory authority before exercising the rights stemming from the authorisation. Upon notification, when required, an undertaking may begin activity'.[61]

Anyone can get such a general authorisation by making:

'a declaration ... to the national regulatory authority of the intention to commence the provision of electronic communication networks or services and the submission of the minimal information which is required to allow the national regulatory authority to keep a register or list of providers of electronic communications networks and services'.[62]

Anyone who is issued with such a general authorisation will be granted the right to 'provide electronic communications networks and services'.[63] The general authorisation may be subject to conditions, but only those that are set out in the annex to the Authorisation Directive. One permitted set of conditions are those 'in relation to the transmission of illegal content'.[64] However, it would appear that ComReg does not impose such restrictions upon Irish providers.[65]

[27.21] Finally, the Television without Frontiers Directive[66] allows for 'freedom of reception' within member states.[67] Again, this right may be restricted, particularly on the grounds of protection of minors. The Television without Frontiers Directive provides that:

'Member States shall take appropriate measures to ensure that television broadcasts by broadcasters under their jurisdiction do not include programmes which might seriously impair the physical, mental or moral development of minors, in particular those that

---

[59] Directive 2002/20/EC of the European Parliament and of the Council of 7 March 2002 on the authorisation of electronic communications networks and services (Authorisation Directive), OJ L 108 , 24/04/2002 p 0021–0032.

[60] 'except where this is necessary for the reasons set out in Article 46(1) of the Treaty', Directive 2002/20/EC, art 3(1).

[61] Directive 2002/20/EC, art 3(2).

[62] Directive 2002/20/EC, art 3(3).

[63] Directive 2002/20/EC, art 4(1)(a).

[64] Directive 2002/20/EC, Annex, para A(9).

[65] ComReg, *General Authorisation*, Doc No 03/81, 25 July 2003.

[66] Council Directive 89/552/EEC of 3 October 1989 on the coordination of certain provisions laid down by Law, Regulation or Administrative Action in Member States concerning the pursuit of television broadcasting activities, OJ L 298 , 17/10/1989 p 0023–0030.

[67] Council Directive 89/552/EEC, art 2(2).

involve pornography or gratuitous violence. This provision shall extend to other programmes which are likely to impair the physical, mental or moral development of minors, except where it is ensured, by selecting the time of the broadcast or by any technical measure, that minors in the area of transmission will not normally hear or see such broadcasts'.[68]

The Television without Frontiers Directive also provides that 'Member States shall also ensure that broadcasts do not contain any incitement to hatred on grounds of race, sex, religion or nationality'.[69]

---

[68] Council Directive 89/552/EEC, art 22.
[69] Council Directive 89/552/EEC, art 22.

Chapter 28

Defamation

Introduction

[28.01] Defamation is a tort, as it is part of the common law and has no statutory definition. Legislation, such as the Defamation Act 1961 and the Defamation Bill 2006, has and will have an impact upon the law, as does the Constitution and the European Convention on Human Rights (ECHR). But the law of defamation is primarily determined by case law. A judge who hears a case involving a new technology or a novel situation will be able to amend precedent to ensure that the tort continues to apply. In the long term there is no need for the Oireachtas to keep updating the tort of defamation, as the judiciary is able to do so. The only problem with this approach is that the judiciary is only able to update the law when a case is heard which involves such a new technology or novel situation. So in the short term, the application of the tort of defamation to that technology or situation will remain unclear. However, this must be read more as an observation than a criticism. Legislating for an area as complex and evolving as defamation can never be easy and may not be helpful. During its passage through the Oireachtas, the Bill that became the Electronic Commerce Act 2000 was amended to purportedly extend the law of defamation to the Internet. The redundancy of this extension was apparent at the time, not least to the Minister who accepted the amendment.[1] On the other hand, the Defamation Bill 2006 appears to give limited consideration to the possibility that defamation can occur online and that defamatory statements may be published in fora which lack the hierarchical management and legal advice needed to process the offers of amends and apology that the Bill will require. At present, Irish defamation law appears to be evolving into a two-tier structure. On the one hand, you have the well established, respectable, 'old media' of newspapers, radio and TV stations. The Defamation Bill 2006 is directed at meeting the needs of this 'old media'. On the other hand, you have the anarchic and unregulated 'new media' of websites, discussion boards, blogs and video uploads. The Defamation Bill 2006 appears to give limited consideration to the application of defamation law to this 'new media'.

[28.02] If anything the Defamation Bill 2006 may encourage the anarchic development of the Irish Internet. If you want to establish a website that will host a discussion about any issue – whether topical or obscure – you may do so in one of two ways. You may structure it in such a way that you become the 'publisher' of the site, and in doing so you must provide the legal structures, purchase liability insurance and seek legal advice so that you may limit your exposure to claims for defamation. Alternatively, you may

---

[1] Seanad Éireann – Volume 163 – 30 June, 2000, Electronic Commerce Bill 2000 [Seanad Bill amended by the Dáil]: Report and Final Stages.

establish the website with yourself as 'intermediary service provider'. The essential criterion for ensuring that you fall into this category is to ensure that you have as little to do with the content of your site as possible. If you are informed that material is defamatory, you must take it down but other than that you must avoid anything that could be construed as editorial intervention.

[28.03] Again, these remarks should be read more as observation than criticism. The law of defamation has long recognised that there is a difference between publishers and distributors. The difference now is that the Internet allows anyone to publish any allegation to a global market. Publishers used to act as gatekeepers; now they do not. Of course, this phenomenon is not unique to Ireland, and it is actually less apparent here than in other jurisdictions such as the USA. But because the Irish law of defamation is so strict and the damages that may be imposed are so punitive, Irish law creates very strong incentives for websites to make qualitative judgments about the material that they distribute. This may have interesting consequences for Irish media; one consequence might be that Irish media would follow the American experience after the abolition of balancing requirements. An explosion in the number of outlets might mean that only the most aggressive and radical voices would have the volume to distinguish themselves from the throng. It is not that websites would ignore alternative voices, but they would not be able to provide such balance as any such editorial involvement would expose the editor to the laws of defamation.

[28.04] Alternatively, the Irish Internet might become an anarchic mess of untruths, half-truths and conspiracy theories. Over time, consumers would come to distrust anything that was produced by this mess, and would instead gravitate back to older, better established media, such as http://www.ireland.com; http://www.rte.ie or http://www.independent.ie. Of course, it is impossible to predict what will happen as Ireland moves online. The development of the Irish Internet has been retarded by the slow roll-out of broadband. By excluding the need for expensive print and distribution processes, widespread internet usage in Ireland should encourage the development of new sites and online media outlets. But Irish defamation law means that those sites will have to develop a 'top-down' hierarchical management structure almost immediately. It is impossible to imagine a site such as http://www.wikipedia.com developing in Ireland. The content of sites such as this is controlled by users; the whole point of the site is that nobody is there checking the content of what goes online. This process has many advantages, but unfortunately the absence of formal editorial structures means that the site has been used to publish untruths. The resulting controversy has seriously damaged the credibility of all information published on http://www.wikipedia.com, but the site's innovative approach to user-generated content has had a revolutionary effect on publishing. Defamation law would seem to preclude the development of such innovative forms of content in Ireland. Wikipedia lacks the formal management structures of a traditional newspaper or encyclopedia, but the operators of the site probably have sufficient control to be viewed as publishers. Again this is more an observation; the Irish law of defamation is well established by common law, legislation and the Constitution. Changing the law would require a radical restructuring of how Irish people view the rights of the individual and the role of the media, but some may consider that it is the function of the Internet to force such a restructuring.

[28.05] The argument can be made that defamation law is now at the stage that copyright was at in 1999 when the Record Industry Association of America decided to shut down Napster. There is no question that Napster was directly breaching copyright; it was furthermore encouraging and facilitating others to do so. Napster controlled the distribution of online music. What Napster was doing was illegal, but it was controlled. Legally, the RIAA were clearly right to close down the site but from a business perspective and with the benefit of hindsight they might have been wiser to have taken over the site on behalf of the music industry. Two things have happened since *Grokster.* Firstly, we have seen the growth in off-shore sites such as http://www.allofmp3.com and its mirror sites. These sites are based in countries like Russia, which are outside the jurisdiction of American and European courts. Secondly, we have seen the growth of systems such as bitTorrent (the peer-to-peer system). The consequence of RIAA trying to completely control the distribution of online music in the USA has been the development of systems and processes whereby music can be distributed outside the control of any person or agency. RIAA is no longer struggling for control of music with Napster, Grokster or even Steve Jobs in a sense it has ceded control to nobody and everybody simultaneously. A similar process may occur if an attempt is made to apply the law of defamation to online discussions as strictly as it applies to discussions in newspapers and on RTÉ. Instead, the discussion will move offshore or underground, outside the control of the Irish courts. Initially the effects of such a move may be limited and individuals may be satisfied that as long as they are not defamed in The Irish Times or on *Prime Time*. But it is submitted that the consequences of such a move might be seriously damaging to Irish society as it would limit process of national discussion. Since *Napster*, a generation of consumers have grown up who rarely, if ever, purchase music legitimately. They acquire their music from offshore sites or underground distribution networks. As a result the CD music format has died and the authors' local music store has closed down. If online discussions are forced offshore, the consequences may be more serious for Ireland. You will not have a national discussion anymore; you will have a diffuse amalgam of cliques and conspiracy theorists and experts propounding their views online. This may prove to be a good thing for Irish society, or it may prove to be bad, but it may prove fatal to Ireland's defamation laws.

The tort of defamation in the context of the Constitution and the ECHR

[28.06] The right to a reputation is one of the unspecified personal rights provided by Article 40.3 of the Constitution.[2] Although the tort of defamation long precedes the Bunreacht na hÉireann, the tort may be regarded as giving effect to the Constitutional right. The right to one's reputation is not absolute; it must be balanced with the right to freedom of expression, the right to communicate and the right to publish one's views. The right to a reputation must also be assessed in the context of Article 10 of the ECHR.

[28.07] As a consequence of the enactment of the European Convention on Human Rights Act 2003 all Irish legislation must be interpreted and applied 'in a manner

---

[2] *The State (Vozza) v Floinn* [1957] IR 227; *Re Haughey* [1971] IR 217; *Goodman International v Hamilton (No 1)* [1992] IR 542, [1992] ILRM 145; and *Goodman International v Hamilton (No 2)* 1993 IR 227, 1993 ILRM 821.

compatible with the State's obligations under the Convention'.[3] Furthermore, 'Judicial notice shall be taken of the Convention provisions'.[4] It remains to be seen how the courts will adapt the Irish law of defamation to the Convention rights.[5]

What is defamatory?

[28.08] A statement about a person will be defamatory if it fulfills the following criterion 'A publication is defamatory of a person if it injures or tends to injure his good reputation in the minds of right-thinking people.'[6] As the Supreme Court acknowledged in *Berry v Irish Times*,[7] the difficulty with this simple definition:

> 'is to discover what is meant by 'right-thinking people.' It does not mean all such people but only some such people, perhaps even only one, because if a plaintiff loses the respect for his reputation of some or even one right-thinking person he suffers some injury.'[8]

Defamation is a complex tort, but there are two key elements. One is that the statement must be defamatory; the other is that it must be published. As of yet, information technology has not affected what is or is not a defamatory statement, although enhanced abilities to create, alter and adjust visual images and audio recordings might be misused to damage the reputations of individuals. Where information technology has had an effect is with regard to the publication of those statements. It has made publication a whole lot easier. Express scepticism of how much real effect the Internet will have in this regard has been made:

> 'In the course of argument much emphasis was given to the fact that the advent of the World Wide Web is a considerable technological advance. So it is. But the problem of widely disseminated communications is much older than the internet and the World Wide Web. The law has had to grapple with such cases ever since newspapers and magazines came to be distributed to large numbers of people over wide geographic areas. Radio and television presented the same kind of problem as was presented by widespread dissemination of printed material, although international transmission of material was made easier by the advent of electronic means of communication.'[9]

Regardless of whether the Internet and information technologies have had a major impact on the jurisprudence of defamation law, they are having very considerable practical impact. Until recently only a major corporation or institution with access to considerable funds and expertise, such as Dow Jones, could aspire to global publication. Now everyone can. At the time of writing,[10] the most popular clip on http://www.youtube.com has been viewed 318,277 times in the past 24 hours. The very vast majority of material on the Internet will never even come close to this level of

---

3   European Convention on Human Rights Act 2003, s 2(1).
4   European Convention on Human Rights Act 2003, s 4.
5   See the discussion of these points in Healy, *Principles of Irish Torts* (Clarus Press, 2006) pp 349–353.
6   *Berry v Irish Times* [1973] IR 368 at 380.
7   [1973] IR 368.
8   [1973] IR 368 at 380.
9   *Dow Jones & Company Inc v Gutnick* [2002] HCA 56, para 38.
10 Midnight (Belgian time), 30 August 2007.

popularity. But the Internet has made it possible for anyone to publish anything. The legal ramifications of this development are only beginning to be worked out.

Defamation, libel and slander

[28.09] Defamation is the term given to the overarching tort of damaging another's reputation. Libel is a defamatory statement published in a permanent format; slander is a transient defamatory statement. A statement is published when it is communicated to third parties. The Defamation Bill 2006, which is apparently to be re-introduced into the 30th Dáil, would have abolished the separate torts of libel and slander and replaced them with a single tort of defamation.[11]

Publication online

[28.10] The Electronic Commerce Act 2000 provides 'All provisions of existing defamation law shall apply to all electronic communications within the State, including the retention of information electronically.'[12] This provision was probably unnecessary, being described as 'an avoidance of doubt type amendment'.[13] The reason why there was no doubt was that the English courts had already clarified that the laws of defamation applied online in *Godfrey v Demon Internet*.[14] This case clarified that the English law of defamation applied to the publication of defamatory statements both by sending emails and by posting messages online.

Publication by email

[28.11] The facts of *Lunney v Prodigy Services Co*[15] *were as follows:*

> "Some infantile practical joker with access to a computer sent an offensive electronic message (hereinafter email) to a boy scout leader, infusing the text of the message with threats more likely to perplex than actually to intimidate an adult recipient. The intended victim of this prank appears to be less the boy scout leader himself than the plaintiff, Alex G. Lunney, who was then a 15-year-old prospective eagle scout, and whose name

---

[11] Defamation Bill 2006, s 5, which proposed that 'The tort of libel and the tort of slander ... shall cease to be so described, and ... shall, instead, be collectively described, and are referred to in this Act, as the "tort of defamation".

[12] Electronic Commerce Act 2000, s 23.

[13] Seanad Éireann – Volume 163 – 30 June, 2000, Electronic Commerce Bill 2000 [Seanad Bill amended by the Dáil]: Report and Final Stages.

[14] *Godfrey v Demon Internet* [2000] 3 WLR 1020. The Minister who was responsible for the Bill (Mary O'Rourke TD) explained the significance of this case in the following terms: 'There is a precedent in the UK – the decision of the English High Court of 26 March 1999 in *Godfrey v Demon Internet* – but we just cannot take such precedent. It is likely that Irish courts will hold that defamation principles apply equally to the Internet. We will have to wait until there is an Irish precedent. In the UK case the judge said the defendant internet service provider was analogous to a bookseller or publishers who sold defamatory materials. The judge said that publication of defamatory matter will occur each time a person accesses it on the Internet ... We do not have Irish case law, and we will see if the English precedent becomes the precedent here. I will accept the amendment' Dáil Éireann – Volume 522 – 29 June 2000, Electronic Commerce Bill, 2000 [Seanad]: Committee Stage (Resumed) and Remaining Stages.

[15] *Lunney v Prodigy Services Co* (1998) 250 AD 2d 230.

appeared as the signatory and author of the email message in question. The charade was, as they say crude but effective, in that the plaintiff was initially suspected of having sent the threatening piece of electronic correspondence ... In his amended complaint, the plaintiff expanded his factual allegations in order to encompass two 'bulletin board' messages posted with the help of Prodigy's service.'[16]

Commenting on the above in *Godfrey v Demon*[17] Morland J stated that 'In my judgment, at English common law Prodigy would clearly have been the publisher of the practical joker's message.'[18]

Publication by posting online

[28.12] In *Godfrey v Demon* the defendant hosted a usenet, which was described by Morland J in the following terns:

> 'Usenet is one to many publication from author to readers round the world. An article (known as a posting) is submitted by its author to the Usenet news-server based at his own local ISP (the originating ISP) who disseminates via the internet the posting. Ultimately it is distributed and stored on the news-servers of every (or nearly every) ISP in the world that offers Usenet facilities to its customers. Internet users world wide can read and download the posting by connecting to their local ISP's news-servers.'

A message was posted to one such usenet, soc.culture.thai, which was hosted by the defendant and was 'squalid, obscene and defamatory of the plaintiff.'[19] The plaintiff sued the Internet service provider successfully, Morland J holding that the defendants were responsible:

> 'whenever they transmit and whenever there is transmitted from the storage of their news server a defamatory posting, publish that posting to any subscriber to their ISP who accesses the newsgroup containing that posting. Thus every time one of the defendants' customers accesses soc.culture.thai and sees that posting defamatory of the plaintiff there is a publication to that customer ... The situation is analogous to that of the bookseller who sells a book defamatory of the plaintiff.'[20]

It should be noted that there have been at least a couple of instances where prosecutions were brought for criminal libel online, and these instances are discussed below.

Publication by repetition

[28.13] The Internet is an environment where statements, whether made in an email[21] or placed on a website,[22] can be quickly transmitted to a wide audience. This means that a

---

16 (1998) 250 AD 2d 230 at 231–232.
17 *Godfrey v Demon* [2000] 3 WLR 1020.
18 [2000] 3 WLR 1020 at 1030.
19 [2000] 3 WLR 1020 at 1023.
20 [2000] 3 WLR 1020 at 1026.
21 The most infamous example being that of Claire Swire, who lost her dignity but kept her job, Eaglesham, 'email lawyer escapes sack' (2000) The Financial Times, 22 December.
22 'A message that the entertainer Twink is purported to have left on her ex-husband's phone has become an Internet phenomenon', Hegarty, 'You can't zip up the web' (2006) The Irish Times, 16 December.

defamatory statement can be repeated to an audience far outside that for which it was originally intended, and this process can exacerbate the defamatory effects of any statement. Every time a defamatory statement is repeated a fresh cause of action will arise, it being 'a well established principle of the ... law of defamation that each individual publication of a libel gives rise to a separate cause of action.'[23] So the original publisher will be liable for his publication, as the subsequent publisher will be liable for his. But what if the original publisher anticipated or knew that his publication would be repeated? If this happens, then the original publisher may be liable for the subsequent publication as well as his own. In *Ewins v Carlton Television Ltd*[24] the first-named defendant had made a programme in which serious allegations were made about the plaintiffs. This programme was then supplied to UTV in Northern Ireland, which broadcast the programme to an audience that included 110,000 viewers in the South. In his judgment Budd J adopted the rule in *Speight v Gospay*:[25]

> 'the original publisher of a defamatory statement is liable for its republication by another person where, inter alia, the repetition or republication of the words to a third person was the natural and probable result of the original publication. The natural and probable consequence of providing the programme complained of to Ulster Television for re-distribution on its network was that it would reach a significant number of viewers in this jurisdiction.'

[28.14] Modern media can repeat, and amplify, statements made to small audiences. This occurred in the English Court of Appeal decision in *McManus v Beckham*.[26] The defendant was the wife of a famous footballer; the plaintiffs ran a shop that sold memorabilia and autographs. The plaintiffs had sued the defendant for defamation alleging that she 'came into their shop and in a rude, loud and unreasonable way advised the three customers present that the autograph on a photograph of her husband ... was a fake'.[27] The plaintiffs sued the defendant in respect of the original publication only, but sought to 'rely on the press coverage in establishing the loss they say they suffered.'[28] The plaintiffs alleged that:

> 'the slander took place on 26 March 2001, there was a loss of business thereafter, and the size of the loss can be explained by the fact that the slander was not only published to those three customers in the shop, but was published outside the shop including receiving wide publicity in the national press.'[29]

The plaintiffs were only claiming a single cause of action relating to the original statement in the shop. They were not claiming two causes of action: one in respect of the original slander; the other in respect of the re-publication in the press.

---

[23] *Loutchansky v Times Newspapers* [2001] EWCA Civ 1805, para 57.
[24] *Ewins v Carlton Television Ltd* [1997] 2 ILRM 223.
[25] *Speight v Gospay* [1891] 60 LJQB 231.
[26] *McManus v Beckham* [2002] EWCA Civ 939, [2002] 4 All ER 497, [2002] 1 WLR 2982.
[27] [2002] EWCA Civ 939, para 1.
[28] [2002] EWCA Civ 939, para 2.
[29] [2002] EWCA Civ 939, para 12.

In *McManus v Beckham* the plaintiffs alleged that the defendant:

> 'routinely and assiduously courts publicity and 'well knew and could and did foresee' that what she said was likely to come to the attention of the national and local media and was likely to be reported widely 'in such media in eye-catching and sensational terms and/or repeated in the specialist celebrity autograph market ... that she thus knew and/or could foresee that the newspapers and the celebrity market would repeat the defamatory sting in whole or in part.'[30]

[28.15] Waller LJ noted that the plaintiff might find it difficult to 'establish actual knowledge or awareness, but difficulty is not the same as impossibility.'[31] But subject to proof, Waller LJ thought it was possible that the plaintiffs might succeed.

> 'What the law is striving to achieve in this area is a just and reasonable result by reference to the position of a reasonable person in the position of the defendant. If a defendant is actually aware (1) that what she says or does is likely to be reported, and (2) that if she slanders someone that slander is likely to be repeated in whole or in part, there is no injustice in her being held responsible for the damage that the slander causes via that publication. I would suggest further that if a jury were to conclude that a reasonable person in the position of the defendant should have appreciated that there was a significant risk that what she said would be repeated in whole or in part in the press and that that would increase the damage caused.'[32]

Given the exceptional level of media interest in the defendant, particularly at the time when she made the statements in question, there are good grounds for arguing that *McManus v Beckham* is very much an exceptional case. If a less well known, or obscure, person were to similarly defame another, then the repetition of that defamatory statement would not be reasonably foreseeable. In *Slipper v BBC*[33] the plaintiff was a police officer who was the subject of a television documentary, which was reviewed in the press. The plaintiff sued contending that 'the following passages from reviews which repeat the defamatory sting of the said film should be taken into account in assessment of general damages.'[34] The defendant sought to have this paragraph struck from the plaintiff's statement of claim by way of an interlocutory motion. The question reached the Court of Appeal, where Stocker LJ held:

> 'In my opinion this is a question of remoteness of damage and not liability and raises an issue of fact for the jury. I have no doubt at all that, to put it no higher, it could not be said that this was a 'plain and obvious case' so as to justify striking out. I would go further and say that the matter cannot be resolved without the findings of fact by the jury, to which I have referred. This includes the question of whether or not it was foreseeable or a natural and probable consequence of the invitation to review that such reviews would include the sting of libel. Accordingly I agree with the trial judge that there was no case for striking out and his decision was correct.'[35]

---

30 [2002] EWCA Civ 939, para 28.
31 [2002] EWCA Civ 939, para 31.
32 [2002] EWCA Civ 939, para 34.
33 *Slipper v BBC* [1990] 3 WLR 967; see also *Weld-Blundell v Stephens* [1918] 2 KB 742, [1919] 1 KB 520, CA, [1920] AC 956, HL(E).
34 [1990] 3 WLR 967 at 971.
35 [1990] 3 WLR 967 at 979.

[28.16] The question then arises of what is reasonably foreseeable as regards the repetition of statements made online. It is clear that the Internet does create an environment where such statements can be repeated – in this regard the case of the unfortunate Clair Swire is instructive. She was a lawyer who sent a lewd (not defamatory) email to her boyfriend. He forwarded the email to another, who forwarded it on and soon it was read nationwide.[36] The forwarding of such emails is not uncommon,[37] but it might be hard to prove that it was so common that it became reasonably foreseeable. That said, a cynic might concur with the view of Sumner LJ in *Weld-Blundell v Stephens*[38] that 'taking men as we find them, few things are more certain than the repetition of a calumny confidentially communicated, even on an honourable understanding of secrecy.'[39] Obviously what is reasonably foreseeable will depend upon the circumstances of any particular case. It is one thing to argue that the maker of a defamatory statement, who publishes in a private email, should not be liable for the repetition of that statement as the repetition is not reasonably foreseeable. It is quite another to argue that someone who publishes a statement on a publicly accessible website such as http://www.youtube.com or http://www.rate-your-solicitor.com should be liable for the repetition. Of course much, indeed virtually all, of the material that is published on such sites will remain obscure and unnoticed. And the publisher might be surprised if such a statement should be repeated, but given the nature of such sites and the reality that they are publicly available, it would be difficult to argue that subsequent repetition was not reasonably foreseeable.

Repetition by linking

[28.17] In the American case of *Steinbuch v Cutler*[40] the defendant created a blog under the name 'Washingtonienne', where she wrote 'about her social and sexual activities with various men'. One of these men was the plaintiff. The better known Wonkette blog then linked to Washingtonienne, whereupon the defendant's claims were 'circulated to a wide audience'. Were similar events to occur in relation to an Irish blog, the question would arise of whether it was reasonably foreseeable that links would be created to a blog created by a staff member of the Houses of the Oireachtas in which she posted 'intimate details about her experience sleeping with six different men, some of whom were paying for her favors … (including) … the married 'Chief of Staff at one of the gov agencies.'[41] It is unlikely that this question would trouble the court for very long.

Repetition in breach of copyright

[28.18] Should the initial publisher be liable for repetition of a defamatory statement where that repetition is in breach of the copyright in the original statement? Such

---

[36] Woods, 'Yum yum: The saucy email that wrecked Claire's life' (2000) The Sunday Times, 17 December.

[37] Sherwood & Larsen, 'Analyst's explicit email puts his job at risk' (2006) The Financial Times, 21 January.

[38] *Weld-Blundell v Stephens* [1920] AC 956.

[39] [1920] AC 956 at 976.

[40] *Steinbuch v Cutler* US District Court for the District of Colombia, 30 October 2006.

[41] Rosen, 'Your blog or mine?' (2004) The New York Times, 19 December.

repetition is not uncommon.[42] On the one hand it may seem unfair to find the initial publisher liable for such unauthorised repetition. On the other hand, the CRRA 2000–2004 ensure that the owners of copyright have a variety of mechanisms, most notably injunctions, by which they may enforce their copyright. So it may be that the courts would expect an initial publisher to at least have tried to prevent such repetition, before finding that the initial publisher was not liable for same. But every case will depend upon its facts.

Publication in an online archive

[28.19] In *Loutchansky v Times Newspapers*[43] the plaintiff claimed that he was initially defamed by a couple of articles published by the defendant newspaper. He also claimed that 'each article was posted on 'The Times' website, where it has since remained accessible and, as ultimately conceded, has from time to time been read.'[44] The question then arose of whether the plaintiff had a single cause of action encompassing both the initial publication and the subsequent replication in the newspaper's Internet archive, or whether the plaintiff had a separate cause of action in respect of each cause of publication. Philips LJ in the English Court of Appeal noted that:

> 'a restriction on the readiness to maintain and provide access to archives that amounts to a disproportionate restriction on freedom of expression. We accept that the maintenance of archives, whether in hard copy or on the Internet, has a social utility, but consider that the maintenance of archives is a comparatively insignificant aspect of freedom of expression. Archive material is stale news and its publication cannot rank in importance with the dissemination of contemporary material.'[45]

Philips LJ noted that the cause of action in respect of the Internet archive was subsidiary to the primary cause of action, namely the initial publication, and that 'the scale of such publication and any resulting damage is likely to be modest compared with that of the original publication.'[46] He therefore dismissed the plaintiff's appeal arguing that the initial publication and the publication in the newspaper's archive should be treated as a single publication.

Jurisdiction

[28.20] The Internet is a global network – an article published in Ireland may be downloaded anywhere from Tokyo, Japan to Toronto, Canada. This means that a defamatory statement may receive worldwide publication. Therefore jurisdiction is an important aspect of Internet defamation. Practical considerations are of great significance when considering how the Irish law of defamation may apply to statements published elsewhere in the world. One such consideration is that it is not enough to get

---

[42] When the New York Times started charging for full access to its site and columnists, popular columns were replicated elsewhere in breach of the newspaper's copyright: 'The top seven searches on Technorati are all searches for blocked-off New York Times columns'; Kaus, 'The Aspens Sleep With the Fishes!' (2005) Slate Magazine, 26 September.

[43] *Loutchansky v Times Newspapers* [2001] EWCA Civ 1805, [2002] QB 783.

[44] [2001] EWCA Civ 1805, para 9.

[45] [2001] EWCA Civ 1805, para 74.

[46] [2001] EWCA Civ 1805, para 75.

an award of damages in the Irish courts; some consideration must also be given to how the award will be enforced.

Jurisdiction under the Brussels Convention

[28.21] The Brussels Convention is implemented into Irish law as the Jurisdiction of Court and Enforcement of Judgments (European Communities) Act 1988. This provides that the Irish courts have jurisdiction in tort cases, provided that the 'harmful event' complained of occurred in Ireland.[47] There are two articles of the Convention that are of relevance. Article 2 provides that:

> 'persons domiciled in a Contracting State shall, whatever their nationality be sued in the courts of that State. Persons who are not nationals of the State in which they are domiciled shall be governed by the rules of jurisdiction applicable to the nationals of that State'.

Article 5(3) provides that, in matters relating to tort, a person domiciled in one contracting state may be sued in the jurisdiction where the harmful event occurred. In *Sheville & Ors v Presse Alliance SA*,[48] the ECJ examined an alleged libel published in *France Soir* which was distributed in the UK. Proceedings were commenced in the UK and the issue arose as to whether the English courts had jurisdiction to deal with the alleged libel.[49] The court held that:

> 'On a proper construction of the expression 'place where the harmful event occurred' in article 5(3) of the Convention, the victim of a libel by a newspaper article distributed in several contracting states may bring an action for damages against the publisher either before the courts of the contracting state of the place where the publisher of the defamatory publication is established which have jurisdiction to award damages for all the harm caused by the defamation or before the courts of each contracting state in which publication was distributed and where victim claims to have suffered injury to his reputation which have jurisdiction to rule solely in respect of the harm caused in the state of the court seized'.[50]

[28.22] In *Ewins & ors v Carlton Television*[51] the plaintiffs claimed damages following a television documentary concerning purported IRA activities. The documentary was made and published by Carlton and disseminated to the public by ITN and UTV in 1995; it allegedly was defamatory of the plaintiffs who commenced an action against the defendants in the Irish courts. The defendant sought to have the proceedings stayed on a number of grounds including: if the proceedings were brought in the UK it would avoid a multiplicity of proceedings; the defendants were domiciled in the UK; the alleged

---

47 See *Casey v Ingersoll Rand* [1966] 2 ILRM 456 and *Short & Ors v Ireland, the Attorney General and BNFL* [1997] 1 ILRM 161.

48 *Sheville & Ors v Presse Alliance SA* [1995] EC 289. See *Murray v Times Newspapers* [1995] 3 IR 244.

49 See s 4 of the Jurisdiction of Courts and Enforcement of Judgments (European Communities) Act 1988: Judicial notice shall be taken of any ruling or decision of or expression of opinion by the European Court on any question as to the meaning or effect of any provision of the Conventions.

50 (7 March 1995) ECJ para 33, quoted on page 6 of the judgment of Barron J.

51 *Ewins & ors v Carlton Television* [1997] 2 IRLM 223.

actions and conduct which constituted the plaintiffs' claim occurred in the UK; and the plaintiff would suffer no injustice as a result. Carlton usually transmitted in the London area but also supplied programmes to other UK companies which were part of ITN and this included Ulster TV. The programme was seen in Ireland in three ways: firstly there was an unavoidable spillage in border areas; secondly, this spillage was extended to other areas by the deliberate tuning of aerials to intercept signals broadcast in Northern Ireland or Wales and finally, there was the unlawful distribution by cable companies and deflector systems. The number of viewers for the programme was estimated by RTE at 111,000. Barr J noted in the High Court that UTV as part of ITN had an interest in broadcasting to as many people as possible whether officially or unofficially. While he referred to the decision in *Sheville & ors v Presse Alliance SA,* he substantially relied on the judgement of Carswell LJ in *Turkington v Barron St Oswald*[52] where a defamatory statement was broadcast by the BBC about the plaintiffs who were solicitors at a press conference.. The plaintiffs sued claiming damages for defamation under the law of England and Wales, Scotland, Northern Ireland and the Republic of Ireland. Oswald sought unsuccessfully to have the proceedings set aside. Carswell LJ refused and applied the rule in *Speight v Gospay*[53] which states that the original publisher of a defamatory statement is liable for its republication by another person where, *inter alia,* the repetition or republication to a third person was the natural and probable result of the original publication. This reasoning was applied by Barr J:

> 'the natural and probable consequence of providing the programme complained of to Ulster Television for re-distribution on its networks was that it would reach a significant number of viewers in this jurisdiction and accordingly, harm (if there was harm) would be done in this State within the meaning of article 5(3) of the Convention'.

The plaintiffs had a choice of jurisdiction and could choose the one they felt was most advantageous to them.[54]

Jurisdiction outside the Brussels Convention

[28.23] Suppose a defamatory statement is published on a server based in the USA or Russia, which is then downloaded to an Irish computer. There are differing approaches to deciding which country will have jurisdiction. One is 'the single publication rule': there was one single publication of the statement, that publication took place in the USA and, therefore, the courts of the USA have exclusive jurisdiction. The other approach is that of the 'multiple publication rule', which is that a separate publication of the statement occurs every time that it is downloaded. Under this rule the courts of Ireland will have jurisdiction, but only in respect of the specific downloading of the statement in Ireland. As of yet, the Irish courts have yet to adjudicate on this point. The Irish courts will permit service out of the jurisdiction where 'the action is founded on a tort committed within the jurisdiction.'[55]

---

52 *Turkington v Barron St Oswald* (6 May 1996, unreported).
53 *Speight v Gospay* [1891]60 LJ QB 231.
54 See Murray, 'Cross border defamation' [1997] Irish Law Times, No 8, Vol 15.
55 Rules of the Superior Courts, Ord 11, r1(f).

In considering the application of this provision in *Grehan v Medical Incorporated*,[56] Walsh J commented that it:

> 'requires the court to determine the issue as to whether or not a tort was committed within the State within the meaning of that rule. It is clear that the issue is not merely a mechanical one because that would inevitably lead to arbitrary results. The court must have regard to the implications for the plaintiff or the defendant if the trial is to take place within the State. The task of the court is to interpret and to apply the rule in a way designed to ensure that justice and practical common sense prevail. The court therefore should interpret the rule in the light of a broad policy and in the light of its choice of law implications. If more than one possible interpretation of the rule is available, the one which serves to encourage the operation of sensible choice of law rules should be followed, rather than one which would tend to frustrate them.'[57]

Walsh J considered that it was sufficient to give the Irish courts jurisdiction in respect of a tort 'if any significant element occurred within the jurisdiction.'[58]

[28.24] If the Irish courts follow the view of the courts of England and Wales and hold that downloading material from the Internet amounts to the publication of an allegedly defamatory statement contained in that material, then this would seem to be a sufficiently significant element of the tort of defamation to give the Irish courts jurisdiction. The procedure for serving a foreign defendant, and thus invoking the jurisdiction of the Irish courts is complex and was reviewed by the Supreme Court in *Analog Devices v Zurich Insurance*,[59] where it was noted that 'international comity of the courts have long required ... that our courts examine such applications with care and circumspection.'[60]

[28.25] Fennelly J held that the plaintiff would have to show that it had a 'good arguable case' before the court could grant leave to serve out of the jurisdiction. Fennelly also thought that when this test was being applied:

> 'it must be borne in mind that the issue of jurisdiction is being determined irrevocably and that a foreign defendant is being summoned involuntarily before our courts. Therefore, I believe that, though disputes of fact cannot always be satisfactorily resolved on affidavit, the court must look at the matter carefully. It is not a case where the applicant's allegations must be presumed to be true. The foreign party's affidavit evidence must also be considered.'[61]

Fennelly J then turned to whether Ireland was the proper forum to hear the case. In essence the defendants had insured the plaintiffs' premises in Ireland and there had been an incident on those premises, which led to the plaintiffs making a claim. There was a dispute about the application of the policy. The defendants wanted the dispute to be litigated in the USA, but the plaintiffs sought to have it litigated in Ireland. The

---

[56] *Grehan v Medical Incorporated* [1986] IR 528 see also *O'Daly v Gulf Oil Terminals Ltd* [1983] ILRM 163.

[57] [1986] IR 528 at 541.

[58] [1986] IR 528 at 542.

[59] *Analog Devices v Zurich Insurance* [2002] 1 IR 272.

[60] [2002] 1 IR 272 at 281.

[61] [2002] 1 IR 272 at 282.

defendants argued that 'the court should ... refuse jurisdiction on the ground that Ireland is not a convenient or proper forum and ... that the United States District Court is the appropriate forum.'[62]

[28.26] Fennelly J considered that the correct balance to be made between the parties when considering whether the national courts offered a *forum conveniens* for hearing a dispute had been set out by Wilberforce, in *Amin Rasheed Corpn. v Kuwait Insurance*:[63]

> 'The intention must be to impose upon the plaintiff the burden of showing good reasons why service of a writ, calling for appearance before an English court, should, in the circumstances, be permitted upon a foreign defendant. In considering this question the court must take into account the nature of the dispute, the legal and practical issues involved, such questions as local knowledge, availability of witnesses and their evidence and expense.'[64]

Fennelly J held that Ireland offered a *forum conveniens* to hear the dispute in *Analog Devices v Zurich Insurance,* noting that:

> 'The claim flows from an incident in a ... plant situated at Raheen, County Limerick. All of the evidence of fact about that incident is almost certainly going to be given by employees and executives of one or other of the plaintiff companies ... No doubt, expert evidence will have to be given and some of the experts may come from the United States, but the evidence relied on by the second defendant for the statement I have just cited is that of an expert with a Dublin address.'[65]

The Australian approach

[28.27] The leading common-law decision on Internet jurisdiction is that of the Australian High Court in *Dow Jones & Company Inc v Gutnick.* The appellant, Dow Jones, published a magazine called *Barron's,* which the respondent alleged had defamed him. The appellant also ran a website, wsj.com, which was based in New Jersey, USA and the article in question was uploaded to this site and that of Barron's Online. The defendant had business and other interests abroad but he lived in the state of Victoria, Australia and 'much of his social and business life could be said to be focused in Victoria.'[66] The respondent sued the appellant for defamation in the Australian courts. He gave an undertaking to the courts not to sue elsewhere and asserted that he sought:

> 'to have his Victorian reputation vindicated by the courts of the State in which he lives [and that he] is indifferent to the other substantial parts of the article and desires only that the attack on his reputation in Victoria as a money-launderer should be repelled and his reputation re-established.'[67]

---

62 [2002] 1 IR 272 at 287.
63 *Amin Rasheed Corpn. v Kuwait Insurance* [1984] AC 50.
64 [1984] AC 50, cited by Fennelly J at [2002] 1 IR 272 at 288.
65 [2002] 1 IR 272 at 293–294.
66 *Dow Jones & Company Inc v Gutnick* [2002] HCA 56, para 2.
67 [2002] HCA 56, para 6.

The appellant contended that the Australian courts lacked jurisdiction to hear the respondent's case, arguing that:

> 'articles published on *Barron's Online* were published in South Brunswick, New Jersey, when they became available on the servers which it maintained at that place ... [68]

> ... Dow Jones submitted that it was preferable that the publisher of material on the World Wide Web be able to govern its conduct according only to the law of the place where it maintained its web servers, unless that place was merely adventitious or opportunistic.'[69]

This approach was supported by the interveners in the case, which included amazon.com. These interveners argued that the alternative to the argument propounded by Dow Jones was that:

> 'a publisher would be bound to take account of the law of every country on earth, for there were no boundaries which a publisher could effectively draw to prevent anyone, anywhere, downloading the information it put on its web server.'[70]

Gleeson CJ did not appear to be impressed by this argument, which he suggested:

> 'may have a greater appearance of certainty than it would have in fact. 'Adventitious' and 'opportunistic' are words likely to produce considerable debate. Does a publisher's decision to have a server in a country where the costs of operation are low, or the benefits offered for setting up business are high, warrant either of these descriptions? Does a publisher's decision to have servers in two, widely separated, states or even countries warrant either description, or is it simply a prudent business decision to provide security and continuity of service? How is the user to know which server dealt with a particular request? Is the fact that one rather than the other server met the request 'adventitious'?'[71]

[28.28] Gleeson CJ considered that when deciding jurisdiction in a tort case:

> 'in the end the question is 'where in substance did this cause of action arise'?'[72]

> ... ordinarily, defamation is to be located at the place where the damage to reputation occurs. Ordinarily that will be where the material which is alleged to be defamatory is available in comprehensible form assuming, of course, that the person defamed has in that place a reputation which is thereby damaged. It is only when the material is in comprehensible form that the damage to reputation is done and it is damage to reputation which is the principal focus of defamation, not any quality of the defendant's conduct. In the case of material on the World Wide Web, it is not available in comprehensible form until downloaded on to the computer of a person who has used a web browser to pull the material from the web server. It is where that person downloads the material that the damage to reputation may be done. Ordinarily then, that will be the place where the tort of defamation is committed.'[73]

---

[68] [2002] HCA 56, para 19.

[69] [2002] HCA 56, para 21.

[70] [2002] HCA 56, para 21.

[71] [2002] HCA 56, para 22.

[72] [2002] HCA 56, para 43, citing *Distillers Co (Biochemicals) Ltd v Thompson* [1971] AC 458 at 468.

[73] [2002] HCA 56, para 44.

Gleeson CJ therefore held that the Australian Courts, specifically those of the State of Victoria, did have jurisdiction to hear the respondent's action for defamation. Gleeson CJ concluded his judgment by noting that, in his view, this decision would not have the terrible consequences anticipated by the applicant and the interveners:

'a claim for damage to reputation will warrant an award of substantial damages only if the plaintiff has a reputation in the place where the publication is made. Further, plaintiffs are unlikely to sue for defamation published outside the forum unless a judgment obtained in the action would be of real value to the plaintiff. The value that a judgment would have may be much affected by whether it can be enforced in a place where the defendant has assets ...'[74]

Finally, if the two considerations just mentioned are not thought to limit the scale of the problem confronting those who would make information available on the World Wide Web, the spectre which Dow Jones sought to conjure up in the present appeal, of a publisher forced to consider every article it publishes on the World Wide Web against the defamation laws of every country from Afghanistan to Zimbabwe is seen to be unreal when it is recalled that in all except the most unusual of cases, identifying the person about whom material is to be published will readily identify the defamation law to which that person may resort.'[75]

The English approach

[28.29] In *Richardson v Schwarzenegger*[76] Eady J noted that it was

'well settled now that an Internet publication takes place in any jurisdiction where the relevant words are read or downloaded ... There is no 'single publication rule' applying to trans-national libels.'[77]

[28.30] Eady J cited *Lewis v King*[78] and *Dow Jones & Company Inc v Gutnick* in support of his view. The facts of *Lewis v King* were 'nothing if not colourful' and related to a dispute between the boxing promoter Don King and world heavyweight boxing champions Lennox Lewis and Mike Tyson. Litigation was initiated before the courts of New York by Lewis, including the complaint that 'King threatened Jeff Wald, a friend

---

74 [2002] HCA 56, para 53.
75 [2002] HCA 56, para 54.
76 *Richardson v Schwarzenegger* [2004] EWHC 2422.
77 [2004] EWHC 2422, para 19. See also *Berezovsky v Forbes Inc* [1999] EMLR 278 in which the English Court of Appeal held that the lower court had erred in principle in approaching his decision as if the global publication was a single tort in respect of which an action could only be brought in a single jurisdiction. The court held that each publication in England had to be treated as a separate tort.
78 *Lewis v King* [2004] EWCA Civ 1329. See also the House of Lords decision of *Berezovsky v Michaels* 2000 1 WLR 1004. The plaintiffs had been described by Forbes magazine as 'criminals on an outrageous scale (2000 1 WLR 1004, 1007)'. It was agreed that this magazine would have been read by about 6000 persons within the jurisdiction of the Courts of England and Wales (2000 1 WLR 1004, 1008). The article was published on the Internet but there was 'not the necessary evidence before the House to consider this important issue satisfactorily. Having come to a clear conclusion without reference to the availability of the article on the Internet it is unnecessary to discuss it in this case' (2000 1 WLR 1004 at 1015).

of Tyson, by stating to Wald that he would 'shove a shotgun up [his] ass', and would 'come out to California and kill [him]' if Wald 'messed with [his] fighter'.[79]

[28.31] This complaint was posted on the Internet by Burstein, an associate of Lewis and a lawyer. Burstein was then interviewed by a couple of boxing publications, and alleged that King had called him a 'shyster lawyer', imitated Hitler at a press conference, and persistently referred to a 'Shelly Finkel' as 'Shelly Finkelstein'. King sued in the English High Court, pleading that 'the meaning of the words complained of in both texts is that he is a persistent, bigoted, and unashamed or unrepentant anti-semite.'[80] These statements were 'stored on websites based in California. In the ordinary way they can be, and have been, downloaded (in the UK)'.[81] The Court held that:

> 'in relation to Internet libel, bearing in mind the rule in *Duke of Brunswick v Harmer* that each publication constitutes a separate tort, a defendant who publishes on the Web may at least in theory find himself vulnerable to multiple actions in different jurisdictions. The place where the tort is committed ceases to be a potent limiting factor.'[82]

In deciding whether or not the UK was a *forum conveniens* to hear this dispute, the Court of Appeal rejected 'out of hand'[83] the submission that:

> 'in deciding, in an Internet case, what is the most appropriate *forum* the court should be more ready to stay proceedings 'where defendants did not target their publications towards the jurisdiction in which they have been sued. That is, it might be argued that for the purposes of *forum non conveniens* enquiries involving material published via the Internet, the intention of the defendant should be taken into account.'[84]

[28.32] The Court of Appeal noted that:

> 'the ascertainment of what is clearly the most appropriate *forum* is to identify the place where the tort has been committed. That will, of course, by definition be England in a defamation case where leave to serve out has been obtained on the basis of publication here. But – and here is our second proposition from the cases – the more tenuous the claimant's connection with this jurisdiction (and the more substantial any publication abroad), the weaker this consideration becomes.'[85]

If an article is published online can a plaintiff assume that it has been downloaded within the jurisdiction? This issue came before the English High Court in *Al Amoudi v Brisard*.[86] The plaintiff described himself as 'a prominent and respected international businessman who is well known in the major financial centres of the world.'[87] The defendant asserted that he was 'an author and international expert and investigator on

---

[79] [2004] EWCA Civ 1329, para 6.

[80] [2004] EWCA Civ 1329, para 6.

[81] [2004] EWCA Civ 1329, para 28.

[82] [2004] EWCA Civ 1329, para 28.

[83] [2004] EWCA Civ 1329, para 34.

[84] [2004] EWCA Civ 1329, para 33.

[85] [2004] EWCA Civ 1329, para 27.

[86] *Al Amoudi v Brisard* [2006] EWHC 1062 (QB), [2006] 3 All ER 294.

[87] [2006] EWHC 1062 (QB), para 4.

terrorism financing.'[88] The plaintiff claimed that the defendant had published defamatory statements about him online, but the defendant pleaded that 'the reports containing the words complained of were not downloaded within this jurisdiction.'[89] The plaintiffs argued that there was a:

> 'rebuttable presumption (of law)[90] ... that the defendants published or caused to be published on the Internet to a substantial number of readers in this jurisdiction the two items complained of.'[91]

[28.33] However, this argument was rejected by the court which was 'unable to accept that under English law a claimant in a libel action on an Internet publication is entitled to rely on a presumption of law that there has been substantial publication.'[92]

If the alleged defamatory statement has only been published by a 'derisory' number of people within the jurisdiction then his claim may fail. In *Jameel (Yousef) v Dow Jones*[93] a statement had been published on the defendant's website which the plaintiff claimed defamed him. The defendant was able to adduce evidence that only five subscribers within the jurisdiction had been able to access the alleged defamatory statement and that three of these were associates of the claimant. The case was dismissed as an abuse of process. The Court of Appeal dismissed the claim, holding that if it had been:

> 'considering an application to set aside permission to serve these proceedings out of the jurisdiction we would allow that application on the basis that the five publications that had taken place in this jurisdiction did not, individually or collectively, amount to a real and substantial tort ... it would not be right to permit this action to proceed. It would be an abuse of process to continue to commit the resources of the English court, including substantial judge and possibly jury time, to an action where so little is now seen to be at stake. Normally where a small claim is brought, it will be dealt with by a proportionate small claims procedure.'[94]

Where an article is published to a small number of persons, a defence of qualified privilege might be raised. In *Gutnick v Dow Jones*[95] an attempt to raise a defence of qualified privilege was made; the defendant arguing that it was engaged in 'the performance ... of subscription contracts entered into between it and those persons who were entitled to download the online version or receive the print version by mail. It pleads that it was a specialist news and information service such that it had a legal, social or moral duty to make available to its subscribers'[96] information of the type complained of. The argument failed.

---

88 [2006] EWHC 1062 (QB), para 5.
89 [2006] EWHC 1062 (QB), para 13.
90 [2006] EWHC 1062 (QB), para 31.
91 [2006] EWHC 1062 (QB), para 21.
92 [2006] EWHC 1062 (QB), para 37.
93 *Jameel (Yousef) v Dow Jones* [2005] QB 946, [2005] 2 WLR 1614.
94 [2005] 2 WLR 1614 at 1634.
95 *Gutnick v Dow Jones* [2004] VSC 138, see previously [2003] VSC 79.
96 [2004] VSC 138, para 18.

Why choose the Irish courts?

[28.34] As noted above, Irish courts have yet to consider the issue of whether an Irish citizen or resident can sue in the Irish courts in respect of a defamatory statement made in a state which is not a signatory to the Brussels Convention, such as the USA or Russia. However, the courts of England and Wales, and also those of Australia, have given some consideration to this issue. Typically, though not always, these decisions have related to a publication in the USA which has allegedly defamed someone in the UK or Australia. This does not just reflect the primacy of the USA as a generator of English language Internet content, it also reflects the impact of the First Amendment of the US Constitution, which provides that 'Congress shall make no law … abridging the freedom of speech, or of the press'.

[28.35] In reality, seeking a relief from an Irish, English or Australian court may be the only realistic option open to someone who believes that they have been defamed on an American website. The difficulty with doing so is that the US Courts will not enforce Irish, English or American court orders that conflict with the US Constitution. In *Yahoo! v La Ligue Contre Le Racisme Et l'Antisemitisme (LICRA)*,[97] Yahoo! ran an auction website that was available in France. Nazi memorabilia was available on this site which was contrary to French anti-racism laws. LICRA obtained an order from the French courts requiring:

> 'Yahoo! to 'take all necessary measures to dissuade and render impossible any access [from French territory] via Yahoo.com to the Nazi artifact auction service and to any other site or service that may be construed as constituting an apology for Nazism or a contesting of Nazi crimes.'[98]

LICRA took a number of steps in relation to this order: it served Yahoo! with a 'cease and desist' order; then served Yahoo! with a court process and initiated further proceedings before the French courts. All of these actions sought to force Yahoo!'s compliance with the French order, as it related to France. The problem was that Yahoo!'s systems made it difficult for Yahoo! to identify every one of its French users, although experts estimated that it could identify about 90% of them.[99] Fines were imposed by the French courts, albeit not enforced. Yahoo!'s response was to seek in the US courts 'a declaratory judgment that the interim orders of the French court are not recognizable or enforceable in the United States.'[100]

[28.36] Initially this application was successful and LICRA's motion to dismiss Yahoo!'s application was dismissed. Judge Fogel of the US District Court for the Northern District of California granted Yahoo! summary judgment, commenting that:

> 'the United States Constitution and implementing legislation require that full faith and credit be given to judgments of sister states, territories, and possessions of the United States … The extent to which the United States, or any state, honors the judicial decrees of foreign nations is a matter of choice, governed by 'the comity of nations.' The French

---

[97] *Yahoo! v LICRA* US Ct of Apps (9th Cir), 12 February 2006.
[98] US Ct of Apps (9th Cir), 12 February 2006, p 413.
[99] US Ct of Apps (9th Cir), 12 February 2006, p 415.
[100] US Ct of Apps (9th Cir), 12 February 2006, p 417.

order's content and viewpoint-based regulation of the web pages and auction site on Yahoo.com, while entitled to great deference as an articulation of French law, clearly would be inconsistent with the First Amendment if mandated by a court in the United States. What makes this case uniquely challenging is that the Internet in effect allows one to speak in more than one place at the same time. Although France has the sovereign right to regulate what speech is permissible in France, this Court may not enforce a foreign order that violates the protections of the United States Constitution by chilling protected speech that occurs simultaneously within our borders ... Absent a body of law that establishes international standards with respect to speech on the Internet and an appropriate treaty or legislation addressing enforcement of such standards to speech originating within the United States, the principle of comity is outweighed by the Court's obligation to uphold the First Amendment.'[101]

[28.37] However, LICRA successfully appealed this ruling on its motion to dismiss to the US Court of Appeals for the Ninth Circuit on the basis that there was no actual dispute between the parties, Yahoo! having altered its systems so that it 'complied "in large measure" with the French court's orders.'[102] But the reality remains that the US Courts will not enforce orders of foreign courts that violate the First Amendment of the US Constitution. In *Bachchan v India Abroad Publications, Inc*[103] the applicant had successfully sued for defamation in the English High Court and a substantial award of damages had been made. The applicant then sought to enforce this award through the New York courts. The Supreme Court for the State of New York noted that there were a variety of differences between the US law of defamation and that of England and Wales[104] and it denied the application for judgment on the basis that:

'a significant difference between the two jurisdictions lies in England's lack of an equivalent to the First Amendment to the United States Constitution. The protection to free speech and the press embodied in that amendment would be seriously jeopardized by

---

[101] *Yahoo! v LICRA*, US District Court for the Northern District of California, Order granting motion for summary judgment, 7 November 2001.

[102] US Ct of Apps (9th Cir), 12 February 2006, p 451. The court concluded with the comment that: 'First Amendment issues arising out of international Internet use are new, important and difficult. We should not rush to decide such issues based on an inadequate, incomplete or unclear record. We should proceed carefully, with awareness of the limitations of our judicial competence, in this undeveloped area of the law ... As currently framed, however, Yahoo!'s suit comes perilously close to a request for a forbidden advisory opinion. There was a live dispute when Yahoo! first filed suit in federal district court, but Yahoo! soon thereafter voluntarily changed its policy to comply, at least in part, with the commands of the French court's interim orders. This change in policy may or may not have mooted Yahoo!'s federal suit, but it has at least come close. Unless and until Yahoo! changes its policy again, and thereby more clearly violates the French court's orders, it is unclear how much is now actually in dispute' *Yahoo! v LICRA* US Ct of Apps (9th Cir), 12 February 2006, 450–451.

[103] *Bachchan v India Abroad Publications, Inc* 154 Misc 2d 228, 585 NYS 2d 661 (Sup Ct NY Co1992). See similarly *Abdullah v Sheridan Square Press, Inc*, No 93 Civ 2515, 1994 WL 419847 (SDNY May 4, 1994); and *Telnikoff v Matusevitch* 702 A.2d 230, 244 (Md. 1997).

[104] In particular: 'we believe that a private-figure plaintiff must bear the burden of showing that the speech at issue is false before recovering damages for defamation from a media defendant. (contd/)

the entry of foreign libel judgments granted pursuant to standards deemed appropriate in England but considered antithetical to the protections afforded the press by the US Constitution.'[105]

[28.38] In *Sarl Louis Feraud Int'l v Viewfinder*[106] the 'plaintiffs maintained that (the) defendant made unauthorized use of their intellectual property and engaged in unfair competition by posting photographs of models wearing clothing of their design at various fashion shows'. The defendant posted these photographs on a website based in the USA and the plaintiffs sued the defendant in the French courts which made an order awarding the plaintiffs substantial damages. The US Federal District Court for the Southern District of New York refused to enforce the order of the French Court, declaring that:

> 'The freedoms of speech and of the press protected by the First Amendment are not mere vagaries of legal policy, matters of legal detail that might as easily have been resolved differently by our legislatures or courts. Freedom of speech is a matter of constitutional command, binding even on the will of the majority as expressed in legislation ... American courts have recognized that foreign judgments that run afoul of First Amendment values are inconsistent with *our* notions of what is fair and just, and conflict with the strong public policy of *our* State'.

[28.39] Given the realities of American law, anyone who can be described as a 'public figure' will not be able to sue for defamation in the USA.[107] This would make the Irish courts more attractive. A public figure that does so might be accused of forum shopping and the Courts take a dim view of such activity. In *Analog Devices v Zurich Insurance*, the High Court refused to adjourn Irish proceedings on the basis that competing proceedings initiated in the courts of Masset were 'no more than forum shopping[108].' However, it seems that the English courts, at least, will not prevent an individual from suing in their jurisdiction because doing so will confer a judicial advantage upon him. In *Lewis v King* Eady J had held that:

> 'In the light of the proposition that no such actions could survive in New York, it would seem that some of the other arguments about whether New York would be a more convenient forum become of theoretical interest only. There would seem to be little point in addressing how much more convenient it would be, or would not be, for people to give evidence there rather than here.'[109]

---

[104] (\contd) To do otherwise could 'only result in a deterrence of speech which the Constitution makes free ... The 'chilling' effect is no different where liability results from enforcement in the United States of a foreign judgment obtained where the burden of proving truth is upon media defendants. Accordingly, the failure of Bachchan to prove falsity in the High Court of Justice in England makes his judgment unenforceable here' *Bachchan v India Abroad Publications, Inc* 154 Misc 2d 228, 585 NYS 2d 661 (Sup Ct NY Co 1992).

[105] 154 Misc 2d 228, 585 NYS 2d 661 (Sup Ct NY Co 1992).

[106] *Sarl Louis Feraud Int'l v Viewfinder Inc* No 04 Civ 9760, 2005 US Dist LEXIS 22242 (SDNY Sept 29, 2005).

[107] *New York Times v Sullivan* (1964) 376 US 254.

[108] [2002] 1 IR 272, 278.

[109] [2004] EWHC 168 , para 37.

On appeal, counsel for the Defendant argued that Eady J had held that the plaintiff 'would enjoy what in the argot of the law of defamation is called a "juridical advantage" if he were allowed to sue in this jurisdiction.'[110] The Court of Appeal found the view of Goff LJ in Goff's speech in *Spiliada Maritime Corp v Cansulex Ltd*[111] 'rather difficult':[112]

> 'We have to consider where the case may be tried 'suitably for the interests of all the parties and for the ends of justice.' Let me consider the application of that principle in relation to advantages which the plaintiff may derive from invoking the English jurisdiction. Typical examples are: damages awarded on a higher scale; a more complete procedure of discovery; a power to award interest; a more generous limitation period. Now, as a general rule, I do not think that the court should be deterred from granting a stay of proceedings ... simply because the plaintiff will be deprived of such an advantage, provided that the court is satisfied that substantial justice will be done in the available appropriate forum.'[113]

[28.40] In spite of their difficulties, the Court of Appeal accepted that this decision and that of *Metall und Rohstoff AG*,[114] undoubtedly state the present law' on this point. The Court of Appeal commented that Eady J's judgment was 'exiguous' and could 'have been more clearly stated'[115] but ultimately the Court of Appeal regarded it 'as simply inconceivable that he failed to give proper consideration to the points urged on both sides.'[116]

[28.41] The great disadvantage with bringing proceedings in the Irish courts is that the judgment of the court may be unenforceable. It is clear that the US courts will apply rigorous standards before enforcing an award of damages that might be viewed as contrary to their Constitution. Injunctions may also be unenforceable against foreign defendants. In *Lakah Group v Al Jazeera Satellite Channel* [117] the defendant had conducted an interview at premises situated in London. The interview was broadcast by the defendant and about a week subsequently the plaintiff successfully applied for an injunction restraining the defendant from broadcasting it further. The plaintiff subsequently returned to court seeking to enforce the injunction, arguing that the defendant 'was continuing to publish via the Internet the audio soundtrack of the television interview containing the words complained of.'[118] Eady J rejected this application, holding that 'it would be in my judgment wholly inappropriate to have resort to the contempt jurisdiction of the English court in respect of these parties who are outside its jurisdiction.'[119]

---

[110] [2004] EWHC 168 , para 20.
[111] *Spiliada Maritime Corp v Cansulex Ltd* [1987] AC 460.
[112] [2004] EWCA Civ 1329, para 38.
[113] [1987] AC 460 at 482–484.
[114] *Metall und Rohstoff AG* [1990] 1 QB 391.
[115] [2004] EWCA Civ 1329, para 41.
[116] [2004] EWCA Civ 1329, para 43.
[117] *Lakah Group v Al Jazeera Satellite Channel* [2002] EWHC 2500 (QB), [2002] All ER (D) 383 (Nov).
[118] [2002] EWHC 2500 (QB), para 12.
[119] [2002] EWHC 2500 (QB), para 36.

Defences

[28.42] The tort of defamation offers publishers of defamatory statements a wide variety of defences, such as justification,[120] privilege[121] and fair comment.[122] To these defences must be added that provided by the European Convention on Human Rights. However, the defences that are of principle interest from an information technology law perspective are those that will be available to service providers and the innocent dissemeninators of defamatory statements, and these are considered below.

Innocent dissemination

[28.43] A defamatory statement must be published by someone for it to be defamatory. Many persons may be innocently involved in the publication of such a statement, for example, a postman may carry a defamatory letter to the addressee, a news agent may sell a defamatory newspaper and an Internet service provider may transmit a defamatory email to its destination. None of these innocent disseminators will be liable for the tort of defamation and a similar exemption will apply online. In *Bunt v Tilley*[123] the plaintiff represented himself in proceedings against three individuals who he alleged had defamed him online, and their respective service providers. The plaintiff sought damages from the service providers on the basis that they had 'published the offending words "via the services provided" by their ISPs'. The three service providers brought a motion seeking to have proceedings against them dismissed. Eady J considered that the case raised 'points of general significance as to the basis upon which a provider of such services could, if at all, be liable in respect of material which is simply communicated via the services which they provide.'[124] The plaintiff relied upon the fact that the:

> 'defendants have provided a route as intermediaries, whereby third parties have access to the Internet and have been able to pass an electronic communication from one computer to another resulting in a posting to the Usenet message board. The Usenet service is hosted by others … such as Google.'[125]

---

[120] Where a plaintiff can show that the statements are indeed defamatory, there is a presumption that the statements are false. The defendant must then show that the statements are true. Truth or justification is a complete defence to the plaintiff's action. See Healy, *Principles of Irish Torts* (Clarus Press, 2006) p 365; McMahon and Binchy, *Law of Torts* (3rd edn, Tottel Publishing, 2000) p 917.

[121] There are two types of privilege: qualified and absolute. Qualified privilege arises where the defendant acted bona fide in making the statement, where he acted in furtherance of a moral or legal duty. Absolute privilege arises with regard to presidential and parliamentary utterances, reports of court proceedings, judicial proceedings, communications between spouses and state communications. See Healy, *Principles of Irish Torts*, (Clarus Press, 2006) p 369; McMahon and Binchy, *Law of Torts* (3rd edn, Tottel Publishing, 2000) p 917.

[122] A defendant may rely on this defence where he can show that what he said was comment as opposed to fact, his comment was on a matter of public importance and the comment was made fairly on true facts. See Healy, *Principles of Irish Torts* (Clarus Press, 2006), p 368; McMahon & Binchy, *Law of Torts* (3rd edn, Tottel Publishing, 2000), p 917.

[123] *Bunt v Tilley* [2006] EWHC 407 (QB).

[124] [2006] EWHC 407 (QB), para 5.

[125] [2006] EWHC 407 (QB), para 8.

In coming to his conclusion, Eady J noted that:

'In determining responsibility for publication in the context of the law of defamation, it seems to me to be important to focus on what the person did, or failed to do, in the chain of communication. It is clear that the state of a defendant's knowledge can be an important factor. If a person knowingly permits another to communicate information which is defamatory, when there would be an opportunity to prevent the publication, there would seem to be no reason in principle why liability should not accrue ...[126]

... to impose legal responsibility upon anyone under the common law for the publication of words it is essential to demonstrate a degree of awareness or at least an assumption of general responsibility, such as has long been recognised in the context of editorial responsibility.'[127]

Eady J went on to review the various authorities, but was unable to extract any useful precedent from them. Eady J concluded that he was:

'prepared to hold as a matter of law that an ISP which performs no more than a passive role in facilitating postings on the Internet cannot be deemed to be a publisher at common law ...[128]

I would not, in the absence of any binding authority, attribute liability at common law to a telephone company or other passive medium of communication, such as an ISP. It is not analogous to someone in the position of a distributor, who might at common law need to prove the absence of negligence ... There a defence is needed because the person is regarded as having "published". By contrast, persons who truly fulfill no more than the role of a passive medium for communication cannot be characterised as publishers: thus they do not need a defence.'[129]

The Directive on e-Commerce

[28.44] The Directive on e-Commerce[130] provides for immunities for what it refers to as 'relevant service providers'. A relevant service provider is defined by the regulations as 'any service normally provided for remuneration,[131] at a distance, by electronic means and at the individual request of a recipient of the service.'[132] The function of a service provider under the Directive on e-Commerce must inevitably intersect with those of innocent disseminator and publisher under the law of e-Commerce. The clear and explicit exemption from liability provided by the Directive on e-Commerce is far

---

[126] [2006] EWHC 407 (QB), para 21.

[127] [2006] EWHC 407 (QB), para 22.

[128] [2006] EWHC 407 (QB), para 36.

[129] [2006] EWHC 407 (QB), para 37.

[130] Directive 2000/31/EC of the European Parliament and of the Council of 8 June 2000 on certain legal aspects of information society services, in particular electronic commerce, in the Internal Market (Directive on electronic commerce) OJ L 178/1, 17 July 2003, implemented in Ireland by the European Communities (Directive 2000/31/EC) Regulations 2003 (SI 68/2003).

[131] The issue of whether this means that Internet access services that are provided free of charge is discussed by: *Gatley on Libel and Slander* (10th edn, Sweet and Maxwell, 2004) at para 6.27; Collins *The Law of Defamation and the Internet* (2nd edn, OUP, 2005) pp 214–215, para 17.03; and by Eady J in *Bunt v Tilley* [2006] EWHC 407 (QB) paras 41–44.

[132] SI 68/2003, reg 3(1).

preferable to the limited exemptions provided by the common law for innocent disseminators and publishers. So any provider of online content would be well advised to configure his systems, where possible, to make him appear as a 'relevant service provider' and not a publisher. As implemented by SI 68/2003, the Directive on e-commerce provides exemptions from liability in three specific instances:

(i)   mere conduits;

(ii) caching; and,

(iii) hosting.

Each of these exemptions is discussed below and all of these exemptions share common features. Firstly, each exemption will: 'not affect the power of any court to make an order against an intermediary service provider requiring the provider not to infringe, or to cease to infringe, any legal rights.'[133] Secondly, where a relevant service provider can avail of an exemption from liability in respect of a particular act, then he will not:

(a)   be liable in damages or ... be liable to be the subject of an order providing for any other form of relief, for infringing, by reason of that act, the legal rights of any natural or legal person or, by reason of that act, for breaching any duty, or

(b)   be liable to be subject to any proceedings (whether civil or criminal) by reason of that act constituting a contravention of any enactment or an infringement of any rule of law.[134]

Intermediary service provider

[28.45] In *Bunt v Tilley* Eady J rejected the plaintiff's submission that as regards the meaning of the term 'intermediary service' provider:

> 'Simple logic dictates that to be an INTERMEDIARY service provider one must be a service provider who is BOTH customer of an upstream service provider and supplier to a downstream service provider.'

Eady J noted that this was not a question of logic but rather one of definition, noting that the restrictive definition asserted by the plaintiff did not apply in the legislation.[135] The Directive on e-Commerce does try to limit the extent to which publishers can reconfigure themselves as 'service providers', stating that:

> 'A service provider who deliberately collaborates with one of the recipients of his service in order to undertake illegal acts goes beyond the activities of 'mere conduit' or 'caching' and as a result cannot benefit from the liability exemptions established for these activities.'[136]

---

133   SI 68/2003, regs 16(2), 17(2) 18(3), recital 45 of the Directive on e-Commerce is relevant, stating that: 'The limitations of the liability of intermediary service providers established in this Directive do not affect the possibility of injunctions of different kinds; such injunctions can in particular consist of orders by courts or administrative authorities requiring the termination or prevention of any infringement, including the removal of illegal information or the disabling of access to it'.

134   SI 68/2003, reg 15.

135   *Bunt v Tilley* [2006] EWHC 407 (QB) para 39.

136   Directive on e-Commerce, Recital 44.

It is of interest that this recital leaves open the possibility that a hosting service might collaborate with its customers – it would seem that a host who does so may still benefit from the liability exemption.

Mere conduits

[28.46] The first exemption is that provided to 'mere conduits' SI 68/2003 provides that:

'An intermediary service provider shall not be liable for information transmitted by him or her in a communication network if ... the information has been provided to him or her by a recipient of a relevant service provided by him or her (being a service consisting of the transmission in a communication network of that information), or ... a relevant service provided by him or her consists of the provision of access to a communication network.'

This exemption will apply provided:

(i)   the intermediary service provider did not initiate the transmission',

(ii)   the intermediary service provider did not select the receiver of the transmission, and

(iii) the intermediary service provider did not select or modify the information contained in the transmission.[137]

SI 68/2003 goes on to provide that references to transmission and the provision of access:

'include references to the automatic, intermediate and transient storage of the information transmitted in so far as this takes place for the sole purpose of carrying out the transmission in the communications network, and provided that the information is not stored for any period longer than is reasonably necessary for the transmission.'[138]

Caching

[28.47] The second exemption is provided for caching. In *Bunt v* Tilley caching was explained to Eady J in the following terms:

'The enormous volume of requests for web pages generated by Internet users has led to the development of technical solutions ... to enable more efficient transmission of that information across the Internet ... Caching is one such ... It is a technical process which enables Internet providers ... to speed up the delivery of web pages to Internet users by making a temporary copy of a web page that is requested by a user. When a subsequent request is made for the same page, the user can be provided with that content from the local 'cached' copy made by the Internet service provider, rather than having to go back to the original web site which is the source of that page ... A web cache ... is not a copy of the Internet – that is neither the purpose of a web cache, nor would it be commercially or technically feasible. In order for web caches not to have to expand in memory size indefinitely the actual content in a web cache is designed to be overwritten in accordance with automatic defined rules ensuring that ... cached content is up to date and ... cached content which is not being searched for (or has been removed or altered) is overwritten.'[139]

---

[137] SI 68/2003, reg 16(1)(b).
[138] SI 68/2003, reg 16(2).
[139] [2006] EWHC 407 (QB) para 52.

[28.48] SI 68/2003 states that an intermediary service provider will not be:

'liable for the automatic, intermediate and temporary storage of information which is performed for the sole purpose of making more efficient that information's onward transmission to other users of the service upon their request.'[140]

To avail of this exemption, the storage in question must be 'done in the context of the provision of a relevant service by the relevant service provider consisting of the transmission in a communication network of information provided by a recipient of that service'.

In addition, the following conditions must be complied with:

(i)   the intermediary service provider does not modify the information,

(ii) the intermediary service provider complies with conditions relating to access to the information,

(iii) the intermediary service provider complies with any rules regarding the updating of the information that have been specified in a manner widely recognised and used by industry,

(iv) the intermediary service provider does not interfere with the lawful use of technology, widely recognised and used by industry to obtain data on the use of the information, and

(v)   the intermediary service provider acts expeditiously to remove or disable access to the information it has stored upon obtaining actual knowledge of the fact that the information at the initial source of the transmission has been removed from the network, or access to it has been disabled, or that a court or an administrative authority has ordered such removal or disablement.[141]

In *Bunt v Tilley* Eady J considered that the purpose of the above provision was:

'to protect Internet intermediaries in respect of material for which they are not the primary host but which they store temporarily on their computer systems for the purpose of enabling the efficient availability of Internet material. Many ISPs and other intermediaries regularly cache, or temporarily store, commonly accessed web pages on their computer systems, so that those pages will be more quickly accessible to their subscribers. This is described[142] … as a 'sort of half way house between mere transmission and hosting'.[143]

Hosting

[28.49] Finally, SI 68/2003 provides an exemption for intermediary service providers which provide hosting services. Such services are described as 'consisting of the storage of information provided by a recipient of the service'. The provider of such a hosting service will not be liable for the information stored at the request of that recipient if the provider can show that he fulfils one of the following criteria.

---

[140] SI 68/2003, reg 17(1).
[141] SI 68/2003, reg 17(1).
[142] In Gatley, p 169, para 6.29.
[143] *Bunt v Tilley* [2006] EWHC 407 (QB) para 51.

(a)   the intermediary service provider does not have actual knowledge of the unlawful activity concerned and, as regards claims for damages, is not aware of facts or circumstances from which that unlawful activity is apparent, or

(b)   the intermediary service provider, upon obtaining such knowledge or awareness, acts expeditiously to remove or to disable access to the information.[144]

This provision will 'not apply where the recipient of the service is acting under the authority or the control of the intermediary service provider referred to in that paragraph'.[145] Collins suggests that content hosts are:

'the operators of computer systems on which Internet content, such as web pages and bulletin board postings, are stored. Content hosts play a part every time the content stored on their computer systems is displayed on the screen of an Internet user ... because they are the primary storage site for that content'.[146]

The Directive on e-Commerce was enacted on 8 June 2000; at that time restricting this exemption to 'intermediaries' would have quite effectively limited the number of service providers who could of it. But this may no longer be the case. A host of successful websites now exists which only function to provide intermediary services such as http://www.youtube.com, http://www.myspace.com and http://www.bebo.com. SI 68/2003 makes it explicitly clear that anyone providing such intermediary services will be exempt from liability provided they comply with all of the criteria set out above. This creates an interesting dichotomy. On the one hand, a site such as http://www.myspace.com is clearly an intermediary, as the operators of the site do not edit or control the content that is placed on their site. On the other hand the operators of http://www.myspace.com are clearly involved in the provision of Internet content, but they are just not involved enough to become liable for it. It may be speculated that if material on a site such as http://www.myspace.com did become sufficiently prominent on the site then, perhaps by receiving an exceptional number of views, 'actual knowledge' of the content might be imputed to the operators of the site.

[28.50] It is not entirely clear how expeditiously the host should act in response to receiving actual knowledge. It should be noted that the service provider must act once it receives actual knowledge; he does not have to wait until he receives a communication from someone who claims that they were defamed.[147] Where the subject of an alleged defamatory statement decides to send a communication to a service provider requesting that the statement be removed, that statement should be clear and definite. In particular,

---

[144] SI 68/2003, reg 18(1).

[145] SI 68/2003, reg 18(2).

[146] Collins, *The Law of Defamation and the Internet* (2nd edn, OUP, 2005).

[147] Unfortunately SI 68/2003 does not explain what will amount to 'actual knowledge', in contrast the UK's Electronic Commerce (EC Directive) Regulations 2002 (SI (UK) 2002/2013), do, providing at reg 22 that: 'In determining whether a service provider has actual...a court shall take into account all matters which appear to it in the particular circumstances to be relevant and, among other things, shall have regard to ... whether a service provider has received a notice through a means of contact ... and ... the extent to which any notice includes ... the full name and address of the sender of the notice...details of the location of the information in question; and ... details of the unlawful nature of the activity or information in question'.

it should clearly identify the precise statement at issue. In *Godfrey v Demon* the subject of a defamatory statement proceeded as follows:

'On 17 January 1997 the plaintiff sent a letter by fax to ... the defendants' managing director, informing him that the posting was a forgery, and that he was not responsible for it and requesting that the defendants remove the posting from its Usenet news server ... the defendants admit ... receipt and that the posting was not removed as requested but remained available on its news server until its expiry on about 27 January 1997.'[148]

As a consequence, the plaintiff was able to recover damages for defamation. In contrast, in *Bunt v Tilley* the plaintiff was unable to prove that he ever informed the defendant service providers that he felt defamed by statements published on their systems. The plaintiff sent one of the Defendants, AOL, the following message:

'One of your (UK) customers has committed an act of libel against my business on our business forums ... and he started a thread entitled 'Be warned about these cheap Batteries! Load of Crap!'... I am emailing you in this instance in order to ask what procedures you need completed by myself before you are able to divulge this individual's name and address to me, so that I can institute legal proceedings against them for libel under UK law as a matter of urgency.'

[28.51] Eady J noted that this message was deficient in a number of aspects. Firstly, the address on which the plaintiff claimed the defamatory statement was made was actually the 'claimant's own website; it was thus within his power to remove them if he wished to do so.'[149] Secondly, the plaintiff 'did not ask AOL to remove the posting or suggest in either of the emails that he believed AOL was responsible for the posting.'[150] Finally, Eady J noted counsel for AOL's point that: 'the words were not on their face defamatory. At most, they could be interpreted as disparaging the product'.[151] Eady J considered that Counsel for AOL made a 'powerful argument' that 'an ISP should not become liable as a publisher (especially for postings on a site which it does not host) simply because it has been previously told of wholly unrelated allegedly defamatory statements, not necessarily even by the same author.'[152] What will amount to actual knowledge would appear to be determined by the facts of any particular case. But in practice it may well be that the courts will treat the time of knowledge as being from when a communication requesting the removal of defamatory words is received. This appeared to be the approach taken by Eady J in *Bunt v Tilley* when he stated that:

'One of the factors I have to consider is whether knowledge has been notified to any of the corporate defendants in such a way as to render the ISP in question responsible for publication from that moment onwards (even assuming 'innocence' up to that point).'[153]

[28.52] In *Godfrey v Demon* Morland J ruled that the defendants' defence was 'hopeless' as 'the defamatory posting was published by the defendants and, as from 17

---

[148] *Godfrey v Demon* [2000] 3 WLR 1020 at 1023.
[149] *Bunt v Tilley* [2006] EWHC 407 (QB) para 27.
[150] [2006] EWHC 407 (QB) para 28.
[151] [2006] EWHC 407 (QB) para 28.
[152] [2006] EWHC 407 (QB) para 31.
[153] [2006] EWHC 407 (QB) para 25.

January 1997 they knew of the defamatory content of the posting.'[154] However, actual knowledge may be imputed to a defendant even where no communication is sent. In *AG (Comer) v Shorten*[155] Davitt P suggested that actual knowledge:

> 'may be proved by direct or circumstantial evidence, or a combination of both; and the fact that the person in question had the means of knowledge is obviously a very important circumstance. It is not by itself, however, necessarily sufficient; and will only become so where the circumstances are such that the only reasonable inference which can be drawn from the fact that the person in question had the means of knowledge is that he in fact must have used them to acquire actual knowledge.'[156]

[28.53] The law of defamation would suggest that the service provider should act instantly or as fast as reasonably possible. But the above provision must be read in the context of the European Convention on Human Rights, and in particular Article 10 thereof, which protects the individual's right to freedom of expression. Article 10(2) does allow for the limitation of this right, but only in accordance with the law. That may suggest that a service provider should consider the legitimacy of any such request for removal or disablement before complying with it. It would seem likely that few, if any, service providers actually undertake such consideration. In 2003 UK researchers undertook a study of how quickly Internet service providers would remove content in response to a 'take-down' notice, even where it should have been obvious that the work was not protected by copyright. The researchers created a webpage which displayed an excerpt from John Stuart Mill's *On Liberty* and which was hosted by a major UK service provider. They then sent an email to the service provider, purporting to be from the non-existent John Stuart Mill Heritage Foundation, requesting that the service provider undertake 'the necessary measures to discontinue any such possible infringement of our intellectual property rights'. The service provider complied with this request with alacrity, without asking any questions of the purported victim. This research has been replicated in the USA[157] and the Netherlands.[158] The penalties for publishing a defamatory statement are severe in Ireland and the law is clear. In contrast, the European Court of Human Rights is parsimonious in its awards of damages and the implementation of the Convention in Irish law is ongoing. As a result, it is likely that many service providers will simply remove any material which they are informed may be defamatory without ever considering whether they should do so.

Monitoring

[28.54] Irish law cannot impose any general obligation to monitor upon Internet service providers who provide 'mere conduit', caching or hosting services. This is made explicitly clear by the Directive on e-Commerce, which provides 'Member States shall not impose a general obligation on providers … to monitor the information which they

---

[154] *Godfrey v Demon* [2000] 3 WLR 1020 at 1030.

[155] *AG (Comer) v Shorten* [1961] IR 304.

[156] [1961] IR 304 at 308.

[157] 'Chilling Effects or Efficient Process? Takedown Notices under the Digital Millennium Copyright Act,' *Santa Clara Computer and High Technology Journal*, co-authored with Laura Quilter (forthcoming, May 2006).

[158] http://www.bof.nl/takedown/.

transmit or store, nor a general obligation actively to seek facts or circumstances indicating illegal activity.'[159] Member states may oblige such service providers to inform 'the competent public authorities of alleged illegal activities', however, Irish criminal law does not normally provide for obligatory reporting of crime. There are exceptions of course. For example a service provider who found that one of its customers was distributing child pornography would be very unwise not to report that individual to the gardaí so that the service provider could not be accused of knowingly facilitating that distribution. The Directive on e-Commerce also provides that member states may oblige service providers to provide their competent authorities with 'information enabling the identification of recipients of their service with whom they have storage agreements.'[160]

[28.55] None of the above sheds much light upon a difficult dilemma for service providers: whether or not they should monitor the content of their site. If a service provider hosts a public area such as a message board, there is a danger that it may be used to publish defamatory statements. Monitoring the board means that the service provider should be able to remove such statements, which lessens the chances that someone will be defamed by such messages. But monitoring means that 'actual knowledge' of what is on the board may be imputed to the service provider.

Relief: injunctions and damages

[28.56] Where defamatory statements are made online, the courts appear to take a pragmatic approach in the relief that they will offer defendants. In *Maguire v Gill* the plaintiff alleged that the defendant had defamed her on a website, but the defendant denied all knowledge of the site in question. In response, the court directed that anyone having knowledge of the injunction should remove the material in question.[161] In the English case of *Cray v Hancock*[162] the plaintiff had successfully acted as solicitor for the defendant's wife in relation to works done to the defendant's home. The defendant's wife subsequently withdrew instructions and the defendant then sent a letter and faxes to the claimant's firm alleging that he was greedy, incompetent and had overcharged his wife. These communications were read by members of staff of the plaintiff's firm. The plaintiff then received numerous emails and became aware of Internet forum postings and spoof websites that repeated the allegations. At hearing, the English court was satisfied that the letter and faxes had been published by being read by members of staff of the plaintiff's firm. The court held that the subsequent campaign against the claimant, which included emails, Internet forum postings and spoof websites, had amounted to harassment. The Court awarded the plaintiff damages of £19,000 for libel and harassment. It is important to realise that a statement does not have to be published on a prominent website for it to be defamatory. In *Keith-Smith v Williams*[163] the plaintiff and defendant were members of a discussion group hosted by Yahoo!:

---

[159] Directive on e-Commerce, art 15(1).
[160] Directive on e-Commerce, art 15(2).
[161] 'Man ordered to remove comments from website' (2006) The Irish Times, 14 September.
[162] *Cray v Hancock* [2005] All ER (D) 66 (Nov).
[163] *Keith-Smith v Williams* [2006] EWHC 860 (QB).

'there were perhaps only a hundred or so members of the discussion group, anybody could access the site over the Internet and read what was upon it. To contribute to the discussion one had to be a paid up member. Thus, anything that was said on the site could be read not only by members, but by the vast numbers of people who found the site on the Internet.'[164]

[28.57] The defendant became abusive towards the plaintiff and published a variety of statements about him. The plaintiff contacted his solicitors, who successfully sought Norwich Pharmacal relief.[165] They wrote to the defendant and then served proceedings against her, actions which had the effect of provoking the defendant into 'more frenzied abuse.'[166] In assessing damages, MacDuff QC[167] held that:

'The published statement upon which reliance is placed in the pleadings is clearly seriously defamatory. In once sense those statements have been made to a restricted audience. In fact, it is very likely that few people have read those statements. However, they were available to the whole world, at least to that part of the world which has a computer or access to a computer and knows how to go on to the internet and to find the various sites upon it. But fortunately, as a matter of fact, few people have likely picked up on these defamatory statements and I suspect that many of those who have read them dismissed them as being the rantings of a person who was not to be believed,'[168]

MacDuff QC awarded the plaintiff 'modest' damages including aggravated damages, commenting that these were low:

'through the good fortune, or her good fortune, that these remarks did not get a wider publication elsewhere and were, happily, only seen by a relatively small number of people, most of whom, in all probability, did not believe what they were reading.'[169]

In *Godfrey v Demon* Morland J noted that 'any award of damages to the plaintiff is likely to be very small.'[170] Of course awards of damages for defamation in the English courts tend to be lower, often far lower, than awards in Ireland. [171]

Reform

[28.58] Substantial proposals have been made to reform the law of libel. The Law Reform Commission published a *Report on the Civil Law of Defamation*[172] in 1991. A bill proposing reform of the tort was published by Michael McDowell TD in 1999. When he became Minister for Justice Equality and Law Reform Michael McDowell appointed an expert group, which published a report, *The Report of the Legal Advisory Group on Defamation*[173] in March 2003.

---

[164] [2006] EWHC 860 (QB) para 5.
[165] See **Anonymity** chapter 18.
[166] [2006] EWHC 860 (QB) para 10.
[167] Sitting as a Deputy Judge of the English High Court.
[168] [2006] EWHC 860 (QB) para 17.
[169] [2006] EWHC 860 (QB), para 24.
[170] *Godfrey v Demon* [2000] 3 WLR 1020 at 1030.
[171] See *De Rossa v Independent Newspapers* [1999] 4 IR 432 where the plaintiff was awarded £300,000.
[172] Law Reform Commission, *Report on the Civil Law of Defamation*, December 1991.
[173] http://www.justice.ie/en/JELR/rptlegaladgpdefamation.pdf/Files/rptlegaladgpdefamation.pdf.

This report made a number of recommendations, including:

(i)   a defence known as 'the defence of reasonable publication;

(ii)   juries should continue to have a role in assessing damages in the High Court;

(iii)   the jurisdiction of the Circuit Court in defamation cases should be set at €50,000

(iv)   all plaintiffs in defamation proceedings should have to file an affidavit which would verify the particulars of their claim;

(v)   a Press Council should be established, on a statutory basis;

(vi)   defendants in defamation actions would be able to make lodgments in court regardless of whether liability is admitted or denied;

(vii) a new fast-track procedure should be introduced so that it would be possible for either of the parties to apply to the court to have a defamation action disposed of in a summary manner by a judge sitting alone;

(viii) a new defence, to be known as 'the defence of innocent publication' should be provided for;

(ix)   only a single cause of action should lie in respect of a multiple publication; and

(x)   the limitation period in respect of defamation proceedings should be one year.

Many of these recommendations were then implemented in the Defamation Bill 2006. This Bill was not enacted by the Oireachtas and the Bill lapsed with the conclusion of the 29th Dáil. But this failure of legislation did not prevent the establishment of the Press Council of Ireland by the newspaper and magazine industry. At the time of writing, a commitment has been given to reintroduce the Bill in the Seanad in the autumn of 2007.[174]

The Defamation Bill 2006

[28.59] The Defamation Bill 2006 would appear to be primarily directed at the application of defamation laws to existing broadcast and newspaper organisations. Websites are unlike newspapers or radio broadcasts in one crucial aspect: allegations can be easily and cheaply retracted from publication online or taken down from websites. People use websites differently from newspapers or radio news broadcasts; someone who relies on RTÉ Radio for their news will tend to listen to a specific broadcast at a precise time. Once a broadcast is made at that time it cannot be retracted. In contrast, someone who relies on a website such as http://www.rte.ie, for their news may consult the site at various times during the day. If they encounter an article of particular interest on the site, they may forward it to friends or colleagues. If an article is removed from publication, publishers may be able to quickly mitigate the worst effect of their publication and will be able to prove this mitigation as they will be able to provide figures of the precise number of persons who viewed the allegedly defamatory material prior to its removal. Unfortunately, the Bill failed to explain how its defences will integrate with those provided by the e-Commerce Directive. The Bill provided for a

---

[174] Cullen, 'Defamation Bill to go before Seanad again in autumn' (2007) The Irish Times, 18 August.

defence of 'innocent publication'. A defendant may avail of this defence if he can prove that:

(a)   he or she was not the author, editor or publisher of the statement to which the action relates;

(b)   he or she took reasonable care in relation to its publication;

(c)   he or she did not know, and had no reason to believe, that what he or she did caused or contributed to the publication of a statement that would give rise to a cause of action in defamation.[175]

The Defamation Bill 2006 went on to provide that:

'A person shall not … .be considered to be the author, editor or publisher of a statement if … in relation to any electronic medium on which the statement is recorded or stored, he or she was responsible for the processing, copying, distribution or selling only of the electronic medium or was responsible for the operation or provision only of any equipment, system or service by means of which the statement would be capable of being retrieved, copied, distributed or made available.'[176]

[28.60] The Defamation Bill created a specific regime for traditional media which would run in parallel with that provided in the e-Commerce Directive; one for 'publishers' and the other for 'relevant service providers'. The Bill allowed for courts to take a publisher's behaviour, present and past, into account:

'The court shall, for the purposes of determining whether a person took reasonable care, or had reason to believe that what he or she did caused or contributed to the publication of a defamatory statement, have regard to … the extent of the person's responsibility for the content of the statement or the decision to publish it, … the nature or circumstances of the publication, and … the previous conduct or character of the person.'[177]

But the above falls far short of the absolute exemption from liability provided by the Directive on e-Commerce. The Defamation Bill 2006 also provided for the abolition of the multiple publication rule, and this proposal may prove to be more controversial. The Bill proposed to change the law so that 'a person has one cause of action only in respect of a multiple publication.'[178] This abolition was recommended by the Legal Advisory Group on Defamation, which considered that:

'in the context of multiple publication, a rule should be formulated to deal with proceedings for defamation based on publication by electronic means. It suggests a provision whereby such proceedings should also give rise to a single cause of action which, in this instance, would mean disregarding the number of times a particular publication might be accessed. The basic idea is that electronic and non-electronic publications should be treated equally insofar as the multiple publication rule was concerned.'

---

[175] Defamation Bill 2006, s 25(1).

[176] Defamation Bill 2006, s 25(2).

[177] Defamation Bill 2006, s 25(3).

[178] Defamation Bill 2006, s 10(1), s 10(3) defines 'multiple publication' as: 'publication by a person of the same defamatory statement to 2 or more persons (other than the person in respect of whom the statement is made) whether contemporaneously or not'.

[28.61] This recommendation was the product of the Group's 'intention to ensure that any recommendations made were technology neutral.'[179] The Group provided the heads of a draft defamation Bill – s 10 of the Defamation Bill 2006 would appear to be based upon Head 32 of the Group's draft. The Group provided an explanatory note to this head, which states:

> 'this Head provides for a general rule that only one cause of action will lie in respect of a multiple publication ... Provision is also made to deal with a cause of action which arises out of a publication by an electronic means of communication. It is made clear a single cause of action will lie notwithstanding the number of times the publication may be accessed.'[180]

The Group did not explain precisely why it felt that the multiple publication rule disadvantaged electronic publishers. But they may have been concerned that the multiple publication rule would discourage the provision of digital archives. The multiple publication rule can enable someone to effectively by-pass the Statute of Limitations by accessing a copy of a statement in an archive. This is what happened in the leading case on the rule, *Duke of Brunswick v Harmer*,[181] which the English Court of Appeal thought provided a 'striking illustration' of this principle:

> 'On 19 September 1830 an article was published in the 'Weekly Dispatch'. The limitation period for libel was then six years. The article defamed the Duke of Brunswick. Seventeen years after its publication an agent of the Duke purchased a back number containing the article from the 'Weekly Dispatch''s office. Another copy was obtained from the British Museum. The Duke sued on those two publications. The defendant contended that the cause of action was time-barred, relying on the original publication date. The Court of Queen's Bench held that the delivery of a copy of the newspaper to the plaintiff's agent constituted a separate publication in respect of which suit could be brought.'[182]

Suppose it came to a man's notice that an article published by *The Irish Times* in 1998 contained a statement that he considered to be defamatory of them. Following the rule set out in *Duke of Brunswick v Harmer* one might arrange for one's friends and acquaintances to download copies of the offending article from the archive supplied by *The Irish Times* on http://www.ireland.com. He might then bring an action for defamation in respect of this recent publication. The action would probably fail. Such an action was brought in *Loutchansky v Times Newspapers*, where the English Court of Appeal ruled that the multiple publication rule did not apply to the extraction of articles from archives.

[28.62] An alternative explanation is that the Group was minded to restrict the jurisdiction of the Irish courts, so that a person who is defamed by a website based in the UK or USA can no longer sue in the Irish Courts in respect of articles downloaded in Ireland. The English and Australian courts have asserted jurisdiction in such cases, and

---

[179] Legal Advisory Group on Defamation, *Report of the Legal Advisory Group on Defamation*, March 2003, p 31.

[180] Legal Advisory Group on Defamation, *Report of the Legal Advisory Group on Defamation*, March 2003, p 85.

[181] *Duke of Brunswick v Harmer* (1849) 14 QB 185.

[182] [2001] EWCA Civ 1805, para 57.

they have done so on the basis of the multiple publication rule. If the Oireachtas abolishes the multiple publication rule, it is difficult to see on what other basis the courts could reassert jurisdiction in respect of such downloads. That the multiple publication rule grounded the assertion by the English courts over defamatory statements downloaded in England and Wales is clear from the judgment of the House of Lords in *Berezovsky v Michaels*. Steyn LJ noted that the English Law of Libel had three distinctive features, one of which was 'that each communication is a separate libel'.[183] Steyn LJ considered that counsel for the defendant had argued that in respect of trans-national libels, the court should proceed on the 'assumption that there is in truth one cause of action'. This approach was rejected by Steyn LJ, who commented that:

> 'The result of such a principle, if adopted, will usually be to favour a trial in the home courts of the foreign publisher because the bulk of the publication will have taken place there. Counsel argued that it is artificial for the plaintiffs to confine their claim to publication within the jurisdiction.'[184]

This decision did not specifically address the publication of defamatory statements online, but that issue was addressed by the English Court of Appeal in *Lewis v King*. The English Court of Appeal held that an action could be brought before the courts of England and Wales in respect of defamatory statements published on a Californian website. The court found that 'in relation to internet libel, bearing in mind ... that each publication constitutes a separate tort, a defendant who publishes on the Web may at least in theory find himself vulnerable to multiple actions in different jurisdictions.'[185] In making this finding, the court referred to the judgment of Gleeson CJ, in *Gutnick v Dow Jones* who stated that:

> 'A publisher, particularly one carrying on the business of publishing, does not act to put matter on the internet in order for it to reach a small target. It is its ubiquity which is one of the main attractions to users of it. And any person who gains access to the internet does so by taking an initiative to gain access to it in a manner analogous to the purchase or other acquisition of a newspaper, in order to read it.[186] ... Comparisons can, as I have already exemplified, readily be made. If a publisher publishes in a multiplicity of jurisdictions it should understand, and must accept, that it runs the risk of liability in those jurisdictions in which the publication is not lawful and inflicts damage.'[187]

[28.63] By abolishing the multiple publication rule and adopting the single one, the Irish courts might be required to depart from the jurisprudence of the English and Australian courts and follow that of the American courts. Adopting a single publication rule could amount to a rejection of Gleeson CJ's finding in *Gutnick v Dow Jones* that:

> 'In defamation, the same considerations that require rejection of locating the tort by reference only to the publisher's conduct, lead to the conclusion that, ordinarily, defamation is to be located at the place where the damage to reputation occurs. Ordinarily that will be where the material which is alleged to be defamatory is available in

---

[183] *Berezovsky v Michaels* [2000] 1 WLR 1004 at 1012.
[184] [2000] 1 WLR 1004 at 1012–1013.
[185] [2004] EWCA Civ 1329, para 28.
[186] [2002] HCA 56, para 181.
[187] [2002] HCA 56, para 192

comprehensible form assuming, of course, that the person defamed has in that place a reputation which is thereby damaged. It is only when the material is in comprehensible form that the damage to reputation is done and it is damage to reputation which is the principal focus of defamation, not any quality of the defendant's conduct. In the case of material on the World Wide Web, it is not available in comprehensible form until downloaded on to the computer of a person who has used a web browser to pull the material from the web server. It is where that person downloads the material that the damage to reputation may be done. Ordinarily then, that will be the place where the tort of defamation is committed.'

[28.64] A single publication rule might deprive the subject of a statement published in New York – which is downloaded in Ireland and damages a person's reputation here – of recourse to the Irish Courts. The Defamation Bill 2006 did provide for some redress in such a situation, stating that 'A court may grant leave to a person to bring more than one defamation action in respect of a multiple publication where it considers that the interests of justice so require.'[188] The difficulty with this provision is that it is inherently contradictory for the Oireachtas to abolish the multiple publication rule on the one hand and expect the courts to re-enact it on the other. The Constitution would seem to prevent the Courts from doing so in any event. The Oireachtas must be aware that the multiple publication rule, has underpinned the decisions of the Australian court in *Gutnick v Dow Jones* and the English Court in *Lewis v King*. These decisions held that the courts of those countries had jurisdiction to hear actions relating to articles which were initially published in the USA, but were downloaded in Australia and England. It would seem to follow that in abolishing the multiple publication rule the Oireachtas intended to deprive Irish Courts of jurisdiction in cases similar to *Gutnick v Dow Jones* and *Lewis v King*.[189] In some exceptional cases, a court might consider that the 'interests of justice' would require that they assert jurisdiction, but the general rule would have to be that the Irish courts did not have jurisdiction.

[28.65] Abolishing the multiple publication rule would not mean that Americans would be free to say whatever they wanted about Irish people on American websites without fear of Ireland's defamation laws. In the main, Americans can do that already, so long as they do not have assets within the reach of the Irish courts. What this change would mean is that an Irish person could make a defamatory statement about another Irish person and so long as they took care to initially publish that statement on an American website or other American outlet, no action for defamation could be brought in the Irish Courts in respect of that statement. Arguably, abolition of the multiple publication rule would mean that the repetition of such a statement on an Irish website, or in an Irish newspaper, would also have to be litigated in the US courts. To all intents and purposes, the US Courts do not allow 'public figures' to sue for defamation,[190] a radically different

---

[188] Defamation Bill 2006, s 10(2).

[189] And so the Irish courts could not develop a new rule, other than the multiple publication rule, to give themselves jurisdiction over defamatory statements initially published in the USA and subsequently downloaded in Ireland.

[190] *New York Times v Sullivan* (1964) 376 US 254.

position to that which presently prevails in Ireland. The *Cogair*[191] website gave Irish politicians some experience of what they might expect in such a scenario. The more recent case of *Maguire v Gill*[192] provided some unfortunate Irish lawyers with a rather similar experience. In both cases, the websites that published the allegedly defamatory statements were unable to continue, because whilst they were outside the jurisdiction of the Irish courts, the persons who were allegedly operating them were not. In any event, the fact that these allegations were being made by anonymous or pseudonymous persons on obscure websites diluted their impact. But if a provision similar to s 10 of the Defamation Bill 2006 is enacted, then such persons would be immune from suit, so long as they were careful to only publish on websites in jurisdictions such as the USA. Furthermore, the persons who made such allegations would be able to disclose their identities, giving their allegations greater impact and allowing them to promote themselves. They might also be able to promote their sites domestically; again, so long as they ensured that they always made sure that any defamatory statements they made were initially published abroad. It is very difficult to see how long Ireland's defamation laws could retain their effect in such a situation.

---

[191] 'For the past eight months a website called Cogair has been publishing articles that Ireland's mainstream media in Ireland wouldn't touch with a 10-foot barge-pole. In its articles and 'secure discussion group'; Cogair purports to expose corruption in high places 'Scandal, rumour or gossip?' (1997) The Irish Times, 20 October; 'Cogair... anonymously published allegations about politicians, dissident republicans and the judiciary that no Irish publication would have taken the risk of carrying. Subsequent court cases and tribunals proved that much of what Cogair said was true'; Collins, 'When online gets out of line' (2006) The Irish Times, 25 November. The authors do not know why the Cogair website disappeared after 8 months, but it would not be hard to imagine that a threat of defamation proceedings had something to do with the disappearance.

[192] 'Man ordered to remove comments from website' (2006) The Irish Times, 14 September.

Chapter 29

Blasphemy, Sedition, Indecency and Criminal Libel

Introduction

[29.01] Blasphemous, seditious and indecent utterances have the dubious distinction of being criminalised by the Constitution itself, which provides that 'The publication or utterance of blasphemous, seditious, or indecent matter is an offence which shall be punishable in accordance with law'.[1]

Given the constitutional mandate, one might expect that the Oireachtas would feel impelled to ensure that the laws of blasphemy, sedition and indecency were clear. However, this has not been the case, and it would seem that an offence of blasphemy does not exist at all. It is highly likely that the offence of obscenity does not exist either. The offence of distributing or possessing seditious matter definitely exists, but will only apply to the Internet if the courts are willing to stretch the definition contained in a statute from 1939 sufficiently far. Frankly, the law in this area is a mess. This mess may reflect Irish history; until very recently strict controls were place upon what Irish people read and watched. Those controls are now both technologically and socially obsolete. However, there is no debate as to what, if anything, should replace them.

Blasphemy

[29.02] The Supreme Court decision of *Corway v Independent Newspapers*[2] dealt with the publication of a cartoon by the defendant following the 1995 divorce referendum. This showed:

> 'a stout comic figure of a priest in an old-fashioned surplice with lace on the sleeves and at the bottom and a stole, holding what was clearly the host in his right hand and chalice in his left hand. To the left of him were three caricatured ministers, namely, from left to right, Mr De Rossa, Mr Ruairí Quinn and the Taoiseach, Mr Bruton, each with a hand up indicating rejection of the host and chalice being offered by the priest. Immediately above the cartoon were the words 'Hello, Progress – Bye-Bye Father.'[3]

The plaintiff sought to prosecute the defendants for blasphemy in respect of this libel. In order to do so, the plaintiff had to overcome the obstacle put in his way by the Defamation Act 1961, which provided that:

> 'No criminal prosecution shall be commenced against any proprietor, publisher, editor or any person responsible for the publication of a newspaper for any libel published therein without the order of a Judge of the High Court sitting in camera being first had and

---

[1] Bunreacht na hÉireann, Article 40.6.1°i.
[2] *Corway v Independent Newspapers* [1999] 4 IR 484.
[3] [1999] 4 IR 484 at 486.

obtained, and every application for such order shall be made on notice to the person accused, who shall have an opportunity of being heard against the application.'[4]

The plaintiff's application was initially refused by Geoghan J in the High Court who doubted that the cartoon was in fact blasphemous.[5] The plaintiff then appealed to the Supreme Court, where Barrington J noted that:

'There is no definition of blasphemy in the Constitution nor is there any Act of the Oireachtas defining blasphemy. Mr Murdoch in his dictionary of Irish Law (Topaz Publications, Dublin, 1988) defines blasphemy as follows:-

'The crime which consists of indecent and offensive attacks on Christianity, or the Scriptures, or sacred persons or objects calculated to outrage the feelings of the community. The Constitution declares that the publication or utterance of blasphemous matter is an offence which shall be punishable in accordance with law ... The mere denial of Christian teaching is not sufficient to constitute the offence.'[6]

[29.03] Barrington J then went on to review the history of the common law offence of blasphemy, up to the disestablishment of the Church of Ireland in 1869, through to the enactment of the Constitution in 1937. Barrington J compared the protections offered by the Constitution to religion with those provided by the House of Lords in *R v Lemon*[7] *in which* the majority of the House held that 'an intention to publish blasphemous matter was sufficient *mens rea* to constitute the offence of blasphemy and that it was not necessary to prove a specific intention to blaspheme.'[8]

Barrington considered that:

'It is difficult to see how the common law crime of blasphemy, related as it was to an established church and an established religion could survive in such a constitutional framework. Certainly it is difficult to see how the view of the majority in the House of Lords in R v Lemon that the mere act of publication of blasphemous matter without proof of any intention to blaspheme is sufficient to support a conviction of blasphemy would be reconciled with a Constitution guaranteeing freedom of conscience and the free profession and practice of religion.'

Barrington J went on to note that:

'There is no doubt that the crime of blasphemy exists as an offence in Irish law because the Constitution says so. It says that the publication or utterance of blasphemous matter 'is an offence which shall be punishable in accordance with the law'. Yet the researches of the Law Reform Commission would appear to indicate that the framers of the Constitution did not intend to create a new offence. This may explain why there is no statutory definition of blasphemy. The Censorship of Films Act 1923 ... and ... the Defamation Act 1961, assume that the crime exists without defining it. It would appear that the legislature has not adverted to the problem of adapting the common law crime of blasphemy to the

---

4   Defamation Act 1961, s 8.
5   [1999] 4 IR 484 at 494.
6   [1999] 4 IR 484 at 495.
7   *R v Lemon* [1979] AC 617.
8   *Corway v Independent Newspapers* [1999] 4 IR 484 at 496.

circumstances of a modern State which embraces citizens of many different religions and which guarantees freedom of conscience and a free profession and practice of religion.'[9]

[29.04] Barrington J pointed out the confused position of different religions under the Irish Constitution: the position of the Christian and Jewish religions seemed clear enough, but what of the Muslim religion, or the Hindu? This led Barrington J to the conclusion that:

'in the absence of any legislative definition of the constitutional offence of blasphemy, it is impossible to say of what the offence of blasphemy consists ... neither the *actus reus* nor the *mens rea* is clear. The task of defining the crime is one for the legislature, not for the courts. In the absence of legislation and in the present uncertain state of the law the Court could not see its way to authorising the institution of a criminal prosecution for blasphemy against the respondent.'[10]

Whilst the Defamation Act 1961 does not provide any direction upon what amounts to a blasphemous libel, it does provide for the imposition of severe penalties should a conviction for the offence be obtained:

'Every person who composes, prints or publishes any blasphemous ... libel shall, on conviction thereof on indictment, be liable to a fine not exceeding five hundred pounds or imprisonment for a term not exceeding two years or to both fine and imprisonment or to penal servitude for a term not exceeding seven years.'[11]

Sedition

[29.05] Groups that are opposed to the state, for whatever reason, can be avid users of the Internet. For example, insurgent groups in Iraq are avid users of the Internet. This material has been analysed to extract 'themes insurgents consider best to mobilise activists or legitimise actions, and gives us information on internal debates and levels of coordination, and about shifts in tactics and strategy.'[12] The online publication of similar material by an unlawful organisation[13] that has been suppressed[14] pursuant to the *Offences against the State Acts* might amount to an offence in Ireland. The Offences Against the State Act 1939 provides that:

'It shall not be lawful to set up in type, print, publish, send through the post, distribute, sell, or offer for sale any document ... which is or contains or includes a treasonable document, or ... which is or contains or includes a seditious document.'[15]

The term document is defined as including 'a book and also a newspaper, magazine, or other periodical publication, and also a pamphlet, leaflet, circular, or advertisement.'[16]

---

9   [1999] 4 IR 484 at 501.
10 [1999] 4 IR 484 at 502.
11 Defamation Act 1961, s 13.
12 International Crisis Group, *In Their Own Words: Reading the Iraqi Insurgency,* Middle East Report N°50, 15 February 2006.
13 Offences Against the State Act 1939, s 18.
14 Offences Against the State Act 1939, s 19.
15 Section 10(1).
16 Section 2(1).

This is not expressed to be an exhaustive definition, and it might, possibly, be stretched to include an electronic document. The term 'treasonable document' is defined as including 'a document which relates directly or indirectly to the commission of treason; the expression.'[17]

[29.06] The term 'seditious document' is defined as including:

> 'a document consisting of or containing matter calculated or tending to undermine the public order or the authority of the State, and ... a document which alleges, implies, or suggests or is calculated to suggest that the government functioning under the Constitution is not the lawful government of the State or that there is in existence in the State any body or organisation not functioning under the Constitution which is entitled to be recognised as being the government of the country, and ... a document which alleges, implies, or suggests or is calculated to suggest that the military forces maintained under the Constitution are not the lawful military forces of the State, or that there is in existence in the State a body or organisation not established and maintained by virtue of the Constitution which is entitled to be recognised as a military force, and ... a document in which words, abbreviations, or symbols referable to a military body are used in referring to an unlawful organisation.'[18]

The maximum penalty that may be imposed for such an offence is a six-month term of imprisonment.[19] Similarly, it is unlawful 'for any person to have any treasonable document, seditious document, or incriminating document in his possession or on any lands or premises owned or occupied by him or under his control.'[20] Upon conviction for this offence a maximum penalty of three months' imprisonment may be imposed.[21]

Indecency

[29.07] Pornography is big business online, albeit not as big as its urban mythical status. According to the US Department of Justice, about 1% of webpages contain pornographic images. Given that Yahoo! claims to have indexed about 24 billion webpages, 240 million webpages is a lot of pornography.[22] The structure of pornography sites tends to be different from sites with less obscene subject matter; for example, there has been a major move in recent years away from sites that charge for access. But pornography sites have moved in the opposite direction. Concerns in the USA about children viewing pornography have encouraged pornography sites to try to restrict access to their wares, at least to those who have access to a credit card.[23] It would appear that only a small number of pornographic webpages are hosted in Ireland,[24] which is just

---

[17] Section 2(1).
[18] Section 2(1).
[19] Section 10(3).
[20] Section 12(1).
[21] Section 12(2).
[22] The validity of any computer-generated count of web-pages is very much open to question because 'as much as a third of the world wide web consists of artificially-generated pages of spam designed to promote commercial web sites.' Orlowski, 'My spam-filled search index is bigger than yours!' 16 August 2005.
[23] Waters, 'Porn found on 1% of web pages' (2006) Financial Times, 15 November.
[24] For example, the domain name porn.ie has been placed in the IEDR's forbidden category.

as well because the Irish law on obscene libel is 'largely redundant in practice.'[25] It is becoming increasingly obvious that Ireland has failed to take the policy decisions that would allow the development of a framework for regulating obscene, indecent and pornographic material.

Obscenity

[29.08] As is noted by the Law Reform Commission, 'obscenity is not prohibited by the Constitution, although indecency is.'[26] Obscenity, indecency and pornography are all different terms, which have different meanings. The Commission explained the difference between obscenity and pornography as follows:

> 'Obscenity in the English language means that which is repugnant to the senses, offensive, foul, repulsive or loathsome. Pornography is by contrast used to refer to sexual lewdness or erotic behaviour. Obscenity therefore, may or may not be pornographic, and vice versa. It is in the law only that the word 'obscenity' of itself has sexual connotations.'[27]

In 1991 the Law Reform Commission was unable to identify more than two prosecutions for obscenity during the twentieth century. The first case identified by the Commission was *DPP v Fleming*[28] in which the defendant pleaded guilty to charges of obscene and criminal libel in respect of 'obscene graffiti scribbled in public places around Ireland by the defendant.'[29] There would not appear to have been any prosecutions for obscene libel since *DPP v Fleming* in 1986, or at least the authors are unable to identify any such prosecutions.[30] The second case was the notorious case of *Attorney General v Simpson*,[31] which related to a production of the Tennessee Williams play *The Rose Tattoo* at a small Dublin theatre.

[29.09] The Law Reform Commission suggested that the test of what is or is not obscene was set out in *Hicklin*[32] by Cockburn CJ:

> 'test of obscenity is this, whether the tendency of the matter charged as obscenity is to deprave and corrupt those whose minds are open to such immoral influences, and into whose hands a publication of this sort may fall.'[33]

---

[25] McGonagle, *Media Law* (Thomson Round Hall, 2006) p 313.

[26] Law Reform Commission, *Consultation paper on the crime of libel,* August 1991, p 92.

[27] Law Reform Commission, p 93.

[28] See Law Reform Commission, *Consultation paper on the crime of libel,* August 1991 and McGonagle, *Media Law,* (Thomson Round Hall, 2006).

[29] Law Reform Commission, p 92. The defendant was a farmer. The graffiti gave his neighbour's phone number and suggested that they were available for sex; the defendant was effectively sentenced to nine months' imprisonment: McGonagle, *Media Law* (Thomson Round Hall, 2006) p 313.

[30] In 2006 a 'detective garda, who was subjected to a two-year campaign by a man who wrote graffiti in toilets and hospitals alleging the detective was a paedophile, secured €51,000'. 'Garda victim of graffiti campaign awarded €51,000' (2006) The Irish Times, 27 June.

[31] *Attorney General v Simpson* 93 ILTR 33.

[32] *Hicklin* (1868) LR 3 QB 360.

[33] Law Reform Commission, *Consultation paper on the crime of libel,* August 1991, p 93.

The Commission acknowledged the highly subjective nature of this test, noting that:

> 'obscenity is a subjective concept … that which disgusts one person leaves a second indifferent and is enjoyed by a third … whether something is obscene is a matter of taste and opinion. The literal meaning of obscenity is inherently a subjective concept. The 'corrupt and deprave' test shifts the centre of gravity away from taste (is this offensive or repulsive?) and on to morality (does this corrupt?). Instead of asking whether the matter is distasteful, one has to enter the speculative realm of deciding whether the viewing of such matter has negative effects in the minds of some members of society. Whether certain matter is commendable or corrupting, or indeed whether certain states of mind are good or bad, is essentially a moral question.'[34]

The reported Irish decision on obscenity is that of District Justice O'Floinn in *Attorney General v Simpson*. Given how much Ireland has changed since 1959, one would hesitate to call this a modern decision, and in any event it is not much use as the District Justice 'used the unlikely test 'Is the play a filthy play? That is the question.'[35] Other than *DPP v Fleming* there have been a variety of prosecutions since 1959 that relate to issues of obscenity. Such prosecutions relate to the making of obscene phone calls, publishing advertisements and the like. But there seems to have been only one prosecution for obscenity. It may well be that the grim atmosphere in which *Attorney General v Simpson* was prosecuted, the alleged interference in the decision to prosecute[36] and the consequences for the defendant, his theatre and his family, has made prosecutors unenthusiastic about approaching the law in this area. Any prosecutor with a mind to try would face a difficult task. Since the enactment of the UK's Obscene Publications Acts the decisions of the UK courts have focused upon the specific definition of obscenity given in those Acts. This means that any Irish prosecutor would face the daunting task of applying nineteenth-century standards to twenty-first-century material. As the Law Reform Commission noted:

> 'If excessive judicial intervention in matters of morality is a matter of concern today, it was less so in the nineteenth century. Furthermore it may well have been easier to identify a unified morality than it is today, and was certainly easier than identifying a unified 'taste' in publications. The necessarily subjective basis of the crime of obscene libel and the moral questions it raises will be returned to later.'[37]

[29.10] And as the Law Reform Commission notes standards of morality, indecency and obscenity are no longer uniform. Irish society is now made up of diverse strands: what might appear obscene to someone who has the moral standards of a 1950s Irish Catholic might seem mundane to a homosexual who is now able to express himself sexually

---

[34] Law Reform Commission, p 94.

[35] Law Reform Commission, p 98.

[36] 'The case … was not about The Rose Tattoo at all, but had its roots in a hidden struggle between the Department of Justice and the Machiavellian Catholic Archbishop of Dublin, John Charles McQuaid': Linehan, 'The thorny affair of the Rose Tattoo' (2002) The Irish Times, 13 November 2002. See, Whelan and Swift, *Spiked: Church-State Intrigue and The Rose Tattoo* (New Island, 2002).

[37] Law Reform Commission, *Consultation paper on the crime of libel,* August 1991, p 98.

without fear of prosecution. No decision of a court could satisfy either group, and there is a very persuasive argument to be made that devising a standard that could satisfy the needs of both groups is a difficult policy decision that must be made by the legislature and not the courts. Of course, the Law Reform Commission's *Consultation paper on the crime of libel* would be of great assistance to the putative prosecutor. But there have been a number of changes since the consultation paper and the Commission's *Report on the Crime of Libel* were published. Firstly, there has been the decision of *Corway v Independent* in which the Supreme Court refused to sanction a prosecution for blasphemous libel because the law was so unclear. Secondly, the enactment of the European Convention on Human Rights Act 2003 requires the courts to apply the Convention, including Articles 10 and 7 thereof. Article 10 allows for the right to freedom of expression to be restricted where such restrictions are 'prescribed by law.'[38] Given the obscurity of the law in this area, it may be argued that the offence of obscenity cannot be said to be 'prescribed by law'. Article 7 of the Convention provides 'No one shall be held guilty of any criminal offence on account of any act or omission which did not constitute a criminal offence under national or international law at the time when it was committed.'[39] If a prosecution were to be brought today on a charge of obscenity, the Court that tried the charge would, in large part, have to reinvent an offence that has not been developed since the nineteenth century. Bringing such a prosecution would leave the court in 'a difficult chicken and egg situation'.[40] It is impossible to say what precisely the modern common law of obscenity would amount to until a court decides upon a case. But any person convicted in such a case could, rightly, argue that the offence did not exist until their prosecution occurred and so their conviction fell foul of Article 7 of the Convention. It therefore seems unlikely that charges of obscenity will be brought under the law as it stands.

[29.11] There are two aspects of obscenity laws that are of particular relevance to the Internet. It may be assumed that the Irish crime of obscenity will apply to the Internet. In the English case of *R v Waddon*[41] the defendant pleaded guilty to obscenity charges in relation to a website called 'xtreme-perversion.' The defendant's guilty plea followed the trial judge's finding that uploading and downloading material to and from a website amounted to publication for the purposes of the UK's Obscene Publications Acts. This finding was upheld by the English Court of Appeal. In an Irish case it might be argued that the Electronic Commerce Act 2000's extension of defamation laws to the Internet[42] includes obscene libels.

Restriction of publication to closed groups

[29.12] A major advantage for online systems over conventional bookshops and newsagents is that they can monitor every person who uses their system. As already noted, the use of credit cards may ensure that only adults can use such systems.

---

[38] ECHR, art 10(2).
[39] ECHR, art 7(1).
[40] *Re Ansbacher (Cayman) Ltd* [2002] 2 IR 517 at 520.
[41] *R v Waddon* (6 April 2000) CA (Eng and Wales).
[42] Electronic Commerce Act 2000, s 23.

Operators may also have passwords and insist that users identify themselves before accessing the system. None of these systems is perfect: credit card numbers may be stolen and the internet being the marketplace that it is, if one operator goes into business with the intention of providing such password control, somebody else will go into business with the intention of providing a means of by-passing it. So if an online operator has a system that although imperfect, ensures that the great majority of those who view his material are adults, will the fact that the occasional adolescent is able to view the material mean that the test of obscenity will have to be decided by examining the effect of the material on the adolescent or on the adults?

[29.13] This question was examined by the House of Lords in *DPP v Whyte*.[43] The defendants ran a bookshop that was open to the public, which sold both pornographic books and books of general interest. The pornographic articles were held in a separate part of the shop but not in a looked case or cupboard. Each such book bore the label 'adults only', which, as the court noted, might act as an attraction rather than a deterrent. The court had no doubt that the pornographic books were of the 'hardest' quality and obscene in the ordinary sense of the word. The police had observed the premises over a period of time and as a result the likely readers were known. They were 'men principally of middle age and upwards who came there regularly to make purchases.'[44] These comprised the large majority of the customers, though occasionally middle-aged women and, from time to time, younger persons would enter the shop. The defendants tried to exclude those aged less than 21 years from the shop.

[29.14] At the initial trial, the Justices made findings of fact as to who the readers of the pornography were. They concluded that young persons were possible and not probable readers. They thought that the persons 'likely' or 'most likely' to purchase them were males of middle age and upwards. Wilberforce LJ was strongly of the view that this approach was incorrect. He felt that the approach of the justices in identifying a category of most likely readers was not permitted or required by the Act. He felt that account should also be taken of other persons who might read the books in question even if it was less likely that they would in comparison with the main category. He stated:

> 'In the case of a general shop, open to all and sundry, and offering all types of books, common sense suggests the conclusion that likely readers are a proportion of all such persons as normally resort to such shops, and it would require strong evidence to justify a conclusion that the likelihood of reading the books was confined to one definable category.'[45]

He had grave doubts regarding whether the evidence in this case, which had a number of gaps in it, justified the limitation of the group of 'likely readers' to middle-aged men. However, he felt that on a fair reading of the facts, the House of Lords was not entitled to reject the finding of the Justices that the likely readers of the books were men of middle age and upwards. Lord Cross agreed with Wilberforce LJ; he felt that although the facts found that the majority of the readers would be middle-aged or elderly men, it

---

[43] *DPP v Whyte* [1972] AC 849.
[44] [1972] AC 849 at 860.
[45] [1972] AC 849 at 861.

did not follow that there could be no other likely readers. It did not follow from the fact that just because members of one group could be the 'most likely' readers that there were no other 'likely' readers of the books. In Lord Cross's view, such other likely readers should only be excluded if they were numerically negligible as compared with the middle-aged and elderly male readers. He felt that if the Justices had appreciated this point, they would not have excluded all other categories, in particular they would not have excluded young men aged over 18 years. However, like Wilberforce LJ, he was unwilling to conclude that the finding of the Justices was one at which no reasonable man would have arrived.[46]

[29.15] Whether in practice cases such as *Whyte* and *Calder and Boyars* will be of any benefit to a supplier of online pornography is open to question. Some of the material on a site may be such that it would corrupt and deprave any users. Many users of the Internet are young and easily corrupted, although they may be sufficiently au fait with the technology to avoid password systems. The courts may doubt the veracity of records kept by suppliers of pornography purporting to show that only middle-aged men accessed their system. More especially, the courts are ill-equipped to assess the effectiveness of particular Internet technologies; judges may be unwilling to permit material which is otherwise obscene to be published on the Internet merely because the suppliers claim to be able to control access to it. In *DPP v Whyte* Pearson LJ did not wish to give booksellers the idea that if he was able to sell a large number of books to those unlikely to be corrupted, he could then sell a small number to readers likely to be corrupted. He stated:

> 'The statutory definition ... refers to persons which means some persons, though I think in a suitable case, if the number of persons likely to be affected is so small as to negligible - really negligible – the *de minimus* principle might be applied. But if a seller of pornographic books has a large number of customers who are not likely to be corrupted by such books, he does not thereby acquire a licence to expose for sale or sell such books to a small number of customers who are likely to be corrupted by them.'[47]

[29.16] A particular problem in this regard is the fact that the swapping and trading of such material on the Internet would appear to be endemic. The courts may be unimpressed by a supplier who claims to be able to ensure that only adults can view his material if he permits other suppliers to peruse his site, copy material and then redisplay it elsewhere on sites that have no such protection. In this situation it is arguable that the person who uses the unprotected system is the person to whom the material is published by the initial supplier. [48]

Jurisdiction

[29.17] The publishers of a website in Ireland that would only be available to persons accessing it from outside the State would not be able to avoid Ireland's obscenity laws,

---

[46] [1972] AC 849 at 869.
[47] [1972] AC 849 at 866.
[48] This question was examined by the Court of Criminal Appeal in *R v Barker* [1962] 1 All ER 748.

such as they are. In the English case of *Gold Star Publications v DPP*,[49] the police raided a warehouse containing magazines that were undoubtedly obscene. The defendant claimed that the articles (150,000 in all) were bound for Europe and the USA. This gave rise to a question of law as to whether the UK's Act applied only to material published in England or whether it also applied to material destined for publication abroad. There were two objections to the view that the Act did apply. The first was that of 'moral imperialism or paternalism'. This was rejected by Wilberforce LJ in the House of Lords. He took the view that 'parliament may not want England to become a "flourishing export trade in pornography" and may have thought that profits made by export could help to sustain the domestic trade.'[50] Furthermore, this objection would prevent the authorities in England from dealing with pornography bound for Scotland and Northern Ireland. This was unlikely to have been the intention of Parliament in his view. The second objection was that if the Act was applied to goods for export this would make the Act unworkable. This objection stems from the fact that obscenity is relative. What may deprave or corrupt some may have no effect or, theoretically, a beneficial effect on others. How can English magistrates decide on the likely effect of pornography on foreigners of different attitudes and mores? Wilberforce LJ held that a magistrate could so adjudicate on this case and the UK Act did apply to publication outside the jurisdiction of the English Courts. Roskill LJ concurred, noting that:

> 'standards of morality vary immensely in different countries and what is forbidden or is obscene in one country may even be thought therapeutic in another ... I am unable to see why he ceases so to publish an obscene article for gain because its ultimate destination is in Scotland, Northern Ireland or anywhere else in the world.'[51]

[29.18] The converse would also seem to be true: websites abroad that provide obscene material that is downloaded in Ireland will be susceptible to Irish law. In the English case of *R v Perrin*[52] the defendant ran a website with the domain name http://www.sewersex.com. This provided a preview page, 'available free of charge to any one with access to the internet'. This page provided images of 'people covered in faeces, coprophilia or coprophagia, and men involved in fellatio.'[53] The defendant was prosecuted under the UK's Obscene Publications Acts and convicted. He appealed. One of the grounds of his appeal was that the site was hosted in the UK. On appeal against his conviction the defendant argued that the English courts did not have jurisdiction. The English Court of Appeal responded that:

> 'there was publication when anyone accessed the preview page, and he rejected entirely Mr Fulford's submission that a prosecution should only be brought against a publisher where the prosecutor could show that the major steps in relation to publication were taken within the jurisdiction of the court. Not only would that lead to publishers taking their major steps in countries with the most relaxed laws, but such countries might also have little interest in prosecuting, especially if the offensive material was targeted elsewhere.'[54]

---

49 *Gold Star Publications v DPP* [1981] 2 All ER 257.
50 [1981] 2 All ER 257 at 259.
51 [1981] 2 All ER 257 at 265.
52 *R v Perrin* [2002] EWCA Crim 747.
53 [2002] EWCA Crim 747, para 2.
54 [2002] EWCA Crim 747, para 51.

Conspiracy to corrupt public morals

[29.19] This common law offence was examined in *AG (SPUC) v Open Door Counselling*[55] where the defendants were involved in the referral of pregnant women to the UK for abortions. The plaintiff objected to this on the basis of the Eighth amendment to the Constitution, which outlawed abortion. Hamilton P held that the supply of such information could be an offence. He cited with approval the decision of the House of Lords in *Knuller v DPP*[56] where a magazine contained advertisements inviting readers to meet others in order to engage in homosexual acts, which were legal in the UK. They were convicted of conspiring to corrupt public morals. Hamilton P noted that, in the *SPUC* case the defendants were reputable organisations providing necessary services to the women. He stated that finding that such activities or conduct was liable to corrupt public morals was not one to be reached lightly. He quoted Simon LJ 'The words "corrupt public morals" suggest conduct which a jury might find to be destructive of the very fabric of society'. In *AG(SPUC) v Open Door Counselling* Hamilton P was unwilling to find that the defendants were engaged in a criminal conspiracy to corrupt public morals as this was a question which should be left to a jury in a criminal trial.

Outraging public decency

[29.20] In *Knuller v DPP*[57] a majority of the House of Lords held that there is an offence of outraging decency and therefore also an offence of conspiring to outrage public decency. Public decency may be outraged in a number of ways, for example by indecent exposure,[58] indecent words[59] or exhibiting pictures.[60] The act must be committed in public,[61] which means that:

> 'The substantive offence (and therefore the conduct the subject of the conspiracy) must be committed in public, in the sense that the circumstances must be such that the alleged outrageously indecent matter could have been seen by more than one person, even though in fact no more than one did see it. If it is capable of being seen by one person only, no offence is committed.'[62]

[29.21] An internet website would probably come within this definition as material is made available to the public.

[29.22] Simon LJ went on to hold that:

> 'It should be emphasised that "outrage" like "corrupt" is a very strong word. "Outraging public decency" goes considerably beyond offending the susceptibilities of, or even shocking reasonable people. Moreover the offence is, in my view, concerned with recognised minimum standards of decency, which are likely to vary from time to time ... notwithstanding that 'public' in the offence is used in a locative sense, public decency

---

55 *AG (SPUC) v Open Door Counselling* [1988] IR 593.
56 *Knuller v DPP* [1973] AC 435.
57 [1973] AC 435.
58 *R v Ruden* [1809] 2 Comp 89.
59 *R v Sauders* [1875] 1 QBD 75.
60 *E v Fewy* [1864] 4 F & F73.
61 *R v Mayling* [1963] 2 QB 717.
62 Per Simon LD in *DPP v Knuller* [1973] AC 435 at 494.

must be viewed as a whole; and I think the jury should be invited, where appropriate, to remember that they live in a plural society, with a tradition of tolerance towards minorities and that this atmosphere of toleration is itself part of public decency'.[63]

Advertisements for prostititues

[29.23] There would appear to be a significant phenomenon of prostitutes, or rather their pimps, advertising their services online:

'The sex industry in Ireland is booming as never before ... On-street prostitution is all but gone, apart from small numbers of more chaotic, drug-using women. The core of the industry has moved indoors, using mobile phones, the internet and private rented apartments to offer a discreet, though surprisingly accessible, 'service' ... Completely legally, anyone can access numerous websites listing mobile-phone numbers for Ballsbridge, Clondalkin and elsewhere in Dublin, as well as Limerick and Galway 'agencies'.'[64]

[29.24] The apparent pervasiveness of such advertisements is surprising, given that it is an offence to publish these. But, unless they are very unwise, the publishers of these sites will ensure that they are hosted in jurisdictions beyond the reach of the gardaí. The Criminal Justice (Public Order) Acts 1994 and 2003 provide that an offence will be committed by any person who:

'publishes or causes to be published[65] or distributes[66] or causes to be distributed an advertisement which advertises a brothel or the services of a prostitute in the State or any premises or service in the State in terms, circumstances or manner which gives rise to the reasonable inference that the premises is a brothel or that the service is one of prostitution shall be guilty of an offence.'[67]

[29.25] This provision would seem to apply to the Internet, the Criminal Justice (Public Order) Acts 1994 and 2003 provides that the term 'advertisement' includes:

'every form of advertising or promotion, whether in a publication or by the display of notices or posters or by the means of circulars, leaflets, pamphlets or cards or other documents or by way of radio, television, computer monitor, telephone, facsimile transmission, photography or cinematography or other like means of communication.'[68]

[29.26] Given that this legislation was enacted in 1994 it may seem surprising that the above does not include any reference to the Internet. But the definition seems broad enough to encompass the placing of an advertisement online. The Criminal Justice (Public Order) Act 1994 and 2003 provide a defence for an accused who can:

'show that he is a person whose business it is to publish or distribute or to arrange for the publication or distribution of advertisements and that he received the advertisement in

---

63 [1973] AC 435 at 495.

64 Holland, 'Trafficking in misery' (2006) The Irish Times, 6 May.

65 'Publish' is defined as 'publish to the public or a section of the public': Criminal Justice (Public Order) Act 1994, s 23(5).

66 'Distribute' is defined as 'distribute to the public or a section of the public': Criminal Justice (Public Order) Act 1994, s 23(5).

67 Criminal Justice (Public Order) Act 1994 and 2003, s 23(1).

68 Criminal Justice (Public Order) Act 1994, s 23(5).

question for publication or distribution in the ordinary course of business and did not know and had no reason to suspect that the advertisement related to a brothel or to the services of a prostitute.'[69]

[29.27] In other words, this is a defence of innocent dissemination and as such it should be read in conjunction with the Directive on e-Commerce. Anyone convicted on indictment of such an offence may be fined a maximum of €12,697 (£10,000). In 2000, a publisher was fined €50,000 after he published advertisements which promoted prostitution.[70] Section 7 of the Criminal Justice (Public Order) Act 1994–2003 also provides that it:

'shall be an offence for any person in a public place to distribute or display any writing, sign or visible representation which is threatening, abusive, insulting or obscene with intent to provoke a breach of the peace or being reckless as to whether a breach of the peace may be occasioned ... . A person who is guilty of an offence under this section shall be liable on summary conviction to a fine not exceeding £500 or to imprisonment for a term not exceeding 3 months or to both'.

Censorship

[29.28] Censorship has a controversial history in Ireland, and a dispute about censorship policy between the Government and the Catholic Church is said to have been the driving force behind *Attorney-General v Simpson*.[71] Ireland has a specific censorship regime for three different technologies:

   (i)   printed matter, such as books and magazines, is dealt with by the Censorship of Publications Acts; [72]

   (ii)   films are dealt with by the Censorship of Films Acts; and

   (iii) videos and DVDs are dealt with by the Video Recordings Act 1989.

[29.29] Of the above, the Video Recordings Act 1989 has the greatest application to information technologies. The Act defines video recording as: 'any disc or magnetic tape containing information by the use of which the whole or a part of a video work may be produced'. A video work is defined as meaning 'any series of visual images (whether with or without sound) ... produced, whether electronically or by other means, by the use of information contained on any disc or magnetic tape, and ... shown as a moving picture.'[73] It is an offence to supply a video work that has not be certified by the Official Censor, unless the supply is a supply or work exempted by the Act.V[74] This offence is punishable by a maximum term of imprisonment of three years.[75] The continuing

---

[69] Criminal Justice (Public Order) Act 1994, s 23(3).

[70] '€50,000 fine for publisher who made €400,000 a year from brothel ads' (2000) The Irish Times, 19 October.

[71] See Whelan and Swift, *Spiked: Church-State Intrigue and The Rose Tattoo* (New Island, 2002).

[72] See *Melton Enterprises Ltd v Censorship of Publications Board* [2003] 3 IR 623 for an analysis of the decision-making processes of the Censorship Board under the Censorship of Publications Act 1946.

[73] Video Recordings Act 1989, s 1(1).

[74] ideo Recordings Act 1989, s 5(1).

[75] Video Recordings Act 1989, s 5(3).

relevance of this enactment must be very much open to question at this stage. Take the example of http://www.youtube.com. At the time of writing, the site contains thousands of video clips, which would seem to fall within the Video Recordings Act 1989 definition of video work. Similarly a very large number of video works will be provided by a host of websites. It is true that http://www.youtube.com does not charge for accessing these clips, but the sites are undoubtedly run as a business, which means that this is not a supply that is exempted by the Video Recordings Act 1989.[76] It would not appear that either of these sites, or any of the many sites that make video works available for download to Irish residents, have certificates for these works. Certainly the sites do not appear to comply with the labeling requirements of the Video Recordings Act 1989.[77] Of course the problem is not with the actions of the operators of these sites, or the Official Censor, but rather with the Video Recordings Act 1989. The Act was never designed to deal with sites such as these. In the highly unlikely event that a prosecution were to be brought against the operators of such sites for breach of the Video Recordings Act 1989, then a very persuasive argument could be made that sites such as http://www.youtube.com could not have been contemplated of the Oireachtas when it enacted the Video Recordings Act 1989.[78]

Sending obscene messages

[29.30] The sending of obscene messages by telephone is an offence under the Post Office (Amendment) Act 1951 as amended by the Communications Regulation (Amendment) Act 2007.[79] Section 13(1) provides that any person who:

(a) sends by telephone any message that is grossly offensive, or is indecent, obscene or menacing,

or

(b) for the purpose of causing annoyance, inconvenience, or needless anxiety to another person—

(i) sends by telephone any message that the sender knows to be false, or

(ii) persistently makes telephone calls to another person without reasonable cause, commits an offence.

[29.31] The term 'message' includes a text message sent by means of a short message service (SMS) facility.[80] Interestingly it does not expressly refer to email; however, if such an email is sent it would probably be covered by other legislation.[81]

[29.32] Where a person is found guilty of such an offence they are liable on conviction on indictment to a fine not exceeding €75,000 or to imprisonment for a term not exceeding 5 years, or to both. Where a person is tried summarily, they are liable to a fine

---

[76] Video Recordings Act 1989, s 2(1)(a) provides that '"xempted supply" means a supply of a video recording ... that is neither a supply for reward nor a supply in the course or furtherance of a business'.

[77] Video Recordings Act 1989, s 12.

[78] http://www.youtube.com was founded in February 2005: http://www.youtube.com/t/about.

[79] Video Recordings Act 1989, Sch 1, Pt 2.

[80] Video Recordings Act 1989, s 13(5).

[81] See **Chapter 21** on Spam.

not exceeding €5,000 or to imprisonment for a term not exceeding 12 months, or to both.[82] In addition to any other penalty imposed for the offence the court order any apparatus, equipment or other thing used in the course of committing the offence to be forfeited to the State.[83]

Criminal Libel

[29.33] The Law Reform Commission described criminal libel as being something that is obviously 'an anomalous and anachronistic survival in our law.'[84] However, there have been a couple of occasions upon which prosecutions have been successfully brought in respect of criminal libel online. In the first such case, a man who had spread Internet messages alleging one of his former teachers was a paedophile was convicted of criminal libel and jailed for 2.5 years. The messages had been sent to Internet bulletin boards and by email to another teacher in the man's former school. One of the defamatory libels falsely alleged that someone had asked up to 10 people to film nude boys for the man's former teacher and that the teacher had also asked the defendant to do the same.[85] In the second, a sandwich-seller was convicted of criminal libel, albeit the probation Act was applied, and required to pay 'substantial' compensation after he posted the name and personal details of a business rival on a website advertising the services of prostitutes. The defendant had 'placed an advertisement headed 'Exclusive Maureen' – a reference to Ms Walker's Exclusive Sandwiches business – on the Escort Ireland website and gave details of the services she would provide.' In the day's that followed, the woman in question received more than 100 phone calls.[86]

[29.34] One of the features of the offence of criminal libel is that the sanction of the High Court must be sought before such a prosecution can be initiated against the proprietor of a newspaper or a magazine. The Defamation Act 1961 provides that:

> "No criminal prosecution shall be commenced against any proprietor, publisher, editor or any other person responsible for the publication of a newspaper for any libel published therein without the order of a judge of the High Court sitting *in camera* being first had and obtained, and every application for such order shall be made on notice to the person accused, who shall have an opportunity of being heard against the application.'[87]

[29.35] The application of this provision to the Internet would seem doubtful, as only the proprietors and publishers of newspapers are protected by it. 'Newspapers' are defined by the Defamation Act 1961 as:

> 'any paper containing public news or observations thereon, or consisting wholly or mainly of advertisements, which is printed for sale and is published in the State or in Northern Ireland either periodically or in parts or numbers at intervals not exceeding thirty-six days.'[88]

---

[82] Video Recordings Act 1989, s 13(2).

[83] Video Recordings Act 1989, s 13(4).

[84] Law Reform Commission, *Report on the Crime of Libel*.

[85] 'Man gets jail for Internet libel of teacher' (1999) The Irish Times, 21 December.

[86] 'Woman to get more than £10,000 for Web slur' (2001) The Irish Times, 11 May.

[87] Defamation Act 1961, s 8.

[88] Defamation Act 1961, s 2.

[29.36] The requirement that a newspaper be 'printed for sale' would seem to mean that this section does not apply to the publisher or proprietor of a website the contents of which are not made available in printed form. However, the only reported Irish court decision to consider what may amount to the offence of criminal libel was *Hilliard v Penfield Enterprises Ltd*,[89] which was brought by the widow of a deceased Church of Ireland rector. Following his death, Phoenix magazine published an article about him, which Gannon J described in the following terms:

> 'I have read the article and consider it to be so scurrilous and contrived in its presentation of dissociated persons and events as to arouse feelings of revulsion towards the author as well as vilifying the subject, namely the applicant's deceased husband ... It would be impossible to describe a libel which accuses a person of having been twenty years ago an intelligence officer for the I.R.A. and of providing contacts to lead to massive bank robberies, or of setting fire to houses and cars on behalf of the I.R.A. as being of a trivial character. A libel of the nature which this article is can only be described as most serious in the nature of the defamation.'[90]

[29.37] Gannon J began his judgment by referring to a previous, unreported, judgment of Finlay P in *Gallagher v Independent Newspapers*,[91] which had analysed the relevant case law. In particular Finlay P set out the following principles, which had been enunciated in *Goldsmith v Pressdram*[92]:

> '(1) Firstly the applicant must establish a clear *prima facie* case in the sense that it is a case which is so clear at first sight that there is beyond argument a case to answer if the matter goes before a criminal court.
>
> (2) The libel must be a serious one, so serious that it is proper for the criminal law to be invoked.
>
> (3) Although it may be a relevant factor that the libel is unusually likely to provoke a breach of the peace, that is not a necessary ingredient.
>
> (4) The question of the public interest must be taken into account on the basis that the judge should ask himself the question: does the public interest *require* the institution of criminal proceedings?[93]

[29.38] Gannon J considered that in citing the above Finlay P 'was clearly adopting and signifying his agreement with the judgment of Wien J in the *Goldsmith case*.'[94] In considering the severity of the alleged libel, Gannon J considered that:

> 'The requirement that the criminal nature of the libel is to be tested by the seriousness or gravity of the libel is not assisted by having regard merely to the penalties prescribed in ... the Defamation Act 1961. The speeches in the House of Lords in *R v Wells Street*

---

89 *Hilliard v Penfield Enterprises Ltd* [1990] 1 IR 138.

90 [1990] 1 IR 138 at 141.

91 *Gallagher v Independent Newspapers* (3 July 1978, unreported) HC.

92 *Goldsmith v Pressdram* [1976] 3 WLR 191.

93 *Hilliard v Penfield Enterprises Ltd* [1990] 1 IR 138 at 142. Finlay P was following the English judgment in *Goldsmith v Pressdram* 1977 QB 83.

94 [1990] 1 IR 138 at 142.

Stipendiary Magistrate, ex p Deakin[95] convey to me that the gravity of the defamatory matter and the gravity of its effect in damaging a character (good or bad) must be put in the balance against the public interest invoked in defence.'[96]

[29.39] Gannon J considered that the test which was to be applied would have to be:

'the likely effect on a significant section of law abiding citizens. I think the likelihood of provoking a breach of the peace would be significant if it should appear affirmative, but if negative would be of marginal significance. It must be borne in mind that the mischief is the damage to the good name and repute of the vilified party in the esteem of other right minded persons, and not the damage to his self-esteem. The latter is more likely to provoke a breach of the peace in the physical sense, but the former could also provoke a physical reaction in the case of a libel of some classes of highly esteemed public personages.'[97]

[29.40] Gannon J considered that the fact that the victim of such a libel might have a civil remedy open to him was irrelevant:

'it is in the public interest that every crime should be properly investigated and every criminal brought to justice. The nature and circumstances of the libel has to be considered in this light, and must not be obscured by the right of a party who has been wronged to find remedy in compensation or other court intervention on the civil side.'[98]

[29.41] Gannon J set out the following analysis of how severe a libel would have to be to amount to a criminal libel, noting that:

'From earliest times the primacy of the preservation of the public peace and order seems to have been emphasised as the key factor in the test of criminality. Formerly the disturbance contemplated was some form of violent physical reaction. But it seems to me that in modern times the disturbance of the public peace and order may manifest itself in no more violent manner than by a substantial volume of protest in the form of public assembly or correspondence to newspapers or protest by other means of mass communication. There are many forms of crime involving deception which so offend the public conscience that it is in the public interest that they be investigated and that the suspected person be charged and prosecuted. The essence of the offence of criminal libel, it seems to me, is its impact on the public conscience as much as its falsity which, when perpetrated by a newspaper, may result in a damaging deception of a significant section of the public sufficiently representative of the current climate of social and moral standards.'[99]

[29.42] Gannon J quoted the following passage from Dilhorne VC to the effect that:

'A criminal libel must be a serious libel. If the libel is of such a character as to be likely to disturb the peace of the community or to provoke a breach of the peace, then it is not to be regarded as trivial. But to hold...that the existence of such a tendency suffices to show that the libel is a serious one, is a very different thing from saying that proof of its existence is

---

[95] *R v Wells Street Stipendiary Magistrate, ex p Deakin* [1980] AC 477.
[96] *Hilliard v Penfield Enterprises Ltd* [1990] 1 IR 138 at 143.
[97] [1990] 1 IR 138 at 143.
[98] [1990] 1 IR 138 at 143.
[99] [1990] 1 IR 138 at 143–144.

necessary to establish guilt of the offence. Evidence of the bad character of the person libeled is irrelevant to question whether the libel has any such tendency.'[100]

[29.43] Gannon J appeared to consider that the libel contained in the Phoenix article was very serious, and might well have been willing to sanction the prosecution. But the problem for the plaintiffs was that the subject of the article was dead, and being dead could no longer suffer any wrongs. Gannon J reviewed the authorities on this point and cited the following passage from *R v Ensor*[101]:

> 'Now to say in general that the conduct of a dead person can at no time be canvassed, to hold that even after ages are past the conduct of bad men cannot be contrasted with the good would be to exclude the most useful part of history; and therefore it must be allowed that such publications may be made fairly and honestly. But let this be done whenever it may, whether soon or late after the death of the party, if it be done with a malevolent purpose to vilify the memory of the deceased and with a view to injure his posterity (as in *R v Critchley*), then it comes within the rule stated by Hawkins – then it is done with a design to break the peace, and then it becomes illegal … a mere vilifying of the deceased is not enough … There must be a vilifying of the deceased with a view to injure his posterity. The dead have no rights and can suffer no wrongs. The living alone can be the subject of legal protection, and the law of libel is intended to protect them, not against every writing which gives them pain, but against writings holding them up individually to hatred, contempt or ridicule.'[102]

[29.44] In *Hilliard v Penfield* Gannon J refused to grant leave to prosecute the defendants because it seemed to him that 'the defamation of the widow and daughter of the deceased … does not have the gravity in law to require prosecution for a criminal offence.'[103] Had the application been successful, the Defamation Act 1961 would have provided further protections for the defendants to the extent that they were newspaper proprietors, publishers or editors. When the charge is heard in the District Court, then the District Court Judge:

> 'may receive evidence as to the publication being for the public benefit, as to the matters charged in the libel being true, as to the report being fair and accurate and published without malice and as to any matter which, under this or any other Act or otherwise, might be given in evidence by way of defence by the person charged on his trial on indictment, and the Justice, if, of opinion after hearing such evidence that there is a strong or probable presumption that the jury on the trial would acquit the person charged, may dismiss the case.'[104]

[29.45] If the Judge decides not to dismiss the charge, then if he:

> 'is of opinion that, though the person charged is shown to have been guilty, the libel was of a trivial character and that the offence may be adequately punished by virtue of the powers conferred by this section, the Justice shall cause the charge to be reduced into writing and read to the person charged and shall then ask him if he desires to be tried by a

---

[100] Cited by Gannon J at *Hilliard v Penfield Enterprises Ltd* [1990] 1 IR 138 at 146.
[101] *R v Ensor* (1887) 3 TLR 366.
[102] Cited at [1990] 1 IR 138 at 146–147.
[103] [1990] 1 IR 138, 147.
[104] Defamation Act 1961, s 9.

jury or consents to the case being dealt with summarily, and, if such person consents to the case being dealt with summarily, may summarily convict him, and impose on him a fine'.[105]

Defences

[29.46] The mere fact that what was published is the truth will not be a sufficient defence to a charge of criminal libel. This may appear extraordinary, but the offence of criminal libel is not directed towards the preservation of an individual's reputation but rather towards the preservation of public order. The Defamation Act 1961 provides that:

> 'On the trial of any indictment for a defamatory libel ... the truth of the matters charged may be inquired into but shall not amount to a defence, unless it was for the public benefit that the said matters charged should be published.'[106]

[29.47] So if a database of convicted pedophiles were to be maintained on the web, the fact that all the entries were true would not be a defence to a charge of criminal libel. The defence would have to argue that it was in the public interest to know the identity of these offendors, while the prosecution might argue that placing this information in the public domain was a threat to public order.

[29.48] Nor can the defence surprise the prosecution by raising the question of truth at trial. If evidence of truth is to be given, the allegation of truth, justification and public benefit must be raised in pleadings as must the facts upon which the defendant intends to rely. The prosecutor will be in the advantageous position of being at liberty to reply generally, denying the whole, so that he or she will not have to give anything away. If this plea is made and the defendant is convicted, the court may take this plea into account in pronouncing sentence, but the sentence may be aggravated or mitigated by the plea. The court may not consider the truth of the matters charged in the alleged libel complained of by such indictment shall in no case be inquired into without such plea of justification.[107] In addition to such plea of justification, the defendant may enter a plea of not guilty.[108] Finally, nothing in this section can take away or prejudice any defence under the plea of not guilty which the defendant is competent to make.[109] A defence which may prove to be of importance in Internet cases is provided by section 7: '...it shall be competent for the person charged to prove that the publication was made without his authority, consent or knowledge and that the publication did not arise from want of due care or caution on his part.'[110] But a mere absence of knowledge or consent would appear to be insufficient, as it must also be shown that the publication did not result from a want of knowledge or consent on the part of an ISP. The jury will have the right to examine the entirety of the offence and the court cannot simply direct them to find the defendant guilty merely on the proof of the publication by him of the paper charged to be a libel and of the sense ascribed to such paper in the indictment.[111]

---

[105] Section 10.
[106] Section 6.
[107] Defamation Act 1961, s 6(a).
[108] Section 6(b).
[109] Section 6(c).
[110] Section 7.
[111] Section 5(a).

However, the court has discretion to give its opinion and directions to the jury on the issues before the court[112] and the jury may find a special verdict.[113]

Penalties

[29.49] The penalties for publishing a defamatory libel are quite severe. Every person who maliciously publishes any defamatory libel will, on conviction thereof on indictment, be liable to a fine not exceeding two hundred pounds or to imprisonment for a term not exceeding one year or to both such fine and imprisonment.[114] Every person who maliciously publishes any defamatory libel, knowing the same to be false, will, on conviction thereof on indictment, be liable to a fine not exceeding five hundred pounds or to imprisonment for a term not exceeding two years or to both such fine and imprisonment.[115] Every person who composes, prints or publishes any blasphemous or obscene libel may on conviction on indictment be liable to a fine not exceeding five hundred pounds or imprisonment for a term not exceeding two years or to both fine and imprisonment or to penal servitude for a term not exceeding seven years.[116]

Pro-ana sites

[29.50] Anorexia and bulimia are dangerous diseases, which can lead to death and disability. The development of 'pro-ana' and 'pro-mia' sites, which promote anorexia and bulimia as legitimate lifestyle choices, are therefore a serious concern.[117] It is likely that such sites are 'damaging deception of a significant section of the public sufficiently representative of the current climate of social and moral standards.'[118] The operators of such sites might therefore be prosecuted for criminal libel. The only problem with bringing such a prosecution is that most, if not all, operators of these sites are themselves sufferers of eating disorders for whom medical treatment may be more appropriate than jail time.

Incitement to hatred

[29.51] As a global information network, the Internet allows all voices to be heard. Unfortunately some of those voices will be those of racists and those who seek to incite hatred against different groups. For example, in January 2007, 'A State-funded advisory body on racism ... condemned a website aimed at taxi drivers in Ireland for carrying offensive and racist material relating to immigrants in Ireland.'[119] Hosting material such

---

[112] Section 5(b).

[113] Section 5(c).

[114] Section 11.

[115] Section 12.

[116] Section 13(1).

[117] See Giles, 'Constructing identities in cyberspace: the case of eating disorders' Br J Soc Psychol (2006) Sep; 45 (Pt 3):463–77; Mulveen and Hepworth, 'An interpretative phenomenological analysis of participation in a pro-anorexia internet site and its relationship with disordered eating' J Health Psychol (2006) Mar; 11(2):283–96; and, Brotsky and Giles, 'Inside the "pro-ana" community: a covert online participant observation' Eat Disord (2007) Mar-Apr; 15(2):93–109.

[118] *Hilliard v Penfield Enterprises Ltd* [1990] 1 IR 143–144.

[119] O'Brien, 'Taxi website asked to remove racist material' (2007) The Irish Times, 23 January.

as this is unwise as it may be an offence to do so contrary to the Prohibition of Incitement to Hatred Act 1989. As its name suggests, this Act is directed at prohibiting the incitement of hatred. Hatred is defined by the Act as 'hatred against a group of persons in the State or elsewhere on account of their race, colour, nationality, religion, ethnic or national origins, membership of the travelling community or sexual orientation.'[120]

The Act provides that it will be:

'an offence for a person … to publish or distribute written material … to use words, behave or display written material … in any place other than inside a private residence, or … inside a private residence so that the words, behaviour or material are heard or seen by persons outside the residence … or … to distribute, show or play a recording of visual images or sounds, if the written material, words, behaviour, visual images or sounds, as the case may be, are threatening, abusive or insulting and are intended or, having regard to all the circumstances, are likely to stir up hatred.'[121]

[29.52] This offence would certainly seem to encompass publishing or distributing such material online. The Prohibition of Incitement to Hatred Act 1989 provides a defence for innocent disseminators[122] in respect of this offence and, again, this defence should be read in conjunction with the Directive on e-Commerce. The Act also makes it an offence to broadcast such material, providing that:

'If an item involving threatening, abusive or insulting visual images or sounds is broadcast … the person providing the broadcasting service concerned … any person by whom the item concerned is produced or directed, and … any person whose words or behaviour in the item concerned are threatening, abusive or insulting[123] … is guilty of an offence if he intends thereby to stir up hatred or, having regard to all the circumstances, hatred is likely to be stirred up thereby.'[124]

[29.53] The Act defines 'broadcast' as meaning:

'the transmission, relaying or distribution by wireless telegraphy or by any other means or by wireless telegraphy in conjunction with any other means of communications, sounds, signs, visual images or signals, intended for direct reception by the general public whether such communications, sounds, signs, visual images or signals are actually received or not.'

[29.54] This definition might extend to Internet transmissions, but the Oireachtas probably intended that it would only apply to television and radio broadcasts. A court might therefore hesitate before extending the definition in this way. In any event the Prohibition of Incitement to Hatred Act 1989 provides other offences that may be

---

[120] Prohibition of incitement to Hatred Act 1989, s 1(1).

[121] Section 2(1).

[122] Section 2(2) provides: 'if the accused person is not shown to have intended to stir up hatred, it shall be a defence for him to prove that he was not aware of the content of the material or recording concerned and did not suspect, and had no reason to suspect, that the material or recording was threatening, abusive or insulting'.

[123] Section 3(2).

[124] Section 3(1).

applied to the Internet. The significance of the offence of broadcasting a message intended to incite hatred is that it explicitly dispenses with the defence of innocent dissemination. The offence is clearly stated to be committed by 'the person providing the broadcasting service concerned ... any person by whom the item concerned is produced or directed'. If such a broadcast were to be broadcast online or through an electronic communications network, it would be interesting to see how this offence would interact with the exemptions from liability provided for service providers by the Directive on e-Commerce.

[29.55] The provision of the Prohibition of Incitement to Hatred Act 1989 that might most easily be applied to information technology is its prohibition on possession of material that may incite hatred. The Act provides that it will be an offence for a person:

> 'to prepare or be in possession of any written material[125] with a view to its being distributed, displayed, broadcast or otherwise published, in the State or elsewhere, whether by himself or another, or ... to make or be in possession of a recording of sounds or visual images with a view to its being distributed, shown, played, broadcast or otherwise published, in the State or else-where, whether by himself or another, if the material or recording is threatening, abusive or insulting and is intended or, having regard to all the circumstances, including such distribution, display, broadcasting, showing, playing or other publication thereof as the person has, or it may reasonably be inferred that he has, in view, is likely to stir up hatred.'[126]

[29.56] Again this provision provides for an innocent disseminator defence.[127] It should be kept in mind that where a person is charged with any of the above offences 'no further proceedings in the matter (other than any remand in custody or on bail) shall be taken except by or with the consent of the Director of Public Prosecutions.'[128] On conviction on indictment a maximum penalty of a fine of up to €12,697 (£10,000), together with a term of imprisonment of up to 2 years, may be imposed.[129]

Reform

[29.57] A number of proposals have been made to reform the law in this area. In 1991 the Law Reform Commission made a number of recommendations; interestingly, the Commission suggested that the defence of innocent dissemination should be abolished in respect of criminal libel.[130] The Commission also recommended that the common law offences of seditious[131] and obscene[132] libel should be deleted and that the Constitution should be amended to delete 'so much of Article 40.6.1° which renders the publication

---

[125] Section 1(1) defines written material as including 'any sign or other visual representation'.
[126] Section 4(1).
[127] Section 4(2).
[128] Section 8.
[129] Section 6.
[130] Law Reform Commission, *Report on the Crime of Libel* August 1991, recommendation 11.
[131] Law Reform Commission, recommendation 18.
[132] Law Reform Commission, recommendation 19.

or utterance of blasphemous matter an offence.'[133] In 2003 the Legal Advisory Group on Defamation made recommendations including the following:

(i)   The common law offences of blasphemous libel, obscene libel and seditious libel should be abolished; and

(ii) The offence of criminal libel should be abolished and replaced by a narrower offence to be known as the offence of publication of gravely harmful statements.[134]

In response to these recommendations, the Defamation Bill 2006 provided that 'The common law offences of criminal libel, seditious libel and obscene libel are abolished.'[135]

[29.58] The Bill also provided for an offence of publishing gravely harmful statements:

'A person who knowingly, and with the intention of causing grave injury to the reputation of a person (other than a body corporate), publishes or causes to be published a statement containing false allegations concerning the second-mentioned person, thereby causing grave injury to the reputation of the second-mentioned person, shall be guilty of an offence.'[136]

This offence would be punishable by a maximum penalty of 5 years' imprisonment together with a fine not exceeding €50,000.[137] A notable difference between this proposed offence and that of criminal libel is that the requirement of applying to the High Court before prosecuting the publisher or proprietor of a newspaper for criminal libel would be abolished. It would be replaced by a general provision that:

'Proceedings for an offence under this section shall not be brought unless, not later than one year after the alleged commission of the offence ... the Director of Public Prosecutions gives his or her consent to the proceedings being brought, or ... the High Court makes an order permitting the bringing of the proceedings.'[138]

---

[133] Law Reform Commission, recommendation 20
[134] Legal Advisory Group on Defamation, March 2003, *Report of the Legal Advisory Group on Defamation* Recommendations XX and XXI, p 41.
[135] Defamation Bill 2006, s 34.
[136] Section 35(1).
[137] Section 35(2).
[138] Section 35(4).

PART VIII: CYBERCRIME

Chapter 30

Cybercrime

Introduction

[30.01] As computers have become ubiquitous, so too has cybercrime. Many international businesses now consider computer crime to be more costly than conventional physical crime.[1] Computer security breaches are estimated to have cost UK businesses some £10bn in 2006.[2] Citizens of the UK fear becoming victims of cybercrimes such as phishing more than they fear mugging, car theft and burglary.[3] Computer crime has not just become more common, however. The perpetrators of cybercrime may now be dedicated professional criminals, as opposed to bored and impressionable teenagers:

> 'The frantic fire-fighting days when large-scale attacks of fast-spreading viruses and worms such as MyDoom and Blaster threatened to disrupt internet communications across the world seem to be over … .The back-bedroom hobbyists who created these threats mainly for fun have been replaced by professional cybercriminals looking to steal data – such as credit cards or personal identity details – from corporate networks'.[4]

The beneficiaries of cybercrime have also changed. Cybercrime is now used as a tool of corporate competition. In October 2006 'Allegations that Russia's largest aluminium producer hacked into the computers of its opponents in a long-running legal dispute'.[5] were sent forward for hearing by the English High Court. In August 2006 Belgian prosecutors issued charges against Suez, a French utility company, accusing it of 'hacking into the computers and trying to intercept the internal communications of Electrabel, a Belgian electricity company'.[6] The tools of cybercrime have become more sophisticated. Viruses and hacking tools may now be used to establish networks of

---

1   A survey undertaken by IBM of 600 businesses in the USA and 2401 businesses in 16 other countries found respondents considered that ' cybercrime (57% of U.S. and 58% of international businesses) is more costly to their organizations than physical crime (43% and 42%, respectively)'. IBM, 'US Businesses: Cost of Cybercrime Overtakes Physical Crime' 14 Mar 2006, http://www-03.ibm.com/press/us/en/pressrelease/19367.wss.

2   PriceWaterhouse Coopers/DTI, *Information Security Breaches Survey 2006,* April 2006, http://www.pwc.com/uk/eng/ins-sol/publ/pwc_dti-fullsurveyresults06.pdf.

3   http://www.getsafeonline.org/nqcontent.cfm?a_id=1424.

4   Palmer, 'Sleuths on the cybercrime trail' (2006) Financial Times, 5 May.

5   Tait, 'Russian hacking case sent to trial by judge' (2006) Financial Times, 21 October.

6   'Companies International: five accused of Hacking in industrial espionage case' (2006) Financial Times, 18 August.

compromised computers known as bot-nets.[7] These bot-nets may then be used to launch distributed denial of service (DDoS) attacks, perhaps as part of an extortion scheme.[8]

[30.02] Irish law provides for a quite considerable number of offences that may be committed with or against information technology systems. These offences are discussed below. Irish cybercrime law encompasses very broad offences, notably s 9 of the Criminal Justice (Theft and Fraud Offences) Act 2001. Other offences are quite specific, such as the offence of unauthorised access contained in the Criminal Damage Act 1991. However, neither offence is likely to prove easy to prosecute and the undeniable difficulty of proving cybercrime offences means that whilst there is good reason to believe that cybercrimes are increasingly commonplace, prosecutions for those crimes are very rare. There would not appear to have ever been a successful prosecution for cybercrime in Ireland. Difficulties of proof are one reason for this rarity. Another may be that victims may be unwilling to have their vulnerabilities publicised. Victims may be concerned that customers will be discouraged or other cybercriminals encouraged if their vulnerabilities become public. Yet it may be unfair to place too much blame upon the victims. In its novelty and complexity, cybercrime may be compared to 'white-collar' crime,[9] which society has dealt with in a similarly ambiguous fashion.[10]

Dishonest operation

[30.03] The Criminal Justice (Theft and Fraud Offences) Act 2001 provides that:

'A person who dishonestly, whether within or outside the State, operates or causes to be operated a computer within the State with the intention of making a gain for himself or herself or another, or of causing loss to another, is guilty of an offence[11]'

Those convicted of the offence upon indictment may be punished by a fine and a maximum term of imprisonment of up to 10 years.[12] A number of elements must be

---

[7]   A bot-net is 'a network made up of independent programs, or bots, acting in concert ... Like viruses, bots spread by installing themselves on Net-connected computers. The difference is that, while viruses act individually according to an inflexible program, bots respond to external commands and then execute coordinated attacks. The operational software, known as command and control, or C&C, resides on a remote server' Berinato, Attack of the Bots (2006) Wired Magazine, November.

[8]   Rigby, 'The whiz-kids and wiseguys of cyber crime' (2005) Financial Times, 9 December.

[9]   'The term was introduced by the American sociologist Edwin Sutherland ... (who) defined white collar crimes as criminal behaviour committed by upper-class individuals in the course of their employment', Jones, *Criminology* (3rd edn, Oxford University Press, 2006) p 42.

[10]   See Nelken, 'White Collar Crime' in Magure, Morgan, Reiner (eds), *The Oxford Handbook of Criminology,* (2nd edn, Oxford, 1997) pp 891–924.

[11]   Criminal Justice (Theft and Fraud Offences) Act 2001, s 9(1). This provision may be compared to art 8 of the Cybercrime Convention, which requires that parties: 'adopt such legislative and other measures as may be necessary to establish as criminal offences under its domestic law, when committed intentionally and without right, the causing of a loss of property to another person by: a any input, alteration, deletion or suppression of computer data; b any interference with the functioning of a computer system, with fraudulent or dishonest intent of procuring, without right, an economic benefit for oneself or for another person'.

[12]   Criminal Justice (Theft and Fraud Offences) Act 2001, s 9(2).

proven before a conviction may be obtained. The term 'operate' is not defined by the Criminal Justice (Theft and Fraud Offences) Act 2001. Computers may be operated in different ways. One method of operation is for an individual to directly enter commands into a computer system. In *R v Governor of Brixton Prison (ex parte Levin)*[13] it was alleged that Mr Levin had operated a computer in St Petersburg in Russia to 'put into execution a scheme to obtain money, credits and assets under the custody of Citibank by entering unauthorised instructions into Citibank's computer'.[14] Directly entering commands into the victim's computer would seem to amount to operating a computer and so could amount to an offence contrary to s 9 of the Criminal Justice (Theft and Fraud Offences) Act 2001. Alternatively, an existing program may be altered or a new program created which will automatically operate a computer to cause a gain to one or a loss to another. This occurred in in *R v Thompson*.[15] The appellant was employed as a computer programmer by the Bank of Kuwait in Kuwait. He was alleged to have 'programmed the bank's computer with a programme of his own devising which caused the computer to debit five ... substantial dormant savings accounts ... and to credit his own savings account ... with a corresponding amount'.[16]

This would amount to causing a computer to operate and so would be an offence contrary to s 9. It is the authors' view that the offence would be committed when the accused's computer program caused the victim's computer to transfer funds into his account. An alternative view would be that the offence would be committed when the accused reprogrammed the victim's computer. However, a gain would not have accrued to the accused and a loss would not have been caused to the victim at this stage. Instead the accused might be charged with causing damage to the victim's data (that is its computer program) in respect of that operation.

[30.04] So the offence of dishonest operation of a computer is quite comprehensive. It would appear to be an all-encompassing offence, and it would seem unnecessary to charge an alleged computer criminal with any other offence. But in practice it is unlikely to be so simple. Computers are complex machines. Proving that a hacker or dishonest employee gained unauthorised access to a computer and damaged the data therein is one thing. Proving a causal connection between those actions and the accrual of a gain or the suffering of a loss, perhaps many months later, is quite another. In particular, proving that the accused had the requisite intent or *mens rea* may prove a challenge. For the s 9 offence to be made out, the accused must be shown to have operated the computer 'dishonestly ... with the intention of making a gain for himself or herself or another, or of causing loss to another'.

A person will be considered to have acted dishonestly if he does something 'without claim of right made in good faith'.[17] The accused must be shown to have acted with the

---

[13] *R v Governor of Brixton Prison (ex parte Levin)* (1996) 3 WLR 657.
[14] (1996) 3 WLR 657 at 661.
[15] *R v Thompson* (1984) 1 WLR 962.
[16] (1984) 1 WLR 964.
[17] Criminal Justice (Theft and Fraud Offences) Act 2001, s 2(1).

intention of making a gain for himself or a loss to another.[18] The Criminal Justice (Theft and Fraud Offences) Act 2001 makes it clear that these terms are quite narrowly defined. It states that these terms 'are to be construed as extending only to gain or loss in money or other property'.

So, doing something dishonest that enhanced one's reputation or reduced that of another[19] might fall outside the ambit of this offence, since a person's reputation is not a proprietary right.[20] However, if such a monetary or proprietary gain or loss results from the dishonest operation of a computer, then it will not matter 'whether any such gain or loss is temporary or permanent'.[21] So the fact that one's gain may only be fleeting is irrelevant. For the purposes of the Criminal Justice (Theft and Fraud Offences) Act 2001 a gain will include 'a gain by keeping what one has, as well as a gain by getting what one has not'[22] and a loss will include 'a loss by not getting what one might get, as well as a loss by parting with what one has'.[23]

Unauthorised access

[30.05] The Criminal Damage Act 1991 makes a distinction between computer hacking which was intended to cause damage to a computer system and that which did not. This distinction was deliberate. The reasoning behind it was set out by the Minister for Justice, when introducing the Criminal Damage Bill 1990 to the Dáil upon its second reading:

> 'It could be argued that hacking activity which does not result in data or programs being modified – the 'looking around' activity I have mentioned – should not be made an offence on the grounds that, first, what is involved is merely a breach of confidentiality and, second, that such breaches are not punishable under the criminal law except in two cases, these being breaches of the Official Secrets Act 1963, or of section 22 of the Data Protection Act 1988, which makes it an offence to disclose personal data that has been improperly obtained. I think that many people would regard the breach of confidentiality

---

18 The Criminal Justice (Theft and Fraud Offences) Act 2001 also provides that at trial 'it shall not be necessary to prove an intention dishonestly to cause a loss to, or make a gain at the expense of, a particular person, and it shall be sufficient to prove that the accused did the act charged dishonestly with the intention of causing such a loss or making such a gain' s 54(1). So it is not necessary to prove that a person intended to act dishonestly for a prosecution to succeed. What is required is that the prosecutor must show that a person did a dishonest act with the intention to making a gain or causing a loss.

19 For example, a spoof entry in Wikipedia, the online encyclopedia, alleged that John Seigenthaler Sr, who served in the Kennedy administration in the USA, had been involved in the assassinations of both John F. and Robert Kennedy. See Hafner, 'Growing Wikipedia Revises Its 'Anyone Can Edit' Policy' (2006) New York Times, 17 June.

20 But what if a person derived their income from their reputation? The courts have been willing to award damages for loss of reputation. It remains to be seen if the courts would allow the offence to be extended in this way.

21 Criminal Justice (Theft and Fraud Offences) Act 2001, s 9(3)(a).

22 Criminal Justice (Theft and Fraud Offences) Act 2001, s 9(3)(b).

23 Criminal Justice (Theft and Fraud Offences) Act 2001, s 9(3)(c).

as sufficient, without more, to justify criminalising this activity and I sympathise with that view but the Government's reason for doing so is based on other grounds.

The fact is that hacking is a matter of major and legitimate concern to users of computer systems. To counter it, ever more sophisticated security measures have to be put in place which reduce their speed and efficiency. In addition, the systems must be monitored regularly to check whether there have been unauthorised attempts at entry. If any instance of hacking, however trivial, is detected, it must be investigated to see if any damage has been caused. Even if it has not, it may be advisable to close down the system and rewrite the software completely as a precaution. In particular, hacking into operational computer systems, such as those I have mentioned — and they include such operations as air traffic control — could have most serious consequences. That is why in recent years any form of unauthorised access to computer systems has been made an offence in many countries, including the US, Canada, the UK, the Netherlands, Germany, Iceland and France'.[24]

[30.06] The Criminal Damage Act 1991 provides that:

'A person who without lawful excuse operates a computer ... within the State with intent to access any data kept either within or outside the state, or ... outside the State with intent to access any data kept within the State, shall, whether or not he accesses any data, be guilty of an offence ...'[25]

Jurisdiction is established by the location of either the alleged offender, who may be within or without the state, or by the location of the data that is allegedly accessed. As with the dishonest operation offence, the *actus reus* of the offence is relatively straightforward. All that is required is that the accused person operates a computer. It is clear from the Act that it is not necessary for that person to actually access the data in question. Hence the entering of an incorrect password into a computer system will be sufficient to establish the offence. The intriguing question then arises as to whether a person could be convicted of this offence in a circumstance where it was not in fact possible for them to access the data concerned. This situation might arise where they entered a password which had been changed. The courts of England and Wales have been willing to convict on charges such as incitement to receive stolen goods which were either not stolen or did not exist,[26] incitement to rob a woman who did not exist[27]

---

[24] Dáil Éireann – Volume 403 – 29 November 1990, Criminal Damage Bill, 1990: Second Stage.
[25] Criminal Damage Act 1991, s 5(1).
[26] *Reg v McDonough* (1962) 47 Cr App R 37.
[27] *R v Fitzmaurice* (1983) 2 WLR 227. The facts were that the appellant's father wished to claim a reward for tipping the police off about a prospective robbery of a security van. To give credence to his story, the appellant recruited two men to snatch a sum of money from a woman. The woman did not exist, but, the men were arrested in the vicinity of the security van, which the appellant's father had informed the police was due to be robbed. The appellant was subsequently convicted of inciting the men to rob the non-existent woman and his conviction was upheld on appeal. See also Haggard v Mason [1976] 1 WLR 187 in which it was held that the offence of offering to supply a controlled drug was committed, even though the drug in fact supplied was not a controlled drug.

and conspiracy to produce non-existent cocaine.[28] In *DPP v Nock*[29] the House of Lords refused to uphold a conviction for conspiring to produce non-existent cocaine, but subsequently upheld a conviction for importing a controlled drug even though the substance which the appellant thought was heroin was in fact snuff.[30] However, unlike its UK equivalent the Irish statute does not go so far as to actually provide that the offence may be committed 'even though the facts are such that the commission of the further offence is impossible'.[31] Computers contain and are parts of complex systems. What may be impossible to a layman may be straightforward for an expert. Hence, a defendant might find it difficult to establish the impossibility of gaining the access in question. However, there are some situations where it cannot be doubted that access is impossible, such as where an attempt is made to use a computer without an Internet connection to access a database that does not exist.

[30.07] This offence would not seem to be limited to Internet or hacking offences. Entering a password into a single computer is sufficient to establish the offence. In the English case of *Attorney General's Reference (No 1 of 1991)*[32] the respondent was a former employee of a wholesale locksmiths. He returned to his old workplace accompanied by his new employer. While the sales assistant was distracted, he helped himself to an expensive key-cutting machine. When challenged, the accused assured the sales assistant that he was going to pay for the machine. The sales assistant then commenced the process of creating an invoice for the respondent using a computer to do so. The sales assistant was again distracted and at that point the respondent entered a code into the computer. This code gave the respondent a 70% discount. The UK equivalent of the Criminal Damage Act 1991 criminalised 'causing a computer to perform any function with intent to secure access to any program or data held in any computer'.[33] And it seemed to the trial judge that 'to be straining language to say that only one computer is necessary' to commit this offence.[34] The Court of Appeal disagreed, being persuaded by the argument that if it were necessary for one computer to be used to hack into another before the offence was committed, then the 'kind of activity of going straight to the in-house computer and extracting confidential information from it could be committed with impunity'[35] at least in so far as this offence was concerned. A similar argument might be made with regard to the unauthorised access offence under the Criminal Damage Act 1991. It does refer to the operation of a computer with the intent of accessing any data. However, the Criminal Damage Act 1991 clearly does not

---

[28] *DPP v Nock* (1978) 3 WLR 57.
[29] *DPP v Nock* (1978) 3 WLR 57. The appellants had sought to extract cocaine from what they thought was a mixture of cocaine and lignocaine hydrochloride, but when the substance was tested by the police laboratory it was found to contain no cocaine. The appellants were initially convicted, and this conviction was overturned by the House of Lords.
[30] *R v Shivpuri* [1986] 2 All ER 334.
[31] UK Computer Misuse Act 1990, s 2(4).
[32] *Attorney General's Reference (No 1 of 1991)* (1992) 3 WLR 432.
[33] UK, Computer Misuse Act 1990, s 1(1)(a).
[34] *Attorney General's Reference (No 1 of 1991)* (1992) 3 WLR 432 at 436.
[35] (1992) 3 WLR 432 at 438.

specify where that data need be. It may be within or without the state and it may be on the computer that is operated directly by the accused or on another computer.

[30.08] The accused must be shown to have acted without a lawful excuse. The Criminal Damage Act 1991 defines lawful on the basis that a person charged shall be treated as having a lawful excuse in the following circumstances:

> 'if at the time of the act or acts alleged to constitute the offence he believed that the person or persons whom he believed to be entitled to consent to or authorise ... the accessing of ... the property in question had consented, or would have consented to or authorised it if he or they had known of ... the accessing and its circumstances'[36], or

> 'if he is himself the person entitled to consent to or authorise accessing of the data concerned'.[37]

In general, the prosecution will have to show that the accused did not believe that he was authorised to access the data in question. If the accused honestly believed that he was authorised to access the data, then he cannot be convicted of the alleged offence. It is immaterial whether or not this belief is justified, so long as it is honestly held.[38]

[30.09] The accused will be deemed to have a lawful excuse where he is the person entitled to issue the consent or authority in question. So, in general, the owner of a computer system will be deemed to have a lawful excuse to access the system. But, it is possible to buy and own goods which are protected by systems such as digital rights management (DRM systems). In this case the owner will own a copy of the data in question, but the DRM will operate to limit how he uses it. So the owner of the data will not be the person entitled to consent to or authorise the accessing of the data in question. That right will be reserved to the owner of copyright or other intellectual property, which is contained in the work. That an offence might be committed by someone who accesses data of which they own a copy on their own computer would seem clear. The offence of unauthorised access is committed by someone who 'operates a computer ... with intent to access any data'.

The accused must have an intention to access 'any data'. There is no need to prove that he intended to access specific data. The Criminal Damage Act 1991 provides that the offence will be committed:

> 'whether or not the person intended to access any particular data or any particular category of data or data kept by any particular person'.[39]

[30.10] There is no requirement that the data be on another computer, or indeed, be owned by someone else. So DRM does create the possibility that a person could be convicted of unauthorised access to their own data. But, the rights of copyright owners are not absolute. Chapter 6 of the CRRA 2000 sets out a number of acts which are permitted in respect of copyright works. The owner of computer data who found that DRM systems were interfering with this ability to undertake a permissible act might

---

[36] Criminal Damage Act 1991, s 6(2)(a).

[37] Criminal Damage Act 1991, s 6(2)(b).

[38] Criminal Damage Act 1991, s 6(3), and s 6 cannot 'be construed as casting doubt on any defence recognised by law as a defence to criminal charges', s 6(5).

[39] Criminal Damage Act 1991, s 5(2).

argue that the owners of copyright would have authorised the bypassing of the DRM to enable him to exercise his statutory rights. Of course, the acts permitted by Chapter 6 of the CRRA 2000 are quite limited. But, it would not be necessary for the individual concerned to show that his belief that his actions were mandated by that Act was justified. He need only show that he honestly believed that to be the case. Whilst this argument might suffice to avoid liability under the Criminal Damage Act 1991 it could not be used to avoid liability altogether. The CRRA 2000 provides that:

> 'A person who ... removes or alters rights management information from copies of copyright works, copies of recordings of performances or copies of databases knowing or having reason to believe that the primary purpose or effect of such removal or alteration is to induce, enable, facilitate or conceal an infringement of any right conferred by this Act ... shall be guilty of an offence'.[40]

So it is an offence to remove DRM and access the data that the DRM protects without authority. But this offence can only be committed by someone who knows or has reason to believe that the removal is for the purpose of breaching copyright. An offence would not be committed by a person who removed DRM in the belief that the work contained in the data protected by the DRM was either not protected by copyright or else that the intended use of the work was permitted by the CRRA 2000. However, many DRM systems will employ encryption and overcoming encryption may be an offence under the Electronic Commerce Act 2000.

[30.11] On the other hand, it is also possible that the offence of unauthorised access could be committed using DRM software. In January 2006 Sony BMG 'settled a series of class-action lawsuits stemming from its use of software that was intended to prevent illegal copying of its CDs but left customers' computers vulnerable to viruses and other attacks'.[41] One of these DRM programs, Mediamax,:

> 'exhibited all the classic signs of "spyware" ... MediaMax installs itself even if you decline the click-through 'agreement' that pops up when you insert a CD. It records your actions and reports them to Sony BMG and, like the rootkit, MediaMax is designed to be difficult to remove from your PC'.[42]

Where a program is designed to disregard a refusal to accept it onto a computer, then any access that the program subsequently gains to the computer is almost certainly unauthorised. Spyware is frequently installed on computers in circumstances where users are not informed of what is happening. A good argument can be made that such installations amount to unauthorised access and thus are an offence.

[30.12] A particularly difficult problem arises where an individual who is authorised to access data for one reason then accesses it for another. In *R v Bow Street Metropolitan Stipendiary Magistrate*[43] the US authorities were seeking the extradition of one Joan

---

[40] CRRA 2000, s 376(1)(a).
[41] Edgecliffe-Johnsonin, 'Sony BMG settles suits over 'flawed' music CDs' (2006) Financial Times, 3 January.
[42] Doctorow, 'Vaudeville offers a music lesson for Sony BMG' (2005) Financial Times, 12 December.
[43] *R v Bow Street Metropolitan Stipendiary Magistrate* (1999) 3 WLR 620.

Ojomo. Ms Ojomo was an employee of American Express, assigned to the credit section. She was able to access the accounts of every customer of American Express, but was only allowed to access those accounts that were assigned to her.

> 'However she accessed various other accounts and files which had not been assigned to her and which she had not been given authority to work on. Having accessed those accounts and files without authority, she gave confidential information obtained from those accounts and files to, among others, Mr. Allison. The information she gave to him and to others was then used to encode other credit cards and supply PIN numbers which could then be fraudulently used to obtain large sums of money from automatic teller machines'.[44]

There was evidence that Ms Ojomo did not have the authority to access the data in question for this purpose. The House of Lords had to consider whether such activity could amount to an offence for the purposes of the UK's Computer Misuse Act 1990 so that Ms Ojomo could be extradited to the USA. The House of Lords held that it would. Although this English decision is of interest, it would not be directly applicable here, not least because the wording of the UK's Computer Misuse Act 1990 differs from that of the Criminal Damage Act 1991. However, it does suggest that just because an individual is authorised to use a computer for one purpose does not mean that use for another purpose will be authorised. In *R v Bow Street Metropolitan Stipendiary Magistrate* the House of Lords held that Ms Ojomo used her computer to gain access 'to data which she knew she was not authorised to access' and that doing so 'came fairly and squarely'[45] within the scope of the unauthorised access offence under the UK's Computer Misuse Act 1990. It is likely that if the Irish courts would come to a similar conclusion if faced with similar circumstances.

[30.13] A different situation would arise where a person who is entitled to access a computer does so on the instructions of another who is exceeding their authority. In *DPP v Bignell*[46] the accused were English police officers. For their own private purposes they requested that a computer operator access certain information on the UK's Police National Computer system. The police officers exceeded their own authority in making this request. But the operator did not exceed his authority in processing the request, as his access was authorised even though he was obtaining that access in accordance with a wrongful request. The police officers' convictions for offences of unauthorised access under the UK's Computer Misuse Act were overturned on appeal.[47] It is likely that the Irish courts would come to a similar conclusion if faced with similar facts. The Irish offence of unauthorised access is committed by someone who 'without lawful excuse operates a computer'. It therefore cannot be committed by someone who instructs another to operate a computer on their behalf. This decision may be compared with the decision of the House of Lords in *R v Browne*.[48] The defendant was a former English

---

[44] (1999) 3 WLR 620 at 623.

[45] (1999) 3 WLR 620 at 626.

[46] *DPP v Bignell* (1998) 1 Cr App R 1.

[47] A decision described as 'probably right' by Hobhouse LJ in the House of Lords in *Regina v Bow Street Magistrates' Court and Allison (AP)* (5 August 1999) HL.

[48] *R v Brown* (1996) 2 WLR 203.

policeman, who had been entitled to gain access to the police national computer for the purposes of policing. However, he abused his privileges and accessed the computer on behalf of a friend who was a debt collector. He was convicted of offences under the UK's Data Protection Act 1984 and his convictions were upheld on appeal to the House of Lords.

[30.14] The offence of unauthorised access may have advantages for prosecutors. It has a comparatively broad application. Furthermore, the elements of the offence are comparatively straightforward and so it may be easier to prove than other offences, although that does not mean that proving an offence will be easy. However, it also has substantial disadvantages. Upon conviction for the offence of unauthorised access, a fine not exceeding £500 or a term of imprisonment not exceeding three months may be imposed. Thus, unauthorised access is unquestionably a minor offence. If an offence is to be prosecuted, then it must be initiated 'within six months from the time when the cause of complaint shall have arisen'.[49] The shortness of this time period may cause difficulties in computer cases, as the crime of unauthorised access may be committed but not noticed until a considerable period of time has passed. The offence may also be technologically obsolete. In 2001, Raphael Gray pleaded guilty to ten counts of computer fraud.[50] Had the matter gone to trial, then Gray was prepared to mount an interesting defence. Both the Irish and UK offences of unauthorised access are essentially based around the concept of the *Prestel* hacking case where two journalists were prompted to enter a username and password, but entered those of the Duke of Edinburgh.[51]

> 'When the (UK's) 1990 Computer Misuse Act was framed, computers were accessed by presenting acceptable authentication credentials. Usually these would be a username and a password ... The entry credentials mediated ... access, and the law was formed on that basis. Intruders were assumed to have pretended to be authorised individuals when in fact they were not.'

[30.15] Systems on the web are not accessed in quite this way. As far as the web server's operating system is concerned, all those browsing pages on the server are the same, anonymous username associated with the web application itself. Provided that the remote user's browser – Microsoft's Internet Explorer, most commonly – presents a

---

[49]   Petty Sessions (Ireland) Act, 1851, s 10(4). In *DPP v Stafford* [2005] IEHC 187 it was held by the Finlay Geoghan J in the High Court that the 'the way in which a period of six calendar months from the date of commission of an offence should be calculated is the following. If the date of offence is to be included in the six month period then the six months expires on the day before the equivalent date to that date in the sixth month. Where the date of offence is at the end of a month such that in the six month there is no day which is equivalent to one day less than the date of offence then it must expire on the last day of the six month. This undoubtedly means for example that six calendar months from an offence committed on the 29, 30 and 31 August 2002, expires on the 28 February 2003. However, this variation in the number of days which comprise six months follows from the months being calendar months. It also provides certainty of computation'.

[50]   Morris, 'Teenage hacker admits fraud' (2001) Financial Times, 7 July.

[51]   *R v Gold, R v Schifreen* (1988) 2 WLR 984.

well formatted request for a valid page, then that page will be transmitted by the server back to the IP address associated with the response'.[52]

Usually a web page will only link to other pages and other files that the administrator of the website has made available in an area of the site often referred to as the web-root. Gray was alleged to have requested files outside the web-root. He was allegedly able to do this without being asked for a username or password. A user will not be held to have committed the offence of unauthorised access

> 'if at the time of the act or acts alleged to constitute the offence he believed that the person or persons whom he believed to be entitled to consent to or authorise ... the accessing of ... the property in question had consented, or would have consented to or authorised it if he or they had known of ... the accessing and its circumstances'.[53]

Suppose that a website is made publicly available. This links to a variety of other material some of which is in the web-root, some of which is not. If a user is able to manipulate those links to call up material, outside the web-root, without overcoming any security, can he be said to have committed the offence of unauthorised access? Arguably he cannot. The website has been made publicly available. It is not unreasonable to assume that all material that can be accessed through that website without encountering security measures is also publically available. This may remain the case even where material on the website is manipulated in some way, provided that no over security measures, such as a prompt for username and password, are overcome. After all, the Internet is a medium undergoing continuous technological development, where manipulation of material and technological innovation are to be encouraged. In such circumstances, defence pleas such as the following may well succeed 'had not been challenged to present access credentials; he had not had to ignore a warning message telling him that the access was not permitted'.[54]

[30.16] Raphael Gray was alleged to have caused in the region of €3m worth of damage and other losses. However, he was sentenced to a three-year term of probation following a guilty plea.[55]

Creating a false instrument

[30.17] If a username and/or password are falsely entered into a computer program, the argument could be made that, in doing so, the perpetrator is making a false instrument. Creating a false password is arguably forgery and this is an offence under the Criminal Justice (Theft and Fraud Offences) Act 2001, which provides:

> 'A person is guilty of forgery if he or she makes a false instrument[56] with the intention that it shall be used to induce another person to accept it as genuine and, by reason of so

---

[52] Barrett, *Traces of Guilt* (2004 Transworld Books), pp 263–264.

[53] Criminal Damage Act 1991, s 6(2)(a).

[54] Barrett, p 263.

[55] Morris, 'Teenage hacker admits fraud' (2001) Financial Times, 7 July.

[56] An instrument 'means any document, whether of a formal or informal character ... and include any ... disk, tape, sound track or other device on or in which information is recorded or stored by mechanical, electronic or other means.' Criminal Justice (Theft and Fraud Offences) Act 2001, s 24(a). This is a similar definition of instrument to that before the House of Lords in *R v Gold, R v Schifreen* (1988) 2 WLR 984.

accepting it, to do some act, or to make some omission, to the prejudice of that person or any other person.'[57]

[30.18] Prosecutions for similar offences were brought in the English case of *R v Gold, R v Schifreen*.[58] The appellants were two journalists who hacked the Prestel information system that was then provided by British Telecom. They did so by entering the usernames and passwords of others without their permission. They were caught, charged and initially convicted of charges that they:

> 'made a false instrument namely a device on or in which information is recorded or stored by electronic means with the intention of using it to induce the Prestel Computer to accept it as genuine and by reason of so accepting it to do an act to the prejudice of British Telecommunications Plc.'[59]

They appealed and their appeal ultimately reached the House of Lords. The problem for the prosecution was that the username and password in question were 'held momentarily in the control area of the user segment while the checking of them was carried out, and then being totally and irretrievably expunged'.[60]

[30.19] The Prestel system did not store username and password combinations because storage was expensive back in 1984, but it is now comparatively cheap. It should thus be relatively inexpensive to store such combinations now. This leaves the possibility open of prosecuting those who falsely enter usernames and passwords for forgery under the Criminal Justice (Theft and Fraud Offences) Act 2001 as opposed to unauthorised access under the Criminal Damage Act 1991. One reason why this might be done is that someone convicted of a forgery offence under the Criminal Justice (Theft and Fraud Offences) Act 2001 may be sentenced to an unlimited fine and a ten-year term of imprisonment.[61] In comparison, upon conviction for the offence of unauthorised access, a fine not exceeding £500 or a term of imprisonment not exceeding three months may be imposed.[62]

Offences under the Electronic Commerce Act 2000

[30.20] The Electronic Commerce Act 2000 established a set of rules for the regulation of electronic signatures and signature-reation devices. The Act defines 'signature verification device' as 'a device, such as configured software or hardware used to generate signature verification data'.[63]

The Act defines 'signature verification data' as 'data, such as codes, passwords, algorithms or public cryptographic keys, used for the purposes of verifying an electronic signature.'[64]

---

[57] Criminal Justice (Theft and Fraud Offences) Act 2001, s 25(1).
[58] *R v Gold, R v Schifreen* (1988) 2 WLR 984.
[59] (1988) 2 WLR 984 at 986.
[60] (1988) 2 WLR 984 at 990.
[61] Criminal Justice (Theft and Fraud Offences) Act 2001, s 25(2).
[62] Criminal Damage Act 1991, s 5(1).
[63] Electronic Commerce Act 2000, s 2(1).
[64] Electronic Commerce Act 2000, s 2(1).

The Act criminalises the misuse of signature-creation devices. Given that such devices may be used to create passwords or other authentication tools such as cryptographic keys, this is an offence that could have some application to unauthorised access offences. Of course, what would be prosecuted would not be the actual unauthorised access, but rather the unauthorised creation of the electronic signature that might be wrongfully used to gain access. It would not be necessary to prove that the accused actually gained access to the victim's system or data. All that would have to be proven is that the accused person faked the victim's electronic signature or signature-creation device.

[30.21] The Electronic Commerce Act 2000 makes it an offence where a person:

> 'knowingly accesses, copies or otherwise obtains possession of, or recreates, the signature creation device of another person ... without the authorisation of that other ... for the purpose of creating or allowing, or causing another person ... to create, an unauthorised electronic signature using the signature creation device'.[65]

For the offence to be proven, it must first, be shown that the accused person accessed, copied or otherwise obtained the signature-creation device of someone else. Alternatively, it may be shown that the accused recreated another's signature creation device. The Electronic Commerce Act 2000 does not make it an offence to possess another's signature-creation device. So, even if the accused person were to be found in possession of, say, copies of their victim's password-creation algorithms, that would be insufficient to make out the offence. What would have to be proven was that the accused had accessed, copied, obtained or recreated that device without authorisation. Proving the offence will be further complicated by the need to prove intent or *mens rea*. What must be shown is that the accused accessed, copied, obtained or recreated the device:

> 'knowingly ... without ... authorisation ... for the purpose of creating or allowing, or causing another person ... .to create, an unauthorised electronic signature.'

The accused must be shown to have acted 'knowingly'. And, it would seem that they have to be shown to have known two things. Firstly, they must be shown to have known that they were acting 'without authorisation'. So, the accused must be shown both to have acted without authorisation and to have known that they were acting without authorisation. Secondly, they must be shown to have known that the signature creation device that they were accessing, copying, obtaining or recreating would be used to create an unauthorised electronic signature.

[30.22] Alteration, disclosure or use of a signature creation device will be an offence. The Electronic Commerce Act 2000 provides that a person who:

> 'knowingly alters, discloses or uses the signature creation device of another person ... without the authorisation of that other person ... or in excess of lawful authorisation, for the purpose of creating or allowing, or causing another person ... to create, an unauthorised electronic signature using the signature creation device'.[66]

---

[65] Electronic Commerce Act 2000, s 25(a).
[66] Electronic Commerce Act 2000, s 25(b).

For the offence to be made out it, must be shown that the accused altered, disclosed or used the signature-creation device of another either without authorisation or exceeding the existing authorisation. The intent that must be proven is that the accused must be shown to have known that they were acting without authorisation or in excess of their authorisation. Again, it must be shown that the accused both acted without authorisation and knew that they were acting without authorisation. The accused must also be shown to have known that the signature-creation device would be used to create an unauthorised electronic signature.

[30.23] The Electronic Commerce Act 2000 makes some, specific, uses of a electronic signature an offence. Electronic signature is defined by the Act as 'data in electronic form attached to, incorporated in or logically associated with other electronic data and which serves as a method of authenticating the purported originator, and includes an advanced electronic signature.'

The Act makes it an offence where a person 'knowingly creates, publishes, alters or otherwise uses a certificate or an electronic signature for a fraudulent or other unlawful purpose.'[67]

So, if a person created a signature for the purpose of gaining unauthorised access contrary to the Criminal Damage Act 1991, they might commit an offence contrary to this provision of the Electronic Commerce Act 2000. There would seem to be no reason not to believe that a computer password could is an electronic signature. Once entered into a computer system, a password will be in electronic form. Once entered into the system, the password will be incorporated or associated with other electronic data and, by definition, a password is 'a method of authenticating the purported originator'.

[30.24] Finally, the Electronic Commerce Act 2000 provides for two offences that are specifically designed to protect certificate service providers. [68] The Act first provides that an offence will be committed by any person who:

> 'knowingly accesses, alters, discloses or uses the signature creation device of a certification service provider used to issue certificates, without the authorisation of the certification service provider or in excess of lawful authorisation, for the purpose of creating, or allowing or causing another … to create, an unauthorized electronic signature using the signature creation device.'[69]

So, the making of certificates without the authorisation of the certification service provider who is purported to have issued them is an offence. This offence would seem to encompass the situation where an employee of the certificate provider creates certificates without authorisation or the provider's systems are compromised by outsiders who then use those systems to produce unauthorised certificates.

---

[67] Electronic Commerce Act 2000, s 25(c).

[68] A certificate service provider is defined by the Act as: 'a person or public body who issues certificates or provides other services related to electronic signatures'. Electronic Commerce Act 2000, s 2(1). At the time of writing, the only Irish provider of such certificates is Post-Trust, a subsidiary of An Post, see http:www.post.trust.ie.

[69] Electronic Commerce Act 2000, s 25(e).

[30.25] The second offence designed to protect certificate service providers would seem to encompass the issuing of 'fake' certificates. The Act provides that an offence will be committed by any person who:

'knowingly publishes a certificate, or otherwise knowingly makes it available to anyone likely to rely on the certificate or on an electronic signature that is verifiable with reference to data such as codes, passwords, algorithms, public cryptographic keys or other data which are used for the purposes of verifying an electronic signature, listed in the certificate, if the person … knows that—

(i)   the certification service provider listed in the certificate has not issued it,

(ii)   the subscriber listed in the certificate has not accepted it, or

(iii)   the certificate has been revoked or suspended, unless its publication is for the purpose of verifying an electronic signature created before such revocation or suspension, or giving notice of revocation or suspension, is guilty of an offence'.[70]

[30.26] Territorial jurisdiction for offences under the Act extends to 'activities that took place partly outside the State'.[71] The Electronic Commerce Act 2000 provides for investigative powers for An Garda Síochána,[72] but specifically provides that:

'Nothing in this Act shall be construed as requiring the disclosure or enabling the seizure of unique data, such as codes, passwords, algorithms, private cryptographic keys, or other data, that may be necessary to render information or an electronic communication intelligible'.[73]

[30.27] The Electronic Commerce Act 2000 provides for corporate offences.[74] Offences under the Electronic Commerce Act 2000 are punishable on summary conviction by the imposition of a fine not exceeding €1904 (£1,500) or a term of imprisonment not exceeding 12 months, or both.[75] On conviction upon indictment, a fine not exceeding €634869 (£500,000) or a term of imprisonment not exceeding 5 years, or both, may be imposed.[76]

Social engineering and phishing

[30.28] A social engineer 'preys on the best qualities of human nature: our natural desire to be helpful, polite, supportive, a team player and the desire to get the job done'. US-CERT,[77] an agency of the US Government describes a social engineering attack in the following terms:

'To launch a social engineering attack, an attacker uses human interaction (social skills) to obtain or compromise information about an organization or its computer systems. An

---

[70]   Electronic Commerce Act 2000, s 25(f).
[71]   Electronic Commerce Act 2000, s 26.
[72]   Electronic Commerce Act 2000, s 27.
[73]   Electronic Commerce Act 2000, s 28.
[74]   Electronic Commerce Act 2000, s 7.
[75]   Electronic Commerce Act 2000, s 8(a).
[76]   Electronic Commerce Act 2000, s 8(b).
[77]   United States Computer Emergency Readiness Team (US CERT), http://www.us-cert.gov/.

attacker may seem unassuming and respectable, possibly claiming to be a new employee, repair person, or researcher and even offering credentials to support that identity. However, by asking questions, he or she may be able to piece together enough information to infiltrate an organization's network. If an attacker is not able to gather enough information from one source, he or she may contact another source within the same organization and rely on the information from the first source to add to his or her credibility'.[78]

[30.29] In essence the term 'social engineering' simply refers to fooling others into disclosing confidential information such as passwords. In the Autumn of 2006 a number of senior officers of Hewlett-Packard resigned after it was revealed that they had employed investigators who had 'used pretexting', or deception, to obtain private telephone records'.[79] The Electronic Commerce Act 2000 also criminalises social engineering. That is it provides that an offence will be committed by any person who 'knowingly misrepresents the person's or public body's identity or authorisation in requesting or accepting a certificate or in requesting suspension or revocation of a certificate.'[80]

[30.30] One particularly pernicious form of social engineering is phishing. In the summer of 2006 seven customers of Bank of Ireland received emails requesting that they re-enter their security details to ensure that their accounts were not de-activated. The victims were directed to a web-page that appeared to be a hosted by the Bank; they entered their details and were promptly defrauded of around €120,000 between them.[81] The theft of this money would clearly be an offence under a variety of laws, most obviously s 4 of the Criminal Justice (Theft and Fraud Offences) Act 2001, which provides that 'a person is guilty of theft if he or she dishonestly appropriates property without the consent of its owner and with the intention of depriving its owner of it'.[82]

[30.31] Upon conviction, a sentence of up to 10 years imprisonment and a fine may be imposed.[83] If it can be shown that the accused sent a phsihing email and induced a person to disclose their confidential bank information with the intention of using that information to access that person's bank account, then the offence of deception may be made out. Section 6 of the Criminal Justice (Theft and Fraud Offences) Act 2001 provides that any person who 'dishonestly, with the intention of making a gain for himself or herself or another, or of causing loss to another, by any deception induces another to do or refrain from doing an act is guilty of an offence'.[84]

[30.32] This offence is punishable by a fine and a term of imprisonment not exceeding five years.[85] Similarly, the offence of unlawful use of a computer contrary to s 9 of the Criminal Justice (Theft and Fraud Offences) Act 2001 might also be committed.

---

[78] US CERT cyber Security tip ST04-014, http://www.us-cert.gov/cas/tips/ST04-014.html.
[79] Allison, 'HP loses fourth senior official in scandal' (2006) Financial Times, 29 September.
[80] Electronic Commerce Act 2000, s 25(d).
[81] Weston, 'Gone phishing' (2006) The Irish Independent, 22 August.
[82] Criminal Justice (Theft and Fraud Offences) Act 2001, s 4(1).
[83] Criminal Justice (Theft and Fraud Offences) Act 2001, s 4(6).
[84] Criminal Justice (Theft and Fraud Offences) Act 2001, s 6(1).
[85] Criminal Justice (Theft and Fraud Offences) Act 2001, s 6(2).

However, to prove both of these offences, it will have to be shown that the phishing email was sent and the link to the fake web-page created for the purpose of causing a loss to the victim. Sending a phishing email and creating a fake website are not offences *per se*. The email and the web-site induce the victim to part with their information and it appears to be the law in Ireland that information cannot be stolen.

Information theft?

[30.33] However, as it currently stands, Irish law does not recognise any offence of the theft of Information, meaning that the owners of confidential information cannot expect the same sorts of protections in Ireland as they may receive in neighbouring jurisdictions. In the USA, the 1996 Economic Espionage Act has led to numerous prosecutions and hundreds of investigations for trade secret misuse. Many individual US states also have similar provisions, and it is a criminal offence to disclose trade secrets without permission in France and Germany. A change in the Irish law was advocated in 1992 by the Law Reform Commission, which recommended that 'property, in the context of dishonesty, be defined to include intellectual property protected by the equitable doctrine of confidentiality'.[86]

[30.34] Similarly, in 1992 the English Law Commission produced a consultation paper on the theft of information, which concluded that 'There can be no doubt that the misuse of trade secrets causes direct and indirect harms to very valuable interests, both private and public'.[87] The Commission cited the English case of *R v Absolom*[88] in support of this argument. In this case, the defendant, a geologist, obtained and then tried to sell the results of a major oil company's exploration for oil off the Irish coast. Some £13m had been spent to get these results and they would have cost between £50,000 and £100,000 to purchase. When the defendant was brought to trial for theft it was accepted by the court that he had acted in 'utmost bad faith', but an acquittal was directed, as the information in the results was not capable of founding such a charge. The English Commission provisionally proposed that 'the unauthorised use or disclosure of a trade secret should, in certain circumstances, be an offence'.[89]

[30.35] However, Irish law already contains a number of offences relating to information. Section 140(4) of the CRRA 2000 makes it an offence where an individual 'provides information ... intended to enable or assist a person to circumvent rights protection measures'. The Offences Against the State Act 1998 created an offence of unlawful collection of information that makes it an offence to 'collect, record or possess information which is of such a nature that it is likely to be useful in the commission by members of any unlawful organisation of serious offences'.[90] Similarly, if confidential information is extracted from a database, then depending on how it is treated subsequently, this may amount to an offence under the CRRA 2000 but, only to the

---

[86] *Law Reform Commission Report on Dishonesty,* 1992, p 181 at para 20.49.
[87] P 23, at para 3.27.
[88] *R v Absolom* (1983) The Times, 14 September.
[89] P 30 at para 3.61.
[90] Offences Against the State Act 1998, s 8(1).

extent that the copyright in the database had been infringed.[91] The main example of this anomaly is where a document is removed from a company's premises, the contents copied and then it is returned.[92]

[30.36] Section 4(1) of the Theft and Fraud Offences Act 2001 provides 'a person is guilty of theft if he or she dishonestly[93] appropriates [94] property without the consent of its owner[95] and with the intention of depriving its owner of it'. This offence is punishable by up to 10 years' imprisonment and an unlimited fine. Although the Bill contains extensive exemptions for the likes of mushroom-pickers and makes it clear that land cannot be stolen for its purposes, there is no specific provision requiring that intellectual property cannot be stolen; it must therefore be assumed that it can be stolen for the purposes of the Act. The issue then is whether or not confidential information can fall within the ambit of the offence. This turns on the interpretation of two terms: firstly, 'property', and secondly, 'with the intention of depriving its owner of it'.

[30.37] This is defined by section 2(1) of the Bill as 'all ... property, real or personal, including ... intangible property'. In *Oxford v Moss*[96] an English Judge, Smith J, held that information did not fall within the definition of property in the UK Theft Act 1968, which is virtually identical to that in the Irish legislation.[97] As noted above, there is no definitive answer to the issue of whether or not confidential information is 'property'. Charleton and Lavery suggest that confidential information cannot be property, although Clark alludes to the existence of property rights in the Irish Constitution.[98] Although at the present time what authorities there are weigh against it, there is no reason to believe that if this issue were to be argued before the Irish courts it would be held that confidential information was in fact property. In *House of Spring Gardens v Point Blank Ltd*[99] Griffin J stated that the defendants had 'misused confidential information the

---

91 See para **[33.30]** below.

92 See *Oxford v Moss* (1979) 68 Cr App R 183.

93 'dishonestly' is defined by s 2(1) of the Act as 'without a claim of right made in good faith'. This term was stated by the Court of Criminal Appeal in *People (DPP) v O'Loughlin* [1979] IR 85 to mean that if a defendant raised a claim of right made in good faith, then the court would have to examine whether he 'believed honestly and whether, with that honest belief, what he did could be excused'.

94 This is defined by s 4(5) as meaning ' usurps or adversely interferes with the proprietary rights of the owner of the property'.

95 Owner is defined by s 2(4)(a): 'a person shall be regarded as owning property if he or she has possession or control of it, or has in it any proprietary right or interest (not being an equitable interest arising only from an agreement to transfer or grant an interest)'.

96 *Oxford v Moss* (1979) Crim App Rep 183.

97 Theft Act 1968, s 4 defined 'property' as including 'money and all other property, real or personal, including things in action and other personal property'.

98 'it is not desirable nor necessary to ascribe property rights to information', Lavery, *Commercial Secrets* (Round Hall, 1996), p 50 'It seems Clear that information is not property for the purposes of larceny', Charleton *et al, Criminal Law* (Tottel Publishing, 2000), para 10.50 at p 794.

99 *House of Spring Gardens v Point Blank Ltd* [1984] IR 611.

property of (the plaintiff)' and in *Boardman v Phibbs*[100] three Law Lords recognised that information could constitute property.[101] Although *Oxford v Moss* appears persuasive, it was decided over twenty years ago, before the advent of the 'information society', when the perceived value and importance of information was far below today's. A specific offence of stealing information already exists. Section 22 of the Data Protection Act 1998 makes it an offence to access and disclose personal data without authorisation; changes in Ireland's economy and society in recent years may mean that the Irish courts place greater weight on precedents from the USA. In particular, the Irish courts might find the decision of the American Federal Courts in *United States v Bottone*[102] persuasive. In that case the defendants removed papers describing manufacturing processes from their workplace and copied and returned them. Their convictions for transporting stolen property in interstate commerce were upheld,[103] Friendly J stating:

> 'when the physical form of the stolen goods is secondary in every respect to the matter recorded in them, the transformation of the information in the stolen papers into a tangible object never possessed by the original owner should be deemed immaterial. It would offend common sense to hold that these defendants fall outside the statute simply because, in efforts to avoid detection, their confederates were at pains to restore the original papers to [their employer] and transport only copies or notes, although an oversight would have brought them within it'.

[30.38] In *Carpenter v United States*[104] the applicant was a reporter for the *Wall Street Journal* who, prior to publication, would inform co-conspirators which stocks he would recommend his readers buy. The co-conspirators would buy stocks prior to publication and benefit from the gains that resulted from the applicant's recommendation. The applicant's employment contract made it clear that his column was the journal's confidential information prior to publication, the US Supreme Court rejected the applicant's contention that he had not taken 'property' from the Journal[105] and upheld the applicant's conviction under the same statute as that which convicted Bottone above.

---

[100] *Boardman v Phibbs* [1967] AC 46.

[101] Dilhorne VC at 89–91, Hodson LJ at 107–111, Guest LJ at 115–116.

[102] *United States v Bottone* 365 F 2d 389 (2d Cir), cert denied, 385 US 974 (1966).

[103] 365 F 2d 389 at 394. The case law in the USA remains divided, see *United States v Brown* 925 F 2d 1301 (10th Cir 1991), where it was held that intangible intellectual property such as computer source code could not be the subject of a prosecution for transporting stolen property interstate. But in *United States v Riggs* 739 F Supp 414, 420 (ND Ill 1990), the court rejected the defendant's 'disingenuous' argument that he merely transferred electronic impulses across state lines. 'This court sees no reason to hold differently simply because [the defendant] stored the information inside computers instead of printing it out on paper. In either case, the information is in a transferrable, accessible, even salable form.' at 421. See also *United States v Belmont* 715 F 2d 459 (9th Cir) cert denied 465 US 1022 (1984); *United States v Gottesman* 724 F 2d 1517 (2d Cir 1984).

[104] *Carpenter v United States* 108 S Ct 316 (1987).

[105] Citing: 3 W Fletcher, *Cyclopedia of Law of Private Corporations* s 857.1, p 260 (rev ed 1986) (footnote omitted): 'Confidential information acquired or compiled by a corporation in the course and conduct of its business is a species of property to which the corporation has the exclusive right and benefit, and which a court of equity will protect through the injunctive process or other appropriate remedy'.

[30.39] Intention is the element which might perhaps cause the greatest difficulty a prosecutor who sought to extend the crime of theft to confidential information. Wrongfully publishing another's confidential information. This is the element of the definition where any attempt to extend the offence of larceny to confidential information would encounter significant difficulty. Wrongfully publishing another's confidential information will not deprive them of their own information; they may still use it as they had intended before the wrongful publication.[106] As was said by Wien J in *Oxford v Moss* p 186 'there was no intention permanently to deprive the owner of it, namely, the so called intangible property'. However, it can be argued that this is incorrect; it is not the information itself that is valuable, it is the exclusivity of it. In *Carpenter v United States*[107] the US Supreme Court stated that 'it is sufficient that the Journal has been deprived of its right to exclusive use of the information, for exclusivity is an important aspect of confidential business information and most private property for that matter'.

It is therefore possible, although not completely certain, that an Irish court would not extend this offence to encompass the theft of information.

Official Secrets Act

[30.40] The Official Secrets Act 1963 protects what it terms 'official information'. This is defined as:

> 'any secret official code word or password, and any sketch, plan, model, article, note, document or information which is secret or confidential or is expressed to be either and which is or has been in the possession, custody or control of a holder of a public office, or to which he has or had access, by virtue of his office, and includes information recorded by film or magnetic tape or by any other recording medium'.[108]

Although it is unsatisfactory in many ways, the Official Secrets Act 1963 creates protections for private information that are far superior to those available to unofficial information such as that held by the public sector. The Act creates an offence of disclosure of official information, providing that:

> 'A person shall not communicate any official information to any other person unless he is duly authorised[109] to do so or does so in the course of and in accordance with his duties as the holder of a public office.'

[30.41] Interestingly, the section goes on to provide that information may be disclosed by such a person 'when it is his duty in the interest of the State to communicate it'.[110]

---

[106] See comments of but the Bill will also criminalise temporary deprivation and again contrast this statement with the decision of US Supreme Court in *Carpenter v US*.

[107] *Carpenter v United States* 108 S Ct 316 (1987).

[108] Official Secrets Act 1963, s 2(1).

[109] The Act defines 'duly authorised' as: 'authorised by a Minister or State authority or by some person authorised in that behalf by a Minister or State authority'. Official Secrets Act 1963, s 4(1).

[110] Official Secrets Act 1963, s 4(1).

Thus, it could be argued that a defence for 'whistle-blowers' exists under the Act.[111] The Act creates an offence.

An interesting obligation is imposed upon duly authorised persons by the Act, which requires that they 'take reasonable care to avoid any unlawful communication of such information'. So, it could be argued that IT support staff in a government Department who fail to properly secure their servers may be committing an offence contrary to the Official Secrets Act 1963 and, upon conviction, would be liable to a term of imprisonment of up to two years.[112]

Data protection offences

[30.42] The DPA 1988–2003 regulates the processing of personal data. It provides for a couple of criminal offences. The broadest offence provided by the DPA 1988–2003 is that:

> 'A person who ... obtains access to personal data, or obtains any information constituting such data, without the prior authority of the data controller or data processor by whom the data are kept, and ... discloses the data or information to another person, shall be guilty of an offence'.[113]

[30.43] To some extent, this offence simply replicates the offence of unauthorised access provided by the Criminal Damage Act 1991. There are differences between the offences, however. Firstly, there is no requirement that the alleged offender operate a computer in the process of accessing the data. So, this offence would apply to social hacking, particularly as it applies not just to data, but also 'information constituting ... data'. Secondly, the authority of the data controller is not defined, so it may be defined more flexibly than in the Criminal Damage Act 1991. Finally, the offence is broader than that of simply gaining access to data; it also applies to subsequent disclosures of that data. However, the scope of this offence is limited to personal data, which is defined by the DPA 1988-2003 as being 'data relating to a living individual who is or can be identified either from the data or from the data in conjunction with other information that is in, or is likely to come into, the possession of the data controller'.[114]

[30.44] So, the offence would be committed by someone who gained access to a list of customers of a credit card company. The customers would be identified by the list and so the list would constitute personal data. But the offence would not be committed by someone who gained access to a list of credit card numbers. Because the list would not identify the individual customers, it could not constitute personal data. The offence will not be committed by 'a person who is an employee or agent of the data controller or data processor concerned'.[115] This exemption does not appear to distinguish between employees who are acting within or without the scope of their employment. So, an

---

[111] The Whistleblowers Protection Bill 1999, a private members bill, was introduced to the Dáil by Pat Rabbitte TD on 24 March 1999. However, it did not progress through the Oireachtas. For a discussion of its provisions see: Kinsella, *Whistle While You Work* 2005 COLRI.

[112] Official Secrets Act 1963, s 13(3).

[113] DPA 1988–2003, s 22(1).

[114] DPA 1988–2003, s 1(1).

[115] DPA 1988–2003, s 22(2).

employee who, without authority, accesses personal data, of which their employer is the data controller, will not commit this offence. This contrasts with the situation in the UK, where in *R v Brown* a police officer was convicted of wrongfully accessing personal data, which was held in the police national computer. The defendant in Brown accessed that data for the purpose of disclosing it to a friend of his, who was a debt collector. Such a disclosure would be an offence under the DPA 1988–2003 which provide that:

> 'Personal data processed by a data processor shall not be disclosed by him, or by an employee or agent of his, without the prior authority of the data controller on behalf of whom the data are processed'.[116]

[30.45] Contravention of this provision is an offence.[117] The difficulty with such an approach is that it will be considerably harder to prove that an employee disclosed personal data without authority than to prove that he accessed it. Punishment for an offence under the DPA 1988–2003 is limited to a fine of up to €100,000[118] where a conviction is obtained on indictment. The DPA 1988–2003 do not provide for terms of imprisonment. Hence, offences under the DPA 1988–2003 are inferior to those provided by other statutes such as the Criminal Damage Act 1991. Offences under the Data Protection Act 1988–2003 may be prosecuted by the DPC, at least summarily.[119]

419 scams or advanced fee fraud

[30.46] In March 2006 an email was circulated claiming to be from an employee of Bank of Ireland. The email claimed that the employee was acting as accounting officer in respect of a victim of the 7 July 2006 London bombings. It claimed that the victim had left €7.5 million in a bank account and offered recipients the opportunity to receive 40% of this sum in return for posing as the deceased man's relatives and providing their bank account details.[120] Of course, neither the supposed employee, nor the victim, nor his money existed. That such an obvious scam should succeed might seem surprising. But such scams are highly lucrative and their success may be attributed to the economics of Internet distribution. Suppose such a scam will be ignored by 99.999% of recipients. Circulating such an email to one million recipients will still generate 10 replies. Circulate it to 10 million and one may expect 100 replies. In truth, the funds that may be extracted from a single willing recipient may be sufficient to justify the entire process. In November 2004 an Australian perpetrator of such a scam was sentenced to over five years in jail after he was convicted of participating in a 419 scam that stole €2.5m (Aus$4m) from his victims.[121] Such scams are known as '419' scams because that is the section of the Nigerian penal code that makes such frauds an offence. Nigeria has become a center for 419 frauds, which are highly sophisticated schemes. The acquisition of bank account details is not the objective of such schemes. Instead, the fraudsters seek to draw the victim into becoming part of a complex and highly dubious scheme. Once

---

[116] DPA 1988–2003, s 21(1).
[117] DPA 1988–2003, s 21(2).
[118] DPA 1988–2003, s 31(1)(b).
[119] DPA 1988–2003, s 30(1).
[120] 'Economic Crime proves a profitable business' (2007) The Irish Times, 5 January 2007.
[121] 'Internet scammer jailed' (2004) The Age, 8 November, http://www.theage.com.au.

the victim is fully involved, he or she will typically be requested to provide funds to ensure that the scheme does not collapse. It is this funding that is the objective of the scheme. An Garda Síochána advise that citizens should 'Avoid these scams like the plague'.[122] At best victims may lose their dignity and considerable sums of money, at worst they may lose their lives.[123] It is important to realise that once victims become embroiled in such scams, they may commit offence, and become criminals themselves.

[30.47] A 419 fraud will involve a number of offences. Again, the offence of making a gain or causing a loss by deception contrary to s 6 of the Criminal Justice (Theft and Fraud Offences) Act 2001 may be committed. The offences of theft contrary to s 4 or unlawful use of a computer contrary to s 9 of that Act may also be committed. By their nature, 419 scams are international. The criminals will often try to entice the victim to travel to Nigeria, where they may be intimidated, murdered or simply disappear.[124] However, if the victims are unable or unwilling to travel then it may be necessary to intimidate them at home.[125] And, in this situation, other offences may be committed such as demanding money with menaces, contrary to Criminal Justice (Public Order) Act 1994,[126] or assault contrary the Non-Fatal Offences Against the Person Act 1997. [127]

Passive hacking

[30.48] It is clear that the offence of unauthorised access was not intended to apply where information held on a computer was gathered without actually accessing the system concerned. As was stated by the Minister for Justice when the Criminal Damage Bill 1990 was read for the second time, this provision:

> 'does not cover what is called electronic eavesdropping, that is, the remote monitoring of electromagnetic emissions from computer equipment. It is possible to pick up the radiation from a computer screen in much the same way as radio or television transmissions are picked up and to convert this radiation into an image on the eavesdropper's own computer screen. But all that can be seen on that screen is whatever

---

[122] http://www.garda.ie/angarda/crimeprev/advance_fee.html.

[123] Dixon, 'The lure of easy money' (2005) The Guardian, 10 November.

[124] 'victims have been threatened with violence unless they cooperate from the start. If they have traveled to Nigeria they have been held hostage until a ransom is paid. Since 1992, 17 people have been killed in Nigeria attempting to recover their funds and the U S State Department has documented over 100 cases in which American citizens have been rescued from Nigeria'. Smith, Holmes and Kaufman, 'Nigerian Advance Fee Fraud', Australian Institute of Criminology, Trends and issues in crime and criminal Justice, No 121, July 1999, p3. http://www.aic.gov.au/publications/tandi/ti121.pdf.

[125] One perpetrator of the scam 'employs seven Nigerians in America to spy on (victims) and threaten any who get cold feet.'If the white guy is getting suspicious...They'll try to scare you that you're not going to get out of it. Or you're going to be arrested and you will face trial in Nigeria. They'll tell you that you are in too deep – you either complete it or you'll be killed.' Dixon, 'The lure of easy money' (2005) The Guardian, 10 November.

[126] Criminal Justice (Public Order) Act 1994, s 17(1).

[127] This Act defines assault as including causing another 'to believe on reasonable grounds that he or she is likely immediately to be subject to any ... force or impact', Non-fatal Offences against the Person Act 1997, s 2(1)(b).

happens to be on the screen that is being monitored at that particular time and, in practice, the results are likely to be unsatisfactory because of the limited strength of the radiation — and consequently the limited area over which it can be received — and also because of its susceptibility to electrical interference. This kind of surveillance is essentially no different from any other kind of electronic eavesdropping of current activities. It is 'passive' and does not have the potential, as hacking does, of reading all the data files of the company being hacked or of going further and manipulating or even rendering useless its entire information system'.[128]

Damage to data

[30.49] Damaging data can be prosecuted under the Criminal Damage Act 1991. Prosecutions pursuant to the Criminal Damage Act 1991 are commonplace,[129] but such prosecutions are typically taken in relation to crimes such as vandalism or arson. The Criminal Damage Act 1991 was based upon the recommendations of the Law Reform Commission in their Report on Malicious Damage.[130] In recommending the whole-scale reform of the law of malicious damage , the LRC commented that:

> 'Advances in technology can also result in new applications of the concept of 'damage'. In *Cox v Riley*,[131] the erasure of programmes from a plastic circuit card used to operate a computerised saw ... constituted damage.'[132]

In recommending reform of the law of malicious damage, the LRC considered that:

> 'the approach ... of providing for a long list of specific offences, should be replaced by one based on a general offence in respect of criminal damage to another person's property. That general offence should be supplemented by a small number of other offences dealing with liability in specific instances'.[133]

[30.50] The Criminal Damage Act 1991 is applied to computers by extending the definition of property to included data. The Act defines property as data, and defines data as 'information in a form in which it can be accessed by means of a computer and including a program.'[134]

At the time of its enactment there was some justification for treating computer crime as being similar to more familiar crimes such as vandalism or arson. However, this justification may no longer exist. At the time of its enactment, the most serious threat posed by computer criminals was that of 'hacking'. Subsequent to the enactment of the Criminal Damage Act 1991, the LRC gave what was an accurate picture of the activities of hackers at that time:

> '(t)he tools of the hacker can be quite simple. All that is needed is a personal computer and a device ... which enables the hacker to gain access to the public communications

---

[128] Dáil Éireann – Volume 403 – 29 November 1990, Criminal Damage Bill 1990: Second Stage.

[129] 'I am informed by the Garda authorities that in 2005 there were 6,159 proceedings commenced for damaging property belonging to another under the Criminal Damage Act 1991, resulting in 1,130 convictions to date'. The Minister for Justice, Dáil Éireann, Written Answers, 21 March 2006, 1514.

[130] Law Reform Commission, 'Report on Malicious Damage' LRC 26-1988.

[131] *Cox v Riley* 83 Cr App R 54 (1988).

[132] Law Reform Commission, para 20, p 13.

[133] Law Reform Commission, para 15, p 10.

[134] Criminal Damage Act 1991, s 1(1).

network. Once a hacker has gained access to the network then all the needs to be done is to access individual computer by breaking their security codes. That may be by a simple password or a set of numbers or some combination. That can be obtained either through underground electronic bulletin boards or by programmes designed to break into the computers of others'.[135]

[30.51] The capabilities and sophistication of information technologies have improved dramatically since 1991 and so have the capabilities and sophistication of computer criminals. Hackers are now:

'taking advantage of programs that secretly install themselves on thousands or even millions of personal computers, band(ing) these computers together into an unwitting army of zombies, and using the collective power of the dragooned network to commit Internet crimes'.[136]

[30.52] By automating the processes of computer crime, these 'botnets' magnify the ability of their controllers to commit computer crimes. The use of botnets makes it more difficult to prove guilt since the controller of a botnet will not directly control each zombie computer, but rather programmes a command and control computer to control the botnet. Furthermore, jurisdictional issues are likely to prove a considerable obstacle to any such prosecution. It might be theoretically possible to prove that an Irish resident directed a computer in a second country to direct a computer in a third country to damage data held on a computer in a fourth country. The drafters of the Criminal Damage Act 1991 were conscious of the potentially international nature of computer crime. The Act provides that proceedings for an offence of damaging data 'alleged to have been committed by a person outside the State in relation to data kept within the State or other property so situate may be taken, and the offence may for all incidental purposes be treated as having been committed, in any place in the State'.[137] However, the practical difficulties of doing so may prove insurmountable.

[30.53] Therefore, the relevance of the Criminal Damage Act 1991 is open to question. The authors understand that no prosecution has ever been brought for an offence of damage to data contrary to the Act. Certainly a professional criminal should be able to evade its provisions with relative ease. If the offence of damaging date is ever to be enforced, then it is unlikely that the accused persons will be professional criminals. The core computer crime offence created by the Criminal Damage Act 1991 is that of damaging data. The Act provides that 'A person who without lawful excuse damages any property belonging to another intending to damage any such property or being reckless as to whether any such property would be damaged shall be guilty of an offence'.[138]

---

[135] Law Reform Commission, 'Report on Dishonesty' LRC 43-1992, para 9.7, p 104.
[136] Markoff, 'Attack of the Zombie Computers Is Growing Threat' (2007) New York Times, 7 January.
[137] Criminal Damage Act 1991, s 7(1).
[138] Criminal Damage Act 1991, s 2(1).

As noted above, data is defined as 'information in a form in which it can be accessed by means of a computer and includes a program'.[139] In relation to data the term 'damage' has the following meaning:

> 'to add to, alter, corrupt, erase or move to another storage medium or to a different location in the storage medium in which they are kept (whether or not property other than data is damaged thereby), or ... to do any act that contributes towards causing such addition, alteration, corruption, erasure or movement.'[140]

[30.54] The Criminal Damage Act 1991 has a separate definition of 'to damage' that applies to property other than data, but includes a storage medium in which data is kept. That is 'to destroy, deface, dismantle or, whether temporarily or otherwise, render inoperable or unfit for use or prevent or impair the operation of'.

Actions that damage a storage medium, such as reformatting a hard disk could fall within this definition. 'To damage' can also include an omission; its definition of 'to damage' includes 'to make an omission causing damage'.

A person will be treated as having a lawful excuse, if at the time the property was damaged:

> 'he believed that the person or persons whom he believed to be entitled to consent to or authorise the damage ... the property in question had consented, or would have consented to or authorised it if he or they had known of the damage or the accessing and its circumstances'.[141]

[30.55] The Act goes on to provide that 'it is immaterial whether a belief is justified or not if it is honestly held'.[142] A person will be deemed to be reckless where 'he has foreseen that the particular kind of damage that in fact was done might be done and yet has gone on to take the risk of it.'[143]

[30.56] The Act creates a number of specific offences. Damaging property with the intention that the damage would endanger the life of another is a specific offence.[144] Damaging property, whether the perpetrator's own or that of another, with the intent to defraud is another specific offence,[145] as is arson.[146] A maximum penalty of 10 years' imprisonment together with a fine limited to €12,697 may be imposed upon an individual convicted of damaging property contrary to the Criminal Damage Act 1991. However, a maximum penalty of life imprisonment may be imposed where the accused is convicted of arson or damaging property with intent to endanger life.[147] Threatening to

---

[139] Criminal Damage Act 1991, s 1(1).
[140] Criminal Damage Act 1991, s 1(1).
[141] Criminal Damage Act 1991, s 6(2)(a).
[142] Criminal Damage Act 1991, s 6(3).
[143] Criminal Damage Act 1991, s 2(6).
[144] Criminal Damage Act 1991, s 2(3).
[145] Criminal Damage Act 1991, s 2(4).
[146] Criminal Damage Act 1991, s 2(5).
[147] Criminal Damage Act 1991, s 2(6).

damage property is a separate offence,[148] as is possessing any thing with intent to damage property[149]

Extortion

[30.57] Extortion is an increasing problem online. The Criminal Damage Act 1991 makes it an offence to threaten to damage property. It provides that:

'A person who without lawful excuse makes to another a threat, intending that that other would fear it would be carried out ... to damage any property belonging to that other or a third person, or ... shall be guilty of an offence'.

The difficulty with this provision is that it only applies to one specific form of threat: a threat made against property. Internet extortions can be based upon a variety of threats, one example applying in the English decision in *Zezev and Yarkmaka v Governor of HM Prison Brixton*.[150] One of the applicants was an employee of a company in Kazakhstan that was provided with services by Bloomberg. The applicants used this legitimate access to gain unauthorised access to the email accounts of Michael Bloomberg himself and his head of security. They then sent emails threatening to reveal that they had compromised Bloomberg's security unless they were paid €200,000. Bloomberg immediately contacted the FBI who directed him to set up accounts in London and request that the applicants travel to London, where the money would be paid. The FBI arranged with the London Metropolitan Police for a hotel room to be placed under covert surveillance and arrested the applicants there. Ultimately, they were extradited to the USA. Although this was undoubtedly a threat, it was a threat to the victim's reputation not their property. Were such a case to arise in Ireland, then it might be more appropriate to bring charges of blackmail, extortion and demanding money with menaces under the Criminal Justice (Public Order) Act 1994, which provides that 'It shall be an offence for any person who, with a view to gain for himself or another or with intent to cause loss to another, makes any unwarranted demand with menaces.'[151]

[30.58] The Criminal Justice (Public Order) Act 1994 provides that 'a demand with menaces shall be unwarranted unless the person making it does so in the belief ... that he has reasonable grounds for making the demand, and ... that the use of the menaces is a proper means of reinforcing the demand'.[152] It does not appear to matter that both the demand and the menace exist online. The Act provides that 'the nature of the act or omission demanded shall be immaterial and it shall also be immaterial whether or not the menaces relate to action to be taken by the person making the demand'.[153]

---

[148] Criminal Damage Act 1991, s 3.
[149] Criminal Damage Act 1991, s 4.
[150] *Zezev and Yarkmaka v Governor of HM Prison Brixton* (2002) Cr App R 33.
[151] Criminal Justice (Public Order) Act 1994, s 17(1). In *DPP v Kavanagh* (18 May 1999) CCA an appeal against a conviction for demanding money with menaces during the kidnapping of a bank official was denied. In *People (DPP) v Ahern* (20 May 2003, unreported), an appeal against a conviction for demanding money with menaces from prostitutes was denied.
[152] Criminal Justice (Public Order) Act 1994, s 17(2)(a).
[153] Criminal Justice (Public Order) Act 1994, s 17(2)(b).

Upon conviction on indictment, a fine and a term of imprisonment of up to 14 years may be imposed.[154]

Distributed denial of service attacks

[30.59] Distributed Denial of Service (DDoS) attacks are an increasing problem online. Such attacks may be related to attempted extortions. Reports indicate that 'more than 20 denial-of-service extortion cases are occurring every week in the US, with financial demands up to $1m a time'.[155] Gambling websites are particularly vulnerable to such extortion demands:

> 'In March 2004, at the time of the UK Cheltenham horse races, several online bookmakers were targeted, including William Hill, Paddy Power and Blue Square. Criminals took control of thousands of home computers, which had been surreptitiously infected by a computer virus. The compromised computers, or 'bots', were used to send thousands of page requests to betting websites in an attempt to overwhelm servers and take their business offline. The bookmakers were then contacted by extortionists: Blue Square ... was ordered to pay €7,000 to cease the attacks'.[156]

[30.60] In the UK an attempt was made to prosecute for such an offence in *DPP v Lennon*.[157] Lennon was accused of sending 5 million emails to his former employer and causing an unauthorised modification to the contents of his employer's computer. This would be the English equivalent of the offence of data damage under the Criminal Damage Act 1991. Lennon's defence was that the purpose of his employer's computer and service connection was to accept emails and that, as such, he had consented to receipt of all 5 million. The Trial Judge agreed. The prosecution appealed. Jack J who heard the appeal agreed that:

> 'the owner of a computer which is able to receive emails is ordinarily to be taken as consenting to the sending of emails to the computer. His consent is to be implied from his conduct in relation to the computer. Some analogy can be drawn with consent by a householder to members of the publish to walk up the path to his door when they have a legitimate reason for doing so ... But ... the householder does not consent to a burglar coming up his path. Nor does he consent to having his letterbox choked with rubbish'.

Jack J did not try to define the objective limits of the consent given by a computer owner who consents to the receipt of emails. Instead he concluded that such consent:

> 'does not cover emails which are not sent for the purpose of communication with the owner, but are sent for the purpose of interrupting the proper operation and use of his system'.

---

[154] Criminal Justice (Public Order) Act 1994, s 17(3).

[155] Ilett, 'The crime gangs that covet your computer network' (2005) Financial Times, 8 November.

[156] Thomas, 'Websites face more attacks' http://www.ft.com, 30 May 2006.

[157] *DPP v Lennon* [2006] EWHC 1201, [2006] 170 JP 532.

Jack J rejected the defendant's contention that each of his 5 million emails should be considered separately. Thus, Lennon's initial acquittal was overturned.[158] But the UK had already responded to the acquittal by drafting an offence of unauthorised acts with intent to impair, or with recklessness as to impairing, the operation of a computer.[159]

Possessing any thing with intent to damage property

[30.61] Hackers have always used tools, although the tools they now use are far more sophisticated than those that were used in the days of Captain Crunch and his eponymous whistle.[160] Such tools, which are sometimes referred to as 'exploits' allow expert hackers to make their expertise available to all. An effect allows even the least adept programmer to hack a system like an expert. As one commentator has noted:

'Today's computer hackers stereotypically young (twenty-something and younger), male and socially on the fringe. They have their own counterculture: hacker names and handles, lingo, rules. And, like any subculture, only a small proportion of hackers are actually smart. The real hackers have an understanding of technology at a basic level, and are driven by a desire to understand. The rest are talentless poseurs and hangers-one, either completely inept or basic criminals. Sometimes they're called *lamers* or *script-kiddies*'.[161]

[30.62] An example of such an exploit is the Trin00 distributed denial-of-service tool.

'The problem starts with the hackers who write hacking tools. These are programs – sometimes called exploits – that automate the process of breaking into systems. An example is the Trin00 distributed denial-of-service tool. Thousands of servers have been brought down because of this attack, and it's caused … companies millions of dollars in time and effort to recover from …

---

[158] 'UK bans denial of service attacks', http://www.theregister.co.uk, 12 November 2006.

[159] Police and Justice Act 2006, s 36.

[160] John T Draper, Captain Crunch, was a 'phone phreak', the name given to early hackers who focused on getting free phone calls. He used a whistle, which he received in a box of Cap'n Crunch breakfast cereal, to make a perfect 2600 hertz tone. This tone caused a phone line to disconnect and enter into operator mode, and from this beginning Draper was able to explore the phone system. He identified other tones, which caused other switches to do other things. Ultimately he packaged his knowledge in the form of his Blue Box, which created a range of tones. See: http://en.wikipedia.org/wiki/John_Draper.

[161] Schneier, *Secrets & Lies* (Wiley Computer Publishing, 2000) p 44. The expansion of online criminality from expert hackers to script kiddies has been noted elsewhere. Lehtine, Russell & Gangemi note that in the 1980s 'businesses and individuals lagged … behind the growing ranks of attackers, many of whom were no longer elite hackers, but an annoying and dangerous breed of vandal known as the *script kiddie*, short on skill, long on desire to interrupt computation for the sake of doing so'. Lehtine, Russell and Gangemi, *Computer Security Basics* (O'Reilly Media Inc, 2006) p 27. The term 'script-kiddies' is defined by wikipedia as: 'a derogatory term for inexperienced crackers who use scripts and programs developed by others, without knowing what they are or how they work, for the purpose of compromising computer accounts and files, and for launching attacks on whole computer systems (see DoS). In general, they do not have the ability to write these kinds of programs on their own'. See also Lemos, 'Script kiddies: The Net's cybergangs' ZDNet, 11 July 2000, http://news.zdnet.com.

The Trin00 serves no conceivable purpose other than to attack systems ... once an exploit is written and made available, any wannabe hacker can download it and attack computers on the Internet. He doesn't even have to know how it works.'[162]

[30.63] Jeffery Lee Parson is an example of a script kiddie. He adapted the Blaster worm, which was released in 2005. He was arrested by the FBI, admitted his offence and was ultimately sentenced to a term of 18 months' imprisonment. However, the actual authors of Blaster have not been identified and remain at large.[163] The Criminal Damage Act 1991 criminalises the possession of such tools, but only in certain circumstances. It provides that:

'A person (... the possessor) who has any thing in his custody or under his control intending without lawful excuse to use it or cause or permit another to use it ... to damage any property belonging to some other person, or ... to damage his own or the intended user's property ... in a way which he knows is likely to endanger the life of a person other than the possessor, or ... with intent to defraud ... shall be guilty of an offence'.[164]

[30.64] Possession of such a thing is punishable on conviction upon indictment by the imposition of a fine not exceeding €12,697 and a term of imprisonment not exceeding 10 years. The difficulty with using this provision to combat script-kiddies is that this provision will only apply where the possessor has the intention of endangering the life of another or engaging in fraud. There is difficulty substantiating reports that the activities of hackers have actually ever endangered the lives of individuals.[165] However, quite a number of cases where hackers intended to defraud individuals have been successfully prosecuted.[166] Thus, it is possible that a prosecution for possession of a thing with intent to use it to hack a computer system could be made. But, such a prosecution could only be brought where it could be shown that what was intended was the damaging of data, not the gaining of unauthorised access. So, a prosecution might succeed where it was brought for possession of a program, such as a computer virus, which was intended to damage the data of another with intent to defraud. A prosecution could not succeed where it was brought in respect of possession of a program, such as Netbus[167] or Back-orifice,[168] which was intended to be used to gain unauthorised access to another's computer, even if it was intended to utilise that access to defraud another.

[30.65] This provision might be effective against someone who was found to be in possession of so-called ransomware and who could be proven to have the intention of sending it to third parties. Ransomware is the term given to a virus that 'grabs copies of documents on a disk and encrypts the original so the rightful owner cannot open them. To unlock such a file or document the user needs a key – basically a set of numbers – for

[162] Schneier, pp 45–46.
[163] Leyden, 'FBI arrests Blaster suspect' http://www.theregister.co.uk, 30 August 2003.
[164] Criminal Damage Act 1991, s 4.
[165] Lemos, 'Cyberterrorism: The real risks, CNET' http://www.news.com, 27 August 2002.
[166] See eg *R v Governor of Brixton Prison (ex parte Levin)* (1996) 3 WLR 657 and *R v Thompson* (1984) 1 WLR 962.
[167] http://en.wikipedia.org/wiki/NetBus.
[168] http://en.wikipedia.org/wiki/Back_Orifice and http://www.symantec.com/avcenter/warn/backorifice.html.

which the hacker demands money laundered through an apparently legitimate operation'.[169] This type of offence is not really defined by the use of a virus, but rather by the purpose, extortion, for which the virus is used.[170] Even if it were possible to locate and prosecute a ransomware extortionist, it would be insufficient to simply prove that they were in possession of such a virus. Obviously, any victim of such an extortion would also be in possession of the virus. In order to succeed in a prosecution, it would be necessary to prove firstly, that the virus concerned was capable of damaging the data of a victim, and secondly, that it was intended to use the virus in this way with the intent of defrauding a victim.

[30.66] A number of agencies now exist, which publish known vulnerabilities of computer systems. The US Government funds or has itself established a variety of agencies dedicated to such work: CERT,[171] US-CERT,[172] CERIAS,[173] Infraguard,[174] IAIP,[175] FedCirc[176] and CIAC.[177] A separate restricted CERT organisation is run by the US Dpartment of Defence. Europe now has the European Network and Information Security Agency (ENISA),[178] which was established by Regulation (EC) No 460/2004 of 10 March 2004 establishing the European Network and Information Security Agency.[179] Individual companies may also notify their customers of vulnerabilities. But swiftness with which hackers will exploit such vulnerabilities, their publication is becoming increasing controversial. The relationship between security, secrecy and openness is complex.[180] There are good arguments to be made that such information should be published, not least because the only way in which the security of information technology products will be improved is if consumers start to demand such improvements. Such demands will only be made if consumers know how vulnerable the products that they buy are; consumers can only gain such knowledge if vulnerabilities

---

[169] Clapperton, 'Hackers who hold users to ransom' (2006) Financial Times, 1 August. However, the use of the term 'ransomware' may be in dispute. Wikepedia defines it as 'proprietary software for which an offer is given to release the software as open source in exchange for a one time payment, or when a certain amount is raised'. http://en.wikipedia.org/wiki/Ransomware.

[170] 'The first example of ransomware is quite old ... In 1989 a hacker sent what was called the AIDS Information Trojan on floppy disk, which encrypted files and demanded money be sent to a PO Box in Panama'; Clapperton, 'Hackers who hold users to ransom' (2006) Financial Times, 1 August.

[171] http://www.cert.org.

[172] http://www.us-cert.gov.

[173] http://www.cerias.purdue.edu.

[174] http://www.infraguard.net.

[175] http://www.llnl.gov/hso/iaip.html.

[176] http://www.fedcirc.gov.

[177] http://www.ciac.org/ciac/index.html.

[178] http://www.enisa.eu.int.

[179] OJ No. L 077 , 13/03/2004 P. 1–11.

[180] Swire, 'A Model for When Disclosure Helps Security: What is Different About Computer and Network Security?' (2004) Journal on Telecommunications and High Technology Law, Vol 2.

are published.[181] Furthermore, it is clear that hackers eagerly share information about vulnerabilities that they have identified. Thus, a policy of non-disclosure of vulnerabilities might prevent victims from gaining access to information about vulnerabilities, but not necessarily prevent hackers from gaining access to that information.[182]

Malware

[30.67] There are now a great number of malicious programs, or malware, in existence. One anti-virus vendor claims to protect against '180,292 different viruses, spyware, worms, Trojan horses and other malware, as well as adware and other potentially unwanted applications'.[183] Infection with this malware can have varied consequences, some are relatively benign, others extremely harmful. The existence of malware has spawned its own industry, comprising anti-virus vendors. Furthermore, some are cynically suggest that this industry has spawned its own 'virus hype'.[184] However, there is no question that viruses have caused costly havoc. Viruses are now the product of organised criminal gangs; research suggests that 'just 5% of malicious programs are now written by bored teenagers. The rest are produced by ever increasing numbers of professional criminals and fraudsters'.[185] Changes in the motivations of the writers of malware have resulted in changes to the targets of malware. It appears that malware creators no longer aim their wares at the general population: 'Financially motivated hackers do not want to infect millions of emails as it draws attention to their malware, and increases the chance that users will take efforts to protect themselves'.[186] Instead malware authors have 'moved away from large, multipurpose attacks on network perimeters and toward smaller, more focused attacks on client-side targets'.[187] As motivations and targets change, the type of malware being created has also changed: 'In

---

[181] Granick, 'The price of restricting vulnerability publications' International Journal of Communications Law and Policy, Issue 9, Spring 2005, http://www.ijclp.org/index.html.

[182] Swire, 'A Theory of Disclosure for Security and Competitive Reasons: Open Source, Proprietary Software, and Government Agencies' Houston Law Review, Vol 42, No 5, January 2006, 1333–1380, at 1340.

[183] Sophos, *Sophos Security Threat Management Report*, July 2006, p 1.

[184] 'The anti-virus industry does quite like to spread a little fear', Robert Schifreen, a security expert and author of *Defeating the Hacker*, quoted in Clapperton, 'Hackers who hold users to ransom' (2006) Financial Times, 1 August. 'Unfortunately, a backlash has recently started against virus alarmists ... Many journalists have noticed that often those who raise loudest the warning cry are owners of companies that publish virus protection software. It makes sense to scare the public into buying protection, but the practice may have questionable ethics'. Lehtine, Russell and Gangemi, 'Computer Security Basics' (O'Reilly Media Inc, 2006), p 93. 'If viruses did not exist, the IT industry might be tempted to invent them', Lex, 'Pest control' (2005) Financial Times, 18 August.

[185] Johnson, 'Of worms and woodpeckers: the changing world of the virus-busters fighting rise in internet crime' (2006) The Guardian, 6 February.

[186] Sophos, *Sophos Security Threat Management Report*, July 2006, p 1.

[187] Symantec, *Symantec Internet Security Threat Report: Trends for July 05–December 05*, Volume IX, March 2006, p 4.

2005, Trojans outnumbered viruses and worms almost 2 to 1; today, computer users are four times more likely to be hit by a Trojan than by a virus or worm'.[188]

[30.68] Possession of a virus might be construed as possession of any thing with intent to damage property.[189] Simply showing that someone possessed a copy of a virus would not be sufficient to prove the offence, since all victims of viruses will possess a copy. Since viruses are designed to be distributed surreptitiously, proving that a person distributed a virus would not be sufficient to prove an offence. Again many victims will distribute viruses without either knowledge or intent. The intent to damage property must be proven. Given their ubiquity the simple possession or distribution of a virus will be insufficient to establish the offence. Where a virus is used or distributed it may damage data, which will be an offence contrary to the Criminal Damage Act 1991.[190] Use of a virus may be an offence contrary to the Criminal Justice (Theft and Fraud Offences) Act 2001.[191] Again it may be difficult to prove intent, that the alleged perpetrator intended to cause the damage or loss or accrue a gain. Again the alleged perpetrator may have a strong argument that he was himself an unwitting victim of the virus. Even if intent may be proven, it may be very difficult to establish an evidential link between the use or distribution of the virus and the actual damage, loss or gain. So whilst the possession, use and distribution of viruses are undoubtedly criminal offences, actual convicting a perpetrator of such offences may prove difficult.

Viruses

[30.69] Symantec, a provider of anti-virus systems, defines a computer virus as follows:

'a small program written to alter the way a computer operates, without the permission or knowledge of the user. A virus must meet two criteria:

It must execute itself. It will often place its own code in the path of execution of another program.

It must replicate itself. For example, it may replace other executable files with a copy of the virus infected file. Viruses can infect desktop computers and network servers alike'.[192]

There are thousands of viruses of different types in existence. Symantec suggest that computer viruses can be divided into five sub-categories: file-infector viruses; boot-sector viruses; master-boot record viruses, multi-partite viruses and macro-viruses. For example, Michelangelo is a boot-sector virus. This means that it resides in the boot sector of a disk, such as the hard drive on a PC, and is designed to run when a user tries to start up the computer from that infected disk. Lehtine, Russell and Gangemi describe the operation of a computer virus in the following terms:

'A virus is a code fragment that copies itself into a larger program, modifying that program ... .a virus is not an independent program but depends upon a host program,

---

[188] Sophos, *Sophos Security Threat Management Report*, July 2006, p 3.
[189] Criminal Damage Act 1991, s 4.
[190] Criminal Damage Act 1991, s 2.
[191] Criminal Justice (Theft and Fraud Offences) Act 2001, s 9.
[192] 'What is the difference between viruses, worms, and Trojans?,' http://www.symantec.com. Wikipedia defines a computer virus as 'a self-replicating computer program that spreads by inserting copies of itself into other executable code or documents', http://en.wikipedia.org/wiki/Computer_virus.

which it infects. The virus then replicates itself, infecting other programs as it reproduces. After seeing to its own reproduction, it then does whatever dirty work it carries in its programming, or payload'.[193]

Worms

[30.70] Worms differ from viruses in that they 'replicate themselves from system to system without the use of a host file'.[194] The love-bug worm was written by a Filipino who was identified but escaped prosecution due to the lack of a computer crime law in the Phillipines.[195] Another example of a worm is 'Sober-Z ... which, at its peak, accounted for one in every 13 emails. The worm, ... masqueraded as an email from the FBI or CIA claiming that the recipient is believed to have accessed illegal websites'.[196] The most famous worm remains that created by Morris, which closed down the Internet in

Trojan Horse

[30.71] A Trojan Horse is a computer program. Its distinguishing feature is that, like the mythological wooden horse used by the Greeks to enter Troy, a Trojan Horse program persuades users to run it by pretending to be something else.[197] Lehtine, Russell and Gangemi describe the operation of a Trojan Horse program as follows:

> 'A *Trojan Horse* is a code fragment that hides inside a program and performs a disguised function ... a Trojan horse hides in an independent program that performs a useful and appealing function – or appears to perform that function. Along with the apparent function, however, the program performs some other unauthorised operation. A typical Trojan horse tricks a user into running a program, often an attractive or helpful one. When the unsuspecting user runs the program, it does indeed perform the expected function. But its real purpose is often to penetrate the defences of the system'.[198]

Failure to prevent the placing of a Trojan Horse program on a system can have serious consequences. In the English case of *Julian Green* charges were brought in respect of 172 images which had been found on the defendant's computer. In the period between his computer being searched and the commencement of his trial, the defendant 'spent one night in police cells, nine days in prison, lived in a bail hostel for three months, and lost custody of his daughter and possession of his house, both to his former wife'. However, the defendant was able to retain an expert who 'established that 11 Trojan

---

[193] Lehtine, Russell and Gangemi, 'Computer Security Basics' (O'Reilly Media Inc, 2006), pp 81–82.

[194] 'What is the difference between viruses, worms, and Trojans?' http://www.symantec.com.

[195] Hayes, 'No "sorry" from Love Bug author' http:www.theregister.co.uk, 11 May 2005.

[196] Sophos, *Sophos Security Threat Management Report*, July 2006, p 3.

[197] Wikipedia suggests that 'the defining characteristics of Trojans are that they require some user interaction, and cannot function entirely on their own nor do they self-propagate/replicate', http://en.wikipedia.org/wiki/Trojan_horse_%28computing%29.

[198] Lehtine, Russell and Gangemi, *Computer Security Basics* (O'Reilly Media Inc, 2006) p 87.

horse programs and one computer virus were present on the machine's hard drive, and that these were most likely responsible for the downloaded images'.[199]

[30.72] Charges against the defendant were dismissed on the basis of this evidence. The significance of the Trojan Horse defence is that it would not appear to be necessary to actually find such a program on a defendant's computer before invoking the defence. In the English case of *Aaron Caffrey* the defendant was accused of launching a DoS attack against a system based in the USA. He admitted that the attack had been launched from his PC, but claimed that the attack had actually been launched by a Trojan. Examination of his PC revealed tools that might be used in a computer attack, but no Trojan. The defendant suggested to the jury that 'it would have been impossible for the experts to have tested every file on his PC. He also said the Trojan might have had a facility to self-destruct, leaving no trace of its existence'.[200] His account was accepted by the jury, which acquitted him of all charges. It would be easy to dismiss such acquittals as the result of gullible juries faced, in the case of *Aaron Caffrey,* with a love-lorn teenager who suffered from Asberger's syndrome. But reports have emerged in the media that extortionists have contacted users and 'threatened to "plant" child pornography on their computers and then call the cops if they didn't agree to pay a small fee'.[201]

Bombs

[30.73] Lehtine, Russell and Gangemi describe a bomb as being:

> 'a type of Trojan horse, used to release a virus, a worm or some other system attack. It's either an independent program or a piece of code that's been planted by a system developer or programmer. A bomb works by triggering some kind of unauthorised action when a particular date, time or condition occurs.

> Technically there are two types of bombs: time and logic. A bomb that's set to go off on a particular date or after some period of time has elapsed is called a time bomb ... A bomb that's set to go off when a particular event occurs is called a logic bomb'.[202]

[30.74] In *R v Thompson*[203] the appellant was 'employed as a skilled computer programmer by the Commercial Bank of Kuwait, in Kuwait'[204]. The appellant began his crime by opening five separate savings accounts in different branches of the Bank of Kuwait. These were opened under his own name.

---

[199] Pinsent-Masons Solicitors, 'Porn charges dropped with Trojan horse defence' (2003) Outlaw News, 5 August, http://www.out-law.com/page-3783; also Leyden, 'Suspected paedophile cleared by computer forensics' http://www.theregister.co.uk, 28 October 2003.

[200] Allison, 'Youth cleared of crashing American port's computer' (2003) The Guardian, 18 October.

[201] Rasch, 'The Giant Wooden Horse Did It!', http://www.theregister.co.uk, 20 January 2004.

[202] Lehtine, Russell and Gangemi, *Computer Security Basics* (O'Reilly Media Inc, 2006) p 88. Wikipedia defines a logic bomb as being 'a piece of code intentionally inserted into a software system that will set off a malicious function when specified conditions are met. For example, a programmer may hide a piece of code that starts deleting files, should he ever leave the company', http://en.wikipedia.org/wiki/Logic_bomb.

[203] *R v Thompson* (1984) 1 WLR 962.

[204] (1984) 1 WLR 962 at 964.

The appellant then:

> 'was able to obtain information about other savings accounts held by other customers of the bank at the same five branches, all of which had two particular features. First, they were ones with substantial credit balances and, secondly, they were what were called dormant accounts – accounts which their proprietors only infrequently operated'.

The appellant then:

> 'programmed the bank's computer with a programme of his own devising which caused the computer to debit five of the substantial dormant savings accounts (one at each of the five branches of the bank) and to credit his own savings account at each of those five branches with a corresponding amount. The appellant's skills were also such, and the operation of modern computers so sophisticated, that he was able to arrange that the relevant entries (debit and credit respectively) were only made by the computer on the records of the accounts at each of the branches after the appellant had left Kuwait and was in an aircraft on the way home to England … the programme went on to cause it then to erase within itself any evidence that they had been made.'[205]

When the appellant arrived in England he opened a number of bank accounts and had some of his illicitly acquired funds transferred to those accounts, gaining some £45,000 in the process. However, his fraud was detected and he was arrested and ultimately extradited to Kuwait.

[30.75] In July 2006, one Roger Duronio was convicted in New Jersey, USA, of planting a logic bomb in 1,000 of his employers' computers. Duronio had spent $23,000 on purchasing 'put option contracts which he bought on the belief that the widespread damage he would inflict with the logic bomb would cause … (his employer's) … stock price to drop steeply'. Although the bomb did work and began deleting files on his employer's computers, his employer's share price remained unchanged and Duronio lost his money. He was convicted of both security fraud and computer crime offences.[206]

Trap doors

[30.76] In the US case of *Creative Computing v Getloaded.com*[207] the parties both operated web-sites that sought to enable trucking companies avoid deadheading, that is 'having to drive a truck, ordinarily on a return trip, without a revenue-producing load'.[208] The plaintiffs had developed a very successful site, http://www.truckstop.com, with which the defendants attempted to dishonestly compete. The defendants used a number of underhand methods to gain access to the plaintiff's information including:

> 'Getloaded's officers also hacked into the code Creative used to operate its website. Microsoft had distributed a patch to prevent a hack it had discovered, but Creative Computing had not yet installed the patch on truckstop.com. Getloaded's president and

---

[205] (1984) 1 WLR 962 at 964.
[206] United States Attorney's Office, District of New Jersey, 'Jury Convicts Former UBS Computer Systems Manager for Unleashing "Logic Bomb" on Company' 19 July 2006, http://www.usdoj.gov/usao/nj/press/files/duro0719_r.htm
[207] *Creative Computing v Getloaded.Com* US Ct of Apps (9th Cir), Seattle, Washington, USA, No 02-35856, 15 October 2004, Kleinfeld, Circuit Judge 14568.
[208] 15 October 2004, Kleinfeld, Circuit Judge, p 14568.

vice-president hacked into Creative Computing's website through the back door that this patch would have locked'.[209]

The plaintiffs sued the defendants for damages under the US Federal Computer Fraud and Abuse Act. The defendant argued that had the plaintiff 'installed Microsoft's free patch that had been distributed before Getloaded hacked in, the hack would have been prevented'.[210] This argument was rejected by Kleinfeld J who suggested that:

'Getloaded's argument that ... (the plaintiff) ... could have prevented some of the harm by installing the patch is analogous to a thief arguing that 'I would not have been able to steal your television if you had installed deadbolts instead of that silly lock I could open with a credit card.' A causal chain from the thief to the victim is not broken by a vulnerability that the victim negligently leaves open to the thief'.[211]

Theft of wi-fi

[30.77] Wi-fi is a technology that allows for wireless access to Internet connections. It has obvious benefits for both domestic and business users. Wi-fi is based upon radio waves. With a typical range of 200 feet,[212] it is often not possible to contain a wi-fi networks within the physical confines of an individual property, particularly in urban areas. This makes wi-fi networks vulnerable to unauthorised access.[213] Such access may be made simply for the purpose of accessing a broadband Internet connection for free,[214] but it may also be made for the purpose of committing further criminal offences.[215] In 2005 a London man who 'piggy-backed' on a wireless broadband connection, using a laptop whilst sitting in his car, was convicted of dishonestly obtaining an electronic communications service under the UK's Communication Act 2003.[216] In Ireland the Postal and Telecommunications Services Act 1983 provides that:

'A person who connects or causes to be connected any apparatus or device to, or places or causes to be placed any apparatus or device in association or conjunction with, the

---

[209] 15 October 2004, Kleinfeld, Circuit Judge, p 14569.

[210] 15 October 2004, Kleinfeld, Circuit Judge, p 14575.

[211] 15 October 2004, Kleinfeld, Circuit Judge, pp 14575–14576.

[212] Although, with the right technology, wi-fi networks can be accessed from up to 300 ft outdooers.

[213] Mortleman, 'Snack Squad' (2002) The Guardian, 21 March. Searching for unsecured wi-fi networks is sometimes referred to as 'war-driving'. Software such as netstumbler is available to help in the identification of wi-fi networks, maps exist on the Internet identifying such networks (see http://www.wigle.net) and devices can be bought which automate the process.

[214] Marriott, 'Hey neighbour, stop piggybacking on my wireless' (2006) The New York Times, 5 March.

[215] In July 2006, a nine-year sentence imposed on a hacker who tried to access, via a wi-fi connection, credit card numbers and other information held on the computers of a DIY store was upheld. See, *USA v Saledo, Poulson, Crazy-Long Hacker Sentence Upheld,* Wired News, http://wired.com/news/technology/0,71358-0.html, 11 July 2006.

[216] Wakefield, 'Wireless hijacking under scrutiny' http://news.bbc.co.uk, 28 July 2005. See similarly in the USA: Green, 'Man fined $250 in first area case of Internet piracy' (2006) The Rockford Register, 23 March.

telecommunications system operated by an licensed operator[217] or any part of the system the effect of which might result in the provision by the company of a service to any person without payment of the appropriate rental, fee or charge shall be guilty of an offence'.[218]

There are a number of reasons why this provision might not prove effective against a Wi-fi thief. Firstly, it only applies to someone who steals telecommunications services from a licensed operator such as Eircom. But wi-fi communications are not typically provided by licensed operators such as Eircom; instead they are used by customers of those licensed operators. Theft of wi-fi from a customer of a licensed operator will not result in that licensed operator providing a service without payment of the appropriate fee. A more fundamental problem is that licensed operators no longer exist. They have been replaced by authorised undertakings. As one of these authors has argued elsewhere, this amendment may not be effective against in relation to criminal offences.

[30.78] Prosecutions could be brought under a number of alternative statutes. If the individual in question entered a username and password combination, even a simple one such as 'guest', he might be prosecuted for unauthorised access of the victim's wi-fi network.[219] He might also be prosecuted for the general offence under the Criminal Justice (Theft and Fraud Offences) Act 2001.[220] When connected to the wi-fi network, the individual would have operated both his own computer and the computer housed in the wi-fi router. Access to the wi-fi network would have conferred the requisite gain upon the individual. He would have been acting dishonestly if he had entered a username and password without being authorised to do so, if he had done so 'without a claim of right made in good faith'. However, if the wi-fi network was made available without the requirement of a username and password, then it is difficult to see how an offence could be committed. A good argument can be made that if a wi-fi network is available without any security, then any user is entitled to assume that they are authorised to use it. This argument could be based on a number of grounds. There is a movement towards making free wi-fi available and in the UK and USA this has led to local councils taking initiatives to organise the provision of such services.[221] An accused person could reasonably claim that he assumed that the provider of wi-fi was deliberately making it available for free.[222]

---

[217] Postal and Telecommunications Services (Amendment) Act 1999, s 9.

[218] Postal and Telecommunications Services Act 1983, s 99(2).

[219] See Hale, 'Wi-fi Liability: Potential Legal Risks in accessing and operation wireless internet' (2004) Santa Clara Computer and High Tech LJ, Vol 21 p 544.

[220] Criminal Justice (Theft and Fraud Offences) Act 2001, s 9(1), which provides: 'A person who dishonestly, whether within or outside the State, operates or causes to be operated a computer within the State with the intention of making a gain for himself or herself or another, or of causing loss to another, is guilty of an offence'.

[221] 'Nobody in Brighton is ever further than 10 minutes from a free wireless broadband hotspot...' see Judge, 'Brighton Rocks' (2005) The Guardian, 16 June. Meyer, 'UK's "biggest" muni Wi-Fi network goes live' (2006) ZD-Net, 1 August.

[222] See Heikkila, 'WiFi activists on free Web crusade' 29 November 2003, http:// archives.cnn.com/2002/TECH/11/21/yourtech.wifis/index.html.

Misconduct/misfeasance of public office

[30.79] Unauthorised access to, or disclosure of, data by a public servant may amount to the common law tort of misfeasance of public office. In *R v Bottrill*[223] the accused pleaded guilty to 'an offence of misconduct in a public office contrary to common law ... Bottrill was ... a sergeant in the Warwickshire Constabulary and the misconduct ... was improperly obtaining and disclosing...information held on the Police National Computer'.[224] Bottrill was sentenced to three months' imprisonment. The constituents of the offence of misconduct of public office were reviewed by the English Court of Appeal in *Attorney General's Reference No 3 of 2003*:[225] 'A public officer acting as such ... Wilfully neglects to perform his duty and/or wilfully misconducts himself ... To such a degree as to amount to an abuse of the public's trust in the office holder ... Without reasonable excuse or justification'.[226]

The court was of the opinion that the phrase 'bad faith' should not be used when summing this offence up for the jury in a criminal trial.[227] Wrongful disclosure of information may also amount to the tort of misfeasance of public office. In *Hanahoe v Hussey*[228] the plaintiff's legal firm 'had and has the highest reputation in legal circles'.[229] A search warrant was executed on the plaintiff's premises, but the information that this was to occur was leaked to the media in advance. When the gardaí arrived to serve the warrant they were met by reporters and a 'media circus' ensued.[230] The leaking of this information was held by to be the tort of misfeasance of public office and damages of €127,149 (£100,000) were awarded.[231]

The theft of electricity

[30.80] The Energy (Miscellaneous Provisions) Act 1995 provides that 'A person who dishonestly[232] uses, or causes to be wasted or diverted, any electricity or gas shall be guilty of an offence.'[233]

In its *Report on the Law Relating to Dishonesty* the Law Reform Commission alluded to the possibility that someone who dishonestly used a computer might be prosecuted for dishonestly using the electricity that powered the computer.[234] The Commission did not

---

[223] *R v Bottrill* (7 May 1999, unreported).

[224] *R v Rees* [2000] EWCA Crim 55 (20 October 2000).

[225] *Attorney General's Reference No 3 of 2003* [2004] EWCA Crim 868 (7 April 2004).

[226] [2004] EWCA Crim 868, para 61.

[227] [2004] EWCA Crim 868, para 63.

[228] *Hanahoe v Hussey* [1997] IEHC 173, [1998] 3 IR 69 (14 November, 1997).

[229] [1997] IEHC 173, [1998] 3 IR 69, para 1.

[230] [1997] IEHC 173, [1998] 3 IR 69, para 65.

[231] See also *Three Rivers District Council and Others v Governor and Co of The Bank of England* [2000] UKHL 33, [2000] 3 All ER 1, [2000] 2 WLR 1220 (18 May 2000).

[232] A person will be deemed to have acted dishonestly where they have committed the act in question 'without claim of legal right': Energy (Miscellaneous Provisions) Act 1995, s 15(2)(b).

[233] Energy (Miscellaneous Provisions) Act 1995, s 15(2)(a).

[234] The Commission referred to the offence of fraudulently abstracting electricity contrary to s 10 of the Larceny Act 1916, which was replaced by s 15 of the Energy (Miscellaneous Provisions) Act 1995.

offer any opinion on whether a conviction might result from such a prosecution, it merely wondered if the Irish courts would apply as strict a construction to the law as the courts of Hong Kong did in the case of *Siu Tak-Chee*.[235] In that case, a hacker was convicted for abstracting electricity worth one-eighth of a Hong Kong cent, but was discharged unconditionally without the conviction being recorded. Whilst such a prosecution is a possibility, its relevance is open to question. Prosecuting a person for dishonestly using a computer is difficult enough, without the added burden of proving that they used or wasted electricity in the process of doing so.

Organised crime

[30.81] The Criminal Justice Act 2006 defines a criminal organisation as being:

> 'a structured group, however organised, that … is composed of 3 or more persons acting in concert … is established over a period of time … has as its main purpose or main activity the commission or facilitation of one or more serious offences in order to obtain, directly or indirectly, a financial or other material benefit'.

The Act goes on to define a structured group as 'a group that … is not randomly formed for the immediate commission of a single offence, and … does not need to have formally defined roles for its members, continuity of its membership or a developed structure'.[236] The definition of a criminal organisation would therefore seem to be quite broad, potentially applying to any group of three or more persons who commit crimes together. The Act makes it an offence for any person who knowingly 'participates in or contributes to any activity of the organisation' where that participation or contribution is 'for the purpose of enhancing the ability of a criminal organisation to commit or facilitate … a serious offence'.[237] It is also make an offence where a person 'commits a serious offence for the benefit of, at the direction of, or in association with, a criminal organisation is guilty of an offence'.[238]

[30.82] Perhaps the most significant change made by the Act is the creation of a statutory offence of conspiracy. The Act provides that:

> 'a person who conspires, whether in the State or elsewhere, with one or more persons to do an act—
>
> (a) in the State that constitutes a serious offence, or
>
> (b) in a place outside the State that constitutes a serious offence under the law of that place and which would, if done in the State, constitute a serious offence, is guilty of an offence irrespective of whether such act actually takes place or not'.[239]

The offence has a broad reach, as it can be committed outside the state where 'the offence, the subject of the conspiracy, was committed, or was intended to be committed, in the State or against a citizen of Ireland'.[240]

---

[235] *Siu Tak-Chee* (August 1984, unreported), which was cited and discussed by the Tasmanian Law Reform Commission.

[236] Criminal Justice Act 2006, s 70(1).

[237] Criminal Justice Act 2006, s 72(1).

[238] Criminal Justice Act 2006, s 73(1).

[239] Criminal Justice Act, 2006, s 71(1).

[240] Criminal Justice Act 2006, s 71(2)(a).

Click fraud

[30.83] Search engines such as Google and Yahoo! have developed a business model in which advertisers pay them whenever an Internet users clicks upon an advertisement. This model has proven highly lucrative:

> 'Advertisers bid on keywords that they believe potential customers will be interested in. This enables internet firms such as Google, the market leader, and Yahoo!, its smaller rival, to display advertisements alongside the results of internet searches. Somebody searching for a particular type of wine, for example, might see advertisements from wine merchants. Google, Yahoo! and other firms also place ads on affiliates' websites—so wine merchants' advertisements might also appear on a wine-appreciation site. The advertiser pays only when a consumer clicks on an ad; the owner of the website where the ad was displayed then receives a small commission'.[241]

This placing of advertising can generate significant revenue. A person who conducts an Internet search for a key word is clearly interested in the subject matter:

> 'American law firms ... are prepared to pay as much as $30 each time someone clicks on an advertisement after searching for 'mesothelioma'—the name of an obscure asbestos-related disease. It is, after all, quite an efficient way to find sufferers who might be interested in launching a money-spinning compensation lawsuit'.[242]

The reason why advertisers are prepared to pay so much is because they assume that anyone who conducts an Internet search for a particular term is genuinely interested in that term. Click fraud arises when individuals click on such advertisements but are not genuinely interested in the products advertised. In *Google v Auction Expert International*[243] the plaintiff successfully sued in respect of allegations that the defendants had paid people to click on ads that appeared on the defendant's site, costing advertisers $50,000.[244]

[30.84] A couple of situations are suggested that might amount to click fraud:

> 'The first exploits the fact that Google, Yahoo! and other firms place ads on the websites of their affiliates, who receive a small cut of the advertising revenue generated by each resulting click. Unscrupulous affiliates can generate a stream of bogus commissions by repeatedly clicking advertisements on their own websites (or getting other people or machines to do so on their behalf). The second form of click fraud is aimed at the competition: click on a rival company's advertisements, displayed on websites or alongside the results of an internet search, and its advertising budget will swiftly be exhausted'.[245]

---

[241] 'Trouble Clicks' (2006) The Economist, 23 November.

[242] 'Truth in advertising' (2006) The Economist, 23 November.

[243] *Google v Auction Expert International* Sup Ct (Cal), Santa Clara, case No 1-04-CV-030560. In March 2006 Google settled a click fraud lawsuit for up to $90m filed against it by companies alleging that they had paid for fraudulent clicks. Nuttall, 'Google to pay $90m in "click fraud" suit' http://www.ft.com, 9 March 2006.

[244] It should be noted that search engines have also faced law-suits from advertisers alleging that they have failed to properly

[245] 'Truth in advertising' (2006) The Economist, 23 November.

Employing persons to impersonate genuine customers clicking on advertisements would seem to be the offence of dishonest use of a computer contrary to s 9 of the Criminal Justice (Theft and Fraud Offences) Act 2001. The offence requires that the accused act 'dishonestly ... with the intention of making a gain for himself ... or of causing a loss to another'. Therefore it would be committed regardless of whether the employee hoped to benefit the business or bankrupt its rivals. Click fraud also amount to the offence of 'making gain or causing loss by deception' contrary to s 6 of the Criminal Justice (Theft and Fraud Offences) Act 2001. This provides that:

> 'A person who dishonestly, with the intention of making a gain for himself or herself or another, or of causing loss to another, by any deception induces another to do or refrain from doing an act is guilty of an offence'.

[30.85] This offence requires that the alleged click fraud has caused another person to do an act by deception. For the purposes of the Criminal Justice (Theft and Fraud Offences) Act 2001 a person will deceive another where he 'creates or reinforces a false impression ... prevents another person from acquiring information which would affect that person's judgment of a transaction, or ... fails to correct a false impression which the deceiver previously created'.[246]

[30.86] The deception is that the employee is impersonating a person with a genuine interest in the subject matter. In doing so, the employee will create a false impression. The act that is done is the payment of the fee by the victim to the affiliate of the search engine. If the click fraud is committed in order to benefit a business directly, then it will have been done with the intention of causing a gain for the business. If the click fraud is committed in order to damage a rival of the business, then it will have been done with the intention of causing a loss to another. These actions must be done 'dishonestly', defined as being 'without a claim of right made in good faith'.[247] An employee who clicks on Internet advertisements might have the right to do so, but if they were engaging in click fraud then they could not be said to be acting in good faith.

[30.87] Additional charges might also be brought. An employer and an employee who conspire together to commit click fraud could be committing the offence of conspiracy contrary to s 71 of the Criminal Justice Act 2006. Alternatively, it could be argued that the business in question was a criminal organisation and the employees were committing criminal offences for its benefit, contrary to s 73 of the Criminal Justice Act 2006.

Terrorism

[30.88] Although the prospect of 'cyber-terrorism' has generated not inconsiderable media interest, its potential as a real threat remains in doubt. There is no question that terrorist or insurgent groups use the Internet, but they tend to do so for communications and propaganda purposes.[248] The concept of hackers using the Internet to wreak havoc

---

[246] Criminal Justice (Theft and Fraud Offences) Act 2001, s 2(2).

[247] Criminal Justice (Theft and Fraud Offences) Act 2001, s 2(1).

[248] International Crisis Group, 'In Their Own Words: Reading the Iraqi Insurgency' 15 February 2006, http://www.crisisgroup.org/home/index.cfm?l=1&id=3953.

has existed for decades.[249] But launching such attacks has proved more difficult in reality. In 2002 the US Naval War College simulated a 'Digital Pearl Harbour'. Although it was estimated that the attack would have cost $200m and taken five years the attack was unable to fulfil objectives such as crashing the Internet.[250] The sole verified example of a successful cyber-attack on physical infrastructure remains the Australian case of *R v Boden*.[251] In this case, an Australian local council had about 150 sewage pumping stations and the controls for these were linked to a computer network. These computers were installed by a private sector contractor. One of the contractor's employees resigned and sought employment from the council. He was told to reapply later. He reapplied and his application was rejected. Upon which:

> 'The sewerage system then experienced a spate of faults. Pumps were not running when they should have been, alarms were not reporting to the central computer and there was a loss of communication between the central computer and various pumping stations'.[252]

The contractor investigated and the accused was identified and ultimately convicted. When sentencing him, 'the trial judge expressed the view that the appellant was actuated by a desire for vengeance'.[253] Although this attack caused some damage, it could hardly be classified as terrorism. If 'cyber-terrorism' should occur in Ireland then the Criminal Justice (Terrorist Offences) Act 2005. This defines 'terrorist activity' as committing any of a number of scheduled offences with the intention of:

> 'seriously intimidating a population, or ... unduly compelling a government or an international organisation to perform or abstain from performing an act, or ... seriously destabilising or destroying the fundamental political, constitutional, economic or social structures of a state or an international organisation'.[254]

[30.89] One such scheduled offence is contained in 'section 2 of the Criminal Damage Act 1991 (damaging property)'. Thus, a person who engages in terrorist activity by damaging data may commit an offence contrary to the Criminal Justice (Terrorist Offences) Act 2006[255]. The Internet is an invaluable research tool. Someone who uses the Internet to conduct research for a terrorist organisation may commit an offence contrary to the Offences Against the State (Amendment) Act 1998, which provides:

> 'It shall be an offence for a person to collect, record or possess information which is of such a nature that it is likely to be useful in the commission by members of any unlawful organisation of serious offences generally or any particular kind of serious offence'.[256]

---

[249] For example, the 1983 film *Wargames* in which a hacker gains access to military computers and almost causes World War III.
[250] A full report of the simulation can be downloaded from http://www.gartner.com/2_events/ audioconferences/dph/dph.html.
[251] *R v Boden* [2002] QCA 164 (10 May 2002).
[252] [2002] QCA 164 (10 May 2002), para 8.
[253] [2002] QCA 164 (10 May 2002), para 48.
[254] Criminal Justice (Terrorist Offences) Act 2005, s 4.
[255] Criminal Justice (Terrorist Offences) Act 2005, s 6.
[256] Offences Against the State (Amendment) Act 1998, s 8(1).

Someone convicted of such an offence may be sentenced to a term of up to 10 years' imprisonment.[257] In the UK case of *R v F*[258] the accused was a native of Libya who claimed to have fled that country after family and friends were murdered by the political regime. He reached the UK and was granted asylum. Some time after he became resident in the UK he was accused of being 'in possession of a document or record containing information of a kind 'likely to be useful to a person committing or preparing an act of terrorism' contrary to the UK's counter-terrorism legislation. One of these was an electronic document saved on a CD entitled: 'A special training course on the manufacture of explosives for the righteous fighting group until God's will is established'. This document had been 'downloaded from a Jihadist website'.[259] The English Court of Appeal ruled that possession of documents such as this was an offence contrary to UK counter-terrorism law. There is no doubt that the Internet can be used to disseminate information that may be of use to terrorist organisations, information on how to make bombs has long been available online.[260] Providing training in explosives is an offence contrary to the Offences Against the State (Amendment) Act 1998, which provides 'A person who instructs or trains another or receives instruction or training in the making or use of firearms or explosives shall be guilty of an offence'.[261]

Again, this offence is punishable by an term of up to 10 years' imprisonment.[262] The Internet may also be used to direct terrorist cells.[263] Directing a terrorist organisation 'at any level of the organisation's structure' is an offence contrary to the Offences Against the State (Amendment) Act 1998.[264]

[30.90] As noted above, the Internet may be used to distribute propaganda. In the words of one expert: 'Blogs are today's revolutionary pamphlets, websites are the new dailies and list-servers are today's broadsides'.[265] The use of the Internet to distribute terrorist propaganda may be contrary to the Offences Against the State Act 1939, which makes it unlawful to: 'publish … .distribute, sell, or offer for sale any document[266] … which is or

---

[257] Offences Against the State (Amendment) Act 1998, s 8(3).

[258] *R v F* [2007] EWCA Crim 243.

[259] [2007] EWCA Crim 243, para 3.

[260] US Department of Justice, *Report On The Availability Of Bombmaking Information*, April 1997, http://www.usdoj.gov/criminal/cybercrime/bombmakinginfo.html.

[261] Offences Against the State (Amendment) Act 1998, s 12(1).

[262] Offences Against the State (Amendment) Act 1998, s 12(3).

[263] Thomas, 'Al Qaeda and the Internet: The Danger of 'Cyberplanning', Parameters, Spring 2003, pp 112–23.

[264] Offences Against the State (Amendment) Act 1998, s 6 and also Criminal Justice (Terrorist Offences) Act 2006, s 6.

[265] 'Dark days, difficult times' (2006) The Economist, 16 November.

[266] Where 'document' is defined as: 'a book and also a newspaper, magazine, or other periodical publication, and also a pamphlet, leaflet, circular, or advertisement'. Offences Against the State Act, 1939, s 2.

contains or includes an incriminating document,[267] or ... which is or contains or includes a treasonable document,[268] or ... which is or contains or includes a seditious document[269] ...'.[270] Possession of such documents will also be an offence.[271]

---

[267] Where an 'incriminating document' is 'a document of whatsoever date, or bearing no date, issued by or emanating from an unlawful organisation or appearing to be so issued or so to emanate or purporting or appearing to aid or abet any such organisation or calculated to promote the formation of an unlawful organisation', Offences Against the State Act, 1939, s 2.

[268] Where a 'treasonable document' includes 'a document which relates directly or indirectly to the commission of treason': Offences Against the State Act, 1939, s 2.

[269] Where a seditious document includes: 'a document consisting of or containing matter calculated or tending to undermine the public order or the authority of the State': Offences Against the State Act, 1939, s 2.

[270] Offences Against the State Act, 1939, s 10(1).

[271] Offences Against the State Act, 1939, s 12.

Chapter 31

International and European Computer Crime

Introduction

[31.01] The Internet is a globalised network. Anyone can log-on from anywhere and access the same content as anyone else:

> 'A globalized Internet running on open protocols meant that users could disregard both their own physical location and that of anyone they traded bits with; an occasional slow-to-respond (even while lightly-trafficked) Web site might be the only betrayal of physical distance online for the average user. Web site operators, in turn, embraced the idea that setting up a single site would expose its contents to the entire Net-connected populace, wherever it might be geographically found'.[1]

[31.02] It is certainly true that the Internet gives the impression of representing a borderless, globalised, world. A Dubliner can check the headlines on the New York Times,[2] the weather in Brussels[3] or an Australian case reference[4] as easily as an American, a Belgian or an Australian. But, this borderless impression is an illusion.[5] A variety of technologies exist for identifying the location of users and once a user's location is identified they can be made subject to local laws and brought before local courts.[6] Or, if they have used the apparently borderless internet to commit offences elsewhere, they may be made accountable to the law and brought before the Courts of the places where they committed their offences. Of course, computer criminals will be aware of these technologies and may utilise counter-technologies to hide their where-abouts. But, as a matter of law, the borderless internet is an illusion. Recent legislative initiatives such as the European Arrest Warrant mean that European computer criminals can be brought to justice with relative ease. Of course, whilst the internet may facilitate

---

[1] Zittrain, 'Be Careful What You Ask For: Reconciling a Global Internet and Local Law' The Berkman Center for Internet & Society Research Publication Series, Research Publication No 2003-03, 5/2003, http://cyber.law.harvard.edu/publications.

[2] http://www.nytimes.com/.

[3] http://www.meteo.be/english/index.php?menu=Menu1_4.

[4] http://www.austlii.edu.au/.

[5] 'Although it is often helpful to think of the internet as a parallel digital universe, or an omnipresent 'cloud', its users live in the real world where limitations of geography still apply'. 'The revenge of geography' (2003) The Economist, 13 May.

[6] 'A number of companies...offer 'geolocation services' that enable websites to determine the physical locations of individual users. This is done using a database that links internet protocol (IP) addresses of users' computers to specific countries, cities or even postcodes'. 'The revenge of geography' (2003) The Economist, 13 May.

the development of international crime, that development is independent of the Internet. As Griffiths LJ noted in *Liangsiriprasert v United States*[7]:

> 'Unfortunately in this century crime has ceased to be largely local in origin and effect. Crime is now established on an international scale and the common law must face the new reality.'

Although the law may change, practical factors may make prosecution difficult. For example, Vasiliy Gorshkov and Alexy Ivanov from Chalyabinsk, Russia were in the habit of using the internet to access the systems of American companies without authorisation. They would use this access to extort money from their victims, threatening to delete their files or post customer details online. As part of this extortion they would remind their victims clients that they were in Russia, beyond the reach of the FBI. This was true. Since the FBI could not go to Russia to get Gorshkov and Ivanov, the FBI got Gorshkov and Ivanov to come to them; setting up an elaborate operation in which the Russians travelled to the USA to pitch for work as a security consultant, identifying security flaws in the networks of American companies. In the course of his work Gorshkov and Ivanov accessed their own systems in Russia, the FBI monitored him doing so, then used the information gathered to access the Russians' systems and use the evidence gathered there to arrest and convict them.[8] International conventions, such as the Cybercrime convention, are facilitating international co-operation in relation to cybercrime, but as one FBI man has noted:

> 'The impediment to fighting botnets is international law ... It's a question of jurisdiction over 100,000 computers all over the world.'[9]

Identifying the jurisdiction of the Irish courts

[31.03] A key problem in prosecuting an Internet crime is deciding the place or locus where the crime occurred. The Courts adopted a pragmatic approach to identifying the locus of a crime in *The People (AG) v Thomas*.[10] The facts were that the appellant and his companion had boarded an Irish registered ferry, the MV Munster, travelling from Liverpool to Dublin. The two men argued and fought on board. When the ferry was about fifteen miles off the coast of Wales they struggled and the appellant threw or caused his companion to fall overboard. His companion fell about 20-24 feet from the deck of the ship to the water below. The appellant was arrested, charged and ultimately convicted of the manslaughter of his companion. He appealed on the grounds, *inter alia,* that his companion:

> 'there was no jurisdiction in the Central Criminal Court to try the appellant for manslaughter as the death did not occur on board the ship and so was not within the jurisdiction of the Court'.[11]

---

7   *Liangsiriprasert v United States* (1991) 1 AC 225.
8   http://www.usdoj.gov/criminal/cybercrime/gorshkovconvict.htm and http://www.usdoj.gov/criminal/cybercrime/ivanovSent_NJ.htm.
9   David Thomas, chief of the FBI's counterterrorism/counterintelligence and criminal computer intrusion investigations, quoted in Berinato, 'Attack of the Bots' (2006) Wired Magazine, November.
10   *The People (AG) v Thomas* [1954] 1 IR 319.
11   *The People (AG) v Thomas* [1954] 1 IR 319 at 329.

[31.04] The appellant argued that his companion was alive when he was within the jurisdiction of the Irish Court, that is when he threw his companion from the deck of the MV Munster. The death of his companion in the Irish sea was not within the jurisdiction of the Irish court. The Supreme Court disagreed, giving judgment for the court Maguire CJ stated that:

> 'The verdict of manslaughter in this case involved a finding of fact that Humphries is dead. The evidence points only to a death by drowning on the high seas. The other ingredient of the crime, the act or omission causing the death, occurred on board the MV 'Munster,' an Irish ship. Thus the event leading to the death also took place upon the high seas. The two elements necessary to give jurisdiction were thus both present. The crime was committed on the high seas and the appellant was at the time of its commission on an Irish ship. The appellant was, therefore, properly triable in the Central Criminal Court'.[12]

In general the Oireachtas must provide jurisdiction

[31.05] In general the Oireachtas will have to specifically provide for an offence to have application outside the State. In *R v Treacy*[13] the appellant had posted a letter in England to a woman in Germany demanding money with menaces. He had been convicted of the blackmail in the English courts. [14] In the House of Lords Reid LJ commented that:

> 'It has been recognised from time immemorial that there is a strong presumption that when Parliament in an Act applying to England, creates an offence by making certain acts punishable it does not intend this to apply to any act done by anyone in any country other than England.'

[31.06] In *Air India v. Wiggins*[15] Diplock LJ commented that:

> 'in construing Acts of Parliament there is a well established presumption that, in the absence of clear and specific words to the contrary, an 'offence creating section' of an Act of Parliament ... was not intended to make conduct taking place outside the territorial jurisdiction of the Crown an offence triable in an English criminal court ... The presumption against a Parliamentary intention to make acts done by foreigners abroad offences triable by English criminal courts is even stronger.'

It seems clear from the decision of the Supreme Court in *FJ McK v GWD*[16] that a similar presumption will be applied by the Courts here and that the Oireachtas will have to explicitly set out the extra-territorial nature of an offence before the courts will give effect to it. *FJ McK v GWD* was a challenge to the orders made pursuant to the Proceeds of Crime Act 1996. The CAB had sought orders pursuant to that act in elation to premises which c were alleged to have been purchased with the proceeds of criminal offences committed in the UK. Fennelly J expressed the opinion of the court that the Proceeds of Crime Act 1996:

> 'like all penal statutes, should be given a strict interpretation. In the absence of a clear and unambiguous contrary indication, there is a presumption that Acts of the Oireachtas do not

---

[12] *The People (AG) v Thomas* [1954] 1 IR 319 at 333.
[13] *R v Treacy* (1971) AC 537.
[14] Contrary to s 21 of the English Theft Act 1968.
[15] *Air India v. Wiggins* 71 Cr App R 213 (HL).
[16] *FJ McK v GWD* [2004] 1 IR 470.

have extra-territorial effect. Where statutes provide for such effect, this can be clearly seen ... Such legislation will normally, as in the case of the Extradition Acts, contain provisions for correspondence between offences contrary to our law and those of other states. An absurd result of the contrary interpretation of the Act of 1996 could be that property could be seized pursuant to the Act if it were the proceeds of activity which was criminal in another state, though perfectly lawful here. This would, in turn, mean that the Act was unconstitutional. The Act should be construed, so far as possible, so as make it consistent with the Constitution'.[17]

So, unless a statute clearly provides that an offence can be committed abroad, then it will be presumed that the statutory offence has no such application. . A variety of statutes do provide for criminal offences with extra-territorial application. An example is the Criminal Law (Jurisdiction) Act 1976. Similarly, s 31(11) of the Criminal Justice Act 1994 clearly provides for application to foreign criminal activity.

Section 9 of the Criminal Justice (Theft and Fraud Offences) Act 2001

[31.07] Section 9 of the Criminal Justice (Theft and Fraud Offences) Act 2001 provides for the following offence.

'A person who dishonestly, whether within or outside the State, operates or causes to be operated a computer within the State with the intention of making a gain for himself or herself or another, or of causing loss to another, is guilty of an offence'.

The Oireachtas has clearly provided that this offence can have some extra-territorial effect. If someone in St Petersburg, Russia, or Kuwait should dishonestly operate a computer within Ireland contrary to this provision then they will commit an offence. So long as a computer within the state is 'operated' in the commission of the offence then the actual location of the accused would seem to be irrelevant. Section 9 provides that the offence may be committed by a person 'whether within or outside the State '.

[31.08] Jurisdiction is established by the location of the computer which is operated to cause a gain to the accused or a loss to the victim. Obviously, it is possible for a computer to be operated from anywhere in the globe. In *R v Governor of Brixton Prison (ex parte Levin)*[18] the applicant's extradition from the UK was sought by the US authorities on charges that he had used a computer based in St. Petersburg, Russia to operate one belonging to Citibank and based in Parsipenny in New Jersey, USA. It is clear that a Russian resident who entered similar unauthorised instructions into computers operated by Citibank in Dublin would commit an offence under section 9. However, what if *R v Governor of Brixton Prison (ex parte Levin)* were to occur in reverse? A computer might be used in Dublin to send instructions to another based in St. Petersburg and cause a gain for the accused or a loss to the victim in Russia. Arguably, the Irish Courts would still have jurisdiction as a computer within the State would still have been operated during the Commission of the offence. The one situation where the Irish Courts would not have jurisdiction would seem to be in the situation that actually arose in *R v Governor of Brixton Prison (ex parte Levin)*. That is where a computer in Russia was used to operate another in the USA. However, even in this situation it might

---

[17]   *FJ McK v GWD* [2004] 1 IR 470 at 482.
[18]   *R v Governor of Brixton Prison (ex parte Levin)* [1997] AC 741.

be possible to argue that if the messages sent from Russia to the USA had been routed through a server based in Ireland then jurisdiction might arise here. The Irish server would have been 'operated' to the extent that it processed the internet traffic between Russia and the USA. However, evidential problems might prove insurmountable in such a case. The decision in *R v Thompson* sets out a quite interesting scenario. As noted above the accused had been employed by the Bank of Kuwait. He had inserted his own computer program into the bank's computer which transferred funds from dormant accounts to his own. But, he took care to ensure that his program only ran when 'he ... had left Kuwait and was in an aircraft on the way home to England '.[19] An employee of an Irish Bank who attempted a similar crime would commit an offence as they would have dishonestly caused a computer within the state to operate whilst they were outside the State.

Criminal Damage Act 1991

[31.09] The offence of unauthorized access contrary to s 5 of the Criminal Damage Act 1991 can clearly have international effect.

> 'A person who without lawful excuse operates a computer ... within the State with intent to access any data kept either within or outside the State, or ... outside the State with intent to access any data kept within the State, shall ... be guilty of an offence'.[20]

So, this offence can be committed by someone within Ireland who intends to access data abroad, or someone outside Ireland who intends to access data within Ireland. But, there must be an Irish link. The offence cannot be committed by someone who operates a computer abroad with intent to access data held abroad. An offence of damaging data contrary to s 2 of the Act may also be committed outside the state. The Act provides that:

> 'Proceedings for an offence under section 2 or 5 alleged to have been committed by a person outside the State in relation to data kept within the State or other property so situate may be taken, and the offence may for all incidental purposes be treated as having been committed, in any place in the State'.[21]

Child Trafficking and Pornography Act 1998

[31.10] Offences contrary to the Child Trafficking and Pornography Act 1998 may not have an extra-territorial effect. The Act prohibits the import and export of child pornogaphy,[22] but both of these actions would be committed within the State. The Act also makes it an offence where any person 'knowingly produces, distributes, prints or publishes any child pornography'.[23] The argument was made in the English case of *Gold Star Publications v DPP*[24] that a pornography business that catered exclusively to the

---

[19] *R v Thompson* (1984) 1 WLR 964.
[20] Criminal Damage Act 1991, s 5(1).
[21] Criminal Damage Act 1991, s 7(1).
[22] Child Trafficking and Pornography Act 1998, s 5(1)(b).
[23] Child Trafficking and Pornography Act 1998, s 5(1)(a).
[24] *Gold Star Publications v DPP* [1981] 2 All ER 257.

export market was not subject to the England's Obscene Publications Act. However, this argument failed.

Non-fatal Offences against the Person Act 1997

[31.11] The Non-Fatal Offences Against the Person Act 1997, created an offence of harassment. This may be committed by a person who:

> 'without lawful authority or reasonable excuse, by any means including by use of the telephone, harasses another by persistently following, watching, pestering, besetting or communicating with him or her'.[25]

The Non-Fatal Offences Against the Person Act 1997 does not make any provision for this offence to have extra-territorial effect. But, it is possible that it may still have such an effect. Or at least, it is suggested by the Australian decision of *DPP v Sutcliffe*[26] that it may have such an effect. The accused was an Australian who harassed a Canadian actress. It was agreed that, amongst other things, he had set up an Australian web-site devoted to the TV programme in which she appeared and had sent emails to persons who he thought were involved in that TV programme. The Trial Judge struck out the case for want of jurisdiction, but a case stated was taken to the Supreme Court of Victoria asking whether the trial judge was:

> 'in error when she ruled that the Magistrates' Court of Victoria did not have jurisdiction to hear or determine the charge of stalking in circumstances where the defendant's acts had occurred wholly in Victoria and the alleged victim was at all material times in Canada[27]?'

The Supreme Court of Victoria held that she had been, noting that:

> 'the respondent is a resident of this State and the acts which constitute the alleged stalking were all perpetrated by him in this State. All the ingredients of the offence save for the final ingredient of harmful effect occurred in this State. The respondent did not have to do anything more to achieve what he set out to do. He set it all in train from this State. His conduct and presence in this State provide a real connection with this State and its laws and clearly the Magistrates' Court has jurisdiction to hear the alleged offence'.[28]

Criminal Justice Act 2006

[31.12] The Criminal Justice Act 2006 provides for a couple of offences which clearly have an extra-territorial effect. The Act provides for an offence of conspiracy which provides that

> 'a person who conspires, whether in the State or elsewhere, with one or more persons to do an act ... in the State that constitutes a serious offence, or ... in a place outside the State that constitutes a serious offence under the law of that place and which would, if done in the State, constitute a serious offence, is guilty of an offence irrespective of whether such act actually takes place or not'.[29]

---

25 Non-Fatal Offences against the Person Act 1997, s 10(1).
26 *DPP v Sutcliffe* [2001] VSC 43 (1 March 2001).
27 *DPP v Sutcliffe* [2001] VSC 43 (1 March 2001), para 19.
28 *DPP v Sutcliffe* [2001] VSC 43 (1 March 2001), para 69.
29 Criminal Justice Act 2006, s 71(1).

This offence will apply to 'a conspiracy committed outside the State if ... the offence, the subject of the conspiracy, was committed, or was intended to be committed, in the State or against a citizen of Ireland, ... the conspiracy is committed on board an Irish ship[30] ... the conspiracy is committed on an aircraft registered in the State, or ... the conspiracy is committed by an Irish citizen or a stateless person habitually resident[31] in the State'.[32] The offence is not limited to these four circumstances, the DPP may bring charges in other circumstances but only if a request has been made for the accused's extradition and that request has been refused, or a European Arrest Warrant has been received but refused endorsement or 'because of the special circumstances ... it is expedient that proceedings be taken against the person for an offence under the law of the State in respect of the act'.[33]

[31.13] The *Criminal Justice Act 2006* also provides for an offence of enhancing the abilities of a criminal organization. This offence will have extra-territorial effect in two circumstances. Firstly, the Act provides that a 'person who, for the purpose of enhancing the ability of a criminal organisation to commit or facilitate ... a serious offence in the State ... whether done in or outside the State ... participates in or contributes to any activity of the organisation is guilty of an offence'.[34] Secondly, it provides that: 'person who, for the purpose of enhancing the ability of a criminal organisation to commit or facilitate ... in a place outside the State, a serious offence under the law of that place where the act constituting the offence would, if done in the State, constitute a serious offence, knowingly, by act ... done in the State, on board an Irish ship or on an aircraft registered in the State, participates in or contributes to any activity of the organisation is guilty of an offence'.[35] Where prosecutions for such offences are brought, it will not be necessary for the prosecution to prove that 'the criminal organisation concerned actually committed a serious offence in the State or a serious offence under the law of a place outside the State where the act constituting the offence would, if done in the State, constitute a serious offence, as the case may be '.[36]

[31.14] Where proceedings are brought for any of the above offences then 'in relation to an act committed outside the State may be taken in any place in the State and the offence may for all incidental purposes be treated as having been committed in that place'.[37] Double jeopardy will apply to prosecutions outside the State. The Act provides that: 'A person who is acquitted or convicted of an offence in a place outside the State shall not

---

[30] The term Irish Ship '... has the meaning it has in s 9 of the Mercantile Marine Act 1955', Criminal Justice Act 2006, s 70(1).

[31] '... A stateless person who has his or her principal residence in the State for the 12 months immediately preceding the commission of a conspiracy is....considered to be habitually resident in the State on the date of the commission of the conspiracy' Criminal Justice Act 2006, s 71(5).

[32] Criminal Justice Act 2006, s 71(2).

[33] Criminal Justice Act 2006, s s 71(3) and 74(3).

[34] Criminal Justice Act 2006, s 72(1).

[35] Criminal Justice Act 2006, s 72(1).

[36] Criminal Justice Act 2006, s 72(2)(a).

[37] Criminal Justice Act 2006, s 74(1).

be proceeded against for an offence … (of conspiracy) … consisting of the act, or the conspiracy to do an act, that constituted the offence, or … (an offence of facilitating a criminal organization) … consisting of the act that constituted the offence, of which the person was so acquitted or convicted'.[38]

European Instruments

[31.15] The European Union has some limited functions in relation to criminal law,[39] the objective of the European Union is to:

'provide citizens with a high level of safety within an area of freedom, security and justice by developing common action among the Member States in the fields of police and judicial cooperation in criminal matters.'[40]

European Instruments: the Council Framework Decision 2005/222[41] on attacks against information

[31.16] The objective of the Council Framework Decision 2005/222[42] *on attacks against information* systems is to approximate the criminal law of the Member States to 'ensure the greatest possible police and judicial cooperation in the area of criminal offences related to attacks against information systems, and to contribute to the fight against organised crime and terrorism'.[43] The Framework Council Decision sets out four separate criminal offences which Member States are expected to implement. These are: illegal access to information systems; illegal system interference; illegal data interference; and, instigation, aiding and abetting and attempt. Member States must have complied with the Framework Decision by 16 March 2007;[44] and have transmit national transposition provisions to the Council and the Commission by that date. Progress on compliance and transposition will be assessed by the Council by 16th September 2007.[45]

Illegal access to information systems

[31.17] The Framework Decision seeks to protect information systems, which are defined as meaning: 'any device or group of inter-connected or related devices, one or more of which, pursuant to a program, performs automatic processing of computer data, as well as computer data stored, processed, retrieved or transmitted by them for the purposes of their operation, use, protection and maintenance'.[46] Member States are expected to 'take the necessary measures to ensure that the intentional access without right to the whole or any part of an information system is punishable as a criminal offence'. Member States are given three explicit derogations from this provision. Firstly,

---

38 Criminal Justice Act 2006, s 77.
39 Treaty on European Union, Title VI, OJ C325 p5, 24.12.2002
40 Treaty on European Union, art 29.
41 OJ L 069 , 16/03/2005 P 67–71.
42 OJ L 069 , 16/03/2005 P 67–71.
43 Framework Decision 2005/222/JHA, Recital 8.
44 Framework Decision 2005/222/JHA, art 12(1).
45 Framework Decision 2005/222/JHA, art 12(2).
46 Framework Decision 2005/222/JHA, art 1(a).

they need only criminalize those cases which are 'not minor'.[47] Secondly, they '... may decide that the conduct ... is incriminated only where the offence is committed by infringing a security measure'.[48] Finally, member states may decide not to create an offence of attempting to gain illegal access.[49] An effectively derogation is also provided by the definition of 'without right'. This is defined by the Framework Decision as meaning 'access ... not authorised by the owner, other right holder of the system or part of it, or not permitted under the national legislation'.[50] Since the National leglislation of Member States are allowed to define what is and is not authorized access, they are in effect allowed to define the application of this provision. Ireland provided for such an offence in section – of the Criminal Damage Act 1991.

Illegal system interference

[31.18] Member States are expected to 'take the necessary measures to ensure that the intentional serious hindering or interruption of the functioning of an information system by inputting, transmitting, damaging, deleting, deteriorating, altering, suppressing or rendering inaccessible computer data is punishable as a criminal offence when committed without right'. Again this offence need only be created for those cases which are 'not minor'.[51] And as with unauthorized access, the definition of 'without right' allows Member States to effectively define the situations where unauthorized interruption will occur.[52]

Illegal data interference

[31.19] The Framework Decision seeks to protect the integrity of computer data which is defined as: 'any representation of facts, information or concepts in a form suitable for processing in an information system, including a program suitable for causing an information system to perform a function'.[53] Member States are expected to '... take the necessary measures to ensure that the intentional deletion, damaging, deterioration, alteration, suppression or rendering inaccessible of computer data[54] on an information system is punishable as a criminal offence when committed without right'. As before, it is only necessary to introduce such an offence 'for cases which are not minor'.[55] The instigation of aiding and abetting such an offence[56] and an attempt to commit such an offence must also be criminalized.[57] At first glance s 2(1) of the Criminal Damage Act 1991 would appear to provide for such an offence. However, the Framework Decision would appear to require a somewhat broader offence than that actually provided by

---

[47] Framework Decision 2005/222/JHA, art 2(1).
[48] Framework Decision 2005/222/JHA, art 2(2).
[49] Framework Decision 2005/222/JHA, art 5(3).
[50] Framework Decision 2005/222/JHA, art 1(d).
[51] Framework Decision 2005/222/JHA, art 3.
[52] Framework Decision 2005/222/JHA, art 1(d).
[53] Framework Decision 2005/222/JHA, art 1(b).
[54] Framework Decision 2005/222/JHA, art 1(b).
[55] Framework Decision 2005/222/JHA, art 4.
[56] Framework Decision 2005/222/JHA, art 5(1).
[57] Framework Decision 2005/222/JHA, art 5(2).

s 2(1). Damaging data is defined by the Criminal Damage Act 1991 as being 'to add to, alter, corrupt, erase or move to another storage medium or to a different storage medium in the same location '.[58] Deletion in the Framework Decision would appear to equate to erase in the Criminal Damage Act 1991. Similarly, deterioration in the Framework Decision would seem to equate to corrupt in the Irish Act. However, the definition of damage in the Criminal Damage Act 1991 would not appear to explicitly provide any equivalent of the Framework Decision's 'suppression or rendering inaccessible of computer data'. Section 9 of the Criminal Justice (Theft and Fraud Offences) Act 1991 does provide an offence of quite general application. But, the specifics of that offence are somewhat different to the offence that is required by the Framework Decision. The Framework Decision requires the creation of an offence of 'intentional deletion ... of computer data'. As discussed above, the Framework Decision does not allow for the limitation of the *mens rea* requirement of the offence other than it requires the criminalization of 'intentional' acts. Section 9 of the Criminal Justice (Theft and Fraud Offences) Act 1991 would appear to be more limited than this. Section 9(1) requires that a computer be dishonestly operated by a person 'with the intention of making a gain for himself or herself or another or of causing loss to another'. This is clearly a more limited offence than is required by the Framework Decision. Again, some amendment of the definition of damaging data in s 1(1) of the Criminal Damage Act 1991 would seem to be required in order to implement this article of the Framework Decision.

Liability of legal persons

[31.20] The Framework Decision requires that MS make legal persons liable for certain offences. A legal person is defined as: 'any entity having such status under the applicable law, except for States or other public bodies in the exercise of State authority and for public international organisations'.[59] The Framework Decision requires that member states 'take the necessary measures to ensure that legal persons can be held liable for (computer crime) offences ... committed for their benefit by any person, acting either individually or as part of an organ of the legal person, who has a leading position within the legal person, based on: ... a power of representation of the legal person, or ... an authority to take decisions on behalf of the legal person, or ... an authority to exercise control within the legal person'.[60] In addition, MS must ensure 'that a legal person can be held liable where ... (a) ... lack of supervision or control ... has made possible the commission of the offences ... .for the benefit of that legal person by a person under its authority'.[61] Finally, liability of a legal person under these provisions will not 'exclude criminal proceedings against natural persons who are involved as perpetrators, instigators or accessories in the commission of the offences'.[62] The Framework Decision specifically requires that Member States 'take the necessary measures to ensure that a legal person held liable pursuant ... (this provision) ... is

---

[58] Criminal Damage Act, 1991, s 1(1).
[59] Framework Decision 2005/222/JHA, art 1(c).
[60] Framework Decision 2005/222/JHA, art 8(1).
[61] Framework Decision 2005/222/JHA, art 8(2).
[62] Framework Decision 2005/222/JHA, art 8(3).

punishable by effective, proportionate and dissuasive penalties or measures'.[63] These penalties are discussed in greater detail below.

Penalties

[31.21] The Framework Decision requires that Member States 'take the necessary measures to ensure that the offences ... are punishable by effective, proportional and dissuasive criminal penalties ... '.[64] In particular, the Framework Decision requires that the offences of Illegal system interference and illegal data interference be punishable by 'punishable by criminal penalties of a maximum of at least between one and three years of imprisonment'.[65] The Framework Decision requires that Member States provide for increased penalties in what it terms 'aggravating circumstances'. Member States must provide that where the offences of gaining illegal access by infringing security measures, illegal system interference or illegal data interference are committed, then 'punishable by criminal penalties of a maximum of at least between two and five years of imprisonment when committed within the framework of a criminal organization'.[66] Member States may also impose such enhanced penalties 'when the offence has caused serious damages or has affected essential interests'.[67] Member States should also provide for the imposition of 'effective, proportionate and dissuasive penalties' on legal persons. Such penalties may include criminal and non-criminal fines, as well as other penalties such as: exclusion from entitlement to public benefits or aid; temporary or permanent disqualification from the practice of commercial activities; placing under judicial supervision; or a judicial winding-up order.[68]

Jurisdiction

[31.22] Council Framework Decision 2005/222/JHA on attacks against information systems requires that Member States establish that computer crimes will fall within their jurisdiction where the offence has been committed 'in whole or in part within its territory; or ... by one of its nationals ... for the benefit of a legal person that has its head office in the territory of that Member State'.[69] An offence will be committed within the territory of a Member State where 'the offender commits the offence when physically

---

[63] Framework Decision 2005/222/JHA, art 9(2).

[64] Framework Decision 2005/222/JHA, art 6(1).

[65] Framework Decision 2005/222/JHA, art 6(2).

[66] Framework Decision 2005/222/JHA, art 7(1). The term criminal organisation is defined by art 1 of Joint Action 98/733/JHA as: 'a structured association, established over a period of time, of more than two persons, acting in concert with a view to committing offences which are punishable by deprivation of liberty or a detention order of a maximum of at least four years or a more serious penalty, whether such offences are an end in themselves or a means of obtaining material benefits and, where appropriate, of improperly influencing the operation of public authorities'.

[67] Framework Decision 2005/222/JHA, art 7(2).

[68] Framework Decision 2005/222/JHA, art 9(1).

[69] Framework Decision 2005/222/JHA, art 10(1). The Framework Decision gives Member States a discretion as to whether they establish jurisdiction over offences committed by their nationals or offences committed fo rhte benefit of legal persons. (contd/)

present on its territory'. It is irrelevant whether or not the offence is actually against an information system on the territory of the Member State'. An offence will also be committed where 'the offence is against an information system' on the territory of the Member State. This Member State will have jurisdiction regardless of whether 'the offender commits the offence when physically present on its territory'.[70] Where a Member State does not permit the extradition or surrender of its citizens, then it must establish its own jurisdiction over its nationals where they commit computer crime offences outside that Member State's territory.[71]

[31.23] Since virtual computer networks can operate without regard for physical borders, problmes of multiple jurisdictions can arise. The Framework Decision tries to deal with such problems by providing that:

> 'Where an offence falls within the jurisdiction of more than one Member State and when any of the States concerned can validly prosecute on the basis of the same facts, the Member States concerned shall cooperate in order to decide which of them will prosecute the offenders with the aim, if possible, of centralising proceedings in a single Member State'.

To facilitate this process the Framework Decision provides that 'the Member States may have recourse to any body or mechanism established within the European Union in order to facilitate cooperation between their judicial authorities and the coordination of their action'. In deciding which Member State should prosecute alleged offenders, the Framework Decision provides that sequential account may be taken of the following factors. In the first place account may be taken of the Member State where the offence actually occurred. Alternatively, account may be taken of the Member State of which the perpetrator is a national. Finally, account may be taken of the Member State in which the perpetrator was found.[72]

Exchange of information

[31.24] The Framework Decision provides for the exchange of information between Member States. It provides that 'Member States shall ensure that they make use of the existing network of operational points of contact available 24 hours a day and seven days a week'.[73] It also provides that MS must 'inform the General Secretariat of the Council and the Commission of its appointed point of contact for the purpose of exchanging information on offences relating to attacks against information systems'. This information will be circulated amongst the MS by the council.[74] The network referred to is that established by the G8; the European Council recommended all MS

---

[69] (\contd) Framework Decision 2005/222/JHA, art 10(5). However, the 'Member States shall inform the General Secretariat of the Council and the Commission where they decide to apply (this) paragraph...where appropriate with an indication of the specific cases or circumstances in which the decision applies'. Framework Decision 2005/222/JHA, art 10(6).

[70] Framework Decision 2005/222/JHA, art 10(2).

[71] Framework Decision 2005/222/JHA, art 10(3).

[72] Framework Decision 2005/222/JHA, art 10(4).

[73] Framework Decision 2005/222/JHA, art 11(1).

[74] Framework Decision 2005/222/JHA, art 11(2).

should join this network in *Council Recommendation of 25 June 2001 on contact points maintaining a 24-hour service for combatting high-tech crime.*[75]

European instruments: the European Arrest Warrant

[31.25] The European Arrest Warrant (EAW) was established by Framework Decision 2002/584/JHA[76] (the EAW Decision). This Decision created 'a system of free movement of judicial decisions in criminal matters … within an area of freedom, security and justice'.[77] The EAW Decision is implemented in Ireland by the European Arrest Warrant Act 2003 (the EAW Act). The EAW Decision applies specifically to 'computer related crime'.[78] An EAW warrant must conform to the format set out in the annex to the EAW Decision,[79] although an arrest may be made without a warrant, in urgent cases, and where other criteria are fulfilled.[80] The entire purpose of the EAW is to facilitate the arrest and transfer of persons suspected or accused of criminal offences from one Member State to another. This facility may surprise some Irish people. For example, in *The Minister for Justice, Equality and Law Reform v McArdle*[81] the respondent's arrest and transfer was sought by the Spanish authorities in relation to the death of his wife. The Respondent argued that:

> 'complains that … his wife's (the victim) body was released to him for repatriation and burial. No conditions or restrictions were placed on the release. He believed at that point that all investigations were concluded. At no time was he informed that an investigation was continuing or that there were any outstanding issues relating to his wife's death or that he was suspected of having murdered or otherwise harmed her'.

The EAW did not issue until almost five years after the death of the respondent's wife. The respondent challenged the EAW on grounds of delay and fair procedures, but Finnegan J directed its execution noting that:

> 'Nothing has been urged upon me to suggest that in surrendering the Respondent for trial in Spain his constitutional rights or the rights enshrined in the European Convention on Human Rights will be abrogated.'

A significant number of EAWs have now been processed by the Irish courts. [82] The EAW Decision has been similarly implemented in the rest of the EU and this means that European computer criminals can no longer frustrate or delay their arrest simply by moving around within the EU. Of course, the Internet is not neatly circumscribed by the boundaries of the EU. Offences may well be committed by computer criminals based in

---

[75] OJ C 187 , 03/07/2001 P 5–6.
[76] OJ L 190 , 18/07/2002 P 1–20.
[77] Framework Decision 2002/584/JHA, Recital 5.
[78] Framework Decision 2002/584/JHA, art 2(2).
[79] EAW Act 2003, s 11(1).
[80] EAW Act 2003, s 14(1).
[81] *The Minister for Justice, Equality and Law Reform v McArdle* (27 May 2005, unreported) HC (Finnegan J).
[82] For example in *Clarke v Governor of Portlaoise Prison* (23 May 2006, unreported) SC, the Supreme Court refused to overturn an order for committal made by the High Court pursuant to s 16 of the EAW Act 2003.

Ireland against computers based outside the EU and *vice versa*. In such circumstances the provisions of bilateral extradition treaties may have to be invoked.

International instruments: The Cybercrime Convention

[31.26] The Council of Europe's Convention on Cybercrime was adopted by the Council of Europe on the 8 November 2001 and was opened for signature in Budapest, on 23 November 2001. It was signed by Ireland on the 2 February 2002, but has yet to be ratified by Ireland. The COE justifies the convention on the basis that it is

> 'necessary to deter actions directed against the confidentiality, integrity and availability of computer systems, networks and computer data, as well as the misuse of such systems, networks and data, by providing for the criminalisation of such conduct, as described in this Convention, and the adoption of powers sufficient for effectively combating such criminal offences, by facilitating the detection, investigation and prosecution of such criminal offences at both the domestic and international level, and by providing arrangements for fast and reliable international co-operation.'[83]

At the national level the Convention requires that Member States ensure that their national laws criminalise certain activities and allow for certain procedures. At the international level the Convention seeks to harmonise extradition and mutual assistance procedures. It also seeks the establishment of a 24/7 network. Of course, the EU could have introduced similar measures, article – of the EU Treaty empowers . Therefore, the EU could have required that its 27 member states introduce harmonise their procedures by means of a Framework Decision. And, the EU is in the process of doing so. What makes the Cybercrime Convention significant is that representatives of the USA participated in its drafting. And, the US President signed the USA's instrument of ratification of the Convention on 22 September 2006.[84] As of October 2006 the Treaty had been signed by 26 States and ratified by 17.[85] This substantial international dimension means that the Cybercrime Convention is of great significance. If Computer crime is an international crime, then the Cybercrime may create the international structures that may ultimately curtail it.

National measures – criminal offences

[31.27] Ratification of the Convention requires that parties to the Convention ensure that their national laws allow for certain offences. These are, firstly, offences against the confidentiality, integrity and availability of computer data. Parties to must criminalise the following intentional act:

> 'the access to the whole or any part of a computer system without right'.

Irish law already provides for this, in section – of the Criminal Damage Act 1991. One variation that Irish law does not allow for is that parties to the Convention may 'require that the offence be committed by infringing security measures, with the intent of

---

[83] Preamble to the Convention.

[84] http://www.state.gov/r/pa/prs/ps/2006/73354.htm the Convention has been signed but not ratified by Canada, Japan and South Africa.

[85] http://conventions.coe.int/Treaty/Commun/ChercheSig.asp?NT=185&CM=7&DF=10/30/2006&CL=ENG.

obtaining computer data or other dishonest intent, or in relation to a computer system that is connected to another computer system'.[86]

[31.28] Parties to the Convention must also criminalise illegal interception, being: 'the interception without right, made by technical means, of non-public transmissions of computer data to, from or within a computer system, including electromagnetic emissions from a computer system carrying such computer data'.[87] Again, parties to the Convention may require that the offence be committed with dishonest intent, or in relation to a computer system that is connected to another computer system. This may be compared to s 98 of the Postal and Telecommunications Services Act 1983. The Convention creates an offence of data interference being: 'the damaging, deletion, deterioration, alteration or suppression of computer data without right'.[88] But, parties may require that this will only be a criminal offence where it results in serious harm.[89] Again, this would appear to be an offence under s 2 (1) of the Criminal Damage Act, 1991. However, the Convention requires that Ireland create two offences that are not already provided for by Irish law. Firstly, Ireland must provide for an offence of system interference. This is the intentional:

'serious hindering without right of the functioning of a computer system by inputting, transmitting, damaging, deleting, deteriorating, altering or suppressing computer data'.[90]

There would not seem to be any existing equivalent to this in Irish law or s 99 of the Postal and Telecommunications Services Act, 1983. Section 9 of the Criminal Justice (Theft and Fraud Offences) Act 2001 might apply. But, only if it could be shown that the serious hindering in question had caused a gain to perpetrator or a loss to another. Whilst it may be possible to show that a person hindered the functioning of a computer system, it is quite another thing to show that this hindering caused a loss or a gain. Furthermore, the section 9 offence must be committed 'dishonestly' whilst the Convention requires that the offence of system interference be committed intentionally and without right.[91] The argument may be made that these terms are equivalent, but it is also arguable that they are not. Similarly, the Convention requires the creation of an offence committed by 'the production, sale, procurement for use, import, distribution or otherwise making available of' devices, including computer programs or 'a computer password, access code, or similar data' for the purpose of committing any of the above offences. This offence must be 'committed intentionally and without right'.[92] Again this has no direct parallel in Irish law at present although s 4 of the Criminal Damage Act 1991, s 25 of the Electronic Commerce Act 2000 and Pt VII of the Copyright and Related Rights Act 2000 might have some application.

---

[86] Cybercrime Convention, art 2.
[87] Cybercrime Convention, art 3.
[88] Cybercrime Convention, art 4(1).
[89] Cybercrime Convention, art 2(2).
[90] Cybercrime Convention, art 5.
[91] Cybercrime Convention, art 6.
[92] Cybercrime Convention, art 6.

[31.29] The Convention allows for the creation of offences of computer related forgery[93] and fraud.[94] The former offence would seem to find an Irish equivalent in section – of the Criminal Justice (Theft and Fraud Offences) Act 2001 whilst the equivalent of the latter would seem to be s 9 of that Act. The Convention also requires the enactment of offences related to child pornography.[95] The Child Trafficking and Pornography Act 1997 goes far beyond what is required by the Convention in this regard. The relatively weak provisions of the Convention in relation to child pornography probably reflect the difficulties of the US position and the need to comply with the First Amendment to the US Constitution.

The Convention requires that parties create offences in relation to copyright infringement,[96] which Ireland has done in the Copyright and Related Rights Act 2000.[97] It also requires the creation of inchoate offences of attempt and aiding and abetting.[98] And, it requires the imposition of corporate liability.[99] Finally, the Convention requires the imposition of 'effective, proportionate and dissuasive sanctions'.[100]

National measures: – procedural law

[31.30] Parties to the Convention must provide for a variety of procedural steps, which are principally directed at the preservation of evidence. However, it is important to realise that these procedural steps cannot be used solely for the purposes of investigating cybercrime. The Convention is very clear on this point. It first provides that parties must: 'adopt such legislative and other measures as may be necessary to establish the powers and procedures provided for in this Section for the purpose of specific criminal investigations or proceedings'.[101] It then provides that these powers and procedures must be applied to 'criminal offences established in accordance with ... this Convention'. And, these same powers and procedures must also be applied to:

> 'other criminal offences committed by means of a computer system; and ... the collection of evidence in electronic form of a criminal offence'.[102]

The Convention does require that parties to its provisions respect the rights of citizens in the establishment and application of these powers and procedures.[103] The Convention requires that parties provide for the expedited preservation[104] and partial disclosure of

---

[93] Cybercrime Convention, art 7.
[94] Cybercrime Convention, art 8.
[95] Cybercrime Convention, art 9.
[96] Cybercrime Convention, art 10.
[97] Copyright and Related Rights Act 2000–2004, ch 13.
[98] Cybercrime Convention, art 11.
[99] Cybercrime Convention, art 12.
[100] Cybercrime Convention, art 13.
[101] Cybercrime Convention, art 14(1).
[102] Cybercrime Convention, art 14(2).
[103] Cybercrime Convention, art 15.
[104] Cybercrime Convention, art 16.

stored computer data.[105] It also requires that parties provide for production orders[106] and the search and seizure of stored computer data.[107] Finally, Member States must provide for the real time collection of traffic data[108] and the interception of content data.[109]

[31.31] Parties to the Convention must establish their jurisdiction over offences required by the Convention that are committed on the territory of the party, on a ship flying its flag, a plane registered with the party or an offence committed by one of its nationals where:

> 'the offence is punishable under criminal law where it was committed or if the offence is committed outside the territorial jurisdiction of any State'.[110]

International co-operation

[31.32] Parties to the Convention commit themselves to co-operate with each other, they must:

> 'co-operate with each other ... to the widest extent possible for the purposes of investigations or proceedings concerning criminal offences related to computer systems and data, or for the collection of evidence in electronic form of a criminal offence'.[111]

In particular, parties must deem Convention offences to be '... extraditable offences in any extradition treaty existing between or among the Parties'.[112] As regards mutual assistance, parties must:

> 'afford one another mutual assistance to the widest extent possible for the purpose of investigations or proceedings concerning criminal offences related to computer systems and data, or for the collection of evidence in electronic form of a criminal offence[113]'

The Convention details how this mutual assistance is to be provided[114] and requires the establishment of a 24/7 network.[115] The Convention also contains two provisions designed to circumvent the absence of structures of co-operation, so that crime may be prevented or investigated. Firstly, parties may forward 'spontaneous information' to each other.[116] Secondly, the Convention allows for the processing of 'mutual assistance requests in the absence of applicable international agreements'.[117]

---

[105] Cybercrime Convention, art 17.
[106] Cybercrime Convention, art 18. See the Criminal Justice (Theft and Fraud Offences) Act 2001, s 52.
[107] Cybercrime Convention, art 19. See the Criminal Justice (Theft and Fraud Offences) Act 2001, s 49.
[108] Cybercrime Convention, art 20. See the Criminal Justice (Terrorist Offences) Act 2005, Pt V.
[109] Cybercrime Convention, art 21. See the Interception of Postal Packets and Telecommunications Messages Act 1993.
[110] Cybercrime Convention, art 22(1).
[111] Cybercrime Convention, art 23.
[112] Cybercrime Convention, art 24(2).
[113] Cybercrime Convention, art 25(1).
[114] Cybercrime Convention, arts 29–34.
[115] Cybercrime Convention, art 35.
[116] Cybercrime Convention, art 26.
[117] Cybercrime Convention, art 27.

International instruments: extradition

[31.33] Extradition in Ireland is subject to the Extradition Act 1965, this Act has been amended on successive occassions.[118] Ireland has a variety of bilateral agreements with other countries, for example the Treaty on Extradition between Ireland and the United States of America signed 13 July 1983. Extradition is an extremely complex process, far more complex than the procedures to be applied under the European Arrest Warrant.

---

[118] See: The Extradition (Amendment) Act 1987; Extradition (European Convention On The Suppression Of Terrorism) Act, 1987; The Extradition (Amendment) Act 1994, Extradition (European Union Conventions) Act, 2001.

Chapter 32

Evidence

Introduction

[32.01] Computers and other storage devices can contain vast amounts of data. In turn this data may contain evidence which may be relevant to criminal investigations or civil actions; but the gathering, analysis and admission of this data into evidence create their own challenges. Just because data has been deleted does not mean that it cannot be reconstructed and entered into evidence:

> 'Digital media store data in different ways at a physical level, such as magnetic particles and laser-created pits, as well as at a logical level, in terms of partitions, drives and sectors … under all file systems data is not necessarily stored in a contiguous manner, but rather will often be fragmented across the media, in blocks, which are only logically associated through addressing information …

> The deletion of files in standard desktop applications will generally only result in the removal of the addressing information associated with each block of data … or the files are simply treated as deleted and are renamed in another directory, such as the 'recycle bin' or 'trash'. As such the data remains on the media and is potentially recoverable, until it has been either completely overwritten by new data, or has been deleted by other means. This residual representation of erased data is sometimes referred to as "data remanence" …'[1]

[32.02] In *R v Porter*[2] the defendant's computers were seized as part of an investigation into child pornography. A large amount of child pornography had been deleted from these computers, which the UK police were able to recover. The ability of the police to recover this data was explained by the trial judge in the following terms:

> 'a file remains on the hard drive even if it has been deleted or lost … A file does not cease to be a file on a hard drive if it has been deleted. It remains a file, albeit a deleted file … Such files may be active or deleted, recovered, lost or unallocated.'[3]

On appeal it was conceded by the Crown that some of these files 'were only retrievable with the use of specialist forensic techniques and equipment provided by the United States Federal Government which would not have been available to the public'. Both sides agreed that 'that the defendant could have acquired software to enable him to retrieve the items which had been emptied from the recycle bin.'[4]

---

[1] I Walden, *Computer Crimes and Digital Investigations* (Oxford University Press, 2007), para 4.38, p 212. See also RG Smith, P Grabosky & G Urbas, *Cyber Criminals on Trial* (Cambridge University Press, 2004); E. Casey, *Digital Evidence and Computer Crime* (2nd edn, Elsevier Academic Press, 2004).

[2] *R v Porter* (2006) 1 WLR 2633.

[3] (2006) 1 WLR 2633 at 2636.

[4] (2006) 1 WLR 2633 at 2635.

[32.03] Once this data is gathered, its analysis may prove problematic; the accuracy of computer data is subject to a whole variety of variables. In one case an individual was alleged to have accessed child pornography in the early hours of the morning because:

> 'The time zone on the ... computer ... was set to the default value: Seattle time, the headquarters of Microsoft. As a result, all of the file data stamps were represented as though they were in Seattle; midday ... became 3 am on the night before it.'[5]

Depending on what examinations are undertaken, considerable expertise may be required. In *Admiral Management Services v Para-Protect Europe Ltd*,[6] a costs application, Burton J accepted that some 'special expertise' might be required where computers were examined and

> 'it was found that files on the hard disks had been erased by the use of proprietary software. The Claimant was however able to retrieve relevant information from the disks by accessing the slack space on the computer hard disk ... it was suggested that special expertise is required to access information on a hard disk without over-writing existing data on the disk.'

On the other hand, Burton J thought that no special expertise would be required for 'someone who did no more than access or examine a file and bring up its 'properties' in Microsoft Word'.

Evidence from computers in criminal cases

[32.04] Computers are now pervasive throughout society and criminals are not adverse to the advantages offered by modern technology. The most obvious situation where evidence may be gathered from a computer is where an offence related to the use of computers, such as criminal damage, has been committed.[7] In fact, computers may contain evidence relevant to a variety of offences. In *R v Coutts*[8] the appellant was convicted of murder, it having been 'the prosecution(s) case that the appellant had deliberately murdered the victim in order to satisfy his macabre sexual fantasies, and that the murder was the manifestation of his long-standing sexual fixation for women who are helpless and being strangled.'[9] In support of its case the prosecution:

> 'called two computer experts to give evidence. Part of the evidence related to the two computers found in the appellant's flat. Records on the computers in the appellant's flat indicated that he had visited a number of pornographic websites at crucial times prior to and after the victim's death. A CD computer disk containing images of violence towards women ... was also found.
>
> A time-line of the appellant's internet usage compiled by one of the experts showed the particular websites he had accessed, and the search terms he had used. These included

---

5 Barrett, *Traces of Guilt* (Corgi Books, 2004), p 64.
6 *Admiral Management Services v Para-Protect Europe Ltd* [2002] EWHC 233 (Ch), [2002] 1 WLR 2722, [2002] EWHC 233 (Ch).
7 See C Davis, A Philipp & D Cowen, *Hacking Exposed, Computer Forensics Secrets and Solutions* (McGraw-Hill/ Osbourne, 2005).
8 *R v Coutts* (2005) 1 WLR 1605.
9 (2005) 1 WLR 1605 at 1607.

words such as 'rape', 'murder' and 'necro'. The websites visited by the appellant could be classified … as: 'genuine deceased appearance'; 'asphyxiation and strangulation'; 'rape torture and violent sex'; and 'general pornographic'. An expert gave evidence that many of the 'asphyxiation and strangulation' images did not appear to be consensual and that the women in these clips and images appeared more like victims.[10]'

The defence claimed that his victim had died in an accident; the Court of Appeal agreed with the trial judge that the evidence of the appellant's internet activities was admissible to rebut this defence.[11] Evidence derived from computer emails and mobile phones featured prominently in the case of *DPP v O'Reilly*;[12] evidence derived from mobile phones featured in the cases of *Murphy v DPP*[13] and also in *DPP v O'Donoghue*.[14] However, Irish law has so far failed to provide an explicit power to search and copy the contents of computer during investigations into offences other than those of theft and fraud.

Search warrants

[32.05] Searches of computers are not the same as searches of homes or businesses; a number of points of difference have been identified:

> 'First, home searches are conducted by physically entering and observing, while computer searches require passing an electric current over rotating magnetic points, processing the data, and then sending it to a monitor or other output device. Second, home searches occur at the suspect's residence, while computer searches typically occur offsite on a government computer that stores a copy of the suspect's hard drive. Third, home searches normally involve a limited amount of property, whereas computer searches involve entire virtual worlds of information. Fourth, unlike home searches, computer searches generally occur at both a physical and virtual level through the use of special programs designed to retrieve evidence.'[15]

Modern statutes that create criminal offences will normally empower the gardaí to apply to the District Court for a search warrant. For example the Criminal Damage Act 1991 provides that a Judge of the District Court may issue a search warrant where he is:

> 'satisfied by information on oath of a member of the Garda Síochána that there is reasonable cause to believe that any person has in his custody or under his control or on his premises any thing and that it has been used, or is intended for use, without lawful excuse—
>
> … to damage property belonging to another,
>
> … to damage any property in a way likely to endanger the life of another or with intent to defraud, or
>
> … to access, or with intent to access, data.'[16]

---

[10] (2005) 1 WLR 1605 at 1614.

[11] (2005) 1 WLR 1605 at 1627.

[12] Sheridan, 'Jury now decides after 20 days of evidence' (2007) The Irish Times, 21 July.

[13] *Murphy v Director of Public Prosecutions* [1989] ILRM 71.

[14] Roche, 'Accused phoned dead boy's mobile' (2005) The Irish Times, 9 December.

[15] Kerr, 'Searches and Seizures in a Digital World' Harvard Law Review, Vol 119, p 531 at 534.

[16] Criminal Damage Act 1991, s 13(1).

[32.06] Such a search warrant will be:

> 'expressed and operate to authorise a named member of the Garda Síochána, accompanied by such other members of the Garda Síochána as may be necessary, at any time or times within one month of the date of issue of the warrant, to enter if need be by force the premises named in the warrant, to search the premises and any persons found therein, to seize and detain anything which he believes to have been used or to be intended for use as aforesaid and, if the property concerned is data … to operate, or cause to be operated by a person accompanying him for that purpose, any equipment in the premises for processing data, inspect any data found there and extract information therefrom, whether by the operation of such equipment or otherwise.'[17]

Obstruction of such a search is a criminal offence punishable by 'a fine not exceeding £1,000 or imprisonment not exceeding 12 months or both.'[18] This power of search is defective in a number of aspects, it gives the gardaí power to operate computers on a premises. However, it does not give them a power to compel the disabling of security or encryption systems that may protect the contents of any such system. It also fails to give the gardaí an explicit power to copy the contents of a system. Best practice requires that the gardaí image the hard-drive of any such system, but doing so requires the copying of material both relevant and irrelevant to an investigation. It is not explicitly clear from the Criminal Damage Act 1991 that the gardaí have the power to undertake such copying. Such a power might be inferred from the grant of a power to operate any computer, but then again it might not, the decision made by a Court on such a point may ultimately depend on the facts of any particular case.

[32.07] Surprisingly, the Child Trafficking and Pornography Act 1998 and 2004 contains a power of entry, search and seizure that is least adapted to the search of computers. The Child Trafficking and Pornography Act 1997 provides for the issue of a warrant by a judge of the District Court 'on the sworn information of a member of the Garda Síochána not below the rank of sergeant.'[19] Such a warrant will authorise 'a named member of the Garda Síochána, alone or accompanied by such other members of the Garda Síochána and such other persons as may be necessary … to enter, within 7 days from the date of the warrant, and if necessary by the use of reasonable force, the place named in the warrant … to search it and any persons found there, and … to seize anything found there, or anything found in the possession of a person present there at the time of the search, which that member reasonably believes to be evidence of or relating to an offence.' Given that the Child Trafficking and Pornography Act 1997 is directed at images of child pornography stored on any 'tape, computer disk or other thing on which data … is stored'[20] it is surprising that the Act does not confer any specific power on gardaí to: operate a computer; copy the contents of a computer; compel a person to operate a computer to enable the gardaí gain access; or compel a person to give the

---

[17] Criminal Damage Act 1991, s 13(2).
[18] Criminal Damage Act 1991, s 13(4).
[19] Child Trafficking and Pornography Act 1998 and 2004, s 7(1).
[20] Child Trafficking and Pornography Act 1998 and 2004, s 2(1).

gardaí the information needed to either operate the computer or gain access to information held within the computer.[21]

[32.08] The Criminal Justice (Theft and Fraud Offences) Act 2001 contains a statutory power of search that is superior, in terms of its application to computer, to any power provided by any statute that pre- or post-dates it. This superiority probably reflects the reality that the computer crime unit of An Garda Síochána is part of the Garda Fraud Squad, and one may assume that the views of the Garda Fraud Squad were canvassed when drafting a statute that is primarily directed at fraud offences. The Criminal Justice (Theft and Fraud Offences) Act 2001 provides for the granting of a search warrant in respect to offences under the Criminal Justice (Theft and Fraud Offences) Act 2001: 'for which a person of full age and capacity and not previously convicted may be punished by imprisonment for a term of five years or by a more severe penalty and to an attempt to commit any such offence.'[22] The Criminal Justice (Theft and Fraud Offences) Act 2001 provides that:

> 'A judge of the District Court, on hearing evidence on oath given by a member of the Garda Síochána, may, if he or she is satisfied that there are reasonable grounds for suspecting that evidence of, or relating to the commission of, an offence ... is to be found in any place, issue a warrant for the search of that place and any persons found there.'[23]

Such warrant will 'authorise a named member of the Garda Síochána, alone or accompanied by such other persons as may be necessary ... to enter, within 7 days from the date of issuing of the warrant (if necessary by the use of reasonable force), the place named in the warrant ... to search it and any persons found there ... to examine, seize and retain any thing found there, or in the possession of a person present there at the time of the search, which the member reasonably believes to be evidence of or relating to the commission of an offence to which this section applies, and ... to take any other steps which may appear to the member to be necessary for preserving any such thing and preventing interference with it.'[24] The authority conferred by this provision 'to seize and retain any thing includes, in the case of a document or record, authority ... to make and retain a copy of the document or record, and ... where necessary, to seize and, for as long as necessary, retain any computer or other storage medium in which any record is kept.'[25] This gives the gardaí a general power to retain and copy computer data. Encryption and other security systems can effectively block a search of a computer; to deal with this potential problem the Criminal Justice (Theft and Fraud Offences) Act 2001 provides that:

> 'A member of the Garda(í) ... acting under the authority of a warrant under this section may ... operate any computer at the place which is being searched or cause any such computer to be operated by a person accompanying the member for that purpose, and ...

---

[21] M Ferraro & E Casey, 'Investigating child exploitation and pornography' (Elsevier Academic Press, 2005).

[22] Criminal Justice (Theft and Fraud Offences) Act 2001, s 48(1).

[23] Criminal Justice (Theft and Fraud Offences) Act 2001, s 48(2).

[24] Criminal Justice (Theft and Fraud Offences) Act 2001, s 48(3).

[25] Criminal Justice (Theft and Fraud Offences) Act 2001, s 48(4).

> ... require any person at that place who appears to the member to have lawful access to the information in any such computer—
>
>> 'to give to the member any password necessary to operate it,
>>
>> ... otherwise to enable the member to examine the information accessible by the computer in a form in which the information is visible and legible, or
>>
>> ... to produce the information in a form in which it can be removed and in which it is, or can be made, visible and legible.'[26]

[32.09] The gardaí are given a power to seize material, other than privileged material, that 'is likely to be of substantial value ... to the investigation for the purpose of which the warrant was issued.'[27] The Criminal Justice (Theft and Fraud Offences) Act 2001 contains a very broadly worded computer crime offence and to a great extent the power of search provided by this Act remedies the defects in the power of search provided by the Criminal Damage Act 1991. However, as its title suggests the Criminal Justice (Theft and Fraud Offences) Act 2001 is directed at offences of theft and fraud that cause a gain for one or a loss for another. As such it is unlikely that the superior powers of search and seizure of the Criminal Justice (Theft and Fraud Offences) Act 2001 could be utilised in an investigation into child pornography or an offence against the person such as murder.

[32.10] The Criminal Justice (Miscellaneous Provisions) Act 1997 confers a general power on the gardaí for a search warrant where an investigation is being taken into an 'arrestable offence.'[28] 'This power of search was amended by the Criminal Justice Act 2006 which provides that:

> 'If a judge of the District Court is satisfied by information on oath of a member not below the rank of sergeant that there are reasonable grounds for suspecting that evidence of, or relating to, the commission of an arrestable offence is to be found in any place, the judge may issue a warrant for the search of that place and any persons found at that place.'[29]

Such a warrant may authorise a named member of the gardaí, accompanied by such persons as he thinks necessary to do the following:

> 'to enter, at any time or times within one week of the date of issue of the warrant, on production if so requested of the warrant, and if necessary by the use of reasonable force, the place named in the warrant,
>
> ... to search it and any persons found at that place, and
>
> ... to seize anything found at that place, or anything found in the possession of a person present at that place at the time of the search, that that member reasonably

---

[26] Criminal Justice (Theft and Fraud Offences) Act 2001, s 48(5).

[27] Criminal Justice (Theft and Fraud Offences) Act 2001, s 48(6).

[28] An arrestable offence is defined as: 'an offence for which a person of full capacity and not previously convicted may, under or by virtue of any enactment or under the common law, be punished by imprisonment for a term of five years or by a more severe penalty and includes an attempt to commit any such offence' Criminal Law Act 1997, s 2(1) as amended by the Criminal Justice Act 2006, s 8.

[29] Criminal Justice (Miscellaneous Provisions) Act 1997, s 10(1) as amended by the Criminal Justice Act 2006, s 6.

believes to be evidence of, or relating to, the commission of an arrestable offence.'[30]

The gardaí will also have the power to arrest any person who obstructs their search,[31] obstruction is an offence punishable by 'on summary conviction to a fine not exceeding €3,000 or imprisonment for a term not exceeding 6 months or both.'[32] The Criminal Justice Act 2006 also provides a power to seize and retain evidence.[33]

[32.11] As noted above searches of computers are not the same as searches of homes or other premises. One key difference is that in a conventional search the gardaí will identify and seize certain items which the gardaí consider may relevant to their investigation. These items may be weapons or drugs, and after they are seized the gardaí may arrange for tests to be taken of those items to confirm or deny the suspicions of the gardaí. However the initial investigation will take place on the premises and may be witnessed by the suspect or his representatives. During a search the gardaí may identify and copy hard-drives and other computer storage devices. The actual investigation of that evidence will occur later out of sight of the suspect and any representatives. This may make investigations of computer evidence more invasive than other types of investigation. It remains to be seen how the Irish courts will treat such investigations. The Courts may follow the approach of the US Tenth Circuit which held in *United States v Carey*[34] that each file on a computer must be treated separately and may require a separate warrant to search. But the Irish Courts may prefer the approach of the US Fifth Circuit in *United States v Runyan*[35] which held that the hard-drive of a computer was a single unit, once one file had been opened legitimately, every file on the drive might be opened in succession.

Execution of 'remote' search warrants

[32.12] It is quite possible to use information technology to conduct searches 'remotely' that is over the Internet.[36] In the American case of *United States v Gorshkov*[37] FBI agents accessed the Internet account of a suspect and downloaded his files without obtaining a warrant. The US Courts concluded that this did not amount to the seizure of the data:

> 'because it did not interfere with defendant's or anyone else's possessory interest in the data. The data remained intact and unaltered. It remained accessible to defendant and any coconspirators or partners with whom he had shared access.'

---

[30] Criminal Justice (Miscellaneous Provisions) Act 1997, s 10(2) as amended by the Criminal Justice Act 2006, s 6.

[31] Criminal Justice (Miscellaneous Provisions) Act 1997, s 10(3)(b) as amended by the Criminal Justice Act 2006, s 6.

[32] Criminal Justice (Miscellaneous Provisions) Act 1997, s 10(4) as amended by the Criminal Justice Act 2006, s 6.

[33] Criminal Justice Act 2006, s 7.

[34] *United States v Carey* 172 F 3d 1268 (10th Cir 1999).

[35] *United States v Runyan* 275 F 3d 449 (5th Cir 2001).

[36] Zittrain 'Searches and Seizures in a Networked World' Harvard Law Review, Vol 119, No Forum, p. 83, 2006.

[37] *United States v Gorshkov* No CR00-550C, 2001 WL 1024026 (WD Wash May 23, 2001).

The possibility that the gardaí could undertake such remote searches is acknowledged by the Criminal Justice (Theft and Fraud Offences) Act 2001, which states that a search warrant issued under that Act will empower the gardaí to:

'operate any computer at the place which is being searched or cause any such computer to be operated by a person accompanying the member for that purpose.'[38]

The Act goes on to define "computer at the place which is being searched' as including: 'any other computer, whether at that place or at any other place, which is lawfully accessible by means of that computer'.[39] A warrant issued under the Criminal Justice (Theft and Fraud Offences) Act 2001 will authorise the gardaí to enter a premises, the Act does not specify that this has to be a physical entry. However, the Constitution provides that:

'The dwelling of every citizen is inviolable and shall not be forcibly entered save in accordance with law.[40]'

[32.13] Arguably a remote search of a persons dwelling, even a portion of that dwelling such as his computer, would have to be authorised by law. The Courts may not be willing to authorise remote searches unless those searches are specifically authorised by statute. Doubts about the legitimacy of remote searches were expressed by the US Supreme Court in *Kyllo v United States*[41] where the police suspected that the plaintiff was growing marijuana at his home. Growing marijuana in this way typically requires the use of high-intensity lamps, so the police used an infrared thermal imager sensor to 'determine whether an amount of heat was emanating from petitioner's home consistent with the use of such lamps'. The scan swiftly led the Police to conclude that the plaintiff 'was using halide lights to grow marijuana in his house' and they used the evidence gathered by the scan to get a search warrant for the plaintiff's home. The plaintiff unsuccessfully sought to suppress the evidence revealed in the resultant search, arguing that the scan was a breach of his right to privacy and ultimately his appeal reached the US Supreme Court. Justice Scalia, delivering the opinion of the Court, commented that:

'It would be foolish to contend that the degree of privacy secured to citizens ... has been entirely unaffected by the advance of technology. For example, as the cases discussed above make clear, the technology enabling human flight has exposed to public view (and hence, we have said, to official observation) uncovered portions of the house and its curtilage that once were private ... The question we confront today is what limits there are upon this power of technology to shrink the realm of guaranteed privacy'

The court accepted that the thermal sensor used in this case was 'relatively crude'. However, the court was more concerned about '... more sophisticated systems that are already in use or in development'. The court concluded that:

'Where, as here, the Government uses a device that is not in general public use, to explore details of the home that would previously have been unknowable without physical

---

38 Criminal Justice (Theft and Fraud Offences) Act 2001, s 48(5)(a).
39 Criminal Justice (Theft and Fraud Offences) Act 2001, s 48(8).
40 The Bunreacht na hÉireann, Art 40.5.
41 *Kyllo v United States* (99–8508) 533 US 27 (2001) 11 June 2001.

intrusion, the surveillance is a 'search' and is presumptively unreasonable without a warrant.'

Drafting such a statute that would withstand Constitutional review may not be easy. Remote searches bring with them the practical difficulty of serving the search warrant. If the courts will be slow to authorise remote searches then they may have a serious difficulty contemplating surreptitious searches.

Defeating encryption

[32.14] Other than 'wiping' the contents of a disk, encryption provides the only other 'true anti-forensic method (which) will defeat forensic analysis of data'.[42] Once a file has been encrypted then it may be useless to investigators:

> 'Encrypted files cannot be read at all; they appear as mere gibberish to forensic tools and cannot provide evidence for law enforcement.'[43]

Encryption has the obvious advantage over wiping in that it preserves the data in question, whilst ensuring that only the person who encrypted the data or anyone whom he told of the encryption key can use that data. If a strong enough encryption program is properly used then it should withstand any efforts to overcome it. That leaves investigators with limited options: one is to 'ask the suspect to supply the encryption key and the method by which he … encrypted the data.'[44] If the suspect refuses, investigators will have limited options. One option will arise where an investigation is being undertaken into an offence contrary to the Criminal Justice (Theft and Fraud Offences) Act 2001 which is punishable by a term of imprisonment of five years or more.[45] A member of the Garda Síochána may give evidence on oath before a Judge of the District Court to the effect that: the gardaí are investigating such an offence; 'a person has possession or control of particular material or material of a particular description' ; and, 'there are reasonable grounds for suspecting that the material constitutes evidence of or relating to the commission of the offence.' If this evidence satisfies the Judge then he may make an order to the effect that the person in question must:

(a) 'produce the material to a member of the Garda Síochána for the member to take away …

(b) … give such a member access to it.' [46]

A Judge of the District Court may subsequently vary or discharge this order.[47]

---

[42] Davis, Philipp & Cowen, *Hacking Exposed; Computer Forensics Secrets & Solutions* (McGraw Hill Osbourne, 2005), p 175.

[43] Kerr, 'Searches and Seizures in a Digital World' Harvard Law Review, Vol 119, p 531 at 546

[44] Davis, Philipp & Cowen, *Hacking Exposed; Computer Forensics Secrets & Solutions* (McGraw Hill Osbourne, 2005, p 180).

[45] Criminal Justice (Theft and Fraud Offences) Act 2001, s 52(1).

[46] Criminal Justice (Theft and Fraud Offences) Act 2001, s 52(2).

[47] Criminal Justice (Theft and Fraud Offences) Act 2001, s 52(7).

Where the material in question 'consists of or includes information contained in a computer' then the Judge's order may:

> 'effect as an order to produce the information, or to give access to it, in a form in which it is visible and legible and in which it can be taken away.'[48]

[32.15] The order cannot be read as conferring 'any right to production of, or access to, any document subject to legal privilege.' It will 'have effect notwithstanding any other obligation as to secrecy or other restriction on disclosure of information imposed by statute or otherwise'. Where such an order empowers the gardaí to take away a document or be given access to it, then the order will empower the gardaí to both copy a document and take a copy of a document away.[49] Where material is taken away by a member of the gardaí, then it 'may be retained by the member for use as evidence in any criminal proceedings.'[50]

[32.16] The information contained in any document produced to a member of the gardaí or to which a member was given access will be admissible as evidence in criminal proceedings, unless the information is privileged, supplied by a person who would not be compellable as a witness or 'was compiled for the purposes or in contemplation of any … criminal investigation … investigation or inquiry carried out pursuant to or under any enactment … civil or criminal proceedings, or … proceedings of a disciplinary nature or the procedural aspects of the provision were not complied with.[51] Failure to comply with such an order will be an offence, punishable by a fine not exceeding £1,500 (€1,904) or imprisonment for a term not exceeding 12 months or both.[52]

[32.17] Other Acts provide powers to order the production of material in specific circumstances, for example, the Criminal Justice Act 1994 provides a power whereby the gardaí may apply to the District Court for an order directing that a person produce to the gardaí or provide them with access to relevant materials.[53] However this provision will only apply where persons are being investigated for drugs trafficking or money laundering offences[54]

If a provision such as this or that provided by the Criminal Justice (Theft and Fraud Offences) Act 2001 does not apply then the gardaí may find it difficult to acquire the information in question. Any person asked to supply such a decryption key may invoke their privilege against self-incrimination. Decrypting such information may pose a considerable technical challenge, but even if such a challenge can be overcome, the Electronic Commerce Act 2000 may not be. The Electronic Commerce Act 2000

---

48 Criminal Justice (Theft and Fraud Offences) Act 2001, s 52(3).
49 Criminal Justice (Theft and Fraud Offences) Act 2001, s 52(4).
50 Criminal Justice (Theft and Fraud Offences) Act 2001, s 52(5).
51 Criminal Justice (Theft and Fraud Offences) Act 2001, s 52(6).
52 Criminal Justice (Theft and Fraud Offences) Act 2001, s 52(8).
53 Criminal Justice Act 1994, s 63(1).
54 Criminal Justice Act 1994, s 63(2).

provides legal protection for electronic signatures. It defines an electronic signature as meaning:

'data in electronic[55] form attached to, incorporated in or logically associated with other electronic data and which serves as a method of authenticating the purported originator, and includes an advanced electronic signature.'[56]

[32.18] The Electronic Commerce Act 2000 provides that an offence will be committed by a person or public body which:

'knowingly accesses, copies or otherwise obtains possession of, or recreates, the signature creation device of another person or a public body, without the authorisation of that other person or public body, for the purpose of creating or allowing, or causing another person or public body to create, an unauthorised electronic signature using the signature creation device.'[57]

Electronic signatures come in a variety of formats, some such signatures will also encrypt the document that they are used to sign.[58] Decrypting that document may involve recreating the signature, this may be an offence if not authorised by the person who created the initial signature. The Electronic Commerce Act 2000 will not protect every type of encryption program, but it creates an incentive for those who want to keep their data secret from the gardaí or other authority to use a signature creation device that will.

[32.19] It should be noted that the privilege against self-incrimination was recognised as a Constitutional right by the Supreme Court in *Heaney v Ireland*.[59] Where a statue purports to abrogate this right the Courts will consider whether that provision: 'is proportionate to the objects to be achieved by the legislation.'[60] But where there is no statutory obligation upon a suspect to provide a password or encryption key to the gardaí it would seem that he may invoke his privilege against self-incrimination and refuse to supply the information.

The duty to preserve evidence

[32.20] As noted above the Criminal Justice (Theft and Fraud Offences) Act 2001 gives gardaí a power to 'make and retain a copy of the document or record, and ... where necessary, to seize and, for as long as necessary, retain any computer or other storage medium in which any record is kept.'[61] There seems to be no question that the gardaí are

---

[55] The Electronic Commerce Act 2000 defines 'electronic' as including '... electrical, digital, magnetic, optical, electro-magnetic, biometric, photonic and any other form of related technology', s 2(1).
[56] Electronic Commerce Act 2000, s 2(1).
[57] Electronic Commerce Act 2000, s 25(a).
[58] Philip J Windley, Digital Identity, O'Reilly Media. See Chapter 6, public key cryptography at 36.
[59] *Heaney v Ireland* [1996] 1 IR 580. See also *Re National Irish Bank Ltd (No 1)* [1999] 3 IR 145 and Article 6 of the European Convention on Human Rights, see *Murray v United Kingdom* (1996) 22 EHRR 29 and *Quinn v O'Leary* [2004] 3 IR 128.
[60] [1996] 1 IR 580 at 589.
[61] Criminal Justice (Theft and Fraud Offences) Act 2001, s 48(4).

under a duty to preserve evidence and make that evidence available to the accused should the need arise. In *Murphy v DPP*[62] the accused was charged with driving a stolen car, his solicitor sought to have the car inspected for finger-print evidence. However, the gardaí parted with possession of the car before the accused's solicitor could do so. Lynch J reviewed the authorities and concluded that:

> 'the applicant has been deprived of the reasonable possibility of rebutting the evidence proffered against him. It is also clear that there is no way in which this loss to the applicant of possibly corroborative evidence, can now be remedied by any further inspection of the car ... evidence relevant to guilt or innocence must so far as is necessary and practicable be kept until the conclusion of the trial. These authorities also apply to the preservation of articles which may give rise to the reasonable possibility of securing relevant evidence.'[63]

[32.21] Hardiman J concurred with this judgment in *Braddish v DPP*.[64] In this case a prosecution was brought following the robbery of a shop which was 'protected by video surveillance' As part of the investigation that followed a member of An Garda Síochána:

> 'viewed the video tape. He believed that the video tape showed the robbery in progress and that the applicant was the person shown committing it.'[65]

The accused's solicitor sought access to the video tape in question, but An Garda Síochána had parted with possession of it. The accused appealed from the trial of these charges, and his appeal reached the Supreme Court, where Hardiman J noted that:

> 'It is well established that evidence relevant to guilt or innocence must, so far as necessary and practicable, be kept until the conclusion of a trial. This principle also applies to the preservation of articles which may give rise to the reasonable possibility of securing relevant evidence.'[66]

[32.22] In *Braddish v DPP* the accused had also confessed to the robbery in question. The prosecution therefore responded to the accused's request for the video tape, that they were not relying on the tape but rather upon the confession. This argument was rejected by Hardiman J who held that:

> 'this is a video tape which purports actually to show the robbery in progress. It is not acceptable, in my view, to excuse the absence of so vital and direct a piece of evidence simply by saying that the prosecution are not relying on it ...
>
> This video tape was real evidence and the gardaí were not entitled to dispose of it before the trial. It is now admitted that they should not have done so ... It is the duty of the gardaí, arising from their unique investigative role, to seek out and preserve all evidence having a bearing or potential bearing on the issue of guilt or innocence. This is so whether the prosecution proposes to rely on the evidence or not, and regardless of whether it assists the case the prosecution is advancing or not.'[67]

---

[62] *Murphy v Director of Public Prosecutions* [1989] ILRM 71.
[63] [1989] ILRM 71 at 76.
[64] *Braddish v DPP* [2001] 3 IR 127.
[65] [2001] 3 IR 127 at 129.
[66] [2001] 3 IR 127 at 131
[67] [2001] 3 IR 127 at 132–133.

Hardiman J pointed out that it clear that this rule would apply not just to items 'with a direct and established evidential significance' but also to those that 'may give rise to the reasonable possibility of securing relevant evidence.'[68] Hardiman J cited the judgment of Kenny J in *Sterling-Winthrop Group Ltd v Farben-Fabriken Bayer AG*[69] *in support of his view that the obligation to preserve extended to* 'material with the capacity to damage the case of an adversary'. Hardiman J went on to state that:

'a member of the Garda Síochána is not entitled to dispose of evidence, or omit to disclose it, simply because he personally has formed the view that it will not be helpful.'[70]

Imaging of hard-drives

[32.23] Gathering evidence from computers is notoriously difficult as the process itself '... may modify the source data or its related meta-data, fatally undermining the evidential value of the forensic material.'[71] To overcome this problem it is now best practice for investigators to initially duplicate the entire contents of the hard-drive, a process known as mirroring or imaging:

'Imaging involves the acquisition and creation of a complete bitstream image of the digital media, such as a hard drive or smart card, in a non-invasive manner and including those areas which are not occupied by data elements. The imaging process by itself will ... generate data ... that may be required at a later stage to verify the authenticity and integrity of the acquisition process and any subsequent copies. A number of copies of the image are generally created, a master copy for evidential purposes, a copy on which the analysis is carried out, and a third that is provided to the suspect for his own verification and analysis purposes. The images are widely accepted as an accurate representation of the original digital media, and the use of such images never appears to have been successfully challenged before the UK courts.'[72]

[32.24] In general the imaging of a hard-drive would not appear to be an overly complicated process, in *Admiral Management Services v Para-Protect Europe Ltd*[73] the parties were themselves computer forensics experts. In a costs application subsequent to the main action Burton J heard evidence that the imaging of a hard disk was a 'straightforward' task:

'The task of imaging was a mundane one which could have been performed by one junior employee. The process of imaging a computer requires a few minutes to configure the imaging computer and hook it to the computer to be imaged. After this set-up, the sole activity consists of sitting there patiently and waiting while the copy is made. Indeed, it is not even necessary to wait: you can go away and come back later when the imaging has been completed.'[74]

---

[68] [2001] 3 IR 127 at 133 citing Lynch J in *Murphy v Director of Public Prosecutions* [1989] ILRM 71 at 76.

[69] *Sterling-Winthrop Group Ltd. v Farben-Fabriken Bayer AG* [1967] IR 97.

[70] [2001] 3 IR 127 at 134.

[71] Walden, para 4.18, p 207.

[72] Walden, para 4.42, p 213

[73] *Admiral Management Services v Para-Protect Europe Ltd* [2002] EWHC 233 (Ch), [2002] 1 WLR 2722, [2002] EWHC 233 (Ch).

[74] [2002] EWHC 233 (Ch), [2002] 1 WLR 2722, [2002] EWHC 233 (Ch) para 42.

But the imaging of a hard-drive means that any evidence derived from that image will not be based upon the original hard-drive but rather on a copy of that drive. This would not seem to create a problem. The Criminal Evidence Act 1992 allows for the admission of copies of evidence, providing that:

> 'Where evidence contained in a document is admissible in evidence in criminal proceedings, the information may be given in evidence, whether or not the document was still in existence, by producing a copy of the document, or of the material part of it, authenticated in such manner as the Court may approve.'[75]

[32.25] The Criminal Evidence Act 1992 goes on to provide that it 'is immaterial … how many removes there are between the copy and the original, or by what means … the copy produced or any intermediate copy was made'. The application of this provision was examined by the Supreme Court in *McFarlane v DPP*.[76] The facts were that in 1998 the accused was arrested in relation to the notorious kidnapping of Don Tidy in 1983. At that time a number of items had been recovered from where Mr. Tidy was being held, namely a milk carton, a plastic container and a cooking pot, on which the accused's fingerprints were found. These items were then lost by the gardaí, but photographs of the fingerprints were retained. The accused claimed that as a result of the loss of these items:

> 'the applicant is not in a position to comprehensively independently evaluate the alleged physical evidence in this case.'

[32.26] However, the gardaí were able to establish 'a chain of evidence covering the identification of the fingerprints on the items, the photographing of the fingerprints on the items and the preservation of the photographs.' As a result the Supreme Court held that the photographs of the applicant's fingerprints could be used, even though the originals were missing. The Court cited *Z v DPP*[77]:

> '[The] onus of proof which is on an accused person who seeks an order prohibiting his trial on the ground that circumstances have occurred which would render it unfair is that he should establish that there is a real risk that by reason of those circumstances … he could not obtain a fair trial.[78]'

The Supreme Court noted that as regards establishing a risk, the applicant did not have to discharge:

> 'a burdensome onus of proof: what is in question, after all, is the demonstration of a real risk, as opposed to an established certainty, or even probability of an unfair trial.'

It would appear from *McFarlane v DPP*, that where the gardaí cannot preserve primary evidence then they are under an obligation to preserve a copy of that evidence:

> 'the gardaí have been in breach of their duty to preserve the evidence, but … this breach has not resulted in the loss of that evidence in an independently verifiable form'.

---

75 Criminal Evidence Act 1992, s 30(1).
76 *McFarland v DPP* [2006] IESC 11.
77 *Z v DPP* [1994] 2 IR 476.
78 [1994] 2 IR 476 at 506.

[32.27] Evidence held on the image of a hard-drive is different from the photographs that were at issue in *McFarlane v DPP* in one aspect. The Supreme Court cited the distinction between primary and secondary evidence set out in Cross on *Evidence:*

> ' 'Primary evidence' is that which does not, by its very nature, suggest that better evidence may be available; 'secondary evidence' is that which, by its very nature does suggest that better evidence may be available. The original of a document is primary evidence, a copy secondary evidence, of its contents.'[79]

Provided that it is properly preserved the master copy of the image of a hard-drive may well be regarded as the best possible evidence of what was on a hard-drive at a particular time; superior even to the original hard-drive. This is because the master-copy should have been preserved which is focused solely upon ensuring that the stability of the master-copy.

Admissibility – Criminal Evidence Act 1992

[32.28] The admission of information that is electronically stored may be governed by the Criminal Evidence Act 1992. This Act provides for the admissibility of documentary evidence, the Act defines a document as including:

> 'a map, plan, graph, drawing or photograph, or ... a reproduction in permanent legible form, by a computer or other means (including enlarging), of information in non-legible form.'

The Act goes on to define 'information' as including: ' any representation of fact, whether in words or otherwise'. The Act defines 'information in non-legible form' as including 'information on microfilm, microfiche, magnetic tape or disk.'[80] Given the broad nature of these definitions there would not seem to be any question that the Criminal Evidence Act 1992 applies to information or data that is stored on a computer or a computer disk such as a CD or DVD. The technological neutrality of this provision may be questioned however; for example the definition does not specifically mention 'flash memory' devices, which are certainly not disk shaped and do not use magnetic tape to store date. These were being marketed at the time of the Acts enactment.[81] Instead of magnetic tapes or disks, flash memory relies upon Dynamic Random Access Memory (DRAMs) and Electrically Programmable Read Only Memories (EPROM) chips. Whether any significance may be attached to the failure of the Criminal Evidence Act 1992 to refer to storage media other than photographic films or fiches and magnetic tapes or disks remains to be seen.

---

[79] Cross on *Evidence,* 5th Edition at page 15.
[80] Criminal Evidence Act 1992, s 2(1).
[81] 'Intel's 'flash memory' chips will play a key role in making lightweight portable computers possible, the company claims ... The flash memory provides a semiconductor alternative to the floppy disk drive as a medium for data storage, Intel claims. The chips are smaller, lighter, and less fragile than a disk drive.' Kehoe, 'PC separates to mix and match' (1990) The Financial Times, 22 March.

[32.29] The Criminal Evidence Act 1992 provides for the admission of the information contained in a document into evidence, the Act provides that:

> 'information contained in a document shall be admissible in any criminal proceedings as evidence of any fact therein of which direct oral evidence would be admissible if the information ...
>
>> ... was compiled in the ordinary course of a business,[82]
>>
>> ... was supplied by a person (whether or not he so compiled it and is identifiable) who had, or may reasonably be supposed to have had, personal knowledge of the matters dealt with, and
>>
>> ... in the case of information in non-legible form that has been reproduced in permanent legible form, was reproduced in the course of the normal operation of the reproduction system concerned.'[83]

[32.30] The application of this provision to phone records was reviewed by the Court of Criminal Appeal in *DPP v Murphy*.[84] The facts were that the appellant had been convicted of conspiracy to cause an explosion, namely the Omagh bombing of 1998. The accused had given two mobile phones to another person, evidence of phone records was produced at trial showing that those two phones had been in the vicinity of Omagh on the day of the bombing. The appellant was convicted and appealed. His conviction was overturned on appeal, but the Court of Criminal Appeal ruled that the phone records in question had been properly admitted into evidence. The Court noted that in the English case of *R. v Wood* [85] Lord Land CJ had stated that:

> 'Witnesses and especially expert witnesses frequently and properly give factual evidence of the results of a physical exercise which involves the use of some equipment, device or machine. Take a weighing machine; the witness steps on the machine and reads a weight of the dial, receives a ticket printed with the weight, or even hears a recorded voice saying it. None of this involves hearsay evidence. The witness may have to be cross-examined as to whether he kept one foot on the ground; the accuracy of the machine may have to be investigated. But this does not alter the character of the evidence which is being given.'[86]

[32.31] The Court of Criminal Appeal noted that in that case the English Court of Appeal had held that evidence was properly allowed of computer results, specifically those provided by a computer that was 'used as a calculator, a tool which did not contribute to its own knowledge but merely carried out a sophisticated calculation which could not have been done manually.'[87]

---

[82] The Criminal Evidence Act 1992 defines 'business' including: 'any trade, profession or other occupation carried on, for reward or otherwise, either within or outside the State and includes also the performance of functions by or on behalf of ... any person or body remunerated or financed wholly or partly out of moneys provided by the Oireachtas, ... any institution of the European Communities, ... any national or local authority in a jurisdiction outside the State, or ... any international organisation' Criminal Evidence Act 1992, s 4.

[83] Criminal Evidence Act 1992, s 5(1).

[84] *DPP v Murphy* [2005] 2 IR 125.

[85] *R v Wood* (1982) 76 Cr App R 23.

[86] (1982) 76 Cr App R 23 at 26.

[87] [2005] 2 IR 125 at 152.

The Court of Criminal Appeal noted that:

> 'Lord Lane CJ was ... of the opinion that the computer printout was not hearsay, but was more properly to be treated as a piece of real evidence, the actual proof and relevance of which depended upon the evidence of others.'[88]

The Court of Criminal Appeal went on to refer to the cases of *Castle v Cross*[89] in which the English Court had 'held that intoximeter evidence was admissible on the basis that it was a tool, albeit a sophisticated one, and that in the absence of any evidence that it was defective, the printout, the product of a mechanical device, fell into the category of real evidence.'[90] Having reviewed these cases the Court of Criminal Appeal expressed the view that:

> 'these principles apply, not only where the device in question processes information supplied to it ... but also where the device itself gathers information.'

[32.32] The Court of Criminal Appeal cited *R v Spiby*[91] in support of this view, in which:

> 'the printout from a computerised machine was used to monitor telephone calls. It automatically recorded information such as the numbers to which the calls were made and the duration of the calls. This was admitted as real evidence. It was held that where information is recorded by mechanical means without the intervention of the human mind the record made by the machine is admissible.'

[32.33] Finally, the Court of Criminal Appeal cited the decision of the House of Lords in *R v The Governor of Brixton Prison, ex p Levin.*[92] The Court of Criminal Appeal analysed the judgment of the House in the following terms:

> 'At issue there was whether the accused had used a computer terminal to gain unauthorised access to the computerised fund transfer services of a bank in order to make fraudulent transfers of funds from accounts of clients of the bank to accounts which he controlled. Each request for a transfer was processed automatically and a record of the transaction was copied to the computer's historical records. The House of Lords held that the printout of screen displays of these records was admissible to prove the transfers of funds they recorded.'

In particular, the Court of Criminal Appeal noted the following statement of Templeman J in respect of these screen displays:

> 'They do not assert that such transfers took place. They record the transfers ... [t]he evidential status of the printouts is no different from that of a photocopy of a forged cheque.'[93]

---

88   [2005] 2 IR 125 at 152–153.
89   *Castle v Cross* [1984] 1 WLR 1372.
90   [2005] 2 IR 125 at 153.
91   *R v Spiby* (1990) 91 Cr App R 186.
92   *R v The Governor of Brixton Prison, Ex p Levin* [1997] AC 741.
93   [1997] AC 741 at 746.

[32.34] The Court of Criminal Appeal concluded its analysis of the authorities by noting that they would have to be read in the light of *R v Cochrane*[94]:

> 'in which it was held ... that before the judge can decide whether computer printouts are admissible, whether as real evidence or as hearsay, it is necessary to call appropriate authoritative evidence to describe the function and operation of the computer.'[95]

The Court of Criminal Appeal went on to decide: 'that the objections made to the admissibility of telephone records in this case are ill-founded.'[96] In *R (O) v Coventry Magistrates Court*[97] it was held that a computer printout recording successful and unsuccessful attempts to enter a website was admissible as real evidence.

[32.35] Whatever system the information is stored upon, it would seem that an accused person may have a right to inspect that system, or have an expert do so. In *Whelan v Kirby*[98] charges of driving whilst intoxicated were brought against the accused. The charges were based upon a reading taken by an intoximeter and the accused sought to have this machine examined by an expert.[99] The Supreme Court agreed that the accused' ... had an arguable case that an inspection was reasonable given the relative novelty of the machine in particular and the fact that for all practical purposes he could be convicted on the say so of a printout.'[100]

[32.36] Evidence will be admissible pursuant to the Criminal Evidence Act 1992 regardless of whether the information in question was supplied 'directly or indirectly'. However, if the information was supplied indirectly, then the above will only apply 'if each person (whether or not he is identifiable) through whom it was supplied received it in the ordinary course of a business.'[101] On the other hand the above will not apply to information that falls into one of the following categories:

> 'information that is privileged from disclosure in criminal proceedings,
>
> ... information supplied by a person who would not be compellable to give evidence at the instance of the party wishing to give the information in evidence by virtue of this section, or
>
> ... information compiled for the purposes or in contemplation of any ... criminal investigation, ... investigation or inquiry carried out pursuant to or under any enactment, ... civil or criminal proceedings, or ... proceedings of a disciplinary nature.'[102]

---

[94] *R v Cochrane* (1993) Crim LR 48.
[95] [2005] 2 IR 125 at 153.
[96] [2005] 2 IR 125 at 153–156.
[97] R (O) v Coventry Magistrates Court, Times Law Reports, 22 April 2004
[98] *Whelan v Kirby* [2005] 2 IR 30.
[99] Expert evidence about the functioning of intoximeter was given to the High Court in *McGonnell v AG and DPP* 16/09/2004 2002, McKechnie J held at para 77 that 'the plaintiffs have failed to demonstrate that the apparatus in question is in any way flawed or incapable of complying with design standards.'
[100] [2005] 2 IR 30 at 42.
[101] Criminal Evidence Act 1992, s 5(2).
[102] Criminal Evidence Act 1992, s 5(3). (contd/)

Where admissible information in question is 'is expressed in terms that are not intelligible to the average person without explanation' then that explanation will also 'be admissible in evidence if either ... it is given orally by a person who is competent to do so, or ... it is contained in a document and the document purports to be signed by such a person.'[103]

Certificates

[32.37] A party to criminal proceedings who wishes to give information contained in a document may give a certificate. Such a certificate may purport 'to be signed by a person who occupies a position in relation to the management of the business in the course of which the information was compiled or who is otherwise in a position to give the certificate.' This certificate shall be evidence of any matter stated or specified therein. Such a certificate may state:

(a)   'that the information was compiled in the ordinary course of a specified business ...

(b)   that the information is not subject to privilege or taken from an non-compellable witness ...

(c)   ... that the information was not compiled for the purposes or in contemplation of any investigation, inquiry or proceedings ...' or if it was compiled for that purpose, specifying which provision of the Criminal Evidence Act 1992 would enable it to be admitted into evidence.

(d)   ... that the information was supplied, either directly or, as the case may be, indirectly through an intermediary or intermediaries (who, or each of whom, received it in the ordinary course of a specified business), by a person who had, or may reasonably be supposed to have had, personal knowledge of the matters dealt with in the information and, where the intermediary, intermediaries or person can be identified, specifying them ...

(e)   That a '... reproduction was effected in the course of the normal operation of a specified system ...' where the information was '... information in non-legible form that has been reproduced in permanent legible form, stating that the reproduction was effected in the course of the normal operation of a specified system ...

(f)   ... that the person who supplied the information cannot reasonably be expected to have any, or any adequate, recollection of the matters dealt with in the

---

[102] (\contd) This will not apply where the information question is a deposition given before a District Court judge in certain circumstances, or the 'document containing the information is ... a map, plan, drawing or photograph (including any explanatory material in or accompanying the document concerned), ... a record of a direction given by a member of the Garda Síochána pursuant to any enactment,...a record of the receipt, handling, transmission, examination or analysis of any thing by any person acting on behalf of any party to the proceedings, or ... a record by a registered medical practitioner of an examination of a living or dead person' Criminal Evidence Act 1992, s 5(4).

[103] Criminal Evidence Act 1992, s 5(6).

information, having regard to the time that has elapsed since he supplied it or to any other specified circumstances,

(g)   ... the date (or, if that date is not known, the approximate date) on which it was compiled ...' unless that date or approximate date was '... already shown on the document ...

(h)   ... any other matter that is relevant to the admissibility in evidence of the information and is required by rules of court to be certified.'[104]

[32.38] It is 'sufficient for a matter to be stated or specified to the best of the knowledge and belief of the person stating or specifying it.'[105] Just because a certificate is given does not mean that a court cannot 'require oral evidence to be given of any matter stated or specified in the certificate.[106] In *Re The Employment Equality Bill 1996*[107] the Supreme Court stated that:

> 'Proof by way of certification is an interference with the norm of a trial viva voce. A certificate is an appropriate form of proof when it is proportionate to the ends to be achieved. It is a justifiable method of proof when the process is, for example, of a technical nature and there are other issues before the court.'[108]

[32.39] A considerable body of jurisprudence has been developed by the Irish Courts in relation to the certification of evidence from intoximeters and other machines designed to measure the amount of alcohol in the body of a person accused of driving whilst intoxicated. Intoximeters are essentially computers specifically designed to measure alcohol levels. The Road Traffic Acts have quite specific provisions on the admission of evidence derived from such machines. Such decisions should not be regarded as automatically applicable to the admission of evidence pursuant to the Criminal Evidence Act 1992. However, these cases provide principles that may be applied to the admission of evidence under the Criminal Evidence Act 1992. In *Director of Public Prosecutions (O'Reilly) v Barnes*[109] the defendant was accused of driving whilst intoxicated. O'Neill J reviewed the authorities and concluded that it was:

> 'clear from the long line of authorities that has evolved that there are two guiding principles which must inform decisions as to the admissibility into evidence of certificates or statements which are admitted into evidence by virtue of statutory provision and in the absence of contradictory evidence prove their content.'[110]

O'Neil J identified the first such principle in the following passage from the dissenting judgment of O'Higgins CJ in *Director of Public Prosecutions v Kemmy*[111]:

> 'Where a statute provides for a particular form of proof or evidence on compliance with certain provisions, in my view it is essential that the precise statutory provisions be

---

[104] Criminal Evidence Act 1992, s 6(1).
[105] Criminal Evidence Act 1992, s 6(2).
[106] Criminal Evidence Act 1992, s 6(3).
[107] *Re The Employment Equality Bill 1996* [1997] 2 IR 321.
[108] [1997] 2 IR 321 at 382–383.
[109] *Director of Public Prosecutions (O'Reilly) v Barnes* [2005] 4 IR 176.
[110] [2005] 4 IR 176.
[111] *Director of Public Prosecutions v Kemmy* [1980] IR 160.

complied with. The courts cannot accept something other than that which is laid down by the statute, or overlook the absence of what the statute requires. To do so would be to trespass into the legislative field. This applies to all statutory requirements; but it applies with greater general understanding to penal statutes which create particular offences and then provide a particular method for their proof.'[112]

[32.40] O'Neill J identified the second principle as being set out in the following passage from the judgment of O'Flaherty J in *Director of Public Prosecutions v Somers*:[113]

'what happened here was that the doctor made a technical slip by not filling out the second paragraph of the prescribed form ... If courts were to allow such flimsy points as this to govern cases, the administration of justice would most likely be brought into disrepute.

It is true that in general the law expects strict compliance with the wording of statutes, especially in a penal context. But this is so that the purposes and objects of the legislation are observed. It is impossible to seek perfection at all stages of life and when there is a tiny flaw in the filling out of a document such as this, which flaw is of no significance and cannot possibly work any injustice to an accused and is not in discord with the purposes and objects of the legislation, then the courts are required to say that such a slip, as we have here, cannot be allowed bring about what would be a manifest injustice as far as the prosecution of this offence is concerned.'[114]

[32.41] O'Neill J noted that Baron J and Lynch J had agreed with the above statement, Baron J had gone on to note that:

'The essence of the criminal law is certainty as to that law. So everyone must know with certainty what conduct will amount to a criminal offence. If the accused is convicted, he must know with certainty of what he has been convicted and the exact nature of his punishment.

It follows that statutes within the criminal law field must be construed strictly to ensure that these aims are achieved. What has to be construed here are provisions to ensure that there will be certainty as to what has been done leading to a prosecution. The accused person is entitled to know at his trial that everything that should have been done had been done. There must be no room for doubt.'[115]

[32.42] Applying these principles to the case before him, O'Neill J. held that:

'A court ... must approach the matter on the basis of being satisfied that there has been a strict compliance with the relevant statutory provision before admitting the statement into evidence against an accused ...

On the other hand where objection has been taken to the statement on the basis of an error in it, if the error is of such an obvious or trivial or inconsequential nature so that it could not be said that it gave rise to any confusion or misleading of the accused or imposed any prejudice on him or in any way exposed him to any injustice, then the court should conclude that the error in question did not detract from the due completion of the

---

[112] [1980] IR 160 at 164.
[113] *Director of Public Prosecutions v Somers* [1999] 1 IR 115 at 119.
[114] [1999] 1 IR 115 at p. 119.
[115] [1999] 1 IR 115 at p. 120.

statement in question and it should be admitted and permitted the force and effect provided for by ... (statute).'[116]

[32.43] This led O'Neill J. to the conclusion that:

'what has to be decided ... is whether the error that was made is one which was plain or palpable or clear and which did not mislead or confuse or cause prejudice or injustice to the accused bearing in mind that ... the accused is entitled to certainty as to the nature of the offence and the nature of the evidence with which he is confronted.'[117]

In this case, a Garda admitted that 'he had in error typed into the intoxilyzer machine the wrong offence.'[118] O'Neill J applied the principles set out above and came to:

'the conclusion that the error which was made in this case does not detract from the due completion of the statement in question ... it does not seem to me to have been possible that the accused was confused let alone misled as to the particular offence for which the specimen was taken. It would appear to me that a suggestion that there was any lack of certainty in the circumstances of this case as to the particular ... is simply unreal and not credible. I am quite satisfied that the error in question did not and indeed could not have imposed any prejudice on the accused or exposed him to any risk of injustice.'

Therefore O'Neill J ruled that a 'typographical error in the ... certificate is not fatal to the successful prosecution of the accused.'[119] A person who makes a statement in such a certificate that 'he knows to be false or does not believe to be true, he shall be guilty of an offence and shall be liable ... on summary conviction, to a fine not exceeding £500 (€635) or imprisonment for a term not exceeding 6 months or both, or ... on conviction on indictment, to a fine or imprisonment for a term not exceeding 2 years or both.'[120]

Procedure

[32.44] The Criminal Evidence Act 1992 sets out the procedures which must be complied with if information in a document is to be admissible in evidence at a trial.[121] The following documents must be served:

(a)   The document containing the information together with any certificate must have been served on the accused.

(b)   Alternatively, the party proposing to give the information in evidence must have served the following documents on the other parties to the proceedings not later that 21 days before the trial:

   (i)   a notice of intention so to give the information in evidence,

   (ii) a copy of the document,

   (iii) a copy of any certificate that is to be given.

---

[116] [2005] 4 IR 176 at p. 181–182.
[117] [2005] 4 IR 176 at p. 182.
[118] [2005] 4 IR 176 at p. 179.
[119] [2005] 4 IR 176 at p. 182.
[120] Criminal Evidence Act 1992, s 6(4).
[121] The Criminal Evidence Act 1992 leaves open the possibility that a court might grant leave to admit information that did not comply with the above, s 7(1).

Once all the above have been served on all the parties, they may consider whether they wish to object to the admissibility of the information contained in the documents. If a party decides to object to the admissibility of a document then they must serve[122] notice of their intention to do so 'not later than 7 days before the commencement of the trial.'[123]

Admission and weight of documentary evidence

[32.45] Ultimately the decision as to whether documentary evidence should be admitted is one for the individual Court. The Criminal Evidence Act 1992 makes this explicitly clear, providing that:

> ' in any criminal proceedings information ... that is admissible in evidence by virtue of (the *Criminal Evidence Act* 1992) ... shall not be admitted if the court is of opinion that in the interests of justice the information or that part ought not to be admitted.'[124]

[32.46] In considering whether such evidence should be admitted then 'the court shall have regard to all the circumstances.' These circumstances may include:

(a)   'whether or not, having regard to the contents and source of the information and the circumstances in which it was compiled, it is a reasonable inference that the information is reliable ...

(b)   ... whether or not, having regard to the nature and source of the document containing the information and to any other circumstances that appear to the court to be relevant, it is a reasonable inference that the document is authentic ...

(c)   ... any risk, having regard in particular to whether it is likely to be possible to controvert the information where the person who supplied it does not attend to give oral evidence in the proceedings, that its admission or exclusion will result in unfairness to the accused or, if there is more than one, to any of them.'[125]

The court will have to estimate the weight to be attached to information that may be given in evidence. Of course the court may decide not to attach any weight at all. In making that estimate 'regard shall be had to all the circumstances from which any inference can reasonably be drawn as to its accuracy or otherwise.'[126]

Credibility of supplier

[32.47] Where information contained in a document is given in evidence pursuant to the Criminal Evidence Act 1992, the following provisions will apply:

(a)   'any evidence which, if the person who originally supplied the information had been called as a witness, would have been admissible as relevant to his credibility as a witness shall be admissible for that purpose ...'

---

[122] Documents may be served in a variety of ways, including delivering it in person to the accused or his solicitor, leaving at the accused's home or place of business or that of his solicitor or sending it registered post to the same address, Criminal Evidence Act 1992, s 7(3). But if the accused is representing himself the document must be served on him personally, Criminal Evidence Act 1992, s 7(4).

[123] Unless they get leave of the Court, Criminal Evidence Act 1992, s 7(2).

[124] Criminal Evidence Act 1992, s 8(1).

[125] Criminal Evidence Act 1992, s 8(2).

[126] Criminal Evidence Act 1992, s 8(3).

(b)   ... evidence may, with the leave of the court, be given of any matter which, if that person had been called as a witness, could have been put to him in cross-examination as relevant to his credibility as a witness but of which evidence could not have been adduced by the cross-examining party ...

(c)   ... evidence tending to prove that that person, whether before or after supplying the information, made (whether orally or not) a statement which is inconsistent with it shall, if not already admissible ... be admissible for the purpose of showing that he has contradicted himself.'[127]

Mandatory reporting?

[32.48] Although anecdotal tales and survey evidence suggests that computer crimes are not uncommon, prosecutions for computer crimes are. One reason for this may be a reluctance of victims to report these crimes. Chang[128] suggests three reasons why the victims of cybercrime may chose not to report those crimes. Firstly, he suggests that victims may have what he terms 'competitive advantage concerns'. He illustrates such concerns with the example of egghead.com. This site suffered an illegal intrusion in December 2000. Management took those intrusions very seriously and hired 'the world's leading computer security experts'. However, investigating this intrusion took far more time than management had initially anticipated. Whilst the investigation was ongoing egghead.com's business took a turn for the worst and ultimately filed for bankruptcy in October 2001. Chang speculates that egghead.com 'consumed with dealing with the hacking incident, was not able to recognize and respond quickly enough to the intense competition within the computer and software marketplace.'[129] Secondly, there is what Chang refers to as 'negative publicity concerns'. He illustrates this with the case of CDUniverse, from which 300,000 credit card numbers were stolen, a hacking incident which was widely publicised at the time. Chang speculates that 'many potential customers declined making purchases from CDUniverse for fear that their own credit card numbers would be stolen by hackers.'[130] Chang quotes Greene[131] in this regard:

'most companies believe that the public relations (PR) costs of being identified with weak security are far greater than the damage that the most malicious hackers can inflict.'[132]

---

[127] Criminal Evidence Act 1992, s 9.

[128] Chang, *Computer hacking: making the case for a national reporting requirement,* The Berkman Center for Internet and Society, Research Publication No. 2004-07, http://www.cyber.law.harvard.edu/publications.

[129] Chang, *Computer hacking: making the case for a national reporting requirement,* The Berkman Center for Internet and Society, Research Publication No. 2004-07, http://www.cyber.law.harvard.edu/publications, p 12.

[130] Chang, *Computer hacking: making the case for a national reporting requirement,* The Berkman Center for Internet and Society, Research Publication No. 2004-07, http://www.cyber.law.harvard.edu/publications, p 13.

[131] Greene, *Is prosecuting hackers worth the bother?* http://www.theregister.co.uk, 21 August 2001.

[132] Greene, *Is prosecuting hackers worth the bother?* http://www.theregister.co.uk, 21 August 2001.

[32.49] Finally, there is what Chang refers to as 'Lack of knowledge by victims that anything can be done'. This actually seems to be a lack of confidence that reporting a computer crime will result in either a prosecution or a conviction.[133]

The Law Reform Commission rejected the argument that there should a statutory duty to disclose computer crime in its 1996 *Report on the Law Relating to Dishonesty*[134]: The Commission considered that:

> 'the strongest arguments against imposing such a statutory duty are that it would be unenforceable as well as unjust to businesses to force them to reveal weaknesses or misfortune to some central agency. Even if anonymity were obtained it could not be guaranteed. Whether such a duty would be efficacious is also to be doubted ... A catalogue of misdeeds relating to computers might serve to increase general awareness among computer users for the need for severity, but that goal can arguably be better served by advertising campaigns and education.'[135]

[32.50] The difficulties that arise in requiring the mandatory reporting of a crime are best illustrated by the debate about the mandatory reporting of child abuse. Obviously, child abuse is an extremely serious crime. The Law Reform Commission recommended the mandatory reporting of child sexual abuse, in its 1990 report on that subject.[136] The issue was not considered in detail by the subsequent Ferns Report. The Catholic Church, which was the subject of that Report, had adopted a mandatory system of reporting. But, although the Church promised 'full disclosure with no guarantee of confidentiality', in reality it was withholding the identities of the individual complainants. The Inquiry noted that this might be 'a valuable factor in persuading the victim to provide information' . But, it also noted that the gardaí would not approach a victim without their consent and that 'not meaningful investigation can be carried out ... without the identity of the complainant being made known.' [137] But, the form of mandatory reporting that was approved of by the Ferns Report fell short of that recommended by the Law Reform Commission. The Commission had recommended that someone, such as a doctor, teacher or nurse, who was required to make such a report should:

> 'be required to make an initial oral report followed by a written back-up report identifying the child.'[138]

[32.51] The reporting of anonymous allegations in the manner approved by the Ferns Report is unusual. Such reporting is justified by the over-riding requirements of child

---

[133] Chang, *Computer hacking: making the case for a national reporting requirement,* The Berkman Center for Internet and Society, Research Publication No. 2004-07, http://www.cyber.law.harvard.edu/publications, p14.

[134] Law Reform Commission, *Report on the Law Relating to Dishonesty,* LRC 43-1992, September 1992.

[135] Law Reform Commission, *Report on the Law Relating to Dishonesty,* LRC 43-1992, September 1992, p 327–328.

[136] Law Reform Commission, *Report on Child Sexual Abuse,* LRC 32–1990, September 1990, para 1.07, p 7.

[137] Murphy J, *The Ferns Report,* October 2005, p 264.

[138] Law Reform Commission, *Report on Child Sexual Abuse,* LRC 32–1990, September 1990, para 1.15–16, p 86.

welfare. The State recognised the validity of that justification by enacting the Protections for Persons Reporting Child Abuse Act 1998.[139] But, it is highly questionable that the anonymous reporting of allegations of criminal conduct could be said to be covered by qualified privilege in other situations. The debate about the mandatory reporting of cyber crime offences turns on the same point as the debate about the mandatory reporting of child sexual abuse. Anonymous complaints of criminal activity are of limited use to the authorities, but requiring the disclosure of victims' identities may dissuade them from coming forward in the first place.

That said, Irish law does require mandatory reporting of at least one form of criminal offence, namely that of market abuse. The Market Abuse Regulations 2005[140] provide that:

> 'Any prescribed person[141] who reasonably suspects that a transaction might constitute market abuse shall notify[142] the Bank[143] without delay (which notification may be a telephone call to a telephone number specified by the Bank provided that a notification in writing to the same effect is made as soon as is practicable after that call).'[144]

[32.52] The Regulations provide an exemption from liability for any prescribed person who provides such notification, stating that a: ... prescribed person shall not be liable for any act done, or purporting to be done, in good faith'.[145] The Regulations go on to provide that such notification will: 'not contravene any restriction on the disclosure of information.'[146] Where the Central Bank receives such a notification it must: 'transmit the notification immediately to the relevant competent authority'.[147] However, the argument may be made that the Regulations are exceptional, as they only apply to financial instruments.[148] A much more general provision is to be found in the Criminal Justice (Theft and Fraud Offences) Act 2001, which provides for the reporting of offences by auditors.[149]

---

[139] The Act provides that a person 'not be liable in damages in respect of the communication ... of his or her opinion that ... a child has been or is being assaulted, ill-treated, neglected or sexually abused'.

[140] SI 342/2005, the regulations implement Directive 2003/6/EC of the European Parliament and of the Council of 28 January 2003 on insider dealing and market manipulation (market abuse), OJ L096, 12.04.2003, p.16.

[141] SI 342/2005, reg 13(8) defines 'prescribed person' as 'any person (including any investment firm, credit institution or market operator) professionally arranging transactions in financial instruments who...is registered in the State, or ... consists of a branch operating in the State of any person (including any investment firm, credit institution or market operator) ... professionally arranging transactions in financial instruments, and ... registered in another Member State'.

[142] SI 324/2005, reg 2(1) specifies that notify means: 'notify in writing'.

[143] SI 324/2005, reg 2(1) defines the bank as: 'the Central Bank and Financial Services Authority of Ireland'.

[144] SI 342/2005, reg 13(1).

[145] SI 342/2005, reg 13(6).

[146] SI 342/2005, reg 13(7).

[147] SI 342/2005, reg 13(3).

[148] SI 342/2005, reg 4.

[149] Criminal Justice (Theft and Fraud Offences) Act 2001, s 59.

Evidence from computers in civil cases

[32.53] Evidence derived from computers can have probative value in a variety of civil cases. *Baigent v Random House Group Ltd*[150] concerned an allegation that the best-seller *The Da Vinci Code* had been copied from the plaintiff's work. Smith J. in the English High Court noted that with regard to one document:

> 'In the 'properties' ... it is stated that it had been edited for a total of 18 minutes. The Defendants rely on this point as showing that it is far more likely that the complete document had been downloaded from the internet which could reflect 18 minutes. That length of time cannot possibly reflect copying out ... and creating.'[151]

[32.54] In *R + V Versicherung AG v Risk Insurance and Reinsurance Solutions*[152] Moore-Bick J in the English Commercial Court found in relation to a certain document that:

> 'One can see from the computer record that the document had originally been created on 20 March 2001, but had subsequently been modified, perhaps on more than one occasion, before reaching its final form.'[153]

[32.55] Evidence derived from computer records can be used to verify the assertions of witnesses. In *Baker v Potter*[154] David Richards J rejected the suggestion that an attendance note of a meeting had not been created until five months afterwards because a secretary recalled creating the note the day after and her recall was verified by: 'computer records (which) show that the relevant file was opened'[155] the day after the meeting. However, the Courts should be cautious before treating computer records as being a complete record of all the facts that they appear to disclose. In *Britannia Zinc Ltd v Southern Electric Contracting*[156] evidence was provided by a computer print-out. Plaintiff's counsel argued that:

> 'there could be no possible doubt that the information recorded in the Print-out was correct.'

[32.56] However, this approach was rejected by Seymour QC[157] as 'superficial':

> ' Errors can be made by those charged with inputting information into a computer in recording the job number. Those whose function it was to decide what job number should be allocated to particular work or goods can make a mistake in determining the appropriate allocation or in recording the allocation when made. Errors can be made in inputting other information ... into the computer. For all these reasons a computer record is not, by itself, a self-proving document. It is necessary in my judgment, if a computer record is to be relied upon as evidence in support of claims such as those in the present

---

[150] *Baigent v Random House Group Ltd* [2006] EWHC 719 (Ch), [2006] All ER (D) 113 (Apr).

[151] [2006] EWHC 719 (Ch), [2006] All ER (D) 113 (Apr) at para 326.

[152] *R + V Versicherung AG v Risk Insurance and Reinsurance Solutions* [2004] EWHC 2682 (Comm), [2006] Lloyd's Rep IR 253, 2003 Folio 413.

[153] [2004] EWHC 2682 (Comm), [2006] Lloyd's Rep IR 253, 2003 Folio 413 at para 16.

[154] *Baker v Potter* [2004] EWHC 1422 (Ch).

[155] [2004] EWHC 1422 (Ch), para 46.

[156] *Britannia Zinc Ltd v Southern Electric Contracting* [2002] EWHC 606 (TCC).

[157] Sitting as a Deputy Judge of the English Technology and Construction Court.

action, for the accuracy of the record to be verified by someone who created it or at least by someone who was responsible for ensuring that it was accurately prepared.'[158]

[32.57] It is important to keep in mind that computers can provide very accurate records, but only of what was entered into the computer. As was said by Hallgarten QC in *Winchester Fruit v American Airlines*[159] in relation to electronic records held by an airline:

'while those records indicate certain events to the nearest minute it is not always clear whether it is the timing of the event or of its entry which is recorded.'[160]

Discovery, production and inspection of computer records

[32.58] There would not seem to be any question that records on a computer can be documents for the purposes of discovery. In *McCarthy v O'Flynn*[161] the Supreme Court held that an X-ray photograph was a document for the purposes of discovery, Kenny J stating:

'Etymologically the word 'document' is derived from the Latin word 'documentum' which in turn comes from the verb 'docere.' Therefore, it is something which teaches or gives information or a lesson or an example for instruction. The main characteristic of a document is that it is something which gives information. An X-ray plate or photograph gives information and so it is a document and the defendant is entitled to discovery of it.'[162]

[32.59] In *Mulcahy v Avoca Capital Holdings*[163] the plaintiff sought to have his expert's examine the computers of the defendant's directors. The plaintiff's expert told the Court that 'he would much prefer unfettered access'. However, it did not seem to Clarke J that the plaintiff was entitled to this. Clarke J made an order permitting the plaintiff's expert to examine the computers in question but only in accordance with the conditions sought by the defendants. Clarke J held that it was clear that if information was relevant then the defendants had no discretion to decline to allow the plaintiff's expert see that documentation and take that information away if necessary. The courts may take a very broad view of what documents should be discovered in an action, in *Sterling-Winthrop Group Ltd v Farbenfabriken Bayer AG*[164] Kenny J cited the following:

'The doctrine seems to me to go farther than that and to go as far as the principle which I am about to lay down. It seems to me that every document relates to the matters in question in the action, which not only would be evidence upon any issue, but also which, it is reasonable to suppose contains information which *may*—not which *must*—either

---

[158] [2002] EWHC 606 (TCC) para 18.
[159] *Winchester Fruit v American Airlines* [2002] 2 Lloyd's Rep 265.
[160] [2002] 2 Lloyd's Rep 265, para 13.
[161] *McCarthy v O'Flynn* [1979] IR 127 at 131.
[162] [1979] IR 127. Notice might also be taken of the decision Hoffman J in the English High Court in *Alliance & Leicester Building Society v Ghahremani and Others* (Times Law Reports, 19 March 1992).
[163] *Mulcahy v Avoca Capital Holdings* [2005] IEHC 136.
[164] [1967] IR 97.

directly or indirectly enable the party requiring the affidavit either to advance his own case or to damage the case of his adversary.'[165]

[32.60] This was cited in *McKenna v Best Travel Ltd*[166] in which Morris J held that it was:

'well settled that it is only documents which would support or defeat an issue that arises in the existing action which are required to be discovered or should be made the subject matter of an order for discovery. Unless the documents in question enable the plaintiff to advance her case or damage the defendants' case, these documents are not discoverable.'[167]

Discovery is governed by the Rules of the Superior Courts which provide that:

'Any party may, without filing any affidavit, apply to the Court for an order directing any other party to any cause or matter to make discovery on oath of the documents which are or have been in his possession or power, relating to any matter in question therein. On the hearing of such application the Court may either refuse or adjourn the same, if satisfied that such discovery is not necessary, or not necessary at that stage of the cause or matter, or make such order on such terms as to security for the costs of discovery or otherwise and either generally or limited to certain classes of documents as may be thought fit.'[168]

[32.61] As an alternative to ordering the filing of an affidavit, the court may order that the party from whom discovery is sought 'shall deliver to the opposite party a list of the documents which are or have been in his possession, custody, or power, relating to the matters in question'. The fact that the court has ordered the delivery of such a list will not prevent the court subsequently ordering the filing of an affidavit of documents.[169] Finally the court may not make an order for discovery if the court is '... of opinion that it is not necessary either for disposing fairly of the cause or matter or for saving costs.'[170] Documents may be produced[171] or inspected[172] and a court may 'make an order for inspection in such place and in such manner as it may think fit'.[173] Where business books are concerned, the court may order that a copy be made available.[174] Orders for discovery may also be made against third parties:

'Any person not a party to the cause or matter before the court who appears to the court to be likely to have or to have had in his possession custody or power any documents which are relevant to an issue arising or likely to arise out of the cause or matter or is or is likely to be in a position to give evidence relevant to any such issue may by leave of the court upon the application of any party to the said cause or matter be directed by order of the

---

[165] [1967] IR 97 at 102.
[166] *McKenna v Best Travel Ltd* [1995] 1 IR 577.
[167] [1995] 1 IR 577 at 580.
[168] Rules of the Superior Courts, Ord 31, r 12(1).
[169] Rules of the Superior Courts, Ord 31, r 12(2).
[170] Rules of the Superior Courts, Ord 31, r 12(3).
[171] Rules of the Superior Courts, Ord 31, r 14.
[172] Rules of the Superior Courts, Ord 31, r 15.
[173] Rules of the Superior Courts, Ord 31, r 18.
[174] Rules of the Superior Courts, Ord 31, r 20.

court to answer such interrogatories or to make discovery of such documents or to permit inspection of such documents.'[175]

[32.62] Penalties may be imposed for failure to comply with such orders:

'If any party fails to comply with any order … for discovery or inspection of documents, he shall be liable to attachment. He shall also, if a plaintiff be liable to have his action dismissed for want of prosecution, and, if a defendant, to have his defence, if any, struck out, and to be placed in the same position as if he had not defended, and the party interrogating may apply to the Court for an order to that effect, and an order may be made accordingly.'[176]

Where parties to an action discuss or seek the inspection of an individual's computer, it is important that they should be clear as to what is being sought. In particular they should be clear as to whether inspection of just the data that may be accessed through the conventional file structure is being made, or whether an inspection of all the data on a disk, deleted and non-deleted, is being offered. In *Smyth v Malakooty*[177] this clarity was not present when the parties agreed the terms upon which such an inspection might take place, subsequently a dispute arose:

'as to whether or not the expert who cannot identify the relevant material should then take what I will call a disk image of each of the computers, or should merely copy such files as are apparent looking at the conventional file system. By disk image, I mean a precise electronic image of the disk in question. Such an image would enable a detailed forensic exercise to be carried out of the material on the computers, but away from the computers by working on a copy of the image, and would, for example, in due course, if permission were given, enable a search to be made for deleted items.'[178]

[32.63] In *Derby v Weldon*[179] the defendants sought:

'an order that the plaintiffs allow inspection of all the … plaintiff's computer records and make facilities available to enable those defendants … to inspect records therein relating to the matters set out in the schedule, to peruse the same, make notes of their contents, and to be supplied with copies thereof on payment of the proper charges.'[180]

Vinelott J began his judgment by noting that:

'The court has a discretion as to the extent to which inspection and copying of documents disclosed on discovery is to be permitted and in the context of a computer database, this discretion can only be exercised in the light of expert evidence as to the extent of the information available online or from backup systems, archival or history files, the extent to which materials stored in history files can be recovered with or without reprogramming, the extent to which reprogramming and transferring data to the online system might damage the history files of the computer, and the extent to which recovery of information and any necessary reprogramming might disrupt the conduct of the plaintiffs' business.'[181]

---

[175] Rules of the Superior Courts, Ord 31, r 29.
[176] Rules of the Superior Courts, Ord 31, r 21.
[177] *Smyth v Malakooty* [2005] EWHC 3373 (Ch).
[178] [2005] EWHC 3373 (Ch), para 9.
[179] *Derby v Weldon* [1991] 1 WLR 652.
[180] [1991] 1 WLR 652 at 653.
[181] [1991] 1 WLR 652 at 654.

[32.64] The dispute in *Derby v Weldon* related to currency and commodity transactions undertaken by two of the defendants whilst they were directors of one of the plaintiffs in a period of time after that plaintiff had been taken over by other plaintiffs. The plaintiffs wished to inspect the certain of the defendants' systems to see what records those systems held in relation to the transactions in question.[182] Inspecting the data on the systems in question posed a considerable technical challenge, the system was based around a number of mainframe computers, this system had been adapted during the period in question and 'No complete record of the programmes in use was maintained and it is not now possible to recreate the programmes in use at any particular time.'[183] The system was described in the following terms:

'... four systems were maintained ... and they were processed each month. Backup files at the month end would be recorded on diskettes which were stored. Selected data was fed into the financial recording system and onto an online inquiry system. Month-end data files can be restored from the backup diskettes though not all backup diskettes can now be found and some have deteriorated to the point where restoration of the data damages the diskette reader. The restoration of this data gives rise to another problem ... System ... will only hold two months' restored backup data in addition to current operational data, and recreating all the backup data would accordingly take a considerable time. Moreover, often when a file has been recreated further time is needed to reprogramme the system so that current programmes can access the recreated data file while continuing to access current data files.'[184]

[32.65] Vinelot J identified a number of difficulties which had arisen in this case.

(a)   'Even when the relevant material is online and capable of being shown on screen or print out, some means will have to be found of screening out irrelevant or privileged material. The party seeking discovery cannot be allowed simply to seat himself at his opponent's computer console and be provided with all necessary access keys'.

(b)   'There may be material on the computer which is not accessible by current programmes but which can be retrieved by reprogramming. Prima facie the powers of the court would extend to requiring that the computer be reprogrammed so as to enable the relevant information to be retrieved. Otherwise an unscrupulous litigant would be able to escape discovery by maintaining his records in computerised form and altering current programmes when litigation was in prospect so that information previously retrievable could not be retrieved without reprogramming. Of course questions may then arise as to who bears the cost of any necessary reprogramming and whether it can be done without affecting current programmes'.

(c)   'If, as will often be the case, the computer is in daily use, the question may arise – it arose acutely in the instant case – whether access can be arranged, in particular whether any necessary reprogramming can be done or whether

---

[182] [1991] 1 WLR 652 at 654–655.
[183] [1991] 1 WLR 652 at 657.
[184] [1991] 1 WLR 652 at 657.

information stored in the archival or history files can be retrieved, without unduly interrupting the necessary everyday use of the computer'.

(d) 'Safeguards may have to be embodied in order to ensure that tapes or diskettes which may have deteriorated in storage are not damaged by use and that the use of them does not damage the computer's reader. In the instant case, the condition of some diskettes was such that read once they would be unreadable or only partially readable a second time and the uses of some old diskettes in fact caused damage to the computer's reader'.

(e) 'In some cases it may be possible for the database to be copied by transfer on to a diskette or tape or directly on to another computer. If that is done the material may be capable of being analysed in ways which were not originally contemplated. Provision may have to be made for the results of any such analysis, and printouts made, to be made available to the other party in good time so that he is not taken by surprise at the trial. In the instant case agreement was recently reached for the provision of further experts' reports dealing with information gleaned from parts of the plaintiffs' computer database which was transferred to Coopers' computer.

Matrimonial proceedings

[32.66] Data recovery will not just be used in criminal and commercial cases, cases have also been reported of its use in the family courts. In *L v L*[185] the parties were engaged in a matrimonial dispute. Tugendhat J began his judgment by noting that in such disputes it was not uncommon:

'for one party ... to suspect that the other party is about to destroy documents, or conceal information which is, or may be, relevant to the proceedings.'[186]

[32.67] The husband used a laptop. Whilst he was away his wife engaged a computer expert who removed the laptop 'made two copies of the hard drive and returned the laptop to the family home'. The wife said that she did this after 'the husband had thrown out a number of documents which had been kept at his home ... and she feared that he was destroying evidence that might assist her case'.[187] Subsequently the husband brought. a motion in the Queen's Bench Division of the English High Court (not the family courts). In doing so the husband sought and order that the wife and her solicitors: 'deliver up ... to the husband's solicitors to be held by ... any and all copies of the hard drive of the laptop which are in their possession, control or power' .[188] The case turned on. the question of whether it would have been possible for the wife to get a search order (the equivalent of an Anton Piller order) for the laptop. Tugendhat J held that it would have been, finding that:

'I would be prepared to assume that the fact that the husband had destroyed some ... would have been sufficient evidence to support a reasonable fear of further destruction as

---

[185] *L v L* [2007] EWHC 140 (QB).
[186] [2007] EWHC 140 (QB), para 1.
[187] [2007] EWHC 140 (QB), para 19.
[188] [2007] EWHC 140 (QB), para 6.

a matter of principle. But even making that assumption in her favour, I have difficulty applying that to the laptop. The husband left the laptop in the house. There is no evidence that he destroyed documents on the laptop. The wife's evidence is that she hopes that there is still evidence to be found on it. It might be thought that if she was concerned about safeguarding it before an application could be made to the court, all that would have been necessary would have been to put it in a safe place pending the application, assuming (which is far from clear) that she had reasonable grounds to fear that the husband or his agents might come back to retrieve it by force. Even if there was evidence sufficient to obtain a preservation order, I can see no basis at all for suggesting, and Miss Skinner did not suggest, that there was sufficient evidence to cross the very high threshold necessary in order to obtain a search order.'[189]

Tugendhat J considered that it was:

'a matter for considerable concern that parties to litigation should conduct searches which lack any of the safeguards built into a search order issued by the court, and all the more so if they do that in circumstances where they could not reasonably expect to obtain any such order from the court.'[190]

He considered that the wife's actions might well have broken the UK's data protection and computer crime laws and that 'if the case were to go to trial there is a real prospect that it might be found that the wife had acted unlawfully.'[191] He made the order sought by the husband, but only on the basis that the husband's solicitors would retain the copies of the hard drive in question.[192]

Anton Piller Order

[32.68] Anton Piller orders permit a party to a civil action to attend on the premises of another and search those premises for relevant documents or articles. They were described by Scott J in *Columbia Pictures Inc v Robinson*[193] as 'Draconian and essentially unfair'.[194] In *Anton Piller KG v Manufacturing Processes Ltd*[195] Denning MR ruled that they should be granted:

'only in an extreme case where there is grave danger of property being smuggled away or of vital evidence being destroyed.'[196]

In the same case Ormond LJ ruled that the orders should only be made when the following conditions were complied with:

'First, there must be an extremely strong prima facie case. Secondly, the damage, potential or actual, must be very serious for the applicant. Thirdly, there must be clear evidence that the defendants have in their possession incriminating documents or things, and that there

---

[189] [2007] EWHC 140 (QB), para 92.
[190] [2007] EWHC 140 (QB), para 93.
[191] [2007] EWHC 140 (QB), para 112.
[192] [2007] EWHC 140 (QB), para 118.
[193] *Columbia Pictures Inc v Robinson* [1986] 3 WLR 542.
[194] [1986] 3 WLR 542 at 570.
[195] *Anton Piller KG v Manufacturing Processes Ltd* [1976] Ch 55, [1976] 1 All ER 779, [1976] 2 WLR 162.
[196] [1976] Ch. 55 at 61.

is a real possibility that they may destroy such material before any application *inter partes* can be made.'[197]

[32.69] Scott J described the orders as follows:

> '*Anton Piller* orders have become established as part of the tools of the administration of justice in civil cases ... they play a part not unlike that played by search warrants in the area of crime and suspected crime ... the legitimate purposes of *Anton Piller* orders are clearly identified by the leading cases which have established the legitimacy of their use ... perhaps the most usual purpose ... is to preserve evidence necessary for the plaintiff's case. *Anton Piller* orders are used to prevent a defendant, when warned of impending litigation, from destroying all documentary evidence in his possession which might, were it available, support the plaintiff's cause of action. Secondly, *Anton Piller* orders are often used in order to track to its source and obtain the possession of the master tape or master plate or blueprint by means of which reproductions in breach of copyright are being made. This purpose is, perhaps, no more than a sub-division of the first.

It is implicit in the nature of *Anton Piller* orders that they should be applied for ex parte and dealt with by the courts in secrecy.

> *Anton Piller* orders and procedure have, therefore, these characteristics: no notice to the defendant of what is afoot, and secrecy ... they are mandatory in form and are designed for immediate execution. The respondent to the order is required by the order to permit his premises to be entered and searched and, under most if not all orders, to permit the plaintiff's solicitors to remove into the solicitors' custody articles covered by the order.'[198]

[32.70] Applicants for an Anton Piller order must give an undertaking as to damages, but the orders have the disadvantage that they: 'produce for the respondents damaging and irreversible consequences without any hearing at which they can be heard.'[199] A further safeguard are 'the duties of full disclosure that the solicitors and counsel acting for the applicant owe to the court and that execution of *Anton Piller* orders is customarily required to be supervised by solicitors.'[200] But in *Columbia Pictures Inc v Robinson* Scott J noted that this placed solicitors and Counsel in an 'unsatisfactory position'.[201] Finally, Scott J noted that: 'an *Anton Piller* order always contains a liberty for the respondent to apply on short notice for the order to be set aside. But this cannot in practice be done until after the order has been executed'.[202] Given these disadvantages Scott J suggested that the orders:

> 'be so drawn as to extend no further than the minimum extent necessary to achieve the purpose for which they are granted, namely, the preservation of documents or articles which might otherwise be destroyed or concealed. Anything beyond that is, in my judgment, impossible to justify ... I do not understand how an order can be justified that allows the plaintiffs' solicitors to take and retain all relevant documentary material and correspondence.' [203]

---

[197] [1976] Ch. 55 at 62.
[198] *Columbia Pictures Inc v Robinson* [1986] 3 WLR 542 at 565.
[199] [1986] 3 WLR 542 at 568.
[200] [1986] 3 WLR 542 at 569.
[201] [1986] 3 WLR 542 at 569.
[202] [1986] 3 WLR 542 at 569.
[203] [1986] 3 WLR 542 at 570.

The second condition that Scott J thought should be imposed was:

'a detailed record of the material taken should always be required to be made by the solicitors who execute the order before the material is removed from the respondent's premises.' [204]

The third condition suggested by Scott J was:

'no material should, in my judgment be taken from the respondent's premises by the executing solicitors unless it is clearly covered by the terms of the order. In particular, I find it wholly unacceptable that a practice should have grown up whereby the respondent to the order is procured by the executing solicitors to give consent to additional material being removed ... I would not ... be prepared to accept that an apparent consent by a respondent had been freely and effectively given unless the respondent's solicitor had been present to confirm and ensure that the consent was a free and informed one.' [205]

Fourthly, Scott J found it inappropriate:

'that seized material the ownership of which is in dispute ... should be retained by the plaintiffs' solicitors pending the trial ... those responsible for the administration of justice might reasonably be expected to provide a neutral officer of the court charged with the custody of the material. In lieu of any such officer ... the plaintiffs' solicitors ought ... as soon as solicitors for the defendants are on the record, to be required to deliver the material to the defendants' solicitors on their undertaking for its safe custody and production, if required, in court.' [206]

Finally, Scott J held that:

'... the nature of *Anton Piller* orders requires that the affidavits in support of applications for them ought to err on the side of excessive disclosure. In the case of material falling into the grey area of possible relevance, the judge, not the plaintiffs' solicitors, should be the judge of relevance.' [207]

[32.71] Anton Piller orders are granted by the Irish Courts on a regular basis. They were granted to the plaintiff in *House of Spring Gardens v Point Blank*[208] and in *N(J) v K(T)*[209] O'Higgins J granted the plaintiff an:

'Anton Piller Order to permit the Plaintiff's solicitors enter and search the premises in Dublin which the first-named Defendant had given as his address and there to seize the items listed in the Schedule to the Order.'[210]

[32.72] In *Microsoft v Brightpoint*[211] the defendant complained that an Anton Piller order: 'was oppressively and excessively executed',[212] but these allegations were rejected

---

[204] [1986] 3 WLR 542 at 570.

[205] [1986] 3 WLR 542 at 570–571.

[206] [1986] 3 WLR 542 at 571.

[207] [1986] 3 WLR 542 at 571.

[208] *House of Spring Gardens v Point Blank* [1984] IR 611.

[209] *N (J) v K (T)* [2002] IEHC 16 (19 February, 2002).

[210] [2002] IEHC 16 (19 February, 2002) at para 7.

[211] *Microsoft v Brightpoint* [2000] IEHC 194, [2001] 1 ILRM 540.

[212] [2000] IEHC 194; [2001] 1 ILRM 540, para 22.

by Smyth J. However, there should be no doubting the intrusive nature of such an order, as was stated by Denning LJ in *Anton Piller KG v Manufacturing Processes Ltd*[213]:

> "Let me say at once that no court in this land has any power to issue a search warrant to enter a man's house so as to see if there are papers or documents there which are of an incriminating nature, whether libels or infringements of copyright or anything else of the kind. No constable or bailiff can knock at the door and demand entry so as to inspect papers or documents. The householder can shut the door in his face and say, 'Get out'[214] ... But the order sought in this case is not a search warrant. It does not authorise the Plaintiffs' solicitors or anyone else to enter the Defendants' premises against their will. It does not authorise the breaking down of any doors, nor the slipping in by a back door, nor getting in by an open door or window. It only authorises entry and inspection by the permission of the Defendants. The Plaintiffs must get the Defendant's permission. But it does do this: it brings pressure on the Defendants to give permission. It does more. It actually orders them to give permission – with, I suppose, the result that if they do not give permission, they are guilty of contempt of court. This may seem to be a search warrant in disguise.[215]

As Smyth J noted *in Microsoft v Brightpoint*:

> 'There is no good time for a Defendant to receive an Anton Piller Order.'[216]

Privilege against self-incrimination

[32.73] One difficulty with an Anton Piller order is that it may be difficult, and probably impossible, to get such an order to search the home of an individual. This is because the State guaranteed the inviobility of the home when the Constitution was adopted in 1937. This guarantee might be limited by statute, but it would be difficult to argue that the guarantee should be limited by a line of caselaw which began in the English courts in 1974.[217] The other problem is the shear amount of information that may be extracted from a computer may create a problem for the use of Anton Piller orders in Ireland. This is because the right to silence and the privilege against self-incrimination has been recognised as a Constitutional right by the Supreme Court in *Heaney v Ireland*.[218] A defendant may be able to claim privilege against self-incrimination in respect of that material and refuse to permit the execution of an Anton Piller order. *IBM v Prima Data International*[219] the plaintiff was endeavouring to discover how the defendant's assets of £650,000 or so had been dissipated. The plaintiff sought to serve an Anton Piller order, Sir Mervyn Davies ruled that the order might be served:

> 'but may not be executed until ... the defendant is told of his privilege right and ... the defendant then expressly declines to claim that right. In short, the order means that the supervising solicitor must say to the defendant, 'I have a search order but I cannot execute

---

[213] [1976] Ch 55, [1976] 1 All ER 779, [1976] 2 WLR 162.
[214] Citing *Entick v Carrington* (1765) 2 Wils 275, [1558-1774] All ER Rep 41.
[215] [1976] 1 All ER 779 at 782–783.
[216] [2000] IEHC 194; [2001] 1 ILRM 540, para 24.
[217] EMI Ltd v Pandit [1975] 1 WLR 302.
[218] *Heaney v Ireland* [1996] 1 IR 580.
[219] *IBM v Prima Data International* [1994] 1 WLR 719.

it if you tell me that the search may result in disclosing matters showing that you have been involved in a conspiracy.' It seems to me that the form of order adequately protects the defendant's privilege while at the same time allowing search if privilege is not claimed. Of course that is not the end of the story. Defendants are bemused by the appearance of solicitors bearing 13-page orders in legal language. A supervising solicitor must ensure that the defendant properly understands his rights as preserved by the order, i.e. that there will be no entry if the defendant claims privilege and the meaning of privilege must be explained. Everyday language must be used.'[220]

[32.74] This privilege was considered by Smyth J in *Microsoft v Brightpoint,* where the defendant argued that the plaintiff had failed to: '... advise the ... as to it's right against self-incrimination' Smyth J rejected this argument, commenting that the defendant's representative:

'... insists that the company is compliant with the law, if he is correct and so found to be on a full hearing then self-incrimination simply cannot arise. Accordingly this is not a basis for setting aside the Anton Piller Order.'[221]

It will be interesting to see how the Irish courts approach the recent decisions of the English Courts in *O Ltd v Z*[222] and *C plc v P.*[223] Both cases have broadly similar facts. In *O Ltd v Z* the plaintiff was a former employer of the defendant. The plaintiff suspected (correctly) that the defendant had taken information confidential to the plaintiff when he left the plaintiff's employment. The plaintiff obtained a search order for the defendant's premises and computers; the defendant's computer was given to an expert employed by the plaintiff. When the expert examined the defendant's computer:

'it was found (as no one except, if anyone, the Defendant, had any reason to expect) to include material completely irrelevant to the Claimant's claim, paedophile pornography of a serious nature. So serious is it that its mere possession can be a crime.'

[32.75] The plaintiff's expert sought to hand this information over to the prosecution authorities. One difficulty with doing so was that:

'... the defendant had never been told of the privilege against self-incrimination either by the words of the Search Order or by the Supervising Solicitor or how to exercise it and, in that the only privilege that was explained to him was a quite different one, he might well have thought that the privilege against self-incrimination was not open to him even had he otherwise been aware of it as a possibility.'[224]

The plaintiff had executed the Anton Piller order on the defendant's premises and had found a large number of PCs, floppy discs and CDs. The plaintiff's expert copied the defendant's hard drive and a number of CD's, when the plaintiff's expert subsequently examined the data he found several hundred images of child pornography, many of which were of the most serious sort. It was this material that the plaintiff's expert sought to hand over to the prosecution authorities. Lindsay J ruled that the defendant had lost

---

[220] [1994] 1 WLR 719 at 730.
[221] [2000] IEHC 194, [2001] 1 ILRM 540, para 27.
[222] *O Ltd v Z* [2005] EWHC 238 (Ch).
[223] *C plc v P* [2006] 3 WLR 273.
[224] [2005] EWHC 238 (Ch), para 1.

the privilege because 'he handed the offensive material to the third party without claiming the privilege.'[225]

[32.76] In *C plc v P* the defendant's computers were placed in the custody of the supervising solicitor, who then transferred it to an expert. That expert found child pornographic images on one of the computers, and the issue came before the Courts to decide whether or not this material should be transferred to the Police. Evans-Lombe J noted that the defendant had:

> '... effectively claimed (the privilege against self incrimination) in respect of the material to be produced as a result of the execution of the search order, before the search started, and an objective consideration of the events occurring after the execution of that order does not result in the conclusion that he lost the benefit of it.'[226]

However, Evans-Lombe LJ went on to hold that that the common-law privilege against self-incrimination was now limited by the European Convention on Human Rights, which required that he balance the privilege with the public interest in being protected from crime. Evans-Lombe LJ therefore held that this was:

> 'a case where the court can modify the application of domestic (the privilege against self incrimination) so as to exclude from its ambit material constituting freestanding evidence which was not created by the respondent to the search order under compulsion.'[227]

He then directed that the expert: 'to pass the computer and associated electronic materials on which the offending material is stored to the appropriate police authority.'[228]

---

[225] [2005] EWHC 238 (Ch), para 70.
[226] [2006] 3 WLR 273 at 284.
[227] [2006] 3 WLR 273 at 307.
[228] [2006] 3 WLR 273 at 308.

PART IX: IT IN THE WORKPLACE

Chapter 33

Privacy at Work

Introduction

[33.01] The workplace reflects society's conflict between privacy and surveillance. The employee has a right to privacy. This right is not absolute. It must be balanced with the rights of the employer, such as the right to a reputation, the right to earn a livelihood and the right to property. The need to maintain this balance can lead to conflict. And, in the workplace this conflict can become acute. As the Article 29 Working Party notes:

> 'Workers do not abandon their right to privacy and data protection every morning at the doors of the workplace. They do have a legitimate expectation of a certain degree of privacy in the workplace as they develop a significant part of their relationships with other human beings within the workplace. However, this right must be balanced with other legitimate rights and interests of the employer, in particular the employer's right to run his business efficiently to a certain extent, and above all, the right to protect himself from the liability or the harm that workers' actions may create. These rights and interests constitute legitimate grounds that may justify appropriate measures to limit the worker's right to privacy'.[1]

[33.02] The Employment Appeals Tribunal (EAT) commented in *Mehigan v Dyflin Publications*[2] that:

> 'Email and the Internet are now an essential means of global business communication. As a result many employees have unlimited access to web and email at their fingertips. This means of communication brings with it a duty on the employee to act responsibly and use it only for legitimate purposes'.

Furthermore, the boundaries between workplace and domestic life are becoming indistinct. One survey found that as of the summer of 2002 found that some 62 per cent of male employees and 38 per cent of female employees were working longer than standard hours.[3] Changes in demographics, economics and society as a whole will make e-working and flexible work practices increasingly commonplace.[4] Mobile phones, BlackBerries, laptop computers and the increasing use of the home office mean that it is often impossible to draw a clear dividing line between what is being done within and without the parameters of an individual's employment.[5]

---

[1] The Article 29, Working Party *Working Document on the surveillance of electronic communications in the workplace*, p 4.

[2] *Mehigan v Dyflin Publications Ltd* (10 December 2002) EAT, UD 582/2001, MN 2032/2001.

[3] Drew, Murphy and Humphreys 'Off the Treadmill – Achieving Work/Life Balance', National Framework Committee on Work/Life Balance, 23 October 2003.

[4] See http://www.familyfriendly.ie.

[5] Professor Steve Barley of Stanford University, California, USA estimates that the average executive in Silicon Valley spends 'the equivalent of three and a half extra weeks a year just communicating outside work'. (contd/)

As has been acknowledged by the ECtHR:

'it is not always possible to distinguish clearly which of an individual's activities form part of his professional or business life and which do not. Thus, especially in the case of a person exercising a liberal profession, his work in that context may form part and parcel of his life to such a degree that it becomes impossible to know in what capacity he is acting at a given moment of time[6] ... it may not always be possible to draw precise distinctions, since activities which are related to a profession or business may well be conducted from a person's private residence and activities which are not so related may well be carried on in an office or commercial premises'.[7]

[33.03] Working from home further complicates the issue of workplace surveillance. In addition to the implicit right of privacy, the Irish Constitution explicitly guarantees that: 'The dwelling of every citizen is inviolable and shall not be entered save in accordance with law'.[8] This guarantee only extends to those parts of a building that are actually used as a dwelling.[9] So, if an employee were to be working from a distinct office in their home, surveillance of this area might not violate the inviolability of their dwelling. However, if they were to be working from their dining room, or another area which was shared with family members, this would be a part of their dwelling and so the constitutional right would come into play. That said, the Constitution only requires that the dwelling 'shall not be entered save in accordance with law'. A contract of employment that explicitly permitted the employer to conduct surveillance of the home office might thus avoid breach of the constitutional guarantee. However, it is submitted that the contract in question would need to contain totally unambiguous wording to avoid that guarantee.[10]

[33.04] One fresh challenge being created by the Internet for employers is the extent to which it can monitor 'blogging' employees. Blogging allows anyone to go online to express everything from intelligent criticism to mindless pontification. A problem may arise where bloggers criticise their employers.[11] Although employers sometimes pay

---

5   (\contd) However, Professor Barley doubts that this time has any benefits in terms of worker productivity, see Waters 'Plugged into it all' FT Magazine, 12/13 November 2005, p24.

6   *Niemietz v Germany* (23 November 1992) ECtHR, para 29.

7   (23 November 1992) ECtHR, para 31.

8   Constitution, Article 40.5.

9   See *DPP v MacMahon* [1986] IR 393: 'The act of entering, as a trespasser, the public portion of a licensed premises which is open for trade does not, of course, constitute any invasion or infringement of any constitutional right of the owner of those premises', per Finlay CJ at 398.

10   And although the contract might be permit the surveillance of the employee at home, it is hard to see how it could be permit the surveillance of others who might dwell in the same premises as the employee.

11   In early 2005 a branch of Waterstone's Bookshop in Edinburgh, Scotland, dismissed an employee who had referred to his employer on his blog. '(He) mentioned his work twice ... ranted about his 'sandal-wearing' manager he nicknamed 'Evil Boss'' In another posting, the employee joked about 'Bastardstone's. He was dismissed for 'gross misconduct' and 'bringing the company into disrepute'. 'Barkham, blogger sacked for sounding off' (2005) The Guardian, 12 January.

employees to blog,[12] the very vast majority of the 8 million blogs now available online are created in their author's own time.[13] Once uploaded to the Internet, most blogs will be available to anyone who wishes to read them. Merely because something is publicly available does not mean that the blogger in question cannot have any right to privacy in it.[14] So, any employer who monitors their employee's blogs as a function of their business, as opposed to reading them for their own enjoyment or education, may have to justify the necessity of doing so. Such necessity may be established on the grounds of protection of the employer's reputation or its intellectual property. Another reason is illustrated by the Employment Appeals Tribunal ('EAT') decision of *Fogarty and O'Connor v IBM*.[15] A complaint had been made to the respondent 'about the existence of a particular website'. This website was known as 'Virtual Vengeance' and was 'a chat site where people could access and type statements about employees ... (of the respondent company). The entries were grossly offensive, sexual, racist and deeply offensive about various employees'. The respondent investigated and was satisfied that the claimants had accessed the site in question. The claimants denied having written anything on the site. However, they were dismissed by the respondents and these dismissals were ruled fair by the EAT.

Who is an employee?

[33.05] A comprehensive discussion of how the law will distinguish between an employee under a contract of service and a contractor under a contract for services is outside the scope of this work. The current law was set out by Keane CJ in *Denny v Minister for Social Welfare*[16]:

> 'It is ... clear that, while each case must be determined in the light of its particular facts and circumstances, in general a person will be regarded as providing his or her services under a contract of service and not as an independent contractor where he or she is performing those services for another person and not for himself or herself. The degree of control exercised over how the work is to be performed, although a factor to be taken into account, is not decisive. The inference that the person is engaged in business on his or her own account can be more readily drawn where he or she provides the necessary premises or equipment or some other form of investment, where he or she employs others to assist in the business and where the profit which he or she derives from the business is dependent on the efficiency with which it is conducted by him or her'.[17]

---

12 For example, Robert Scoble who styles himself 'The Microsoft Geek Blogger', see http:// radio.weblogs.com/0001011/. Sun Microsystems also encourages employees to blog, see http:/ /www.blogs.sun.com and Zeller 'When the blogger blogs, can the employer intervene?' (2005) New York Times, 18 April.

13 As of 21 March 2005. CNET news.com 'The Future of Blogging' 5 April 2005.

14 For example, see the ECtHR decision in *Von Hannover v Germany* (24 June 2004) in which the ECHR ruled that the plaintiff's privacy was breached by photographing her on the public road and in a restaurant. See similarly, the decision of the House of Lords in *Campbell v MGN* [2004] UKHL 22.

15 *Fogarty and O'Connor v IBM* UD771/2000 UD661/2000, unreported EAT decision.

16 *Denny v Minister for Social Welfare* [1998] 1 IR 34.

17 *Denny v Minister for Social Welfare* [1998] 1 IR 34 at 50, see also *Tierney v An Post* [2000] 1 IR 536.

[33.06] So, in every case, the employee must be identified having regard to the particular facts and circumstance of their particular case. If it is ascertained that an individual is in fact an employee, the next issue which arises is to what functions that employee discharges in the course of their employment. The employer will only be responsible for the actions of the employee that are discharged in the course of his or her employment. Therefore, the employer will not need to monitor activities undertaken outside the scope of employment. Where the employer does not need to monitor certain activities, then its right to monitor them will be curtailed. Again, this issue can only be decided having regard to the particular facts and circumstances of each case. An employer whose Internet usage policy forbade employees using the Internet for personal purposes might be permitted to monitor the fact that an employee had clicked onto an Internet travel site. However, he would not necessarily be allowed to monitor the details of what pages the employee viewed on the site.[18]

Vicarious liability

[33.07] An employer may be vicariously liable for the actions of its employee,[19] even where those actions will amount to a criminal offence.[20] The test for vicarious liability is:

> 'summarized in the second edition of McMahon and Binchy ... where it is suggested that the test is by looking to see if the acts complained of are so closely connected with the employment of the primary wrongdoer as to make the employer vicariously liable'.[21]

---

[18]   The employer might claim that it needed to monitor the individual pages viewed to ascertain whether the employee was in fact booking a work-related trip. However, this information could be better ascertained by the employer checking whether or not the employee had a work-related trip in prospect and whether or not the employee would be responsible for booking their own accommodation.

[19]   Employer and employee may be concurrent wrongdoers under s 11(2) of the Civil Liability Act 1961 'persons may become concurrent wrongdoers as a result of vicarious liability of one for another'.

[20]   See *Johnson and Johnson (Ireland) Ltd v CP Security Ltd* [1985] IR 362. The defendant employed a security guard to protect the premises of the plaintiff. The defendant was held to be vicariously liable when the security guard assisted others in stealing van loads of goods from the plaintiff's premises. However, see *Reilly v Ryan* [1991] ILRM 449 where the defendant was held not to be liable where the defendant's bar manager used a customer as a human shield to protect himself during a robbery. And *Health Board v BC and The Labour Court* [1994] ELR 27 where the defendant was held not to be liable for a sexual assault committed by two employees upon another. See also: *Poland v John Parr and Sons* [1927] 1 KB 236; *Lloyd v Grace Smith and Co* [1912] AC 716; *Morris v CW Martin and Sons Ltd* [1966] 1 QB 716; *Harrison v Michelin Tyre Co Ltd* [1985] 1 All ER 918; *Aldred v Nacanco* [1987] IRLR 292; *Lister v Hesley Hall Ltd* [2002] 1 AC 215.

[21]   Per Hederman J in, *McIntyre v Lewis* [1990] IESC 5, [1991] 1 IR 121. What O'Higgins J (in *Delahunty v South Eastern Health Board and Ors* [2003] IEHC 132) referred to as the 'classic formulation of the test' is contained in *Salmond and Heuston's Law of Torts* (21st edn), at p 443: 'If it is either (1) a wrongful act authorised by the master or (2) a wrongful and unauthorised mode of doing some act authorised by the master, it is clear that the master is responsible for acts actually authorised by him; (contd/)

Each case will depend upon its facts.[22] The issue of whether an employee's use of her employer's phone was within the scope of her employment was examined in *Crofter Properties v Genport*.[23] The plaintiff owned a hotel, which was let to the defendant. The plaintiff brought an action seeking, *inter alia*, to recover possession of the hotel. The defendant counterclaimed for injurious falsehood, negligent misstatement and defamation. The facts were such that McCracken J could only describe them as 'bizarre'[24] in that 'officers of the South East Regional Crime Squad in England began to get telephone calls from a lady described as having an Irish accent who would not identify herself'.

In the course of these telephone calls, the lady in question made various serious allegations about the defendant's business, involving references to IRA money laundering operations. These calls were traced back to the plaintiff's home. McCracken J had 'no doubt ... that ... (an employee of the plaintiff) ... made these telephone calls'.[25] However, McCracken J held that 'he was not satisfied that the plaintiff can be made vicariously liable for the effect of these calls'.[26] This judgment was appealed to the Supreme Court. Giving judgment for the court, Murray J stated that:

> 'Having regard to all the facts and circumstances, I am satisfied that the only proper inference to be drawn from the actions of...(the plaintiff's employee)...is that she was a person deeply involved in a responsible position for the affairs of the plaintiff company and in the furtherance of its interests sought to damage the defendant in the hope that this would somehow assist the plaintiff in its objective of regaining possession of the hotel which it had leased to the defendant'.[27]

Murray J was satisfied that the defendant had established that 'as a matter of probability, that ... (the plaintiff's employee) ... had made those phonecalls in her capacity as a

---

[21] (\contd) the liability will exist in this case even if the relationship between the parties was one of agency and not one of service at all. But a master, as opposed to the employer of an independent contractor, is liable even for acts which he has not authorised provided they are so connected with the acts that he has authorised that they might rightly be regarded as modes – although improper modes – of doing them.' See the judgment of Gilligan J in *Fanning v University College Cork* [2005] IEHC 264 'when determining whether an act or omission has been committed within the 'course of employment' for the purpose of imposing vicarious liability upon an employer, the fact that the act or omission is closely connected to the employment is not the only factor which the court must take into account. It is also necessary to consider the damage suffered by the plaintiff and the undesirability of foisting an undue burden on the defendant'.

[22] And: '(t)he application of the doctrine of vicarious liability to the facts of a particular case can often be a matter of great difficulty. The difficulty arises in determining whether a particular act has been committed in the scope of employment so as to render the employer vicariously liable for the torts.' *Per* O'Higgins J in *Delahunty v South Eastern Health Board and Ors* [2003] IEHC 132 (30 July 2003).

[23] *Crofter Properties v Genport* [2002] 4 IR 73.

[24] *Crofter Properties v Genport* [2002] 4 IR 73 at 79.

[25] *Crofter Properties v Genport* [2002] 4 IR 73 at 82.

[26] *Crofter Properties v Genport* [2002] 4 IR 73 at 88.

[27] *Crofter Properties v Genport* [2002] 4 IR 73 at 92.

person with an important position in the affairs of the company for the purpose of furthering its interests and in such a manner as to engage the responsibility of the plaintiff company for her actions'.[28]

Does the constitutional right to privacy apply in the workplace?

[33.08] The constitutional right to privacy almost certainly extends to the workplace. Certainly, other constitutional rights have been found to extend into the workplace, such as the right to earn a livelihood[29] and the right to dissociate oneself from a trade union.[30] In *Hanahoe v Hussey*,[31] the gardaí executed a search warrant and entered the plaintiff's workplace, a solicitor's office. The fact that the office in question was a workplace, not a private home, did not prevent Kinlen J in the High Court from finding that the privacy of those premises had been breached 'a warrant is a very serious interference with the right to privacy. The courts must protect this privacy and only allow invasion of that right under strict interpretation of any constitutional law which seeks to demean it'.[32]

Does art 8 of the ECHR extend to the workplace?

[33.09] It is clear that the ECHR extends to the workplace, and so individuals may invoke art 8 of the ECHR in relation to breaches of their privacy which occur in work. In *Niemietz v Germany*,[33] the applicant's law office was searched by the German Authorities on foot of a search warrant. The applicant argued that the search was in breach of art 8 of the ECHR.[34] The German Authorities disagreed, asserting that 'the Convention drew a clear distinction between private life and home, on the one hand, and professional and business life and premises, on the other'.[35] The ECtHR held in favour of the applicant, stating that:

> 'To deny the protection of Article 8 … on the ground that the measure complained of related only to professional activities – as the Government suggested should be done in the present case - could moreover lead to an inequality of treatment, in that such protection would remain available to a person whose professional and non-professional activities were so intermingled that there was no means of distinguishing between them'.[36]

[33.10] Although significant, it could still be argued that the decision in *Niemietz v Germany* was peculiar to its facts, that it only applied to those 'exercising a liberal profession' whose 'work may form part and parcel of his life to such a degree that it

---

[28] *Crofter Properties v Genport* [2002] 4 IR 73 at 93.
[29] *Attorney General v Paperlink* [1984] ILRM 373 and *Greally v Minister for Education* [1999] 1 IR 1.
[30] See *Educational Co of Ireland v Fitzpatrick (No 2)* [1961] IR 345 and *Meskell v CIE* [1973] IR 121.
[31] *Hanahoe v Hussey* [1998] 3 IR 69.
[32] [1998] 3 IR 69 at 108.
[33] *Niemietz v Germany* (23 November 1992) ECtHR.
[34] Article 8 of the ECHR is discussed in detail in Chapter – above. Article 8(1) provides: 'Everyone has the right to respect for his private and family life, his home and his correspondence'.
[35] *Niemietz v Germany* (23 November 1992) ECtHR, para 26.
[36] (23 November 1992) ECtHR, para 29.

becomes impossible to know in what capacity he is acting at a given moment of time'.[37] This was not the case in *Halford v United Kingdom*.[38] The applicant had been 'appointed to the rank of Assistant Chief Constable with the Merseyside police'.[39] However, she was refused a further promotion to Deputy Chief Constable. She then initiated proceedings before the UK's Industrial Tribunal. She alleged that:

> 'certain members of the Merseyside Police Authority launched a "campaign" against her in response to her complaint to the Industrial Tribunal. This took the form, inter alia …(of) interception of her telephone calls[40] … She allege(d) that calls made from her home and her office telephones were intercepted for the purposes of obtaining information to use against her in the discrimination proceedings'.[41]

The applicant claimed that this interception was in breach of art 8 of the ECHR. The respondent disagreed, submitting that:

> 'telephone calls made by Ms Halford from her workplace fell outside the protection of Article 8 … because she could have had no reasonable expectation of privacy in relation to them. At the hearing before the Court, counsel for the Government expressed the view that an employer should in principle, without the prior knowledge of the employee, be able to monitor calls made by the latter on telephones provided by the employer.'[42]

[33.11] The ECtHR held in favour of the applicant, finding that:

> 'it is clear from its case-law that telephone calls made from business premises as well as from the home may be covered by the notions of 'private life' and 'correspondence' within the meaning of Article 8[43]… There is no evidence of any warning having been given to Ms Halford, as a user of the internal telecommunications system operated at the Merseyside police headquarters, that calls made on that system would be liable to interception. She would, the Court considers, have had a reasonable expectation of privacy for such calls[44] …(therefore) the Court concludes that the conversations held by Ms Halford on her office telephones fell within the scope of the notions of 'private life' and 'correspondence' and that Article 8 … is therefore applicable.'[45]

[33.12] In *Copland v United Kingdom*[46] the applicant was employed as a personal assistant to the members of the senior management of a college in Wales. The college intensively monitored the applicant's phone, email and internet browsing. The ECtHR found that:

> 'telephone calls from business premises are *prima facie* covered by the notions of 'private life' and 'correspondence' for the purposes of Article 8 (1).… It follows logically that

---

[37]   (23 November 1992) ECtHR, para 29.
[38]   *Halford v United Kingdom* (25 June 1997) ECtHR.
[39]   (27 May 1997) ECtHR, para 9.
[40]   (27 May 1997) ECtHR, para 12.
[41]   (27 May 1997) ECtHR, para 17.
[42]   (27 May 1997) ECtHR, para 43.
[43]   (27 May 1997) ECtHR, para 44.
[44]   (27 May 1997) ECtHR, para 45.
[45]   (27 May 1997) ECtHR, para 46.
[46]   *Copland v United Kingdom* (3 April 2007).

emails sent from work should be similarly protected under Article 8, as should information derived from the monitoring of personal internet usage'.[47]

Citing *Halford v United Kingdom*, the ECtHR went on to find that:

> 'The applicant in the present case had been given no warning that her calls would be liable to monitoring, therefore she had a reasonable expectation as to the privacy of calls made from her work telephone ... The same expectation should apply in relation to the applicant's email and internet usage'.[48]

[33.13] The college had no internet usage policy in place at the time that the monitoring took place, but it is not clear from the judgment that the existence of such a policy would have ensured that the monitoring was 'in accordance with the law'. The court noted that to be in accordance with the law

> 'there must be a measure of legal protection in domestic law against arbitrary interferences by public authorities with the rights safeguarded by Article 8(1). This is all the more so in areas such as the monitoring in question, in view of the lack of public scrutiny and the risk of misuse of power'.[49]

[33.14] The ECtHR was of the view that any law that permitted monitoring would have to be compatible with the rule of law, this means that in order to fulfill the requirement of foreseeability a law must:

> 'be sufficiently clear in its terms to give individuals an adequate indication as to the circumstances in which and the conditions on which the authorities are empowered to resort to any such measures'.[50]

The ECtHR noted that there was no domestic law regulating monitoring in the UK at the time. This led the ECtHR to the conclusion that the interference was not in accordance with the law in this case. The ECtHR was careful to make it clear that it was not saying that monitoring of employees was illegal unless the monitoring was regulated by a domestic law such as the Communications (Lawful Business Practice) Regulations 2000, which was enacted by the UK in the years after the events gave rise to this action. The ECtHR stated that:

> 'The Court would not exclude that the monitoring of an employee's use of a telephone, email or internet at the place of work may be considered 'necessary in a democratic society' in certain situations in pursuit of a legitimate aim'.[51]

But the ECtHR declined to pronounce further on this issue. The ECtHR might consider that monitoring where an employer had an acceptable use policy, of which employees were aware and to which they had agreed, to be one where was 'necessary in a democratic society' and thus permitted by Article 8(2) of the ECHR. But the ECtHR would appear to prefer that workplace monitoring be regulated by legislation. The ECtHR did not rule out the possibility that workplace monitoring could occur where

---

[47] (3 April 2007), para 41.
[48] (3 April 2007), para 42.
[49] (3 April 2007), para 45.
[50] (3 April 2007), para 46.
[51] (3 April 2007), para 48.

regulations had not been enacted, but such monitoring would only occur in 'certain situations'. The ECtHR did not define what these situations might be. The decision in *Copland v United Kingdom* means that Ireland might prudently consider legislating for monitoring in the workplace.

Monitoring of communications

[33.15] In *Mehigan v Dyflin Publications* the EAT noted that:

> 'email and the internet have become an invaluable means of business communication for companies throughout Ireland. Effective use of these systems can transform a company's profitability, which is evident from the recent explosion of e-commerce.
>
> As a result, in many companies, employees have unlimited use to the Internet and sending and receiving emails fro their own personal use. A number of issues have therefore begun to emerge regarding the unauthorised use of business equipment, the monitoring of email and Internet use by employees, the harassment of employees by sending offensive and possibly defamatory emails and the implementation of work place policies regulating the use of business equipment'.

[33.16] Employees have a right of privacy when using the phone, Internet or email. This right has to be balanced with other rights. The employer has a right to monitor employee communications, for example, to ensure that employee privileges are not being abused or to monitor employee performance. Furthermore, the rights of the person or persons with whom an employee communicates must also be taken into account. It is clear from the decision of the High Court in *Kennedy and Arnold v Ireland*[52] that the courts will distinguish in the award of damages between breaches of privacy that are 'deliberate and conscious' and those that are 'incidental'.[53] However, the courts will award damages for 'incidental' privacy breaches. In *Case Study 2/2002*, the DPC recounts that he was contacted by a woman who, in the course of her employment 'received a telephone call from one of the major international banking organisations based in Ireland. In the course of the call, she heard 'pips' on the line and, on enquiring, was informed that the call was being recorded but no explanation for the recording was given by the person representing the bank'.[54] The DPC investigated and found that the bank:

> 'operated an automated telephone recording system. Under this system, calls are automatically recorded and the recordings are retained for one year. Access to these recordings, permitted only under strictly controlled conditions, is limited either to where evidence is required in the case of a dispute by a customer as to an instruction or confirmation given, or where there is an investigation of suspected fraud or other criminal

---

52 *Kennedy and Arnold v Ireland* [1987] IR 587.

53 'the injury done to the plaintiffs' right to privacy was serious, the distress suffered by them as a result thereof significant and in the case of the first and second plaintiffs was done consciously, deliberately and without justification. In the case of the third plaintiff, who is the spouse of the second plaintiff, the injury was not done consciously or deliberately but incidentally. In all the circumstances of this case, I will award to the first plaintiff the sum of €20,000 damages, to the second plaintiff the sum of €20,000 damages and to the third plaintiff the sum of €10,000 damages' [1987] IR 587 at 595.

54 DPC *Annual Report* 2002, p 24.

activity. Only a limited number of senior individuals had access to the recordings, which are kept in a secure room in a secure locked cabinet and then only where documentation had been completed and approved'.

The DPC considered that:

'a legitimate interest basis exists for the recording of calls in business critical areas in the financial services sector, subject to the proviso that callers should be clearly informed that recording is taking place and the caller can then either go on with the call or not'.[55]

[33.17] The DPC considered that the bank had addressed the issue satisfactorily by 'introducing automated messages within the telephone system which would advise that the call was being recorded and the purpose of the recording', and 'limiting the recording of calls to business critical areas'.[56]

In this context, the Article 29 Working Party suggests that:

'If access to ... (an) ... email's content is absolutely necessary, account should be taken of the privacy of those outside the organisation receiving them as well as those inside. The employer, for instance, cannot obtain the consent of those outside the organisation sending emails to his workers. The employer should make reasonable efforts to inform those outside the organisation of the existence of monitoring activities to the extent that people outside the organisation could be affected by them. A practical example could be the insertion of warning notices regarding the existence of the monitoring systems, which may be added to all outbound messages from the organisation'.[57]

That staff might have legitimate concerns with the introduction of a call recording system was accepted by the Labour Court in *Irish Life v Amicus*.[58] The employer wished to install a customer call recording system arguing that: '(c)all-recording is a well established tool in service industries and essential to the Company's retail business where customers want to do business over the phone rather than in writing or in person'. The union argued that '(t)he recording of telephone calls (particularly private calls) is an extremely sensitive issue for workers not least from the perspectives of privacy and trust'. The Labour Court was satisfied that a sustainable case had been made out for the introduction of the system, subject to the following conditions:

(a)   The provision of a facility 'which would allow staff to make private calls, in the circumstances in which such calls are allowed, on phone extensions which are not subject to recording';

(b)   The modification of the 'Code of Practice on the use of the system ... so as to distinguish between the frequency of and circumstances in which calls will be monitored as between new staff and long-serving staff. This should reflect the different training and coaching requirements of those respective categories of staff'.

---

55   DPC *Annual Report* 2002, p 25.
56   DPC *Annual Report* 2002, p 25.
57   Article 29, Working Party, *Working Document on the surveillance of electronic communications in the workplace*, p 17–18.
58   *Irish Life v Amicus* CD/05/627 Recommendation No 18349, (10 October 2005).

Monitoring and SI 535/2003

[33.18] Directive 58/2003 provides that:

'Member States shall ensure the confidentiality of communications and the related traffic data by means of a public communications network and publicly available electronic communications services, through national legislation. In particular, they shall prohibit listening, tapping, storage or other kinds of interception or surveillance of communications and the related traffic data by persons other than users, without the consent of the users concerned'.[59]

As is argued above, the implementation of this provision in SI 535/2003 may mean that employees will not be able to enforce its provisions against employers who intercept communications on their own communications systems.

Section 98(4)(a) of the Postal and Telecommunications Services Act 1983 does provide that:

'The Minister may make regulations prohibiting the provision or operation of overhearing facilities in relation to any apparatus (including private branch telephone exchanges) connected to the network of the company otherwise than in accordance with such conditions as he considers to be reasonable and prescribes in the regulations'.

Such regulations have yet to be made.[60]

The Article 29 Working Party working document on the surveillance of electronic communications in the workplace

[33.19] The Article 29 Working Party suggests that '(b)efore being implemented in the work place, any monitoring measure must pass a list of tests …'.[61]'. The Working Party summarises those tests as follows:

(a)   Is it necessary? Couldn't the employer obtain the same result with traditional methods of supervision?

(b)   Is the processing of personal data proposed fair to the workers?

(c)   Is it proportionate to the concerns that it tries to ally?

(d)   Is the monitoring activity transparent to the workers?

Is monitoring necessary?

[33.20] The Working Party suggests that: '(i)t would only be in exceptional circumstances that the monitoring of a worker's mail or Internet use would be considered necessary'. The Working Party suggests that:

'the employer must check if any form of monitoring is absolutely necessary for a specified purpose before proceeding to engage in any such activity. Traditional methods of supervision, less intrusive for the privacy of individuals, should be carefully considered

---

[59]   Directive 2002/58, art 5(1).

[60]   And, if they were to be made, they would have to comply with the decision of the Supreme Court in *Mulcreevy v Minister for the Environment* [2004] 1 IR 72.

[61]   Article 29 Working Party, *Working Document on the surveillance of electronic communications in the workplace*, p 4.

and where appropriate implemented before engaging in any monitoring of electronic communications'.[62]

Some of the grounds that may necessitate monitoring are discussed below.

Defamation

[33.21] Defamatory statements made in a phone call will be as actionable as those made face-to-face. In *Crofter Properties v Genport,*[63] the Superior Courts were satisfied that an employee of the plaintiff had made a number of phone calls which made serious allegations about the defendant. The Supreme Court held that the employer was vicariously liable for the actions of its employee and the matter was then remitted back to the High Court for an assessment of damages. In the High Court, general damages were assessed as being in the sum of IR£50,000 (€63,486). The award of exemplary or punitive damages in the sum of IR£250,000 (€317,434) was appealed to the Supreme Court, which reduced this to IR£100,000 (€126,973).[64] So, in total the plaintiff was awarded IR£150,000 or €190,460. There is no reason to believe that the law of defamation does not apply to internet communications.[65] However, for the avoidance of any doubts,[66] the Electronic Commerce Act 2000 provides that: 'All provisions of existing defamation law shall apply to all electronic communications within the State, including the retention of information electronically.[67]' Actions have been commenced before the English courts in respect of defamatory statements made in emails. Most notably, in *Western Provident Association v Norwich Union Healthcare*[68] the parties were competing medical insurance companies. Employees of the defendant sent emails alleging that the plaintiff was insolvent and being investigated by the UK's Department of Trade and Industry. The settlement was reported to be in the region of £450,000.[69]'

---

[62] Article 29 Working Party *Working Document on the surveillance of electronic communications in the workplace*, p 13.

[63] *Crofter Properties v Genport* [2002] 4 IR 73.

[64] See *Crofter v Genport* [2005] IESC 20.

[65] See *Godfrey v Demon Internet* [1999] EWHC QB 244 'There is a precedent in the UK – the decision of the English High Court of 26 March 1999 in *Godfrey v Demon Internet* – but we just cannot take such precedent. It is likely that Irish courts will hold that defamation principles apply equally to the Internet'. The Minister for Public Enterprise, Mary O'Rourke TD, Dáil Éireann – Volume 522 – 29 June, 2000 Electronic Commerce Bill 2000 [Seanad]: Committee Stage (Resumed) and Remaining Stages. '… if you are a 'player' in the business or financial world and are trying to attract international investment what is said about you or your companies on the Internet obviously assumes considerable importance.' Per Keane CJ in *O'Brien v Mirror Group Newspapers Ltd* [2000] IESC 70 (25 October 2000) SC.

[66] '… this was an avoidance of doubt type amendment which clarified that defamation law applies to electronic communications within the State …', The Minister for Public Enterprise, Mary O'Rourke TD, Seanad Éireann – Volume 163 – 30 June 2000 Electronic Commerce Bill 2000 [Seanad Bill amended by the Dáil]: Report and Final Stages.

[67] Electronic Commerce Act 2000, s 23.

[68] *Western Provident Association v Norwich Union Healthcare* (unreported), see Price and Duohu *Defamation* (3rd edn, Thomson Sweet and Maxwell, 2004), para 35–16, p 426.

[69] See also *Exoteric Gass Solutions and Duffield v BG Plc* (23 June, unreported), Eady J; (contd/)

Passing off/protection of business reputation

[33.22] In *Mulvany v Compaq Computer*[70] the applicant, an employee of the respondent, was dismissed on the basis that she had 'abused the company facility by using it to promote a business, a commercial venture in which she was involved at the time'. The EAT was satisfied that the applicant:

> 'misused company property in so far as she advertised on her business card a telephone number the property of the company and communicated by emails in circumstances where the company name appeared on these communications which could have been to the detriment of the company'.

Although concerns about a company's reputation might justify some monitoring, those concerns would not necessarily justify the dismissal of an employee. The EAT also ruled that 'the fact that the company knew of this activity for a considerable period before they initiated these disciplinary procedures indicates that the company themselves were not treating it with the same gravity that they subsequently attributed to the behaviour'. The EAT ruled that the dismissal 'was unfair in circumstances where no warning was given'.

Fraud and theft

[33.23] The monitoring of employees may be necessary to prevent fraud and theft. But the system installed will have to be proportionate to the threat posed. A number of decisions of the Labour Court have analysed the introduction of CCTV monitoring in the workplace for the purposes of preventing theft. These decisions suggest that such systems should only be introduced in consultation with the workforce. Where such systems do gather evidence of an alleged theft, then this evidence will still have to be processed in a fair manner that accords due process to the employee. In *McCollum v Dunnes Stores (Oakville) Ltd*,[71] the respondent's security manager stated that in '2001 there were stock loss issues … relating to minerals and chocolate. Empty packets were found in the stockroom of the off-licence'. She therefore 'arranged for the installation of a covert camera'. The claimant was then allegedly 'observed drinking a bottle of diet cola'. The claimant was called to a meeting with the management of the respondent and her shop steward at which she was questioned about her diet cola drinking and subsequently dismissed. The EAT ruled that her dismissal was unfair as the 'video evidence should have been shown to her without comment at the beginning of the inquiry and she should then have been asked to explain her actions'. Even if an employer is certain that it has clear evidence of employee's gross misconduct or dishonesty that does not mean that it does not have to bother with fair procedures. Should it dismiss that employee without regard to procedural proprieties and should the matter find its way to

---

[69] (\contd) see Price and Duohu *Defamation* (3rd edn, Thomson Sweet and Maxwell, 2004), para 35–16. The second-named plaintiff was a former employee of the defendant. An email circulated to the defendant's employees which 'stated that there had been a complaint against the (plaintiffs) concerning the misuse of confidential information … and instructing employees not to have any dealings with them. Price and Duohu *Defamation* (3rd edn, Thomson Sweet and Maxwell, 2004), paras 35–16.

[70] *Mulvany v Compaq Computer* (22 July 2000), EAT, UD 935/1999, MN1305/99.

[71] *McCollum v Dunnes Stores (Oakville) Ltd* (2 October 2003) UD424/2002, MN820/2002.

the EAT, that tribunal will not have any regard to the guilt or innocence of the employee. The EAT will only concern itself with the procedures followed by the employer. The test was set out in *Looney and Co Ltd v Looney*[72]:

> 'It is not for the Tribunal to seek to establish the guilt or innocence of the claimant, nor is it for the Tribunal to indicate or consider whether we, in the employer's position, would have acted as he did in his investigation, or concluded as he did or decided as he did, as to do so would substitute our mind and decision for that of the employer. Our responsibility is to consider against the facts what a reasonable employer in the same position and circumstances at that time would have done and decided and to set this up as a standard against which the employer's action and decision be judged'.

Pornography and child pornography

[33.24] Pornography causes a number of concerns for employers. Firstly, if sent from the employer's system to customers or other third parties it might damage the employer's reputation. As the EAT noted in *Mehigan v Dyflin Publications Ltd*,[73] the sending of pornographic material 'had the potential to put the viability of the company, and the continued employment of ..., at risk'. Secondly, there is what the EAT referred to in *Mehigan v Dyflin Publications Ltd* as the 'the harassment of employees by sending offensive ... emails.' In *Mehigan v Dyflin Publications Ltd*, the EAT noted the evidence of a coworker of the claimant that 'he had seen hardcore pornographic images and cartoon characters in a sexual position'. The EAT determined that actions such as this meant that the claimant had made 'an enormous contribution' to his own dismissal. The EAT suggested that:

> 'The exposure of co-employees to this, if left unchecked could be seen as a hostile working environment that could have wider employment ramifications for the respondent. In the UK case of Morse and Future Reality (1996) the company was held liable in a case of constructive dismissal brought by Ms Morse who shared a room with four male colleagues who regularly downloaded pornographic material from the Internet'.

Finally, there is the danger that the possession or distribution of pornographic emails could expose the employer to criminal charges. A distinction has to be made between material that is simply pornographic and that which is obscene, or in the most extreme case, child pornography. Although the material in *Mehigan v Dyflin Publications Ltd* was described as hardcore pornography, there is no suggestion in the determination of the EAT that possession or distribution of it might amount to a criminal offence.[74] The justification for the claimant's dismissal was the harm that the sending of pornographic emails might do to his employer's business and the hostility that such material might engender in his working environment. The EAT did find that his dismissal was unfair but only after 'much discussion'.

---

[72] *Looney and Co Ltd v Looney* UD843/984, cited in EAT decision *Connolly v Carey Glass Ltd* 11/03/2004 UD45/2003, MN488/2003.

[73] *Mehigan v Dyflin Publications Ltd* (10 December 2002, unreported) EAT, UD 582/2001, MN 2032/2001.

[74] The claimant was accused of being in possession of pornographic images, receiving 'hard-core pornographic' emails and downloading an 'an Internet icon that was of a sexual nature'.

[33.25] Perhaps the most extreme situation is where the employer might discover that its systems are being used for the wholesale storage and distribution of pornography or child pornography. This is what happened to the Birmingham University in *R v Fellows and Arnold*.[75] The first named defendant:

> 'used the computer of his employers ... to store data which enabled it to display indecent pictures of children on the computer screen and to produce prints. He also made this data available on the Internet, so that other computers world-wide could receive and display similar screen images and produce identical prints'.[76]

Both defendants were convicted under the UK's Protection of Children Act 1978. In Ireland, the Child Trafficking and Pornography Act 1998 prohibits 'the production, dissemination, handling or possession of child pornography''.[77] Of particular relevance to employers is that the Act makes it an offence to knowingly encourage or facilitate any person who:

(a)   'knowingly produces, distributes, prints or publishes any child pornography';

(b)   'knowingly imports, exports, sells or shows any child pornography';

(c)   'knowingly publishes or distributes any advertisement likely to be understood as conveying that the advertiser or any other person produces, distributes, prints, publishes, imports, exports, sells or shows any child pornography'.[78]

[33.26] These offences are quite broad and would cover almost any interaction with child pornography. Therefore, any employer who comes into the knowledge that one of its employees is using its systems to produce, disseminate, handle or possess child pornography must report the matter to An Garda S'och‡na. To do otherwise is to invite charges that the employer is knowingly facilitating the employee's activities. Even an employer who quietly asks such an employee to leave without a fuss may be knowingly encouraging or facilitating the employee's activities and so committing an offence under the Act. The duty that the Child Trafficking and Pornography Act 1998 imposes upon employers is therefore quite draconian. However, this duty would seem justified given the harm that the production and use of child pornography can do.

Incitement to hatred

[33.27] The sending of a racist communication may amount to an offence under the Prohibition of Incitement to Hatred Act 1989.[79] That Act makes it an offence to 'publish or distribute written material ... if the written material, words, behaviour, visual images or sounds, as the case may be, are threatening, abusive or insulting and are intended or, having regard to all the circumstances, are likely to stir up hatred''.[80] So, an employee who used their employer's systems to publish or distribute such material might commit an offence. So too might an employer who permitted their system to be used for that

---

[75] *R v Fellows and Arnold* (1997) 1 Cr App R 244.

[76] (1997) 1 Cr App R 244 at 245.

[77] Child Trafficking and Pornography Act 1998, preamble.

[78] Child Trafficking and Pornography Act 1998, s 5(1).

[79] In particular s 2 which provides that it will be an offence 'to publish or distribute written material '.

[80] Prohibition of Incitement to Hatred Act 1989, s 2(1)(c).

purpose. If a single isolated incident were to occur, then the employer could argue that although the publication and distribution had occurred using its systems, this activity was clearly outside the scope of the employee's employment. However, this argument would be harder to make if the distribution and publication were to occur recurrently and the employer ignored or condoned it. It should be noted that in *Fogarty and O'Connor v IBM* the EAT ruled fair the dismissal of employees who accessed a website containing content that was 'grossly offensive, ... sexual, racist and deeply offensive'.

Intellectual property

[33.28] Employers may wish to monitor to ensure that their own intellectual property does not exit their systems. The danger that employees may inadvertently disclose a company's confidential information by Internet or email use should not be overstated. A survey of UK employees found that just 4 per cent had 'accidentally sent out confidential company information to someone who should not have seen it, in an email or as an email attachment', and 1 per cent didn't know if they had done so.[81] That said, any employer who controls particularly sensitive information may feel that a one-in-twenty risk is sufficiently serious to warrant monitoring. The DPC's *Case Study 3/2003* is an example of how an inadvertent disclosure of confidential information can easily occur. The information in question was details of visa and asylum applicants which had been disclosed by the Department of Justice, Equality and Law Reform. The DPC investigated and found that 'through an unfortunate and accidental breach in operating procedures, visa decisions for 506 applicants were posted live on the website with the inadvertent inclusion of the applicants' name and nationality'.[82]

[33.29] The DPC found that this was in contravention of the DPA, as it was an 'incompatible disclosure of personal data'. It could also be argued that this disclosure was a breach of the controller's duty to keep personal data secure, and the department did alter its procedures to 'avoid a recurrence'. However, the monitoring of employee communications is not necessarily an effective method of identifying or preventing the disclosure of confidential information. Controls on the use and communication of that information may offer more effective protections against disclosure than blanket monitoring of all employee communications. Therefore, an issue of proportionality might arise if concerns about the disclosure of confidential information were used to justify the monitoring of all employee communications. This is illustrated by the decision of the Labour Court in *AIBP Ltd v A Worker*.[83] The court found that the employee in question was dismissed for 'the accessing of sensitive company information'. The employee informed the court that she 'carried out most of her work on a computer and was never informed that certain files were not to be accessed as they contained sensitive company information'. The court accepted the employee's explanation that 'her accessing of the particular file was based on curiosity in relation to

---

81 YouGov survey conducted for Brands2life 'Internet Access at Work' 5–8 November 2004, http://www.yougov.com.

82 DPC *Annual Report 2003*, p 32.

83 *AIBP Ltd v A Worker* (24 November 1998), Labour Court, CD/98/267 Recommendation No LCR16023.

the technology rather than ... for commercial reasons'. The Labour Court concluded that it:

> 'finds it strange that this sensitive company information was so accessible and that the password to it seems to have been known within the plant.

> While accepting the need for confidentiality on sensitive information, the Court finds that the manner of dismissal of the complainant was unfair'.

[33.30] Employers may also need to monitor to ensure that the intellectual property of others does not enter their systems. The Irish Recorded Music Association (IRMA) has settled legal actions with 'at least one firm that did not know that one of its employees was using its network to illegally upload music'.[84] On the face of it is hard to see why any employer would settle such a claim. IRMA's legal actions were directed at 'people who have illegally uploaded hundreds or thousands of music tracks onto peer-to-peer file-sharing networks'. It would seem self evident that the activities of such 'serial file sharers' are far outside the scope of any legitimate employment. Their employer might therefore have argued that it was not vicariously liable for this activity. Unfortunately for employers, the CRRA 2000 may impose liability in such a situation. Section 45(d) of the CRRA 2000 provides:

> 'A person infringes the copyright in a work where he or she without the licence of the copyright owner ... otherwise than in the course of a business, trade or profession, makes available to the public to such an extent as to prejudice the interests of the owner of the copyright, a copy of the work which is, and which he or she knows or has reason to believe is, an infringing copy of the work'.[85]

Presumably, the employees in question were using their employers' systems to make music available over the peer-to-peer networks 'to such an extent as to prejudice the interests of the owner of the copyright'. It may be argued that s 45(1) makes it irrelevant that the employee was acting 'otherwise than in the course of a business'. If it is assumed that an employer is managing its ICT systems effectively and securely, then only the employer's system administrator would be capable of acting as a 'serial file sharer'. And it may be that the courts would find that the actions of the system administrator were 'closely connected' with his employment. So, it is important that employers are able to trust their system administrators not to engage in activities of this type. However, it is relatively straightforward for system administrators to ensure that other employees are not acting in this way. An effective administrator should be able to monitor the system to ensure that other employees do not start uploading large amounts of data to unfamiliar networks. They might configure the system's firewall to ensure that such unauthorised activity was not possible. Such precautions can all be taken without

---

[84] Cassidy 'IRMA takes legal action against 50 file-sharers' http://www.ireland.com, 15 November 2005.

[85] See also s 46(2) of the Copyright and Related Rights Act 2000, which provides: 'A person infringes the copyright in a work where he or she, without the licence of the copyright owner, transmits the work by means of a telecommunications system ... knowing or having reason to believe that infringing copies of the work may be made by means of the reception of the transmission in the State or elsewhere'.

monitoring the actual content of communications sent or received by employees. Therefore, the level of monitoring that may be justified on this ground may be limited.

Performance management

[33.31] Monitoring of employees can have a significant effect upon their performance. This effect, which is sometimes called the 'Hawthorne Effect', was first identified in the 1930s.[86] The legitimacy of monitoring for the purposes of productivity has been acknowledged by the Labour Court in a number of recommendations. The Labour Court has been willing to countenance the use of cameras as a method of monitoring production, but only if it can be shown to have 'real benefits'. In *Thermo King Europe v AEU*[87] in 1986 the employer sought to introduce 'a synthetic industrial engineering technique which uses video equipment to record work activities'. In a 1990 decision the Labour Court concluded that:

> 'It is clear that the use of a video camera is not a familiar tool of measurement and the trail period has not removed employee disquiet nor indeed established the reality of the benefits envisaged by the Company. The Court therefore recommends that there should be a further trial period of 12 months during which particular attention should be paid to the employees comments regarding studies being conducted under "ideal conditions".'

[33.32] However, as surveillance of production has become more sophisticated, and the benefits of such surveillance have been accepted, the Labour Court has become more willing to accept the use of such technologies as a means of monitoring production. In *Crown Equipment v Amicus/AEEU*[88] the Court was:

> 'of the view that the proposed use of video recording in this instance is part of normal ongoing change and recommends that the Union should cooperate fully with its use as part of the Process Improvement Programme. After a period of six months the process should be reviewed to evaluate benefits achieved and with a view to sharing the savings made. These benefits should be measured in terms of the improvements achieved in the levels of efficiency and competitiveness'.

---

[86] 'During the Great Depression, a Harvard Business School Professor name George Elton Mayo conducted a series of experiments on human behaviour and workplace productivity at Western Electric's Hawthorne Plant ... From a massive factory floor full of workers hunched over telephone relay devices, Elton May choose half a dozen women and monitored their behaviour and productivity for several weeks, without them knowing the was watching. Having ascertained a base productivity level, Elton Mayo then segregated his six women in a special room, under the eye of a supervisor, and adjusted the hours in their workday, the days in their workweek, the hour of their lunch break, the frequency of breaks and so forth. Looking for the effects of monotony and fatigue on the job, he tinkered with the conditions and monitored the women's productivity. But as he conducted his experiment, Elton Mayo noticed ... that what made the difference in the smaller room was not the breaks or any other change Elton May could have imposed. It was the fact that somebody was watching'. Patrick Radden Keefe *Chatter* (Random House, New York, 2005), p 41.

[87] *Thermo King Europe v AEU* Case LCR12966.

[88] *Crown Equipment v Amicus/AEEU* CD/03/571 Recommendation No 17568. See also *Dubarry Shoes Ltd v SIPTU* CD/97/98 Recommendation No LCR15492.

[33.33] The introduction of monitoring systems for the purposes of making production more efficient may be legitimate for the purposes of the DPA, but, only if it can be shown to have tangible benefits and only if all aspects of the DPA are complied with. Furthermore, the surveillance of production in the manufacturing sector is one thing, it is quite another to monitor the provision of services. Factories are by their nature closed environments to which an employer may control entry and exit. This allows employers to ensure that everyone within their premises is an employee discharging their duties under their contract of an employment. Services, however, will be provided to members of the public, and any monitoring of how efficiently an employee interacts with a customer must also by its nature monitor the customer. The legitimacy of monitoring in such circumstances will not be so easily established and heed should be paid to *Case Study 2/2002*, which considered the monitoring of customer calls to a bank's call centre and is discussed above.

Is monitoring fair?

[33.34] The Article 29 Working Party notes that all data processing operations can only commence if they comply with one of the criteria for making data processing legitimate. The Working Party draws particular attention to the criterion that 'processing is necessary for the purposes of the legitimate interests pursued by the controller or by the third party or parties to whom the data are disclosed, except where such interests are overridden by the interests for fundamental rights and freedoms of the data subject'.[89] The Working Party suggests one such legitimate interest might be: '(t)he need of the employer to protect his business from significant threats, such as to prevent transmission of confidential information to a competitor'.[90]

Is monitoring proportionate?

[33.35] The Working Party suggests that:

> 'The proportionality principle … rules out blanket monitoring of individual emails and Internet use of all staff other than where necessary for the purpose of ensuring the security of the system Where the objective identified can be achieved in a less intrusive way the employer should consider this option'.

So '(t)he monitoring of emails should, if possible, be limited to traffic data on the participants and time of a communication rather than the contents of communications if this would suffice to allay the employer's concerns'.

Is monitoring wise?

[33.36] The installation of powerful monitoring computer systems in the workplace is now commonplace. For example, Dublin City Council has published a tender for a system that would monitor the Internet use, email and telephone calls of its 6,500 employees.[91] However, just because an employer can monitor the workplace does not

---

[89] Directive 95/46, art 7(f), implemented as DPA, s 2A(1)(d).

[90] Article 29 Working Party *Working Document on the surveillance of electronic communications in the workplace*, p 17.

[91] 'Staff members fixed line and mobile phone calls will all be monitored in terms of cost effectiveness to ensure that people are not wasting the council's money on personal calls. (contd/)

mean that it should. It is not uncommon for employers to regret their decision to monitor what happens at work. US President Nixon is the seminal example of the chief executive who came to regret the installation of monitoring devices in his workplace. Presidents previous to him had installed recording systems.[92] President Eisenhower installed such a system, but took the sensible precaution of including an on/off switch that he was able to control from behind his desk.[93] When Nixon arrived, he installed an upgrade. Unfortunately (for him), he omitted the on/off switch.[94] The resulting 'Nixon Tapes' were a key part of the scandal that caused his presidency to implode. Perhaps coincidentally, modern US Presidents appear quite technologically adverse, and neither President Clinton nor the present President Bush used or use email.[95]

[33.37] Irish and European law may place limitations on the objectives that may be pursued by email monitoring policies. For example, in March 2005, Harry Stonecipher, the boss of Boeing, was forced to resign after emails that he had sent to a female employee were disclosed to the Boeing Board. Stonecipher had sent emails to the object of his affections, which were forwarded by a 'whistleblower' to the Chairman of Boeing's Board'.[96] There was no allegation of sexual harassment in this case. A similar case in Ireland would raise issues such as whether it is permissible for employers to intrude into the personal lives of their employees in this way. With specific regard to data protection, an email that contains details of an affair being conducted between employees will contain data relating to those employees' sexual lives. As such, it will be sensitive data and can only be processed in accordance with the restrictions imposed by s 2B of the DPA.

Is monitoring transparent?

[33.38] The Article 29 Working Party is of the opinion that 'an employer must be clear and open about his activities…no covert email monitoring is allowed by employers

---

[91] (\contd) The system will also incorporate an alarm mechanism if a staff member dials a banned telephone number or visits a non-work related website. It will also enable managers to view Web content that is downloaded or uploaded by Council employees', Smyth 'Dublin City Council to give its staff the 'Big Brother' treatment' (2004) The Irish Times, 23 January.

[92] 'The wiring of the White House … had begun as early as 1940, when Roosevelt had his office space and phone rigged with primitive recording devices'. Summers *The Arrogance of Power: The Secret World of Richard Nixon* (Victor Gollancz, 2000), p 315.

[93] 'two decades before Nixon was to install secret recording equipment in his White House, Eisenhower had recording equipment set up in the Oval Office, a device he activated with the flip of an unseen switch under his desk'. Summers *The Arrogance of Power: The Secret World of Richard Nixon* (Victor Gollancz, 2000), p 146.

[94] Initially, Nixon who 'had been perennially anxious about electronic surveillance' removed the 'extensive, really extensive' taping system from the White House 'But toward the end of Nixon's first term … microphones would again be sown around the presidential quarters – this time with devastating results'. Summers *The Arrogance of Power: The Secret World of Richard Nixon* (2000) Victor Gollancz, p 314–315.

[95] President Bush told reporters that: 'I don't email. And there's a reason. I don't want you reading my personal stuff. MacMillan 'Bush: The email stops here' (2005) The Washington Post, 15 April.

[96] 'The end of the office affair?' (2005) The Economist, 10 March.

except in those cases where a law in the Member State under art 13 of ... Directive (95/46) allows for (it)'. This clarity and openness may be attained in three ways. Firstly, the Working Party recommends registration with the DPC. Secondly, the Working Party suggests that workers' right of access 'without constraint at reasonable intervals and without excessive delay or expense is a powerful tool that workers individually can exercise to make sure that the monitoring activities in the workplace remain lawful and fair to the worker'.[97] Finally, the employer may provide workers with 'a readily accessible, clear and accurate statement of his policy with regard to email and Internet monitoring...Workers need to be provided with full information as to what specific circumstances would justify such an exceptional measure and as to the breadth and scope of such monitoring'.[98]

The Working Party suggests that this information should include, at least, the following elements:

(a) 'email/Internet policy within the company describing in detail the extent to which communication facilities owned by the company may be used for personal/private communications by the employees (eg limitation on time and duration of use)';

(b) 'Reasons and purposes for which surveillance, if any, is being carried out. Where the employer has allowed the use of the company's communication facilities for express private purposes, such private communications may under very limited circumstances be subject to surveillance, eg to ensure the security of the information system (virus checking)';

(c) 'The details of surveillance measures taken, ie who? what? how? when?';

(d) 'Details of any enforcement procedures outlining how and when workers will be notified of breaches of internal policies and be given the opportunity to respond to any such claims against them'.[99]

[33.39] Where the employer detects a misuse of the electronic communications systems in the company, then the Working Party recommends that the worker in question should be informed immediately. This information might be given by a 'warning window', displayed on a computer screen. The requirement of transparency is consistent with the decision of the ECtHR in *Halford v United Kingdom*. In this case, the ECtHR held that monitoring of the applicant's office telephone had been a breach of her right to respect for her private life under art 8 of the ECHR. As an Assistant Chief Constable, the applicant had been:

'provided with her own office and two telephones, one of which was for private use. These telephones were part of the Merseyside police internal telephone network, a

---

97 Article 29 Working Party *Working Document on the surveillance of electronic communications in the workplace*, p 16. Although the Working Party does acknowledge that: '(a)ccess to employer's files, however, might be problematic in exceptional circumstances as for example access to the so-called evaluation data'.

98 Article 29 Working Party *Working Document on the surveillance of electronic communications in the workplace*, p 14.

99 Article 29, Working Party *Working Document on the surveillance of electronic communications in the workplace*, p 15.

telecommunications system outside the public network. No restrictions were placed on the use of these telephones and no guidance was given to her, save for an assurance which she sought and received from the Chief Constable shortly after she instituted the proceedings in the Industrial Tribunal that she had authorisation to attend to the case while on duty, including by telephone'.[100]

Although the respondent did not admit that the applicant's phones had been monitored, it did concede 'that the applicant had adduced sufficient material to establish a reasonable likelihood that calls made from her office telephones had been intercepted'.[101] The ECtHR held that this interception amounted to an interference in the applicant's rights under art 8 of the ECHR on the grounds, *inter alia*, that:

> 'There is no evidence of any warning having been given to Ms Halford, as a user of the internal telecommunications system operated at the Merseyside police headquarters, that calls made on that system would be liable to interception. She would, the Court considers, have had a reasonable expectation of privacy for such calls, which expectation was moreover reinforced by a number of factors. As Assistant Chief Constable she had sole use of her office where there were two telephones, one of which was specifically designated for her private use. Furthermore, she had been given the assurance, in response to a memorandum, that she could use her office telephones for the purposes of her sex-discrimination case.[102]'

It is worth reiterating that in coming to its decision the ECtHR rejected the view of the respondent that 'an employer should in principle, without the prior knowledge of the employee, be able to monitor calls made by the latter on telephones provided by the employer'.[103]

Internet and email use policies

[33.40] As well as the general suggestions discussed above, the Working Party makes a number of more specific recommendations with regard to email and Internet usage policies. With specific regard to email, the Working Party recommends that the points set out below should be addressed:

(a)   'Whether a worker is entitled to have an email account for purely personal use, whether use of web-mail accounts is permitted at work and whether the employer recommends the use, by workers, of a private web-mail account for the purpose of using email for purely personal use';

(b)   'The arrangements in place with workers to access the contents of an email, ie when the worker is unexpectantly absent, and the specific purposes for such access;'

(c)   'When a backup copy of messages are made, the storage period of it';

(d)   'Information as to when emails are definitively deleted from the server';

---

[100] *Halford v United Kingdom* (25 June 1997) ECtHR, para 16
[101] (25 June 1997) ECtHR, para 47.
[102] (25 June 1997) ECtHR, para 45.
[103] (25 June 1997) ECtHR, para 43.

(e)   'Security issues';

(f)   'The involvement of representative of workers in formulating the policy'.[104]

The Working Party enthuses about the possibility that workers could be allowed access to web-based email accounts.[105] However, the DPA places employers under a statutory duty to keep the personal data that they control secure. In effect this will require employers to maintain a firewall of some description. Web-based emails can compromise firewalls and other security measures, as they allow them to be bypassed. Therefore, employers should seek technical advice before pursuing this option. That said, a survey undertaken in the UK in November 2004 found that 44 per cent of employees surveyed had used 'web-mail account(s) to send personal emails from work'.[106]

[33.41] As regards the monitoring of Internet use, the Article 29 Working Party suggests that:

> 'prevention should be more important than detection... the interest of the employer is better served in preventing Internet misuse through technical means rather than in expending resources in detecting misuse. ...Internet policy should rely on technical means to restrict access rather than on monitoring behaviour'.

In particular the Working Party suggests that the following elements should be present in an employer's Internet Use Policy, which should:

(a)   'set out clearly to workers the conditions on which private use of the Internet is permitted as well as specifying material, which cannot be viewed or copied';

(b)   'inform ... about the systems implemented both to prevent access to certain sites and to detect misuse. The extent of such monitoring should be specified, for instance, whether such monitoring may relate to individuals or particular sections of the company or whether the content of the sites visited is viewed or recorded by the employer in particular circumstances';

(c)   'specify what use, if any, will be made of any data collected in relation to who visited what sites'; and

(d)   'Inform workers about the involvement of their representatives, both in the implementation of this policy and in the investigation of alleged breaches'.[107]

---

[104] Article 29 Working Party *Working Document on the surveillance of electronic communications in the workplace*, p 22.

[105] Such as those provided by http://www.ireland.com, http://www.gmail.com or http://www.hotmail.com. It recommends that 'employers may consider providing workers with two emails accounts'. One such account would be 'for only professional purposes, in which monitoring within the limits of this working document would be possible'. The other would be 'only for purely private purposes ... which would only be subject to security measures and would be checked for abuse in exceptional cases'. See Article 29 Working Party *Working Document on the surveillance of electronic communications in the workplace*, p 5.

[106] YouGov survey conducted for Brands2life 'Internet Access at Work', 5–8 November 2004, http://www.yougov.com.

[107] Article 29 Working Party *Working Document on the surveillance of electronic communications in the workplace*, p 25.

The DPC's policy

[33.42] The EAT noted in *Mehigan v Dyflin*[108] that: 'Increasingly, companies are introducing policies, which clearly specify that company email is not for private purposes and that email should not be used for any purpose other than company business'.[109] The DPC has made the acceptable use policy that he applies within his own office available on the Internet. The policy instructs employees to 'think before you send', not to 'deliberately perform acts which waste your own and your colleagues time or computer resources' and warns that 'the Internet is an unregulated, world wide environment'. It contains provisions relating to:

   (a)   potentially dangerous material;

   (b)   obscenity, child pornography and incitement to hate;

   (c)   other offensive and time wasting material;

   (d)   misleading information;

   (e)   material that is sent by employees;

   (f)   screening procedures;

   (g)   time wasting and resources;

   (h)   financial implications;

   (i)   security;

   (j)   blogs;

   (k)   personal use; and

   (l)   freedom of Information and Archives Acts (which the DPC points out only apply to public bodies).

Undoubtedly, the DPC's policy is a useful template. However, it does not set out to employees how an allegation that they have contravened the policy may be investigated and what sanctions may be imposed if that allegation should be upheld. It is would seem clear from decisions of the EAT that a policy should provide such information if it is to be implemented in practice.

Enforcement of Internet and email usage policies

[33.43] Employers cannot simply dismiss employees at will. Dismissal of an employee for breach of an email policy may prove difficult to justify, particularly where employees are able to rely upon the provisions of the Unfair Dismissals Acts.[110] The

---

[108] *Mehigan v Dyflin Publications Ltd* (10 December 2002, unreported) EAT, UD 582/2001, MN 2032/2001.

[109] However, a survey by the Small Firms Association determined that 57 per cent of small firms have no such policy, see Creaton 'Net abuse a growing problem for firms' (2004) The Irish Times, 3 May.

[110] See the exclusions in the Unfair Dismissals Act 1977, s 2, but see also the Protection of Employees (Part-time Work) Act 2001, s 8. Even where the does not apply, employers may still have to follow the rules of fair procedures when dismissing for misconduct, see *Phelan v BIC (Ireland) Ltd* [1997] ELR 208 and *Hickey v Eastern Health Board* [1991] 1 IR 208; also, *Anthony Philpott v Ogilvy and Mather Ltd* [2000] 3 IR 206.

Unfair Dismissals Acts state that 'the dismissal of an employee shall be deemed…not to be an unfair dismissal, if it results wholly or mainly from … the conduct of the employee'.[111] However, the employer will have to establish that its employee's conduct has been such as to justify that dismissal. In doing so, the employer will be bound by the normal rules of fair procedures. The employer should ideally establish a disciplinary code which accords with the Code of Practice on Grievance and Disciplinary Procedures drafted by the Labour Relations Commission.[112]

[33.44] As a matter of both fair procedures and prudence, any Internet and email usage policy should clearly state the consequences of failure to comply with its provisions. Furthermore, great care should be taken by employers to both inform employees of the contents of such policies and also to ensure that the employer can establish that employees have been given the necessary information. Many employees will be expected to use the Internet extensively in the course of their work. In such situations, it may not be sufficient to simply stick a lengthy document under their nose and have them sign a paper indicating that they have read it. It would be preferable to immediately warn employees if they are suspected of breaching the policy in question. If an employer intends that its employees may be disciplined for breaches of its Internet usage policy then it is essential that its policy document should indicate how that disciplinary process may be initiated and what the outcome of that process may be. The consequences of an employer failing to clearly inform employees of what sanctions they might face should they breach an Internet or email usage policy are illustrated by the decision of the EAT in *Colum O'Leary v Eagle Star*.[113]

[33.45] The EAT described *Colum O'Leary v Eagle Star* as a case that 'exhibited peculiar features which ranged from the sublime to the ridiculous'. The claimant was one of a number of employees who had joined a fraternity which styled itself as 'The Legends'. This group was alleged to be 'harassing staff and forming hit lists of people within the company that they identified as 'company men'. The claimant claimed that 'there was nothing vindictive about the group ... it was just lads having a joke'. The respondent considered them to be 'a sinister group of intimidating thugs'. The respondent was able to produce emails that threatened violence towards individuals and declared 'war towards company men'. However, the EAT found that: 'The misuse or abuse of emails has not been defined within the company structure as 'gross misconduct' and accordingly warrants a warning, verbal or written, but does not warrant dismissal as a course of first instance'.

[33.46] The EAT found that:

> 'Epithets such as '*company men*' and '*brown-nosers*' and such like, may be unpalatable but they should not result in provoking gross indignation to the extent that a company feels rightly that it can unleash the ultimate punishment of terminating a contract of employment. In relation to the emails the respondent company failed to prove malice or

---

[111] Unfair Dismissals Act 1977, s 6(4)(b).
[112] This was published as Industrial Relations Act 1990 (Code of Practice on Grievance and Disciplinary Procedures) (Declaration) Order 2000 (SI 146/2000).
[113] *Colum O'Leary v Eagle Star* 2003 ELR 223.

malicious intent. In law there must be a wilful injuria and the company failed to substantiate same'.

The EAT concluded that the company should have recollected the 'the commonplace but trite couplet which runs: 'Sticks and stones may break your bones but words will never hurt you''. Although the emails in question contained a variety of expletives, the EAT was of the view that only rarely would 'the use of such coarse terms ... justify dismissal in the absence of warnings'. The EAT appeared of the view that where employers need to maintain 'a certain decorum' then a 'telling off' might be sufficient to curtail the 'tactless blunderbuss' of the 'F word'. The EAT concluded that the dismissal of the claimant was unfair, as it was inordinately disproportionate to the offence complained of. This decision was based in part upon the fact that 'in relation to the plethora of documents concerning the use and abuse of IT systems, not one was identified to the satisfaction of the Tribunal as clearly signposting the likely consequences of departing from approved procedures'.

[33.47] The procedure to be followed when enforcing Internet and email policies was examined by the EAT in *Mehigan v Dyflin Publications Ltd.*[114] The claimant was employed by the respondent for twelve years and was dismissed for using his company email to disseminate pornographic material on the grounds that these 'activities constitute not just a breach of the bond of trust but an act of gross misconduct which could reflect very badly on the respondent company'. The EAT noted the phenomenon of increased availability and use of Internet and email in the workplace and the challenges that this use created. In its determination the EAT stated that:

> 'It is highly desirable for employers to include in their email policy/Internet policy a statement to the effect that the sending of offensive emails is prohibited and will be dealt with in accordance with the companies email procedures.

> Any disciplining or dismissal of staff for unauthorised use or misuse of company email systems and the internet must be carried out having regard to the employee's fundamental rights to fair procedures and natural justice. Therefore, where the 'offence' is not sufficiently serious to justify dismissal, employers are expected to apply the different stages in the company disciplinary procedure. Where there is no disciplinary procedure then the employer must act in a fair and reasonable manner. Where an employer feels that an employee's conduct is sufficiently serious to justify summary dismissal then the fairness of the dismissal will be judged against the standard of what the reasonable employer would have done in the circumstances; whether the punishment fits the crime and whether there were any mitigating circumstances in favour of the employee. Under the Unfair Dismissals Acts 1977–2001, the burden of proof falls on the employer to justify a dismissal as not being unfair.

> The Tribunal is likely to deem any dismissal unfair unless due process is afforded to the employee. A typical disciplinary investigation would involve a meeting or meetings during which the employee is granted the right to reply to the allegations against him/her and the right to be represented at meetings'.

---

[114] *Mehigan v Dyflin Publications Ltd* (10 December 2002, unreported) EAT, UD 582/2001, MN 2032/2001.

Clearly the Employment Appeals Tribunal or any other third party will be heavily influenced by the existence of a written email and internet policy where the employer reserves the right to dismiss for breaches of policy. It is unlikely that the use of the internet for unauthorised purposes will amount to a sufficient reason justifying an employer from dismissing an employee without notice in the absence of a clear written statement to this effect in the company's policy. An exception to this, perhaps, would be a situation where an employee was using the company's facilities to download obscene pornography from the Internet'.

[33.48] The facts in *Mehigan v Dyflin Publications Ltd* were that a computer disk containing pornographic material had been found in or around the computer used by the claimant on the employer's premises. The EAT found that the respondent employer:

'failed to have in place clear policies and a code of practice on employee use of email and the internet. The consequences of its misuse should have been made absolutely clear to all employees. After much discussion, the Tribunal decided that the onus was on the employer to have a clear policy in place to deal with the use of email and the consequences for its misuse/abuse. Because of this the Tribunal has to hold the dismissal unfair'.

However, the EAT went on to determine that the claimant was not without blame in this situation. The EAT was satisfied that:

'the claimant made an enormous contribution to his dismissal. Having been employed for twelve years and being the person responsible for overseeing advertisements he should have known that his behaviour was unacceptable and had the potential to put the viability of the company, and the continued employment of his fellow workers, at risk. The Tribunal does not accept that this was once off incident (sic) and notes the evidence of a fellow employee that he had seen hardcore pornographic images on the claimant's computer and cartoon characters in a sexual position'.

[33.49] Whatever penalty is imposed on an employee should be proportionate to the gravity of the breach of policy that has occurred. In *Cable and Wireless v A Worker*[115] the employee in question was suspended for a month and given a final written warning following an investigation into what the company described as 'obscene, disgusting and pornographic material that had been found within the Company's email/internet system'. However, the employee argued that 'The email clip was sent by the ... (employee) ... to only one staff member who did not find it offensive and there was a warning attached saying that its contents may be offensive to others'. The Labour Court reviewed the evidence and concluded that 'in the particular circumstances of this case, the offence committed warrants a lesser sanction than a final written warning and accordingly recommends that this final warning should be removed and replaced by a written warning'.

[33.50] Finally, it is crucial that any policy should be consistently applied to all employees. In the Labour Court decision of *Citibank v Massinde Ntoko*[116] the complainant was a native of the Democratic Republic of the Congo. He had made a personal phone call from his workplace and as a consequence he was summarily

---

[115] *Cable and Wireless v A Worker* (10 October 2001) Recommendation of the Labour Court.
[116] *Citibank v Massinde Ntoko* (8 March 2004) The Labour Court.

dismissed. The complainant was able to satisfy the court that 'other staff had used the phones for private use'. and had not been dismissed. The Labour Court was:

> 'satisfied that the complainant has proved as a matter of probability that he was singled out for special unfavourable treatment by his manager, that another agency employee of a different racial origin would not be so treated and that his dismissal arose as a direct consequence of the special treatment to which he was subjected'.

The court found that the Mr Ntoko had been discriminated against on the grounds of his race contrary to s 8 of the Employment Equality Act 1998.

Access and location monitoring

[33.51] The location of employees may be monitored in a variety of different ways. In *Mac Rental Ltd v AGE & MOU*[117] an employer wished to introduce a 'Vehicle Management System to track vehicles using a Global Positioning Satellite (GPS) system'. The employees Union 'raised serious objections to the proposal and expressed their fears and anxieties concerning the use of such a system; explaining that it represented an intrusion and invasion of drivers' privacy'. The employer outlined the system to the Labour Court and gave the Court 'assurances regarding its use'. In particular the employer stated that it did not intend to use the system as a 'performance management mechanism or a monitoring too'. The employer also assured the court that it would introduce a Code of Practice would provide the necessary protection for both sides in that regard. The Labour Court found in favour of the employer and recommended that the parties enter into negotiations with regard to the introduction of the GPS system and the contents of the Code of Practice. Another-method of monitoring the location of employees is by installing access control devices.[118] The most basic such device may be a key or keycard that is issued to every employee and allows employees to gain access whilst excluding others. However, more advanced systems are now available. The National Gallery is, or was, in the process of introducing a biometric clocking-in system, which would compare the fingerprints of clocking-in workers with those on a centralised data-base. The office of the DPC suggested that '(i)n a time-management context, thee creation of a central database would be excessive and involve a contravention of (the DPA)'. In *Abbey Theatre v BATU*[119] the Labour Court recommended that employees of the Abbey Theatre co-operate with the introduction of a new time and attendance system which required 'a fingertip to be inserted into a reader which converts the fingerprint into an encrypted algorithm and the worker then enters their unique pin number onto a pad'. The employees' trade union contended 'that the system would impinge on the fundamental rights of each worker using the system as it

---

[117] *Mac Rental Ltd v Automobile, General Engineering And Mechanical Operatives Union Technical, Engineering And Electrical Union (AGE & MOU)*, The Labour Court, Cd/05/1109 Recommendation No 18460.

[118] Another form of location monitoring may be provided by Global Positioning System (GPS) enabled systems. The introduction of such a system by an employer was examined by the Labour Court in *Mac Rental Ltd v AGEMOU* (CD/05/1109 Recommendation No 18460, (25 January 2006).

[119] *Abbey Theatre v Building and Allied Trades Union (BATU)*, The Labour Court, CD/06/1125 Recommendation No 18914.

may store their fingerprint'. The Data Protection Commissioner was asked for his views and he stated that he could:

> 'neither give a general approval to nor a general condemnation of Biometric Systems'.

[33.52] However, the Data Protection Commissioner examined the specific system being proposed by the Abbey Theatre and found it compliant with Data Protection legislation. The Labour Court noted that the system contained certain, unspecified safeguards. The Labour Court regarded:

> 'use of the system as normal ongoing change and recommends that the Union's members comply with the use of the system'.

The successful introduction of this biometric system may reflect the introduction by the Data Protection Commissioner of his guidelines on 'Biometrics in the Workplace'. These suggest that particular data protection issues may arise with regard to biometrics: the biometrics must be fairly obtained; they must be accurate; kept securely; and processed in a transparent manner. The DPC suggests that biometric systems should not involve 'excessive' processing of data: 'an employer must conduct some assessment of the need for a system and evaluation of the different types of system before introduction'. This assessment should be undertaken on a case-by-case basis and should take the following factors into account:

(a) *'Environment*. The nature of the workplace may require high levels of security. Areas containing sensitive information, high value goods or potentially dangerous material may warrant a higher level of security than would areas with low value goods or areas with complete public access';

(b) *'Purpose*. Can the intended purpose be achieved in a less intrusive way? A system used to control access for security purposes might be more legitimate than a system used by the same employer purely for time management purposes';

(c) *'Efficiency*. Ease of administration may necessitate the introduction of a system where other less invasive systems have failed, or proved to be prohibitively expensive to run'; and

(d) *'Reliability*. If a employer suffers as a result of untrustworthy staff, impersonating each other for various reasons, then a system may be justified as long as other less invasive ones have been assessed and reasonably rejected'.

[33.53] The DPC recommends that an employer should undertake a 'Privacy Impact Assessment' before introducing biometric control systems into the workplace. This assessment would seek answers to the questions set out below.

(a) Do I have a time management and/or access control system in place?

(b) Why do I feel I need to replace it?

(c) What problems are there with the system?

(d) Are these problems a result of poor administration of the system or an inherent design problem?

(e) Have I examined a number of types of system that are available?

(f) Will the non-biometric systems perform the required tasks adequately?

(g)   Do I need a biometric system?

(h)   If so, what kind do I need?

(i)   Do I need a system that identifies employees as opposed to a verification system?

(j)   Do I need a central database?

(k)   If so, what is wrong with a system that does not use a central database?

(l)   What is the biometric system required to achieve for me?

(m)   Is it for time management purposes and/or for access control purposes?

(n)   How accurate will the data be?

(o)   What procedures are used to ensure accuracy of data?

(p)   Will the data require updating?

(q)   How will the information on it be secured?

(r)   Who shall have access to the data or to logs?

(s)   Why, when and how shall such access be permitted?

(t)   What constitutes an abuse of the system by an employee?

(u)   What procedures shall I put in place to deal with abuse?

(v)   What legal basis do I have for requiring employees to participate?

(w)   Does the system used employ additional identifiers (eg a PIN numb or smart card) along with the biometric?

(x)   If so, would these additional identifiers be sufficient on their own, rather than requiring operation in conjunction with a biometric?

(y)   How shall I inform employees about the system?

(z)   What information about the system need I provide to employees?

(aa)   Would I be happy if I was an employee asked to use such a system?

Job applicants

[33.54] The resumes that job applicants submit to prospective employers may well contain sensitive data within the definition of the DPA. And it is certainly true that an applicant will consider their application to be information of the utmost sensitivity. In *Case Study 6/2003*, an engineer had decided to seek a career change, so he submitted his CV to a recruitment agency. The agency then circulated his CV to a number of employers, including the engineer's current employer. The DPC concluded that 'the individual's personal data was disclosed by the company to a third party without his consent and that the company also breached the security requirements of the Acts as adequate measures were not in place'. A similar issue was reported in the DPC's *Annual Report 2004* in which a recruitment agency disclosed the 'the personal data of some 260 employees and former employees of a major financial institution ... to more than 100 prospective job applicants'. The DPC concluded that 'recruitment agencies must be extra vigilant and I intend to conduct a review of their data protection systems in the coming years'.[120]

---

[120] DPC *Annual Report 2004*, p 22

[33.55] In *Case Study 3/2004*, the DPC: 'received a complaint from an individual who had applied for a specialized medical post with a major hospital'. The complainant had:

'forwarded his CV accompanied by a letter in which he stated that he withheld consent to the organisation contacting the referees listed on his CV until 'mutual interest' had been established and he had time to appraise the referees of his intentions. He was subsequently contacted by the Human Resources section informing him that they had already contacted the referees'.

The DPC investigated and concluded that 'insufficient care appears to have been taken by the organisation to ensure that appropriate guidance was provided to staff involved in the recruitment process and that clear procedures were in place which reflects best data protection practice in regard to the contacting of referees'. The DPC advised that 'written consent should be obtained to have reference enquiries taken up and that this should be exercised only in respect of candidates who are being short listed or to whom a provisional offer is being made'.[121]

[33.56] In recent years, a practice has emerged of employers requiring that prospective employees avail of their right of access to enable the employer, ascertain whether they have a criminal record. The DPA now provides that a person shall not in connection with 'the recruitment of another person as an employee, … the continued employment of another person, or … a contract for the provision of services to him or her by another person' require that person make an access request or supply the information obtained as a result of that access request.[122] At the time of writing this provision had yet to be commenced.[123]

[33.57] In *Case Study 10/2000*, the DPC received a complaint from taxi drivers whose Personal Public Service Number (PPSN) had been sought when they applied for a permit to operate from Dublin Airport. The DPC:

'contacted Aer Rianta and informed it that only public bodies that are designated under the Social Welfare Acts may request a person's PPSN. As Aer Rianta are not a specified body under the Social Welfare Acts, they therefore had no authority to seek the PPSN. Indeed, it is an offence under the Acts to do so. Aer Rianta immediately agreed to omit the request for the PPSN from their form'.

Medical reports

[33.58] When a job applicant is successful, they may be required to attend a medical examination before they take up employment. This issue was referred to by the DPC in *Case Study 1/2002*. The DPC noted that: 'Generally, an employer will have the right under the contract of employment to refer an employee for a medical report'.[124] However, a medical report must, by its nature, contain medial data, which is sensitive data. Therefore the DPC is of the view that the employer 'must obtain 'explicit' consent from a data subject before sensitive data may be processed'.[125] The DPC does

---

[121] DPC *Annual Report 2004*, p 21.

[122] DPA, s 4(13).

[123] See Data Protection (Amendment) Act 2003 (Commencement) Order 2003 (SI 207/2003).

[124] DPC *Annual Report 2004*, p 19.

[125] DPA, s 2B(1)(b)(i).

acknowledge that a medical report might be processed where 'the processing is necessary for the purpose of exercising or performing any right or obligation which is conferred or imposed by law on the data controller in connection with employment'.[126] All employers have a duty of care towards their employees. If an employer worked in a particularly dangerous environment, or if its employees were to be exposed to particular risks and dangers then the employer might be justified in its processing health data in relation to his employees to ascertain that they were not at risk or to manage their exposure to risk.

References

[33.59] The giving of references by employers in relation to current or future employees is an important function. As was stated by the House of Lords in *Spring v Guardian Assurance*:

> 'The employer is possessed of special knowledge, derived from his experience of the employee's character, skill and diligence in the performance of his duties while working for the employer. Moreover, when the employer provides a reference to a third party in respect of his employee, he does so not only for the assistance of the third party, but also, for what it is worth, for the assistance of the employee. Indeed, nowadays it must often be very difficult for an employee to obtain fresh employment without the benefit of a reference from his present or a previous employer. It is for this reason that, in ordinary life, it may be the employee, rather than a prospective future employer, who asks the employer to provide the reference; and even where the approach comes from the prospective future employer, it will (apart from special circumstances) be made with either the express or the tacit authority of the employee. The provision of such references is a service regularly provided by employers to their employees; indeed, references are part of the currency of the modern employment market'.[127]

[33.60] In *Spring v Guardian Assurance,*[128] the plaintiff's former employer gave him a reference. This stated that the plaintiff's 'former superior has ... stated that he is a man of little or no integrity and could not be regarded as honest'.[129] Unsurprisingly, this reference was described by plaintiff's counsel as administering 'the kiss of death'.[130] to the plaintiff's career. The plaintiff sued and the House of Lords held that:

> 'an employer who provides a reference in respect of one of his employees to a prospective future employer will ordinarily owe a duty of care to his employee in respect of the preparation of the reference ... when such a reference is provided by an employer, it is plain that the employee relies upon him to exercise due skill and care in the preparation of the reference before making it available to the third party'.[131]

---

[126] DPA, s 2B(1)(b)(ii).
[127] Per Goff LJ in *Spring v Guardian Assurance* (1995) 2 AC 596 at 319.
[128] *Spring v Guardian Assurance* (1995) 2 AC 596.
[129] *Spring v Guardian Assurance* (1995) 2 AC 596 at 307
[130] (1995) 2 AC 596 at 342.
[131] (1995) 2 AC 596 at 319.

This judgment was applied by the English Court of Appeal in *Bartholomew v London Borough of Hackney*[132] which it was held that 'a reference must not give an unfair or misleading impression overall, even if its discrete components are factually correct'.[133]

[33.61] Unsuccessful job applicants, or even successful job applicants, will therefore have an interest in accessing references given by previous employers, whilst those previous employers will have a similar interest in keeping those references confidential. The DPA provides that:

'Where personal data relating to a data subject consists of an expression of opinion about the data subject by another person, the data may be disclosed to the data subject without obtaining the consent of that person to the disclosure'.[134]

However, this does not apply if 'the expression of opinion ... was given in confidence or on the understanding that it could be treated as confidential'.[135]

[33.62] What is meant by 'confidential' is not defined by the DPA or indeed any other statute. In *House of Spring Gardens v Point Blank*,[136] Costello J stated that: 'All the cases show that there is no simple test for deciding what circumstances will give rise to an obligation of confidence'.[137] He went on to state that:

'The Court ... is being asked to enforce what is essentially a moral obligation. It must...decide whether there exists from the relationship between the parties an obligation of confidence regarding the information which has been imparted'.[138]

[33.63] A test for deciding what was, or was not, confidential was proposed by Megarry J in *Coco v An Clark (Engineers) Ltd*[139]:

'It may be that the hard-worked creature, the reasonable man, may be pressed into service once more; for I do not see why he cannot labour in equity as well as at law. It seems to me that if the circumstances are such that any reasonable man standing in the shoes of the recipient would have realised upon reasonable grounds the information was being given to him in confidence, then this should suffice to impose upon him an equitable obligation of confidence'.[140]

Arguably, an employer who receives a reference from a prospective employee's former employer owes that former employer a duty of confidence. That duty might be implied by common law or equity. Alternatively, the duty might be explicitly stated in

---

[132] *Bartholomew v London Borough of Hackney* (23 October 1998) CA(Eng), Civil Division.

[133] Per Walker LJ. See also *Cox v Sun Alliance* (9 May 2001) CA (Eng), [2001] EWCA Civ 649; *Brown v Las Direct* [2001] EWCA Civ 1798.

[134] DPA, s 4A(4)(a).

[135] DPA, s 4A(4)(b).

[136] *House of Spring Gardens v Point Blank* [1984] IR 611.

[137] *House of Spring Gardens v Point Blank* [1984] IR 611 at 662. Noting that the courts had held that such an obligation arose 'when inventors had communicated information in the course of business negotiations with a view to joint ventures'.

[138] *House of Spring Gardens v Point Blank* [1984] IR 611 at 663–664. This passage was quoted in full by O'Higgins CJ, who stated that he agreed entirely with it. [1984] IR 611 at 696.

[139] *Coco v An Clark (Engineers) Ltd* [1969] RPC 41.

[140] [1969] RPC 41 at 420–421.

correspondence, which might state 'Strictly Confidential'. However, the obligation of confidence will not necessarily arise from any such words used by either party, but rather will arise where the reference was communicated in circumstances importing an obligation of confidence.[141]

Sensitive data and the Employment Equality Acts

[33.64] The DPA limits the circumstances in which sensitive data may be processed. At the same time, the Employment Equality Acts prohibit discrimination by employers against employees[142] on a number of grounds.[143] The processing of sensitive data may result in employees becoming the victims of discrimination and so be contrary to the Employment Equality Acts. Some examples of where the processing of sensitive data might result in discrimination under the Employment Equality Acts are:

(a)   The processing of data as to 'racial or ethnic origin' might amount to discrimination 'on the ground of race' under the Employment Equality Acts;

(b)   The processing of data as to 'religious or philosophical beliefs' might amount to discrimination on 'the religion ground' under the Employment Equality Acts;

(c)   The processing of data as to 'sexual life' might amount to discrimination on the 'the sexual orientation ground' under the Employment Equality Acts;

(d)   The processing of data as to 'physical or mental health' might amount to discrimination on 'the disability ground' under the Employment Equality Acts.

[33.65] An employer should first consider whether it is permissible to process the relevant category of sensitive data under s 2B of the DPA. However, if such processing would amount to discrimination under the Employment Equality Acts then it could be argued that it is excessive and so contrary to the principles of data protection.[144] Reference should be made in this context to the decision of the Labour Court in *Citibank v Massinde Ntoko*,[145] in which it was held that the employee had been discriminated against on the grounds of race in relation to the monitoring of his use of his employer's phone system.

Reuse of employee data

[33.66] The relationship between employee and employer can change. For example, employees may engage in industrial action. This occurred in the DPC's *Case Study 2/00.* Teachers who were members of the Association of Secondary Teachers, Ireland ('ASTI') withdrew from supervision for three days.[146] The Department of Education and Science

---

[141] [1969] RPC 41 at 47, referred to by Costello J in *House of Spring Gardens v Point Blank* [1984] IR 611 at 662.
[142] Employment Equality Acts 1998–2004, s 8.
[143] Employment Equality Acts 1998–2004, s 6. It should be noted that the Acts make an employer vicariously liable for the discriminatory practices of its employees, see ss 23 and 32.
[144] Specifically, s 2(1)(c)(iii).
[145] *Citibank v Massinde Ntoko* (8 March 2004), The Labour Court.
[146] Oliver and Flynn 'Deducting teachers' pay over strike was not legal' (2001) The Irish Times, 22 February.

then stopped the pay of ASTI members for those days. The department identified ASTI members by using its payroll database to identify those teachers who were paying subscriptions to the ASTI. These entries would have been created when the employee filled in a form entitled 'Authorisation of subscription from salary'. This form 'simply mandated the Department to deduct union membership subscriptions from salary, and forward the moneys to the trade union. The form made no mention about other uses by the Department of the individual's trade union membership data'. This satisfied the DPC that:

> 'the purpose for which the data had been obtained by the Department, and for which the data were kept, was quite plain; and that this purpose did not encompass the use to which the Department had actually put the data.'.

The DPC therefore concluded that the Department was in breach of the DPA. This case study should be compared with *Case Study 7/2003* in which:

> 'Three employees of Aer Lingus complained that information held on the Aer Lingus payroll database regarding their authorisation to allow deductions at source in respect of their union subscriptions was used by Aer Lingus to identify and single them out as IMPACT members and deny them pay increases and refuse them staff travel privileges ...'.

[33.67] The DPC investigated and 'established that Aer Lingus did not refer to the payroll database in this instance'. The dispute related to an agreement made between Aer Lingus and SIPTU. IMPACT was not a party to this agreement. In implementation of this agreement SIPTU supplied a list of its members to Aer Lingus. Therefore the DPC concluded that 'the complaints were without foundation and that no contravention of the Data Protection Acts had occurred in this instance'.

[33.68] Another change that can occur between employer and employee is where one initiates a court action against the other. In *Case Study 1/2004*:

> 'An employee of a major national company had been requested to attend a doctor nominated by the employer in the context of his on-going sick leave. His employment was subsequently terminated and he made an access request ... for a copy of the medical report. The company refused him access on the grounds that the employee had initiated legal proceedings against the company and that the report was privileged and that it did not have to be released ...'.

The DPC investigated. He found that 'the first formal notification of court proceedings was sent by the data subject's solicitors many months (after the medical appointment in issue)'. Therefore, the DPC concluded that the medical examination was not conducted in relation to court proceedings. And, that: 'The employee in this case was clearly under the impression that the referral was related to assessing his fitness for work only'. Therefore, the employer was not able to refuse access to the report in question on the basis that it was personal data 'in respect of which a claim of privilege could be maintained in proceedings in a Court in relation to communications between a client and his professional legal advisers or between those advisers.'[147] The DPC concluded that:

> 'when the employee agrees to attend the doctor, what is important is that the employee clearly understands that s/he is required to attend the medical assessment for a particular

---

[147] DPA, s 5(1)(g).

purpose eg to determine whether s/he is fit to return to work and attends on that basis alone. On the other hand, if the purpose is connected with anticipation of or defence of legal proceedings then the employee should know that this is the basis for the referral'.[148]

The duty to secure personal data

[33.69] The DPA obliges employers to apply 'appropriate security measures' to secure the privacy of their employee's personal data.[149] In DPC's *Case Study 1/98*, a 'large organisation, whose staff are employed at several locations throughout the country, used a central database to record information relating to its employees and their work'. An employee complained that 'there had been a breach of security because the laptops were without any password protection for a period during the development of the system' and, he 'objected to certain of his personnel data and details of his work activity being generally available to staff, and argued that such data should only be available to those who needed them to perform their managerial functions'. As regards the first complaint, the employer in question had developed a very powerful security system which required the entry of three different passwords. This system proved cumbersome. Instead, a single individual password was issued to each member of staff. This had the effect of giving access to the entire system from certain laptops. As soon as the DPC commenced his investigation, the employer took steps to rectify the system. Therefore, this element of the complaint was not upheld. As regards the second complaint, the DPC suggested that:

'one would expect a Human Resources Manager to have access to personal data not necessarily available to the manager of a client database, and vice versa. Data controllers should, in my view, take reasonable steps to prevent personal data from being made available to employees who may have no work-related interest in the data'.

He concluded that 'an appropriate balance must be struck between the concerns of the employee as data subject, the real operational requirements of the organisation and the costs to the organisation'.

Employee evaluation data

[33.70] In *Recommendation 1/2001*[150] the Article 29 Working Party considered the issue of employee evaluation data. The Working Party recommended that:

'Personal data can be ... found in subjective judgments and evaluations which can actually include elements specific to the physical, physiological, psychical, economic, cultural or social identity of data subjects. This is equally true if a judgment or a evaluation is summarised by a score or rank or is expressed by means of other evaluation criteria.

The fact that under national law a few of these subjective data cannot be always accessed and rectified directly, or that they can be rectified by the inclusion of statements or notes made by data subjects, does not prevent them from being personal data, with a view to transparency of processing and the exercise of right of access.

---

[148] DPC *Annual Report 2004*, p 19.
[149] DPA, s 2(1)(d).
[150] Article 29 Working Party, *Recommendation 1/2001 on Employee Evaluation Data*, 22 March 2001.

Similar considerations apply in respect of the fact that direct access to the data included in subjective judgments or evaluations can be deferred or limited under national law'.[151]

Evaluation documents must inevitably contain personal data relating to the individuals evaluated. As is clear from s 4 of the DPA, employees have a right of access to those documents. The DPA does provide for some limitation on the right of access if an employee evaluation were to be provided in confidence.[152]

[33.71] Fair procedures require that employers should properly investigate allegations made against employees and others. In *Case Study 03/04*, the DPC received a complaint from an employee who 'had made an access request ... for personal data contained in a human resources division investigation file concerning a bullying and harassment complaint which he had lodged against another member of staff'. The DPC investigated and found that 'the complaint was of a serious nature and that the matters were being investigated under the employer's policy on bullying and harassment in the workplace'. The employer was withholding the data in question 'until such time as the investigation was completed'. This was because:

> 'documentation prepared in connection with the investigation would, if disclosed at a juncture not provided for in the process itself, be likely to prejudice the effectiveness and fairness of the investigative process and that it is therefore not liable to be disclosed'.

[33.72] The employer was only withholding data created in conjunction with the ongoing manner and the DPC therefore determined that it was permissible to withhold this data, as it was data:

> 'kept for the purpose of preventing, detecting or investigating offences, apprehending or prosecuting offenders or assessing or collecting any tax, duty or other moneys owed or payable to the State, a local authority or a health board, in any case in which the application of that section to the data would be likely to prejudice any of the matters aforesaid'.

Unfortunately, the DPC did not specify how the investigation of an allegation of bullying could fall within one of these categories. The DPA does exempt data kept for the purpose of 'investigating offences' but only a very serious allegation of bullying could amount to an offence, and an allegation of such severity should properly be investigated by An Garda Síochána, not the employer itself. The last of the DPC's conclusions on this matter was that: '(o)n completion of the investigation, this section however would no longer be applicable'.

[33.73] Employee evaluations can be a powerful tool for managing human resources. Given their utility, management may wish to make evaluations available throughout their organisation. However, such availability may compromise the privacy of employees. In *Case Study 3/2001*, the DPC received a complaint from employees of a company which had 'created a computer file setting out performance assessment reports for individual members of staff'. The DPC investigated and found that 'the line manager of a particular unit had created a file, setting out performance ratings for staff under his supervision. However, the 'access permissions' on this file had inadvertently been set to

---

[151] Article 29 Working Party, *Recommendation 1/2001*, p 2–3.
[152] DPA, s 4(4A).

allow numerous people outside of his management team to read it'. The company and the DPC investigated the matter and on foot of these investigations introduced the following safeguards:

(a) 'an immediate training programme in IT security for all managers and staff, together with regular refresher programmes;

(b) all remaining hard- and soft-copies of the file in question to be destroyed as a matter of the utmost urgency, with all company systems swept to confirm this;

(c) HQ policies on security should be reissued to all managers and staff;

(d) standards for holding sensitive data, both personal and commercial, to be reviewed and published'.

The DPC 'accepted that, in an employment context, staff members may not automatically have the option of objecting to their data being used for appraisal purposes – this would naturally depend on conditions of employment and industrial relations norms'. He concluded that 'staff should be made fully aware of new appraisal initiatives which involve the use of their personal data ... The performance appraisal file in this case had not met these standards, and so its creation entailed a contravention of the Act.' Personality and psychological tests, such as Myers-Briggs,[153] are now available to employers to evaluate existing or prospective employees.[154] A strong argument can be made that such tests, and the results of such tests, are health data and so sensitive data. If this is so, then the processing of such data by employers would have to be very seriously limited. It is submitted that under the DPA, data of this type could probably only be processed by employers with the 'explicit consent' of their employees.[155] Where tests are administered by computer systems, then the prohibition by automated means[156] should also be taken into account.

CCTV surveillance of employees

[33.74] It would seem to be beyond question that the processing of data derived from CCTV footage of employees amounts to the processing of personal data. Personal data is 'data relating to a living individual who is or can be identified ... from the data'. It would be unrealistic for an employer to claim that it, or one of its managers, could not identify each of its employees. Therefore, CCTV monitoring of the workplace must be in accordance with the DPA. It is submitted that the decision as to whether CCTV equipment is to be installed or used should be made on a similar basis to that upon which electronic communications may be monitored.

---

[153] The Myers Briggs test is supposed to only be administered in accordance with certain ethical rules. These rules should limit abuse of the test, as they provide that: 'Indicator results ... (of Myers-Briggs should) ... never be used to label, evaluate, or limit the respondent in any way', http://www.myersbriggs.org., Ethics for Administering the Myers-Briggs Type Indicator Instrument.

[154] See also the DPA's prohibition on automated decisions in certain circumstances, DPA, s 6B.

[155] DPA, s 2B(1)(b)(i).

[156] DPA, s 6B.

In particular, the employer should have regard to the following questions:

(a) Is it necessary? Couldn't the employer obtain the same result with traditional methods of supervision?

(b) Is the processing of personal data proposed fair to the workers?

(c) Is it proportionate to the concerns that it tries to allay?

(d) Is the monitoring activity transparent to the workers?

[33.75] The legitimacy of the use of CCTV cameras may depend upon the purpose for which they are installed, the location in which they are installed and the information that is disclosed to employees. The installation of hidden or covert CCTV cameras for the purposes of identifying the perpetrators of theft or vandalism will be particularly controversial. This is particularly so where workers or their representatives are not informed of the existence of the cameras. In the Labour Court decision of *Tytex v SIPTU*[157]:

> 'what appeared to be a concealed video camera was discovered in a wall clock in a canteen. At a meeting on 6th March, the Union confronted management and asked to know what the camera was for. It emerged that there were 8 cameras, 1 in each canteen, 5 on the factory floor and 1 in the car park and that they had been installed 2 years previously'.

[33.76] Work stopped at the factory in protest for a period of two hours, and a considerable amount of media attention followed. The union was concerned at the secret manner in which the cameras were installed; the company responded that 'it installed the cameras because of ongoing theft of company property'. The company claimed that 'the cameras were pointed at doors and windows so that any theft of property could be filmed'. The union responded that this '(wa)s not true. The cameras in the canteen were pointed directly at the dining area. The company was, in effect, spying on the workforce. One camera was located in a small tea room which a number of female workers had used as a changing room. This (wa)s a gross invasion of privacy'. The Labour Court did not adjudicate on these different claims and allegations but commented that:

> 'given the efforts being made to improve the efficiency and competitiveness of industry generally, and the exhortations to the social partners to establish partnerships to this end, ... the actions of the Company in installing a security system, particularly of the type indicated, without consultation, was not acceptable and was detrimental to the maintenance or development of a climate of good industrial relations'.

[33.77] The company 'accept(ed) that their action should not have been taken, and they ... agree(d) to pay to a charity, nominated by the Union, the sum of £3,000'. The Company also 'offered to change to an open camera system provided it will not be interfered with'. Similarly, in the Labour Court decision of *Johnson Brothers Ltd v SIPTU*,[158] management had initially 'informed the Union of its intention to install internal security cameras in the dispatch/warehouse area'. However, a problem with stock losses developed and '(i)n February, 1997, the Company identified discrepancies

---

[157] *Tytex v SIPTU* CD/97/132 Recommendation No LCR15502.
[158] *Johnson Brothers Ltd v SIPTU* CD/98/6 Recommendation No LCR15802.

in a particular area of the warehouse and installed an additional security camera without the Union's knowledge'. Management argued that:

'It would not have been practical to discuss the installation and location of the camera in February, 1997, as the person responsible for the theft may have been alerted.

... There was no viewing monitor attached to the camera and tapes were only viewed by Management when a stock discrepancy occurred. The Company dismantled the camera when the cause of the discrepancy had been identified. Due to the nature of the problem and the fact that it could have been carried out by a member of staff or by an outside contractor, the Company was justified in its use of the camera'.

A dispute arose which was investigated by the Labour Court.[159] The court concluded that it was 'regrettable that the Company did not consider advising the Union of its intention to extend the system, in a way which could not have undermined its effectiveness, thus avoiding the current dispute'.

[33.78] The installation of a CCTV system in an area where workers might expect some privacy may also be controversial. There is an argument to be made that installation of a 'video camera ... in (a) female changing room' amounts to discrimination'.[160] In *Meadow Meats v SIPTU*,[161] the company had 'introduced two cameras in the locker rooms'. The workers objected, claiming this was 'an invasion of privacy'. The company claimed that:

'The main reasons for the security cameras were health and safety, pilferage of employees' property and damage to Company lockers. The two locker rooms have been upgraded at a considerable cost. One incident of 'horse-play' in the locker room resulted in a worker being 'stabbed'.'

The Labour Court recommended that:

'While it is clear that problems exist in relation to the locker room, given the sensitivity involved, the Court recommends that a camera is not put in this area but that the Union meets with the Company in order to agree how the problems raised can be addressed'.

[33.79] A particularly difficult issue may arise for employers where it is alleged that an employee has placed a locker room under surveillance. In such a situation it is very important that the employer should investigate the allegations fully and carefully. In *Giblin v Borderland Imports Ltd*,[162] an allegation was apparently made that the claimant had placed a camera in a storeroom and then instructed female employees to change their clothes there. The EAT considered the evidence and concluded:

'The employer failed to conduct any or any proper investigation into the matter. Had he done so he would have come to the conclusion that there was no evidence that the claimant had placed a camera in the storeroom as alleged. What the witness for the respondent had seen in the storeroom is a matter for conjecture as no one attempted to discover what in fact the witness had seen after the incident by going into the storeroom and inspecting the

---

[159] Pursuant to the Industrial Relations Act 1990, s 26(1).

[160] See Labour Court Decision *Powers Supermarkets Ltd and Helen Farell, Olive Reddy, Martha Byrne, Angela Toomey et al; The Employment Equality Agency*, REE906 EET791.

[161] *Meadow Meats v SIPTU* CD/98/72 Recommendation No LCR15878.

[162] *Giblin v Borderland Imports Ltd* (25 May 2004) UD857/2003, MN2050/2003.

place where the purported camera was said to be placed. The claimant stated that he did not own a camera and he and his vehicle had been searched by the gardaí subsequent to the incident and no camera was found. In the circumstances the Tribunal find that the claimant was unfairly dismissed by the Respondent'.

[33.80] The purpose for which CCTV surveillance is undertaken will determine whether or not it is legitimate. As discussed in the context of communications monitoring above, such purposes may include the need to enhance productivity or to prevent theft. Other justifications may include the need to prevent accidents. In *Fair Oak Foods v SIPTU*,[163] the dispute concerned:

'the installation of video cameras by the Company in production areas of its meat processing plant in Clonmel, Co. Tipperary. The Company claims that the need for such cameras has arisen due to the number of occupational injuries and claims at the plant in recent years, some of the injuries involving cutting with butchers' knives, allegedly, deliberately inflicted by a colleague, or self-inflicted. The Company considers that the frequency and nature of the claims justifies a suspicion of fraud. The Company states that the installation of video cameras is at the insistence of its insurers who share the Company's concern about the claims profile, and who would withdraw insurance cover in the event of the non-instalment of video cameras. The Company would, accordingly, be forced to cease production'.

[33.81] The Union objected:

'strongly to the proposed use of cameras in the production areas, claiming that this would represent an unwarranted and unnecessary intrusion on the workers. The Union holds that the bad accident record in recent years arose due to failings on the Company's part in terms of training and the issue of protective kit. The Union states that the addressing of those issues in recent months has resulted in a substantial decrease in the accident rate'.

The Labour Court reviewed the matter and commented that: 'Although the Union has expressed its total opposition, in principle, to the use of cameras, as required by the Company, it has failed to suggest any viable alternative and has failed to address the issue in any meaningful way'. The court recommended 'that the Company should make every effort to obtain employer liability insurance based on recent accident records rather than on past records'. If the company was unable to do this then:

'this position must be made clear to the Union. The Union should then accept the Company guarantees that the use of video recordings will be restricted to viewing incidents where an accident has already occurred. A guarantee should be also given that the viewing of such recordings should only take place following an invitation to a shop steward or Union official to be present'.

[33.82] Similarly, the Labour Court viewed video evidence of a worker's interactions with passengers and supervisors in *Aer Rianta v SIPTU*.[164] In *Hall v Crowe*,[165] the EAT requested that the respondent bring a video of a work-related incident to the hearing. The monitoring of an employee outside the hours of work may be more difficult to justify. The Labour Court did examine video evidence taken of an employee playing

---

[163] *Fair Oak Foods v SIPTU* CD/00/198 Recommendation No LCR16531.
[164] *Aer Rianta v SIPTU* CD/911/20 Appeal Decision No AD7291.
[165] *Hall v Crowe* (24 February 2004) UD1288/2002.

golf in *Patrick Power Supermarkets t/a Quinnsworth v A Worker*.[166] At issue was the dismissal of the worker following:

'monitoring of the individual by the Company while he was on sick-leave with a 'bad back'. Methods of surveillance included the use of video equipment which recorded the worker playing golf on a number of occasions at the Old course in Lahinch'.[167]

[33.83] Reference might also be made to the decisions of the courts in *Shelly-Morris v Dublin Bus*[168] and *Conor O'Connor v Dublin Bus*.[169] In the latter case, Hardiman J commented that:

'A significant number of personal injury claims feature injuries which are not, or not wholly, capable of being proved or negatived by the normal processes of clinical medicine. The credibility of the plaintiff is central in such cases, some of which are very substantial ones. Video surveillance of the kind featured in this case is often resorted to as a check or control of the plaintiffs' account'.[170]

However, these decisions may have to be reconsidered in the context of the DPA and the ECHR. This issue is discussed at Chapter 10 above.

---

[166] *Patrick Power Supermarkets t/a Quinnsworth v A Worker* CD9334 Recommendation No LCR14164, see similarly the decision of the EAT in *Connolly v Carey Glass Ltd* (11 March 2004) UD45/2003, MN488/2003.

[167] The company 'maintain(ed) that if the worker could engage in the type of activity such as playing golf that he could have attended his work 'which is far less physically demanding'. The worker argued that: 'Golf is not a robust, physical sport. It is a means of getting plenty of fresh air, especially in Lahinch'.

[168] *Shelly-Morris v Dublin Bus* [2003] 1 IR 232.

[169] *Conor O'Connor v Dublin Bus* [2003] 4 IR 459.

[170] *Conor O'Connor v Dublin Bus* [2003] 4 IR 459.

Chapter 34

IT Misuse at Work

Introduction

[34.01] Whilst the use of information technology can boost the productivity of employees, the abuse of that technology may expose employers to significant risk. A dishonest employee may use IT systems to steal from his employer. This is an ongoing problem. During the debate on the Criminal Damage Bill 1990 the Minister of State for what was then the Department of Tourism, Transport and Communications offered the following analysis to the Seanad:

> 'Hacking ... can be done ... from inside ... an organisation ... (i)nsider hacking takes place when an employee with legitimate access to the data equipment either uses it for a wrongful purpose or exceeds his level of authorisation in accessing particular data. The insider may, of course, be using a terminal that is located far from the central processing system of the organisation concerned'.[1]

A survey undertaken for the Dublin Chamber of Commerce suggested that fraud costs Irish businesses some €2.5bn a year and that '34 per cent of the businesses surveyed said that they had taken disciplinary action against employees who had committed offences'.[2] An earlier survey found that fraud costs Irish small firms some €100m a year and that 'more than 80 per cent of fraud cases are internal'.[3] Information technology can provide both the tools and the motivation for employees to commit fraud.[4]

[34.02] A dishonest employee may use his employer's IT system to steal from others, possibly leaving the employer vicariously liable for his misconduct. In *Johnson and Johnson (Ireland) Ltd v CP Security Ltd*[5] the defendant provided security guards for the plaintiff's premises under contract. One of the guards employed by the defendant then stole the plaintiff's stock. The plaintiff sued the defendant for compensation for the stolen stock. The High Court rejected the plea of the defendant that it 'was not

---

[1] Minister of State at the Department of Tourism, Transport and Communications, Seanad Éireann – Volume 130 – 17 December 1991, Criminal Damage Bill 1990: Committee Stage. 'There's this great myth that people sit in darkened rooms hacking, which they do ... [but] the biggest threat is still the staff' Mike Dalton, vice-president for Europe at McAfee quoted in Braithwaite, 'Media companies failing to secure IT systems, says study', (2006) Financial Times, 21 June.

[2] O'Halloran, 'Corporate crime costing €2.5bn' (2005) Irish Times, 17 June.

[3] Coyle, 'Fraud costs small firms €100m a year' (2004) Irish Times, 5 June.

[4] An addiction to online gambling sites led a junior accountant in a UK-based building firm to embezzle over €1m from his employer and ultimately send it into receivership, see 'Online gambler spent £1m of bosses' money' (2006) Daily Telegraph, 10 July.

[5] *Johnson and Johnson (Ireland) Ltd v CP Security Ltd* [1985] IR 362.

responsible for the criminal act of his servant, the same not having been done within the scope of his employment'.[6] Egan J was 'cautious in committing myself to a completely general proposition that a master would in every conceivable circumstance be held vicariously liable for the tort or criminal act of his servant committed in the course of his employment'. However, he held that the employer would be liable in a case where '... the employers were specifically engaged to safeguard the plaintiff's property'.[7]

[34.03] An employee may use his employer's IT systems to abuse or harass others. In *X v European Central Bank*[8] one employee harassed another 'more or less continuous(ly) from the time of his recruitment ... until his suspension'.[9] Such harassment may disrupt the workplace.[10] Furthermore, if damage is caused by it, then the employer may be liable for it. In *Western Provident Association v Norwich Union*[11] the parties were competing medical insurance companies. Employees of the defendant sent emails alleging that the defendant was insolvent and under investigation. The resulting defamation action was settled for a sum reported to be in the region of £450,000. In *Crofter Properties v Genport*[12] an employee of the plaintiff had made a number of phone calls which made serious allegations about the defendant. The plaintiff was ultimately awarded damages of €190,460 against the plaintiff's employer.

[34.04] An employee may use his employer's IT systems to download or distribute illegal or objectionable content. In 2005 IRMA, which represents the Irish record industry, settled a threatened court action with 'at least one firm that did not know that one of its employees was using its network to illegally upload music'.[13] In *R v Fellows and Arnold*[14] one of the defendants:

> 'used the computer of his employers ... to store data which enabled it to display indecent pictures of children on the computer screen and to produce prints. He also made this data

---

6   Egan J in *Johnson and Johnson (Ireland) Ltd v C Security Ltd* [1985] IR 362 at 365, citing *Cheshire v Bailey* [1905] 1 KB 237.
7   [1985] IR 362 at 366.
8   *X v European Central Bank* Case No. T-333/99, (18 October 2001) ECJ, European Court reports 2001 Page II-03021; Page IA-00199; Page II-00921.
9   (18 October 2001) ECJ, para 223.
10 The Equality Acts 1998–2004, s 14A provide that 'Where ... an employee ... is harassed or sexually harassed in the course of his or her employment by a person who is ... employed at that place or by the same employer ... the victim's employer, or ... a client, customer or other business contact of the victim's employer and the circumstances of the harassment are such that the employer ought reasonably to have taken steps to prevent it...the harassment or sexual harassment constitutes discrimination by the victim's employer in relation to the victim's conditions of employment'. See also *Majrowski v Guy's and St Thomas's NHS Trust* (2005) 2 WLR 1503 on the vicarious liability of employers for harassment in the workplace.
11 *Western Provident Association v Norwich Union Healthcare* (unreported), see Price and Duohu, *Defamation* (3rd edn, Thomson Sweet & Maxwell, 2004), paras 35–16.
12 *Crofter Properties v Genport* [2002] 4 IR 73.
13 Smyth, 'Web users made to pay by music industry' (2005) Irish Times, 4 August.
14 *R v Fellows & Arnold* (1997) 1 Cr App R 244.

available on the Internet, so that other computers world-wide could receive and display similar screen images and produce identical prints'.[15]

[34.05] An employee may install unauthorised software on his employer's systems. In the EAT decision of *Scally v First Class Productions Ltd T/A Storm Cinemas*[16] the claimant was the manager of the defendant's Portlaoise outlet. The defendant's operations manager transferred from Dublin to Portlaoise, something that the claimant felt restricted his autonomy. Subsequently the respondent's operations manager had a discussion with the claimant about the installation of a key-logger onto the respondent's computers. The claimant indicated that he knew what a key-logger was, but he was not asked to install one. The EAT described a key-logger in the following terms:

'A key-logger is a device that, unbeknownst to a user of the computer, records every keystroke made on the computer. It therefore makes the controller of the device privy to everything done on the computer. It is an intrusive device. The Claimant acknowledged that it is an intrusive device. It is, effectively, a piece of spy software.'

The claimant installed a key-logger without permission and doing so gave him 'access to potentially sensitive information to which he was not entitled to have access.'

The EAT accepted that the installation of the key-logger 'caused no damage to the respondent's computer system. However the respondent's operations manager subsequently installed a second key-logging system and the 'installation of the second key logger caused some difficulties in the application of both programs. The claimant then told the operations manager 'what he had done after unsuccessfully attempting to un-install his key logger. The claimant was suspended on full pay; the respondent investigated and then dismissed the claimant. The claimant initiated a claim before the EAT for unfair dismissal. The EAT dismissed this claim holding that:

'the claimant acted without the authority or knowledge of the Respondent in installing a key-logger. He did not tell the Respondent's management until it became clear that his own device would be discovered. For this reason, the Tribunal is satisfied that he did not install the key-logger on the company's behalf. That he did so was a serious breach of discipline and one for which it was reasonable for the Respondent to dismiss him.'

Unauthorised access

[34.06] As noted above unauthorised access of a computer is a criminal offence. Unauthorised access may occur in different ways in the employment context. One form of unauthorised access occurs where an employee exceeds his access privileges to a computer system. Another occurs where an employee is entitled to access information, but not for the purpose for which he accesses it. In the UK case of *Denco v Johnson*[17] the respondent was a trade union shop steward and sheet metal worker. He had access to his employer's computer system, but only to those parts that were relevant to his job. His daughter was also employed by the same employer. She worked in the Marketing Department and had access to those parts of the system that were relevant to her job.

---

[15] (1997) 1 Cr App R 244 at 245.
[16] *Scally v First Class Productions Ltd T/A Storm Cinemas* 20/07/2006 UD 1231/2004, RP656/2004, MN960/2004, FL12789 (EAT).
[17] *Denco v Johnson* (1991) 1 WLR 330.

During a period where the respondent was working on the nightshift, his employer noticed that at 03.58 in the morning the respondent's daughter's name was entered into the system. An incorrect password was entered initially, before the correct password was entered; the UK EAT considered that this '... clearly shows an intent deliberately to obtain access to that menu'.[18] A list of customers was then obtained and printed out. The respondent was dismissed. His dismissal was found to be unfair, and an appeal was then made to the EAT. The employer argued that to justify dismissal on the grounds of gross misconduct it was 'quite sufficient to prove that an employee has deliberately used an unauthorized password to enter (a) computer'.[19]

The employer succeeded in getting a rehearing of the case. However the decision was complicated by the fact that the employer had not made the seriousness of gaining unauthorised access to sections of a computer clear to the employee. The UK EAT commented that:

> 'It must surely be common sense that where a system such as the present has been instituted that the unauthorised use of a password is a very serious matter indeed ... Unauthorised use of or tampering with computers is an extremely serious industrial offence. However it is clearly desirable to reduce into writing rules concerning the access to and use of computers and not only to post them but to leave them near the computers for reference'.[20]

[34.07] In *Ellis (claimant) v Decisions Ltd & Career Decisions International Ltd*[21] the claimant had assisted a fellow employee to instruct a solicitor with a copy of that employee's 'job description and contract of employment, which was password protected, were attached to a covering email which contained the password and sent to her solicitor from the claimant's personal email address. A difficulty arose because:

> 'The copy email was quarantined by the respondent's spans system because the computer did not recognise the claimant's personal email address. On Monday, 14th June 2004, MD was given a copy of it. She was concerned because the email contained a confidential company password, which would give access to employees' contracts of employment.

Disciplinary charges were initiated, on foot of which the claimant was dismissed. He invoked the Unfair Dismissals Acts. The respondent conceded that assisting a fellow employee to instruct a solicitor was not a breach of company discipline. However, the respondent claimed that assisting a fellow without informing the respondent had resulted in a 'breach of trust, which sundered the relationship of trust and confidence' between the parties. The EAT found that the employee was unfairly dismissed, but that the claimant had contributed to his own dismissal.

---

[18]   (1991) 1 WLR 330 at 333.
[19]   (1991) 1 WLR 330 at 334.
[20]   (1991) 1 WLR 330 at 336.
[21]   *Ellis (claimant) v Decisions Ltd & Career Decisions International Ltd* 24/01/2007 UD766/ 2004 [FL13418] (EAT).

Dismissal of a dishonest employee

[34.08] An employee may be dismissed for misconduct. The Unfair Dismissals Acts 1977–2005 provide that 'the dismissal of an employee shall be deemed ... not to be an unfair dismissal, if it results wholly or mainly from ... the conduct of the employee'.[22]

The decision as to whether or not an employee's conduct is such as to justify his dismissal is a serious one. It is also highly subjective. In *Pacelli v Irish Distillers*[23] it was the view of the EAT that the judgment as to what is serious misconduct justifying dismissal and what is not, is a subjective judgment to be made by the employer concerned:

> 'The conduct or misconduct does not have to constitute a major or minor departure from acceptable standard practice. The nature and extent of the departure is one element and its impact on the employment relationship is another. It might possibly be imagined that some precise definition could readily be given, or some test be applied, whereby the more serious misconduct, namely gross misconduct, might be at once marked out and distinguished alike from minor infringements and dismissible behaviour. The Tribunal believes that the assessment of the conduct, and whether or not that amounts to gross misconduct, rests with the employer, however, the employer must act reasonably and prudently in qualifying conduct as amounting to a trivial departure from standards and gross misconduct, together with consistency in indiscriminately enforcing penalties for breaches thereof in accordance with its practices and procedures no matter who the person is or the position he holds in the company.

[34.09] In *Glover v BLN Ltd*[24] Kenny J stated that:

> 'It is impossible to define the misconduct which justifies immediate dismissal. ..There is no fixed rule of law defining the degree of misconduct which justify dismissal... What is or is not misconduct must be decided in each case without the assistance of a definition or a general rule. Similarly, all that one can say about serious misconduct is that it is misconduct which the court regards as being grave and deliberate. And the standards to be applied in deciding the matter are those of men and not of angels'.[25]

[34.10] In *Mahon v Noyeks*[26] the EAT commented that:

> 'It is not possible to provide a list of the types of conduct which will be judged by the Tribunal as being so serious as to justify dismissal without prior warnings. A list will depend on such factors as the nature of the work involved and the level of responsibility of the Employee in question. Misconduct must be measured in the context of the Employee's act not just its consequences or potential consequences to the employer. The reasons for the act have to be evaluated and put into the context of his employment and responsibility. It is well established that each case of unfair dismissal must be judged on its merits and what may justify dismissal in one situation may not in another. The role of the Tribunal is not to establish as objective standard but to ask whether the decision to dismiss came with

---

[22] Unfair Dismissals Acts 1977–2005, s 6(4).
[23] *Pacelli v Irish Distillers* 23/01/2003 UD57I/2001 [FL7404] (EAT).
[24] *Glover v BLN Ltd* [1973] IR 388.
[25] [1973] IR 388 at 405.
[26] *Mahon v Noyeks* 09/06/2005 UD681/2004 [FL11501] (EAT).

the band of responses a reasonable employer might be expected to take having regard to the particular circumstances of the case.

Procedure

[34.11] A key aspect of any procedure is that the employee in question must be asked for an explanation for any suspicious conduct and that no decision must be taken in relation to an employee until he has been offered an opportunity to provide the explanation sought. An explanation must be sought even where an employee is observed removing goods from his employer's premises and the incident in question is recorded on CCTV. In *McGuinness v Shomar*[27] the respondent's manager observed on CCTV that the claimant, an employee of the respondent, was placing a box in the back of his car. This box was found to contain electrical goods from the respondent's shop. The claimant initially failed to give an explanation and the EAT concluded that 'In the circumstances it was reasonable for the general manager to believe that the claimant was guilty of gross misconduct.'

[34.12] The evidence in *McGuinness v Shomar* appears to have been quite clear. It is not necessary for an employer to have such clear evidence before an employee is dismissed. What an employer must do is fairly conduct a rigorous investigation and offer the employee in question an opportunity to explain the conduct at issue and consider that explanation before making any decision. If this is done, then an employer may even dismiss on the basis of circumstantial evidence. In *Pacelli v Irish Distillers*[28] the respondent company was suffering 'shrinkage' of its stock. This was a particularly serious problem for the respondent as it had to 'pay duty on such missing product, and the monetary amounts involved may be considerable'. Although the EAT considered that '(t)he Claimant ... cannot be said to have been responsible for the shortages with scientific certainty' it was still willing to deem the claimant's dismissal fair as the respondent had 'conducted a far-reaching, fair and proper investigation of the malpractices associated with the stock-shortages'. A large number of instances had occurred when the claimant was on duty and in the area of the respondent's premises where the plaintiff was supposed to be working. The EAT held that:

> 'The happenings and/or occurrences are in such number as to warrant and dictate a proper and adequate explanation from the Claimant as they occurred when he was on duty and took place within his precinct of the company premises; to hold otherwise would be to defy logic.'

[34.13] However, the claimant failed to provide such an explanation. The EAT noted that it was not for it to say whether or not the claimant was in fact guilty of any wrongdoing.[29] Rather, the issue for the EAT was 'much narrower than that ... did the Respondent Company act fairly, properly and justly in reaching it decision to dismiss the Claimant?.

---

27 *McGuinness v Shomar Ltd* 12/05/2004 UD1038/2003 MN2385/2003 [FL9412] (EAT).
28 *Pacelli v Irish Distillers* 23/01/2003 UD57I/2001 [FL7404] (EAT).
29 Citing *Hennessy v Read & Write Shop Ltd* (UD 192/1978).

[34.14] The EAT considered the test for what would be regarded as reasonable action by an employer had been set out in the *Hennessy v Read & Write Shop Ltd*[30]:

'1.   Did the company believe that the employee mis-conducted himself as alleged: If so,

2.   Did the company have reasonable grounds to sustain that belief? If so,

3.   Was the penalty of dismissal proportionate to the alleged mis-conduct?'

The EAT held that '(t)he circumstances in the instant case ... are capable of supporting a suspicion with more than reasonable accuracy, and accordingly ... the Tribunal finds that the respondent company acted fairly and having regard to the grave nature of the misconduct the penalty was proportionate'. On that basis the EAT concluded that that the respondent 'had a reasonable belief and suspicion that the claimant was involved and that grounds existed to support such an honest belief in the absence of an adequate explanation from the claimant.

[34.15] The painstaking investigation undertaken prior to dismissal in *Pacelli v Irish Distillers* may be compared with the rather rapid dismissal of an employee in *Mahon v Noyeks*. The EAT expressed dissatisfaction with the procedure by which the employee was dismissed; he was given only two days within which to explain himself. However, the EAT concluded that dismissal was reasonable in the circumstances. The circumstances were the employee in question was employed to collect the respondent's bad debts and had failed to pass on a number of cheques to his employer. These decisions may be compared with that in *Maher v Eamonn Thompson T/A Thompson Transport*.[31] A serious allegation of theft had been made against the claimant. A more senior member of the respondent's staff had conducted an investigation of a sort but had refused to put the allegation to the claimant directly as he 'believed it to be a complete waste of time ... (and) ... believed the claimant was guilty of an offence from the outset'. The respondent also failed to interview other relevant personnel. The EAT ruled that 'the dismissal of the claimant by the Respondent was procedurally unfair in that no proper investigation had been carried out'.

[34.16] The ECJ decision in *X v European Central Bank*[32] illustrates the painstaking investigation and careful procedure that prudent employers should adopt when considering whether or not to dismiss an employee. The applicant was an employee of the respondent. An investigation of the applicant was commenced after another employee lodged a complaint against him. A couple of months after this investigation was commenced the applicant was suspended on full pay and informed that disciplinary proceedings had been opened against him. The applicant was also informed of the charges being laid against him. Two such accusations had been made. Firstly, that he 'repeatedly procured through the internet documents of a pornographic and political nature and ... sent them to third parties by electronic mail'. and secondly, that he had 'importuned the colleague who had submitted the complaint by sending him numerous

---

[30]   *Hennessy v Read & Write Shop Ltd* (UD 192/1978).

[31]   *Maher v Eamonn Thompson T/A Thompson Transport* 23/01/2007 UD537/2006 RP273/2006 MN346/2006 [FL13408] (EAT).

[32]   *X v European Central Bank* Case No T-333/99 (18 October 2001) ECJ.

messages by electronic mail containing material of a pornographic and/or ideologically extreme nature'.[33] The ECB then commenced the next stage of its investigation: 'it ... heard a series of witnesses'; ensured that 'certain checks were carried out concerning the internet sites consulted by the applicant and the electronic mail messages sent by him and 'the applicant's computer was disconnected from the ECB network and placed under seal'.[34] The ECB then sent the applicant 'three files containing approximately 900 pages of documents ... together with a CD-ROM on which were saved the pornographic images ... which the applicant had distributed by electronic mail within and outside the ECB'. The applicant, accompanied by his lawyer, then attended a hearing.[35] Following this, the administration of the ECB issued a reasoned opinion, which set out the evidence gathered and which it was proposed would be laid before the Executive Board of the ECB.[36] This reasoned opinion reached the conclusion that the applicant had harassed his colleague by sending inappropriate emails and had otherwise disregarded the procedures of the ECB and compromised its image.[37] It advocated the dismissal of the applicant.[38] The reasoned opinion was sent to the applicant's lawyer[39] who made a number of observations. In particular, he claimed that: 'there was no proof that the applicant had been the only person having access to the computer issued to him'[40]. Some correspondence then commenced between the applicant's lawyer and the EC[41]B, but the Executive Board of the ECB ultimately concluded that the applicant was to be dismissed. With regard to the applicant's observation that the ECB could not prove that his computer had been used by him alone, the ECB came to the following conclusion:

> 'the use of computers within the ECB was controlled by the use of personal and confidential passwords ... given the substantial number of messages sent by electronic mail during office hours over a period of 18 months from the applicant's computer, which was located in an open-plan office occupied by six persons, it was hardly likely that that computer could have been used by a third party without attracting attention.'

The ECJ agreed with the ECB and considered that the applicant's observation was 'manifestly unfounded'.[42] On appeal to the ECJ, the applicant argued that dismissal was a disproportionate response to the applicant's actions.[43] The ECJ disagreed, concluding that:

> 'The very considerable number and frequency of the incidents recorded demonstrate offensive and violent behaviour on the part of the applicant towards the victim. It cannot seriously be denied that, under the labour law of most of the Member States, such

---

[33] Case No T-333/99 (18 October 2001) ECJ, para 8.
[34] Case No T-333/99 (18 October 2001) ECJ, para 9.
[35] Case No T-333/99 (18 October 2001) ECJ, para 11.
[36] Case No T-333/99 (18 October 2001) ECJ, para 12.
[37] Case No T-333/99 (18 October 2001) ECJ, para 13.
[38] Case No T-333/99 (18 October 2001) ECJ, para 14.
[39] Case No T-333/99 (18 October 2001) ECJ, para 15.
[40] Case No T-333/99 (18 October 2001) ECJ, para 16.
[41] Case No T-333/99 (18 October 2001) ECJ, paras 17–22.
[42] Case No T-333/99 (18 October 2001) ECJ, para 217.
[43] Case No T-333/99 (18 October 2001) ECJ, para 220.

behaviour would have justified summary dismissal[44] ... Having regard to the particular seriousness of the applicant's non-compliance with his obligations, as illustrated by those myriad complaints, the penalty imposed does not appear to be manifestly disproportionate.'[45]

Misconduct of employees

[34.17] It would seem that an employee, or at least a manager, may be dismissed for disregarding basic security procedures. In *O'Brien v Mundania*[46] the claimant was employed as duty manager in a public house operated by the respondent. One night the claimant went home, without securing all the doors to the pub. Another of the respondent's employees noticed that a door to the pub was open and called the garda. The claimant was subsequently dismissed by the respondent. He appealed to the EAT, which unanimously found that:

> 'in leaving a door of the respondent's premises not only unlocked but open and leaving the lights on in the respondent's premises the claimant was guilty of a serious dereliction of duty, amounting to conduct which justified his dismissal'.[47]

[34.18] However, whilst the EAT did conclude that the claimant 'was guilty of serious negligence' it was also of the view that the claimant's admission of fault and previously exemplary record meant that he should not have been deprived of notice. [48] The claimant's negligence was very clear in this case: he was the duty manager and so was clearly responsible for the security of the pub. This decision would suggest that a manager with a responsibility for security, who disregards a basic security precaution, may be dismissed. However, not all IT-based security precautions will be as glaringly obvious as securing all the doors to a pub was located in an area where crime was not uncommon and containing some €70,000 of takings and stock. Furthermore, the claimant's defence was that he 'asked someone whom he trusted to lock the back door and he felt that if he checked it afterwards it would question that trust'. There is no indication from the decision in *O'Brien v Mundania* that any disciplinary action was taken against that employee. Arguably, the decision in *O'Brien v Mundania* is more about the dismissal of a manager who failed to properly manage a security risk, rather than that of an employee who failed to follow an instruction.

[34.19] Merely because an employee has disregarded procedures will not justify their dismissal, and certainly not where the individual employee is singled out as an example. In *Carey v Docket and Form International Ltd*[49] the respondent was 'a printing company that produces documents that requires a high level of security'. To this end 'various and rigorous security measures' were employed. These included: keeping documents in a

---

44   Case No T-333/99 (18 October 2001) ECJ, para 224.
45   Case No T-333/99 (18 October 2001) ECJ, para 226.
46   *O'Brien v Mundania* 23/09/2005 MN1006/2004, UD1307/2004 [FL11711] (EAT).
47   Pursuant to s 6(4)(a) of the Unfair Dismissals Acts. Accordingly the claim under the Unfair Dismissals Acts 1977–2005
48   Pursuant to s 8 of the Minimum Notice and Terms of Employment Acts 1973–2001.
49   *Carey v Docket and Form International Ltd* 08/04/2005 UD302/2004, MN255/2004 [FL10787] (EAT).

vault, use of CCTV cameras, destroying used materials and documents. The claimant was an employee of long standing who sought to bring some waste-paper home with him. He failed to go through the proper procedures in doing so: he sought permission from another junior employee and brought the paper out a side door. The respondent responded by dismissing him. The EAT concluded that this was an overreaction. It considered that the respondent was '… correct to place high regard and due attention to security but this incident did not threaten or challenge the security of the enterprise'. The claimant erred in that he failed to obtain formal and authorised permission to remove this material and the timing and location of the deposited material could legitimately give rise to suspicion. Ultimately, the EAT considered that 'the Respondent wished to make an example of the claimant which was in the Tribunal's opinion unfair. It follows that the dismissal was unfair'.

And the EAT awarded the claimant some €27,000 in compensation.

Chapter 35

Restraint of Trade Clauses

Introduction

[35.01] Employees can learn a lot from their employers and when their employment ceases, they will bring that knowledge with them. In the information, knowledge or learning society that Ireland has become, the knowledge that is acquired by an employee is increasingly valuable. In a competitive environment an employer may wish to restrict a former employee's ability to utilise that knowledge to compete with his former boss. In general the law will not permit such a restriction. Even where a restriction will be permitted, that restriction will be limited and one which the courts will enforce only in very clear circumstances. This chapter examines the enforceability of such restraints in two situations. These are:

(a) Restraints of trade that are explicitly set out in contracts of employment. These may protect the employer's goodwill or his confidential information or both. The courts may enforce such clauses but only where the restriction is clear and reasonable.

(b) Restraints that will be implied in a contract of employment. These can usually protect only the employer's trade secrets.

Contractual restraints of trade

[35.02] Many of the Irish cases on restraint of trade focus on the preservation of goodwill as opposed to intellectual property or confidential information. In other words, Irish restraint of trade actions tend to be brought to prevent former employees contacting or poaching the customers of their former employers. For example, in *Murgitroyd & Co Ltd v Purdy*[1] the plaintiff was a firm of patent agents. The defendant was a patent agent himself and a former employee of the plaintiffs. When he commenced employment with the plaintiffs, the defendant had made the following undertaking:

> 'The executive will not within the Republic of Ireland during the period of 12 months following determination of his employment hereunder on his account and in competition with the company carry on any business which competes with the business of the company or any associated company having intellectual property work as one of its principal objects existing as of the date of termination of the executive's employment hereunder and with which the executive shall have been directly or indirectly concerned PROVIDED THAT nothing contained in this clause shall preclude the executive from holding at any time any shares or loan capital (not exceeding one *per centum* of the shares or loan capital of the class concerned for the time being in issue) in any company whose shares are listed or dealt in on a recognised stock exchange and nothing in this agreement

---

[1] *Murgitroyd & Co Ltd v Purdy* [2005] 3 IR 12.

will affect the executive's right to accept employment as an employee in another firm of patent attorneys'.[2]

Clarke J noted that it was 'well settled' that the above clause would only be enforceable if it met the following two-part test 'it is reasonable as between the parties; and ... it is consistent with the interests of the public'.

[35.03] Regarding what might be regarded as reasonable between the parties, Clarke J cited the view of Wilberforce LJ in *Stenhouse Ltd v Phillips*[3]:

> 'The accepted proposition that an employer is not entitled to protection from mere competition by a former employee means that the employee is entitled to use to the full any personal skill or experience even if this has been acquired in the service of his employer: it is this freedom to use to the full a man's improving ability and talents which lies at the root of the policy of the law regarding this type of restraint. Leaving aside the case of misuse of trade secrets or confidential information ... the employer's claim for protection must be based upon the identification of some advantage or asset inherent in the business which can properly be regarded as, in a general sense, his property, and which it would be unjust to allow the employee to appropriate for his own purposes, even though he, the employee, may have contributed to its creation.'

Clarke J considered that:

> 'The test seems to be ... as to whether in all the circumstances of the case both the nature of the restriction and its extent is reasonable to protect the goodwill of the employer ... But it is clear that the duration of the prohibition and the geographical scope of same are important matters to be considered having regard to the nature of the work in question and the structure of the business'.[4]

[35.04] Clarke J cited Halsbury's view that: 'where a business is carried on by a small number of people and with customers widely distributed, a very large area will be allowed and a wider restraint may be reasonable in a business carried on by agents or correspondence than in one necessitating constant attendance in person.'[5] Clarke J was:

> 'satisfied that there are only 10 ... patent attorneys operating in Ireland and that they all operate from Dublin. No difficulty would appear to be encountered in servicing the demands of the Irish business from Dublin. In those circumstances it does not seem to me that a geographical restriction based upon the jurisdiction of the Irish state is unreasonable having regard to the way in which the business operates in Ireland'.

Furthermore Clarke J was satisfied that having regard to the 'specialised nature of the business' of being a patent agent a period of 12 months was not unreasonable.[6]

---

[2]   [2005] 3 IR 12 at 15.

[3]   *Stenhouse Ltd v Phillips* [1974] AC 391.

[4]   *Murgitroyd & Co Ltd v Purdy* [2005] 3 IR 12 at 21.

[5]   (47) *Halsbury's Laws of England* (4th edn), para 31 cited by Clark J at [2005] 3 IR 12 at 21.

[6]   The length of time that will be regarded as reasonable will vary from industry to industry. In *Societa Esplosivi Industriali v Ordnance Technologies Ltd* [2004] EWHC 48 (Ch) a period of 9.5 years was held to be 'not a long one in the context of a defence project using and developing cutting edge technology' [2004] EWHC 48 (Ch), para 146.

But he noted that:

'Covenants against competition by former employees are never reasonable as such. They may be upheld only where the employee might obtain such personal knowledge of, and influence over, the customers of his employer as would enable him, if competition were allowed, to take advantage of his employer's trade connection.'[7]

[35.05] However, the anti-competition clause in this case went too far as it prevented the former employee from competing with his former employer at all. Clarke J was of the view that:

'A prohibition on dealing with (in addition to soliciting of) customers of the plaintiff would, in my view, have been reasonable and sufficient to meet any legitimate requirements of the plaintiff. The wider prohibition which restricts dealing with those who might be, but are not, such customers is excessive ...

There may be types of business where it is not practical to distinguish between customers and non-customers. This is not one of them. On the evidence, the number of customers is small and identifiable. A prohibition on dealing with those identified customers would be sufficient to prevent the defendant taking advantage of the plaintiff's trade connections. The wider restriction which prohibits competing for business in which the plaintiff might have an interest but where the client was not an existing customer, could not be directed to that end but to the wider aim of restricting competition as such ... that is not a permissible end'[8].

[35.06] The courts may be unwilling to imply a non-compete clause into a contract which does not expressly provide for one. *Wallis Bogan & Company v Cove*[9] concerned three solicitors who had left their former employer to set up their own firm and compete for their own clients. The English Court of Appeal ruled that:

'The essential question is: whether the solicitor is entitled to canvass clients of the firm. In so doing, the solicitor is, indeed, taking advantage of a professional connection with the client. But that connection is no different in principle from the trade connection that, for instance, a milk roundsman may acquire with his employer's customers. Clients and customers alike represent the employers' goodwill which the employers are entitled to protect by an express covenant in reasonable restraint of trade, but which is not protected for them by an implied term if they do not bother to exact an express covenant'.

[35.07] Clarke J cited the above passage in *The Pulse Group Ltd and Pulse Marketing Services Ltd v Ciaran O'Reilly and Eye Gen Ltd Trading as 'Brando'*.[10] The first-named defendant was a former chief executive of the plaintiff, who had resigned from the plaintiff and set up the second named defendant. The plaintiffs sought injunctive relief and an order restraining the defendants from 'interfering with or otherwise contacting suppliers, contractors, distributors or employees'. However, Clarke J held that there

---

[7]   *Murgitroyd & Co Ltd v Purdy* [2005] 3 IR 12 at 21, citing *Kores Manufacturing Co Ltd v Kolok Manufacturing Co. Ltd* [1959] Ch 108.

[8]   *Murgitroyd & Co Ltd v Purdy* [2005] 3 IR 12 at 21–22.

[9]   *Wallis Bogan & Co v Cove* (1997) IRLR 453.

[10] *The Pulse Group Ltd and Pulse Marketing Services Ltd v Ciaran O'Reilly and Eye Gen Ltd Trading as 'Brando'* [2006] IEHC 50.

were no 'arguable grounds for implying any ... covenant'[11] and so refused the order. Clarke J held that:

> ' ... the law is clear. In the absence of an express term in a contract of employment the only enduring obligation on the part of an employee after his employment has ceased is one which precludes the employee from disclosing a trade secret'.[12]

[35.08] In contrast, Peart J was willing to grant injunctive relief in *European Paint Importers Ltd v O'Callaghan, O'Mahony, Complete Coatings Ltd*.[13] The plaintiff was seeking to enforce the following restraint of trade clause against a former employee:

> 'The employee covenants with the Company that he will not for the period of one year after ceasing to be employed by the Company, in connection with the carrying on of any business similar to or in competition with the business of Heavy Duty Coating, and Industrial Paint Sales, on its own behalf or on behalf of any person, firm or company, directly or indirectly seek to procure orders from or do business with any person, firm or company who has any time during the One Year immediately preceding such cessation of employment done business with the Company'

However, Peart J interpreted the above as meaning that the defendants should not 'take any positive step to seek business from existing customers of the plaintiff for a period of twelve months'. Peart J was unwilling to rule the above clause as meaning that the defendants should refuse to do business with customers of their former employer, even where the customer made the initial approach.

The restraint of knowledge workers

[35.09] Employers in technology industries may protect the knowledge acquired by employees as confidential information. Employees will typically have to agree to clauses such as the following in their contracts of employment:

(a)   The employee is aware that in the course of employment under this agreement he will have access to and be entrusted with information in respect of the business and financing of the Company and its dealings transactions and affairs all of which information is or may be confidential.

(b)   The employee shall not (except in the proper course of his duties) during or after the period of his employment under this agreement divulge to any person whatever or otherwise make use of (and shall use his best endeavours to prevent the publication or disclosure of) any trade secret or any confidential information concerning the business or finances of the Company or any of its suppliers, agents, distributors or customers.

(c)   All notes and memoranda of any trade secrets or confidential information concerning the business of the Company or any of its suppliers, agents, distributors or customers which shall be acquired received or made by the Employee during the course of his employment shall be the property of the

---

[11]   [2006] IEHC 50, para 3.2.

[12]   [2006] IEHC 50, para 3.4.

[13]   *European Paint Importers Ltd v O'Callaghan, O'Mahony, Complete Coatings Ltd* [2005] IEHC 280.

Company and shall be surrendered by the Employee to someone duly authorised in that behalf at the termination of his employment or at the request of the company at any time during the course of his employment.[14]

[35.10] In *Balston Ltd v Headline Filters Ltd*[15] Scott J have been expressed strong doubts about the appropriateness of applying clauses such as the above to high technology:

'Technology based industries abound. All have what they regard as secrets. Employees particularly those employed on the scientific or technical side of the manufacturing business, necessarily acquire knowledge of the relevant technology. They become associated with technological advances and innovations. Their experience, built up during their years of employment naturally equips them to be dangerous competitors if and when their employment ceases. The use of confidential information restrictions in order to fetter the ability of these employees to use their skills and experience after determination of their employment to compete with their ex-employer is, in my view, potentially harmful. It would be capable of imposing a new form of servitude or serfdom, to use Cumming-Bruce LJ's words on technologically qualified employees. It would render them unable in practice to leave their employment for want of an ability to use their skills after leaving. Employers who want to impose fetters of this sort on their employees ought in my view to be expected to do so by express covenant. The reasonableness of the covenant can then be subjected to the rigorous attention to which all ex-employee covenants in restraint of trade are subject. In the absence of an express covenant, the ability of an ex-employee to compete can be restricted by means of an implied term against use or disclosure of trade secrets. But the case must in my view, be a clear one. An employee does not have the chance to reject an implied term. It is formulated and imposed on him subsequently to his initial entry into employment. To fetter his freedom to compete by means of an implied term can only be justified, in my view, by a very clear case'.[16]

[35.11] If applied, the above dicta would mean that post-employment restraints would be even more difficult to apply in industries such as the software one where intellectual property is particularly valuable. A view might be taken that if an employer does not consider information to be of sufficient value that it should be protected by an express clause, then the court should not consider it of sufficient value for it to be protected as a trade secret. Scott J's dicta was expressly echoed by Mummery J in *Ixora Trading v Jones*[17] who gave judgement in the Court of Appeal in the case of *FSS Leisure v Johnson*.[18] This concerned a programmer who had left his previous employer and commenced work with a competitor. His previous employer sued, alleging breach of confidential information. It claimed that its computerised booking system was confidential information. This system contained 2,852 separate programs of which the employee had worked on 395. Mummery J rejected the employer's claim holding that 'It is not sufficient for the employer to assert a claim that he is entitled to an accumulated

---

[14] Butterworths, *The Encyclopedia of Forms and Precedents* (5th edn, 1994) Reissue Vol 14, pp 79–80, para 315.

[15] *Balston Ltd v Headline Filters Ltd* [1987] FSR 330.

[16] [1987] FSR 330 at 351.

[17] *Ixora Trading v Jones* [1990] FSR 251 at 261.

[18] *FSS Leisure v Johnson* [1999] FSR 505.

mass of knowledge which he regards as confidential'[19] and refused an injunction on the basis that:

> 'neither the pleaded case nor the oral evidence ... is sufficiently specific, precise or cogent to establish the entitlement (of the plaintiffs) to identifiable trade secrets. (The plaintiffs) are essentially claiming to be able to control the exercise, after the termination of the employment relationship, of the skill, experience, know-how and general knowledge inevitably gained by (the defendant) while employed as a programmer with (the plaintiffs).'[20]

[35.12] If employment is terminated as a result of a repudiatory breach by an employer, any contractual obligations of confidence owed by the employee may then end, but the employer may still succeed in equity.[21] It is also possible that an employer may be able to enforce an implied duty of confidence more broadly against an employee who is not applying the information concerned as part of his general skill or knowledge, but using it maliciously.[22]

Non-contractual restrictions: trade secrets

[35.13] In *Mahon v Post Publications*[23] the Supreme Court noted that:

> 'The law of confidence has ... developed ... in a commercial context. Dismissed or defecting employees have not infrequently purloined their former master's technical or commercial information. While employees can be restrained in contract without resort to the equitable doctrine, the latter becomes relevant when the information is conveyed to third parties who are on notice of the confidential character of the information'.[24]

[35.14] So in *Meadox Medicals v VPI Ltd*[25] Hamilton J granted an injunction where the defendant's 'use of such knowledge and confidential data ... were in breach of their express agreement with Meadox'.[26] Where there is no confidentiality clause in the contract of employment, the courts may still protect the employer's confidential information, but only where they can be defined as trade secrets. An employee will always owe his employer a duty of confidence while he is employed and the courts will imply a term to this effect into the contract of employment.[27] The Courts may be willing

---

19. [1999] FSR 505 at 513.
20. [1999] FSR 505 at 516.
21. See Toulson & Phipps, *Confidentiality* (Sweet & Maxwell, 1996) p 177; *SBJ Stephenson v Keith Anthony Mandy* [2000] FSR 286.
22. See Toulson and Phipps' criticism of the judgment in *Mainmet Holdings v Austin* [1991] FSR 538 (Sweet & Maxwell, 1996), p 175.
23. *Mahon v Post Publications* [2007] IESC 15.
24. [2007] IESC 15, para 71.
25. *Meadox Medicals v VPI Ltd* (27 April 1982, unreported) HC (Hamilton J).
26. (27 April 1982, unreported) HC at p 57.
27. The principle is an ancient one going back to *Tipping v Clark* (1843) 2 Hare 383 at least. For a more recent Irish example, see *Kehoe v McCaughan and McCaughan* (9 March 1993, unreported) HC, decisions of Lardner J. It should of course be kept in mind that employers also owe an obligation of confidence to their employees and prospective employees. See the Australian case of *Smith Kline Laboratories v Department of Community Services* [1991] 28 FCR 291. See *Prout v British Gas PLC* [1992] FSR 478 on when the obligation owed may terminate.

to protect the employer's secrets after the employee has ceased employment but the protection will be more limited, as it cannot be used to restrict the employee from using his general skill and knowledge in his subsequent employment. In *Meadox Medicals v VPI Ltd*[28] former employees of the plaintiff had joined the defendant. The subject matter of the action included a programming technique. Pumfrey J held that if this technique was disclosed during the course of employment then that disclosure would amount to a breach of the contract of employment and of confidentiality. But as it was not inherently confidential, an ex-employee would not be prevented from using it after his employment ceased.[29]

[35.15] In *Faccenda Chicken Ltd v Fowler*[30] the English Court of Appeal approved Goulding J's categorisation of the types of information which can be protected when an employee leaves as follows:

'First, there is information which, because of its trivial character or its easy accessibility from public sources of information cannot be regarded by reasonable persons or by the law as confidential at all … Secondly there is information which the servant must treat as confidential (either because his is expressly told it is confidential or because from its character it is obvious it is so) but which once learned necessarily remains in the servant's head and becomes part of his own skill and knowledge applied in the course of his master's business … Thirdly, there are to my mind, specific trade secrets so confidential that, even though they may necessarily have been learned by heart, and even though the servant may have left the service they cannot lawfully be used for anyone's benefit but the master's'.[31]

[35.16] This issue arose before the English Court of Appeal in *AT Poeton v Michael IKEM Horton*[32] where it was held that an employer's trade secrets could be protected but only if the following three stage test was satisfied:

(a)   The information could only be protected if it was not in the public domain.[33]

(b)   If the information was not in the public domain, then it had to be decided if the information was a 'trade secret'. This would be decided by the nature of the information itself, but if the information was not a trade secret, then it would not be protected.

(c)   Even if it was a trade secret the court would have to decide whether or not it had become part of the employee's own skill and knowledge, which he would be free to use unless expressly restrained by convenant.[34]

---

[28]   *Meadox Medicals v VPI Ltd* [2000] RPC 95.
[29]   [2000] RPC 95, para 36, p 110.
[30]   *Faccenda Chicken Ltd v Fowler* [1987] Ch 117, [1985] FSR 105.
[31]   Quoted with approval by the Court of Appeal at [1987] Ch 117 at p 133.
[32]   *AT Poeton v Michael IKEM Horton* [2001] FSR 169.
[33]   [2001] FSR 169 at 181.
[34]   [2001] FSR 169 at 182. See *Coco v AN Clark (Engineers) Ltd* [1969] RPC 41; *Printers and Finishers ltd v Holloway* [1965] RPC 239 and *Faccenda Chicken Ltd v Fowler* [1987] Ch 117.

The court held that the plaintiff's action could not succeed as it had not satisfied the above test. In both these cases the Court of Appeal used the following criteria for identifying what is and is not a trade secret:

(a)   the nature of the employment and whether the employee habitually handles confidential information so as to heighten his appreciation of its confidential nature;

(b)   the nature of the information itself, such as information of a highly confidential nature, examples of which might be secret processes of manufacture, or information which was only circulated to a restricted group of people;

(c)   the employer must have impressed on the employee the confidentiality of the information to the extent that it shows the information can properly be regarded as a trade secret; and

(d)   finally, the issue of whether or not the information can be easily isolated from other information the employee is free to use or disclose.[35]

[35.17] However, there is no universal formula for determining what is or is not a trade secret.[36] In *Lansing Linde Ltd v Kerr*[37] Staughton LJ preferred the following definition of a trade secret:

'a trade secret is information which, if disclosed to a competitor, would be liable to cause real (or significant) harm to the owner of the secret ... it must be information used in a trade or a business, and ... the owner must limit the dissemination of it or at least not encourage or permit widespread publication'.[38]

The use of source codes by an ex-employee may be a breach of confidence.[39]

---

[35]   [2001] FSR 169 at 185–186.

[36]   See Toulson and Phipps *Confidentiality* (Sweet & Maxwell, 1996) p 31.

[37]   *Lansing Linde Ltd v Kerr* (1991) 1 WLR 251.

[38]   (1991) 1 WLR 251 at 260. Lavery sets out some general principles on what factors will be taken into account by the courts in deciding whether information is capable of protection after the employer/employee relationship is terminated. Lavery, *Commercial Secrets* (Sweet & Maxwell, 1996), ch 7.

[39]   *Cantor Fitzgerald v Tradition* [2000] RPC 95 at paras 86–87 and *Ibcos Computers v Barclays Finance Ltd* [1994] FSR 275 at 314.

Chapter 36

Health, Safety and Disposal

Introduction

[36.01] The use of information technology in the workplace gives rise to a variety of health and safety issues. In addition, when information technology devices such as computers come to the end of their lives they will have to be disposed of. Such disposal must be undertaken in accordance with Irish and European legislation on the management of waste.

Safety, Health and Welfare at Work Act 2005

[36.02] The Safety, Health and Welfare at Work Act 2005 (SHWWA 2005) provides that 'Every employer shall ensure, so far as is reasonably practicable, the safety, health and welfare at work of his or her employees.'[1] This duty extends to:

'(a) managing and conducting work activities in such a way as to ensure, so far as is reasonably practicable, the safety, health and welfare at work of his or her employees;

(b) managing and conducting work activities in such a way as to prevent, so far as is reasonably practicable, any improper conduct or behaviour likely to put the safety, health or welfare at work of his or her employees at risk;

(c) as regards the place of work concerned, ensuring, so far as is reasonably practicable ... the design, provision and maintenance of it in a condition that is safe and without risk to health ...

(d) ensuring, so far as it is reasonably practicable, the safety and the prevention of risk to health at work of his or her employees relating to the use of any article or substance or the exposure to noise, vibration or ionising or other radiations or any other physical agent;

(e) providing systems of work that are planned, organised, performed, maintained and revised as appropriate so as to be, so far as is reasonably practicable, safe and without risk to health;

(f) providing and maintaining facilities and arrangements for the welfare of his or her employees at work;

(g) providing the information, instruction, training and supervision necessary to ensure, so far as is reasonably practicable, the safety, health, and welfare at work of his or her employees;

(h) determining and implementing the safety, health and welfare measures necessary for the protection of the safety, health and welfare of his or her employees when identifying hazards and carrying out a risk assessment ... or when preparing a

---

[1] SHWWA 2005, s 8(1).

safety statement ... ensuring that the measures take account of changing circumstances and the general principles of prevention specified in *Schedule 3*;

(i)   having regard to the general principles of prevention ... where risks cannot be eliminated or adequately controlled or in such circumstances as may be prescribed, providing and maintaining such suitable protective clothing and equipment as is necessary to ensure, so far as is reasonably practicable, the safety, health and welfare at work of his or her employees;

(j)   preparing and revising, as appropriate, adequate plans and procedures to be followed and measures to be taken in the case of an emergency or serious and imminent danger;

(k)   reporting accidents and dangerous occurrences;

(l)   obtaining, where necessary, the services of a competent person (whether under a contract of employment or otherwise) for the purpose of ensuring, so far as is reasonably practicable, the safety, health and welfare at work of his or her employees.'[2]

[36.03] Whatever measures are taken by the employer in discharge of these duties, they cannot impose costs on his employees.[3] Employers must provide their employees with information, which must be 'given in a form, manner and, as appropriate, language that is reasonably likely to be understood by the employees concerned'.[4] They must also provide their employees with training, which must be provided 'on recruitment ... in the event of the transfer of an employee or change of task assigned to an employee ... on the introduction of new work equipment, systems of work or changes in existing work equipment or systems of work, and ... on the introduction of new technology'.[5] The employer is under the same duty towards fixed-term and temporary employees as he is under in respect of his permanent staff.[6] And the duty of the employer will extend to other persons who may be present in the workplace:

'Every employer shall manage and conduct his or her undertaking in such a way as to ensure, so far as is reasonably practicable, that in the course of the work being carried on, individuals at the place of work (not being his or her employees) are not exposed to risks to their safety, health or welfare.'[7]

[36.04] The employer is not the only person under a duty in respect of health and safety. Employees are under duties including to 'take reasonable care to protect his or her safety, health and welfare and the safety, health and welfare of any other person who may be affected by the employee's acts or omissions at work ... attend such training and, as appropriate, undergo such assessment as may reasonably be required by his or her employer'.[8] The SHWWA 2005 provides a number of enforcement mechanisms. Part 5 of the Act creates the Health and Safety Authority, which continues the work of the old

---

2   SHWWA 2005, s 8(2).
3   SHWWA 2005, s 8(5).
4   SHWWA 2005, s 9(1)(a).
5   SHWWA 2005, s 10(3).
6   SHWWA 2005, s 8(3)–(4).
7   SHWWA 2005, s 12.
8   SHWWA 2005, s 13.

National Authority for Occupational Safety and Health.[9] This Authority and its authorised officers are given a variety of powers.[10] However, the Act makes it clear that the primary duty of ensuring a safe place of work is imposed on employers and, to a lesser extent, on their employees. The employer is under a duty to:

'identify the hazards in the place of work under his or her control, assess the risks presented by those hazards and be in possession of a written assessment … . of the risks to the safety, health and welfare at work of his or her employees, including the safety, health and welfare of any single employee or group or groups of employees who may be exposed to any unusual or other risks.'[11]

Employers have a duty to appoint someone to undertake certain duties in respect of health and safety, employees may also select a person to represent their views on health and safety to their employers. The employer must appoint:

'one or more competent persons to perform such functions as are specified by the employer, relating to the protection from and the prevention of risks to safety, health and welfare at work.'[12]

At the same time, the employees may:

'select and appoint from amongst their number at their place of work a representative … to represent them at the place of work in consultation with their employer on matters related to safety, health and welfare at the place of work.'[13]

Keyboards, display units and repetitive strain injury

VDU regulations

[36.05] The VDU regulations are provided by the Safety, Health and Welfare at Work (General Application) Regulations 1993.[14] The regulations apply to what it terms 'workstations', which are defined as:

'an assembly comprising display screen[15] equipment, which may be provided with a keyboard or input device or software (or a keyboard or input device and software) determining the operator and machine interface, and includes optional accessories and peripherals such as a diskete drive, telephone, modem, printer, document holder, work chair and work desk or work surface and the immediate work environment of the display screen equipment'.[16]

---

[9]   SHWWA 2005, s 32(1)(a).
[10] SHWWA 2005, Pt 6, Ch 2.
[11] SHWWA 2005, s 19(1).
[12] SHWWA 2005, s 18(1).
[13] SHWWA 2005, s 25(1).
[14] Safety, Health and Welfare at Work (General Application) Regulations 1993 (SI 44/1993), Pt VII. These regulations are continued in force pursuant to SHWWA 2005, s 4(4).
[15] Where 'display screen' is defined as: 'any alphanumeric or graphic display screen, regardless of the display process involved,' SI 44/1993, reg 29.
[16] SI 44/1993, reg 29.

The regulations do not apply to:

'drivers' cabs or control cabs for vehicles or machinery ... computer systems on board a means of transport ... computer systems mainly intended for public use ... portable display screen equipment not in prolonged use at a workstation ... calculators, cash registers and any equipment having a small data or measurement display required for direct use of the equipment; and ... typewriters of traditional design'.[17]

In respect of the 'workstations' to which the regulations do apply, the employer must:

'(a) perform an analysis of the workstations in order to evaluate the safety and health conditions to which they give rise for his employees, particularly as regards possible risks to eyesight, physical problems and problems of mental stress;

(b) take appropriate measures to remedy any risks found ... and taking account of any additional or combined effects of any such risks so found ...

(c) plan the activities of his employees in such a way that daily work on a display screen is periodically interrupted by breaks or changes of activity which reduce workload at the display screen;

(d) provide information to his employees in relation to the measures applicable to workstations which have been implemented;

(e) provide training to employees in the use of workstations before commencing this work with display screen equipment and whenever the organisation of the workstation is substantially modified'.[18]

[36.06] In addition, employers must ensure:

'that an appropriate eye and eyesight test, carried out by a competent person, is made available to every employee ... before commencing display screen work ... at regular intervals thereafter.'[19]

If such tests show it to be necessary, then 'an ophthalmological examination' of the employee must be undertaken.[20] If on foot of those tests it is found to be necessary to supply the employee with 'special corrective appliances appropriate to his work', then those shall be supplied.[21]

Electrical equipment

[36.07] Information technology relies upon electrical equipment to work, and the Safety, Health and Welfare at Work (General Application) Regulations 1993 impose specific obligations upon employers with regard to the safe use of such equipment, for example, 'All electrical equipment and electrical installations shall at all times be so ... constructed ... installed ... maintained ... protected and ... use(d) ... so as to so as to prevent danger.'[22]

---

[17] SI 44/1993, reg 31.
[18] SI 44/1993, reg 31(1).
[19] SI 44/1993, reg 32(a).
[20] SI 44/1993, reg 32(b).
[21] SI 44/1993, reg 32(c).
[22] SI 44/1993, reg 36.

The law of torts

[36.08] The law of torts imposes a duty upon employers to supply their employees with safe equipment[23] and to warn their employees of any risks associated with the use of workplace equipment.[24] In relation to the use of information technology, this issue has most prominently arisen with regard to Repetitive strain injuries and other related injuries that affect the wrist, upper limbs, back and neck. The Personal Injuries Assessment Board (PIAB)'s Book of Quantum sets out the parameters which will guide it in assessing the damages to be paid in respect of 'the specific wrist injuries of Repetitive Strain Injury (Tenosynovitis), Carpal Tunnel Syndrome, Cubital Tunnel Syndrome and Radial Tunnel Syndrome':

Substantially recovered	up to €26,200
Significant ongoing	€15,500 to €70,100
Serious and permanent conditions	€26,000 to €88,600

[36.09] In the English case of *Fifield v Denton Hall Legal Services*[26] the plaintiff was a secretary employed by the defendant. Her case was that:

> 'although she had ... suffered intermittent pain in her wrists ... she slowly developed a build up of pain in her hands, mostly in the morning, and that this caused some difficulty typing. The pain also moved up to her elbows and shoulders, and eventually to her neck. She is right-handed and the symptoms were worse on her right side.'[27]

The plaintiff sued for damages and was awarded £157,341 (sterling) at hearing. The defendant appealed, arguing that her injuries were not work related. The appeal was dismissed by the Court of Appeal, where Wall LJ held that the evidence that the plaintiff's injuries were work related was 'overwhelming'.[28]

Disposal

[36.10] Computers are pieces of electrical equipment, which may contain a variety of hazardous substances such as battery chemicals. When computers and other electrical equipment come to the end of their lives they must be disposed of in accordance with a variety of legislation including:

1.   Council Directive 2002/96/EC1 on waste, electrical and electronic equipment;[29]

---

23   See, for example, *English v Anglo-Irish Meat* Co (2 December 1988, unreported) HC.

24   *Nagle v Tipplers Tavern Ltd* (11 October 1991, unreported) HC. See generally, Healy, *Principles of Irish Torts* (Clarus Press, 2006) Ch 7.

25   Personal Injuries Assessment Board, *Book of Quantum*, Version 1, June 2004, p 11.

26   *Fifield v Denton Hall Legal Services* [2006] EWCA Civ 169. See also *Pickford v Imperial Chemical Industries plc* [1997] ICR 566, [1996] IRLR 622.

27   [2006] EWCA Civ 169, para 5.

28   [2006] EWCA Civ 169, para 45.

29   OJ L37, 13.02.2003, p 24, amended by Council Directive 2003/108/EC2 of 8 December 2003, OJ L 345, 31.12.2003, p 106.

2. The Waste Management (Waste Electrical and Electronic Equipment) Regulations 2005;[30] and

3. The Waste Management Acts 1996 and 2001.

It should also be noted that a variety of legislation will apply to the use of hazardous and other chemicals in the manufacture and use of electronic equipment, such as the Waste Management (Restriction of Certain Hazardous Substances in Electrical and Electronic Equipment) Regulations 2005.[31]

---

[30] SI 340/2005.

[31] Waste Management (Restriction of Certain Hazardous Substances in Electrical and Electronic Equipment) Regulations 2005 (SI 341/2005).

Chapter 37

Equality

Introduction

[37.01] In recent years, Ireland has enacted equality legislation in the form of the Equal Status Acts 2000–2004 and the Employment Equality Acts 1998–2004. These enactments broadly prohibit discrimination on many grounds, both in the disposal of goods and the provision of services and in the workplace.

> 'discrimination shall be taken to occur where ... a person is treated less favourably than another person is, has been or would be treated in a comparable situation on any of the grounds specified.'[1]

Such discrimination may occur on a number of different grounds, one of which may be that one employee: 'is a person with a disability and the other either is not or is a person with a different disability'.[2] In *A Technology Company v A Worker*[3] the complainant applied to the respondent for employment as an IT support specialist. It was agreed between the parties that the complainant was visually impaired and as a result was disabled for the purposes of The Employment Equality Acts. The complainant underwent a telephone interview. In the course of that interview the complainant asked if he could undertake a skills test in an electronic format, as he was unable to read from a page. The complainant subsequently attended a face-to-face interview, but was not offered the opportunity to take the written test. He was subsequently informed that his application was unsuccessful; he rang the respondent's HR unit and was told that he had not got the job because he could not read from a page. The case reached the Labour Court, which held that as the complainant was unable to take the written test he:

> 'was denied an opportunity to undertake an integral and otherwise essential part of the selection process because of his disability. This meant that the whole selection process was tainted with discrimination.'

The Labour court went on to find that the complainant was discriminated against contrary to the Employment Equality Acts and awarded him €12,000.

---

[1] Employment Equality Acts 1998–2004, s 6(1).

[2] Employment Equality Acts 1998–2004, s 6(2)(g).

[3] *A Technology Company v A worker,* The Labour Court, ADE/07/1 Determination No 0714, 11 September 2007. The reference to the Technology Company as the respondent and the Worker as the claimant is made by the Labour Court, and reflects the fact that the case was first heard by an Equality Officer.

As regards the disposal of goods and the provision of services:As regards the disposal of goods and the provision of services:

> 'discrimination includes a refusal or failure by the provider of a service to do all that is reasonable to accommodate the needs of a person with a disability by providing special treatment or facilities, if without such special treatment or facilities it would be impossible or unduly difficult for the person to avail himself or herself of the service.'[4]

[37.02] Given the provision of websites and access terminals and the pervasiveness of information technology in the workplace, employers and the providers of information technology services to the public cannot ignore the needs of the disabled. Member states of the EU have given a commitment that:

> 'Public sector web sites and their content in Member States and in the European institutions must be designed to be accessible to ensure that citizens with disabilities can access information and take full advantage of the potential for e-government.'[5]

The European Commission responded to this commitment with a *Communication on Accessibility of Public Web Sites and their Content*,[6] which noted that: 'accessing Internet Web pages and their content presents a variety of problems for persons with physical, sensory or cognitive impairments.'[7] The European Commission then followed up with a *Communication on eAccessibility*, which found that:

> 'making the benefits of ICT available to the widest possible number of people is a social, ethical and political imperative.'[8]

[37.03] Accessibility issues have arisen in a number of cases of the Irish Equality Tribunal. In *Wellard v Educational Building Society and Allied Irish Banks*[9] the applicant was a visually impaired lady. She asked for her ATM pin number to be sent to her in Braille, but her request was refused. She claimed discrimination, which was denied by the respondents, who:

> 'explained that all ATM Pin Nos are generated in a closed encrypted environment by computer for security reasons and that there is no manual input involved by staff. The EBS generates a Pin No for its customers in an encrypted format. This is then sent to the AIB whose own encrypted system produce the Pin No in a sealed EBS envelope which is then sent directly to the customer.
>
> The whole system is encrypted internally to ensure that details of an individual's Pin No are not disclosed to anyone including staff members...

---

4   Equal Status Acts 2000–2004, s 4(1).
5   European Union, *Conclusions of the Feira Council*, June 2000.
6   European Commission, *Communication on Accessibility of Public Web Sites and their Content*, Brussels, 25 September 2001, COM(2001) 529 final.
7   EC Commission, *Communication on Accessibility of Public Web Sites and their Content*, Brussels, 25 September 2001, COM(2001) 529 final, p 3, http://eur-lex.europa.eu/LexUriServ/site/en/com/2001/com2001_0529en01.pdf.
8   EC Commission, *Communication on eAccessibility, Brussels*, 13 September 2005 COM(2005) 425, para 1.
9   *Wellard v Educational Building Society and Allied Irish Banks* Equality Tribunal, Case No DEC-S2005/093.

To ensure confidentiality, ATM cards and Pin Nos are sent to the customer under separate cover. The Pin No itself is automatically generated by computer and sent directly to the customer in a tamper-proof format. The whole process is designed from start to finish to protect the confidentiality of customers' Pin Nos.'[10]

The respondents appeared to have argued that their system was designed to ensure that the pin numbers were generated automatically, without human intervention. The first person to see a pin number would be the customer. changing the system to provide for the creation of pin numbers in Braille would compromise this security:

'The system as it stands cannot generate Braille Pin Nos and the respondents say that technically it is unlikely that this can be done without compromising existing security arrangements and that there would be a huge cost factor involved.

The respondents state that any attempt to re-engineer the existing system to accommodate Braille Pin Nos would require "man-years" of work and, even then, the need for manual intervention could not be ruled out.'[11]

[37.04] However, at hearing, the banks were able to suggest that there was a possible solution to this problem. The Equality Officer was of the view that a case of discrimination had not been made out, as rectifying the problem would cost more than a nominal sum and the banks were therefore exempted by the Equal Status Acts 2000–2004.[12] The Equality Officer concluded with the remark that:

'As outlined above, the respondents have now identified a practice whereby a Braille version of a person's Pin No can be issued without any breach of security or customer confidentiality and that this service could be provided at a 'nominal cost'. I would, therefore, recommend that the respondents make this service available as soon as possible to those visually impaired customers who wish to avail of it. I also trust that this service will be offered to Ms Wellard should she decide to seek a new Pin No in the future.'[13]

[37.05] Access to information was at issue in *Kwiotek v NUI Galway*[14] where the applicant was a PhD student at the respondent university. She was also visually impaired and sought to have library materials provided to herself in a Braille format, but 'was very dissatisfied with the amount of material she had received in Braille'.[15] However, the Equality Officer rejected the complaint on the basis that the respondent had sought to reasonably accommodate the applicant and to do more than a nominal sum.[16]

---

[10] Equality Tribunal, Case No. DEC-S2005/093, para 5.1.
[11] Equality Tribunal, Case No. DEC-S2005/093, para 5.1.
[12] Equal Status Acts 2000–2004, s 4.
[13] Equality Tribunal, Case No DEC-S2005/093, para 8.2.
[14] *Kwiotek v NUI Galway* Equality Tribunal, Case No. DEC-S2004-176.
[15] Equality Tribunal, Case No. DEC-S2004-176, para 2.2.
[16] Equality Tribunal, Case No. DEC-S2004-176, para 6.

Index

All references are to *paragraphs* numbers

Computer data (contd)
matrimonial proceedings, 32.66, 32.67
retrieval, 32.02
search warrants, 32.05–11
Computer programs
artistic works, as, 4.35–44
back-up copies, 4.28, 4.29
computer programs, back-up copies, 4.28, 4.29
copying or storage, 2.05
copyright, 1.19, 4.01, 4.04
   Council Directive 91/250 provisions, 4.01, 4.02, 4.12
   CRRA provisions, 4.01, 4.03
copyright infringement
   Irish cases, 4.26, 4.27
   UK law, 4.18–25
copyright infringement, adaptations, 4.48, 4.49
cut and paste function, 5.13, 5.14
damages, project abandonment, 22.06, 22.07
decompilation, 4.51–64
defects, limitation clauses, 22.23
definition, 4.06
design materials, 4.10, 4.11
dramatic work, as, 4.45, 4.46
films, as, 4.47
harmonised protection, Directive 91/250, 4.12
intellectual creation, 4.07–09
non-literal copying, 4.30
non-text copying, 4.31–34
patentability, 9.06–11
reverse engineering, right of repair, 4.65–74
translation or adaptation, right of, 4.50
Computer Security Basics, 30.71–73
Computer system contracts
parties, unequal bargaining power, 22.23
performance bonds, 22.24–26
Computer-generated works
authorship, 1.45
copyright duration, 1.77

Computer-implemented inventions
patentability, 8.05, 8.06
proposed Directive, 9.12–14
Confidential information
assertion of rights in, 13.01
communication, need for, 13.05, 13.10
confidence, obligation, 13.05, 13.11–13
confidence, statutory obligations, 13.31–34
duration, 13.18
employment references, 33.59–63
encryption, 13.08
freedom of expression
   constitutional right, 13.20
   ECHR Art.10, 13.21–27
IT employees, contractual restraint, 35.09–12
jurisdiction, 13.02
legal catergorisation, 13.02, 13.03
locus standi, 13.17
proprietary rights in, 13.02, 13.03
public domain, entry, 13.18
secrecy, need for, 13.06
State information, 13.28–30
technological development, 13.09
third party liability, 13.19
three requirements for, 13.05
trade secrets, non-contractual restrictions, 35.13–17
unauthorised use or disclosure, 13.07, 13.14–16
wrongful publication, offence, 30.39
Conspiracy to corrupt public morals, 29.19
Constitutional rights
communication, right of, 27.07, 27.08
confidential information, 13.20
freedom of expression, 27.01–06
   ECHR Art.10, and, 27.10–12
privacy, workplace, 33.01, 33.02, 33.08, 33.16
self-incrimination, privilege against, 32.73–76

N/L

T

Taxation
e-Commerce, 20.71
Taylor, Max, Professor, 26.04
Technological protection measures,
2.56–59
CRRA measures, 2.64–71
Directive on Harmonisation of Copyright
provisions, 2.72, 2.73
encrypted broadcasts, 2.60–63
Telecom Eireann
alpha-numeric phone number,
administration, 11.07, 11.10–19
Television without Frontiers Directive,
27.21
Texting
censorship, obscene messages, 29.31
DPC, action against, 21.01
spim, 21.01
unsolicited, 21.13
Theft of electricity, 30.80
Third parties
confidential information, liability, 13.19
Trade mark infringement
mark owner, rights of, 10.07
Trade marks
assignment, 10.07
definition, 10.02
descriptiveness, 8.02
distinctive character, acquisition, 10.03
domain names, similarities and
differences, 10.01
domain names, use as, 10.12, 10.13
internet usage, 10.09–11
    MySpace and YouTube, 10.14, 10.15
    search engines, 10.16–21
licensing, 10.07
passing off, refusal, 10.06
refusal, grounds for, 10.04–06
Trade secrets, employment,
non-contractual restrictions, 35.13–17
Trade union membership
sensitive data, 15.25

Transient or incidental copying,
2.05–08
Trojans, 21.08
Typographical arrangements
copyright, 1.34

U

Unfair terms, consumer contracts,
22.30–32
Unregistered designs
infringement, copying, 6.04
protection periods, 6.04

V

VAT
e-Commerce, 20.72
Viruses, 21.08, 30.67, 30.68
definition, 30.69
infection, 'all risks' insurance cover,
22.11–13
worms, difference, 30.70
Visual impairment
bank customers, 37.03, 37.04
students, 37.05
Voice over Internet Protocol (VoIP),
21.01
surveillance and, 17.51

W

Waste electrical and electronic
equipment (WEEE)
  computer disposal, 36.10
Websites
access, discrimination, 37.02
copying, 5.02
hypertext links
    picture links, 5.15–19
    text links, 5.14
intermediary service provider, 28.02
publisher, legal structure provision, 28.02
structure and layout, 5.03–07
WiFi
theft of, 30.77, 30.78
unauthorised access, 30.77
Wikipedia
Irish defamation law and, 28.04
prank posting, 22.02